FIFTH INTERNATIONAL SYMPOSIUM ON
STRATIFIED FLOWS

VOLUME II

UNIVERSITY OF BRITISH COLUMBIA
VANCOUVER, 10-13 JULY, 2000

EDITORS:

G. A. LAWRENCE
R. PIETERS
N. YONEMITSU

DEPARTMENT OF CIVIL ENGINEERING, UNIVERSITY OF BRITISH COLUMBIA
VANCOUVER, CANADA V6T 1Z4

SCIENTIFIC ADVISORY COMMITTEE

L. ARMI	U.S.A.	S. KOMORI	JAPAN
T. ASAEDA	JAPAN	J. LEE	CHINA
K. AYOTTE	AUSTRALIA	P. LINDEN	U.S.A.
R. BADDOUR	CANADA	E. LIST	U.S.A.
P. BAINES	AUSTRALIA	T. MAXWORTHY	U.S.A.
R. BREIDENTHAL	U.S.A.	T. MCCLIMANS	NORWAY
F. BROWAND	U.S.A.	S. MONISMITH	U.S.A.
J. BÜHLER	SWITZERLAND	K. NAKATSUJI	JAPAN
I. CASTRO	U.K.	G. PARKER	U.S.A.
Y. CHASHECHKIN	RUSSIA	W. PELTIER	CANADA
G. CHRISTODOULOU	GREECE	W. RODI	GERMANY
A. COTEL	U.S.A.	J. ROTTMAN	U.S.A.
P. DAVIES	U.K.	G. SPEDDING	U.S.A.
D. FARMER	CANADA	C. STEVENS	NEW ZEALAND
J. FERNANDO	U.S.A.	G. SWATERS	CANADA
M. GARCIA	U.S.A.	P. TAYLOR	CANADA
M. GREGG	U.S.A.	P. VIOLLET	FRANCE
P. HAMBLIN	CANADA	B. VOISIN	FRANCE
E. HOPFINGER	FRANCE	I. WOOD	NEW ZEALAND
H. HUPPERT	U.K.	A. WÜEST	SWITZERLAND
J. IMBERGER	AUSTRALIA	H. YAMAZAKI	JAPAN
G. IVEY	AUSTRALIA	H. YEH	U.S.A.
M. JAMALI	IRAN	S. YOSHIDA	JAPAN
G. JIRKA	GERMANY		

LOCAL ORGANISING COMMITTEE

G. LAWRENCE (CHAIR)	S. ALLEN	D. STEYN
N. YONEMITSU (VICE-CHAIR)	R. PIETERS	P. WARD

TECHNICAL SUPPORT

C. SEWELL   J. YONEDA

SPONSORS

INTERNATIONAL ASSOCIATION FOR HYDRAULIC RESEARCH
AMERICAN SOCIETY OF CIVIL ENGINEERS
CANADIAN SOCIETY FOR CIVIL ENGINEERING
CANADIAN METEOROLOGICAL AND OCEANOGRAPHIC SOCIETY
PACIFIC INSTITUTE FOR THE MATHEMATICAL SCIENCES
UNIVERSITY OF BRITISH COLUMBIA, DEPARTMENT OF CIVIL ENGINEERING

ISBN 0-88865-344-1

PRINTED IN VANCOUVER BY WEST COAST REPRODUCTION CENTRES

INVITED PRESENTATIONS

Laurence Armi
Three-layer hydraulics, virtual controls and generalizations to continuous stratification

Burkard Baschek
Kayaking on stratified flows

Herbert E. Huppert
Solidification in multi-component geological fluids

Jörg Imberger
Buoyancy effects in stratified lakes

Gerhard H. Jirka
On integral models of buoyant jets

Joseph H. W. Lee
On the deformation of duckbill valves

Paul F. Linden
The application of MTT plume theory to building ventilation

Trevor J. McDougall
Parameterizing the adiabatic effects of eddies in stratified fluids

Owen M. Phillips
The Ruddick-Turner experiment: A beautiful puzzle

James W. Rottman
The Scientific Life of John E. Simpson

Geoffrey R. Spedding
Stratified Wakes

Craig L. Stevens
The influence of turbulence on phytoplankton photoadaptation in coastal embayments

Gordon E. Swaters
Interaction of cold domes with topographic Rossby waves

Alfred J. Wüest
Deep mixing in Lake Baikal – low replacement and high turbulence

Shizuo Yoshida
Flow structures and mixing processes in highly stratified rivers

VOLUME I

VOLUME II

CONTENTS

2 JETS, PLUMES AND THERMALS

3 BIOLOGICAL INTERACTIONS

4 LAKES

5 DEEP LAKES AND MINE PITS

6 RESERVOIR INFLOW AND OUTFLOW

7 HYDRODYNAMIC STABILITY

8 DAVID WILKINSON MEMORIAL SESSION

9 J. STEWART TURNER SESSION

VOLUME II

10 INTERNAL WAVES

11 RIVERS AND ESTUARIES

12 COASTAL FLOWS

13 OCEANIC FLOWS

14 ATMOSPHERIC FLOWS

15 JOHN E. SIMPSON SESSION

16 TURBULENCE AND MIXING

9

TURNER SESSIONS

The role of frontal processes in air-sea gas exchange

Burkard Baschek, David Farmer, and Svein Vagle

Institute of Ocean Sciences, Sidney, B.C., Canada V8L 4B2
baschekb@maelstrom.seos.uvic.ca, farmerd@dfo-mpo.gc.ca, vagles@dfo-mpo.gc.ca

1. Abstract

The role of strong vertical motions associated with plunging jets over a sill on air-sea gas exchange was studied in the estuarine regime of Haro Strait, B.C., in October 1999. Measurements were carried out with an acoustic resonator for measuring bubble size distributions at different depths, towed CTD, vessel-mounted ADCP, and Echo Sounder. In addition, air photos were taken in order to map the extent of the tidal fronts in the region.

In these fronts, small breaking waves generate gas bubbles at the sea surface which are then trapped by highly energetic eddies and drawn down to depths of up to $120\,m$. The vertical current speed in these downwelling regions sometimes exceeded $0.5\,m\,s^{-1}$. These violent processes may play an important role in the aeration of the water masses exchanged between semi-enclosed basins and the open ocean.

2. Introduction

As part of the estuarine circulation of the coastal waters of southern British Columbia (Figure 1), the fresh water from the Fraser River flows into the Pacific ocean. Especially in the tidal fronts of Haro Strait, it is mixed by strong tidal activity with the more saline water from the Pacific ocean which lies beneath it.

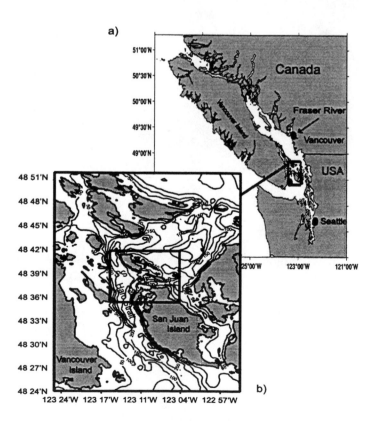

Figure 1: Map of a) southern British Columbia, Canada, and b) Haro Strait.

In order to study these mixing processes and their dynamics, a research cruise was carried out in Haro Strait in October 1999 by the Institute of Ocean Sciences, Sidney. Ship-board measurements with CTD, towed CTD, vessel mounted ADCP, echo sounder, vertical Doppler, and a Resonator Package for measuring size distributions of gas bubbles provided information about the tidal fronts and associated eddies at Battleship and Stuart Islands (Figure 2) .Repeated stations and sections were occupied in both frontal zones so as to gain a better understanding of the temporal evolution of the processes. In particular, the research objectives of the Haro Strait Experiment 1999 were:

- to measure flow and water mass properties during strong ebb tide in order to understand the structure and evolution in tidal fronts.
- to study the effect of mixing in tidal fronts.
- to map the locations of the fronts at Stuart and Battleship Islands.
- to measure bubble size distributions and calculate the role of mixing in the aeration of the water.

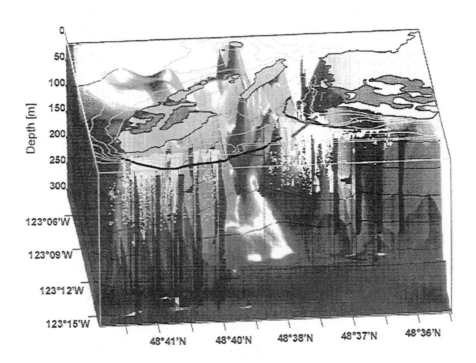

Figure 2: The topography of Haro Strait. The black lines show the location of the tidal fronts at Stuart and Battleship Islands during a strong ebb tide. The white dots indicate high intensity of the acoustic backscatter (mostly gas bubbles). The gray arrows show the mean current speed during strong ebb tide as measured with a vessel-mounted ADCP and the position of the transect shown in Figure 4 is marked by the gray line.

3. Tidal fronts

During ebb tide, the strong tidal flow in Spieden Channel forms two frontal lines at Battleship Island as it enters Haro Strait (Figure 3). These two front lines meet as the denser water of Spieden Channel sinks rapidly under the slowly moving water of Haro Strait. At intermediate depths of $50 - 100\,m$ (Figure 4) the water then spreads and mixes with the resident water mass.

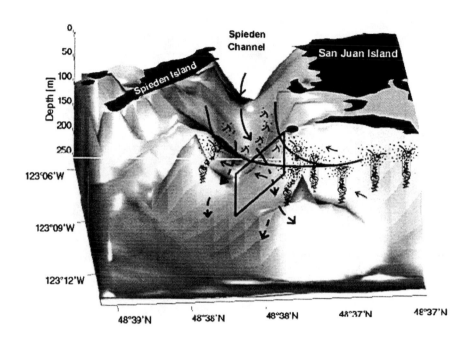

Figure 3: Sketch of the tidal front at Battleship Island, Haro Strait. For explanations see text.

The boundary between the two water masses tilts and stretches with time due to effects of the density gradient and the strong currents. The eddies, which are generated in the frontal zone, are stretched by these processes. This increases their rotational speed, while the corresponding vortex tilting transforms horizontal into vertical circulation.

The mixing processes are enhanced by highly energetic eddies, which are formed in the frontal zone. Gas bubbles, which are generated at the sea surface by small breaking waves are trapped by the eddies and drawn down by strong vertical currents of up to $0.5\,m\,s^{-1}$ to depths of more than $120\,m$. This violent mixing may play a significant role in the modification and aeration of the water masses in Haro Strait and other locations where water masses are exchanged between semi-enclosed basins and the open ocean.

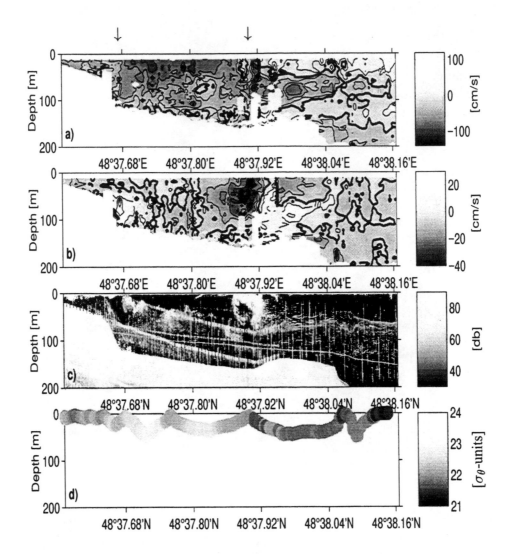

Figure 4: A cross section through the tidal front at Battleship Island (Figure 2) measured with vessel-mounted ADCP, Echo Sounder, and towed CTD. The location of the tidal fronts is marked by the arrows. a) east-west (along-strait) component of the current speed [$cm\ s^{-1}$], b) vertical component [$cm\ s^{-1}$], c) intensity [dB] of the acoustic backscatter, d) density [σ_θ-units].

4. Size distributions of gas bubbles

The size distribution of gas bubbles in the upper $60\ m$ of the water column was measured with an acoustic resonator, which was attached to a CTD and towed behind the boat.

It has to be noted that location of the vessel (echo sounder, Figure 5), does not exactly match the location of the resonator. The volume scaled bubble size distribution may be compared to open ocean measurements; the peak is shifted towards greater bubble sizes. This is likely to be caused by the different entrainement mechanisms in tidal fronts and by the associated high vertical current speeds. The measurement of bubble size distributions can therefore provide useful information about the mechanisms important for aeration of the water.

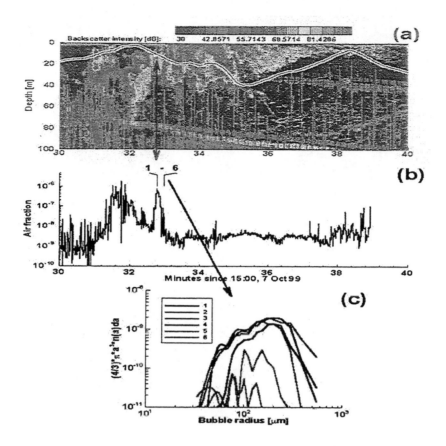

Figure 5: Measurements of size distributions of gas bubbles in approx. 18 m depths. a) Intensity of acoustic backscatter [dB] measured with an echo sounder (the location is indicated by the white line), b) fraction of air in water, c) volume scaled bubble size distribution as function of the bubble radius a.

5. References

D.M Farmer, E.A. D'Asaro, M.V. Trevorrow and G.T. Daikiri (1995): Three-dimensional structure in a tidal convergence front. Continental Shelf Res., 1995, Vol. 15, 13, pp.1649-1673.

D.M. Farmer, S. Vagle and A.D. Booth (1998): A free-flooding acoustical resonator for measurement of bubble size distributions. J. of Atm. and Oceanic Tech., Vol. 15, pp. 1132-1146.

C. Garrett (1995): Flow seperation in the ocean. In Topographic effects in the ocean, Hawaiian Winter Workshop, ed. P. Müller and D. Henderson.

R. Pawlowicz and D.M. Farmer (1998): Diagnosing vertical mixing in a two-layer exchange flow. J. Geophys. Res., Vol. 103, C13, pp. 30695-30711.

H.E. Seim and M.C. Gregg (1994): Detailed observations of a naturally occuring shear instability. J. Geophys. Res.,Vol. 99, C5,pp. 10049-10073.

H. Takeoka, A. Kaneda and H. Anami (1997): Tidal fronts induced by horizontal contrast of vertical mixing efficiency. J. Oceanogr., Vol. 53, pp.563-570.

P.J. Thomas and P.F. Linden (1996): A laboratory simulation of mixing across tidal fronts. J. Fluid Mech.,Vol. 309, pp. 321-344.

Mixing induced by a finite mass flux plume in a ventilated room

C. P. Caulfield[1], A. W. Woods[2], A. McBurnie[3] & J. C. Phillips[3]

[1]: Department of Mechanical and Aerospace Engineering, U.C.S.D., La Jolla, California, 92093-0411, USA
cpc@mae.ucsd.edu
[2]: B.P. Institute, Bullard Laboratories, University of Cambridge, Madingley Road, Cambridge CB3 OEZ, U.K.
[3]: School of Mathematics, University of Bristol, University Walk, Bristol BS8 1TW, U.K.

1. Abstract

Continuous isolated releases of dense turbulent fluid within an enclosed ventilated space occur in a range of industrial and geophysical contexts. Frequently, there is a significant flux of mass at the source. We analyse both numerically and experimentally the effect of a dense turbulent plume with finite source mass flux (and hence a finite source density difference) on the transient evolution of the ambient density within a confined ventilated space (or room). We consider in detail flows with a single vent.

For ventilation through a single opening, we find that the position of the vent relative to the source strongly influences the mixing in the room. For finite source mass fluxes, we find that the ambient density approaches the source plume fluid density at a depth-dependent rate. For the flows we consider, we develop simple reduced models which capture quantitatively the evolution of the bulk characteristics of the flow. The predictions of our models agree well with data obtained from a sequence of analogue laboratory experiments measuring the behaviour of salt plumes within enclosed spaces.

2. Fundamental Model

There has been considerable interest in the mixing produced by a localised source of buoyancy in a confined space since the pioneering work of Baines and Turner (1969). The problem is of central importance for modelling the natural ventilation of large buildings, where convective flows may dominate, and for processes such as LNG storage where the mixing of new, volatile-rich and older, volatile-poor LNG is crucial to avoid explosions (Germeles, 1975). Baines and Turner examined the mixing produced by a plume in a confined region whose density was initially uniform. Their model focused on the motion of the so-called first front, which descends through the environment and across which there is an abrupt division between the original fluid in the room and the fluid which has been cycled through the plume. They also showed how the density profile of the fluid behind this front could be determined by numerical solution of the advection equation in the environment. Germeles (1975) developed a more detailed numerical scheme, including effects of a non-zero source mass flux to explore the filling box process in more detail. Later, Worster and Huppert (1983) introduced a simplified model by assuming that, behind the first front, the rate of change of density in the environment was independent of height. This simplification was shown to give a good analytical approximation to Germeles' numerical solutions in the idealised case of a point source of buoyancy with no mass or momentum flux.

However, in many real applications, there is a non-zero mass flux associated with the source of buoyancy, for example a dense gas leak, hot-air underfloor heating and recharge in a magma chamber. Here, we show that such a mass flux can have a profound influence on the longer term mixing and density evolution in an enclosed region, especially in open systems in which the reservoir is ventilated thereby preventing pressure build-up associated with the mass source. As time increases, the density within the region contaminated by the plume approaches the density of the fluid issuing from the source. As the contaminated region is typically vertically stratified at finite times, this asymptotic approach to the source density implies that the local (time) rate of change of the density within the contaminated region must be a function of depth, as the depth varying densities must all ultimately attain the same maximum value, that of the source fluid.

It is crucial to retain this vertical stratification, and it is typically not appropriate to make a well–mixed assumption for flows with finite source mass flux.

Furthermore, since the density of the ambient fluid in the vicinity of the source increases towards the density of the fluid issuing from the source, the influence of buoyancy in driving the motion of the plume diminishes. Indeed, ultimately, irrespective of the flow conditions provided the source volume flux is non-zero, the plume ceases to be buoyancy driven, but instead becomes momentum driven, with density variations within the room only playing a higher order role. In such a circumstance, the evolution of the plume decouples from the evolution of the ambient cconcentration, and so momentum flux within the plume can be considered as being close to constant both in time and space, given by its source value.

By using the method of characteristics, it is possible to develop a reduced model for the ultimate evolution of the mean concentration within the room irrespective of the vent location. The concentration of the fluid which is being vented can be related to the total concentration within the room at some (usually earlier) time, and thus the total concentration satisfies a simple delay equation. By comparison with a full numerical calculation of the flow defined by the underlying partial differential equations (using a slight modification of the scheme developed by Germeles 1975) and analogue laboratory experiments, (where the density differences between the room and plume fluid are modelled using saline solutions) solutions of the delay equation accurately track the time evolution of the concentration within the room.

We are interested in modelling the descent and mixing of dense fluid, issuing from a source with a finite initial mass flux and then entraining ambient fluid as it descends towards the "floor" of an enclosed space or room. We assume that the density differences between the plume fluid and the ambient fluid are always sufficiently small so that the Boussinesq approximation may be made. We follow the classical model of a turbulent buoyant plume (Zeldovich 1937, Morton, Taylor and Turner 1956). Throughout our discussion, dimensional quantities are denoted with an asterisk. Turbulence closure is achieved by using the "entrainment assumption", which states that the characteristic inflow velocity at any height due to turbulent entrainment is proportional to a characteristic downward velocity $W^*(z^*)$ within the plume at that height, with a universal constant of proportionality ϵ, the so–called "entrainment constant" (see Turner 1986 for a fuller discussion). We assume also that the plume is axisymmetric, with radial profiles of velocity $w_p^*(r^*, z^*)$ and density $\rho_p^*(r^*, z^*)$ within the plume that are self–similar with height. Under these assumptions, the motion of the plume may be described using horizontal averages of three quantities, namely the volume flux, the specific momentum flux and the specific buoyancy flux:

$$Q^*(z^*) \equiv b^{*2}W^* = 2\int_0^\infty w^* r^* dr^* , \tag{1}$$

$$M^*(z^*) \equiv b^{*2}W^{*2} = 2\int_0^\infty w^{*2} r^* dr^* , \tag{2}$$

$$F^*(z^*) \equiv G^{*\prime}b^{*2}W^* = 2\int_0^\infty \frac{g^*(\rho_p^* - \rho_a^*)}{\rho_a^*(0,0)} w^{*2} r^* dr^* , \tag{3}$$

where ρ_a^* is the ambient density, ρ_p^* is the distribution of density within the plume, $\rho_a^*(0,0)$ is the reference density of the ambient fluid initially at the source height $z^* = 0$, $G^{*\prime}(z^*)$ is the characteristic value of the reduced gravity of the plume, and a factor of π has been suppressed.

The constant ϵ parameterises the rate of mixing of ambient fluid into the plume and has value $\epsilon \sim 0.1$. In a confined environment, with cross-sectional area A^*, the ambient density evolves as a result of the entrainment since mass conservation requires an opposite upflow outside the plume to balance the flux of entrained fluid. If this has speed $\mathcal{W}^*$ then the ambient density is time–dependent, and evolves according to

$$\frac{\partial \rho_a^*}{\partial t^*} = -\mathcal{W}^* \frac{\partial \rho_a^*}{\partial z^*} . \tag{4}$$

If we assume that the environment is sufficiently large that $A^* \gg \pi Q^{*2}/M^*$, where $\pi Q^{*2}/M^* = \pi b^{*2}$

represents the cross-sectional area of the plume (c.f. Baines and Turner, 1969), then

$$\mathcal{W}^* \approx -(Q^* - Q_n^*)/A^* , \tag{5}$$

where Q_n^* is the net downward flux through the room at that level. This net flux Q_n^* is determined by the location, number and effective area of the vents within the room, and plays a crucial role in the flow dynamics.

We assume that the density, ρ_s^*, and volume flux, Q_s^*, of the fluid issuing from the source are constant, and non–zero. Thus, the reduced gravity $g_s'^*(t^*)$ at the source $z^* = 0$ has (time–dependent) value

$$g_s'^*(t^*) = \frac{[\rho_s^* - \rho_a^*(0, t)]g^*}{\rho_a^*(0, 0)} . \tag{6}$$

The ambient density at the height of the source may vary from its initial value, and so the source specific buoyancy flux F_s^* is time–dependent, and is defined by

$$F_s^*(t^*) = Q_s^* g_s'^*(t^*) . \tag{7}$$

Initially $F_s^* = F_0^*$ when ρ_a^* has its initial value at the source. We define a reference (dimensional) volume flux Q_H^* as the volume flux of a plume with zero source mass flux and specific buoyancy flux F_0^* after it has descended through the room over the distance H^* between the source and the floor.

For simplicity, and to isolate the effects of initial non-zero volume flux from any initial adjustments due to an excess or deficiency of initial specific momentum flux, we require the source specific momentum flux to be constant with time, and to be determined by requiring that the plume is initially in "pure plume balance" (see Caulfield and Woods 1995 for a fuller discussion). Similarly to Q_H^*, we may define a reference specific momentum flux M_H^* as the specific momentum flux at the floor associated with a notional point source with specific buoyancy flux equal to the initial specific buoyancy flux of the actual source.

We use Q_H^*, M_H^*, F_0^* and $\rho_a^*(0, 0)$ to define nondimensional fluxes. It is natural for flows with finite non–zero source volume fluxes $Q_s > 0$ to define a "concentration" $C(z, t^*)$ for the ambient fluid:

$$C(z, t^*) = \frac{\rho_a(z, t^*) - 1}{\rho_s - 1} . \tag{8}$$

$C = 0$ when the ambient fluid has its initial density, and so $C = 0$ for all z at $t = 0$. Conversely, $C = 1$ corresponds to the ambient fluid having exactly the same density as the source fluid. If the concentration at the source evolves with time, the source conditions which we have chosen imply that, near the source, the plume departs from pure plume balance, and becomes "forced".

Using (8), the source specific buoyancy flux for flows with non–zero initial volume flux may be written as

$$F_s = 1 - C(0, t^*) = 1 - C_s(t^*) , \tag{9}$$

defining implicitly the ambient concentration at the source C_s. In general, at all heights in the plume:

$$F = (C_p - C)\frac{Q}{Q_s} , \tag{10}$$

where C_p is the concentration of plume fluid:

$$C_p(z, t^*) = \frac{\rho_p(z, t^*) - 1}{\rho_s - 1} , \tag{11}$$

where ρ_p is the (nondimensional) plume density.

Using these definitions, the equations for the evolution of the plume with non–zero initial volume flux become

$$\frac{\partial}{\partial z}Q = \frac{5}{3}M^{1/2} \, , \tag{12}$$

$$\frac{\partial}{\partial z}(M^2) = \frac{8}{3}FQ \, , \tag{13}$$

$$\frac{\partial}{\partial z}F = -\frac{Q}{Q_s}\frac{\partial C}{\partial z} \, . \tag{14}$$

To complete our numerical scheme, equation (4) needs to be nondimensionalized appropriately. For a filling box, the natural characteristic time is the notional time τ_f^*, over which the actual dimensional volume flux πQ_H^* at the floor would fill the room's volume A^*H^*, where A^* is the cross–sectional area, i.e.

$$\tau_f^* = \frac{A^*H^*}{\pi Q_H^*} \, . \tag{15}$$

This time is commonly referred to as the "filling box time". Using (15), and the definition of the concentration C, (4) may be reposed as

$$\frac{\partial C}{\partial t} - (Q - Q_n)\frac{\partial C}{\partial z} = 0 \, , \tag{16}$$

for flows with finite source volume flux, where Q_n is the net downward flux of fluid at any level, and corresponds to the net out flow through any vent between the present location and the floor of the room. When it is non-zero, $Q_n = Q_s$. Equations (12)–(14) and (16), together with source conditions $Q = Q_s$, $M = M_s$ and $F = F_s(t)$ given by (9) and initial condition $C = 0 \, \forall z$ now specify a closed set of equations.

To solve the full problem, we utilize a slight modification of the conservative numerical integration scheme of Germeles (1975). The scheme relies on a discretization of the ambient density field (or equivalently the concentration field) into a finite number of "layers" separated by sharp "interfaces" or "levels". In general, the ith "layer" lies between the ith and $i + 1$th "interface". Fundamentally, the evolution of the plume through the depth of the room is assumed to occur significantly more rapidly than the evolution of the ambient density field within the room. Therefore, during any time interval, the plume equations (12)–(14) are solved with a concentration gradient approximated using the discretized layerwise density field, which is assumed to be constant during the plume evolution. In particular, the volume flux through each interface is recorded. Once the plume calculation has extended to the full depth of the room, the volume flux through the furthermost interface from the source is recorded. Each of the layers is then advected towards the source by using a discretization of (16), with the appropriate value for Q_n determined by the vent location. Using this equation at each of the interfaces automatically conserves volume within the room. A final new layer is introduced at the floor of the room, with volume given by the appropriate volume flux through the (previous) interface most distant from the source multiplied by the time step. The depth of this layer can then be calculated, defining a new furthermost interface from the source.

3. Results

Since we are interested in sources with finite volume flux, we investigated the effect of varying Q_s, and the (nondimensional) vent location h_v relative to the source location (which is chosen to be at $z = 0$). Numerical solutions for the concentration profile demonstrate that at all heights within the room as $t \to \infty$, $C \to 1$, and so $\rho_a \to \rho_s, \forall z$. Since at all finite times the ambient fluid was found to be stably stratified, it is apparent that the concentration within the room does indeed increase at a depth–dependent rate. Irrespective of the source volume flux, provided it is finite, when $h_v \leq 0$, and hence the vent is above, or at the same level as the source, the first front arrives at the source in a finite time τ_s. The time τ_s is a natural time of development for the plume solutions. Once the first front has passed the source, the first front propagates at a constant rate to the height of the vent. Conversely, if $h_v > 0$, and hence the vent is below the source, the first front only approaches the vent asymptotically.

Increasing the source volume flux Q_s increases the rate of propagation of the first front at all stages of its evolution. Interestingly, increasing Q_s also increases the effect of the variation of the vent location h_v on the evolution of the first front. For example, if the source volume flux is "small" compared to the volume flux $Q(1)$ which the developed plume has when it reaches the floor, i.e. when $z = 1$, the location of the vent has little effect on the development of the first front. On the other hand, if the volume flux of the plume increases due to entrainment by a relatively small amount compared to its initial values, the effect of variation in the location of the vent (where significant volumes of fluid leaves) is very large.

The time evolution of the fluid which leaves the room through the vent is also a strong function of vent location and source volume flux. Once the first front has passed the vent, in all cases the vent concentration jumps discontinuously to a nonzero value. The vent concentration then continues to grow until it ultimately asymptotes to the value $C = 1$, when the room is completely contaminated with fluid of the density issuing from the source. This continuous increase from its initial value is due to the process of reentrainment by the rising plume of higher and higher concentration contaminated fluid as the ambient concentration field evolves.

However, there is significant variability due to both the vent location and the source volume flux in the time evolution of the vented concentration distributions. In general, increasing the source volume flux increases the vented concentration C_v. The process of entrainment reduces the concentration C_p within the plume by a proportionally smaller amount as the source volume flux Q_s increases. Therefore, when the plume reaches the floor of the room, the plume fluid which forms a new layer of ambient fluid has proportionally higher concentration as Q_s increases.

There is also significant variation in the concentration with the location of the vent. If the vent is near the floor of the room, contaminated fluid (with concentration $C > 0$) leaves the room significantly earlier than for flows with the vent further from the floor of the room, where the vented fluid is initially pure ambient fluid, with concentration $C = 0$. Therefore, for vents further from the floor of the room, more of the released source fluid (with density ρ_s) remains in the room. When the contaminated fluid actually reaches the level of the vent, the concentration of the vented fluid increases more rapidly than for flows with vents nearer to the floor of the room. Ultimately, although for all vent locations $C_v \to 1$ as $t \to \infty$, at sufficiently late time C_v actually increases at any particular instant as h_v decreases, (i.e. as the vent height increases within the room.)

In flows with finite source volume flux, there is eventually always an outflow of contaminated fluid from the room, so it is necessary to model carefully the evolution of the total quantity of source fluid between the source and the floor of the room I_{10} as defined as

$$I_{10} = \int_0^1 C dz ,\qquad (17)$$

This quantity is the important measure of the quantity of contaminant remaining inside a room. The crucial question to answer is whether useful reduced models can be developed which accurately capture the evolution of I_{10} within the room. For brevity, we concentrate here on the case where $h_v = 0$, and so $\tau_v = \tau_s$ and the vent and source are at the same height, although other circumstances have also been considered. In this case, $I_{10} = \bar{C}$, the mean concentration between the vent and the floor of the room.

The evolution of $\bar{C}$ satisfies

$$\frac{d\bar{C}}{dt} = Q_s(1 - C_s) .\qquad (18)$$

Therefore, $\bar{C}$ increases linearly with time until time τ_s, when C_s discontinuously becomes nonzero as contaminated fluid starts to be vented from the room. Since the room is always stratified, $C_s < \bar{C}$ for all finite times, and for flows with finite source volume fluxes it is not appropriate to make a well-mixed assumption to model the evolution of $\bar{C}$ (identifying C_s with $\bar{C}$, and supposing that $\partial C/\partial t$ is depth-independent, as in the zero source volume flux calculations of Worster and Huppert 1983). Instead it is necessary to develop a reduced model for the evolution of C_s.

Such a model can be developed since, for flows where $h_v = 0$, within a finite time (i.e. $t \geq \tau_s$), the buoyancy flux at the source reduces from its initial value towards zero, while the source volume flux and source specific momentum flux remain fixed at their initial constant non-zero values Q_s and M_s. This has the crucial implication that ultimately the right-hand side of equation (13) is approximately zero, and so $M(z) \simeq M_s$ a constant, and the "plume" is essentially momentum driven. This implies that the evolution of the specific momentum flux and the volume flux decouples from the evolution of the concentration, both within the plume, and in the ambient. Equation (12) can then be simply integrated to yield

$$Q = Q_s + \frac{5M_s^{1/2}z}{3} = z_e^{5/3}\left(1 + \frac{5z}{3z_e}\right), \tag{19}$$

where z_e is the nondimensional effective origin of a plume with source volume flux Q_s^* and buoyancy flux F_0^* (see Caulfield and Woods 1995 for a fuller discussion.) Since the volume flux is now known explicitly, it is possible to solve (16) (with $Q_n = 0$) by the method of characteristics, and thus derive a simple reduced model for the concentration at the vent/source C_s in terms of the mean concentration at some earlier time, and thus the time evolution of $\bar{C}$ for all times $t > \tau_s$. Since $\bar{C}$ is trivially determined before τ_s (as no contaminated fluid is vented), a reduced model for the complete evolution of $\bar{C}$ can be developed. It can be shown that

$$\frac{d}{dt}\bar{C}(t) = \frac{5Q_s}{5+3z_e}\left[1 - \bar{C}(t - \tau_m)\right], \tag{20}$$

$$\tau_m = \frac{3z_e}{5Q_s}\log\left[\frac{(5+3z_e)}{3z_e}\right]. \tag{21}$$

Results from this reduced model agree very well with solutions of the full governing equations. Through comparison with analogue laboratory experiments, this reduced model is quantitatively superior to "well-mixed" models for plumes with finite source volume flux, and allows us to model simply not only the evolution of the mean concentration within the room, but also time-dependent variation in the vertical concentration profiles.

4. References

BAINES, W. D. & TURNER J. S. 1969 Turbulent buoyant convection from a source in a confined region. *J. Fluid Mech.* **37**, 51-80.

CAULFIELD, C. P. & WOODS A. W. 1995 Plumes with non-monotonic mixing behaviour. *Geophys. Astrophys. Fluid Dyn.* **79**, 173-199.

GERMELES, A. E. 1975 Forced plumes and mixing of liquids in tanks. *J. Fluid Mech.* **71**, 601-623.

MORTON, B. R., TAYLOR, G. I. & TURNER, J. S. 1956 Turbulent gravitational convection from maintained and instantaneous sources. *Proc. R. Soc. Lond.* **A234**, 1-23.

TURNER, J. S. 1986 Turbulent entrainment: the development of the entrainment assumption, and its application to geophysical flows. *J. Fluid Mech.* **173**, 431-471.

WORSTER, M. G. & HUPPERT, H. E. 1983 Time-dependent density profiles in a filling box. *J. Fluid Mech.* **132**, 457-466.

ZELDOVICH, Y. B. 1937 The asymptotic laws of freely-ascending convective flows. *Zhur. Eksper. Teor. Fiz.* **7**, 1463-1465 (in Russian). English transl. in *Selected Works of Yakov Borisovich Zeldovich*, Vol. 1 1992 (ed. J. P. Ostriker), pp. 82-85. Princeton University Press.

Stratified and Rotating Critical Flows

Benoit Cushman-Roisin

Thayer School of Engineering, Dartmouth College, Hanover NH 03755-8000
Benoit.R.Roisin@Dartmouth.edu

1. Abstract

In the absence of rotation, marginal stability according to individual-particle displacements corresponds to density homogeneity, while in the absence of stratification, it yields zero vorticity. But, in the simultaneous presence of rotation and stratification, marginal stability according to individual-particle displacements holds interesting possibilities.

This paper reviews the theory, establishes a set of equations governing critical flows and derives some general classes of nonlinear solutions. A family of solutions with relevance to coastal flows is presented. Finally, the theory is extended to axisymmetric and arbitrary 3D flows.

Along the way, the paper also proposes a dimensionless ratio as a measure of the "distance" to criticality in observed flows. A connection with the Richardson number is established in a limiting case.

2. Introduction

Critical flows are defined here as flows in which an individual particle displacement is everywhere marginally stable. In a critical flow, therefore, an individual particle, once displaced slightly while everything around it has remained unchanged, is neither pulled back toward its original position or pulled further away from it.

If a situation is unstable according to this definition, all particles rapidly re-arrange themselves, creating a situation that evolves rather catastrophically into a new configuration. An example is the rapid mixing undergone by an initially top-heavy fluid. The new configuration will no longer be unstable to individual particle displacements but may nonetheless become unstable to less dramatic and more organized types of instabilities. For example a bottom-heavy thermal-wind flow may be stable with respect to individual particle displacements and yet be baroclinically unstable to fluctuations of certain wavelengths.

Since mixing occurs frequently in the atmosphere and oceans, we can expect a number of flow situations to be critical in the sense stated above. Knowing the properties of critical flows can then enable us to anticipate certain relations that exist in freshly mixed flows. Being able to detect how "close" a certain observed situation is to criticality can also helps us determine its degree of vulnerability in the face of future perturbations.

3. Governing Equations and Solution

We shall consider here three-dimensional, non-hydrostatic flows, with ambient rotation (on an *f*-plane), ambient stratification and no friction. The Boussinesq approximation is invoked. Under these assumptions, the governing equations are:

$$\frac{du}{dt} - fv = -\frac{\partial p}{\partial x}, \quad \frac{dv}{dt} + fu = -\frac{\partial p}{\partial y}, \quad \frac{dw}{dt} = -\frac{\partial p}{\partial z} + b, \quad \frac{db}{dt} = 0,$$

where the time derivative is the material derivative, the hydrostatic pressure in equilibrium with the reference density has been subtracted, the remaining pressure is divided by the reference density for convenience, and b is the buoyancy (gravitational acceleration time relative density difference). The continuity equation is not listed because it will not be needed in the following analysis.

The previous set of equations admits a number of trivial steady states: Stratification at rest [$u = v = w = 0$ and $b(z)$], homogeneous rectilinear flow [$u = w = b = 0$, $v(x)$], homogeneous 2D flows [$u(x,y)$, $v(x,y)$, $w = b = 0$], stratified rectilinear flow [$u = w = 0$, $v(x,z)$, $b(x,z)$ with $f\partial v/\partial z = \partial b/\partial x$], axisymmetric flow, etc.

Consider now the particle at an arbitrary position (x, y, z) in one such steady-state flow and imagine that it has been displaced to the new position $(x+\xi, y+\eta, z+\zeta)$, with everything else around it remaining the same. At this new position, the particle will most likely find itself out of equilibrium. For example, having conserved its buoyancy (last governing equation), the particle may find itself too heavy or too light for the local vertical pressure gradient $\partial p/\partial z$. Or, having conserved its geostrophic momentum ($v+fx$, $u-fy$), it will have acquired a new velocity that may not be balanced by the local horizontal pressure force ($-\partial p/\partial x$, $-\partial p/\partial y$). Being out of equilibrium, the particle will be subjected to forces and be accelerated, either back toward its original position or further away from it. Criticality as defined here corresponds to the boundary between these two possible outcomes.

If we assume that the displacement vector is short, then the pressure gradient at the new position can be approximated by a Taylor expansion. Subtraction of the basic-state flow then leads to a set of equations governing the temporal evolution of the displacement vector [$\xi(t)$, $\eta(t)$, $\zeta(t)$] in which x, y and z are viewed as parameters. Because all coefficients of the preceding equations are time-independent, we may seek a solution including a factor $\exp(i\omega t)$, with a fixed frequency ω. After this series of transformations, the equations reduce to the following set:

$$\left(\frac{\partial^2 p}{\partial x^2} - \omega^2\right)\xi + \left(\frac{\partial^2 p}{\partial x \partial y} - if\omega\right)\eta + \frac{\partial^2 p}{\partial x \partial z}\zeta = 0$$

$$\left(\frac{\partial^2 p}{\partial x \partial y} + if\omega\right)\xi + \left(\frac{\partial^2 p}{\partial y^2} - \omega^2\right)\eta + \frac{\partial^2 p}{\partial y \partial z}\zeta = 0$$

$$\frac{\partial^2 p}{\partial x \partial z}\xi + \frac{\partial^2 p}{\partial y \partial z}\eta + \left(\frac{\partial^2 p}{\partial z^2} - \omega^2\right)\zeta = 0.$$

Since the displacement vector cannot have all its components simultaneously zero, the determinant of this algebraic system must vanish. This yields a polynomial equation of third degree for ω^2. If all six possible ω values are real, then the displaced particle executes finite oscillations, but if some ω values are found to be complex, these occur in pairs of complex conjugates and one element of the pair leads to exponential growth. Therefore, stability occurs when all ω values are real, for which it is sufficient to have all three ω^2 values real and positive. Criticality occurs when one of these values reaches zero. Because the general case is rather elaborate, let us consider particular cases of increasing complexity.

4. Particular Cases

4.1 Stratification at rest

The basic state [$u = v = w = 0$, $b = b(z)$] implies a pressure distribution depending on z only. The determinant of the problem reduces to:

$$\omega^2(\omega^2 - f^2)(\omega^2 - N^2) = 0$$

where $N^2 = d^2p/dz^2 = db/dz$. The root $\omega^2 = 0$ implies criticality with respect to horizontal displacement (obvious!), the root $\omega^2 = f^2$ implies the possibility of inertial oscillations (stable), while the root $\omega^2 = N^2$ represents vertical oscillations if the fluid is bottom heavy and instability if the fluid is top heavy. Criticality occurs when $N^2 = 0$, namely when the fluid has homogeneous density. There is no new result here, but the approach is far more general.

4.2 Homogeneous rectilinear flow

The basic state $[u = w = b = 0, v = v(x)]$ implies a pressure function of x only, and the determinant becomes:

$$\omega^4(\omega^2 - L^2) = 0$$

where $L^2 = d^2p/dx^2 + f^2 = f(f + dv/dx)$. Criticality now occurs when $L^2 = 0$, namely when the total vorticity, $f + dv/dx$, vanishes. The flow is stable when $L^2 > 0$, which occurs when the total vorticity has the same sign as the ambient vorticity f. This is inertial stability (see Holton, 1992, page 207).

4.3 Stratified rectilinear flow

The basic state is now generalized to include both horizontal and vertical variations of a rectilinear flow and density stratification: $u = w = 0$, $v = v(x,z)$, $b = b(x,z)$, in thermal-wind balance $f\,\partial v/\partial z = \partial b/\partial x = \partial^2 p/\partial x\partial z$. The determinant admits the set of roots:

$$\omega^2 = \frac{1}{2}\left[(L^2 + N^2) \pm \sqrt{(L^2 - N^2)^2 + 4M^4}\right],$$

where $L^2 = \partial^2 p/\partial x^2 + f^2 = f(f + \partial v/\partial x)$, $M^2 = \partial^2 p/\partial x\partial z = f\partial v/\partial z = \partial b/\partial x$, and $N^2 = \partial^2 p/\partial z^2 = \partial b/\partial z$. Those roots are always real. The flow is critical when the lowest of the two roots (obtained by selecting the minus sign) vanishes, namely: $M^4 = L^2 N^2$ in the quadrant where $L^2 > 0$ and $N^2 > 0$; for higher values of M^4, the flow is unstable. This instability has been called "symmetric instability" (see Holton, 1992, pages 277-281). Here, it is worth insisting that it is not enough to have $L^2 > 0$ and $N^2 > 0$, in agreement with the previous conditions, but that $L^2 N^2 > M^4$ is also required. In other words, when geostrophy and gravity act simultaneously, the requirement for stability is more stringent than if each were acting separately. Finally, it can also be demonstrated that, when the flow is unstable, the exponentially growing displacements are those that occur in the wedge defined by the horizontal plane and the local sloping density surface. It is erroneous to view this instability as the "basic mechanism" of baroclinic instability (Pedlosky, 1987, pages 518-521.)

Expressed in terms of original variables, the condition for criticality becomes:

$$\left(f + \frac{\partial v}{\partial x}\right)\frac{\partial b}{\partial z} - \frac{\partial v}{\partial z}\frac{\partial b}{\partial x} = 0$$

which implies vanishing potential vorticity. Criticality and the thermal-wind balance

$$f\frac{\partial v}{\partial z} = \frac{\partial b}{\partial x}$$

combine to form a coupled nonlinear system for the variables v and b. Accompanying conditions are $f(f + \partial v/\partial x) > 0$ and $\partial b/\partial z > 0$. Because the latter inequality implies that buoyancy varies monotonically with depth, we can use buoyancy as a substitute vertical variable. The set of equations is then transformed into the linear system:

$$f + \frac{\partial v}{\partial x} = 0, \qquad f\frac{\partial v}{\partial b} = -\frac{\partial z}{\partial x}.$$

The solution is rather immediate:

$$v(x,b) = V(b) - fx, \qquad z(x,b) = Z(b) - fx\frac{dV}{db},$$

where $V(b)$ and $Z(b)$ are two arbitrary functions. The nonlinearities have been relegated to the inversion of these functions to extract the buoyancy b as a function of x and z. Also, since $V(b)$ and $Z(b)$ are totally arbitrary, the number of solutions is rather vast.

5. Distance to Criticality and Richardson Number

Let us define the dimensionless ratio

$$\mu = \frac{M^4}{L^2 N^2} = \frac{(\partial v/\partial z)(\partial b/\partial x)}{(f + \partial v/\partial x)(\partial b/\partial z)}.$$

Since criticality occurs for $\mu = 1$ and stability is on the side $\mu < 1$, the proximity of this ratio to unity can be used as a measure of the "distance" of a flow to criticality.

In the large-scale limit (very small Rossby number, i.e. $|\partial v/\partial x| \ll |f|$), this ratio becomes:

$$\mu = \frac{(\partial v/\partial z)(\partial b/\partial x)}{f(\partial b/\partial z)} = \frac{(\partial v/\partial z)^2}{(\partial b/\partial z)} = \frac{1}{Ri}.$$

Therefore, only in this limiting case is the Richardson number a measure of the proximity to criticality.

6. Coastal Flows

If we choose linear expressions for the preceding functions $V(b)$ and $Z(b)$, inversion is immediate, and a family of solution is

$$v(x,z) = \frac{fN^2 H^2 L}{f^2 L^2 + N^2 H^2}\left(1 - \frac{x}{L} + \frac{z}{H}\right)$$

$$b(x,z) = b_0 + \frac{fN^2 HL^2}{f^2 L^2 + N^2 H^2}\left(-1 + \frac{x}{L} + \frac{N^2 H^2}{f^2 L^2}\frac{z}{H}\right),$$

where all parameters are arbitrary constants. As illustrated below (Figure 1), this corresponds to a coastal flow of surface width L and shore depth H, which matches smoothly with a resting stratification of strength N offshore and below. Physically, such situation with reduced stratification toward the coast and a current flowing (in the Northern Hemisphere) with the coast on its left would be associated with the effect of a past coastal-upwelling event.

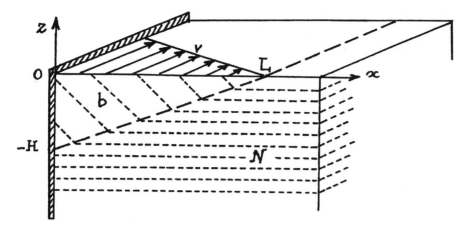

Figure 1. Schematic structure of a critical coastal flow.

7. Stratified Axisymmetric Flow

The analysis can be extended to circular-symmetric flow (vortex), and the main result is similar to the preceding one, namely that stability requires simultaneously $L^2 > 0$, $N^2 > 0$ and $L^2N^2 > M^4$, except that the quantities L^2 and M^2 are now defined in terms of the azimuthal velocity $v(r,z)$ as

$$L^2 = \left(f + \frac{2v}{r}\right)\left(f + \frac{\partial v}{\partial r} + \frac{v}{r}\right) \quad \text{and} \quad M^2 = \left(f + \frac{2v}{r}\right)\frac{\partial v}{\partial z} = \frac{\partial b}{\partial r}.$$

The ratio $\mu = M^4/L^2N^2$ can still be defined as the distance to criticality. At criticality and with buoyancy used as the vertical variable, the equations governing the flow are:

$$f + \frac{\partial v}{\partial r} + \frac{v}{r} = 0 \qquad \left(f + \frac{2v}{r}\right)\frac{\partial v}{\partial b} = -\frac{\partial z}{\partial r}.$$

This set of equations admits the general solution

$$v(r,b) = \frac{1}{r}A(b) - \frac{fr}{2} \qquad z(r,b) = Z(b) + \frac{A(b)}{r^2}\frac{dA}{db},$$

where the functions $A(b)$ and $Z(b)$ are arbitrary. The structure of vortices obeying these relations remains to be explored.

8. Arbitrary 3D flows

For an arbitrary but steady, three-dimensional flow, the vanishing determinant is rather difficult to discuss in all generality. However, we can take advantage of the fact that vertical variations in the pressure field are much larger than the horizontal variations. Using ε as the vertical- to length-scale ratio ($\varepsilon = f/N \ll 1$) and writing all double derivatives of the pressure as follows, we have:

$$\frac{\partial^2 p}{\partial x^2} = af^2 \qquad \frac{\partial^2 p}{\partial x \partial y} = bf^2 \qquad \frac{\partial^2 p}{\partial y^2} = cf^2$$

$$\frac{\partial^2 p}{\partial x \partial z} = \frac{d}{\varepsilon} f^2 \qquad \frac{\partial^2 p}{\partial y \partial z} = \frac{e}{\varepsilon} f^2$$

$$\frac{\partial^2 p}{\partial z^2} = \frac{f^2}{\varepsilon^2} \qquad (= N^2)$$

Writing ω/f as a power of ε yields two asymptotic solutions, namely $\omega/f \sim \varepsilon$ and $\omega/f \sim 1$ at the leading orders. The first solution, to its leading and first orders, is:

$$\left(\frac{\omega}{f}\right)^2 = \frac{1}{\varepsilon^2} + \left(d^2 + e^2\right) + O(\varepsilon^2) \quad \rightarrow \quad \omega^2 = N^2 + \frac{1}{N^2}\left[\left(\frac{\partial^2 p}{\partial x \partial z}\right)^2 + \left(\frac{\partial^2 p}{\partial y \partial z}\right)^2\right] + O\left(\frac{f^2}{N^2}\right)$$

This solution is real positive as long as $N^2 > 0$, and this pair of roots cannot therefore cause an instability. The other asymptotic roots are obtained at the leading order from:

$$\left(\frac{\omega}{f}\right)^4 + \left(1 + a + c - d^2 - e^2\right)\left(\frac{\omega}{f}\right)^2 + \left(b^2 + cd^2 + ae^2 - ac - 2bde\right) = 0$$

Criticality occurs when one root vanishes while the other is positive, which is when the product of roots (last term) is zero and the sum of roots (minus middle coefficient) is positive. The criteria are thus:

$$b^2 + cd^2 + ae^2 = ac + 2bde \quad \text{and} \quad d^2 + e^2 \geq 1 + a + c.$$

The implications of these relations have yet to be explored.

9. References

Holton, J. R., 1992: *An Introduction to Dynamical Meteorology*, 3rd ed. Academic Press, 507 pp.

Pedlosky, J., 1987: *Geophysical Fluid Dynamics*, 2nd ed. Springer-Verlag, 710 pp.

The Wave-Turbulence Transition in Stratified Flows

Eric A. D'Asaro
Applied Physics Laboratory and School of Oceanography
Ren-Chieh Lien
Applied Physics Laboratory
University of Washington,Seattle, Washington 98105

May 4, 2000

1 Abstract

Measurements of the Lagrangian trajectories of neutrally buoyant floats in a variety of oceanographic boundary layers and hydraulic flows, and results from microstructure profilers in the open ocean, are used to study the interaction of waves and turbulence in stratified flows. Lagrangian frequency spectra of vertical and horizontal velocity suggest a distinct separation between internal waves, at Lagrangian frequencies below the buoyancy frequency N, and turbulence, at Lagrangian frequencies above N. The anisotropy of "stratified turbulence", in this view, is due entirely to internal waves; the turbulence remains nearly isotropic. The dynamics of the flow is controlled by a Froude number: the ratio of the velocity to the phase speed of the lowest internal wave mode. For small Froude number, waves dominate and the dissipation and mixing rates are controlled by wave-wave interactions. At large Froude number, the dissipation and mixing rates are controlled by turbulent interactions, even though there may still be a significant wave component present. The transition between these regimes is found to be marked by singularities in the Lagrangian and Eulerian spectral forms which can be used to diagnose whether wave-wave or turbulent interactions are controlling.

2 Introduction

Two very different classes of models have been used to understand turbulence and mixing in stratified geophysical flows. One approach attempts to extrapolate the physics of unstratified turbulence into the stratified regime. Such "Stratified Turbulence" models (Mellor and Yamada 1982, Luyten et al. 1996) work well if the stratification is not too strong and the flow remains highly turbulent, but fail if the stratification is too strong (Simpson et al. 1996). A second approach attempts to extrapolate the physics of waves into a partially turbulent regime. Such "Wave-Wave Interaction" models (Müller et al. 1986) work well in the weakly turbulent ocean thermocline (Gregg 1989; Polzin et al. 1995) and have not been well tested in other regimes. The two classes of models are fundamentally different in physical assumptions and mathematical form and will yield very different results if applied to the same flow.

The two different classes of models are designed to operate in different Froude number regimes. Wave-wave interaction models assume that the flow can be expressed as the sum of interacting internal waves, each of which is a solution to the inviscid linear internal wave equations. Energy transfer and fluxes occur through the interactions of these waves. This approach is appropriate at low Froude number, where the waves are stable and interact only weakly. Stratified turbulence models generally parameterize fluxes by assuming a local turbulent eddy viscosity, or similar closure, whose strength depends on the local length and time scales of the flow. This approach is appropriate at low Froude number where the flow is mostly turbulent and waves play only a minor role. A transition from the low Froude number wave physics to the high Froude number turbulent physics should occur at some intermediate Froude number. In this paper we describe some advances in understanding this *Wave to Stratified Turbulence Transition* or W-T transition

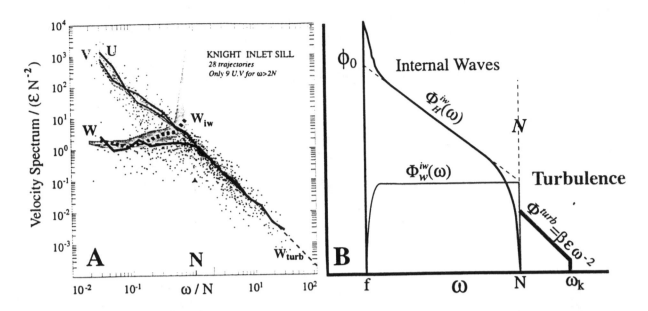

Figure 1: A. Normalized east (U), north (V), and vertical (W) velocity spectra from the Knight Inlet sill. Dots are individual spectral estimates corrected for instrumental response; lines are average of these; shading represents the 95% confidence interval. Heavy dashed line (W_{iw}) is the vertical velocity spectrum computed from (1) assuming that horizontal spectra are entirely due to internal waves. Thin dashed line (W_{turb}) is the spectral form for isotropic turbulence. B. Model Lagrangian frequency spectra of vertical ($\Phi_w(\omega)$) and horizontal ($\Phi_H(\omega)$) velocity as a function of Lagrangian frequency ω. The model consists of an internal wave component ($f < \omega < N$), extending from the Coriolis frequency f to the buoyancy frequency N, and a turbulent component ($N < \omega < \omega_k$), extending to the Kolmogorov frequency ω_k and proportional to the turbulent dissipation rate ε

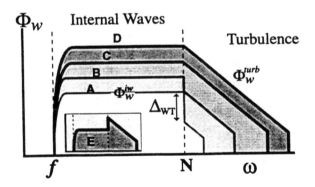

Figure 2: Evolution of Lagrangian frequency spectrum of vertical velocity with increasing energy. Spectra A and B are below the W-T transition energy. Spectrum C is just at the transition energy. Spectra D and E are two possible spectra above the transition energy. Spectrum E is not observed to occur.

based on the observed forms of Eulerian and Lagrangian spectra. More detailed discussions are in D'Asaro and Lien (2000a) and D'Asaro and Lien (2000b)[1].

3   Lagrangian Frequency Spectrum

Lien et al. (1998) and D'Asaro and Lien (2000a) describe frequency spectra ($\Phi_u(\omega)$, $\Phi_v(\omega)$, $\Phi_w(\omega)$) [m^{2}s^{-1}] of velocity (u,v,w) as a function of Lagrangian frequency, ω [s^{-1}], as observed by neutrally buoyant floats in

---

[1]All figures are modified from these papers and copyrighted by the American Meteorological Society, 2000

regions of both strong and weak turbulence. Their key diagnostic is the internal wave consistency relationship (Fofonoff 1969, Calman 1978)

$$\frac{\Phi_w^{iw}}{\Phi_H^{iw}} = \frac{\omega^2(\omega^2 - f^2)}{(N^2 - \omega^2)(\omega^2 + f^2)} \tag{1}$$

where $\Phi_H^{iw} = \Phi_u^{iw} + \Phi_v^{iw}$. Spectra of horizontal and vertical velocity from open ocean sites typically lie close to the Garrett-Munk spectrum for frequencies below N and obey (1). This is the major reason why we think internal waves dominate these scales in the ocean.

Figure 1A shows 28 spectra of vertical and horizontal velocity taken near the sill of Knight Inlet, a region of strong turbulence and mixing. The dashed line marked W_{iw} shows the vertical velocity spectrum computed from (1) assuming that the horizontal velocity spectrum is entirely due to internal waves. If (1) is true, W_{iw} should equal W. The motions with frequencies below N have the properties expected of internal waves: they are anisotropic, approximately as specified by (1), and they have approximately the Garrett-Munk spectral shape characteristic of internal waves. This is truly remarkable; the sill of Knight Inlet is not where you would expect to find a Garrett-Munk spectrum!

The motions with frequencies above N have the properties expected of homogeneous turbulence: their spectra are isotropic, and they have the -2 spectral slope characteristic of homogeneous turbulence (W_{turb}). Based on these results D'Asaro and Lien (2000a) hypothesize that the buoyancy frequency, measured in Lagrangian coordinates, separates waves and turbulence.

Based on these observations, we propose the Lagrangian frequency spectrum for stratified turbulence shown in Figure 1B. It is the sum of internal wave and turbulent components. Motions with frequencies below N are modelled as internal waves. We model the internal wave horizontal velocity spectrum following GM76 (Gregg and Kunze 1991). Motions with Lagrangian frequencies above N are due to turbulence. We assume isotropic turbulence and the Lagrangian inertial subrange (Corrsin 1963, Lien et al. 1998)

$$\Phi^{turb}(\omega) = \frac{\beta\varepsilon}{\omega^2}, \qquad (\omega > N) \tag{2}$$

with a Kolmogorov constant β, which has a value between 1 and 2 (Lien et al. 1998). We use $\beta = 1.8$. The inertial subrange form should be correct only for frequencies much larger than a "Large-Eddy" frequency, here taken to be N, and much less than a Kolmogorov frequency $\omega_k = (\varepsilon/\nu)^{(1/2)}$. D'Asaro and Lien (2000a) give analytical forms for the exact spectral shape of the spectrum near N.

Figure 2 shows the evolution of the model Lagrangian frequency spectrum as a function of internal wave energy. For typical oceanic, i.e., Garrett-Munk or GM, energy levels, (spectrum A), the internal wave spectrum has far more energy than the turbulence spectrum. This results in the sharp drop in the spectrum near N. This drop is particularly sharp when observed from neutrally buoyant floats (Cairns 1975, D'Asaro and Lien 2000a, Kunze et al. 1990), i.e. for Lagrangian spectra. However, since the value of ε increases quadratically with wave energy (Gregg 1989; Polzin et al. 1995) the ratio $\Phi_w^{turb}(N)/\Phi_w^{iw}(N)$ will be proportional to $\Phi_w^{iw}(N)$. At low energies (spectrum A), the ratio will be small. As the internal wave energy increases (spectrum B), the ratio will increase until it reaches 1 (spectrum C). At this energy, which will turn out to mark the W-T transition, the drop in spectral level at N has disappeared.

If the energy is increased above the W-T transition level there are two possibilities: Φ_w^{turb} could continue to increase quadratically, as shown in spectrum E (Fig.2, insert), leading to a sharp increase in spectral level at N, or it could remain at the same level as Φ_w^{iw} as shown in spectrum D. D'Asaro and Lien (2000a) (Fig.1A) find no spectra which look like E, but many spectra which look like D. We therefore assume that only spectrum D occurs. D'Asaro and Lien (2000a) assume this and using the analytical spectral shapes near N, find

$$\varepsilon = 1.2\,\beta^{-1}\Phi_w^{iw}N^2 = 0.6\,\beta^{-1}\sigma_w^2 N \tag{3}$$

where σ_w^2 is the total vertical velocity variance. This relationship, valid at or above the W-T transition, shows a linear relationship between energy and dissipation. Thus the W-T transition marks a change from a quadratic to a linear relationship between energy and turbulent dissipation rate.

One consequence of this spectral form is that waves contribute much more to horizontal velocity than to vertical velocity, while turbulence contributes equally. Thus the well known anisotropy of stratified turbulence is due entirely to its wave component. The turbulence itself remains isotropic, but imbedded within an anisotropic wave field.

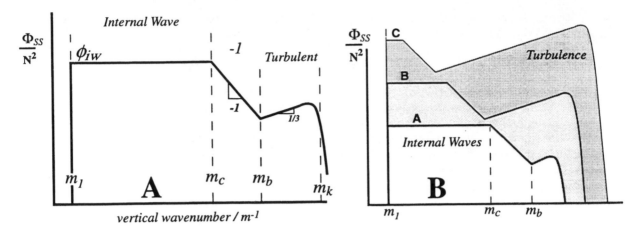

Figure 3: A. Model spectra of vertical wavenumber spectrum of shear. B. Evolution of model vertical wavenumber spectra of shear with increasing energy. Spectrum A is close to GM energy. With increasing energy the bandwidth of the internal waves shrinks and the bandwidth of turbulence increases. Spectrum D is close to the Wave-Turbulence transition.

4 Eulerian Wavenumber Spectrum

The vertical wavenumber spectrum, $\Phi_{SS}(m)$, of horizontal shear, S, in the ocean thermocline has been measured by many investigators using vertical profilers (Gregg 1991). Measurements have been mostly at near-GM energy levels. The basic form, first proposed by Gargett et al. (1981), is shown in Figure 3A. There are three wavenumber bands: a low wavenumber "Internal Wave" band, a high wavenumber "Turbulence" band and an intermediate "-1" band named for its spectral slope. We will extrapolate this form to energies much higher than GM and show how it eventually fails.

The low wavenumber band is believed to be dominated by internal waves (Müller et al. 1978). We assume a white normalized shear spectrum, $\Phi_{SS}(m)/N^2$ with a level ϕ_{iw}, consistent with numerous observations (Gregg et al. 1993; Polzin et al. 1995). The lower end of the internal wave band is set by the WKB-stretched wavelength of the gravest internal wave mode, m_1. This is set by the thermocline depth; for the open ocean we assume the GM76 value $m_1 = 2\pi/b$ [m^{-1}] with $b = 1300\,m$. For the continental shelf, this is set by the water depth; we will use $b = 100\,m$. In the Garrett-Munk spectrum the shear spectral slope changes from white to $+2$ below vertical mode number $j*$ but we ignore this based on evidence that $j*$ becomes small at high energy (D'Asaro and Lien 2000a).

The upper end of the internal wave band is set by a critical wavenumber, m_c (Munk 1981, Sherman and Pinkel 1991) at which the Froude number becomes small. More formally, the value of m_c is set so that the Froude function

$$Fr(m) = \int_{m_1}^{m} \frac{\Phi_{SS}(m)}{N^2} dm \tag{4}$$

equals a critical value, i.e. $Fr(m_c) = Fr_c$. Polzin et al. (1995) uses $Fr_c = 0.7$. This yields

$$\phi_{iw}(m_c - m_1) = Fr_c. \tag{5}$$

Previous investigators have ignored the finite depth of the ocean, assuming $m_1 \ll m_c$, and thus written (5) with $m_1 = 0$. We will show that the W-T transition occurs when m_1 and m_c become comparable.

At wavenumbers above m_c the spectral slope changes to -1. At wavenumbers above $m_b = (N^3/\varepsilon)^{1/2}$, corresponding to the inverse Ozmidov and overturning (Dillon 1982) length scales, the spectrum assumes the form of the turbulent "-5/3" inertial subrange

$$\Phi_{SS}^{turb} = m^2 \Phi_u^{turb} = \alpha_E \varepsilon^{2/3} m^{1/3} \tag{6}$$

out to the Kolomogorov (viscous) wavenumber $m_k = (\varepsilon/\nu^3)^{1/4}$. The Kolmogorov constant is $\alpha_E = 0.5$, to an accuracy of 10% (Sreenivasan 1995).

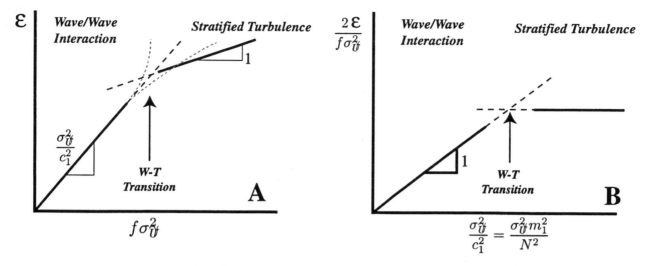

Figure 4: The W-T transition energy defined as the intersection of the wave-wave interaction and stratified turbulence model predictions of ε as a function of the variance of horizontal velocity, σ_U^2. The coordinates are log-log. Grey dashed lines show possible extrapolation errors near the transition. (A) dimensional (B) nondimensional. c_1 is the phase speed of the lowest mode.

Figure 3B shows the evolution of the vertical wavenumber spectrum with increasing energy as in Fig.2. At the GM level (spectrum A), the internal wave bandwidth, $m_c - m_1$ is large, since $m_c \gg m_1$ and the turbulence bandwidth is small, since m_k is not very much bigger than m_b. With increasing energy (Spectra B-C), the internal wave bandwidth shrinks as m_c approaches m_1 and the turbulence bandwidth increases. The theory fails when m_c and m_1 become comparable so that the internal wave bandwidth becomes small. This will occur at the W-T transition.

5   Results

D'Asaro and Lien (2000b) compute the internal wave energy at which the transitions in wavenumber and frequency spectra occur. They use the quadratic relationship between the internal wave energy and the energy dissipation rate ε from Henyey et al. (1986) as implemented by Polzin et al. (1995). Combining this with the spectral shapes shown above yields our main results: The "wave-turbulence" transition is marked by

- An rms velocity approximately equal to the phase speed of the lowest internal wave mode

- The merging of the internal wave and turbulence spectra near Lagrangian frequency N (Fig. 2)

- The reduction of the internal wave vertical wavenumber bandwidth to a small value (Fig. 3B)

- A change from a quadratic relationship between wave energy and dissipation rate at low energies to a linear relationship at high energies (Fig. 4).

Existing parameterizations of the Lagrangian and Eulerian wavenumber spectral shapes (Figs. 1 and 3), combined with the Polzin et al. (1995) parameterization of dissipation rate predict that all of the above will occur at nearly the same energy. The shape of the Lagrangian and Eulerian spectra (Figs. 1B and 3) may be a useful diagnostic as to whether a given flow is above or below the W-T transition.

The W-T transition is predicted to occur at a lower average dissipation rate and internal wave shear, but similar energy density, in shallow water than in deep water. This occurs because the phase speed of the lowest mode is smaller in shallow water. The open ocean thermocline is likely to remain below the transition, but flow on the continental shelves may often rise above it. The upper atmosphere appears to be close to the transition, judging from the small range of wavenumbers below m_c.

Turbulence parameterization schemes that ignore internal waves will be accurate only for energies above the transition. A crucial question for models of stratified flows is whether the flow is mostly above or mostly below the transition. If it is above, then stratified turbulence models such as (Mellor and Yamada 1982) are appropriate. If not, then internal wave dynamics will be important and the sources, sinks and internal transfers of the internal wave field will need to be modelled.

References

Cairns, J. (1975). Internal wave measurements from a midwater float. *J. Geophys. Res. 80*(3), 299–306.

Calman, J. (1978). On the interpretation of ocean current spectra. II: Testing dynamical hypotheses. *J. Phys. Oceanogr. 8*, 644–652.

Corrsin, S. (1963). Estimates of the relations between Eulerian and Lagrangian scales in large Reynold's number turbulence. *J. Atmos. Sci. 20*, 115–199.

D'Asaro, E. A. and R. C. Lien (2000a). Lagrangian measurements of waves and turbulence in stratified flows. *J. Phys. Oceanogr. 30*(3), 641–655.

D'Asaro, E. A. and R. C. Lien (2000b). The wave-turbulence transition in stratified flows. *J. Phys. Oceanogr. in-press.*

Dillon, T. M. (1982). Vertical overturns: A comparison of Thorpe and Ozmidov length scales. *J. Geophys. Res. 87*, 9601–9613.

Fofonoff, N. P. (1969). Spectral characteristics of internal waves in the ocean. *Deep-Sea Res. 16S*, 59–71.

Gargett, A. E., P. J. Hendricks, T. B. Sanford, T. R. Osborn, and A. J. Williams, III (1981). A composite spectrum of vertical shear in the upper ocean. *J. Phys. Oceanogr. 11*, 1258–1271.

Gregg, M. (1991). The study of mixing in the ocean: A brief history. *Oceanography 4*, 39–45.

Gregg, M. and E. Kunze (1991). Shear and strain in Santa Monica Basin. *J. Geophys. Res. 96*, 16,709–16,719.

Gregg, M. C. (1989). Scaling turbulent dissipation in the thermocline. *J. Geophys. Res. 94*, 9686–9698.

Gregg, M. C., D. P. Winkel, and T. B. Sanford (1993). Varieties of fully resolved spectra of vertical shear. *J. Phys. Oceanogr. 23*, 124–141.

Henyey, F. S., J. Wright, and S. M. Flatté (1986). Energy and action flow through the internal wave field: An Eikonal approach. *J. Geophys. Res. 91*, 8487–8495.

Kunze, E., M. G. Briscoe, and A. J. Williams III (1990). Interpreting shear and strain fine structure from a neutrally buoyant float. *J. Geophys. Res. 95*(C10), 18,111–18,125.

Lien, R. C., E. A. D'Asaro, and G. T. Dairiki (1998). Lagrangian frequency spectra of vertical velocity and vorticity in high-Reynolds number oceanic turbulence. *J. Fluid Mech. 362*, 177–198.

Luyten, P., E. Deleersnijder, J. Ozer, and K. Ruddick (1996). Presentation of a family of turbulence closure models for stratified shallow water flows and preliminary application to the Rhine outflow region. *Cont. Shelf Res. 16*(1), 101–130.

Mellor, G. L. and T. Yamada (1982). Development of a turbulence closure model for geophysical fluid problems. *Rev. Geophys. Space Phys. 20*, 851–875.

Müller, P., G. Holloway, F. Henyey, and N. Pomphrey (1986). Nonlinear interactions among internal gravity waves. *Rev. Geophy. 24*, 493–536.

Müller, P., D. J. Olbers, and J. Willebrand (1978). The IWEX spectrum. *J. Geophys. Res. 83*, 479–500.

Munk, W. H. (1981). Internal waves and small-scale processes. In B. A. Warren and C. Wunsch (Eds.), *Evolution of Physical Oceanography*, pp. 264–291. Cambridge, MA: MIT Press.

Polzin, K., J. Toole, and R. Schmitt (1995). Finescale parameterizations of turbulent dissipation. *J. Phys. Oceanogr. 25*, 306–328.

Sherman, J. and R. Pinkel (1991). Estimates of the vertical wavenumber-frequency spectrum of vertical shear and strain. *J. Phys. Oceanogr. 21*(2), 292–303.

Simpson, J. H., W. R.Crawford, T. P. Rippeth, A. R. Campbell, and J. V. S. Cheok (1996). The vertical structure of turbulent dissipation in shelf seas. *J. Phys. Oceanogr. 26*(8), 1579–1590.

Sreenivasan, K. (1995). On the universality of the Kolmogorov constant. *Phys. Fluids 7*, 2788–2784.

Excitation of Large-Amplitude Internal Waves from a Turbulent Mixing Region

Kathleen Dohan and B. R. Sutherland*

*Mathematical Sciences, University of Alberta, Edmonton, Canada   T6G 2G1

bruce.sutherland@ualberta.ca   http://taylor.math.ualberta.ca/~bruce

1. Introduction

In laboratory experiments, Linden (1975) and E and Hopfinger (1986) examined the deepening of a grid-generated turbulent mixed layer above a stratified fluid. Internal waves were observed to be generated on the scale of eddies at the base of the mixing region. Although the amplitude of the waves could not be determined directly, by comparing their results with mixing in two-layer fluids, E and Hopfinger concluded that the waves were not of sufficiently large amplitude to affect the deepening rate.

In both cases cited above, the experiments were performed in a tank with square horizontal cross-section. Here we report on experiments performed in a tank with large aspect ratio. As a consequence of this geometry mean circulations develop in the mixing region that excite relatively large amplitude internal wave modes on the scale of the tank.

2. Experimental Set-up

Experiments are performed in an acrylic tank of cross-sectional area 9.7×47.5 cm and depth 49 cm. The horizontal cross-section has a much higher aspect ratio than conventional experiments performed in tanks with square cross-sections. A metal mixer is placed 5 cm from the top of the tank, and 3 cm below the level of the water. The mixer is composed of a square grid of cylindrical bars of diameter 0.6 cm spaced 3.2 cm apart. The stroke length of the grid is set at 1 cm with a stroke frequency of 7 Hz.

The experimental set-up is shown schematically in Fig. 1. The tank is initially filled with uniformly salt-stratified water using the standard "double-bucket" technique. In a range of stratified fluid experiments the buoyancy frequency, $N = -(g/\rho_0)d\bar{\rho}/dz$, is as low as 0.3 and as large as $1.4\,\mathrm{s^{-1}}$.

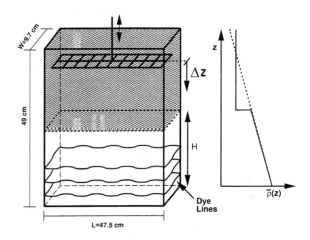

FIGURE 1: The experimental set-up and the corresponding initial (dashed line) and final (solid line) density profile. The shaded region of the tank represents the turbulent mixing region.

To visualize the internal waves, while the tank is being filled Rhodamine dye is added to mark three isopycnal layers. The turbulent region is visualized using pearlescent dye which is injected along the top surface of the tank. The particles align themselves in the direction of strong shear and brightly reflect any incident light. The tank is illuminated from the short side of the tank by a bank of fluorescent lights. A digital camera records the full field of motion through the wide side of the tank and the images are analyzed for both the turbulence characteristics and the internal wave motions with the use of the image processing software, DigImage (Dalziel 1993).

3. Theory

In the analysis of experiments, the characteristics of the turbulent mixing region and the internal waves beneath it are studied separately.

The characteristics of turbulent eddies are

determined in terms of the their time-scale, recorded as a function of depth. If the grid is assumed to supply energy evenly across the horizontal, the only length-scale involved in the turbulence is distance from the energy source. Dimensional arguments then predict that $\ell \propto \delta z$ where ℓ is the integral length-scale of turbulent eddies and δz is the distance from a virtual origin (Thompson 1969; Thompson and Turner 1975). The experiments of (Thompson and Turner 1975; E and Hopfinger 1986) indicate a linear decay of the root mean square turbulent velocity, u, with distance from the virtual origin such that $u \propto \delta z^{-1}$. Combining these results, the integral time-scale, τ, for homogeneous 3-D turbulence is expected to obey the scaling law

$$\tau \propto z^2 \qquad (1)$$

The internal waves observed in the experiments typically are a superposition of standing mode. In general, the frequency and wavelength of Boussinesq internal waves are related by the dispersion relation

$$\omega^2 = N^2 \frac{\alpha^2 + \beta^2}{\alpha^2 + \beta^2 + \gamma^2} \qquad (2)$$

where α, β and γ are the along-tank, across-tank and vertical wavenumbers, respectively.

In a bounded domain the range of wavenumbers is limited to a discreet number of modes. Requiring no normal flow out of the bottom or side walls of the tank, the vertical displacement field is given in a co-ordinate system with the origin at the bottom corner of the tank as follows:

$$\xi = A_\xi \cos(\alpha_n x) \cos(\beta_n y) \sin(\gamma_m z) e^{-i\omega t}. \qquad (3)$$

Here A_ξ is the amplitude and the wavenumber components now hold the discreet values

$$(\alpha_n, \beta_m, \gamma_p) = (n\frac{\pi}{L}, m\frac{\pi}{W}, (p+1/2)\frac{\pi}{H}), \qquad (4)$$

with n, m, and p being non-negative integers. Here L and W are the length and width of the tank, respectively, as shown in Fig. 1. The top of the stratified region, at $z = H$, is bounded by a turbulent region. In deriving (3) and (4) it is assumed that the amplitude of the waves with

respect to z is largest at the base of the mixing region.

4. Image Analysis

For time-discretized signals $x(n)$ and $y(n)$, the cross-correlation is defined as a function of shift τ

$$r_{xy}(\tau) = \sum_{n=-\infty}^{\infty} x(n)y(n-\tau), \quad \tau = 0, \pm 1, \pm 2... \qquad (5)$$

A vertical time series, taken at a horizontal location x_0, over the depth of the turbulent region for a typical experiment is given in Fig. 2 a). Because the bright and dark streaks in the image correspond to coherent structures in the turbulence, the local slope around position z_0 and time t_0 provides a measure of the local vertical velocity. To extract this information, a reference signal $F_0(t)$ is chosen as the horizontal section of the time series at z_0. Neighbouring signals $F_n(t)$, at positions z_n, are cross-correlated with $F_0(t)$. The value δt at which there is a peak in the cross-correlation is the time shift of the signal from t_0 to $t_0 + \delta t$ corresponding to the position shift from z_0 to $z_n = z_0 + \delta z$. In this way, a series of $(\delta z, \delta t)$ pairs are assembled, and an average velocity $\delta z / \delta t$ around (x_0, z_0, t_0) is obtained.

In cases for which the mixing region exhibits a mean circulation on a time-scale longer than that of the turbulent eddies, the above method may also be used to measure the velocity of the mean flow (though this analysis is not shown herein). The technique effectively filters the fast time-scale of the eddy motions and so provides an efficient method for determining the mean long-time behaviour of the flow.

The width along the time axis of a bright feature in a time series measures the duration of that motion. A time-scale of the motions in the turbulent flow at a position (x_0, z_0) is defined as the rate of de-correlation of the signal $F_0(t)$

$$T = \left| \frac{dR_{FF}(\tau)}{d\tau} \right|^{-1} \quad at \ \tau = 0 \qquad (6)$$

where $F_0(t)$ is the signal taken from a time series as described above, and R_{FF} is the normalised autocorrelation of F.

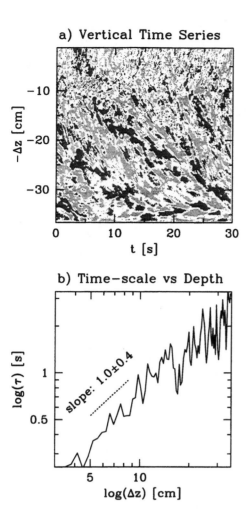

a) Vertical Time Series

b) Time-scale vs Depth

slope: 1.0±0.4

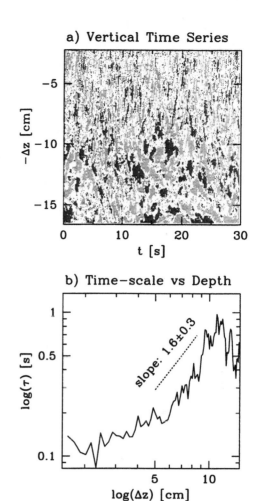

a) Vertical Time Series

b) Time-scale vs Depth

slope: 1.6±0.3

FIGURE 2: Time-scale results for a homogeneous fluid experiment. a) The vertical time series of the turbulence, taken one-third of the horizontal distance from the side wall. Δz is the distance from the midplane of the grid. b) Log-log plot of eddy time-scales τ as a function of Δz. The dashed line is the best-fit line through the plot between $\Delta z = 5.0\,\mathrm{cm}$ and $8.5\,\mathrm{cm}$. The line is offset above the data.

A similar method to determine the horizontal length-scale for turbulence at a position (z_0, t_0).

5. Results

a. Mixing Region Analyses

The time-scale analyses reported upon here is given for three distinct experiments: mixing in homogeneous, weakly stratified and strongly stratified fluid. As evident by observing the experiment in motion and by cross-correlation analyses (not shown) an pronounced mean circulation is observed in the homogeneous fluid experiments. The circulation consists of two

FIGURE 3: As in Fig. 2, for a weakly stratified experiment with $N = 0.5 \pm 0.1\,\mathrm{s}^{-1}$.

counter-rotating vortices with vorticity vectors directed out of the long side of the tank. The circulation fills the depth of the tank down to 40 cm from the grid.

Fig. 2 shows the results of the time-scale analyses on a vertical time series for a homogeneous fluid experiment. Fig. 2b is a log-log plot of the dependence of the time-scale, τ on the distance from the mixer, Δz. The vertical time series on which analyses were performed were taken 17 cm from the left wall. The duration for the time series is chosen to be 30 s, sufficiently long to gather adequate statistics but short enough to resolve the small-scale structures.

Over the range $\Delta z = 5.0\,\mathrm{cm}$ to $8.5\,\mathrm{cm}$, the best-fit line through the log-log plot has slope of 1.0 ± 0.4,

The same time-scale analysis is applied to a

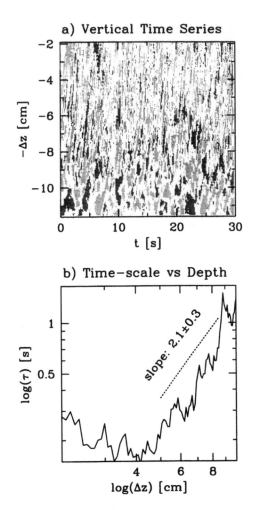

a) Vertical Time Series

b) Time-scale vs Depth

slope: 2.1±0.3

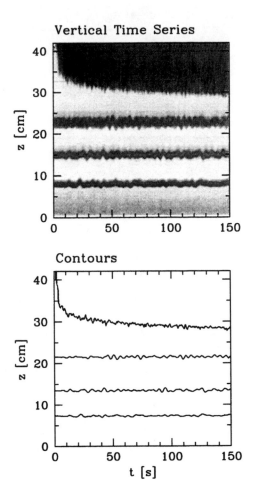

Vertical Time Series

Contours

FIGURE 4: As in Fig. 2, for a strongly stratified experiment with $N = 1.4 \pm 0.1\,\mathrm{s}^{-1}$.

FIGURE 5:
a) Vertical time series for the strongly stratified experiment taken one-third of the tank width from the side wall, covering both the turbulent region and the internal wave region. b) Contours taken of the vertical time series. The top contour traces the deepening of the base of the mixing region, and the bottom three contours are the vertical displacements of the three isopycnal layers marked by dye lines.

weakly stratified experiment in which the buoyancy frequency is $N = 0.5\,\mathrm{s}^{-1}$. The results are given in Fig. 3. The vertical time series in Fig. 3a) covers the vertical extent of the turbulent mixing region which deepened to 16.4 cm from the mixer. The logarithmic plot in Fig. 3b) shows that there exists a relation between the turbulence time-scale and the distance from the mixer, but this persists only for a small distance in the turbulent region. There is some variability in the data close to the mixer due to the jets generated by the ladder configuration. The slope of the best-fit line through $\Delta z = 5.0\,\mathrm{cm}$ to $\Delta z = 8.5\,\mathrm{cm}$ is 1.6 ± 0.3.

In the strongly stratified fluid experiments The depth of the mixing region is less than 11.4 cm over the duration of the experiment so that the ratio of width to depth of the mixing

region is approximately 1 : 1. The mean circulation observed in the homogeneous fluid experiments does not occur in the strong stratified case.

Fig. 4 shows the strongly stratified time-scale analysis results when the buoyancy frequency is $N = 1.4\,\mathrm{s}^{-1}$. Again there exists a dependence of time-scale on distance from the mixer in the centre of the turbulent region but the best-fit line taken through the previous region has a slope of 2.1 ± 0.3.

b. Internal Wave Analyses

Vertical time series are used to measure the vertical motions of the internal waves generated by the turbulence in the underlying stratified region. Fig. 5a shows a vertical time series over 150 s of the strongly stratified experiment. The vertical motions are tracked by the three dye lines at isopycnal layers with mean vertical positions 7.5, 13 and 22 cm above the bottom of the tank. Both the deepening of the mixed layer and the vertical motion of the base of mixing region are clearly seen in a time series. Fig. 5b shows the corresponding contours taken of the dye lines and the base of the mixing region.

Each contour in Fig. 5b is Fourier transformed and from this the time-averaged amplitude is determined as a function of frequency. The results determined from the strongly stratified experiment are shown in Fig. 6. The time-averaged amplitudes are found to be an order of magnitude smaller than the maximum displacement observed during the transient excitation of large-amplitude waves.

The base of the mixing region exhibits a broad band of frequencies including those well above the buoyancy frequency. The excitation frequencies are filtered by the allowed motions in the stably stratified region. In Fig. 6b amplitudes are peaked at distinct frequencies and there is relatively little energy in motions with frequencies greater than N.

The largest peaks occur for frequencies close to N near the base of the mixing region. Interestingly, at mid-depth, the most significant motions occur for smaller frequencies, corresponding to modes with more complex vertical structure.

The vertical dashed lines in Figs. 6b-d indicate the predicted frequencies of modes with wavenumbers given by equation (4) such that $(n, m, p) = (1, 0, 0)$, $(2, 0, 0)$, and $(1, 0, 1)$. The diagnostic indicates that the peak may be associated with mode with more complex vertical structure than that with $p = 0$. Further analyses are required to elucidate these dynamics.

Comparing the amplitudes of the waves in a range of experiments, it is found that the waves are larger amplitude in fluid with weaker stratification. This result is not obvious. Though weaker stratification can support larger ampli-

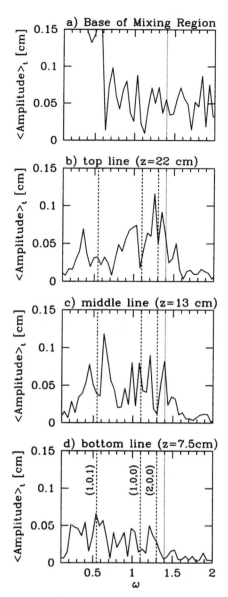

FIGURE 6: Average amplitudes as a function of frequency, as determined from power spectra of time series for the four contours shown in Fig. 5b. The vertical dotted line denotes the value of the buoyancy frequency. The three vertical dashed lines indicate the predicted frequencies of the internal wave modes as specified.

tude waves with the same energy input, the base of the mixing region is also farther from the grid in weakly stratified experiments, and so motions at the base of the mixing region are less energetic.

6. Discussion and Conclusions

Mixing-box experiments have been performed

to study the structure of turbulence and internal waves in a tank whose horizontal cross-section has approximately a 5:1 aspect ratio. If the tank is filled with homogeneous fluid, the time-scale of eddies grows linearly with distance from the grid over a large vertical range. If fluid is stratified, a power law relationship is found between the eddy time-scale and distance from the grid, but only over a limited range. In particular, the scaling behaviour of the eddies is modified over a significant distance from the base of the mixing region, a result that brings into question the suitability of theories that suppose scaling behaviour persists over the whole range between a virtual source and the base of the mixing region.

Furthermore, the power law exponent is different in unstratified and stratified experiments. For the strongly stratified case, in the (albeit small) scaling range, the time-scale varies as the square of the distance from the grid, as predicted for homogeneous turbulence. For the unstratified case, the linear scaling of time-scale with distance from the grid implies that the root mean square velocity u is approximately constant, which is a direct consequence of the observed mean vorticular circulation in the tank.

In stratified fluid experiments, the longest observed eddy time-scale is approximately 1 second. This is an order of magnitude shorter than the buoyancy period of the ambient fluid. Thus the individual eddies are unable to excite internal waves directly. Nonetheless, large-amplitude wave excitation occurs. The amplitudes are large in the sense that the vertical displacement can be as great as 2 percent of the horizontal wavelength. In numerical simulations of propagating waves with these amplitudes, weakly nonlinear effects are found to be non-negligible (Sutherland 2000).

Apparently the mean circulation in the mixing region is responsible in part for the wave excitation. Thus in the weakly stratified experiments, because there exists a mean circulation (as indicated by the 1.6 power law for the eddy time-scales as a function of depth) larger amplitude wave excitation is anticipated. Indeed this is observed.

The mean circulation itself is believed to be established as a consequence of the up-scale transfer of energy in the effective two-dimensional turbulence acting over length-scales greater than the width of the tank.

Though the structure of the waves is certainly affected by the lateral boundaries of the tank, we propose these results may be geophysically relevant. For example, the results may point toward a new mechanism for internal wave generation beneath Langmuir cells where the mean circulation in the mixing region is established by pairs of counter-rotating vortices overlying a thermocline. Work is in progress to investigate this connection.

References

Dalziel, S. B. 1993. Rayleigh-Taylor instability: experiments with image analysis. *Dyn. Atmos. Oceans*, 20:127–153.

E, X. and Hopfinger, E. J. 1986. On mixing across an interface in stably stratified fluid. *J. Fluid Mech.*, 166:227–244.

Linden, P. F. 1975. The deepening of a mixed layer in a stratified fluid. *J. Fluid Mech.*, 71:385–405.

Sutherland, B. R. 2000. Internal wave reflection in uniform shear. *Q.J.R.M.S.*, in press.

Thompson, S. M. 1969. *Turbulent Interfaces Generated by an Oscillating Grid in a Stably Stratified Fluid*. PhD thesis, University of Cambridge.

Thompson, S. M. and Turner, J. S. 1975. Mixing across an interface due to turbulence generated by an oscillating grid. *J. Fluid Mech.*, 67:349–368.

Baroclinic effects in separated boundary layers: a mechanism for intense vertical mixing in the coastal ocean

David M Farmer[1], Richard Pawlowicz[2] and Burkard Bashek[1]

[1]Institute of Ocean Sciences, 9860 West Saanich Road, Sidney, BC, V8L 4B2
[2]Oceanography, Department of Earth and Ocean Sciences, University of British Columbia, 6870 University Blvd., Vancouver, BC CANADA V6T 1Z4
farmerd@dfo-mpo.gc.ca, rich@ocgy.ubc.ca, baschekb@maelstrom.seos.uvic.ca

Boundary layer separation due to flow past headlands and islands generates shear layers accompanied by strong horizontal mixing. Are such flows responsible for vertical mixing of density stratified water masses? Observations of flow past Stuart Island in Haro Strait, British Columbia, shows a well defined frontal structure originating near the western tip of the island and separating the primary tidal current from a back eddy in the island wake. The shear zone begins as an almost vertical but unstable vortex sheet. Instabilities form a sequence of eddies which subsequently grow and merge to form a spreading shear zone. Approximately 4km downstream of the separation this lateral spreading of the shear zone is inhibited by a baroclinic effect. Horizontal transverse density gradients across the shear zone exist as a result of differential mixing of the stratified water passing around each end of the island. The horizontal gradients cause the shear zone to tilt and stretch. The rate at which the interface tilts on its passage from its origin to the active zone appears consistent with a simple loch exchange model viewed as a two-dimensional process orthogonal to the shear zone and advected downstream at the speed of the tidal current. As the interface tilts the shear zone is stretched, generating intense circulation, whirlpools and vertical motions. Broad regions of upwelling alternate with narrow downdraughts characterised by persistent vertical currents of order $0.5ms^{-1}$. Even in calm conditions, small waves on the turbulent air-sea interface break and inject bubbles that are observed acoustically to penetrate to depths of 120m. Further downstream, the shear zones diffuses laterally. It is proposed that this is a common mechanism along irregular coasts subject to strong tidal currents which can mix and otherwise modify water masses exchanged between semi-enclosed basins and the open ocean.

Thermal Circulation in Complex Terrain: A Case of *Urban Fluid Mechanics*

By

H.J.S. Fernando, M. Princevac, J.C.R. Hunt and E. Pardyjak
Environmental Fluid Dynamics Program/ Mechanical & Aerospace Engineering
Arizona State University, Tempe, AZ 85287-9809

1. Abstract:

Studies of flow and dispersion in areas of large human settlements (cities) have received increased attention, particularly in light of recent awareness on improving the "Livability" of cities. These studies are encapsulated in an emerging research area called "Urban Fluid Mechanics," which include the study of urban air and watersheds encompassing supply, transport, cleanliness, health effects and management of air and water resources in cities. An important example of Urban Fluid Mechanics is the thermal (atmospheric) circulation within cities located in complex terrain that are prone to serious air pollution problems. Some experimental and theoretical studies carried out to investigate such thermally driven flows in the absence of background (synoptic) winds are summarized in this paper.

2. Introduction:

Many large human settlements are located in areas abutting transportation corridors built upon waterways, which are characterized by mountains, valleys and escarpments (referred to as complex terrain). These areas are typically sheltered from background (synoptic) wind systems, causing their micrometeorology to be dependent on local thermal forcing. The most prominent thermally driven winds in complex terrain include up-slope (anabatic) and up-valley winds during the day and down-slope (katabatic or drainage) and down-valley winds at night. The so-called valley winds blow parallel to the longitudinal axis of a valley whilst slope winds occur along the side slopes. Previous studies indicate that the valley winds are driven by horizontal (hydrostatic) pressure gradients that are built up by the variation of temperature within or at the edge of the valley (McKee & O'Neil 1989). Conversely, the nocturnal (radiative) cooling of a slope produces dense down-slope (also known as *katabatic or drainage*) winds whereas the daytime heating produces up-slope (or *anabatic*) winds. In the absence of synoptic flow, the local flow in complex terrain cities such as Phoenix, Arizona can be recurring and largely dependent on the thermal forcing on the topography; see Figure 1. Laboratory, theoretical, field experimental and numerical simulation programs are being carried out at Arizona State University to investigate flow phenomena characteristic of complex-terrain airsheds, and this paper summarizes some preliminary laboratory and theoretical results obtained during these research efforts.

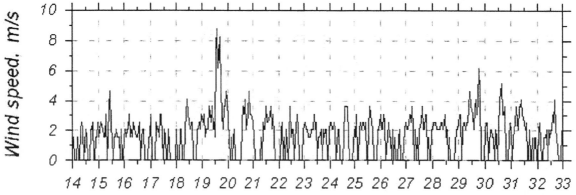

Figure 1: Hourly atmospheric surface layer wind observations made during 19 days in the Phoenix Sky Harbor International Airport during January 14 to February 2, 1998, at a height of 9.14m.

3. Background

Numerous studies have been carried out to investigate flows in complex topographies, which are reviewed in Thyer (1966), Atkinson (1981), Vergeiner & Dreiseitl (1987), Blumen (1990), Whiteman (1990), Ruffieux (1995) and Baines & Condie (1998). Perhaps the most studied case is the katabatic flows along sloping boundaries, for which many different approaches have been used. In the approach of Manins & Sawford (1979), full two-dimensional unsteady equations for momentum and potential temperature were integrated in the direction normal to the slope over a large depth H to obtain layer-averaged equations, for which solutions were obtained using closure assumptions. The layer averaging reduces the complexity of equations and yields representative along-slope velocity (U), buoyancy (Δ), length scale (h) of the flow and the net inflow velocity $(-w_H)$ into the current, as defined by

$$Uh = \int_0^H u\,dn \qquad\qquad U^2 h = \int_0^H u^2 dn\,;$$

$$U\Delta h = \int_0^H ug'dn\,; \qquad\qquad S_1\Delta h^2 = 2\int_0^H g'n\,dn\,; \qquad (1)$$

$$S_2\Delta h = \int_0^H g'dn \qquad\qquad \int_0^H w\,dn = w_H.H - S_3 w_H h\,.$$

Here (u,w) are the along-slope (s) and normal (n) velocities, $g' = (\theta_a - \theta)g/\theta_r$ the reduced gravity, g the gravity, θ the potential temperature, θ_a the ambient potential temperature and θ_r a reference temperature. This procedure, however, introduced new unknowns, the "shape" factors S_1, S_2 and S_3, and the "surface" shear stress $-\overline{(u'w')}_0$ or the drag coefficient C_D [defined as $-\overline{(u'w')}_0 = C_D U^2 = u_*^2$, where u_* is the friction velocity] which needed to be parameterized in modeling. The relevant forcing parameter is the "surface" buoyancy flux $B = g[(R_H - R_0) - Q]/\rho_r C_p\theta_r$, where C_p is the specific heat at constant pressure, ρ_r the reference density, $R_H - R_0$ is the radiation divergence over the height H (which is zero for laboratory experiments) and Q is the "surface" heat flux. Hitherto, S_1, S_2 and S_3 have been estimated either using rudimentary field observations (Manins & Sawford 1979; Horst & Doran 1986) or laboratory observations of gravity currents on simple slopes (Ellison & Turner 1959).

By using simple parameterizations for C_D and $-w_H = EU$, where $E = E(Ri)$ is the entrainment coefficient and Ri is the relevant Richardson number $Ri = h\Delta\cos\alpha/U^2$ of the flow, where, α is the slope angle, Manins & Sawford (1979) obtained stationary solutions for the case of neutrally stratified ($N = 0$) ambient fluid. The variation of h, U and Δ with the stream-wise coordinate s was proposed to be

$$h = C_1(\sin\alpha)^{2/3}s \qquad U = C_2(\sin\alpha)^{2/3}(\overline{B}s)^{1/3} \qquad \Delta = C_3(\sin\alpha)^{-8/9}(\overline{B}^2/s)^{1/3}, \qquad (2)$$

where C_1, C_2 and C_3 are constants and $\overline{B}$ is the slope-averaged value of B. On the other hand, simple solutions could not be found for the unsteady case and for buoyancy frequency $N \neq 0$.

The work reported on up-slope flows, on the other hand, is much less. Hunt et al. (2000) developed theoretical models for up- and down-slope winds over a simple slope, driven by surface heating. The (potential) temperature structure of the along-slope flow was considered as $\theta = \theta_a(s, n = h)$ $+ \Delta\theta(s,n)$, where $\theta_a(s,n)$ here is the ambient temperature above the up-slope flow of thickness h. Near the surface, the temperature varies rapidly, above which the temperature is nearly uniform up to the top of the layer. The steady case with $\Delta\theta(s,0) = \Delta\theta_s$ was analyzed using a three-layer analysis (Figure 2), consisting of a surface layer [S] near the ground of thickness h_s, a middle layer [M] in which $h_s < n < h - h_I$ and an inversion layer [I] where $h - h_I < n < h$.

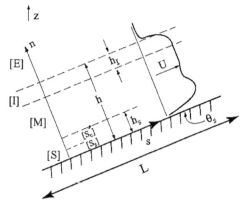

Figure 2: Flow configurations considered by Hunt et al. (2000)

Region [S] was subdivided into two layers, a region $[S_S]$ dominated by the surface shear stress τ_0 and $[S_C]$ dominated by the convective velocity $w_* = (|\bar{B}|h)^{1/3}$, with the demarcation height being the Monin-Obukhov length scale $n = L_*$. Using the equations of motion for each sublayer of [S]; assuming self-similar profiles of mean velocity in [M], determined by a balance between the inertia and shear stress gradients; and accounting for the entrainment of external fluid into [I] from the outer layer [E] determined by buoyancy, inertia and shear stresses, an expression was derived for the layer-averaged steady up-slope flow in [M] using an asymptotic analysis, viz.

$$U_M = \lambda_u \alpha^{1/3} w_*, \tag{3}$$

where λ_u is a constant. The driving term for the entire flow was the horizontal buoyancy gradient (baroclinicity). By estimating $\lambda_u \sim 10$, the typical up-slope wind speed in the Phoenix valley was predicted as 2m/s, which agreed well with the observations of Ellis et al. (2000).

The model was extended to the case of ground cooling, with $\Delta\theta(s,0) = \Delta\theta_0(1 - t / \Delta t_0)$, where t is the time and Δt_0 is the time scale of cooling, to study the evening transition from up-slope to down-slope flow. The solution for U_M at the transition took the form

$$U_M{}^2 = U_0^2 \left(1 - \frac{\alpha\Delta b_0 s}{U_0^2} - \beta \frac{s^2}{2} \right), \tag{4}$$

where U_o is the initial layer-averaged velocity corresponding to the buoyancy jump of $\Delta b_0 = g\Delta\theta_0 / \theta_r$ and $\beta = 2\alpha\Delta b_0 / \Delta t_0 U_0^3$. Further analysis of this solution shows that the transition from heating to cooling is associated with a *front*, which forms at a distance,

$$s_f \approx \sqrt{\frac{2}{\beta}\left(\frac{\Delta t_0 U_0^3}{\alpha \Delta b_0}\right)^{1/2}} . \qquad (5)$$

For $s < s_f$, the entire flow moves up slope and at $s > s_f$ the katabatic flow is initiated near the ground while the flow aloft still flowing up slope! The front is not stationary and propagates until the entire slope surface is covered by the drainage flow.

4. Experiments

To investigate the nature of thermally driven flows in complex topographies and to verify the theoretical ideas presented above, a series of laboratory experiments were carried out with $N = 0$ and using two generic topographies. These include a simple (variable) slope and a two-dimensional sinusoidal basin. Provisions were made so that the bottom surfaces of the apparatuses can be subjected to periodic heating and cooling or can be maintained at a fixed temperature using a computer-controlled heat exchanger. Since katabatic flows found in laboratory settings tend to be laminar, some artificial stirring of the bottom was introduced to enhance turbulence, as was done by Noh & Fernando (1992); artificial roughness elements were attached to the slope bottom and the entire plane was oscillated with a specified frequency. Rakes of thermistors traversing perpendicular to the sloping walls were used to determine the temperature structure and standard digital particle tracking velocimetry based on DigImage software was used for velocity measurements.

In the katabatic flow experiments, the cooling of the ground was first introduced and the flow was allowed to establish (which typically took 30-45 minutes). Thereafter, temperature and velocity profiles were measured and were used to evaluate the profile factors S_1, S_2 and S_3 defined in (1). These measurements are shown in Figure 3, which shows that at least S_1 and S_2 can be considered as constants at large Ri; this is a very useful result in the context of katabatic flow modeling. The data for S_3 are rather scattered, which can be attributed to the difficulty of evaluating S_3 via measurements of various governing terms in (1).

The transition between up-slope flow and down-slope flow was also of interest, given the theoretical prediction that the transition should be accompanied by the formation of a front. Although this new flow phenomenon is evident in the field observations of Keon (1982) and Papoudopoulous & Helmis (1999), it was not recognized and hence no attempt was made to identify the phenomenon. Therefore, a series of experiments were conducted in the basin-shaped tank by first heating the tank and then cooling it to impose a smooth temperature cycle. Figure 4 shows a sequence of photographs taken during this transition. Note the initial along-slope flow and then the formation of a stagnant region in the domain during cooling. Above the stagnation region, the katabatic downward flow can be seen whereas below the region the flow is still up the slope. The flow in the stagnation region is characterized by rapid overturning, much the same way as the frontal region of a gravity current; the vertical thickness in the present case, however, is comparatively larger. Flow visualization studies and measurements show that the turbulence (and hence vertical mixing) in the overturning region is intense.

5. Conclusions

This paper presented some preliminary results of an on-going research program to study thermally driven flows in complex terrain. The focus herein was on laboratory results, but the research program includes theoretical, numerical and field experimental components. Some of the model parameters used in integral models of katabatic flows were evaluated using laboratory results. Experimental support for the new theoretical prediction that the transition from up-slope to down-slope flows is associated with the formation of frontal zones characterized by intense vertical mixing was also presented. Many other new results are available, which will be published elsewhere.

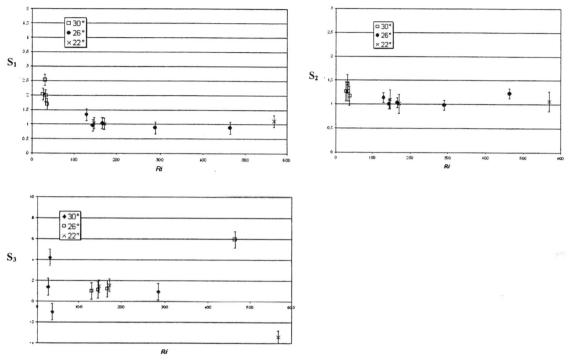

Figure 3: Measurements of parameters S_1, S_2 and S_3 in (1) using laboratory experiments performed by cooling a simple slope. The results are presented as a function of Ri.

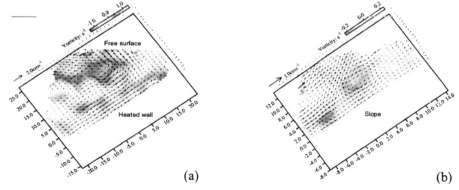

(a)   (b)

Figure 4: (a) The up-slope flow observed during the heating period of the basin-shaped topography ($\overline{B} = 6.13 \cdot 10^{-7} \mathrm{m^2/s^3}$) (b) The frontal structure observed during the transition period wherein the topography was cooled gradually.

6. Acknowledgements

Urban Fluid Mechanics research at Arizona State University is funded by the Environmental Meteorology Program of the Department of Energy (under the VTMX Program) and the National Science Foundation. Also Marko Princevac was supported by a fellowship from the "Graduate Assistance in Areas of National Need" Program of the Department of Education.

7. References

Atkinson, R.W. 1981: Mesoscale atmospheric circulations, Academic Press Inc., London, 495pp.

Baines, P.G. and Condie, S. 1998: Observations and modeling of Antarctic down slope flows: a review. In: Ocean, Ice and Atmosphere: Interactions at the Antarctic Continental Margin (Eds: S. S. Jacobs & R. Weis), *AGU Antarctic Research Ser.* **75**, 29-49.

Blumen, W. (Ed.) 1990: Atmospheric processes over complex terrain. *Meteor. Monogr.* **23** (45). *Am. Meteor. Soc.*, Boston, MA.

Ellis, A.W., Hilderbrandt, M.L., Thomas, W. and Fernando, H.J.S. 2000b: A case study of the climatic mechanisms contributing to the transport of lower atmospheric ozone across metropolitan Phoenix area. *J. Climate Res.* (Accepted for publication).

Ellison, T.H. and Turner, J.S. 1959: Turbulent entrainment in stratified flows. *J. Fluid Mech.* **6**, 423-448.

Horst, T.W. and Doran, J.C. 1986: Nocturnal drainage flow on simple slopes. *Boundary- Layer Meteor.* **34**, 263-286.

Hunt, J.C.R., Fernando, H.J.S., Grachev, A.A., Pardyjak, E.P., Berman, N.S. and Anderson, J. 2000: Slope –Breezes and weak air movements in a wide enclosed valley. Submitted to *J. Atmos Sci.*

Keon, T.L. 1982: Recurrent nocturnal temperature rises in the Salt River valley, Arizona. Master of Arts Thesis, Arizona State University, May 1982, 90p.

Manins, P.C. and Sawford, B.L.1979: A model of katabatic winds. *J. Atmos. Sci.* **36**, 619-630.

McKee, T.B. and O'Neal, R.D. 1989: The role of valley geometry and energy budget in the formation of nocturnal valley winds. *J. Appl. Meteor.* **28,** 445-456.

Noh, Y. and Fernando, H.J.S. 1992: The motion of a buoyant cloud along an incline in the presence of boundary mixing. *J. Fluid Mech.* **235**, 557-577.

Papadopoulous, K.H. and Helmis, C.G. 1999: Evening and morning transition of katabatic flows. *Boundary-Layer Meteor.* **92**, 195-227.

Ruffieux, D. 1995: Climatology and meteorology in complex terrain. *Theor. Appl. Climatol.* **52**, 1-134.

Thyer, N.H. 1966: A theoretical explanation of mountain and valley winds by a numerical method. *Arch. Meteor. Geophys. Bioklin.* **A15**, 318-348.

Vergeiner, I. and Dreiseitl, E. 1987: Valley winds and slope winds-observations and elementary thoughts. *Meteor. Atmos. Phys.* **36**, 264-286.

Whiteman, D.C. 1990: Observations of thermally developed wind systems in mountainous terrain. Atmospheric Process Over Complex Terrain. *Meteor. Monogr.* **23** (45), 5-42. *Am. Meteor. Soc.,* Boston, MA.

Laboratory Studies of Plume Interactions with Stratified Shear Interfaces

Andrew Folkard

Hydrodynamics & Sedimentology Laboratory, Institute of Environmental & Natural Sciences, University of Lancaster, Lancaster LA1 4YB, United Kingdom
E-mail: a.folkard@lancaster.ac.uk

1. Abstract

Plumes of fluid are often observed in nature to interact with stratified shear interfaces (i.e. quasi-discontinuous stratified shear layers). Examples of this include chimney plumes hitting inversion-layer ceilings; sewage plumes impinging on unmixed fresh/saltwater interfaces; descending plumes of cold water formed at ice-leads interacting with the oceanic thermocline; and volcano plumes interacting with atmospheric interfaces. Laboratory studies of these phenomena have not previously been described in the literature, and as a result there is a lack of understanding regarding their morphology and dynamics. Thus a novel set of experiments are described here in which the behaviour of a turbulent plume is observed in the presence of a two-layer ambient. The lower layer, into which the plume initially emerges, is quiescent and at a relatively-high density. The upper layer is forced to flow uniformly across the top of the lower layer, and has a lower density. The flow of the resulting plume is characterised by (a) the extent to which it penetrates into the upper layer; and (b) the nature of its extension upstream and downstream at the interface. The behaviour is found to be governed by three non-dimensional parameters: the initial gradient Richardson number of the interface Ri_G, the ratio of the upper layer crossflow speed to the speed of the plume when it first impinges on the interface U_F/U_{PI}, and the ratio of the plume Monin-Obukhov lengthscale to the lower layer depth L_{MO}/H_L. Regime diagrams are presented showing the effect of changing these parameters on the plume flow and quantitative relationships are determined. Further details of this work are given in Folkard (2000).

2. Introduction

Turbulent fluxes of momentum and buoyancy from point sources - forced plumes - are common in environmental and industrial fluids, and have been of research interest for many years (e.g. List, 1982). Particular applications lie in predicting the dispersion of marine discharges and atmospheric emissions, and in modelling oceanic deep water convection, volcanic plumes, and convection in the Earth's liquid core.

Often in nature, plumes interact with interfaces between ambient fluid layers whose density and velocity characteristics both differ. These are referred to herein as stratified shear interfaces. A non-exhaustive list of examples includes cases in estuaries and coastal waters, where sewage effluent plumes impinge on fresh/saltwater interfaces; in the troposphere, where chimney plumes impinge on the ceilings of inversion layers; and at larger scales in the atmosphere where volcanic plumes strike interfaces. The dynamics of these interactions vary greatly, but the generic concept of a plume interacting with a stratified shear interface is common to all.

Studies of stratified shear interfaces in the absence of plumes abound in the literature. Originally, these were aimed at deducing a universal entrainment law (see Fernando, 1991, for a review) and have more recently been concerned with determining the way in which the presence of the interface alters the spectrum of turbulent energy above or below it (e.g. Cortesi et al, 1999; Atsavapranee and Gharib, 1997). The current work develops that cited above in a novel direction by studying a physical laboratory model of the interaction of a buoyant plume with a stratified shear layer. It is intended as an initial, largely-descriptive study which deduces the evolution of macroscopic characteristics of the plume, and relates them to parameters which describe the initial conditions and ambient flow field.

3. Apparatus and Procedure

The experiment was carried out in a perspex tank as shown in Figure 1. The tank was filled with a two-layer density stratified fluid, the interface being coincident with the dividing plate. An initial density profile was recorded, and the upper layer was then set in motion by pumping fluid through the cross-flow inlet and outlet pipes. The initial transient flow was allowed to pass and a steady-state flow set up. The plume fluid was then allowed to enter the tank. Each experimental run continued until the downstream nose of plume fluid reached the end of the tank. Four independent parameters were varied between runs: the densities of the two ambient layers ρ_U and ρ_L, the upper layer flow rate U_F, and the pressure head driving the plume Δh. In each run, only one of these parameters was varied from a standard set of values.

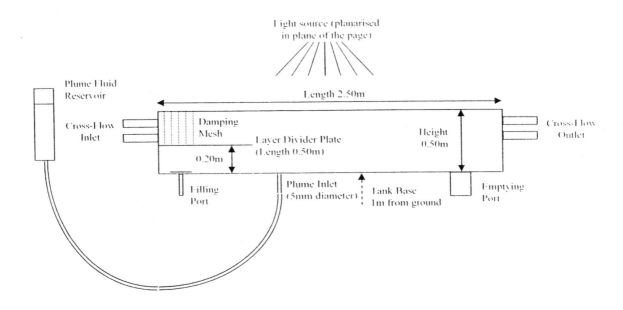

Figure 1: Schematic diagram of experimental apparatus. The tank width (normal to the page) is 0.35m.

4. Results

The plume fluid initially rose through the lower layer about a vertical centre line. On reaching the interface, it rose above it for a short distance in an oscillatory fashion. Thereafter, it typically spread out up and downstream at approximately the level of the interface. Three different configurations of upstream flow were observed. In the first - Category 1 flow - the fluid forms a gravity current which flows steadily along the interface. In the second - Category 2 flow - the upstream nose is attenuated and becomes stationary, suggesting a balance between buoyancy forces driving it upstream and advective forces due to the upper layer cross-flow acting downstream. In the third case - Category 3 flow - the upstream nose is destroyed, and the whole plume turns downstream on reaching the interface.

The downstream flow can also be categorised into three different cases. The first - Category A - behaves as if there were no upper layer cross-flow, namely flowing as a sharp-nosed gravity current at the approximate depth of the interface. In the second case - Category B - the plume initially barely breaks through the interface. Thus a small volume of plume fluid interacts with the cross-flow and is skimmed off, forming a narrow, advection-dominated ribbon of plume fluid. Thereafter a gravity current similar to that in Category A is formed. However, the quantitative mesaurements of downstream position are determined by the initial ribbon of fluid, hence they differ significantly from those for Category A. In the final case – Category C - the interface is relatively weak, and the plume breaks through it so that most of the plume fluid reaches the upper layer. It then forms a wide, and highly turbulent band of fluid which is advection-dominated.

In the following quantitative discussion, the characteristics of the plume are referred to according to Figure 2. The external parameters which are considered are as follows:

- the initial gradient Richardson number of the interface $Ri_G = \Delta b_{UL} \Delta z_I / U_F^2$. Here, $\Delta b_{UL} = g\Delta\rho_{UL}/\rho_L$ is the buoyancy jump across the interface, where $\Delta\rho_{UL}$ is the density jump across the interface.
- the Monin-Obukhov lengthscale $L_{MO} = (U_P^4 a / \Delta b_{PL}^2)^{1/4}$ where U_P is the initial plume speed, and $\Delta b_{PL} = g\Delta\rho_{PL}/\rho_L$ is the initial buoyancy difference between the plume fluid and the lower layer. This is normalised by the lower layer depth H_L, giving a measure of the extent to which the plume is momentum-dominated or buoyancy-dominated when it impinges on the interface.
- the ratio of the upper layer cross-flow speed U_F to the speed U_{PI} at which the plume hits the interface.

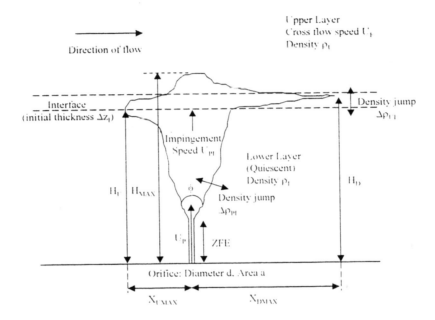

Figure 2: Diagram defining the parameters and symbols used in the description of the plume in the text

4.1. Plume Penetration

Here, penetration is defined as H_{MAX} - H_U (see Fig. 2) and normalised using the initial interface thickness Δz_I, to give the non-dimensional penetration $P^* = P/\Delta z_I$. *A priori* two parameters are expected to cause variations in P^*: Ri_G, which indicates the tendency of the interface to allow penetration; and U_F/U_{PI}. P^* is expected to increase with decreasing Ri_G and decreasing U_F/U_{PI}. Figure 3 shows the results obtained for this parameter. Both expected trends are corroborated by this plot. Furthermore, the data suggest the quantitative relationship $P^* = \mu_1/Ri_G + \kappa_1$ (where $\mu_1 = 0.57 \pm 0.07$ and $\kappa_1 = 1.12 \pm 0.09$) for $U_F/U_{PI} \le 2$. This can be translated into an approximate rule of thumb such that $P^* \sim 1$ when $1/Ri_G = 0$ and increases by ~0.5 for every unit increase in $1/Ri_G$ in the range shown. This relationship will clearly be dependent on the value of the layer Richardson number.

4.2. Upstream Flow

Categories 1, 2, and 3 as defined above can be described qualitatively as "flowing", "attenuated" and "destroyed". The aim here is to identify limitations of the flow regimes in which each type of flow is observed. Their occurrence is considered in terms of $1/Ri_G$, which once again serves to describe the nature of the interface. However, U_F/U_{PI} is not sufficient to distinguish between momentum-dominated and buoyancy-dominated plumes, which will be expected to exhibit different upstream behaviours. Therefore these two types of flow are distinguished using the Monin-Obukhov lengthscale L_{MO} normalised by the depth of the lower layer H_L, as described above. A high value of L_{MO}/H_L indicates that the plume is momentum-dominated when it reaches the interface, and a low value that it is buoyancy-dominated. Thus "flowing" upstream configurations would be expected at low values of L_{MO}/H_L and high values of Ri_G and vice versa. This expectation is borne out and quantified by Figure 4. A similar figure in which L_{MO}/H_L is replaced by U_F/U_{PI} shows the data points interwoven, corroborating the prediction given above that this parameter does not sufficiently distinguish between plumes which will give different flow configurations.

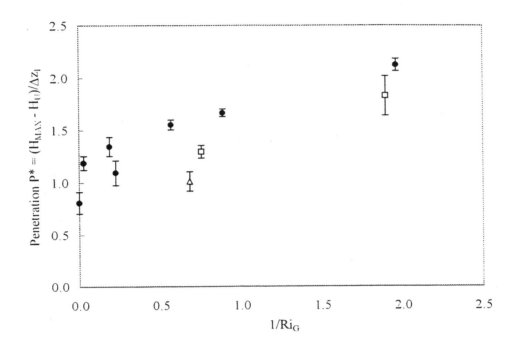

Figure 3: Relationship between Plume Penetration $P*$ and initial gradient Richardson number Ri_G. Note variation with U_F/U_{PI} (filled circles: $U_F/U_{PI} < 2.0$; squares: $2.0 < U_F/U_{PI} < 3.0$; triangles: $U_F/U_{PI} > 3.0$)

4.3. Downstream Flow

Figure 5 shows how the different categories of flow fall into different areas of the parameter space defined by Ri_G and U_F/U_{PI}. The results are as expected in that weak interfaces (the data suggest $Ri_G < \gamma_1$ where $1.0 < \gamma_1 < 1.5$) result in Category C flows, strong interface with relatively weak plume impingement speeds (the data suggest $U_{PI} < \gamma_2 U_F$ where $0.1 < \gamma_2 < 0.15$) results in Category B flows and strong interfaces with stronger plume impingement speeds result in Category A flows.

The appropriate scaling for the downstream flow speed may also be considered. This arises from considering the balance of an advective term $\partial(u^2/2)/\partial x$ with a pressure gradient term $\rho^{-1}\partial p/\partial x$. Integrating this between the interior of a gravity current travelling at U_D, and a moving ambient travelling at U_F, the expression $U_D^2 - U_F^2 = \alpha_1 g'_{UL}\Delta z_I$ emerges where α_1 is a coefficient of proportionality. In order to determine this coefficient, the downstream flow speed U_D is considered for the runs with no upper layer cross-flow, which give a figure of $\alpha_1 = 0.0129$ (that this is much lower than the O(1) value expected may be a result of the relatively crude method of measuring interface thickness leading to an overestimation of Δz_I). Thus the downstream flow speed is normalised by $\sqrt{(U_F^2 + 0.0129\ g'_{UL}\Delta z_I)}$. This is plotted against U_F/U_{PI} in Fig. 6. Rather than remaining at the predicted value of $U_D/(U_F^2+\alpha g'_{UL}\Delta z_I) = 1$,

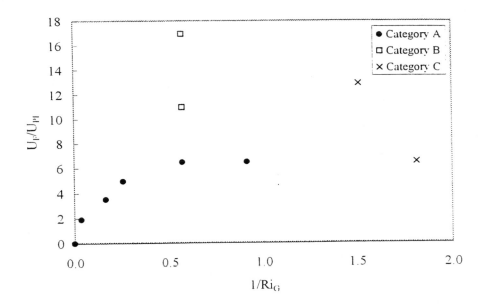

Figure 4: Regime diagram showing parameter values that result in each of the three categories of upstream flow described in the text

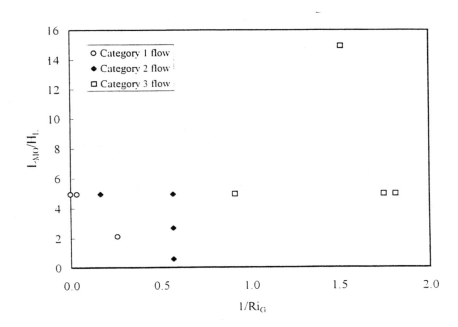

Figure 5: Regime diagram showing parameter values which results in each of the three categories of downstream flow described in the text

the data for Category A follow closely the curve for a pure gravity current. This suggests that, for these cases, the plume fluid flows within the interface, relatively unaffected by the upper layer flow. Category C flows have values close to those for pure advection, confirming that they flow almost fully within the upper layer. Category B flows show intermediate values, which suggest that the thin wisp of fluid which is initially skimmed off these plumes flows further into the upper layer than the Category A flows.

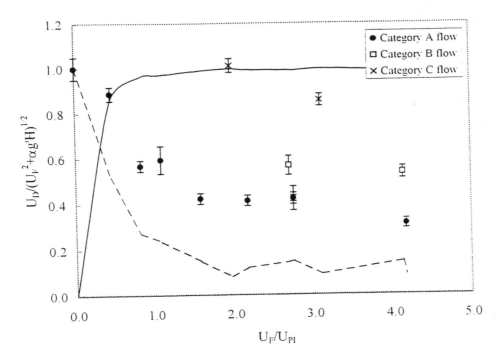

Figure 6: Variation of downstream flow speed U_D with U_F/U_{PI}. U_D is normalised by the value predicted by the model described in the text. Solid line represents pure advection, dashed line pure buoyancy current

5. Discussion

The results obtained provide a bulk, semi-quantitative description of this novel flow configuration. The standard parameter describing the state of the interface, namely the gradient Richardson number Ri_G is found to be one of the dominant factors in determining the nature of the flow observed. The non-dimensional vertical penetration P^* and downstream speed U_D are also shown to be dependent on the ratio of the upper layer cross-flow to the speed at which the plume impinges on the interface, U_F/U_{PI}. In the case of the upstream flow, however, the latter parameter is inappropriate. We suggest that this is because buoyancy driven flows will tend to be driven upstream within the interface more than momentum-driven flows. Here, therefore, we find the flow classified in terms of Ri_G and the normalised Monin-Obukhov lengthscale. The types of upstream and downstream flow do not necessarily coincide. A weak, buoyancy-driven plume (low L_{MO}/H_L, high U_F/U_{PI}) impinging on a relatively strong interface (high Ri_G) would be expected to form a Category 2 flow upstream, and a Category B flow downstream. However, if the plume was similarly weak but momentum driven (high L_{MO}/H_L, high U_F/U_{PI}), it would form the same downstream flow but a destroyed upstream flow (Category 3).

References

Atsavapranee, P, and Gharib, M, 1997, Journal of Fluid Mechanics, 342, 53-86
Cortesi, AB, Smith, BL, Yadigaroglu, G, & Banerjee, S, 1999, Physics of Fluids, 11(1), 162-185
Fernando, HJS, 1991, Annual Review of Fluid Mechanics, 23, 455-493
Folkard, AM, 2000, Fluid Dynamics Research, 26 (6), 355-375
List, EJ, 1982, Annual Review of Fluid Mechanics, 14, 189-212

Multiple Steady States in Natural Ventilation

Joanne M. Holford and Gary R. Hunt

Department of Applied Mathematics and Theoretical Physics, Silver Street,
Cambridge, CB3 9EW, U. K.

1. Abstract

There has been increasing interest in recent years in the natural ventilation of buildings in temperate climates. This method harnesses the forces of buoyancy and ambient wind, bringing advantages of low maintenance costs and energy efficiency. However, careful initial design is necessary to ensure adequate ventilation. In particular, it is necessary to have accurate estimates of the heat fluxes and external pressure variations, and then model the coupling between the flow rate through the building and the stratification within. Over the diurnal timescale it is appropriate for many buildings to consider steady-state flows, in which the rate of heating is balanced by the removal of heat by the ventilation flow.

Laboratory studies, of a single space ventilated by the opposing effects of buoyancy and wind, show that such a steady state is not necessarily unique, but depends on the time history of the flow. The existence of multiple steady states has also been observed in operational heat recovery systems and in numerical ventilation modelling. There are parallels with the thermohaline overturning of the oceans in which surface buoyancy fluxes may, in certain parameter regimes, support one of several overturning patterns. Here we present results from modelling and laboratory experiments in a generic two-storey atrium building, which also supports multiple steady states. Each of the three linked internal spaces has high- and low-level openings, favouring displacement ventilation.

The existence of multiple steady states stems from the possibility of flow reversals through the upper storey, or of stagnant fluid in this storey if it is unheated. Often one possible steady state does not provide adequate ventilation to this storey. Hence, in even a well-designed building, care may be needed in ordering the opening of ventilation pathways as the building heats up, to ensure that the most appropriate steady state is reached and adequate ventilation is obtained.

2. Introduction

Occupied buildings require a supply of fresh air to maintain a comfortable internal environment. In many regions, except for those with hot climates or high pollution levels, the ambient air outside the building is a suitable source of fresh air. The ventilation must be sufficient to prevent a build-up of carbon dioxide or odours. In temperate climates, the ventilation should also remove any excess heat generated by equipment and occupants, and from solar gains.

Traditionally built, compact buildings are ventilated by leakage and through open windows. In modern, large, well-sealed buildings, one ventilation solution is to install air conditioning, but this can be costly to maintain and run. An alternative is to design the building for natural ventilation, so that pressure differences caused by the thermal stratification inside the building (stack pressure), and by any incident wind, drive a flow through the building. An efficient natural ventilation strategy is displacement ventilation, in which the space has inlet and outlet openings separated by as great a vertical distance as possible, in order to maximise the driving force of the stack pressure. We shall concentrate on the ventilation of heated spaces with openings in the floor and ceiling.

Most modelling of natural ventilation has concentrated on steady flows, in which the rate of heat supply to the air inside the building is balanced by the rate of heat removal by the ventilation flow. Linden, Lane-Serff & Smeed (1990) showed that the steady flow driven by a point buoyancy source on the floor produces a two-layer stratification. Ambient air is drawn in through the lower opening and entrained into a rising plume above the point source. The plume supplies a warm upper layer, from which fluid exits out of the upper opening. Studies by Hunt & Linden (2000) of the ventilation of a similar enclosure in an oncoming flow show that this displacement flow is not always attained. If the incident wind reduces the pressure difference between points outside the two openings sufficiently, ambient air can be forced in through the upper opening to mix in the room, while warm air leaves through the lower opening. For a range of wind speeds both this mixing flow and the usual displacement flow can occur, depending on the time history of the flow. The possibility of multiple stable steady flows result from the existence of two possible directions for the flow. Models of convection in a loop, such as Keller (1966), and of the thermohaline ocean circulation, such as Stommel (1961), also show multiple steady flow patterns for some parameter ranges. In common with ventilation flows, the boundary conditions in these models are represented as fluxes rather than as fixed values.

Real buildings are more complex than a single enclosure and comprise many linked compartments. An increasingly common feature of naturally-ventilated buildings is a tall atrium, designed to allow a warm layer of air to build up over a significant height, creating large stack pressures to drive a flow. Hunt and Holford (1998) studied steady displacement flows in an atrium building in which each storey is a single space connected to the ambient at low level and to the atrium at high level. Each compartment of the building can be represented as a generic room which has arbitrary pressures and densities outside the openings. The merging of different flowpaths through these compartments increases the complexity of modelling the flow and introduces the possibility of multiple steady flows.

Studies of natural ventilation often focus on the flow generated by a particular distribution of heat sources. In a real building, this distribution is complex and not usually well-known, although an estimate can often be made of the total heat input. In section 3 we investigate the range of flow rates that can occur in a generic room, for a given heat input. In section 4 we consider the development of mixing flows in the generic room. The range of parameters for which multiple steady flows can occur is investigated. In addition, the dynamics of the transient flow near the stable steady flows can be used to estimate a timescale for the approach to the steady flow. In section 5, the existence of multiple steady ventilation flows in a two-storey atrium building are confirmed by laboratory experiments. Conclusions are drawn in section 6.

3. Bounds on Natural Ventilation Flow Rates Through a Generic Room

Consider a room of height H and cross–sectional area S, with an opening of effective area A_1^* in the floor and another of effective area A_2^* in the ceiling. A constant buoyancy flux B is supplied to the fluid of density $\rho(z,t)$ within the room, and the pressure and density of fluid outside the openings, p_1, p_2, ρ_1 and ρ_2, are specified. Two main assumptions are made. The first is that the volume flow rate Q is unidirectional through both openings, which requires the pressure drop across each opening to be sufficiently large. The second is that the pressure distribution inside the room is hydrostatic, which requires the opening areas to be sufficiently small. We take $Q > 0$ to represent 'forward' flow through the room, as sketched in figure 1.

For forward flow, the assumption of hydrostatic pressure, combined with the pressure-driven flow through the openings, gives

$$(p_1 - p_2) - g\int_0^H \rho \; dz = \rho_0 \frac{Q^2}{A^{*2}}, \tag{1}$$

where ρ_0 is a reference density, A^* is the combined effective area of both openings ($A^{*-2} = A_1^{*-2} + A_2^{*-2}$) and the Boussinesq approximation has been made. For this forward flow to occur, the left-hand side of (1) must be positive. If the left-hand side is negative, the flow is a 'reverse' flow in the opposite direction through both openings. In terms of the buoyancy $b = -g(\rho - \rho_0)/\rho_0$,

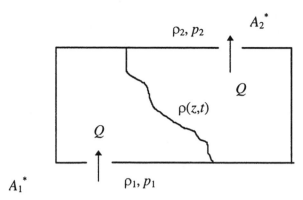

Figure 1 Sketch of the generic heated room supporting a forward ($Q > 0$) ventilation flow

$$Q = A^* \sqrt{\frac{\Delta p}{\rho_0} + M} \qquad \text{and} \qquad Q = -A^* \sqrt{-\frac{\Delta p}{\rho_0} - M} \qquad (2,3)$$

for forward and reverse flow, respectively. Here $p = p_1 - p_2 - \rho_0 g H$ is the excess pressure drop (above hydrostatic pressure in a fluid of density ρ_0) applied between the openings, and $M = \int_0^H b \, dz$ is the total buoyancy per unit cross-sectional area in the room. Conservation of buoyancy gives

$$S\frac{dM}{dt} = B - Q\big[b(H) - b_1\big] \qquad \text{and} \qquad S\frac{dM}{dt} = B + Q\big[b(0) - b_2\big] \qquad (4,5)$$

for forward and reverse flow, where b_1 and b_2 are the buoyancies outside the lower and upper openings, respectively. The locus of possible values for the stratification parameters $b(0)$, $b(H)$ and M for a steady flow are shown in figure 2. For a forward flow, the maximum flow rate (at minimum $b(H)$) is attained with a well-mixed stratification, while the minimum flow rate (at maximum $b(0)$) is attained when the buoyancy is collected in a thin layer at the ceiling. For a reverse flow, both minimum and maximum attainable flow rates correspond to well-mixed stratifications.

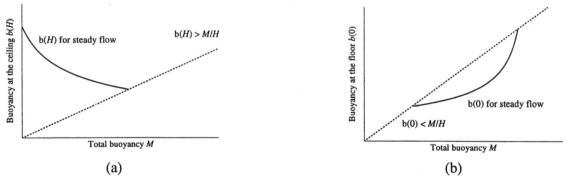

(a)   (b)

Figure 2 Locus of possible steady states of the stratification for (a) forward flow with $p/\rho_0 + M > 0$ and (b) reverse flow with $p/\rho_0 + M < 0$.

This analysis provides a justification for the use of both point source models of buoyancy input, and of well-mixed models, as these represent limiting cases for the flow rate. The analysis confirms the existence of multiple steady ventilation flows due to the reversal of the flow direction, and suggests further opportunity for multiple steady flows if the structure of the stratification can vary. However, these steady flows will only be realised if they are stable to small perturbations in the flow parameters.

4. Multiple Steady Mixing Flows in a Generic Room

In a mixing flow, the buoyancy $b(z,t) = b(t)$ inside the room is uniform in space. We non-dimensionalise using scales appropriate for the forward flow through a room immersed in a homogeneous hydrostatic ambient, which has the steady solution $b = (B^2/A^{*2}H)^{1/3}$. For the transient flow, there are two competing timescales, representing the heating of a room with no ventilation, $T_1 = SHb(0)/B$, and the flushing of a room with no heating, $T_2 = (S/A^*)\sqrt{H/b(0)}$. For the situation with heating and flushing, we expect that the time to approach the steady state does not depend strongly on the initial conditions, and eliminate $b(0)$ to give the timescale $T = (T_1 T_2^2)^{1/3}$. In terms of non-dimensional (overbar) variables, (2) to (5) give

$$\frac{d\bar{b}}{dt} = 1 - (\bar{b} - \bar{b}_1)\sqrt{\bar{b} + \bar{E}} \qquad \text{and} \qquad \frac{d\bar{b}}{dt} = 1 - (\bar{b} - \bar{b}_2)\sqrt{-\bar{b} - \bar{E}} , \qquad (6,7)$$

for forward and reverse flow, respectively. The external non-dimensional parameters are

$$\bar{E} = \left(\frac{A^{*2}}{HB}\right)^{2/3} \frac{\Delta p}{\rho_0} , \qquad (8)$$

the excess pressure difference between the openings, and $\bar{b}_1$ and $\bar{b}_2$, the buoyancies outside the two openings. We will now drop the overbar notation from non-dimensional variables.

Analysis shows that there is always a steady forward flow $b = b_f$, and there may be zero, one or two steady reverse flows $b = b_r$. There are two solutions for b_r if $E < -b_1 - 3/4^{1/3}$. In order to investigate the stability of these steady flows, we consider the evolution of a small perturbation ε away from the buoyancy in the steady flow. For forward flow,

$$\frac{d\varepsilon}{dt} = -\varepsilon\left(\frac{1}{b_f - b_1} + \frac{1}{2(b_f + E)}\right) + O(\varepsilon^2) , \qquad (9)$$

and so the steady flow is stable as both factors in the bracket are positive. However for reverse flow,

$$\frac{d\varepsilon}{dt} = -\varepsilon\left(\frac{1}{b_r - b_2} - \frac{1}{2(-b_r - E)}\right) + O(\varepsilon^2) , \qquad (10)$$

and only the steady flow with smaller b is stable. Figure 3 shows the steady solution curves in b, E space, for the situations $b_2 > b_1$ and $b_2 = b_1 = 0$. Changing the relative buoyancy of the fluid outside the openings only shifts the forward and reverse solutions relative to each other, and two steady stable solutions are always possible for sufficiently negative values of the excess pressure E.

Phase plane analysis can determine which steady flow will be realised in practice from any initial condition, without calculating the flow evolution. In this simple flow, the phase space is one-dimensional, and the unstable reverse solution $b = b_u$ separates the regions of attraction of the two stable fixed points, as shown in figure 4a. If the initial value $b(0) > b_u$, or there is no second solution b_u, then $b(t) \to b_f$, the forward flow. Alternatively, if $b(0) < b_u$, then $b(t) \to b_r$, the reverse flow. Close to the unstable reverse solution, the pressure drop across each opening is small, and exchange flows through the openings alter the structure of the solution, removing the steady forward and unstable reverse solutions.

One important characteristic of the transient evolution is the time taken for the flow to approach the steady state, which may be estimated from the linear stability analysis. From integration of (9) and (10), the close approach to each steady state is approximately $\varepsilon \sim c \exp(-t/\tau)$, for some constant c, where

$$\tau = (b_f - b_1)\left[1 + (b_f - b_1)^3/2\right]^{-1} \qquad \text{and} \qquad \tau = (b_r - b_2)\left[1 - (b_r - b_2)^3/2\right]^{-1} \qquad (11,12)$$

are the timescales for approach to the forward and reverse flow, respectively. The time for the departure of the buoyancy from the steady-state value to reduce by a factor of n, t_{adjust}, is then approximately $t_{adjust} \sim \tau \ln(n)$. When a close approach to the steady state is required, i.e. for n large, t_{adjust} is dominated by motion close to the steady state, and the approximation is good. Figure 4b compares the estimate $\tau \ln(n)$ with calculated values of t_{adjust}, for the time histories shown in figure 4a.

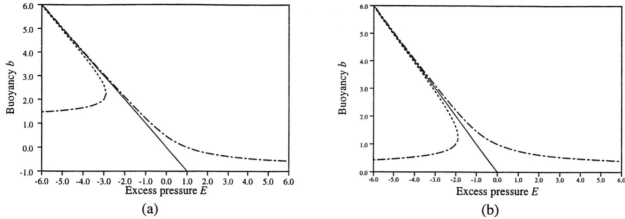

(a)   (b)

Figure 3 Steady solutions in b, E parameter space for two situations: (a) $b_1 = -1$ and $b_2 = 1$, and (b) $b_1 = b_2 = 0$. The dot-dash lines indicate stable solutions, while the dotted line indicates an unstable solution. The solid line indicates the boundary between forward and reverse flow.

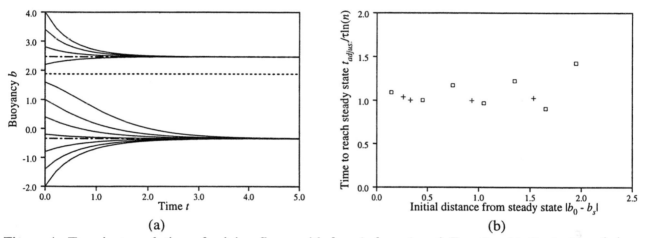

(a)   (b)

Figure 4 Transient evolution of mixing flows with $b_1 = 1$, $b_2 = -1$ and $E = -2$. (a) Evolution of the buoyancy b with time, with the stable (dot-dash) and unstable (dotted) steady states and (b) comparison of the time to reach the larger (+) and smaller (□) steady state t_{adjust} with the timescale $\ln(n)$, for $n = 4$.

5. Laboratory Investigation of a Two-Storey Atrium Building

A model of a simple two-storey atrium building has been used to investigate multiple steady flow patterns in the laboratory. A Perspex model is immersed upside down in a tank of fresh water, and dyed salt solution from a constant head tank is released from a point source to supply a (negative) buoyancy input. The small-scale flow in water has approximate dynamical similarity to a full-scale flow in air. The experiments will be described in an inversion of the lab frame, as for a real heated building. A top-down chimney (essentially a siphon for ambient fluid, see Gage, Hunt & Linden 2000) links the lower levels of each storey to the ambient. Each storey is also connected by a vent in the ceiling to the atrium, which also has a vent in the ceiling.

Figure 5 shows two steady ventilation patterns in which all external parameters, including the opening areas and the supplied buoyancy flux, are the same. Buoyancy is supplied in the lower storey while the upper storey is unheated. In order to reach the flow in figure 5a, all openings were set to the final values before the buoyancy was supplied. As buoyant fluid rose from the lower storey and collected in the atrium, the stack pressure drew ambient fluid through the upper storey. The flow rate through both storeys increased until the steady state was reached. In figure 5b, buoyancy was first supplied with a smaller upper atrium opening. Buoyant fluid rose into the atrium and left the building both through the atrium ceiling and through the upper storey. Once a steady flow was attained, the upper atrium vent area was increased to the same size as in figure 5a. Although the ratio of flow rates through the atrium and upper storey altered, the flow through the upper storey remained reversed.

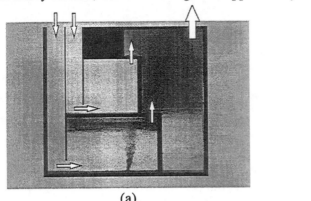 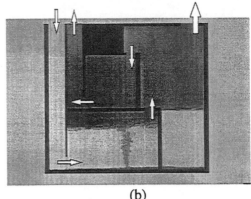

(a)   (b)

Figure 5 Steady ventilation flows in an identical model showing (a) forward and (b) reversed flow in the upper (unheated) storey of a two-storey atrium building.

6. Conclusions

Any multi-compartment linked building can be considered as a set of generic rooms for which the fluid pressures and densities outside the openings are specified by either the external ambient or the conditions in the adjoining rooms. Multiple steady flow patterns can occur due to the possibility of flow reversals in one or more rooms. The range of possible forward and reverse flows for arbitrary stable stratification in a generic room has been investigated. The maximum and minimum flow rates occur when the stratification is well-mixed, or when heat is confined to a thin layer under the ceiling. A stability analysis for the simplest mixing flows gives the region of attraction for each stable steady flow, and can be used to estimate the time for close approach to the steady state. Multiple steady flow patterns are observed, for some parameters, in laboratory experiments in a two-storey atrium building. The time delay between opening different vents can be used to control which steady flow pattern is attained. Ventilation control strategies in real buildings can make use of this feature to try to ensure that unfavourable steady ventilation patterns are avoided.

The authors would like to thank the technical staff D. Page-Croft, B. Dean and D. Lipman. The financial support of the Leverhulme trust (JMH), and the E.P.S.R.C. (GRH) is gratefully acknowledged.

References

Gage, S.A., Hunt, G.R. & Linden, P.F. (2000) Top down ventilation and cooling. *J. Architectural and Planning Research,* in press.

Hunt, G. R. & Holford, J. M. (1998) Top-down natural ventilation of multi-storey buildings. *Proc. of 19th AIVC Conf.: Ventilation Technologies in Urban Areas,* 197 – 205.

Hunt, G. R. & Linden, P. F. (2000) Multiple steady airflows and hysteresis when wind opposes buoyancy. *Air Infiltration Review,* **21**(2), 1 – 3.

Hunt, G. R. & Linden, P. F. (1998) Time-dependent displacement ventilation caused by variations in internal heat gains: application to a lecture theatre. *Proc. of RoomVent '98,* **2**, 203 – 210.

Keller, J. (1966) Periodic oscillations in a model of thermal convection. *J. Fluid Mech.,* **26**, 599 – 606.

Linden, P. F., Lane-Serff, G. F. & Smeed, D. A. (1990) Emptying filling boxes: the fluid mechanics of natural ventilation. *J. Fluid Mech.,* **212**, 300 – 335.

Stommel, H. M. (1961) Thermohaline convection with two stable regimes of flow. *Tellus,* **13**, 224 – 230.

Localized mixing associated with a turbulent region in a stratified shear flow

G. O. Hughes[1,2] and P. F. Linden[1,3]

[1]Department of Applied Mathematics and Theoretical Physics, University of Cambridge, Silver Street, Cambridge CB3 9EW, U.K.
[2]Research School of Earth Sciences, The Australian National University, Canberra, ACT 0200, Australia
[3]Department of Mechanical and Aerospace Engineering, University of California (San Diego), 9500 Gilman Drive, La Jolla, CA 92093-0411, USA
graham.hughes@anu.edu.au, pflinden@mae.ucsd.edu

Abstract

We present results of novel laboratory experiments that examined the mixing due to an isolated two-dimensional turbulent region in a stratified shear flow. The region of turbulence was generated mechanically in a racetrack-shaped tank, which allowed a flow to develop with very small vertical to horizontal aspect ratio. In all experiments the turbulent region expands rapidly at initial times until the height of the region is limited by the ambient stratification. Localized mixing then produces a horizontal density gradient that drives intrusive flows of fluid from the turbulent region into the ambient fluid. A quasi-steady-state is reached where ambient fluid is drawn into the turbulent region at the same rate as mixed fluid escapes from this region. Complete homogenization of fluid in the region was never achieved – the residual stratification during mixing was typically 20-50% of the ambient value. Of the total mechanical energy supplied to the localized turbulence, the proportion used for mixing was in the range 0.18-0.25, which is consistent with those proportions previously found to characterize high efficiency mixing processes in a stratified fluid.

1. Introduction

In density-stratified environments such as the atmosphere and oceans a variety of mechanisms exist that produce localized regions of turbulent overturning and mixing. Typical mechanisms include Kelvin–Helmholtz billows, internal wave breaking and overturning rotors associated with topography. As many geophysical flows are, on average, stable to shear (*i.e.* have Richardson number $Ri > 0.25$), mixing events tend to be both spatially and temporally intermittent. Consequently, it is important to understand the mixing due to localized turbulence in a stratified fluid.

Many previous studies have examined the mixing due to stratified turbulence (see the review by Fernando, 1991, for a summary). A number of studies have considered more specifically the mixing in a localized turbulent region. Fernando (1988) and De Silva & Fernando (1992) studied the evolution of a turbulent region in a linear stratification. The turbulence was produced by vertical oscillations of a horizontal grid which occupied the tank cross-section. De Silva & Fernando (1998) extended their earlier work by oscillating a grid, which spanned the tank width but not the tank length, in a linear stratification. Folkard, Davies & Fernando (1997) also conducted similar experiments but in a rotating tank. The results of most previous laboratory studies have been influenced significantly by tank end-walls. In contrast, Hughes & Linden (2000) studied the evolution of an isolated turbulent region in a quiescent stratified fluid in a racetrack-shaped tank which minimizes these effects.

In this paper, we consider the mixing due to an isolated turbulent region in an ambient shear flow. In §2 we describe the experimental apparatus, followed in §3 by our qualitative observations. Measurements are presented in §4 showing the evolution of the density field due to mixing. Our conclusions are given in §5.

2. Experiments

The experiments were conducted in the stratified-shear-flow tank in the Department of Applied Mathematics and Theoretical Physics (DAMTP) in Cambridge. This tank consists of open channel sections connected in a racetrack geometry, around which the flow is recirculated. Experiments were conducted in the working section, which was 2.4m in length, 20cm in width, and up to 40cm in depth. The working section channel was made of Perspex in order to allow experimental observation. The tank was stratified with salt solution to a depth of 26cm. The density of the salt solution was made to vary linearly with depth using the 'double-bucket' system.

A localized turbulent region was generated using an in-situ spindle fitted with a row of plastic strips in a single plane and supported horizontally across the tank. A stepper motor was used to rotate the spindle, thus agitating fluid in its immediate proximity. The stepper motor movement was controlled from a computer, allowing the nature of the agitation to be easily varied (*i.e.* the speed, direction and agitation angle of the spindle). The plastic strips, 50mm long and 5mm wide, were arranged on the spindle at equal intervals and occupied about 40% of the total area in the plane cross-section. By aligning this plane with the horizontal before the mixer agitation was started, the disturbance to the ambient flow around the spindle was minimized. The mixing generated using this method was close to two-dimensional across the tank width. Attention in these experiments was restricted to studying turbulent regions that were nominally two-dimensional, since the narrow width of the working section in the stratified-shear-flow tank limited the range of three-dimensional effects that could be considered. The ambient flow in the tank was bidirectional and the spindle was placed at the nominal level of zero velocity, 12.6cm above the tank bottom. Therefore, the centroid of the turbulent region remained stationary in the laboratory frame during an experiment. The region of approximately linear shear in the ambient velocity profile extended at least 6cm above and below the spindle centre.

Light-attenuating food dye was introduced to the tank during the filling process so that the dye concentration varied linearly with height in the unperturbed stratification. Perturbations to the density field during the experiments were determined with an image-processing system by measuring the change in attenuation of light passing through the flow (Holford & Dalziel, 1996). A conductivity probe was used to measure the ambient density profile.

Two parameters were varied in the experiments described here. These were the dimensionless mixer rotation speed Ω/N and the Richardson number $Ri = N^2/(du/dz)^2$ that characterizes the ambient shear du/dz, where $N^2 = -g/\rho_0(d\rho_a/dz)$ is the buoyancy frequency of the ambient stratification $d\rho_a/dz$, g is the gravitational acceleration and ρ_0 is a reference density. The dimensionless mixer speed Ω/N was varied between 1.16 and 9.35 and the Richardson number Ri between 7 and 130. The direction of mixer rotation was anticlockwise to match the sense of the ambient shear. Dimensional considerations show that the rate of energy input from the mixer into the turbulence was proportional to $(\Omega/N)^3$.

3. Observations

The evolution of the turbulent region after mixer agitation began (see Figure 1) was qualitatively similar in all experiments. Initially, turbulent eddies entrained surrounding fluid and the region expanded rapidly. A sharp boundary was evident between the turbulent region and the surrounding ambient fluid. Vertical expansion of the localized turbulence was soon suppressed at a height where the largest turbulent eddies could no longer overturn against the stratification. While the mixer continued to supply energy to the turbulence, the limiting height of the region remained approximately constant. For a given Richardson number, this limiting height increased with the dimensionless mixer rotation speed Ω/N. In the absence of any imposed shear, the initial region of active turbulence was approximately cylindrical across the tank. Nevertheless, the active turbulence led to large fluctuations in the boundary of this region, where numerous wave-breaking and entrainment events were observed to engulf ambient non-turbulent fluid. The region of active turbulence became visibly asymmetric as the ambient shear was increased, tending to be slightly elliptical with the longer axis inclined at a small angle to the horizontal.

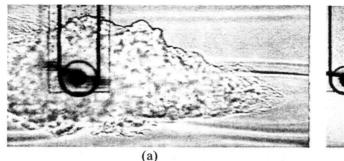 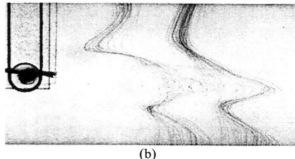

(a)   (b)

Figure 1. Photographs of localized turbulent mixing in an ambient (approximately linear) shear flow – (a) shadowgraph showing the region of active turbulence and one intrusion, and (b) the vertical profile of horizontal velocity showing the perturbation due to localized mixing; dye lines, which were initially vertical, were produced by dropping crystals of potassium permanganate through the flow. Above the level of the mixer the ambient flow was from right to left, while below the mixer, the flow was from left to right.

After the initial times, localized mixing produced a horizontal density gradient that drove intrusive flows of mixed fluid away from the turbulent region (cf. similar observations by De Silva & Fernando, 1998, and Hughes & Linden, 2000, for localized mixing in a quiescent stratification). The turbulence was observed to decay rapidly with distance from the mixer. Eventually the wedge-shaped intrusions reached a very elongated and asymmetric form. The centres of the intrusions tended to be vertically offset from the horizontal axis so that their propagation was partly assisted by the local flow. In the absence of ambient shear, the intrusions were approximately symmetrical about the horizontal axis and consisted of fluid from both halves of the turbulent region, above and below the horizontal. The presence of ambient shear appeared to force a greater proportion of fluid from either the upper or lower half of the turbulent region into the accompanying intrusion.

Return flows towards the turbulent region were also evident on either side of the intrusions. In contrast to observations of localized mixing in a quiescent stratification, the introduction of ambient shear also forced an asymmetry to develop in the return flows – see Figure 1b. The velocity field has the qualitative form that would be obtained by the superposition of the ambient shear profile with the mixing-induced flow in a quiescent stratification (cf. Hughes & Linden, 2000). Consequently, the return flows assisted by the local flow are stronger than those opposed by the local flow. The rates at which ambient fluid is entrained into the turbulent region from each of the return flows is thus no longer equal. However, we were unable in our experiments to completely suppress the opposed return flows (in a laboratory frame of reference) by increasing the mean shear.

A new and robust feature observed with the introduction of ambient shear was a 'secondary intrusion'. This type of intrusion resulted from weak mixing both some distance above and below the main intrusions, but only propagated from the vicinity of the turbulent region in the direction of the local flow once the main intrusive flow was established. The fluid between the main intrusion and the secondary intrusion was flowing in the opposite direction, towards the mixer, as part of the opposed return flow. It was not clear what mechanism led to the formation of secondary intrusions, but we suggest that shear instability is the most likely candidate owing to the large velocity gradient in this region.

In addition to the energy supplied to the turbulence by agitation of the mixer, the ambient shear is another potential source of energy for mixing. Ambient shear forced non-turbulent fluid to be entrained in an asymmetric fashion. On the intrusion boundaries where the outflow opposed the local shear the wave-breaking activity was noticeably enhanced. In addition, mixing events were observed on the boundary of the secondary intrusion adjacent to the return flow. Barenblatt (1990) conjectured that a relatively weak ambient shear might be able to sustain turbulence in regions where the density gradient had been reduced by mixing. However, even in the case of the experiments conducted with the strongest shear (*i.e.* $Ri \approx 7$), the turbulence was observed to decay with distance from the mixer. On the basis of this observation, it is

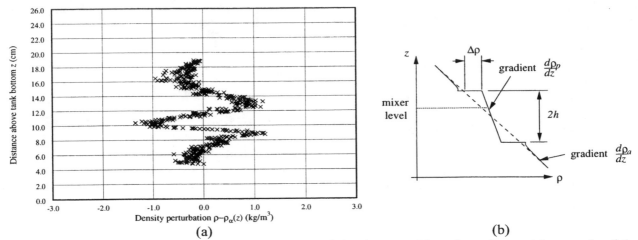

Figure 2. Density profiles due to localized turbulent mixing in an ambient shear flow – (a) example of the measured profile of perturbations about the ambient stratification, (b) idealized profile used as a fit to the measurements.

very difficult for localized turbulent mixing to reduce the local Richardson number below the critical value for shear instability (*i.e.* $Ri_{cr} \approx 0.25$) by sufficient homogenization of the local density field. Measurements in §5 of the density field in the flow suggest that very strong ambient shear $Ri \approx O(1)$ would be required for the maintenance of localized turbulence.

4. Results

In our experiments we assume that the flow is antisymmetric with respect to the vertical (and horizontal) axis. Hence we chose to make measurements only to the right of the mixer; the ambient flow is directed from right to left above the spindle and from left to right below the spindle. The use of optically-attenuating food dye to mark isopycnal surfaces allowed in-situ measurement of irreversible changes to the density field during an experiment, from which the amount of mixing could be evaluated directly (Winters *et al.*, 1995). It is assumed in this calculation that the reversible density fluctuations sampled by a light ray average to zero across the tank width. An example of the permanent perturbation to the initially linear density profile at one horizontal position in an experiment is shown in Figure 2a. A number of asymmetrical features are due to the ambient shear; the mixed region centre is offset from the level of the mixer, the upper density interface is less sharp than the lower interface because of enhanced mixing and, for the same reason, the density perturbations above the mixed region are smaller and more variable than those below the mixed region. In order to compare a number of such profiles, we define the mixed region height $2h$ and mixedness $\gamma = 1-(d\rho_p/dz)/(d\rho_a/dz)$ based on the idealized approximation in Figure 2b. This approach inevitably introduces some errors into our data because the measured profile does not always closely match the idealized profile. Results are presented here for the evolution of the mixedness only. Note that $\gamma = 0$ and $\gamma = 1$ correspond to the respective limits of no mixing and complete homogenization of the density field within the turbulent region.

The typical time evolution of the mixedness during an experiment is plotted in Figure 3 at several dimensionless distances x/l from the mixer, where l is the mixer radius. After an initial delay the mixedness at a given position increases suddenly to a maximum value, which is approximately constant thereafter. This quasi-steady-state is reached by about $Nt \approx 20$ for the range of positions shown. The initial delay increases with distance from the mixer, consistent with the propagation of mixed fluid away from the mixer in an intrusion. The variation in the maximum mixedness value gives some idea of the noise present in these measurements. Spurious values of γ in excess of one are probably due to the idealized linear fit not being appropriate for the measured density profile. Nevertheless, it can be seen that the maximum attained mixedness tended to decrease with distance from the mixer, consistent with the

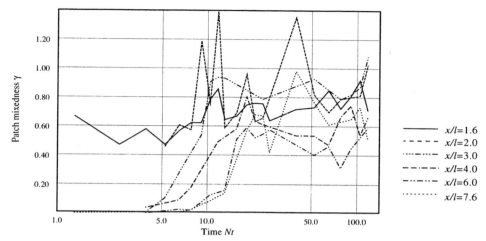

Figure 3. Example of the time evolution of the mixedness at several positions relative to the mixer.

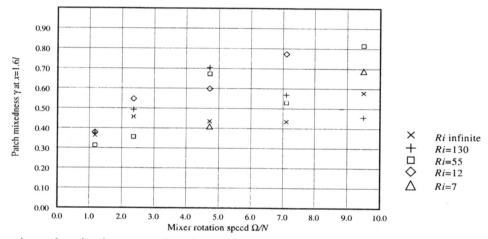

Figure 4. Quasi-steady mixedness as a function of dimensionless mixer speed Ω/N for different Ri.

physical idea of incompletely mixed fluid escaping from the turbulent region into intrusions that restratify with distance from the mixer.

In order to determine the effect upon localized mixing of the mixer rotation speed and the ambient shear, we compare in Figure 4 the quasi-steady-state mixedness observed in the turbulent region for a number of different experiments. We use the average steady-state mixedness at $x/l = 1.6$ for this purpose since it was impractical to take measurements closer to the mixer. Although we expect some noise through the use of such 'point values', the mixedness is seen to increase with Ω/N and possibly with decreasing Ri. Neither of these trends are perhaps intuitive since increasing Ω/N also increases the volume of active turbulence, while decreasing Ri tends to decrease the residence time of fluid in that volume. A rough estimate of the noise in Figure 4 can be made by comparing the points corresponding to $Ri \rightarrow \infty$ and $Ri \approx 130$, as the observed difference between these experiments was typically small, particularly at larger values of Ω/N.

The flux Richardson number R_f is defined as the ratio of energy used for mixing to that supplied to the turbulence. Using a combination of dimensional arguments and the results of Winters *et al.* (1995), Hughes & Linden (2000) predict that R_f and the mixedness γ of the turbulent region are related by the curve in Figure 5. The largest turbulent overturns are assumed to fill the region of active turbulence, which requires that $\gamma > 0.5$. This plot is also applicable to localized mixing in the presence of ambient

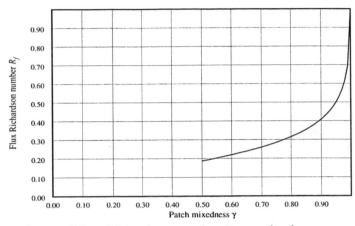

Figure 5. Predicted dependence of flux Richardson number R_f on mixedness γ.

shear; note, however, that γ is a function of Ri. The flux Richardson number varies weakly over the typical range of measured γ taking values in the range 0.18-0.25, which are consistent with those values of R_f previously found (Linden, 1979; Fernando, 1991) to characterize high efficiency mixing processes in a stratified fluid.

5. Conclusions

We have examined the mixing due to a single localized turbulent region in a stratified shear flow using a simple experiment. The amount of mixing increased as both the ambient shear and the energy supplied to the turbulent region increased. Complete homogenization of the fluid within the turbulent region was never achieved because horizontal density gradients drive partially-mixed fluid from this region into outward-flowing intrusions, where the turbulence decays rapidly. Unmixed ambient fluid is entrained into the turbulent region at the same rate as the partially-mixed fluid escapes. The Reynolds number characterising our laboratory scale turbulence is of $O(10^3)$, which is perhaps an order of magnitude less than that characterising oceanic turbulence. Nevertheless, we expect these conclusions to have relevance in the oceans, and possibly also to the higher Reynolds number flows characteristic of the atmosphere.

6. References

BARENBLATT, G.I. 1990 Evolution of turbulence in a stably stratified shear flow, *Izv. Atmos. Ocean. Phys.* **26**, 928–932.

DE SILVA, I.P.D. & FERNANDO, H.J.S. 1992 Some aspects of mixing in a stratified turbulent patch, *J. Fluid Mech.* **240**, 601–625.

DE SILVA, I.P.D. & FERNANDO, H.J.S. 1998 Experiments on collapsing turbulent regions in stratified fluids, *J. Fluid Mech.* **358**, 29–60.

FERNANDO, H.J.S. 1988 The growth of a turbulent patch in a stratified fluid, *J. Fluid Mech.* **190**, 55–70.

FERNANDO, H.J.S. 1991 Turbulent mixing in stratified fluids, *Ann. Rev. Fluid Mech.* **23**, 455–493.

FOLKARD, A.M., DAVIES, P.A. & FERNANDO, H.J.S. 1997 Measurements in a turbulent patch in a rotating, linearly-stratified fluid, *Dyn. Atmos. Oceans* **26**, 27–51.

HOLFORD, J.M. & DALZIEL, S.B. 1996 Measurements of layer depth during baroclinic instability in a two-layer flow, *Appl. Sci. Res.* **56**, 191–207.

HUGHES, G.O. & LINDEN, P.F. 2000 The mixing due to a turbulent patch in a stratified fluid, *J. Fluid Mech.*, in preparation.

LINDEN, P.F. 1979 Mixing in stratified fluids, *Geophys. Astrophys. Fluid Dyn.* **13**, 2–23.

WINTERS, K.B., LOMBARD, P.N., RILEY, J.J. & D ASARO, E.A. 1995 Available potential energy and mixing in density-stratified fluids, *J. Fluid Mech.* **289**, 115–128.

Approximate analysis of turbulent entrainment in an inclined plume using k- ε model equations based on similarity assumption

Tadaharu Ishikawa[1], Akira Moribayashi[2], Fengyi Gao[1], Xin Qian[1]

[1]Department of Environmental Science and Technology, Tokyo Institute of Technology,
4250 Nagatsuda, Midori-ku, Yokohama, Japan 226-8502
[2]Integrated Technology Services IBM Japan, LTD. ,
19-21,Nihonbashi hakozaki-cho, Chuo-ku, Tokyo, Japan 103-8510

1. ABSTRACT

A purely mathematical approach is undertaken to the *E-Ri* relation of a steady density under flow over a constant slope: A set of the $\kappa-\varepsilon$ model equations including buoyancy effect is simplified based on the boundary layer approximation and the dynamic similarity assumption. Then, the Galerkin method is applied to the equations so as to obtain the relation efficiently for wide ranges of the slope angle and the bottom roughness. The obtained *E-Ri* relation shows the tendency as follows: With small surface roughness, *E* decreases rapidly as *Ri* approaches to unity just as an empirical relation proposed by Turner (1986). On the other hand, with large surface roughness, *E* decrease in proportion to $Ri^{-1.0\sim1.2}$ just as an empirical relation proposed by Parker et al.(1987).

2. INTRODUCTION

Inclined plumes appear in many situations in the natural environment, playing an important role in heat and mass transport. Several empirical formulae have been proposed for a relation between the entrainment coefficient, *E*, and Richardson number, *Ri*, mostly based on laboratory data. However, it has not been concluded yet which formula is most appropriate. Since the ranges of experimental parameters are limited due to restrictions of facility scale and available working fluid, experimental data are grouped in a restricted area of the *E-Ri* map, so that most of the empirical formulae pass through the "cloud of data" and then diverge from one another. However, information of entrainment rate at conditions out of the cloud (at large *Ri* and/or small *E*) becomes significant when we consider the scale of plumes appearing in the natural environment.

In this study, a purely mathematical approach is undertaken to the *E-Ri* relation of two-dimensional inclined plumes to gain knowledge on the basic characteristics of the relation. The analytical method adopted here is a hybrid of the standard k- ε turbulent model and a kind of integral methods for the turbulent mixing layer analysis.

3. BASIC EQUATIONS

Let us consider a steady density under flow of an incompressible fluid on a constant slope as shown in **Figure-1**, where the negative buoyancy flux is kept constant along the slope, but the volume flux is on the increase because of the entrainment at the interface. The governing equations used here are the continuity equation, conservation equations of momentum, buoyancy, turbulent kinetic energy and dissipation rate, and an expression of kinetic eddy viscosity on the basis of the $\kappa-\varepsilon$ model.

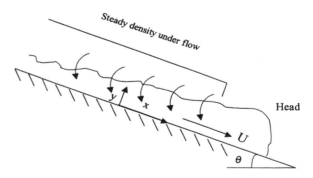

Fig. 1   Schematic view of an inclined plume

From these equations, Fukushima (1988) deduced a set of dimensionless equations through the following procedures. In this study, the equations almost the same as Fukushima's are used for analysis but with some mathematical correction: Applying the boundary layer approximation to the governing equations, we obtain,

$$u\frac{\partial u}{\partial x}+v\frac{\partial u}{\partial y}=eg\sin\theta-g\cos\theta\frac{\partial}{\partial x}\int_y^\infty edy+\frac{\partial}{\partial y}\left(v_e\frac{\partial u}{\partial y}\right) \tag{1-a}$$

$$\frac{\partial u}{\partial x}+\frac{\partial v}{\partial y}=0 \tag{1-b}$$

$$u\frac{\partial(eg)}{\partial x}+v\frac{\partial(eg)}{\partial y}=\frac{\partial}{\partial y}\left\{\frac{v_e}{\sigma_g}\frac{\partial(eg)}{\partial y}\right\} \tag{1-c}$$

$$u\frac{\partial k}{\partial x}+v\frac{\partial k}{\partial y}=\frac{\partial}{\partial y}\left(\frac{v_e}{\sigma_k}\frac{\partial k}{\partial y}\right)+v_e\left(\frac{\partial u}{\partial y}\right)^2+\cos\theta\frac{v_e}{\sigma_g}\frac{\partial(eg)}{\partial y}-\varepsilon \tag{1-d}$$

$$u\frac{\partial\varepsilon}{\partial x}+v\frac{\partial\varepsilon}{\partial y}=\frac{\partial}{\partial y}\left(\frac{v_e}{\sigma_\varepsilon}\frac{\partial\varepsilon}{\partial y}\right)+C_1\frac{\varepsilon}{k}\left\{v_e\left(\frac{\partial u}{\partial y}\right)^2+(1-C_3)\cos\theta\frac{v_e}{\sigma_g}\frac{\partial(eg)}{\partial y}\right\}-C_2\frac{\varepsilon^2}{k} \tag{1-e}$$

$$v_e=C_\mu\frac{k^2}{\varepsilon} \tag{1-f}$$

where x = the distance along the slope; y = the distance perpendicular to the slope; e = relative density difference; u, v = flow velocity in the x and y direction, respectively; k = turbulent kinetic energy; ε = dissipation rate; g = acceleration of gravity; θ = slope angle; and v_e = kinetic eddy viscosity. The model parameters are set to their standard values,

$$\sigma_g=1/1.2,\quad \sigma_k=1.0,\quad \sigma_\varepsilon=1/0.77,\quad C_1=1.44,\quad C_2=1.92,\quad C_\mu=0.09 \tag{2}$$

Let us assume that a dynamic similarity is developed and that all the physical quantities are expressed by the form, $S_i\propto x^p f_i(\eta)$, where S_i = a physical quantity; p= a constant; $\eta=y/x$; $f_i(\eta)$ = a dimensionless function of η. Then, the following equations can be obtained through dimensional considerations.

$$u=U_0f_u(\eta)\quad(3-a),\qquad v=V_0f_v(\eta)\quad(3-b),\qquad eg=G_0x^{-1}f_g(\eta),\quad(3-c)$$

$$k=K_0f_k(\eta)\quad(3-d),\qquad \varepsilon=E_0x^{-1}f_\varepsilon(\eta)\quad(3-e),\qquad v_e=N_0xf_n(\eta)\quad(3-f)$$

$$\eta f_uf_u'-f_vf_u'+f_g-\cot\theta\,\eta f_g+(f_nf_u')'=0 \tag{4-a}$$

$$\eta f_u'-f_v'=0 \tag{4-b}$$

$$f_uf_g+\eta f_uf_g'-f_vf_g'+\frac{1}{\sigma_g}(f_nf_g')'=0 \tag{4-c}$$

$$\eta f_uf_k'-f_vf_k'+\frac{1}{\sigma_k}(f_nf_k')'+f_nf_u'^2+\frac{1}{\sigma_g}(\cot\theta f_nf_g')-f_\varepsilon=0 \tag{4-d}$$

$$f_uf_\varepsilon+\eta f_uf_\varepsilon'-f_vf_\varepsilon'+\frac{1}{\sigma_\varepsilon}(f_nf_\varepsilon')'+C_1\frac{f_\varepsilon}{f_k}f_nf_u'^2+C_1(1-C_3)\frac{1}{\sigma_g}\cot\theta f_n\frac{f_\varepsilon}{f_k}f_g'-C_2\frac{f_\varepsilon^2}{f_k}=0 \tag{4-e}$$

$$f_n=C_\mu f_k^2/f_\varepsilon \tag{4-f}$$

where $'$ (prime) = differentiation by η; U_0, V_0, G_0, K_0, E_0 and N_0 are scale factors, which can be assumed arbitrarily. Then, the following relations have already been assumed in Eqs.(4) for the simplicity.

$$\frac{G_0 \sin\theta}{U_0^2} = 1, \qquad \frac{V_0}{U_0} = 1, \qquad \frac{K_0}{U_0^2} = 1, \qquad \frac{E_0}{U_0^3} = 1, \qquad N_0 = \frac{K_0^2}{E_0} \qquad (5)$$

Note that there still remains one freedom parameter for scaling because five relations are assumed in Eqs.(5) for six physical quantities. In Eq.(4-a), the underlined term is the one Fukushima dropped incorrectly.

4. APPLICATION OF WEIGHTED RESIDUAL METHOD

The weighted residual method (WRM) solves differential equations approximately by assuming the unknown variables as a linear combination of some known functions (trial functions), and determining the amplitudes of the functions so that the residuals of the differential equations are minimized in a sense of weighted average: Suppose a governing equation is $[D\{z(\xi),\xi\}=0]$, where ξ is an independent valuable, $z(\xi)$ is a dependent valuable on ξ, and $D\{\cdot\}$ is some differential operator. $z(\xi)$ is replaced by an approximated form of $\hat{z}(\xi) = \Sigma a_i \cdot \varphi_i(\xi)$ where $\varphi_i(\xi)$s are trial functions and a_is are their amplitudes. Then, the a_is are obtained from the set of equations, $[\int D\{\hat{z}(\xi),\xi\} \cdot w_i(\xi)d\xi=0]$ where the distribution of residuals is kept orthogonal to the weight functions, $w_i(\xi)$s. This mathematics is a general form including integral methods that have often been used for the analysis of turbulent boundary layers, surface mixed layers, or plumes.

Applying WRM to Eqs.(4) and using partial integration, the following equations are obtained:

$$\int_0^\infty (\eta \hat{f}_u \hat{f}_u{'} - \hat{f}_v \hat{f}_u{'} + \hat{f}_g - \cot\theta\eta \hat{f}_g)w_u d\eta - \int_0^\infty \hat{f}_n \hat{f}_u{'} w_u{'} d\eta + | \hat{f}_n \hat{f}_u{'} w_u |_0^\infty = 0 \qquad (6-a)$$

$$\int_0^\infty (\eta \hat{f}_u{'} - \hat{f}_v{'})w_v d\eta = 0 \qquad (6-b)$$

$$\int_0^\infty (\hat{f}_g \hat{f}_u + \eta \hat{f}_u \hat{f}_g{'} - \hat{f}_v \hat{f}_g{'})w_g d\eta - \frac{1}{\sigma_g}\int_0^\infty \hat{f}_n \hat{f}_g{'} w_g{'} d\eta + \frac{1}{\sigma_g}| \hat{f}_n \hat{f}_g{'} w_g |_0^\infty = 0 \qquad (6-c)$$

$$\int_0^\infty (\eta \hat{f}_u \hat{f}_k{'} - \hat{f}_v \hat{f}_k{'} + \hat{f}_n \hat{f}_u{'}{^2} + \frac{\cot\theta}{\sigma_g}\hat{f}_n \hat{f}_g{'} - \hat{f}_\varepsilon)w_k d\eta$$

$$- \frac{1}{\sigma_k}\int_0^\infty \hat{f}_n \hat{f}_k{'} w_k{'} d\eta + \frac{1}{\sigma_k}| \hat{f}_n \hat{f}_k{'} w_k |_0^\infty = 0 \qquad (6-d)$$

$$\int_0^\infty \left\{ \hat{f}_u \hat{f}_\varepsilon + \eta \hat{f}_u \hat{f}_\varepsilon{'} - \hat{f}_v \hat{f}_\varepsilon{'} + C_1 \frac{\hat{f}_\varepsilon}{\hat{f}_k}\hat{f}_n \hat{f}_u{'}{^2} + C_1(1-C_3)\frac{1}{\sigma_g}\cot\theta \hat{f}_n \frac{\hat{f}_\varepsilon}{\hat{f}_k}\hat{f}_g{'} - C_2 \frac{\hat{f}_\varepsilon^2}{\hat{f}_k} \right\}w_\varepsilon d\eta$$

$$- \frac{1}{\sigma_\varepsilon}\int_0^\infty \hat{f}_n \hat{f}_\varepsilon{'} w_\varepsilon{'} d\eta + \frac{1}{\sigma_\varepsilon}| \hat{f}_n \hat{f}_\varepsilon{'} w_\varepsilon |_0^\infty = 0 \qquad (6-e)$$

$$\hat{f}_u = C_\mu \hat{f}_k^2 / \hat{f}_\varepsilon \qquad (6-f)$$

where $\hat{f}_i$ = a trial function of quantity i; w_i = a weight function; and $|\cdot|$ means the values at the boundary. Eq.(6-f) is same as Eq.(4-f) because it is an algebraic equation to which WRM is not applied.

How to assume the trial functions and weight functions is a key issue of WRM. The trial functions must be able to resemble the profiles of the quantities and also be easy to calculate. For the inside of a plume, they are assumed as the following on the basis of numerical experiments by Fukushima (1988) and

675

authors (unpublished). For the outside of a plume, $\hat{f}_i = v_0$ and all other functions are zero:

$$\hat{f}_u = u_0(1-\xi) \qquad (7-a), \qquad\qquad \hat{f}_v = v_0\xi^2 \qquad (7-b),$$

$$\hat{f}_g = g_0(1-\xi) \qquad (7-c), \qquad\qquad \hat{f}_k = k_0\xi(1-\xi)+k_1(1-\xi) \qquad (7-d),$$

$$\hat{f}_\varepsilon = \varepsilon_0\{\xi(1-\xi)+k_1/k_0(1-\xi)\} \qquad\qquad\qquad\qquad\qquad\qquad (7-e)$$

$$w_v = 1, \qquad w_u = 1-\xi, \qquad w_g = 1-\xi, \qquad w_{k0} = 1, \qquad w_{k1} = 1-\xi, \qquad w_\varepsilon = 1 \qquad (8)$$

where ξ is a new dimensionless distance normalized by the dimensionless layer thickness, that is, $\xi = \eta/\delta$, $\delta =$ the dimensionless thickness of the plume layer; and u_0, v_0, g_0, k_0, k_1, ε_0 are dimensionless amplitudes which are to be determined by solving the equations. Each profile of u, v, and g is represented by a single function for which only the magnitude is the object of study. On the other hand, the profile of k is composed of two trial functions based on the following considerations: There are two sources of turbulence in an inclined plume; the shear on the bottom surface and the shear at the density interface. Accordingly, the profile of k can be changed reflecting the ratio of them. The profile of ε is coupled with that of k, and only the amplitude is questioned. The assumptions of Eqs.(7) are somewhat intentional in order to describe the essential parts of the phenomenon with the smallest load of calculation, as is usual in WRM.

It should be noted that the existence of the wall boundary layer is neglected in the trial functions for the simplicity of calculation. In other words, the wall layer is assumed to be far thinner than the whole layer of the plume as shown in **Figure-2**. The dynamic effects of the wall boundary layer are taken into account through the specification of boundary conditions described below.

Boundary conditions are introduced through the flux terms indicated with $|\cdot|$. For the upper boundary, the conditions have already been taken into account in the assumption of trial functions. At the bottom boundary, fluxes of momentum, turbulent kinetic energy and dissipation rate from "the wall boundary layer of zero thickness" must be taken into account. If the dynamic similarity must be held in the plume layer, dimensional argumentation leads to the following forms of expression for these fluxes.

$$\hat{f}_u{}' = -C_D u_0^2, \qquad \hat{f}_v{}' = 0, \qquad \hat{f}_g{}' = 0, \qquad \hat{f}_k{}' = \alpha(C_D)u_0^3, \qquad \hat{f}_\varepsilon{}' = \frac{\varepsilon_0}{k_0}\beta(C_D)u_0^3 \qquad (9)$$

where $C_D =$ the surface drag coefficient; and $\alpha(C_D)$, $\beta(C_D) =$ some functions of C_D. These functions can be obtained numerically from the analysis of an ordinary boundary layer. The description of this process is, however, eliminated here because of limited space, and only the results are shown in **Figure-3**.

After substituting Eqs.(7) into Eqs.(6) and executing the integrations, six algebraic equations are

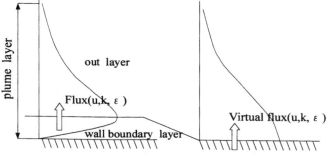

Fig. 2.   Replacement of the wall boundary layer
with virtual fluxes at the boundary

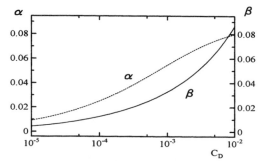

Fig. 3.   Dependency of α and β on C_D

obtained for the seven unknowns; dimensionless layer thickness, δ, and the dimensionless amplitudes, u_0, v_0, g_0, k_0, k_1, ε_0. Because one freedom of scaling has been remained at the step of Eqs.(5), one of the amplitudes can be set arbitrarily here. In this study, u_0 is set as unity. The algebraic equations are left out on this text because of the restriction of space.

The algebraic equations are solved for a given slope angle, θ, and a surface drag coefficient, C_D, by using the Newton–Raphson method.

5. RESULTS AND DISCUSSIONS

The form of Richardson number defined by Ellison and Turner (1959) is used herein.

$$R_i = \frac{A\cos\theta}{V^3} \tag{10}$$

where V = the characteristic velocity; and A is the relative buoyancy flux along the slope. Their definitions are as follows:

$$V = \int_0^\infty u^2 dy \bigg/ \int_0^\infty u \, dy, \qquad A = \int_0^\infty egu \, dy \tag{11}$$

On the other hand, the entrainment coefficient is written as,

$$E = \frac{1}{V}\frac{d}{dx}\left(\int_0^\infty u \, dy\right) \tag{12}$$

Substituting Eqs.(3-a), (3-c), (7-a) and (7-c) into Eqs.(10) and (12), we obtain the following expressions.

$$Ri = \frac{9}{8}\cot\theta\,\delta\,g_0, \qquad E = \frac{3}{4}\delta \tag{13}$$

Then the pairs of E and Ri for given θ and C_D can be obtained by substituting the solution of the algebraic equations into Eqs.(13).

Calculation results are shown with solid lines in **Figure-4** in which are also plotted some data of flume experiments as well as field experiments. With small bottom roughness, E decreases rapidly as Ri approaches to unity just as an empirical relation proposed by Turner (1986). On the other hand, with large bottom roughness, E decrease in proportion to $Ri^{-1.0\sim1.2}$ just as an empirical relation proposed by Parker et al. (1987).

This result suggests that if the bottom roughness is very small, an inclined plume cannot exist stably under a condition in which Richardson number exceeds some critical value. The existence of this critical condition can be explained from a consideration of TKE balance: The second term on the right hand side of Eq. (1-d) means the production rate of the turbulent kinetic energy, Pr, and the third term means the rate of energy transfer from the turbulent kinetic

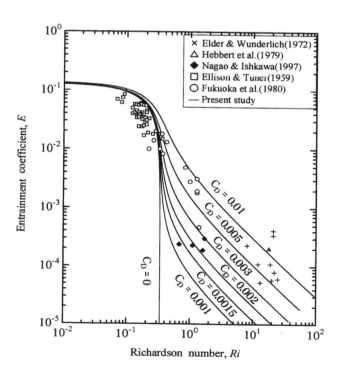

Fig. 4.   The E-Ri relation

energy to the potential energy, Pt. On average, Pr must be larger than Pt, otherwise the mean dissipation rate becomes negative. Note that the advection terms and diffusion terms contribute only to the redistribution of TKE but neither to the production nor dissipation. Accordingly, the following equality must be satisfied on average.

$$\nu_e \frac{U^2}{H^2} > \cos\theta \frac{\nu_e}{\sigma_g} \frac{B}{H} \quad \Rightarrow \quad R_i = \frac{BH}{U^2} < \frac{\sigma_g}{\cos\theta} \tag{14}$$

where U = a characteristic velocity; B = a characteristic relative buoyancy; H = the plume layer thickness; and Ri = an overall Richardson number whose definition is somewhat different from Eq.(10). Then, Eq.(14) suggests that there is a critical value of Ri which is in the order of unity, although this argument is not very strict because of the inconsistency of the definition of Ri.

In the case of large bottom roughness, TKE is produced at the bottom surface and supplied into the plume layer. As a result, the turbulent mixing can be sustained even in the condition of large Ri in which TKE production in the plume is not enough. The TKE balance in this case must be similar to the one in the surface mixed layer of lakes or oceans. If some constant fraction of the energy supplied through the boundary is transformed into a potential energy, the following relation might be established:

$$BgW_g \propto \alpha(C_D)U_0^3 \quad \Rightarrow \quad E \propto R_i^{-1} \tag{15}$$

This relation of a power function is shown at the lower right side of the figure.

6. CONCLUSION

There are two sources of turbulence for the entrainment of an inclined plume; the shear at the density interface, and the shear at the bottom surface. This fact suggests that the entrainment coefficient depends not only on Richardson number but also on some dimensionless parameter indicating the effect of the bottom roughness, such as the drag coefficient, C_D. In this study, this situation is sketched with an integral methods based on the $\kappa-\varepsilon$ model equations: With small bottom roughness, E decreases rapidly as Ri approaches to unity, because the TKE production in a plume layer becomes too short to sustain the mixing. Then, the E-Ri relation shows the tendency similar to the one proposed by Turner (1986). With large bottom roughness, E decreases in proportion to a power function of Ri, the exponent of which approaches to unity as Ri becomes large.

REFERENCES

Ellison, T.H. and Turner, J.S. (1959): Turbulent entrainment of stratified flows, J. Fluid Mech., Vol.6, pp.423-448.

Elder, R.A and Wunderlich, W.O. (1972): Inflow density currents in TVA reservoirs, Proc., Int. Symp. on stratified flow, ASCE, pp.221-236.

Fukuoka, S., Fukushima, Y. and Nakamura, K. (1980): Study on the plunging depth and interface form of density currents in a two-dimensional reservoir, Proc., JSCE, No.302, pp. 55-65.

Fukushima, Y. (1988): Analysis of inclined wall plume by turbulent model, Proc., JSCE, No.399, pp.65-74.

Hebbert, B., Imberger, J., Loh, I. And Patterson, J. (1979): Collie river underflow into the Wellington Reservoir, J. Hydraulic Div., ASCE, Vol.105, pp.533-545.

Nagao, M., Ishikawa, T. and Nagashima, S. (1997): Entrainment coefficient of an inclined plume in Lake Ogawara, Proc., JSCE, No.579, pp.105-114.

Parker, G., Garcia, M., Fukushima, Y. and Yu, W. (1987): Experiments on turbidity currents over an erodible bed, J. Hydraulics Res., IAHR, Vol.25, No.1, pp.123-147.

Turner, J.S. (1986): Turbulent entrainment: the development of the entrainment assumption and its application to geophysical flows, J. Fluid Mech., Vol.173, pp.431-471.

Modelling upwelling in the coastal ocean

G.N. Ivey, K.B. Winters[1] and M.J. Coates[2]

Centre for Water Research, The University of Western Australia, Nedlands, Western Australia. 6907
[1] also at Applied Physics Laboratory, University of Washington
[2] School of Ecology and Environment, Deakin University, Warrnambool, Victoria. 3280
ivey@cwr.uwa.edu.au, winters@cwr.uwa.edu.au, mcoates@deakin.edu.au

1. Abstract

Models of upwelling have usually focused on the steady state situation which arises after an along-shore constant wind stress has been applied for sufficiently long time that a steady frontal situation has developed with cold dense lower layer water confined between the coast and the offshore front. In many regions of the coastal ocean, such as the south-western corner of Western Australia, for example, upwelling does occur but is highly transient in nature. Unsteady winds lead to variability in the formation time and offshore position of upwelling fronts. In addition, the ambient density cannot usually be described by a simple two or even multi-layered density stratification and the bottom topography is often complex in nature.

We describe a series of combined laboratory and numerical studies which focus on the transient development of the flow as it evolves following the initiation of a surface stress. We consider the case where the fluid is continuously stratified and investigate the effects of stratification, bottom slope, wind speed (or surface stress) and latitude. The laboratory experiments use a combination of particle image velocimetry techniques and measurements of the density field to quantify the evolving flow. The numerical experiments are based on direct numerical simulations of the laboratory-scale flow and are performed in a parameter range both comparable to the laboratory experiments and in ranges not accessible in the laboratory set-up. The results of the study provide a description of both the kinematics and dynamics of the flow field during upwelling in both the inner shelf region adjacent to the coast and the region offshore of the upwelling front.

2. Introduction

Wind driven upwelling in the coastal ocean leads to the transport of cold, nutrient rich water to the surface, supporting the high biological productivity found in many coastal regions. This has lead to considerable interest in the dynamics of coastal upwelling on sloping continental shelves with satellite imagery in particular showing the richly detailed nature of the upwelling process. Most studies have focussed on the dynamics of steady upwelling systems, such as those that occur off the coasts of Oregon, California, Peru and South Africa (e.g. Smith, 1995; Allen et al, 1995). Most models have focussed on steady state dynamics in fluids that can be described by layered ambient density stratification. In many regions of the coastal ocean, such as the South-Western corner of Western Australia, for example, upwelling occurs in the summer months but is highly transient in nature (Gersbach et al, 1999). Unsteady winds lead to variability in the formation time and offshore position of upwelling fronts.

The purpose of the work is to examine the way in which oceans and lakes respond to the onset of upwelling-favorable wind forcing in such situations. Our goal is to understand the dynamical processes involved, and answer such questions as how long does it take for upwelling to develop? What is the nature of any frontal zones that develop separating the inner shelf region from the outer shelf region? What are the mechanisms of exchange across these frontal zones? How are the these processes influenced by the wind speed, ambient density stratification, bottom slope and latitude? We describe here a series of coordinated laboratory and numerical experiments which are designed to investigate these issues in a situation where the fluid has a continuous ambient density stratification.

3. Experiments

The laboratory experiments were conducted in a 0.976 m internal diameter by 0.5 m deep circular Perspex tank, double walled for insulation and to provide undistorted horizontal views. The tank was mounted on a rotating turntable revolving at a prescribed rotation rate Ω in a Northern Hemisphere (anti-clockwise) sense. For convenience, the experiments were performed in an inverted sense from the geophysical case, and the surface wind stress was modeled by differentially rotating a false bottom in the tank at a rate $\Delta\Omega$ with respect to the tank (e.g. Ivey et al, 1995). A conical lid of height 0.088 m and radius L of 0.488 m was inserted into the tank to represent a uniformly sloping continental shelf. In operation, there was a 17 mm gap between the rotating false bottom and the bottom of the cone, to permit entrance of a horizontal laser light sheet for flow visualization and Particle Image Velocimetry (PIV), leading to a total maximum working depth of $H = 0.105$ m. All experiments were conducted with an initially linearly stratified fluid, with temperature as the stratifying agent. A vertically traversing rack containing six thermistors spaced over the tank radius enabled the measurement of the time-dependent temperature field following the initiation of the surface forcing.

The numerical modeling was done at the laboratory scales to provide a detailed representation of the underlying physical processes. The numerical scheme and its testing is described in detail by Winters et al (2000), but basically is a fully three-dimensional, non-hydrostatic, direct numerical simulation scheme with enhanced grid resolution in the near-shore, near-surface region. Numerical experiments are impulsively started by applying a surface boundary condition to the along-shore component of motion of an initially linearly stratified fluid.

4. Results

A total of 30 laboratory and 15 numerical experiments have been conducted. Figure 1 shows the temperature contours from a vertical section at one azimuthal position from a typical laboratory experiment. Note that the figure is drawn in the geophysical sense, hence the apparent contradiction of having the temperatures increase with depth. On initiation of the surface stress, an offshore Ekman transport is established drawing a compensating upwelling flow up the bottom slope to replace the offshore transport. Even at early times, there is evidence of both tilting of the isotherms and a developing surface mixing region which increases in depth as time progresses. The mixing region remains confined to the inner shelf region, however, and a distinct frontal region has developed at $x/L \approx 0.45$ by about $t = 7T_f$, where $T_f = 2\pi/f$ is the inertial period.

Figure 2 shows time series from the row of offshore thermistors placed at a fixed depth of $z/H = 0.16$. Four distinct regimes can be defined. In Regime 1, corresponding to times up to $3T_f$, there is a steady increase in nearshore temperature (corresponding to a decrease in temperature in the field environment) as water is transported up the slope towards the driven surface. Further offshore, there is a steady decrease in temperature as fluid is "downwelled" to conserve volume flux. In Regime 2, for times from $3T_f$ to $7T_f$, high frequency oscillations are now observed at the inner shelf locations as the depth of the surface mixing region penetrates to the depth of the fixed thermistors. These instabilities are convective in nature as unstable fluid parcels stir over the depth. Locations further offshore also show evidence of weaker, high-frequency temperature oscillations. In Regime 3, for times from $7T_f$ to $10T_f$, the nearshore region reaches a near steady mean temperature and oscillations of lower frequency than those in Regime 2 now start to appear in the offshore regions. Note that these low frequency oscillations cannot be observed in the near-shore stations. A strong lateral temperature gradient is observed at $x/L \approx 0.45$. Finally, in Regime 4 for $t > 10T_f$, no trends in the mean temperature records are observed anywhere, but large amplitude, low frequency temperature oscillations are observed in a limited range offshore and centered around the region of maximum lateral temperature gradient.

Velocity fields obtained during this experiment show that there is a transition zone where the mean along shore or azimuthal velocity increases rapidly from zero at the coast to a maximum at a finite distance offshore, then decreases approximately linearly towards the center of the tank. The peak in the azimuthal velocity coincides with the frontal position and moves slowly offshore as the flow develops and the velocity profile tends to broaden in long time. The low frequency fluctuations in temperature described above in Figure 2 appear to be associated with the unstable eddy structures superimposed on this mean azimuthal swirling flow.

In Figure 3 we show the results from a typical numerical experiment. The panel shows the surface density at a fixed long-shore location, as a function of time and distance offshore. For times less than $3T_f$, dense fluid is brought to the surface near $x/L = 0$ to replace the fluid moved offshore in the surface Ekman layer. After $3T_f$, a banded or striated pattern, most pronounced in the offshore zone, appears and this is the surface signature of gravitational instabilities in the surface Ekman layer which is attempting to move dense water offshore above lighter surface layer water (cf. Zang and Street, 1995). The whole pattern tends to mover slowly offshore with increasing time and there is a clear trend towards lower frequency oscillations in the surface density field. Winters et al (2000) describe the evolution of the density and associated velocity fields in some detail, and show the along-shore scale of these features is consistent with large scale baroclinic instabilities associated with the cross-shelf density gradients established by the stress driven upwelling.

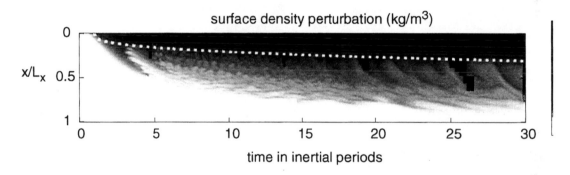

Figure 3. Surface density field as a function of time and distance offshore. The total density range is 7 kgm^{-3}, $f = 0.21$ s^{-1}, $N = 1.445$ s^{-1}, $\Delta\Omega = -0.075$ s^{-1}. The dotted reference line represents a growth rate of frontal scale $l \sim t^{1/3}$(see below).

5. Discussion

The laboratory and numerical experiments suggests a complex time-dependent response. A schematic model of the process is shown in Figure 4 and shows at some time t there will be a region of mixed fluid adjacent to the coast of width l, separated from the ambient fluid offshore which still retains the initial density gradient, characterized by buoyancy frequency N. In the region $0 \le x \le l$, the only energy source available for mixing is the surface stress $\tau_s = \rho u_*^2$, where ρ is a reference density and u_* the friction velocity.

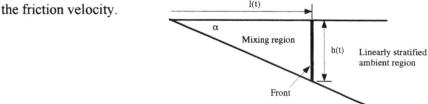

Figure 4. Vertical cross-sectional schematic of front of width l growing into stratified environment.

Over time t the work done by the wind W_s, per unit width along the shoreline, can be written as

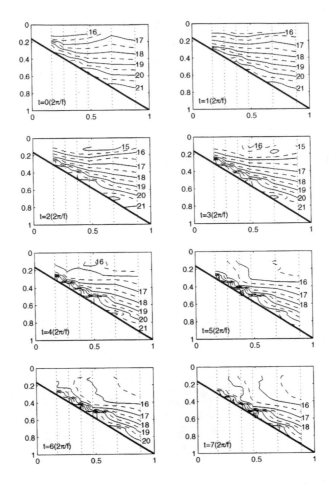

Figure 1. Temperature contours obtained at a fixed azimuthal position using six profiling thermistors. The thick sloping line marks the bottom. Parameters are $f = 0.21$ s^{-1}, $N = 0.38$ s^{-1}, $\Delta\Omega = -0.15$ s^{-1}.

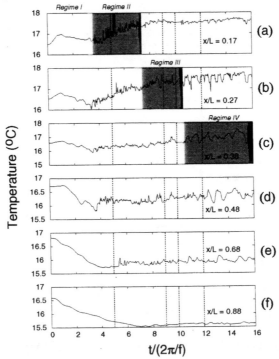

Figure 2: Time series of temperatures for experiment where parameters are $f = 0.21$ s^{-1}, $N = 0.34$ s^{-1}, $\Delta\Omega = -0.075$ s^{-1}.

$$W_s = \beta \rho u_*^3 lt \qquad (1)$$

where the surface drift velocity is taken as $u_d = \beta u_*$, with coefficient β. Within the region $0 < x < l$, if the fluid were to be mixed by this wind stress, then the increase of potential energy ΔPE, per unit width along the shoreline, is given by

$$\Delta PE = \frac{\gamma}{12} \rho N^2 \left(\frac{h}{2}\right)^3 l \qquad (2)$$

where coefficient γ in the range $0 \leq \gamma \leq 1$ expresses the degree of mixing in the near shore region ($\gamma = 0$ corresponds to no mixing, while $\gamma = 1$ corresponds to the well-mixed case). Equating (1) and (2) and noting that only a part of the wind energy will be used for mixing (some goes into driving the mean flow and some is dissipated), yields the depth at the front h as

$$h(t) = c \left(\frac{u_*}{N^{2/3}}\right) t^{1/3} \qquad (3)$$

Now from the geometry $\tan \alpha \approx \alpha = h/l$ for small slopes, hence the frontal width l is predicted to be

$$l(t) = c \left(\frac{u_*}{N^{2/3}\alpha}\right) t^{1/3} \qquad (4)$$

and coefficient c must be determined. This simple energy model thus reveals that under a constant surface stress the front will grow in width like $t^{1/3}$.

In the field, the friction velocity u_* can be specified from a knowledge of wind speed and sea surface state. In the laboratory model, this stress is applied by rotating the circular false bottom of the tank with velocity $U_s(r) = r\Delta\Omega$, and the radius r is $0 < r < L$. The stress applied to the water surface is

$$\tau_s = \rho u_*^2 = \rho v \left.\frac{du}{dz}\right|_{z=0} \sim \rho v \frac{U_s}{\delta} \qquad (5)$$

where δ is the boundary layer thickness. For a laminar Ekman layer, $\delta \sim (v/f)^{1/2}$, and this implies from (5) that $u_* \sim \left(v(r\Delta\Omega)^2 f\right)^{1/4}$. For a turbulent Ekman layer, $\delta \sim u_*/f$, hence from (5)

$$u_* \sim \left(vr\Delta\Omega f\right)^{1/3} \qquad (6)$$

Note that by analogy with the viscous sub-layer in open channel flow, it is still appropriate to use a laminar viscosity in (5) at z=0, even if the Ekman layer is fully turbulent. In the laboratory experiments described above, it is clear that the Ekman layer is turbulent due to both shear generation but also due to convective stirring down from the free surface. Convective turbulence will tend to increase the boundary layer scale beyond the estimate $\delta \sim u_*/f$, implying that (6) is an *upper* bound estimate for u_*. On the other hand, as the boundary is insulated in both the laboratory and numerical models, the convective turbulence is driven by the stress from the driven surface and associated Ekman layer pumping continually attempting to lift heavy fluid over light. Thus (6) is likely a conservative estimate of the stress. Substituting (6) into (4) we obtain the prediction

$$l(t) = c\left(\frac{vr\Delta\Omega f}{N^2\alpha^3}\right)^{1/3} t^{1/3} \qquad (7)$$

We plot the laboratory results in Figure 5 where we have taken $r \approx L$, since in the lab experiments upwelling occurs close to the outer boundary of the tank. We have taken the position of the peak in the alongshore mean velocity as the estimator for l (CF Allen et al, 1995). While the data are scattered, the best estimate line shown suggests the coefficient $c \approx 9$ in equation (7). Indeed one point to note from this exercise is the difficulty in defining what a front is.

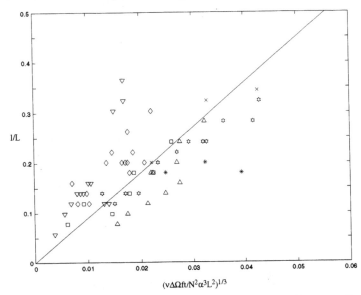

Figure 5. Plot of frontal width l versus time from several experiments. Parameters range from $f = 0.21 - 0.42$ s^{-1}, $N = 0.34 - 0.46$ s^{-1}, $\Delta\Omega = -(0.075 - 0.15)$ s^{-1}.

Equation (7) predicts the front continues to grow like $t^{1/3}$. This appears to be consistent with the observations in both the laboratory experiments in Figure 5 and the numerical results shown in Figure 3. While there are large amplitude baroclinic instabilities beyond times $t \sim 10T_f$, this does not appear to have a first order effect on the growth rate of the upwelling region, although clearly some energy must be expended in maintaining the wave field. Perhaps the most difficult issue to quantify is in fact the definition and location of the front itself.

References

Allen, J.S., P.A. Newberger and J. Federiuk (1995) Upwelling circulation on the Oregon Continental Shelf. Part 1: Response to idealized forcing, *Journal Physical Oceanography*, 25, 1843-1866.

Gersbach, G.H., Pattiaratchi, C.B., Ivey, G.N. and G.R. Cresswell (1999) Upwelling on the south-west coast of Australia - source of the Capes Current? *Continental Shelf Research*, 19, 363-400.

Ivey, G. N., J.R. Taylor, and M.J. Coates (1995) Convectively driven mixed layer growth in a rotating, stratified fluid. *Deep Sea Research*. 42: 331-349.

Smith, R.L. (1995) The physical processes of coastal ocean upwelling systems, *Upwelling in the modern ocean: modern processes and ancient records*, C. Summerhayes, K. Emneis, M.V. Angel, R.L. Smith and B. Zeitzschel (editors), 39-64, John Wiley.

Winters, K., M. Coates, G. Ivey and J. Sturman (2000) A laboratory and numerical study of the transient development of wind-driven coastal upwelling. *Journal Physical Oceanography*, submitted.

Zang, Y. and R.L. Street(1995) Numerical simulation of coastal upwelling and interfacial instability of a rotating, stratified fluid, *J. Fluid Mech.*, 305, 47-75.

The behaviour of turbulent fountains in a stratified fluid

Ross C. Kerr and Lynn J. Bloomfield

Research School of Earth Sciences, Australian National University, Canberra, ACT, Australia
Ross.Kerr@anu.edu.au, Lynn.Bloomfield@anu.edu.au

Abstract

We present a combined experimental and theoretical investigation of turbulent fountains produced when dense fluid is injected from below into a stratified fluid. The experiments show that the injected fluid rises to a maximum height before the flow reverses direction, and then intrudes either along the base of the tank or at an intermediate height in the environment. For both axisymmetric and two-dimensional fountains, we determine the initial and steady-state heights of the fountain, the height of intermediate intrusion and the critical condition for spreading to occur along the base. With the continued injection of fluid into a confined region, both the fountain and the environment are observed to evolve with time. We determine expressions for the increase in the height of the fountain, and for the motion of the ascending and descending 'fronts' that mark the vertical extent of the spreading layer of mixed fluid. We also develop a new theoretical model of fountains in an arbitrary ambient density gradient.

Introduction

Turbulent fountains and plumes occur in a number of important environmental and geophysical applications, including: the improvement of water quality by forced mixing in reservoirs, harbors and small lakes (Larson & Jönsson 1994); the disposal of brines, sewerage and industrial waste into the ocean (Koh & Brooks 1975); the heating or cooling of buildings (Baines, Turner & Campbell 1990); the replenishment of large chambers of magma in the Earth's crust (Campbell & Turner 1989); the evolution of volcanic eruption columns (Woods & Caulfield 1992; Woods, Bursik & Kurbatov 1998); and the exit snow from snowplows (Lindberg & Petersen 1991). In many of these examples, both the flow and environment evolve with time as the presence of confining boundaries results in the accumulation of injected fluid.

The continuous flow of a plume into a confined region containing an initially homogeneous fluid was first analysed by Baines & Turner (1969). They determined the changes to the environmental density profile resulting from the continuous addition of buoyant fluid from both point and line sources. This problem subsequently became known as a 'plume filling box' model. Similar filling box models have since been applied to axisymmetric plumes in an initially stratified fluid (Cardoso & Woods 1993) and to fountains in initially homogeneous surroundings (Baines et al. 1990).

In this paper, we summarize the results of our investigations of axisymmetric turbulent fountains in a stratified fluid; further details can be found in Bloomfield & Kerr (1998, 1999, 2000), which also study the behaviour of two-dimensional turbulent fountains. We first examine the initial flow of the fountain, and quantify how the strength of the stratification determines whether the falling fluid either spreads along the base of the tank, or whether it intrudes at an intermediate height in the environment. We then develop a 'stratified filling box' model which quantifies the subsequent evolution of the fountain and the environment when either basal or intermediate spreading occurs. Finally, we describe an approximate theoretical model of a turbulent fountain.

Experimental Method

The experiments were carried out in an acrylic tank which was 38 cm × 38 cm in internal cross section and 80 cm deep. An ambient linear density gradient, of approximately 25 cm depth, was

Figure 1: Photograph of an axisymmetric fountain where the density of the input fluid is equal to that at the base of the stratified environment. The flow rises like a jet and then falls before intruding into the environment at an intermediate height (upper photo). With the continued input of fluid, ascending and descending fronts are created in the environment (lower photo).

established with NaCl solutions using the double bucket method. The source fluid was placed in a 20 l bucket elevated 1.5 m above the tank. The flow rate resulting from this gravitational head, which was kept constant throughout an experiment, was measured with a flow meter. The source fluid was injected upwards from the base of the tank through a tube with an 8.8 mm inner diameter. Two sets of cross hairs of 0.5 mm diameter were positioned 3 mm and a further 44 mm upstream of the tube outlet to ensure that the flow was turbulent from the source. Using a method outlined by Baines *et al.* (1990), measurements of the position of the descending front formed by a weakly buoyant jet indicated that the position of the virtual point source was a distance $z_v = 1.0 \pm 0.2$ cm below the base of the tank, and the effective source radius was $r_e = 4.16 \pm 0.23$ mm. The flows were observed using the shadowgraph method, and dye was introduced into the input fluid to mark the extent of the spreading layer. Recording the flows on video enabled the mean fountain height to be measured to within 0.5 cm, or 2–4%.

Qualitative Observations

In our experiments, the dense injected fluid entrains environmental fluid and rises until gravity brings it to rest at an initial height. This height is then reduced to a lower, final value as the flow reverses direction and the downflow interacts with the continued upflow. In a weakly stratified environment with a sufficiently large buoyancy flux at the source, the subsequent behaviour is qualitatively similar to that observed in a homogeneous environment (Baines *et al.* 1990). The downflow spreads along the base until it reaches the walls, and an *ascending front* is formed that rises as ambient fluid from above it is entrained into the downflow. At the same time, the presence of the dense layer reduces the density difference between the source fluid and its immediate environment, and thus causes the fountain height to rise. The front rises faster than the fountain height, and eventually overtakes the top of the fountain. After this point, the fountain interacts only with the stratified layer, and the rise of the front is controlled only by the rate at which source fluid is added.

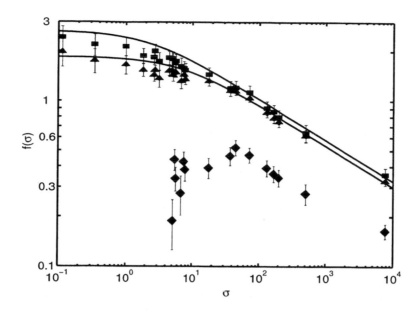

Figure 2: Dimensionless initial fountain height (■), final fountain height (▲) and spreading height (♦) as a function of σ.

However, in a more strongly stratified environment with a sufficiently small buoyancy flux at the source, the downflow intrudes into the interior of the tank (see figure 1). As a result, an additional *descending front* at the bottom of the spreading layer moves towards the base of the tank as fluid from below it is entrained into the upflow of the fountain. The formation of a second front in a stratified fluid is analogous to the 'plume filling box' models in which one front is observed in a homogeneous environment (Baines & Turner 1969) while two form in a stratified fluid (Cardoso & Woods 1993).

Initial, Final and Spreading Heights

During the first stages of the flow in a stratified fluid, dimensional analysis indicates that the initial, final and spreading heights of the fountain are given by $z = f(\sigma)M_o^{3/4}F_o^{-1/2}$, where the dimensionless parameter, σ, is defined by $\sigma = M_o^2N^2/F_o^2$, $\rho_i M_o = Q_o^2/(\pi r_e^2)$ is the initial momentum flux, $\rho_i F_o = \rho_i \Delta_o Q_o$ is the initial buoyancy flux and $N^2 = -(g/\rho_o)(\mathrm{d}\rho/\mathrm{d}z)$ is the square of the buoyancy frequency. In these expressions, Q_o is the initial volume flux, $\Delta_o = g(\rho_i - \rho_o)/\rho_o$, g is the gravitational acceleration, z is the height above the source and ρ is the ambient fluid density, with ρ_o the density at the base of the tank and ρ_i the density of the input fluid. Our experimental determination of the functions $f(\sigma)$ are given in figure 2.

In the limits of small and large σ, the appropriate $f(\sigma)$ for the initial, final and spreading heights, respectively, is given by:

$$f_i(\sigma) = \begin{cases} 2.65 & \sigma < 0.1 \\ 3.25\,\sigma^{-1/4} & \sigma > 40, \end{cases} \tag{1}$$

$$f_f(\sigma) = \begin{cases} 1.85 & \sigma < 0.1 \\ 3.00\,\sigma^{-1/4} & \sigma > 40, \end{cases} \tag{2}$$

and

$$f_s(\sigma) = \begin{cases} 0 & \sigma < 5 \\ 1.53\,\sigma^{-1/4} & \sigma > 40. \end{cases} \tag{3}$$

At intermediate values of σ, the simple functions $f_i(\sigma) = (2.65^{-4} + 3.25^{-4}\sigma)^{-1/4}$ and $f_f(\sigma) = (1.85^{-4} + 3.0^{-4}\sigma)^{-1/4}$ are a good fit to the experimental results for all values of σ.

Model of the Fronts and Fountain

The motion of the descending front is determined by calculating the volume flux of environmental fluid entrained into the upflowing fountain in the region below the front. If we introduce the dimensionless heights $\tilde{z} = z/r_e$, and time $\tilde{t} = Q_o t / A r_e$, the height of the descending front above the base of the tank is given by

$$(\tilde{z}_d - \tilde{z}_v) = (\tilde{z}_s - \tilde{z}_v)e^{-2\alpha\tilde{t}}, \tag{4}$$

where A is the cross-sectional area of the tank, $z_d(t)$ is the height of the front above the virtual point source, $\alpha = 0.076 \pm 0.004$ is the jet entrainment coefficient and t is time. This exponential decrease in the height of the descending front contrasts with the algebraic decrease in the height of the descending fronts formed by an axisymmetric plume in either a homogeneous (Baines & Turner, 1969) or a stratified fluid (Cardoso and Woods, 1993).

The position of the ascending front, $\tilde{z}_a(t)$, is determined by the initial volume flux plus the volume flux Q_e of environmental fluid entrained into the downflowing fountain in the region above the front. Baines et al. (1990) found that, in a homogeneous fluid, the entrained volume flux per unit height into the downflow of the fountain is constant and is given by

$$\frac{dQ_e}{dz} = B\frac{Q_o}{r_e}, \tag{5}$$

where B was found experimentally to be $B \approx 0.25$. Baines et al. (1990) also explained that the observation of constant entrainment per unit height can be understood by viewing the downflow as a line plume which encircles the upflow. In a linearly stratified environment, the behaviour of a plume is little different to that in a uniform fluid until close to the spreading height (Cardoso & Woods, 1993). As a result, (5) also accurately predicts the entrainment into the downflow of a fountain in a stratified fluid, and the rise of the ascending front is given by

$$\frac{d\tilde{z}_a}{d\tilde{t}} = 1 + B(\tilde{z}_f - \tilde{z}_a). \tag{6}$$

After the ascending front has reached the top of the fountain at a time $\tilde{t}^*$, the position of the front increases at the same rate as which the free surface rises due to the addition of fluid to the tank, so that $d\tilde{z}_a/d\tilde{t} = 1$. To integrate (6) for times $\tilde{t} < \tilde{t}^*$, we need an expression for the change in the fountain height with time.

To determine the height of the fountain as a function of time, we must consider both that its environment evolves with time from being stratified to being homogeneous, and that the addition of dense source fluid increases the average ambient density. We therefore derived two approximate expressions for the fountain height: $\tilde{z}_{fs}(\tilde{t})$, which gives the fountain height in a stratified environment whose mean stratification is decreasing with time, and $\tilde{z}_{fh}(\tilde{t})$, which gives the fountain height in a homogeneous fluid of whose mean density is increasing with time (see Bloomfield & Kerr (1999) for details). To quantify the fountain height at all times, we then combined these two expressions into a single expression for the fountain height which characterizes the transition from $\tilde{z}_{fs}$ at small times to $\tilde{z}_{fh}$ as $\tilde{t} \to \tilde{t}^*$. A suitable expression for $\tilde{z}_f(\tilde{t})$ is therefore $\tilde{z}_f(t) = (1 - w(\tilde{t}))\tilde{z}_{fs} + w(\tilde{t})\tilde{z}_{fh}$, where the weighting function $w(\tilde{t})$ is chosen to be $w = (\tilde{z}_a - \tilde{z}_d)/(\tilde{z}_f - \tilde{z}_v)$.

The position of the fountain height and the fronts were measured in a series of experiments performed for a range of values of σ. The data from one of these experiments is shown in figure 4 along with the result of integrating (6) for the ascending front, the predicted position of the

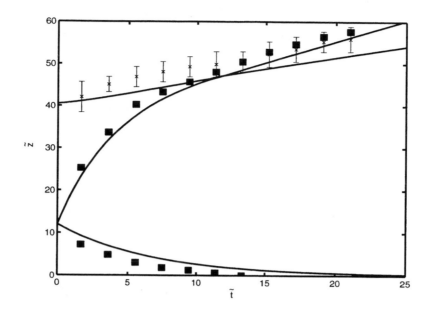

Figure 3: Experimental measurements of the fountain height ($\times$) and the fronts ($\blacksquare$) along with the theoretical predictions of our model. In this experiment, $\sigma = 14$ and $f_s(14) = 0.4$.

fountain height and, where applicable, the expression for the descending front (4). The good agreement between theory and experiment for the fountain height and ascending front indicates that the assumptions made, and the simple weighting function used, describe the actual fountain behaviour well. The experimental results indicate that the descending front falls slightly faster than predicted by (4). This faster descent is almost certainly due to the additional entrainment into the overshooting fluid below the front, which is not included in our model.

A Theoretical Model of a Fountain

Recently, we have developed a new theoretical model of axisymmetric turbulent fountains in both homogeneous and stratified environments. The model, which builds on a model developed by McDougall (1981), uses a set of entrainment equations to quantify the fluxes of volume, momentum and buoyancy in the upflow and downflow of the fountain. Four different formulations were considered, comprising two formulations of the body forces acting on the central upflow, and two formulations of the rates of entrainment between the upflow, the downflow, and the environment. These equations were integrated numerically to obtain predictions for the fountain height, the width of the upflow and downflow, the upflow and downflow velocity, and the upflow and downflow buoyancy. The numerical calculations were then compared with experimental measurements in a homogeneous fluid (figure 4), and gave reasonably good agreement. The calculations were also consistent (within 5%) with our experimental measurements of the fountain height in a linearly stratified fluid. The fountain model can also be used to obtain an improved prediction of $\tilde{z}_{fs}(t)$ in our model of the ascending front.

Acknowledgements

We thank Tony Beasley, Derek Corrigan and Ross Wylde-Browne for their technical assistance with the experiments, and Stewart Turner for his helpful comments. The financial support of an Australian Research Council Fellowship (for R.K.) and that of a Jaeger Scholarship and Australian Postgraduate Award (for L.B.) are gratefully acknowledged.

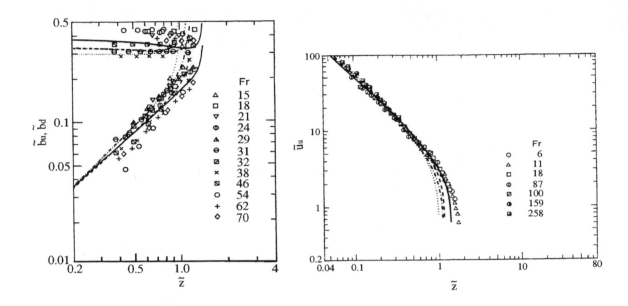

Figure 4: Comparison of four theoretical model formulations with the experimental data of Mizushina *et al.* (1982) for the upflow and downflow radius (left figure) and the upflow velocity (right figure).

References

BAINES, W.D. & TURNER, J.S. 1969 Turbulent buoyant convection from a source in a confined region. *J. Fluid Mech.* **37**, 51-80.

BAINES, W.D., TURNER, J.S. & CAMPBELL, I.H. 1990 Turbulent fountains in an open chamber. *J. Fluid Mech.* **212**, 557-592.

BLOOMFIELD, L.J. & KERR, R.C. 1998 Turbulent fountains in a stratified fluid. *J. Fluid Mech.* **358**, 335-356.

BLOOMFIELD, L.J. & KERR, R.C. 1999 Turbulent fountains in a confined stratified environment. *J. Fluid Mech.* **389**, 27-54.

BLOOMFIELD, L.J. & KERR, R.C. 2000 A theoretical model of a turbulent fountain. *J. Fluid Mech.* submitted.

CARDOSO, S.S.S. & WOODS, A.W. 1993 Mixing by a turbulent plume in a confined stratified region. *J. Fluid Mech.* **250**, 277-305.

CAMPBELL, I.H. & TURNER, J.S. 1989 Fountains in magma chambers. *J. Petrol.* **30**, 885-923.

KOH, R.C.Y. & BROOKS, N.H. 1975 Fluid mechanics of waste-water disposal in the ocean. *Ann. Rev. Fluid Mech.* **7**, 187-211.

LARSON, M. & JÖNSSON, L. 1994 Efficiency of mixing by a turbulent jet in a stably stratified fluid. *Proc. 4th Inter. Symp. on Stratified Flows, Grenoble, France.*

LINDBERG, W.R. & PETERSON, J.D. 1991 Negatively buoyant jet (or plume) with application to snowplow exit flow behaviour. *Transportation Research Record* **1304**, 219-229.

McDOUGALL, T.J. 1981 Negatively buoyant vertical jets. *Tellus* **33**, 313-320.

MIZUSHINA, T., OGINO, F., TAKEUCHI, H. & IKAWA, H. 1982 An experimental study of vertical turbulent jet with negative buoyancy. *Wärme-und Stoffübertragung* **16**, 15-21.

WOODS, A.W., BURSIK, M.I. & KURBATOV, A.V. 1998 The interaction of ash flows with ridges. *Bull. Volcanol.* **60**, 38-51.

WOODS, A.W. & CAULFIELD, C.P. 1992 A laboratory study of explosive volcanic eruptions. *J. Geophys. Res.* **97**, 6699-6712.

Parameterizing the Adiabatic Effects of Eddies in Stratified Fluids

Trevor J McDougall[1]

[1]CSIRO Marine Research, GPO Box 1538, Hobart, Tasmania 7001, Australia.
Trevor.McDougall@marine.csiro.au

1. Abstract

Mesoscale eddies act to mix fluid parcels in a way that is highly constrained by the stratified nature of the fluid. The residual-mean theory provides the link between the different views that are apparent from averaging these turbulent flow fields in height coordinates and in density coordinates. It reduces the parameterization problem from three dimensions to two dimensions and it shows how the eddy fluxes are skew-symmetric in height coordinates so that the total advection velocity can be adiabatic.

2. Introduction

Mesoscale eddies are responsible for causing significant fluxes of density and tracer, particularly in the Southern Ocean. The effects of mesoscale eddies still need to be parameterised in climate models because of the present and foreseeable limitations of computer power. For twenty years in ocean modelling mesoscale eddies have been parameterized as horizontal diffusion and in the past six years we have learnt how to improve on this scheme and also what damage this horizontal mixing was doing to the model results. Horizontal mixing implies an uncontrolled amount of diapycnal mixing and it is this unwanted diapycnal mixing that needs to be avoided in ocean modelling. What was needed was a formulation for mesoscale mixing that is the three-dimensional extension of the successful zonal-residual-mean theory of atmospheric science. This paper outlines the extra difficulties that are encountered on performing the residual-mean approach in three dimensions under a temporal or ensemble averaging operator compared with the simpler task of performing a zonal average.

3. The Temporal-Residual-Mean Density Equation

In what follows the averaging operator (the overbar) is defined to be an ensemble average, or a low-pass temporal average and primed quantities are the deviations from this ensemble or low-passed value. In developing the theory it is convenient to deal with the density conservation equation and to ignore any non-linearity in the equation of state. The usual conservation equations for Eulerian-averaged density and for half the density variance are

$$\overline{D_t}\,\overline{\gamma} = \overline{Q} - \nabla \cdot \left(\overline{\mathbf{U}'\gamma'} \right) \tag{1}$$

and

$$\overline{D_t}\,\overline{\phi} = \overline{Q'\gamma'} - \overline{\mathbf{U}'\gamma'} \cdot \nabla\overline{\gamma} + O\!\left(\alpha^3\right). \tag{2}$$

Here $\overline{\phi} \equiv \frac{1}{2}\overline{\gamma'^2}$, is half the density variance measured at a fixed point in space, and the terminology $O\!\left(\alpha^3\right)$ indicates terms that are of cubic or higher order in perturbation amplitude.

In order to develop residual-mean conservation equations that apply to unsteady flows we need to admit the possibility that the Eulerian-mean density may not be the most appropriate mean density to appear in the mean density conservation equation. For example, the Eulerian-mean density, $\bar{\gamma}(x,y,z,t)$, describes a density surface whose average height is not that of the original Eulerian averaging, z. The appropriate mean density is the one whose surface is, on average, at the height of the averaging. This density can be expressed in terms of $\bar{\gamma}$ and $\bar{\phi}$ by

$$\tilde{\gamma} = \bar{\gamma} - \left(\frac{\bar{\phi}}{\bar{\gamma}_z}\right)_z + O(\alpha^3). \tag{3}$$

The distinction here is between averaging density at a given height, z, versus averaging the height of a specific density surface $\gamma = \tilde{\gamma}$. Near the sea surface and the ocean floor, the accuracy of the Taylor series expansion that underlies (3) degrades so that the error term becomes linear in perturbation quantities.

Combining (3) and (1), a conservation equation can be written for the modified density, $\tilde{\gamma}$, namely

$$\tilde{\gamma}_t + \nabla \cdot \left(\overline{U} \tilde{\gamma}\right) = \overline{Q}^{\#} - \nabla \cdot \mathbf{F}^M + O(\alpha^3) \tag{4}$$

where the modified density flux, $\mathbf{F}^M$, is

$$\mathbf{F}^M = \overline{U'\gamma'} + \overline{U}\left(\frac{\bar{\phi}}{\bar{\gamma}_z}\right)_z + \mathbf{k}\left\{\left(\frac{\bar{\phi}}{\bar{\gamma}_z}\right)_t - \frac{\overline{Q'\gamma'}}{\bar{\gamma}_z} + \frac{\overline{Q}_z}{\bar{\gamma}_z}\left(\frac{\bar{\phi}}{\bar{\gamma}_z}\right)\right\} \tag{5}$$

and

$$\overline{Q}^{\#} \equiv \overline{Q} + \left[-\frac{\overline{Q'\gamma'}}{\bar{\gamma}_z} + \frac{\overline{Q}_z}{\bar{\gamma}_z}\left(\frac{\bar{\phi}}{\bar{\gamma}_z}\right)\right]_z. \tag{6}$$

Now the density variance equation, (2), is used to eliminate $\overline{w'\gamma'}$ from the expression, (4), and after much algebra, the modified density flux, can be expressed as

$$\mathbf{F}^M = \tilde{\gamma}\,\mathbf{U}^+ + \mathbf{M} + O(\alpha^3) = -\mathbf{A}\nabla\tilde{\gamma} + \mathbf{N} + O(\alpha^3). \tag{7}$$

The quasi-Stokes velocity, $\mathbf{U}^+$, is defiined in terms of the quasi-Stokes streamfunction,

$$\boldsymbol{\Psi} \equiv -\frac{\overline{\mathbf{V}'\gamma'}}{\bar{\gamma}_z} + \frac{\overline{\mathbf{V}}_z}{\bar{\gamma}_z}\left(\frac{\bar{\phi}}{\bar{\gamma}_z}\right) \tag{8}$$

by

$$\mathbf{U}^+ \equiv \nabla \times (\boldsymbol{\Psi} \times \mathbf{k}) = \boldsymbol{\Psi}_z - \mathbf{k}\left(\nabla_H \cdot \boldsymbol{\Psi}\right), \tag{9}$$

and the density flux, is non-divergent and is defined by

$$\mathbf{M} \equiv \nabla \times \left[\left(-\boldsymbol{\Psi}\tilde{\gamma} + \frac{\overline{\mathbf{V}\phi}}{\bar{\gamma}_z}\right) \times \mathbf{k}\right]. \tag{10}$$

Also, the asymmetric matrix $\mathbf{A}$ is defined in terms of the two components of the quasi-Stokes streamfunction, $\boldsymbol{\Psi} = \left(\Psi^x, \Psi^y\right)$, as

$$A \equiv \begin{bmatrix} 0 & 0 & \Psi^x \\ 0 & 0 & \Psi^y \\ -\Psi^x & -\Psi^y & 0 \end{bmatrix}$$ (11)

and the non-divergent density flux, N, is given by

$$N \equiv \left(\frac{\overline{V\phi}}{\overline{\gamma}_z} \right)_z - k \nabla_H \cdot \left(\frac{\overline{V\phi}}{\overline{\gamma}_z} \right) = \nabla \times \left[\left(\frac{\overline{V\phi}}{\overline{\gamma}_z} \right) \times k \right].$$ (12)

4. Features of the TRM Density Equation

It can be shown that the quasi-Stokes streamfunction, Ψ, has a very simple physical interpretation: it is the contribution of perturbations (or eddies) to the horizontal transport of fluid that is denser than the modified density, $\tilde{\gamma}$. Hence, the horizontal transport of fluid that is more dense that this density can be found by adding the quasi-Stokes streamfunction to the horizontal transport below this height that can be obtained from the Eulerian-averaged velocity. In this way it can be shown that the thickness-weighted velocity that is found by thickness-weighted averaging the horizontal velocity in density coordinates is the sum of the Eulerian-mean velocity and the quasi-Stokes velocity, $\overline{V} + \Psi_z$.

Similarly, $\overline{Q}^\#$ can be shown to be the thickness-weighted value of the density source term, Q.

The rearrangement of the Reynolds-averaged density equation, (1), into the form (4)–(5) and the subsequent two simplified forms of the modified density flux, (7), lie at the heart of the Temporal-Residual-Mean theory. Substituting the two alternative expressions, (7), into the mean density equation, (4) gives the following two versions of the mean density equation.

$$\begin{aligned}
\tilde{\gamma}_t + \nabla \cdot \left(\overline{U}\tilde{\gamma} \right) &= \overline{Q}^\# - \nabla \cdot \left(U^+ \tilde{\gamma} \right) - \nabla \cdot M + O\left(\alpha^3 \right) \\
&= \overline{Q}^\# + \nabla \cdot \left(A\nabla \tilde{\gamma} \right) - \nabla \cdot N + O\left(\alpha^3 \right).
\end{aligned}$$ (13)

When the non-divergent fluxes M and N are ignored, the top line of (13) shows how mesoscale eddies may be regarded as causing an extra three-dimensional advection velocity, namely the quasi-Stokes velocity, U^+. The second line of (13) shows that an alternative explanation of the effects of eddies is that they cause a skew-diffusion of density, that is, a diffusive flux of density that is directed parallel to density surfaces. The important practical feature of both interpretations is that all one needs to know in order to be able to incorporate the effects of mesoscale eddies into an ocean model's density equation is the two-dimensional quasi-Stokes streamfunction, and (8) is an expression for this streamfunction in terms of quantities that are available in an eddy-resolving height-coordinate model. In this way, the TRM theory has reduced the task of parameterization from three dimensions in (1) to just two dimensions.

The top line of (13) shows that when the flow is instantaneously adiabatic, (hence $\overline{Q}^\# = 0$), the TRM velocity, $\overline{U}^\# = \overline{U} + U^+$, has no component through $\tilde{\gamma}$ surfaces. This result is the "adiabatic" result that we desire. The "adiabatic" nature of the tracer advection velocity is a highly prized feature in ocean modelling. Note that this result is in stark contrast to the Eulerian-mean velocity, where from (1) or (13) it is seen that the Eulerian-mean velocity has a large component through mean isopycnals.

When the tracer equations are examined in the light of this TRM approach one finds that there is only one interpretation for the tracers that are carried by eddyless coarse resolution models:- they are the thickness-weighted mean tracer values that would be found by averaging the tracer between density surfaces. This dictates the way in which ocean observations should be compared with the output of coarse-resolution ocean models and also the way in which ocean observations should be averaged before performing inverse calculations.

5. Boundary Conditions on the Quasi-Stokes Streamfunction

The physical interpretation of the quasi-Stokes streamfunction, as described above, provides guidance on the boundary conditions that should be imposed at the top and bottom of the ocean. Any density surface which is less dense than any in the ocean at a particular time is assumed to reside at the sea surface. The modified density, $\tilde{\gamma}$, appropriate to each height has the property (by definition) that the height of this $\tilde{\gamma}$ surface averages to zero. The contribution of eddies to the transport of water that is more dense than $\tilde{\gamma}$ can therefore be shown to reduce to zero as the sea surface (or ocean floor) is approached. By definition, this transport is the quasi-Stokes streamfunction and so it must approach zero smoothly at the top and bottom boundary.

In the absence of a horizontal boundary one would estimate that a fluid parcel in a mesoscale eddy would undergo vertical excursions (of height) that would scale with the Rossby radius, R, multiplied by the magnitude of the slope of the density surface, $|\mathbf{L}| = \left| -\nabla_H \tilde{\gamma} / \tilde{\gamma}_z \right|$. Both R and $|\mathbf{L}|$ can be estimated locally at every point in an ocean model. One would estimate that if $R|\mathbf{L}|$ were greater than the depth of a certain grid-point, then the density surface, $\tilde{\gamma}$, appropriate to that point would have begun to clip the sea surface at some times. This suggests that the quasi-Stokes streamfunction (or a diffusivity that is used to parameterize the quasi-Stokes streamfunction) should be tapered to zero according to the scaled height, $z/(R|\mathbf{L}|)$.

6. Conclusions

The TRM approach tells us how we should interpret the variables that are carried in an eddyless model, and it also reduces the task of parameterizing the most important eddy effects from being a three-dimensional task to being a two-dimensional task. The task is now quite specific:- we must learn how to parameterize the quasi-Stokes streamfunction, (8). If we are successful in doing this we will be able to run an eddyless height-coordinate model while knowing that it is equivalent to running a density coordinate model at high resolution and averaging over the mesoscale eddies.

This short paper has concentrated on the density equation and the implicit assumption has been that the Eulerian-mean velocity is available as an output of the momentum equations. This is usually though to be a good assumption because of the dominance of the geostrophic balance at the large scales of relevance to the global ocean circulation.

There is however an alternative way of implementing such a TRM parameterization. One can apply the TRM averaging approach to the horizontal momentum equations, thereby obtaining a forcing term on the right of these equations that looks a little similar to the Eliassen-Palm flux of the zonal-averaging literature. The key result of that literature is that while the Eliassen-Palm flux is of second order in perturbation quantities, its divergence is one order higher and so can often be ignored or at least assumed to be equal to the northward flux of potential vorticity. No such result has been proven for the three-dimensional problem under temporal or ensemble averaging. Indeed, it seems very likely that the divergence of this flux is still of second order in perturbation quantities. Nevertheless, one can boldly assume this result by a crude analogy with the zonal averaging literature. The results of this approach are expected to be very similar to the more conventional method of implementing the TRM scheme in the tracer equations.

Inclined Wall Plume Generated by Buoyancy Flux from Sloping Bed

Kohji Michioku[1], Ken-ichi Matsushita[2] and Toshiyuki Takahashi[3]

[1]Department of Civil Engineering, Kobe University, Kobe 657-8501, JAPAN
[2]Osaka Gas Co. Ltd., Osaka 541-0046, JAPAN
[3]Fukken-Chosa-Sekkei Co. Ltd, Hiroshima 732-0052, JAPAN
michioku@kobe-u.ac.jp

1. Abstract

An inclined plume generated by a buoyancy flux on a sloping boundary was examined. The flow is a free convection; a driving force is a pure buoyancy flux from the slope surface and no mass flux discharge is supplied. The present system is to simulate a sloping benthic layer in a reservoir surrounded by anaerobic waters in which dissolved matters are released from the bed due to anaerobic reduction. A heavy and salty water mass is then produced right above the bed and gravitationally runs down the sloping bed. The plume transports dissolved constituents such as nutrients and metals to deep region, which promotes eutrophication in the bottom layer. This flow configuration was reproduced in a laboratory experiment. For technical convenience of flow generation and measurements in the experimental model, buoyancy was supplied by heat flux instead of salinity discharge. Through measurements of velocity and buoyancy profiles, it was confirmed that the flow has a self-similar structure. A theoretical analysis was also performed and the solutions of velocity and buoyancy show good agreement with the experiment. Streamwise development of the plume was well reproduced by the theory as well.

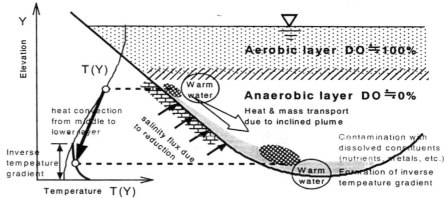

Figure 1 Generation of an inclined plume and construction of an inverse temperature gradient in a eutrophic reservoir.

2. Introduction

In eutrophic lakes and reservoirs dissolved oxygen is significantly consumed while organic matters are decomposed, which makes impounded water anaerobic. Bed sediments surrounded by the anaerobic water are then reduced and dissolved constituents such as nutrients and metals are released from the benthic layer. The ionic matters generally increase salinity and specific weight of water. A plume is generated in a way that the heavy water mass slides down the perimeter where the bed is inclined, as

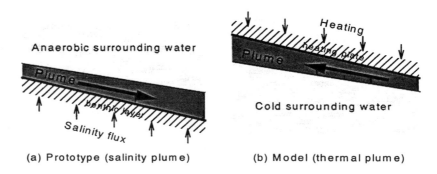

Figure 2 Prototype plume and experimental model

illustrated in Fig.1. It was found through the authors' field measurements (Michioku and Kanda, 1999) that this plume transports nutrients and metals from the inclined perimeter to the bottom, which brings serious eutrophication of the bottom layer. An inverse temperature gradient was also constructed by transporting warm water weighted with salinity from shallower regions to the lake bottom. This heat transfer is schematically shown in the left diagram in Fig.1.

The present study is to investigate hydrodynamics of the inclined plume that is generated by buoyancy flux supplied from a sloping boundary. In a sense that there is no mass flux supply, the flow is a free convection and very different from ordinary plumes that are initiated usually by combination of mass, momentum and buoyancy flux discharges. Although the plume in the prototype is driven by salinity buoyancy, a modeling was made by thermal buoyancy for the sake of experimental convenience. This situation is close to a gravity flow around a heat radiator. Among previous studies of heat exchanger, Sparrow et al. (1959) examined a forced convection around a heated plate with varied titling angle. The prototype and the model systems are compared in Fig.2. In the model an inclined boundary is uniformly heated from above, below which a plume is generated. Therefore, buoyancy or specific gravity is directed upward in the model, while it is downward in the prototype. Nevertheless, both of the systems are completely equivalent in a dynamic sense.

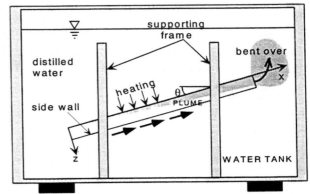

Velocity and buoyancy profiles and streamwise flow development were investigated in the laboratory experiment. A theoretical analysis was also made to describe the flow structure. Since there is no difference between the thermal and salinity plumes in a normalized coordinate system, the theory can be directly compared with the laboratory data. The analysis will be verified through comparison with the experiment. Application possibility of the present theory to a reservoir system will be finally discussed.

Figure 3 Experimental apprautus

3. Experimental setup

Figure 3 shows our experimental equipment. A plastic-walled test channel was installed with an inclined angle θ in a 110cm-deep water tank with a horizontal dimension of $150\text{cm} \times 100\text{cm}$. The test section is 80cm long and has a rectangular cross section of 15cm wide and 5cm deep. A constant power was supplied to an aluminum heating plate that is installed on the channel's bottom. Given a constant temperature flux H_S (cm°C/sec) and a slope angle θ, a steady plume motion was generated along the sloping channel. Flow visualization was made for velocity measurements by use of hydrogen bubbles. Temperature was measured at 6 cross sections with twenty thermocouples and processed by a data logger. The experimental conditions were varied in ranges of $2.86° < \theta < 76.0°$ and $0.0053 < H_S < 0.079\,\text{cm°C/sec}$. A two dimensional coordinate system is defined such that x is taken from the upstream end to downstream and z is originated from the bottom surface to vertically downward. Although the heater is actually located at the top surface of the channel, we call this the "bottom" for convenience of comparing with the salinity plume system.

4. Velocity and temperature

Examples of velocity and temperature profiles are respectively shown in Figs.4 and 5. Fig.5(a) shows that the plume is heated up in the downstream direction. This increases plume's buoyancy and then the fluid motion is accelerated as shown in Fig.4(a). Fig.5(c) indicates that the plume looses more heat energy when the slope is steeper. This is because more heat is transported downstream by the more rapidly increased velocity in a case of steeper slope, which is recognized from Fig.4(c).

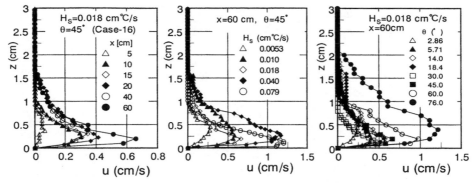

(a) Dependency of U(z) on x   (b) Dependency of U(z) on H_S (c) Dependency of U(z) on θ

Figure 4 Measured velocity profiles $U(z)$

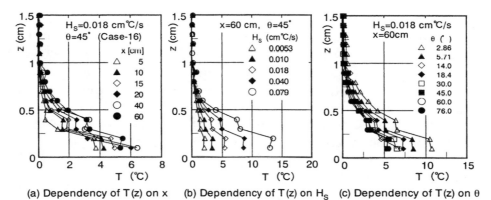

(a) Dependency of T(z) on x   (b) Dependency of T(z) on H_S (c) Dependency of T(z) on θ

Figure 5 Measured temperature profiles $T(z)$

5. Theory

(1) Governing equations and boundary conditions
Note that the present system is well approximated to be a boundary layer along a sloping bed. For a steady plume system in Fig.6 conservation of mass, momentum and concentration is written as follows.

$$\frac{\partial u}{\partial x} + \frac{\partial w}{\partial z} = 0 \tag{1}$$

$$u\frac{\partial u}{\partial x} + w\frac{\partial u}{\partial z} = g\sin\theta - \frac{1}{\rho}\frac{\partial p}{\partial x} + \nu\frac{\partial^2 u}{\partial z^2} \tag{2}$$

$$0 = -g\cos\theta - \frac{1}{\rho}\frac{\partial p}{\partial z} \tag{3}$$

$$u\frac{\partial C}{\partial x} + w\frac{\partial C}{\partial z} = \kappa_C\frac{\partial^2 C}{\partial z^2} \tag{4}$$

Boussinesq approximation is used in the formulation. Here, (u, w): vector velocities in the direction of (x, z), C: concentration, g: gravity acceleration, p: pressure, ν: kinematic viscosity and κ_C: coefficient of diffusivity. Fluid density ρ is related to C by an equation of state as

$$\rho = \rho_0(1 + \beta C) \tag{5}$$

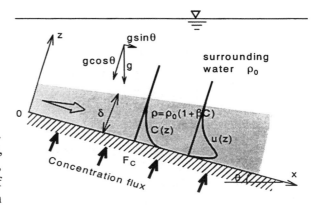

Figure 6 Coordinate system in the analysis

where β is a proportional coefficient. This set of equations is directly applicable to the thermal plume system by replacing βC with $-\alpha T$ and κ_C with κ_T, respectively. α and κ_T are a thermal expansion coefficient and heat diffusivity.

Elimination of p between Eqs.(2) and (3) leads to a momentum balance in the x-direction as

$$u\frac{\partial u}{\partial x} + w\frac{\partial u}{\partial z} = \underbrace{\beta Cg\sin\theta}_{[G1]} - \underbrace{\frac{\partial}{\partial x}\int_z^\infty \beta Cg\cos\theta dz}_{[G2]} + \nu\frac{\partial^2 u}{\partial z^2} \qquad (6)$$

For a constant concentration flux from the bottom F_C, the boundary conditions are written as follows.

$$u=w=0, \quad F_C = -\kappa_C(\partial C/\partial z)\big|_{z=0} = (\partial/\partial x)\int_0^\infty uCdz \qquad \text{at } z=0 \qquad (7)$$

$$u=C=0 \qquad \text{at } z=\infty \qquad (8)$$

(2) Self-similarity analysis

A self-similarity of flow structure is assumed in a way same to a plume analysis done by, for instance, Ellison and Turner (1959) and Parker et al. (1986) etc.. Introducing a stream function ψ defined by $(u,w) = (\partial\psi/\partial z, -\partial\psi/\partial x)$, variables are assumed to have the following self-similar functional forms,

$$\eta = azx^{-l}, \qquad (9), \qquad \psi = bx^m F(\eta) \qquad (10), \qquad C = ex^n G(\eta) \qquad (11)$$

where, $F(\eta)$ and $G(\eta)$ are unknown functions of a variable η. (a,b,e,l,m,n) are undetermined coefficients.

Substituting the variables in Eqs.(9)-(11) into Eqs.(4) and (6) and Eq.(7)$_{-2}$, a set of algebraic equations for (l,m,n) are obtained from a condition that $F(\eta)$ and $G(\eta)$ should be independent of x. They are

$$2m-2l-1=n=n+l-1=m-3l \qquad (12), \qquad m+n-l-1=n-2l \qquad (13), \qquad 0=n-l=m+n-1 \qquad (14)$$

No combination of (l,m,n) satisfies all of the Eqs.(12)-(14). An order estimation, however, fortunately leads to possibility that the second gravity term [G2] in Eq.(6) would be negligibly small compared to the other terms. This was also suggested by and Mahrt (1982). This approximation brings little significant error for practical use in a range of the present system. The coefficients are finally identified to be

$$l = 1/5, \, m = 4/5, \, n = 1/5 \qquad (15)$$

Substituting Eqs.(9)-(11) and Eq.(15) into Eqs.(4) and (6) with the boundary condition of Eq.(7), partial differential equations Eqs.(4) and (6) are converted to the following two ordinary differential equations.

$$\frac{3}{5}F'^2 - \frac{4}{5}FF'' - G - \Pr F''' = 0 \qquad (16), \qquad \frac{1}{5}F'G - \frac{4}{5}FG' - G'' = 0 \qquad (17)$$

In the course of formulation, the coefficients (a,b,e) in Eqs.(9), (10) and (11) are determined to be

$$a = \left(I^{-1}\kappa_C^{-3}\beta gF_C\sin\theta\right)^{1/5}, \quad b = \left(I^{-1}\kappa_C^2\beta gF_C\sin\theta\right)^{1/5}, \quad e = F_C I^{-1}\left(I^{-1}\kappa_C^2\beta gF_C\sin\theta\right)^{-1/5} \qquad (18)$$

where $I \equiv \int_0^\infty F'Gd\eta$ and $\Pr = \nu/\kappa_C$ is Prandtl number.

Next, introducing the following characteristic scales of length, velocity and concentration (L_0, U_0, C_0),

$$L_0 = I^{1/4}\kappa_C^{3/4}(\beta gF_C\sin\theta)^{-1/4}, \quad U_0 = I^{-1/4}(\kappa_C\beta gF_C\sin\theta)^{1/4}, \quad C_0 = I^{-3/4}F_C(\kappa_C\beta gF_C\sin\theta)^{-1/4}$$

and substituting (a,b,e) in Eq.(18) into Eqs.(9)-(11) the variables are normalized as,

$$\eta = \tilde{z}\tilde{x}^{-1/5}, \quad \tilde{u} \equiv U_0^{-1}u = U_0^{-1}(\partial\psi/\partial z) = \tilde{x}^{3/5}F'(\eta), \quad \tilde{C} \equiv C_0^{-1}C = \tilde{x}^{1/5}G(\eta) \qquad (19)$$

where $(\tilde{x} \equiv x/L_0, \tilde{z} \equiv z/L_0)$ are normalized coordinates. Note that the scales (L_0, U_0, C_0) have been determined so as to satisfy the following relationship.

$$\Pe \equiv U_0 L_0/\kappa_C = 1.0, \quad U_0 C_0 = F_C/I \qquad (20)$$

Normalized boundary conditions corresponding to Eqs.(7) and (8) are now

$$F(0) = F'(0) = 0, \quad G'(0) = -I, \quad F'(\infty) = 0, \quad G(\infty) = 0 \qquad (21)$$

Because the factor I can be determined without any restriction, $I=1$ is used here.

6. Similarity profiles of velocity and buoyancy

The solutions for $F(\eta)$ and $G(\eta)$ are obtained by numerically integrating Eqs.(16) and (17) with use of the conditions, Eq.(21). Eq.(19) suggests that experimental velocity and buoyancy are normalized in a way of

$$
\left.
\begin{array}{l}
\tilde{u} \cdot \tilde{x}^{-3/5} \\
\equiv (u/U_0) \cdot (x/L_0)^{-3/5} \\
\tilde{C} \cdot \tilde{x}^{-1/5} \\
\equiv (C/C_0) \cdot (x/L_0)^{-1/5}
\end{array}
\right\}
$$

(22)

and

$$
\eta = \tilde{z}\tilde{x}^{-1/5} = (z/L_0)(x/L_0)^{-1/5}
$$

(23)

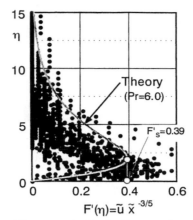

Figure 7 Self-similar profile of velocity $\tilde{u} \cdot \tilde{x}^{-3/5}$

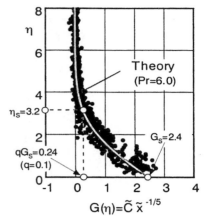

Figure 8 Self-similar profile of buoyancy $\tilde{C} \cdot \tilde{x}^{-1/5}$

The normalized experimental data can now be compared with the solutions of $F'(\eta)$ and $G(\eta)$, respectively. In the normalization, thermal buoyancy is related with salinity buoyancy as $\alpha T \Leftrightarrow \beta S$ and $\alpha H_s \Leftrightarrow \beta F_c$. The results are shown in Figs.7 and 8. The experimental data are from all measurement points and from all cases of experimental conditions. Because the velocity data shown were obtained by tracing hydrogen bubbles, their distribution is flatten than the theoretical profile due to the bubbles' buoyancy effect. They also show considerable scattering. After this experiment, flow visualization was made by using fine nylon particles of 10μm in diameter and a specific weight of 1.02 in an experiment with a

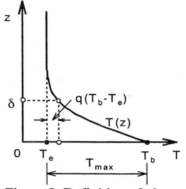

Figure 9 Definition of plume layer thickness δ.

boundary condition of a constant bottom temperature. A PTV analysis was rather successful and the velocity data show much less experimental errors than the present experiment, although they are not shown here. Nevertheless, it is confirmed that the normalized velocity and buoyancy have self-similar profiles independently of experimental conditions and streamwise distance. Considering the buoyancy effects of hydrogen bubbles in the velocity profile, one can say that agreement between the experiment and the theory is fairy satisfactory.

7. Streamwise development of plume

In order to discuss streamwise development of the plume, a plume layer thickness δ is defined from a temperature profile as shown in Fig.9. T_b and T_e are temperature of the bottom and the surrounding water, respectively. q is a fraction of a temperature anomaly at a certain depth, $\{T(z)-T_b\}$, to that at the bottom, (T_b-T_e). The thickness δ is here defined to be a height z corresponding to $\{T(z)-T_b\} = q(T_b-T_e)$ It was found through a careful examination of the data that a power law dependency of δ on x is mostly unchanged between a range of $0.01<q<0.2$. Therefore, the fraction q is set to be $q=0.1$. The theoretical curve of $G(\eta)$ in Fig.8 shows that the variable $\eta \equiv \eta_s = 3.2$ for $q=0.1$. A normalized relationship between δ and x is then obtained by putting $\eta=3.2$ in Eq.(19).₁ as

$$
\tilde{\delta} \equiv \delta/L_0 = \eta_s \tilde{x}^{1/5} = 3.2\tilde{x}^{1/5}
$$

(24)

where $\tilde{\delta} \equiv \delta / L_0$, $\tilde{x} \equiv x / L_0$. Referring theoretical curve of $F'(\eta)$ and $G(\eta)$ and Eqs.(19)$_{-2}$ and (19)$_{-3}$, dependencies of the maximum velocity U_{max} and the maximum temperature T_{max}, on x are obtained in dimensionless forms as well. They are

$$\tilde{U}_{max} \equiv U_{max} / U_0 = F'_S \tilde{x}^{3/5} = 0.39 \tilde{x}^{3/5} \quad (25)$$

$$\tilde{C}_{max} \equiv C_{max} / C_0 = G_S \tilde{x}^{1/5} = 2.4 \tilde{x}^{1/5} \quad (26)$$

The solutions Eqs.(24)-(26) are compared with the laboratory data in Figs.10, 11 and 12. The data points well fit the power laws estimated by the theory.

8. Concluding remarks

An inclined plume developed on an aerobic benthic layer was experimentally and theoretically examined. Prototype phenomena considered are that a plume is generated through anaerobic reduction and release of dissolved matters from an anaerobic benthic boundary in a reservoir. This is responsible for constructing a highly polluted water mass in the reservoir bottom. The plume's driving force is a pure buoyancy flux supplied from the sloping surface and there is no mass flux discharge. A laboratory experiment was carried out with respect to a plume driven by thermal buoyancy instead of salinity buoyancy. An analysis was also made assuming that the plume has a self-similar flow structure. The experimental profiles of the plume's velocity and buoyancy are confirmed to be very self-similar, which well agree with the proposed theory. Streamwise development behaviors of the plume are also in good agreement between the theory and the experiment. Prediction accuracy of reservoir eutrophication would be much improved by applying the present theory to water quality analysis in fields.

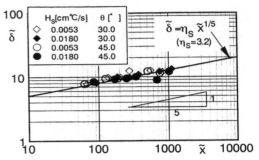

Figure 10 Dimensionless plume layer thickness $\tilde{\delta}$ versus, $\tilde{x}$.

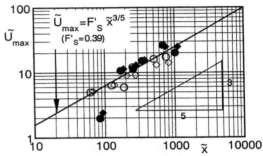

Figure 11 Dimensionless maximum velocity $\tilde{U}_{max}$ versus, $\tilde{x}$.

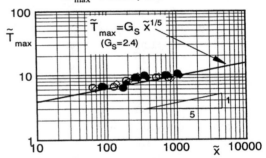

Figure 12 Dimensionless maximum temperature $\tilde{T}_{max}$ versus, $\tilde{x}$

The authors are grateful to the financial support from the Grant-in Aid for Scientific Research, the Japan Ministry of Education (Project No. 10650505, Leader: Dr. K. Michioku).

References

Ellison,T.H. and Turner,J.S.: Turbulent entrainment in stratified flows, *J. Fluid Mech.*, Vol.6, pp.423-448, 1959.

Mahrt,L.: Momentum balance of gravity flows, *J. Atmos. Sci.*, Vol.39, pp.2701-2711, 1982.

Michioku,K. and Kanda,T.: Nutrient transport due to heat-salt convection in a eutrophic reservoir, *Proc. 28th Conf. IAHR*, 1999.

Parker,G., Fukushima,Y. and Pantin,H.M.: Self-accelerating turbidity currents, *J. Fluid Mech.*, Vol.171, pp.145-181, 1986.

Sparrow,E.M., Eichhorn,R. and Gregg,J.L.: Combined forced and free convection in a boundary layer flow, *Physics Fluids*, Vol.2, No.3, pp.319-328, 1959.

Formation and Growth of Layers in an Infinite Stably Stratified Fluid due to Diffusive Convection

Takashi Noguchi and Hiroshi Niino

Ocean Research Institute, University of Tokyo, Tokyo 164 8639, Japan
noguchi@ori.u-tokyo.ac.jp, niino@ori.u-tokyo.ac.jp

1. Abstract

Formation of layers due to diffusive convections in an infinite fluid with linear vertical gradients of salt and temperature is investigated numerically, where all the density, salinity, and temperature decrease as the height increases. The fluid is initially at rest, but small random temperature perturbations are added over the whole calculation domain to trigger convective motions. Periodic conditions are imposed both at the lateral and vertical boundaries. When the ratio of the initial vertical gradients of temperature and salt falls into the range in which diffusive convections have a positive growth rate according to a linear theory, multi-layer structure in which convective layers are sandwiched by sharp diffusive interfaces is formed spontaneously. The average thickness of layers increases with time by repeating merging among the adjacent layers. Two different types of layer merging were found: one was caused by a weakening of the interface and the other by a migration of the interface.

2. Introduction

It is known that step-like vertical structures of salinity and temperature are fairly common features observed in many regions of the oceans (Neshyba et al., 1971; Tait and Howe, 1968). In these structures, nearly neutrally-stratified layers are sandwiched by very sharp and stable density (and concentration) gaps both from above and below. Observations suggest that each layer has a typical vertical dimension of about 10m and possesses horizontal coherency over several kilometers (Tait and Howe, 1968). The fact that sharp gradients of density and concentrations are often observed suggests that there must be some mechanism to maintain them against possible molecular and turbulent diffusion processes. The existence of the neutrally-stratified layer, on the other hand, suggests the presence of some mixing process.

One of the most promising candidates to produce these observed features of the step-like structures is the double-diffusive convection. In fact, there have been several studies on this process. However, most of the previous studies examined the development of the convective layers driven by some buoyancy flux through vertical boundaries: e.g. a linear gradient of salinity is heated from the bottom (Turner, 1968; Huppert and Linden, 1979; Fernando, 1987), or linear gradients of salinity and temperature are located between homogeneous layers (Linden, 1976).

In this paper, we will demonstrate by the use of a two-dimensional numerical model that layers can be generated in a stably-stratified infinite fluid without boundary fluxes but at the expense of the potential energy stored in the inner temperature field as expected theoretically by Linden(1976).

In what follows we will describe our numerical simulation on the diffusive convections and resulting layer formation. In section 3, basic equations and model configuration are described. Results are presented in section 4, and summary and conclusions are given in section 5.

3.Basic Equations and Model

Set-up. Consider two-dimensional convective motions in an infinite two-components incompressible fluid. The initial density field is homogeneous in the horizontal direction but varies linearly in the vertical direction.

The density ρ_* of the fluid depends on both salinity S_* and temperature T_*, and is given by

$$\rho_* = \rho_{0*}(1 - \alpha T_* + \beta S_*),\qquad(1)$$

under the Boussinesq approximation, where the constants ρ_{0*}, α, and β are the reference density, the thermal expansion coefficient, and the saline contraction coefficient, respectively and the asterisks denote dimensional quantities.

Both the vertical gradients of salinity $\overline{S_{z*}}$ and that of temperature $\overline{T_{z*}}$ are assumed to be negative. The vertical gradient of density $\overline{\rho_{z*}} = \rho_{0*}(-\alpha\overline{T_{z*}} + \beta\overline{S_{z*}})$ is also negative, so that the density stratification is stable. The contribution of temperature to the density gradient, $-\rho_{0*}\alpha T_{z*}$ will be hereafter denoted by ρ_{T_z*}, and that of salinity, $\rho_{0*}\beta S_{z*}$ by ρ_{S_z*}. Because of the difference in the diffusion coefficients of temperature and salinity, double-diffusive convection may be possible if the density gradient ratio $\gamma \equiv \rho_{T_z*}/\rho_{S_z*}$ falls into a certain range.

Nondimensionalization.   In the numerical model, all variables are nondimensionalized. Although there is no externally-given length scale in this problem, there exists one internal length scale,

$$\delta_* \equiv \left| \frac{1}{\rho_0} \frac{g\overline{\rho_T}_{z*}}{\kappa_T \nu} \right|^{-\frac{1}{4}},$$

where g is the gravity acceleration, κ_T the thermal diffusion coefficient, and ν the kinematic viscosity. By using this length scale, the following scaling has been introduced: time $t_* = (\delta_*^2/\kappa_T) \cdot t$, temperature and salinity $(T_*, S_*) = \delta_*(\overline{T_{z*}}\cdot T, \overline{S_{z*}}\cdot S)$, horizontal and vertical coordinates $(x_*, z_*) = \delta_*(x, z)$, horizontal and vertical velocities $(u_*, w_*) = (\kappa_T/\delta_*)\cdot(u, w)$, and pressure $p_* = (\kappa_T/\delta_*)^2 \cdot p$.

Model.   The present numerical model solves the two-dimensional Navier-Stokes equations

$$\frac{Du}{Dt} = -\frac{\partial p}{\partial x} + Pr\nabla^2 u,\qquad(2)$$

$$\frac{Dw}{Dt} = -\frac{\partial p}{\partial z} + Pr\nabla^2 w - Pr(T - \gamma^{-1}S),\qquad(3)$$

together with the conservation equations of T and S

$$\frac{DT}{Dt} = \nabla^2 T,\qquad(4)$$

$$\frac{DS}{Dt} = \tau\nabla^2 S,\qquad(5)$$

and the continuity equation

$$\frac{\partial u}{\partial x} + \frac{\partial w}{\partial z} = 0,\qquad(6)$$

where $D/Dt \equiv \partial/\partial t + u\,\partial/\partial x + w\,\partial/\partial z$, $\tau \equiv \kappa_S/\kappa_T$, and Pr the Prandtl number. For a salinity-temperature system, $\tau = 10^{-2}$ and $Pr = 7$.

These equations are cast in a finite difference form, in which variables are configured in square staggered grid: *i.e.* vorticity and stream function are taken at the vertex, while T and S at center. The upstream scheme was used in the advection terms, since it is capable of coping with very sharp interfaces. Although the scheme is known to have spurious numerical diffusion, it turned out that the model succeeded to make quite a realistic prediction of the flow characteristics.

The grid interval is 1.2 in non-dimensional unit (δ_* in dimensional unit) both in the horizontal and vertical directions. The computational domain is a right square with 256×256 grid points. In order to consider convective motions in an infinite fluid, periodic boundary conditions are imposed both at the horizontal and vertical boundaries of the domain for all variables except for T and S. For T and S that have the basic linear stratification, however, only the deviations from the basic stratification are calculated.

Before starting the calculation, a two-dimensional white noise is imposed as initial temperature disturbances. The amplitude of the disturbances is no more than 1/10000 of the domain's top - bottom temperature difference, and is uniform over the whole two-dimensional wavenumber space. The phase of the disturbance, however, is randomized. The time integration is made with a time step of $\Delta t = 2 \times 10^{-3}$, and is continued until $t = 800$.

4.Results

Flow evolution. A linear stability analysis for a salinity-temperature system shows that the basic state is unstable with respect to diffusive convections if the density gradient ratio γ is larger than 0.876.

For $\gamma = 0.88$, the small initial random perturbations cause oscillations that resemble stationary internal gravity waves (Fig.1A,B). The oscillation frequency is about 0.45 in non-dimensional time. The amplitude of the vertical velocity, however, remains small until $t \sim 130$. After $t \sim 130$, the quasi-steady oscillations are taken over by rapidly growing convective motions (Fig.1C,D). At the same time, heat and salt transports abruptly start to increase (Fig.2).

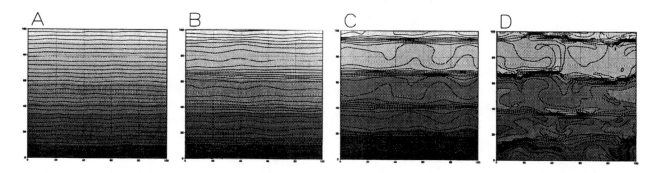

Figure 1: Net density distribution for times A–D indicated in Figure 2. Note that only $\frac{1}{9}$ of the entire calculated domain is displayed.

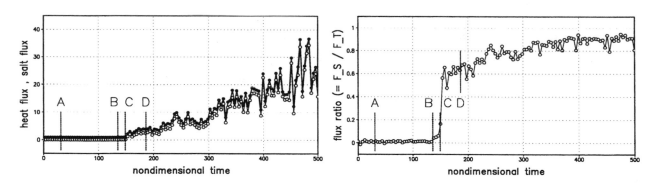

Figure 2: Time evolution of (a)vertical fluxes of heat (solid circle) and salt (open circle), and (b)their flux ratio.

Figure 3 shows the time evolution of the horizontally averaged non-dimensional density $\bar{\rho}$ as a function of vertical coordinate. The vertical profile of $\bar{\rho}$ remains almost linear until $t \sim 130$ before the convections initiate. After $t \sim 130$, however, it starts to show indentations, and by $t \sim 200$, remarkable step-like structures of density that resemble the one observed commonly in the oceans are established. Each step has a structure in which a layer of nearly homogeneous density

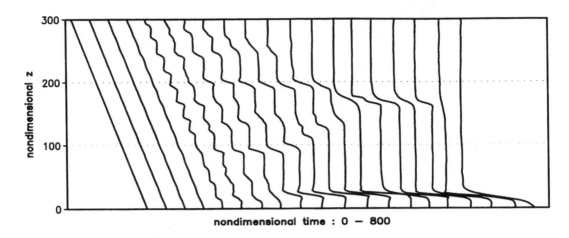

Figure 3: Time evolution of horizontally averaged density as a function of vertical coordinate. The density profiles are plotted every 40 non-dimensional time from left to right. Each profile is offset by 25% of the density difference between the top and bottom.

is sandwiched by thin diffusive interfaces with a sharp and very stable density gradients.

Figure 4 shows the streamlines and vertical density gradients at $t \sim 250$. It is seen that convective cells whose aspect ratio is of the order of 1, contribute to mix the density in the homogeneous layer. These convective motions are driven by the dominating molecular flux of heat at the diffusive interfaces.

Critical density ratio. The spontaneous generation of convections and step-like structures do not always occur: there is a critical value of density gradient ratio γ_{cr} above which convections and step-like structures are formed. Figure 5 shows the time evolution of disturbance kinetic energy for $\gamma = 0.87$ and 0.88. The critical value appears to be located between 0.87 and 0.88, which is very close to the critical value of 0.876 for diffusive convections to grow according to a linear stability analysis.

5. Summary and Conclusions

Formation of step-like structures due to diffusive convections in an infinite fluid with linear gradients of temperature and salinity are investigated numerically. When the density gradient ratio exceeds a critical value, which is close to the one for diffusive convections to grow according to the linear stability analysis, spontaneous layer formation occurs. The process of the layer formation can be divided into three stages:

At the first stage, nearly steady oscillating motions arise. The horizontal scale of the motions remains almost constant and is close to the buoyancy boundary layer scale $d = (\kappa_T \nu / N^2)^{1/4}$, where N is the buoyancy frequency.

After several tens of the oscillation period, a transition to the second stage occurs. In this stage, overturning convective motions develop and form well-mixed regions. The convective motions resemble Rayleigh-Bénard convection cells at a high Rayleigh number. The well-mixed regions gradually start to be organized into layers, a typical thickness of which is of the order of d.

At the third stage, the layers develop in a quasi-self-similar manner: Their average thickness increase with time by repetition of merging of the adjacent layers. Finally, the layers grow up to fill the whole depth of the calculation domain. It is likely that, if the calculation domains would be larger, a deeper layer would result in the final stage.

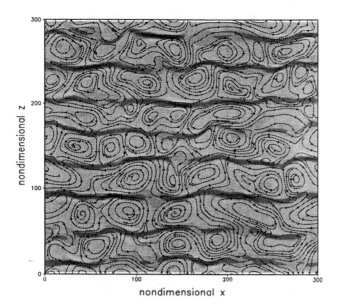

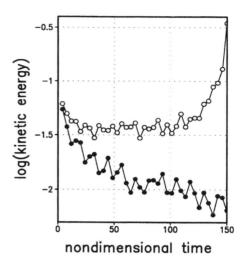

Figure 4: Vertical density gradient and streamlines at $t \sim 250$. Darker shade means sharper density gradient. Parameters are same as in Figure 1.

Figure 5: Time evolution of logarithm of volume averaged kinetic energy for two different density gradient ratios: one for $\gamma = 0.87$ (solid circle), and the other for $\gamma = 0.88$ (open circle).

Finally, it is of interest to compare the present results with the oceanic observations. Based on the typical stratification in the Arctic ocean (Neshyba et al., 1971), the characteristic length and time scales δ_* and δ_*^2/κ_T are of the order of 1cm and 10min, respectively. Thus once layers of thickness of several centimeters are generated initially, it takes about a week for them to grow to a thickness of 10m, which is a typical layer depth observed in the oceans (Kelley, 1984).

6.References

Fernando, H. J. S., 1987. The formation of a layered structure when a stable salinity gradient is heated from below. *J. Fluid Mech.*, **182**, 525–541.

Huppert, H. E. and P. F. Linden, 1979. On heating a stable salinity gradient from below. *J. Fluid Mech.*, **95**, 431–464.

Kelley, D. E., 1984. Effective diffusivities within oceanic thermohaline staircases. *J. Geophys. Res.*, **89**, 10484–10488.

Linden, P. F., 1976. The formation and destruction of fine-structure by double diffusive processes. *Deep-Sea Res.*, **23**, 895–908.

Neshyba, S., V. T. Neal and W. Denner, 1971. Temperature and conductivity measurements under upper Ice Island T-3. *J. Geophys. Res.*, **76**, 8107–8120.

Tait, R. I. and M. R. Howe, 1968. Some observation of thermohaline stratification in the deep ocean. *Deep-Sea Res.*, **15**, 275–280.

Turner, J. S., 1968. The behaviour of a stable salinity gradient heated from below. *J. Fluid Mech.*, **33**, 183–200.

Interleaving in the equatorial Pacific

Kelvin J. Richards[1] and Neil Edwards

[1]Southampton Oceanography Centre, European Way, Southampton, UK, SO14 3ZH
kelvin@soc.soton.ac.uk

The equatorial ocean plays a major role in the El Nino/Southern Oscillation. Mixing processes in the upper ocean contribute to the dynamics and thermodynamics of the system, with the mean state and variability of the ocean being dependent on the strength and form of the mixing. Here we consider the effect of lateral interleaving of water masses across the equator. Observations of interleaving will be presented showing layers of alternately high and low salinity, a few tens of metres thick, extending several hundred kilometres in the north/south direction. Estimates of the salt and heat fluxes associated with the interleaving suggest the interleaving fluxes are as strong, if not stronger, than eddy fluxes. A linear stability analysis demonstrates the formation mechanism to be a mixed double-diffusive/inertial instability. Results from a numerical model of the interleaving process show double diffusive processes are important at finite amplitude. The effective lateral diffusion coefficient of the interleaving is found to be O(1000 m2/s) and sometimes higher. Based on the results of the theory a parametrization scheme has been developed to include the effects of interleaving in ocean GCMs. The scheme has been implemented in a GCM of the Pacific Ocean. Early results suggest that the scheme can have a significant effect on the model sea surface temperature.

Laboratory models of double-diffusive sources in closed regions: the production of stratification and large-scale circulations

J. Stewart Turner

Research School of Earth Sciences, Australian National University,
Canberra, ACT 0200, Australia.

1. Abstract

Many observations of layering and intrusions in the ocean now suggest that such structures and motions depend on the presence of compensating horizontal and vertical gradients of temperature and salinity i.e. on double-diffusive processes. A surprising result of double diffusion is that it increases vertical density gradients and can even produce strong stratification in an initially homogeneous region. Most attention has in the past been given to one-dimensional transport processes but the focus of this paper is on the effects produced by multiple, spatially separated double-diffusive sources in closed regions. These have been studied in laboratory experiments using both heat and salt and the analogue salt-sugar system in various simple geometries. The aim has been first to understand the basic physical principles and then to relate these two-dimensional models to particular observations in the ocean.

2. Introduction

Double diffusion is no longer just an oceanographic curiosity   - layering and step-like distributions of T and S are now documented by many observations which have been explained in terms of these concepts. It has also been accepted that both the stratification of the ocean and the thermohaline circulations within it must be ultimately determined by the action of all the localized and distributed sources and sinks of heat and salt near the surface. The bottom water in the world s oceans is formed by the sources having the largest buoyancy flux, and the mean stratification adjusts to this influx, through a filling box process, with the effects of upwelling being balanced by distributed downward fluxes from the surface. Sources having a smaller buoyancy flux (or more mixing) cannot penetrate to the bottom of this density gradient set up by the major sources of bottom water, but instead spread out as mid-depth intrusions.

Even a superficial look at the T-S properties of ocean water masses and smaller scale intrusions shows, however, that these are distinguished not by their density differences alone but also by (often compensating) temperature and salinity differences, so that they are inherently double-diffusive. Yet there have been relatively few laboratory studies of double-diffusive processes in two-dimensional geometries, compared with those of one-dimensional transports through interfaces. Several of these earlier experiments will be discussed briefly before concentrating on the more recent work; some of them were begun many years ago, but they have a fresh relevance in the present context.

3. Previous two-dimensional laboratory experiments

An inflow of concentrated sugar solution released into a tank of homogeneous salt solution of the same density immediately separates, because of differential molecular diffusion, to form strong upward and downward convecting plumes, which spread out along the top and bottom boundaries (see Fig. 1).   This is very different from a laminar plume of salt flowing into salt solution of almost the same density, and it illustrates several counter-intuitive features of double-diffusive processes. Many phenomena occur when the system is hydrostatically stable or neutrally stratified, and the vertical density difference actually increases (rather than decreasing as it does with mechanical mixing); and the rates of convective transport can be large, even though the ultimate cause is molecular diffusion.

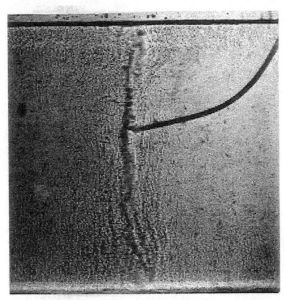

Figure 1. Convection produced by a source of sugar in
uniform salt solution of the same density.

Line sources of fluid released continuously into a density gradient also behave quite differently depending on their composition relative to their environment (Turner 1978). A source of salt solution released into a salinity gradient spreads as a single intrusion at its own density level. However when a sugar source having the same density and flowrate is injected into the same salinity gradient there is strong vertical convection near the source, though the vertical spread is now limited by the stratification (c.f. Fig. 1). Several intrusions spread out at levels above and below the source; since these contain an excess of sugar, diffusive interfaces form above and salt fingers below them. There is a slight upward tilt to the layers as they extend, implying that the rate of density flux due to fingers is larger than that at diffusive interfaces.

Horizontal property gradients set up when the side-wall boundary conditions do not match those in the interior of a fluid can produce instabilities without the injection of any fluid from a source. Heating a salinity gradient through a vertical wall produces a series of equally-spaced extending layers. Turner and Chen (1974) investigated the equivalent process in a salt-sugar system by setting up a stable density gradient composed of smooth opposing gradients of salt and sugar solutions, with a maximum of salt at the top and of sugar at the bottom. With vertical side walls the system was stable since the surfaces of constant concentration were normal to the boundaries and the no-flux condition was satisfied. When a sloping boundary was inserted, however, diffusion distorted these surfaces and upset the hydrostatic equilibrium, producing counterflows parallel to the slope and intrusions propagating into the interior. Huppert and Turner (1980) studied the melting of an ice wall into a salinity gradient, a case where both temperature and salinity are unmatched to the interior properties. Colder, fresher intrusions extended into the ambient fluid along the whole depth of the vertical ice wall, with no fresh water at all reaching the surface.

Conditions at oceanic fronts have also been modelled, using a geometry which removed the solid wall present in the experiments described above. Ruddick and Turner (1979) set up identical vertical density gradients on either side of a vertical barrier, using salt solution on one side and sugar on the other. When the barrier was removed the large horizontal property gradients drove a series of inclined intrusions across the front, consisting of layers of fingers separated by diffusive interfaces, with the velocity and scale both proportional to the horizontal gradients at the depth of the layer. A recent paper by Ruddick, Phillips and Turner (1999) has led to a greatly improved understanding of these observations, using the concept of continuous hydrostatic adjustment. Intrusions driven by temperature and salinity differences, showing

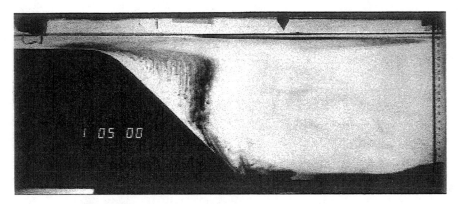

Figure 2. Convection and motions produced by heating and evaporation on a shelf.
Sheared salt fingers form below a warm salty outflow near the surface;
dense fluid is deposited on the slope, leading to a downslope flow
and diffusive layering near the bottom.

the same features, have been observed in the ocean A remarkable general implication of such oceanic measurements is that not only can differential molecular diffusion affect convective motions on the layer scale (tens of metres in the vertical) but it can also, by driving intrusions across fronts, influence the large-scale mixing between water masses.

Some earlier experiments designed to explore the circulation on a shelf or in an inverse estuary have been followed up by Turner (1998), using the heat-salt system directly. A tank 1.8m long, 80mm wide and 250mm deep was filled to a depth of about 220mm with salt solution in the range 1.03 — 1.10 SG. One end of the tank was fitted with a plane shelf about 500mm long and slope 1:30, placed so that the minimum water depth was about 10mm, with a curved transition region leading to a slope of 45^0 inclination extending to the bottom. The shelf region was heated using infrared lamps, and this produced evaporation and an increase in salinity on the shelf. Fresh water was added at the other end of the tank to keep the water level (and thus the mean salinity) constant. Typically, steady counter-flows developed near the surface about 30min after the heating was begun, and these were observed using dye streaks, as shown in Fig. 2. There was a warm, salty outflow from the shelf and below this a return flow, with strong salt-finger convection between these layers. The fingers deposited denser fluid on the slope and this produced a flow down the slope and out along the bottom, leading in time to a strong stratification of T and S (in the diffusive sense) and intrusions at various levels. Features that can be interpreted in terms of comparable double-diffusive processes at a shelf and slope in the ocean have been identified in unpublished CTD profiles obtained across the Australian NW shelf in 1995 (Dr P.E. Holloway, personal communication 1997).

4. Sloping layers produced by diagonal gradients

Two other previous experiments will be discussed in more detail, since they provide a direct laboratory analogue of the extensive series of layers documented in the C-SALT observations, and summarized by Schmitt (1994). That study revealed a series of very strong temperature and salinity steps in the main thermocline over an area of 1 million sq km, separating well-mixed layers 5-30m thick. The vertical T and S gradients were in the finger sense, and indeed sheared fingers were observed in the interfaces. The layers had strong horizontal coherence and persisted over several years; they were warmer, saltier and denser in the north, and cooler fresher and lighter in the south. They had a systematic slope, and the property gradients can be interpreted in terms of a constant lateral density ratio $\alpha Tx/\beta Sx = 0.85$. Thus we have called the overall gradients diagonal, in the sense that they have both vertical and horizontal components.

Schmitt (1994) has compared this system to tilted sheared layers described in the exploratory paper by Turner and Chen (1974) already referred to. While a long tank was being filled from the top with vertical gradients of salt and sugar in the finger sense (salt stable, sugar unstable), shearing motions were observed which sometimes broke down to form well-mixed layers. Usually the filling took place using the double-bucket technique and three floats extending over the whole of the surface to make the distributions as uniform horizontally as possible. But when only a single float was used at one end of the tank, horizontal as well as vertical gradients were set up and these generated the strongest shears and instabilities.

A subsequent experiment, unpublished but documented with a movie, is even more directly related to the C-SALT observations. An experimental tank was constructed with three compartments, separated by horizontal barriers which extended along most of the length but leaving small gaps, with removable covers, on the right of the upper and the left of the lower barrier. In a typical run the bottom compartment was filled with salt solution, the centre with crossed gradients of salt and sugar in the finger sense, and the top with sugar solution. When the covers were removed to allow communication between the three compartments, diagonal gradients of salt and sugar were set up. These rapidly produced strong shearing motions in the central fingering region, leading to breakdown and the establishment of inclined well-mixed layers. Several variations on this experiment were also studied, including starting with three or four layers in the central chamber rather than a continuous gradient, and with the stratification in the diffusive as well as the finger sense.

5. Horizontally separated buoyancy sources in a long tank

Another oceanographic phenomenon will be described first, to provide a further specific motivation for the recent laboratory experiments to be described next. Observations in the Arctic Ocean since 1990 (first brought to my attention by Dr E.C. Carmack) have shown that a major and continuing warming has taken place, due to the influx of anomalously warm water from the Atlantic. The transition is occurring via persistent multiple intrusions, 40-60m thick, extending laterally in a coherent manner through the Atlantic water and upper deep waters of the Arctic. The distributions of T and S can support both diffusive and finger convection, and it seems highly probable that the layers are self-organizing and self-propelled by double-diffusive transports.

The analogue laboratory experiments used sources of salt and sugar solutions, fed in at opposite ends of a tank (750mm long, 75mm wide and filled to a depth of 150mm), at constant rates controlled by a peristaltic pump. An overflow tube drew fluid from a point at the centre of the tank to keep the depth constant. Many experiments have been carried out using different depths of the inflows and withdrawal (Turner and Veronis 2000), and only a selected few of these will be described here.

A control experiment was conducted using homogeneous salt solution in the tank, SG 1.11, and two sources of salt solution, one lighter, SG 1.10, and one denser, SG 1.12, than the tank fluid, flowing in at the same rate (5.3ml/min) near the surface at the two ends; the overflow was also near the surface, in the centre. (This control run is similar to the experiment reported by Pierce and Rhines (1996).) As the stratification evolved, the fluid at the bottom became steadily denser, while that at the top at first became lighter, reflecting the density of the lighter input, and then denser again, eventually reaching the mean density of the two inputs. Note also that the density range in the tank never went outside that of the two inputs in this experiment. In a non double-diffusive system, with ordinary turbulent mixing, there is no mechanism for it to do so.

These results clearly cannot explain the Arctic observations described above. However when one salt source (SG 1.104, input at the bottom) and one sugar source (SG 1.100, input at the top at the other end of the tank), were injected into a tank containing a 50:50 mixture of the source fluids the behaviour was

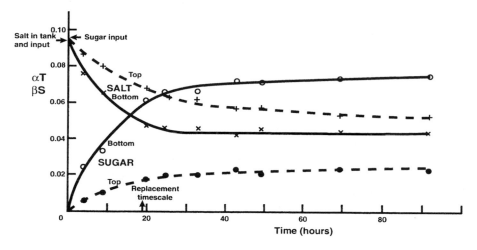

Figure 3. Development of the density contributions of salt (αT) and sugar (βS) (in units of g cm^{-3}) to the densities of the top and bottom layers in a run with salt solution initially in the tank.

very different from the salt/salt case. The density of the bottom fluid increased steadily and rapidly became greater than that of the input, and at first the top became lighter for the same reason. As the withdrawal of fluid (from the top in this case) became more significant the overflow density again approached the mean density of the inputs, but the final vertical density difference was much larger than the original small difference between them. Dye streaks revealed vigorous double-diffusive intrusive motions, and the level of the outflows changed in time in response to the evolving density structure. These features are indeed analogous to the ocean observations.

An instructive series of experiments was conducted under nominally identical conditions, but making different measurements in each run. The tank fluid was salt solution, SG 1.11. The inputs and withdrawal were all at the top, with the salt input being a denser turbulent plume, SG 1.12, and the sugar input at the other end laminar and lighter, SG 1.10. The time history of intrusions and plumes was monitored using photos and video recordings of dye streaks. Initially the salt outflow along the bottom behaved as it would in a non double-diffusive filling box , while there was vigorous convection near the sugar input. A sugar-rich intrusion moved across the top of the salt flow (the bottom water) and in fact this provides a simple analogue of the Mediterranean outflow into the Atlantic, with fingers forming below it. Polarimeter records (measuring the total sugar in a light beam shone through the tank) showed rapid fluctuations due to fingers, and also variations with a 45-60 minute timescale, corresponding to the passage of fronts and confirming the observations made using dye streaks. Samples were withdrawn at discrete times and various positions and depths, and their density and refractive index measured. These values were inverted using the Ruddick and Shirtcliffe (1979) results to give the separate salt and sugar contributions to the density. These showed that the vertical differences over the bottom half of the tank evolved from the initial finger sense to the diffusive sense after several days, with excursions due to the passage of fronts.

Three closely related experiments were monitored over many days using the analysis of withdrawn samples. These were all started with the tank fluid and the input salt and sugar solutions having exactly the same density, SG 1.100, and both inputs and withdrawal at mid-depth. The only difference was that in the three experiments the tank fluid was pure salt, pure sugar or a 50:50 mixture, respectively. The most remarkable result is that although the detailed behaviour and rate of evolution was very different, specially in the early stages when the sources produced a different local double-diffusive behaviour, all three runs evolved to an asymptotic state in which the overall mean vertical differences of salt and sugar were the same. The stratification developed a clear two-layer structure, with a sharp central interface and weakly stratified upper and lower layers. Fig. 3 shows the time history of the density contributions of salt and sugar in the run started with salt in the tank. The top to bottom density difference increased steadily from zero to the asymptotic maximum of about 0.05 g cm^{-3} after about 100 hours. Strong shears and intrusive motions persisted, however, even when the mean density was no longer evolving.

From Fig. 3 we see that in the final state the overall salt distribution was unstable, with a slightly higher value in the top layer, while the sugar was strongly stable. The sugar concentration in the top layer was lower than the two salt concentrations, and in the bottom layer it was larger than either salt concentration. This state corresponds quite closely to the one-dimensional diffusive run down of a layer of salt solution above sugar solution. It cannot be produced by finger run down, (which leads to a much smaller density change) and it corresponds to the maximum release of potential energy. It is, however, achieved through the action of many intrusions, above and below which both fingers and diffusive interfaces are observed. These remain active in the final dynamic state, which is driven by the remaining potential energy in the salt field. The key to the explanation of the evolution lies in the nature of the plumes which form near the sources of salt and sugar (see Fig. 1), and the differences between the two, and further detailed studies of these are in progress.

6. Summary and discussion

The laboratory experiments described above have shown how horizontally separated sources and sinks with different double-diffusive properties can produce complex effects in closed regions, even in simple geometries. The evolution to an asymptotic state having the maximum vertical density difference may not be steady or monotonic, and it is certainly sensitive to the boundary conditions. The final state of stratification may have complicated horizontal velocities superimposed on it, with unsteady intrusions and interleaving motions. These and the other exploratory experiments discussed earlier were motivated by ocean observations. No direct application is possible or appropriate at this time, but the results do shed light on the comparable two-dimensional phenomena in the ocean, where temperature and salinity are the relevant double-diffusive properties. Many observations of layers and intrusions (notably in the C-SALT area and the Arctic) cannot be interpreted without introducing double diffusion. Density differences alone are not enough, nor are one-dimensional double-diffusive transports; the observed intrusive motions and layers must be driven by horizontal gradients of T and S.

7. References

Huppert, H.E. and Turner, J.S. 1980 Ice blocks melting into a salinity gradient. *J. Fluid Mech.* **100**, 367-384.

Pierce, D.W. and Rhines, P.B 1996 Convective building of a pycnocline: laboratory experiments. *J.Phys. Oceanogr.* **26**, 176-190.

Ruddick, B.R. and Shirtcliffe, T.G.L. 1979 Data for double diffusers: physical properties of aqueous salt-sugar solutions. *Deep-Sea Res.* **26**, 775-787.

Ruddick, B.R. and Turner, J.S. 1979 The vertical length scale of double-diffusive intrusions. *Deep-Sea Res.* **26**, 903-913.

Ruddick, B.R., Phillips, O.M. and Turner, J.S. 1999 A laboratory and quantitative model of finite-amplitude thermohaline intrusions. *Dyn. Atmos. Oceans* **30**, 71-99.

Schmitt, R.W. 1994 Double diffusion in oceanography. *Ann. Rev. Fluid Mech* **26**, 255-285.

Turner, J.S. 1978 Double-diffusive intrusions into a density gradient. *J. Geophys. Res.* **83**, 2887-2901.

Turner, J.S. 1998 Stratification and circulation produced by heating and evaporation on a shelf. *J. Marine Res.* **56**, 885-904.

Turner, J.S. and Chen, C.F. 1974 Two-dimensional effects in double-diffusive convection. *J. Fluid Mech.* **63**, 577-592.

Turner, J.S. and Veronis, G. 2000 Laboratory studies of double-diffusive sources in closed regions. *J.Fluid Mech.* **405**, 269-304.

Internal waves and shear layers driven by turbulent plumes

A.B.D. Wong, R.W. Griffiths and G.O. Hughes

Research School of Earth Sciences, The Australian National University, Canberra 0200, Australia
Ross.Griffiths@anu.edu.au, Graham.Hughes@anu.edu.au

Abstract

When a turbulent buoyant plume is released in a long rectangular tank, the flow is observed to be more complex than that suggested by the traditional "filling-box" model. A quasi-steady-state density stratification develops in the tank, as predicted by Baines & Turner (1969). However, a series of horizontal counterflowing "shear layers" are superposed on the slow horizontal entrainment-driven flow. The shear layer velocities are sufficient to direct surrounding fluid away from the plume at some levels. We develop a theory that explains the observed shear layer structure in terms of internal wave modes in a viscous stratified fluid. The internal wave modes are excited by the horizontal outflow of dense plume fluid along the tank bottom. The nonlinear density gradient produced by the plume convection causes the vertical scale to decrease with increasing height. A travelling-wave solution in a uniform density gradient shows that the energy of the propagating internal waves is attenuated by viscosity, causing the velocity maxima to decrease with height. The vertical scale of the quasi-stationary shear layers is set by the depth of the plume outflow, which in turn is fixed by a match of the downward phase speed of waves with the upward advection velocity.

1. Introduction

Baines & Turner (1969) gave solutions for the large-time steady state flow in which the outflow from a descending turbulent plume generates a relatively slow upwards motion in a finite box and establishes a stable stratification. Entrainment into the plume was assumed to draw water towards the plume at all depths above the outflow at a rate given by the "entrainment assumption". The outflow layer from the plume source at the bottom has been found to occupy one-quarter of the water depth (Manins, 1979). This "filling-box" model with various modifications has since been employed in many studies including the filling of containers of liquefied natural gas (Germeles 1975), turbulent flows down sloping boundaries in the oceans (Killworth 1977), the effects of time-dependent plume fluxes on production of ocean bottom waters (Killworth & Turner 1982), development of stratification in magma chambers (Turner 1980) and ventilation in buildings (Cooper & Linden 1996; Linden & Cooper 1996).

During its descent a dense plume entrains surrounding water and therefore increases in radius and decreases in density. The first plume water to reach the bottom spreads in an outflow layer, the top of which forms the "first front" (a discontinuity in density separating the overlying homogeneous water from water that has passed through the plume). At later times the plume entrains some of the dense water from below the first front, making the outflow progressively denser. This generates a vertical advection throughout the environment; the first front is therefore lifted upwards and a stable stratification is established. On recognising this fundamental process Baines & Turner (1969) found a power series solution for asymptotically large times when the plume radius, vertical velocity and density anomaly relative to the environment no longer vary with time at a given depth, but the plume and environment densities increase linearly in time at all depths. The variation with depth of both the buoyancy frequency N and the vertical velocity V in the environment are both important to the flow structure reported here (see schematic profiles in figure 1).

The "filling-box" process has generally been studied in boxes having lengths and widths comparable to the water depth. The horizontal entrainment into the plume was assumed to be slowing varying with depth and the slow vertical advection in the plume environment was assumed to be uniform over the area of the box. In this paper, we summarise experiments of Wong et al. (2000) which show that in long tanks a series of strong counterflowing shear layers is established in the stratification

Figure 1. A photograph of shear layers revealed by dye streaks in a long channel. The plume is at the left hand end of the tank. Profiles of the buoyancy frequency and vertical advection in the environment are also shown.

produced by the "filling-box" mechanism. We present evidence that the layers are produced by internal gravity wave normal modes excited by the plume outflow. They are similar in nature to columnar modes generated by internal intrusions into density gradients (Manins 1976).

2. Experiments

We carried out experiments in which a constant flux of dense salt solution was released at a steady rate through a small nozzle protruding just below the free surface of a long tank of water. The nozzle was positioned near one end of the tank and equidistant from three side walls. Two tanks were used. The first was 1.1m long, 0.3m wide and 0.24m deep while the second was 2.0m long, 0.2m wide and 0.4m deep. A number of depths from source-to-base were used. Conductivity profiles and time records at a fixed point were used to calculate density profiles and perturbations. Dye streaks were used to measure vertical profiles of horizontal velocity.

The entrainment constant E was measured by comparing the progress of the first front with the analytical solution of Baines & Turner (1969). The value that we use for a top hat profile is $E = 0.129$, which corresponds to 0.0912 for a Gaussian profile (see Turner 1973 and 1986) and is therefore consistent with those used in other studies. It appears that the shear layers do not significantly influence the entrainment into the plume.

A strong and persistent series of layers appeared as dominant features in the profiles of horizontal velocity, as seen in figure 1, but corresponded to extremely small perturbations in the density gradient. Hence we call these "shear layers" in order to distinguish them from density layering. Figure 2 shows characteristic horizontal velocity profiles taken halfway along the tank at a number of times and normalised by the entrainment velocity scale $U_e = 2^{4/3}\pi^{2/3}E^{4/3}F^{1/3}H^{2/3}B^{-1}L^{-1}(L-x)u_e$, where F is the buoyancy flux at the plume source and x is the horizontal distance from the source in a tank with dimensions $H \times B \times L$ (depth $\times$ width $\times$ length). The bottom outflow layer thickness was approximately one-quarter of the tank depth. Immediately above the outflow layer there was a layer of similar thickness moving towards the plume. In the upper half of the tank there were several layers. Both vertical scales and the magnitudes of the horizontal velocities in the shear layers generally decreased with height. Horizontal velocities towards the plume decreased with increasing horizontal distance from the plume. Parcels of water did not necessarily traverse the tank from end to end during their residence time in each layer in the presence of the mean vertical advection, but those that were not entrained into the plume migrated upwards through the series of shear layers, experiencing an oscillatory horizontal velocity.

The shear layer structure was observed to approach a quasi-steady-state on a time scale that was proportional to the travel time $L/\bar{N}H$ ($\bar{N}$ the depth-averaged buoyancy frequency) of internal waves through the length and depth of the tank. Establishment time scales in the range $12\text{--}15L/\bar{N}H$ are consistent with the dominance of higher vertical modes that have smaller phase speeds. At large times after the quasi-steady-state stratification had developed slow oscillations of the flow structure were observed (see variations between profiles in figure 2). These continued velocity fluctuations were most visible in the region $0.55 < y/H < 0.85$, where the positions of the extrema in horizontal velocity shifted vertically.

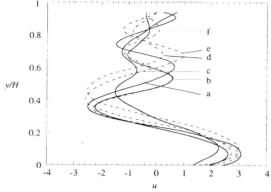

Figure 2. Profiles of horizontal velocity taken from dye streaks in one experiment and at a number of times during a single cycle of the long-period oscillation (H = 0.235m, L = 1.1m).

3. Analysis of inviscid baroclinic normal modes of the "filling-box"

The full problem is complex and involves a turbulent bottom outflow, mean vertical and horizontal transport throughout the tank, a nonlinear density gradient that gives a large increase in buoyancy frequency with height, possible effects of viscosity and poorly determined boundary conditions. We approach this problem by first investigating the structure of baroclinic normal modes supported by the nonlinear density gradient with inviscid laminar flow. More detail is given in Wong et $al.$ (2000).

Following Gill (1982) we find separable solutions for vertical velocity and pressure perturbations of the form $w = \omega W(y)\cos(kx + \omega t)$ and $p' = P(y)\sin(kx + \omega t)$, where the frequency is related to the horizontal wavenumber k by $\omega^2 = c_n^2 k^2$ and c_n is the phase speed of the nth mode. Figure 3a gives the functional dependence of u on the dimensionless depth y/H for columnar baroclinic ($\omega = 0$) modes 2, 4, 6 and 8 in an infinitely long tank. It shows that for the nth mode there are $n + 1$ shear layers (or velocity extrema) whose thicknesses decrease toward the top of the tank as a result of the increasing buoyancy frequency. In the experiments it appears that the modes most strongly excited at large times are those with vertical scales (at the bottom of the tank) similar to the plume outflow depth. The observed structure is similar to modes 6, 7 and 8, except that the observed velocity amplitude decreases with height in stark contrast to the predicted increasing amplitude. This difference will be attributed to viscosity acting on the decreasing vertical scales.

4. Analysis of viscous internal waves in a linear density gradient

Here we consider the case of a constant buoyancy frequency N and look for solutions to the viscous linearised equations of motion corresponding to a travelling wave propagating in the vertical direction and a standing wave in the horizontal, $i.e.$ a streamfunction $\psi = \psi\exp[i(my+\omega t)]$. We choose the horizontal wavenumber $k = \pi/L$ to correspond to the lowest mode that satisfies the boundary conditions of zero horizontal velocity at $x = 0, L$ in the tank. The vertical wavenumber m takes complex values in order to describe the attenuation of the wave motion with height due to viscosity. Since the shear layers are excited at the base of the tank by the plume outflow we consider only internal wave modes that decay with height ($i.e.$ Im(m) > 0). Moreover, only modes that radiate energy upward from the plume outflow are permissible (i.e. downward phase velocity, Re(m) > 0).

The solution for the vertical wavenumber, in dimensionless terms, depends on the Reynolds number $Re = NH^2/\nu$, the tank aspect ratio $L' = H/L$ and the frequency $\omega' = \omega/N$. However, only the trivial solution satisfies the boundary conditions. We therefore introduce a steady and spatially uniform vertical velocity field V representing the advection in the "filling-box". Travelling wave solutions, normalised to remove the dependence on distance along the tank and to give each mode a similar amplitude, then take the form shown in figure 3b for particular values of Reynolds number and aspect ratio. Increasing Re has the effects of reducing the attenuation with height and shifting the frequency

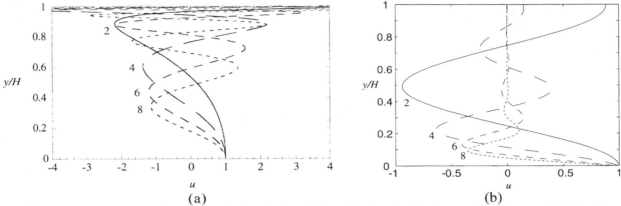

(a)   (b)

Figure 3. Normal modes 2, 4, 6 and 8 calculated by (a) the inviscid analysis for a "filling-box" density gradient with no vertical advection, and (b) the viscous analysis in a fluid with linear density gradient and uniform vertical advection ($Re = 9000$, $H/L = 0.214$).

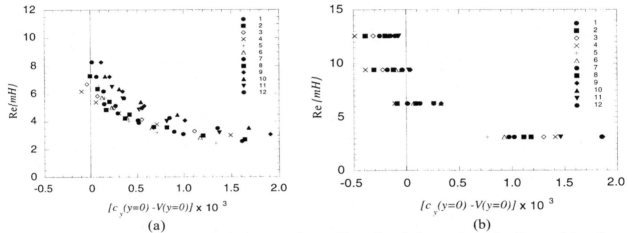

(a)   (b)

Figure 4. The dimensionless vertical wavenumber mH predicted for each mode (denoted by discrete symbols) under the experimental conditions from the analyses of (a) the inviscid baroclinic modes in a "filling-box" density gradient with no advection, and (b) the viscous modes in a linear density gradient with uniform advection. The vertical line indicates modes for which the phase speed and vertical advection are approximately balanced.

spectrum towards that given by the inviscid analysis above. Decreasing the aspect ratio decreases the frequency of a given mode and hence increases the attenuation. Thus viscous attenuation renders more rapidly varying modes unimportant for the flow structure.

In figure 4 we plot the difference of the downward phase speeds $c_y = \omega/m$ and the uniform upward advection speed $V(y = 0)$ (evaluated at the bottom of the tank where the motions are excited by the plume outflow) as a function of the dimensionless vertical wavenumber for the conditions (Re, L', H/B) in 12 experiments. The results indicate that a matching of the speeds and a quasi-stationary mode will be achieved at wavenumbers of 6 to 9 (corresponding to modes $n > 7$ for the "filling-box" density profile and to $n = 2 - 4$ for the linear gradient). Thus we conclude that vertical advection is crucial in selecting the dominant vertical scale of shear layers.

5. A heuristic theory for viscous internal wave modes in a nonlinear stratification

In order to investigate the combined influence of vertical advection, viscous attenuation and the nonlinear density gradient, we develop a simpler heuristic theory in which the upward energy flux in internal waves is attenuated as a result of the vertical diffusion of momentum. The frequency of an

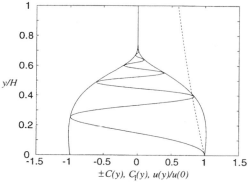

Figure 5. The amplitude envelope $\pm C(y)$ and normalised horizontal velocity $u(y)/u(0)$ predicted by (1) and (4) for one set of experimental conditions (experiment 10 of Wong *et al.* 2000). The broken line shows for contrast the amplitude attenuation (3) predicted for the case of a linear density profile and constant vertical advection speed (*i.e.* constant vertical wavenumber).

internal wave remains constant along a ray ($\omega = -\omega_f + mV$ = constant) and we consider only long-period waves ($\omega = 0$), so that $c_y = \omega_f/m = V$. Since $k \ll m$ it follows from the dispersion relation for internal waves (i.e. $\omega_f(y) = N(y)k/[k^2+m^2(y)]^{1/2}$) that

$$m(y)/m(0) \approx \left[N(y)V(0)/N(0)V(y)\right]^{1/2}. \tag{1}$$

Thus both increase in N and decrease in V with height lead to a decreasing scale of the shear layers. By assuming that the velocity structure has the form

$$u(y)/u(0) = C(y)\cos\left[m(y)y\right], \tag{2}$$

where $m(y)$ is given by (1), the amplitude envelope $C(y)$ can be found by estimating the decrease with height, due to viscosity, of the upward energy flux. Wong *et al.* (2000) find $C(y)$ for the general case (figure 5), but here we give the expression for only the simpler case in which both N and V are taken as constant with height:

$$C_1(y) = \exp\left[-\left(m^4(0)H^4/2\pi ReL'\right)y/H\right], \tag{3}$$

where $Re = N(0)H^2/v$. Thus smaller tank aspect ratios and smaller Reynolds numbers (due to weaker buoyancy fluxes) give greater attenuation. This result is expected to accurately represent the more complete solution near the base of the tank. The vertical wavenumber at the bottom is

$$m(0)H = \left[N(0)H/V(0)\right]^{1/2}(kH)^{1/2} = 1.01E^{-1}(B/H)^{1/2}. \tag{4}$$

In previous discussions of the "filling-box" process the depth of the plume outflow has remained unspecified and unexplained, although Manins (1979) noted that in his experiments its depth was $0.15H$. We suggest that the outflow is in fact controlled by the dominant internal wave mode and predict that its depth corresponds to the height of the first zero velocity level. In figure 6 we plot the height y/H of this zero velocity level as a function of $(c_y - V)(y = 0)$ and find that the bottom layer depth is in the range $(0.15 - 0.26)H$ in a linear stratification. The nonlinear gradient may decrease these values slightly, in close agreement with measurement. Thus we conclude that coupling of the plume outflow with the wavefield causes preferential excitation of modes whose half-wavelength is similar to the outflow depth. In turn, given the vertical advection speed imposed by the plume buoyancy flux and tank aspect ratio, the outflow depth adjusts to make the wavefield stationary in the vicinity of the outflow.

6. Conclusions

The stratified environment produced by a turbulent plume supports a series of shear layers superimposed on the steady vertical advection and horizontal entrainment flows driven by the plume. These layers are the result of a continuous excitation of baroclinic wave modes whose downward phase speed approximately balances the upward advection in the "filling-box". The

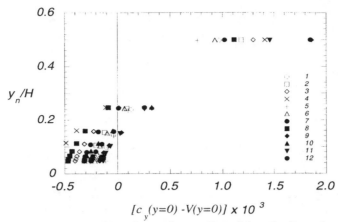

Figure 6. The depth of the bottom outflow layer is predicted by finding the height from the base at which each internal wave mode (discrete symbols) has a downward phase speed equal and opposite to the upward advection speed. For all modes this height lies in the range $0.15 < y/H < 0.28$.

dominant wave mode is found to have a vertical scale near the tank bottom that is comparable with the observed turbulent outflow from the dense plume. We suggest that the outflow is not independent of the wave field and that the dominant baroclinic mode is responsible for setting the outflow depth. The baroclinic modes are established on the time scale for the propagation of internal waves through the box and develop rapidly compared to either the ventilation of the box by vertical advection or the rate of change of the "filling-box" stratification in its transient stages.

Experiments and analysis suggest that viscosity becomes a controlling influence on the upward momentum flux and causes the amplitude of horizontal velocities in the shear layers to decrease with increasing height. Owing to both the increase in buoyancy frequency and the decrease in vertical advection towards the top of the gradient, the shear layer depths decrease with height. At large times, when the stratification has achieved its constant shape, the baroclinic modes are observed to undergo a very low frequency oscillation (between the five-layer and six-layer states for our experimental conditions) and the cause of this behaviour is currently the subject of further work.

7. References

BAINES, W.D. & TURNER, J.S. 1969 Turbulent buoyant convection from a source in a confined region. *J. Fluid Mech.* **37**, 51–80.

COOPER, P. & LINDEN, P.F. 1996 Natural ventilation of an enclosure containing two buoyancy sources. *J. Fluid Mech.* **311**, 153–176.

GILL, A.E. 1982 *Atmosphere-Ocean Dynamics.* Academic Press, 662pp.

GERMELES, A.E. 1975 Forced plumes and mixing of liquids in tanks. *J. Fluid Mech.* **71**, 601–623.

KILLWORTH, P.D. 1977 Mixing on the Weddell Sea continental slope. *Deep-Sea Res.* **24**, 427–448.

KILLWORTH, P.D. & TURNER, J.S. 1982 Plumes with time-varying buoyancy in a confined region. *Geophys. Astrophys. Fluid Dyn.* **20**, 265–291.

LINDEN, P.F. & COOPER, P. 1996 Multiple sources of buoyancy in a naturally ventilated enclosure. *J. Fluid Mech.* **311**, 177–192.

MANINS, P.C. 1976 Intrusion into a stratified fluid. *J. Fluid Mech.* **74**, 547–560.

MANINS, P.C. 1979 Turbulent buoyant convection from a source in a confined region. *J. Fluid Mech.* **91**, 765–781.

TURNER, J.S. 1973 *Buoyancy effects in fluids.* Cambridge University Press, 368pp.

TURNER, J.S. 1980 Differentiation and layering in magma chambers. *Nature* **285**, 213–215.

TURNER, J.S. 1986 Turbulent entrainment: the development of the entrainment assumption, and its application to geophysical flows. *J. Fluid Mech.* **173**, 431–471.

WONG, A.B.D., GRIFFITHS, R.W. & HUGHES, G.O. 2000 Shear layers driven by turbulent plumes. *J. Fluid Mech.* (SUBMITTED).

10

INTERNAL WAVES

Three-Dimensional Disturbances of an Internal Solitary Wave: A Numerical Simulation

Brian C. Barr,[1] Daniel T. Valentine, [1,2] and Timothy W. Kao[3]

[1]Mechanical and Aeronautical Engineering, Clarkson University, Potsdam, NY 13699-5725 USA
[2]Computational Mechanics, Applied Research Laboratory, State College, PA 16804-0030 USA
[3]Civil Engineering, The Catholic University of America, Washington, DC 20064 USA
barrb@clarkson.edu, clara@clarkson.edu, kao@cua.edu

1. Abstract

This paper describes two computational simulations of three-dimensional effects of internal solitary waves on a pycnocline in a rectangular channel of equal width and depth. The first simulation is the generation of a line solitary wave with an asymmetric initial disturbance. Because the channel is relatively narrow, the wave that emerges is essentially two dimensional. The wave speed and other properties are compared with previously reported, two-dimensional results. The second simulation is the encounter of a solitary wave with a rectangular sill that spans half the width and half the depth of the channel. The results of this simulation are compared with a similar two-dimensional simulation. The induced transverse flow weakens the effect of the three-dimensional interaction.

2. Introduction

Internal solitary waves on pycnoclines are ubiquitous in coastal seas. They have been observed in many locations from the Andaman Sea to the Arctic Ocean; see, e.g., Apel et al. (1975), Osborne and Burch (1980), and Liu et al. (1998). Since internal waves are a major mechanism for the transport of mass, heat, momentum and salinity, a better understanding of internal solitary waves would help to quantify these processes. They are generated by tidal action at the corners of continental shelves and propagate towards the shore and towards the open sea. The waves have been called solitary waves because significant aspects of their behavior are describable by nonlinear equations that have solitary wave solutions.

Three-dimensional internal solitary wave interaction phenomena have been observed in field studies by Hsu et al. (2000), among others. The field studies indicate the occurrence of oblique wave-wave and wave-shelf interactions, three dimensional interaction with topographical features, and diffraction. Numerous features of wave-wave interactions need elaboration, such as phase and direction shifts, merging of solitary waves, and changes in the size and amplitude of wave packets. We have developed a three dimensional viscous flow code to study some of these problems; some of our results were recently presented by Barr, Valentine and Sipcic (1999).

In the present investigation internal solitary waves in a channel whose width and depth are equal are examined. With this relatively narrow channel, the waves generated tend towards two-dimensional motion. This is because the three-dimensional interaction of the waves with their images associated with the side walls causes them to move in such a way as to produce a tendency for the waves to move parallel to the side walls of the channel. This idea is elaborated in this paper via an examination of two, numerical simulations of internal solitary waves on a pycnocline.

3. Analysis

The basic fluid configuration investigated is that of a two-layered stably stratified fluid with the density changing continuously across a region between the two layers, known as the pycnocline, in a rectangular channel with width and depth d, and length L. The x coordinate is the lengthwise direction; the y coordinate is the transverse direction; the z coordinate is in the vertical direction, opposite the direction of gravitational acceleration. The shallow upper layer of depth h_1 has density ρ_1 and the deeper lower layer of depth h_2 has density ρ_2 with $\rho_2 < \rho_1$.

The model equations for the flow of an incompressible, viscous, diffusive, Boussinesq fluid are the continuity, Navier-Stokes and diffusion equations. Using d as the reference length and U, the linear two-layered wave speed as the reference velocity, these equations can be written as

$$\nabla \cdot \boldsymbol{u} = 0 \tag{1}$$

$$\frac{\partial \boldsymbol{u}}{\partial t} + \boldsymbol{u} \cdot \nabla \boldsymbol{u} = -\nabla p + \frac{1}{Fr^2}(\theta - \bar{\theta})\boldsymbol{k} + \frac{1}{Re}(\nabla \cdot \nabla \boldsymbol{u}) \tag{2}$$

$$\frac{\partial \theta}{\partial t} + u\frac{\partial \theta}{\partial x} + v\frac{\partial \theta}{\partial y} + w\frac{\partial \theta}{\partial z} = \frac{1}{ReSc}\left(\frac{\partial^2 \theta}{\partial x^2} + \frac{\partial^2 \theta}{\partial y^2} + \frac{\partial^2 \theta}{\partial z^2}\right) \tag{3}$$

$$\frac{\partial \bar{\theta}}{\partial t} = \frac{1}{ReSc}\frac{\partial^2 \bar{\theta}}{\partial z^2} \tag{4}$$

where

$$\theta = \frac{\rho_2 - \rho(x, z, t)}{\rho_2 - \rho_1}, \bar{\theta} = \frac{\rho_2 - \bar{\rho}(z,t)}{\rho_2 - \rho_1}, Re = \frac{Ud}{\nu}, Sc = \frac{\nu}{D_{ab}}, Fr^2 = \frac{h_1 h_2}{d^2},$$

and where ν is the kinematic viscosity, and D_{ab} is the diffusivity.

Equations (1), (2), (3), and (4) are solved numerically subject to the following boundary conditions. The tank bottom, end walls and sill faces, if present, are no-slip, insulated walls. The upper surface of the channel is a pure slip, rigid lid. The side walls are also pure-slip, rigid boundaries.

The initial condition is a state of rest with a pool of upper fluid suspended down into the lower layer. The initial depths of the upper and lower layers, the width of the pycnocline, along with the size and shape of the displaced pool of upper layer fluid used to generate the wave are specified as

$$\theta = \frac{1}{2} + \frac{1}{2}\tanh(\alpha[z - (A_1 - A_2 y)\operatorname{sech}^2(\lambda x) - h_2]). \tag{5}$$

The dimensions of the displaced pool are selected so as to generate only one solitary wave [see Whitham (1974)]. At time t=0, the pool is released and motion ensues. The initial condition for the reference-density stratification is given by $\bar{\theta} = 1/2 + (1/2)\tanh(\alpha[z - h_2])$ where α controls the pycnocline width, A_1 and A_2 control the amplitude of the displaced pool in the transverse direction and λ is its width.

The computational solution method that was developed is an implicit, control-volume derived, iterative method based on a split time step ADI (Alternating Direction Implicit)/SIMPLE (Semi-IMplicit Pressure Linked Equations) algorithm. It is second order accurate in both space and time. All spatial derivatives are center differenced. The time splitting/ADI portion of the method breaks up the solution of the momentum equations and density transport equations into a series of sweeps along a coordinate direction. Each sweep results in a tridiagonal system of equations that can be efficiently solved. The second component of the algorithm is a system to progressively move the estimated velocity fields towards simultaneously satisfying the momentum and continuity equations, as well as advancing the pressure field to the new value. The scheme is iterated until continuity is satisfied to within a small positive value.

4. Results and Discussion

The parameters selected for the two cases computed are Re = 10,000, Sc = 833, Fr = 0.3, h_1 = 0.1 and h_2 = 0.9. The initial value of the pycnocline width is α = 60. These selections are consistent with the experimental conditions of Kao et al. (1985). The time step and grid size selected for the numerical solutions are Δt = 0.01, Δx = 0.1, Δy = 0.05, and Δz = 0.025. The solutions are summarized next.

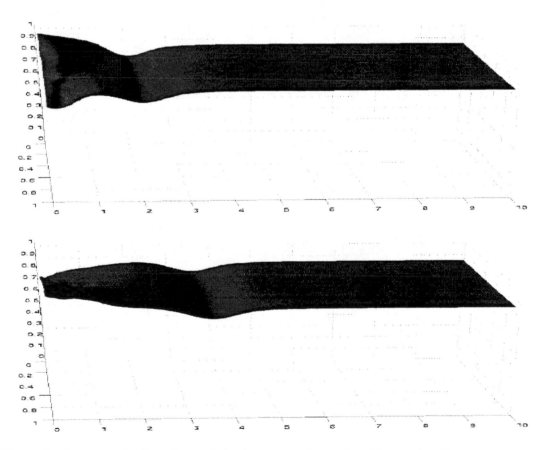

Figure 1. Asymmetric disturbance inducing a two-dimensional internal solitary wave.

Figure 1, plots of the θ = 0.5 isosurface at time t= 2.9 and 3.9, illustrates the generation of an internal solitary wave by an asymmetrical initial condition where in equation (5) A_1= 0.5 and A_2=0.5. The resulting generated wave sorts itself from the sloshing tail that gets left behind. The wave speed of the leading solitary wave at t=3.9 is equal to 1.2, with an amplitude of 0.08. This speed is consistent with the two-dimensional, finer-grid results reported by Valentine et al. (1999).

Any small transverse disturbance contained in the main leading wave decays. The wave at t = 3.9 is essentially two-dimensional. This is confirmed by comparing the shape of the contour of the 0.5 isopycnal at several locations in the transverse direction at t = 1.9, 2.9 and 3.9 as shown in Figure 2. Thus, for a seemingly strong three-dimensional initial condition, the generated internal solitary wave that emerges is two dimensional.

The second simulation involves the interaction of an internal solitary wave with a three-dimensional step sill. For this case, $A_1 = 0.375$ and $A_2 = 0$, so a line solitary wave is generated, without a sloshing tail. The wave generated is moving at speed 1.3 and it has an amplitude

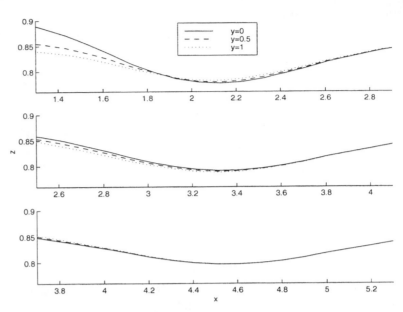

Figure 2. θ=0.5 isopycnals at t=1.9, 2.9 and 3.9 for oblique initial condition

of 0.17 between t = 2.5 and t=3 from the onset of motion. It is this wave that encounters the step. As can be seen in Figure 3, the onset wave is two dimensional in the transverse direction. As the wave encounters the step, the wave face steepens. However, the transmitted wave, the portion of the onset wave that propagates over the step sill, is not strongly three dimensional. Because of the pure slip side wall boundaries, the topography encountered by the wave is actually a periodic series of step sills in y of height d/2 and width d, spaced a distance d apart. The length of the incident wave is roughly two and a half times larger than the distance between the sills. Figure 4, showing the θ=0.5 isosurface at times t=1.8, 3.6, and 6.4, shows a more global representation of this interaction.

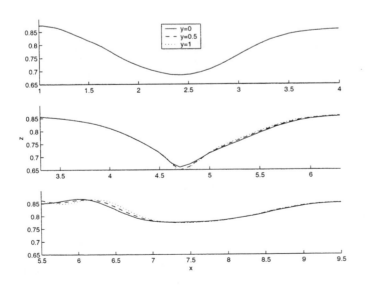

Figure 3. θ=0.5 isopycnals for step sill simulation, at t=1.8, 3.6, and 6.4

Valentine et al. (1999) found that the interaction with a two dimensional step sill causes an increased return flow over the top of the sill. Figure 5 illustrates the difference in vertical velocity induced by the incident wave on the three-dimensional sill at t = 3.5 and on a similar two dimensional step-shelf case for an incident wave with an amplitude of 0.11. Comparing a slice of the vertical component of velocity in the region with the step (specifically at y = 0.75) to a similar two-dimensional case shows that the three-dimensional case has a downward velocity near the corner of the step only half as large as that in the two-dimensional case. Thus, the third dimension provides relief when a solitary wave encounters this topographical feature.

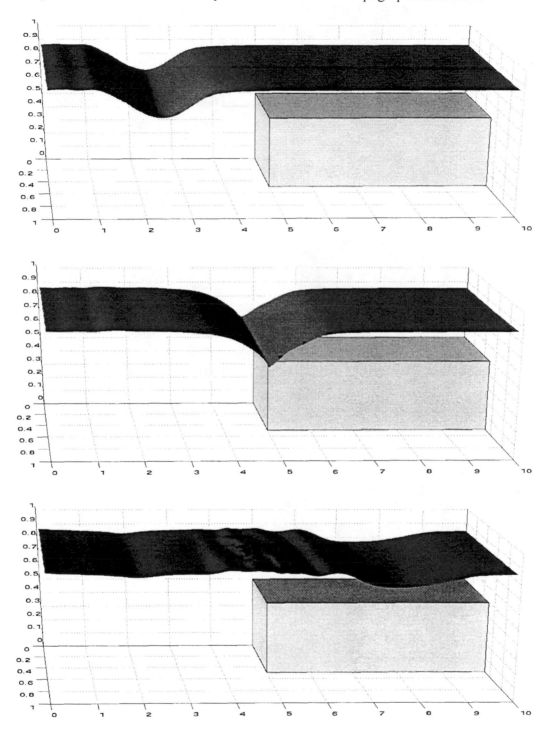

Figure 4. Internal solitary wave on a pycnocline encountering a step-sill.

Because of the length of the onset wave, the periodic nature of the obstacle, and the relief provided to the return flow over the step sill by the induced transverse flow, the effect of the obstacle is significantly less than may have been anticipated.

729

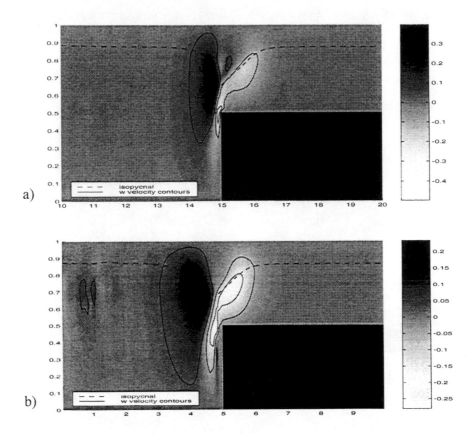

Figure 5. Comparison of velocity field induced by a solitary wave encountering (a) a step-shelf (a two-dimensional flow) and (b) a step-sill (a slice of the three-dimensional velocity field at y = 0.75).

5. References

Apel, J. R. et al. 1975 Observations of oceanic internal and surface waves from the Earth Resources Technology Satellite. *J. Geophys. Res.* **80**, 865-881.

Barr, B. C. 1997 Internal solitary waves: a numerical simulation. *MS Thesis*, Clarkson University.

Barr, B.C., Valentine, D.T., and Sipcic, R. 1999 Computational Analysis of Three-dimensional Internal Solitary Waves. *Bull. Am. Phys. Soc.* **44**, 90.

Hsu M.-K., Liu, A. K., and Liu C. 2000 A study of internal waves in the China Seas and Yellow Sea using SAR. *Continental Shelf Research* **20**, 389-410

Kao, T. W., Pan F.- S., and Renouard, D. 1985 Internal solitons on the pycnocline: generation, propagation, and shoaling on breaking over a slope. *J. Fluid Mech.* **159**, 19-53.

Liu, A. K., Chang, Y. S., Hsu, M.-K., and Liang, N. K. 1998 Evolution of nonlinear internal waves in the East and South China Seas. *J. Geophys. Res.* **103**, 7995-8008.

Lynett, P., and Liu, P. L.-F. 1998 Numerical modeling of internal wave-wave interactions. *Workshop on nonlinear internal waves.*

Osborne, A. R. and Burch, T. L. 1980, Internal Solitons in the Andaman Sea. *Science* **208**, 451-460.

Valentine, D. T., Barr B., and Kao, T. W. 1999 Large Amplitude Solitary Wave on a Pycnocline and Its Instability, Chapter 15 in the book dedicated to C.-S. Yih entitled *Fluid Dynamics at Interfaces* (eds. W. Shyy and R. Narayanan). Cambridge University Press, 227-239.

Whitham, G. B. 1974 *Linear and Nonlinear waves*, J. Wiley and Sons, Inc.

Periodic internal wave beams: explicit solutions and laboratory experiments

Yuli D. Chashechkin,

Institute for Problems in Mechanics of the RAS, 101/1 prospect Vernadskogo, Moscow, 117526, Russia, E-mail: chakin@ipmnet.ru

1. Abstract

Linear problems of generation of a periodic internal wave beam, its propagation, reflection off a solid surface or off a critical level and scattering on interfaces in a continuously stratified viscous fluid are solved asymptotically in the Boussinesq approximation and studied experimentally using schlieren and probe techniques. Complete solution of any particular wave problem, satisfying to the exact boundary conditions, contains, besides wave beams, internal boundary currents. These currents are formed on solid surfaces and propagate in a fluid interior as a thin interfaces. Their thickness is determined by appropriate kinetic coefficient (viscosity for velocity ant salt diffusion coefficient for density) and buoyancy frequency. Transverse moving internal boundary currents generate internal waves directly. Calculated parameters of periodic internal waves are in reasonable agreement with laboratory experiments.

2. Introduction

The atmosphere, lakes and oceans are examples of stratified systems with a fine structure where internal waves exist. As far as internal waves is difficult to observe, to measure, to calculate, their quantitative description is not yet complete and laboratory experiments are used both for qualitative observations and to a theory. Internal waves are divided into several types depending on their formation conditions. Transient (Cauchy-Poisson) waves are produced by compact instantaneous source and lee (attached) waves are generated by uniform flow over topography. The most significant role is attributed to periodic internal waves, which are fundamental in the linear theory (Lighthill). Due to a mathematical complexity most of theoretical results are produced by asymptotic methods and do not satisfy exact boundary conditions.. The aim of given paper is to present a method to construct exact solutions of different linear and slightly non-linear periodic internal problems in a viscous continuously stratified fluid satisfying exact boundary conditions and to compare with experimental data. Detailed analysis shows that viscosity and salt diffusivities lead to damping of waves in consequence of energy dissipation, to entrainment of ambient fluid into wave motion, and to generation of *internal boundary currents* in a fluid interior and on solid surfaces (Kistovich, Chashechkin, 1998). These currents are characterized by different transverse length scales for spatial variations of velocity and density that equals to those of transient flows, induced by diffusion on a topography, that is $\delta_v = \sqrt{\nu / N}$ for velocity and $\delta_s = \sqrt{\kappa_s / N}$ for salinity (Kistovich, Chashechkin, 1993; Baydulov, Chashechkin.). This theory of internal waves and boundary currents is closed and self-consistent.

3. Theoretical background

Motions of a continuously stratified liquid of which a density ρ depends on a salinity S in a gravity field with an acceleration g are studied. An initial density profile $\rho(z)$ is characterised by a buoyancy length scale $\Lambda = |d \ln\rho / dz|^{-1}$, buoyancy frequency $N = \sqrt{g / \Lambda}$ and buoyancy period $T_b = 2\pi / N$. Since the stratification is weak and viscosity and diffusivity are small, there are strong inequality $\Lambda \gg \lambda \gg \delta_v \gg \delta_s$. Taking into account these ratios, the basic set of governing equations is transformed into set of linearized (Kistovich, Chashechkin, 1998) or sequence of coupled non-linear equations (Kistovich, Chashechkin, 1999, Doklady), containing traditional operator of internal waves (for ideal and viscous fluids) and additional operators, produced by expansions in powers on the small parameters, containing viscosity and diffusivity coefficients. The boundary conditions are no-slip for velocity, impermeability for matter and attenuation of all disturbances at infinity in a fluid at rest. Solutions of the first equation give the propagating internal waves and additional solutions describe thin flows, which are called *internal boundary currents*. Three frames of reference are employed: a basic laboratory co-ordinate system (x,y,z) where axe z is directed upward in opposition to gravity acceleration, attached co-ordinate system (ξ,ζ) where axe ξ is directed along an emitting (reflecting) surface and concomitant system (q,p), where axe q is directed along a propagating wave ray.

3.1 Generation of periodic waves by an oscillating plane strip

Neglecting by diffusivity of an exponentially stratified fluid and calculating at the attached frame of co-ordinate one can see that the solution of dispersion equation corresponding to ordinary differential equation for spectral function $f(z,k)$ of a vertical displacement η (Kistovich, Chashechkin, 1998)

$$i\omega\nu f^{(4)} - \left[\omega^2 + 2i\omega k^2\right]f^{(2)} + \left[\omega^2 - N^2(z) + i\omega\nu)k^2\right]f = 0$$

contain four roots (time-dependent factor $\exp(-i\omega t)$ is omitted here and below). Two of roots describe the propagating wave beams

$$\Psi_w = \pm(1+i\mu)\sqrt{\frac{\nu\sin\theta}{2N}\left|\frac{\sin(\theta\mp\varphi)}{\sin(\theta\pm\varphi)}\right|}\int\limits_0^\infty V(\pm k\sin(\theta\mp\varphi))\exp\left[ikp_\pm - \frac{\nu k^3 q}{2N\cos\theta}\right]dk$$

and two other roots describe internal boundary currents formed on an emitting surface

$$\Psi_b = -(1+i\mu)\sqrt{\frac{\nu\sin\theta}{2N\left|\sin^2\theta - \sin^2\varphi\right|}}U(\xi)\exp\left(-i\frac{\mu\zeta}{\lambda_b}\right)\exp\left(-\frac{\zeta}{\lambda_b}\right),$$

where $V(k)$ is spectral function of the source velocity $U(\xi)$ and $\lambda_b = \sqrt{2\nu\sin\theta / N\left|\sin^2\theta - \sin^2\varphi\right|}$ is the thickness of the boundary current, $\mu = \text{sign}(\sin^2\theta - \sin^2\varphi)$, $\theta = \arcsin(\omega / N)$ is the direction of wave propagation (Kistovich, Chashechkin, 1999, JAMM).

The spectral velocity function of the plane strip of width a oscillating with a small amplitude b is $V(k) = (U / \pi k)\sin(ka / 2)$, $U = -i\omega b$, and for vertical displacement we have

$$\eta = -(1+i\mu)\frac{\alpha b\sin\theta}{6\pi}\sqrt{\frac{\nu\sin\theta}{2N}\frac{\sin(\theta-\varphi)}{\sin(\theta+\varphi)}}\left\{F(p+\frac{a^*}{2},q) - F(p-\frac{a^*}{2},q)\right\}$$

where $\alpha = \sqrt[3]{2N\cos\theta / \nu q}$, $a^* = a\sin(\theta-\varphi)$ is the projection of the width of the plate on the direction

of the beam propagation; and $F(p,q) = \int\limits_0^\infty y^{-2/3}e^{-y}\exp(i\alpha py^{1/3})dy = \sum\limits_{m=0}^\infty \frac{(i\alpha p)^m}{m!}\Gamma\left(\frac{m+1}{3}\right)$.

These expressions are regular functions of all physical parameters of the problem and tend to zero as $\omega \to 0$ or $\omega \to N$. In the limiting case $\nu \to 0$ the solutions go to zero. The envelope of a fluid particle displacement across a beam is described by the a function

$$\Phi(p,q) = \left\{F(p+\frac{a^*}{2},q) - F(p-\frac{a^*}{2},q)\right\}.$$ In a far-field region the waves look like those generated by

two sources localized on the extreme points of the body. The transverse centralised uni-modal or bi-modal structure of the beam near a generator depend of the ratio of generator size by viscous wave scale $L_\nu = \sqrt[3]{g\nu} / N$. Due to the viscous widening bi-modal profile of the beam with distance is transformed into uni-modal one. Calculations of distance of the beam transformation are presented in (Kistovich, Chashechkin, 1999, JAMM). Practically if $a << L_\nu$ the uni-modal wave beams are produced. A wide plate ($a >> L_\nu$) generates bi-modal beams.

Calculations show that the internal wave field predicted by the force-source model (Lighthill) coincides with the exact solution only in two cases: for the horizontal plane and for plane inclined only at the particular angle. The boundary currents are described incorrectly by both a force and mass source model. Thus, in general case the formal procedure of replacing an oscillating body by force (and mass) sources borrowed from the equivalent theory of homogeneous fluid is not valid.

3.2 Propagation of periodic wave beams

In an exponentially stratified fluid periodic internal waves propagate along a straight lines and a source located at the point ($p = 0$, $q = -L_1$) in concomitant system generates waves of amplitude

$$\eta(p,q) = \int_0^\infty A_1(k) \exp\left\{ ikp - \frac{\nu k^3 (L_1 + q)}{2N\cos\theta} \right\} dk .$$

In a fluid with an arbitrary smooth profile of buoyancy frequency $N(z)$ the amplitude is

$$\eta(p,q) = \sqrt{\frac{\mu(z_0)}{\mu(z_1)}} \int_0^\infty A_1(k) \exp\left\{ ikp - \frac{\nu k^3 (Q(z_1) + q)}{2N(z_1 \cos\theta)} \right\}) dk ,$$

where $A_1(k)$ is a spectral function of a source of waves located at the point z_0, point of observation is

$(x_1 ; z_1)$;   *concomitant current length scale*   is $Q(z) = \dfrac{\mu(z)}{(1+\mu^2(z))^{3/2}} \int_{z_0}^z \dfrac{(1+\mu^2(z'))^2}{\mu(z')} dz'$;

$\mu^2(z) = (N^2(z) - \omega^2)/\omega^2$ and current scale $Q(z)$ is related with geometrical length of a beam by the

formula $Q(z) = \dfrac{\sqrt{(dL(z')/dz)^2 - 1}}{(dL(z')/dz)^3} \int_{z_0}^z - \dfrac{(dL(z')/dz)^4}{\sqrt{(dL(z')/dz)^2 - 1}} dz'$ and $L(z) = \int_{z_0}^z \sqrt{1+\mu^2(z')} dz'$.   So any

smooth stratification is equivalent to exponential stratification with appropriate length Q and amplitude being multiplied by $\sqrt{\mu(z_0)/\mu(z_1)}$.

3.2 Reflection of a periodic wave beam off a sloping plane

The linear problem of the reflection of a periodic internal wave beam off a rigid inclined plane in an exponentially stratified fluid is solved with accuracy to the terms of the first order of magnitude on the viscosity ν (Kistovich, Chashechkin, 1995) over the whole range of parameters, including the critical angle $\varphi = \theta$. Compression of a wave beam is described by a geometrical factor

$M = -\dfrac{\sin(\varphi - \theta)}{\sin(\varphi + \theta)}$ everywhere except the critical angle at which the viscosity constrains wave length

and removes singularity due to the formation of the internal boundary current. The length scales of the current are exactly the same as for the boundary current formed on a generating surface. An energy loss coefficient that is defined as ratio of energy flux in the boundary current by the incident energy flux is calculated for the vertical and horizontal reflection wall:

$$K_v = \frac{4\sin^4\theta}{\cos^3\theta} \sqrt{\frac{\nu^3 \sin\theta}{2N^3}} \left(\int_0^\infty k^2 |H(k)|^2 dk \Big/ I_1 \right); \qquad K_h = 4\cot\theta \sqrt{\frac{\nu}{2N\sin\theta}} \left(\int_0^\infty |H(k)|^2 dk \Big/ I_1 \right), \qquad \text{and}$$

$K = \dfrac{4\cot\varphi \sin^4\theta \cos\theta}{N|\sin^2\varphi - \sin^2\theta|} \left(\int_0^\infty k |H(k)|^2 dk \Big/ I_1 \right)$ in an arbitrary case except critical angle $\theta = \varphi$, here

$I_1 = \int_0^\infty \dfrac{|H(k)|^2}{k} dk$. Energy loss coefficient is maximal for the horizontal reflection surface and mini-

mal for the vertical wall. Reflection of periodic wave beam from a critical level in a fluid at rest where $\omega = N$ is also studied (Kistovich, Chashechkin, 1998).

An internal wave beam incident of the surface of discontinuity of a buoyancy frequency produces internal boundary current in it directly. To ensure the required smoothness of a wave spectral function it is necessary to take into account all solutions of the singular disturbed operator of internal wave which, including propagating and reflected internal waves and internal boundary currents on the both sides of discontinuity. Detailed calculations show, that the spatial structure of the current depends on the number of a dissipative coefficients of the problem. Each boundary current is characterized by its own intrinsic length scale ($\delta_v = \sqrt{\nu/N}$ for velocity field and $\delta_s = \sqrt{\kappa_s/N}$ for salinity). Efficiency of direct energy transformation depend on the fine structure of the density field of the medium. If the buoyancy frequency and/or its first derivative are singular, the amplitude of the reflected beam is of the same order as the amplitude of the incident beam, whereas the amplitude of the boundary current is small and determined by the viscosity of the medium ($\sim\nu$). If the buoyancy frequency and its first derivative are continuous but its second derivative is discontinuous then both the reflected beam and the boundary current have the same order of smallness ($\sim v$). If only the third derivative is discontinuous, the reflected beam is order of ($\sim v$). and boundary current is an order of $v^{3/2}$.

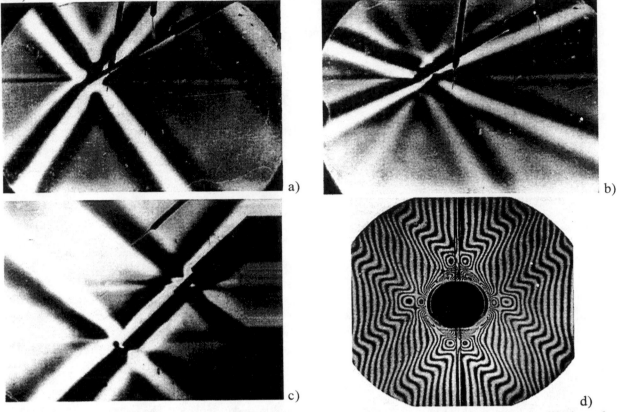

Fig. 1 Schlieren and interferometric images of periodic internal waves generated by oscillating plate (a, b, c: N = 1.14 rad s^{-1}; a = 1, 1, 6 cm, φ = 33^0, 33^0, 45^0; ω = 1.01; 0.53; 0.81 rad s^{-1}, θ = 63^0, main beam ω_1 = 0.53 rad/s, θ_1 = 27^0, second harmonic − ω_2 = 1.06 rad/s, θ_2 = 68^0; θ = 45° (critical case), A$_0$ = 0.15 cm) and by a cylinder (d = 4 cm)

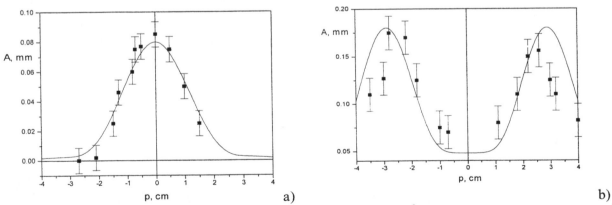

Fig. 2. Wave amplitudes across a beam (a, b − a = 1, 6 cm, φ = 50^0, N = 0.84 rad/s, ω = 0.64 rad s^{-1}, θ = 50^0, A$_0$ = 0.15 cm, q = 5 cm, k$_f$ = 0.7; 1.5). Solid curve − theory, points − experiment

3.1 Non-linear generation of periodic waves by boundary currents on a periodically rotating horizontal disk

On the surface of a disk of radius R rotating with an outer edge velocity $U_0\, e^{i\omega t/2}$ in a viscous exponentially stratified fluid the internal boundary current with velocity u is formed

$u = \dfrac{U_0 r}{2R} \vartheta(R-r)\left[e^{i\kappa|z|-i\omega t/2} + e^{i\kappa^*|z|+i\omega t/2} \right]$, where $\kappa^2 = \dfrac{i\omega}{2\nu} - k^2$, $\operatorname{Im} k > 0$, $\vartheta(x)$ is unit function. The current creates centripetal acceleration, which acts as a force source and generates internal waves with a frequency ω and vertical displacement

$$\eta(p,q) = -\frac{U_0^2 e^{-i\omega t}}{8(1+\sqrt{2})\omega^2 R} \sqrt{\frac{\nu}{\pi N r}} \int_0^\infty \frac{2J_1(kR') - kR'J_1(kR')}{\sqrt{k}} \exp\left(ikp - \frac{\nu k^3 p}{2N\cos\theta} \right) dk + c.c.$$

, where $c.c.$ is complex conjugate, J is Bessel function and $R' = R\sin\theta$. On the centre plane of the beam wave amplitude is quadratic function both of velocity and radius of the disc

$$\eta(q) = \frac{U_0^2 R^2 \sin\theta}{48(1+\sqrt{2})} \left(\frac{2\cos^4\theta}{\pi^3 \nu^4 N^8 q^{10}} \right)^{1/6} \Gamma\left(\frac{7}{6}\right).$$

If the disc performs periodic rotating oscillations on the background of a uniform rotation waves with the main frequency $\omega/2$ and its second harmonic are generated (Kistovich, Chashechkin, 1999).

4. Experimental Technique

The test is carried out in a $9000 \times 60 \times 60$ cm³ tank with optic windows, filled with linearly stratified brine. Side view of a flow is observed by schlieren instrument IAB-451. Density variations are measured by a home made conductivity probe which is dynamically calibrated by sweep oscillations or "jump up-down" on a height around 1 cm.

5. Main results

Typical schlieren and schlieren interferometric images of periodic internal waves generated by an oscillating plate and a vertically oscillating cylinder are shown in Fig. 1. Transverse profiles of wave displacements are presented in Fig. 2. Sloping wide bands visualize periodic internal waves of the main frequency in Fig. 1, a c, d and main and second harmonics in Fig.1, c. There is a conductivity probe on the photo. Thin horizontal strips represent internal boundary currents separated from an oscillating plate and propagating inside a fluid producing extended irregularity of a density. Direct visualization by density markers shows that these boundary currents act as a pump and form general circulation of a fluid ascending on the left side of the strips and descending on the right side in the direction corresponding to diffusion induced boundary currents on a motionless strip (Kistovich, Chashechkin,1993). The transverse structure of the beam near the generator depend on the ratio of generator size by wave viscous scale. Centralised uni-modal beams are formed by a narrow strip ($a < L_v$, Fig.1 a, b)) and b-modal beams are produced by a wide body ($a > L_v$, Fig.1 c, d). There is no singularity on a critical angle $\varphi = \theta$ (right upper beam in Fir. 1, c). Transverse profiles are described by the theory rather good with fitting coefficient $k_f = 0.7$ for narrow strip and $k_f = 1.5$ for the wide generator. Pattern of the 3D periodic wave beam reflecting from a sloping solid surface is shown in Fig 3, a. The change in bands brightness is prescribed by anisotropy of the schlieren instrument with vertical slit and knife. In accordance with the theory the wave induced boundary current is separated from the reflecting surface.

Periodic wave beams produced by a rotating oscillations of the disc are shown in Fig. 3, b. Thin horizontal interfaces – transversally moving internal boundary currents are closed by a tip circular rotating vortices. At small velocities (U < 3 cm/c) wave amplitudes are quadratic functions ($D = 2$; 4 cm, $\eta = 0,005U^2$; $0,04U^2$ [η] = mm, [U] = cm/s, curves 1 и 2), and when U > 8 cm/c a saturation is observed. Theoretical decreasing of amplitudes with distance is $h = 1,29q^{-5/3}$, [h] = mm, [q] = cm, laboratory data satisfy $h = 1,14q^{-1,54}$ at q < 7 cm.

Calculations and laboratory data show that any source in a viscous fluid generates simultaneously periodic internal wave beams and boundary currents. Internal boundary currents arising on a reflecting surface limit geometrical compression. Moving internal boundary currents generate periodic internal waves on a horizontal disc performing rotating oscillations in a continuously stratified fluid. Results of analytical calculations are in reasonable agreement with the laboratory experiments.

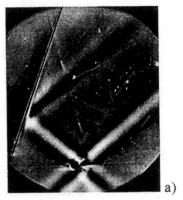 

a)   b)

Fig. 3. Reflection of 3D periodic waves off the wall and non-linear generation of periodic waves
by the disc

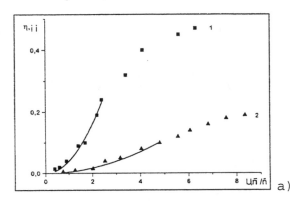 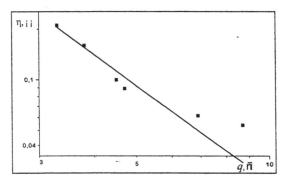

Fig. 4. The centreplane wave amplitudes versus the disc velocity (a) and distance from the source (b).

The research is supported by the Ministry of Science and Technology of the Russian Federation
(Program of support of unique experimental set-ups), by the Ministry Education of the Russian Federation (Federal Program "Integration", Grant 2.1-304) and the Russian Foundation for Basic Research (Grant 99-05-64980).

List of References

1. Baydulov V.G., Chashechkin Yu.D. A boundary current induced by diffusion near a motionless horizontal cylinder in a continuously stratified fluid // Izvestiya AS USSR, Atmospheric and Oceanic Physics. 1996. V. 32. No. 6. P. 818-823.
2. Il'inykh Yu. S., Kistovich A.V., Chashechkin Yu.D. Comparison of an exact solution to a certain problem of periodic internal wave generation with experiment // Izvestiya AS, Atmospheric and Oceanic Physics. 1999. V. 35. No. 5. P. 649-655.
3. Kistovich A.V., Chashechkin Yu.D. The structure of transient boundary flow along an inclined plane in a continuously stratified medium // J. Appl. Maths. Mechs. 1993.V. 57. No. 4. P. 633-639.
4. Kistovich A.V., Chashechkin Yu.D. The reflection of beams of internal gravity waves at flat rigid surface // J. Appl. Maths. Mechs. 1995.V. 59. No. 4. P.579-585.
5. Kistovich Yu.V., Chashechkin Yu.D. Geometry and Energetics of Beams of Internal Waves // Izvestiya, Atmospheric and Oceanic Physics // 1997. V. 33. No. 1. P. 36-41.
6. Kistovich Yu.V., Chashechkin Yu.D Linear theory of the propagation of internal wave beams in an arbitrary stratified liquid // J. Appl. Mech. and Techn. Physics. 1998. V. 39. No. 5. P. 729-737.
7. Kistovich Yu.V., Chashechkin Yu.D. Exact solution of certain linearized problem of monochromatic internal wave generation in a viscous fluid // J. Appl. Maths. Mechs. 1999.V. 63. No. 4. P. 611-619.
8. Kistovich Yu.V., Chashechkin Yu.D. Non-linear generation of periodic internal waves by boundary current on a rotating axially symmetric body // Doklady-Physics. 1999. Vol. 367. P. 636-639.
9. Lighthill J. Waves in fluids. CUP.Cambridge.1978.

Modeling of Strongly Nonlinear Internal Waves in a Multilayer System

Wooyoung Choi
Theoretical Division and Center for Nonlinear Studies
Los Alamos National Laboratory, Los Alamos, NM 87545, USA
wychoi@lanl.gov

Abstract

We consider strongly nonlinear internal gravity waves in a multilayer fluid and propose a mathematical model to describe the time evolution of large amplitude internal waves. Model equations follow from the original Euler equations under the sole assumption that the waves are long compared to the undisturbed thickness of one of the fluid layers. No small amplitude assumption is made. Both analytic and numerical solutions of the new model exhibit all essential features of large amplitude internal waves, observed in the ocean but not captured by the existing weakly nonlinear models. Differences between large amplitude surface and internal solitary waves are addressed.

1 Introduction

Two fundamental physical mechanisms, nonlinearity and dispersion, play important roles in the evolution of long internal gravity waves commonly observed in the ocean, more generally in any stratified fluids. Under the assumption of weakly nonlinear and weakly dispersive, the balance between these two effects leads to a remarkable phenomenon of solitons, very localized disturbances propagating without any change in form. However there have been a number of observations of large amplitude internal waves for which the weakly nonlinear assumption is far from being realistic. For example, in the northwestern coastal area of the Unites States, Stanton & Ostrovsky (1998) observed the train of tidally-generated internal waves in the form of solitary waves depressing the 7m deep pycnocline up to 30m. Evidently the weakly nonlinear models like the Korteweg-de Vries (KdV) equation commonly used in the community of geophysical fluid dynamics are completely irrelevant in such cases and new models need to be developed. The theory to be desired is of course one being able to account for full nonlinearity of the problem but this simple idea has never been successfully realized. Recently Choi and Camassa (1996, 1999) have derived various new models for strongly nonlinear dispersive waves in a simple two-layer system, using a systematic asymptotic expansion method for a natural small parameter in the ocean, that is the aspect ratio between vertical and horizontal length scales. Analytic and numerical solutions of the new models describe strongly nonlinear phenomena which have been observed but not been explained by using any weakly nonlinear models. This indicates the importance of strongly nonlinear aspects in the internal wave propagation. An interesting point to make is that the including strong nonlinearity does not simply add new nonlinear terms but change dispersive characters, from linear to nonlinear.

Despite of recent progress, the two-layer system is often too simplified to be useful for practical applications. For instance, the two-layer model has not only its limited despcription of smoothly stratified ocean but also the lack of higher-order baroclinic wave modes. Therefore the theory needs

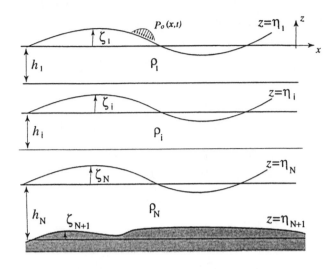

Figure 1: A multi-layer system

be extended to the more general situation relevant for real oceanic applications. Here we will study a continuously stratified fluid approximated by a stack of several homogeneous layers.

2   Nonlinear Dispersive Model

For an inviscid and incompressible fluid of density ρ_i, the velocity components in Cartesian coordinates (u_i, w_i) and the pressure p_i $(i = 1, \cdots, N)$ satisfy the continuity equation and the Euler equations:

$$u_{ix} + w_{iz} = 0, \tag{1}$$

$$u_{it} + u_i u_{ix} + w_i u_{iz} = -p_{ix}/\rho_i, \tag{2}$$

$$w_{it} + u_i w_{ix} + w_i w_{iz} = -p_{iz}/\rho_i - g, \tag{3}$$

where g is the gravitational acceleration and subscripts with respect to space and time represent partial differentiation. For a stable stratification, $\rho_i < \rho_{i+1}$ is assumed . The boundary conditions at the upper and lower interfaces of the i-th layer require the continuity of normal velocity and pressure:

$$\eta_{it} + u_i \eta_{ix} = w_i, \qquad p_i = p_{i-1} \quad \text{at} \quad z = \eta_i(x, t), \tag{4}$$

$$\eta_{i+1t} + u_i \eta_{i+1x} = w_i, \quad \text{at} \quad z = \eta_{i+1}(x, t), \tag{5}$$

In (4)–(5), $\eta_i(x, t)$ $(i = 1, \cdots, N)$ is the location of the upper interface of the i-th layer given by

$$\eta_i = \zeta_i - \sum_{j=1}^{i-1} h_j, \tag{6}$$

where h_i is the undisturbed thickness of the i-th layer and $\zeta_i(x, t)$ is the interfacial displacement. The position of the bottom, $\eta_{N+1}(x, t)$ can be written as

$$\eta_{N+1} = \zeta_{N+1} - \sum_{j=1}^{N} h_j = \zeta_{N+1} - h, \tag{7}$$

where $\zeta_{N+1}(x, t)$ is the bottom topography and h is the total depth.

Under the assumption that the thickness of each layer is much smaller than the characteristic wavelength, we have the following scaling relation between u_i and w_i, from (1),

$$w_i/u_i = O(h_i/L) = O(\epsilon) \ll 1 \,, \tag{8}$$

where L is a typical wavelength. For finite-amplitude waves, we also assume that $u_i/U_0 = O(\zeta_i/h_i) = O(1)$, where U_0 is a characteristic speed chosen as $U_0 = (gh)^{1/2}$.

The derivation of model is very similar to that for the two-layer model in Choi & Camassa (1999) and will not be shown here. The final set of equations for the i-th layer can be written, in dimensional form, as

$$H_{it} + \left(H_i\overline{u}_i\right)_x = 0, \qquad H_i = \eta_i - \eta_{i+1} \,, \tag{9}$$

$$\overline{u}_{it} + \overline{u}_i\overline{u}_{ix} + g\eta_{ix} + P_{ix}/\rho_i = \frac{1}{H_i}\left(\tfrac{1}{3}H_i^3 a_i + \tfrac{1}{2}H_i^2 b_i\right)_x + \left(\tfrac{1}{2}H_i a_i + b_i\right)\eta_{i+1x} \,, \tag{10}$$

where the layer-mean horizontal velocity $\overline{u}_i$ is defined as

$$\overline{u}_i(x,t) = \frac{1}{H_i}\int_{\eta_{i+1}}^{\eta_i} u_i(x,z,t)\,\mathrm{d}z \,, \tag{11}$$

and $P_i(x,t) = p_{i-1}(x,\eta_i,t)$ is the pressure at the upper surface of the i-th layer. In (10), a_i and b_i are defined as

$$a_i(x,t) = \overline{u}_{ixt} + \overline{u}_i\,\overline{u}_{ixx} - (\overline{u}_{ix})^2 \,, \qquad b_i(x,t) = -D_i^2\eta_{i+1} \,, \tag{12}$$

where $D_i = \partial_t + \overline{u}_i\partial_x$ stands for material derivative.

For $1 \le i \le N$, (9)–(10) determines the evolution of $2N$-unknowns, $\overline{u}_i$ and η_i, while P_i is given by the following recursion formula:

$$P_{i+1} = P_i + \rho_i\left(gH_i - \tfrac{1}{2}a_iH_i^2 - b_iH_i\right) \,, \tag{13}$$

where P_1 is the known atmospheric pressure at the free surface. These equations have been derived under the sole assumption that the waves are long compared with the water depth and we have imposed no assumption on wave amplitude. The kinematic equation (9) is exact, while the dynamic equations given by (10) and (13) have non-hydrostatic contributions correct up to $O(\epsilon^2)$. Even for rigid-lid approximation ($\zeta_1 = 0$), the system of (9)–(10) is still valid if P_1 is regarded as unknown pressure at the top boundary.

3   One-layer System

For the case of a homogeneous layer ($N = 1$), equations (9)–(10) reduce to the system of equations derived by Green & Naghdi (1976) by using the director sheet theory. Without any topography at the bottom and external pressure at the free surface ($\zeta_2 = P_1 = 0$), equations (9)–(10) possess the solitary wave solution given by

$$\zeta_1(X) = a\,\mathrm{sech}^2(kX), \qquad X = x - ct \,, \tag{14}$$

$$k^2 h_1^2 = \frac{3a}{4(h_1 + a)}, \qquad \frac{c^2}{gh_1} = 1 + \frac{a}{h_1} \,, \tag{15}$$

where a and c are wave amplitude and speed, respectively.

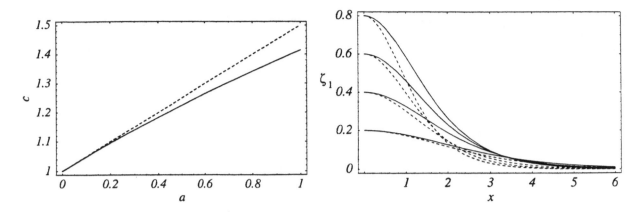

Figure 2: (a) Wave speed $(c/\sqrt{gh_1})$ versus wave amplitude (a/h_1) curves for surface solitary waves: ———, strongly nonlinear theory given by (15); – – –, weakly nonlinear (KdV) theory given by (17). (b) Surface solitary wave solutions (———) given by (14) for $a/h_1 =$ (0.2, 0.4, 0.6, 0.8) compared with KdV solitary waves (– – –) of the same amplitude. Here we show only half of the wave profile

For weakly nonlinear unidirectional waves of $a/h_1 = O(\epsilon^2)$, (9)–(10) can be reduced to the KdV equation for ζ_1:

$$\frac{1}{\sqrt{gh_1}} \zeta_{1t} + \zeta_{1x} + \frac{3}{2h_1}\zeta_1\zeta_{1x} + \frac{h_1^2}{6}\zeta_{1xxx} = 0 . \tag{16}$$

It is interesting to notice that the solitary wave solution of the KdV equations has the same form as that of the GN equations give by (14) with

$$k^2h_1^2 = \frac{3a}{4h_1}, \qquad \frac{c}{\sqrt{gh_1}} = 1 + \frac{a}{2h_1} , \tag{17}$$

which is the small amplitude limit of (15).

As shown in figure 2a, the solitary wave speed from the strongly nonlinear theory increases with wave amplitude at a much slower rate than that from the KdV theory. In figure 2b, one can see that the strongly nonlinear solitary wave solution given by (14) is certainly wider than the KdV soliton of the same amplitude. In §4, we will make the similar observations for interfacial solitary waves in a two-layer system and these features seem to be generic in strongly nonlinear waves.

4 Two-layer System

As shown in Choi & Camassa (1999), with rigid lid approximation ($\zeta_1 = 0$), the coupled system of (9)–(10) for $i = 1, 2$ can be reduced, for traveling waves at the interface, to

$$(\zeta_{2x})^2 = \frac{3\zeta_2^2\left[c^2(\rho_1 H_2 + \rho_2 H_1) - g(\rho_2 - \rho_1)H_1 H_2\right]}{c^2(\rho_1 h_1^2 H_2 + \rho_2 h_2^2 H_1)} , \tag{18}$$

where $H_1 = h_1 - \zeta_2$ and $H_2 = h_2 + \zeta_2$. This particular form of equation has been obtained earlier by Miyata (1985) using conservation laws, for steay flows. When replacing ζ_2 by wave amplitude a in (18), the numerator has to vanish and this gives wave speed c in terms of wave amplitude a as

$$\frac{c^2}{c_0^2} = \frac{(h_1 - a)(h_2 + a)}{h_1 h_2 - (c_0^2/g) a} , \tag{19}$$

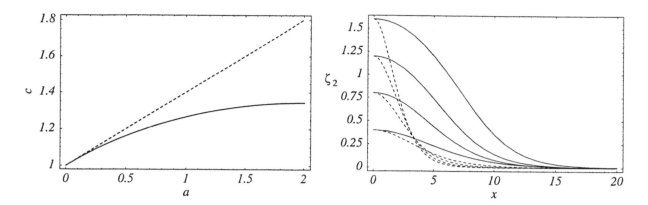

Figure 3: (a) Wave speed (c/c_0) versus wave amplitude (a/h_2) curves for internal solitary wave ($\rho_1/\rho_2 = 0.99$, $h_1/h_2 = 5$): ———, strongly nonlinear theory given by (19); – – –, weakly nonlinear (KdV) theory given by (23). (b) Internal solitary wave solutions (———) of (18) for $\rho_1/\rho_2 = 0.99$, $h_1/h_2 = 5$ and $a/h_2 =$ (0.4, 0.8, 1.2, 1.6) compared with KdV solitary waves (– – –) of the same amplitude given by (23).

where c_0 is the linear first baroclinic wave speed given by

$$c_0{}^2 = \frac{g h_1 h_2 (\rho_2 - \rho_1)}{\rho_1 h_2 + \rho_2 h_1}. \tag{20}$$

For uni-directional weakly nonlinear waves of $a/h_2 = O(\epsilon^2)$, (9)–(10) for $i = 1, 2$ can be further simplified to the KdV equation for ζ_2 as before:

$$\zeta_{2t} + c_0 \zeta_{2x} + c_1 \zeta_2 \zeta_{2x} + c_2 \zeta_{2xxx} = 0, \tag{21}$$

where

$$c_1 = -\frac{3 c_0}{2} \frac{\rho_1 h_2^2 - \rho_2 h_1^2}{\rho_1 h_1 h_2^2 + \rho_2 h_1^2 h_2}, \qquad c_2 = \frac{c_0}{6} \frac{\rho_1 h_1^2 h_2 + \rho_2 h_1 h_2^2}{\rho_1 h_2 + \rho_2 h_1}. \tag{22}$$

The solitary wave solution of (21) is given by (14) with

$$k^2 = \frac{a c_1}{12 c_2}, \qquad c = c_0 + \frac{c_1}{3} a. \tag{23}$$

Figures 3a and 3b clearly show that strongly nonlinear solitary waves are slower and broader than weakly nonlinear waves of the same amplitude. In fact Choi & Camassa (1999) have demonstrated that the strongly nonlinear theory yields excellent agreement with available expeimental data or numerical solutions of the Euler equations.

For a two-layer system, since wave amplitude cannot be greater than the total depth, there is a maximum wave amplitude beyond which no solitary wave solution exists. As wave amplitude approaches to the limiting value, the solitary wave becomes broader and finally degenerates into a front-like, or internal bore, solution, as shown in figure 4. In this interesting limit, the amplitude and speed can be found, from (18) and (19), as

$$a_m = \frac{h_1 - h_2 (\rho_1/\rho_2)^{\frac{1}{2}}}{1 + (\rho_1/\rho_2)^{\frac{1}{2}}}, \qquad c_m{}^2 = g(h_1 + h_2) \frac{1 - (\rho_1/\rho_2)^{\frac{1}{2}}}{1 + (\rho_1/\rho_2)^{\frac{1}{2}}}. \tag{24}$$

For an inviscid homogeneous layer, front solutions are impossible without the loss of energy which is often contributed to the effects of viscosity. On the other hand, for internal waves, the front-like solutions of (18) hold the conservation law for energy.

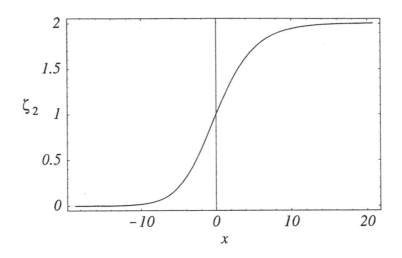

Figure 4: A front solution of (18) for maximum wave amplitude given by (24) for $\rho_1/\rho_2 = 0.99$ and $h_1/h_2 = 5$.

The limiting behaviours of highest waves are completely different between surface and internal waves. As shown by Stokes (1880), surface waves of maximum amplitude have a sharp peak of 120°, which cannot be captured by the present long wave theory. Therefore one can see that the GN theory for long surface waves ceases to be valid when the waves become too high. On the other hand, as wave amplitude increases, internal solitary waves becomes broader and broader, leading to internal bore. Therefore the long wave theory for internal waves is expected to be valid even for large wave amplitude. This explains why the strongly nonlinear theory for internal waves gives much better agreement with experimental data or numerical solutions of the Euler equations (Choi & Camassa 1999) compared to that for surface waves.

This work was supported by the U.S. Department of Energy.

References

[1] Choi, W. & Camassa, R.: Weakly nonlinear internal waves in a two-fluid system. *J. Fluid Mech.* **313**, (1996), 83–103.

[2] Choi, W. & Camassa, R.: Fully nonlinear internal waves in a two-fluid system. *J. Fluid Mech.* **396**, (1999), 1–36.

[3] Green, A. E. & Naghdi, P. M.: A derivation of equations for wave propagation in water of variable depth. *J. Fluid Mech.* **78**, (1976), 237–246.

[4] Miyata, M.: An internal solitary wave of large amplitude. *La mer* **23**, (1985), 43–48.

[5] Stanton, T. P. & Ostrovsky, L. A.: Observations of highly nonlinear internal solitons over the continental shelf. *Geophys. Res. Lett.* **25**, (1998), 2695–2698.

[6] Stokes, G. G.: Supplement to a paper on the theory of oscillatory waves. *Mathematical & Physical Papers* **1**, (1880), 314–326.

Synthetic schlieren measurements of internal waves generated by oscillating a square cylinder

Stuart B. Dalziel

Department of Applied Mathematics and Theoretical Physics,
University of Cambridge, Silver Street, Cambridge CB3 9EW, UK
s.dalziel@damtp.cam.ac.uk

1. Abstract

This paper presents new results showing the similarities and differences in the internal wave field produced by oscillating circular and square cylinders in a linear stratification. For a square cylinder, each of the four wave beams has the same structure, but this structure differs qualitatively from that from a circular cylinder. As with the waves from a circular cylinder, the wave beams are unimodal in the far field, but show more than one peak close to the cylinder. In each beam, the portion of the wave beam not crossing the plain normal to the direction of oscillation has an almost identical structure (quantitatively) to that for a circular cylinder, whereas the portion of the beam crossing this plane has a very different structure resulting from separation at the corners of the square cylinder. The experimental measurements presented in this paper are obtained using the recently developed 'synthetic schlieren', and an outline the basic principles is given.

2. Introduction

Internal gravity waves are an important dynamical feature of most density-stratified flows and play particularly crucial rôles in the atmosphere and oceans. As a consequence, there have been many theoretical, numerical and experimental studies of the waves, their generation by flow over obstacles, by the collapse of turbulence, and excitation through other fluid dynamical and mechanical means.

The classical experiments of Mowbray & Rarity (1967), where a small circular cylinder was oscillated either vertically or horizontally in a linear stratification, demonstrate the basic dispersive properties of the waves. Linear theory predicts the motion should be aligned along beams of infinitesimal width for inviscid fluids (Makarov, Neklyudov & Chashechkin 1990), but that viscosity would broaden this, reducing the shear to finite values.

For a finite size cylinder, the beams are of a width comparable with the diameter of the cylinder (Appleby & Chrighton 1986, 1987; Voisin 1991; Hurley & Keady 1997). If the diameter of the cylinder is larger than the viscous scale $(g\nu)^{1/3}/N$ then there is a gradual transition from a bimodal distribution near the cylinder to a unimodal distribution in the far field. Here g is the acceleration due to gravity, ν is the kinematic viscosity,

$$N = \sqrt{-\frac{g}{\rho_0}\frac{\partial\rho}{\partial z}} \qquad (1)$$

is the buoyancy frequency, and ρ is the density. This transition is described by the theory of Hurley & Keady (1997), and the validity of which has been demonstrated by the experiments of Sutherland et al. (1999).

This paper provides new results comparing the structure of the wave field produced by a circular cylinder with that produced by a square cylinder of comparable size. As with the work by Sutherland et al. (1999), the density perturbations resulting from the waves are measured using the recently developed 'synthetic schlieren' technique. However, whereas Sutherland et al. (1999) used a pattern of lines to obtain measurements of the vertical density gradient, the present paper uses a pattern of random dots to extract both components of the in-plane density gradient. The synthetic schlieren variant referred to as 'pattern matching refractometry' in Dalziel *et al.* (2000) is employed.

Section 3 outlines the basic optical principle for synthetic schlieren and gives some details of the processing algorithms. Results of the wave fields produced by a circular cylinder and by a square cylinder are presented in section 4, with the conclusions in section 5.

3. Synthetic schlieren

The basic principle involved is that there is a one to one relationship between density ρ' and refractive index n' fluctuations within the fluid, and that these fluctuations cause the features visible on the mask located on the far side of the tank to appear to move horizontally and/or vertically. For the optical arrangement shown in figure 1, these apparent movements are given by

$$\Delta \xi = \tfrac{1}{2} W (W + 2B) \frac{1}{n_0} \frac{\partial n'}{\partial x}, \tag{2a}$$

$$\Delta \zeta = \tfrac{1}{2} W (W + 2B) \frac{1}{n_0} \frac{\partial n'}{\partial z}, \tag{2b}$$

where W is the width of the tank and B the distance from the tank to the mask. The displacements $\Delta \xi$ (in the x direction along the tank) and $\Delta \zeta$ (in the vertical z direction) are relative to the *world* coordinates of the mask. The nominal refractive index is n_0 and the light rays are nominally parallel to the cross-tank coordinate y.

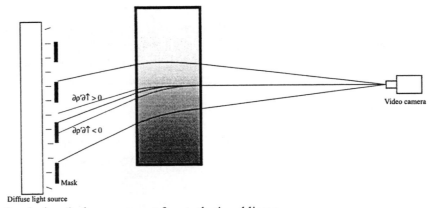

Figure 1: Sketch of typical optical arrangement for synthetic schlieren.

For salt water the relationship between salinity, density and refractive index are approximately linear, allowing us to write

$$\nabla n = \frac{dn}{d\rho} \nabla \rho = \beta \frac{n_0}{\rho_0} \nabla \rho, \tag{3}$$

where $\beta = (\rho_0/n_0)(dn/d\rho) \approx 0.184$. For the purposes of this paper we shall ignore the deflection of light rays due to the refractive index contrasts associated with entering and exiting the experimental apparatus.

3.1 QUALITATIVE MODE

In its simplest form, synthetic schlieren simply requires images of the mask placed on the far side of the flow. The absolute value of the difference between an image with a density perturbation and one without a density perturbation can be shown to be proportional to the apparent movement of the mask, at least while the apparent movement is small. Figure 2 plots the magnitude of this absolute difference, $|P_{ij}(t) - P_{ij;0}|$, as a function of the apparent shift for a mask of randomly located dots. Here, $P_{ij;0}$ is the pixel intensities of the unperturbed mask, and $P_{ij}(t)$ the pixel intensities of the perturbed mask.

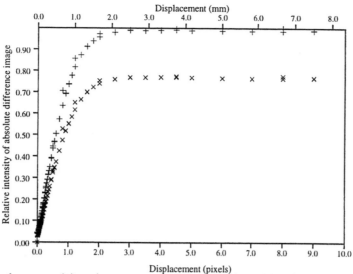

Figure 2: Variations in the mean (+) and root mean square (×) value of $|P_{ij}(t) - P_{ij;0}|$ as the mask is displaced by a milling machine traverse.

Figure 3 shows a typical example of the internal wave patterns visualised using this mode of synthetic schlieren. Note the waves emanating from the tangents to the 40mm diameter circular cylinder, and the gradual reduction in the intensity of the pattern of the pattern away from the cylinder. At the same time, there is a transition within each of the four wave beams from a bimodal distribution aligned with the tangents, to a unimodal distribution centred on the beam. The use here of $|P_{ij}(t) - P_{ij;0}|$ discards the sign of the perturbation, resulting in both positive and negative perturbations giving a dark colour in this figure.

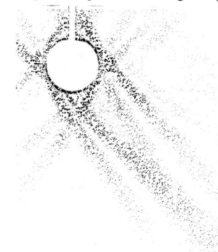

Figure 3: Qualitative synthetic schlieren using a mask of two-dimensional objects to visualise the internal wave field from a circular cylinder oscillating at a frequency $\omega/N \sim 2^{-1/2}$.

3.2 QUANTITATIVE MODE

Quantitative mode synthetic schlieren attempts to measure the apparent displacement of the features found on the mask. Three distinct methods for achieving this have been described by Dalziel *et al.* (2000): line refractometry, dot tracking refractometry and pattern matching refractometry. The first (and simplest) of these was employed by Sutherland *et al.* (1999) in their experiments of the structure of internal waves from a circular cylinder, while this paper adopts the third which arguably represents the most powerful of the variations.

For those familiar with the group of techniques often referred to as PIV or Particle Image Velocimetry, the ideas behind pattern matching refractometry will need little explanation. In passing, we note that the name PIV is itself misleading, as common usage applies this title to what would be more appropriately described as 'pattern matching velocimetry' as there is no need for the patterns to be from particles *and* there are other techniques (such as particle tracking velocimetry) which fall under this description.

The basic idea with pattern matching refractometry is to look to see how the patterns present on the mask appear to move with the changes in the density field. The random dot pattern selected here was chosen to ensure there was an approximately uniform density of dots at the same time as providing a pattern that is locally unique. The procedure for identifying the apparent shift is simply one of optimising some measure of the difference between a region of the unperturbed image and a corresponded shifted region in the perturbed image. In particular, we choose here to minimise

$$f_{abs}\left(\Delta\xi,\Delta\zeta;x_i,z_j\right)=\left\langle\left|P(x+\Delta\xi,z+\Delta\zeta;t)-P_0(x,z)\right|\right\rangle, \qquad (4)$$

although we note that a range of other functions (such as the cross-correlation function normally used in PIV) may be used instead. The search algorithm for the apparent displacements $\Delta\xi$, $\Delta\zeta$ uses a combination of biquadratic fitting of f_{abs} and bilinear interpolation of P to obtain the required subpixel accuracy. This procedure is embedded in a multigrid framework for improved efficiency. Further details of this process may be found in Dalziel *et al.* (2000).

4 Results

Using the pattern matching refractometry mode of synthetic schlieren to obtain $\nabla\rho'$ is straightforward and only takes a few minutes to set up and calibrate. Figure 4 shows typical images of the internal wave field measured in this way for a circular (figure 4a) and square (figure 4b) cylinder. In both cases the frequency of oscillation is close to $\omega/N=2^{-1/2}$. To assist comparison with the results of Sutherland *et al.* (1999), only the vertical component of the density field is shown. The field of view extends over most of the depth of the tank, allowing the reflections from the tank floor and the free surface to be observed. While a knowledge of the horizontal component allows us to invert $\nabla\rho'$ and thus obtain ρ' to within a single arbitrary constant, the relatively small size of the tank used here ($605\times100\times400$mm) leads to multiple reflections of the internal waves and a complex structure for ρ' that is beyond the scope of this paper. The measurements of $\nabla\rho'$ are less sensitive to these reflections (smaller ρ' and larger length scales combine to make $\nabla\rho'$ from the reflected waves much weaker than that from the directly radiated waves).

While the structure of the waves is broadly similar in the two cases, there are a number of important differences. For the circular cylinder, each of the four wave beams are clearly split into two bands close to the cylinder, emanating tangentially from the cylinder, with viscous diffusion leading to a gradual increase in the perturbation between these bands prior to reflection from the tank floor or free surface.

In contrast, the four wave beams emanating from the circular cylinder appears to have an additional, broader band originating at the corner of the square, approximately half way between the two tangential bands. The positioning and form of this broader band suggests that it originates from the separation of the boundary layer on the vertical faces of the square cylinder, the resulting disturbance to the flow being confined to the region immediately above and below the cylinder (for the present vertical oscillation). Additionally, there is some suggestion of horizontal banding from the top and bottom faces of the cylinders. More detailed experiments suggest that this is the result of mixed fluid being generated primarily by the initial transients of the cylinder, but also from the on-going boundary layer separation and the vanishing of the diffusive flux on the top and bottom faces of the cylinder.

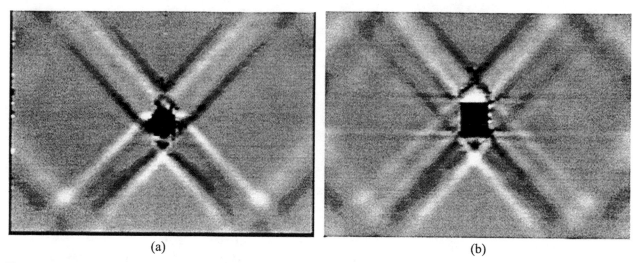

(a)   (b)

Figure 4: Quantitative mode synthetic schlieren measurements of the vertical gradient of the density perturbation for (a) a circular cylinder and (b) a square cylinder.

Figure 5 shows the cross-beam structure of the internal wave field for the lower left-hand beam at a distance of 8 radii from the cylinder as the cylinder reaches the bottom of its stroke. This figure presents the perturbation in the vertical density gradient normalised on the oscillation amplitude (in s^{-2}/cm) as a function of the cross-beam position (in cm). Curves are shown for the circular cylinder (solid line), the square cylinder (dashed line), and the viscous theory of Hurley & Keady (1997; dot-dash line).

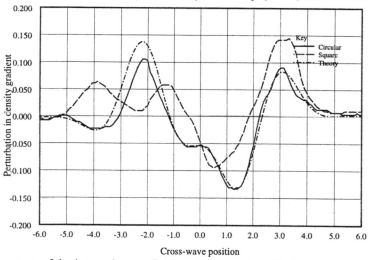

Figure 5: Cross-beam structure of the internal wave field 8 radii from the cylinder.

As found by Sutherland *et al.* (1999), there is good agreement between the theoretical predictions of the wave field and experimental measurements for a circular cylinder. The level of agreement found in figure 5 is comparable with the earlier results, and is maintained across all phases of the waves.

The wave field from the square cylinder is broadly similar for the upper band of this beam (*i.e.* the band that starts at the upper corner of the cylinder and crosses the mid-plane normal to the direction of cylinder oscillation), a feature that is again observed for all phases of the waves. The somewhat larger amplitude found in the square cylinder is due in part to the absence of any normalisation based on the size of the cylinder (the square cylinder was sized approximately midway between the inscribed and circumscribed square for the circular cylinder). Identical results are found for the comparable band in the other beams.

The lower band of this beam (*i.e.* the band that does not cross the mid-plane) shows two peaks rather than the single peak found for the circular cylinder. Each of these peaks is slightly more than half the amplitude of that found for the circular cylinder, and is broader in width, suggesting a higher energy flux is carried away from the cylinder, and we may therefore expect the square cylinder to have a larger drag than its circular counterpart. Again, identical behaviour is found for the corresponding bands in the other beams, and similar differences are found for other phases of the oscillation, and for oscillations at different frequencies.

5 Conclusions

The internal gravity wave field produced by a square cylinder oscillating in a linear stratification shows similarities in the near field with that generated by the oscillation of a circular cylinder. In both cases the motion is confined to four beams forming a Saint Andrew's cross centred on the cylinder and bounded by the tangents to the cylinder at an angle $\cos\theta = \omega/N$ to the vertical. Within each beam, the structure of parts of the wave field crossing the mid-plane of the oscillation are very close to that of a circular cylinder, whereas the parts of the wave beam that emanate from the horizontal faces (for a vertical oscillation) show significant differences, creating what is essentially a trimodal distribution across each beam.

These differences in the near field are believed to be primarily due to the separation of the viscous boundary layer found on the vertical faces of the vertically oscillating cylinder, and the subsequent disturbance to the flow caused by the development of a weak separated wake immediately above and below the cylinder.

The near-field differences will, in turn, lead to a modified structure over the whole of the beam further from the cylinder, as viscous effects kill off the higher wavenumber components, but ultimately details will be lost with the development of a unimodal distribution. However, these preliminary results suggest that the energy flux carried by the waves will be greater from a square cylinder, and that we may expect the cylinder to experience a larger drag.

The author wishes to thank Mr. Franck Rodriguez for his assistance in running some of the experiments.

References

Appleby, J.C. & Crighton, D.G. (1986) Non-Boussinesq effects in the diffraction of internal waves from an oscillating cylinder. *Q. J. Mech. Appl. Maths* **39**, 209-231.

Appleby, J.C. & Crighton, D.G. (1987) Internal gravity waves generated by oscillations of a sphere. *J. Fluid Mech.* **183**, 439-450.

Dalziel, S.B., Hughes, G.O. & Sutherland, B.R. (2000) Whole-field density measurements by 'synthetic schlieren'. *Exp. in Fluids* **28**, 322-335.

Hurley, D.G. & Keady, G. (1997) The generation of internal waves by vibrating cylinders, Part 2: Approximate viscous solution for a circular cylinder. *J. Fluid Mech.* **351**, 119-138.

Kistovich, A.V., Neklyudov, V.I. & Chashechkin, Y.D. (1990) Spatial structure of two-dimensional and monochromatic internal-wave beams in an exponentially stratified liquid. *Izv. Atmos. Oceanic Phys.* **26**, 548-554.

Mowbray, D.E. & Rarity, B.S.H. (1967) A theoretical and experimental investigation of the phase configuration of internal waves of small amplitude in a density stratified liquid, *J. Fluid Mech.* **28**, 1-16.

Sutherland, B.R., Dalziel, S.B., Hughes, G.O. & Linden, P.F. (1999) Visualisation and measurement of internal waves by "synthetic schlieren". Part 1: Vertically oscillating cylinder; to *J. Fluid Mech.* **390**, 93-126.

Voisin, B. (1991) Internal wave generation in uniformly stratified fluids. Part 1. Green's function and point sources. *J. Fluid Mech.* **231**, 439-480.

Direct Numerical Simulation of Unstable Finite Amplitude Progressive Interfacial Waves

O. B. Fringer[1], S. W. Armfield[1,2], and R. L. Street[1]

[1]Civil and Environmental Engineering, Stanford University, Stanford, CA 94301, U.S.A.
[2]Mechanical and Mechatronic Engineering, The University of Sydney, N.S.W. 2006, Australia
fringer@stanford.edu,armfield@mech.eng.usyd.edu.au,street@cive.stanford.edu

1   Abstract

We use a finite volume formulation to perform two dimensional direct numerical simulations of progressive finite amplitude interfacial breaking waves. Steep interfacial waves with ka as high as 1.86 are generated by decreasing the buoyancy frequency in the horizontal direction, so that long waves shorten as they propagate into a region with decreased reduced gravity. By generating short waves, we show that interfacial waves can break in the absence of a background shear. The primary instability results from a convective nonlinearity when the horizontal velocity induced by the wave exceeds its phase speed. The results prove that large amplitude progressive interfacial waves do not necessarily succumb to shear instabilities before they reach their critical convective breaking amplitude.

2   Introduction and Objectives

The mechanism by which a progressive interfacial wave breaks in the absence of topographic effects has long been a subject of much debate. A large amplitude progressive wave can break due either to shear or to nonlinear overturning when the fluid velocity induced by the wave exceeds its phase speed. Whether or not nonlinear overturning dominates the breaking process is the subject of this paper.

Holyer (1979) applied potential theory to two infinitely deep fluid layers separated by a vortex sheet to calculate the maximum steepness of an interfacial wave to 31st order in ka, where k is the wavenumber and a is the wave amplitude. While convergence for expansions of this kind are questionable since ka is $\mathcal{O}(1)$ and the horizontal velocity field is discontinuous at the interface, she computed the critical wave amplitudes at which the fluid velocity induced by the wave is greater than its phase speed for different density ratios. She found that in the limit of a Boussinesq interfacial wave the horizontal fluid velocity exceeds the phase speed at the interface half way between the crest and trough when $ka = 1.1$. Tsuji and Nagata (1973) had performed a similar analysis to lower order, but postulated that a real interfacial wave would break much sooner than predicted by potential theory because of the onset of shear instabilities at the interface.

In his experiments with finite amplitude interfacial waves, Thorpe (1978) showed that they break at much lower steepnesses when subjected to a mean shear or when the layer thicknesses differ. He computed the maximum steepness for interfacial waves in two fluid layers of different depths in the absence of mean shear, and showed that the fluid velocity exceeds the wave phase speed when $ka = 0.33$ and the lower layer depth is 1/3 that of the upper layer. Troy and Koseff (2000) have reported that deep water interfacial waves can break forward or backward when several wavelengths interact in a nonlinear manner. Their experiments generated large amplitude interfacial waves by focusing different wave components via dispersion to a point at which the steepness reaches a critical value and generates a breaking instability. Whether or not the waves break forward or backward depends on the initial phase distribution of the components in the wave packet. A small amplitude wave breaks backward if it encounters a region of negative shear at the crest of a longer background wave, and breaks forward if it encounters a region of positive shear in the trough of a longer background wave.

The results in the literature have generally been inconclusive. Potential theory can only predict overturning due to a convective nonlinearity because no shear is present that can prevent this instability. The answer can only be obtained with a direct numerical simulation of the breaking process. While a host of numerical studies have been performed on breaking gravity waves in a continuously stratified fluid (Lin et al. , 1993; Lombard & Riley, 1996; Andreassen et al. , 1998; Slinn & Riley, 1998a), few, if any, have been performed on waves breaking at an interface between two miscible fluids of different densities. Chen et al. (1999) used an interface tracking method to simulate breaking surface waves. While they performed simulations of interfacial waves to validate their results, their simulations, as with all multi-fluid simulations, do not capture mixing across the interface, because the fluids are immiscible. Simulation of a realistic breaking interfacial wave must allow for diffusion across the interface because this diffusion process plays a significant role in the breaking dynamics.

In this paper we report on the initial findings of the breaking mechanism with two dimensional simulations, and demonstrate conclusively that the dominant mechanism can be a forward overturning nonlinear instability. In Section 3 we cover the numerical method, while Section 4 describes the breaking dynamics, and Section 5 concludes with a brief description of our intended future work.

3   Numerical Method

We implement a direct numerical simulation to solve the two dimensional Navier-Stokes and scalar transport equations using a finite volume formulation on a nonstaggered grid with a rigid lid. The grid is stretched both in the horizontal and vertical to resolve the shorter waves in the right half plane of the domain as well as the thin interface between the two layers. Momentum is advanced with a pressure correction method (Armfield & Street, 2000) and the viscous and diffusive density terms are advanced semi-implicitly using approximate factorization (Zang et al. , 1993). Advection of momentum is computed with the QUICK scheme (Leonard, 1979) and scalar transport is computed with the SHARP formulation (Leonard, 1987). The bulk of the computation involves solution of the pressure with a multigrid Poisson solver, and the scheme is both second order accurate in space and time. Boundary conditions are free slip everywhere except at the rightmost boundary, where we implement a Sommerfeld radiation condition (Javam et al. , 1999) in order to minimize interfacial wave reflection.

Interfacial waves are generated at the left boundary of a rectangular domain with dimensions $L = 1$m and $d = 0.2$m with 256×80 grid points. These waves are generated with a vertical momentum source which is zero everywhere except near $x = 0$ of the form

$$F(x, z, t) = F_0 \exp\left[-\left(\frac{x}{L_x}\right)^2 - \left|\frac{z + d/2}{L_z}\right|^3\right] \sin(\omega t), \qquad (1)$$

where $F_0 = 4.0 \times 10^{-7}$m/s^2 is the forcing amplitude, $\omega = 1.5$rad/s is the forcing frequency, and $L_x = 0.1$m and $L_z = 0.322$m are the forcing length scales. We initialize the two-layer density stratified domain with a stable stratification given by

$$\frac{\rho}{\rho_0}(x, z) = -\frac{\Delta\rho(x)}{2\rho_0} \tanh\left[\frac{2(z + d/2)}{\delta} \tanh^{-1}(\alpha)\right], \qquad (2)$$

where $\delta = 0.01$m is the interface thickness, $\alpha = 0.99$, and $-d < z < 0$. In order to generate large amplitude interfacial waves, large values of F_0 cause substantial stirring at the wave generation zone. Reduction of stirring due to forcing at the generation zone is accomplished by generating small amplitude waves at $x = 0$ and reducing the density difference $\Delta\rho(x)$ horizontally with

$$\Delta\rho(x) = \Delta\rho_1 + \frac{\Delta\rho_2 - \Delta\rho_1}{2}\left[1 + \tanh\left(\frac{2(x - x_\rho)}{L_\rho}\tanh^{-1}(2\alpha - 1)\right)\right], \qquad (3)$$

where $L_\rho = 0.25$m is the thickness of the horizontal density variation, $\alpha = 0.99$, $x_\rho = 0.375$m, $\Delta\rho_1$ is the initial density difference between the two layers, and $\Delta\rho_2$ is the final density difference between the two layers, as shown in Figure 1.

The wave Reynolds number $Re = c\lambda/\nu$ based on the forcing wave is approximately 2280, while the ratio $\omega/N_{max} = 0.22$, where N_{max} is the maximum buoyancy frequency of the initial stratification in the forcing region. The Prandtl number based on the physical parameters is 7. However, the numerical Prandtl number is likely an order of magnitude smaller due to the diffusive nature of SHARP in the advection of density. The longest waves in the domain have wavenumbers given by $kH = 1.67$, where $H = 0.1$m is the layer depth, and are hence close to deep water waves since $\tanh(kH) = 0.93$. For the shortest waves, $k\delta = 0.5$, where δ is the interface thickness.

4 Results and Discussion

4.1 Effects of Varying the Horizontal Density Field

We performed runs with ten different density differences in the range $0.25 \leq \frac{\Delta\rho_2}{\Delta\rho_1} \leq 1.0$ with $\Delta\rho_1/\rho_0 = 0.030$, and forced ten waves through the domain for each run. Assuming that the wave period remains unchanged as the wave traverses into the region of weaker stratification, a linear modal analysis predicts that the wavelength for deep water waves decreases in proportion to the change in density ratio. The leading edge of a long wave encounters a weaker stratification and hence slows down, causing a decrease in wavelength and an increase in amplitude, as shown in Figure 1. In Figure 2a, the dashed line depicts the results of linear theory using a modal analysis. The slight deviation from the solid line occurs because of the finite depth of the layers. The $\times$ depict the results from the numerical simulations. For small density ratios the deviation from linear theory results from a significant increase in the steepness parameter ka, which grows to 1.86 for the largest horizontal density change, as shown in Figure 2b. When $\Delta\rho_2 \sim \Delta\rho_1$, the numerical results

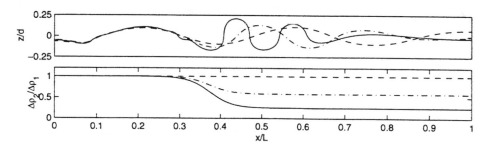

Figure 1: Effects of varying the stratification longitudinally, showing the decrease in wavelength after two waves have entered the weakly stratified region. The upper figure depicts the interface profiles, while the lower figure depicts the longitudinally varying density ratio $\Delta\rho(x)/\Delta\rho_1$. solid: $\Delta\rho_2/\Delta\rho_1 = 0.25$ $ka_2 = 1.86$, dash-dot: $\Delta\rho_2/\Delta\rho_1 = 0.58$ $ka_2 = 0.72$, dash: $\Delta\rho_2/\Delta\rho_1 = 1.0$ $ka_2 = ka_1 = 0.35$.

deviate from the linear theory because of contamination from the exit boundary. For the case in which $\Delta\rho_2 = \Delta\rho_1$, the wavelength does not change as the wave propagates, and only 2.6 waves can fit in the 1.0m domain. While the radiative boundary condition can radiate most of the energy, some of it is reflected and contaminates the longer wave results. In order to keep the horizontal resolution constant, we did not increase the domain length for the longer waves.

Figure 2b depicts the interface profiles with increasing steepnesses obtained after 2 waves have entered the weakly stratified region. The potential theory of Holyer (1979) bears a striking resemblance to the profiles shown, in that the steepness at a quarter wavelength becomes close to vertical. The steepest profile with $ka = 1.86$ in this figure eventually breaks roughly three periods later. All of the other waves remain stable and do not break.

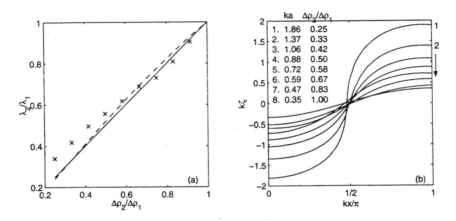

Figure 2: (a) Wavelength increase of a nonlinear interfacial wave as a function of the longitudinal decrease in the density ratio between the two layers. solid: deep water linear theory, dash: linear modal analysis, ×: numerical experiments. (b) Interfacial wave profiles with varying steepnesses, showing the horizontal density ratio as well as the steepness for each wave.

4.2 Breaking Dynamics

Increasing the wave amplitude to a critical point generates a peak in the horizontal velocity field at the wave nodes that exceeds the phase speed of the wave when $ka = 1.86$. Holyer (1979) predicted that this condition would arise when $ka = 1.10$. The discrepancy most likely is due to the finite interface and finite layer depths present in our simulations as well as a lack of resolution necessary to generate the instabilities required to break a wave with a lower steepness. The ensuing breaking dynamics are shown in Figure 3. Here we show the contours of constant density between $-0.015 < \rho/\rho_0 < 0.015$. Because these waves are in the weakly stratified region, the background stratification no longer varies in the horizontal. Once the fluid velocity exceeds the wave speed, a jet of fluid moves out ahead of the wave and begins to sink toward the trough at $t_b = 0.38T$. This resembles the description of Thorpe (1978) in his experiments of breaking in the presence of a background shear. The jet of heavier fluid is then sheared off and pulled back over the crest, leaving behind a smaller secondary forward breaker that is visible at $t_b = 0.67T$, which also ejects a jet of heavier fluid that falls into its own trough.

In Figure 4 we present a more detailed picture of the breaking dynamics. At $t_b = 0.0T$, the horizontal velocity just exceeds the phase speed of the wave. This occurs half way between the crest and the trough, just as Holyer (1979) predicted. Throughout the rest of the process, the horizontal velocity continues to exceed the phase speed, except that the peak moves down towards the trough, and causes another secondary breaker to overturn. This secondary breaker is most likely the result of the influence of the wave just ahead of this sequence, which is breaking backwards due to shear.

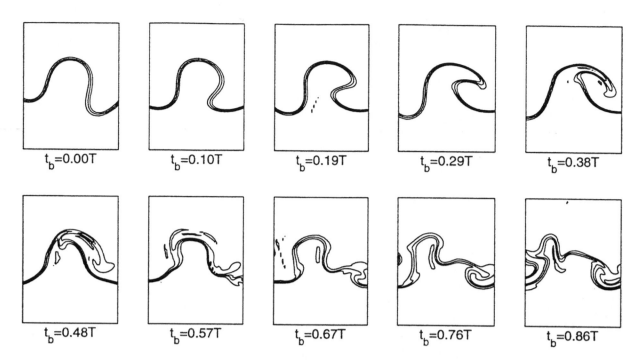

Figure 3: Time evolution t_b of a breaking interfacial wave with $ka = 1.86$. Here, $T = 4.2s$ is the forcing wave period, and we plot 5 contour lines between $-0.015 < \rho/\rho_0 < 0.015$. This time series was obtained by only showing the first in a train of five progressive waves that all broke as well.

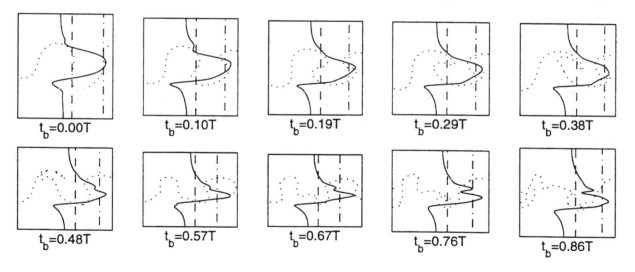

Figure 4: Time evolution t_b of the maximum horizontal velocity profile within a breaking interfacial wave. The dotted line indicates the $\rho = 0$ interface and the dashed line indicates the slice across which we show the horizontal velocity profile (solid). The dash-dot line indicates the point at which the horizontal velocity in the profile is equal to the wave speed, which in this case is roughly $c = 0.03\text{m/s}$.

5 Conclusions and Future Work

Despite speculation to the contrary in the literature, we have shown conclusively that a finite amplitude progressive interfacial wave can break forwards due to a convective nonlinearity before it is overtaken by a shear instability. The forward breaking occurs when the horizontal fluid velocity within the wave exceeds the phase speed of the wave. The actual steepness at which the wave breaks is a function of the numerical resolution and the maximum buoyancy frequency N_{max}, which is a function of the interface thickness parameter $k\delta$ as well as the stratification. In future work, in order to refine our predictions, we will carry out higher resolution studies for longer time in order to determine the exact steepness at which an interfacial wave with a fixed set of parameters breaks. This will help us to determine whether or not the critical steepness of $ka = 1.86$ obtained with the present simulations is physical, or depends to some degree on the resolution.

6   Acknowledgments

OBF acknowledges his support as a Computational Science Graduate Fellow, DOE. SWA and RLS acknowledge support of ONR Grant N0014-99-1-0413 (Scientific Officer: Dr. Louis Goodman, Physical Oceanography Program).

References

Andreassen, O., Hvidsten, P. O., Fritts, D. C., & Arendt, S. 1998. Vorticity dynamics in a breaking gravity wave. 1. Initial instability evolution. *J. Fluid Mech.*, **367**, 27.

Armfield, S. W., & Street, R. L. 2000. Time accuracy of fractional-step methods for the Navier- Stokes equations on non-staggered grids. *Computational Techniques and Applications Conference-CTAC99*, in press.

Chen, G., Kharif, C., Zaleski, S., & Li, J. 1999. Two-dimensional Navier-Stokes simulation of breaking waves. *Phys. Fluids*, **11**, 121–133.

Holyer, J. Y. 1979. Large amplitude progressive interfacial waves. *J. Fluid Mech.*, **93**, 433–448.

Javam, A., Armfield, S. W., & Imberger, J. 1999. Numerical study of internal waves generation in the stratified fluid. *J. Fluid Mech.*, **396**, 183–201.

Leonard, B. P. 1979. A stable and accurate convective modelling procedure based on quadratic upstream interpolation. *Comp. Meth. App. Mech.*, **19**, 59–98.

Leonard, B. P. 1987. SHARP Simulation of discontinuities in highly convective steady flow. *NASA Technical Memorandum*, **100240**.

Lin, C. L., Ferziger, J. H., Koseff, J. R., & Monismith, S. G. 1993. Simulation and stability of two-dimensional internal gravity waves in a stratified shear flow. *Dyn. Atmos. Oceans*, **19**, 325–366.

Lombard, P. N., & Riley, J. J. 1996. On the breakdown into turbulence of propagating internal waves. *Dyn. Atmos. Oceans*, **23**, 345–355.

Slinn, D. N., & Riley, J. J. 1998a. Turbulent dynamics of a critically reflecting internal gravity wave. *Theoret. Comput. Fluid Dyn.*, **11**, 281–303.

Thorpe, S. A. 1978. On the shape and breaking of finite amplitude internal gravity waves in a shear flow. *J. Fluid Mech.*, **85**, 7–31.

Troy, C. D., & Koseff, J. R. 2000. Laboratory Experiments on Breaking Interfacial Waves. *Fifth International Symposium on Stratified Flows*, in press.

Tsugi, Y., & Nagata, Y. 1973. Stokes' expansion of internal deep water waves to the fifth order. *J. of Ocean. Soc. Japan*, **29**, 61–69.

Zang, Y., Street, R. L., & Koseff, J. R. 1993. A dynamic mixed subgrid-scale model and its application to turbulent recirculating flows. *Phys. Fluids A*, **5**, 3186–3196.

Generation of Long Internal Waves in a Fluid Flowing over a Localized Topography at a Periodically Varying Velocity

Mitsuaki Funakoshi[1] and Yasuo Ohsugi[2]

[1]Department of Applied Analysis and Complex Dynamical Systems, Graduate School of Informatics, Kyoto University, Yoshida-Honmachi, Kyoto, 606-8501, JAPAN
[2]Department of Applied Mathematics and Physics, Graduate School of Engineering, Kyoto University, Yoshida-Honmachi, Kyoto, 606-8501, JAPAN
mitsu@acs.i.kyoto-u.ac.jp

1. Abstract

The generation of long internal waves in a two-layer fluid flowing over a localized topography is examined numerically using the forced KdV equation under the assumption that the velocity U of the fluid far from the topography is close to the phase speed of a linear long interfacial wave and varies periodically with period T. For T within a few regions, we observe the $1 : n$ entrainment of the wave motion near the topography to period T, in which n upstream-advancing waves are generated in period T. These regions extend and shift to larger T as the amplitude of the variation of U increases. Furthermore, when the entrainment occurs, the spatial region where time-periodic evolution is almost attained extends toward both upstream and downstream directions with increasing time, and often has an aperiodic spatial structure.

2. Introduction

Forced Korteweg-de Vries (fKdV) equation has been established as a mathematical model capable of describing the generation of long surface or internal waves in a fluid flowing over a localized topography at a velocity U close to the phase speed c_p of linear long waves (Grimshaw and Smyth, 1986; Wu, 1987). By the numerical computations of this equation, it was shown that upstream-advancing waves are generated periodically at the topography for U sufficiently close to c_p and that these waves are close to a train of soliton solutions of the Korteweg-de Vries (KdV) equation for appropriate values of U (Grimshaw and Smyth, 1986; Wu, 1987; Smyth, 1987; Lee et al., 1989). Furthermore, the extension of a flat depression followed by downstream-advancing modulated wave-trains was observed downstream the topography.

Although most of the studies based on the fKdV equation are for constant U, there is also a study for U varying slowly with the time. Grimshaw et al. (1996) examined the case in which U is a linear function of the time, that is, the case with a constant acceleration. In the present paper, we study the case in which U varies periodically. Our purpose is to examine the effect of the variation of U on the generation of waves at a localized topography and to examine the spatial and temporal behaviors of the generated waves.

3. Forced Korteweg-de Vries equation

We consider a two-layer fluid with a rigid lid flowing over a localized topography. Here the velocity of this flow far from the topography is expressed by U. We assume that the upper fluid of depth h_1 and density ρ_1 and the lower fluid of depth h_2 and density ρ_2 are inviscid and incompressible and that their motions are irrotational and two-dimensional with the velocity potentials Φ_1 and Φ_2.

Let x be the horizontal coordinate fixed to the bottom, z the vertical upward coordinate, t the time, $\zeta(x,t)$ an interface displacement, and $z = -h_2 + b(x)$ the bottom. Using the gravitational acceleration g and h_1, the following dimensionless variables are defined:

$$\tilde{x} = \frac{x}{h_1}, \quad \tilde{z} = \frac{z}{h_1}, \quad \tilde{t} = \sqrt{\frac{g}{h_1}}\, t, \quad \tilde{b} = \frac{b}{h_1}, \quad \tilde{\zeta} = \frac{\zeta}{h_1}, \quad \tilde{\Phi}_i = \frac{\Phi_i}{\sqrt{gh_1^3}} \quad (i = 1, 2). \tag{1}$$

Here we assume that U is close to the phase speed $\hat{c}_{\mathrm{p}} = \sqrt{gh_1 h_2(\rho_2 - \rho_1)/(h_2 \rho_1 + h_1 \rho_2)}$ of linear long interfacial waves. Therefore, the Froude number $F = U/\hat{c}_{\mathrm{p}}$ is assumed to be close to 1. Next, the stretched coordinates $\xi = \epsilon^{\frac{1}{2}}\tilde{x}$ and $\tau = \epsilon^{\frac{3}{2}}\tilde{t}$ are introduced using a small parameter ϵ characterizing the non-dimensional amplitude of waves. Furthermore, the relations

$$\tilde{b} = \epsilon^2 H(\xi), \quad F = 1 + \epsilon\lambda(\tau), \tag{2}$$

are assumed. Here $H(\xi)$ represents the bottom topography, whereas $\lambda(\tau)$ expresses the small and slow variation of U around $\hat{c}_{\mathrm{p}}$. We also assume the following expansions of $\tilde{\zeta}$ and $\tilde{\Phi}_i$ with respect to ϵ :

$$\begin{aligned}
\tilde{\zeta} &= \epsilon\tilde{\zeta}^{(1)}(\xi,\tau) + \epsilon^2\tilde{\zeta}^{(2)}(\xi,\tau) + O(\epsilon^3), \tag{3} \\
\tilde{\Phi}_i &= F\tilde{x} + \epsilon^{\frac{1}{2}}\tilde{\Phi}_i^{(1)}(\xi,\tilde{z},\tau) + \epsilon^{\frac{3}{2}}\tilde{\Phi}_i^{(2)}(\xi,\tilde{z},\tau) + \epsilon^{\frac{5}{2}}\tilde{\Phi}_i^{(3)}(\xi,\tilde{z},\tau) + O(\epsilon^{\frac{7}{2}}) \quad (i = 1, 2). \tag{4}
\end{aligned}$$

Using these assumptions in the Laplace equation for velocity potentials and the boundary conditions at the interface, bottom, and lid, we obtain a sequence of equations in successive orders of ϵ.

In $O(\epsilon^{\frac{5}{2}})$, we obtain the fKdV equation for $\tilde{\zeta}^{(1)}$. This equation is expressed as

$$\frac{\partial \eta}{\partial \tau} + \lambda\frac{\partial \eta}{\partial \xi} - \frac{3}{2}\eta\frac{\partial \eta}{\partial \xi} - \frac{1}{6}\frac{\partial^3 \eta}{\partial \xi^3} = \frac{1}{2}\frac{dH}{d\xi}, \tag{5}$$

after a certain scale transformation of variables, where η is used in place of $\tilde{\zeta}^{(1)}$. Equation (5) is solved numerically in order to examine the wave generation by the localized bottom topography

$$H(\xi) = 0.1\,\mathrm{sech}^2\left(\frac{\xi}{2}\right). \tag{6}$$

Furthermore, the periodic boundary condition with sufficiently large period L is assumed. As the initial condition, we use $\eta(\xi, 0) = 0$ for all ξ.

In the present study, we mainly examine the case in which velocity U varies periodically. That is, we assume that the function λ defined by eq. (2) is expressed as

$$\lambda(\tau) = f_0 + f_1 \sin\left(\frac{2\pi\tau}{T}\right). \tag{7}$$

The parameters f_0, f_1 and T characterize the departure of the averaged value of U from $\hat{c}_{\mathrm{p}}$, the amplitude and period of the variation of U, respectively.

In the numerical integration of eq. (5), the pseudo-spectral method suggested by Fornberg and Whitham (1978) is used because of the high accuracy in the approximation of spatial derivatives. We also use the second-order leap-frog scheme for the time evolution. The computations were usually performed up to $\tau = 3000$ with $L = 6000$ or more. We used a grid size $\Delta\xi = 0.5$ or 0.4 and a time increment $\Delta\tau = 0.025$ or 0.01.

4. Results for constant U

In this section, we show a few results on the generation of waves at localized bottom topography (6) for constant U, that is for $f_1 = 0$ in eq. (7). If f_0 is sufficiently close to zero, it is widely known that upstream-advancing waves are generated periodically at the localized topography and that a flat depression followed by a modulated wavetrain forms downstream. It is also known that, after a sufficient time, these upstream-advancing waves are generated with a constant period $\hat{T}_s$ and have the same time-independent local maximum (minimum) of η expressed by $\hat{\eta}_{max}$ ($\hat{\eta}_{min}$) when their distance from the topography is sufficiently large. Furthermore, it is known that no upstream-advancing wave is generated periodically if f_0 is sufficiently apart from zero.

For topography (6), periodic generation of upstream-advancing waves is observed for f_0 within the range $-0.14 \leq f_0 \leq 0.312$. We find that, for larger f_0, $\hat{\eta}_{max}$ ($\hat{\eta}_{min}$) is larger(smaller) and $\hat{T}_s$ is larger. The upstream-advancing waves observed for relatively large f_0 within this range are approximated well by a train of solitons of the KdV equation. If $\hat{\eta}_{min}$ is not close to zero, these waves are approximated well by the cnoidal wave solution of the KdV equation. We define $f_{0c} = 0.312$ as the upper limit of f_0 for which upstream-advancing waves are periodically generated.

5. Results for sinusoidally varying U

5.1 Temporal behavior of waves near the localized topography

We first examine the generation of upstream-advancing waves for various T with the fixed values of $f_0 = 0$ and $f_1 = 0.2$. For all T within the region $2 \leq T \leq 100$, the repetitive generation of these waves is observed similarly to the case of constant U. In order to examine the characteristics of this generation for varying U, we calculate from $\eta(\xi, \tau)$ at each τ the values of $\xi = \xi_{max}(\xi_{min})$ which give local maxima (minima) of η, and the values of these maxima (minima) called $\eta_{max}(\eta_{min})$. Figure 1 shows the dependence of η_{max} of each upstream-advancing wave on τ for a few T. Here, since η_{max} is plotted only when the condition $-30 \leq \xi_{max} \leq 1$ is satisfied, the curve corresponding to each upstream-advancing wave ends at a certain τ when ξ_{max} reaches -30.

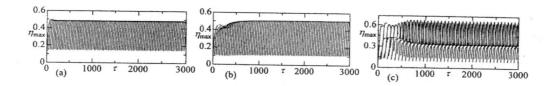

Figure 1: Time-dependence of η_{max}. $f_0 = 0$ and $f_1 = 0.2$. (a) $T = 10$, (b) $T = 36$, (c) $T = 75$.

For small T satisfying $2 \leq T \leq 10$, η_{max} of each wave increases at the initial stage and then tends to a value, as shown in Fig. 1(a). After a transient time, the waves of almost the same height are shed upstream. Furthermore, the period of the wave generation fluctuates only slightly, and its averaged value is close to $T_0 = 33.4$ independent of T. Here T_0 is the generation period $\hat{T}_s$ for constant U with $f_0 = 0$. Therefore, when T is considerably smaller than T_0, the influence of the variation of U on the wave generation is weak.

However, if T increases up to around T_0, the wave generation becomes strongly affected by the variation of U. For $T = 36$, after a sufficient time, a train of upstream-advancing waves of the same time-independent height are generated with constant period T, as shown in Fig. 1(b). Since T can be interpreted as the period of the variation of a forcing, we call this behavior 1 : 1 entrainment. We find that this 1 : 1 entrainment occurs for all T within the range $35 \leq T \leq 37$. This range of T is called a 1 : 1 entrainment region. For T just outside this entrainment region, the periodic variations of the height and generation interval of upstream-advancing waves with a long period are observed.

Next, for $T = 75$ which is slightly larger than $2T_0$, after a sufficient time, the generated waves are again periodic with period T, in which upstream-advancing waves are generated twice in period T, as shown in Fig. 1(c). We call this behavior 1 : 2 entrainment. The 1 : 2 entrainment is observed for all T within the range $75 \leq T \leq 79$. For T just outside this entrainment region, the modulation of the heights of upstream-advancing waves with a long period is again observed after a transient time. For T not close to these two entrainment regions, we usually observe an aperiodic wave motion near the topography.

In order to show the above entrainment more clearly, we calculate the averaged generation period T_s of upstream-advancing waves. In Fig. 2(a), the value of T/T_s is plotted for each T within the range $2 \leq T \leq 100$. This T/T_s usually increases monotonically with T except for two regions of T in which T/T_s takes constant values 1 and 2. These regions correspond to the two entrainment regions introduced before. That is, for all T within these regions, the behavior of waves near the topography is periodic with period T. This behavior is similar to the entrainment of the free oscillation of a nonlinear oscillator to the frequency of a periodic external force.

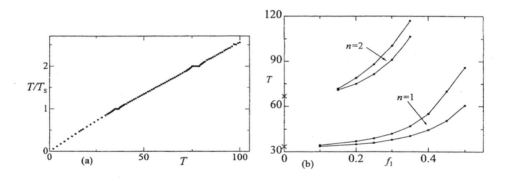

Figure 2: (a) Dependence of T/T_s on T. $f_0 = 0$ and $f_1 = 0.2$. (b) 1 : n entrainment regions for $f_0 = 0$. Two crosses on the vertical axis denote $T = T_0$ and $2T_0$.

The dependence of the 1 : n entrainment regions on f_1 is also examined. Figure 2(b) shows the 1 : 1 and 1 : 2 entrainment regions for $f_0 = 0$ obtained for several f_1. Each entrainment region shifts to larger T with increasing f_1. This direction of the shift is the same as that in the entrainment of the motion of a soft-spring nonlinear oscillator with the increase in the amplitude of a forcing of period T. As f_1 decreases to zero, the 1 : 1 entrainment region shrinks and seems to approach T_0. We also obtain a tendency that the 1 : 2 entrainment region shrinks and approaches $2T_0$ as f_1 decreases to zero. For $f_1 \geq 0.2$, the width of the 1 : 1 entrainment region is smaller than that of 1 : 2 entrainment region.

5.2 Temporal and spatial behavior of entrained wave motion

In this subsection, we examine the spatial structure and temporal evolution of the generated waves when the 1 : 1 or 1 : 2 entrainment occurs. For T within the 1 : 1 entrainment region, the generated waves near the topography asymptote to a periodic time evolution. This tendency toward a periodic time evolution is observed also at the locations far from the topography after a sufficient time. The spatial region composed of the locations where time-periodic evolution is almost attained, expressed by $\xi_u \leq \xi \leq \xi_d$, is called a periodic domain hereinafter, and is defined by the following way: at time τ, $\xi_d(\xi_u)$ is determined as the value of ξ at which $d(\xi, \tau) = |\eta(\xi, \tau) - \eta(\xi, \tau + T)|$ first reaches a threshold value ϵ_p as ξ increases(decreases) from zero. Under this definition with $\epsilon_p = 0.01$, we find that this domain appears near the topography after a certain time and extends toward both upstream and downstream directions with increasing τ. That is, both $|\xi_u|$ and $|\xi_d|$ increase monotonically with τ. Figure 3(a) shows an example of the periodic domain. From the two wave profiles at $\tau = 1080$ and $\tau = 1116$, we find that $\xi_u = -62$ and $\xi_d = 138$ at $\tau = 1080$.

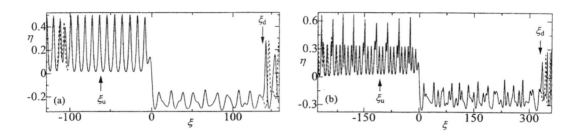

Figure 3: Wave profiles for $f_0 = 0$ and $f_1 = 0.2$. (a) $T = 36$. Profiles at $\tau = 1080$ (solid line) and $\tau = 1116$ (dashed line). (b) $T = 75$. Profiles at $\tau = 2700$ (solid line) and $\tau = 2775$ (dashed line).

Within the periodic domain, the values of η_{max} (and η_{min}) of all the upstream-advancing waves are time-independent and the same when they are sufficiently far from the topography, as illustrated in Fig. 3(a). This value is expressed by $\hat{\eta}_{max}$ (and $\hat{\eta}_{min}$). Furthermore, these waves propagate at the velocity which changes periodically with period T. In the downstream part of the periodic domain, although the waves of small amplitude around a minus value are shed downstream periodically with period T, no spatial periodicity is recognized even far from the topography, as found from Fig. 3(a). This temporal periodicity and spatial aperiodicity are compatible when the velocity of each downstream-advancing wave changes irregularly as it propagates owing to the interaction with neighboring waves.

The dependences of $\hat{\eta}_{max}$ and $\hat{\eta}_{min}$ on T and f_1 are examined for fixed $f_0 = 0$. As shown in Fig. 4(a), $\hat{\eta}_{max}$ is larger and $\hat{\eta}_{min}$ is smaller for larger T, irrespective of the value of f_1. Furthermore, except for the case in which f_1 is small or T is close to the lower end of the entrainment region, generated waves are approximated by a train of solitary waves because $\hat{\eta}_{min}$ is close to zero. Equation (5) with $H = 0$ has a soliton solution $\eta = a \operatorname{sech}^2 \left[\sqrt{3a} \left(\xi + \frac{1}{2} a\tau - \int_0^\tau \lambda(\tau') d\tau' - \xi_0 \right) /2 \right]$, where $a(> 0)$ and ξ_0 are constants. The velocity of the above solitary waves is time-periodic and agrees well with that of this soliton solution with $a = \hat{\eta}_{max}$. Moreover, as f_1 decreases to zero, $\hat{\eta}_{max}$ and $\hat{\eta}_{min}$ tend to their values for constant U expressed by crosses. On the other hand, the range of $\hat{\eta}_{max}$ shifts to the lower direction as f_1 increases to 0.5, whereas the dependence of the range of $\hat{\eta}_{min}$ on f_1 is weak for large f_1.

Next, for T within the 1 : 2 entrainment region, the generated waves near the localized topography asymptote to a periodic time evolution. Similarly to the case of the 1 : 1 entrainment, we observe the tendency toward a periodic time evolution also at the locations far from the topography after a sufficient time. An example of this tendency is shown in Fig. 4(b). The time evolution of η for $\xi = -30$ is almost periodic with period T for $\tau > 1300$. Therefore, we can define the periodic

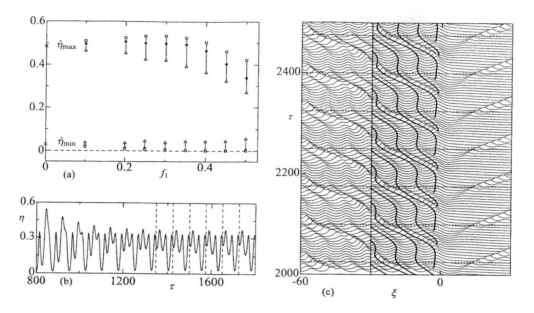

Figure 4: (a) Ranges of $\hat{\eta}_{max}$ and $\hat{\eta}_{min}$ for T within the $1:1$ entrainment region. $f_0 = 0$. $\square$, $\bullet$ and $\triangle$ denote the values for T at the upper end, middle and lower end of this region. $\bullet$ and $\square$ are sometimes located at almost the same position in $\hat{\eta}_{min}$. $\times$ denotes the values of $\hat{\eta}_{max}$ and $\hat{\eta}_{min}$ for constant U. (b) Time evolution of η. $f_0 = 0$ and $f_1 = 0.2$. $\xi = -30$. $T = 75$. Dashed lines are drawn with the interval of T. (c) Time evolution of the wave profile for $f_0 = 0$, $f_1 = 0.2$ and $T = 75$. Thick lines denote the locations of the peaks of the upstream-advancing waves.

domain in the same way. We then observe again its appearance near the topography after a certain time and extension toward both upstream and downstream directions with increasing τ. Figure 3(b) shows an example of the periodic domain. From this figure, we find that spatial periodicity is recognized neither in the upstream part nor the downstream part even far from the topography. The time evolution of the wave profile corresponding to Figs. 3(b) and 4(b) is shown in Fig.4(c). The motion of the peaks of the upstream-advancing waves expressed by thick lines is time-periodic, whereas the wave profile is not periodic at any time.

6. References

Fornberg, B., Whitham, G.B., 1978. Phil. Trans. R. Soc. London, Ser. A 289, 373-404.

Grimshaw, R., Pelinovsky, E., Sakov, P., 1996. Stud. Appl. Math. 97, 235-276.

Grimshaw, R.H.J., Smyth, N., 1986. J. Fluid Mech. 169, 429-464.

Lee, S., Yates, G.T., Wu, T.Y., 1989. J. Fluid Mech. 199, 569-593.

Smyth, N.F., 1987. Proc. R. Soc. London, Ser. A 409, 79-97.

Wu, T.Y., 1987. J. Fluid Mech. 184, 75-99.

Laboratory modelling of the motion of an internal solitary wave over a finite amplitude bottom ridge

Yakun Guo[1], Peter A Davies[1], Kristian Sveen[2], John Grue[2] and Ping Dong[1]

[1] Department of Civil Engineering, University of Dundee, Dundee DD1 4HN, UK
[1] Department of Mathematics, University of Oslo, N-0316 Oslo, Norway
y.guo@dundee.ac.uk, p.a.davies@dundee.ac.uk, jks@math.uio.no,
johng@math.uio.no, p.dong@dundee.ac.uk

1.   Abstract

Parametric laboratory experiments has been carried out to investigate the propagation of an internal solitary wave of depression and its distortion by a bottom ridge in a 2-layer stratified fluid system. Wave speeds, wave profiles of the solitary wave and density fields and velocity fields induced by the wave propagation have been measured upstream, downstream and over the ridge. The results show that the internal solitary waves can be distorted appreciably by the bottom ridge, provided that the solitary wave amplitude is sufficiently large for blockage effects to be significant. In extreme cases involving a solitary wave with large amplitude and large blockage ratio, the solitary wave is distorted sufficiently for mixing to take place as a result of passage over the bottom ridge. The attenuation of the solitary wave amplitude due to the passage over the topography has been investigated for a wide range of model parameters. and the laboratory results have been compared favourably with the prediction of a recently-developed theoretical model.

1.   Introduction

Internal solitary waves (ISWs) that propagate along density interfaces have been observed at many oceanic locations (Ostrovsky & Stepanyants, 1989), with the amplitudes of such waves occasionally exceeding several tens of metres (e.g Osborne et al, 1978). Due to their practical importance and theoretical interest, the dynamics and properties of ISWs propagating in a fluid of constant depth have been well documented over the past decades, both theoretically and experimentally (Koop & Butler, 1981; Kao et al., 1985; Michallet & Barthélemy, 1998). Experimental studies show that KdV theory is valid for solitary waves with small amplitude; more recently, Grue et al (1999) have modelled large amplitude internal solitary waves by means of fully non-linear theory and have obtained good agreement with their laboratory experimental results. Kao et al (1985) observed that solitary waves of sufficiently high amplitude were able to break on a slope and Helfrich (1992) was able to estimate the energy loss associated with the shoaling of internal solitary waves on a uniform slope. Michallet & Ivey (1999) subsequently examined by means of laboratory experiments the mixing process and energy loss due to internal solitary waves breaking over a uniformly-sloping bottom. Few investigations have been carried out for internal solitary waves of depression passing over a bottom ridge, though Wessels & Hutter (1996) conducted similar experiments for internal waves of elevation over a bottom sill. In the latter experiments, no measurements were made of the wave velocity fields, though estimates of the energy dissipated by the interaction of the waves with the sill were deduced from measurements of the relevant waveforms.

2.   Experimental configuration.

The experiments were conducted in a channel having dimensions 6.4 m x 0.4 m x 0.6 m (see Fig 1). The channel was partially filled with salt water of density ρ_2 to a depth h_2, with a layer of lighter salt water of density ρ_1 and thickness h_1 being added to a total depth $H (= h_1 + h_2)$ by means of a floating sponge arrangement. A watertight movable gate was installed at one end of the channel, allowing waves to be generated by the step-like pool technique (Kao *et al.*, 1985; Michallet & Barthélemy, 1998; Grue *et al.*, 1999; Michallet & Ivey, 1999) with a reservoir of light salt water contained initially behind the gate. By adjusting the position of the gate and the excess volume of the lighter salt water behind it, a solitary internal wave of prescribed amplitude a could be generated.

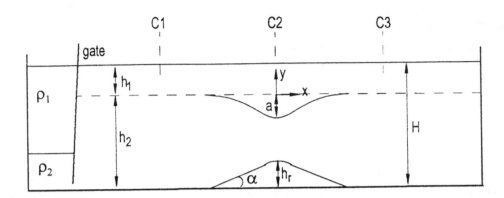

Fig 1: Schematic representation of experimental arrangement. See text for notation details.

The velocity fields induced by the propagation of the solitary wave were measured using the *Digimage* particle tracking technique (Dalziel, 1992) at three camera locations, namely 3.20 m (C1), 4.05 m (C2) and 4.90 m (C3) downstream of the gate. Before and during the experiments, vertical density profiles were also measured at several locations, by means of a computer-controlled array of fast-response microconductivity probes (Head, 1983). For those experiments performed with a ridge in position, the crest of the ridge was located at C2 position. Reference experiments were also run with no ridge in position, for a wide range of the model parameters (see Table 1 for a complete parameter list).

$2\Delta\rho/(\rho_2 + \rho_1)$	h_2/h_1	H (cm)	α (°)	h_r (cm)	$(h_2 - h_r - a)/h_2$
1.25% → 2.15%	4 → 8.5	30 → 38	11.3 → 18.4	10 → 15	0.13 → 0.94

Table 1. Experimental parameters (see Fig 1 for symbols)

3.   Results
3.1   Qualitative observations

Experiments have been conducted with a range of different wave amplitudes and different ridge dimensions. Three distinct wave motion patterns have been observed, namely;

<u>Type I</u>: for relatively small wave amplitudes a and the higher values of $(h_2 - h_r - a)/h_2$, propagation of a solitary waves is not altered significantly by the presence of the ridge.
<u>Type II</u>: for moderate values of the wave amplitude and $(h_2 - h_r - a)/h_2$, the blocking effect applied by the ridge causes steepening of the back of the wave and significant distortion, though without breaking.
<u>Type III</u>: as the wave amplitude increases and the value of $(h_2 - h_r - a)/h_2$ decreases, the ridge applies significant blocking, resulting in steepening and eventual breaking of the wave. As a result of wave breaking, internal wave trains are generated downstream of the ridge and the amplitude of the leading solitary wave is significantly reduced compared with the no ridge case. For strong wave break events, overturning and mixing take place (see density measurements below) and for all Type II and III flows, vortices are observed to be generated around the ridge as a wave propagates over it.

762

3.2 Velocity profiles at the wave trough

For the reference cases in which no ridges are present, many of the properties of the internal solitary waves have already been well-documented in earlier investigations (see, for example, Grue et al., 1999) and confirmed here. Figs 2a, b show typical Type I velocity profiles measured at C1 and C3 respectively, for experiments with and without the ridge and nominally identical initial conditions. The solid line indicates the prediction of the fully nonlinear theory (Grue et al., 1999) and the velocity data are shown normalised by the wave speed c_0, defined (within the Boussinesq approximation) as:

$$c_0 = [g'h_1h_2/(h_1 + h_2)]^{1/2} \tag{1}$$

where $g'(= g\Delta\rho/\rho_1)$ and g are the reduced and normal values respectively of the gravitational acceleration and $\Delta\rho = (\rho_2 - \rho_1)$. The results shown in Fig 2a indicate that for this case (i) the experimentally-determined velocities in the lower layer exceed slightly those predicted by the above theory and (ii) there is no significant effect of the ridge upon the velocity profile. As with the counterpart data in Fig 2b, small differences in velocity values in the lower part of the water column between ridge and no-ridge cases may be ascribed to small differences in initial conditions. Data of the type shown in Fig 2b confirm that the ridge has little influence on the upstream and downstream velocity fields induced by the propagation of Type I waves (though modifications are seen in the region directly above the ridge).

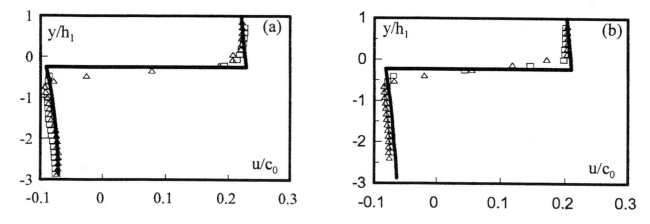

Fig 2: Type I velocity profiles at (a) C1 and (b) C3 for (□) without and (Δ) with the ridge. See text.

As the values of a and $(h_2 - h_r - a)/h_2$ increase and decrease respectively, the flow pattern turns from Type I into Type II and III and the influence of the ridge on the propagation of waves becomes more and more pronounced. Fig 3 shows the velocity profiles at stations C1-3 for an extreme Type III case in which strong wave breaking takes place at C2 (over the ridge). For such cases, the contraction of the lower layer cross section over the ridge causes the magnitude of the lower layer velocity over the ridge to be significantly increased (see the C2 profile on Fig 3). In consequence, the solitary wave is decelerated as it encounters the front part of the ridge, with the back portion of the wave steepening progressively as the wave adjusts to the contraction. Eventually, the wave breaks and, as a result of the encounter, both the layer velocities are reduced significantly (see Fig 3). For such a strong Type III encounter, the thickness of the velocity shear layer separating the upper and lower layer motions increases significantly both above (C2) and downstream (C3) of the ridge, as a result of wave breaking and mixing over the ridge.

3.3 Wave profile

Wave profiles were determined from the video record by measuring the vertical displacement of the interface between the consituent layers as a function of time at a fixed horizontal position. Such

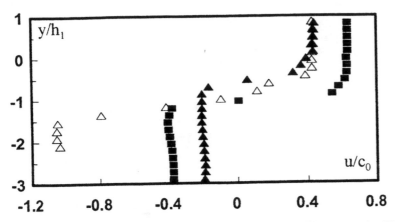

Fig 3: Type III velocity profiles with ridge for C1 (■), C2 (Δ), C3 (▲)

measurements were found to be in good agreement with the results obtained directly from sequential density profile measurements using the microconductivity probes. Fig 4a shows a wave profile obtained in this way, for waves of Type I with and without the ridge in place; in this dimensionless plot, the displacement η (normalised by h_1) is shown in terms of the parameter $c_0 t/\lambda$, where c_0 is the wave velocity defined in (1), t is the elapsed time (relative to some arbitrary origin) and λ is the characteristic length estimated from KdV theory and defined as:

$$\lambda = 2h_1 h_2/[3(h_2 - h_1)a]^{1/2} \tag{2}$$

For Type I cases, Fig 4a illustrates that (i) at both of the reference stations, data points coincide for the ridge and no ridge cases and (ii) the profile at the upstream location (C1) shows an amplitude significantly greater than that measured at the downstream location (C3) for both ridge and no-ridge configurations. Such measurements confirm that the presence of the ridge does not affect significantly the propogation and form of the solitary wave for Type I flows; the reduction of wave amplitude between the two measurement profiles is ascribed to viscous attenuation. In contrast, for waves falling in the Type II and III categories, the ridge exerts a significant effect upon the wave propagation and structure. For the extreme cases in which strong wave breaking is observed, not only are the velocity and amplitude of the leading solitary wave greatly attenuated (see Fig 3), but the wave profile is also significantly distorted. Fig 4b illustrates this property for a Type III flow, with the wave profiles measured at stations upstream (C1) and downstream (C3) of the ridge showing the damping of the wave amplitude and the distortion of the wave profile due to the strong influence of the ridge on the wave. As indicated above, during the Type III wave breaking process over the ridge, mixing and overturning events are observed to take place. These phenomena are quantified conveniently by processing the sequential density profile measurements (Fig 5a) in terms of the instantaneous buoyancy anomaly profile $g^*(y_i)$ (see Fig 5b) defined (De Silva, Imberger & Ivey, 1997) here as:

$$g^*(y_i) = g[\rho(y_i) - \rho_T (y_i)]/\rho_m \tag{3}$$

where g is the gravitational acceleration, $\rho(y_i)$ the measured instantaneous density profile over the ridge crest, $\rho_T (y_i)$ the corresponding Thorpe-ordered density profile and ρ_m the mean density. For the station considered (in this case, the ridge crest), the non-zero values of the buoyancy anomaly at particular vertical positions indicates and quantifies the mixing and overturning processes occurring at such sites.

3.4   Wave amplitude damping

As seen, the wave amplitude is an important parameter of the wave. Thus, it is interesting to investigate the variation and attenuation of this property as the wave propagates along the density interface.

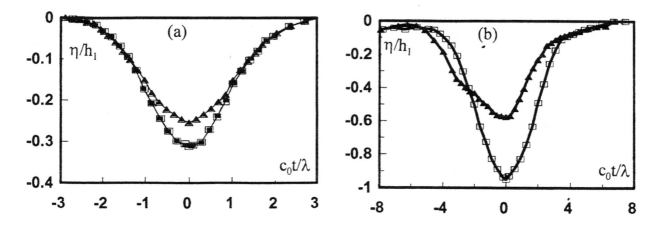

Fig 4: Wave profiles for (a) Type I, with (solid) and without (open) ridge for C1 (□), C3 (Δ) and (b) Type III at C1 (□) and C3 (▲). See text.

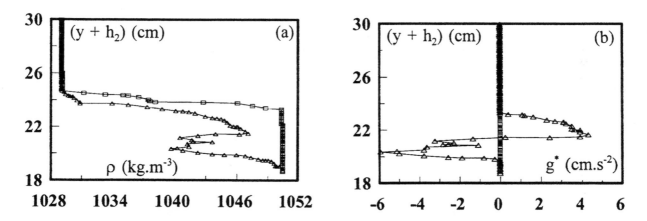

Fig 5: Instantaneous vertical profiles of (a) density and (b) buoyancy anomaly for Type III. In (a) □ and Δ denote initial and perturbed profiles respectively. See text.

In the present study, the wave amplitude attenuation is caused by a combination of viscous effects and processes associated with the encounter between the wave and the bottom topography. A convenient measure of the integrated wave amplitude attenuation for the present geometry is provided by the wave amplitude difference $(a_1 - a_3)$ between C1 and C3, normalised by the amplitude a_1 at C1. The results for all experiments analysed by this method are shown in Fig 6 in terms of the dimensionless blockage factor $(h_2 - h_r - a_1)/h_2$. For the experiments without the presence of the ridge, the average attenuation of the wave amplitude is about 4.8% per metre, a value that agrees well with the results of Kao $et\ al$ (1985). For the waves in Type I encounters, the ridge has no significant effect on the wave and the attenuation of the wave amplitude shows values that do not differ significantly from those without the ridge present. There is a sharp increase of the (leading) wave amplitude attenuation when the wave is broken by the encounter with the ridge for the smallest values of the blockage parameter $(h_2 - h_r - a_1)/h_2$.

4.   Conclusions

The results presented above show the properties of an internal solitary wave in a 2-layer fluid and the interaction of such a wave with a bottom ridge topography. The studies show that the effects of the ridges on the wave can be either significant or trivial, depending on the input parameters. Three general wave encounters have been classified, namely (i) Type I, where the ridge has no significant effect on the wave propagation away from the ridge, (ii) Type II, where the wave is distorted significantly by the interaction with the ridge and vortices are formed around the ridge and (iii) Type III, where the wave breaks over the ridge and wave trains are generated after the ridge. When the wave breaks, overturning and mixing processes take place, causing a thickening of the pycnocline and significant attenuation of the velocity and amplitude of the leading solitary wave.

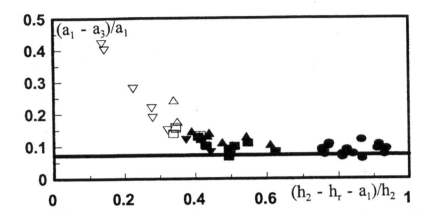

Fig 6: Composite plot of amplitude difference $(a_1 - a_3)/a_1$ versus blockage factor $(h_2 - h_r - a_1)/h_2$.

Acknowledgements

The authors are grateful for the support of this work by the UK Engineering and Physical Science Research Council (EPSRC) and the Research Council of Norway.

References

Dalziel, S B., 1992. Decay of rotating turbulence: some particle tracking experiments. *Appl. Sci. Res.*, 49, 217-235.

De Silva I P D, Imberger, J & Ivey, G N., 1997. Localized mixing due to a breaking internal wave ray at a sloping bed. *J. Fluid Mech.*, 350, 1-27.

Grue, J, Jensen, A, Rusås, P-O & Sveen, J K., 1999. Properties of large-amplitude internal waves. *J. Fluid Mech.*, 380, 159-177.

Head, M J., 1983. The use of four-electrode conductivity probes for high-resolution measurement of turbulent density or temperature variation in salt-stratified water flows. *PhD Dissertation*, UCSD, USA.

Helfrich, K R., 1992. Internal solitary wave breaking and run-up on a uniform slope. *J. Fluid Mech.* 243, 133-154

Kao, T W, Pan F-S & Renouard, D., 1985. Internal solitons on the pycnocline: generation, propagation and shoaling and breaking over a slope. *J. Fluid Mech.*, **159**, 19-53.

Koop, C G & Butler, G., 1981. An investigation of internal solitary waves in a two-fluid system. *J. Fluid Mech.*, **112**, 225-251.

Michallet, H & Barthélemy, E., 1998. Experimental study of interfacial solitary waves. *J. Fluid Mech.*, **366**, 159-177.

Michallet, H & Ivey G N., 1999. Experiments on mixing due to internal solitary waves breaking on uniform slopes. *J. Geophys. Res.*, **104**, C6, 13467-13477.

Osborne, A R, Burch, T L & Scarlet, R I., 1978. The influence of internal waves on deep water drilling. *J. Petroleum Tech.*, **30**, 1497-504.

Ostrovsky, L A & Stepanyants, Yu A., 1989. Do internal solitons exist in the ocean? *Rev. Geophys.*, 27(3), 293-310.

Wessels, F & Hutter, K., 1996. Interaction of internal waves with a topographic sill in a two-layer fluid. *J. Phys. Oceanogr.*, **26**, 5-20.

Making Waves...in Nonlinearly Stratified Fluids

David F. Hill[1]

[1]Department of Civil and Environmental Engineering, The Pennsylvania State University,
University Park, PA 16802
dfhill@engr.psu.edu

1 Abstract

The great interest in stratified flows has of course resulted in a tremendous variety of laboratory investigations over the past decades. These controlled laboratory studies have led to the identification and quantification of numerous important phenomena fundamental to stratified fluid mechanics.

In the past, most studies have been of simple stratifications, such as two-layer, linear, or piecewise linear systems. The advantages of this are that these density profiles are easy to construct in the laboratory and they also allow for analytic tractability in terms of solving the equations of motion and making scaling arguments. However, most stratified fluids exhibit density profiles which deviate appreciably from these simple approximations.

The current work is motivated by the desire to generate and study stratified fluids whose density profiles more accurately reflect those observed in the field. This is accomplished using a modified version of the familiar two-tank method. The unsteady conservation equations are solved to find the flow rates needed to provide a specified density profile. The execution of this is then implemented using computer-controlled peristaltic pumps.

As an example of a potential application, this technique is currently being employed in experiments on internal wave breaking and dissipation. A horizontal shaking table is used to resonate internal waves to the point of breaking, with the goal of understanding the sensitivity of the breaking process to the background stratification.

2 Introduction

The very earliest laboratory studies of stratified flows were carried out for the case of discrete fluid layers. In the case of immiscible fluids, this is especially easy, but, even for miscible fluids, a sharp interface can be obtained with some care. Most common was to consider a two-layer system, but three layers and more were certainly possible. Thorpe (1968) carried this approach to the extreme by carefully layering a tank (in 1cm increments) with progressively heavier fluid layers. After completing this task, a wait of a few hours yielded a fluid of more or less linear density gradient, thanks to diffusion. In the same vein, an ambitious work by Stillinger et al. (1983) created a remarkably linear density profile in a closed-loop water tunnel by bringing together a total of *ten* fluid layers via splitter plates.

The important and heavily cited work of Fortuin (1960) provided the fluid mechanics community with a much easier method of obtaining linearly stratified fluids. Known familiarly as the 'two-tank method,' it essentially requires establishing and maintaining constant flow rates between three containers of fluid. It is this method that the current study generalizes.

Finally, it should be noted that it is possible to 'create' more complex density profiles by disturbing two-layer profiles in a host of ways. For example, Linden (1980) found that, by dropping a grid vertically through a density interface, the interface would thicken considerably, yielding a diffuse pycnocline. Alternatively (e.g. Prych et al. (1964)), towing an object, such as a flat plate, horizontally at a density interface can yield a similarly altered density profile.

3   Experimental Procedure

Consider the experimental schematic shown in Figure 1. At the bare minimum, three tanks and a mixer are required. To provide the flow between the tanks, it is, in principle, possible to use gravity, but this is not terribly practical. As such, two pumps will be required to deliver the required flow rates.

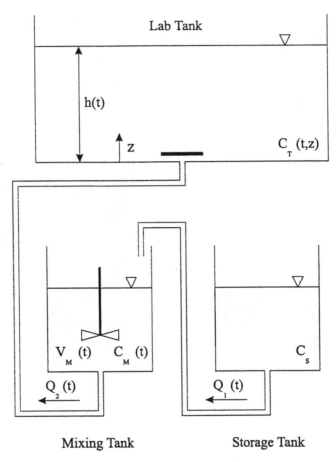

Figure 1: Schematic of the experimental apparatus for the proposed experiments.

Looking at the configuration in detail, there is a storage tank, which contains salty water of some known concentration C_S (kg/m^3). This water is pumped at a flow rate of $Q_1(t)$ into a second tank, called the mixing tank. As indicated, in this general case, Q_1 is unsteady and therefore shown as a function of time. In the mixing tank, an electric (or air) mixer is used to blend the incoming salty water with the (initially) fresh water. As a result, the concentration of salt in the mixing tank will be a monotonically increasing function of time and is given by $C_M(t)$. Additionally, the volume of the mixing tank will be time-varying and is given by $V_M(t)$. The initial concentration and volume of the mixing tank are given by C_{M_i} and V_{M_i}.

The mixed fluid is then pumped at a flow rate of $Q_2(t)$ from the mixing tank into the laboratory, or *test section*, tank. This third and final tank will of course be specific to the experiment. While this lab tank can be of any shape and size in principle, the following analysis makes the assumption that the planform area of the tank, A, is not a function of the vertical coordinate z. Generalizing the analysis to allow for this variation is straightforward.

The mixed fluid is introduced into the lab tank by way of a diffuser plate, which spreads out the fluid gently and minimizes mixing in the tank. It should be noted that some researchers use the approach of introducing the fluid by way of a *floating* diffuser plate, which remains on the free surface of the lab tank, rather than the bottom. In this approach, the fresh water tank is the storage tank and the (initially) salty water tank is the mixing tank. While the subsequent analysis is for the case of the bottom diffuser, the two problems are essentially mirror images of each other and solution of the surface diffuser case is a simple extension.

The main equations in the analysis are the conservation of salt and water in the mixing tank. These are given by

$$C_M(t)\frac{dV_M(t)}{dt} + V_M(t)\frac{dC_M(t)}{dt} = C_S Q_1(t) - C_M(t)Q_2(t) \tag{1}$$

$$\frac{dV_M(t)}{dt} = Q_1(t) - Q_2(t). \tag{2}$$

Additionally, use will be made of the equations of volume and salt conservation in the lab tank.

$$A\frac{dh(t)}{dt} = Q_2(t) \tag{3}$$

$$\frac{d}{dt}\left[A\int_0^{h(t)} C_T(t,z)dz\right] = C_M(t)Q_2(t). \tag{4}$$

There are other parameters of interest, such as the total fill time (T) of the lab tank and the final depth (H) of the lab tank. The *forward* problem, in which the flow rates, storage tank concentration and initial mixing tank volume are specified and the resulting lab tank density profile is computed is quite easy, but not terribly helpful. After all, the stated goal is to be able to specify the final density profile and then figure out what it takes to accomplish this. This *inverse* problem is far more complicated, due to the many free parameters, and there is no unique solution.

Eventually, an optimization technique will be developed to more effectively solve this inverse problem. In the meantime, a cruder method can be used as follows:

- Specify $C_T(T,z)$, A, H, V_{M_i}, and V_{M_f}. Furthermore, specify $Q_2(t)$ to be some known vector of values, possibly even a constant. Depending upon the particular geometry (i.e. the diffuser size and gap height) of an individual experiment, there will be a fairly optimal value of Q_2. If the flow rate through the diffuser is much faster than this, there will be significant local mixing at the diffuser exit; much slower and it will take prohibitively long to fill the lab tank. For the current experiments, $\sim 0.5 gpm$ proves to be fairly ideal.

- Compute the volume of the lab tank as well as the mass of salt in the lab tank at the conclusion of filling:

$$V_T = AH$$

$$M_T = A\int_0^H C_T(T,z)dz.$$

- Compute the required concentration of salt in the storage tank:

$$C_S = \frac{M_T + C_T(T,0)V_{M_f}}{V_T + V_{M_f} - V_{M_i}}.$$

- Convert $C_T(T,z)$ to $C_M(t)$, using (3) and the fact that $C_T(T,z) = C_M(T-t)$.

- Finally, numerically integrate the mixing tank equations to find $V_M(t)$. With this known, $Q_1(t)$ is immediately known!

4 Experimental Apparatus

Having determined the flow rates necessary to create a desired density profile, the second step is the delivery of these flow rates, for which there are several options. Benielli and Sommeria (1998) used stepper motors to advance what amounted to the plungers of large syringes in their study of the Faraday resonance of internal waves in linearly stratified fluids. This is a fine and precise method, but one that does not lend itself well to *large* volumes of water.

A second alternative is to utilize controlled proportional solenoid valves. A number of vendors offer integrated flow control devices, which consist of a valve and an electronic flow sensor to provide feedback in the system. In these cases, a $4-20mA$ input control signal will open or close the valve, thereby controlling the flow. As these controllers do not include any means for driving the flow, an external pump will have to be included in the system. Special care must be exercised, therefore, in selecting an appropriate pump so as not to overload the controller.

A third option, and the one adopted in this study, is to control the flow by controlling the pumps directly. Controlling standard centrifugal pumps is difficult for a variety of reasons, so peristaltic pumps were chosen instead. Specifically, two Masterflex pumps (Cole-Parmer, Model #07549-52), which accept a $4-20mA$ input and each deliver a flow rate of $0.2-2gpm$ were used. While peristaltic pumps have the distinct advantage of being quite linear in operation, initial tests indicated that they were not nearly as linear as the manufacturer claimed. Therefore, a simple calibration between current input and flow rate output was performed.

The rest of the experimental apparatus consists of components familiar to those who work with stratified flows: a MSCTI (Head (1983)), a computer-controlled translation stage for traversing the probe, and associated data acquisition equipment.

5 Sample Results

To test the ability of the designed system to faithfully reproduce specified density profiles, two trials were carried out. Both were facilitated by stratifying a laboratory tank having a length of $61.0cm$, a width of $45.7cm$, and a total depth of $30.5cm$. The goal of the first trial was to create a density profile having a hyperbolic tangent shape. This is an improvement upon the two-layer profile in that the buoyancy frequency profile displays a moderately diffuse, rather than an infinitely thin, pycnocline. As demonstrated by Figure 2, the agreement between the specified and the measured density profiles is exceptional. Also shown are the flow rates of the two pumps that were required to achieve this profile.

With this as an encouraging first attempt, a second and even more challenging profile was attempted. Lamb (2000) recently demonstrated that numerical simulations of internal solitary wave breaking are extremely sensitive to the shape of the density profile. Specifically, he indicated that the presence of a mixed layer at the free surface had a profound effect upon the dynamics. As indicated by Figure 3, an attempt was made at creating a density profile characterized by a thin mixed layer, fairly sharp pycnocline, and slow decay of $N(z)$ (the buoyancy frequency) below that. Essentially, this profile is two hyperbolic tangent profiles matched at the depth of the pycnocline. Again, the agreement between the requested and measured density profiles is excellent.

6 Future Work

With this technique established as a successful means of creating arbitrarily stratified fluids, attention has been turned to understanding the dynamics of breaking internal waves in these fluids. To this end, a horizontal shaking table (Figure 4a) has been designed and can be used to linearly resonate waves to the point of breaking.

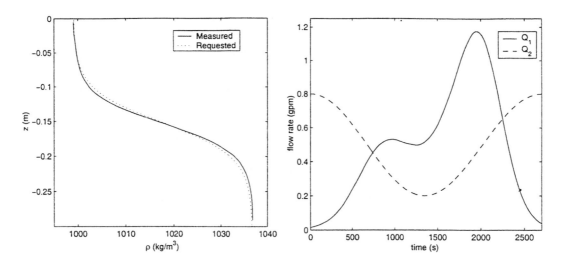

Figure 2: (a). Comparison between requested and measured density profiles for a hyperbolic tangent shape. (b). Required flow rates.

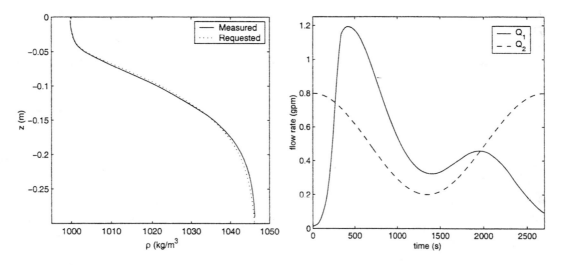

Figure 3: (a). Comparison between requested and measured density profiles for a *double-tanh* shape. (b). Required flow rates.

This apparatus has already been tested successfully for the simple case of breaking interfacial waves. As illustrated by Figure 4b, the breaking process weakens the initial density profile as fluid is mixed vertically. Simple potential energy arguments can be used to quantify, therefore, the efficiency of the breaking process.

The balance of this research effort, therefore, will focus on an investigation of both the structure and the breaking characteristics of internal waves in arbitrarily stratified fluids. Of paramount interest is how the *shape* of the background density profile affects the mixing efficiency of the breaking event. Initially, experiments are to be conducted in a domain with vertical walls, representing breaking in the fluid interior, but later work will utilize this technology to investigate boundary mixing as well.

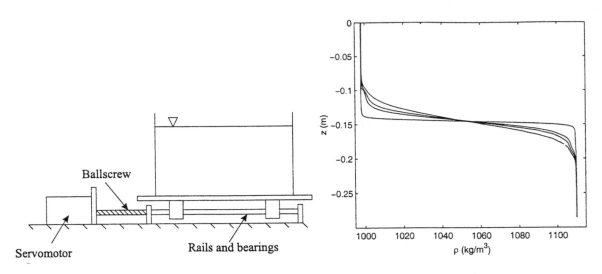

Figure 4: (a). Apparatus for internal wave breaking experiments. (b). Evolution of two-layer profile due to breaking.

References

[1] D. Benielli and J. Sommeria. Excitation and breaking of internal gravity waves by parametric instability. *Journal of Fluid Mechanics*, 374:117–144, 1998.

[2] J.M.H. Fortuin. Theory and application of two supplementary methods of constructing density gradient columns. *Journal of Polymer Science*, XLIV:505–515, 1960.

[3] M.J. Head. *The use of miniature four-electrode conductivity probes for high resolution measurement of turbulent density or temperature variations in salt-stratified water flows.* PhD thesis, University of California at San Diego, 1983.

[4] K.G. Lamb. Shoaling solitary waves and the formation of waves with trapped cores. In *AGU Ocean Sciences 2000 Meeting (abstract only)*, 2000.

[5] P.F. Linden. Mixing across a density interface produced by grid turbulence. *Journal of Fluid Mechanics*, 100(4):691–703, 1980.

[6] E.A. Prych, F.R. Harty, and J.F. Kennedy. Turbulent wakes in density stratified fluids of finite extent. Technical report, Massachussets Institute of Technology, 1964.

[7] D.C. Stillinger, M.J. Head, K.N. Helland, and C.W. Van Atta. A closed-loop gravity-driven water channel for density-stratified shear flows. *Journal of Fluid Mechanics*, 131:73–89, 1983.

[8] S.A. Thorpe. On standing internal gravity waves of finite amplitude. *Journal of Fluid Mechanics*, 32(3):489–528, 1968.

Transport across a dynamical barrier by breaking inertia-gravity waves

G. Huerre and C. Staquet

LEGI, B.P. 53, 38041 Grenoble Cédex 9 France

Chantal.Staquet@hmg.inpg.fr

Abstract

We investigate the conditions under which inertia-gravity waves may break in the neighbourhood of a dynamical barrier and whether breaking, if occuring, results in a significant transport of mass across the barrier. Three-dimensional direct numerical simulations of a simple physical model of the wave/barrier interaction are carried out for this purpose. We show that inertia-gravity waves may indeed break near the barrier, thereby inducing a turbulent transport across it, through a mechanism that *increases* the intrinsic frequency of the waves.

1 Introduction

The interaction of internal gravity waves with a horizontally inhomogeneous current has been studied using a linear theoretical analysis (Ivanov & Morozov 1974), within the WKB approximation (Basovich & Tsimring 1984, Badulin, Shrira & Tsimring 1985, Badulin & Shrira 1993). When the wave enters the current so that its intrinsic frequency increases by Doppler effect, the analysis shows that the wave amplitude increases as well (due to the conservation of wave action along ray paths), the component of its wave vector along the direction of inhomogeneity goes to infinity and its group velocity along that same direction goes to zero. If there exists a location in the flow where the intrinsic frequency equals the Brunt-Väisälä frequency N, the wave becomes trapped at that location: it cannot propagate beyond the trapping plane so that its energy may accumulate there. In the context of linear theory, the wave needs an infinite time to reach the trapping location. Since the amplitude of the wave increases as it propagates, nonlinear effects may actually dominate the dynamics and the wave may even break before reaching the trapping location. The work by Badulin *et al.* (1985) shows that horizontal inhomogeneties of density, namely fronts, result in the same trapping process. The effect of the Coriolis force does not change these conclusions (Olbers 1981).

In a stably-stratified fluid, a current with horizontal inhomogeneities is a dynamical barrier (in the sense that the potential vorticity gradient in the direction of inhomogeneity possesses extremal values). It is therefore of interest to investigate the conditions under which an inertia-gravity wave propagating toward such a barrier may break: the breaking process yields a turbulent flow, with enhanced transport properties and one may wonder whether the barrier could become locally permeable because of breaking. In the present paper, a very simplified model of the interaction of inertia-gravity waves with a dynamical barrier is considered, as a first step. The conditions under which breaking may occur are examined using three-dimensional direct numerical simulations of the Boussinesq equations in a rotating reference frame. An equation for the transport of a passive scalar is coupled to the equations so as to quantify the possible resulting transport process. The breaking of inertia-gravity waves, without any barrier, has been investigated using three-dimensional numerical simulations by Lelong & Dunkerton (1998a, 1998b).

The outline of the paper is the following. In the next section, we describe the physical and numerical models we use to study the interaction of an inertia-gravity wave with a dynamical barrier. Section 3 reports about the breaking process and the resulting transport properties. Conclusions are drawn in the final section.

2   A simplified model of the wave-barrier interaction

Physical model

We consider a uniformly stably stratified medium of Brunt-Väisälä frequency N within a rotating frame of reference with Coriolis frequency f. The barrier is a horizontal shear flow whose shear is also horizontal: $\mathbf{U}(x, y, z, t = 0) = U(y)\mathbf{i_x}$. The barrier is thus barotropic, as a first step: any variation of U along the vertical direction z would yield a horizontal inhomogeneity of the density field, according to the thermal wind balance, which would complicate the problem. The use of a shear flow models either a horizontal current or a vortex whose horizontal extent is much larger than the wave horizontal wavelength. Two different shear flows have been considered, a shear layer $U(y) = U_{max} \tanh((y - y_1)/a))$ and a jet; results for the former flow are presented in this paper. The parameters of the shear layer have been chosen so that it remains stable during the evolution and breaking of the wave.

An unforced monochromatic inertia-gravity wave is emitted at a fixed frequency ω_0 at a location $y = y_0 < y_1$ away from the barrier and propagates toward it. Its energy is confined about the y_0 plane so that a wave packet is actually considered. As the wave enters the current, its intrinsic frequency Ω is modified by Doppler effect ($\Omega = \omega_0 - \mathbf{k}.\mathbf{U}$) so that Ω will increase as y increases when k_x is negative, since dU/dy is positive. When a jet is considered, this means that the wave packet propagates *against* the current. In the present barotropic case, the trapping location, if it exists, is a vertical $y = y_t$ plane. The value of y_t is computed by writing that Ω is equal to N in the Doppler relation:

$$U(y_t) = (\Omega(y_0) - N)/k_x + U(y_0). \tag{1}$$

$\Omega(y_0)$ and $U(y_0)$ respectively are the intrinsic frequency and the value of the shear flow at the location the wave packet is emitted and k_x is the horizontal component of its wavevector. From (1), y_t can be of either sign.

Numerical model

The numerical domain is a parallelepipedic box of side (L_x, L_y, L_z). We solve the Boussinesq equations within a rotating frame of reference in this domain, using periodic boundary conditions along the x and z directions and free slip ones along the inhomogeneous y direction. A pseudo-spectral method is used along all three directions and time advancement is performed using a third order Adams-Bashforth scheme. The resolution of the computations is $(200, 201, 100)$ along the (x, y, z) directions respectively.

The results presented below correspond to the following numerical values: $N/f = 4$; $N = U_{max} = a = 1$; $y_0 = -2$, $y_1 = 1$; $L_x = L_y = 2L_z = 12a$; $k_x = -k_y = -k_z/4 = -(\pi/3)a^{-1}$. These values have been designed so that a trapping plane exists within the computational domain, to which the wave gets close in a few Brunt-Vaisala periods only to save computer time. The trapping plane is located at $y_t = 0.55$ and the wave amplitude is equal to $U_{max}/10$.

3   Results

Breaking process

The overall dynamics of the wave packet is illustrated in figure 1, through contours in a vertical x-plane at successive times. The density fluctuation ρ' about the linear hydrostatic density profile is plotted in the left column and the enstrophy Z (half the squared modulus of the vorticity) is plotted in the right column. The shear flow being horizontal, it does not displace the isopycnals and is therefore not visible in the left column. By contrast, both the wave packet and the barrier appear in the right column. The shear flow has no component in a vertical x-plane so that the intrinsic group velocity is parallel to the isopycnals.

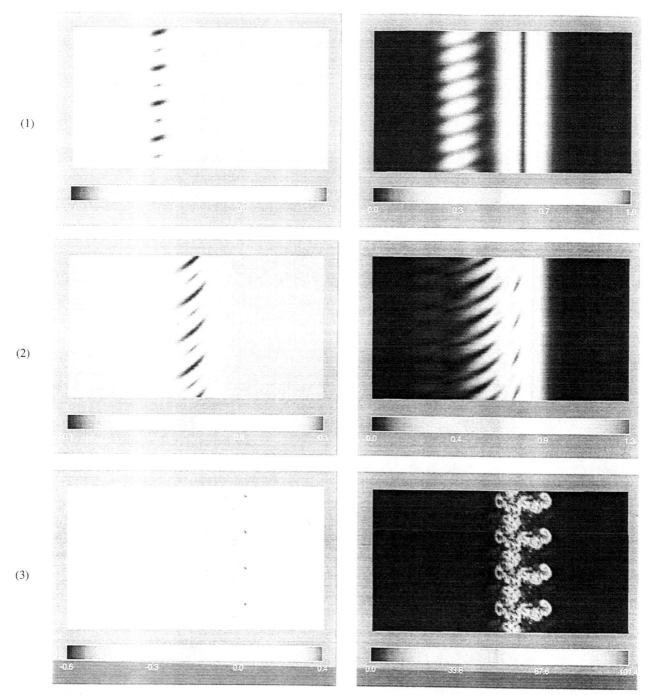

FIGURE 1: Visualization in a vertical x-plane of an inertia-gravity wave propagating toward a dynamical barrier. Contours of the fluctuating density (left column) and enstrophy (right column) are plotted at successive times: (1) t=0; (2) t=1.75 T_{BV}; (3) t=6.2 T_{BV}. $T_{BV} = 2\pi/N$ is the Brunt-Väisälä period.

The upper row displays ρ' and Z at initial time while these contours are plotted at $t = 1.75\ T_{BV}$ in the middle row. $T_{BV} = 2\pi/N$ is the Brunt-Väisälä period. At the latter time, the isopycnals have tilted toward the vertical as the intrinsic frequency has increased. The last row is plotted at $t = 6.2\ T_{BV}$, just after breaking has occured. The occurence of breaking is manifested as the appearance of very small density and vorticity scales, and by the maximum enstrophy to have increased by a factor 100 from its initial value.

The temporal evolution of the volume averaged enstrophy Z is plotted in figure 2. The enstrophy remains nearly constant up to $t \simeq 5.6\ T_{BV}(= 35\ a/U_{max})$. The dramatic increase from this time on signals that breaking has started.

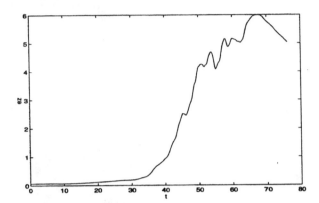

Figure 2: Volume averaged enstrophy as a function of time. The time unit is a/U_{max}.

The energy gained by the wave packet as it propagates toward the barrier is of course provided by the horizontal shear since the fluid system is not forced. The extraction of energy occurs through the action of the wave Reynolds stress upon the horizontal shear, $-u'v'dU/dy$. Since dU/dy is positive, the Reynolds stress $u'v'$ has to be negative for energy to be extracted from the current to the wave. This condition is equivalent to the wave intrinsic frequency to increase as the wave propagates toward the barrier. The volume averaged value of $-u'v'dU/dy$ is plotted as a function of time in figure 3. One would expect this term to remain very small as long as the wave propagates in an irrotational medium and to increase when it enters the shear. However, wave fluid motions are tilted toward the vertical by the shear through Doppler effect. Figure 3 shows that $-u'v'dU/dy$ displays a very sharp increase when the wave breaks near the trapping plane, while remaining very small before that time. The accumulation of the energy of the wave near the trapping plane is very likely responsible for this sudden increase but the precise underlying mechanisms need to be clarified. The breaking process occurs through a buoyancy induced instability, resulting from the strong streamwise shear $\partial w'/\partial y$ that develops as the wave approaches the trapping plane.

Transport across the barrier

A passive scalar located on the opposite side of the trapping plane with respect to the waves was added to the initial condition in order to quantify the transport resulting from breaking. The scalar has a gaussian distribution about the $y = y_c$ plane; the value of y_c was varied from 0.65 to 1.65 without any change to be observed in the scalar behavior. We describe the results for $y_c = y_1(= 1)$ below.

The evolution of the distribution remained nearly gaussian as time elapses, thereby indicating that a diffusive process has occured. Diffusion started earlier on the left side (first affected by the breaking waves) than on the right one so that, at a given time, each side of the distribution was fitted by a gaussian function with a different variance. Figure 4 displays the temporal evolution of the scalar distribution (fig. 4a) and the left and right variances $\sigma^2(t)$ resulting from fitting (fig. 4b). The variance remains constant as long as breaking has not occured. When breaking starts, σ^2 grows linearly in time, up to a value equal to 7: σ is therefore nearly three times larger than half the shear layer thickness a, meaning that transport occurs across the barrier. The diffusion coefficient is defined by $\kappa_t = 0.25 \, d\sigma^2/dt$, which yields a value of 0.04 in the present case. When divided by a turbulent horizontal length scale and a typical velocity associated with the turbulent regime resulting from wave breaking, a value of 0.7 is obtained for the normalized κ_t: the transport induced by the waves is therefore of turbulent nature. This conclusion is confirmed by the value of 0.7 to remain unchanged when the molecular viscosity is decreased by a factor 10.

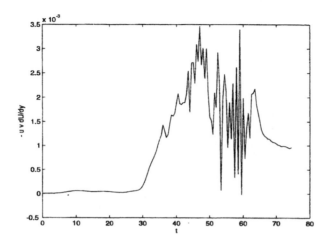

Figure 3: Temporal evolution of the rate of the wave energy due to energy exchange with the horizontal mean shear. The time unit is a/U_{max}.

4   Conclusions

Using three-dimensional numerical simulations of the Boussinesq equations in a rotating reference frame, we have shown that an inertia-gravity wave packet may break in the neighbourhood of a dynamical barotropic barrier and transports mass (and momentum) across the barrier. The basic mechanism is the increase of the wave intrinsic frequency Ω by Doppler shifting, which leads to the formation of a trapping plane where $\Omega = N$. The wave energy increases as the wave propagates toward the plane and accumulates in its neighbourhood, which triggers breaking. The existence of such a breaking process may account for the finding by Jacobitz & Sarkar (1998) that turbulence production in a stably stratified fluid is strongly increased when the flow involves a horizontally sheared horizontal mean flow.

The barotropic model used in the present study is too simple for its predictions to have any input to the current debate about the possible permeability of such barriers. We are currently investigating the more realistic situation of the interaction of inertia gravity waves with a baroclinic barrier.

Acknowledgements

This work benefitted from discussions with Jan-Bert Flor and Claude Sidi. Support was provided by the PNCA research program of CNRS/INSU. Computer time was allocated by the Computer

Center of CNRS (IDRIS) under contracts n° 990580 and 000580.

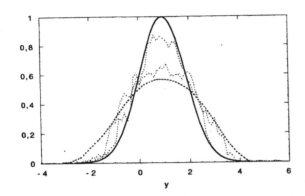 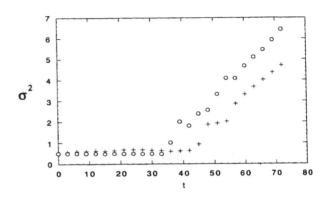

Figure 4: (a) Distribution of the passive scalar (averaged over x and z) as a function of time: $t = 0$, 6.7 (42), 9 (57) and 11.5 (72), expressed in Brunt-Väisälä periods (and in units of a/U_{max}). Note the dissymmetry between the left and right sides of the distribution. (b) Variance of the scalar distribution obtained by fitting the left and right sides by a gaussian function. The upper curve corresponds to the left side. The time unit is a/U_{max}.

References

Badulin S.I., V.I. Shrira & L.S. Tsimring 1985 The trapping and vertical focusing of internal waves in a pycnocline due to the horizontal inhomogeneities of density and currents. *J. Fluid Mech.*, **158**, 199-218.

Badulin S.I. & V.I. Shrira 1993 On the irreversibility of internal-wave dynamics due to wave trapping by mean flow inhomogeneities. Part1. Local analysis. *J. Fluid Mech.*, **251**, 21-53.

Basovich A.Y. & L.S. Tsimring 1984 Internal waves in a horizontally inhomogeneous flow. *J. Fluid Mech.*, **142**, 233-249.

Ivanov Y.A. & Y.G. Morozov 1974 Deformation of internal gravity waves by a stream with horizontal shear, *Oceanology*, **14**, 457-461.

Jacobitz F.G. & S. Sarkar 1998 The effect of nonvertical shear on turbulence in a stably stratified medium. *Physics of Fluids*, **10**, no. 5, 1158-1168.

Lelong M.-P. & T.J. Dunkerton 1998a Inertia-gravity wave breaking in three dimensions. Part I: Convectively stable waves. *J. Atmos. Sci.*, **55**, no. 15, 2473-2488.

Lelong & Dunkerton 1998b Inertia-gravity wave breaking in three dimensions. Part II: Convectively unstable waves. *J. Atmos. Sci.*, **55**, no. 15, 2489-2501.

Olbers D.J. 1981 The propagation of internal waves in a geostrophic current. *J. Phys. Oceanogr.*, **11**, 1224-1233.

Generation of Oblique Internal Waves by a Surface Wave

Mirmosadegh Jamali[1], Greg Lawrence[2], Michael Quick[2]

[1]Department of Civil Engineering, Sharif University of Technology, Teheran, Iran
[2]Department of Civil Engineering, The University of British Columbia, Vancouver, Canada
mjamali@sina.sharif.ac.ir, lawrence@civil.ubc.ca, mquick@civil.ubc.ca

1. Abstract

The results of a theoretical and experimental investigation of resonant interaction of a surface wave with two internal waves are presented. The interaction takes place in a two-layer fluid in three dimensions. A standard weakly nonlinear wave interaction analysis is performed, and the evolution equations of the internal waves are derived. The results indicate the more oblique the internal waves with respect to the surface wave, the higher the growth rate of the internal waves. The maximum growth rate occurs when the internal waves form a symmetric configuration with respect to the surface wave. Some results of a series of experiments are presented. The observations indicate the interaction leads to the generation of oblique internal waves. The internal waves are reflected from the side-walls of the flume resulting in formation a three-dimensional standing-wave pattern at the interface.

2. Introduction

At the bottom of many lakes, estuaries, and coastal waters, a fluid-mud layer forms beneath an upper, clear layer. Re-suspension of material from this layer can be of significant practical importance. In coastal waters it can lead to the need for substantial dredging or sediment replenishment. Re-suspension can be the result of surface wave action triggering instabilities at the interface between the fluid mud and the overlying water.

To investigate the interfacial instabilities, the model of surface wave motion in a two-layer fluid can be adopted. This simplified problem was first studied by Wen (1995) in the context of surface wave motion over a highly viscous sub-layer. Wen's (1995) study was motivated by her qualitative observations of interfacial wave generation by a surface wave over a fine-sediment bed in a laboratory flume. Wen (1995) studied the problem theoretically in two dimensions and showed that a resonant interaction between the surface wave and two opposite-travelling internal waves leads to the growth of the internal waves, and hence the instability of the interface. Consistent with the experimental results, Wen's (1995) theoretical results indicated that the internal waves are short, and their frequencies are nearly equal to the half of the surface-wave frequency. Moreover, the internal waves have opposite propagation directions. The interaction was subsequently investigated by Hill and Foda (1996), Jamali (1997), and Hill (1997). The first two works were limited to a two-dimensional analysis of the interaction, whereas in the last the focus was on the three-dimensional interaction. In this paper, the results of a theoretical and experimental investigation of the three-dimensional problem are discussed.

3. Resonant Triad

The present study considers a triad consisting of a surface wave (denoted as wave 0) and two internal waves (denoted as waves 1 and 2) as shown in figure 1. The three waves satisfy the resonance conditions:

$$\vec{k}_0 = \vec{k}_1 + \vec{k}_2$$
$$\omega_0 = \omega_1 + \omega_2 \tag{1}$$

where for each wave i the wave number k_i and the frequency ω_i are related by a dispersion relation. For a two-layer inviscid fluid the dispersion relation is given by

$$\frac{\dfrac{\rho'}{\rho}(\omega^4 - g^2 k^2)\,tanh(kh)}{(gk\,tanh(kh) - \omega^2)} + gk - \omega^2\,coth(kd) = 0 \tag{2}$$

(e.g., see Jamali, 1998) where the parameters are defined in figure 1.

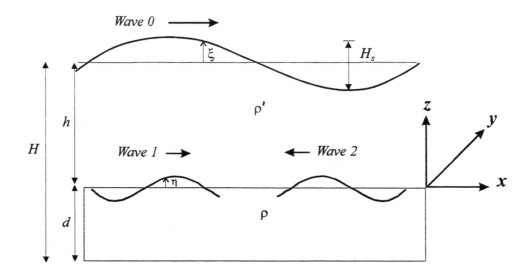

Figure 1 Configuration of the problem in three-dimensional interaction analysis.

The resonance conditions (1) and the individual dispersion relations of the waves form a system of algebraic equations from which the wave numbers and frequencies of the interacting waves can be determined. The existence of the solution to this system of equations is demonstrated graphically in figure 2. The triad shown is just one of the possible solutions. In general, there exists infinite number of the internal wave pairs that can be in resonance with a given surface wave. Given that the two internal waves in a pair have nearly opposite directions (e.g., see Hill, 1997; and Jamali, 1998), a pair is distinguished from the others by its angle from the surface wave. In a real situation, the pair having the maximum growth rate has the highest chance to appear.

4. Theory

To investigate the interaction, a standard three-wave interaction analysis (e.g., see Craik, 1985) is performed. Consider the two-layer fluid system shown in figure 1. The system is assumed to be infinite horizontally and three-dimensional. The coordinate system xyz is located on the interface. The depth of the upper layer is denoted by h, the depth of the lower layer by d, and the total depth by H. The densities of the upper and lower layers are ρ' and ρ respectively. The layers are assumed inviscid. The surface wave is denoted as wave 0 and the two opposite-traveling internal waves as waves 1 and 2. Without loss of generality, wave 0 is assumed to travel in the positive x direction and the two internal waves in the x - y plane. The internal wave 1 has an arbitrary directional angle θ_1 relative to the surface wave. Note that from the resonance conditions the direction angle of the internal wave 2 is obtained as a function of θ_1.

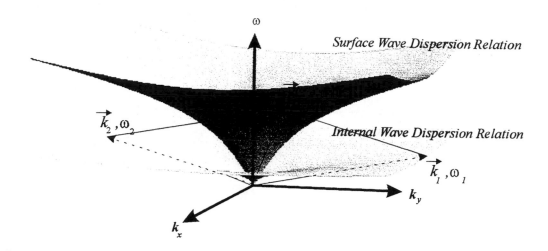

Figure 2. Demonstration of existence of the resonant triad in the interaction of a surface wave (denoted by subscript 0) with two internal waves (denoted by subscripts 1 and 2).

With the assumption of incompressible fluid layers and irrotational flows in the layers, the fluid motion can be described by velocity potentials $\phi'(x,y,z)$ and $\phi(x,y,z)$ in the upper and lower layers respectively. The potentials satisfy Laplace's equation in the corresponding layers.

$$\nabla^2\phi' = 0, \qquad\qquad 0 < z < h \qquad\qquad (3)$$

$$\nabla^2\phi = 0, \qquad\qquad -d < z < 0 \qquad\qquad (4)$$

The above equations are subject to the boundary conditions at the free surface, the interface of the layers, and the solid bed. On the free surface, the boundary conditions are

$$\xi_t + \phi'_x\xi_x + \phi'_y\xi_y = \phi'_z, \qquad\qquad z = h + \xi(x,y,t) \qquad\qquad (5)$$

$$\rho'[\phi'_t + \frac{1}{2}(\phi'^2_x + \phi'^2_y + \phi'^2_z) + gz] = C'(t), \qquad z = h + \xi(x,y,t) \qquad\qquad (6)$$

where $\xi(x,y,t) =$ the displacement of the free surface. The first equation represents a kinematic boundary condition while the second equation corresponds to a dynamic one. On the two-layer interface, the kinematic boundary conditions are

$$\eta_t + \phi'_x\eta_x + \phi'_y\eta_y = \phi'_z, \qquad\qquad z = \eta(x,y,t) \qquad\qquad (7)$$

$$\eta_t + \phi_x\eta_x + \phi_y\eta_y = \phi_z, \qquad\qquad z = \eta(x,y,t) \qquad\qquad (8)$$

where $\eta(x,y,t) =$ the displacement of the interface, and the dynamic boundary condition is

$$\rho'[\phi'_t + \frac{1}{2}(\phi'^2_x + \phi'^2_y + \phi'^2_z) + gz - C'(t)] = \rho[\phi_t + \frac{1}{2}(\phi^2_x + \phi^2_y + \phi^2_z) + gz - C(t)],$$

$$z = \eta(x,y,t) \qquad\qquad (9)$$

On the bed, the problem is subject to a kinematic boundary condition requiring the normal velocity be zero, i.e.,

$$\phi_z = 0, \qquad\qquad z = -d \qquad\qquad (10)$$

Next, a standard weakly nonlinear interaction analysis is performed. For this purpose, the wave amplitudes are assumed to be small. The dependent variables are expanded as perturbation series in ε, where ε is a typical non-dimensionalized wave amplitude. With the assumption that the wave amplitudes are functions of time, and their time derivatives are $O(\varepsilon^2)$, the perturbation analysis is carried out to second order. The following forms are assumed for the time derivatives of the amplitudes.

$$\frac{da_0}{dt} = O(b_1 b_2), \qquad \frac{db_1}{dt} = O(a_0 \bar{b}_2), \qquad \frac{db_2}{dt} = O(a_0 \bar{b}_1) \qquad (11)$$

where a_i and b_i are half of the amplitudes of wave i at the free surface and the interface respectively. At first order, the linear wave theory for a two-layer fluid is obtained. At second order, the time derivatives of the wave amplitudes are obtained as follows.

$$\frac{da_0}{dt} = \alpha_0 b_1 b_2, \qquad \frac{db_1}{dt} = \alpha_1 a_0 \bar{b}_2, \qquad \frac{db_2}{dt} = \alpha_2 a_0 \bar{b}_1 \qquad (12)$$

where α_0, α_1 and α_2 are interaction coefficients. Considering that the surface wave has much more energy than the internal waves, time variation of the surface wave amplitude is negligible. Consequently, the first equation in (12) is neglected, and a_0 is taken constant in the next two equations. The analysis indicates that α_1 and α_2 are approximately equal. The expressions for α_1 and α_2 were found to be quite long, so they are not presented here. For a detailed discussion of the analysis, the interested reader is referred to Jamali (1998).

Combining the last two equations in (12) gives second-order, constant coefficient differential equations for $b_1(t)$ and $b_2(t)$. The solution to the internal-wave amplitudes at large times varies as

$$b_1(t) \sim b_2(t) \sim e^{\gamma t}, \qquad (13)$$

where

$$\gamma = \alpha |a_0|, \qquad (14)$$

and $\alpha = \sqrt{\alpha_1 \alpha_2}$. The quantity α is a measure of the forcing for growth of the internal waves. From the analysis, α turns out to be a positive real number.

5. Results

To examine some properties of the interaction, a numerical example is presented. Consider a test case where $d = 4.0\,cm$, $H = 16.0\,cm$, $\rho' = 1.00\,gr/cm^3$, $\rho = 1.04\,gr/cm^3$, $\omega_0 = 2\pi / 0.8$ rad/sec, and $\theta_1 = 75°$. From the solution of the resonance conditions, the kinematic properties of the waves are obtained as

$(k_0)_x = 7.54\,rad/m$, $\qquad (k_0)_y = 0$, $\qquad |\vec{k}_0| = 7.54$ rad/m

$(k_1)_x = 21.00\,rad/m$, $\qquad (k_1)_y = 78.35\,rad/m$, $\qquad |\vec{k}_1| = 81.11$ rad/m, $\quad \omega_1 = 3.95$ rad/s,

$(k_2)_x = -13.45\,rad/m$, $\quad (k_2)_y = -78.35\,rad/m$, $\qquad |\vec{k}_2| = 79.5$ rad/m, $\quad \omega_2 = 3.91$ rad/s

It can be seen that the internal waves are short with opposite travel directions, and their frequencies are approximately half of the surface wave frequency.

The interaction analysis yields the following values for α's:

$$\alpha_1 = -17.32i \ (m.s)^{-1}, \qquad\qquad \alpha_2 = -17.14i \ (m.s)^{-1}$$

It can be seen that α's are nearly equal. From the above values, $\alpha = 17.23\,(m.s)^{-1}$.

The variation of $\alpha H / \omega_0$ with θ_1 is shown in figure 4. The forcing increases with θ_1 until it reaches a maximum around $\theta_1 = 90^\circ$. Note that the graph is symmetric about this maximum point.

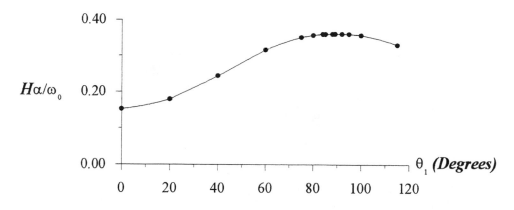

Figure 3 Variation of $\alpha H / \omega_0$ with θ_1.

Jamali (1998) shows that the maximum point corresponds to the case where k_1 and k_2 are symmetric with respect to, and nearly perpendicular to, k_0. At this symmetric configuration, the frequencies of the internal waves are exactly equal to $\omega_0 / 2$. This suggests that in a medium like an open ocean, the excited internal waves appear as a standing wave across the surface wave. It can be shown that the amplitude of this standing wave pattern varies as $sin(k_0 x - \omega_0 t)$ with x and t.

6. Experimentation

A series of experiments were carried out in a wave flume 3 meters long, 21 cm wide, and 35 cm deep. Salt water was used as the lower layer and fresh water as the upper layer. In a typical experiment, a three-dimensional standing internal wave was observed at the interface a few minutes after the surface wave was generated in the flume. An example of the three-dimensional pattern is shown in figure 4. At the start of each experiment, initially there was no interfacial wave, but as the experiment proceeded, the internal-wave pattern appeared with growing amplitude. The time of the first appearance (visibility level), the geometric properties, and the growth rate of the standing internal wave were found to be functions of the experimental parameters.

In the formation of the three-dimensional standing pattern, the flume side-walls play an important role. It is recalled from the theoretical analysis that the internal waves have a higher growth rate when they are oblique to the surface wave. However, the flume has finite width, and the oblique internal waves are reflected from the side-walls. This leads to the generation of the image internal waves besides the original internal waves. Since the internal waves have the same wave numbers normal to the surface wave, see the resonance conditions (1), the four internal waves combine to form a standing wave across the wave flume. On the other hand, the wavelengths of the internal waves along the flume are nearly equal, e.g., refer to the preceding numerical example. Consequently, the combination of the two excited internal waves and their images lead to the observed three-dimensional standing wave pattern at the interface. It is interesting to note that according to figure 4, the internal waves are observed to be short compared to the surface wave, consistent with the theoretical results. Other experimental results along with a full description of the experiments are given in Jamali (1998).

Figure 4 Three-dimensional internal waves at the interface of the two layers.

7. Conclusions

In a three-dimensional interaction of a surface with two internal waves, the internal waves are short and their frequencies are close to half of the frequency of the surface wave. The interaction analysis indicates the more oblique the internal waves to the surface wave, the higher the growth rate of the internal waves. In a wave flume, the excited oblique internal waves are reflected from the flume side-walls resulting in a three-dimensional standing wave.

8. References

1. Craik, A. D. D. (1985) *Wave Interactions and Fluid Flows,* Cambridge University Press.

2. Hill, D. F., and Foda, M. A. (1996) "Subharmonic resonance of short internal standing waves by progressive surface waves," *J. Fluid Mech.,* V 321, p 217.

3. Hill, D. F. (1997) *The Subharmonic Resonance of Interfacial Waves by Progressive Surface Waves,* Ph.D. Thesis, University of California at Berkeley.

4. Jamali, M. (1997) "Resonant excitation of internal waves by a surface wave," *Proc. XXVIIth Conf. IAHR,* San Francisco, p 1334.

5. Jamali, M. (1998) *Surface Wave Interaction with Oblique Internal Waves,* Ph.D. Thesis, The University of British Columbia.

6. Wen, F. (1995) "Resonant generation of internal waves on the soft sea bed by a surface water wave", *Phys. Fluids,* V 7, p 1915.

Surface Wave Interaction with Internal Waves on a Diffuse Interface

Mirmosadegh Jamali[1], Brian Seymour[2]

[1]Department of Civil Engineering, Sharif University of Technology, Teheran, Iran
[2]Department of Mathematics, The University of British Columbia, Vancouver, Canada
mjamali@sina.sharif.ac.ir, seymour@math.ubc.ca

1. Abstract

A two-dimensional analysis of the generation of internal waves by a progressive surface wave on a thin diffuse interface is presented. The fluid system is modeled as a combination of upper and lower layers, divided by a thin third layer. A standard weakly nonlinear wave interaction analysis is performed. By taking the non-dimensional density difference δ as a small perturbation parameter and assuming a thin interface thickness, the evolution equations of the internal waves are derived asymptotically. Two possibilities for the interaction are found: 1- interaction between a surface wave and two first-mode internal waves, 2- interaction between a surface wave, a first-mode and a second-mode internal wave. The asymptotic analysis indicates that the internal waves have a higher growth rate in the first case.

2. Introduction

The resonant interaction of a surface wave with two internal waves was first studied by Wen (1995) in the context of surface wave motion over a sediment bed. She found that the internal waves are short, and their frequencies are nearly equal to the half of the surface-wave frequency. According to her laboratory observations, the internal waves were two-dimensional with opposite propagation directions. The interaction was subsequently investigated by Hill and Foda (1996), and Hill (1997). The first work was limited to a two-dimensional analysis of the interaction. In the second, Hill (1997) investigated the interaction experimentally and theoretically and showed that the interaction has in fact a three-dimensional nature. More recently, Jamali (1998) studied the interaction theoretically and experimentally in an attempt to investigate the phenomenon in more detail and to address some issues surrounding Hill's (1997) results.

One experimental observation of Jamali (1998) concerned the effect of interface diffusion on the interaction. He found that in the experiments the diffuse interface of the two layers had an affect on the growth rate of the internal waves. In this paper, a two-dimensional analysis of the generation of internal waves by a progressive surface wave on a thin diffuse interface is presented.

3. Resonance Triad

The present study considers a two-dimensional triad consisting of a surface wave (denoted as wave 0) and two internal waves (denoted as waves 1 and 2) as shown in figure 1. Without loss of generality, wave 0 is assumed to travel in the positive x direction.
The three waves satisfy the resonance conditions

$$k_0 = k_1 + k_2$$
$$\omega_0 = \omega_1 + \omega_2 \tag{1}$$

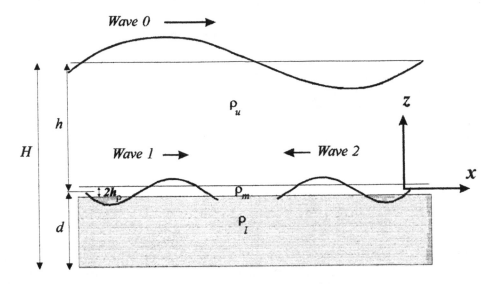

Figure 1 Configuration of the problem.

where for each wave i the wave number k_i and the frequency ω_i are related by a dispersion relation. The resonance conditions (1) and the individual dispersion relations of the waves form a system of algebraic equations from which the wave numbers and the frequencies of the interacting waves can be determined. A three-layer system with a free surface admits a surface-wave mode and two internal-wave modes. A plot of the dispersion relations for the surface and internal waves in a typical three-layer system is given in figure 2. It can be seen that there are two possible resonant triads: one composed of a surface wave and two first-mode internal waves, and the other composed of a surface wave and a pair of internal waves of different mode. Later, this point will be confirmed analytically.

4. Equations of Motion

Consider a three-layer inviscid fluid system with a thin middle layer as shown in figure 1. The system is assumed to be two-dimensional and horizontally infinite. The coordinate system xyz is located on the mid-height of the interface. The surface of the upper layer, and the bottom of the lower layer are located at $z = h$ and $z = -d$ respectively. The middle (diffuse) layer has a thickness of $2h_\rho$ as indicated. The total depth is denoted by H. The density of the upper, the middle, and the lower layer is ρ_u, ρ_m, and ρ_l respectively. It is assumed that each layer has a constant density, and $\rho_m = \left(\rho_u + \rho_l\right)/2$.

With the assumption of incompressible fluid layers and irrotational flows in the layers, the fluid motion can be described by velocity potentials $\phi'(x,z)$, $\phi''(x,z)$, and $\phi(x,z)$ in the upper, middle, and lower layer respectively. The potentials satisfy Laplace's equation in the corresponding layers.

$$\nabla^2 \phi' = 0, \qquad\qquad h_\rho < z < h \qquad\qquad (2)$$

$$\nabla^2 \phi'' = 0, \qquad\qquad -h_\rho < z < h_\rho \qquad\qquad (3)$$

$$\nabla^2 \phi = 0, \qquad\qquad -d < z < -h_\rho \qquad\qquad (4)$$

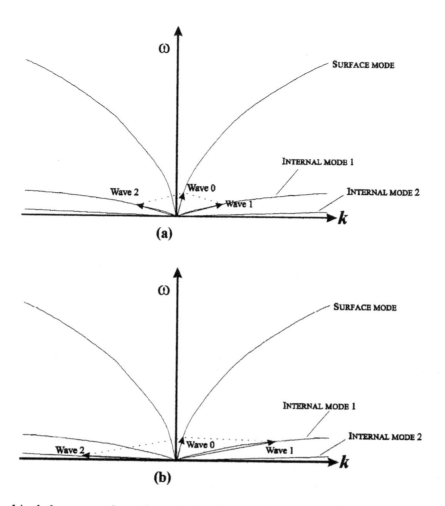

Figure 2 Graphical demonstration of resonant triads: **a)** Interaction of a surface wave with first-mode internal waves; **b)** Interaction of a surface wave with internal waves of different modes.

The above equations are subject to the boundary conditions at the free surface, the interfaces of the layers, and the solid bed. On the free surface, the boundary conditions are:

$$\xi_t + \phi'_x \xi_x = \phi'_z, \qquad\qquad z = h + \xi(x,t) \qquad\qquad (5)$$

$$\rho_u [\phi'_t + \frac{1}{2}(\phi'^2_x + \phi'^2_z) + gz] = C'(t), \qquad z = h + \xi(x,t) \qquad\qquad (6)$$

where $\xi(x,t)$ = the displacement of the free surface. The first equation represents a kinematic boundary condition while the second equation corresponds to a dynamic condition. At the interfaces, $z = h_\rho + \eta_u(x,t)$ and $z = -h_\rho + \eta_l(x,t)$ where η_u and η_l are the displacements of the upper and the lower interfaces respectively, there are four boundary conditions. Transferring these boundary conditions to the corresponding undisturbed interfaces yields the following, correct to $O(\varepsilon^2)$ where ε is a typical non-dimensional wave amplitude:

$$\phi'_z - \phi''_z = \{ (\phi' - \phi'')_x \eta_u \}_x, \qquad z = h_\rho \qquad\qquad (7)$$

$$(1-\delta/2)(\phi'_{tt}+g\phi'_z)-(\phi''_{tt}+g\phi''_z)=\{((1-\delta/2)\phi'-\phi'')_x g\eta_u\}_x + \tfrac{1}{2}\{(\phi'^2_x+\phi'^2_z)-(1-\delta/2)(\phi'^2_x+\phi'^2_z)\}_t$$
$$-\{((1-\delta/2)\phi'_z-\phi''_z)\eta_u\}_t$$

$$z=h_\rho \qquad\qquad (8)$$

$$\phi_z-\phi''_z=\{(\phi-\phi'')_x\,\eta_l\}_x, \qquad z=-h_\rho \qquad\qquad (9)$$

$$(1+\delta/2)(\phi_{tt}+g\phi_z)-(\phi''_{tt}+g\phi''_z)=\{((1+\delta/2)\phi-\phi'')_x g\eta_l\}_x + \tfrac{1}{2}\{(\phi''^2_x+\phi''^2_z)-(1+\delta/2)(\phi^2_x+\phi^2_z)\}_t$$
$$-\{((1+\delta/2)\phi_z-\phi''_z)\eta_l\}_t$$

$$z=-h_\rho \qquad\qquad (10)$$

where $\rho_m=(\rho_u+\rho_l)/2$. At the bed, the problem is subject to a kinematic boundary condition requiring the normal velocity be zero, i.e.,

$$\phi''_z=0, \qquad\qquad z=-d \qquad\qquad (11)$$

5. Perturbation Solution

For the purpose of the interaction analysis, it is assumed that the amplitudes of the waves are sufficiently small that a standard weakly nonlinear interaction (Craik, 1985) can be performed. Performing the interaction analysis (Jamali, 2000), at first order the linear solutions of the waves are obtained. At second order, the following equations for the time variations of the wave amplitudes are derived.

$$\frac{da_0}{dt}=\alpha_0 b_1 b_2, \qquad\qquad \frac{db_1}{dt}=\alpha_1 a_0 \bar{b}_2, \qquad\qquad \frac{db_2}{dt}=\alpha_2 a_0 \bar{b}_1 \qquad\qquad (12)$$

where a_0 is the amplitude of the surface wave at the free surface, and b_1 and b_2 are the amplitudes of the internal waves 1 and 2 at $z=0$ respectively. The constants α_0, α_1 and α_2 are interaction coefficients.

Considering that the surface wave has much more energy than the internal waves, surface wave variation with time can be neglected. This implies that a_0 can be assumed constant in the last two equations of (12). Simultaneous solution of the last two equations yields the internal wave amplitudes as functions of time. In the following, the parameter δ is taken as a small perturbation parameter, and by assuming $h_\rho=O(\delta^2)$, the interaction coefficients as well as the kinematic properties of the interacting waves are obtained asymptotically.

6. Solution of Resonance Conditions

Having dispersion relations for the interacting waves, the solutions to (1) are obtained asymptotically in terms of δ with the assumption $h_\rho=O(\delta^2)$. When both internal waves are primary, simultaneous solution of (1) and the corresponding dispersion relations yields the following leading-order solution for ω_1, ω_2, k_1, and k_2.

$$\omega_1 \sim \omega_2 \sim \frac{\omega_0}{2} \qquad\qquad (13)$$

$$k_1 \sim -k_2 \sim \left(\frac{\omega_0^2}{2g}\right)\frac{1}{\delta} \qquad\qquad (14)$$

It is seen that in this mode of interaction $\omega_1, \omega_2 = O(1)$ and $k_1, k_2 = O(1/\delta)$.

When the internal waves are of different mode, e.g., when internal wave 1 is primary, and wave 2 is secondary, simultaneous solution of (1) with the corresponding dispersion relations yields the following leading-order solution for ω_1, ω_2, k_1, and k_2.

$$\omega_1 \sim \omega_0 \tag{15}$$

$$\omega_2 \sim \frac{\sqrt{2}\omega_0^2 \sqrt{h_\rho}}{\sqrt{g\delta}} \delta^{1/2} \tag{16}$$

$$k_1 \sim -k_2 \sim \left(\frac{2\omega_0^2}{g}\right)\frac{1}{\delta} \tag{17}$$

From the above it can be seen that in this mode of interaction $\omega_1 = O(1)$, $\omega_2 = O(\delta^{1/2})$, and $k_1, k_2 = O(1/\delta)$.

Since second-mode internal waves have frequencies of order $\delta^{1/2}$ whereas a surface wave has a frequency of order 1, the second equation of (1) can never be satisfied by two second-mode internal waves. This indicates that interaction between a surface wave and two second-mode internal waves is impossible.

7. Second-order Solution

At second order the evolution equations of the waves are obtained. As discussed, two modes of interaction are found possible. The interaction between a surface wave and two first-mode internal waves is referred to as mode 1, and the interaction between a surface wave and two internal waves of different mode is referred to as mode 2. For the first mode the leading-order term of α_2 is obtained as

$$\alpha_2 \sim \frac{i\omega_0 \left(\omega_0^2 \, sinh(k_0 d) - g k_0 \, cosh(k_0 d)\right)}{4g \, sinh(k_0 H)}. \tag{18}$$

It is interesting to note that the effect of the diffuse interface does not appear at leading order. It can be shown that the above is also the leading order solution of α_2 in a purely two-layer fluid system. To obtain α_1, use is made of the following relation between α_1 and α_2 (Jamali, 1998).

$$\frac{\alpha_1}{\omega_1} = \frac{\alpha_2}{\omega_2} = \frac{\alpha_0}{\omega_0 \delta} \tag{19}$$

Since $\omega_1 \sim \omega_2 = O(1)$, correct to leading order, the leading term of α_1 is also given by (18).

Having α_1 and α_2, the last two equation of (12) can be combined to yield the equation for b_1. At large times, the solution for $b_1(t)$ is given by

$$b_1(t) \approx C_1 e^{\alpha |a_0| t}, \tag{20}$$

where

$$\alpha = \sqrt{\alpha_1 \overline{\alpha}_2}. \tag{21}$$

It can be shown that (20) is the long-term solution for b_2 as well. The parameter $\alpha|a_0|$ is referred to as the growth parameter of the internal waves. Since α_1 and α_2 are equal at the leading order, it follows that the growth parameter $\alpha|a_0|$ is of order 1 in this mode of interaction.

For the second mode of interaction, the leading-order term of α_2 is obtained to be of order δ :

$$\alpha_2 \sim \frac{i(\cosh(k_0 d) + \sinh(k_0 d))\left(\frac{26 h_\rho \omega_0^4}{\delta^2} - g^2 k_0\right)^2}{\omega_0 g^3 \sinh(k_0 H)} \delta \tag{22}$$

Knowing that in this mode of interaction $\omega_1 = O(1)$ and $\omega_2 = O(\delta^{1/2})$, from (19) it follows that $\alpha_1 = O(\delta^{1/2})$. Consequently, α turns out to be $O(\delta^{3/4})$, and hence it goes to zero when $\delta -> 0$. This implies that in this mode of interaction the internal waves have a lower growth rate than that in the previous mode, and hence in a real situation the interaction is most anticipated between a surface wave and two first-mode internal waves.

8. Conclusions

A two-dimensional analysis of the generation of two internal waves by a surface wave on a thin diffuse interface was presented. A three-layer system admits two modes of internal wave motion, and similarly two modes of interaction were found possible. These were interaction between a surface wave and two first-mode internal waves, and the interaction between a surface wave, a first-mode and a second-mode internal wave. The case of interaction between a surface wave and two second-mode internal waves was shown to be impossible. The asymptotic analysis indicated that the growth rate in the first mode is higher than in the second. This implies that in a real situation the interaction emerges as between a surface wave and two first-mode internal waves.

9. Acknowledgement

The first author would like to acknowledge the financial support received from Sharif University of Technology to attend the symposium.

10. References

1. Craik, A. D. D. (1985) *Wave Interactions and Fluid Flows*, Cambridge University Press.

2. Hill, D. F., and Foda, M. A. (1996) "Subharmonic resonance of short internal standing waves by progressive surface waves," *J. Fluid Mech.*, V 321, p 217.

3. Hill, D. F. (1997) *The Subharmonic Resonance of Interfacial Waves by Progressive Surface Waves*, Ph.D. Thesis, University of California at Berkeley.

4. Jamali, M. (1998) *Surface Wave Interaction with Oblique Internal Waves*, Ph.D. Thesis, The University of British Columbia.

5. Jamali, M. (2000) *Asymptotic Analysis of Interaction of a Surface Wave with Two Internal Waves*, M.Sc. Thesis, The University of British Columbia.

6. Wen, F. (1995) "Resonant generation of internal waves on the soft sea bed by a surface water wave", *Phys. Fluids*, V 7, p 1915.

Evolution Equation for Nonlinear Internal Waves in Stratified Liquid of an Arbitrary Depth

Georgy A. Khabakhpashev and Oleg Yu. Tsvelodub

Department of Physical Hydrodynamics, Institute of Thermophysics
Siberian Branch of the Russian Academy of Sciences, Novosibirsk 630090, Russia
geshev@otani.thermo.nsk.su

1. Abstract

A second-order differential model for three-dimensional perturbations of the interface of two fluids of different density is constructed. An evolution equation for traveling quasistationary waves of arbitrary length and small but finite amplitude is obtained. In the case of the horizontal bottom and lid, there are perturbations of the Stokes-wave type among the steady-state periodic solutions. For moderately long perturbations, solutions in the form of solitary waves which are in agreement with the available experimental and analytical results are found.

2. Introduction

Borisov and Khabakhpashev proposed a very simple differential model capable of describing the dynamics of long and short three-dimensional, weakly nonlinear perturbations of the interface of two fluids of different density confined fy a rigid horizontal bottom and lid. However, the derivation of the wave-type equation for quasistationary disturbances was not quite correct. In addition, formally, even a linearized equation can have unstable solutions. The purpose of this work is to obtain a second-order differential model and a corresponding evolution equation that is free from the above-mentioned diadvantages with no requiring the layers to be of constant depth.

3. Second-Order Differential Model

It is assumed that the fluids are ideal, incompressible, and immiscible, the stationary components of the fluid motion equal zero, the occurring oscillating flows are potential, and the waves are weakly nonlinear (i. e., $\eta_a k/\text{th}(kh_m) \sim \varepsilon$, where η_a is the amplitude of the disturbance at the interface, k is the wave number, h_m is the depth of the smaller layer, and ε is a small parameter). Third-order infinitesimals are omitted with capillary effects ignored. The initial system of hydrodynamic equation was reduced by Borisov and Khabakhpashev to the equations:

$$\frac{\partial \eta}{\partial t} + \nabla \cdot \{\langle \mathbf{u}_l \rangle [\eta + (-1)^l h_l]\} = 0; \tag{1}$$

$$\frac{\partial \mathbf{u}_{li}}{\partial t} + \nabla \left(g\eta + \frac{u_{li}^2}{2} + \frac{p_i}{\rho_l} \right) + \frac{\partial^2 \eta}{\partial t^2} \nabla \eta = 0. \tag{2}$$

by integrating over the vertical coordinate and by using the standard kinematic and dynamic boundary conditions on the lid, the bottom, and the interface. Here t is the time, $\mathbf{u}$ is the vector of the horizontal component of the fluid velocity, the angular brackets indicate its value averaged over the layer depth, g is the acceleration of gravity, ρ is the density, p is the pressure, $l = 1$ for the upper fluid, and $l = 2$ for the lower one; the subscipt i indicates the values of the quantities related to the interface and the gradient operator ∇ is determined in the horizontal plane.

Then, using the dependences for the vertical profiles $\mathbf{u}_l$ (see, for example, Lamb) one may related

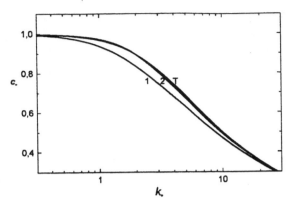

Figure 1. The dimensionless phase velocity c_* as a function of the dimensionless wave number k_* for $h_2/h_1 = 3$ and $\rho_2/\rho_1 = 1.25$: curves 1 and 2 refer to calculations by the approximation (5) for $\alpha = 0$ and $2/3$, respectively, and curve T to calculation by the exact dispersion relation (4).

the Fourier components of the boundary and averaged velocities of the fluids:

$$u_{li}(\omega, k) = kh_l \operatorname{cth}(kh_l)\langle u_l(\omega, k)\rangle, \tag{3}$$

where ω is the cyclic frequency. If $\nabla h \sim \varepsilon^{3/2}$, the formulas for waves in a liquid of constant depth are also locally true for a weakly inclined bottom and lid. In this connection, we give the dispersion relation for linear monoharmonic vortex-free waves in a two-layer liquid in the form (Lamb):

$$\omega^2[\rho_1 \operatorname{cth}(kh_1) + \rho_2 \operatorname{cth}(kh_2)] = gk(\rho_2 - \rho_1). \tag{4}$$

We replace approximately this transcendental equation by the following Padé approximation:

$$\omega^2(1/A_\omega + \omega_*^2) = \omega^2/c_*^2 = k^2 c_0^2 = k^2 g\delta, \qquad A_\omega = 1 + \alpha\omega_*^2, \qquad \omega_*^2 = \omega^2\beta/g_+^-, \tag{5}$$

$$g_+^- = g\frac{\rho_2 - \rho_1}{\rho_1 + \rho_2}, \qquad \beta = h_1 h_2\frac{\rho_1 + \rho_2}{\chi}, \qquad \delta = h_1 h_2\frac{\rho_2 - \rho_1}{\chi}, \qquad \chi = \rho_1 h_2 + \rho_2 h_1.$$

Here c is the phase velocity (the subscipt 0 indicates its value for the waves of infinitely small frequency) and α is the numerical coefficient. If $\alpha = 0$, we have the simplest polynomial approximation suggested by Borisov and Khabakhpashev. In this case, the long-wave ($\omega_*^2 \ll 1$) and short-wave ($\omega_*^2 \gg 1$) asymptotic curves coincide with the exact dispersion curve. In addition, in the range of intermediate frequencies the approximation error is determined by the ratios of the layer depths and the fluid densities. In particular, for $h_2/h_1 = 3$ and $\rho_2/\rho_1 = 1,25$ (the experiment by Gavrilov was performed for these values), the maximum relative deviation of the exact relation (4) from the approximate (1.5) with $\alpha = 0$ is 8,5 % and it is reached for $k_* = kH \approx 4$ ($H = h_1 + h_2$ is the distance between the bottom and the lid). If $\alpha = 2/3$, the approximation error does not exceed 2 %, and the corresponding maximum is attained for $k_* \approx 6$ (Fig. 1). A comparison of relations (4) and (5) leads to the expressions $kh_l \operatorname{cth}(kh_l) = 1/A_\omega + \omega^2 h_l/g_+^-$, by means of which we write Eqs. (3) in the form:

$$A_\omega u_{li}(\omega, k) = (1 + A_\omega\omega^2 h_l/g_+^-)\langle u_l(\omega, k)\rangle. \tag{6}$$

Application of the inverse Fourier transform to (6) yields the differential relations for the velocities

$$A_t\mathbf{u}_{li} = \langle \mathbf{u}_l\rangle - A_t\frac{h_l}{g_+^-}\frac{\partial^2\langle \mathbf{u}_l\rangle}{\partial t^2}, \qquad A_t = 1 - \alpha\frac{\beta}{g_+^-}\frac{\partial^2}{\partial t^2}. \tag{7}$$

In contrast to formulas (7), relations (3) and (6) also remain valid in the case of weakly nonlinear perturbations. Therefore, we can use the generalization of expressions (7)

$$A_t\mathbf{u}_{li} = \langle \mathbf{u}_l\rangle - A_t\left\{\left[\frac{h_l}{g_+^-} + \frac{(-1)^l}{g_+^-}\left(\eta + \frac{3h_l}{g_+^-}\frac{\partial^2\eta}{\partial t^2}\right)\right]\frac{\partial^2\langle \mathbf{u}_l\rangle}{\partial t^2} - 4\mathbf{u}_{li}'\right\}, \tag{8}$$

792

where $\mathbf{u}'_{li}$ are the velocities of translational motion of the fluid particles near the interface of the infinitely deep layers in the direction of wave motion. These values are the second-order infinitesimals and depend neither on the horizontal coordinates nor on time. Thus, in the approximation considered (without including the third-order infinitesimals) the terms $\partial \mathbf{u}_{li}/\partial t$ and ∇u_{li}^2, which enter Eqs. (2), does not contain $\mathbf{u}'_{li}$. However, the presence of $\mathbf{u}'_{li}$ in Eqs. (8) is necessary for obtaining a solution of the Stokes-wave type for two infinitely deep layers (see, for example, Thorpe or Turner). We note that relations (8) are also in agreement with the results available for the long-wave range.

4. Evolution Equation for Quasistationary Waves

Now we differentiate Eqs. (2) twice with respect to time, multiply all the terms by $\pm\alpha\beta/g_+^-$ and add it again to Eqs. (2). As a result, the following equation is obtained:

$$A_t \frac{\partial \mathbf{u}_{li}}{\partial t} + A_t \left[\nabla \left(g\eta + \frac{p_i}{\rho_l} \right) + \frac{\partial^2 \eta}{\partial t^2} \nabla\eta \right] + \frac{1}{2} A_t \nabla u_{li}^2 = 0. \tag{9}$$

The first terms in Eqs. (9) are replaced by means of expressions (8). Owing the nonlinearity of the last terms of Eqs. (9), in the substitution one can confine oneself to the first order of accuracy and the third-order infinitesimals can be ignored, i.e., one can assume that $\mathbf{u}_{li} = \langle \mathbf{u}_l \rangle - (h_l/g_+^-)(\partial^2 \langle \mathbf{u}_l \rangle /\partial t^2)$. Therefore, the conservation laws for the horizontal components of the momentum in the layers do not contain the values of the fluid velocities at the interface:

$$\frac{\partial \langle \mathbf{u}_l \rangle}{\partial t} + A_t \left\{ \nabla \left[g\eta + \frac{1}{2} \left(\langle u_l \rangle - \frac{h_l}{g_+^-} \frac{\partial^2 \langle u_l \rangle}{\partial t^2} \right)^2 + \frac{p_i}{\rho_l} \right] + \frac{\partial^2 \eta}{\partial t^2} \nabla\eta \right\} -$$

$$-A_t \frac{\partial}{\partial t} \left\{ \left[\frac{h_l}{g_+^-} + \frac{(-1)^l}{g_+^-} \left(\eta + \frac{3h_l}{g_+^-} \frac{\partial^2 \eta}{\partial t^2} \right) \right] \frac{\partial^2 \langle u_l \rangle}{\partial t^2} \right\} = 0. \tag{10}$$

To reduce the system of four Eqs (1) and (10) to one equation for the perturbation of the interface, we apply the operator ∇ to Eqs. (10) in a scalar manner, multiply them by $(-1)^{l+1} h_l$, and substitute the mass conservation laws (1) into the first linear terms of Eqs. (10):

$$\left(1 - \frac{h_l}{g_+^-} A_t \frac{\partial^2}{\partial t^2} \right) \frac{\partial}{\partial t} \left[\frac{\partial \eta}{\partial t} + \nabla \cdot (\langle \mathbf{u}_l \rangle \eta) \right] + \frac{h_l}{g_+^-} A_t \frac{\partial}{\partial t} \nabla \cdot \left[\left(\eta + \frac{3h_l}{g_+^-} \frac{\partial^2 \eta}{\partial t^2} \right) \frac{\partial^2 \langle u_l \rangle}{\partial t^2} \right] -$$

$$-(-1)^l A_t \left[gh_l \nabla^2 \eta + \frac{h_l}{\rho_l} \nabla^2 p_i + h_l \nabla \cdot \left(\frac{\partial^2 \eta}{\partial t^2} \nabla\eta \right) + \frac{h_l}{2} \nabla^2 \left(\langle u_l \rangle - \frac{h_l}{g_+^-} \frac{\partial^2 \langle u_l \rangle}{\partial t^2} \right)^2 \right] + \tag{11}$$

$$+(-1)^l \left[\frac{\partial \langle \mathbf{u}_l \rangle}{\partial t} \cdot \nabla h_l + \frac{\alpha\beta h_l}{g_+^- h_1 h_2 \chi} \frac{\partial^2}{\partial t^2} \left(g\nabla\eta + \frac{\nabla p_i}{\rho_l} - \frac{h_l}{g_+^-} \frac{\partial^3 \langle u_l \rangle}{\partial t^3} \right) \cdot (\rho_1 h_2^2 \nabla h_1 + \rho_2 h_1^2 \nabla h_2) \right] = 0.$$

In this equation the averaged velocities of the fluids enter only the second-order infinitesimal terms. To eliminate $\langle \mathbf{u}_l \rangle$ from these terms, it is necessary to make an additional assumption.

We assume that in the reference system moving together with the wave the form of perturbation varies slowly. Then, with accuracy up to the first-order infinitesimal terms from Eqs. (1) we have equalities $h_l \nabla \cdot \langle \mathbf{u}_l \rangle = -(-1)^l \partial \eta/\partial t$ or $\langle \mathbf{u}_l \rangle = (-1)^l \mathbf{U}\eta/h_l$, where $\mathbf{U}$ is the characteristic velocity of the wave propagation. By means of these formulas we substitute $\langle \mathbf{u}_l \rangle$ into Eqs. (11). Hence, $\mathbf{U}$ will entire only into the scalar products $\mathbf{U} \cdot \nabla h_l$ and $\mathbf{U} \cdot \nabla\eta$. In the considering approximation the last one may be replaced by $-\partial \eta/\partial t$. As a consequence, we rewrite Eqs (11) in the form:

793

$$\frac{\partial^2 \eta}{\partial t^2} - \frac{h_l}{g_+^-} A_t \frac{\partial^4 \eta}{\partial t^4} - (-1)^l \frac{h_l}{\rho_l} A_t \nabla^2 p_i - (-1)^l h_l A_t \left[g \nabla^2 \eta + \nabla \left(\frac{\partial^2 \eta}{\partial t^2} \nabla \eta \right) \right] -$$

$$- \frac{(-1)^l}{h_l} \left(1 + \frac{1}{2} A_t \right) \frac{\partial^2 \eta^2}{\partial t^2} - \frac{(-1)^l}{g_+^-} A_t \frac{\partial^4 \eta^2}{\partial t^4} - \frac{7 h_l (-1)^l}{2(g_+^-)^2} A_t \frac{\partial^2}{\partial t^2} \left[\left(\frac{\partial^2 \eta}{\partial t^2} \right)^2 \right] + \qquad (12)$$

$$+ \frac{1}{h_l} \frac{\partial \eta}{\partial t} \mathbf{U} \cdot \nabla h_l + \frac{\alpha \beta h_l}{g_+^- h_1 h_2 \chi} \left[(-1)^l \left(g \frac{\partial^2 \nabla \zeta}{\partial t^2} + \frac{\nabla p_i}{\rho_l} \right) - \frac{\mathbf{U}}{g_+^-} \frac{\partial^5 \eta}{\partial t^5} \right] \cdot (\rho_1 h_2^2 \nabla h_1 + \rho_2 h_1^2 \nabla h_2) = 0.$$

Here the third-order infinitesimal terms are omitted. We obtained a system of two equations for two desired η and p_i. To reduce them to one equation, we multiply Eq. (12) by h_2/ρ_2 for $l = 1$ and by h_1/ρ_1 for $l = 2$, and add them. As a result, we find the following evolution equation

$$\delta A_t \nabla \cdot \left[\left(g + \frac{\partial^2 \eta}{\partial t^2} \right) \nabla \eta \right] = \frac{\partial^2 \zeta}{\partial t^2} - \frac{\beta}{g_+^-} A_t \frac{\partial^4 \eta}{\partial t^4} - \zeta \left(1 + \frac{1}{2} A_t \right) \frac{\partial^2 \zeta^2}{\partial t^2} - \frac{7\delta}{2(g_+^-)^2} A_t \frac{\partial^2}{\partial t^2} \left[\left(\frac{\partial^2 \eta}{\partial t^2} \right)^2 \right] +$$

$$+ \frac{\gamma \beta}{g_+^-} A_t \frac{\partial^4 \zeta^2}{\partial t^4} + \frac{1}{h_1 h_2 \chi} \left[\mathbf{U} \frac{\partial \eta}{\partial t} + \alpha \beta^2 \frac{\partial^2}{\partial t^2} \left(\nabla \eta - \frac{\mathbf{U}}{(g_+^-)^2} \frac{\partial^3 \eta}{\partial t^3} \right) \right] \cdot (\rho_1 h_2^2 \nabla h_1 + \rho_2 h_1^2 \nabla h_2). \qquad (13)$$

for perturbations of the interface of a two-layer fluid. In this equation all the coefficients are determined only by the physical (ρ_1, ρ_2, g) and geometrical (h_1, h_2) parameters of the system:

$$\zeta = \frac{\rho_2 h_1^2 - \rho_1 h_2^2}{h_1 h_2 \chi}, \qquad \gamma = \frac{\rho_2 h_1 - \rho_1 h_2}{h_1 h_2 (\rho_1 + \rho_2)}.$$

The expressions for quantities β, δ, χ and g_+^- are given after formula (5).

5. Plane Progressive Stable Solutions of the Model Equation

Now we shall assume that the layer depths are constant and the plane wave travel in the direction of increase of the x-coordinate. Then, Eq. (13) is noticeably simplified:

$$\delta A_t \frac{\partial}{\partial x} \left[\left(g + \frac{\partial^2 \eta}{\partial t^2} \right) \frac{\partial \eta}{\partial x} \right] = \frac{\partial^2 \eta}{\partial t^2} + \zeta \left(1 + \frac{1}{2} A_t \right) \frac{\partial^2 \eta^2}{\partial t^2} -$$

$$- \frac{\beta}{g_+^-} A_t \frac{\partial^4 \eta}{\partial t^4} - \frac{\gamma \beta}{g_+^-} A_t \frac{\partial^4 \eta^2}{\partial t^4} - \frac{7\delta}{2 g_+^-} A_t \frac{\partial^2}{\partial t^2} \left[\left(\frac{\partial^2 \eta}{\partial t^2} \right)^2 \right]. \qquad (14)$$

We emphasize that for linear perturbations, this evolution equation gives only the neutral-stable solutions. If a progressive stable wave occurs, one can use the equalities $\partial \eta / \partial x = d\eta / d\xi$ and $\partial \eta / \partial t = -U d\eta / d\xi$, where $\xi = x - Ut$. Then Eq. (14) can be integrated over the variable ξ. In this case, the integration constant should be set equal to zero in order to eliminate nonphysical solutions. Therefore, we obtain the nonlinear standard differential equation in the following form:

$$(U^2 - g\delta A_\xi) \frac{d\eta}{d\xi} - \beta \frac{U^4}{g_+^-} A_\xi \frac{d^3 \eta}{d\xi^3} - \zeta U^2 \left(1 + \frac{1}{2} A_\xi \right) \frac{d\eta^2}{d\xi} + \gamma \beta \frac{U^4}{g_+^-} A_\xi \frac{d^3 \eta^2}{d\xi^3} -$$

$$- \frac{\delta}{2} U^2 A_\xi \frac{d}{d\xi} \left[\left(\frac{d\eta}{d\xi} \right)^2 + \frac{7 U^4}{(g_+^-)^2} \left(\frac{d^2 \eta}{d\xi^2} \right)^2 \right] = 0, \qquad A_\xi = 1 - \alpha \beta \frac{U^2}{g_+^-} \frac{d^2}{d\xi^2}, \qquad (15)$$

One of the partial periodic solutions of Eq. (15) is a solution of the Stokes-wave type:

794

$$\eta = a \cos(k\xi) + \mu a^2 \cos(2k\xi).$$

Substituting this relation into Eq. (15) and grouping the terms to the first power of a we find that $U = c = \omega/k$. The terms that are quadratic in a lead to a Padé approximation of the coefficient μ:

$$\mu = \frac{3\zeta + \omega_*^2(8\gamma - \delta/\beta^2) + \omega_*^4 6\delta/\beta^2 + \alpha\omega_*^2[4\zeta + 32\gamma\omega_*^2 + 3\omega_*^2(9\omega_*^2 - 1/c_*^2)\delta/\beta^2]}{12\omega_*^2[1 + \alpha(5\omega_*^2 - 1/c_*^2)]}.$$

In the case where the fluids are very deep or the waves are moderately long (for $\alpha = 2/3$ and $h_1 = h_2$), this formula yields the results given by Thorpe (see also Turner).

We integrate Eq. (15) once more over the variable ξ. (To satisfy the zeroth boundary conditions at infinities it is assumed that the integration constant is zero.) Thus, we are led to the equation

$$(U^2 - g\delta A_\xi)\eta - \beta \frac{U^4}{g_+^-} A_\xi \frac{d^2\eta}{d\xi^2} - \zeta U^2 \left(1 + \frac{1}{2}A_\xi\right)\eta^2 +$$

$$+\gamma\beta \frac{U^4}{g_+^-} A_\xi \frac{d^2\eta^2}{d\xi^2} - \frac{\delta}{2} U^2 A_\xi \left[\left(\frac{d\eta}{d\xi}\right)^2 + \frac{7U^4}{(g_+^-)^2}\left(\frac{d^2\eta}{d\xi^2}\right)^2\right] = 0. \quad (16)$$

We consider the case of sufficiently long perturbations ($kh_m < \varepsilon^{1/2}$). Then, we can consider that $A_\xi = 1$ in the second and third terms of Eq. (16) and omit the last two terms. Here, all the corrections that are ignored are not smaller than the third-order infinitesimals. If $\alpha = 2/3$, we obtained a simple equation that takes into account a nonlinearity and dispersion of perturbations:

$$(U^2 - g\delta)\eta - \frac{3}{2}\zeta U^2\eta^2 - \beta\frac{U^2}{g_+^-}\left(U^2 - \frac{2}{3}g\delta\right)\frac{d^2\eta}{d\xi^2} = 0.$$

The solutions of this equation can be expressed in terms of the Jacobi elliptic functions, i.e., they are cnoidal waves. In particular, for solitary perturbations we seek the solution in the form

$$\eta = \eta_a/\cosh^2\xi_s, \qquad \xi_s = \xi/L, \qquad \eta_a^* = \zeta\eta_a. \quad (17)$$

$$U = \frac{c_0}{\sqrt{1 - \eta_a^*}}, \qquad L = \frac{2h_1h_2(\rho_1 + \rho_2)}{\chi}\sqrt{\frac{1 + 2\eta_a^*}{3\eta_a^*(1 - \eta_a^*)}}. \quad (18)$$

The dependencies (18) are close to the respective equalities for the solitary solutions of the Korteweg–de Vries equation (for internal waves in fluid with a density jump, see Djordjevic and Redecopp)

$$U_1 = c_0\left(1 + \frac{\eta_a^*}{2}\right) = U[1 + O(\varepsilon^2)], \qquad L_1 = 2\sqrt{\frac{h_1h_2(\rho_1h_1 + \rho_2h_2)}{3\chi\eta_a^*}}.$$

Note also that formulas (18) are in agreement with the characteristics of the solitary perturbations of the modified Boussiesq equation for two-layered liquid (Khabakhpashev)

$$U_2 = c_0\sqrt{1 + \eta_a^*} = U[1 + O(\varepsilon^2)], \qquad L_2 = L_1\sqrt{1 + \eta_a^*}. \quad (19)$$

Thus, the soliton velocities in the Koteweg–de Vries and Boussinesq equations nearly coincide with the value for the wave found (for the same amplitudes), and some discrepancies between their lengths are due to the values of the ratios between the densities and depths of the layers. The previous studies of stationary waves have also shown that the solitary perturbation is determined by velocity U and length L_1 (Long) or by equations (19) (Benjamin).

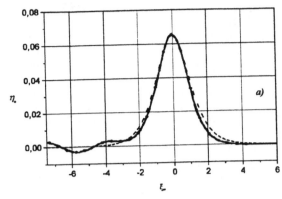

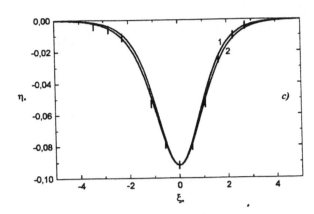

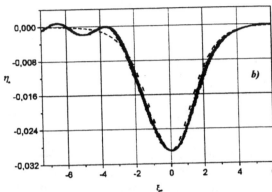

Figure 2. Profiles of the solitary wave ($\eta_* = \eta/H$, $\xi_* = \xi/H$): in Fig. a) and b) solid curves refer to experimental data and dotted lines refer to calculations by Eqs. (17) and (18); in Fig. c) curve 1 refers to calculation by Eqs. (17) and (19) and curve 2 refers to calculation by Eqs. (17) and (18), vertical sections refer to the experimental data by Gavrilov with account of the measurements error.

The experimental forms of the solitary perturbations [a) Maurer and others, b) Wessels and Hutter, c) Gavrilov] is compared with the analytical dependences in Fig. 2. One can see that all the results are in good agreement. The analogous picture is observed for experimental data by Segur and Hammack (see, Borisov and Khabakhpashev).

Some periodic and solitary solutions of the model differential equation were found numerically using the method proposed by Tsvelodub.

6. Acknowledgements

The work was supported by the Russian Foundation for Basic Research (Project No. 00-05-65441), the Russian Council of State Support for Leading Scientific Schools (Grant No. 00-15-96810), and the Siberian Branch of the Russian Academy of Science (Integration Program No. IP-01-00).

7. References

T. B. Benjamin, *J. Fluid Mech.*, **25**, No. 2, 241–270 (1966).

A. A. Borisov and G. A. Khabakhpashev, *Fluid Dynamics*, **29**, No. 1, 97–102 (1994).

V. D. Djordjevic and L. G. Redecopp, *J. Phys. Oceanogr.*, **8**, No. 6, 1016–1024 (1978).

N. V. Gavrilov, *J. Appl. Mech. Tech. Phys.*, **29**, No. 4, 503–506 (1988).

G. A. Khabakhpashev, *Fluid Dynamics*, **25**, No. 6, 909–913 (1990).

H. Lamb, *Hydrodynamics*, Cambridge University Press (1931).

R. R. Long, *Tellus*, **8**, No. 4, 460–471 (1956).

J. Maurer, K. Hutter, and S. Diebels, Eur. J. Mech. B/Fluids, **15**, No. 4, 445-470 (1996).

H. Segur and J.L. Hammack, J. Fluid Mech., **118**, 285-304 (1982).

S. A. Thorpe, *Philos. Trans. Roy. Soc. London, Ser. A*, **263**, 563–614 (1968).

O.Yu. Tsvelodub, Fluid Dynamics, **30**, No. 5, 782-786 (1995).

J. S. Turner, *Buoyancy Effects in Fluids*, Cambridge University Press (1973).

F. Wessels and K. Hutter. J. Phys. Oceanogr., **26**, No. 1, 5-20 (1996).

Shoaling solitary internal waves and the formation of waves with trapped cores.

Kevin G. Lamb

Applied Mathematics, University of Waterloo, Waterloo, Ontario, Canada, N2L 3G1
kglamb@math.uwaterloo.ca

1. Abstract

The shoaling behaviour of large oceanic solitary internal waves in two stratifications is considered via numerical simulation. For the first stratification, the density gradient increases exponentially towards the surface. The second is a modification of the first so as to include a thin surface mixed layer. This change in stratification has a profound effect on the properties of large solitary waves and behaviour of shoaling waves. For the exponential stratification, as a solitary wave propagates into shallower water it steepens at the back and ultimately breaks. A wave with a trapped, recirculatory core is formed which can propagate large distances, providing an efficient means for transporting fluid and trapped particles. The presence of an upper mixed layer significantly changes the behaviour of large solitary waves and waves with trapped cores are no longer formed as the waves shoal.

2. Introduction

Solitary-like waves are common occurences in the stratified coastal ocean where they are generated by tidal flows over topographic features. These waves propagate through water of variable depth and it is of interest to know what happens to them. Here we consider the fate of solitary waves propagating into shallower water. As waves shoal they get larger relative to the local water depth (barring dissipative effects), and can overturn, resulting in significantly enhanced local mixing. As is shown here, waves with recirculating cores can be formed, albeit only for special stratifications, not commonly observed, for which there is significant stratification near the surface.

3. Time-stepping model

The time stepping numerical model used is described in Lamb (1994). Rotation is not included for these simulations. The model equations are the inviscid, incompressible Euler equations with the Boussinesq approximation:

$$\vec{U}_t + \vec{U} \cdot \vec{\nabla}\vec{U} = -\vec{\nabla}p - \rho g \hat{k}, \tag{1a}$$

$$\rho_t + \vec{U} \cdot \vec{\nabla}\rho = 0, \tag{1b}$$

$$\vec{\nabla} \cdot \vec{U} = 0. \tag{1c}$$

Here $\vec{U}(x, z, t) = (u, w)$ is the velocity vector in the vertical plane with u the horizontal velocity in the x direction and w the vertical velocity in the upward z direction, $\vec{\nabla}$ is the gradient operator $(\frac{\partial}{\partial x}, \frac{\partial}{\partial z})$, t is time, ρ and p are the density and pressure respectively scaled by the reference density ρ_o, $g = 9.81$ m s^{-2} is the gravitational constant and $\hat{k}$ is the unit vector in the upward direction.

The time-stepping model is initialized with a single solitary water in water 100 m deep and the wave then propagates over a narrow bank edge into water 40 m deep. The computational domain extends from $x = -4000$ m to $x = 4000$ with the bottom boundary at

$$z = h(x) = 30 \left(1 + \tanh\left(\frac{x}{200}\right)\right). \tag{2}$$

A rigid lid is employed with the surface at $z = 100$ m. The model uses terrain following (sigma) coordinates. The horizontal grid size is $\delta x = 2$ m, and 150 evenly spaced grid points are used in the vertical.

4. Large Amplitude Solitary Waves

The time-stepping model is initialized with a single mode-one solitary wave propagating in a fluid at rest. The initial wave is computed using a separate numerical model. To compute a solitary wave a reference frame moving with the wave is used. In this reference frame the flow is steady and the equations of motion yield the nonlinear solitary wave eigenvalue problem

$$\nabla^2 \eta + \frac{N^2(z - \eta)}{c^2} \eta = 0, \tag{3}$$

where $\eta(x, z)$ is the vertical displacement of the streamline passing through (x, z) relative to its far-field height, the eigenvalue c is the wave propagation speed, and

$$N^2(z) = -g \frac{d\bar{\rho}}{dz}(z) \tag{4}$$

is the square of the buoyancy frequency outside the wave. Here $\bar{\rho}(z)$ is the undisturbed density field nondimensionalized by the reference density. Once η is known, the density field is given by

$$\rho(x, z) = \bar{\rho}(z - \eta(x, z)). \tag{5}$$

Equation (3) is the Dubreil-Jacotin-Long (DJL) equation written in terms of the streamline displacement rather than in terms of a velocity potential. The solution procedure used here (Turkington et al. 1991) uses a variational technique to minimize the kinetic energy for a specified value A of a functional $F(\eta)$ which can be interpreted as a potential energy. Other authors (Davis and Acrivos 1967), Tung et al. 1982, Brown and Christie 1998) have used different techniques to solve the DJL equation. Only mode-one solitary waves can be computed. Higher mode solitary-like waves are accompanied by trailing, lower mode, dispersive wave fields with the same phase speed. These imply a continual energy loss from the solitary-like wave and hence non-steadiness (Akylas and Grimshaw 1992).

The solitary waves with open streamlines which can be calculated are limited in amplitude in one of three ways. First, consider very small waves. For these waves, the wave propagation speed c is close to the linear long-wave propagation speed and, in a reference frame fixed with the fluid at infinity, and the maximum horizontal velocity in the direction of wave propagation, U_{max}, is much smaller than c. As the wave amplitude increases U_{max} increases more rapidly than the c does. For some stratifications a wave amplitude is reached at which $U_{max} = c$. This point is reached when a streamline, in a reference frame in which the wave is steady, first becomes vertical. This is one limiting amplitude for waves with open streamlines. It will be called the breaking limit. Larger waves, with closed streamlines in a recirculating wave core, can be computed. They are convectively unstable because for these waves $z - \eta$ goes above/below the fluid domain for waves of depression/elevation and the density in the centre of the core is lighter/denser than the surrounding fluid. This occurs because only for stratifications with nonzero density gradients at the upper/lower boundary has the breaking limit been reached. Attempts to compute waves with N^2 decreasing to zero rapidly at the upper/lower boundary have been unsuccessful due to failure of the numerical scheme to converge.

Wave amplitudes can also be limited by the conjugate flow limit. In this situation large waves become flat in the centre and simply become longer as the energy in the wave increases. Wave properties such as the maximum isopycnal displacement $\eta_{\max}$ (taken positive for waves of depression and elevation), c and $U_{\max}$ asymptotically approach constant limiting values as the waves flatten in the centre. This limiting behaviour is typical of stratifications with broad pycnoclines well removed from the upper or lower boundaries. The horizontally uniform flow in the centre of long flat waves is called a conjugate flow and can be found by solving the conjugate flow eigenvalue problem

$$\eta''(z) + \frac{N^2(z - \eta(z))}{c^2}\eta(z) = 0 \qquad (6)$$

along with an auxiliary condition

$$\int_0^H \eta'^3(z)\,dz = 0, \qquad (7)$$

(Lamb and Wan 1998). In addition, a conjugate flow solution must satisfy the condition that $\eta'(z) < 1$ in order that all streamlines extend to $\pm\infty$. Stratifications for which the amplitude of solitary waves of elevation/depression is limited by the breaking limit do not have conjugate flow solutions of elevation/depression. (For some stratifications both solitary waves of elevation and depression are possible. Then, for example, if the waves of depression are limited by the breaking limit and waves of elevation are limited by the conjugate flow limit, only conjugate flows of elevation exist)

The third way in which wave amplitudes can be limited is what will be called the stability limit. As solitary wave amplitudes increase the minimum Richardson number in the wave decreases. We have found that for some stratifications the interation procedure used to solve (3) fails to converge before either the breaking limit or the conjugate flow limit is reached. The minimum Richardson number is typically between 0.27 and 0.29 when this occurs. As is well know a minimum Richardson number of less than 0.25 is necessary for a parallel stratified flow to be unstable. While it is not sufficient condition, the lack of convergence for Richardson numbers close to 0.25 suggests that convergence of the numerical iteration procedure breaks down because waves are close to being unstable. The stability limit is reached for stratifications with thin pycnoclines centred away from the mid-depth.

The numerical procedure will converge to solutions with closed streamlines giving a convectively unstable wave with a recirculating core, however it does not appear to converge to solutions with a shear instability. This is attributed to the different energy sources for these two instabilities, being potential and kinetic energy respectively, and the fact that the solution technique is based on minimizing the kinetic energy for a specified potential energy. Note that the conjugate flow eigenvalue problem is not subject to the same instability limit as the solitary wave eigenvalue problem is. Thus, conjugate flows with arbitrarily low minimum Richardson numbers can be computed.

5. Results

Results for two stratifications are presented. The first stratification considered is

$$\bar{\rho}_1(z) = 1 + 0.01\frac{1 - e^{(z-H)/15}}{1 - e^{-H/15}}. \qquad (8)$$

The surface is at $z = H$ where H, taken to be 100 m, is the deep water depth. Because the strength of the stratification increases monotonically up to the surface it is physically not very realistic. In general one would expect to have an upper mixed layer. The second stratification considered is obtained from the first by modifying it to include an upper mixed layer. This modified density is given by

$$\bar{\rho}_{m1}(z) = 1 + 0.005\frac{1 - e^{(z-H)/15}}{1 - e^{-H/15}}\left(1 - \tanh\left(\frac{z - H + 3.0}{2}\right)\right)$$

$$+ 0.0005\left(1 - 0.02(z - H)\right)\left(1 + \tanh\left(\frac{z - H + 3.0}{2}\right)\right).$$

(9)

Both stratifications, henceforth referred to as the exponential and mixed-layer stratifications, are shown in figure 1 (only the stratification in the upper 40 m is shown). They have approximately the same total mass. Both densities have a value of 1.01 at $z = 0$ and the functions asymptotically approach slightly larger values as $z \to -\infty$. The upper mixed layer is thin by oceanographic standards but its presence has a large effect on large solitary waves and it significantly modifies their shoaling properties. Stratifications with various upper mixed layer thicknesses have been investigated. Results for an extreme case with a very thin upper mixed layer approximately 2 m thick are presented in order to illustrate the sensitivity of the results to the near surface stratification.

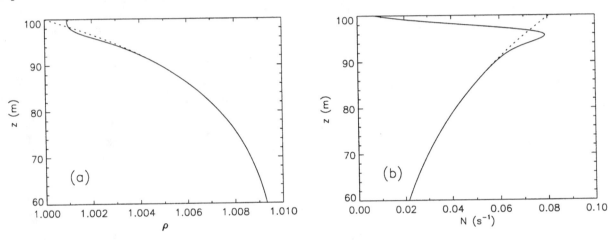

Figure 1.   (a) Density and (b) buoyancy frequency profiles in upper 40 m. (dotted — $\bar{\rho}_1$, solid — $\bar{\rho}_{m1}$).

Solitary mode-one waves are waves of depression for both stratifications. The properties of small solitary waves are similar for the two stratifications, however, the differences increase with amplitude. Some properties of very large waves are quite different for the two stratifications. This can be attributed to the fact that the volume of modified water in the wave increases with wave amplitude. For the exponential stratification, solitary waves are limited in amplitude by the breaking limit in water of all depths. For the mixed-layer stratification, wave amplitudes are limited by the stability limit in the deep water (100 m depth) and by the conjugate flow limit in the shallow water (40 m depth). This has a direct bearing on the shoaling characteristics for the waves.

In figure 2 the wave propagation speed and U_{max} are plotted as functions of the wave amplitude (maximum downward isopycnal displacement). In water of 100 m depth c and U_{max} are similar for both stratifications for amplitudes up to about 10 m, whereafter the propagation speeds remain similar but the maximum current is significantly smaller for the waves in the mixed-layer stratification. The breaking limit is reached at $\eta_{max} \approx 14.7$ m for the exponential stratification. Values for waves beyond the breaking limit are plotted as well, however these waves are convectively unstable and not physically relevant. The cutoff amplitude of these waves is arbitrary — it does not signify the maximum such wave which can be calculated with the solitary wave calculator. For waves in the mixed-layer stratification, the stability limit in water 100 m deep is reached at an amplitude of about 22 m. In water of 40 m depth, c and U_{max} are similar in both stratifications for amplitudes up to about 5 m after which the propagation speeds again remain similar but the rate of increase in U_{max} is greatly reduced for the mixed layer stratification. The breaking limit is reached at $\eta_{max} \approx 9$ m and the conjugate flow limit is reached at $\eta_{max} \approx 14$ m for the exponential and mixed layer stratifications respectively.

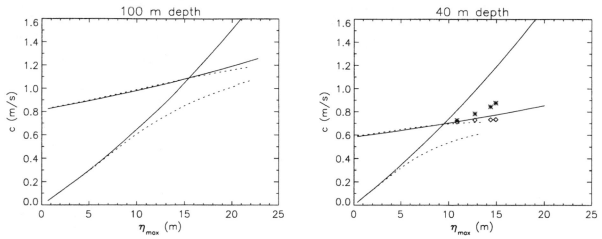

Figure 2.   Solitary wave propagation speeds c and maximum horizontal velocity U_{max} as a function of wave amplitude in water of 100 and 40 m depth (solid — c and U_{max} for density $\bar{\rho}_1$; dotted — c and U_{max} for density $\bar{\rho}_{m1}$). Symbols are average c (diamonds) and U_{max} (stars) for unsteady waves with recirculating cores in the time-stepping model. Values obtained by averaging over approximately 35 min.

For both stratifications, shoaling solitary waves steepen at the back of the wave and, if the waves are sufficiently large, overturn. In the case of the exponential stratification the forward plunging fluid reaches the front of the wave and a wave with a recirculating core (rotating counterclockwise) is formed. Figure 3 shows the resulting wave for an initial wave with an amplitude of 14.3 m. Waves with recirculating cores are formed for initial wave amplitudes as small as 7.6 m. These waves have the form of an unsteady core of trapped fluid, surrounded by an unsteady layer of lighter surface fluid (which passes over and beneath the fluid in the trapped core). Outside this thin layer the flow is relatively steady. In figure 2 the average propagation speed and average maximum horizontal velocity in waves with recirculating cores on top of the bank are plotted as a function of wave amplitude and compared with the properties of the convectively unstable waves computed with the solitary wave calculator. Results from four model runs, with initial deep water wave amplitudes of 8.7, 10.8, 13.2, and 14.3 m are shown. Larger initial waves form larger shoaled waves. The propagation speeds of waves in the time-stepping model are slightly less than those of the exact unstable solitary waves, while the maximum horizontal velocity is significantly smaller. Wave propagation speeds and maximum horizontal velocities increase with wave amplitude and are greater than the corresponding value for a solitary wave at the breaking limit.

The presence of a surface mixed-layer layer causes the shoaling wave to be much wider and the forward plunging fluid at the back of the wave only affects the back portion of the wave. A broad solitary wave, near the maximal wave amplitude, emerges leaving the remnants of the overturning behind. A wave with a recirculating core is not formed in this case. Figure 4 shows the resulting wave field for an initial wave amplitude of about 21.2 m, this being close to the deep water stability limit. Breaking at the rear of the shoaling wave occurs for initial wave amplitudes larger than about 14.0 m.

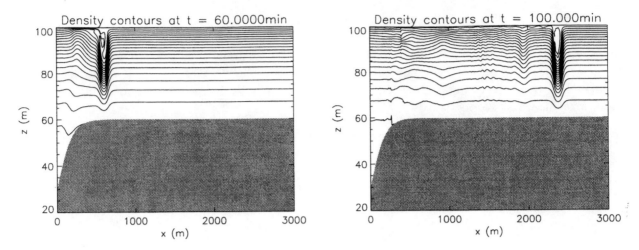

Figure 3. Breaking and formation of a solitary wave with a recirculating core. Initial wave amplitude 14.3 m. Exponential density $\bar{\rho}_1$.

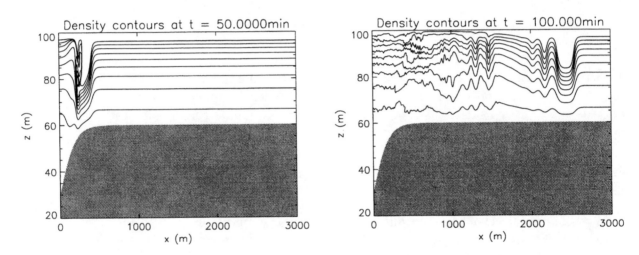

Figure 4. Shoaling wave for mixed layer density $\bar{\rho}_{m1}$. Initial wave amplitude 21.2 m.

6. References

Akylas, T. R., & Grimshaw, R. H. J. 1992. Solitary internal waves with oscillatory tails. *J. Fluid Mech.* **242**, 279–298.

Brown, D. J. & Christie, D. R. 1998 Fully nonlinear solitary waves in continuously stratified incompressible boussinesq fluids. *Phys. Fluids* **10**, 2569–2586.

Davis, R. E. & Acrivos, A. 1967 Solitary internal waves in deep water. *J. Fluid Mech.* **29**, 593–607.

Lamb, K. G. 1994 Numerical experiments of internal wave generation by strong tidal flow across a finite amplitude bank edge. *J. Geophy. Res.* **99**, 843–864.

Lamb, K. G. & Wan, B. 1998 Conjugate flows and flat solitary waves for a continuously stratified fluid. *Phys. Fluids* **10**, 2061–2079.

Sandstrom, H., and Elliott, J. A. 1984 Internal tide and solitons on the Scotian Shelf: A nutrient pump at work. *J. Geophys. Res.* **89**, 6415–6426.

Tung, K.-K., Chan, T. F. & Kubota, T. 1982 Large amplitude internal waves of permanent form. *Stud. Appl. Math.* **66**, 1–44.

Turkington, B., Eydeland, A. & Wang, S. 1991 A computational method for solitary internal waves in a continuously stratified fluid. *Stud. Appl. Math.* **85**, 93–127.

Flat Solitary Waves in a Two-Layer Fluid

J. L. Maltseva

Lavrentyev Institute of Hydrodynamics,
Novosibirsk, Russia, 630090
maltseva@hydro.nsc.ru

1. Introduction

Ovsyannikov (1985) classified possible types of stationary waves in a two-layer fluid under a rigid lid within the second approximation of the shallow water theory. Funakoshi (1985) classified these waves using the Korteweg–de Vries equation with quadratic and cubic nonlinearities.

Funakoshi&Oikawa (1986) and Turner&Vanden-Broeck (1988) studied numerically solitary waves in two-layer flows without velocity shift that become a bore as their amplitude and velocity tend to critical values. Mirie&Pennell (1989) analyzed this situation by semianalytical methods for a long–wave approximation of ninth–order accuracy in amplitude. Bore-like waves, whose existence in exact formulation was proved by Makarenko (1992) and Mielke (1995), was observed in laboratory conditions for a two-layer fluid and was described by Gavrilov (1994).

2. Statement of the Problem

Steady two-dimensional irrotational flow of an inviscid incompressible two-layer fluid in a gravity field is considered. It is assumed that at infinity the velocities of the layers are U_i, where $i = 1$ and 2 (subscript 1 refers to the lower layer and subscript 2 refers to the upper layer), the densities of layers are ρ_i, $\rho_2 < \rho_1$. This piecewise-constant flow with velocities U_i in long-wave limit is stable [8] only if

$$\frac{|U_1 - U_2|}{\sqrt{gH}} < \sqrt{\frac{\rho_1 - \rho_2}{\rho_2}} \left(1 - \frac{\rho_1 - \rho_2}{\rho_1} \frac{H_1}{H}\right)^{3/2}.$$

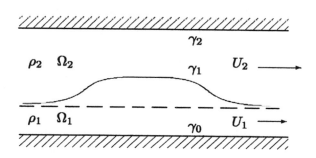

Fig. 1

The flow domain is a strip of width $H = H_1 + H_2$ divided by a contact discontinuity line γ_1 into two curvilinear strips Ω_i. The fluid is bounded by a flat bottom (γ_0: $y = 0$) and a flat rigid lid (γ_2: $y = H$) (see Fig. 1). In the plane of semi-lagrangian dimensionless variables (x, ψ), where ψ is the stream function, double strip $\Pi = \Pi_1 \cup \Pi_2$, $\Pi_1 = (-\infty, +\infty) \times (0, 1)$, $\Pi_2 = (-\infty, +\infty) \times (1, h)$, corresponds to the flow domain. Here $h = 1 + r$ is full dimensionless depth of the fluid, r is the ratio of the undisturbed depths of the layers.

We seek streamlines of the form $y = \psi + \varepsilon w(\varepsilon x, \psi)$, where ε is a long–wave parameter, which is defined below. In this variables the system of steady Euler equations and boundary conditions reduces to the following form:

$$\begin{cases} \varepsilon^2 w_{xx} + w_{\psi\psi} = f & 0 < \psi < 1, \quad 1 < \psi < h, \\ w = 0 & \psi = 0, \quad \psi = h, \\ [w] = 0, \quad [\mathrm{Fr}^2 w_\psi] + h^{-1}w = \varphi & \psi = 1, \\ w \to 0, \quad \nabla w \to 0 & |x| \to \infty, \end{cases} \tag{1}$$

where $f = \operatorname{div} \mathbf{Q}$, $\varphi = \left[\mathrm{Fr}^2 \mathbf{Q_2}(\nabla w)\right]$,

$$\mathbf{Q} = (\mathbf{Q_1}, \mathbf{Q_2}) = \left(\frac{\varepsilon^3 w_x w_\psi}{1 + \varepsilon w_\psi}, \frac{1}{2} \frac{\varepsilon^3 w_x^2 + 3\varepsilon w_\psi^2 + 2\varepsilon^2 w_\psi^3}{(1 + \varepsilon w_\psi)^2}\right).$$

Here brackets denote a jump of a corresponding quantity at the interface between the layers; $\mathrm{Fr}(\psi) = \mathrm{Fr}_i$ in Π_i, where

$$\mathrm{Fr}_i^2 = \frac{U_i^2}{gH} \frac{\rho_i}{\rho_1 - \rho_2}$$

are densimetric Froude numbers.

3. Parametrization of the Froude Numbers Plane

The problem (1) linearized over the piecewise-constant flow with specified Fr_i and r has solutions in the form

$$w(x, \psi) = A(\psi)\, e^{-i\mathfrak{X}x},$$

if $\mathfrak{x}$ is connected to the parameters of the main flow by the dispersion relation

$$\Delta(\mathfrak{x}) \equiv \mathrm{Fr}_1^2\, \mathfrak{x} \coth \mathfrak{x} + \mathrm{Fr}_2^2\, \mathfrak{x} \coth(r\mathfrak{x}) - h^{-1} = 0. \qquad (2)$$

Real roots of Eq. (2) exist only if

$$\mathrm{Fr}_1^2 + r^{-1}\mathrm{Fr}_2^2 \le h^{-1}. \qquad (3)$$

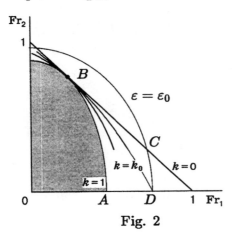

Fig. 2

This inequality defines a spectrum of linear waves. The shaded region in Fig. 2 corresponds to inequality (3). The boundary of the spectrum consists of bifurcation points for solutions of the problem. At these points branching of long stationary waves from the piecewise–constant flow occurs. In particular, it is shown [4, 8] that for

$$|\mathrm{Fr}_1| + |\mathrm{Fr}_2| = 1 \qquad (4)$$

there exists a one-parameter solution of the problem in the form of a bore. We shall consider the family of solutions for pairs of Froude numbers $(\mathrm{Fr}_1, \mathrm{Fr}_2)$ placed in the supercritical region (outside the ellipse) in the neighborhood of the point

$$(\overset{0}{F_1}, \overset{0}{F_2}) = (h^{-1}, rh^{-1}), \qquad (5)$$

which is common for square (4) and ellipse (3). At other points of the ellipse, solitary waves have weakly nonlinear KdV-asymptotics (whose amplitude is of second order with respect to long wave parameter), but in the neighborhood of point (5) this approximation is not uniform. Therefore Mirie&Pennel (1989) considered approximation up to ninth-order term using the symbolic manipulation software package REDUCE. We propose the construction of directly expansion in the neighborhood of this critical point. So, the broadening effect is already observed in the leading order term of the constructed solution. The wave amplitude near this point, in contrast to the classical KdV-asymptotics, is of the same order as the small parameter.

Let us introduce the parametrization $(\mathrm{Fr}_1, \mathrm{Fr}_2) \mapsto (\varepsilon, k)$ by the following rule. Let ε be the minimal positive root of the equation

$$\mathrm{Fr}_1^2 \varepsilon \cot \varepsilon + \mathrm{Fr}_2^2 \varepsilon \cot (r\varepsilon) - h^{-1} = 0. \tag{6}$$

For the points $(\mathrm{Fr}_1, \mathrm{Fr}_2)$ outside the ellipse (3) the dispersion function $\Delta(\ae)$ has only purely imaginary conjugate roots, and $\ae = \pm i\varepsilon$ are the roots that are the nearest to the real axis. The parameter ε is the decay exponent of the solution at infinity. Equation (6) is an analog of the Stokes relation for solitary surface waves $\mathrm{Fr}^2 = \tan \varepsilon / \varepsilon$. The family of level curves of the second parameter k consists of the ellipses

$$\left(k\mathrm{Fr}_1 + (1-k)h^{-1}\right)^2 + r^{-1}\left(k\mathrm{Fr}_2 + r(1-k)h^{-1}\right)^2 - h^{-1} = 0, \tag{7}$$

each of which is tangent to the square (4) at the point (5). As k varies from 0 to 1, these ellipses fill out the curvilinear sectors between the straight line $\mathrm{Fr}_1 + \mathrm{Fr}_2 = 1$ and the ellipse (3) (see Fig. 1). The parametrization (6), (7) has a singularity at the point (5), which is a consequence of a specific character of the solution behavior in the neighborhood of this point. The power series in ε for the Froude numbers

$$\mathrm{Fr}_i = \sum_{n=0}^{\infty} \varepsilon^n \overset{n}{F_i}$$

have the coefficients $\overset{n}{F_i}$ containing the factor $(1-k)^{-n/2}$.

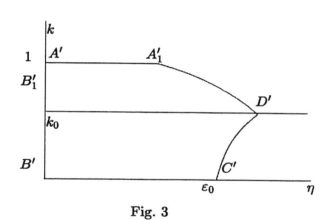

Fig. 3

From this fact one can suggest that there is an expansion on new parameter $\eta = \varepsilon/\sqrt{1-k}$ not on ε. The image of domain $ABCD$ marked in Fig. 2 in the (η, k)-plane is shown in Fig. 3. The distance $A'A_1'$ is equal to $\sqrt{6 - 6h^{-1/2}}$. The interval $A'A_1'$ corresponds to the part of spectrum boundary AB, the interval $B'B_1'$ corresponds to the critical point B. One can show that Froude numbers are analytic on η and Froude numbers $\mathrm{Fr}_i = \mathrm{Fr}_i(\eta, k)$ expansion is converge, so the singularity disappears. As η is small the Froude numbers are

$$\mathrm{Fr}_1 = h^{-1} + \eta\vartheta + O(\eta^2), \qquad \mathrm{Fr}_2 = rh^{-1} - \eta\vartheta + O(\eta^2),$$

where $\vartheta = h^{-1}\sqrt{(r^3 + r^2 + r)/3}$. The smallness of η leads to the smallness of ε.

4. Perturbation Series

We use the following power series for w in ε

$$w = \sum_{n=0}^{\infty} \varepsilon^n w_n.$$

Then (1) leads to the set of boundary problems for w_n.

The two first terms of this approximation for $n = 1$ and $n = 2$ are

$$w_0(x, \psi) = C_0(x)W(\psi), \qquad w_1(x, \psi) = C_1(x)W(\psi),$$

where $W(\psi)$ is piecewise-linear function, $W(0) = W(h) = 0, W(1) = 1$ and the functions $C_0(x)$ and $C_1(x)$ remain undetermined and are obtained from the compatibility conditions for equations of higher–order approximations. So, the equation for the function $C_0(x)$ is obtained from the compatibility condition of the boundary problem for $n = 2$:

$$C_0'' = P_3(C_0), \qquad P_3(C_0) = 2C_0^3 - \frac{3}{\sqrt{1-k}}C_0^2 + C_0. \tag{8}$$

Hence,

$$C_0 = a\,\frac{1 - \tanh^2(x/2)}{a^2 - \tanh^2(x/2)},$$

where $a + 1/a = \pm 2/\sqrt{1-k}$. The plus sign corresponds to a wave of elevation, and the minus sign corresponds to a wave of depression.

The functions C_n for higher-order approximations are obtained from the recurrence formula

$$C_n'' - P_3'(C_0)C_n = f_n(C_0, \dots, C_{n-1}). \tag{9}$$

For $n = 1$, we have $f_1 = k_4 C_0^4 + k_3 C_0^3 + k_2 C_0^2$ with the coefficients k_i which are rational functions of k and r. Hence, we obtain the following representation for C_1:

$$C_1 = \frac{\alpha_1 \cosh x + \alpha_2 \sinh x \cdot (\ln\left[(a - \tanh(x/2))/(a + \tanh(x/2))\right] + \alpha_3}{(a^2 - 1)\alpha_4 (a^2 + 1 + (a^2 - 1)\cosh x)^2},$$

where α_i $(i = 1, 2, 3, 4)$ are rational functions of k and r.

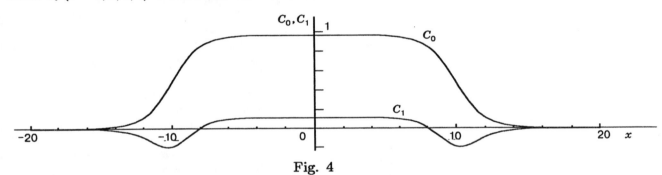

Fig. 4

Plots of the functions C_0 and C_1 for $r = 1.2$ and $a = 1.0001$ are shown in Fig. 4.

5. Limiting Forms of the Waves

We consider the flow regimes corresponding to the limiting values of the parameter k. In the approximation obtained, the interface between the layers is given by the formula

$$y = 1 + \varepsilon C_0(x) + \varepsilon^2 C_1(x) + O(\varepsilon^3).$$

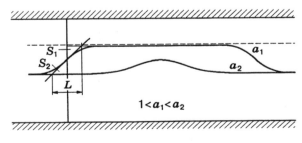

Fig. 5

For fixed a or k, the wave amplitude is of the same order of magnitude as ε. In the limit $a \to 1$, as the point $(\mathrm{Fr}_1, \mathrm{Fr}_2)$ in the plane of Froude numbers approaches the straight line $\mathrm{Fr}_1 + \mathrm{Fr}_2 = 1$, the amplitude remains bounded. The crest of the solitary wave flattens, and its front near the point $x = a\ln[(a - 1)/(a + 1)]$ transforms into a bore (see Fig. 5). Here a_1 and a_2 are different values of the parameter a.

In the limit $a^{-1} \sim \varepsilon \to 0$, we obtain a Korteweg — de Vries solitary wave

$$y = 1 + \varepsilon^2 \mathcal{A}(r) \cosh^{-2}(\varepsilon x) + o(\varepsilon^2).$$

It is possible to relate the parameters (ε, k) to the geometric parameters of the flow, e.g., to the amplitude A. As an additional parameter, it is convenient to use the width L of the wave front, which is defined as the difference of the abscissas of the points at which the inflectional tangent to the wave intersects the lines $y = 0$ and $y = 1/a$ (see Fig. 5), $0 < L \le 4$. We note that if we draw a vertical line through the point of tangency, the areas of the curvilinear triangles S_1 and S_2 bounded by the plot of the function C_0 and by its asymptotes are equal. As a first approximation, we have

$$a = 2 - L/4, \qquad \varepsilon = A(2 - L/4)\sqrt{3(r+1)/(r^4 + r)}.$$

In terms of (A, L), the Froude numbers are given by

$$\mathrm{Fr}_1 = \frac{1}{r+1} + \frac{1}{32}\frac{80 - 16L + L^2}{r+1} A + O(A^3),$$

$$\mathrm{Fr}_2 = \frac{r}{r+1} - \frac{1}{32}\frac{80 - 16L + L^2}{r+1} A + O(A^3).$$

For parameter value $L = 4$ which corresponds to the bore, we get

$$\mathrm{Fr}_1 = \frac{1}{r+1} + \frac{1}{r+1} A + O(A^3), \quad \mathrm{Fr}_2 = \frac{r}{r+1} - \frac{1}{r+1} A + O(A^3).$$

The effective length of the solitary wave that represents the distance between the points of inflection at the edges of the wave is given (in these variables) by

$$l = \frac{8 - L}{2} \ln \frac{12 - L}{4 - L}.$$

6. Summary

An asymptotic solution to the problem of internal waves in a two-layer fluid under a rigid lid near the critical point of Froude numbers was constructed. The approximation obtained was used to prove the existence of an exact solution [5], which substantiates the technique employed herein. The family of internal solitary waves considered here is of interest because for a fixed amplitude there are no restrictions on the effective wavelength. The broadening effect observed numerically as, for ex. by Turner&Vanden-Broeck (1988), is already described with high accuracy by the leading order term.

A uniform asymptotic expansion is constructed for internal solitary waves with flat crests (of the plateau type) that degenerate into a bore in the limit. It is shown that in this case, in contrast to the Korteweg — de Vries wave, the wave amplitude is of the same order as the decay exponent.

The author is grateful to Prof. N. I. Makarenko for his interest in this work and for useful discussions.

The work was supported by Russian Foundation for Basic Research (N 00-01-00850, 00-01-00911) and Council "Leading Scientific Schools" (grant N 00-15-96163).

References

[1] *M. Funakoshi*, "Long internal waves in a two-layer fluid," *J. Phys. Soc. Jpn.*, **54**, No. 7, 2470–2476 (1985).

[2] *M. Funakoshi and M. Oikawa*, "Long internal waves of large amplitude in a two-layer fluid," *J. Phys. Soc. Jpn.*, **55**, No. 1, 128–144 (1986).

[3] *N. V. Gavrilov*, "Internal solitary waves and smooth bores which are stationary in a laboratory coordinate" *Applied Mechanics and Theoretical Physics*, **35**, No. 1, 29–33 (1994).

[4] *N. I. Makarenko*, "Smooth bore in a two-layer fluid," *Int. Ser. Numer. Math.*, **106**, 195–204 (1992).

[5] *J. L. Maltseva*, "On asymptotic properties of internal waves in a two-layer fluid" *Computational Technoligies* [in Russian], **5**, No. 1, 85–92 (2000).

[6] *A. Mielke*, "Homoclinic and heteroclinic solutions in two-phase flow" Adv. Series in Nonlinear Dynamics, 1995, v. 7. Proc. IUTAM/ISIMM Symposium on Structure and Dynamics of Nonlinear Waves in Fluids, World Scientific, p. 353–362.

[7] *R. M. Mirie and S. A. Pennell*, "Internal solitary waves in a two-fluid system," *Phys. Fluids A*, **1**, No. 6, 986–991 (1989).

[8] *L. V. Ovsyannikov, N. I. Makarenko, V. I. Nalimov, et al.*, Nonlinear Problems of the Theory of Surface and Internal Waves [in Russian], Nauka, Novosibirsk (1985).

[9] *R. E. L. Turner and J.-M. Vanden-Broeck*, "Broadening of interfacial solitary waves," *Phys. Fluids*, **31**, No. 9, 2486–2490 (1988).

Second Mode Internal Solitary Waves I – Integral Properties

Nathan Philip Schmidt[1], Robert Hays Spigel[2]

[1]Golder Associates Ltd., Calgary, Alberta, Canada T2P 3T1
[2]National Institute for Water and Atmospheric Research, Christchurch, New Zealand
nschmidt@golder.com, b.spigel@niwa.cri.nz

1. Abstract

The external circulation characteristics of large amplitude second mode internal solitary waves, including relationships between geometry and celerity, were examined using experimental and theoretical methods. Previous studies have based theoretical derivations on the assumption of small dimensionless wave amplitude ($a/h < 1$) and attempted to apply the results to waves of large amplitude. Theoretical considerations for this study assume a large amplitude wave ($a/h \gg 1$).

Second mode internal solitary waves were generated in the laboratory using exchange flow, forced inflow and gravity collapse methods. The gravity collapse method was found to be the most effective for rapid and repeatable wave generation. Particle seeding and laser sheet illumination were used with video and streakline photography to visualize and record wave motion. Waves as large as $a/h = 11.6$ were generated and measured. It was found that wave geometry was described well by existing relationships over the entire range of amplitudes, but that existing equations describing wave celerity were accurate only up to $a/h \cong 3$. Prior work based on assumptions of small amplitude indicated that dimensionless wave celerity, c/c_0, was proportional to a/h. This study, based on the Bernoulli equation and a potential flow solution, predicts a dimensionless wave celerity proportional to $(a/h)^{1/2}$. The resulting theoretical relationship provides a good fit to experimental data for very large amplitude waves and this good fit extends down to waves as small as $a/h = 1$.

Measurements of wave dissipation confirmed that wave decay rates are linear and vary with densimetric factor. The present study made use of calculated wave energies to further examine dissipation rates and it was found that wall shear and fluid drag are the primary mechanisms responsible for wave decay.

2. Introduction

Large amplitude second mode internal solitary waves are gravity waves that travel along interfaces in density-stratified fluids. They carry fluid within the wave, and thus transport both energy and mass. Second mode waves were first described by Benjamin (1967) and Davis and Acrivos (1967). They are able to propagate in deep water because their amplitude scales on the thickness of the density interface rather than on the total depth of fluid. This study examined the integral properties of the wave, including wave geometry, celerity and decay.

3. Background

The stratified ambient is characterized by its upper and lower layer densities, ρ_1 and ρ_3, interfacial half-thickness, h, half-depth, H, and densimetric factor, ω. Wave geometry is defined by amplitude, a, and wavelength, λ. Wavelength and amplitude are rendered dimensionless by dividing by the interfacial half-thickness. Stratified ambient and wave geometry quantities are illustrated in Figure 1. Wave celerity, c, is rendered dimensionless by dividing by the celerity of an infinitesimal first mode wave, c_0. This is a function of the densimetric factor and interfacial half-thickness, and for deep ambients ($H/h > 40$) is calculated as shown in Figure 1.

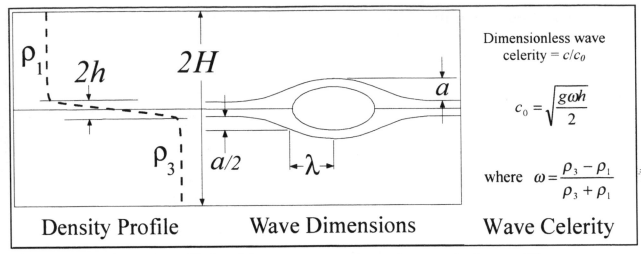

Figure 1 – Definition of stratified ambient, wave geometry and wave celerity quantities

The distinction between waves of large and small amplitude was addressed in Davis and Acrivos (1967). Large amplitude waves were identified by 'closed streamline' regions in which fluid was carried along at the same celerity as the wave, while small amplitude waves propagated faster than any individual fluid component. These observations were confirmed by Tung, Chan and Kubota (1982) and Stamp and Jacka (1995), and both studies noted that approximate analytic solutions based on weakly non-linear theory were not valid in this large amplitude region. The numerical model of Tung, Chan and Kubota (1982) predicted that as the wave amplitude approached the interfacial half-thickness, the wavelength would begin to increase with amplitude. The most comprehensive experimental observations of second mode waves, examining waves as large as $a/h = 3.1$, was presented by Stamp and Jacka (1995). That study recognized a linear relationship between wavelength and amplitude for large amplitude waves.

Several previous studies (Benjamin 1967; Davis and Acrivos 1967; Tung, Chan and Kubota 1982; Stamp and Jacka 1995) indicated that dimensionless wave celerity is related to dimensionless amplitude and presented the relationships that are shown on Figure 5. The experimental data of Davis and Acrivos (1967), Hurdis and Pao (1975) and Stamp and Jacka (1995) all show good agreement with the relationships presented by Tung, Chan and Kubota (1982) and Stamp and Jacka (1995). However, all of the studies noted that the theoretical relationships were not necessarily valid for large amplitude waves.

Stamp and Jacka (1995) also observed that wave amplitude decayed linearly with distance and that the decay rate was larger for waves in ambients with smaller densimetric values.

4. Experiments

Figure 2 illustrates the experimental setup for the present study. Experiments were undertaken in a 600 mm deep x 250 mm wide x 5200 mm long glass-walled flume. A 6 watt scanning beam laser system was used to generate a light sheet to illuminate the flow. The light sheet was directed vertically downwards through the tank, using a 45° mirror, to avoid refraction by the density interface.

The stratified ambient, shown on the left in Figure 2, was set up using layers of saline (ρ_3) and fresh (ρ_1) water, and density profiles were measured using a profiling conductivity probe. Waves were generated by pulling a gate to release a volume of intermediate density fluid ($\rho_2 = (\rho_1 + \rho_3)/2$). The gravity-driven collapse of this fluid generated a second mode wave in a very short distance. A moving frame of reference was established by mounting photographic and video cameras on a motorized trolley. The wave was then tracked as it propagated. The 45° mirror was mounted on a second trolley, slaved to the first, so that the illumination also tracked the wave.

All fluids used in the experiments were seeded with neutrally buoyant particles to enable flow visualization. Images of the flow were recorded using still photographs, time-exposure photographs, and video. The experimental method is described in detail elsewhere (Schmidt 1998).

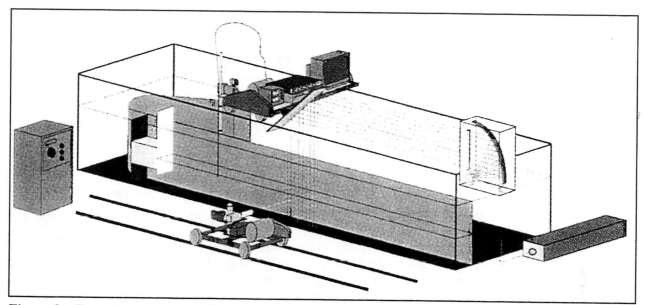

Figure 2 – Experimental Setup Showing Flume Insert and Measuring Equipment

5. Wave Geometry

Streakline images, acquired from videotape using a frame grabber, were used to measure wavelengths and amplitudes. The results of the present study, as well as those of Stamp and Jacka (1995), are presented in Figure 3.

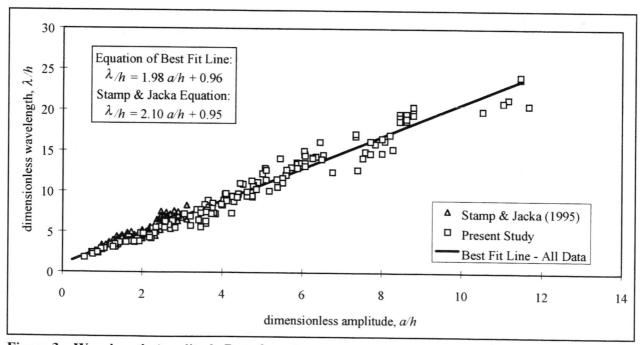

Equation of Best Fit Line:
$\lambda/h = 1.98\ a/h + 0.96$
Stamp & Jacka Equation:
$\lambda/h = 2.10\ a/h + 0.95$

△ Stamp & Jacka (1995)
□ Present Study
— Best Fit Line - All Data

Figure 3 – Wavelength-Amplitude Data from Present and Past Studies

The experimental results indicate that a linear relationship between wave amplitude and wavelength exists for large amplitude waves up to $a/h \cong 12$. This agrees with the conclusion of Stamp and Jacka (1995) that all second mode waves of $a/h > 1$ are similar in shape and differ only by a scaling factor. A regression line fit to the entire body of data returns an equation which is essentially identical to the one presented in that study. The present study examined deep water waves with densimetric factors ranging from $\omega = 0.0028$ to 0.0176. Waves with amplitudes up to $a/h = 11.6$ were measured, extending the body of data from Stamp & Jacka (1995) which observed a maximum value of $a/h = 3.1$.

6. Wave Celerity

Wave celerities were calculated using elapsed times and displacements acquired from the video record of the experiments. A quadratic regression equation was then fit to the position-time (x-t) data. The use of a quadratic equation was arbitrary and based on observations that an excellent fit was provided over the entire range of experiments. This choice is also consistent with subsequent experimental observations and derived relationships that show celerity to vary linearly with time. Once an equation was ascertained, it was differentiated to determine the wave celerity as a function of time.

Early theoretical derivations of propagation celerity have involved weakly nonlinear solutions (Benjamin 1967; Davis and Acrivos 1967) of the governing equations and involve the assumption of small amplitudes and long wavelengths. The fully nonlinear numerical solution of Tung, Chan and Kubota (1982) is also noted as being limited to amplitudes that are "not too large" and wavelengths that are "not too short". All studies recognized that large amplitude waves violate key assumptions of the derivations.

In this study the theoretical derivation proceeded from the assumption of a large amplitude wave. The wave was approximated by a stationary ellipse in a two-dimensional flow, and the solution was based on two methods of calculating the flow velocity at a point on the surface of the ellipse. The first method involved applying the Bernoulli equation along the ellipse's boundary, as illustrated in Figure 4(a), while the second made use of a potential flow solution, as shown in Figure 4(b). By equating the two solutions, it was possible to solve for the magnitude of a uniform flow far upstream of the stationary ellipse, which is equivalent to the velocity of the ellipse in a still fluid. Both solutions involve assumptions of two-dimensional, irrotational, inviscid and incompressible flow, with sharp density interfaces.

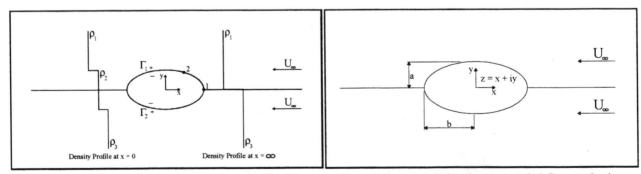

Figure 4 – Problem formulations for (a) the Bernoulli equation; and (b) the potential flow solution

The required derivations are laborious and are detailed elsewhere (Schmidt 1998). However, the Bernoulli equation and potential flow solutions for flow velocity at any point on the ellipse can be equated and rearranged to produce Equation 1, where the coefficient of the dimensionless amplitude varies depending on the point on the surface of the ellipse where the solution is calculated

$$\frac{c}{c_0} = \frac{2\sqrt{\varepsilon}}{\gamma}\sqrt{\frac{a}{h}} = \frac{4}{3}\sqrt{\frac{a}{h}} \tag{1}$$

It has been shown (Schmidt 1998) that the dimensionless amplitude coefficient has a value of approximately 4/3 at all points except those very close to the nose of the ellipse. If this value is adopted, the resulting relationship provides a good fit to the experimental data for large amplitude waves. It also appears to provide a good agreement with both the experimental data and the relation of Stamp and Jacka (1995) over the lower range of amplitudes, down to a value of approximately $a/h = 1$. This is despite the assumption of a small ($a \gg h$) density interface in the analysis.

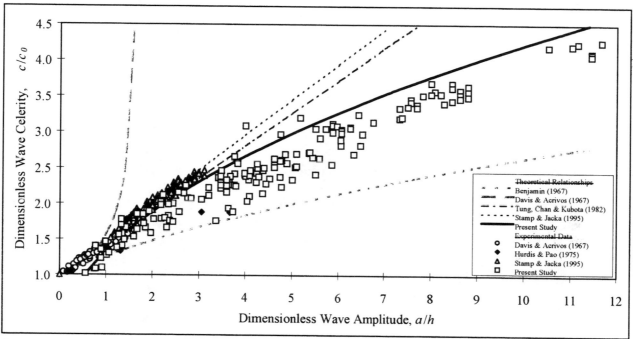

Figure 5 – Amplitude-Celerity Data from Present and Past Studies

The fact that most data points fall on or below the theoretical curve may indicate that the wave celerity is slightly overestimated by the theoretical relationship of Equation 1. In examining this, it is difficult to identify any single cause. Although waves examined were classed as deep-water ($H/h > 40$), the large amplitude waves (a/h up to 11.6) examined may have been influenced by the finite depth of the fluid. In fact, values of H/a fall as low as 7 in some cases, and this explains the tendency of data points to fall below the theoretical curve (i.e., travel slower than predicted). The data presented here are from experimental runs with densimetric factors ranging from $\omega = 0.0028$ to 0.0176.

7. Wave Decay

Wave decay was examined by defining and analyzing the decay of wave energy rather than wave amplitude as was done by Stamp and Jacka (1995). The energy decay rates for each experiment were calculated by three methods: differentiation of curves fit to experimental energy decay data; direct calculation of decay rates based on the differentiated energy equation; and an independent estimate of the retarding force on the wave using a momentum balance that accounted for an accelerating, deformable control volume with a net outward flux. Good agreement between all methods was observed.

Four potential mechanisms for wave decay, as identified by Stamp and Jacka (1995), were then examined. Wall shear was estimated based on the Blasius solution for shear on a flat plate in a laminar boundary layer, and was found to be significant. Fluid drag and turbulent mixing were combined as a single mechanism and quantified using a drag force equation. This drag force was identified as significant, and it was found that the drag coefficient varies with densimetric factor. A scaling analysis indicated that wave radiation was not responsible for a significant portion of wave decay.

8. Conclusions

Large amplitude waves, which exist for amplitudes above $a/h = 1.2$, contain what has been described as a 'closed streamline' region in which fluid is carried along with the wave at its propagation celerity. Existing numerical models, as well as experimental observations, show that when waves become large, the wavelength necessarily increases to allow the expansion of the interior region of the wave. The experiments of Stamp and Jacka (1995) presented a linear relationship between amplitude and wavelength for large amplitude waves. The applicability of this linear relationship has been extended from $a/h = 3.1$ to 11.6.

Previous analytic and numerical models have expressed wave celerity (c/c_0) as a function of amplitude (a/h). The weakly nonlinear analyses of Benjamin (1967) and Davis and Acrivos (1967) fit the experimental data well for small amplitude waves, but rapidly diverge for larger amplitudes. The relationships presented by Tung, Chan and Kubota (1982) and Stamp and Jacka (1995) match the data well for amplitudes up to $a/h \cong 3$. The present study examined waves of amplitudes up to $a/h \cong 12$, and provided the opportunity to examine the validity of the latter relationships for very large amplitude waves, and a significant divergence from the experimental data was observed for amplitudes above $a/h \cong 3$.

A new solution for wave celerity, based on energy methods and the assumption of two-dimensional, irrotational, inviscid and incompressible flow, with a sharp density interface, produced a solution that is applicable to large amplitude waves, and provides a good fit to experimental data.

Wave decay was examined using energy and momentum considerations, and it was found that wall shear and fluid drag (including turbulent mixing) are the two significant contributors to wave decay. Wave radiation was found to be insignificant.

9. Acknowledgements

The authors gratefully acknowledge the New Zealand Vice Chancellor's Committee and the University of Canterbury for providing financial support for this study. Bruce Hunt, Ian Wood and David Wilkinson are thanked for their advice on theory and experimental methods, as are Ian Sheppard and Alan Poynter for their efforts in the laboratory.

10. References

Benjamin, T.B., 1967. Internal Waves of Permanent Form in Fluids of Great Depth. Journal of Fluid Mechanics, vol 29, pp 559-592.

Davis, R.E. and A. Acrivos, 1967. Solitary Internal Waves in Deep Water. Journal of Fluid Mechanics, vol 29, pp 593-607.

Hurdis, D.A. and H.-P. Pao, 1975. Experimental Observation of Internal Solitary Waves in a Stratified Fluid. Physics of Fluids, vol 18, pp 385-386.

Schmidt, N.P., 1998. Generation, Propagation and Dissipation of Second Mode Internal Solitary Waves. Ph.D. Thesis, The University of Canterbury, 406 p.

Stamp, A.P. and M. Jacka, 1995. Deep-Water Internal Solitary Waves. Journal of Fluid Mechanics, vol 305, pp 347-371.

Tung, K.K., T.F. Chan and T. Kubota, 1982. Large Amplitude Internal Waves of Permanent Form. Studies in Applied Mathematics, vol 66, pp 1-44.

Second Mode Internal Solitary Waves II – Internal Circulation

Nathan Philip Schmidt[1], Robert Hays Spigel[2]

[1]Golder Associates Ltd., Calgary, Alberta, Canada T2P 3T1
[2]National Institute for Water and Atmospheric Research, Christchurch, New Zealand
nschmidt@golder.com, b.spigel@niwa.cri.nz

1. Abstract

The internal circulation characteristics of large amplitude second mode internal solitary waves, including internal circulation, fluid entrainment and mass transport, were examined experimentally. Second mode internal solitary waves were generated in the laboratory using a gravity collapse method and were tracked with cameras mounted on a moving trolley to provide a lagrangian frame of reference. Particle seeding and laser sheet illumination were used with video and streakline photography to visualize and record wave motion. Laser Induced Fluorescence (LIF) techniques were also used to observe mixing, entrainment and mass transport characteristics of the wave.

Existing numerical models of second mode internal solitary waves are based on the assumption of small dimensionless amplitude ($a/h < 1$) but the models have been applied to large amplitude waves to predict internal circulation. The resulting circulation pattern resembles two flattened, counter-rotating rotors, symmetrical about the horizontal centreline of the wave, with flow forwards along the centreline. Streakline and dye circulation data from the present study indicate that this is not the case, and that for large amplitude waves, the interior structure is composed of an assemblage of smaller, more circular vortices with flow directed backwards along the centreline of the wave.

Early studies of second mode waves recognized the decay of second mode waves but made no mention of fluid entrainment. More recent studies have made qualitative observations but failed to identify the mechanism by which entrainment occurs. The present study used dye visualization to examine and identify the entrainment mechanism as a non-symmetric Holmboe instability. LIF techniques were also used to examine rates of dye flushing from the wave and to quantify the wave's mass transport capacity.

2. Introduction

Existing numerical models of large amplitude second mode waves describe a mass of fluid with closed streamlines, yet several experimental studies describe observations of fluid entrainment and expulsion. The latter observations point to significant cross-streamline movement of fluid and a complex circulation pattern within the wave. In examining the internal motion of the wave, there are several issues which must be addressed. The first is the pattern of circulation within the wave and the comparison of experimental observations to established theoretical solutions. The second is the question of entrainment of external fluid into the wave and the mechanism by which it is achieved, and the third is an examination of the capacity of the wave for mass transport.

3. Background

Relevant wave parameters include amplitude, a, and celerity, c. The stratified ambient is characterized by its upper and lower layer densities, ρ_1 and ρ_3, interfacial half-thickness, h, densimetric factor, ω, and infinitesimal first mode wave celerity, c_0. These quantities were defined in the accompanying paper.

Figure 1(a) shows the results of wave modeling by Tung, Chan and Kubota (1982), which are in agreement with those presented by Davis and Acrivos (1967). The wave is composed of two counter-rotating cells located above and below its centreline. Flow along the centreline within the closed streamline region is directed forwards, towards a stagnation point at the nose of the wave. It would seem sensible that rearward shear exerted on the wave by the external flow would result in rearward flow in the outer portions of the wave, and that continuity would require that flow along the wave centreline proceed forwards towards the stagnation point.

Observations by Maxworthy (1980) and Stamp and Jacka (1995) indicate that this description of the internal structure of the wave is not wholly accurate. Waves in the former study were observed to continuously eject fluid from the rear of the wave, pointing to flow across the streamlines in this region. The observed gradual loss of wave amplitude was attributed to this loss of fluid, but no mention was made of any entrainment of fluid into the wave. The latter study observed that along the open streamlines of Figure 1(a), the "flow [was] laminar and the fluid stratified" but within closed streamlines "the flow was turbulent and the fluid well mixed". Upper and lower recirculating cells, as described by the numerical solutions, were also recognized. It was noted that there was no defined boundary between the cells and fluid was continuously entrained into and ejected from this area, with entrainment appearing to be distributed evenly along the boundary of these cells. Turbulent mixing was indicated by the rapid spread of dye throughout the region, and it was also observed that turbulent shear instabilities in the lee of the wave occasionally resulted in the entrainment of fluid in that region.

4. Experiments

Experiments were performed using the apparatus described in the accompanying paper. Two methods were used for flow visualization. A Laser Induced Fluorescence technique (LIF) was used to measure concentrations of Rhodamine 6G tracer and to observe entrainment of fluid into the wave, and a neutrally buoyant particle tracer was used to measure fluid velocities and to observe the weak circulation within the wave. The experimental method is described in detail elsewhere (Schmidt 1998).

5. Internal Circulation

Figure 1(b) shows the circulation pattern as observed in a typical wave. Selected streaklines from the internal and external flow were superimposed with light colored arrows to clarify the magnitude and direction of flow. Dark colored arrows were superimposed to clarify the location of vortices and to highlight the rearward flow in the wave. The superposition was accomplished by examining the enlarged graphic image in conjunction with recorded video footage of the flow and describes what was typically observed during the experimental study. The wave pictured had an amplitude of 39 mm and a celerity of 74 mm/s, and the ambient had an interfacial half-thickness of 20.0 mm and a densimetric factor of 0.0172.

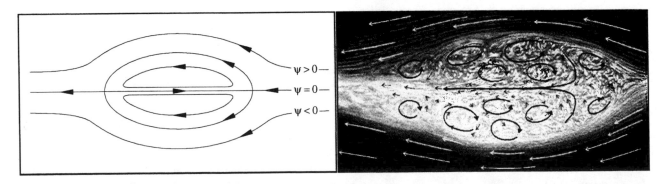

Figure 1 – (a) Streamline plot of second mode internal wave (after Tung, Chan and Kubota, 1982); (b) Streakline image of second mode wave (present study); both with moving frame of reference.

Instead of a vortex pair following the closed streamlines shown on Figure 1(a), it appears that smaller vortices near the boundary of the wave are driven by the external flow, and these in turn drive counter-rotating vortices near the centreline of the wave. The result is a net forward flow within the region midway between the wave boundary and its centreline, with a relatively strong rearward flow (in this case equal to slightly less than 25% of the wave celerity) along the centreline of the wave.

The wake of the wave is the only place where turbulent mixing is observed. This is in conflict with the conclusion of Stamp and Jacka (1995) that "the rapid spread of dye through the [upper and lower recirculating] cells was indicative of turbulent mixing." Similar circulation patterns are observed in the vortex street present in the wake of a cylinder. In a description of the vortex street, Tritton (1988) notes that the counter-rotating vortices produced are not turbulent, as the term turbulence "implies the existence of highly irregular rapid velocity fluctuations." Additionally, Tennekes and Lumley (1972) state that "turbulence is rotational and three-dimensional... the random vorticity fluctuations that characterize turbulence could not maintain themselves if the velocity fluctuations were two-dimensional." The circulation within the wave was observed to be predominantly two-dimensional, with particles staying within the 3 mm wide light sheet for many wavelengths. In a flow with a significant three-dimensional component, particles would be expected to move in and out of the light sheet.

6. Fluid Entrainment

Figure 2 shows fluid entrainment into a second mode wave. The four component images are spaced at two second intervals, and show a wave approaching three separate bodies of dyed, miscible, neutrally buoyant fluid which were present in the interfacial region. The images were scanned from photographic negatives and filtered for intensity threshold and contrast to highlight the dyed regions. Areas of low intensity, corresponding to low dye concentrations, are without color, so the reader may note that conservation of mass appears to be violated. This is because the mixed fluid's fluorescence intensity did not exceed the filter threshold. The wave in Figure 2 had an amplitude of 52 mm and a celerity of 62.5 mm/s, and the ambient had an interfacial half-thickness of 24.9 mm and a densimetric factor of 0.0110.

At $x/h = 95$, the wave emerged from behind one of the tank supports. Two diluted lobes of dyed fluid are evident, with little dye present on the wave's outer boundaries or along its centreline. The first region of interfacial dye is stretched along the outer boundary of the wave, and the second is thickened due to the influence of the approaching wave. At $x/h = 100$, the first region is stretched further and its thickness appears to be less regular. The first sign of what resembles a cusping of this line of fluid is apparent. The second region begins to stretch about the body of the wave as the first had, and the third region of dye appears. At $x/h = 105$, the first dyed region on the boundary of the wave seems to thicken and be drawn into the wave at some locations, while at others it is stretched thinner and stays on the boundary of the wave. The second dyed region exhibits the first signs of this distortion, while the third begins to thicken and envelop the nose of the wave. At $x/h = 110$, the first region of dye has been incorporated into the body of the wave, and the entrainment of the second region is underway. It should be noted that dye did not enter at the nose of the wave, where a stagnation point exists, but at points above and below the nose.

A shear instability, thought to be a form of Holmboe wave, appears to be responsible for the entrainment of fluid into the wave. Whereas a Kelvin-Helmholtz shear instability can occur only at Richardson numbers (J_{local}, as defined in Equation 1) of less than 0.25, the Holmboe instability may exist for any positive value. Measurements of velocity and density gradients undertaken during this study indicate that $J_{local} < 0.25$ only in the lee of the wave, but larger, positive values exist along the forward portions of the wave boundary. Asymmetric Holmboe instabilities of the type observed here were described by Haigh and Lawrence (1996).

$$J_{local} = \frac{g\dfrac{d\rho}{dy}}{\rho\left(\dfrac{du}{dy}\right)^2}\;; \quad J_{bulk} = \frac{g\dfrac{(\rho_3 - \rho_1)}{h}}{\rho\left(\dfrac{c}{h}\right)^2} = \frac{g\,\omega\,h}{c^2} = \frac{2c_0^2}{c^2} \tag{1}$$

Some entrainment of fluid was also observed in the lee of the wave, where mixing in the wake brought fluid into the wave. This turbulent entrainment was also noted by Stamp and Jacka (1995). Fluid incorporated in this fashion did not advance forward in the wave and was soon expelled.

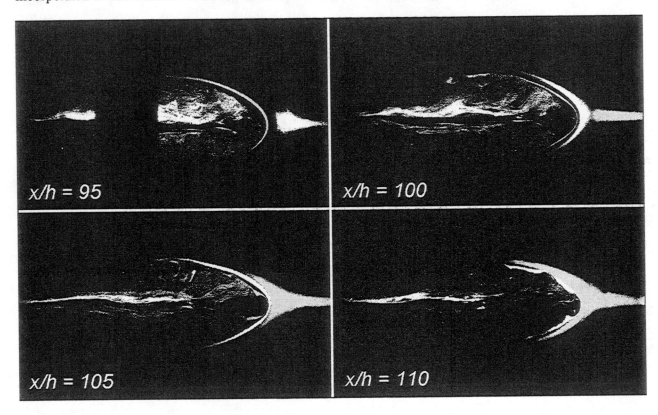

Figure 2 – Fluid entrainment into a second mode wave.

7. Mass Transport

The second mode wave's capacity for mass transport is one of its most striking characteristics, but this capacity is limited by the entrainment and expulsion of fluid described in the previous section. Stamp and Griffiths (1992) stated that "at large amplitude they carry mass over large distances. The fluid being transported is, however, continually exchanged through addition from ahead of the wave and ejection at the rear, so that passive tracer is transported only a finite difference." The present study examined the transport of a tracer using an LIF technique to concentrations of dye within the wave.

Observations of the flushing behavior of large amplitude second mode waves showed that once a wave develops, strong flushing occurs as external fluid is entrained into the wave and internal fluid is expelled. The wave appears to discharge tracer at a constant rate until recently entrained fluid starts to be expelled from the wave. After this point, any remaining, diluted dye is carried only in the vortex lobes above and below the centreline of the wave, and the discharge of dye from the wave slows dramatically.

An examination of flushing data showed that the rate of flushing was proportional to the bulk Richardson number (J_{bulk}, as defined in Equation 1). The bulk value tended to increase as the wave decayed, so a value equal to the mean value over each experimental run was adopted as representative.

Figure 3 shows data from eleven experiments, with densimetric factors ranging from 0.0033 to 0.0371. The data show that dye is initially flushed from the wave at a constant rate which is proportional to the bulk Richardson number. This "primary flushing" occurs until the dye concentration decreases to approximately 10% of the wave's initial maximum concentration. This point was observed to coincide with the first expulsion from the wave of recently entrained, tracer-free fluid. During "residual flushing", diluted dye retained in the two lobes above and below the centreline of the wave, is gradually expelled at a slower rate. The relationship between Richardson number and flushing rate is seems to be counterintuitive, but a similar relationship was seen in a study of the mixing of dense river inflows into lakes (Leong 1988).

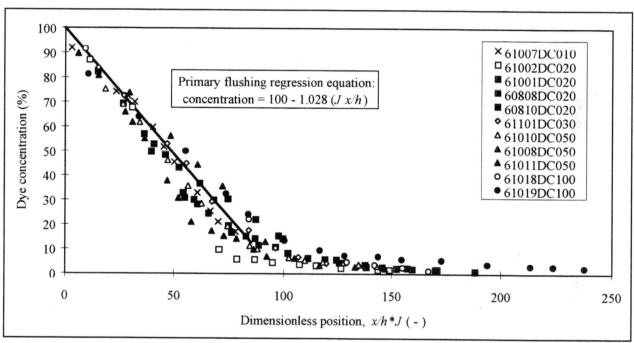

Figure 3 – Tracer flushing from a second mode wave.

8. Conclusions

This study examined circulation within, entrainment into, and mass transport by, large amplitude second mode internal solitary waves.

Circulation patterns within the wave appear to be more complex than the closed streamline, counterrotating vortex structure predicted by previous numerical solutions. It appears that an assemblage of vortices exists on either side of the centreline of the wave. Vortices adjacent to the wave boundary are driven by the external flow, while those away from the boundary are driven by the former, and thus rotate in the opposite direction. The latter vortices drive a rearward flow along the centreline of the wave which expels fluid from the lee of the wave.

The boundary-proximate vortices within the wave play a vital role in the entrainment of external fluid into the wave. Interfacial fluid which is split apart by the propagating wave and stretched along the wave boundary is brought into the wave in cusp-like structures where these vortices rotate inwards. This motion appears to be typical of an asymmetric Holmboe instability.

The entrainment and expulsion of fluid into and out of the wave indicates that the wave has a limited capacity for mass transport. There appear to be two phases in the flushing of passive tracer from a wave. Primary flushing occurs until the dye concentration decreases to approximately 10% of its initial maximum concentration. The end of this phase coincides with the first expulsion from the wave of recently entrained, tracer-free fluid. Diluted dye, retained in two lobes located above and below the centreline of the wave, is then gradually expelled during residual flushing.

9. Acknowledgements

The authors gratefully acknowledge the New Zealand Vice Chancellor's Committee and the University of Canterbury for providing financial support for this study. David Wilkinson, Ian Wood and Bruce Hunt are thanked for their advice on theory and experimental methods, as are Ian Sheppard and Alan Poynter for their efforts in the laboratory.

10. References

Davis, R.E. and A. Acrivos, 1967. Solitary Internal Waves in Deep Water. Journal of Fluid Mechanics, vol 29, pp 593-607.

Haigh, S.P. and G.A. Lawrence, 1996. The Evolution of Symmetric and Non-symmetric Holmboe Waves. Paper submitted to the Journal of Fluid Mechanics, 27 p.

Hurdis, D.A. and H.-P. Pao, 1975. Experimental Observation of Internal Solitary Waves in a Stratified Fluid. Physics of Fluids, vol 18, pp 385-386.

Leong, D.C.K., 1988. Mixing of Dense River Inflows to Lakes. Master of Engineering Research Project, The University of Canterbury, 81 p.

Maxworthy, T., 1980. On the Formation of Nonlinear Internal Waves from the Gravitational Collapse of Mixed Regions in Two and Three Dimensions. Journal of Fluid Mechanics, vol 96, pp 47-64.

Schmidt, N.P., 1998. Generation, Propagation and Dissipation of Second Mode Internal Solitary Waves. Ph.D. Thesis, The University of Canterbury, 406 p.

Stamp, A. and R.W. Griffiths, 1992. Large Amplitude Mode 2 Deep-Water Internal Solitary Waves. 11th Australasian Fluid Mechanics Conference, University of Tasmania, Hobart, 14-18 December 1992, pp 315-317.

Stamp, A.P. and M. Jacka, 1995. Deep-Water Internal Solitary Waves. Journal of Fluid Mechanics, vol 305, pp 347-371.

Tennekes, H. and J.L. Lumley, 1972. A First Course in Turbulence. The M.I.T. Press, Cambridge, 300 p.

Tritton, D.J., 1988. Physical Fluid Dynamics, 2nd Edition, Oxford University Press, Oxford, 519 p.

Tung, K.K., T.F. Chan and T. Kubota, 1982. Large Amplitude Internal Waves of Permanent Form. Studies in Applied Mathematics, vol 66, pp 1-44.

Internal Solitary-like Waves with Recirculating Cores

Marek Stastna, Kevin G. Lamb

Dept. of Applied Math, University of Waterloo, Waterloo, ON, N2L-3G1
mmstastn@barrow.uwaterloo.ca, kglamb@math.uwaterloo.ca

1. Abstract

In this paper we discuss internal solitary wave-like objects with recirculating cores. We develop a self-consistent method to initialize a time-stepping model with a wave past breaking, then utilize this method along with a second-order time stepping model to investigate the evolution of the objects. It is found that outside the core the object behaves like a solitary wave, while inside the core the object is dynamically active. The latter may play a role in sediment resuspension.

2. Introduction

The role of large, vertically trapped internal solitary waves (henceforth ISWs) in mixing has been a topic of interest for some time (Sandstrom and Elliot (1984), Haury et al. (1979)). In recent work Lamb (1999) has shown that large, mode one ISWs shoaling onto the continental shelf can develop trapped, recirculating cores provided the ambient density profile exhibits stratification right up to the surface. If a mixed surface layer overlies the stratified fluid the shoaling ISWs break but an ISW with a recirculating core is not formed. Observations by Bogucki, Dickey and Redekopp (1997) off the California coast show an increase in sediment resuspension associated with the passage of ISW-like events. Most of the density change in the measured background density profile occurs in the bottom half of the water column and hence ISWs are waves of elevation. Furthermore the water column is stratified over its entire bottom third, thus allowing for the possibility of trapped cores. In this article we study the evolution of ISW-like waves with trapped cores for an ambient density profile which approximates that observed by Bogucki et al. Such waves are not steady, but as we will show, consist of a dynamically active core and a wave body that is nearly a solitary wave after an initial period of adjustment. We outline a self-consistent technique for preparing initial waves, present numerical results from a 2-D inviscid, time-stepping model, and finally comment on the relevance of the results to sediment resuspension. Throughout we assume the existence of recirculating cores. In fact, in independent work (not presented here) we have confirmed that recirculating cores may be formed, for the present and similar stratifications, either by shoaling or by adjustment to an externally imposed shear current.

3. Methods

We will consider an inviscid, 2-D model ocean with Cartesian coordinates set up so that $z = 0$ corresponds to the ocean bottom and $z = 60$ to the ocean surface. We neglect rotation for all runs presented. All length measurements are given in meters, all time measurements are given in seconds and all velocity measurements are given in meters per second. At the surface we make the rigid lid approximation. We make the Boussinesq approximation throughout. We consider an ambient density profile given by

$$\begin{aligned}
\rho_0\bar{\rho}(z) &= 1024.735 + C(\ln(\cosh(z-20)) - z) \\
C &= 0.0093 \\
\rho_0 &= 1024.8 \text{kg m}^3.
\end{aligned} \quad (1)$$

ands plotted in figure 1. The initial ISW profile is computed using the direct variational method of Turkington et al. (1991). We do not include a background current, though this is possible.

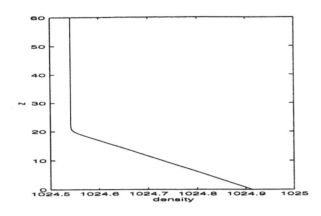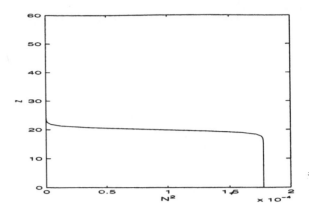

Figure 1: Density and $N^2(z)$ vs. z

The variational method can be used to compute a sequence of ISWs of increasing amplitude. It is found that these waves have an increasing propagation speed and a decreasing half-length. It has been confirmed using the time-stepping model that all resulting waves with open streamlines are indeed solitary waves. Beyond a certain amplitude the objects produced by the variational method have closed streamlines. The region of closed streamlines corresponds to locations in which the mathematical algorithm sets the density in the wave to be equal to values found below the ocean bottom, or since the ambient density is a strictly decreasing function of z, to values larger than the value of the ambient density at the bottom. While this presents no problem for the algorithm it is clearly unphysical and the region of closed streamlines must be modified to yield physically valid objects. Derzho and Grimshaw (1997) have argued, using a weakly nonlinear technique, that the trapped core should be stagnant to leading order, in a frame moving with the wave. We have chosen to avoid introducing discontinuities in the velocity field. Instead we keep the velocity field given by the variational method as it is and to set the density inside the core to be equal to $\bar{\rho}(0)$. This is a self-consistent choice since we do not expect the initial conditions to provide an exact solution of Euler's equations. We do expect that after an initial period of adjustment an ISW-like object with a recirculating core will form, and that this object will evolve slowly. The variational method allows us to have some control over the size of the core and to setup an initial state quickly and inexpensively (in numerical terms).

The time-evolution is performed using Lamb's numerical solver for Euler's equations. The solver uses a second-order projection method and is described in Lamb (1994). For the runs presented here we used a 1000 by 100 point grid, regularly spaced in the horizontal direction and quadratically spaced in the vertical direction. The quadratic spacing was used to allow better resolution of the dynamically active core region. The grid spacing was chosen to have 40 of the 100 points in the bottom 10m. We used a domain 1500m long and 60m deep, or in other words one with a horizontal resolution of 1.5m and a vertical resolution ranging from less than 0.1m near the bottom to about 1.2m at the surface. The results were compared with runs using a regular grid in the vertical (not shown here). We found that the qualitative features of the ISW-like objects were unchanged, but that the quadratic grid allowed better representation of small scale features within the core.

4. Results

For all cases considered the initial waves were centered in the middle of the computational domain and were propagating to the left. A constant rightward background current was added to hold the wave still. This current was given by the wave propagation speed as computed by the variational method. The actual ISW-like object that finally emerges from the initial state has a slightly smaller propagation speed and hence slowly drifts rightward.

Two examples of an initial wave's evolution are shown in figures 2 and 3, for initial cores approximately 20m tall, 50m wide and 12m tall, 40m wide, respectively. The figures show only a subdomain of the full computational domain. The subdomain is approximately centered on the ISW-like object and is 200m long and 20m high. Only the bottom third of the water column is shown. The figures show shaded density contours, one density contour (with a value of $\bar{\rho}(0)$), as well as two velocity contours. The $w = 0.01$ contour is plotted to show the variation of vertical velocity in the evolving core. The $u = 0$ contour is included for two reasons. First, for the initial wave it shows the location of the stagnation points found at $z = 0$. Second, for later times the $u = 0$ contour along with the bottom density contour given an idea of the complex evolution of the core.

The evolution of the initial wave proceeds qualitatively as follows. First the core tilts against the direction of propagation until plunging sets in. The wave breaks backwards (to the right in this case). The plunging high density fluid entrains lighter fluid from outside the core which begins to fill up the core region. By 4000s, in both figure 2 and 3, a region of anomalously high positive vertical velocity is setup at the front of the core, extending into the bottom 2m of the water column (even lower for the large core). After this initial adjustment phase the larger core experiences a further large adjustment first seen at 16000s and continuing to 32000s. This adjustment is marked by nearly vertical regions of anomalously strong updrafts and downdrafts leading to intrusions of lighter fluid into the core as seen in figure 2 at 28000s. Eventually (clearly seen in figure 2 at 32000s) the region where $u = 0$ is completely lifted away from the the ocean bottom. The smaller core exhibits the same qualitative behaviour, however due to the smaller size of the core some of the details are not as clear. In particular the vertical bands of anomalously strong vertical velocity do not seem to be nearly as dominant in figure 3. The final state is reached later for the smaller core. It should be noted that for both cases some of the heavy fluid which initially forms the core is expelled during the adjustment process in a thin (less than 1m) layer behind the wave and directly overlying the ocean bottom. The layer is not shown in the figures.

Figure 4 shows vertical profiles of the horizontal velocity down the middle of the wave for the larger initial core. We can see that above the recirculating region the vertical profile of horizontal velocity retains the profile of the original ISW to a very good approximation throughout the core evolution process. In the core region the initial adjustment occurs over nearly the entire bottom 20m of the water column. Near the bottom the horizontal velocity initially increases in magnitude. Up to 24000s u is generally an increasing function of z in the bottom 20m. After about 24000s the shape of the u vs. z curve changes and by 32000s it can be seen that u decreases with z over the bottom 10m and only then begins to increase. This can be associated with the lifting of the region where $u < 0$ seen in figure 2.

Larger initial cores lead to more wave shedding behind the main object and experience a more violent initial transition. Nevertheless it was possible to calculate cores for the initial wave whose initial height extended past $z = 20.0$m, the top of the ambient stratified layer. The cores ranged in height from under 10m to over 20m and width from under 40m to just over 80.0m. It would have been possible to calculate even larger cores.

In figure 5 we show the propagation speed versus maximum isopycnal displacement. The linear longwave speed is included by labelling it as having a maximum isopycnal displacement of 0m. The post adjustment propagation speed is calculated as the average propagation speed of the ISW-like object over the period between 12000 and 20000s. The post adjustment isopycnal displacement is calculated using the vertical profile of the density down the middle of the ISW-like object at 16000s. Both quantities vary weakly with time. Their variation with time will be investigated in the future. From figure 5 it can be seen that all ISW-like objects with recirculating cores propagate faster and have larger maximum isopycnal displacements than non-breaking ISWs, both initially and after adjustment. It is also clear that for breaking waves the initial propagation speed versus

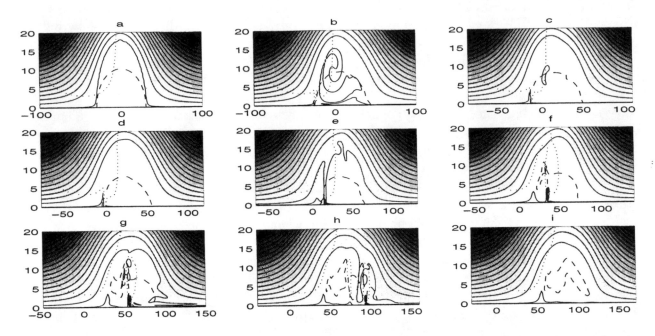

Figure 2: Evolving ISW-like object with a large initial core. Shading and solid lines denote density contours, dashed line denotes $u = 0$ contour, dotted line denotes $w = 0.01$ contour. Times in seconds: a) 0, b) 4000, c) 8000, d) 12000, e) 16000, f) 20000, g) 24000, h) 28000, i) 32000.

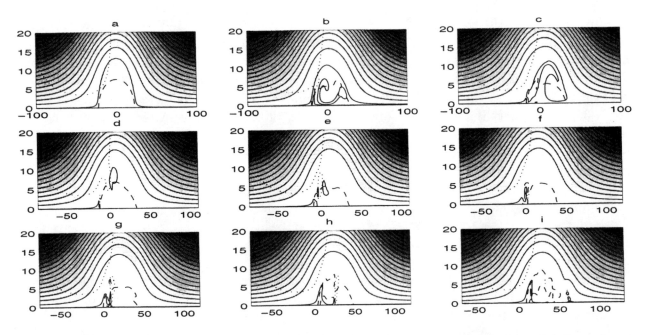

Figure 3: Evolving ISW-like object with a smaller initial core. Shading and solid lines denote density contours, dashed line denotes $u = 0$ contour, dotted line denotes $w = 0.01$ contour. Times as in figure 2

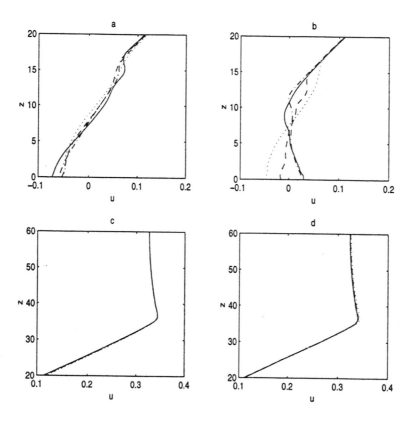

Figure 4: Vertical profile of horizontal velocity u through the centre of the ISW-like object. a) and b) lower 20m (core), c) and d) upper 40m. Times in seconds: a) and c) dotted 4000, dashed 8000, dash-dot 12000, solid 16000, b) and d) dotted 20000, dashed 24000, dash-dot 28000, solid 32000. Note different velocity scales for upper and lower panels.

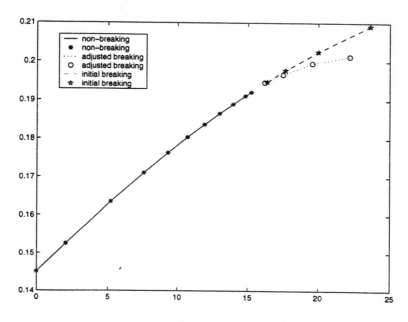

Figure 5: Propagation speed vs. Maximum Isopycnal Displacement. Solid line: non-breaking ISWs, Dashed line: Initial breaking waves, Dotted line: Recirculating cores after 16000s

maximum isopycnal displacement curve is different from the post adjustment propagation speed versus maximum isopycnal displacement curve.

5. Conclusions and Extensions

The technique we have outlined could be used to prepare numerical runs with ISW-like objects with recirculating cores for any stratification for which Turkington's variational method allows the calculation of waves past breaking. We have shown that in the core, the ISW-like objects are dynamically active and hence not solitary waves in the classical sense. In particular, the adjustment of the recirculating cores induces large, positive vertical currents at the front of the core. This could play a significant role in resuspension and will be investigated further. Outside the core the objects behave much like ISWs in the sense that the objects propagate unchanged.

It should be noted that for ambient density profiles which do not exhibit stratification right to the bottom (for waves of elevation) it is not possible to calculate recirculating cores. See article by Lamb in this volume.

Future work will address the interaction of the ISW-like objects with a bottom boundary layer and the possibility of instability therein, as conjectured by Bogucki and Redekopp (1999). Our preliminary results, using a quadratic stress law bottom boundary condition, have shown no instability, but further investigation is needed.

6. References

Bogucki, D., Dickey, T., Redekopp, L.G. (1997) Sediment resuspension and mixing by resonantly generated internal solitary waves, *Journal of Physical Oceanography*, **27**, 1181.

Bogucki, D.J., Redekopp, L.G. (1999) A Mechanism for sediment resuspension by internal solitary waves, *Geophysical Research Letters*, **26**, 1317.

Derzho, O., G., Grimshaw, R. (1997) Solitary waves with a vortex core in a shallow layer of stratified fluid, *Physics of Fluids*, **9**, 3378.

Haury, L., R., Briscoe, M., G., Orr, M., H. (1979) Tidally generated internal wave packets in Massachusetts Bay, *Nature*, **278**, 312.

Lamb, K.G. (1994) Numerical experiments of internal wave generation by strong tidal flow across a finite amplitude bank edge, *Journal of Geophysical Research*, **99**, 843.

Lamb, K.G. (1999) Shoaling, large-amplitude solitary internal waves and the formation of waves with trapped cores, submitted to *Journal of Fluid Mechanics*

Sandstrom, H., Elliot, J.A. (1984) Internal tide and solitons on the Scotian Shelf: a nutrient pump at work, *Journal of Geophysical Research*, **89(C4)**, 6415.

Turkington, B., Eydeland, A., Wang, S. (1991) A computational method for solitary internal waves in a continuously stratified fluid, *Studies in Applied Mathematics*, **85**, 93.

Radiation and diffraction problems for the circular cylinder in a layer of a linearly stratified fluid

Sturova I.V.

Lavrentyev Institute of Hydrodynamics, Novosibirsk, Russia 630090
sturova@hydro.nsc.ru

1. Abstract

The theoretical analysis of the 2-D linear problems on radiation and diffraction of the internal waves by a horizontal cylinder is presented. The circular cylinder is immersed entirely within a linearly stratified layer located between the layers of homogeneous fluids having different densities (model of pycnocline). An inviscid incompressible fluid bounded from above and below by rigid horizontal lids is considered. The linear theory of internal waves within the Boussinesq approximation is used. The boundary integral equation for the disturbance pressure is formulated by introducing a Green function. The extended mass sources over a cylinder surface are used for the solution of this equation. The added mass and damping coefficients are computed.

2. Introduction

In the linear wave theory the wave motions produced by small-amplitude vibrations of a cylinder (radiation problem) and scattering of an incident wave by a restrained cylinder (diffraction problem) have been the most thoroughly studied for a homogeneous fluid with a free surface and recently investigated for a stratified fluid. The boundary condition of fixed normal velocity on the cylinder surface presented a considerable challenge to the solution of these problems. The solution of radiation problem for an elliptic cylinder oscillating in an unbounded exponentially stratified fluid is presented by Hurley (1997). The radiation and diffraction problems for a circular cylinder located beneath a pycnocline in a constant-density layer have been considered by Sturova (1999). Sharp and smooth pycnoclines are simulated by two- and three layer fluids, respectively; in the latter the middle layer is linearly statified. The reciprocity relations are derived for the solution of radiation and diffraction problems.

In this paper the model of smooth pycnocline is used. It is assumed that the inviscid incompressible fluid occupies the region $|x| < \infty, -H < y < H_1$, and there are three layers: homogeneous upper and lower ones and a linearly stratified middle one. The horizontal coordinate is x whilst the vertical coordinate is y measured upwards from the undisturbed interface between the upper and middle layers. Thus, the density distribution at the undisturbed state $\rho_0(y)$ takes the form

$$
\rho_0(y) = \begin{cases} \rho_1 & (0 < y < H_1), \\ \rho_1(1 - \varepsilon y/H_2) & (-H_2 < y < 0), \\ \rho_2 = \rho_1(1 + \varepsilon) & (-H < y < -H_2), \end{cases}
$$

where $\varepsilon > 0$, and $H_1, H_2, H_3 = H - H_2$ are depths of the upper, middle and lower layers, respectively.

2. Radiation problem

The circular cylinder is situated entirely within the middle layer and undergoes small oscillations in the two possible degrees of freedom (surge and heave) at a frequency ω. The disturbed oscillatory motion of the fluid is assumed to be steady and the flow within the upper and lower layers is potential.

In homogeneous layers the velocity potentials can be written as

$$\Phi^{(s)}(x, y, t) = \mathrm{Re}[\exp(i\omega t) \sum_{j=1}^{2} \eta_j \phi_j^{(s)}(x, y)] \quad (s = 1, 3),$$

where $\phi_j^{(s)}$ $(j = 1, 2)$ are radiation potentials due to motions of the cylinder with an unit amplitude in either degree of freedom; η_j are corresponding motion amplitudes; the superscript s is equal to 1 for the upper layer and 3 for the lower one. The radiation potentials satisfy the Laplace equation

$$\nabla^2 \phi_j^{(1)} = 0 \quad (0 < y < H_1), \quad \nabla^2 \phi_j^{(3)} = 0 \quad (-H < y < -H_2). \tag{1}$$

In the middle layer the fluid pressure can be represented as

$$P^{(2)}(x, y, t) = \rho_1 \mathrm{Re}[\exp(i\omega t) \sum_{j=1}^{2} \eta_j p_j^{(2)}(x, y)].$$

The internal wave equation within the Boussinesq approximation has the form

$$\nabla^2 p_j^{(2)} = \frac{N^2}{\omega^2} \frac{\partial^2 p_j^{(2)}}{\partial x^2} \quad (-H_2 < y < 0), \tag{2}$$

where the buoyancy frequency $N = \sqrt{-(g/\rho_1)\mathrm{d}\rho_0/\mathrm{d}y} = \sqrt{\varepsilon g / H_2}$ is constant, g is the gravitational acceleration.

The upper layer is assumed to be bound by a rigid lid. This approximation allows one to 'filter off' the surface waves without considerable distortions of the internal waves.

The boundary conditions are the following

$$\partial \phi_j^{(1)} / \partial y = 0 \quad (y = H_1), \quad \partial \phi_j^{(3)} / \partial y = 0 \quad (y = -H),$$

$$\left(\frac{\partial \phi_j^{(1)}}{\partial y}, \frac{\partial^2 \phi_j^{(1)}}{\partial y^2} \right) = \frac{i\omega}{\omega^2 - N^2} \left(\frac{\partial p_j^{(2)}}{\partial y}, \frac{\partial^2 p_j^{(2)}}{\partial y^2} \right) \quad (y = 0), \tag{3}$$

$$\left(\frac{\partial \phi_j^{(3)}}{\partial y}, \frac{\partial^2 \phi_j^{(3)}}{\partial y^2} \right) = \frac{i\omega}{\omega^2 - N^2} \left(\frac{\partial p_j^{(2)}}{\partial y}, \frac{\partial^2 p_j^{(2)}}{\partial y^2} \right) \quad (y = -H_2).$$

The exact boundary condition on the circular contour $S : x^2 + (y + h)^2 = a^2$ is

$$\frac{n_1}{\omega^2} \frac{\partial p_j^{(2)}}{\partial x} + \frac{n_2}{\omega^2 - N^2} \frac{\partial p_j^{(2)}}{\partial y} = n_j \quad (x, y \in S),$$

where $\vec{n} = (n_1, n_2)$ is the inward normal to the contour S, a is the cylinder radius, and h is the distance between the cylinder axis and the upper interface, $a < h < H_2 - a$. In the far field the radiation condition requires the radiated waves to be outgoing.

The radiation forces $F_{1,2}$ may be obtained by integration of pressure over the body surface. By omitting the hydrostatic term, we have

$$F_k = \sum_{j=1}^{2} \eta_j \tau_{kj} \quad (k = 1, 2), \tag{4}$$

where

$$\tau_{kj} = \omega^2 \mu_{kj} - i\omega \lambda_{kj} = \rho_1 \int_S p_j^{(2)} n_k \mathrm{d}s.$$

828

The coefficients τ_{kj} represent the complex force exerted in the direction k and caused by a sinusoidal motion of the body with an unit amplitude in the direction j; μ_{kj} and λ_{kj} are the added mass and damping coefficients, respectively.

Introducing an unknown distribution of mass sources $\sigma_j(\vec{x})$ over the body surface, we can write for the pressure

$$p_j^{(2)}(\vec{x}) = \int_S \sigma_j(\vec{\xi}) G^{(2)}(\vec{x}, \vec{\xi}) \mathrm{d}s, \quad \vec{x} = (x, y), \ \vec{\xi} = (\xi, \eta),$$

where $G^{(2)}(\vec{x}, \vec{\xi})$ is the Green function in the middle layer. Using Green's theorem, we obtain the boundary integral equation (Wu $et\ al$, 1990)

$$2\pi\sigma_j(\vec{x}) = \mathbf{pv} \int_S \sigma_j(\vec{\xi}) \left(n_1 \frac{\partial G}{\partial \xi} + \frac{\omega^2 n_2}{\omega^2 - N^2} \frac{\partial G}{\partial \eta} \right) \mathrm{d}s + \omega^2 n_j, \tag{5}$$

where the symbol $\mathbf{pv}$ indicates the principal-value integration.

The Green function $G^{(s)}(\vec{x}, \vec{\xi})$ satisfies the equations

$$\nabla^2 G^{(1)} = 0 \quad (0 < y < H_1), \quad \nabla^2 G^{(3)} = 0 \quad (-H < y < -H_2),$$

$$\frac{\partial^2 G^{(2)}}{\partial y^2} - \beta^2 \frac{\partial^2 G^{(2)}}{\partial x^2} = 4\pi\beta^2 \delta(\vec{x} - \vec{\xi}) \quad (-H_2 < y < 0), \tag{6}$$

with the boundary conditions

$$\partial G^{(1)}/\partial y = 0 \quad (y = H_1), \quad \partial G^{(3}/\partial y = 0 \quad (y = -H),$$

$$G^{(1)} = G^{(2)}, \quad \beta^2 \partial G^{(1)}/\partial y = -\partial G^{(2)}/\partial y \quad (y = 0),$$

$$G^{(2)} = G^{(3)}, \quad \beta^2 \partial G^{(3)}/\partial y = -\partial G^{(2)}/\partial y \quad (y = -H_2).$$

and the radiation condition in the far field. Here δ is the Dirac delta-function, $\beta^2 = N^2/\omega^2 - 1$.

When $\omega < N$, the occurring waves will be internal gravity ones, and the Green function in the middle layer $G^{(2)}$ will satisfy the hyperbolic equation (6). The solution for $G^{(2)}$ may be present in the form

$$G^{(2)} = 4i\pi\beta \sum_{l=1}^{\infty} \alpha(k_l) C(k_l, y) C(k_l, \eta) \exp\left(-ik_l|x - \xi|\right), \tag{7}$$

where

$$\alpha(k) = \frac{(1 + \beta^2 t_3^2)}{k_l(1 - \beta^2 t_1 t_3) D'(k_l)}. \quad C(k, \zeta) = \cos(k\beta\zeta) + \beta t_1 \sin(k\beta\zeta),$$

$t_1 = \tanh kH_1$, $t_3 = \tanh kH_3$, $D(k) = (\beta^2 t_1 t_3 - 1) \tan(k\beta H_2) - \beta(t_1 + t_3)$, the prime denotes the differentiation with the respect to k. The values k_l ($k_1 < k_2 < ...$) are positive real roots of the equation $D(k) = 0$ and present the wave numbers of internal waves, $k_l \to l\pi/(\beta H_2)$ at $l \to \infty$.

The similar form of the Green function has been used by Robinson (1969) in solving the diffraction problem for an internal wave propagating in a channel filled with an uniformly stratified fluid into which a vertical barrier extending to the channel bottom has been placed.

When $\omega > N$, $G^{(2)}$ will satisfy the elliptic equation (6) for all real values of ω, and no waves are produced. The solution to $G^{(2)}$ may be presented in the form

$$G^{(2)} = -2\gamma \left[\ln R - \int_0^{\infty} \frac{\cos k(x - \xi)}{kT(k)} Q(k) \mathrm{d}k \right],$$

where $R^2 = (x - \xi)^2 + \gamma^2(y - \eta)^2$, $\gamma^2 = -\beta^2$, $Q(k) = \cosh[k\gamma(y + \eta + H_2)](1 - \gamma^2 t_1 t_3) +$

$\gamma \sinh[k\gamma(y + \eta + H_2)](t_3 - t_1) + \exp(-k\gamma H_2)\cosh[k\gamma(y - \eta)](1 - \gamma t_1)(1 - \gamma t_3),$

$$T(k) = (1 + \gamma^2 t_1 t_3) \sinh(k\gamma H_2) + \gamma(t_1 + t_3) \cosh(k\gamma H_2).$$

When $\omega < N$, it is necessary to use an extended source because the point source may produce the infinite radiated energy in a linearly stratified fluid (Gorodtsov & Teodorovich, 1986). Introducing polar coordinates r, θ by $x = r \sin \theta$, $y = r \cos \theta - h$, we assume the distribution of the sources over the cylinder surface in the form

$$\sigma_1(a, \theta) = \sum_{m=1}^{\infty} a_m \sin m\theta, \quad \sigma_2(a, \theta) = \sum_{m=1}^{\infty} b_m \cos m\theta. \tag{8}$$

Substituting the relation (4) in the equation (1), sequentially multiplying it by $\sin n\theta$ ($\cos n\theta$) and integrating over the cylinder surface, we obtain the infinite system of linear equations for determination of unknown coefficients a_m (b_m)

$$a_n + \frac{a}{2\pi^2} \sum_{m=1}^{\infty} a_m A_{mn} = -\frac{\omega^2}{2\pi} \delta_{1n}, \quad b_n + \frac{a}{2\pi^2} \sum_{m=1}^{\infty} b_m B_{mn} = -\frac{\omega^2}{2\pi} \delta_{1n}, \tag{9}$$

where

$$A_{mn} = \int_0^{2\pi} \sin m\tau \int_0^{2\pi} \sin n\theta \left(n_1 \frac{\partial G^{(2)}}{\partial \xi} - \frac{n_2}{\beta^2} \frac{\partial G^{(2)}}{\partial \eta} \right) d\theta d\tau,$$

$$B_{mn} = \int_0^{2\pi} \cos m\tau \int_0^{2\pi} \cos n\theta \left(n_1 \frac{\partial G^{(2)}}{\partial \xi} - \frac{n_2}{\beta^2} \frac{\partial G^{(2)}}{\partial \eta} \right) d\theta d\tau,$$

$\tau = \arctan[\xi/(\eta + h)]$, δ_{1n} is the Kroneker delta. These systems may be numerically solved by the reduction method.

Once the coefficients a_m, b_m are obtained, we can find all the characteristics of the fluid motion. Far from cylinder, as $x \to \pm\infty$, the flow represents the superposition of an infinite number of wave modes. For example, the pressure in the middle layer has the form

$$p_1^{(2)} = \pm \sum_{l=1}^{\infty} E_1(k_l) C(k_l, y) \exp(\mp ik_l x), \quad p_2^{(2)} = -\sum_{l=1}^{\infty} E_2(k_l) C(k_l, y) \exp(\mp ik_l x),$$

where

$$E_1(k) = 4\pi^2 a\beta\alpha(k) \sum_{m=1}^{\infty} a_m J_m(q)(I_m^- C_m + I_m^+ S_m), E_2(k) = 4i\pi^2 a\beta\alpha(k) \sum_{m=1}^{\infty} b_m J_m(q)(I_m^+ C_m + I_m^- S_m),$$

$C_m = (h_c - \beta t_1 h_s) \cos(m\phi)$, $S_m = (h_s + \beta t_1 h_c) \sin(m\phi)$, $h_c = \cos(k\beta h)$, $h_s = \sin(k\beta h)$, $\phi = \arctan \beta$, $q = akN/\omega$, $I_m^{\pm} = 1 \pm (-1)^m$. J_m is the Bessel function of the first kind of order m.

The radiation loads are equal

$$\omega^2 \mu_{11} - i\omega \lambda_{11} = -\rho_1 a^2 \sum_{m=1}^{\infty} a_m \int_0^{2\pi} \sin m\tau \int_0^{2\pi} \sin \theta G^{(2)} d\theta d\tau,$$

$$\omega^2 \mu_{22} - i\omega \lambda_{22} = -\rho_1 a^2 \sum_{m=1}^{\infty} b_m \int_0^{2\pi} \cos m\tau \int_0^{2\pi} \cos \theta G^{(2)} d\theta d\tau.$$

Nondiagonal added mass and damping coefficients are equal to zero.

Gorodtsov & Teodorovich (1986) have proposed the approximate solution of the given problem, wherein the coefficients a_m, b_m are taken from the solution for an unbounded homogeneous fluid. In this case we have $a_1 = b_1 = -\omega^2/(2\pi)$, $a_m = b_m = 0$ at $m \geq 2$. Then for determination of the damping coefficients at $\omega < N$ we can use only the imaginary part of the Green function (7). This is a generalization of Kochin's results to the case of a stratified fluid. However, this approximation is inadequate for the motion of a body submerged within the stratified layer. For example, the radiation loads for the circular cylinder oscillating in the unbounded uniform stratified fluid are equal to (Hurley, 1997)

$$\mu_{11} = \mu_{22} = 0, \quad \lambda_{11} = \lambda_{22} = \pi\rho_1 a^2 \sqrt{N^2 - \omega^2} \quad (\omega < N), \tag{10}$$

$$\mu_{11} = \mu_{22} = \pi\rho_1 a^2 \sqrt{\omega^2 - N^2}/\omega, \quad \lambda_{11} = \lambda_{22} = 0 \quad (\omega > N). \tag{11}$$

An approximate solution for the diagonal damping coefficients has the form

$$\lambda_{11} = 4\pi\rho_1 a^2 \omega^2 \sqrt{N^2 - \omega^2}/N^2, \quad \lambda_{22} = 4\pi\rho_1 a^2 (N^2 - \omega^2)^{3/2}/N^2 \quad (\omega < N). \tag{12}$$

There is an essential qualitative disagreement between the exact solutions (10), (11) and the approximate one (12).

The numerical results for radiation loads are shown in Fig. 1 where the solid lines represent the Hurley solution (10), (11). The calculations are performed for the 20 first terms in the series (8) and 200 modes of internal waves. At $\omega \to \infty$ the limiting values of the added masses are equal to ones for the cylinder which oscillates in a constant-density layer confined between two rigid horizontal walls owing to the use of the Boussinesq approximation.

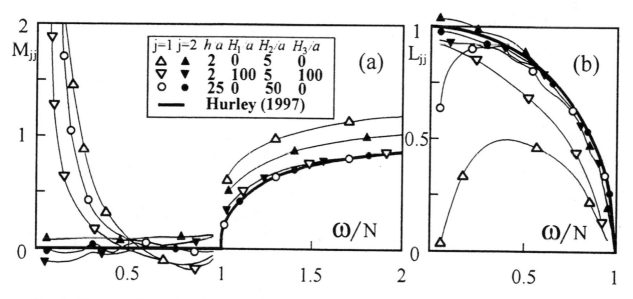

Fig. 1. The non-dimensional added masses $M_{jj} = \mu_{jj}/(\rho_1\pi a^2)$ (a) and damping coefficients $L_{jj} = \lambda_{jj}/(\rho_1\pi a^2 N)$ (b) versus the non-dimensional oscillation frequency ω/N.

With increasing of the middle layer thickness, the calculated radiation loads approach the solutions (10), (11) except small frequencies of the cylinder oscillations. The sharp increase of the added masses at small frequency is attributable to the phenomenon of blocking (Voisin, 1999).

3. Diffraction problem

Let us consider the scattering of the internal wave with prescribed mode number ν by a restrained cylinder. The pressure of the incident wave in the middle layer has the form

$$P_0^{(2)}(x, y, t) = \rho_1 \eta_0 g \text{Re}\{C(k_\nu, y) \exp[i(k_\nu x + \omega t)]\},$$

where η_0 is the amplitude of the internal wave.

In order to find the pressure of diffracted waves in the middle layer

$$P_d^{(2)}(x, y, t) = \rho_1 \eta_0 g \operatorname{Re}[p_d^{(2)}(x, y) \exp(i\omega t)]$$

it is necessary to determine the function $p_d^{(2)}(x, y)$ satisfying the equations and boundary conditions similarly to (1)-(3) and the condition on the contour S

$$n_1 \frac{\partial p_d^{(2)}}{\partial x} - \frac{n_2}{\beta^2} \frac{\partial p_d^{(2)}}{\partial y} = -ik[\cos(k\beta y)(n_1 + it_1 n_2) + \sin(k\beta y)(\beta t_1 n_1 - \frac{in_2}{\beta})] \exp(ikx) \quad (x, y \in S). \quad (13)$$

In the far field the radiation condition should be satisfied.

We seek the distribution of the sources over the cylinder surface in the form

$$\sigma(a, \theta) = \sum_{m=1}^{\infty} (a_m \sin m\theta + b_m \cos m\theta).$$

For determination of unknown coefficients a_m and b_m we have the infinite systems of linear equations (9) in which the right sides represent the Fourier coefficients of sine and cosine transforms (13), respectively.

The exciting forces $\Pi_{1,2}$ can be determined similarly to (4)

$$\Pi_k = \rho_1 \eta_0 g \int_S [C(k_\nu, y) \exp(ik_\nu x) + p_d^{(2)}(x, y)] n_k ds \quad (k = 1, 2).$$

An energy balance exists between the incident wave and the scattering waves (Robinson, 1969; Sturova, 1999).

Acknowledgments

This research is supported by Council "Leading Scientific Schools", grant N 00-15-96162 and by SD RAS Integrate Project N 1-2000.

References

Gorodtsov V.A. & Teodorovich E.V., 1986, "Energy characteristics of harmonic internal wave generators", J. Appl. Mech. Techn. Phys., Vol. 27, N 4, pp. 523-529.

Hurley D.G., 1997, "The generation of internal waves by vibrating elliptic cylinders. Part 1. Inviscid solution", J. Fluid Mech., Vol. 351, pp. 105-118.

Robinson R.M., 1969, "The effect of a vertical barrier on internal waves", Deep-Sea Res., Vol. 16, pp.421-429.

Sturova I.V., 1999, "Problems of radiation and diffraction for a circular cylinder in a stratified fluid", Fluid Dyn., Vol. 34, N 4, pp. 521-533.

Voisin B., 1999, "Internal wave generation. From theory to applications", Final Scientific Rep., TMR Grant N ERBFMBI CT97 2653, 36 p.

Wu J.-h., Wu X.-h. & Li S.-m., 1990, "A theory of wave diffraction and radiation by a large body in stratified ocean (III) Boundary element method", J. Hydrodyn., Ser. A, Vol. 5, N 1, pp. 74-80.

Transmission of Large-Amplitude Internal Waves Across a Reflecting Level in Uniform Shear

B. R. Sutherland

Mathematical Sciences, University of Alberta, Edmonton, Canada   T6G 2G1

bruce.sutherland@ualberta.ca   http://taylor.math.ualberta.ca/~bruce

1. Introduction

It is generally accepted that internal waves propagating vertically in continuously stratified fluid reflect from a level where their Doppler shifted frequency becomes greater than the background buoyancy frequency. Beyond such a level the waves are evanescent. In agreement with linear theory (*e.g.* Lighthill (1978) §4.6), the reflection of small-amplitude internal waves has been demonstrated both by way of laboratory experiments (Koop 1981) and numerical simulations (Sutherland 1996; Sutherland 1999b). However, the dynamics of large-amplitude internal waves near a reflecting level is less well understood. Recent numerical simulations have examined the transmission and reflection of large-amplitude internal waves incident upon a shear layer, for which the background velocity profile has a hyperbolic tangent form (Sutherland 1999b). The simulations have been performed for waves in uniformly stratified Boussinesq fluid. Small-amplitude, vertically compact wavepackets partially transmit and reflect due to transient effects, the measured reflection coefficients agreeing well with linear theory. However, the measured reflection coefficients are found to be significantly different for large-amplitude waves. This has been shown to occur because the wave-induced mean flow changes the intrinsic frequency of the waves in a way that enhances the transmission of a large-amplitude wavepacket across a reflecting level.

This work reports upon the results of simulations of (Boussinesq) internal wavepackets that propagate in uniform shear and uniform stratification. The sign of the shear is established so the intrinsic frequency of the waves increases with height.

In order to ease the interpretation of the re-sults, a brief review is first provided of the stability characteristics of large-amplitude waves in fluid with no background shear.

2. No Background Shear

In the absence of background shear, plane periodic internal waves are unstable to the growth of superharmonic waves (Mied 1976; Drazin 1977; Klostermeyer 1991; Lombard and Riley 1996). However, if the waves are vertically compact, interactions between the waves and the wave-induced mean flow dominate over the effects of superharmonic excitation. For example, Figure 1 shows that in a simulation of doubly periodic waves, the rate of energy transfer between the fundamental waves and superharmonics is comparable with the rate of energy transfer to the mean flow. If the wavepacket is vertically compact, negligible energy is transferred to superharmonics in comparison with that transferred the mean flow.

At larger amplitude, instabilities arise as a result of interactions between the waves and wave-induced mean flow. If the frequency of the waves is close to the background buoyancy frequency, the waves are modulationally unstable (Whitham 1974; Sutherland 1999a). Such waves grow in amplitude initially. Eventually (according to weakly nonlinear theory) this energy is transferred to energy at sideband frequencies (Fermi, Pasta and Ulam 1974; Benjamin and Feir 1967). The wavepackets are stable if their frequency is sufficiently small that $\omega < \sqrt{2/3}N$. The critical frequency corresponds to waves moving at the fastest allowed vertical group velocity. (See the first row of Table 1.)

Figure 2 shows the vertical propagation of a horizontally periodic, vertically compact wavepacket visualised by computing the wave-

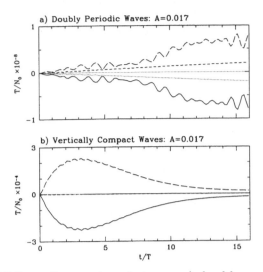

FIG. 1. Comparison between a) doubly periodic and b) horizontally periodic, vertically compact wavepackets of energy transfers between waves and the mean flow for waves with $k_z = -0.4k_x$. In both cases the wave amplitude is $A = 0.017$ The energy transfer rates are shown from waves to the mean flow (solid line), from the mean flow to waves with horizontal wavenumber k_x (long-dashed line), from all waves to waves with horizontal wavenumber k_x (short-dashed line), and from all waves to waves with horizontal wavenumber $2k_x$ (dotted line).

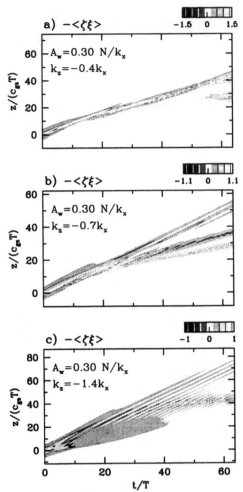

FIG. 2. Time series of the normalised wave-induced mean flow in three simulations of large-amplitude wavepackets in flow with no shear (see text). The amplitude, A_w, and vertical wavenumber, k_z, corresponding to each simulation are shown.

induced mean flow $- \langle \xi \zeta \rangle$ over time. (Here the angle-brackets denote averaging over one horizontal wavelength.) The increase in amplitude of the wavepacket in the case with $k_z = -0.4k_x$ is evident. In the case with $k_z = -1.4k_x$ the wavepacket is predicted to be modulationally stable, and indeed the amplitude decreases over time.

If the amplitude of the wavepacket is larger still, the waves can become convectively unstable. Simulations show that waves that initially are convectively stable are driven to instability due to interactions between the waves and the wave-induced mean flow. Using an estimate based on linear theory, the critical amplitude above which a compact wavepacket ultimately becomes unstable is given by the so-called "self-acceleration condition", listed in the third row of Table 1. This should be compared with the amplitude required for initially overturning waves, given in the second row of Ta-

ble 1.

Simulations of vertically compact, horizontally periodic waves show that the self-acceleration condition does a remarkably good job of predicting at what amplitude the waves are ultimately unstable. Figure 3 shows the stability regime for vertically compact waves. The stability is assessed by computing the change in the squared buoyancy frequency due to waves, $\Delta N^2 = -(g/\rho_0)\partial\rho(x,z,t)/\partial z$, and comparing this with the background squared buoyancy frequency $N^2 = -(g/\rho_0)d\bar\rho(z)/dz$. When $\Delta N^2 < -N^2$ overturning occurs somewhere in the wave-field. Solid triangles and circles are

834

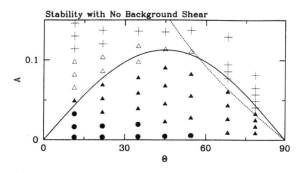

Stability with No Background Shear

vert. modulations	$|\Theta| > \tan^{-1}(2^{-1/2}) \simeq 35°$
overturning	$|A_w| < \frac{N}{k_x}\cos^2\Theta/\sin\Theta$
self-accel.	$|A_w| < \sqrt{2}\frac{N}{k_x}\sin\Theta\cos^2\Theta$
reflection	$|A_w| < \frac{1}{\sqrt{2}}\frac{N}{k_x}\sin\Theta\cos^2\Theta$
transmission	$|A_w| > \sqrt{2\frac{N}{k_x}\sigma_z\overline{U}_z\cos^3\Theta}$

Table 1. Stability characteristics of finite-amplitude internal waves. Values are given in terms of the amplitude, A_w, of the vertical velocity field. N is the buoyancy freqency, k_x is the horizontal wavenumber, σ_z is the vertical extent of the wavepacket, and $\overline{U}_z$ is the background shear.

FIG. 3. Stability regimes compared with simulation results of horizontally periodic waves with vertical extents $\sigma_z k_x = 10$. Each points represents the results of a single simulation for a wavepacket with $\Theta = \tan^{-1}(|k_z/k_x|)$ and amplitude $A = A_\xi/\lambda_x$. A solid circle denotes simulations for which $\min\{\Delta N^2\}/N_0^2 > -0.1$ over the duration of the simulation ($0 \le t < 16T$). A solid triangle is plotted if $-1 < \min\{\Delta N^2\}/N_0^2 < -0.1$ over the duration of the simulation. An open triangle is plotted if $\min\{\Delta N^2\}/N_0^2 < -1$ between times $5T$ and $16T$. A cross indicates simulations in which $\min\{\Delta N^2\}/N_0^2 < -1$ before time $5T$. Superimposed on the regime diagram are the theoretically predicted stability regimes for self-acceleration (below thick solid line) and initially overturning waves (below dashed line).

plotted if overturning never occurs during the simulation time (about 16 buoyancy periods). Note, in agreement with the self-acceleration condition, waves are unstable at surprisingly small amplitudes if their frequency is close to N. The results are relatively insensitive to the vertical extent of the waves. For wavepackets that are both horizontally and vertically compact, the waves are found to be stable at moderately large amplitudes if their frequency lies between N and $\sqrt{2/3}N$.

3. Wave Propagation in Uniform Shear

a. Horizontally periodic waves

A variety of simulations have been performed of horizontally periodic, vertically compact waves in uniform (negative) shear. Typically the shear strength is set so the waves reflect after approximately 15 buoyancy periods.

Whether the wavepackets are stable or unstable to modulations, if they are of sufficiently large amplitude the waves are found to reflect well below the reflection level predicted by linear theory. For example, see Figure 4. In the case with $k_z = -0.4k_x$ superharmonic waves are found to be excited due to nonlinear interactions between the incident and reflected waves (Sutherland 2000). In the cases with $k_z = -0.7k_x$ and $k_z = -1.4k_x$ the interactions are sufficient to lead to overturning and permanent deposition of momentum to the mean flow.

In a simplistic theory, one might assume that wave-breaking occurs if the amplitude of the superimposed incident and reflected waves is so large that waves break due to self-acceleration. This condition, given in the fourth row of Table 1, does provide an adequate measure of stability. Because of the inherently nonlinear nature of the interaction, a more sophisticated theory would be required to improve upon this linear theory prediction.

Particularly interesting is the case with $k_z = -1.4k_x$ in which the waves propagating in shear reflect well below the reflection level even if the shear is relatively weak. Figure 5 shows profiles of the Reynolds stress per unit mass for simulations of large-amplitude waves in a background flow with shear strength $s = -0.016N$, $-0.008N$ and $-0.004N$. In all three cases, a significant proportion of the incident wavepacket reflects after approximately 15 to 20 buoyancy periods. In the last case this portion of the wavepacket reflects at one quarter the distance

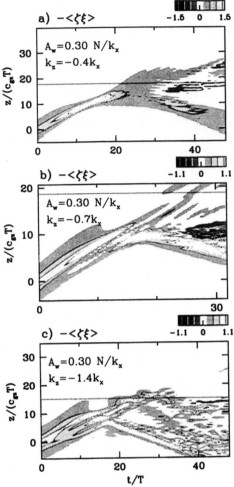

FIG. 4. Time series of the normalised wave-induced mean flow in three simulations of large-amplitude wavepackets in flow with uniform shear: a) $k_z = -0.4k_x$ and $s = -0.002N$, b) $k_z = -0.7k_x$ and $s = -0.004N$, c) $k_z = -1.4k_x$ and $s = -0.016N$. The dotted line indicates the vertical position of the reflecting level predicted by linear theory.

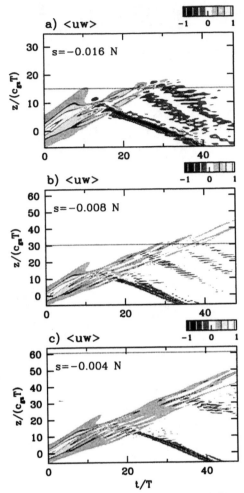

FIG. 5. Time series of the normalised Reynolds Stress per unit mass in three simulations of large-amplitude wavepackets in flow with $k_z = -1.4k_x$ and in uniform shear with strength a) $s = -0.002N$, b) $s = -0.004N$, c) $s = -0.016N$. The dotted line indicates the vertical position of the reflecting level predicted by linear theory.

below the reflection level (Fig. 5c).

b. Horizontally compact waves

The change between small- and large-amplitude dynamics is attributable to interactions between the waves and the wave-induced mean flow. However, if the waves are horizontally compact, the "mean flow" is substantial only over the horizontal extent of the wavepacket. Indeed the evolution of the wavepacket as a whole changes significantly, even if the envelope's horizontal extent is an

order of magnitude larger than the horizontal wavelength (Sutherland 1999b; Sutherland 1999a; Sutherland 2000).

In simulations of compact wavepackets with frequency close to the buoyancy frequency, the waves are found to evolve in such a way that they propagate at approximately constant group velocity well above the reflection level. Figure 6 shows time series of the wave-induced mean flow in three simulations of waves with $k_z = -0.4k_x$ and amplitude $A_w = -0.2N/k_x$, $-0.3N/k_x$ and $-0.4N/k_x$. In the

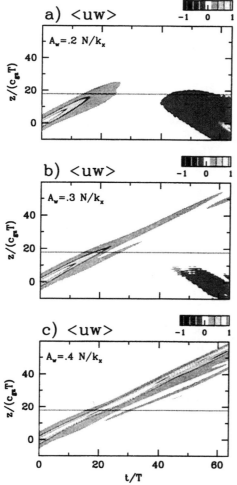

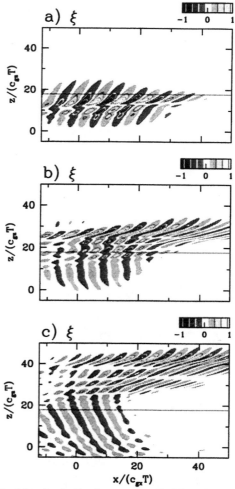

FIG. 6. Time series of $\langle uw \rangle$ for simulations with $k_z = -0.4k_x$ and amplitude A_w equal to a) $0.2N/k_x$, b) $0.3N/k_x$ and c) $0.4N/k_x$. In each simulation the background shear is $s = -0.002N$. The horizontal dashed line on each plot indicates the predicted reflection level.

FIG. 7. Vertical displacement fields after a) 16, b) 32 and c) 48 buoyancy periods, determined from a simulation of a horizontally and vertically compact wavepacket with $k_z = -0.4k_x$ and amplitude $A_w = 0.40N/k_x$. The background shear is $s = -0.002N$. The horizontal dashed line on each plot indicates the reflection level predicted by linear theory.

small-amplitude cases the waves reflect but, if $A_w > 0.3N/k_x$, a significant proportion propagates upward for long times at approximately the speed of the vertical group velocity of linear theory.

The structure of the waves in the case with $A_w = 0.4N/k_x$ are shown at three times in Figure 7. The wavepacket above the reflection level maintains approximately the same structure as it propagates. It is proposed that the structure is established so that the shear associated with the wave-induced mean flow locally shields the wavepacket from the background shear. On this basis, the transmission condition

has been proposed (see the last row of Table 1) which is derived by assuming that the maximum shear strength associated with the wave-induced mean flow is equal and opposite in sign to the background shear. Waves are transmitted across a reflection level if their amplitude is larger than this critical value.

The results of a range of simulations are in agreement with the transmission condition. In simulations with smaller frequency wavepackets, the waves become overturning at amplitudes close the critical amplitude for transmission.

4. Conclusions

Numerical simulations show that upward propagating small-amplitude wavepackets reflect downward at the depth predicted by linear theory. For horizontally periodic waves of large-amplitude, they reflect well below this depth.

The structure of the reflecting large-amplitude waves is quite complex. Reflecting waves with frequency close to the buoyancy frequency excite superharmonic waves. Reflecting waves with smaller frequency and comparable amplitudes evolve to become overturning. Thus momentum may be permanently deposited to the mean flow through wave reflection!

Surprisingly, large-amplitude horizontally compact waves with frequency close to the buoyancy frequency are found to propagate well above the reflection level. Weakly nonlinear effects continuously modulate the waves so that they propagate steadily upward with negligible reflection. Simple analytic theories are derived, and listed in Table 1, that predict at what amplitude transmission through a reflecting level should occur. The simulation results are in accordance with this prediction.

References

Benjamin, T. B. and Feir, J. E. 1967. The disintegration of wavetrains on deep water. *J. Fluid Mech.*, 27:417–430.

Drazin, P. G. 1977. On the instability of an internal gravity wave. *Proc. Roy. Soc. London*, 356:411–432.

Fermi, E., Pasta, J., and Ulam, S. 1974. Studies of nonlinear problems i, Los Alamos Report LA 1940, 1955. In Newell, A. C., editor, *reproduced in Nonlinear Wave Motion*, Providence, RI. Amer. Math. Soc.

Klostermeyer, J. 1991. Two- and three-dimensional parametric instabilities in finite amplitude internal gravity waves. *Geophys. Astrophys. Fluid Dyn.*, 64:1–25.

Koop, C. G. 1981. A preliminary investigation of the interaction of internal gravity waves with a steady shearing motion. *J. Fluid Mech.*, 113:347–386.

Lighthill, M. J. 1978. *Waves in Fluids.* Cambridge University Press, Cambridge, England.

Lombard, P. N. and Riley, J. J. 1996. On the breakdown into turbulence of propagating internal waves. *Dyn. Atmos. Ocean*, 23:345–355.

Mied, R. R. 1976. The occurrence of parametric instabilities in finite-amplitude internal gravity waves. *J. Fluid Mech.*, 78:763–784.

Sutherland, B. R. 1996. Internal gravity wave radiation into weakly stratified fluid. *Phys. Fluids*, 8:430–441.

Sutherland, B. R. 1999a. Internal wave breaking due to self-acceleration. *J. Fluid Mech.*, submitted.

Sutherland, B. R. 1999b. Propagation and reflection of large amplitude internal gravity waves. *Phys. Fluids*, 11:1081–1090.

Sutherland, B. R. 2000. Internal wave reflection in uniform shear. *Q.J.R.M.S.*, in press.

Whitham, G. B. 1974. *Linear and Nonlinear Waves.* John Wiley and Sons, Inc., New York.

A laboratory investigation of breaking interfacial waves

Cary Troy[1], Jeffrey Koseff[2], and Chris Rehmann[3]

[1,2]Environmental Fluid Mechanics Laboratory, Stanford University, Stanford, CA 94305-4020
[3]Department of Civil and Environmental Engineering, University of Illinois, Urbana, IL 61801
carytroy@stanford.edu,koseff@cive.stanford.edu,rehmann@uiuc.edu

Abstract

A miscible, two-layer stratification laboratory experiment is used to examine the nature of interfacial wave breaking. In our technique, we use a wave focusing technique to generate a dispersive packet of waves which focus at a specified location in the tank. The use of the wavemaker transfer function is found to be key in generating repeatable breaking waves with the focusing technique. Results are presented which show that the background weak mean shear, provided in our case by low-wavenumber waves in the wave packet, is an important agent in wave breaking. Specifically, this background shear appears to induce wave breaking and the direction of this background shear seems to dictate whether the waves break by shear (backward-breaking) or convective (forward-breaking) instability.

Introduction

Our ability to accurately predict mass and momentum transfer in the ocean environment is dependent on accurately modeling of the small scales comprising oceanic turbulence (Gregg, 1987, Caldwell and Moum 1995). Of much use are relations between the small scale (unresolved) motions and their effects on the overall flow energetics. For example, the mixing efficiency (the ratio of net buoyancy flux to turbulent dissipation) provides an estimate of the irreversible effect of turbulent mixing on the surrounding density profile. Our study hopes to improve the understanding of small scale turbulence by examining one such oceanic turbulence-producing mechanism: breaking internal waves. Specifically, this study focuses on properties of breaking internal waves produced in a stratification that we approximate with a two-layer (miscible) laboratory experiment.

Work on breaking interfacial waves away from boundaries was first performed by Woods (1967) who carried out dye experiments of waves breaking on an oceanic thermocline. This experiment first suggested how the presence of a background weak mean shear could enhance wave breaking (Phillips, 1968). Thorpe (1978) and Holyer (1979) later found that progressive interfacial waves are susceptible to both shear (backward breaking) and convective (forward-breaking) instabilities. They showed analytically that the breaking conditions for forward-breaking (wave particle speed exceeding phase speed) and backward-breaking ($Ri < 0.25$, where Ri is the local Richardson number) can more easily be met in the presence of a weak background shear, the direction of which can determine the nature of the breaking.

The energetics of breaking standing interfacial waves have been studied by, among others, McEwan (1983) and later by Taylor (1992), who examined the mixing efficiencies of the events. Generally it is found that breaking internal waves have much higher mixing efficiencies than other forms of stratified turbulence, ranging between 20-35% (Rehmann, 1996). Since the mixing efficiency in stratified sheared turbulence peaks when the turbulent Froude number of the mixing event ($Fr_t \equiv \frac{u'N}{L}$) is about 1 (Ivey and Imberger, 1987), following Taylor (1992), we hypothesize that an interfacial wave breaking away from boundaries will exhibit similar behavior and have $Fr_t \sim 1$ in the mixing patch. The present study hopes to closely examine the precise nature of how an interfacial wave breaks, producing a turbulent patch which then loses its energy to viscosity (dissipation) and mixing (net increase in the background potential energy).

Experimental Methods

Stratification

The experiments were conducted at Stanford University's Environmental Fluid Mechanics Laboratory (EFML), in a 4.8m (long) by 0.3m (wide) by 0.6m (tall) Plexiglas tank (see Figure 1). A semi-spherical ("plunger type") wavemaker that is driven up and down vertically by a linear actuator (Industrial Devices Corporation) is located at one end of the tank. The linear actuator is controlled with an analog position controller that allows us to drive the wavemaker with any time-varying signal desired (e.g. a simple sinusoidal signal for monochromatic wave trains). This time-varying wavemaker control signal is composed and generated with a desktop computer. The wavemaker produces progressive interfacial waves that travel to the opposite end of the tank, where a 1:7 sloped synthetic horsehair beach is in place to prevent wave reflections. It is important to keep the amplitude of the wavemaker motions small ($< 3cm$), otherwise unwanted mixing is produced by the wavemaker head. We are further constrained by the Brunt-Vaisala frequency of the interface ($N^2 = \frac{g}{\rho_0}(\frac{\Delta\rho}{\delta})$)), where $\Delta\rho$ is the density difference between the layers and δ is the interface thickness), which sets the upper frequency limit of waves that can be generated in the tank.

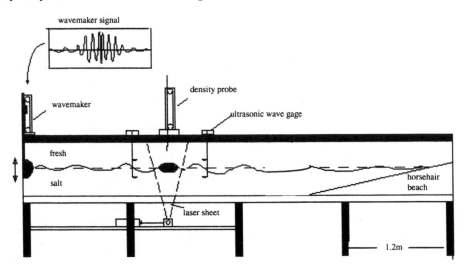

Figure 1. Experimental facility

When we conduct an interfacial wave experiment, the tank is filled with a two-layer salt-stratified solution. Each layer is $28cm$ deep. For all but the longest waves generated in the tank, this layer thickness is sufficiently deep to make the waves dispersive. The density difference between the two layers ranges from $1 - 3\%$, depending on the experiment, and care is taken to avoid temperature differences between the layers (in order to avoid conductivity-temperature mismatch errors when taking a density profile). During the course of an experiment, some unwanted diffusion naturally occurs between the two (miscible) layers. To maintain a sharp density interface between the two layers, a thin slotted pipette is located at the interface as a selective withdrawal device (see density profile in Figure 2). Fluid from the diffuse interface is pumped out of the tank through the slotted pipette, and a sharpened interface is obtained. The overall layer depths are maintained in the midst of the selective withdrawal by adding appropriate water to the bottom and top layers through bottom and surface diffusers, respectively. In this fashion, we can run a two-layer experiment for several days, continually re-sharpening the stratification as needed. Generally, the interface thickness is maintained at between 0.5 and 1.5 cm, which, for layer density differences of up to 3.0%, produce a maximum interfacial buoyancy frequency in our experiments of about $1Hz$. However, we generally find that the limiting factor to generating high-frequency waves is viscosity, which causes the high-frequency waves to decay rapidly with distance away from the wavemaker.

Instrumentation

Density is measured using a Precision Measurements Engineering Model 125 Micro Scale Conductivity and Temperature Instrument (PME125), which consists of a fast-response thermister mounted next to a four-electrode conductivity sensor. The output voltages are collected and analyzed using a data acquisition board and a personal computer. The PME125 probe is calibrated against a Sea-Bird SBE-04 conductivity sensor and a Rosemount platinum resistance thermometer. To obtain the density profile in the tank, the probe is traversed vertically through the water column at $10cm/s$.

Wave heights are measured using the ultrasonic interfacial wave gages described in Michallet and Barthelemy (1997). These wave gages emit an ultrasonic pulse across the density interface; this ultrasonic pulse hits a reflector and is bounced back to the instrument. Processing electronics output a voltage that is dependent on the travel time of the ultrasonic pulse, and this output voltage is compared to a static calibration record of voltage and interface location. In this way, wave height records are easily obtained with resolution of less than $1mm$. Since density profile changes affect the wave gage's calibration, it is important to recalibrate the gage between most experiments and ensure that no density intrusions enter the wave gage measurement volume during the experiment.

For ordinary experiments, we visualize the flow with industrial grade food coloring in one of the layers (usually the bottom). In flow visualization experiments, one layer is colored with Rhodamine dye and illuminated from below with a vertically-oriented laser light sheet. We use a Coherent Innova 305 laser with a programmable scanning mirror mounted below the tank to create the light sheet. Pictures are obtained using a digital camera or a digital video camera.

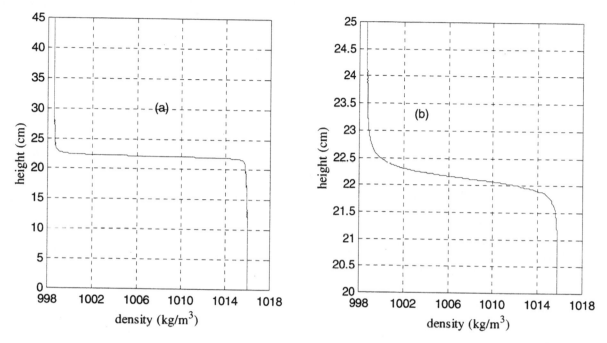

Figure 2. Typical measured density profile maintained during an experiment (a) and close-up of interface (b).

Generation of the breaking wave

We generate the breaking wave following the technique of Longuet-Higgins (1974) which was used later by Rapp and Melville (1990). In this technique, a linear packet, or "chirp" of (necessarily dispersive) waves is generated such that the individual waves in the packet all come into phase at a single location (x_B) and time (t_B). At this location, adding constructively, the waves form a large amplitude wave which then, ideally, becomes unstable and breaks. The wave packet's interfacial displacement, $\eta(x,t)$, is described by linear theory (Rapp and Melville, 1990):

$$\eta(x,t) = \sum_{i=1}^{N} a_i \cos(k_i x - \omega_i t - \phi_i) ,\tag{1}$$

where $a_i, k_i, \omega_i,$ and ϕ_i are the individual waves' amplitudes, horizontal wavenumbers, radian frequencies, and phases, respectively. The phases ϕ_i of the wave packet are chosen such that $(k_i x - \omega_i t - \phi_i) = 0, \pm 2\pi, \pm 4\pi$. The wavenumber k_i (computed) and frequency ω_i (specified) are related by the dispersion relation $k(\omega)$ for the stratification present in the tank. It is normal in the course of our experiments to experience slight, but measurable changes, in the background density profile. To maintain an accurate dispersion relation, we can use the measured profile of $N^2(z)$ to obtain the exact linear dispersion relation by solving the two-dimensional non-hydrostatic normal modes equation (see Gill (1982), for example)

$$\left(\frac{N^2(z) - \omega^2}{\omega^2} \right) k^2 \, \hat{w}(z) + \frac{d^2 \hat{w}}{dz^2} = 0 ,\tag{2}$$

subject to $\hat{w}(0) = \hat{w}(H) = 0$. In equation (2), $N^2(z)$ is the measured profile of buoyancy frequency, and $\hat{w}(z)$ is the eigenfunction of vertical velocity for the first internal mode of the stratification. The $\hat{w}(H) = 0$

condition is the imposed rigid lid condition at the free surface ($z = H$). In practice, the dispersion relation does not deviate much from a two-layer, linear solution (see figure 2).

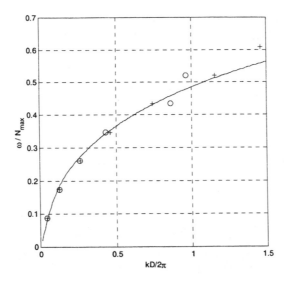

Figure 3. Measured dispersion relation $\omega(k)$ for 2.0% density difference and 1.5*cm* interfacial thickness (wavemaker dia. $D = 15.2cm$). The solid line represents the two-layer linear dispersion relation with finite interface correction presented by Phillips (1966). (o: wavemaker stroke 1cm;+:wavemaker stroke 2cm)

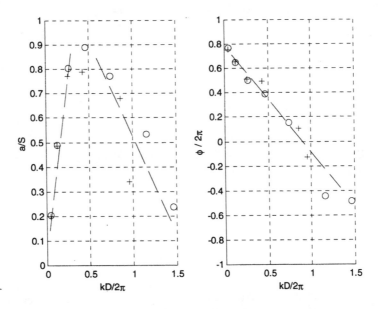

Figure 4. Measured wavemaker transfer function for 2.0% density difference: wave amplitude (a/S) and phase response ($\phi/2\pi$) as a function of wavenumber ($kD/2\pi$) for two different stroke to interface thickness ratios (o: $S/\delta = 1$; + : $S/\delta = 2$). S and D are the wavemaker stroke amplitude and diameter, respectively.

A final, important step in producing a repeatable breaking wave using the focusing technique is the determination of the wavemaker transfer function (Pidgeon, 1999). While the linear theory readily predicts the necessary forcing of the interface to create a focused packet, it remains to be empirically determined how to use the wavemaker to achieve the necessary forcing. The phase and amplitude responses of the wavemaker are needed in order to keep all chirp components of equal steepness (a_ik_i) and to correct for wavemaker-induced phase shifts among different frequency components. To obtain the transfer function of the wavemaker, experiments were conducted which measured the phase and amplitude response of the wavemaker for a range of frequencies, at the density difference of interest (see Figure 4). The wavemaker appears most efficient in generating waves with wavelength about twice the diameter of the wavemaker head. In applying the empirically determined transfer function, the wavemaker is assumed to act as a linear system (all frequencies acting independently).

(a)   (d)

(b)   (d)

(c)   (e)

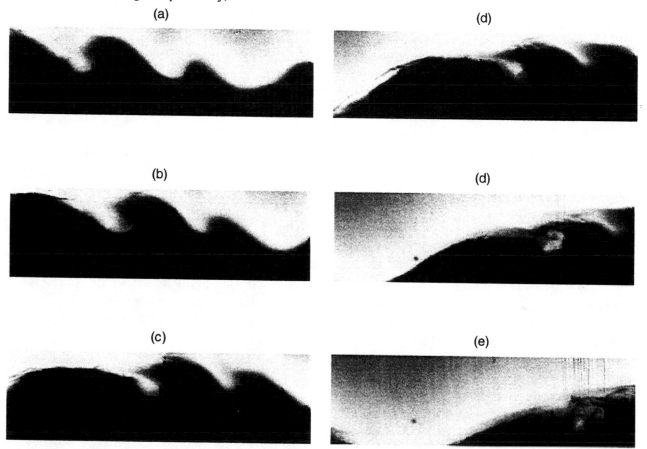

Figure 5. A backward breaking wave induced by the crest of a lower wavenumber wave. Wave propagation is to the right; the images proceed downward from the upper left; the aspect ratio has been preserved and the images are $6cm$ by $20cm, 0.67s$ apart.

Results

The focusing technique was successful in creating unstable interfacial waves. Generally the instability occurs at the prescribed location within a wavelength of the central chirp component's wavelength. However, near the focal location the waves appear to interact non-linearly and do not sum linearly; this is not unexpected since linear assumptions are not valid near the breaking location (Rapp and Melville, 1990). We observe both forward-breaking and backward-breaking instabilities, but backward-breaking is more common, which suggests that the criteria for convective instability is more difficult to meet. It appears that the background mean shear of the wave field does play an important role in determining how the wave breaks. In our experiment, there is no background mean shear; instead, it is the low wavenumber components in the chirp that act as a background shear and induce the wave to break accordingly. For example, a steep high frequency wave atop the crest of a low frequency wave is sheared into breaking backward since the low frequency wave field has similar vorticity at the crest. Similarly, we see convective instabilities originating in the troughs of larger waves, where the shear is in the correct direction for forward breaking. Figure 5 shows a typical backward breaking event that begins breaking when it is overtaken by the crest of a low frequency wave. The striking features of the first frames are the steep (stable) slopes of the progressing wavelets (higher frequency waves). They are visually estimated as $ak \sim 1.2$. These waves propagate without breaking until the shear associated with the crest of the underlying, longer wave overtakes them. The last images in Figure 5 show the development of the instability, and the pairing of two unstable waves, which we see frequently. It seems that a single wave breaking often triggers nearby waves to break, suggesting that a single wavelet breaking can trigger a "catastrophic" breaking if the waves are only marginally stable.

Future Work

We plan to estimate the mixing efficiency of the breaking wave with a control volume approach where interfacial wave gages are used to infer the turbulent kinetic energy production and density profiles yield the net buoyancy flux of the breaking wave. Digital particle tracking in conjunction with laser fluorescence will allow us to measure instantaneous Richardson numbers and buoyancy flux. Overturn lengths can also give us an idea of the energetics of the breaking wave. Depending on the repeatability of the breaking wave produced by our technique, it may be possible to infer turbulent quantities such as Fr_t, which could then be correlated with the measured mixing efficiencies to see if $Fr_t \sim 1$ in the mixing patch of the breaking wave; we want to understand why breaking internal waves are such efficient mixing agents in the ocean.

Acknowledgments

This research was supported by the Physical Oceanography program of the National Science Foundation research grant OCE-9871808. The authors gratefully acknowledge the assistance of Robert Brown in constructing the facility.

References

Caldwell, D.R., and Moum, J.N. 1995. Turbulence and Mixing in the Ocean, *Rev. Geophys.*, Vol 33 Supplement.

Gill, A.E. 1982. *Atmosphere-Ocean Dynamics*. Academic Press.

Gregg, M.C. 1987. Diapycnal mixing in the thermocline: a review. *J. Geophys. Res.*, 92, No. C5, 5249-5286.

Holyer, J.Y. 1979. Large amplitude progressive interfacial waves. *J. Fluid Mechanics*, 93, 433-448.

Ivey, G.N. and Imberger, J. 1991. On the nature of turbulence in a stratified fluid. Part I: the energetics of mixing. J. Phys. Ocean., 21, 650-658.

Longuet-Higgins, M.S. 1975. Breaking waves in deep or shallow water. In *Proc. 10th conf. on Naval hydrodynamics*, pp. 597-605. M.I.T.

Michallet, M., and Barthelemy, E. 1997. Ultrasonic probes and data processing to study interfacial solitary waves. *Experiments in Fluids*, 22, 380-386.

McEwan, A.D. 1983. The kinematics of stratified mixing through internal wavebreaking. *J. Fluid Mechanics*, 128, 47-57.

Phillips, O.M. 1966. *The Dynamics of the Upper Ocean*. Cambridge University Press.

Pidgeon, E.J. 1999. *An experimental investigation of breaking wave induced turbulence*. Ph.D. thesis, Department of Civil and Environmental Engineering, Stanford University, CA.

Rapp, R.J. and Melville, W.K. 1990. Laboratory experiments of deep-water breaking waves. *Proc. Roy. Soc. London Ser. A*, 351, 735-800.

Rehmann, C.R. 1995. *Effects of stratification and molecular diffusivity on the mixing efficiency of decaying grid turbulence*. Ph.D. thesis, Department of Civil Engineering, Stanford University, California.

Taylor, J.R. 1992. The energetics of breaking events in a resonantly forced internal wave field. *J. Fluid Mechanics*, 239, 309-340.

Thorpe, S.A. 1978. On the shape and breaking of finite amplitude internal gravity waves in shear flow. *J. Fluid Mechanics*, 85, 7-31.

Woods, J.D. 1968. Wave-induced shear instability in the summer thermocline. *J. Fluid Mechanics*, 32, 791-800.

II

RIVERS AND ESTUARIES

A laboratory study on the flushing of a blocked estuary

Michael Coates[1], Yakun Guo[2] and Peter Davies[2]

[1]School of Ecology and Environment, Deakin University, P.O. Box 423, Warrnambool, Victoria, 3280, Australia.
[2]Department of Civil Engineering, The University, Dundee, DD1 4HN, Scotland.

1. Abstract

Results are presented from a series of laboratory model studies of flushing of saline water from an estuary with its mouth fully-closed by a sediment bar. Experiments have been carried out to determine the response of the trapped saline water as a function of the fresh water discharge Q, the density difference between the saline and fresh water $\Delta\rho$, and the estuary bed slope α. Data from flow visualizations confirm that the position x_w of the tip of the trapped salt wedge initially migrates downstream according to

$$x_w = 1.3(q^3/g'\alpha^2 hL)^{1/3}t^{1/3}.$$

(The remaining symbols are defined in the text.) However, after a period of time that systemmatically depends on the discharge, the trapped salt wedge migrates more slowly downstream according to

$$x_w = 0.0026(q^{13}/g'^5)^{1/18}(1/H_s\alpha^2)^{1/6}t^{1/6}.$$

2. Introduction

The microtidal estuaries in southern Australia (ones that are subject to very small tides) are unique in that they also have a Mediterranean climate in which very low river flows occur over summer and autumn. Consequently, during this period, a sandbar can form across their mouths that completely isolates these estuaries from the ocean for extended periods. Under such circumstances, saline or brackish water becomes trapped in the estuary, with significant implications for the estuarine ecology. Conditions in these estuaries are such that variations in water quality are determined primarily by the strength of the river inflow (Kurup et al. 1998) and the flushing of this saline water can then only take place naturally by the restoration of a purging flow. The purging flow can arise from storm events in the catchment area or from the regular water releases from upstream feeder reservoirs. The latter are particularly important as they are currently used to provide the water allocation for the environment.

The flushing of such estuaries is the subject of the present paper. A laboratory model has been built to simulate many of the essential features of these estuarine dynamics, and the motion of the trapped salt wedge within the estuary has been measured for various external forcing parameters. Only steady purging flows are considered here although some periodic flows have been investigated by Debler and Imberger (1996), Debler and Armfield (1997) and Coates et al. (1999).

3. The physical system

Figure 1 shows a schematic view of the problem under investigation. Most experiments were run in a long rectangular U-section channel with a width b of 82 mm and working length L of 6.2 m. (The total length of 8.2 m incorporated a 2-m long horizontal lead-in that represented the river bed and allowed the freshwater inflow to become uniform.) Some earlier experiments used a channel of width b of 100 mm and working length L of 3.8 m. A sloping false bottom, of slope α, was inserted into the flume and the cavity filled with a volume of salt water of prescribed initial density $\rho_0 + \Delta\rho$.

With the system at rest, a surface flow of fresh water of density ρ_0 and discharge Q, having depth h, was initiated in the channel. By an elapsed time t, a salt wedge had formed with the tip at position $x = x_w(t)$ relative to its undisturbed upstream location and nominal interface height $z = \xi(x,t)$ relative to the base of the channel (figure 1). It is convenient to describe the behaviour in terms of the drop $\delta(x,t) = H_s - \xi(x,t)$ of the interface level. Since the interface was essentially level over most of its length L, we can write $\delta \approx \alpha x_w$.

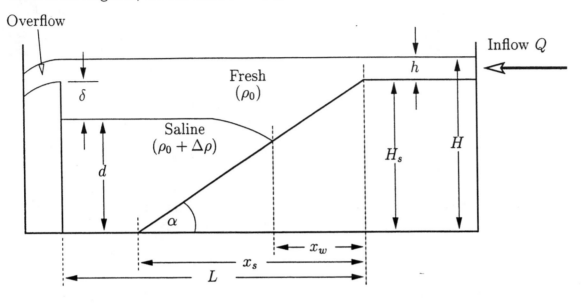

Figure 1: *A schematic of the experiment showing the definition of the various parameters.*

Measurements were made over time of the displacement x_w of the wedge nose caused by the purging flow for a range of values of Q, $\Delta\rho$ and α. Table 1 lists the range of these experimental parameters. An example of such measurements is shown in figure 2 for run 5 ($\Delta\rho = 10\,\mathrm{kgm^{-3}}$ and $\alpha = 0.04$). In each case, there was a clear tendency for the tip of the wedge to migrate downstream at a rate that was systematically dependent upon Q, $\Delta\rho$ and α.

Table 1: *A table of the experimental parameters.*

Expt.	α (radians)	L (m)	b (m)	$\Delta\rho$ (kgm^{-3})	Q ($\times 10^{-3}\,\mathrm{m^3 s^{-1}}$)
1	0.02	6.2	0.082	10	0.15, 0.37, 0.55, 0.97
2	0.02	6.2	0.082	30	0.20, 0.53, 1.02
3	0.02	6.2	0.082	50	0.22, 0.51, 1.00
4	0.04	6.2	0.082	5	0.12, 0.39, 0.57, 1.03
5	0.04	6.2	0.082	10	0.12, 0.40, 0.58, 0.99
6	0.04	6.2	0.082	20	0.12, 0.41, 0.59, 1.04
7	0.04	6.2	0.082	30	0.13, 0.40, 0.51, 1.06
8	0.04	6.2	0.082	50	0.17, 0.41, 0.56, 0.85
9	0.05	3.8	0.100	13	0.50, 0.75, 1.00
10	0.05	3.8	0.100	35	0.50, 0.75, 1.00
11	0.09	3.8	0.100	37	0.50, 0.75

What is apparent from these results is that the entrainment rate of salt water, and thus the migration of the tip of the salt wedge, appears to have two distinct regimes. The initial phase is

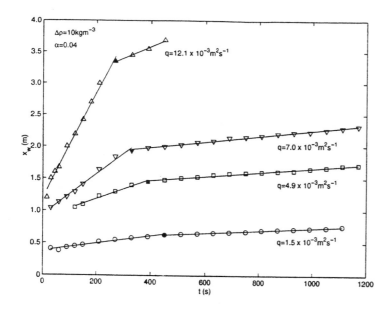

Figure 2: *The displacement x_w of the salt wedge tip as a function of time t for the various flow rates q in run 5. The filled symbols mark the transition between the two entrainment regimes.*

marked by a relatively rapid migration downstream by the salt wedge. After a period of time that is systematically dependent on the flow rate, there is a sudden reduction in the entrainment rate and the salt wedge migrates more slowly downstream.

4. Discussion

We initially look at the first regime. In order to parameterize the entrainment, it is convenient to analyse the data in terms of the energy balance taking place as the wedge moves down the slope, that is, the conversion of the kinetic energy of the incoming freshwater into potential energy required to lift the saline layer. Such conversions can be expressed in terms of a proportionality factor $k(t)$ (Debler and Imberger 1996) that relates the partial conversion of the kinetic energy into potential energy. The potential energy U required to lift a saline layer that after time t has a nominal length $L - x_w/2 \approx L$, provided that $x_w \ll L$ as was the case here, and depth $\delta = \alpha x_w$ is

$$U = mg(\delta/2) = \tfrac{1}{2}g\Delta\rho(\alpha x_w)^2 bL. \tag{1}$$

During this time, a mass $\rho_0 Qt$ of freshwater enters at velocity $u = Q/bh$, providing the required kinetic energy

$$K = \tfrac{1}{2}(\rho_0 Qt)(Q/bh)^2 = \tfrac{1}{2}\rho_0 q^3 t/b^2 h^2 \tag{2}$$

where the discharge per unit width is $q = Q/b$. Equating (1) and (2), we can write

$$x_w^2 = k(t)\frac{q^3 t}{g'\alpha^2 h^2 L} \tag{3}$$

where the reduced gravity is $g' = g\Delta\rho/\rho_0$.

It is convenient to normalize the nose displacement x_w with h (so that $x_* = x_w/h$). However, there is no preferred time scale in this problem and thus we use the scale $t' = g'\alpha^2 h^4 L/q^3$, set by the problem. Defining the non-dimensional time by $t_* = t/t'$, (3) reduces to the simple form

$$x_* = k(t)^{1/2} t_*^{1/2}. \tag{4}$$

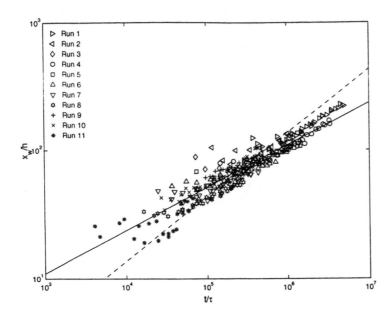

Figure 3: *A plot of the dimensionless salt wedge position x_* against the dimensionless time t_*. The solid line is the line of best fit while the dashed line is $x_* \sim t^{1/2}$.*

Figure 3 shows a plot of x_* against t_* for all the measured data in the first regime. It is clear from this figure that the data show a good fit to a power law relation between x_* and t_* but with a different exponent to that suggested by (4). An analysis of figure 3 indicates that the actual relation is

$$x_* = 1.3t_*^{1/3}. \tag{5}$$

The deviation of these data from (4) gives a horizontally-averaged measure for the conversion efficiency $k(t)$. However, while the energy conversion changes with time, the time dependency is not actually explicit but rather implicit through the increasing thickness $\delta(t)$ of freshwater overlying the saline layer. Consequently, it is more instructive to find $k = k(\delta_*)$, where $\delta_* = \delta/h$. Eliminating t_* in (4) and (5) gives, in dimensional form,

$$k = 2.2\alpha h/\delta. \tag{6}$$

This suggests that the conversion efficiency is inversely proportional to the thickness of the overlying freshwater layer, as might be expected. It is proportional to the flow rate and to the slope angle but is inversely proportional to g' through $h = q^{2/3}/g'^{1/3}$.

In the second regime, the scaling (5) breaks down, but the data do suggest that another power law is valid, as illustrated in figure 4. If we renormalize all the data in the second regime using the general length and time scales $\chi = (q^2/g')^{1/3}$ and $\tau = (q/g'^2)^{1/3}$ respectively, the data suggest a very good agreement to a power law exponent of $n = 1/6$, so that

$$x_* = Ct_*^{1/6}, \tag{7}$$

but where the coefficient of proportionality $C = C(q, g', \alpha)$ is not a constant.

However, the data suggest an empirical relationship between C and the dimensionless parameter $\mathcal{N} = f(q, g')$ defined by

$$\mathcal{N} = \left(\frac{q^2}{g'H_s^3} \right)^{1/3}. \tag{8}$$

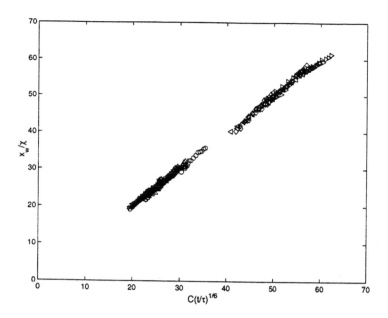

Figure 4: *A plot of the normalized wedge position x_w/χ against $C(t/\tau)^{1/6}$ in the second regime.*

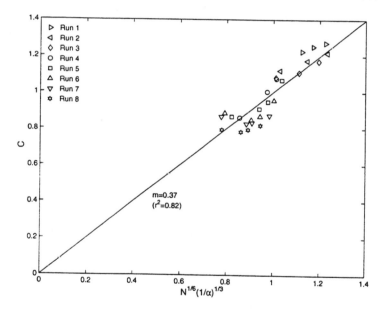

Figure 5: *A plot of the coefficient of proportionality C in terms of the dimensionless parameter* $\mathcal{N} = (q^2/g'H_s^3)^{1/3}$.

This relation is illustrated in figure 5 and a least squares fit suggests that

$$C = 0.37 \left(\frac{\mathcal{N}}{\alpha^2}\right)^{1/6} \qquad (9)$$

is consistent with the data. Using these relations, the normalized salt wedge position in the second regime can determined by

$$x_* = 0.37 \left(\frac{\mathcal{N}}{\alpha^2}\right)^{1/6} t_*^{1/6}, \qquad (10)$$

as shown in figure 6.

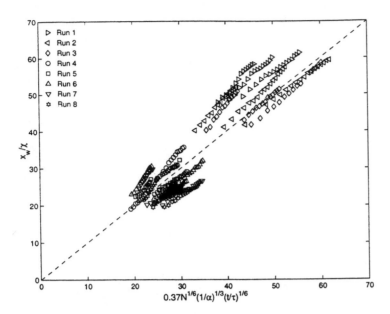

Figure 6: *The normalized salt wedge position as a function of the normalized time in the second regime.*

Unlike the first regime, there is no longer a simple relation for the energy conversion efficiency k in the second regime. If we eliminate t_* using (4) and (10), we obtain, in dimensional form,

$$k = 0.0026\alpha^2 \mathcal{N} h^4 / \delta^4. \tag{11}$$

The conversion efficiency is now proportional to $q^{10/3}$ and inversely proportional to $g'^{1/3}$ through $\mathcal{N}h^4$. It is also inversely proportional to the fourth-power of δ. It is not clear why there should be such a marked fourth-power decrease in the conversion efficiency with the increasing thickness of the overlying freshwater layer.

Acknowledgements. The initial experiments reported in this study were carried out during a summer visit to the Dundee laboratory by one of us (MJC) as part of the Exchange Programme of the Australian Academy of Science and the Australian Academy of Technological Sciences and Engineering with the Royal Society of London. The authors are grateful for this support. Jacqueline Cremers participated in the early stages of this study as part of her undergraduate project for the Department of Physics, Eindoven University of Tecnology, The Netherlands. Technical support from Mr. David Ritchie is gratefully acknowledged.

5. References

COATES, M. J., P. A. DAVIES and Y. GUO, 1999. Laboratory model studies of flushing of trapped salt water from a blocked tisal estuary. Submitted to *ASCE J. Hydraul. Eng.*.

DEBLER, W., and S. W. ARMFIELD, 1997. The purging of saline water from rectangular and trapezoidal cavities by an overflow of turbulent sweet water. *J. Hydraul. Res.*, **35(1):** 43–62.

DEBLER, W., and J. IMBERGER, 1996. Flushing criteria in estuarine and laboratory experiments. *ASCE J. Hydraul. Eng.*, **85(1,2):** 65–96.

KURUP, G. R., D. P. HAMILTON and J. C. PATTERSON, 1998. Modelling the effect of seasonal flow variations on the position of [the] salt wedge in a microtidal estuary. *Coastal Shelf Sci.*, **47:** 191–208.

INTERFACIAL LAYER DEVELOPMENT DUE TO TURBULENT MIXING AT A DENSITY INTERFACE

B. Donnelly , G.A. Hamill , D.J. Robinson , P. Mackinnon and H.T. Johnston

School of Civil Engineering, The Queen's University of Belfast,
Belfast, Ireland, BT7 5AG

brendan.donnelly@qub.ac.uk, g.hamill@qub.ac.uk, des.robinson@qub.ac.uk,
p.mackinnon@qub.ac.uk, h.johnston@qub.ac.uk

Abstract

The development and characteristics of the interfacial layer developed between freshwater overflowing an entrapped saltwater impoundment have been studied experimentally. The density and thickness characteristics of this layer have been reported with respect to freshwater velocity and depth. A CFD model of the interfacial problem is in development and the current findings are reported.

1 Introduction

The construction of weirs and barrages to control water levels at river estuaries has created a specialised case of salt water intrusion, the 'entrapped' salt water wedge. The typical arrested saline wedge, (Figure1) develops when the freshwater river overrides the denser saltwater body; frictional forces along the interface then create the characteristic wedge shape. This wedge is quasi stationary, advancing and retreating depending on tidal conditions freshwater velocity, freshwater depth and density difference between layers.

It is essential that the river systems affected by saline intrusion maintain dissolved oxygen levels capable of supporting the marine life that live within its boundaries. Dispersion of dissolved oxygen through the water column is hampered however by the density interface. This means that the riverbed under the saltwater layer relies upon circulation currents from the ocean source to replenish any stagnated salt water.

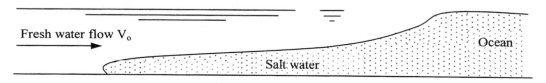

Fresh water flow V_o

Ocean

Salt water

Figure 1. Arrested saline wedge

Control structures such as the Thames Barrage or Belfast's Lagan Weir create an obstruction across the river mouth and effectively isolate the wedge tip from its ocean source (Fig. 2); such intrusions are referred to as entrapped. These entrapped wedges becomes oxygen deprived and grow in size each time the weir is over topped at high tide levels. The removal of this entrapped salt water becomes dependent upon mixing with the overlying freshwater and is essential if a river system low in dissolved oxygen content is to be prevented.

Grubert (1980) states that, 'mixing occurs when a critical velocity capable of disrupting the interface between the stratified layers arises. Interfacial instability leads to the formation of a third or interfacial layer across which the density changes'. The present study concentrates on the development and stability of the interfacial layer associated with an entrapped saline impoundment.

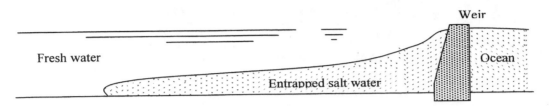

Figure 2. Entrapped saline wedge

2 Review

Christodoulu (1986) stated that the work of Ellison and Turner (1959) was the first study of buoyant overflows specifically concerned with determination of interfacial mixing. The present study uses a variation on the apparatus used by Walker (1996) which was similar to that of Ellison and Turner. The apparatus consists of freshwater overflowing saltwater trapped between two weirs. Work carried out by Walker (1996) using this set-up described two types of interfacial layer development. The first whereby the interfacial layer grew to a certain thickness and then descended slowly through the water column as the saline impoundment was eroded, Figure 3. The second classified as oscillating saw the interfacial layer develop to a certain thickness and then thin or strip down to a lower value, on reaching this point the layer grew again, this process was repeated until the saline impoundment was eroded, Figure 4.

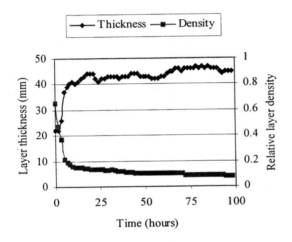

Figure 3. Steady erosion mechanism   Figure 4. Oscillating erosion mechanism

No connection to any parameter; freshwater velocity, freshwater depth or density difference between layers could be determined as to which mechanism of erosion would occur. Further tests similar to Walkers have been undertaken for the present study. This experimental programme has also been run concurrently with the development of Computational Fluid Dynamics (CFD) models of stratified flows using a commercial CFD package FLUENT.

3 Experimental Apparatus and Procedure

Physical experiments of freshwater overflow have been carried out in a 20 m long by 0.75 m square sectional flume at The Queen's University of Belfast. Experimental tests performed by Walker used a 17m long saltwater impoundment. The current work uses an 8.5 m long saltwater impoundment of depth 0.25 m. A false floor 4.5 m long has been installed at the entrance of the tank to allow the overflowing freshwater to fully develop before reaching the salt water impoundment, Figure 5.

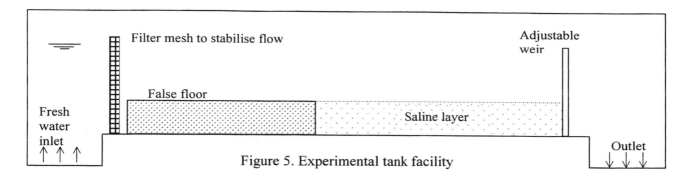

Figure 5. Experimental tank facility

Density and velocity measurements are recorded at the centre of the saline impoundment using a twin wire conductivity probe and a two component Laser Doppler Anemometry (LDA) system with a fibre optic attachment. Three times per hour the laser and conductivity probe complete one vertical traverse of the stratified flow with density and velocity measurements being recorded at 5mm intervals. A full scan of the combined depth of the salt and fresh water layers is not completed but a section 150 mm high centred around the interfacial layer. As the interfacial layer moves downwards the probes are programmed to follow the layer so as to maintain readings in the fully saline, interfacial and freshwater layers.

Eighteen experimental tests covering a range of freshwater depths and velocities have been carried out for the current study, Table 1.

Table 1 – Experimental Test Programme

Velocity mm/s	Freshwater Depth (mm)	$\Delta\rho$ kg/m^3
70	400, 300, 200	25
60	400, 300, 200	25
50	400, 300, 200	25
40	400, 300, 200	25
30	400, 300, 200	25
20	400, 300, 200	25

4 Results

4.1 Erosion Mechanism

One possible explanation for the oscillating mechanism of erosion encountered by Walker was that of an aspect size ratio problem with the experimental facility. Thus the author shortened the saline impoundment length for the current tests from 17 m to 8.5 m. A test with freshwater velocity 50 mm/s and depth 400 mm was then performed, this test also carried out by Walker resulted in an oscillating mechanism. Figure 6 represents the upper and lower boundary positions of the interfacial layer for this test. This shows how once the layer has established it then moves downwards at a constant thickness with no oscillation in interfacial layer thickness or density (Figure 7) occurring.

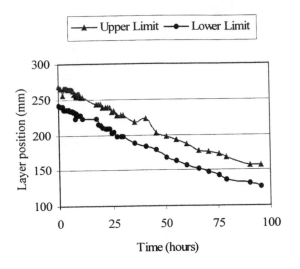

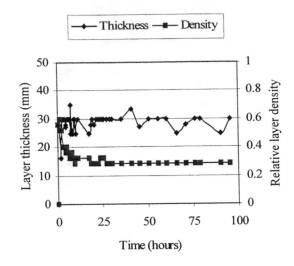

Figure 6. Interfacial layer boundaries

Figure 7. Interfacial layer density & thickness

In changing the length of the impoundment a number of factors where changed in the experimental set-up, these included the weir gate and the length of the false floor to aid in stabilising the freshwater overflow. The current work would suggest that one of these factors influenced the erosion mechanism experienced by Walker. It is therefore concluded that the oscillating mechanism observed by Walker (1996) was a function of the test apparatus and not a natural phenomenon. All tests carried out using the shortened saline impoundment exhibited a steady state of erosion.

4.2 Influence of Freshwater Depth and Velocity

Interfacial layer density, thickness and velocity has been recorded and analysed for each test. All tests produced an interfacial layer of similar thickness regardless of freshwater depth or velocity. Figure 8 shows the affect of varying velocity on interfacial layer density; as velocity decreased so did the interfacial layer density. Varying depth however, had little effect on the interfacial layer density, (Fig. 9). The interfacial density depends therefore upon velocity and not freshwater depth.

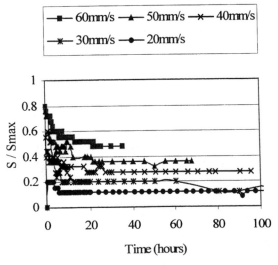

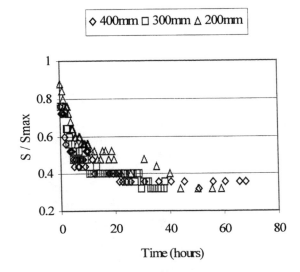

Figure 8. Constant depth, varying velocity

Figure 9. Constant velocity, varying depth

4.3 Computational Fluid Dynamics

A finite volume CFD code (FLUENT5) has been used to try and replicate interfacial layer development by creating models of the experimental test facility (Fig. 10) on a Sun Ultra 1170 workstation. These models involve the use of SPECIES modelling to create two chemically independent phases for each of the two water bodies (freshwater and saltwater). Further information on SPECIES modelling can be obtained from the Fluent user's guide (Volume 2, 1998).

Initially a Volume of Fluid (VOF) model was used to replicate the free surface involved with such flows (a description of VOF methods can be found in Hirt and Nichols (1981)). However, due to limitations on the computational power available for processing, the free boundary is currently replicated using a symmetry plane as this allows for an approximation of the free surface to be modelled without the associated costs.

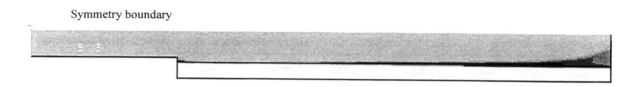
Symmetry boundary

Figure 10. Computational model with initial wedge development

The generation of a definitive mixing layer with a reasonably constant density has proved difficult to reproduce by passing freshwater over the entrapped saltwater layer. The model predicts the slow erosion of the saline impoundment over time with density profiles like those of Figure 11. Although a change between the salt and freshwater layers is clearly visible the assertion of an independent mixing layer is hard to quantify.

Initially an examination of a number of the CFD model parameters was investigated to determine their affect on interfacial layer creation. Particular attention was paid to the diffusion coefficient term between the salt and freshwater layers. CFD models were built to model diffusion tests of a column of stationary stratified water. From these tests a value of 1.2×10^{-9} m^2/s correlated well with physical tests.

Turbulence modelling was also enabled, with the current models using a variation of the standard k-ε model known as realizable k-ε. This relatively new model is better suited to flows involving rotation but most importantly more accurately predicts the spreading rate of both planar and round jets. The turbulence model parameters were set using intensity and length scales. An investigation into the influence of turbulence intensities was undertaken as it was thought that the initial model values were too low. The LDA system had been used to obtain an estimate of experimental values for the computational models. The computational model also used values either side of these values to monitor their affect. The study suggested that varying the inlet turbulence intensity had a relatively small effect on the mixing layer.

Within the computational models a short interfacial layer with a stable density of approximately 1003 kg/m^3 will initially form at the exit weir (Fig. 12) however, unlike experimentally, this does not spread backwards as time progresses to develop into a full interfacial layer. The author feels that the interfacial layer does not develop further due to turbulent eddies being overly damped within the computational model. Further testing with other turbulence models continues. CFD velocity profiles have also been compared with experimental results and these compare favourably, showing a small negative flow, which also occurs experimentally near the density boundary.

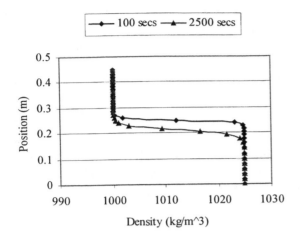

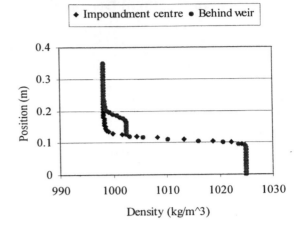

Figure 11. CFD density profiles   Figure 12. Density profile behind weir

5. Conclusion

An experimental programme of freshwater overflowing entrapped saltwater has taken place. The development of thickness and density of an interfacial layer between the two original water bodies has been shown. Contrary to earlier work by Walker (1996) no oscillating mechanism of erosion for the interfacial layer was encountered. For all experimental tests the thickness of the interfacial layer remained constant regardless of freshwater depth or velocity. The freshwater velocity however affected the density of the interfacial layer.

Computational Fluid Dynamics models of the experimental set-up were tested to examine whether an interfacial layer will form in the computational model. Results show the development of an initial interfacial layer, which is limited to a region near the exit weir.

6. References

Christodoulou, G. C. (1986). "Interfacial mixing in Stratified Flows." J. of Hyd. Research Vol. 24 No. 2: pp. 77-92.

Ellison, T. H. and J. S. & Turner (1959). "Turbulent entrainment in stratified flows." J. of Fluid Mech. Vol. 6 Part 3.

FLUENT5, (1998). Users guide, Volume 2, Chapt. 11.

Grubert, J. P. (1980). "Experiments on Arrested Saline Wedge." J. of Hyd. Div ASCE Vol. 106 (HY6) Paper no. 15484: pp. 945-960.

Hirt, C.W. and Nichols, B.D. (1981). "Volume of Fluid (VOF) Method for the Dynamics of Free Boundaries" J. of Computational Physics, Vol. 39, pp. 201-255.

Walker, S.A. (1996). "The effect of time on interfacial mixing in density stratified flows", PhD Thesis, The Queen's University of Belfast.

Salinity Stratification from a Navigation Canal into a Shallow Lake

Ioannis Y. Georgiou, Alex J. McCorquodale
Department of Civil Engineering, University of New Orleans, New Orleans, Louisiana, 70148
igeorgiou@uno.edu, jmccorqu@uno.edu

Abstract

This paper demonstrates the behavior of a dense plume originating in a navigation canal and intruding into a shallow lake. The navigation canal, being connected to Gulf of Mexico brings saline water (>20 ppt) into the brackish lake (~6 ppt). This higher density plume descends and spreads radially in a thin layer at the bottom of the lake. The plumes' interface sustains high density gradients often resulting in low oxygen transfer to the bottom waters near the lake bed. The density gradients are relatively stable and vertical mixing is at minimum under fair wind shear. Plume stability analysis indicates that wind shear induced by wind speeds of 11 m/s and a fetch of 30 Km can produce plume instability, therefore promote vertical mixing throughout the water column. Wind observations in the area have shown that required winds for destratification of the plume are primarily during winter months.

Introduction

The Inner Harbor Navigational Canal (IHNC) is part of the Mississippi River Gulf Outlet (MRGO), which permits ships to navigate from the Gulf of Mexico to Lake Pontchartrain and the Mississippi River at New Orleans (Figure 1). The IHNC is a deep channel with a mean depth near its connection to the Lake of about 10 m. Lake Pontchartrain is a relatively shallow, brackish estuarine lake with a mean depth of less than 4 m and a mean salinity of 4 ppt. At times, the IHNC brings highly saline water (>20 ppt) into Lake Pontchartrain. Under certain conditions, this higher density water has been observed to form a layer of high salinity water over a large area of the bottom of the Lake (300 km^2). This layer is often associated with low dissolved oxygen (DO) and at times becomes hypoxic, a condition that is harmful to shellfish. The salinity wedge in the IHNC had a depth that was typically greater than 60 – 80 % of the canal depth (10 m) while outside of the canal entrance the depth of the density layer was of the order of 0.5 m compared to the mean lake depth of 4 m. The elevation of the saltwater wedge in the canal is typically 2 – 3 m higher than the lake bottom. This difference in the density plume elevation causes a saltwater flux into Lake Pontchartrain.

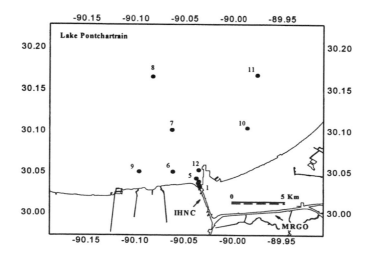

Figure 1 Aerial view of the plume area showing the points for the field sampling program

The summer observations usually showed hypoxia within the stratified layer, but no hypoxia outside of this layer. Data during winter showed high salinity stratification, but no hypoxia. It is thought that the dominant winds out of the north, north-west, and north-east in the winter cause greater vertical mixing and more frequent destabilization of the plume thus resulting in an increase in the bottom DO. The low winter water temperatures also result in higher saturation values for the DO and a reduced bacterial demand for DO. In the summer there are more southerly winds which have a short fetch with respect to the plume location and therefore result in smaller waves and less vertical mixing. The Princeton Ocean Model (POM) is being applied to study the dynamic behavior of the saltwater plume. Forcing functions for the POM model include tide and wind effects. In the future, this model will be applied to study the effect of Lake currents on the location and stability of the plume. In addition, a physical model has been constructed and operated to assess the spreading behavior of the density wedge and the effect of introducing a sill to control the saltwater flux into Lake Pontchartrain.

Background

The stability of a saltwater-freshwater interface, among other things, is related to the gradient Richardson number through the expression shown in Eq. 1 (Yih, 1980).

$$Ri = \frac{g}{\rho} \frac{\left(\frac{\partial \rho}{\partial y}\right)}{\left(\frac{\partial u}{\partial y}\right)^2} \qquad [1]$$

where Ri = gradient Richardson number, ρ = density of fluid, y = water depth, u = total velocity component near the bed (includes u_{cur} = near-bed current velocity, u_s = wave orbidal velocity), and g = acceleration of gravity. In general, mixing is inhibited at and below the interface of the saltwater lens. At high values of the Richardson number, there is no mass exchange taking place across the shear interface, but there is exchange of momentum even if the shear produces perturbations without breaking (Kjerfve, 1988). High velocities induced by wind shear, associated wave action, and near-bed current velocities can destabilize the interface. In shallow water, wind speed, fetch, and depth greatly affect the development of waves (Laenen and Tourneau, 1996). Using wave forecasting equations used by the U.S. Army Corps of Engineers (1984) along with orbital velocities based on linear wave theory, and by obtaining information on near-bed current velocities from numerical models (Haralampides, 2000), values for the total near-bed velocities were obtained by superposition. Eqs. 2, 3, 4 and 5 were used to calculate the wave height (H_s), wave length in shallow water (L_s), and the wave period (T_s).

$$T_s = 7.54 \left(\frac{U_A}{g}\right) \tanh\left[0.833\left(\frac{gh}{U_A^2}\right)^{0.375}\right] \tanh\left[\frac{0.0379\left(\frac{gF}{U_A^2}\right)^{0.333}}{\tanh\left[0.833\left(\frac{gh}{U_A^2}\right)^2\right]}\right] \qquad [2]$$

$$L_s = \left(\frac{gT^2}{2\pi}\right) \tanh\left[\frac{2\pi h}{\left(\frac{gT^2}{2\pi}\right)}\right] \qquad [3]$$

$$H_s = 0.283 \left(\frac{U_A^2}{g}\right) \tanh\left[0.530\left(\frac{gh}{U_A^2}\right)^{0.75}\right] \tanh\left[\frac{0.00565\left(\frac{gF}{U_A^2}\right)^{0.5}}{\tanh\left[0.530\left(\frac{gh}{U_A^2}\right)^{0.75}\right]}\right] \qquad [4]$$

$$u_s = \frac{\pi H}{T_s \sinh\left(\dfrac{2\pi h}{L_s}\right)}$$

[5]

where T_s is the significant wave period, U_A is the effective wind speed, g is the acceleration of gravity, F is the effective fetch, h is the water depth, Ls is the wave length in shallow water, and Hs is the significant wave height. Values for the effective fetch were determined using typical fetches along the directions of frequent prevailing winds (north, north-east, and north-west) with respect to the location of the saltwater wedge. Results from the above calculations are summarized in Table 1.

Methodology

Field Sampling: A field sampling program was developed in order to obtain information on the plumes physical characteristics. The program has been in progress since the summer of 1998, and includes sampling along radial paths starting in the canal and proceeding into the lake. Initial sampling data only included surface and bottom readings. An extensive survey carried out in 1999 included data collection throughout the water column at intervals based on the intensity of stratification. This was achieved by collecting concentrated readings near the lake bed, where the saltwater wedge was evident. The data included readings for salinity, DO, and temperature at 12 stations near the IHNC and in the Lake Pontchartrain at the locations shown in Figure 1.

Physical Model: A physical model was also constructed to assess the spreading characteristics of the saltwater plume. The model has also been used to examine management scenarios for prevention of saltwater intrusion. Such scenarios include the introduction of a sill at the mouth of the canal at the entrance to the lake. Figure 2 shows an elevation snapshot of the plume as it enters the lake. There is a sill in place at an elevation of 1/3 of the lake depth.

Figure 2 Profile view of the saltwater plume entering the lake; Δ_{sal}=6 ppt; ΔT=0°C; sill at 1/3 of lake depth

Results and Discussion

Systematic observations in the lake have shown frequent salinity, temperature, and DO stratification due to saltwater intrusion from the IHNC. The 1998 and 1999 field data showed higher density gradients during summer seasons, when there is little fresh water input in the lake due to drought conditions, low river flows, and increased evaporation. Figures 3 and 4 show typical vertical distribution of salinity and temperature through the water column of the lake. At times, the water temperatures in the salt wedge were found to be higher than the upper layer temperatures. With the specific heat of saltwater being higher than freshwater, the wedge sustained and carried these temperatures in the lake. Figure 3 illustrates the vertical temperature structure. Salinity profiles shown in Figure 4 are typical of the observed summer conditions and have very high maximum salinity gradients at about 4 m (average depth in the area is 4.6 – 5 m). Figures 5 – 6 show respectively the vertical profiles of temperature and salinity after a strong wind from the north; noticeable destratification of the salinity plume has occurred. The mixing process is assisted by bathymetry at the canal-lake junction (Figure 7). A scour hole and a dredge hole are present and extend radially at the mouth of the canal near the lake entrance. These holes provide a step-up in the bathymetry that serve as obstacles to the wedge propagation. Figure 7 also shows the profile view of the arrested saline wedge as it was measured on August 31, 1999. In determining values for the Richardson number, total velocity components were estimated. This included the use of a calibrated numerical model to estimate the current velocities (Haralampides, 2000), RMA2, and information from 3-D simulations using the POM model and field surveys performed by the United States Geological Survey (USGS) during 1996 in the area (Signell, 1995). The wave orbital velocities were estimated using Eqs. 2, 3, 4, and 5, and were added to the current velocities. The densities for both the upper and lower layer were calculated using local temperature and salinity values (Thomann and Mueller, 1987). For simplicity, the salt wedge was assumed to have zero velocity and a characteristic depth of 0.6 m, which is the average plume depth at half the intrusion length. Results for the Richardson number calculations are shown in Table 1, and in Figure 8.

Table 1 Summarized results for stability analysis. Values shown are averaged for wind direction and fetch

Wind Speed [ms^{-1}]	H$_s$ [m]	T$_s$ [m]	L$_s$ [m]	u$_{cur}$ [ms^{-1}]	u$_s$ [ms^{-1}]	u [ms^{-1}]	Ri
5.36	0.17	1.58	3.90	0.03	0.00	0.03	43.88
10.73	0.50	2.57	10.20	0.06	0.15	0.21	1.09
14.31	0.76	3.15	14.62	0.09	0.35	0.44	0.25

A plume stability analysis was performed to determine what physical conditions are required to produce plume instability. A set of three wind speeds were selected representing mild, medium and gusty wind components for the area of study. Respectively, estimates of wave height, period, and wave length velocities were performed in order to get a relationship between wind speed and the Richardson number. Figure 8 clearly shows that wind velocities of approximately 11 ms^{-1} will in fact produce instability on the wedge interface and as a result mixing between the layers will occur. The same conditions also produce wave heights of nearly 0.5 m with a wave period of about 3 s. Field data from the fall of 1999 to the winter of 2000 confirmed that the plume was destabilized by winds from NW to NE between 10 - 12 ms^{-1}.

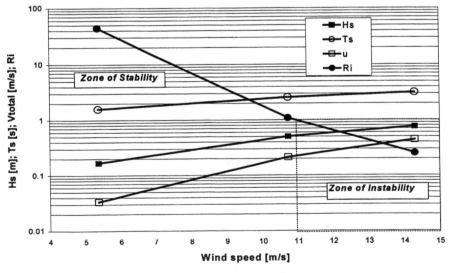

Figure 8 Plume stability analysis. Instability zone defined at: Ri<1; Ua>11 ms^{-1}.

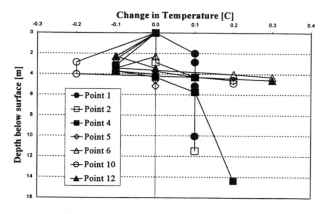

Figure 3 Selected temperature vertical profiles. Wind speeds < 11ms⁻¹

Figure 4 Selected salinity vertical profiles. Wind speeds < 11ms⁻¹

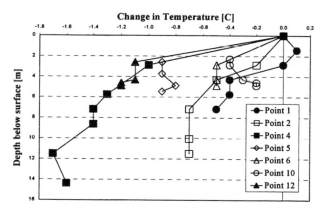

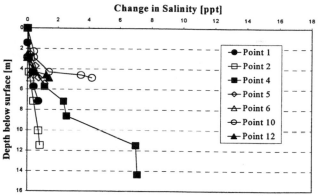

Figure 5 Selected temperature vertical profiles. Wind speeds > 11ms⁻¹

Figure 6 Selected salinity vertical profiles. Wind speeds > 11ms⁻¹

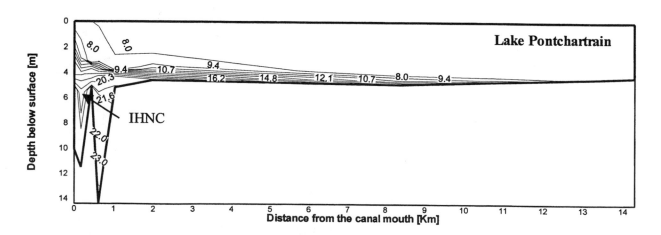

Figure 7 Typical plot of the summer observations of the arrested saline wedge. Salinity in ppt

Conclusions

This study illustrates the formation and expansion of a saltwater wedge from a navigation canal into a shallow lake, as well as the required conditions for plume instability. The stability analysis shows that wind shear induced by wind speeds of approximately 11 ms^{-1} can produce instabilities at the interface and eventually, at higher speeds, produce completely mixed fluid layers. Field data collected near the canal-lake junction show that the irregular bathymetry of the location increases the potential for instability and promotes mixing during inflow conditions. In addition, the stepwise increase in the depth from the canal to the lake serves as a sill and reduces the intrusion length. Laboratory experiment simulations performed using a sill at the canal mouth also reveal that such scenario produces local interface instability and higher entrainment of ambient water into the saltwater wedge. A combination of ongoing field surveys and laboratory experiments, and the future introduction of a three-dimensional numerical model will provide us with essential information on the plume dynamics. In addition, the numerical model will allow us to understand and study the effectiveness of proposed management scenarios for saltwater intrusion control.

References

Haralampides, K., 2000, *A Study of the Hydrodynamics and Salinity Regimes of the Lake Pontchartrain System*, Ph.D Dissertation, University of New Orleans, New Orleans, LA.

Kjerfve, Björn, 1988, *Hydrodynamics of Estuaries*, Volume I, Estuarine Physics, CRC Press, Florida.

Laenen, A., and Le Tourneau, A., P., 1996, *Upper Klamath Basin Nutrient-Loading Study – Estimate of Wind-Induced Resuspension of Bed Sediment During Periods of Low Lake Elevation*, U.S. Geological Survey, Report 95-414, Portland, Oregon.

Signell, Rich, 1995, *Three-Dimensional Circulation Modeling of Lake Pontchartrain*, Online Document, Obtained from www.crusty.er.usgs.gov on May, 9, 2000.

Thomann, V., R., and Mueller, J., A., John, 1987, *Principles of Surface Water Quality Modeling and Control*, Harper Collins Publishers Inc., New York, NY.

U.S. Army Corps of Engineers, 1984, *Shore Protection Manual*, Coastal Engineering Research Center, Department of the Army, Waterways Experiment Station, Vicksburg, Mississippi.

Yih, Chia-Shun, 1980, *Stratified Flows*, Academic Press, New York, NY.

The Control of Coastal Current Transport

Alexander R. Horner[1], Derek A. Fong[1], Jeffrey R. Koseff[1],
Tony Maxworthy[2], and Stephen G. Monismith[1]
[1]Environmental Fluid Mechanics Laboratory, Stanford University
[2]Department of Aerospace and Mechanical Engineering, University of Southern California

We carry out two sets of laboratory experiments to investigate the mechanisms that determine transport in coastal river plumes. In contrast to the steady state models that are typically used, recent work suggests that a bulge region forms at the river mouth and grows in time. Consequently, volume flux in the coastal current is less than the river flow. In this paper we confirm this result and show how different river inflow angles influence the formation of the bulge and, in turn, the character and flow rate of the coastal current. At low inflow angles or high inflow Froude numbers we find that a supercritical plume forms and has no bulge. In contrast, at high inflow angles or low inflow Froude number, a subcritical plume forms and has a bulge at the source and a coastal current flow rate that is lower than the source flow rate.

1 Introduction

Rivers play a critical role in the the exchange of materials between the land and the ocean. They collect the products of terrestrial processes such as erosion, biological decay and human activity and transport them to the coast. At the coast, the actions of the river water determine where, in what concentrations, and how quickly these products move. Whether the river water and its constituents mix rapidly offshore or remain in the near shore region is of considerable importance to the fishing industry, the oil industry, the tourist industry, and anyone interested in maintaining the function and appearance of the coastal environment.

The dynamics of river plumes has been the focus of a considerable amount of study over the past two decades. It is well established that, for most large-scale, mid-latitude rivers in the northern hemisphere, the river water turns to the right at the river mouth and forms a current parallel to the coast (Garvine, 1995). The direction of the coastal current flow, with the coast on its right, will hearafter be referred to as downstream.

Most models assume that, without any other forcing such as wind or an ambient current, river plumes reach a steady state. This implies that the coastal current flow rate matches the river flow rate. Recent work by Fong (1998), however, shows that this is not true. Fong finds that the freshwater flow rate in the coastal current is always less than the river flow rate and is nearly constant in time. As a result, river water accumulates in a growing anticyclonic eddy or bulge at the mouth. Evidence of a turning region at the mouth has also been documented by a number of other researchers (Chao & Boicourt, 1986; Masse & Murthy, 1992), although it is considered to be a steady state feature in each of these studies.

Fong finds that the coastal current flow rate is highly correlated with the potential energy in the coastal current and with the inflow Rossby number. We seek a more complete understanding of how the flow rate in the coastal current is influenced by the source conditions.

Using the method of characteristics, Garvine(1987) constructed a steady state model of supercritical, buoyant plumes with an ambient cross-flow. He shows that the coastal current is supercritical when the angle between the inflow and the coast is small ($< 30^o$) and subcritical when it is large. There is a turning region near the mouth, but it does not grow in time since the model assumes a steady state.

In Garvine's low angle runs the transport must be set by the river flow rate, and we expect a steady state. For higher inflow angles it is possible that the coastal current transport is locally determined and, if it is less than the river flow rate, the difference may be 'backed up' in the turning region. This model also suggests dependence on the densimetric Froude number.

To test the theory we carry out two sets of laboratory experiments. In the first set of experiments we fix the inflow perpendicular to the coastal wall and do runs at a range of inflow Rossby and Froude numbers. In all the runs we find that the coastal current flow rate is constant and less than the river flow rate and that a growing bulge forms at the source. In the second set of experiments we fix the Rossby number while varying the inflow angle and the Froude number. We find that a bulge forms at the source for high inlet angles but not for low angles. The minimum angle at which a bulge forms increases with Froude number.

2 Experiments

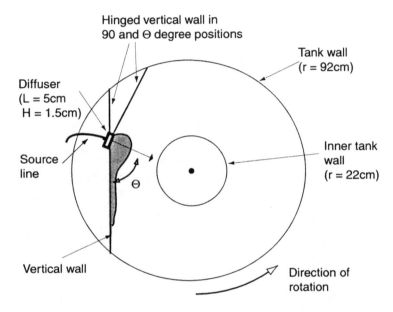

Figure 1: **Schematic of the rotating table as seen from above.** The camera and other instrumentation is not shown. The shaded area shows a typical plume.

Figure 1 shows the experimental facility. The rotating tank is circular and has a vertical wall across one side to form the coastal wall. We attach a diffuser at water level close to the left end of the wall and supply buoyant water from a constant head tank off the table. The flow rate is controlled off the table and measured with a variable diameter flow meter to within 0.5 ml/s. The tank has a sloping bottom with an angle of 15°. In the second set of experiments we remove the sloping bottom so that the tank has a deeper, flat bottom. The water depth at the source is 9 cm with the sloping bottom and 19.5 cm without it. For each run, salty water in the tank is spun up for at least 1.5 hours and then the source is turned on. A video camera in the frame of reference of the rotating table records the motion of the buoyant water. The inflow water is dyed blue to distinguish it from the denser ambient water.

For the first set of experiments the inflow is perpendicular to the wall and we vary the flow rate $(1.5 \leq Q_i \leq 19\,cm^3/s)$, density difference $(5.6 \leq g' \leq 10\,cm/s^2)$, and rotation period $(9.4 \leq T \leq 26.5\,s)$ over a range of inflow Froude $(0.05 \leq Fr_i \leq 2.0)$ and Rossby $(0.04 \leq Ro_i \leq 0.7)$ numbers. Here we define the inflow Froude and Rossby numbers as, $Ro_i = \frac{Q_i T}{4\pi H_i L_i^2}$, and $Fr_i = \frac{Q_i}{L_i H_i \sqrt{g' H_i}}$. We use video images to measure the width of the plume at the mouth.

In the second set of experiments we hold the Rossby number constant by fixing the table rotation period at 12.5 s and the source flow rate at 16.1 ± 1 ml/s. We vary the density difference $(1.5 \leq g' \leq 10.3\,cm/s^2)$ and inflow angle $(30^o \leq \theta \leq 90^o)$. To vary the inflow angle we rebuilt the wall with a hinge immediately to the right of the diffuser(see Figure 1). For these experiments we define the inflow angle, θ, as the angle between the initial direction of the in-flowing buoyant water and the coastal wall to the right. According to this definition, inflow which is directed parallel to the wall in the direction of Kelvin wave propagation has an inflow angle of zero. To vary the angle we rotate the left, hinged section of the wall including the diffuser and then lengthen this section such that it extends all the way to the outer tank wall. In this way there is a continuous path around the circumference of the tank with only one sharp angle possible at the source. We put a Plexiglas grid above the plume which has a resolution of 1 cm and 2 cm in the cross-shore and along-shore directions respectively.

3   Results

90° Inflow For each of the 90° runs there appear to be three phases in the plume evolution. The first is a spin-up phase. When the source is first turned on the buoyant water follows a circular trajectory to the right and returns to the coastal wall 5-10cm from the source. This is about 1 Rossby radii. For the first 0.5-1 rotation periods all of the buoyant water accumulates in this growing, circular bulge and no coastal current forms. In Figure 2(a) the offshore extent of the bulge squared ($L_B{}^2$) is plotted against time. Since the bulge is close to circular, $L_B{}^2$ is proportional to the area of the bulge. We normalize time by the rotation period, T, and $L_B{}^2$ by the initial area $A_i = w^2 R_o$ where w is the width of the diffuser outlet and R_o is the source Rossby number. The initial area corresponds to the area of buoyant water that comes out of the diffuser in one rotation period for each flow rate assuming that it maintains the depth of the diffuser opening. In Figure 2(a) the spin-up phase corresponds to the initial non-linear growth of the bulge. When the same non-dimensional variables are plotted for 6 runs in Figure 2(b) we see that this spin-up phase is self similar. This implies that the assumption of only small variations in depth is reasonable for these runs.

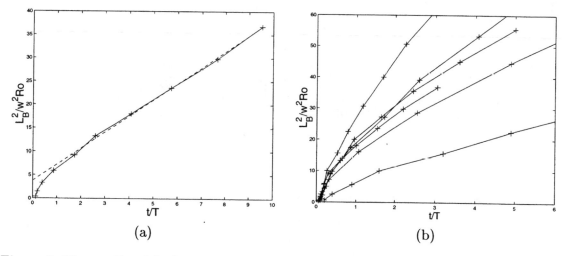

(a)	(b)

Figure 2: **Normalized bulge area vs time** (a) Fr=0.23 and Ro=0.23. The dotted line is a linear fit to all but the first 5 points. (b) Each line represents 1 of 6 runs with Froude and Rossby numbers in the following ranges: $0.23 \leq Fr_i \leq 0.76$, and $0.23 \leq Ro_i \leq 0.68$, respectively

During the second phase the coastal current appears steady, but the bulge continues to grow in time. The best fit line plotted in Figure 2(a) demonstrates that the growth of the bulge is linear. This is true for a large range of Froude and Rossby numbers. Since the volume of buoyant water in the bulge is a weak function of the depth, this result indicates that there is a constant accumulation of water in the bulge. Also, since the source flow rate is constant, the coastal current flow rate must be constant and less than the source flow rate.

After the linear growth phase the bulge often becomes unstable. This instability usually occurs 7-10 rotation periods after the source is turned on and has a frequency of about 6 periods. At the onset of the instability a kink forms on the outer, upstream edge of the bulge. This forms a backward breaking wave which travels clockwise around the bulge until it hits the coastal wall. When it hits the wall, a blob of fluid is pinched off from the bulge and transported downstream in the coastal current. Since the width of the bulge oscillates in the unstable phase, it is not recorded in the plots in Figure 2. This appears to be an important and interesting mechanism by which the bulge loses buoyant water; a more thorough analysis will follow in subsequent experiments.

The coastal current has a relatively constant width. Immediately downstream of the bulge, however, it forms a neck that is about half as wide as the rest of the current. At the neck, the downstream side of the bulge and the outer edge of the coastal current form an angle or cleft that is usually less than 90°. As the unstable bulge waves travel around its perimeter, however, the cleft varies between about 60° and 90°.

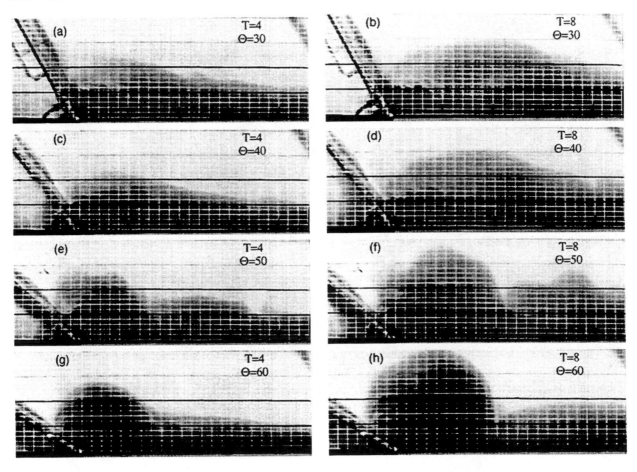

Figure 3: **Increasing inflow angle** Images of 4 runs with inflow angles of (a) 30°, (c) 40°, (e) 50° and (g) 60° after 4 rotation periods. The right column shows the same runs after 8 periods. ($Ro = 0.6 \pm 0.5, Fr = 1.6 \pm 0.5$)

Angled Inflow As anticipated, when we decrease the inflow angle we observe a different flow regime. Figure 3 (a) and 3 (b) show a typical plume with a low inflow angle (30°) after 4 and 8 rotation periods respectively. The bulge does not form at the source. Instead, the buoyant water turns immediately and flows parallel to the wall. The coastal current width is typically about 6cm and remains constant for at least 20cm down the wall. There is a strong shear along the offshore edge of the coastal current and we observe short shear instabilities on this interface. Much further downstream the current appears less energetic and these instabilities are not evident.

Figure 3 (c) and 3 (d) show the same plume with an inflow angle of 40°. We observe a turning region near the source but it does not grow in time or appear to accumulate buoyant water. Further downstream, however, a feature that looks similar to a bulge does form. It often grows and is held immediately upstream of an obtuse (135°) corner where the coastal wall meets the outer wall. Downstream of this bulge the coastal current is only 3-4 cm wide, and much of the transport appears to be blocked.

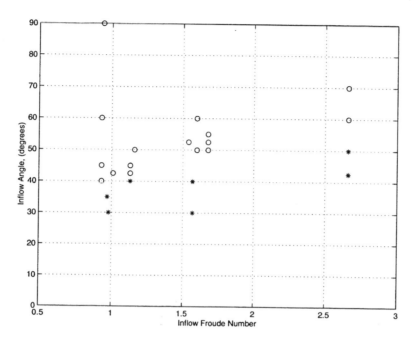

Figure 4: **Bulge formation** Each point is a unique run. Circles represent plumes that form a bulge, and stars represent plumes that do not.

In Figures 3 (e) and 3 (f) the inflow angle is 50°. We begin to see a bulge form that grows in time and accumulates buoyant water. The transition between these two regimes spans 5° − 10° but is nonetheless obvious. At angles from 60° to 90° a bulge forms that is qualitatively similar to the runs in the first set of experiments. Figures 3 (g) and 3 (h) show the 60° run. The growing bulge is evident in this run.

Figure 4 shows all of the runs plotted in terms of inflow Froude number, Fr_i, and angle, θ. Each point represents a unique run. Circles represent runs for which a bulge forms, and the stars are runs with no bulge. For fixed inflow Froude numbers (0.9, 1.1, 1.6, 2.7) we increase the angle from 30° − 40° to 60° − 70°. In each case a bulge does not form for the low angle runs but does form for the high angle runs. We define a critical angle, θ_c, as the minimum angle for which a bulge forms. When Fr_i is 1.6, for example, θ_c is about 45°. θ_c appears to increase from approximately 35° at $Fr_i = 0.9$ to 55° at $Fr_i = 2.7$.

4   Discussion

This relatively simple series of laboratory experiments illustrates two mechanisms that may be important in determining the transport in actual river plumes. According to these experiments, two different regimes are possible for plumes.

The first regime exists when the inflow angle is low or the inflow Froude number is high. For plumes in this regime we observe that no bulge forms near the source and that the in-flowing water turns immediately parallel to the coastal wall. Such plumes appear to be supercritical and steady since no limiting flow rate can be imposed downstream in the coastal current. It should be possible, therefore, to predict the coastal current flow rate based entirely on conditions at the source. In some cases, a large bulge forms downstream along the coastal wall in these supercritical plumes. This bulge appears to be a transition or jump to subcritical flow and is usually stationary and immediately upstream of a bend in the wall. It is possible that this downstream bulge is similar to the meanders and blocking waves documented by McClimans(1981) and Stern(1980), respectively.

The second regime exists when the inflow angle is high or the inflow Froude number is low. For these plumes a bulge forms and grows at the source. The growth is constant in time after an initial spin-up and until it becomes unstable. This implies that the coastal current flow rate is also constant. We conclude that the difference between the coastal current flow rate and the source flow rate accounts for the fluid that accumulates in the bulge, consistent with Fong(1998). The coastal current in this regime appears to be subcritical since information is propagated upstream to the bulge in order to maintain the coastal current flow rate. These plumes do not reach a steady state since the bulge continues to accumulate water. After 7-10 rotation periods, however, the bulge becomes unstable and begins to shed buoyant eddies into the coastal current. We anticipate that the mean flow rate in the coastal current remains constant in the unstable stage and that the volume of these eddies accounts for the discrepancy in flow rates.

The physical mechanism responsible for the transition from supercritical to subcritical in the high angle runs is not clear. In his model, Garvine(1987) suggests that vertical shear instability and mixing occur in the turning region at the mouth. For higher inflow angles more mixing occurs and so the plume water loses energy and becomes subcritical. Our result, however, suggests that, for a given inflow angle, the turning region is more likely to become subcritical and form a bulge at lower inflow Froude numbers. This implies that mixing may not necessarily determine the transition. Instead, we hypothesize that there may be an inviscid condition at the point where the bulge water returns to the wall that determines the state of the flow. In this case, the Rossby number may also be an important parameter.

Acknowledgements We gratefully acknowledge Bob Brown's help in building the rotating table and the support of National Science Foundation grant number DMS-9318166.

References

Chao, S-Y., & Boicourt, B. 1986. Onset of estuary plumes. *J. Phys. Oceanogr.*, **16**, 2137–2149.

D.A.Fong. 1998. *Dynamics of Freshwater Plumes: Observations and Numerical Modelling of the Wind-forced Response and Alongshore Freshwater Transport.* Ph.D. thesis, Woods Hole Oceanographic Institute/Massachusetts Institute of Technology.

Garvine, R.W. 1987. Estuary plumes and fronts in shelf waters:a layer model. *J.Phys.Oceanogr.*, **17**(11), 1877–1896.

Garvine, R.W. 1995. A dynamical system for classifying buoyant coastal discharges. *Cont. Shelf Res.*, **15**(13), 1585–1596.

Masse, A.K., & Murthy, C.R. 1992. Analysis of the Niagra River Plume. *J.Geophys.Res.*, **97**(C2), 2403–2420.

Stern, M.E. 1980. Geostrophic fronts, bores, breaking and blocking waves. *J. Fluid Mech.*, **99**, 687–703.

Vinger, Å, McClimans, T.A., & Tryggestad, S. 1981. Laboratory observations of instabilities in a straight coastal current. *Pages 553–582 of: The Norwegian Coastal Current*, vol. 2. Norway: University of Bergen.

Modeling Salinity Intrusion and Density Current in Partially Mixed Estuaries

Ming-His Hsu[1], Wen-Cheng Liu[2] and Albert Y. Kuo[3]

[1] Professor and Senior Research Fellow, Department of Agricultural Engineering and Hydrotech Research Institute, National Taiwan University, Taipei, Taiwan.

[2] Senior Research Engineer, Hydrotech Research Institute, National Taiwan University, Taipei, Taiwan.

[3] Professor, School of Marine Science / Virginia Institute of Marine Science, The College of William and Mary, Gloucester Point, VA, U.S.A.
mhhsu@flood.hy.ntu.edu.tw, wcliu@hy.ntu.edu.tw, kuo@vims.edu

Abstract

Estuaries, in the traditional sense, are regions of transition from river to ocean. They are characterized by the possibility of tidal motions communicated from the sea, and by gradients of salinity and density associated with the progressive admixture of river water and seawater. Flow conditions in an estuary are primarily influenced by tide, seasonally varying freshwater discharge and intrusion of salt water from the ocean.

A laterally averaged two-dimensional numerical model was developed and expanded for an estuarine system with tributaries as well as mainstream. A series of comprehensive field data was used to calibrate and verify the model for the Tanshui estuarine system which is a partially mixed estuary. Reasonable agreement was obtained between model results and observed data. The model was applied to investigate the salinity intrusion, residual current and estuarine circulation under various hydrological conditions in Tanshui estuary system. The results show that, under very low flow conditions, if the wastewater is totally cut-off by wastewater interception systems, the salinity will increase by 2 to 4 parts per thousand in the middle portion of the mainstem and the lower portion of the tributaries. The computed residual currents in the Tanshui estuary system show the two-layer flow characteristics, particularly under low river discharge conditions.

Introduction

Tidal estuaries comprise the lowest reaches of the river where they enter the sea. Mixing in estuaries results from a combination of various effects such as tide, wind, and inflow from rivers. The interaction between dense saline waters entering from the sea and the fresh water derived from the upland discharge gives rise to a wide spectrum of circulation pattern and estuarine mixing.

In recent years, many numerical models were developed to simulation tide forced and density induced estuaries using one-dimensional, two-dimensional, and even three-dimensional numerical model. Although the full three-dimensional models (e.g. Oley et al., 1985; Sheng, 1987; Casulli and Cheng, 1992, Johnson, 1993; Wang and Ikeda, 1996; Muin and Spaulding, 1997; Blumberg et al., 1999) are available in use, the laterally averaged model is an efficiency and economic tool to study estuarine dynamics in a qusi-3D view, considering narrow transverse section and neglecting lateral variation of physical processes. Physically, this kind of model is able to describe major estuarine phenomena, since tides, tidal currents, salt, and sediment transports, as well as ecological processes.

The work presented in this paper is the part of our series of studies on the Tanshui River environment. In this study, a laterally integrated, two-dimensional, real-time model of hydrodynamics and salinity is developed and expanded to handle tributaries as well as the mainstream of an estuarine system, and applied to the Tanshui River estuary. The Tanshui River estuary is the largest estuarine system in Taiwan, with drainage basin including the city of Taipei. It consists of there major tributaries: the Tahan Stream, Hsintien Stream and Keelung River (Figure 1). The downstream reaches of all three tributaries are influenced by tide. The upriver reaches are affected by daily varying freshwater discharges. The river system has a total drainage area of $2726\,km^2$, and a total channel length of $327.6\ km$.

The dynamic processes involving the interaction between river discharge and tidal currents are complex and lead to estuarine circulation in the Tanshui estuary. The numerical model is calibrated and verified with field data. Then the model is applied to investigate the salinity intrusion and density circulation. Simulations of the combined freshwater and tidal flow in the Tanshui estuary under various hydrological conditions are carried out.

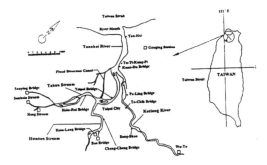

Figure1. Map of the Tanshui River System

Description of the Model

The hydrodynamic and transport equations are based on the principles of conservation of volume, momentum and mass. The model solves the governing equations with a finite difference scheme. The numerical scheme of the simulation model applied a horizontal grid spacing of $\Delta x = 1$ km and a vertical grid spacing of $\Delta z = 2$ m for the top layer and $\Delta z = 1$ m for the layers below. The thickness of the surface layer varied with time and depends on the actual calculated water level.

A time step, Δt, is limited by Courant-Fredrick-Levy (CFL) stability condition $\Delta t \leq \dfrac{\Delta x}{\sqrt{gh}}$. A time step increment (Δt) of 108 seconds, which guaranteed stability, was used for all model runs.

Model Validation

Sufficient data for this investigation were available from a comprehensive field survey of the Tanshui River system carried out in 1994 and 1995 by the Water Conservancy Agency Ministry of Economic Affairs. The measured data were collected and analyzed for the model validation.

Manning's friction coefficient is the most important calibration parameter affecting the calculation of surface elevation, velocity and flow. Since tidal flow constitutes the major portion of energy in estuarine flows, the Manning's coefficient was adjusted based on comparison of the predicted tidal wave propagation with measured data. Both the spatially varying tidal range and phase were calibrated, with results presented in Hsu et al. (1999).

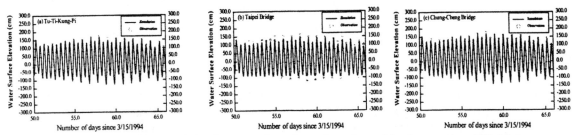

Figure 2. Comparison of the Computed surface elevation with observational field data.

The friction coefficient was verified with the simulation of prototype conditions during the period March 15, 1994 to September 30, 1994. Hourly measurements of water surface elevation at river mouth and daily freshwater discharges upriver of tidal limits were used as boundary conditions. All the tidal gauge data available during the simulation period were compared to the model output time series. Below the results from three representative stations respectively located in Tu-Ti-Kung-Pi, Taipei Bridge, and Chung-Cheng Bridge are presented only (Figure 2). The comparison shows that the model can faithfully reproduce tidal propagation, tidal flow and river flow.

The comparison between the outputs from the two-dimensional, laterally averaged model and the observed tidal heights from the shore gauge is quite favorable. The physical explanation is that the

872

laterally averaged model captures the major physical processes that occur primarily along the main channel. The tidal height is such an example, because it is derived from the volume transports in continuity equation. The along-channel volume transport dominates this process. Thus, although the cross-channel velocity (v) is neglected which may be as important as the along-channel velocity in the estuary with comparable spatial scale in both x and y directs, this two-dimensional, laterally averaged model can capture the correct physics in an estuarine system with narrow, deep channel.

An intensive survey was conducted by Taiwan Provincial Government Water Resources Department on April 12, June 24, 1994, and April 14, 1995. Half-hourly measurements of velocity and hourly salinity were made continuously for 13 daylight hours. The model predictions are compared with the field measurements on April 14, 1995 in Figure 3. Both field data and model simulation indicate that the vertical salinity difference varies with tidal phase from nearly zero to as much as 5 ppt at Kuan-Du. Hsu *et al.* (1997) also showed that the spatial distribution of tidal average salinity has a vertical difference of one to two parts per thousand. Therefore the Tanshui estuary may be classified as a partially mixed estuary. The model reasonably well reproduces all three prognostic variables: tides, tidal current, and salinity in mainstream and tributaries.

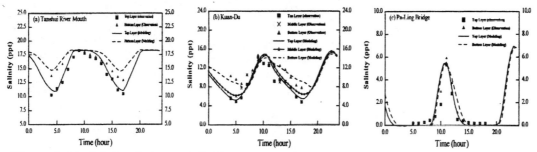

Figure 3. Model simulation and field measurement of salinity distributions on April 14, 1994.

All available velocity data in the Tanshui River system lasted for only 13 hours in this survey. No time varying residual velocity may be deduced through standard low-pass filtering to discern if the two-layer estuarine circulation exists in the Tanshui River system. However, theoretical analysis indicated that two-layer estuarine circulation may exist in the lower portion of the Tanshui estuary (Hsu et al. 1999).

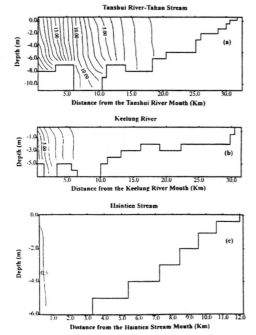

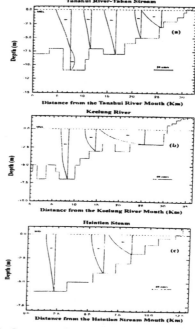

Figure 4. Computed salinity distributions under mean flow conditions.

Figure 5. Computed residual current profiles under mean flow conditions

Model Application

The validated model was used to perform a simulation of combined freshwater and tidal flows under various hydrological conditions to investigate salinity intrusion and density current (or estuarine circulation) in the Tanshui River estuarine system. A harmonic tide of nine constitutes at the river mouth were used to force the model.

Three hydrological conditions were investigated: mean freshwater discharge, Q_{90} discharge and Q_{90} with wastewater interception. The table also shows the lateral inflow from watershed below gauging stations and from wastewater. Historical long-term mean discharges were used for the upriver boundary conditions in the tributaries for the first simulation. The mean discharges at the tidal limits of the three major tributaries are 62.1 m^3/s, 72.7 m^3/s and 26.1 m^3/s for the Tahan Stream, Hsintien Stream and Keelung River, respectively. A high tide salinity of 25 ppt at river mouth was used for the mean flow simulation. The model simulated one-year (705 tidal cycles) hydraulic and salinity conditions. Figures 4 presents the salinity distributions averaged over two spring-neap cycles. The limit of salt intrusion is represented by 1 ppt isohaline. The most stratification occurs near 7 to 10 km from river mouth in the Tanshui River-Tahan Stream. There is little salt intrusion in the Hsintien Stream. Figure 5 shows the residual current averaged over two spring-neap cycles. The estuarine circulation occurs only at deeper waters around Kuan-Du under mean flow condition. An important capability of the coupled hydrodynamic and salinity model is the ability to calculate the residual circulation. The residual circulation arises from the pressure gradient generated by the longitudinal salinity variation, a baroclinic forcing which increases with the depth as well as salinity gradient. Consequently the residual circulation tends to be the strongest in deep sections of the estuary, and in regions where the salinity gradient is the largest.

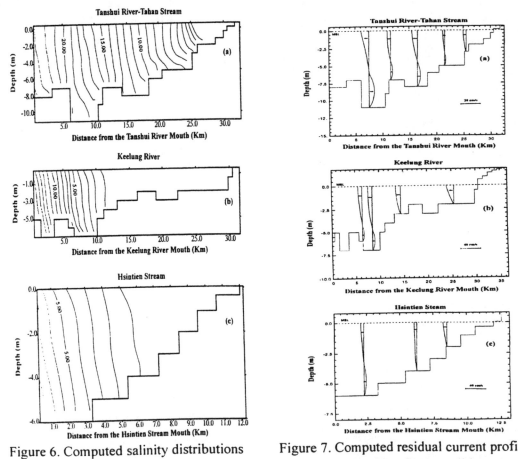

Figure 6. Computed salinity distributions under Q_{90} flow conditions.

Figure 7. Computed residual current profiles under Q_{90} flow conditions

874

To study the responses of residual velocity and salinity distribution to varying river discharge, another model simulation was conducted using Q_{90} flow (Q_{90} is the flow that is equaled or exceeded 90% of time). Q_{90} represents the very low flow condition but has the probability of 10% to occur. The 25 *ppt* of high tide salinity at river mouth was employed for simulation. All other conditions were kept the same as mean flow simulation. Figure 6 presents salinity distributions averaged over two spring-neap cycles. They show that Q_{90} flow condition pushes the limit of salt intrusion farther upriver than mean flow condition. The limit of salt intrusion is located at Hsin-Hai bridge in the Tahan Stream, 14 km from Keelung River mouth in the Keelung River, and Chung-Cheng bridge in the Hsintien Stream. This extensive intrusion of saline water introduces a significant baroclinic forcing and induces a strong residual circulatory system in the estuary. Figure 7 presents residual current profiles averaged over two spring-neap cycles. They indicate that estuarine circulation exists in all three tributaries as well as the mainstream Tanshui River.

The third model simulation was run for one-year (705 tidal cycles) with Q_{90} flow as upstream boundary condition while the lateral inflow from wastewater along the river was totally cut-off by the interception system which is being implemented. Due to the diversion of a large amount of wastewater to the ocean outfall system, the freshwater flow in the river significantly decreases. Figure 8 shows the average salinity distribution over two spring-neap cycles. The limit of salt intrusion is located near Hsin-Hai bridge in the Tahan Stream, 15 *km* distances from Keelung River mouth in the Keelung River, and 7 km distances from Hsintien Stream mouth in the Hsintien Stream. Comparison of the simulation results between no wastewater cut-off (shown in Figure 6) and total wastewater cut-off indicates that salinity increases about 2 *ppt* in most part of the estuary as a result of wastewater diversion. The most increase occurs in the Keelung River with an increase of 4 *ppt* around 5 km from the Keelung River mouth. However the limit of salt intrusion moves only slightly upriver if the wastewater is totally cut-off. Model results indicate that the limits of salt intrusion stay near topographic sills. The sills at the upriver end play an important role in preventing further salt intrusion as freshwater input diminishes.

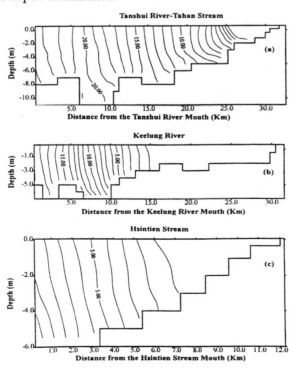

Figure 8. Computed salinity distributions under Q_{90} flow conditions while the wastewater was totally cut-off.

Conclusions

Using a vertical (laterally averaged) two-dimensional numerical model and calibrated values for model constants, an analysis have been made of the computed residual (density) circulation and salinity distribution in the Tanshui estuary under both mean and Q_{90} freshwater discharge conditions. The results show current velocity in estuaries may be decomposed into two components, tidal and residual. In a partially-mixed estuary, the dominant residual velocity is characterized by the upriver movement of more saline water in the lower layer and downriver movement of fresher water in the upper layer. The computed residual velocity profiles in the Tanshui estuary show this two-layer flow characteristics, particularly under low river discharge conditions.

The magnitude of river discharge is the dominant factor affecting salinity distribution in the Tanshui River estuary system. Under mean flow condition, sea water barely intrudes into the Hsintien Stream. In the Keelung River, the limit of salt intrusion is at 5 km as averaged over two spring-neap cycles. Reduction of river discharge to Q_{90} flow increases the distance of salt intrusion by about 6 km, 6 km and 7 km in the Tahan Stream, Keelung River and Hsintien Stream, respectively.

The total diversion of wastewater under Q_{90} flow condition has only slight change in the limit of salt intrusion, since it is limited by shallow depth in the upriver regions. However, there is significant salinity increase in the middle reach of the Tanshui River and lower portions of all tributaries. The most severe impact is noted in the Keelung River where a salinity increase as high as 4 ppt is predicted. This may be attributed to the more gentle bottom slope in this tributary.

Acknowledgment

The research reported here was supported in part by the National Science Council, R.O.C., under grant No. NSC 89-2213-E-002-075.

References

Blumberg, A. F., Khan. L. A. and John, J. P. St., Three-dimensional hydrodynamic model of New York harbor region. J. Hydr. Engrg., ASCE, 125(8), 799-816, 1999.

Casulli, V., and Cheng R. T., Semi-implicit finite difference methods for three-dimensional shallow water flow. Int. J. Numer. Methods Fluids, 15, 629-648, 1992.

Hsu, M. H., Kuo, A. Y., Kuo, J. T., and Liu, W. C., Study of tidal characteristics, estuarine circulation and salinity distribution in Tanshui River system. Tech. Rep. No. 273, Hydrotech Res. Inst. National Taiwan University, Taipei, Taiwan, 1997.

Hsu, M. H., Kuo, A. Y., Kuo, J. T., and Liu, W. C., Procedure to calibrate and verify numerical models of estuarine hydrodynamics. J. Hydr. Engrg., ASCE, 125(2), 166-182, 1999.

Johnson, B. H., Kim, K. W., Heath, R. E., Hsieh, B. B., and Butler, H. L., Validation of three-dimensional hydrodynamic model of Chesapeake Bay. J. Hydr. Engrg., ASCE, 119(1), 2-20, 1993.

Muin M., and Spaulding M., Three-dimensional boundary-fitted circulation model. J. Hydr. Engrg., ASCE, 123(1), 2-12, 1997.

Oley, L. Y., Millor, G. L., and Hires, R. I., A three-dimensional simulation of the Hudson-Raritan Estuary. Part I: description of the model and model simulation. J. Phys. Oceanography, 15, 1676-1692, 1985.

Sheng, Y. P., A three-dimensional mathematical model of coastal, estuarine and lake currents using boundary-fitted grid. Tech. Rep. No. 585, Aeronautical Research Associates of Princeton, Princeton, N. J., 1986.

Wang, J., and Ikeda, M., A 3-D ocean general circulation model for mesoscale eddies, I. Meander simulation and liner growth rate. Acta Oceanol. Sin., 15, 31-58, 1996.

Control of Saline Water Intrusion by Air Bubbles with Changing Tidal Range

Makoto Ifuku

Department of Civil and Environmental Eng., Ehime University, Matsuyama, 790-8577 Japan
ifuku@dpc.ehime-u.ac.jp

1. Abstract

An analysis of saline water intrusion caused by the propagation of tides is carried out using two-dimensional Reynolds and diffusion equations as the governing equations. The boundary condition is that tide is transmitted through the upstream boundary. Reynolds stress is evaluated using the eddy viscosity of the SGS (subgrid-system). In addition, an analysis of the control of saline water intrusion by air bubbles is carried out using the continuity equation for air in an air-water flow. The bubble rise velocity in a density-stratified body of water is evaluated using the formula suggested by Comolet(1979). Turbulent diffusivity is assumed to depend on the temporal flow velocity. The numerical analysis was verified using experiments conducted by Perrels and Karelse(1976) and Komatsu et al.(1996) for comparison.

2. Introduction

In recent years the upstream intrusion of saline water into tidal estuaries has become a serious problem for river environments. With a view to preserving water quality, an artificial control method for preventing such saline water intrusion is required.

Several exploratory experiments on controlling of the ambient boundary layer by introducing local non-uniformities were performed with the objective of achieving stable density-current forms with limited intrusion lengths. These methods include a small step, a barrier, and suction and are applied for intrusions at either the bottom or surface of the ambient water flow.

Jirka and Arita (1987) developed a technology by which the salt wedge is made to undergo changes in density current using a small step positioned at the bottom. However, placing such a step in a river with a comparatively low flow capacity introduced a new problem: flood control. Bubble plumes have been used for a variety of purposes: as bubble breakwaters, as an antifreeze measure in harbours, for the destratification of lakes, and as bubble curtains for the containment of oil spills (Wilkinson 1979, Cheung and Epstein 1987).

A bubble plume entrains the ambient fluid as it rises. The quantitative evaluation of this entrainment process is very important to the prediction of the behavior of the bubble plume. A physical model for analysis of the behavior of bubble plumes has been proposed by Asaeda and Imberger(1993). However, it is merely a qualitative representation of the phenomenon. In particular, there are few analysis applicable to two-dimensional investigations. However, understanding this the control method is not only of fundamental interest in the study of density currents, but also has important engineering applications whenever the prevention of long-distance wedge-like intrusions is desired.

The aim of the present study was to develop a numerical model of a bubble plume in a density-stratified flow with the aim of controlling long intrusions of saline water.

3. Numerical analysis

3.1 Governing Equations
Flow
After integrating over the width of the channel and using the shallow water approximation, the

equations for vertical two-dimensional density current can be outlined as below.
The equation for the conservation of longitudinal momentum reads

$$\left.\begin{array}{l} \partial u/\partial t + \partial/\partial x(u^2) + \partial/\partial z(uw) = -(1/\rho_0)\partial p/\partial x + (1/\rho_0)\partial\tau_{xx}/\partial x + (1/\rho_0)\partial\tau_{zx}/\partial z \\ \partial w/\partial t + \partial(uw)/\partial x + \partial(w^2)/\partial z = -g - (1/\rho)\partial p/\partial z + (1/\rho_0)\partial\tau_{zx}/\partial x + (1/\rho_0)\partial\tau_{zz}/\partial z \end{array}\right\} \quad (1)$$

where t is time; x is the longitudinal coordinate (positive upstream); z is the vertical coordinate (positive upward); u and w are the longitudinal and vertical velocities, respectively; ρ_0 is the fresh water density, ρ is the density; p is the pressure, and g is the gravitational acceleration. Moreover, τ_{xx}, τ_{zx} and, τ_{zz} are the Reynolds stresses and are expressed in Cartesian tensor notation as follows;

$$\tau_{ji}/\rho_0 = (\nu_w + \nu_t)\left(\partial u_i/\partial x_j + \partial u_j/\partial x_i\right), \qquad \nu_t = (c_s\Delta)^2 \left[(\partial u_i/\partial x_j + \partial u_j/\partial x_i)\,\partial u_i/\partial x_j\right]^{1/2} \quad (2)$$

where ν_w is kinematic viscosity; ν_t is the SGS (subgrid-scale) diffusivity suggested by Smagorinsky(7); c_s is the Smagorinsky constant; and $\Delta = (\Delta x\Delta z1)^{1/3}$(with Δx and Δz the londitudinal and vertical grid intervals, respectively).
The continuity equation reads

$$\partial u/\partial x + \partial w/\partial z = 0 \quad (3)$$

Salt Content
The equation for conservation of salt content reads

$$\partial S/\partial t + \partial(uS)/\partial x + \partial(wS)/\partial z = \partial(K_x\partial S/\dot{\partial}x)/\partial x + \partial(K_z\partial S/\partial z)/\partial z \quad (4)$$

where S is the salinity, and K_x, K_z are turbulent diffusivities which are assumed to be as follows (Bear(1979)):

$$K_x = \gamma_x(a_L u^2 + a_T w^2)/q, \;\; K_z = \gamma_z(a_T u^2 + a_L w^2)/q, \;\; q = (u^2 + w^2)^{1/2} \quad (5)$$

where γ_x, γ_z are constants of proportionality; and a_T, a_L are characteristic lengths defined as follows:

$$a_T = \Delta \; ; \; a_L = c_1 \cdot a_T \quad (6)$$

where c_1 is an empirical constant.
Air bubbles
The continuity equation for air bubbles in the air-water flow reads

$$\partial C/\partial t + \partial(uC)/\partial x + \partial(wC)/\partial z = \partial(K_x\partial C/\partial x)/\partial x + \partial(K_z\partial C/\partial z)/\partial z - \partial(u_aC)/\partial x - \partial(w_aC)/\partial z \quad (7)$$

where C is the concentration of air bubbles, and u_a, w_a are the velocities of an air bubble in the x and z directions.
Velocity of air bubble
At equilibrium, the balance of forces yields:

$$-V_{ab}(\partial p/\partial x) - \rho_w c_{DX} u_a \mid u_a \mid A_{ab}/2 = 0, \qquad \mp\rho_w c_{DZ} w_a \mid w_a \mid A_{ab}/2 - \rho_a g V_{ab} \pm F_b = 0 \quad (8)$$

where c_{DX} and c_{DZ} are the drag coefficients, A_{ab} and V_{ab} are the projected area and volume of air bubbles, F_b is a buoyancy force, and sign $\mp$ depends on the motion direction.
Drag coefficients are calculated by the following equations:

$$c_{DX}, c_{DZ} = \begin{cases} 240 & 0.1031 \geq Re \\ 24/Re(1 + 0.15Re^{0.687}) & 0.1031 < Re < 989 \\ 0.44 & 989 \leq Re \end{cases} \quad (9)$$

878

where $Re = |u_a - u|\, d_a/\nu_w$ or $Re = |w_a - w|\, d_a/\nu_w$.

Free surface equation

Integrating eq.(3) over the water depth and substituting the kinematic boundary condition yields

$$\partial \xi/\partial t + \partial(\int_{z_b}^{\xi} u\,dz)/\partial x = 0 \qquad (10)$$

where ξ and z_b are the height of the free water surface and the bottom from the reference datum, respectively.

Density

In this model, water is treated as a homogeneous fluid with the apparent density of an air bubble and water mix. Thus, the apparent density is evaluated by the following equation:

$$\rho = \rho_w/(1 + \beta_1 C), \quad \rho_w = \rho_0/(1 - \beta_2 S), \quad \beta_1 = (\rho_w - \rho_a)/\rho_a, \quad \beta_2 = (\rho_s - \rho_0)/\rho_s \qquad (11)$$

where ρ_w, ρ_s, and ρ_a are the densities of water, sea water, and air bubbles, respectively.

3.2 Boundary Conditions
The boundary conditions are set as in Figure 1.

3.3 Coordinate Transformation
In the physical domain, the water surface is a moving boundary because of tides, and the bottom also changes in space. Further, the longitudinal area of interest is not, in general, rectangle, because of variations in the bottom and the free surface. To obtain a good representation of the flow, an accurate description of the form of the free surface and the bottom is necessary. For a numerical approach based on finite differences, however, a rectangular grid that is coincident with the boundaries is

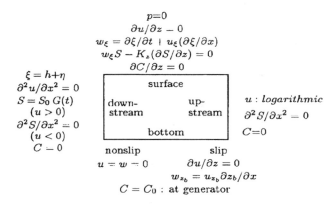

Fig.1 Boundary conditions

preferable. Therefore, the area of interest is modified by a simple transformation into a rectangle. The coordinate transformation is applied to the governing equations, and the spatial and temporal behavior of flow, salinity, and air bubbles are then simulated.

4. Numerical Results

4.1 Analysis based on Experiment by Perrels and Karelse (1978)
The results of a flume test conducted by Perrels and Kareles were used to verify the numerical model. It was assumed that the density difference between river water and seawater, $\Delta\rho(\Delta\rho = \rho_s - \rho_0)$, is 23.8 kg/m^3. At the downstream boundary, the surface elevation was computed using Airy wave theory with a wave amplitude of 2.5 cm and a period of 558.7 s. The river discharge was set to 2.9×10^{-3} m^3/s at the upstream boundary. The length, width, and depth of the channel were 101.5 m, 0.672 m, and 0.216 m, respectively. A no-slip condition was imposed at the bottom. The horizontal grid interval was set to 1.83 m and the water depth was divided into 13 planes. The time increment was $T/2000$. The Smagorinsky constant in eq.(2) was set to 0.1 or 0.2.

Vertical distribution of horizontal velocity

Figure 2(a) shows the vertical distribution at point $x = 7.32$ m for the phase at which the velocity reaches a minimum (referred to as MEV). When the Smagorinsky constant was set to 0.1, the simulated velocity was slightly larger than the experimental value from the bottom to a height equivalent to one-fifth of water depth. The simulated results agree well with the experimental ones at intermediate depths. Overall, the difference between the experimental and simulated results is very small. When the Smagorinsky constant was set to 0.2, the simulated results were slightly larger than the experimental ones at intermediate depths. Further, the simulated results were smaller than the experimental ones near the free surface.

Figure 2(b) shows the vertical distribution at point $x = 7.32$ m for the phase at which the velocity reaches a maximum (referred to as MFV) in the slack phase. When the Smagorinsky constant was set to 0.1, the simulated velocity was slightly smaller than the experimental value at intermediate depths. However, the difference is very small. So the simulated values agree well with the experimental ones near the free surface and near the bottom. When the Smagorinsky constant was set to 0.2, the simulated results were lower than the experimental values near the bottom and larger than the experimental values near the free surface. Judging from these results, the flow structure of density-stratified flow can be represented by the SGS-eddy viscosity. Also it is appropriate to set the Smagorinsky constant at 0.1. Thus the Smagorinsky constant is set to 0.1 in the following numerical analysis.

4.2 Analysis based on Experiment by Komatsu et al.

The results of a flume test by Komatsu et al.(5) were also used for verification of the numerical model. The salinity at the downstream boundary was set at about 1 and 3 g/kg. At the downstream boundary, the surface elevation was computed by Airy wave theory for wave amplitudes of 0.25 and 0.7 cm and a period of 240 s. Meanwhile, the river discharge was set at 3.5×10^{-5} and 5×10^{-5} m^3/s at the upstream boundary. The length and width of the channel were 20 m and 0.25 m, respectively, and the water depth at the downstream boundary was 0.133 m. The bottom slope was 0.005 and the air bubble generator was mounted on the bottom at $x = 3$, 5, and 8.5 m from the river mouth. The horizontal grid interval was set to 5 cm and the water depth was divided into 11 planes. The time increment was $T/2000$. The constants of proportionality, γ_x and γ_z, in eq.(5) and the empirical constant, c_1, in eq.(6) were set to 1.5×10^{-3}, 1×10^{-5}, and 100, respectively. The volumetric concentration of air bubbles was set to 1.5×10^{-3} at the generator.

Vertical distribution of salinity

Figure 3 shows the vertical distribution of salinity at point $x = 3$ m for a river water discharge of 3.5×10^{-5} m^3/s. The closed squares and circles represent the experimental and simulated results, respectively. S_0 is the maximal salinity at the downstream boundary, $x = 0$ m. Where the water is shallower than 8.5 cm, the simulated results are higher than the experimental result by about 10 percent. Meanwhile, at positions which are deeper than $z = 8.5$ cm, the simulated results compare favorably with the experimental results. Figure 3(b) shows the case

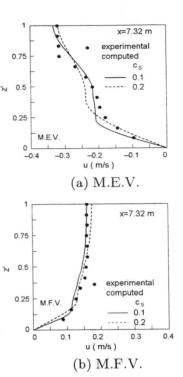

(a) M.E.V.

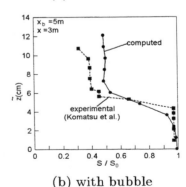

(b) M.F.V.

Fig.2 Vertical distribution of horizontal velocity

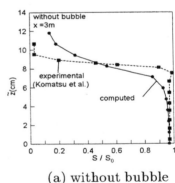

(a) without bubble

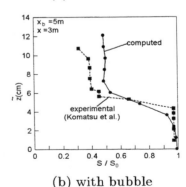

(b) with bubble

Fig.3 Vertical distribution of salinity

where air bubbles were generated 5 m from the river mouth. Where the water is shallower than 5.2 cm, the simulated results are higher than the experimental ones by about 10 percent. It seems that the difference between experimental and simulated results somehow from the evaluation of air-bubble velocity.

Spatial distribution of salinity and flow velocity
Figure 4 shows isohaline and flow velocity at the high water and slack phases around the air-bubble generator, in a case where air bubbles were generated 5 m from the river mouth. The tidal amplitude and river discharge were 0.25 cm and 3.5×10^{-5} m^3/s. The intrusion of isohalines greater than 0.6 is considerably controlled by the upwelling flow caused by the air bubbles. Mixed water with relatively higher density was swept downward by the effect of gravity and the 0.3-0.5 isohaline was finally advected horizontally as an intrusion. Near the downstream and upstream positions where the normalized height is 0-0.4 and 0-0.2, respectively, the vertical component of velocity increases. And near the air-bubble generator, an upwelling flow is caused by air-bubble generation, setting up a counterclockwise circulation upstream and downstream of the air-bubble generator. The mixing caused by upstream circulation seems to affect the intrusion of saline water.

Meanwhile, at the slack phase, the fluid flows downstream with falling tidal level over the whole region except fluid near the bottom downstream of the generator, which flows upstream. The vertical velocity induced by air-bubble generation is reduced in comparison with that at the high water phase. As a result, the dense isohalines formed upstream of the generator moves downstream and the intervals between isohalines increase slightly. The isohalines near the surface upstream of the generator move slightly downstream and their intervals widens slightly.

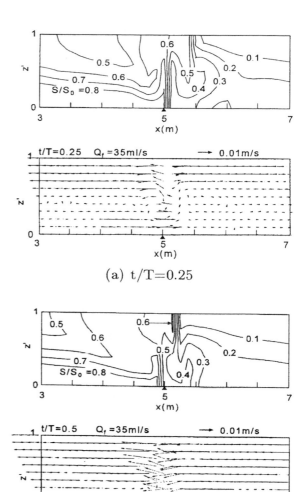

(a) t/T=0.25

(b) t/T=0.5

Fig.4 Isohaline and velocity around
the air−bubble generator

Spatial distribution of time and depth-averaged salinity
Figure 5 shows the spatial distribution of salinity averaged over a tidal cycle and water depth. The closed circles, triangles, and squares represent experimental values and the solid, broken, and dot-dashed lines represent simulated ones for cases where the slip condition is imposed at the bottom. Without air-bubble generation, the cases with amplitudes 0.25 and 0.7 cm correspond to the salt wedge and partially mixed types, respectively. When the amplitude, river discharge, and salinity at the downstream boundary are 0.25 cm, 3.5×10^{-5} m^3/s, and 1 g/kg, the agreement between the experimental and simulated values is highly satisfactory without air-bubble generation. When the air-bubble generator is placed 5 m from the river mouth, the experimental values agree well with the simulated ones at the downstream of generator but the simulation overestimates the experimental results at the upstream of generator. Meanwhile, when the air-bubble generator is 7 m from the river mouth, the experimental and simulated results agree well at the downstream of generator

but the simulation overestimates the experimental results 10 m upstream. Under these simulated conditions, when the generator is near the river mouth, the decrease in salinity is large; that is, control efficiency by air-bubble is good. When the amplitude, river discharge, and salinity at the downstream boundary are 0.7 cm, 5×10^{-5} m^3/s, and 3 g/kg, respectively, agreement between the experimental and simulated values is highly satisfactory without air-bubble generation. In cases where air bubbles are generated, the fall in salinity around the generator is low in comparison with Figure 4(a). This is why the salinity at the downstream boundary is three times that in Figure 4(a) and why the relative high-density water, which rises up with the air bubbles, intrudes upstream of the generator. In cases where the volumetric concentration of air bubbles is set to 3×10^{-3} at the generator, the upstream salinity is approximately one fifth to three tenths that in the case where the volumetric concentration of air bubbles is 1.5×10^{-3} and the control efficiency is slightly higher.

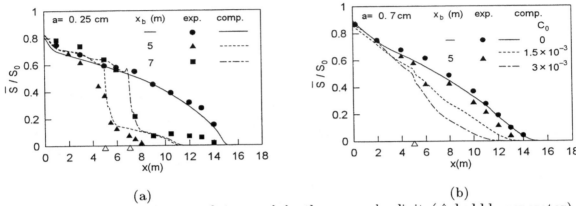

(a)   (b)

Fig.5 Spatial distribution of time and depth averaged salinity($\triangle$:bubble generator)

5. Conclusions

The control efficiency of air-bubble generation in a density-stratified flow is examined numerically. In cases where salinity at the downstream boundary is relatively low, the control efficiency around the generator is high. However, in cases where the salinity at the downstream boundary is relatively high, the control efficiency is considerably reduced.

References

Asaeda, T. and J.Imberger : Structure of bubble plumes in linearly stratified environments, J.F.M., Vol.249, pp.35-57, 1993.

Bear, J. : Hydraulics of Groundwater, McGraw-Hill, pp.225-239, 1979.

Cheung, F.B. and M.Epstein: Two-phase gas bubble-liquid boundary layer flow along vertical and inclined surface, Nucl.Eng.Design, Vol.99, pp.93-100, 1987.

Comolet, R.: Sur le Mouvement d'une bulle de gaz dans un liquide, Jl La Houlle Blanche, No.1, pp.31-42, 1979.

Jirka, G.H. and M.Arita: Density currents or density wedge−boundary layer influence and control method, J.F.M., Vol.177, pp.187-206, 1987.

Komatsu, T., S.Sun, T.Adachi, Y.Kawakami and K.Komesu: Study on the artificial control method for preventing salinity intrusion in a tidal estuary, Ann.J.Hydraul.Eng., JSCE, Vol.40, pp.517-524, 1996. (in Japanese)

Perrels, P.A.J. and M.Karelse : A two-dimensional numerical model for salt intrusion in estuaries, in J.C.J.Nihoul (editor), Hydrodynamics of Estuaries and Fjords, Elsevier Scientific Publishing Company, pp.107-125, 1978.

Smagorinsky, J.: General circulation experiments with primitive equations, Month Weather Rev., Vol.9, No.3, pp.99-164, 1963.

Wilkinson, D.L.: Two-dimensional bubble plumes, J.Hydraul.Div., ASCE, Vol.105, No.HY2, pp.139-154, 1979.

Moving Boundary Level Model for Calculation of Stratified Flow with Large Water Level Change

Hirohide KIRI[1], Hideto FUJII[1] and Tetsuo NAKAYA[1]

[1]National Research Institute of Agricultural Engineering, Tsukuba, Ibaraki,305-8609 Japan
kiri@nkk.affrc.go.jp, fhideto@nkk.affrc.go.jp, tnakaya@nkk.affrc.go.jp

1. Abstract

In quasi-three-dimensional analysis by the Level Model, it is difficult to reproduce the phenomenon whose flow becomes stratification with water level change, because the thickness of the 1st level changes according to the water level change. In this paper, the Moving Boundary Level Model was proposed for quasi-three-dimensional analysis of salinity in the area where the water level changes by tide.

The wave propagation analysis in a straight channel was carried out for the verification of the present method. Then, it was confirmed that the present method was able to reproduce flow velocity near the surface which the Level Model was not able to reproduce. Moreover, the change of salinity according to the tidal change was analyzed for Ariake Bay, in Japan.

2. Introduction

The Level Model is often used for quasi-three-dimensional analysis of salinity in saltwater. However, the Level Model is not suitable for analyzing the salinity of the area where the water level largely changes by tide. This is because that level thickness of the 1st level depends on the range of the water level change. And this change of the level thickness lowers analytical accuracy. To solve the problem, the authors developed the Moving Boundary Level Model which changes its level thickness over a small range even if the water level is changed.

This paper explains the calculation method of the Moving Boundary Level Model and presents the validity of this method by numerical analysis of flow in a straight channel and its application in salinity analysis in Ariake bay.

3. The Moving Boundary Level Model

The Moving Boundary Level Model is the method based on the finite element method and applies the Moving Boundary Technique (Kawahara and Umetsu,1986), used in flood analysis, to quasi-three-dimensional analysis. Figure 1 shows an outline and variable arrangement of the present method.

In the present method, the area the water level is expected to reach is divided into finite element mesh, and elements are classified into three types: an "empty element", a "surface element" and an "underwater element". As a result, the movement of the water surface exceeding the boundary of levels becomes possible and the surface level thickness changes within the thickness of the surface element. Here, the classification of elements is carried out whenever the water surface exceeds the boundary of levels.

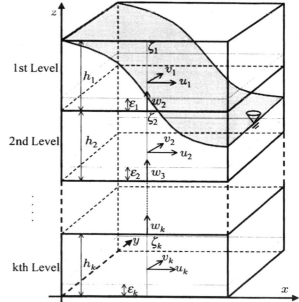

Figure 1. Outline and Variable Arrangement of the Moving Boundary Level Model

Table 1. The Classification Method of Element

Element	Nodes in the element	Element above
Empty element	A part of node is in the empty region	—
Surface element	All nodes are in the water region	Empty element
Underwater element	All nodes are in the water region	Surface element, Underwater element

Table 1 shows the classification method of elements. A "water region" in Table 1 means the area where the water depth exists and in an "empty region", the water depth does not exist. The classification method of these elements according to the water level change and the treatment on the numerical analysis are described as follows.

Determination of the "empty region" and the "water region": In the present method, determination of the empty region and the water region is needed for classification of elements. The empty region and the water region are determinated with the water depth at node. But, the water depth is not permitted to become zero while calculating. Then, the basis water depth (ε_k) is introduced to each level as shown in Figure 2. And determination of the empty region and the water region is carried out by regarding the basis water depth as a boundary of each level. As a result, the longest range that the water surface actually moves in the surface element becomes $-h_k + \varepsilon_k < \zeta_k \leq \varepsilon_{k+1}$. Here, the basis water depth is assumed 25% of the thickness of each level ($\varepsilon_k = 0.25 h_k$) in consideration of the stability of calculation.

Treatment of the "empty element": The element in which the water depth at nodes do not exceed the basis depth is classified as the "empty element".

The empty element is not included in the matrix assembly on the finite element method, and is excluded from the calculation. At nodes in the empty element, $-h_k$ m and 0.0m/sec are substituted for water level and flow velocity, respectively. The classification of elements is judged from the relation between total wave height (ζ_T) and the thickness of levels.

Treatment of the "surface element": As for the "surface element", all nodes in the element are in the water region and the element above is classified as the empty element.

When the water level rises and exceeds the basis depth at all nodes of the empty element, classification of the element is switched from the empty element to the surface element. In this case, because flow velocity at nodes on the switched surface element are 0.0m/s, it is assumed to give flow velocity of nodes on the level below. On the other hand, when water level rise and exceed the basis depth only at a part of a node of the element, it is assumed that element is classified as the empty element (Element by which slash is applied in Figure 2).

Treatment of the "underwater element": As for the "underwater element", all nodes in the element are in the water region and the element above is not classified as the empty element.

In the underwater element, the water level is assumed to be 0.0m. And the flow velocity in the horizontal and vertical direction are calculated by the momentum equations and the continuty equations, respectively.

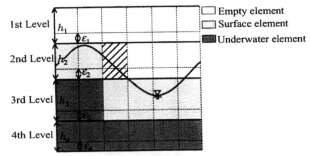

Figure 2. Relation Between the Basis Depth and Classification of Element

4. Basic Equations

On the present method, the basic equations are shown as follows.

Continuity equations

empty element:
$$\zeta_k = -h_k \tag{1}$$

surface element:
$$\frac{\partial \zeta_k}{\partial t} + \frac{\partial}{\partial x}\{(h_k + \zeta_k)u_k\} + \frac{\partial}{\partial y}\{(h_k + \zeta_k)v_k\} - w_{k+1} = 0 \tag{2}$$

underwater element

(middle level):
$$\frac{\partial}{\partial x}(h_k u_k) + \frac{\partial}{\partial y}(h_k v_k) + w_k - w_{k+1} = 0, \quad \zeta_k = 0 \tag{3}$$

(bottom level):
$$\frac{\partial}{\partial x}(h_k u_k) + \frac{\partial}{\partial y}(h_k v_k) + w_k = 0, \quad \zeta_k = 0 \tag{4}$$

Momentum equations

surface element
$$\frac{\partial u_k}{\partial t} + u_k \frac{\partial u_k}{\partial x} + v_k \frac{\partial u_k}{\partial y} + w_{k+1} \frac{u_k + u_{k+1}}{2(h_k + \zeta_k)} + g\frac{\partial \zeta_T}{\partial x} - A_\ell \left(\frac{\partial^2 u_k}{\partial x^2} + \frac{\partial^2 u_k}{\partial y^2}\right) - \frac{1}{\rho_k(h_k + \zeta_k)}(-\tau_{xz}^\ell) = 0 \tag{5}$$

$$\frac{\partial v_k}{\partial t} + u_k \frac{\partial v_k}{\partial x} + v_k \frac{\partial v_k}{\partial y} + w_{k+1} \frac{v_k + v_{k+1}}{2(h_k + \zeta_k)} + g\frac{\partial \zeta_T}{\partial y} - A_\ell \left(\frac{\partial^2 v_k}{\partial x^2} + \frac{\partial^2 v_k}{\partial y^2}\right) - \frac{1}{\rho_k(h_k + \zeta_k)}(-\tau_{yz}^\ell) = 0 \tag{6}$$

underwater element (middle level)
$$\frac{\partial u_k}{\partial t} + u_k \frac{\partial u_k}{\partial x} + v_k \frac{\partial u_k}{\partial y} + \frac{1}{h_k}\{(wu)^s - (wu)^\ell\} + g\frac{\partial \zeta_T}{\partial x} - A_\ell \left(\frac{\partial^2 u_k}{\partial x^2} + \frac{\partial^2 u_k}{\partial y^2}\right) - \frac{1}{\rho_k h_k}(\tau_{xz}^s - \tau_{xz}^\ell) = 0 \tag{7}$$

$$\frac{\partial v_k}{\partial t} + u_k \frac{\partial v_k}{\partial x} + v_k \frac{\partial v_k}{\partial y} + \frac{1}{h_k}\{(wv)^s - (wv)^\ell\} + g\frac{\partial \zeta_T}{\partial y} - A_\ell \left(\frac{\partial^2 v_k}{\partial x^2} + \frac{\partial^2 v_k}{\partial y^2}\right) - \frac{1}{\rho_k h_k}(\tau_{yz}^s - \tau_{yz}^\ell) = 0 \tag{8}$$

underwater element (bottom level)
$$\frac{\partial u_k}{\partial t} + u_k \frac{\partial u_k}{\partial x} + v_k \frac{\partial u_k}{\partial y} + w_k \frac{u_{k-1} + u_k}{2h_k} + g\frac{\partial \zeta_T}{\partial x} - A_\ell \left(\frac{\partial^2 u_k}{\partial x^2} + \frac{\partial^2 u_k}{\partial y^2}\right) - \frac{1}{\rho_k h_k}\tau_{xz}^s = 0 \tag{9}$$

$$\frac{\partial v_k}{\partial t} + u_k \frac{\partial v_k}{\partial x} + v_k \frac{\partial v_k}{\partial y} + w_k \frac{v_{k-1} + v_k}{2h_k} + g\frac{\partial \zeta_T}{\partial y} - A_\ell \left(\frac{\partial^2 v_k}{\partial x^2} + \frac{\partial^2 v_k}{\partial y^2}\right) - \frac{1}{\rho_k h_k}\tau_{yz}^s = 0 \tag{10}$$

where, u_k, v_k : kth level flow velocity in x, y (horizontal)-direction, w_k : kth level flow velocity in z (vertical)-direction, ζ_k : water level in kth level, h_k : level thickness in kth level, ρ_k : water density in kth level, τ : internal friction, A_ℓ : horizontal kinematic eddy viscosity, g : gravity acceralation, t : time, and ζ_T means the total wave height shown by the following equation.

$$\zeta_T = \sum_{k=1}^{m} \zeta_k \tag{11}$$

The salinity is evaluated by the chlorinity and its diffusion equation is the same as the one used with the Level Model. Here, Knudsen's equations are employed for exchanging the chlorinity to water density. The finite element formulation of the basic equations are omitted in this paper.

5. Verifying the validity of the Moving Boundary Level Model

To verify the validity of the present method, numerical analysis of flow in a straight channel was carried out. The finite element mesh of the straight channel used for the analysis is shown in Figure 3. The value of the parameters are listed in Table 2.

The progress wave condition and the sin wave (wave height:H, frequency:T) were employed for the boundary condition at the end and the top of the channel, respectively.

Table 2. List of Parameters

Parameter	Value
H	4.47 m
T	12 hour
A_ℓ	0.0855 m^2/sec
A_v	0.0001 m^2/sec
Δx	50.0 m
Δy	50.0 m
Δt	2.0 sec
h_i	30.0 m

A_v : coefficient of internal friction
h_i : initial depth

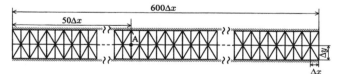

Figure 3. The Finite Element Mesh of the Straight Channel

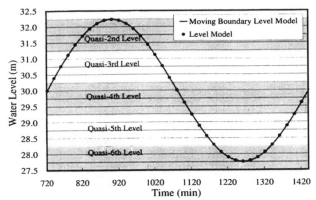

Figure 4. The Time Series of Water Level

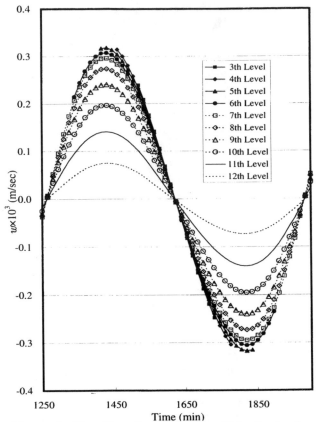

Figure 5. The Time Series of Flow Velocity in the Vertical Direction

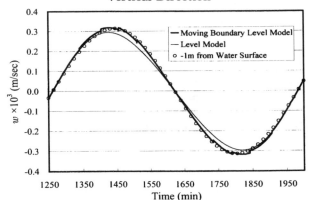

Figure 6. The Comparison of Flow Velocity in the Vertical Direction

The time series of the water level is shown in Figure 4. In this case, the water level moves from 27.765 to 32.255m with the progression of the wave. However, because the basis depth of each level is assumed 25% of level thickness, the bottom boundary of the quasi-1st level is at 32.250m. As a result, the surface element moves from the 2nd level to the 6th level.

The time series of flow velocity in the vertical direction is shown in Figure 5. The vertical flow velocities from the 3rd level to the 7th level cannot be calculated with time change. Figure 4 and 5 show the fact that analysis can be carried out without any numerical vibration even when the water surface exceeds the boundary of the levels.

The flow velocity in the vertical direction at the bottom of the surface element analyzed with the present method is compared with the result at the top of the 2nd level analyzed with the Level Model and is shown in Figure 6. In Figure 6, ∘ shows the flow velocity in the vertical direction at the point of 1.0m beneath the water surface calculated with equation (12).

$$ w = \frac{H\pi}{2T} \left(1 + \frac{-1}{h_i + \zeta_T} \right) \cos 2\pi \left(\frac{t}{T} - \frac{x}{L} \right) \qquad (12) $$

The result analyzed with the present method is not a smooth line, because the surface element changes when the water surface exceeds the boundary of the levels. However, from comparison with equation (12), the flow velocity in the vertical direction near the water surface can be analyzed using the present method but not with the Level Model.

6. The salinity distribution in Ariake Bay

Ariake Bay is a long curved shape 96km in length and 18km in width, located in the western part of Kyusyu island, Japan. The northern part of Ariake Bay is one of the two large production districts of food laver and its cultivation is an important industry in this area. The laver cultivators pay much attention to salinity of seawater during the cultivation period because growing laver is strongly influenced by it. Therefore, in Ariake Bay, it is important to forecast the area where salinity at the surface is low accurately.

However, Ariake Bay has another main characteristic itself. The water level change by tide is extremely large. The tide range in Ariake Bay is the largest one in Japan and it reaches as much as six meters at the spring tide. The large tide range in Ariake Bay becomes obstructive to forecasting the salinity of seawater by the Level Model. Thus, the salinity was forecast by using the present method in Ariake Bay.

The analysis area was the northern part of the bay from Miike port, which corresponds to 1/3 of Ariake Bay (Figure 7).

The analysis area was divided into trianglar elements. Here, the interval of nodes was about 30-350m. The depth data on each node was given by lincar interpolation based on the value read from the chart published by the Hydrographic Department, Maritime Safety Agency.

The analysis was carried out assuming the raising seedling period of laver cultivation. The

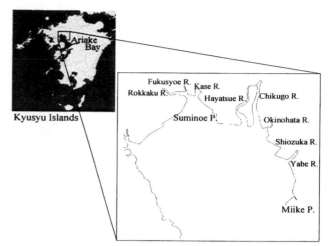

Figure 7. Analysis Area

Table 3. List of Parameters

Parameter	Value
Number of levels	12
Neap range	1.76 m
Frequency	12 hour 25 minutes
A_ℓ	$0.01L^{3/2}\,\mathrm{cm}^2/\mathrm{sec}$
A_v	$5\times(1+3.33R_i)^{-1.5}\,\mathrm{cm}^2/\mathrm{sec}$
L	$\sqrt{2S_e}$

S_e : area of each element
R_i : Richardson number

six typical rivers (the Yabe, the Shiozuka, the Okinohata, the Chikugo, the Rokkaku, and the Kase river) were selected from the rivers which flow into the anlysis area, and the average discharges calculated from the discharge chronology in October 1996, were given as boundary conditions. The model neap tide was assumed to the boundary condition of the tide, because in the neap tide, the destruction of the stratification is small and the lowest salinity at the surface of the water is shown. Moreover, the other parameters used for the calculation are listed in Table 3. The diffusion coefficient in horizontal and vertical direction used an equal value to A_ℓ and A_v, respectively.

Because there was insufficient data for the initial condition, the river water was thrown from the stationary state in the whole analysis area. Then, the analysis result from the 8th period was examined.

The analysis results of salinity at three hours from low tide, high tide, three hours from high tide and low tide in the 8th period from stationary state are shown in Figure 8-11. In Figure 8-11, contour lines are drawn every one permil of the chlorinity.

At high tide, the area where the salinity is low is pushed to the north. And the area extends to the south with the flow of the river water and it is thrown to the west according to the passage of time. Because the discharge of rivers and tide range are not so large, it is small, but the circulated flow of counterclockwise which is said to occur in the northern part of Ariake Bay is observed.

The salinity at the mouth of the Hayatsue river which diverged from the Chikugo river is higher than that at the mouth of the Chikugo river. It is caused that the discharge from the Hayatsue river is smaller than that of the Chikugo river. The salinity at low tide is most reduced in the area around the Chikugo river mouth, because the Chikugo river occupies about 80% of the discharge of rivers which flow into the analysis area.

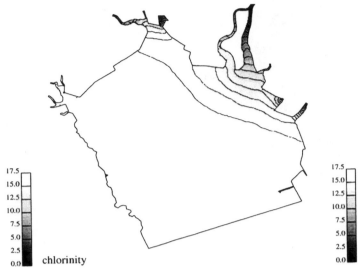

Figure 8. The Salinity Distribution at 3 hour from Low Tide

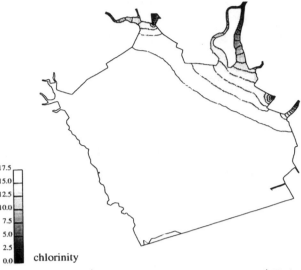

Figure 9. The Salinity Distribution at High Tide

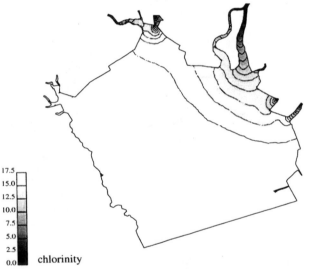

Figure 10. The Salinity Distribution at 3 hour from High Tide

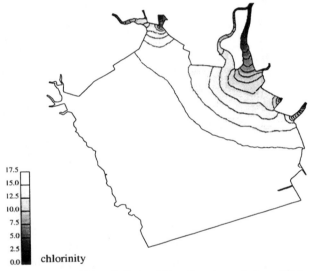

Figure 11. The Salinity Distribution at Low Tide

7. Conclusions

In this report, the Moving Boundary Level Model was proposed as a technique which improves the accuracy of quasi-three-dimensional analysis of stratified flow in an area with water level change. From the results of the wave propagation analysis in the straight channel, it was confirmed that the present method can analyze flow velocity near the water surface which is difficult to analyze with the Level Model. Moreover, the change of salinity in the northern part of Ariake Bay was carried out as an application example of an actual phenomenon.

This technique is expected to be useful in the analysis of the stratified flow not only in salinity analysis in a coastal area with tide but also in water quality analysis in the dam reservoir.

References

Kawahara M. Umetsu T.(1986) Finite Element Method for Moving Boundary Problems in River Flow Int. Jour. for Numerical Methods in Fluids Vol.6,365-386

Measurements of Stratified water quality parameters in a tidal canal

Chan-Ji Lai[1], Chen Hsing Ting[1], Ming Ching Li[1], Shin Chan Chuan[1]

[1]Hydraulic and Ocean Engineering, Cheng Kung University, Tainan, Taiwan., 70700
[1]laicj@mail.ncku.edu.tw , Phone:001886-6-2757575-63268, Fax:001886-6-2741463

1. Abstract

Tainan Canal is a looped shallow tidal channel with one harbor entrance. Tide at the measurement point MS1;MS2 are both semi-diurnal and tidal range were from 0.5 and 1.5m. Average amplitude of tide at MS2 is 1.8 times of that at MS1. Water quality profile measurements were conducted at both sites at summer, winter and spring seasons, without upstream influents. Equipment used were HYDROLAB Minisonde and Datasonde 4 water quality multiprobes. Parameters measured were temperature (TEMP), salinity (sal), DO, pH, ORP, transparency and chlorophyll.

Measured salinity and temperature distributions at MS1 and MS2 indicate that stratification is stronger at MS1, and thermal stratification was not strong at both sites. The DO concentration and ORP were strongly related to the phytoplankton which was much active at the –20~-40cm layer during flood tide. The DO concentrations near bottom were low and contributed very little to the improvement of sediment quality. These findings suggest that a 3-d water quality model should be used in modeling the flow and water quality of the canal and the previously proposed water purification scheme has to be modified accordingly.

2. Introduction

Tainan Canal is a looped shallow tidal channel with one harbor entrance as shown in Fig.1. It surrounds the reclaimed land in which a new city hall is located. This canal has been receiving domestic effluent for a long time. Non-treated effluent pollutes the water body and channel bed. Even so the famous dragon boat racing is held at the north reach every year. Many efforts including construction of intercepts at outlets of the combined sewer system, bio-chemical treatment of the water and dredging of the polluted bed material. Detail information of the water quality parameters (WQP) will help greatly those efforts. Unfortunately most of the previous WQP studies, including numerical modeling of the canal system, did not take the stratification factor into account. Since this canal is tide influenced and has low rate of water exchange, how this density stratification affects WQP is the concerns of our study.

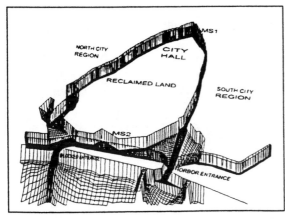

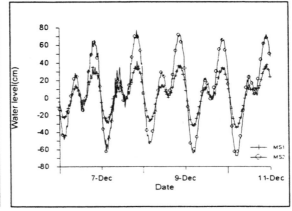

Figure 1. 3-d view of the canal and the measurement points MS1; MS2.

Figure 2. Typical tide records at MS1 and MS2, amplitude ratio of MS1 to MS2 1.8.

3. Method of measurement
3.1 Site selection
Financial reason restricted us from doing full channel survey. Two measuring sites MS1 and MS2 shown in Fig.1 were chosen. MS1 is at the east end of the canal, where both water and channel bed are very polluted. MS2 is near the harbor entrance, where water exchange rate is large and effluent pollution is small.

3.2 Equipment
(1) Water level: Water levels at both sites were self-recorded using pressure type sensors powered by bateries. Data banks recorded tide elevation at an interval of 10 minutes.

(2) WQP: HYDROLAB Minisonde and Datasonde 4 water quality multiprobes were used for profiling the WQPs. The following sensors were mounded into the system for continuous recording, of WQPs. Temperature T ($^\circ$C), salinity Sal (ppt), dissolved oxygen, DO (mg/ℓ), oxidation-reduction potential, ORP (mV), pH, transparency and chlorophyll-a sensors. The sensors were calibrated according the HYDROLAB (1997) standard procedure, before deploying the systems for measurement. In addition, one portable DO sensor, WTW OXI330 and one pH/ORP probe, AQUACYTIC PH21BNC, were also used for cross checking the measurements. The recorded data were stored in data bank and subsequently were retrieved using portable PC.

3.3 Procedures
At each measurement the water surface was used as the reference. The probes were mounted on a cable on which marking was made at 10cm. The probes were then deployed into water at 5-20 cm interval for measurement. Tidal records were retrieved every month. All the measurements were taken at the period when there were no rainfall or runoff effluents.

4. Results and analysis
4.1 Tide records
Figure.2 shows a typical tidal record for the measurement sites MS1 and MS2. Normally the tide ranges in the canal are 1.5m and 0.3m for spring and neap tides respectively. Tidal amplitude attenuates at MS1 and the amplitude ratio between both sites is 1:1.86.

4.2 Salinity distribution and Stratification
Vertical salinity distributions for MS1 and MS2 are given in Figure 3(a)-(e) respectively. In each diagram dates of measurement are shown. Notations "LOW" and "HIGH" representing the data were taken at high or low tides respectively. It is clear from Fig.3 (a)(b) and (c) that stratification and weak mixing exist in MS1. At MS1 the bottom salinity are all greater than 25ppt except at high runoff seasons, they can reduce to less than 20ppt. The salinity at MS2 in Fig.3 (d) and (e), however, show that they are all at the range of 31-33ppt. Near the surface the values are slightly smaller but in overall there is no stratification at MS2.

4.3 WQP at MS1
Figures 4 and 5 are the plots of WQPs (pH, ORP, DO and temperature) distributions for summer and winter seasons and for winter season respectively. Temperature distributions in Figs.4 (d) and 5(d) indicate that thermal stratification is nearly negligible at MS1. In winter there is very little DO concentration but in summer and autumn there are super-saturated concentrations exist at the depth of 20-40 cm. ORP at the date of super-saturated DO also have positive values. At other dates ORP are negative, especially in winter. Distributions of pH shown in Fig.4 (a) vary from 6.5-8.5. The high pH values occur at the date when DO are super-saturated.

Figure 6(a)(b)(c) and (d) show the continuous measurements results at noon of 10/24. At this period, it was ebbing tide as indicated in Fig.6 (e). Fig.6 (a) and (b) are distributions of transparency and chlorophyll-a concentration. At noon, 12:00 the chlorophyll-a are around 10 μg/L from the surface to bottom. Increasing of chlorophyll-a at 13:30 greatly reduces the transparency. The higher chlorophyll-a is exist at −20~-40cm where DO also have high values.

4.4 WQP at MS2
Distributions of WQPs for the winter measurements are shown in Figure 7. Those of the continuous measured results are given in Figure 8 respectively. All the distributions show very

little vertical variation, except DO and ORP's of the 1/11 measurements. On 1/11 ORP becomes negative at the depth above −50cm. All the DO profile measured at flooding tide shows an increase of concentration at depth above −50cm. Distributions of WQP of 10/24 shown in Figure 8 also indicate litter vertical variation, except those of the pH and ORP's at 10:00am.

5 Discussion

It is well known, Harper (1992), that photosynthesis/respiration process of phytoplankton, the nutrients, predation and biomanipulation in an aquatic environment result in the dynamical WQP that can be observed. For example, Chlorella consumes NH_3 and CO_2 and produce O_2 when there is sunlight. Without sunlight, it conducts endogenous metabolism and reversely produces NH_3 and CO_2. Reduction of NH_3 and CO_2 increases pH value and vice versa. This explains the high pH value in the distributions when there is a DO super-saturated concentration. It appears that density stratification has no direct contribution to the vertical distribution of WQPs, even they are stratified alike.

6   Concluding Remarks

Measurements of water quality vertical distribution were conducted in a tidal canal. Results revealed that density stratification has less direct effect on these WQP distributions in an aquatic environment. These WQP can be more easily interpreted if the information related to the ecological interaction is detected. In the future if a model should be used to compute the WQP in the canal, a two layers or 3-d model should be considered, even if the water is not density stratified.

7 References

1. Harper, David, "Eutrophication of freshwaters" , Chapman&Hall, 1992.
2. HYDROLAB, "Datasonde 4/ Minisonde user's manual", rev., 1997.

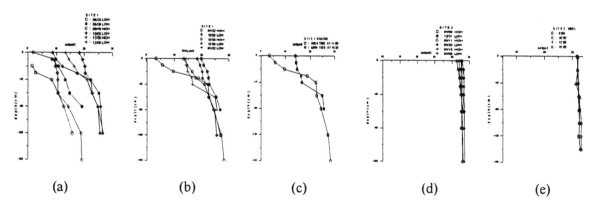

Figure 3 Salinity distribution at (a)(b)(c) MS1 and at (d)(e) MS2 for various seasons

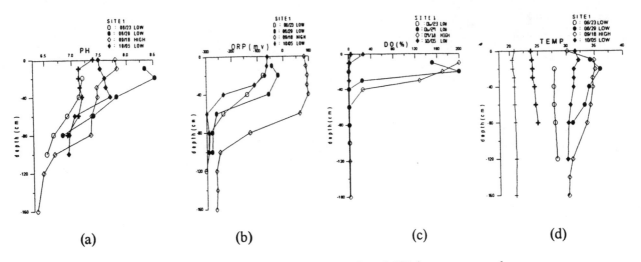

(a)   (b)   (c)   (d)

Figure 4. Profiles of pH、ORP、DO and TEMP at MS1 in summer and autumn

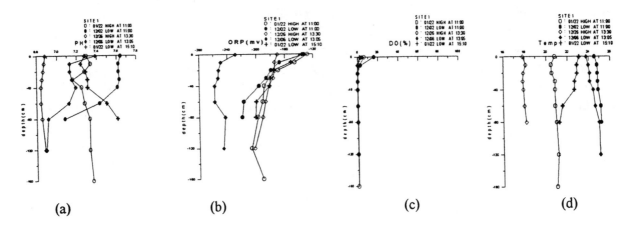

(a)   (b)   (c)   (d)

Figure 5 Profiles of pH、ORP、DO and TEMP at MS1 in winter

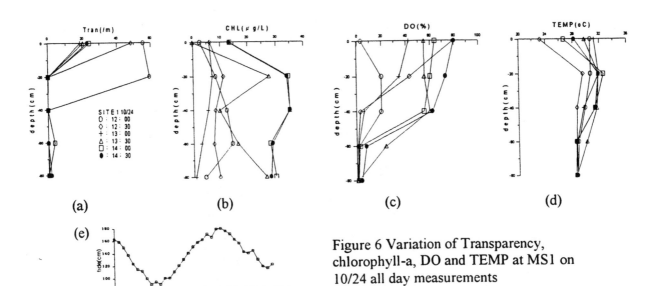

(a)   (b)   (c)   (d)

(e)

Figure 6 Variation of Transparency, chlorophyll-a, DO and TEMP at MS1 on 10/24 all day measurements

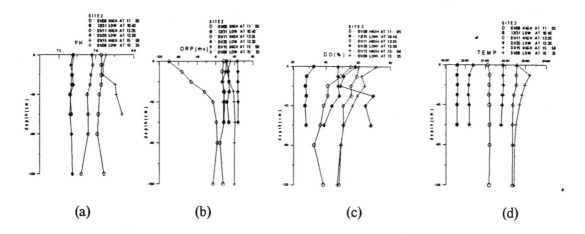

(a)   (b)   (c)   (d)

Figure 7 Profiles of pH、ORP、DO and TEMP at MS2 in winter

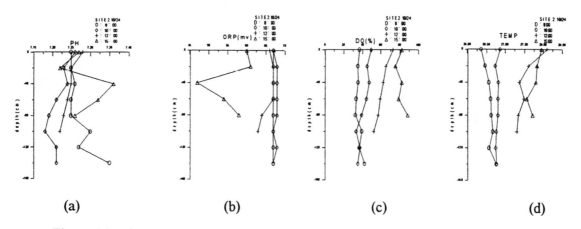

(a)   (b)   (c)   (d)

Figure 8 Profiles of pH、ORP、DO and TEMP at MS2 on 10/24 all day measurements

Observations of Shear-Induced Mixing in a Salt Wedge Estuary

Daniel G. MacDonald[1], and W. Rockwell Geyer[1]

[1]Woods Hole Oceanographic Institution, Woods Hole, MA, USA, 02543
dmacdonald@whoi.edu, rgeyer@whoi.edu

1. Abstract

The Fraser River estuary, British Columbia, exhibits a highly stratified shear flow during the spring/summer freshet, driven by high river flows (on the order of 10^4 cubic meters per second) and large tidal oscillations (typically 2.5 to 4 meters). This paper describes observations from a July 1999 field study, focusing on the entrainment processes across the pycnocline. Measurements were collected primarily from two ship mounted acoustic doppler current profilers (ADCPs), and a towed conductivity, temperature, and depth probe (CTD). The evolution of the internal Froude number across the salt wedge front was calculated from layer-averaged quantities, and indicated a peak in the value of the Froude number in the immediate vicinity of the front. Turbulent kinetic energy (TKE) dissipation rates were estimated by an integral salt balance method as well as a layer-averaged momentum balance approach. Results generally show good agreement between the salt-flux and momentum balance estimates, and indicate that dissipation rates across the interface during the late ebb are on the order of 10^{-3} m^2s^{-3}.

2. Introduction

Turbulence within a highly stratified system can result in an exchange of momentum and mass across what could otherwise be considered two separate and distinct layers of fluid. The importance of this exchange on the kinematics and dynamics of the flow has been recognized for decades, yet the nature of this relationship has yet to be adequately characterized in natural estuarine environments. Such information could enable increased effectiveness in modeling coastal river plumes, which are strongly affected by conditions at the river mouth. At the mouth the depth of the freshwater layer decreases rapidly, and interfacial mixing is intense.

Following the inviscid theory of Armi and Farmer (1986), river discharge through a highly stratified (salt-wedge) estuary could be characterized as two-layer flow through a contraction. An internal Froude number, G, can be defined as:

$$G^2 = F_1^2 + F_2^2, \qquad F_j^2 = \frac{u_j^2}{g'h_j}, \tag{1}$$

where the subscripts 1 and 2 refer to the upper and lower layers, respectively, F_j represents an individual layer Froude number, h_j is the layer thickness, and $g' = g(\rho_2 - \rho_1)\rho_o^{-1}$ is the reduced gravity. According to Armi and Farmer (1986), a critical value of G, equal to 1, would be expected at the point of impingement of the fresh river discharge upon the salt water mass, with continuously increasing supercritical values in the seaward direction. Garvine (1981) used similar assumptions in modeling coastal river plumes. Conversely, several early field studies (Wright and Coleman, 1971; Kashiwamura and Yoshida, 1978) have found, based on fairly limited data, that the Froude number reaches a maximum value slightly exceeding 1, and then decreases in the seaward direction, indicating that dissipation is significant.

The objective of the current research was to investigate the dynamics and kinematics of flow across this crucial transition, referred to as the "lift-off" zone, by developing estimates of Froude number and

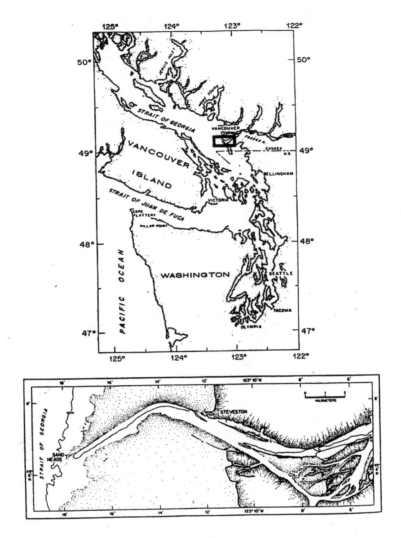

Figure 1: Location and plan of the Fraser River Estuary.

turbulent kinetic energy (TKE) dissipation. Data was collected in the Fraser River Estuary on July 25, 1999 from shipboard instrumentation. Measurements of velocity structure were obtained with two Acoustic Doppler Current Profilers (ADCPs), with frequencies of 300 and 1200 Khz, and salinity data was obtained with a towed conductivity, temperature, and depth (CTD) probe.

3. The Fraser River Estuary

The Fraser River flows into the Strait of Georgia in the southwestern corner of British Columbia, approximately 20 km south of the City of Vancouver (Figure 1). With a total length of 1,368 km, the Fraser River is the longest river in British Columbia, and together with the Columbia and Peace Rivers, drains the lion's share of the western slopes of the Canadian Rockies and the majority of the Coast Range mountains. The watershed of the Fraser encompasses 234,000 km^2, making the Fraser the dominant source of freshwater to the inland sea created by the Strait of Georgia, the Strait of Juan de Fuca, and Puget Sound. The freshet in the Fraser typically occurs in late May or early June as snow pack at the higher elevations of the inland mountains begins to melt. Average freshwater discharge during the freshet is in the vicinity of 8,000 cubic meters per second.

Bathymetry within the estuary is relatively uniform due to maintenance of the channel for navigation. The main stem of the channel, which is dredged regularly and confined by jetties, varies from 600 to

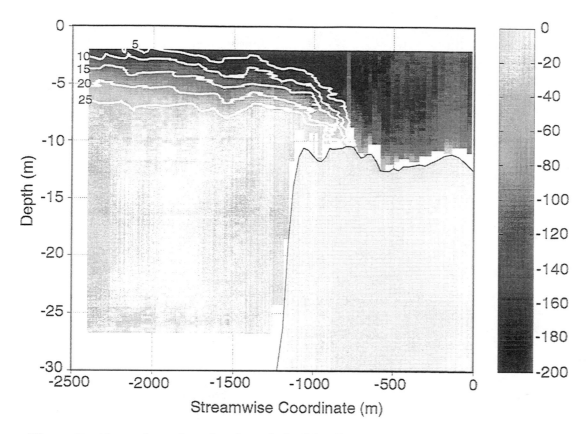

Figure 2: Along-channel section through the lift-off zone (Pass B, July 25, 1999). Shading represents streamwise velocity in cm/s (landward positive). Salinity is represented by the contours in increments of 5 psu.

1,000 m in breadth, with a fairly uniform depth of approximately 10 to 15 m. Depths increase rapidly to over 50 m outside the river mouth. Local tides are characterized by large amplitudes, typically ranging from 2.5 to 4.0 meters, with a pronounced diurnal component. The interaction of these tides with the Fraser discharge, particularly during freshet conditions, results in a highly energetic estuarine environment and intense stratification. The resulting salt wedge typically intrudes some 10 to 20 km landward on each tidal cycle. The data discussed below focuses on the lift-off zone established at the end of the ebb tide, as the salt wedge is forced back to the river mouth, and the position of the salt wedge can be considered steady for several hours during the late ebb.

4. Data Analysis

Data from 6 along-river "passes" through the lift-off zone on July 25, 1999 (passes A through F) were used to directly calculate Froude numbers, and to generate estimates of TKE dissipation through both salt balance and momentum balance approaches. A representative cross section through the lift-off zone (Pass B) is shown in Figure 2, with along stream velocities represented in grayscale, and salinities indicated by contours (5 psu). During the first three passes (A through C), the position of the front is relatively stable, located between 600 and 800 meters seaward of the river mouth. The salt wedge is observed to begin its landward progression during the last three passes, with the front located at 100 meters seaward, 100 meters landward, and 1000 meters landward, respectively. The passes are separated by approximately 40 minutes.

Froude numbers were calculated from (1) using layer-averaged velocities and densities, based on a layer interface defined to be coincident with the 21 psu isohaline. The composite Froude number profiles for the six passes are shown in Figure 3, split into two frames for clarity. It should be noted that hydraulic

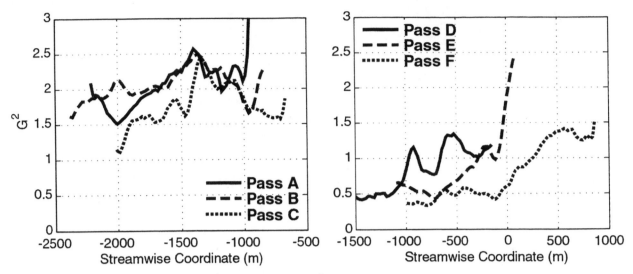

Figure 3: Internal Froude number, plotted as G^2, as a function of along channel coordinate. The internal Froude number represents the sum of the individual layer Froude numbers. In most cases, the upper layer is the active layer, with the exception of landward portions of passes E and F.

theory is based on the presence of two distinct fluid layers. Given that the salinity transition actually occurs across a finite depth, the numerical value of the Froude number is dependent on the method used to define an idealized layer interface ($S=21$ psu in this case), although the general trends are consistent regardless of the interface definition. The profiles in Figure 3 for the early passes indicate a general increase in the value of G^2 towards a maximum supercritical value of approximately 2.5, located roughly 500 meters beyond the front, with values decreasing seaward of the maximum. Later passes find the maximum value located immediately behind the front, with a similar decrease in the seaward direction, towards a minimum value of approximately 0.5. The observed decrease in Froude number is inconsistent with the inviscid theory of Armi and Farmer (1986), and Garvine (1982), and is indicative of momentum exchange (i.e., turbulent mixing) and dissipation between the two layers. The mixing can be quantified further by deriving estimates of TKE dissipation from the data set.

Salt mass was used as a means to estimate TKE dissipation, ε, as:

$$\varepsilon = \left(\frac{g\beta}{\gamma_{mix}} \right) \overline{S'w'}, \tag{2}$$

where $\beta = \Delta\rho(\rho_o\Delta S)^{-1} = 0.77\times10^{-3}\ psu^{-1}$, γ_{mix} is a mixing efficiency, or flux Richardson number (assumed equal to 0.2), and $\overline{S'w'}$ is the vertical Reynolds salt transport. A control volume approach was used to estimate $\overline{S'w'}$, based on an integration of the salt transport equation expressed with respect to salinity:

$$\overline{S'w'} = \int_{0}^{S} \left(\frac{\partial h_s}{\partial t} + \frac{\partial q_i}{\partial x} \right) dS, \tag{3}$$

where q_i is the along isopycnal volume flux (corrected for lateral spreading of the plume), and h_s represents the vertical dimension associated with a given isopycnal. For this analysis, each control volume was taken to have a horizontal dimension, Δx, of 500 m. The dissipation estimates derived from the salt-flux analysis are shown in Figure 4, as ×'s, connected by dashed lines. Values represent the maximum dissipation observed across the pycnocline at a given location.

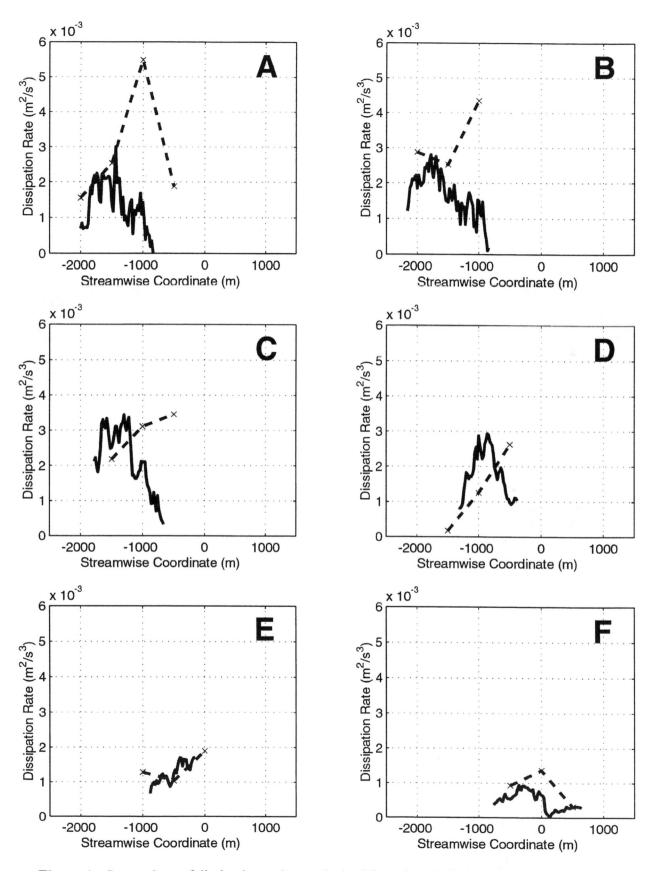

Figure 4: Comparison of dissipation estimates derived from the salt-flux analysis (dashed line, with ×'s), and momentum balance approach (solid line).

An alternative method of estimating dissipation was through the use of a momentum balance approach. Combining the layer averaged momentum equations to remove the barotropic forcing term yields:

$$\frac{\partial u_1}{\partial t} - \frac{\partial u_2}{\partial t} + u_1 \frac{\partial u_1}{\partial x} - u_2 \frac{\partial u_2}{\partial x} = g' \frac{\partial h_i}{\partial x} + \frac{\tau_b}{\rho h_2} + \frac{\tau_i}{\rho} \frac{\left(h_1 + h_2\right)}{h_1 h_2}. \tag{4}$$

where τ_b is a bottom stress, which can be parameterized as $\tau_b = \rho C_D \left| u_2 \right| u_2$, with $C_D = 3 \times 10^{-3}$, and τ_i is the interfacial stress, which can be related to TKE dissipation as:

$$\varepsilon \approx \frac{\tau_i}{\rho} \frac{\partial u}{\partial z}. \tag{5}$$

Dissipation estimates generated by the momentum approach are compared to the salt flux results in Figure 4, for the six passes of July 25. The two methods are in good agreement, particularly across the seaward portion of the lift-off zone, with dissipation rates on the order of 10^{-3} m^{2}s^{-3}. These dissipation rates are 3 to 7 orders of magnitude higher than similarly derived estimates for the oceanic thermocline at mid-latitudes, which range from 10^{-10} to 10^{-6} m^{2}s^{-3} (Gregg, 1989), and 1 to 4 orders of magnitude larger than those found within an energetic tidal channel (Grant et al., 1962). This is, perhaps, not surprising, given the large influx of momentum associated with the river discharge. It is, however, in sharp contrast with existing inviscid theories. Notable discrepancies between the two methods in the immediate vicinity of the front are likely attributable to a breakdown of the formulation of the interfacial stress term when the lower layer depth becomes small and lower layer velocities are negligible. If this is the case, it is likely that the salt-flux derived estimates are more representative of the turbulent conditions.

5. Conclusions

Preliminary analysis of data from the lift-off zone in the Fraser River Estuary indicate a peak in internal Froude number near the front, and evidence of strong TKE dissipation (on the order of 10^{-3} m^{2}s^{-3}) across the zone. These results imply that the inviscid model of Armi and Farmer (1986), and the similar model used by Garvine (1981), are not valid for modeling the near field dynamics of coastal river plumes. The effects of shear-induced, stratified turbulence and interfacial mixing must be taken into account in the vicinity of the lift-off zone over scales greater than a few hundred meters. The existing data set adequately characterizes the streamwise dynamics of the lift-off zone, but it remains unclear what role secondary flows and the three-dimensional structure of the lift-off play. Further studies are planned to focus on the three-dimensional aspects of the lift-off zone.

6. References

Armi, L., and D.M. Farmer, 1986: Maximal two-layer exchange through a contraction with barotropic net flow. *J. Fluid Mechanics*, vol. 164, 27-51.

Garvine, R.W., 1982: A steady state model for buoyant surface plume hydrodynamics in coastal waters. *Tellus*, vol. 34, 293-306.

Grant, H.L., R.W. Stewart, and A. Moilliet, 1962: Turbulence spectra from a tidal channel. *J. Fluid Mechanics*, vol. 12, 241-268.

Gregg, M.C., 1989: Scaling turbulent dissipation in the thermocline. *J. Geophysical Research*, vol. 94 (C7), 9686-9698.

Kashiwamura, M., and S Yoshida, 1978: Outflow Dynamics at a River Mouth. *Proceedings of the 16th Coastal Engineering Conference, A.S.C.E.*, 2925-2944.

Wright, L.D. and J.M. Coleman, 1971: Effluent expansion and interfacial mixing in the presence of a salt wedge, Mississippi River delta. *J. Geophysical Research*, vol. 36, 8649-8661.

Fortnightly modulation of the estuarine circulation in Juan de Fuca Strait

Diane Masson and Patrick F. Cummins

Institute of Ocean Sciences, 9860 W. Saanich Rd, Sidney B.C., Canada V8L 4B2
Email: massond@dfo-mpo.gc.ca Tel: (250) 363-6521 Fax: (250) 363-6746

Riverine discharge into the Strait of Georgia sets up a well defined estuarine circulation within Juan de Fuca Strait, the main path for the freshwater outflow to the continental shelf. At the landward end of Juan de Fuca Strait, the water flows through narrow channels in which strong tidal currents are known to induce significant mixing of the water column, and a spring-neap modulation of the estuarine exchange. A three-dimensional prognostic numerical model has been developed to study the circulation around Vancouver Island, British Columbia. In a series of simulations, the estuarine circulation within Juan de Fuca Strait is established by the Fraser River freshwater discharge. A fortnightly modulation is imposed on the mixing over the various sills to simulate the spring-neap tidal mixing regime. The resulting variation in the estuarine circulation is found to be largely limited to the eastern section of Juan de Fuca Strait, in the vicinity of the sills. Data from current meter moorings and surface salinity data from lighthouse stations compare favorably with the model results.

The effect of local wind forcing on the estuarine exchange is also examined. The model is capable of simulating those rare events during which a concurrence of river freshet, neap tide and northwest wind allows a stronger pulse of fresh surface water to escape relatively unmixed into the eastern end of Juan de Fuca Strait. The disturbance then propagates along the northern shore of the strait as a first mode internal Kelvin wave. Finally, the effect of the fortnightly modulation on the export of fresh water onto the continental shelf is examined. It is found that small amplitude coastal trapped waves are generated near the mouth of Juan de Fuca. However, this fortnightly signal is weak in comparison to the energetic wind-induced variations typically found over the shelf.

Influence of sea-land breeze on change of current and water quality in a stratified semi-enclosed sea

Masayuki Nagao[1], Xiao-Hua Zhu[1], Eisuke Hashimoto[1], Miyuki Yoshida[2] and Yoshio Takasugi[1]

[1]Marine Dynamics Section, Marine Environmental Science and Technology Division,
Chugoku National Industrial Research Institute, Kure, Hiroshima, 737-0197 Japan
[2]Graduate School of Biosphere Sciences, Hiroshima University
nagao@cniri.go.jp, xhzhu@cniri.go.jp, hashimot@cniri.go.jp, yoshida@cniri.go.jp, takasugi@cniri.go.jp

Abstract

To find the best monitoring system for remediation and enhancement of a polluted marine environment, a floating environmental monitoring laboratory has been placed in Kaita Bay, in the Seto Inland Sea of Japan. The monitoring includes meteorological observation, current profiling and water quality measurement. The results indicate that the sea-land breeze, which is a common phenomenon around the coast of the Seto Inland Sea, greatly affects the marine environment of Kaita Bay. Specifically, the time variation of chlorophyll-a at 4 m depth has an apparent diurnal oscillation that has good correlation with the movement of thermal stratification, which might be driven by the sea-land breeze.

1. Introduction

The Seto Inland Sea of Japan is one of the most famous inland seas in the world. But about 200 km^2 of coastal sea has been reclaimed and the percentage of natural shoreline has fallen 38% because of industrial development during the period from the 1960s to 1970s, a period of high economic growth in Japan (Water Quality Bureau of Environment Agency of Japan, 1997). Because of this loss of tideland and underwater forest, the Seto Inland Sea now does not have enough water capacity for purification. Furthermore, huge amounts of nutrient salts whose sources are catchment areas or excess fish/oyster farming cause red tide, lack of dissolved oxygen at the bottom and deposition of sludge to the inner part of the Seto Inland Sea. Now, research and development on remediation and enhancement of this polluted marine environment is becoming our urgent task (Ueshima, 1998).

From 1998 to 2001, Chugoku National Industrial Research Institute (CNIRI) is conducting a research and development project on environment mitigation and renovation for the polluted semi-enclosed sea in order to develop physical process control and bioremediation techniques (Hashimoto et al., 1999). Before applying these, we should understand meteorology, oceanographic phenomena, water quality and inflow from the river as much as possible. Therefore, CNIRI has deployed a special floating laboratory (MARINLABO) that has been moored in Kaita Bay since February 1999.

First this paper will describe the operation of MARINLABO and give an overview of the environment of Kaita Bay deduced from observational data. Next, after showing how the sea-land breeze greatly affects the current and variation of stratification and water quality in Kaita Bay, we will discuss the correlation between the time variation of chlorophyll-a at the middle depth point and the sea-land breeze.

2. Overview of Kaita Bay and MARINLABO

(1) Overview of Kaita Bay

Figure 1 shows the location of Hiroshima Bay and Kaita Bay. The length of Kaita Bay is 3.5 km and the width is 0.8 km. Its surface area is 2.5 km^2, mean water level 8 m and total volume 2.2×10^6 m^3. Because it is completely surrounded with an artificial concrete complex, there isn't any natural shoreline or tideland around it. And because this bay is located in the innermost part of Hiroshima Bay, it is nearly closed and the water exchange rate is very low. As a result, the bottom of the sea is so heavily damaged with organic matter that no life exists in summer except *polychaetes* which is resistance to eutrophication (Mishima et al., 1999).

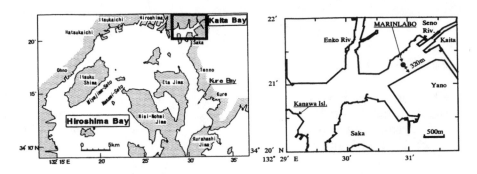

Fig.1 : Location of Hiroshima Bay and Kaita Bay

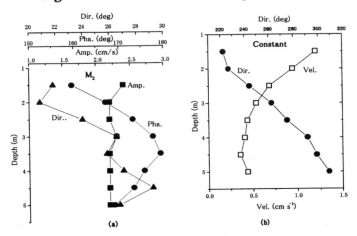

Fig.2 : (a)M2 tidal component and (b)tidal residual current.

Kaita Bay is also markedly affected by inflow from rivers. This bay has two large inflows; one is the Enko River that flows into the bay mouth from the north. The other is the Seno River that flows into the inner part of Kaita Bay. Nagao(2000) estimated that the typical total flow rate for both the Enko and Seno rivers is 2.7 m³/s indicating that the water exchange time is almost 100 days, in other words, 3.5 times in a year.

Also, a sea-land breeze strongly influences the environment of Kaita Bay. Because the coastal region around the Seto Inland Sea is surrounded by mountains, the sea-land breeze is well developed in this region and a lot of scientific work already has been published on the sea-land breeze around the Seto Inland Sea (Miyata, 1982). For example, Yuasa (1994) reported that the vertical profile of horizontal velocity at the river mouth in the Seto Inland Sea varied between daytime and night, and showed that the cause of this was the sea-land breeze. And he also suggested that the movement of nutrient salts in this river mouth reversed between daytime and night in summer. His result is based on observation of drifting buoys.

(2) Overview of MARINLABO

MARINLABO was deployed in Kaita Bay February 10, 1999. We started observation of current and water quality February 12, 1999 (Hashimoto et al., 1999).

It is important to take into account the tidal current, because the tidal range of the Seto Inland Sea exceeds 3 m at spring tide. Therefore, using ADCP we conducted harmonic analysis of tidal current collected over one month starting March 26, 1999. **Figures 2a** and **2b** show the vertical distribution of the amplitude of the M2 component and tidal residual current, respectively. According to **Fig. 2a,** the vertical profile of amplitude of the M2 component from 1.5 m to 5 m depth ranges from 2.0 to 2.5 cm/s. Thus, in Kaita Bay, in terms of the M2 component, the magnitude of tidal current is almost uniform and very small. On the other hand, the direction of the M2 component ranges from 20 to 30° corresponding to the longitudinal direction of this bay. More precisely, from the surface to the bottom, the direction turns slightly to the east. The maximum difference in phase of the M2 component is 20° and in the middle layer (3.5 m depth) the time lag reaches maximum.

On the other hand, according to **Fig. 2b**, the magnitude of residual tidal current reaches its maximum value of 1.25 cm/s at 1.5 m depth, and decreases going from the surface to the bottom. Its direction is 220° at the surface and increases 90° clockwise at the bottom. This clearly shows that the surface water is flowing out from the inner part of the bay to the outer part corresponding to the outflow from the Seno River.

3. Variation of stratification caused by sea-land breeze

Here, we present typical variations of the current, stratification and chlorophyll-a from 1 to 24 August, 1999. **Figure 3** shows the data from the weather station. **Figure 4** shows the flow rate of the Seno River and **Fig. 5** shows the horizontal velocities near the water surface collected by an electromagnetic current

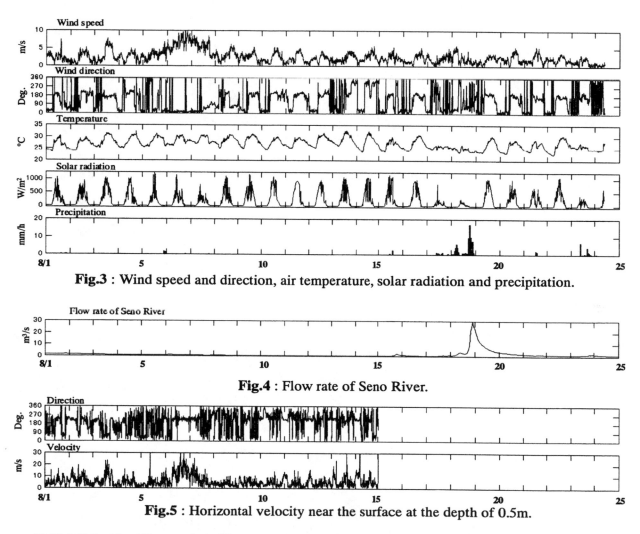

Fig.3 : Wind speed and direction, air temperature, solar radiation and precipitation.

Fig.4 : Flow rate of Seno River.

Fig.5 : Horizontal velocity near the surface at the depth of 0.5m.

meter(ACM-8M, Alec Electronics). **Figure 6** shows the isothermal time variation of water temperature at several depths taken at MARINLABO. **Figures 7a** and **7b** show the salinity at depths of 0.5 m and 3 m, respectively. **Figures 8a** and **8b** show the chlorophyll-a at depths of 1 m and 4 m, respectively. **Figure 9** shows the variation of water depth measured from 1 m above the bottom. This variation corresponds with the variation in tidal level.

From 5 to 8 August 1999, there was little rain. But, the northerly wind continued. The maximum wind speed reached 10 m/s. In this period, the thermal stratification, as shown in **Fig. 6**, tended to be uniform. Because the thermal stratification quickly returned to the previous situation, vertical mixing by the northerly wind didn't cause this vertical uniformity. We that this phenomenon was caused by following mechanism: [1] At first, a northerly wind pushed the surface water to the mouth of the bay. [2] Simultaneously, the water below the middle layer came up to the surface to replace the water moved by the wind [1]. As a result of [1] and [2], the thermal stratification trended toward uniform over this short time.

From 17 to 18 August, there was a hard rainfall with a total amount of 81 mm measured in Hiroshima. Because of this, the maximum discharge of the Seno River was 30 m³/s at midnight on 18 August. But, this discharge was not sufficiently large to destroyed the density stratification, because the salinity at a depth of 3 m didn't vary, but the salinity did vary at a depth of 0.5 m. Additionally, thermal stratification didn't seem to be uniform.

Now let's look from **Fig. 3** to **Fig. 8** to study the daily pattern. At first glance the wind speed and direction for a typical day consists of a southerly wind of 5 m/s speed starting in the afternoon. By comparison, the northerly wind, from late night into morning, is a light breeze. Thus, the horizontal velocity at the surface seems to be affected not only by tidal current, which mainly consists of M2, S2, K1

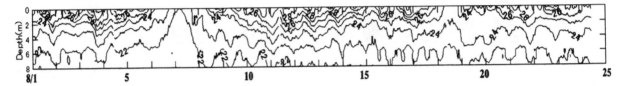

Fig.6 : Time variation of water temperature shown by isotherm

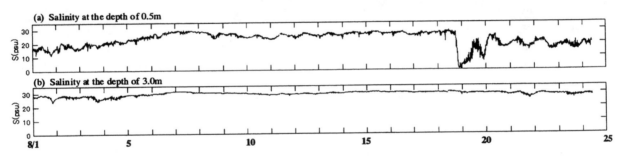

Fig.7 : Time variation of salinity at the depth of (**a**)0.5m and (**b**)3.0m.

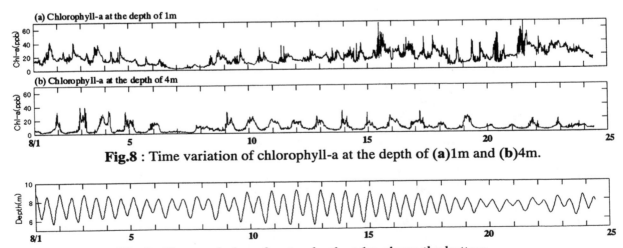

Fig.8 : Time variation of chlorophyll-a at the depth of (**a**)1m and (**b**)4m.

Fig.9 : Time variation of water depth at 1m above the bottom.

906

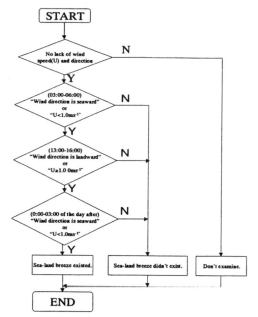

Month	Frequency of the sea-land breeze(day)	Frequency of the peak of chlorophyll-a(day)	Frequency of the sea-land breeze at the day before when the peak existed(day)
Feb. (13th–28th)	10	16	9
Mar.	13	6	4
Apr.	16	3	1
May.	22	17	12
Jun.	16	10	7
Jul.	17	10	7
Aug.(1st–23th)	16	20	15
Total	110	82	55

Fig.10 : Criterion to judge the sea-land breeze, originally suggested by Miyata(1982).

Table 1: Frequency of the sea-land breeze and the peaks of chlorophyll-a at the depth of 4m.

and O1 components in the Seto Inland Sea, but also by this wind variation.

The pattern of variation in chlorophyll-a as shown in **Fig. 8** is different between the surface layer and the middle. The chlorophyll-a in the surface layer (depth of 1 m) is decreased during an environmental disturbance such as a strong wind or flood. But except in these cases, it seems to oscillate with a diurnal cycle. On the other hand, the chlorophyll-a in the middle layer (depth of 4 m) peaks at midnight, and has a minimum value in the daytime. Note that the semi-diurnal component, which can be seen in **Fig. 9**, can't be found in **Fig. 8b**. Therefore, this oscillation in the middle layer may not be caused by tidal motion.

Why does the chlorophyll-a in the middle layer make a diurnal oscillation? If the reason is the diurnal vertical motion of phytoplankton, the chlorophyll-a in the middle layer must decline quickly at sunrise because the phytoplankton swim to the surface, while increasing rapidly at sunset because the phytoplankton sink down to the bottom. But, comparing solar radiation, shown in **Fig. 3**, with chlorophyll-a, shown in **Fig. 8b**, there is no correlation between solar radiation and chlorophyll-a.

One possible reason is that phytoplankton move up or down by means of local fluid motion, such as the displacement of isothermal and internal wave motion, in order to move to the appropriate depth for their growth. The evidence for this possible explanation is that the isothermal lines for 23°C or 24°C that cross 4 m depth decrease sharply at midnight. The cause of this may be as follows. The sea breeze in the daytime pushes the fresh water of the Seno River to the inner part of the bay. This sea breeze also brings the water in the surface layer to the bay mouth near MARINLABO. Simultaneously, the surface water is inclined by the wind and the thickness of the surface layer is increased. Even though the sea breeze stops and the land breeze begins blowing, the thickness of the surface layer remains. Then, chlorophyll-a at a depth of 4 m appears to peak at midnight. On the other hand, when the land breeze starts blowing, the fresh water pushed to the inner part of the bay flows out to the mouth of the bay. As a result, the thickness of the surface layer becomes thinner and the salinity in the surface layer rapidly diminishes. Additionally, the cold water, whose concentration of chlorophyll-a is low, appears in the middle layer.

Because we have not done a physical analysis over a continuous stratification for the case of a sea-land breeze, the above discussion is only our estimate of the situation. For the next step, we plan to confirm our estimate of the situation by means of a 3D numerical model.

4. Correlation between sea-land breeze and oscillation of chlorophyll-a

We have shown the relation between the sea-land breeze and the surface velocity, displacement of stratification and oscillation of chlorophyll-a. In order to confirm this relation and start quantifying it, we should next focus on the data for the times when the sea-land breeze actually exists. But, with the wind speed and direction as shown in **Fig. 3**, it is difficult to know the basic mechanism of the sea-land breeze and describe a pattern (Miyata, 1982). Thus, we need some criteria to judge whether a particular wind is the sea-land breeze or not. Here, we adopt the criterion proposed by Miyata (1982) that only takes into account the pattern of the wind.

Figure 10 shows the criterion. We have made a modification of his criterion as follows. Miyata proposed a threshold wind velocity for the land breeze of 0.5 m/s. Because MARINLABO is moored in the sea and it is on the longitudinal course of the Seno River, and even at night, the wind speed frequently exceeds 0.5 m/s, we raised the threshold value from 0.5 m/s to 1.0 m/s.

By means of the criterion described in **Fig. 10**, we classified the wind data from 13 February to 23 August of 1999 as to whether a sea-land breeze existed or not. As a result, in the entire 192 days there were 110 days in which the both sea and land breeze existed. Both the sea and land breeze occurred on 57% of the 192 days. Additionally, the frequency by month is shown in **Table 1**.

Next, we need to decide whether the peak of chlorophyll-a, which might be caused by the sea-land breeze, was observed or not. Because the average chlorophyll-a is different depending on the season, we adopted the following two criteria for recording the observation of a peak in chlorophyll-a: [1] the peak of chlorophyll-a occurs at midnight and [2] the peak is large. As a result, in the entire 192 days there were 82 days in which the peak of chlorophyll-a occurred at a depth of 4 m. The percentage of peak chlorophyll-a occurrence was 43%.

Finally, we assumed that the peak of chlorophyll-a at a day (the Jth day) was caused by what happened on the previous day (the [J-1]th day). As a result, in the 81 days in which the peak of chlorophyll-a occurred there were 51 days in which the sea-land breeze occurred on the previous day. The correlation of previous day sea-land breeze and chlorophyll-a peak was 68%. In **Table 1**, this result is also shown by month. In addition, we conducted a goodness-of-fit test of symmetry on a 2x2 table with a level of significance of 5%. As a result, there was a definite correlation between the sea-land breeze and the peak of chlorophyll-a.

5. Conclusion

As the result of long-term environmental monitoring, we obtained the following result.
[1] The smallest value of M2 component was 2 cm/s.
[2] The storm and the flood observed in August of 1999 turned the stratification for only a short time. Those environmental disturbances didn't have sufficient power to mix or exchange all of the water in Kaita Bay.
[3] The sea-land breeze strongly affected the marine environment of Kaita Bay.

References

Hashimoto, E., Zhu, X.H., Nagao, M., Takasugi, Y. and Ueshima,H.(1999), New try for marine environmental — long period measurement by MARINLABO in Kaita Bay, Rep. of CNIRI, **53**, 15-21.

Mishima, H., Hoshika, A., Tanimoto, T. and Ueshima, H.(1999), R & D of environment mitigation and renovation in Kaita Bay. Part III., Proc. of autumn meeting in 1999 of Oceanogr. Soc. of Japan, 108.

Miyata, K.(Ed.)(1982): Sea-land breeze in the Seto Inland Sea, Keisui-sha.

Nagao, M., Zhu, X.H., Hashimoto, E., Yoshida, M. and Takasugi, Y.(2000), Response of chlorophyll-a to sea-land breeze in a semienclosed sea, Annual J. of Hydr. Eng., JSCE, **44**, 1173-1178.

Oota River Work Office(1999), Overview of Oota River and Kose River in fiscal 1999.

Ueshima, H.(1998), Mitigation, in *Marine Coastal Environment*, Fuji Technosystem, 933-943.

Ueshima, H., Takasugi, Y., Zhu, X.H., Hashimoto, E., Hoshika, A., Mishima, H., Tanimoto, T. and Nagao, M.(1999), R & D of environment mitigation and renovation in Kaita Bay. Part I., Proc. of autumn meeting in 1999 of Oceanogr. Soc. of Japan, 106.

Water Quality Bureau of Environment Agency of Japan(1997), Environmental conservation of the Seto Inland Sea in fiscal 1996, Assoc. for Environmental Conservation of the Seto Inland Sea, 161.

Zhu, X.H., Hashimoto, E., Nagao, M. and Takasugi, Y.(1999), R & D of Environment Mitigation and Renovation in Kaita Bay. Part II., Proc. of autumn meeting in 1999 of Oceanogr. Soc. of Japan, 107.

Tidal Fronts in the Tay Estuary, Scotland

Neill, S.P.[1], Copeland, G.J.M.[1] and Folkard, A.M.[2]

[1]Department of Civil Engineering, University of Strathclyde, Glasgow, UK G4 0NG
[2]Department of Geography, University of Lancaster, Lancaster, UK LA1 4YB
simon.neill@strath.ac.uk, g.m.copeland@strath.ac.uk, a.folkard@lancaster.ac.uk

Abstract

Frontal systems, caused by lateral variations in stratification and bathymetry, are a consistent feature of the Tay Estuary, Scotland. ADCP and temperature/salinity measurements have been made through a front which occurs on the flood tide, in an attempt to resolve the velocity/density shears in the front. Typical surface density changes across the front are $1.0 - 1.5$ kg m^{-3}. Using initial conditions from the in-situ density measurements, a two-dimensional buoyancy-driven numerical model (TEXSM – Tay Estuary cross-sectional model) has demonstrated that the observed velocity shears are probably not driven by density changes. The front studied is located in an area of high bathymetric gradient between sandbanks and the main channel. Outputs from a 2D depth-averaged numerical model of the estuary have indicated that the surface elevation varies considerably across the sandbanks due to cross-channel phase differences in the flood tide. Using TEXSM, this variation in pressure gradient has been modelled to produce a barotropic flow across the sandbanks and into the main channel, reproducing velocities more characteristic of those observed in the ADCP data.

1 Introduction

Estuarine fronts are widely reported in the literature (see, for example, reviews by Simpson and James, 1986, Bowman, 1988, and O'Donnell, 1993). Due to the secondary circulations invariably associated with estuarine fronts, they can be an important dispersion mechanism for pollutants. Two-dimensional depth-averaged numerical models of estuaries do not generally take the existence of fronts into consideration. Therefore, the results of hydrodynamic and water quality models in regions where fronts are known to exist must be used with caution.

Ferrier and Anderson (1997a,b) have noted the existence of various types of buoyancy-driven tidal fronts in the Tay Estuary including tidal intrusion fronts (Largier, 1992), axial convergent fronts (Nunes and Simpson, 1985) and longitudinal (or shear) fronts (Huzzey and Brubaker, 1988). They also proposed that some of the fronts in the estuary are not buoyancy-driven, but due to flow over and around topographic features such as sandbanks (flow separation fronts).

In this paper, the study zone is introduced in Chapter 2. In-situ data of velocity and density are presented in Chapter 3, and modelling studies made in Chapter 4. After some discussion of the results, a few simple conclusions are drawn for the front observed in the Tay Estuary.

2 The Tay Estuary

The Tay Estuary is located on the east coast of Scotland, flowing 50 km from Perth (the limit of tidal motion) to the North Sea (Figure 1). The fresh waters of the rivers Tay and Earn provide the highest freshwater inflow into an estuary in the UK, regularly exceeding 1000 m^3 s^{-1} (Buck, 1993, Owens and Balls, 1997). At low water, extensive mudflats are exposed on the uppermost parts of the Tay Estuary. The Tay Estuary is constrained to a width of 1.1 km between mudflats at the entrance at Buddon Ness, and again at Tayport Narrows to a width of 1.4 km. The maximum width is 3 km between the entrance and Tayport Narrows, and the width is generally around 2 km. At Dundee, the tidal range varies between 2.4 m (neap) and 4.7 m (spring). The deepest part of the estuary is 30 m in the main channel at Tayport

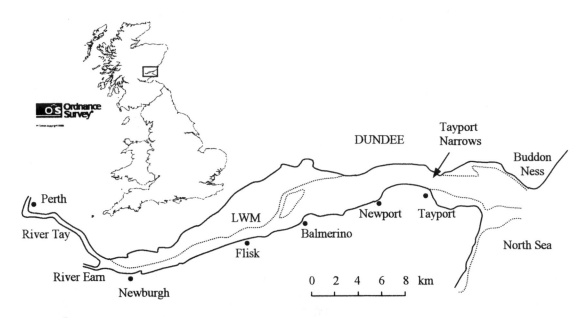

Figure 1 The Tay Estuary

Narrows but depth is generally between 5 and 10 m, where mudflats are not present. The Tay has been classified as a partially mixed estuary (Williams and West, 1975), where the rivers discharge into a sea with moderate tidal range.

The Tay Estuary has been studied fairly extensively in the literature. Early studies focussed on salinity distribution from fieldwork (Williams and West, 1975), a physical model of the estuary (Charlton, 1980) and one-dimensional numerical tidal models (Williams and Nassehi, 1980). Two-dimensional hydrodynamic models have been developed by Gunn and Yenigun (1987) and more recently by Nassehi and Kafai (1999), who have included moving boundaries over the mudflats. Of most interest to this research, however, are the reports of fronts on the Tay Estuary (Ferrier and Anderson, 1997a,b). They have combined aerial remote sensing with in-situ fieldwork to catalogue the various types of front occurring in the estuary, producing temporal maps (with respect to tidal time) of the positions of some of the main fronts.

3 Field Measurements

Data for five in-situ fieldwork days have been collected for the Tay Estuary between 1998 and 1999. Velocities were recorded in three-dimensions using a 300 kHz Workhorse ADCP with bin depths of 25 cm and a ping rate of 5 seconds, mounted at the surface from an anchored boat. Temperature and salinity measurements were recorded using a hand-lowered temperature/conductivity probe. There were two major problems with the fieldwork. Firstly, the ADCP could not measure velocities in the top 2.5 m due to the ADCP shadow zone. Secondly, drag on the temperature/conductivity probe cable was very high, hence depth was measured along a curve and this data had to be post-processed to correct for depth. Despite these problems, some useful data of the fronts has been collected. The main location studied was near the entrance to Tayport harbour, 200 m from the southern shore of Tayport Narrows, as this is a location known for frequent and repeatable frontal activity (Figure 2).

During each of the fieldwork days at Tayport Narrows, the front shown in Figure 2 was observed during the flood tide, consistently in the same location. The front had a very strong foam line of width 1 – 2 m, indicating a surface convergence, and was accompanied by a surface water roughness change across the front. On the shoal side, the surface was generally rougher and on the channel side, the surface was

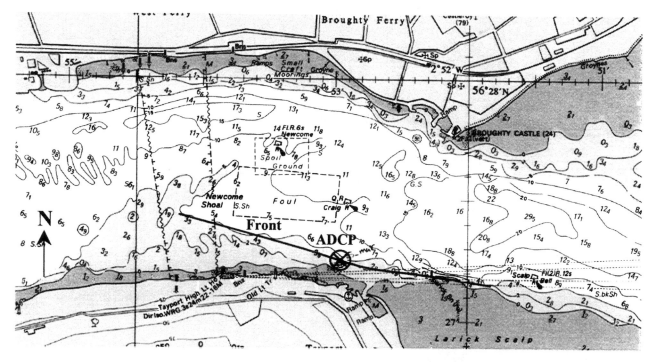

Figure 2 Position of front and ADCP location, Tayport Narrows

generally smoother. The density changes have been confirmed by salinity/temperature data taken either side of the front and are given in Figure 3. Shears are also visible in the lateral (cross-channel) and vertical ADCP data taken vertically through the front (Figure 4). The data presented are only examples of the frontal velocity profiles. Many other profiles were observed in the data but all had the same characteristic shear, with the changes in velocity direction being consistent (i.e. south/upwards above the front, north/downwards below the front). For the data presented, the combined discharge of the rivers Tay and Earn was 239 $m^3 s^{-1}$, considerably lower than the long-term average January flow of 348 $m^3 s^{-1}$ (Anderson *et al*, 1997), and the tidal range was 4.5 m (spring).

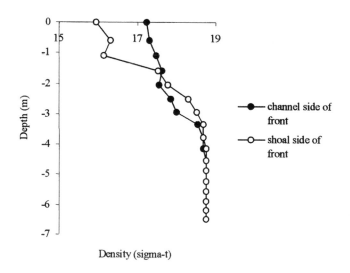

Figure 3 Density profiles either side of front

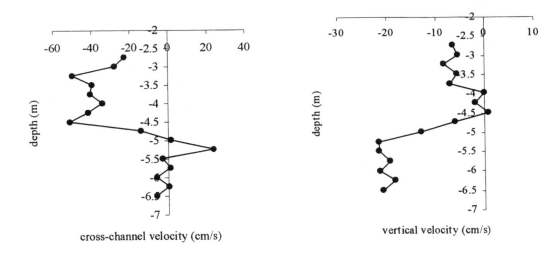

Figure 4 ADCP Velocity profiles through front

4 Numerical Modelling

A two-dimensional buoyancy-driven *k*-epsilon model has been developed to simulate the fronts in a cross-section of the Tay Estuary, based on the SOLA algorithm (Hirt *et al*, 1975, Griebel *et al*, 1998). The model has been calibrated and validated using the lock exchange experiment (Barr and Hassan, 1963) and lid driven cavity flow (Ghia *et al*, 1982). Initial conditions for the model are prescribed by the in-situ density measurements taken on either side of a front (Figure 3), in an attempt to reproduce the velocities observed in the ADCP data. A typical output of the buoyancy generated flow field is given in Figure 5. Maximum velocities produced by the buoyancy-driven model were in the order of 10 cm s^{-1}, considerably less than those observed by the ADCP data, which were more in the order of 50 cm s^{-1} for the cross-channel velocities. The model was unable to produce the surface convergence clearly present due to the intense foam line, and hence the fronts are assumed not to be buoyancy-driven.

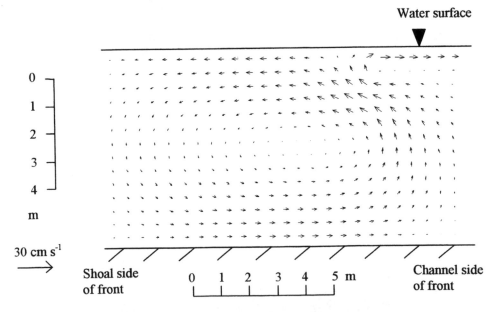

Figure 5 Buoyancy-driven circulation

A different approach was used to examine the fronts by firstly using a calibrated two-dimensional depth-averaged model of the estuary based on the work by Couch and Copeland (1999). During the flood tide, it was discovered that the water surface elevation varied from the main channel to the sandbanks by approximately 15 cm over a horizontal distance of 400 m. This change in water surface elevation, and the associated pressure change, was used as the surface pressure boundary condition for the cross-sectional model, with water density now taken as constant. The resulting barotropic flow modelled leaves the sandbanks and enters the main channel at a velocity in the region of $40 - 50$ cm s^{-1}. Although the flow structure has not yet resembled the ADCP data, the strength of velocities are similar to those observed.

5 Discussion and Conclusions

Estuarine fronts are generally considered to be created and driven by buoyancy forces. This may be true of the majority of cases in the Tay Estuary, but for the front studied the mechanism is likely to be non-buoyancy driven, since the observed velocities were much higher than would be expected by density gradients alone. Although density differences are observed across the front, it appears that the density gradient is not driving the secondary circulation; rather the secondary circulation is creating the density gradient in the first place. In this case, although the processes are not yet fully understood, it appears that the front is created by cross-channel phase differences in the flooding tide between the sandbanks and the main channel, seaward of the restriction at Tayport Narrows. A pressure gradient is set up across the sandbanks, which then creates a barotropic flow into the main channel. It is likely that the lower salinity water observed on the shoal side of the front is due to this laterally advected water meeting the flow in the main channel.

The secondary flows observed in the ADCP data have not yet been reproduced since the bathymetry is thought to be more complex than that presented on the admiralty charts for the area. Shiono and Knight (1991) have studied a physical model for an analogous case of flow along a straight open channel with flood plains which has reproduced the key transverse velocity features observed in the Tay Estuary, particularly the shears. A profile based on their results has been sketched in Figure 6 which demonstrates how a barotropic flow jet from the sandbanks to the main channel can entrain fluid from below to produce a two celled circulation system. By taking a vertical profile of the cross-channel velocity through the circulation system, it can be seen how the cross-channel ADCP profile of Figure 4 may occur (remembering that the ADCP data begins at 2.5 m depth).

The conclusion of this study on the Tay Estuary is that when estuarine fronts are being studied, it is important to consider the non-buoyancy forces that may be present. The bathymetry and topography may often be the dominant factors in determining secondary flows and generating estuarine fronts.

6 References

Anderson, C., Anderson, J. & Proctor, W. 1997. Freshwater inputs an pollutant loads to the Tay Estuary. In *Coastal Zone Topics 3: The Estuaries of Central Scotland.* Joint Nature Conservation Committee.

Barr, D.I.H. & Hassan, A.M.H. 1963. Density exchange and flow in rectangular channels. II. Some observations of the structure of lock exchange flow. *Houille Blanche,* 7/1963, 757-766.

Bowman, M.J. 1988. Estuarine fronts. In *Hydrodynamics of Estuaries, Vol. I, Estuarine Physics* (Kjerfre, B., ed.).

Buck, A.L. 1993. *An Inventory of UK Estuaries: Volume 4. North and East Scotland.* Peterborough, Joint Nature Conservation Committee.

Charlton, J.A. 1980. The tidal circulation and flushing capacity of the outer Tay Estuary. *Proc. Royal Soc. Edinburgh* **78**, 33-46.

Couch, S.J. & Copeland, G.J.M. 1999. Generation of eddies, scour holes and shoals by tidal flow past a headland. Conf. Tidal Action, Tidal Processes and Tidal Effects on Coastal Evolution, Intl Geographical Union, Salvador, Bahia, Brazil, 5-6 Oct. 1999.

Ferrier, G. & Anderson, J.M. 1997a. A multi-disciplinary study of frontal systems in the Tay Estuary, Scotland. *Estuarine, Coastal and Shelf Science* **45**, 317-336.

Ferrier, G. & Anderson, J.M. 1997b. The application of airborne remotely sensed data in the study of frontal systems in the Tay Estuary. *Int. J. Remote Sensing* **18**, 2035-2065.

Ghia, U., Ghia, K.N. & Shin, C.T. 1982. High-Re solutions for incompressible flow using the Navier-Stokes equations and a multigrid method. *Journal of Computational Physics* **48**, 387-411.

Griebel, M., Dornseifer, T. & Neunhoeffer, T. 1998. *Numerical Simulations in Fluid Dynamics: A Practical Intoduction.* SIAM, Philadelphia.

Gunn, D.J. & Yenigun, O. 1987. A model for tidal motion and level in the Tay Estuary. *Proc. Royal Soc. Edinburgh* **92**, 257-273.

Hirt, C., Nichols, B. & Romero, N. 1975. *SOLA – a Numerical Solution Algorithm for Transient Fluid Flows.* Technical Report LA-5852, Los Alamos, NM: Los Alamos National Lab.

Huzzey, L.M. and Brubaker, J.M. 1988. The formation of longitudinal fronts in a coastal plain estuary. *Journal of Geophysical Research* (C2) **93**, 1329-1334.

Largier, J.L. 1992. Tidal intrusion fronts. *Estuaries* **15**, 26-39.

Nassehi, V. & Kafai, A. 1999. A moving boundary computer model for hydrodynamics and salt transport in the Tay Estuary. *Advances in Environmental Research* **3** (3), 293-308.

Nunes, R.A. & Simpson, J.H. 1985. Axial convergence in a well-mixed estuary. *Estuarine, Coastal and Shelf Science* **20**, 637-649.

O'Donnell, J. 1993. Surface fronts in estuaries: a review. *Estuaries* **16**, 12-39.

Owens, R.E. & Balls, P.W. 1997. Dissolved trace metals in the Tay Estuary. *Estuarine, Coastal and Shelf Science* **44**, 421-434.

Shiono, K. & Knight, D.W. 1991. Turbulent open-channel flows with variable depth across the channel. *Journal of Fluid Mechanics* **222**, 617-646.

Simpson, J.H. & James, I.D. 1986. Coastal and estuarine fronts. In *'Baroclinic Processes on Continental Shelves'* (Mooers, N.K., ed.). pp. 63-93. American Geophysical Union, Washington.

Williams, D.J.A. & Nassehi, V. 1980. Mathematical tidal model of the Tay Estuary. *Proc. Royal Soc. Edinburgh* (B) **78**, 171-182.

Williams, D.J.A. & West, J.R. 1975. Salinity distribution in the Tay Estuary. *Proc. Royal Soc. Edinburgh* (B) **75**, 29-39.

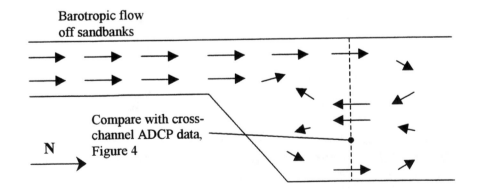

Figure 6 Theoretical flow across bathymetry gradient

The Effect of Wind on Interfacial Mixing in a Highly Stratified River

Shuzo Nishida[1], Shizuo Yoshida[2] and Keiji Nakatsuji[1]

[1]Civil Engineering, Osaka University, 2-1 Yamadaoka, Suita, Osaka 565-0871, Japan
[2]Physics of Fluid, Hokkaido University, N13-W8 Kitaku, Sapporo 060-0813, Japan

Abstract

Field observations were conducted at a highly stratified river with a salt wedge to clarify mixing processes and the effect of wind on the mixing. The measurements were carried out at the tidal portion of the Ishikari River flowing into Japan Sea. An ADCP was settled on the riverbed to measure velocity profiles and recorded the profiles of 0.25m depth step for about three weeks in summer. The interface level was evaluated by the echo intensity of the ADCP data; so that the mean shear between the two layers was obtained. To evaluate the salt diffusion, time series data of salinity in upper layer were collected at five points from the mouth to 20km upstream.

It is shown that the amount of the salinity increase in the upper layer depends on the wind speed, and that the chief factor influencing mixing is the disturbance due to the waves induced by wind. Furthermore an entrainment coefficient was formulated as a function of overall Richardson number and non-dimensional wind speed, and the measurement results show a similar tendency to the derived formula.

1. Introduction

The Ishikari River we have investigated has the second largest basin in Japan, and forms a highly stratified two-layer flow in the vicinity of the river mouth because it flows into the Japan Sea where the tidal range is very small, about 0.1 to 0.3m. In dry season the salt wedge intrudes to 20km or more from the river mouth, and often causes environmental issues such as salt damage of agricultural water.

Research on the processes of stratification and mixing in river mouths or estuaries has a long history, and significant findings are presented by Dyer(1973), Officer(1976) and many other researchers. However, there are few field works on highly stratified rivers like the Ishikari River.

In general an amount of the salinity diffusion of two-layer flow can be estimated by an entrainment

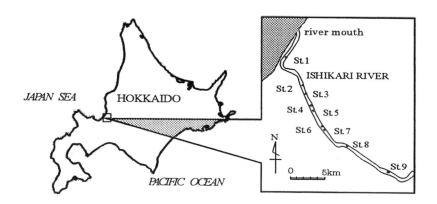

Fig. 1 Ishikari River and observation points

915

coefficient related to the Richardson number (*e.g.*, Tamai 1987, Grubert 1990). In actual rivers, however, the mixing and salt diffusion are depend on discharge rate, sea level change, surface and interfacial waves and wind induced shear, and it is found that the dominant factor in the Ishikari River is wind velocity (Yoshida *et al.* 1998). In this research, the effect of the wind on the salinity diffusion is analyzed by field measurement data, and entrainment coefficient is formulated considering the wind velocity.

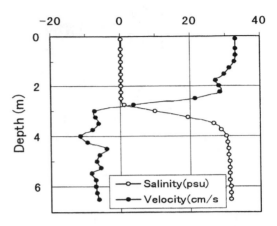

Fig.2 Velocity and salinity profile

2. Methods of observations

Figure 1 shows a map of the Ishikari River and measurement points. Measured variables and locations are as follows.
1) Salinity and temperature at surface layer : St.1(4.4km from the mouth), St.3(9.0km), St.5(11.7km), St.6(14.0km), St.7(14.5km) and St.8(20.0km).
2) Salinity and temperature profile : St.2 (7.8km from the mouth) and St.4(10.8km).
3) Velocity profile using ADCP: St.7(14.5km from the mouth).
4) Interface level using sonar : St.1(4.4km from the mouth) , St.7(14.5km) and St.9(26.6km).

The ADCP(1200kHz) was settled horizontally on the riverbed by diver, and recorded the velocity profiles of 0.25m depth step. Each variable was measured at every 5 or 30min and recorded for about three weeks in summer of 1997 and 1998.

3. Observation results

An example of the salinity and velocity profile measured at 14.5km from the mouth is shown in Fig.2. It is found that there exist the interface at 3m depth, and that the strongly stratified two-layer is formed; so

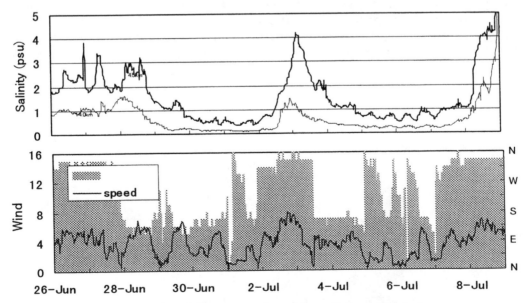

Fig.3 Time series of surface salinity and wind

that the velocity has changed remarkably in the vicinity of the interface.

Figure 3 shows time series of the salinity of surface layer(1.0m depth) at each point, and changes of wind speed and direction divided into 16. The wind blew almost parallel to the river course of the straight section (from St.2 to St.9). It is found that the salinity increases as the wind speed increases, and in particular there is a good correlation when the wind speed exceeds 3m/s. Moreover, the salinity is higher downstream than upstream due to the consecutive entrainment of salt water.

Figure 4 shows a longitudinal change of the surface salinity on July 31 in 1997 when the tip of salt wedge reached to about 20km. The salinity increases linearly toward the river mouth as well as the analytical results for the steady state obtained by Yoshida *et al.* (1995).

Figure 5 shows the measurement results using a multi salinity sensor settled at 10.8km from the river mouth. The sensor was set and measured at each depth of 1.0, 2.0, 2.5, 3.0, 3.5, and 4.0m from the surface by using floating buoy. In the figure the measurement results of four sensors set up in the upper are illustrated. As the wind speed increases, transition layer of salinity above the interface disappears gradually and the salinity in the upper layer is homogenized; so that the surface increases. On the other hand, when the wind speed is weak, the salinity does not diffuse to the surface layer and the transition layer is formed again.

From the above-mentioned results, the salinity diffusion mechanism is considered as follows. First, salt water diffuses in the

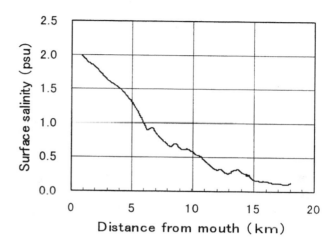

Fig.4 Longitudinal change of surface salinity

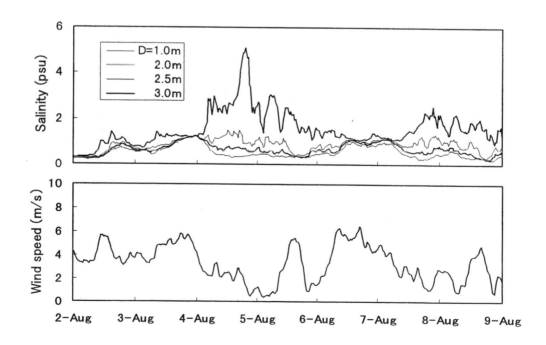

Fig. 5 Time series of salinity at each depth and wind speed

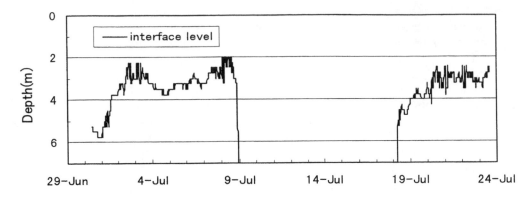

Fig.6   Change of interface level at 14.5km from mouth

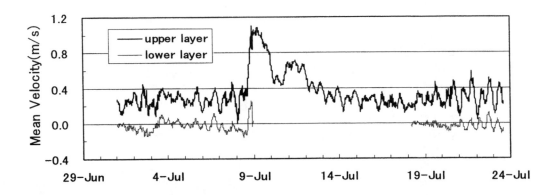

Fig.7   Change of mean velocity in each layer at 14.5km from mouth

vicinity of interface caused by turbulence and breaking of interfacial waves, and the transition layer is formed above the interface.   The salinity saved in this transition layer diffuses uniformly in the upper layer by disturbance generated by wind, and raises the surface salinity.   A direct entrainment of salt water through the interface occurs when the strong wind keeps blowing, and the salinity of surface layer increases further.

Figure 6 shows the long-term change of interface level at 14.5km from the mouth where the riverbed level is depth of about 8m.   The interface level was evaluated by the profile of echo intensities measured by ADCP settled on riverbed, and done the adjustment confirmation with the result measured by a sonar settled to be near the ADCP.   The reason why the interface disappears for the period from July 9 to July 18 is that the salt wedge retreats with rainfall.   Although a small range of interface fluctuation cannot be caught because the vertical resolution of the ADCP is 0.25m, the process of a rapid descent of the interface level caused by flood and gradually re-intrusion of salt wedge is expressed well in the figure.

Figure 7 shows the mean velocities of the upper and the lower layer evaluated from the velocity profile and the interface level measured by the ADCP.   It is found that the velocity of the upper layer changes rapidly and exceeds 1m/s on July 9.   Moreover, the periodic change of the velocity of each layer corresponding to tide is found, and the velocity of the upper layer changes greatly 0.1 to 0.4m/s.

Although such large velocity fluctuation occurs, salinity fluctuation corresponded to the tidal cycle is extremely small.   This means that entrainment and diffusion increasing the surface salinity does not occur only by the tidal current.   Calculated values of the overall Richardson number were not so small as to cause the shear instability though the values changed greatly by ten times or more.

4. Entrainment coefficient

In the following, the amount of a salinity increase in the 2.8km long between St.5 and St.7 is calculated to estimate the entrainment coefficient. A travelling time in the section calculated by mean velocity in the upper layer was used to evaluate the amount of the salinity increase, and also other hydraulic quantities were averaged by the time.

The relation between the entrainment coefficient E and the overall Richardson number Ri is shown in Fig.8, where the upper layer thickness h_1 and the upper layer velocity U_1 are used as length scale and velocity scale, respectively. The entrainment coefficient has been considered as a function of the Richardson number and to be proportional to the -3/2 power of Ri for the salt-fresh water system, i.e. $E = CRi^{-3/2}$. However, present results show that the entrainment coefficient hardly depends on the Richardson number and increases as the wind speed increases, though the lower envelope tends to nearly the -3/2 power of Ri. This suggests two different entrainment mechanisms existing.

The entrainment phenomena are classified into two type mechanisms (Price et al. 1978), i.e. turbulent erosion type (diffusion type) and dynamic instability type (shear type). It is considered that the two kinds of entrainments exist together also on the salt wedge.

Figure 9 shows the dependence of the entrainment parameter C of -3/2 power law on the wind. W/U_1 in the figure represents the dimensionless wind speed. The wind direction during the observation period was almost along the river course as mentioned above. It is found that the parameter C which has been considered to be a constant value (2×10^{-3} for salt wedge) increases as the wind speed increases, and that obviously there is a correlation between them.

Considering that the salinity diffusion is due to shear at the interface and disturbance supplied from the surface, we derive a relational formula of the entrainment coefficient in the coexistence field. Using h_1 as length scale and the following u as velocity scale (e.g., Atkinson et al. 1990), It is assumed that the entrainment phenomenon follows the -3/2 power low of the Richardson number non-dimensionized by h_1 and u.

$$u = (U^3 + \beta \cdot u_*^3)^{1/3} \qquad (1)$$

, where U is a overall velocity such as a mean velocity in upper layer and u_* is a turbulent velocity scale such as a turbulent intensity.

Because the turbulent intensity in the surface layer is considered to be almost in a linear relation with wind speed W except for the case of weak wind from

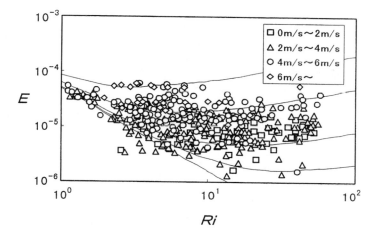

Fig.8 Relation between Ri and entrainment coefficient

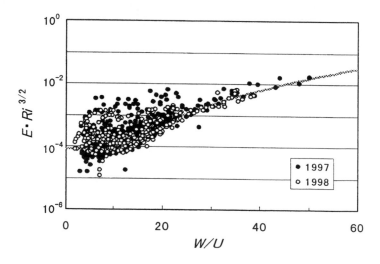

Fig.9 Dependence of entrainment parameter on wind speed

past observation results(Nishida *et al.* 1996), if we replace u_* with W and change the formula, the following relation is obtained.

$$E = \alpha \left[1 + \beta \left(W / U \right)^3 \right]^{4/3} Ri^{-3/2} \qquad (2)$$

where E is the overall Richardson number using h_1 and U, which has been used as a factor of the diffusion on salt wedges.

The solid line in Fig.9 represents the relation (2), and the solid lines in Fig.8 show the relations for the cases of different wind speed. The measurement results show a similar tendency to the formula (2), though there is scatter at low wind speed. The following are considered as a cause of scattering. 1) Surface waves are so hardly generated at a low wind speed less than about 3m/s that the linear relationship between the wind speed W and the turbulent velocity scale u_* does not consist, and 2) the transition layer in the vicinity of the interface grows upward during low wind speeds.

5. Conclusions

The major results and conclusions are summarized as follows.
1) Although the salinity transition layer above the interface grows upward when the wind is weak or rests, the vertical salinity gradient decreases to uniform salinity as wind speed increases and exceeds about 3m/s.
2) The amount of the salinity increase in upper layer between longitudinal two points has good correlation with the wind speed.
3) The chief factor influencing mixing across the density interface in the river channel is the disturbance due to the waves induced by wind, except at the outlet of the river where the shear instability is dominant.
4) The entrainment coefficient on the salt wedge is proportional to the -3/2 power of overall Richardson number only in the region of low Richardson number, and in the region of high Richardson number the entrainment coefficient is depend on non-dimensional wind speed.
5) The entrainment coefficient was formulated as a function of Richardson number and the non-dimensional wind speed, and the measurement results show a similar tendency to the formula.

References

1) Atkinson, J. F., and S .B. Wolcott : Interfacial mixing driven by mean shear and oscillating grid, Journal of Hydraulic Engineering, Vol.116, pp.397-413, 1990.
2) Dyer, K.R. : *Estuaries*, A Physical Introduction, John Wiley & Sons, 1973.
3) Grubert, J. P. : Interfacial mixing in estuaries and fjords, Journal of Hydraulic Engineering, Vol.116, pp.176-195, 1990.
4) Nishida, N. : Field measurements for salinity diffusion in the mouth of Ishikari River, Annual Journal of Hydrailic Engineering, JSCE, Vol.40, pp.487-492, 1996 (in Japanese).
5) Officer, C.B. : *Physical Oceanography of Estuaries*, John Wiley & Sons, 1976.
6) Price, J.F., C.N.K.Mooers and J.C.V.Leer : Observation and simulation of storm-induced mixing-layer deepening, Journal of Physical Oceanography, Vol.8, pp.582-599, 1978.
7) Tamai, N. : Unification of entrainment concept and formulae of the entrainment coefficient, Proceedings of JSCE, No.381, pp.1-11, 1987 (in Japanese).
8) Yoshida, S., M.Ohtani and S.Nishida : Unsteady factors affecting salt diffusion in the stratified flow system at a river mouth, Report of Research Project of a Grant in Aid Scientific Research (B), The Ministry of Science and Culture, Japan, Under Grant No.04452231, 1995.
9) Yoshida, S., M.Ohtani, S.Nishida and P.F.Linden : Mixing Processes in a Highly Stratified River, *PHYSICAL PROCESSES IN LAKES AND OCEANS, COASTAL AND ESTUARINE STUDIES*, Vol.54, the American Geophysical Union, 389-400, 1998.

The Physics of River Plumes:
Physical understanding or numerical artifacts?

Julie Pietrzak

Fluid Mechanics Section, Faculty of Civil Engineering and Geosciences, Stevinweg 1,
Delft University of Technology, 2628 CN, Delft
J.Pietrzak@ct.tudelft.nl

1. Abstract

Rivers, discharging their typically fresher water into saltier coastal waters are an important source of momentum and buoyancy for coastal seas. Understanding the dynamics of river plumes and the factors influencing their spreading is an important objective of coastal ocean research. It is also of direct relevance to studies of sediment and pollutant transport. However, the physics associated with river plume formation and evolution involves a complex interaction between geostrophic adjustment, friction and mixing, topographic effects and ambient forcing. How then can we study these processes? The answer to this question increasingly relies on numerical modelling. In fact, numerical models provide one of the few research tools with which to study these non-linear physical processes. Therefore in this study results are presented from an idealised numerical modelling study of river plume formation and evolution. However, it is still unclear how suitable the current generation of three dimensional primitive equation models are for research into the physics of density fronts and plumes. Unfortunately the non-linear dynamics of river plumes and the large gradients of temperature and salinity found in these regions present a number of challenging modelling issues. Attention is therefore paid to one important aspect of coastal ocean modelling, that of accurate advection. Advection is an important geophysical process and plays a major role in the physics of river plumes. Therefore this study investigates the effect of using different numerical schemes for the advection of scalars in ocean modelling. Since the success of the river plume classification schemes is highly dependent upon the quality of the numerical model results particular attention is paid to the influence of the chosen advection schemes on the resulting model solutions. Comparisons are made between simulations using the upstream and second order central difference schemes with more sophisticated higher order schemes employing total variation diminishing flux limiters. River plume classification schemes are then addressed and the results from a number of numerical experiments are described.

2. Introduction

River plumes, resulting from the discharge of river water into coastal seas form important transport routes. Understanding the dynamics of river plumes is an important task, however river plumes are inherently non-linear. This was realized in many of the early studies, see for example, Csanady, (1984), Kao (1981), Ikeda (1984) and Wang (1984). These studies generally involved two-dimensional numerical studies of density driven flows, concentrating on the density adjustment immediately after release. McClimans (1986) identified three major processes characterizing the seaward expansion of the river flow. These are acceleration, related to a hydraulic control at the river mouth resulting from a balance of inertia and gravity (buoyancy) forces, mixing processes governed by turbulence due to bottom and interfacial friction and geostrophic processes. As the low salinity water moves offshore the resulting cross shore pressure gradient is balanced by the Coriolis force and sets up an alongshore current in geostrophic balance. Therefore river plumes tends to deflect anticyclonically in the Northern Hemisphere, forming baroclinic boundary currents which keep the coast on their right hand side. The dominant force balance of coastal buoyancy plumes appears to be cross-shore geostrophy, for example, the Rhine Plume, the Delaware coastal current and many others. However, basin wide regions of freshwater influence also exist where in contrast the river water spreads out and fills the receiving basin. Plumes that detach themselves from the coast also exist, examples are the Mississippi and the Columbia River.

More recent studies have utilized three-dimensional numerical models in an attempt to increase our knowledge about the physical processes controlling the formation, evolution and subsequent destruction of river plumes. Consequently numerical models have become invaluable tools with which to study the physics of coastal plumes. Indeed, numerical modeling provides one of the few research tools with which to study the diverse range of plume behavior and their associated nonlinear physical processes. Unfortunately, it is unclear how suitable are the current generation of three-dimensional primitive equation models for research into the physics of density fronts and plumes. Here, attention is paid to one aspect of numerical modeling, that of advection.

Advection is an important geophysical process and plays a major role in the physics of river plumes. Recent studies, Hecht *et al.* (1995), James (1995), Pietrzak (1998) highlight the importance of the numerical solution technique for the advection of scalars such as temperature and salinity in ocean models. The latter two studies have paid attention to the coastal environment. This study investigates the effect of using different numerical schemes for the advection of salinity in coastal river plume modeling. In this paper, comparisons are made between simulations using the upstream and second order central difference schemes with more sophisticated higher order forward in time advection schemes. These schemes include the multi-dimensional positive definite advection transport algorithm, MPDATA, (Smolarkiewicz, 1984, 1986,1990,1991) and a total variation diminishing (TVD) flux limited version of the constant grid flux scheme, P2_PDM, Pietrzak (1998). See Hirsch (1990) for a description of TVD methods and Tremback *et. al.* (1987) for a discussion of the constant grid flux schemes. The PDM limiter described in Zalesak (1987) is similar to the Ultimate limiter described by Leonard (1991). Through a number of idealized river plume tests it is demonstrated that significantly different results can be obtained with a numerical model by simply changing the advection routines. Reasons for the differences are explored.

3. Methods

An objective of this study is to understand which type of plume will develop in response to a specified buoyant inflow. Tides and mean flows are neglected. The waters are initially assumed to be at rest and there is no wind forcing. The details of the plume within the estuary are only considered in so far as the magnitude of the freshwater discharge and the ambient stratification are concerned. Instead the plume is driven by a buoyant discharge through a gap in the coast of width L into a coastal sea with a constant depth H of 20 m. The buoyant inflow has constant discharge and density at the river mouth. The numerical model used for the three-dimensional simulations is a hybrid version of the Princeton Ocean Model, (Blumberg and Mellor, 1985) which has been modified to allow for the use of forward in time schemes for tracer advection while retaining central differences for momentum. Specific details of the hybrid model can be found in Pietrzak (1995, 1998). The forward in time schemes discussed in this paper, include the CGF schemes and the MPDATA scheme for the advection of temperature and salinity.

The f-plane approximation is adopted and a latitude of $\phi=45°$ is used, ($f=2\Omega\sin\phi$, where $\Omega=7.292\times10^{-5}$). The vertical eddy diffusivities for momentum and heat and salt are calculated from a second order turbulence closure scheme. Time stepping is implicit in the vertical. The horizontal viscosity and diffusivity is parameterised using the Smagorinsky formulation. The full equation of state is used, temperature was held constant. The external time step is 30 s and the internal time step is 300 s. A constant grid spacing of 2 km is employed. The domain is 56 grid points wide in the offshore direction, 86 grid points in the along-shore direction and has 11 evenly spaced sigma levels in the vertical. The normal and tangential velocities are zero at the side-walls. At the bed the salt flux is zero while momentum is balanced by quadratic bottom stress computed using u_b nearest the bed. C_D was set to a constant value of 2.5×10^{-3}. A freshwater source was implemented in the continuity equation. The river discharge is thus modeled as a volume of zero salinity water in the form of a coastal mound. It is introduced into a one grid cell wide estuary into a coastal sea with a salinity of 35 PSU. The river discharge is 2000 m³s⁻¹.

4. Results and Plume classification

A number of experiments have been performed to assess the sensitivity on the plume response to the type of advection scheme selected. Fig. 1 shows the simulated surface salinity for a number of advection schemes for the river plume test cases. The Kelvin number, the ratio of width to internal wave speed is about 1. Results were also obtained with the MPDATA scheme, which are not shown here. A sensitivity test was carried out and inflow conditions were also tested. (A detailed description of these results will be made available in a separate paper.) The distances are kilometers along and across shore. The results presented here suggest that there is a strong sensitivity to the scheme used. The geostrophic type plume under study here, exhibits excessive damping with the upstream scheme and (for the grid resolution used here) leads to a front that diffuses and propagates more slowly. In contrast the central leap-frog scheme leads to increased baroclinicity, resulting in a front that propagates along the coast much more quickly. The high order schemes appear to offer a result that is a compromise between the two schemes. A well defined geostrophoic front is seen that maintains it structure along the coast. At the mouth of the estuary a well defined bulge is seen with a sharp alongshore front.

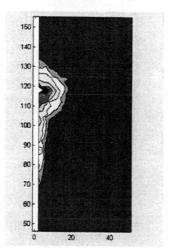 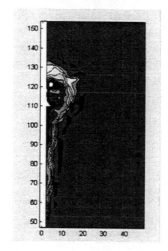 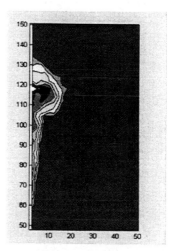

Fig. 1 Surface salinity contours after 2.5 days, using from left to right, the first order upstream, the second order leap-frog and the TVD limited CGF schemes. 1 PSU contour intervals are shown with the offshore contour corresponding to 35 PSU.

The upstream scheme is excessively damping and decreases the propagation speed of the front. Consider the case of simple one dimensional advection, $\dfrac{\partial \psi}{\partial t} = -\dfrac{\partial}{\partial x}(u\psi)$, where ψ (x, t) is a non-diffusive quantity, u is the velocity field assumed constant in the following, t is time and x is the horizontal coordinate. Using the upstream method, the flux form on a staggered grid is given by,

$\psi_j^{n+1} = \psi_j^n - \dfrac{\Delta t}{\Delta x}\left[F_{j+\frac{1}{2}}^n - F_{j-\frac{1}{2}}^n\right]$ where ψ_j^n is the value of ψ at grid point j after n time steps and

$F_{j+\frac{1}{2}}^n = F(\psi_j^n, \psi_{j+1}^n, u_{j+\frac{1}{2}}^n)$, $F_{j-\frac{1}{2}}^n = F(\psi_{j-1}^n, \psi_j^n, u_{j-\frac{1}{2}}^n)$ are the ψ fluxes through the right and left boundary of the grid box respectively. For simplicity constant grid spacing Δx and time increment Δt is assumed. The ψ flux through the right boundary is given by $F''_{j+\frac{1}{2}} = \frac{1}{2}\left[\left(u + |u|\right)\psi''_j + \left(u - |u|\right)\psi''_{j+1}\right]$.

The rate of implicit diffusion can be determined for the case of uniform velocity by expanding $\psi_j^{n+1}, \psi''_{j+1}, \psi''_{j-1}$ in a second order Taylor series about the point $\psi(x_j, t'')$. Substituting into the above, the following equation is approximated with second order accuracy

$$\frac{\partial\psi}{\partial t} + \frac{\partial}{\partial x}(u\psi) = \frac{\partial}{\partial x}\left(K_{impl}\frac{\partial\psi}{\partial x}\right)$$ **Eq. 1**

where $K_{impl} = 0.5\left(|u|\Delta x - \Delta t u^2\right)$ is the implicit numerical diffusion. The numerical diffusion can be very large for typical ocean modelling problems. For example, an ocean model with a grid spacing of 2 km, internal time step of 600 s, and velocities of the order $0.2 ms^{-1}$, implies a numerical diffusion coefficient of about $K_{impl} = 200^2 m^2 s^{-1}$, which can dominate the environmental diffusion. Thus the upstream scheme not only advects ψ but it slowly distorts its shape. In contrast the central leap-frog scheme exhibits not only stronger vertical and horizontal plume density gradients it also unrealistically accentuates these gradients, highlighting the problem of numerical dispersion. The numerical dispersion leads to significant under and over shooting errors. A common modeling practice is to increase the numerical diffusion in order to control this problem, however this damps and smears precisely the sharp discontinuities that are of interest in regions dominated by buoyantly driven flows and fronts. The leap frog scheme involves a central, second order discretisation and a separate second order time integration

and can be discretised as $\dfrac{\psi_j^{n+1} - \psi_j^{n-1}}{2\Delta t} = -u\dfrac{\psi''_{j+1} - \psi''_{j-1}}{2\Delta x}$. In order to elucidate the problem of

computational dispersion substituting a single harmonic wave $\psi_j = \mathrm{Re}\left[\psi(t)e^{ik_j\Delta x}\right]$ into the one-

dimensional advection equation, where k is the wavenumber gives $\dfrac{\partial\psi}{\partial t} + iku\psi = 0$. Substituting the

same equation into the leap-frog scheme gives, $\dfrac{\partial\psi}{\partial t} + ik\left[u\dfrac{\sin k\Delta x}{k\Delta x}\right]\psi = 0$, where the phase velocity of

the wave is now given by the term in brackets. It is no longer a constant value equal to u but is now a function of wavenumber k. Therefore, the numerically calculated waves display a dispersive character. In contrast, the higher order schemes reduce the numerical errors identified with the lower order schemes, yielding an improved ability to retain sharp density gradients in the primitive equation experiments. Of these schemes the P2_PDM exhibited an approximately monotone solution with sharper frontal gradients than the MPDATA schemes. The P2_PDM scheme appears to be a good compromise between shape preservation and computational expense for studies of river plume formation and evolution.

The upstream scheme is positive definite and monotonicity preserving. Unfortunately it is the most diffusive of all the advection schemes suffering from significant amplitude truncation errors. The second order leap-frog is not diffusive but suffers from numerical dispersion. It was implemented in a number of widely used ocean and coastal models, because its lack of amplitude error was considered an important property for conservation of energy and potential vorticity. The main disadvantage of this scheme is that it suffers from numerical dispersion, which can corrupt the flow with non-physical oscillations. It is neither positive definite nor monotonicity preserving. The greatest errors occur in areas where the largest gradients of the advected quantity exist. Unfortunately river plumes provide just such environments, here large gradients of temperature and salinity usually exist because the fresher and generally colder river water discharges into the saline and warmer coastal waters.

5. Discussion

The complexity of plume dynamics requires the use of three dimensional primitive equation models. Chao and Boicourt (1986) carried out an idealised numerical study and found that a coastal plume developed in response to a discharge onto the shelf. They concluded that strong (supercritical) plumes had a near field bulge with an anticyclonic turning region and a thin southward flowing coastal jet downstream. Garvine (1987) also found similar results in a reduced gravity model study, pointing out that all supercritical plumes had this shape. Chao (1988) extended his work to include weak and moderate plumes. He used a modified Froude number together with a dissipation parameter to classify the resulting plumes. The Froude number is the ratio of river discharge to internal wave speed and is a function therefore of the density difference between river and sea. The ratio of the width of the bulge to the width of the coastal current λ was used by Chao (1988) to characterise the shape of the plume. If the width of the bulge is less than (greater than) the width of the coastal current the flow is supercritical (subcritical). In addition if $\lambda = 1$ then the plume is diffusive and tends to spread offshore. Kourafalou et al. (1996 extended this classification system to include a plume number. This is a measure of the ratio of the discharge to the shear velocities and acts as an indicator of the amount of mixing. However, very few studies have assessed the influence of the underlying numerical techniques on the resulting solution. Significantly the river plume classification schemes were derived from numerical results. In particular the diffusive classification was based on simulations that varied the horizontal diffusion. It is worth noting that the amount of horizontal diffusion typically controls the under and over shooting of the second order central leap-frog difference scheme. In the above it has been shown that merely altering the choice of advection scheme affects the type of plume response observed in the numerical simulations and that it is important to take this into account when developing future plume classification systems.

In general, broad agreement is found with the supercritical plume classification. However, consider a supercritical coastal buoyancy plume, where the dominant force balance is geostrophic in the cross-shore direction. In this case the along shore velocity field can be approximately described by the thermal wind relation and it can easily be seen that excessive numerical diffusion will decrease the geostrophic velocities attained by the plume and hence alter the plumes properties. Conversely numerical schemes that act to artificially increase the salinity (and hence density) gradient will increase the geostrophic velocities attained by the plume and hence again alter the plumes properties. In either case this will affect the stability of the plume and its likelihood to meander and shed eddies. The plume response is a measure of the relative imbalance between geostrophic adjustment and along shore mixing. Therefore it is important to use high order non-dissipative advection schemes. In some of the previous studies the meandering of the coastal current was thought to be real rather than due to a numerical artifact. This paper suggests that the role of the advection schemes in reaching these conclusions should be further investigated. Specifically future experiments should address how to isolate the physics from the numerical influences, in particular what is the influence of implicit numerical diffusion on the resulting simulations.

6. References

Blumberg, A. and G. Mellor, A Description of a Three-Dimensional Coastal Ocean Circulation Model. In *Three-Dimensional Coastal Ocean Models*. Coastal and Estuarine Sciences, **4**. Ed. N. Heaps, 1997.

Chao, S.Y., River forced estuarine plumes, *J. Phys. Oceanogr.*, **18**, 72-88,1988.

Chao, S.Y., and W.C. Boicourt , Onset of estuarine plumes, *J. Phys. Oceanogr.*, **16**, 2137-2149,1986.

Csanady, G. T. 1984: Circulation induced by river inflow in well mixed water over a sloping continental shelf. *J. Phys. Oceanogr.*, **14**, 1703-1711,1984.

Garvine, R. W., Estuary plumes and fronts in shelf waters: A layer model, *J. Phys. Oceanogr.*, 17, 1877-1896, 1987.

Hecht, M. W., W. R. Holland and P. J. Rasch 1995: Upwind-weighted advection schemes for ocean tracer transport: An evaluation in a passive tracer context. *J. Geophys. Res.* **100**, 20,763-20,778.

Hirsch,C., *Numerical Computation of Internal and External Flows. Vol. 2: Computational Methods for inviscid and viscous flows*. John Wiley and Sons, 691 pp., 1990.

Ikeda, M., Coastal flows driven by a local density flux, *J. Geophys. Res.* **89**, 8008-8016, 1984.

James, I. D., Advection schemes for shelf sea models. *Journal of Marine Systems*, 8, 237-254, 1996.

Kao, T.W., The dynamics of small scale fronts, I, Shelf water structure due to freshwater discharge, *J. Phys. Oceanogr.*, **11**, 1215-1223, 1981.

Kourafalou, V. H., Oey, L.Y. Wang, J. . and T. . Lee, The fate of river discharge on the continental shelf, 1. Modeling the river plume and the inner shelf coastal current. *J. Geophys. Res.*, **101**, 3415-3434, 1996.

Leonard, B. P., The ULTIMATE conservative difference scheme applied to unsteady one-dimensional advection. *Comput. Methods Appl. Mech. Eng.*, **88**, 17-74, 1991.

McClimans. T.A., Estuarine fronts and river plumes, in *Physical Processes in Estuaries*, ed. J. Dronkers and W. van Leussen, pp. 55-69, Springer-Verlag, New York, 1986.

Pietrzak, J. D., A comparison of several advection scheme for ocean modelling. *Scientific Report*. **95_8**, Danish Meteorological Institute. 45 pp, 1995.

Pietrzak, J.D., On the Use of TVD Flux Limiters for Forward in Time Upstream Biased Advection Schemes in Ocean Modelling. *J. Mon. Wea. Rev.* **126**, 812-830,1998.

Smolarkiewicz, P. K. 1984: A fully multidimensional positive definite advection transport algorithm with small implicit diffusion. *J. Comput. Phys.*, **54**, 325-362.

Smolarkiewicz, P. K., and T. L. Clark, 1986: The multidimensional positive definite advection transport algorithm: Further development and applications. *J. Comput. Phys.*, **67**, 396-438.

Smolarkiewicz, P. K., and W. W. Grabowski, 1990: The multidimensional positive definite advection transport algorithm: Non oscillatory option. *J. Comput. Phys.*, **86**, 355-375.

Smolarkiewicz, P. K., 1991: On forward-in-time differencing for fluids. Mon. Wea. Rev. 119, 2505-2510.

Tremback C. J., J. Powell, W. R. Cotton and R. A. Pielke, 1987: The forward in time upstream advection scheme: Extension to higher orders. *Mon. Wea. Rev.*, **115**, 540-555.

Wang, D.P., Mutual Intrusion of a gravity current and density front formation, *J. Phys. Oceanogr.*, **14**, 1191-1199, 1984.

Zalesak, S. T., A preliminary comparison of modern shock capturing schemes: Linear Advection. *Advances in Computational Methods for Partial Differential Equations*. IMACS, **VI**, 15-22, 1987.

Exchange coefficients for stratified flow in open channel.

K.Shiono, R.N.Siqueira and T. Feng

Department of Civil and Building Engineering, Loughborough University, LE11 3TU, UK,
Tel: 01509-222936, Fax: 01509-223981, Email:K.Shiono@lboro.ac.uk.

1. Abstract

Turbulence measurements were carried out in a narrow rectangular channel to investigate exchange coefficients for stratified flow. Turbulent data at the centre of the channel were only used for the analysis. The distributions of mean velocity with various degrees of stratification over the water depth show the effects of stratification on flow. The exchange coefficient, Cμ, commonly used in the k-e model, eddy viscosity, eddy diffusivity and mixing length were investigated in terms of stratification parameters.

2. Introduction

There is a number of turbulence damping functions with empirical constants in stable stratified flow, and a common use of empirical formulae in numerical models is the Munk /Anderson's formula for the eddy viscosity and diffusivity. Most empirical constants were obtained from atmospheric boundary layer and laboratory data in temperature stratified flows, e.g. Webster (1964), Ueda et. al. (1981), Mizushina et. al.(1978). A few measurements have been also carried out in saline water, e.g. Ellison and Turner (1960), West and Shiono (1988) and Shiono, et. al. (1995). West and Shiono's obtained the mixing length formulae with the empirical constants from turbulent data in estuaries. Shiono et. al. (1995) examined both formulae using the flow in an open compound channel and the result showed a better agreement with those obtained by West and Shiono (1988) than by Munk and Anderson (1948). This paper examines these empirical constants using the experimental data of narrow rectangular channel flow with various degrees of stratification.

3. Turbulence dumping formulae

The transport of the momentum and solutes given by Reynolds stresses and fluxes may be related to the gradients of mean velocity and solutes by exchange coefficients using the Bousinesq's hypothesis. The exchange coefficients commonly used in numerical models are eddy viscosities, eddy diffusivities and mixing lengths. For uniform and steady flow in an open channel, the Reynolds stress, $\tau = \rho \overline{u'w'}$, arising from the horizontal shear and the vertical Reynolds flux, $F = \overline{\rho'w'}$, can be expressed as:

$$\rho\overline{u'w'} = -\rho\varepsilon_m \frac{\partial \overline{U}}{\partial z} = -\rho l_m^2 \frac{\partial \overline{U}}{\partial z}\left|\frac{\partial \overline{U}}{\partial z}\right| \quad and \quad \overline{\rho'w'} = -\varepsilon_s \frac{\partial \overline{\rho}}{\partial z} = -l_m l_s \left|\frac{\partial \overline{U}}{\partial z}\right| \frac{\partial \overline{\rho}}{\partial z} \quad (1)$$

where z are the longitudinal and vertical directions respectively, u', w' and ρ' are the turbulent fluctuations of velocity and salinity in the x and z directions respectively, $\overline{U}$ is the temporal averaged longitudinal velocity, ε and l are the eddy viscosity or diffusivity and mixing length respectively.

For homogeneous density 2-D flow in a wide open channel, the eddy viscosity and the mixing length can be written in the form

$$\varepsilon_{mo} = \kappa u_* z(1 - z/h) \quad and \quad l_{mo} = \kappa z(1 - z/h)^{1/2} \qquad (2)$$

where κ = von Karman constant (≈ 0.41), and h=water depth.

For stratified flow, either the eddy viscosity or mixing length is given as

$$(1 + \beta_m R_i)^{\alpha_m} \quad for \quad \frac{\varepsilon_m}{\varepsilon_{mo}} or \frac{l_m}{l_{mo}} \quad and \quad (1 + \beta_s R_i)^{\alpha_s} \quad for \quad \frac{\varepsilon_s}{\varepsilon_{mo}} or \frac{l_s}{l_{mo}} \qquad (3)$$

where α and β are empirical constants. Ri is the local gradient Richardson number usually defined in the form:

$$R_i = \frac{-g \frac{\partial \overline{\rho}}{\partial z}}{\rho \left(\frac{\partial \overline{U}}{\partial z} \right)^2} \qquad (4)$$

The empirical constants commonly used amongst numerical modellers are the Munk and Anderson (1948)'s empirical constants, $\alpha_m, \beta_m, \alpha_s$ and β_s for the eddy viscosity and diffusivity which are –0.5, 1.0, -1.5 and 3.33 respectively. The empirical constants, $\alpha_m, \beta_m. \alpha_s$ and β_s, for the mixing lengths obtained by West and Shiono (1988) are –0.5, 87.0, -1.5 and 7.48 respectively.

4. Experiment and results

The rectangular channel has dimensions of 100mm width, 250mm height and 12m length in which two ducts were built in the first 2.5m of the channel in order to make two-layer density flow. The lower channel was to discharge saline water and the other was for fresh water. The flow rates were 75l/min in the both ducts. The same total discharge and the same water depth were kept when the density differences between saline water and fresh water changed to 1kg/m^3, 3kg/m^3, and 5kg/m^3. The water depth was 105mm. Turbulence measurements of 3 components of velocity and salinity were conducted using a combined Laser Doppler Anemometer (LDA) and Laser Induced Fluorescence (LIF) system. Fluorescent dye, Rodamine 6G, mixed with saline water was used as a tracer and as a surrogate for salinity concentration. The measurements were undertaken at 6.4m downstream. The detail measurement technique is given by Feng and Shiono (2000).

Vertical distributions of velocity, density, Reynolds stress and flux
The distributions of longitudinal velocity, Reynolds stress and flux are shown in Figs. 1-4 at the centre of the channel 6.4m downstream from the outlet of the two ducts. It can be seen from Fig. 1 that, for the fresh water case, the location of maximum velocity is significantly below the water surface, which indicates the flow being 3 dimensional since the aspect ratio is 1.0. As the density difference at the outlet of the two ducts increases, the location of maximum velocity clearly moves towards the water surface. The detailed flow structure in the whole cross section can be seen in Feng and Shiono (2000). The distribution of saline water density over the water depth in Fig. 2 is more or less a linear variation except in the vicinity of the water surface. However it is noticed that there is a wavy form along the linear trend line for the 5 kg/m^3. The distributions of the Reynolds stress due to the horizontal plane shear for the various density differences in Fig. 3 show that the magnitude of the Reynolds stress reduces over the water depth as the density difference increases. The locations of zero shear stress corresponds well with the peak locations of maximum velocity, hence the Bousinesq's expression of the Reynolds stress may be valid. The distributions of the Reynolds in Fig. 4, clearly indicate that the flux increases as the density difference increases.

Flux Richardson number, turbulent Schmidt number Kolmogorov/ Prandtl empirical constant

The flux Richardson number, Rf, turbulent Schmidt number, Kolmogorov and Prandtl empirical constant, Cμ, over the water depth with Ri are shown in Figs. 5-7. A third order of polynomial equation was used to fit on the density and velocity distributions for the Ri and Rf calculations. The distribution of Rf in Fig. 5 shows that Rf increases to 1.0 as Ri, also increases to 1.0. This indicates that the production of turbulent kinetic energy (TKE) due to the buoyancy approaches the same magnitude of the production of TKE due to the Reynolds stresses, hence the total production of TKE gained from the Reynolds stresses and buoyancy approaches zero. This means that the turbulence is substantially reduced consequently the mixing of solute should be reduced.

Fig. 6 shows the distribution of the reciprocal of the turbulent Schmidt number, Tsc, against Ri, ($Tsc = \varepsilon_m / \varepsilon_s$) together with the data obtained by Webster (1965) and the equation of Bloss (1985). There is peak around Ri=0.1, and when Ri becomes smaller, the value approaches 1.0, however as Ri increases more than 1.0 the value becomes smaller than 1.0. The trend of our data agrees well with those obtained by Webster (1965), however the magnitude is larger than the equation of Bloss (1985).

The exchange coefficient, Cμ, commonly used in the k-ε model was calculated using the assumption of turbulence equilibrium (Production of TKE =Dissipation of TKE) with the following equation:

$$C_\mu = \left(\frac{\overline{u'w'}}{k}\right)^2 \left(1 - \frac{Ri}{Tsc}\right) \tag{5}$$

where k = turbulent kinetic energy.

It can be seen from Fig. 7 that Cμ decreases as Ri increases. And at the lowest Richardson number (~0), Cμ is between 0.06 and 0.07, which is smaller than that of 0.09 normally used in the k-ε models. According the turbulence data in open channel flow published by Nezu and Rodi, (1986), Cμ is around 0.07 in the turbulence equilibrium region. Our data also confirms this. The value decreases as Ri increases as expected.

Damping functions for eddy viscosity and mixing length

The normalised eddy viscosity, $\varepsilon_m/\varepsilon_{mo}$, and the normalised mixing length, lm/lmo, together with the empirical formulae obtained by Munk and Anderson (1948), West and Shiono (1988) and the others were plotted in Fig. 8. Both exchange coefficients decrease rapidly from Ri=0 to Ri=0.1 and seem to become more or less constant beyond Ri=0.1. From the various empirical formulae plotted in the figure, in the range of Ri between 0 and 0.1, the mixing empirical formulae of Rossby and Montgomery (1935) and West and Shiono (1988) are definitely closer to the measured data. The Munk and Anderson formula does not agree well with this data.

5. Conclusions

The flux Richardson number increases as the gradient Richardson number increases, and the total production of turbulent kinetic energy due to the Reynolds stresses and buoyancy is substantially reduced in the high Richardson number. The trend of our *1/Tsc* agrees well with those obtained by Webster (1965), however the magnitude of 1/Tsc is larger than the equation of Bloss (1985). Our data also confirms that the Kolmogorov and Prandtl empirical constant, Cμ, is smaller than 0.09 being used in the k-e model when Ri=0. The value, Cμ, decreases as Ri increases when the turbulence equilibrium is assumed. The value is less 0.01 beyond Ri=0.1. Our data for momentum exchange coefficients agree well with Rossby and Montgomery (1935) and West & Shiono (1988) but not the Munk and Anderson (1948) and Bloss (1985) formulae.

References

1. Bloss, S. (1985), see Abraham, 1988, Physical Processes in Estuaries.
2. Ellison, T.H., and Turner, J.S., (1960), Mixing of dense fluid in a turbulent pipe flow, Part 2, Dependence of transfer coefficient on local stability, J. Fluid Mech, 8:529-544.
3. Feng T. and Shiono, K. (2000), Turbulence measurements in a narrow rectangular channel for two-layer stratified flow, 5th International Symposium on Stratified flows, Vancouver, Canada, 10-13 July.
4. Kent, R.E. and Pritchard, A., (1959), A test of mixing length theories in coastal plain estuary, J. Mar. Res. 18:62-72.
5. Mizushina,T., Ogino,F., Ueda, H. and Komori, S., (1978), Buoyancy effect on diffusivities in thermally stratified flow in open channel, Proc. 6th Int. Heat Transfer Conf., Toroto, 1:91-98.
6. Munk, W.H. and Anderson, E.R., (1948), Notes on a theory of the thermocline, J. Mar. Reş. 7:276-295.
7. Shiono, K., Falconer, R. A., Berlamont, J., Elzier, M. and Karelse, M., (1995), A note on stratified flow in a compound channel, Proc. 26th IAHR Congress, London, September, 3:134-139.
8. Rossby, C.G. and Montgomery, R.B. (1935), The layer of friction influence in wind and ocean currents, Pap. Phys. Oceanog. Meteorol. 3, (3):110.
9. Ueda, H., Mitsumoto, S. and Komori, S., (1981), Buoyancy effect on the turbulent transport processes in lower atmosphere, Q.J.R. Meteorol. Soc. 107:561-578.
10. Webster, C.A.G., (1964), An experimental study of turbulence in a density stratified shear flow, J. Fluid Mech. 19:221-245.
11. West, J.R. and Shiono, K. (1988), Vertical turbulent mixing processes on ebb tides in partially mixed estuaries, Estuarine, Coastal and Shelf Science, 26: 51-66.

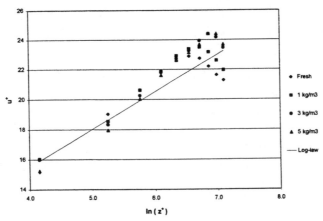

Fig. 1 Distributions of longitudinal velocity

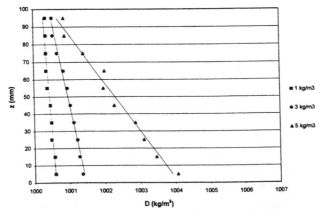

Fig. 2 Distributions of saline water density

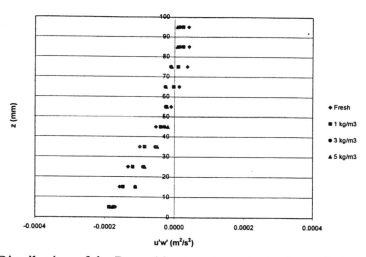

Fig.3 Distribution of the Reynolds stress term for horizontal plane shear.

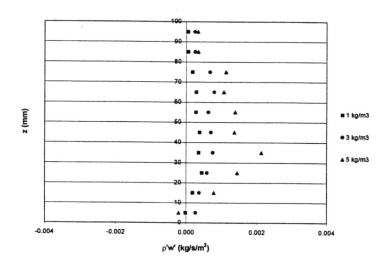

Fig. 4 Distributions of vertical Reynolds flux.

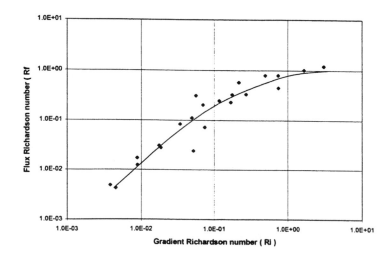

Fig. 5 Flux Richardson number against gradient Richardson number

931

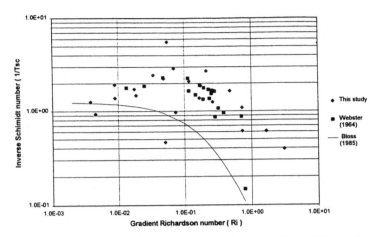

Fig. 6 Inverse turbulent Schmidt number against gradient Richardson number

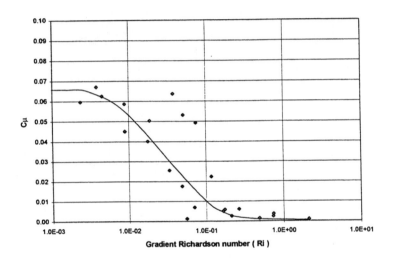

Fig. 7 Kolmogorov/Prandtl constant against gradient Richardson number

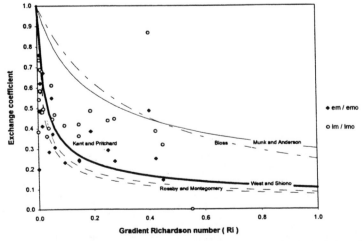

Fig. 8 Exchange coefficients for momentum against gradient Richardson number

Numerical and Experimental Modeling of Intrusive Salt Fronts

I. M. Skarvelis

Civil Engineering, Aristotle University of Thessaloniki, Thessaloniki 540 06, Greece
iskarvel@tee.gr

1. Abstract

A quasi-two dimension two-layer model was developed to analyze the salt front movement into an estuarine river. The finite-difference numerical procedure of the two-layer model and the introduction of a velocity profile, which simulate the main flow characteristic (the density interface and the zero velocity line), are present in detail. The important role of the critical condition at the river mouth and the changes in the river discharge, into the circulation and the geometry of the front and its steady-state form of the saline wedge, are also investigated. Laboratory experiments have been performed to simulate the front movement and its steady-state form, and calibrate the numerical model parameters.

2. Introduction

The intrusion of a saline front in a river, which communicates with the sea, caused by the density difference between the two fluids. The front is formed at the bed of the river and moves forwards or backwards as the tide or upland discharge change. There are some other features, like suspended particles or greater concentration of phytoplakton, that enabling to be detected visually. The steady-state form is the so-called arrested saline wedge, where force equilibrium is maintained between internal buoyancy pressure, shear stress and convective acceleration.

The reason of the experimental studies was to investigate the parameters governing the motion, the shape and the length of the front and the still form of it, the arrested saline wedge. The first extensive experiments of Keulegan (1966) over a wide range of densimetric Froude numbers and Reynold number, include front velocity, wedge characteristic length and shape, patterns of velocity and mixing rates. Recent experimental work of Grubert (1980), Sargent and Jirka (1987), the arrested saline wedge length and shape, velocity or density profile, interfacial stability and entrainment rates are investigated.

The quantitative indication of the dynamic structures, of the arrested saline wedge, is presented from Arita and Jirka (1987). The geometry of the arrested saline wedge is characterized by two major internal lines, the density interface and the zero velocity line (ZVL). The first line divided the flow in an active with high kinetic energy upper layer zone and a passive lower zone, and the second line in the lower zone, across which we have net entrainment.

The numerical models are formulated on the basis of the simulation of the physical dynamics, for a realistic front formation and propagation. The recent understanding of the two internal lines of the still state of arrested saline wedge, are introduced to the quasi one dimension two layer model, giving as a result not only the length and the shape but also the velocity profile during the front movement and its steady-state.

3. Derivation of the equation

The widely used, one dimension model of Schijf and Schonefeld (1953), was used to describe the flow of a two homogeneous layer (salt and fresh water) separated by a sharp interface. The integration of the continuity and motion equation over the depth of each layer (upper layer, h_o and lower layer, h_u), gives the following one dimension two layer model (Abbot and Grubert (1972), Bowden (1983) and Koutitas (1993)).

The computational flow domain, Fig. 1, is divided horizontally into two parts, where in the first part, there is only the ambient fluid and in the second part there is the dense bottom layer and the upper layer

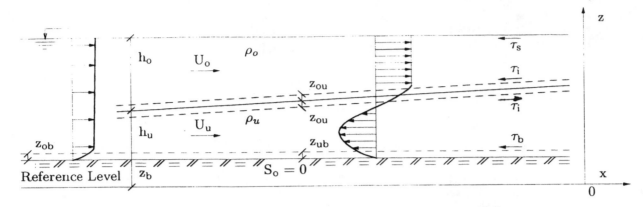

Fig. 1. Schematic representation of the quasi-one dimension two-layer numerical model

of the ambient fluid. The first part is divide vertically into two layers, the bottom layer, and the main layer of the ambient fluid, with a thickness z_{ob} and $h_o - z_{ob}$, respectively. The second part is also divide vertically into four layers with specific thickness, the bottom layer, z_{ub}, the dense layer, $h_u - z_{ub} - z_{ou}$, the interface layer, $2z_{ou}$, and the layer of the ambient fluid, $h_o - z_{ou}$, where $z_{ub} = z_{ob}$.

The equations of continuity and motion for the upper layer are respectively written, as follows:

$$\frac{\partial h_o}{\partial t} + \frac{\partial (U_o h_o)}{\partial x} = 0, \qquad \frac{\partial U_o}{\partial t} + U_o \frac{\partial U_o}{\partial x} = -\frac{1}{\rho_o}\frac{\partial p}{\partial x} - g\frac{\partial (h_o + h_u + y_b)}{\partial x} + \varepsilon_{ho}\frac{\partial^2 U_o}{\partial x^2} + \frac{\tau_s - \tau_i}{\rho_o h_o} \qquad (1)$$

and for the lower layer as:

$$\frac{\partial h_u}{\partial t} + \frac{\partial (U_u h_u)}{\partial x} = 0, \qquad \frac{\partial U_u}{\partial t} + U_u \frac{\partial U_u}{\partial x} = -\frac{1}{\rho_u}\frac{\partial p}{\partial x} - g\frac{\partial (h_u + z_b)}{\partial x} + \varepsilon_{hu}\frac{\partial^2 U_u}{\partial x^2} + \frac{\tau_i - \tau_b}{\rho_u h_u} \qquad (2)$$

where: h_o, h_u, the depth of the upper and lower layer, U_o, U_u, the mean average velocity of the upper and lower layer, p, the pressure is assumed to be hydrostatic, z_b, the distance between the bed and the reference level, ε_{ho}, ε_{hu}, the mean horizontal eddy viscosity of the upper and lower layer, τ_b, τ_i, τ_s, the shear stress at the bottom, the interface, and the surface of the river.

According to the experimental conclusions, the profile suggested for the second part of the computational domain is present in Fig.1. The velocity distribution in the layers, it assumed to be linear at the bottom layer, parabolic at the lower layer, linear at the interfacial layer and logarithmic at the upper layer following the relationships:

upper layer: $\qquad u_o(z) = A_o \ln\left(\dfrac{z}{h_u + z_{ou}}\right) + B_o$ $\hfill (3)$

interfacial layer: $\qquad u_i(z) = A_i z + B_i$ $\hfill (4)$

lower layer: $\qquad u_u(z) = A_u(z - z_{mu})^2 + B_u(z - z_{mu}) + C_u$ $\hfill (5)$

bottom layer: $\qquad u_b(z) = A_b z + B_b$ $\hfill (6)$

where: z the distance from the bottom, z_{mu} the distance of the maximum velocity from the river bottom, in the dense layer and is a function of the lower layer depth.

The calculation of the nine coefficients of the above equations (A_o, B_o, A_i, B_i, A_u, B_u, C_u, A_b, B_b) will be done from the seven equations of the proposed velocity profile boundary conditions:

934

for $z = h_u + z_{ou}$ then $\dfrac{du_o(z)}{dz} = \dfrac{du_i(z)}{dz}$ and $u_o(z) = u_i(z)$ (7)

for $z = h_u - z_{ou}$ then $\dfrac{du_i(z)}{dz} = \dfrac{du_u(z)}{dz}$ and $u_i(z) = u_u(z)$ (8)

for $z = z_{oo}$ then $\dfrac{du_u(z)}{dz} = \dfrac{du_b(z)}{dz}$ and $u_u(z) = u_b(z)$ (9)

for $z = 0$ then $u_b(z) = 0$ (10)

and other two equations from the integration of the velocity distribution in each layer:

$$U_o = \frac{1}{z_{ou}} \int_{h_u}^{h_u - z_{ou}} u_i(z)dz + \frac{1}{h_o - z_{ou}} \int_{h_u - z_{ou}}^{h_u + h_o} u_o(z)dz \qquad (11)$$

$$U_u = \frac{1}{z_{ub}} \int_0^{z_b} u_b(z)dz + \frac{1}{h_u - z_{ub} - z_{ou}} \int_{z_b}^{h_u - z_{ub} - z_{ou}} u_u(z)dz + \frac{1}{z_{ou}} \int_{h_u - z_{ub} - z_{ou}}^{h_u} u_b(z)dz \qquad (12)$$

The profile suggested for the first part of the computational domain, it assumed to be linear at the bottom layer and logarithmic at the upper layer, following the relationships:

upper layer: $u_o(z) = A_o \ln\left(\dfrac{z}{z_{ob}}\right) + B_o$ (13)

bottom layer: $u_b(z) = A_b z + B_b$ (14)

The calculation of the four coefficients of the above equations (A_o, B_o, A_b, B_b) will be done from the three equations of the proposed velocity profile boundary conditions:

for $z = z_{ob}$ then $\dfrac{du_o(z)}{dz} = \dfrac{du_b(z)}{dz}$ and $u_o(z) = u_b(z)$ (15)

for $z = 0$ then $u_b(z) = 0$ (16)

and other equation from the integration of the velocity distribution in each layer:

$$U_o = \frac{1}{z_{ob}} \int_0^{z_b} u_b(z)dz + \frac{1}{h_u - z_{ob}} \int_{z_b}^{h_u - z_{ob}} u_o(z)dz \qquad (17)$$

The shear stresses are defined through the relationships:

$$\frac{\tau_s}{\rho_o} = \varepsilon_s \frac{du_o}{dz}, \qquad \frac{\tau_i}{\rho_o} = \varepsilon_i \frac{du_i}{dz}, \qquad \frac{\tau_b}{\rho_u} = \varepsilon_b \frac{du_b}{dz} \qquad (18)$$

where ε_s, ε_i, ε_b, the eddy viscosity coefficients in the vertical direction, at the free surface, the interface, and the bottom of the river. The derivatives will be calculated from the relationship of the velocity distribution. equations (3,4,5,6), and will be a function of the mean velocity of the upper, U_o, and lower U_u, layer and the thickness, the bottom, z_{oo}, and interfacial, z_{ou}, layer.

The numerical solution of the set equations (1, 2), was applied on a staggered grid (Arakawa's C type), where the standard center and upwind finite difference approximations used for the space and the time derivatives. The boundary condition, upstream of the computational domain, is characterized by the inflow of a constant velocity, U_o, while downstream the flow is critical.

4. Experimental apparatus and procedure

The laboratory apparatus, Fig. 2, has been build to study one dimension stratified flow and consist of a channel and four basins from steel and plexiglass to allow flow visualization and camera recording.
The fresh water was introduced first to the stilling basin Δ3 (0.5 m wide, 0.8 m height and 2.34 m long) at the front of the channel and through a screen system to the main channel, which is 0.5 m wide, 0.5 m

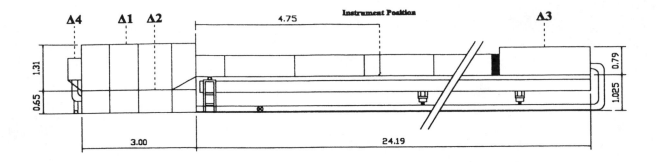

Fig. 2. Schematic representation of the experimental apparatus

height and 24.16 m long. At the back of the channel, there is the gate $\theta 1$, which split it from the stratified basin $\Delta 1$, (1.41 m wide, 1.31 m height, and 3 m long) contain the dense fluid. The fresh or the diluted water pass through the overflow at the back of the stratified, to the regulator basin $\Delta 3$ (1.41 m wide, 0.68 m height and 0.35 m long), and then routed through pipes to the recirculation basin $\Delta 2$, or to the drainage system of the laboratory, respectively. The dimensions of the recirculation basin $\Delta 2$ are 1.65 m wide, 0.65 m height and 3 m long and the inflow freshwater pass trough the pump system and the orifice plate and return at the upstream stilling basin $\Delta 4$.

Salt solution is used as the dense fluid and the initial concentration of the salt solution is measured by weighting salt in a known volume of water. The solution is prepared and hold in a round steel tank (diameter 3m and 1m height), dyed using fluorescene and subsequently pumped though a calibrate valve into the stratified basin $\Delta 1$.

The experimental procedure divided into two stages and the measurements were conduct using two hot film sensors, a temperature and a conductivity sensor, in a place 4.75 m from the stratified basin $\Delta 1$. In the first stage, the gate $\theta 1$ was opened and the salt front intruded near the bottom of the channel against the direction of the overflow freshwater flow. During the front movement, point measurements of the velocity, the temperature and the salinity inside the front and the velocity above freshwater were conducted. After reaching its steady state, and form an arrested saline wedge, measured the profile of the velocity, temperature and salinity. In the second stage, the pumping of salt solution to the stratified basin $\Delta 1$ cause the rise of the solution level and the upstream movement of the front until it reached a new position. During the front movement, point measurements of the velocity, the temperature and the salinity inside the front and the velocity in the above freshwater were also conducted. After reaching its new steady state, an arrested saline wedge, measured again the profile of the velocity, temperature and salinity.

5. Result and discussion

Ten experiments were run in the above described apparatus, while the upstream water height, H_o, varied from 0.1 to 0.2 m and the upstream velocity, U_o, from 0.02 to 0.06 m/sec. The lengths of the arrested saline wedges, in the present limited experimental work, are predicted by Keulegan formula for $H/B = 2$, while the other formulas overestimate it.

The experimental case of $H_o = 0.1$ m, $U_o = 0.02$ m/sec and $\Delta\rho/\rho = 0.007$ were selected to run the quasi-two dimension two-layer model and to compare the result for the length of the steady state of the arrested saline wedge. At the end of the first stage of the experiment, the saline front after 1020 sec from the open of the gate $\theta 1$, reached its still form and its length is 12.5 m. As a result, the distance step for the model could be $\Delta x = 0.5$ m and from the Courant-Fredrichts-Lewy criterion the time step derived, is $\Delta t = 0.3$ sec. Observations from the density profile measurements, show that the thickness of the

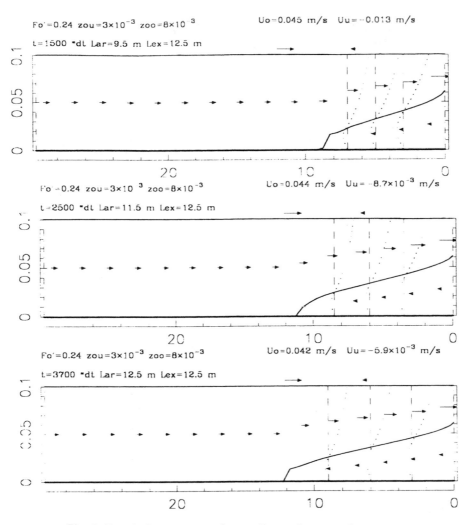

Fig. 2. Result from the quasi-two dimension two-layer model

interfacial layer is $2z_{ou} = 0.006$ m and for this reason, in the model the variable is $z_{ou} = 0.003$ m, and for the bottom layer thickness is $z_{ou} = 0.008$ m.

The eddy viscosity coefficients, ε_i, ε_b, of the shear stress term are depended on the scale of the computational domain and are estimated after a numerical sensitivity analysis of the model. The numerical result for the salt front movement, present in Fig. 3, where the value of the eddy viscosity coefficients is $\varepsilon_i = \varepsilon_b = 3.5E^{-6}$ and the mean horizontal eddy viscosity is $\varepsilon_{hu} = \varepsilon_{hu} = 0.005$.

The introduction of the present vertical velocity distribution and the implication of the density line and zero velocity line could simulate the front movement and there are not only characteristic of the steady state of the saline front. It is also important to note that using this model the friction coefficient in the interface is not constant but varies along the front. The estimation of the parameters, z_{ub} and z_{ou}, could be done from experiments in the field or in the laboratory.

6. Bibliography

1. Abbott M. B. and Grubert J. P., Towards a design system for stratified flows, Proc. International Symposium on Stratified flows, Novosibirsk, 1972.

2. Arita M. and Jirka G. H., Two layer model of saline wedge I: entrainment and interfacial friction, J. Hydr. Engrg. ASCE, 113(10), 1229-1248, 1987.
3. Arita M. and Jirka G. H., Two layer model of saline wedge II: prediction of mean properties, J. Hydr. Engrg. ASCE, 113(10), 1229-1248, 1987.
4. Bowden K., Physical Oceanography of Coastal Waters, Ellis Horwood, 1983.
5. Grubert J. P., Experiments on arrested saline wedge, J. Hydr. Engrg. ASCE, 106(6), 945-960, 1980.
6. Keulegan, G. H., The Mechanism of an Arrested Saline Wedge, Estuary and Coastline Hydrodynamics, A. T. Ippen, ed., McGraw-Hill Book Co., New York, 546-574, 1966.
7. Koutitas Ch., Chasiltzoglou N., Triantafilou G., Krestenitis I., Scientific Calendar of Polytechnic School, Aristotle University, Thessaloniki, IG'(B'), 1993.
8. Sargent F. H. and Jirka G. H., Experiments on the saline wedge, J. Hydr. Engrg. ASCE, 113(10), 1307-1324, 1987.
9. Schijf J. B. and Schoenfeld J. C., Theoretical consideration on the motion of salt and fresh water, Proc. International Hydraulics Convection, Minneapolis, 321-333, 1953.
10. Skarvelis I. M. Study of the hydrodynamic behavior of thermal and saline fronts, thesis presented to the Aristotle University, Thessaloniki, Greece, 2000.

Spring-Neap Variations in Stratification and Turbulent Mixing in a Partially Stratified Estuary

Mark T. Stacey[1], Jon R. Burau[2], Matthew L. Brennan[3], Jessica Lacy[3], Stephen G. Monismith[3], Cara C. Tobin[3],

[1]Civil & Environmental Eng., University of California, Berkeley, CA 94720-1710
[2]United States Geological Survey, WRD, Sacramento, CA 95819-6129
[3]Environmental Fluid Mechanics Laboratory, Stanford University, Stanford, CA 94305

1. Abstract

Variability in stratification and turbulent mixing at the tidal and spring-neap timescales is examined in a partially stratified estuary using direct field observations. A two-week data set of mean current and turbulent Reynolds stress profiles is analyzed in conjunction with a ten-day data set of density profiles collected in San Francisco Bay in October, 1999. The stratification data indicates a transition in the dynamics of the estuary, from a periodically stratified period during the neap tides to a well-mixed condition during the spring tides. The mean currents show both an increase in magnitude and a decrease in the diurnal inequality of the tides as the flow transitions from neap to spring. The stratification and the mean currents result in a significant transition in the turbulent Reynolds stresses occurring between neap and spring tides. During the neaps, the Reynolds stresses are near zero throughout the tidal cycle, with the exception of every other flood tide, due to the periodic stratification of the water column on the 24-hour timescale. During the springs, the Reynolds stresses are in phase with the tidal currents and vary on the 12-hour timescale. The change in dynamics between neap and spring tides are consistent with the horizontal Richardson number, with the neaps showing strain-induced stratification with a 24-hour period and the springs having sufficient mixing energy to remain well-mixed.

2. Introduction

The interaction of turbulent mixing and density stratification is critical to the dynamics of estuarine flows. Recent studies have addressed the balance between these two competing forces in more detail than ever before, but our ability to model such flows is still limited by our understanding of the fundamental physics of this interaction. This interaction is made particularly difficult to study due to the range of timescales that are relevant to the balance between mixing and stratification. At the tidal and sub-tidal timescales, shear in the tidal currents actively produces turbulence and mixing due to turbulence breaks down stratification. The balance between the stratifying effects of advection and the destratifying effects of the turbulence produced by the tidal currents creates important variation at the tidal timescale in the level of stratification (strain-induced periodic stratification, SIPS) as discussed by Simpson et al. (1990). The tidal energy, however, is modulated on the two-week spring-neap cycle, which imposes an additional, longer timescale to the problem (Jay and Smith, 1990).

The details of the interaction between turbulence and stratification have been examined extensively in laboratory studies (Rohr et al. 1988), numerically (Holt et al. 1992) and observationally in the open ocean (Gregg 1987) and in lakes (Imberger and Ivey 1991). Direct observations of turbulence and stratification in estuaries, however, have been limited until recently. Stacey, et al. (1999a) used an acoustic Doppler current profiler (ADCP) to examine turbulence and stratification over a 24-hour period in San Francisco Bay. At the spring-neap timescale, Peters (1997) measured dissipation rates and stratification in the Hudson River during neap and spring conditions and the evidence indicated a reduction in stratification from neap to spring tides, which was tied to increased mixing distributed throughout the water column during the spring tides. The current study extends these two previous estuarine studies by extending the ADCP data collection to an entire two-week spring-neap period. The objective of the study is to fully examine the dynamics of estuarine mixing at the relevant timescales, from the semi-diurnal and diurnal tidal timescales to the spring-neap timescale.

3. Experiment Description

In October 1999 (Julian days 288-300), a suite of instruments was deployed for two weeks in Suisun Cutoff, a straight channel in northern San Francisco Bay (Figure 1) to examine the balance between stratification and turbulence on the spring-neap and tidal timescales. The deployment location was chosen to minimize the effects of lateral variability, while providing a region that is subject to a periodically and partially stratified water column. The centerpiece of the study was a set of instruments deployed near the centerline of the channel. Two acoustic Doppler current profilers (ADCPs, RD Instruments) were mounted on the bottom: one in a 2-meter high frame sampling mode back towards the bed (downwards-looking), the other mounted 40 centimeters above the bed sampling the entire water column (in an upwards-looking configuration). Both ADCPs were cabled to laptops in a houseboat anchored nearby and collected every ping (approximately 2 Hz) for the 2-week deployment. This paper will discuss the upwards-looking data set, which was collected in mode 1 (RD Instruments) with a spatial resolution of 25 centimeters. A 10-minute window was used to define the mean currents ($<u>$) and the variances of the along-beam velocity data within each 10-minute window was used to calculate the turbulent Reynolds stresses ($<u'w'>$) and turbulent kinetic energy using the technique outlined in Stacey et al. (1999a, 1999b). The result was a two-week data set of mean currents and turbulent Reynolds stresses with a vertical resolution of 25 centimeters and a temporal resolution of 10 minutes.

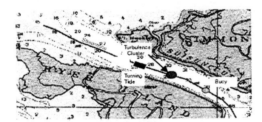

Figure 1: Study location. "Turbulence Cluster" indicates location of data discussed here. R/V Turning Tide (rectangle) is location of dissipation measurements (Gregg et al.)

Adjacent to the up-down frame (deployed from the houseboat), an Ocean Sciences OS200 conductivity-temperature-depth (CTD) profiler was deployed from an autonomous profiling winch. Every 15 minutes the winch would lower the CTD through the water column to collect a profile and the data was uploaded every 2 days throughout the deployment. With the exception of a battery failure that resulted in a short data gap on day 293, the configuration resulted in a continuous record of density profiles throughout a 10-day period (day 289.5 to day 299). This data was block averaged, with a vertical resolution of about 15 centimeters throughout a 7-meter profile.

4. Observations

The data sets collected during the turbulence experiment consisted of two weeks of velocity (mean and turbulent) data and 10 days of density data. In figure 2, the neap (Julian days 289.5 to 291.5) and spring (Julian days 296.5 to 298.5) periods have been extracted from this data set in order to examine the spring-neap variability of the tidal timescale currents and salinity distributions. The tidally driven mean currents (figure 2a) show a transition from a period characterized by a strong diurnal inequality (neap) to a nearly symmetric tidal signal during the spring. This is most evident in the weak ebb tide at Julian day 290.7 (during the neap), which is not evident during the spring (i.e., the ebb tides at 296.8, 297.3 and 297.8 are all nearly equivalent in magnitude). The transition between neap and spring tides in the mean currents, therefore, is characterized by both an increase in tidal energy and a decrease in the diurnal inequality of the tides.

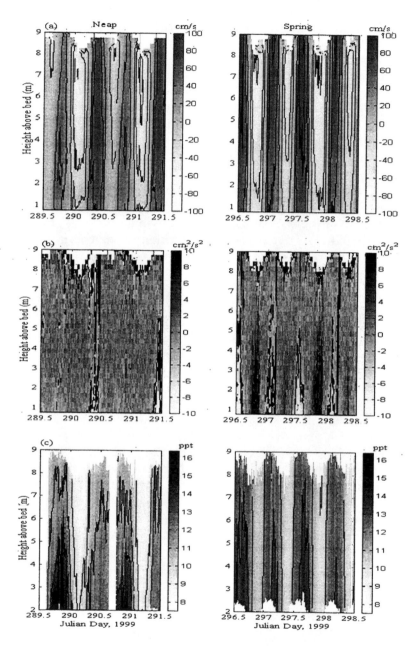

Figure 2: Neap and spring periods of (a) mean velocity; (b) Reynolds stresses ($<u'w'>$); and (c) salinity.

The turbulence, however, shows an even more extreme transition between neap and spring tides. In figure 2b, the Reynolds stresses are seen to be almost non-existent during the neap tide, with the exception of each flood tide that follows a large ebb tide (days 290.4 and 291.5). During the spring tide, the Reynolds stresses are much more symmetric, both between ebbs and floods (compare days 296.8 to 297.1, e.g.) and between consecutive floods (days 297.6 and 298.1, e.g.). The diurnal inequality is still evident in the small Reynolds stresses at hour 297.3 (ebb tide), but is considerably reduced relative to the neap tide. Although much more pronounced, this transition is similar to that seen in the mean currents, with both an increase in mixing energy and a decrease in the 24-hour component of the variability. As we will see, however, this transition is due to more than just the change in the tidal current magnitudes, but is instead tied to the stratification dynamics.

The salinity fields (which dominate the calculation of density for this data set) collected from the automatic CTD profiler deployed adjacent to the upwards-looking ADCP are shown in Figure 2c. During the neap tide, significant stratification develops periodically, with 16 ppt salinity at the bed and 10-11 ppt at the surface (days 289.8 and 290.9). The timing of these stratification events coincides with the end of the weak ebb tides and extends into the ensuing flood tide. During the strong ebb tides (day 290.1, e.g.), the stratification is considerably smaller, resulting in a strong 24-hour variation in the stratification. Comparing this result to the Reynolds stresses in figure 2b, we see that the period of significant turbulent mixing (flood tide following a strong ebb) coincides with the unstratified portion of the tidal cycle. During the spring tide, the salinity distribution is more uniform over the depth, and the stratification has been significantly reduced. The water column is much more well-mixed (on both floods and ebbs) during the spring tide than the neap, resulting in a more symmetric level of turbulent mixing (figure 2b). Taken together, the data indicates that the estuary transitions from a periodically stratified water column (SIPS dominated) during the neap tide to a well-mixed water column during the spring tide.

5. Discussion

In order to examine more closely the transition between neap and spring tidal conditions, time series of the near-bed measurements of the velocity and density are displayed in figure 3. In figure 3a, the transition from neap to spring is clear in the mean currents (upper line), with the magnitude increasing and the diurnal inequality decreasing during the spring tide. The Reynolds stress (figure 3a, lower, bold line) shows an even more pronounced transition from neap to spring. During the neap tide, as was mentioned above, the Reynolds stresses are near zero except for every other flood tide, so that the primary variability in the turbulence is occurring with a 24-hour period. This diurnal variability could also be characterized as an asymmetry in the turbulent mixing, when comparing flood tides and ebb tides, or consecutive tidal periods. As the tides transition into a spring period (starting at about day 292), more turbulence is evident during the intervening flood tide and during the ebbs, but the asymmetry remains. Not until well into the spring tide (days 296-298) is the asymmetry between ebbs and flood eliminated. By the center of the spring tide (day 297), the magnitude of the Reynolds stress is strongly tied to the semi-diurnally varying tidal currents (12-hour cycle) and the asymmetries seen during the neap tides are nearly completely erased.

As discussed above, the stratification also shows a transition from a 24-hour variability during the neap, with significant stratification developing late in the small ebb tides, to a more symmetric, well-mixed condition during the spring. To examine this transition more closely, time series of salinity at two different heights above the bed (2.5 meters and 3.5 meters) are shown in figure 3b and the associated Brunt-Vaisala frequency is shown in figure 3c. During the neap tide, the near-bed salinity (figure 3b) is seen to have a wider range than during the spring tide; but, more importantly, shows significantly larger stratification (the two lines diverge late in the weak ebb tides, e.g. at day 291.8). During the spring tide, the two salinities are completely consistent (only 1 line is visible in figure 3b during the spring tide), suggesting a well-mixed water column. This transition between a periodically stratified period and a well-mixed period is captured in the time series of the Brunt-Vaisala frequency squared, calculated over the region between 2 and 4 meters above the bed (figure 3c). During the neap tides, the Brunt-Vaisala frequency shows strong pulses of stratification occurring every 24 hours, in phase with the end of the small ebb tides (day 290.8, e.g.). The strong ebb tides (day 291.3, e.g.) are characterized by small values of the buoyancy frequency and appear to be well-mixed. This is consistent with the variation of the Reynolds stresses, and the spikes of Reynolds stresses seen during every other flood tide correspond to the well-mixed periods. During the transition to spring conditions, the magnitude of the spike in the buoyancy frequency is reduced (day 293, e.g.) and finally eliminated (days 294-299). Under spring tidal conditions, stratification does not develop, so the tidal currents along should determine the magnitude of the Reynolds stresses. This is once again completely consistent with the Reynolds stresses (figure 3a), which clearly are in phase with the semi-diurnal tidal currents during the spring tide.

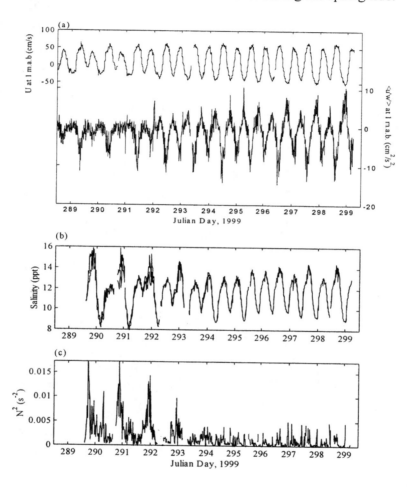

Figure 3: Time series of (a) mean velocity and Reynolds stress at 1 meter above bed (m.a.b.); (b) salinity at 2.5 and 3.5 m.a.b.; (c) mean Brunt-Vaisala Frequency squared from 2-4 m.a.b.

6. Summary and Conclusions

Taken together, the data indicates that this channel transitions from a period of significant periodic stratification (neaps) to a period of persistently well-mixed conditions (springs). Further, the periodic stratification that occurs during the neaps is not periodic on the 12-hour timescale, but rather on the 24-hour timescale. This variation is closely tied to the strong diurnal inequality seen in the tides in this estuary. During the weak ebb tides, turbulent mixing is insufficient to break down the stratification being produced through advection by the tidal currents. During the strong ebb tides in the neaps – and throughout the springs – mixing is sufficient to preserve a well-mixed water column. Previous studies (Monismith et al., 1996; Stacey, et al., *in prep.*) suggest that the horizontal Richardson number, Ri_x, represents the balance between the stratifying effects of advection and the destratifying effects of turbulence; the transition is clear in the stratification data. At day 293, the mixing energy during the weak ebb tide is nearly sufficient to breakdown the stratification created by advection (figure 3c). Day 293 corresponds to the first day in which the weak ebb tidal current reached a maximum of 50 cm/s (figure 3a); it appears that the critical value of Ri_x is reached at that point. Once that threshold is reached (Ri_x goes sub-critical), the stratifying effects of the ebb tides are overcome by the turbulence produced, and the estuary remains well-mixed during the spring tides.

7. Acknowledgements

The authors would like to acknowledge the support of the Office of Naval Research and the Inter-agency Ecological Program during the field experiment.

8. References

Gregg, M. C. (1987) "Diapycnal mixing in the thermocline: A review," *J. Geophys. Res.*, **92**, 5249-5286.

Holt, S. E., Koseff, J. R. and Ferziger, J. H. (1992) "The evolution of turbulence in the presence of mean shear and stable stratification," *J. Fluid Mech.*, **237**, 499-539.

Imberger, J. and Ivey, G. N. (1991) "On the nature of turbulence in a stratified fluid. Part II: Application to lakes," *J. Phys. Oceanogr.*, **21**, 659-680.

Jay, D. A. and Smith, J. D., (1990) "Circulation, density structure and neap-spring transitions in the Columbia River Estuary," *Prog. Oceanogr.*, **25**, 81-112.

Monismith, S. G., Burau, J. R. and Stacey, M. T. (1996) "Stratification dynamics and gravitational circulation in Northern San Francisco Bay", in *San Francisco Bay: The Ecosystem*, J. T. Hollibaugh, ed., Pacific Division, Am. Assoc. Adv. Sci., 123-153.

Peters, H. (1997) "Observations of stratified turbulent mixing in an estuary. Neap-to-spring variations during high river run-off," *Estuar., Coastal Shelf Sci.*, **45**(1), 69-88.

Rohr, J. J., Itsweire, E. C., Helland, K. N. and Van Atta, C. W. (1988) "Growth and decay of turbulence in a stably stratified shear flow," *J. Fluid Mech.*, **195**, 77-111.

Simpson, J. H., Brown, J., Matthews, J. and Allen, G. (1990) "Tidal straining, density currents, and stirring in the control of estuarine stratification," *Estuaries*, **13**, 125-132.

Stacey, M. T., Monismith, S. G. and Burau, J. R. (1999a) "Observations of turbulence in a partially stratified estuary," *J. Phys. Oceanogr.*, **29**, 1950-1970.

Stacey, M. T., Monismith, S. G. and Burau, J. R. (1999b) "Measurements of Reynolds stress profiles of in unstratified tidal flow," *J. Geophys. Res.*, **104**(C5), 10,933-10,949.

Stratification in Fine-grained Sediment-laden Turbulent Flows

Erik A. Toorman

Hydraulics Laboratory, Civil Engineering Department
Katholieke Universiteit Leuven, De Croylaan 2, B-3001 Leuven, Belgium
erik.toorman@bwk.kuleuven.ac.be

1. Introduction

The interaction between fine-grained suspended particles and turbulence is studied within the context of cohesive sediment transport behaviour in estuaries (Berlamont & Toorman, 1998), where stratification continuously changes during the tidal cycle. When the flux Richardson number becomes larger than 1 at the bottom, the flow laminarises, the suspended particles settle and subsequently a fluid mud layer is formed. These dense, non-Newtonian suspensions can flow as a gravity current and cause rapid siltation. Under certain conditions, during deceleration a temporary stable two-layer system of low and high concentrated suspensions with a distinct lutocline as interface (resulting from hindered settling) can be formed (e.g. Wolanski et al., 1988). Turbulence damping around the lutocline may be so strong that laminarisation occurs locally. Many numerical experiments have been carried out to obtain better understanding of these processes.

Results have been obtained with the fully-implicit, 2nd order accurate finite element code "FENST-2D", developed by the author. The numerical model solves the hydrodynamic equations (continuity and Navier-Stokes), together with a turbulence closure model, either Prandtl mixing length (PML) or k-ε, and the sediment transport equation (mass conservation of suspended sediment). The k-ε turbulence model applies the PML approximation in the wall layer, which allows the model to integrate down to the bottom itself. Hindered settling effects are neglected since the concentrations remain small, but viscosity changes of the suspension as a function of concentration are accounted for.

2. Modelling Buoyancy Damping

The effect of buoyancy damping in the PML model is accounted for by correction factors, i.e. the damping functions, applied to the neutral eddy viscosity (ν_0) and eddy diffusivity (or mixing coefficient, K_0). Hence, for stratified conditions the eddy viscosity is written as $\nu_t = F_m \nu_0$ (with F_m = the momentum damping function) and the eddy diffusivity as $K_s = F_s K_0$ (with F_m = the sediment mixing damping function). K_s is generally assumed to be proportional to ν_t, and the proportionality factor in the case of particle-laden flows is known as the Schmidt number $\sigma_s = \nu_t / K_s = \sigma_0 F_m / F_s$, where: σ_0 = the neutral Schmidt number, having a value of ± 0.7, based on experimental data (Turner, 1973).

The k-ε turbulence model takes into account buoyancy effects by a specific buoyancy destruction term G in the k-equation (conservation of turbulent kinetic energy):

$$\frac{\partial k}{\partial t} + u_i \frac{\partial k}{\partial x_j} = \frac{\partial}{\partial x_i}\left((\nu + \frac{\nu_t}{\sigma_k}) \frac{\partial k}{\partial x_i} \right) + P + G - \varepsilon \tag{1}$$

where: ε = turbulent energy dissipation rate, ν = kinematic viscosity of the suspension, $\nu_t = c_\mu k^2/\varepsilon$, and P = the shear production term:

$$P = \nu_t \left(\frac{\partial u_i}{\partial x_j} + \frac{\partial u_j}{\partial x_i} \right) \frac{\partial u_i}{\partial x_j} \qquad G = \frac{g}{\rho} \frac{\nu_t}{\sigma_s} \frac{\partial \rho}{\partial y} \tag{2}$$

where: u_i = the components of the velocity vector, ρ = the suspension density and g = the gravity constant. The ratio $-G/P$ defines the flux Richardson number Rf. Despite the presence of the G-term, the Schmidt number is still required in the buoyancy term (see eq.2) and in the diffusion term of the sediment transport equation.

Several simplified theories have been proposed to be able to describe the damping functions as a function of Rf or the gradient Richardson number $Ri = \sigma_s Rf$ (see Turner, 1973). Experimental data in the literature for various forms of stratification (mainly by temperature or salinity, rarely by suspended particles, e.g. Munk & Anderson, 1948; Ellison & Turner, 1960; Odd & Rodger, 1978) seem to confirm this trend and several (semi-)empirical functions have been proposed, even though they show much scatter, which can be attributed to various sources of error (e.g. Odd & Rodger assume that the neutral eddy viscosity profile is the PML parabolic profile, which is not correct; see e.g. Nezu & Nakagawa, 1993). The most popular form is: $F_m = (1 + \alpha\, Ri)^{-a}$ and $F_s = (1 + \beta\, Ri)^{-b}$. In particular the damping functions proposed by Munk & Anderson (1948) ($\alpha = 10$, $\beta = \alpha/3$, $a = 0.5$, $b = 1.5$) have become widely used. Results in the present study are obtained with the Munk-Anderson (MA) functions and with an empirical Schmidt number variation following:

$$\sigma_s = \sigma_0 \left(1 + \xi\, Ri\right)^n \tag{3}$$

which for $\xi = 21$ and $n = 0.8$ fits best (r = 0.88) the data from Ellison & Turner (1960) and Odd & Rodger (1978) (figure 3).

3. Bottom Boundary Treatment

When buoyancy damping occurs, one obtains wrong results when the traditional boundary conditions for the flow and turbulence field are employed (i.e. the shear velocity is overestimated). When the model uses damping functions as defined above, the corresponding velocity profile can be reconstructed (Toorman, 2000):

$$u = \frac{u_*}{\kappa_0} \ln\left(\frac{y}{c\, y_0}\right) \tag{4}$$

where: κ_0 = the von Karman constant (= 0.41), u_* = the shear velocity, y_0 = the roughness parameter, and c = an apparent roughness modification factor, which is related to the momentum damping function by:

$$F_m = \left(1 - \frac{y}{c}\frac{\partial c}{\partial y}\right)^{-1} \tag{5}$$

Preliminary numerical experiments (using the PML model) suggest that c can be parameterised by:

$$c = \exp\left(-\left(1 + A w_s/u_*\right)\left(1 - \exp(-B Ri^m)\right)\right) \tag{6}$$

with A, B and m empirical parameters. This apparent roughness modification is confirmed by the observation of drag reduction in turbulent suspension flow of fine particles (e.g. Gust, 1976). The present model employs a new boundary treatment method which predicts the correct bottom shear stress (Toorman, 2000), which is very important for the estimation of transport, erosion and deposition rates. The drag reduction predicted by the model is of the same order of magnitude as in the experiments by Li & Gust (2000).

4. Steady State Sediment-laden Open-channel Flow

Steady state 1D calculations for various constant values of total sediment load, particle settling velocities (w_s) and shear velocities (u_*) have been run. Two types of damping functions have been used, MA and (3). A few typical results, obtained with the MA damping functions, where u_* has been varied, are shown in figure 1. It is important to realise that the interpretation of these results only reflects the physics in the model, which may not correspond to the reality. Unfortunately, no validation of the model is possible by lack of any good data set.

The results show that stratification (i.e. Rf) increases in the lower half of the water column with decreasing u_*. The slope of the velocity log-law increases, which implies an (apparent) decrease of the von Karman coefficient. The eddy viscosity profile clearly deviates from the (more or less) parabolic profile obtained in unstratified conditions, but becomes parabolic again at the smallest shear velocity for which $Rf \approx 1$ at the bottom. The numerical model fails as soon as $Rf \geq 1$ at the bottom, because turbulence production by shear (P) is completely destroyed by buoyancy (G), i.e. the flow laminarises and the k-ε model is no longer valid. This condition is reached with a small decrease of u_* as soon as $\partial Rf/\partial y < 0$. However, the turbulent flow can be maintained near the water surface, even when $Rf > 1$. Analysis of the numerical data shows that the production of k in this layer is dominated by diffusion and not shear production. The difference between bottom and surface is the sign of $\partial Rf/\partial y$. Therefore, $Rf > 1$ is not a sufficient condition for laminarisation, which seems to require also that $\partial Rf/\partial y < 0$, and the condition $\partial Rf/\partial y = 0$ seems to imply some sort of stability condition, which meaning remains uncertain.

An interesting feature is the tendency of the Richardson number to homogenize over the depth (except near the free surface, but this layer is not considered as the deviations are related to the boundary conditions which are not strictly correct for real 3D channels). It can be shown (Toorman, 1999) that a constant Rf (i.e. $\partial Rf/\partial y = 0$), assuming a logarithmic velocity profile, a constant κ, a constant σ_s and sediment concentration $C \ll$ the fluid density ρ_w, implies a parabolic eddy viscosity distribution, given by:

$$\nu_t = \sigma_s w_s y \left(1 - y/h\right) \tag{7}$$

This can also be interpreted as a change of the value of κ from 0.41 (the original von Karman constant for a homogeneous fluid) to a smaller value equal to:

$$\kappa_s = \sigma_s w_s / u_* \tag{8}$$

which also corresponds to a Rouse parameter value of 1. The corresponding approximate logarithmic velocity profile and profiles for ε and k can easily be reconstructed with this new value of κ (Toorman, 1999). These theoretical results are all confirmed by the numerical model (figure 1). Apparently, the eddy viscosity distribution of eq.(7) represents a minimal state, which cannot be exceeded without total collapse of turbulence (i.e. laminarisation).

A value Ri_c can be associated to the "critical" condition $\partial Rf/\partial y = 0$. The neutral eddy viscosity ν_0 in steady open-channel flow as predicted by the k-ε model can well be approximated by:

$$\nu_0 = \kappa_0 u_* y \frac{(1 - y/h)^{1/2}}{(1 + y/h)^{4/3}} \tag{9}$$

Equating eq.(7) to $F_m(Ri_c)\nu_0$, using (9), results into:

$$\frac{F_m(Ri_c)}{\sigma_s(Ri_c)} = \frac{1}{F_s(Ri_c)} = \frac{w_s}{\kappa_0 u_*} (1 - y/h)^{1/2} (1 + y/h)^{4/3} \tag{10}$$

This suggests that the sediment flux damping function is not just a function of Ri alone, but is also dependent on y. The dependence on y would disappear if the neutral eddy viscosity profile was parabolic, as is often assumed in the PML models for open-channel flow; then Ri_c would have been determined by the ratio w_s/u_*. The traditional PML model indeed yields this result. However, this is not in agreement with the results obtained with the k-ε model, which rather suggest that the Ri_c is independent on u_* (for a certain sediment load and w_s; figure 1.d). In the case illustrated $Ri_c = 0.21$ and $Rf_c = 0.24$ (when no buoyancy term occurs in the ε-equation, as is recommended for stable stratified shear flow; Rodi, 1980). Additional simulations with other settling velocities reveal little sensitivity to w_s on the value of Ri_c.

The results are very sensitive to the chosen damping functions. Several differences are observed between the results obtained with the two types of damping functions. When eq.(3) is used for the Schmidt number variation, the "critical" condition rather approaches a constant F_m distribution, which yields an eddy viscosity distribution as given by (9), multiplied by F_m.

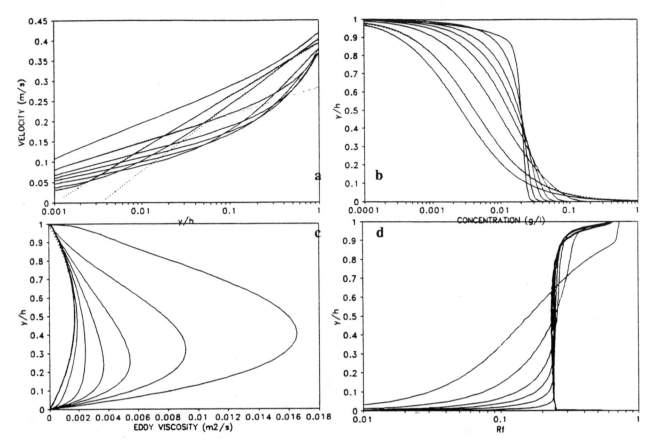

Figure 1: Numerical results for fully-developed sediment-laden turbulent open-channel flow ($h = 16$ m, $w_s = 0.5$ mm/s, mean concentration $C_m = 37$ mg/l) for various shear velocities ($u_* = 15.6, 11.8, 9.9, 8.6, 7.9, 6.9, 5.6$ and 5 mm/s), using the Munk-Anderson damping functions and the k-ε turbulence model. Profiles of (a) velocity (... : $\kappa = 0.41$, --- : $\kappa = \sigma_s w_s/u_*$), (b) sediment concentration (--- : Rouse profile with $Z = 1$), (c) eddy viscosity (--- : $\sigma_s w_s/y$ $(1-y/h)$, and (d) flux Richardson number.

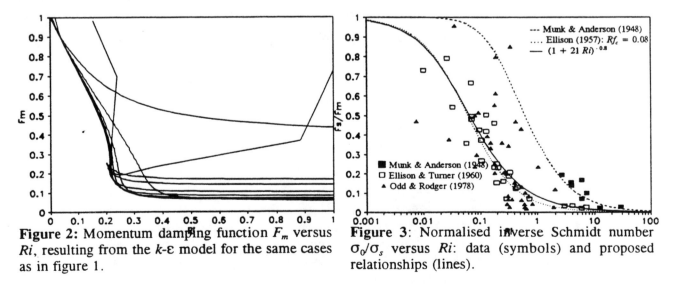

Figure 2: Momentum damping function F_m versus Ri, resulting from the k-ε model for the same cases as in figure 1.

Figure 3: Normalised inverse Schmidt number σ_0/σ_s versus Ri: data (symbols) and proposed relationships (lines).

For the MA damping function Rf does not exceed the value $\alpha^{0.5}/\beta^{1.5}/\sigma_0 = 0.743$, which causes unrealistic deviations at the free surface: a layer of constant Rf is being formed at the surface for low values of w_s/u_*, because the damping at high Ri is too strong, forcing the concentration to become zero at the free surface. These problems do not occur when eq.(3) is employed (fig.3). Therefore, the latter Schmidt number variation seems preferable.

The momentum damping function F_m (fig.2) has been calculated as v_t/v_0. The decrease of F_m with Ri is approximately linear for small Ri, similar to the Monin-Obukov damping function ($F_m = 1-\beta Ri$; Rodi, 1980). However, around Ri_c its decrease is steeper to end asymptotically at a constant value for $Ri > Ri_c$. This result may involve that several data, particularly at high Ri may need to be reinterpreted (such as the data in Munk & Anderson, 1948). Furthermore, the damping for the points where $\partial Rf/\partial y < 0$ seems to be quite different. Data analysis of the recent experiments with fine sand by Cellino & Graf (1999) seem to confirm these trends of F_m as found by the k-ε model.

5. Unsteady Flow

Various scenarios for unsteady flow have been investigated, part of which is described in (Toorman, 1999). When the shear velocity is gradually reduced, there is a non-equilibrium between vertical fluxes of settling and turbulent diffusion, resulting in sedimentation. In the simulations, the sediment is not allowed to attach to the bed, but is forced to remain mobile, neither erosion is considered (i.e. no mass exchange with the bottom). Depending on the conditions, temporarily a step may appear in the density profile, creating a two-layer system. Mixing across the interface (or lutocline) can then enormously be reduced. Again numerical problems may be encountered as laminarisation may occur around the lutocline. By lack of a good model than can handle the local low-Reynolds flow, this can be kept under control by applying locally artificial diffusion in the k-ε equations in order to keep the model running (Toorman, 1999). Other problems occur near the bottom, where the viscous sublayer is thickening and enters the domain which is solved as turbulent flow. Much work remains to be done to improve the numerical performance of the present approach. Future work will include mass exchange with the bottom (erosion and deposition).

6. Discussion & Conclusions

Results of numerical experiments on the interaction of suspended sediment and turbulence in open-channel flow have been presented. Several features are observed, some of which are still not well understood. The von Karman coefficient is found to decrease with increasing Ri. The Munk-Anderson damping functions yield too much damping at high Ri. Another empirical Schmidt number variation is proposed. A critical condition is defined by $dRf/dy = 0$. The exact physical meaning of this condition remains uncertain, but may be related to stability of turbulence generation, or to the capacity of the turbulent flow to keep sediment in suspension. A mathematical investigation might help to understand this. A critical value of Rf can be associated to this condition, which is found to be a function of w_s. The k-ε model results indicate that the damping does no longer increase with Ri above this critical condition and that the damping is different when the sign of dRf/dy changes.

The ratio w_s/u_* is a characteristic parameter for particle-laden turbulent flows and the corresponding features in the limit of $w_s/u_* \rightarrow 0$ (i.e. non-buoyant particles) should become similar as for temperature and salinity stratification. However, in the latter case the flow would show no stratification in the same 1DV steady state conditions as above.

As far as known, no suitable experimental data are available to confirm the numerical results, which should be interpreted with great care as the turbulence model has many deficiencies: invalid for low turbulent Reynolds numbers, not taking into account anisotropy expected near large concentration gradients, assuming an unvalidated Schmidt number variation. Particularly, the laminarisation around lutoclines remains a big challenge for the numerical simulation of time-dependent cases. Some useful data may be generated in the future with direct numerical simulation (DNS, e.g. Boivin et al., 1998), but this method presently has too many restrictions (e.g. low turbulent Reynolds number, low concentrations). Future work will be focusing on the simulation of the integral problem of cohesive sediment transport in real estuaries, including sediment exchange with the bottom.

7. References

Berlamont, J. & E.A. Toorman (1998). "Prediction of COhesive Sediment transport and bed dynamics in estuaries and coastal zones with Integrated NUmerical Simulation models (COSINUS)". *Third European Marine Science and Technology Conf.* (K.G. Bartel et al., eds.), Project Synopses, Vol.2:585-589, European Commission, DG XII/D-03, Brussels.

Boivin, M., O. Simonin & K.D. Squires (1998). "Direct numerical simulation of turbulence modulation by particles in isotropic turbulence". *J. Fluid Mechanics*, 375:235-263.

Cellino, M. & W.H. Graf (1999). "Sediment-laden flow in open-channels under noncapacity and capacity conditions", *J. Hydraulic Engineering*, 125(5):455-462.

Ellison, T.H. (1957). "Turbulent transport of heat and momentum from an infinite rough plane". *J. Fluid Mechanics*, 2:456-466.

Ellison, T.H. & J.S. Turner (1960). "Mixing of dense fluid in a turbulent pipe flow", *J. Fluid Mechanics*, 8:514-544.

Gust, G. (1976). "Observations on turbulent drag reduction in a dilute suspension of clay in seawater", *J. Fluid Mechanics*, 75(1):29-47.

Li, M.Z. & G. Gust (2000). "Boundary layer dynamics and drag reduction in flows of high cohesive sediment suspensions". *Sedimentology*, 47:71-86.

Munk, W.H. & E.A. Anderson (1948). "Notes on a theory of the thermocline", *J. Marine Research*, 3(1):276-295.

Nezu, I. & H. Nakagawa (1993). "*Turbulence in open-channel flow*", IAHR Monograph Series. Balkema, Rotterdam.

Odd, N.V.M. & J.G. Rodger (1978). "Vertical mixing in stratified tidal flows", *ASCE J. Hydraulics Div.*, 104(3):337-351.

Rodi, W. (1980). "*Turbulence models and their application in hydraulics*", IAHR, Delft.

Toorman, E.A. (1999). "Numerical simulation of turbulence damping in sediment-laden flow. Part 1. The Siltman testcase and the concept of saturation", Report HYD/ET99.2, Hydraulics Laboratory, Katholieke Universiteit Leuven.

Toorman, E.A. (2000). "Parameterisation of turbulence damping in sediment-laden flows", Report HYD/ET00.1, Hydraulics Laboratory, Katholieke Universiteit Leuven.

Turner, J.S. (1973). "*Buoyancy effects in fluids*", Cambridge University Press.

Wolanski, E., J. Chappell, P. Ridd & R. Vertessy (1988). "Fluidization of mud in estuaries", *J. Geophysical Research*, Vol.93(C3):2351-2361.

Acknowledgements: The author holds the position of Post-doctoral Researcher, funded by the Fund for Scientific Research Flanders. This work has been carried out within the framework of the MAST3 project COSINUS, funded in part by the European Commission, Directorate General XII for Science, Research & Development under contract no. MAS3-CT97-0082.

Flow structures and mixing processes in highly stratified rivers

Shizuo Yoshida[1], Shuzo Nishida[2], Keisuke Yokoo,
[1]Division of Mechanical Science, Hokkaido University, N13 W8, 060-8628, Sapporo, Japan
[2]Division of Civil Engineering, Osaka University, 565-0871, Yamadaoka, Suita, Osaka, Japan
[3]Fukuda Hydrologic Center Corp., 001-0024, N24W15, Sapporo, Japan
yoshidas@eng.hokudai.ac.jp, nishida@civil.eng.osaka-u.ac.jp, k-yokoo@f-suimon.co.jp

Abstract

A typical stratified flow is observed near the mouth of a river flowing into the sea, where the lighter fresh water temporarily forms a layer atop the heavier salt water. Studies of these flows consist of direct observations, model experiments and theoretical examinations of stratified flow mechanics. Stratified river flow forms many structures in response to flowrate, tide and other conditions. The first author has concentrated on the structures formed by and mixing processes in the highly stratified rivers characterized by extremely low mixing across the salt-fresh interface. The following results are based on 35 years of studies of Hokkaido rivers, particularly the Ishikari, which flows into the Japan Sea, where the tidal difference is about 0.3 m.

1. Introduction

Most of the reports on river mouth flows around the world describe partially mixed or well mixed flows as they occur in tidal estuaries or fjords. There have been relatively few publications on highly stratified flows in river estuaries such as are common among rivers emptying into the Japan Sea, where mixing is extremely weak. When the wind is calm, the halocline in Japan Sea river estuaries is no more than 20 cm thick. Dyer's(1973) definition of 'highly stratified flow' allowed haloclines over 1 meter in thickness. Flows with such thick haloclines would probably not be classed as two-layer flows today. This report describes flows in the 45-km long Ishikari River estuary, which has been observed by the first author of this report for many years, as well as in some other rivers in Hokkaido, in order to discuss some of the structures and mixing characteristics of highly stratified two layer flow

The studies of the salt wedge in Japan date from the first observations of this phenomenon in the Ishikari River published by Fukushima(1942). Many Japanese researchers took an interest in the salt wedge after that, focussing mainly on the shape of the salt wedge. As reported in 1998 by the present authors(1998), nearly all the elements affecting mixing in the Ishikari river estuary have been identified. All the data used for the studies were gathered by the first author, but since some duplicate data taken by the first observers, it may not be inappropriate to consider our results as based on a 60-year period of observations.

River currents are often seen in the littoral zone off the Ishikari mouth, but this report will focus on flow in the Ishikari Estuary.

2. Characteristics of Highly Stratified Flows at River Mouths

Highly stratified river flows are affected by flowrate, topography, tide, wind, waves, atmospheric pressure and other factors. River currents in the littoral zone are particularly susceptible to the wind, since they form shallow, spreading layers over the ocean surface. In the absence of wind, however, their spread pattern is a function of flowrate and channel width. When flowrate is low and the channel is wide, the spread pattern is semicircular; when flowrate is large, it becomes a jet. Yoshida(1995) showed that when the river channel makes a right angle to the shoreline, an empirical relation, $\alpha\beta^{0.147} = C$, predicts the spread pattern. Here $\alpha = \varepsilon g \sqrt{b_0 h_0} / U_0^2$, $\beta = \nu / U_0 \sqrt{b_0 h_0}$ are derived from dimensionless forms of averaged equations of motion for the upper and lower layers, b is the river width, h, upper or lower layer thickness, C, a constant, U the mean flow velocity, ν, the coefficient of dynamic viscosity, and ε, the difference of the upper layer and lower layer densities divided by the upper layer density. Subscripts 0, 1 and 2 mean the river mouth, the upper layer and lower layer, respectively. By the way, jet flow is observed under the condition C <0.67. Also, an approximate relation between the river flowrate and spread distance" under low wind- or wave-driven mixing has been established. For example, if the distance to the "flow center", where 50% of the ebb current consists of river water, and 50%, of sea water, is written as D in km, the spread of the flow can be expressed as $D_{max} > 0.024Q^{0.70}$. Here D varies with time and D_{max} is its maximum value. The minimum value of D_{max} is an empirical value observed in highly stratified flow. No values have been established for other flow conditions yet. Kashiwamura and Yoshida(1972) showed that as the flowrate increases, there is a zone of the river current in the littoral zone where the densimetric Froude number with upper layer parameters increases to a value greater than 1.

3. Characteristics of Highly Stratified Flows in River Channels

As described above, many phenomena have been observed in stratified flows in oceans. The most important phenomena in stratified density flows in channel are changes in the shape of the interface, the processes of diffusion of salt across the interface, and shear instabilities at the interface.

3.1 Factors in Variations of the Interface Shape

3.1.1 Flowrate

Estuarine stratified flow assumes a variety of forms as a function of river flowrate, topography and tidal range. When the flowrate is high and F_{1i} exceeds 1 at all locations in the channel, salt water is unable to enter or remain in the channel. Here F_{1i} corresponds to the square root of α in which $b_0 h_{10}$ and U_0 are replaced by $h_1{}^2$ and U_1, respectively. Thus, $F_{1i} < 1$ is always satisfied when we can see salt wedge in the channel. The relation between flowrate and the length of the invading salt wedge is shown in Figure 1. The data for the Ishikari River are scattered upstream of a location about 8 km upriver from the mouth; this occurs because there is a 'bottleneck' in the river bottom. The 'bottleneck' prevents salt invasion when the flowrate is above a certain level.

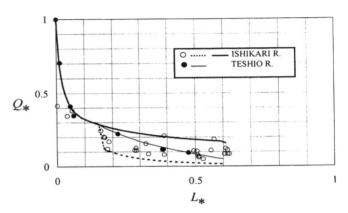

Figure 1 Relationship between river flowrate and salt wedge length. Q_*: River flowrate divided by Q_c, rate of outflow of salt water at river mouth. L_*: Salt wedge length divided by distance L_* from river mouth to location where deepest riverbed elevation is zero.

3.1.2 Topography

As attested to by the reference in the previous section to the 'bottlenecked' portion of the Ishikari River bottom which prevents smooth upstream flow of the tidal wave, variations in the river bottom topography due to sand or other materials change key boundary conditions for estuarine flows. For example, if the channel depth at slack water is sufficiently greater than the tidal range, such as in the Ishikari and Teshio Rivers, the salt water begins to enter the estuary at flood, and the effect of the depth itself on the flow structure is minimal. On the other hand, some Hokkaido rivers emptying into the Pacific Ocean and the Okhotsk Sea (Chiribetsu, Abira, Sarufutsu) include substantial sections whose elevations are above sea level at low water. These rivers see no salt invasion until well after slack water. When invasion occurs, the gradient of the interface is high and invasion proceeds quickly. The vortices caused by river bottom roughness mix river water into the salt wedge, and the density distribution in the vertical direction is not uniform. This structure can no longer be called two-layer; it approaches the partially mixed condition. As the salt wedge is expelled from the estuary during ebb, the invasion length generally remains low.

3.1.3 Tide

When the tidal range is low, the fluctuations in the river surface and interface elevations occur at a period equal to the tidal period, and there appear two modes of waves with distinct phase velocities: a surface wave mode and an interfacial gravity wave mode. However, when the salt wedge is extremely long, the interfacial gravity waves are severely attenuated as they move upstream. Each of these modes causes its own mode in flow speed and a periodic change in the surface salinity. More details on the latter phenomenon will be provided in a later report, but it does not have much influence on flows under a low tidal range.

It is useful to characterize highly stratified flows at a river mouth with the time-averaged densimetric Froude number at the tip of the salt wedge, $F_{1/m}$ and the dimensionless variable K. K is obtained by dividing the actual cross-section average tidal flow speed at the mouth with the cross-section average flow speed at the mouth calculated using the flowrate observed at an upstream point which is unaffected by the tide. Flows can be ranked into 6 classes on the basis of the two criteria, as shown in Figure 2. The Hansen-Latley method is also useful for classifying flows, but the present method is more accurate for characterization of irregular flows.

3.2 Observations of Interface Fluctuations and Salt Diffusion

As an actual example of a highly stratified flow structure, Figure 3 shows several time series observed in the Ishikari River in July and August, 1997: Atmospheric pressure, deviation in sea level due to atmospheric pressure, river surface elevations and interface elevations at several data collection platforms (DCP), salinity 1 m below the river surface, wind speed and wind direction. Salt wedge conditions can be compared with flowrate and tide while considering simultaneous wind and surface salinity conditions.

Figure 4 shows fluctuations by the interface. They

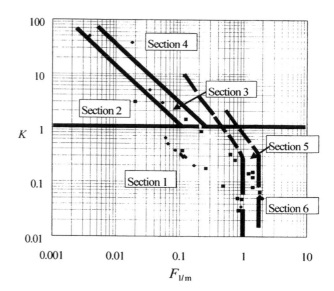

Figure 2   Classification of Two-layer flows. Plotted points are measured data. Thick lines denote boundaries between classifications. Section 1: Non-reversing current; perfectly stratified flow observed at all times. Section 2: River reverses current for some time during flood; upper layer front appears in river water. Section 3: Partially mixed flow. Section 4: Well mixed flow. Section 5: Position of tip of time mean salt wedge is just at river mouth. Section 6: Sea water does not intrude into river channel at any phase of tide.

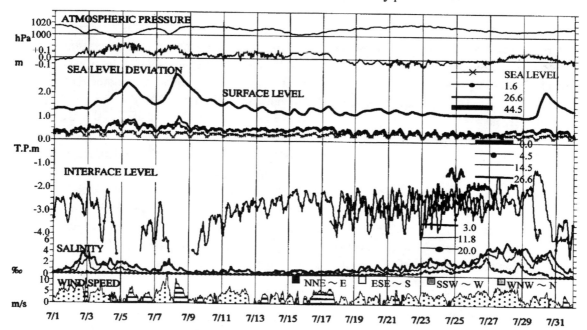

Figure 3 Results of observations taken by hand on Ishikari River in 1997: Time series of surface level, interface level, surface salinity, and wind speed and direction. Numerals in figure are distances (km) upstream from river mouth.

propagate according to interfacial wave motion. The phases of the interface elevations observed at each DCP have been adjusted by the time lags noted in the figure caption to show how closely they fit each other. These data show that: (i) the amplitude of interfacial fluctuation is several times as large as the tidal difference; (ii) the amplitude reaches a maximum several kilometers inland from the river mouth; (iii) the fluctuation leads tide in the downstream portion of the estuary, and lags in the upstream portion; and (iv) fluctuation is almost undetectable near the tip of the salt wedge.

The solid line in Figure 5 connects the average measured amplitudes of interface fluctuation at positions 0.1, 3.0, 4.5, 8.0, 14.5, 20.0 and 26.6 km upstream of the river mouth. The dashed line is the result of calculations; this will be discussed below. Values on the solid line were observed in two surveys, when the flowrate was 120 m^3/sec and 164 m^3/sec.

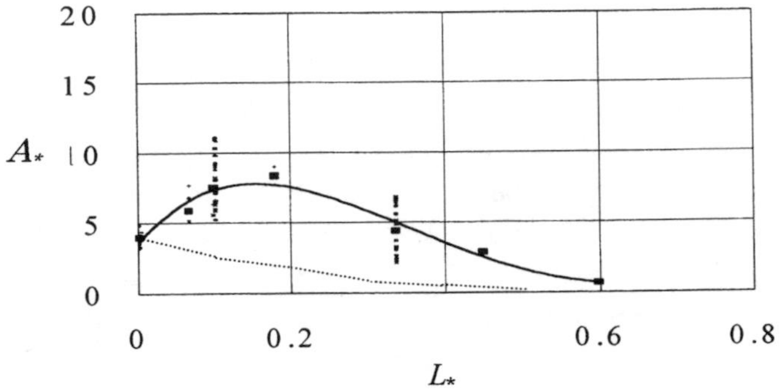

When the tide transitions from semidiurnal to diurnal, the interface shows an "overshoot" downward, as though the slack water which would ordinarily have appeared, actually had appeared.

It is also visible in Figure 3 that, in the vicinity of

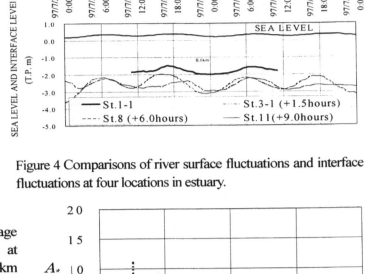

Figure 4 Comparisons of river surface fluctuations and interface fluctuations at four locations in estuary.

Figure 5 Longitudinal distribution of interface fluctuation amplitude. A: Interface fluctuation amplitude divided by tidal range.

the river mouth, surface salinity is 180° out of phase with tide, peaking around slack water and troughing around high water. A relation between surface salinity and wind speed has been found, but this is not clear from a examination of Figure 3 alone; just because salt entrained through wind action into the river layer remains there, it does not necessarily mean that high winds always raise surface salinity. Yoshida et al.(1998) showed that the entrainment coefficient can be expressed as a function of the wind speed when it is blowing in the direction of the river course, and that using that entrainment coefficient, a time history of wind speed over several hours and the average speed of the river current, it is possible to predict the surface salinity at any given time and location along the estuary.

The mechanisms of entrainment have yet to be explained, however. Presently, the authors are observing interfacial waves, which are created by wind action and driven by changes in surface waves and river current speed. Only the following observations have been confirmed under the condition that the river layer is about 3 m thick: (i) wind speed is below 2 m/sec, interfacial waves do not arise; (ii) when wind speed is 6.5 m/sec, interfacial waves with a period of about 30 sec and a height of 50 cm arise; (iii) when wind speed exceeds 7 m/sec, the interfacial waves begin to break. Past surveys of the Teshio and Tokoro rivers have found interfacial waves with periods of 20 – 30 sec in river layers 1.5 – 2 m in thickness. It seems likely that periods of 20 – 30 sec are common for interfacial waves. Interfacial waves with 100 – 110 sec periods and heights of 20 – 50 cm were also observed in the Teshio and Tokoro rivers. Future research themes will include whether these interfacial waves are observed throughout the interface, and the mixing effect of the Langmuir vortices arising above wind speeds of 7 m/sec.

3.3 Shear Flow Instabilities in Highly Stratified Flow at River Mouths

At most points in a highly stratified estuary, when there is no wind or underwater topological features or structures to disturb river or tidal currents, there are no shear flow instabilities to cause interfacial waves. At the mouth, however, shear is quite high, so the Richardson number is small; thus, shear flow instabilities do give rise to interfacial waves there. For example, the "one-sided overturn" predicted by Lawrence et al.(1991) has been observed at slack water, and Kelvin-Helmholz overturn has been observed at high water. It was found from observations of the Ishikari in 1999 that the critical Richardson number for occurrence of flow instabilities near the interface was 0.33. The ϵ relative water depth between the shear center and the interface (see Lawrence et al.(1991) was 0.02. The authors have also made the first observations of another one-sided overturn mode just below the interface, but the dynamic analysis of this is not yet complete.

4 Numerical Analysis of the Shape of the Interface

It is not always necessary to carry out three-dimensional analysis of highly stratified river flow, as the horizontal and vertical distributions of salinity in both the river and sea water layers are quite uniform when mixing is low. To keep the problem as simple as possible, the governing equations have been written to allow changes in the channel cross-sectional area, but river flow is assumed only to proceed toward the mouth. The x axis points in the direction of flow. The cross-section average flow speeds of the river layer and salt water layer are written U_1 and U_2, and their depths are h_1 and h_2, respectively. $B(x)$ is the channel width and $z(x)$ is the river bottom elevation. Thus, the continuity and motion equations take a quasi-one-dimensional form:

$$B\frac{\partial h_1}{\partial t} + \frac{\partial}{\partial x}(BU_1 h_1) = 0 \quad (1), \qquad\qquad B\frac{\partial h_2}{\partial t} + \frac{\partial}{\partial x}(BU_2 h_2) = 0 \quad (2),$$

$$\frac{1}{g}\frac{\partial U_1}{\partial t} + \frac{U_1}{g}\frac{\partial U_1}{\partial x} = -\frac{\partial z}{\partial x} - \frac{\partial h_1}{\partial x} - \frac{\partial h_2}{\partial x} - \frac{f_i}{2gh_1}(U_1 - U_2)|U_1 - U_2| \quad (3),$$

$$\frac{1}{g}\frac{\partial U_2}{\partial t} + \frac{U_2}{g}\frac{\partial U_2}{\partial x} = -\frac{\partial z}{\partial x} - (1-\varepsilon)\frac{\partial h_1}{\partial x} - \frac{\partial h_2}{\partial x} + \frac{f_i}{2gh_2}(U_1 - U_2)|U_1 - U_2| - \frac{f_b}{2gh_2}U_2|U_2| \quad (4).$$

Here, g is the gravitational constant and f_b is the coefficient of friction of the river bottom. Using Manning's roughness constant, n can be rewritten as $f_b = 2gn^2/h_2^{1/3}$. In the present analysis, n has been set at 0.035. ε was defined in part 2; in the Ishikari River, this takes values between 0.024 and 0.027. f_i is the coefficient of friction of the interface; here we will use the empirical expression $f_i = 0.25(R_1 F_1^2)^{-0.5}$ which has been used successfully in Japanese rivers. In this equation, $R_1 = U_1 h_1/\nu$ and $F_1 = \sqrt{U_1^2/\varepsilon g h_1}$ are the Reynolds and densimetric Froude numbers of the river layer. As boundary conditions, the river flowrate at the tip of the salt wedge (upstream flowrate) is assumed constant, and at the river mouth, the water surface is assumed to follow the level of the tide. The elevation of the interface at the river mouth is assumed to obey the following:

$$F_1^2 + F_2^2 - \varepsilon F_1^2 F_2^2 = 1. \quad (5)$$

Here, F_2 is the densimetric Froude number of the salt water layer.

The above expressions were differentiated and the river mouth levels in the period 11:00, 24 July – 11:00, 25 July, in the range of Figure 3, were used to generate the predicted salt wedge shape shown in Figure 6. The above period had semidiurnal tides; upstream flowrate was 120 m³/sec. Figure 7 shows the time series of the same calculations from the viewpoint of a fixed location on the riverbank. Several quantitative results in these figures match well with observations of actual flows: (a) There is almost no damping in the amplitude of fluctuation of the river water surface above the salt wedge, and the

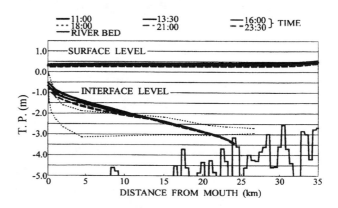

Figure 6 Unsteady solutions for surface and interface. Solid line: Calculated solution. Dashed lines: Extremes of observed data.

955

levels at all locations rise and fall nearly in parallel; (b) the amplitude of interface fluctuations decreases as the observer moves upstream; (c) interface fluctuations lead tidal fluctuations in phase at locations between the river mouth and 5 km inland; and (d) interface fluctuations lag tidal fluctuations in phase at locations between 5 km inland from the river mouth and 15 km inland. Clearly, the interfacial fluctuation is occurring as a wave propagating at the velocity of an interfacial wave.

There is not enough room to show it here, but the overshoot mentioned in section 3.2 was also reproduced by the numerical model.

The model differed significantly from the actual estuary on the following points: (a) It overestimated the elevation of the interface during ebb at locations between 2 and 10 km upstream of the mouth. Comparing with the two dashed lines in Figure 6 representing the upper and lower extremes of measured salt wedge elevations, the model result was quite close to the upper extreme. (b) The results of longitudinal surveys of the interface fluctuation during diurnal tides are shown by dashed lines in Figure 5. The model reproduces the quadrupling of tidal range near the mouth and attenuation with distance up the river described earlier, but between the mouth and the salt wedge tip, the predictions of interface fluctuation range diverge from the results of observations. The maximum in fluctuation range seen at 6 km is not even quantitatively predicted.

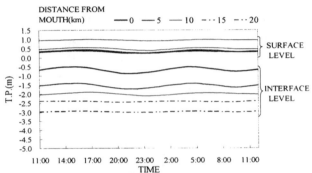

One reason for these shortfalls may be inaccuracy of the empirical value for the interfacial friction coefficient. Future research should attempt to refine this parameter.

Conclusions

1..Flow structures can be qualitatively classified using the time-averaged densimetric Froude number at the tip of the salt wedge and the dimensionless variable K.

2. When the elevation of the river bottom is greater than that of sea level at low tide, the condition for salt invasion at the river mouth can be represented by F_{1i} <1.

Figure 7 Predicted interface fluctuation amplitudes along estuary.

3. Generally, the amplitude of the elevation fluctuation by the interface which is in phase with the tide is several times the tidal difference.

4. When the upper layer in highly stratified flow at a river mouth is about 3 m thick and the wind is blowing at about 6.5 m/sec in the direction of the river, there occur interfacial waves of about 50 cm amplitude and 30 sec period. If the wind speed increases above 7 m/sec, the interfacial waves begin to break.

5. The critical Richardson number for occurrence of flow instabilities near the interface at the mouth of the Ishikari River is 0.33.

Acknowledgments

This research project was financed by a Grant-in-aid for Scientific Research (B) (2) from the Ministry of Education, Science and Culture, Japan, under Grant No.04452231 (1992 – 1995). The authors express their appreciation to the Ministry.

References

1) Dyer, K. R.: Estuaries. A Physical Introduction, John Wiley & Sons, 1973

2) Fukushima, H.: J. Oceanographical Society of Japan, 1(1), 57-73, 1942

3) Yoshida, S.: Research project report of a grant-in aid for Scientific Research (B), the Ministry of Education, Science and Culture, Japan, under Grant No.04452231 (1992 – 1995), 1995

4) Kashiwamura, M. and S. Yoshida: Proceedings of ISF, Novosibirsk, 14, 1-6, 1972

5) Yoshida, S., M. Ohtani, S. Nishida and P. F. Linden: Coastal and Estuarine Studies, 54, 389-400, 1998

6) Lawrence, G. A., F. K. Browand and L.G. Redekopp,: Phys. Fluids, A 3, 2360-2370, 1991

12

COASTAL FLOWS

Using circulation over a coastal submarine canyon to compare numerical and physical modelling.

S. E. Allen[1], M.S. Dinniman [2], J.M. Klinck [2], B.M. Hickey [3], D.D. Gorby [1], A.J. Hewett [1] & J. She [2]

[1] Department of Earth and Ocean Sciences, University of British Columbia, Vancouver, Canada.
[2] Center for Coastal Physical Oceanography, Old Dominion University, Norfolk, USA.
[3] School of Oceanography, University of Washington, Seattle, USA.
allen@ocgy.ubc.ca, msd@ccpo.odu.edu, klinck@ccpo.odu.edu, bhickey@u.washington.edu

1. Abstract

Coastal submarine canyons which cut the continental shelf are frequently regions of steep (up to 45°), three-dimensional topography. Recent observations have delineated the flow over several submarine canyons during 2-4 day long upwelling episodes. The flow has very small (order half the canyon width, say 3 km) horizontal scales and very small (order 100 m) vertical scales. The dynamics are dependent on pressure gradient, Coriolis, and advection terms. Thus upwelling episodes over submarine canyons provide an excellent flow regime for evaluating numerical and physical models of stratified flow over steep topography.

Here we compare a physical and numerical model simulation of an upwelling event over a simplified submarine canyon with the goal of assessing the models limitations. The physical model uses a 1-m horizontally rotating table with variable rotation speed. A 1-m cylindrical tank sits on the table. It has a continental shelf-slope topography against the outside wall. A steep v-shaped canyon cuts into the shelf. The numerical model is the S-coordinate Rutgers University Model 3.1 (SCRUM). The numerical model uses cylindrical coordinates, and viscosity and diffusion set to molecular values. The horizontal coordinate is stretched in the numerical model by a factor of 10 to reduce the exaggerated slopes necessary in the physical model. All time-scales are adjusted so that Rossby, Froude, and Burger numbers match between the models. Careful matching between the models was necessary for a good comparison.

Results show good overall (particle trajectories within the expected error) agreement between the numerical and laboratory models. However there is a systematic difference between the numerical model (less cyclonic vorticity) and the laboratory model (more cyclonic vorticity). This difference cannot be attributed to non-hydrostatic effects in the laboratory and is shown to be due to grid-size errors in vertical advection.

2. Introduction

Both laboratory and numerical models have been used to study processes in coastal ocean circulation. Recent studies have compared test simulations from different numerical models with the disquieting result that the solutions differ not only quantitatively but, in some cases, qualitatively [Haidvogel and Beckmann, 1998]. Given the wide variety of processes and parameterizations in these models, the causes(s) of these differences have not been identified.

The traditional method for verifying numerical models is to compare to an analytical solution. However, only a limited number of analytic solutions exist for stratified flow over steep topography. An alternative evaluation method is to compare results from different models. However disagreements between the models frequently tend to raise questions instead of answering them. We chose to compare results from numerical simulations to those from a physical (laboratory) model of a stratified fluid flowing over a submarine canyon on a continental shelf. This problem activates a number of physical processes (discussed below) making it a good test case [*Haidvogel and Beckmann*, 1998].

Overview of Circulation Over Coastal Canyons

Submarine canyons are common features of the continental shelf. A typical canyon cuts from the continental-slope into the continental shelf about half-way to the coast. Submarine canyons are regions of enhanced upwelling during upwelling favourable conditions. The problem used to compare the two models is a short duration upwelling event. Previous numerical studies have shown good qualitative agreement with the observations [*Klinck* 1996, *Allen*, 1996,]. After acceleration of the shelf-break current (in the field due to the wind or shelf waves) a flow pattern forms over the canyon with the following characteristics: 1) the near surface current is not affected or is only weakly affected by the canyon and travels straight over the canyon; 2) flow just above the canyon rim moves over the canyon, descends into the canyon, turns towards the canyon head and crosses the downstream canyon rim near the head; 3) slightly deeper flow over the continental shelf bends into the canyon near the mouth, traverses up the canyon and crosses the downstream canyon rim near the head; and in 4) deep flow within the canyon turns cyclonically. Observations [*Hickey*, 1997, *Vindeirinho*, 1998] show a trapped eddy over the canyon (level 2 above).

3. Model Details

Laboratory scale Model

The laboratory experiments were performed on a 1-m diameter, rotating table at the University of British Columbia. The outside tank is a cylindrical Plexiglas tank of radius 50 cm. It was fitted with a Plexiglas insert to give a generic coastal bathymetry consisting of a flat abyssal plane, a steep continental slope (slope 45° in laboratory) and a continental shelf (slope 5° in laboratory). The continental shelf and slope were fitted to the outside of the tank with the abyssal plane in the center. A 22° slice was cut out of the generic bathymetry to allow insertion of a canyon shape (Figure 1a).

The table was first accelerated to its starting rotation speed ($f = 0.4$ s^{-1}). Then the tank was filled by gravity feed using the Osler method of stratification. Due to the geometry of the shelf-slope topography, the stratification is stronger near the top. The table was allowed to rotate until the fluid reached solid-body rotation and was stationary with respect to the tank.

The flow was forced by accelerating the table from $f = 0.4$ s^{-1} to $f = 0.52$ s^{-1} linearly over 27.3 s. This period is about one revolution of the tank and is comparable to a wind event of one day in the real world. This forcing results in flow at the shelf-break of about 1.2 cm s^{-1}. The flow in the vicinity of the canyon was visualized using neutrally buoyant particles (pliolite) which were added upstream of the canyon during the acceleration phase of the experiment. The tank was lit by two horizontal sheets of light: green light illuminated depths of 1.2 to 2.2 cm and red light illuminated depths of 2.2 to 3.2 cm. A video camera mounted above the tank recorded the movement of the particles.

The flow was analyzed for a 5 s interval, 2.7 s after the acceleration of the tank was complete. Using frame capture software, frames from the video were captured onto computer at 0.5 s intervals. Composite photos of all the frames were generated and digitized versions of these composite figures are used for model comparison.

Numerical Model Configuration

The S-Coordinate Rutgers University Model Version 3.1 [SCRUM, *Hedström*, 1997] developed by D. Haidvogel and coworkers at Rutgers University was used for the numerical modeling part of this study. SCRUM is a hydrostatic primitive equation ocean circulation model with a free surface using a vertical s (terrain-following) coordinate well suited for use in simulations with variable bathymetry. The model also allows for a curvilinear horizontal coordinate system which enabled us to represent a cylindrical model geometry.

The large slopes of the tank canyon were too steep for the model to accurately compute horizontal pressure gradients. Therefore, the length scale was increased to ten times that of the tank. To use the same bathymetry, stratification and flow velocity as the tank, the Coriolis parameter was reduced (from 0.52 s^{-1} to 0.052 s^{-1}) and the vertical viscosity was reduced (from the molecular value of 10^{-6} m^2 s^{-1} to 10^{-7} m^2 s^{-1}) by a factor of 10 in order to maintain the same Rossby, Burger and Ekman numbers. The duration of the forcing was increased by a factor of 10 so that the model, like the tank, was accelerated over approximately one pendulum day.

The model domain included 242 points in the azimuthal direction, 81 points in the radial, and 16 vertical levels. The grid spacing in the vicinity of the canyon was about 6.2 cm. The domain did not cover the entire 2π radians in the azimuthal direction, but rather $0.6 \times 2\pi$ (in order to save computation time) with a periodic continuation in that direction. The duration of the simulations were much less than the time required for disturbances to wrap around the domain. In the radial direction, the model domain was based on a tank with an inner wall 1 m from the center, an outer wall 5 m from the center (10 x the actual tank dimensions) and a no-slip condition for momentum at both lateral walls. The grided model bathymetry was derived from digitized tank depth contours using an objective analysis scheme.

At the start of the simulation the flow was zero and the free surface was level. The water was forced to move relative to the canyon by a body force over the entire water column. The forcing was zero at the start, increased to a maximum value over six seconds, held constant until 273 seconds and then set to zero. The forcing was in the angular direction only and increased linearly with radial distance in order to simulate the situation in the tank where the water is initially in rigid body rotation before the tank is accelerated with respect to the rotating water.

4. Results

To compare the numerical and laboratory results, tracer particles were placed in the numerical simulation at the time and position tracer particles were observed to start in the laboratory experiment (Figure 1b). In the laboratory, particle depths were determined, by colour, only to within 1 cm depth. This resolution proved inadequate because of the strength of the vertical shear. Therefore in the numerical simulation, particles were seeded throughout the 1 cm depth interval and the track that finished closest to the laboratory track was chosen for comparison.

As discussed in the introduction, flow in the canyon can be divided into three layers. Near-surface flow is not affected or only weakly affected by the canyon. Flow deep within the canyon turns cyclonically. Active upwelling onto the shelf occurs between these two layers. The upwelling layer includes water from both the shelf and slope which turns cyclonically in the vicinity of the canyon, flows up the canyon and exits the canyon near the head.

The deep flow (below 2.5 cm) shows the expected trapped cyclonic eddy within the canyon. The exact position of the eddy appears to be different between the numerical and laboratory realizations: the eddy is narrower and longer in the lab, and shorter and wider in the numerical simulations. Also in the region of the mouth of the canyon, the laboratory flow appears to slow more than the numerical flow.

Agreement between the numerical simulation and the laboratory experiment is generally good in the actively upwelliing layer (1.55 cm to 2.2 cm depth) with one notable exception near the mouth of the canyon. The flow offshore of the shelf-break generally travels past the mouth of the canyon. At the downstream side of the canyon, the flow slows as it advects over the downstream

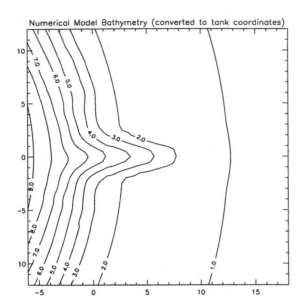

Numerical Model Bathymetry (converted to tank coordinates)

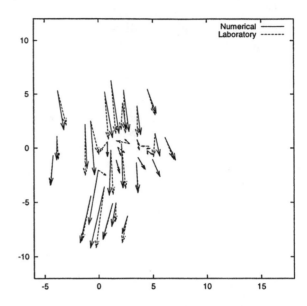

Figure 1: a) Bathymetry over the canyon region. b) Comparison of particle tracks from the laboratory model and the numerical model. Tracks at all depths are superimposed.

edge of the deep part of the canyon. In one case, the tank particle turns cyclonically as if it were within an extension of the deep cyclonic eddy, whereas the numerical particle does not. As seen in the deep tracks, the laboratory eddy is longer (extending further towards the mouth) than the numerical eddy. The flow above the canyon (between 1.8 and 2.0 cm depth) is greatly slowed over the canyon and is turned strongly up-canyon. Flow between 1.55 and 1.75 cm depth bends up-canyon upstream and over the canyon and bends back downstream of the canyon.

5. Discussion

Although the large majority of the tracks are within the expected experimental error (0.5 cm), the tracks show systematic differences between the models. Upstream of the canyon, the laboratory results show weak but definite offshore flow. This flow (observed in the field as well) is absent in the numerical model. Similarly, the numerical flow is more strongly offshore downstream of the canyon. Thus at rim level the laboratory model has stronger cyclonic vorticity over the canyon than does the numerical model.

The one possible source of "error" in the laboratory model is non-hydrostatic effects. The numerical model is hydrostatic and the ocean prototype is expected to be hydrostatic. The strong vertical exaggeration in the laboratory can cause non-hydrostatic effects. The strength of these effects can be evaluated from the governing equations. Scaling the equations to retain the largest terms we find that the largest non-hydrostatic term in the vertical momentum equation is $u\partial w/\partial x$ where u, w are the alongshore and vertical velocity, respectively and x is the alongshore coordinate. Using the geostrophic equations to estimate the vorticity, the non-hydrostatic term leads to a vorticity error of $\partial\zeta/\partial z = -\nabla^2(u\partial w/\partial x) \approx 1.5 \times 10^{-3}\text{cm}^{-1}\text{ s}^{-1}$ where ζ is the vorticity, z is the vertical coordinate and ∇^2 is the horizontal Laplacian. Integrating down from the surface this gives an anti-cyclonic error; that is non-hydrostatic effects reduce the vorticity in the laboratory not increase it. (The magnitude is about 2 orders two small to explain the observed error).

The vertical velocity over the canyon was not determined in the laboratory. The numerical vertical velocity looks suspect (Figure 2 a). First it is very strong and second has very small scale over both the upstream and downstream rim of the canyons. There is no physical reason for very

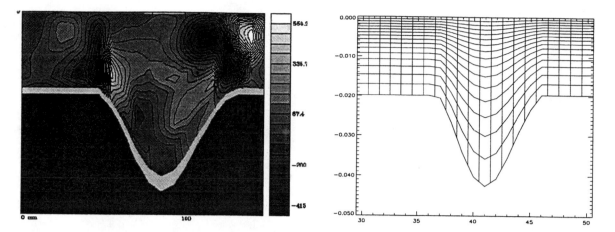

Figure 2: a) Vertical velocity from the numerical model. Units are cm/day. You are looking up the canyon. Positive velocities are up-canyon. b) The numerical grid for the same cross-section.

strong upwards velocities near the upstream rim of the canyon. The numerical vertical velocity is not a dynamic variable in an s-coordinate model (Figure 2 b). But the vertical velocity calculation is identical to the calculation used to advect the density in a stratified fluid. Thus, getting the vertical velocity correct is necessary to get the density field correct.

The error in the vertical velocity field is due to errors at the grid size in the calculation of the vertical velocity in a horizontal flow with vertical shear passing over sharp changes in grid-cell orientation. Consider the single grid-cell shown in Figure 3 and no variation and no flow in the up-canyon (y) direction. The velocity at the lower depth is taken as zero and the velocity at the upper depth is U where

$$U = -\frac{\partial u}{\partial z}\frac{\partial z}{\partial x}dx$$

and from the diagram $\partial z / \partial x = -\tan\bar{\alpha}$. The vertical sigma velocity $\omega = \Omega H_z$ where $\Omega = Ds/Dt$ and $H_z = dz/ds$. The value of ω at the top of the cell is found from

$$\omega = -\int \nabla \cdot (uH_z)ds \qquad (1)$$

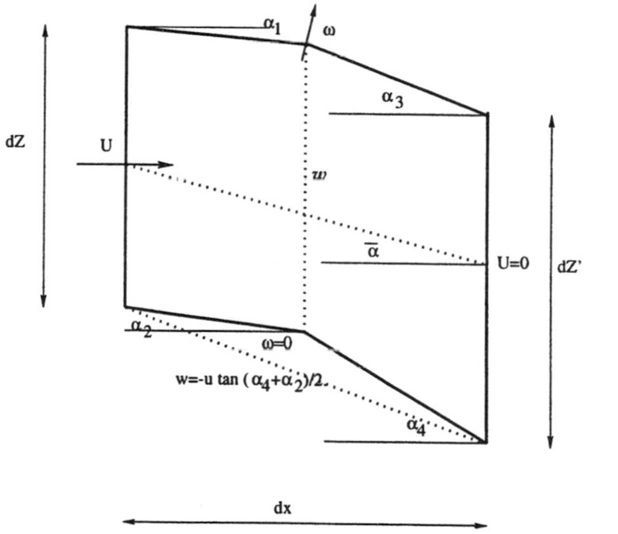

which using the expansion formula [Hedström, 1997] gives (assuming $v = 0$):

Figure 3: Sketch of a single grid cell with a sharp change in orientation.

$$\omega|_s = \omega|_{(s-ds)} + \frac{\left((udz)|_{(x+dx/2)} - (udz)|_{(x-dx/2)}\right)}{dx} = U\frac{dZ}{dx}$$

The vertical velocity is calculated at the centre point as

$$w = \frac{(\omega|_{(s+ds/2)} + \omega|_{(s-ds/2)})}{2} + \frac{\left((u\frac{\partial z}{\partial x})|_{(x+dx/2)} + (u\frac{\partial z}{\partial x})|_{(x-dx/2)}\right)}{2} = \frac{UdZ}{2dx} + \frac{U}{2}\frac{\partial z}{\partial x}\Big|_{(x-dx/2)} \qquad (2)$$

963

substituting for U gives an expression for w:

$$w = \frac{1}{2}\frac{\partial u}{\partial z}\tan\bar{\alpha}\,(dZ - dx\tan\alpha_\ell)$$

where $\alpha_\ell = 1/2(\alpha_1 + \alpha_2)$.

Now w at the bottom (here taken on the straight-line between the two u-grid points) is $u\tan\alpha_b$ where $\alpha_b = 1/2(\alpha_2 + \alpha_4)$ and as there is no horizontal change in u, w is constant with depth. So

$$w = \frac{1}{2}\frac{\partial u}{\partial z}(-dZ' + dx\tan\alpha_b)\tan\alpha_b$$

Taking the worst grid cell in the domain, at the upstream corner, the four angles can be found. The angles are: $\alpha_1 = 0.0094, \alpha_2 = 0.012, \alpha_3 = 0.086, \alpha_4 = 0.105$. With $\partial u/\partial z = 1.6$ s^{-1}, $dx = 6.2$ cm, and $dZ = 0.31$ cm: $w_{num} = 0.0103$cms^{-1}. The length $dZ' = dZ + dx/2(\tan(\alpha_2) + \tan(\alpha_4) - \tan(\alpha_1) - \tan(\alpha_3))$ is 0.373 cm. So $w_{real} = 0.0047$cms^{-1}. So we get a positive error of 480 cm/day. This positvie vertical velocity error at the upstream canyon edge gives a positive density anomaly and therefore positive (up-canyon) flow error upstream of the canyon. This is the sign of the observed error. Without any flow compensation, the estimated error is 10 times too large.

6. Conclusions

Sharp changes in topographic slopes lead to sharp changes in s-coordinate grid-box orientation. Coupled with vertically sheared flows such orientation changes can lead to large errors in the interpolated vertical velocity and thus in the vertical density advection.

Acknowledgements

This work was supported by a National Science and Engineering Research Council of Canada Strategic Grant and by National Science Foundation Grant numbers OCE 96-18239 and OCE 96-18186.

7. References

Allen, S. E.: 1996a, Topographically generated, subinertial flows within a finite length canyon, *J. Phys. Oceanogr.* **26**, 1608–1632.

Haidvogel, D. B. and Beckmann, A.: 1998, Numerical models of the coastal ocean, *in* K. H. Brink and A. R. Robinson (eds), *The Sea*, 10, John Wiley and Sons, chapter 17, pp. 457–482.

Hedström, K. S.: 1997, (draft) user's manual for an s-coordinate primitive equation ocean circulation model (scrum) version 3.0. *Institute of Marine and Coastal Sciences, Rutgers University Contribution #97-10*.

Hickey, B. M.: 1997, The response of a steep-sided narrow canyon to strong wind forcing, *J. Phys. Oceanogr.* **27**, 697–726.

Klinck, J. M.: 1996, Circulation near submarine canyons: A modeling study, *J. Geophys. Res.* **101**, 1211–1223.

Vindeirinho, C.: 1998, *Water properties, currents and zooplankton distribution over a submarine canyon under upwelling-favorable conditions*, Master's thesis, Univ. of B. C., Vancouver, B.C., Canada.

Frontal Instabilities and Coherent Structures in Large-Eddy Simulations of Coastal Upwelling

Anqing Cui and Robert L. Street

Environmental Fluid Mechanics Laboratory
Stanford University, Stanford, CA 94305-4020, USA
cui@stanford.edu, street@ce.stanford.edu

1. Abstract

We created a high-performance parallel code for three-dimensional, unsteady, incompressible flow governed by the Navier-Stokes equations and carried out large-eddy simulations of laboratory-scale realizations of coastal upwelling in an annular rotating tank with a sloping bottom. The upwelling process and the interfacial instabilities of the rotating and stratified fluid were studied in this work.

2. Introduction

Upwelling occurs mostly from spring to summer near the eastern boundary of oceans where prevailing winds carry the surface water away from the coast because of the Coriolis effect. Because upwelling brings cold and nutrient-rich deep water into the surface layer, it affects fishery productivity, ecology and climatology in the coastal regions. We were intended in conducting numerical simulation studies of the phenomena. Two relevant series of laboratory-scale experiments of shear-driven coastal upwelling were conducted by Narimousa and Maxworthy (hereafter referred to as NM) at the University of Southern California and by the Environmental Fluid Mechanics Laboratory (hereafter referred to as EFML) at Stanford University. On the other hand, a common difficulty with previous numerical studies of coastal upwelling flow is insufficient grid resolution. The advent of massively parallel processing provides the possibility to perform large-scale computations of turbulent flows for complex geometries. The objective of this study was to conduct large-eddy simulations on a distributed-memory massively-parallel computer to complement the experimental studies of NM and EFML in investigating the fundamental mechanisms of laboratory-scale coastal upwelling flow.

3. Governing equations and numerical method

The governing equations in the present study are the grid-filtered continuity, Navier-Stokes and scalar transport equations under the Boussinesq approximation:

$$\frac{\partial \overline{u}_j}{\partial x_j} = 0 \tag{1}$$

$$\frac{\partial \overline{u}_i}{\partial t} + \frac{\partial}{\partial x_j}\left[\overline{u}_i \overline{u}_j + \overline{p}\delta_{ij} - \nu \frac{\partial \overline{u}_i}{\partial x_j} + \tau_{ij} \right] = -g(\overline{\rho}_* - \rho_b)\delta_{i2} + f(-\overline{u}_3 \delta_{i1} + \overline{u}_1 \delta_{i3}) \tag{2}$$

$$\frac{\partial \overline{\rho}_*}{\partial t} + \frac{\partial}{\partial x_j}\left[\overline{u}_j \overline{\rho}_* - \kappa \frac{\partial \overline{T}}{\partial x_j} + \chi_j \right] = 0. \tag{3}$$

In the above equations, a variable with an over-bar indicates a grid-filtered quantity, t is the time, u_i ($i = 1,2,3$) are the Cartesian velocity components in the direction of (x_1, x_2, x_3), where x_1 and x_3 are the horizontal coordinates and x_2 is the upward vertical direction, $\overline{p}$ is the reduced dynamic pressure, which is obtained by subtracting the effects due to gravity and centrifugal force from the pressure, g is the gravitational constant, f is the Coriolis parameter, $\overline{\rho}_*$ is the relative density deviation from a reference state, ρ_b denotes the relative background density, ν and κ are, respectively, the kinematic viscosity and thermal diffusivity of the fluid, and τ_{ij} and χ_j represent, respectively, the subgrid-scale stress and the subgrid-scale sclar flux. The Einstein summation rule applies to all the terms of the above equations. The two subgrid-scale quantities (τ_{ij} and χ_j) are modeled using the dynamic mixed subgrid-scale model described in Zang *et al.* (1993). The dynamic mixed subgrid-scale model is able to calculate the model coefficient locally using the resolved quantities by filtering the governing equations at two different spatial scales.

The governing equations are transformed into a generalized coordinate system and discretized using a finite-volume formulation on a single non-staggered grid. The equations are discretized in time with a semi-implicit scheme with the Crank-Nicholson method for the diagonal viscous and diffusive terms and the Adams-Bashforth method for all the other terms. All the spatial derivatives are approximated with second-order central differences with the exception of the convective terms. The convective terms in the momentum equation are discretized using QUICK (Leonard 1979) and the convective term in the scalar transport equation is discretized using SHARP (Leonard 1988).

The fractional step, non-staggered solution technique of Zang *et al.* (1994) is used to advance the discretized equations in time. An estimate of the velocity field is obtained with a second-order accurate factorization by solving the momentum equation with the pressure term omitted. Continuity is then enforced by solving a pressure Poisson equation with a multi-grid method. Zang *et al.* (1994), Zang and Street (1995) and Yuan *et al.* (1999) showed the quantitative accuracy of the numerical schemes for laboratory scale simulations.

The numerical code was implemented on a distributed-memory, massively-parallel computer - the IBM SP2, using the message passing interface (MPI). The use of MPI enables good portability of the code among a broad class of parallel computers. A code performance of about forty MFLOPS per node was achieved, which was the reported peak rate in a recent retrospective study of codes run on NASA-Ames' IBM SP2 (Bergeron 1998). Details of the code implementation can be found in Cui (1999). This parallel code has been validated against a variety of laboratory-scale flows (Cui 1999), such as lid-driven cavity flow, rotating convective flow and flows induced by source-sink pairs in a rotating stratified fluid.

4. Simulation results

large-eddy simulations (LES) were carried out under exactly the same conditions as the experiments to simulate the laboratory-scale coastal upwelling flows. The simulations of NM's and EFML's experiments are denoted as Case NM and Case EFML, respectively. An extensive grid resolution study was conducted and led to the use of up to ten million grid points in each of the simulations. The grid study also shows that the Ekman layer is well resolved and the friction velocity $u^* = \sqrt{\tau_*/\rho}$ can be determined quite precisely in this study. Initially, a stably-stratified two-layer system with fluids of slightly different densities is brought to solid-body rotation inside an annular tank with a conical bottom. At time $t=0$s, the top disk is set to rotate clockwise relative to the system at disk rotation rate $\Delta\Omega$ after the two-layer fluid system is brought to counter-clockwise solid-body rotation at tank rotation rate Ω. A stress is thus applied to the top surface of the upper-layer of fluid by the differentially rotating disk, which is in analogy to the wind stress at the air-sea interface. The fluid below the top disk which moves with the disk is driven radially inward by the Coriolis force and forms the top Ekman layer. The resulting Ekman flux causes the density interface to rise near the outer wall and descend near the inner wall. Figure 1 shows that the density interface reaches the top disk and an axisymmetric surface front is formed at $t=40$s. The surface front migrates away from the outer wall after its formation and allows the lower-layer fluid to contact the top disk in a narrow strip of width λ around the outer edge of the tank, as shown in Figure 2. From Figure

2, which gives the density field from LES at $t=80$s, one can see that a thin layer of the mixed fluid, which is slightly heavier than the upper-layer fluid develops under the top disk. Zang and Street (1995) denoted this layer as the 'top inversion layer'. The side view of the density field at

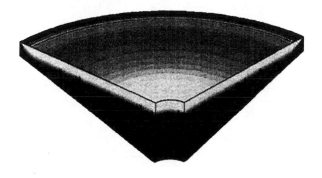

Figure 1: A section of the density field at $t=40$s (Case NM).

Figure 2: A section of the density field at $t=80$s (Case NM).

$t=100$s (Figure 3) shows that a Rayleigh-Taylor type of instability takes place in the top inversion layer due to the unstable stratification, the heavier mixed fluid in the top inversion layer begins to sink to the lower level and thus deepens the top inversion layer. In the process of the migration

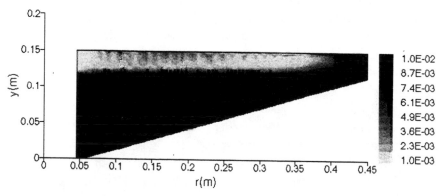

Figure 3: Side view of the density field at $t=100$s (Case NM).

of the surface front, the Coriolis force tends to increase the distance λ from the outer edge of the tank to the front, while the radial pressure gradient caused by the front deformation opposes the Coriolis force, and tends to stop the front. Eventually, geostrophic balance is reached and the front becomes stationary, so that λ reaches its steady-state value λ_s. Before the front becomes stationary, at some time when $\lambda < \lambda_s$, the front becomes unstable to small perturbations and small amplitude azimuthal frontal waves appear at the axisymmetric front. The developed instabilities are believed to be baroclinic instabilities (Narimousa *et al.* 1991). The potential energy contained in the density field is the source of kinetic energy for the baroclinic instabilities. At $t=80$s, such small amplitude frontal waves are already seen at the axisymmetric front (Figure 2). When the waves first appear at the front, they have their smallest wavelength. As time proceeds, neighboring waves combine to create waves of larger size. The process continues until the waves reach their maximum (saturated) size L_w. Figure 4 shows a nearly axisymmetric wave pattern at $t=100$s. The smaller frontal waves at $t=100$s grow into larger waves at $t=200$s (Figure 5). Due to the existence of the frontal wave drift velocity, the velocity vectors in this study are plotted in a reference frame traveling with the maximum drift velocity u_θ in order to reveal the vortex-like structure of the frontal waves. The

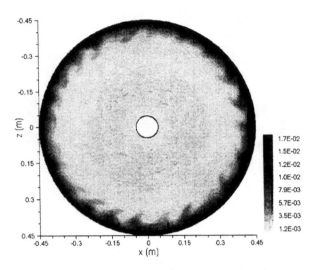

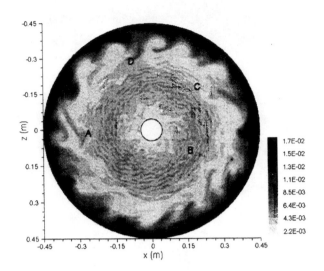

Figure 4: Top view of the density field at y/H=0.9 and t=100s (Case NM).

Figure 5: Top view of the density field at y/H=0.9 and t=200s (Case NM).

differences for λ_s, u_θ and L_w between the LES-computed and the experimentally-measured values are all under 18% of the LES values. A close look at the density and velocity fields around the four marked points (points A, B, C and D) on Figure 5 reveals the rich flow structures in the upwelling flow (Figure 6). Figure 6 shows that a cyclone is about to pinch off at location C. Meanwhile, a cyclone just pinches off at location D. At locations A and B (Figure 6), the pinched-off cyclone interacts with its neighboring frontal anticyclone and leads to generation of an outward meandering jet transferring a filament of heavier fluid towards the center of the tank. The corresponding vertical vorticity and velocity fields for the same four locations (Figure 7) show that a meandering, jet-like wave motion is produced around the outer edge of the upwelled front, with cyclones to the offshore side (at a wave trough) and anticycloclones to the inshore side (at a wave crest). In other words, the frontal waves appear in the form of cyclone/anticyclone pairs when the axisymmetric front becomes unstable. These wave troughs propagate in the direction of the applied surface stress and eventually detach from the wave troughs. The flow structures observed here closely resemble those observed in one of the NM's experiment (1987) with similar parameters.

The non-dimensional parameter $\theta_* = g'h_0/u_*f\lambda_s$, which was introduced by Narimousa and Maxworthy (1987), combines the effects of stratification, rotation and surface stress. Narimousa and Maxworthy (1985 and 1987) found in their experimental study that the upwelling flow field can be characterized by θ_*. NM (1987) reported that the frontal instabilities are much more intense and the upwelling front itself display strong unsteadiness and cyclonic eddies containing the lower-layer fluid pinches off from the front at low θ_* values ($\theta_* \leq 6$). At large values of θ_* ($\theta_* > 6$), the frontal waves are large, and they tend to remain at the front and consequently no pinch-off process is observed. The θ_* value for Case EFML (θ_*=5.8) is more than four times bigger than that of Case NM (θ_*=1.4), which is mainly due to the slow rotation of both the tank and the disk. Accordingly, flow field features different from those observed in Case NM are expected. Compared to Case NM (Figure 5), the frontal instabilities in Case EFML are less intense at the same non-dimensional time. Unlike in Case NM (θ_*=1.4), the frontal waves remain at the front and no pinch-offs are observed for Case EFML (θ_*=5.8). Likewise, no pinch-offs were found in the EFML physical experment either under the same conditions. This finding is also consistent with the observation of NM's experiments (1987).

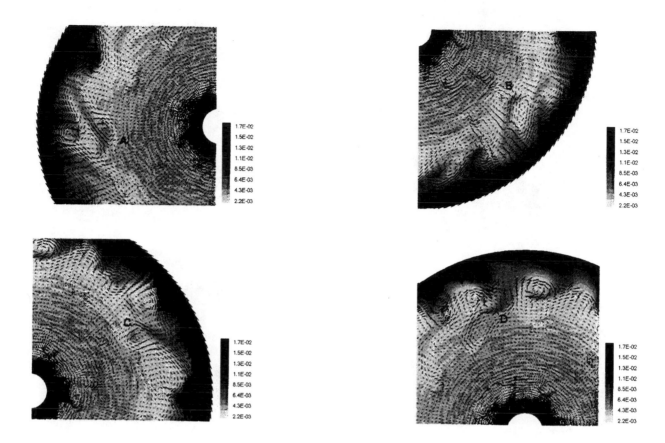

Figure 6: Expanded top view of the density and the velocity fields at four different locations at y/H=0.9 and t=200s (Case NM).

5. Conclusions

Large-eddy simulations of two different full tank configurations were carried out. The friction velocity can be determined quite precisely by the well-resolved simulations in this study. The three-dimensional LES results are able to reveal the complex upwelling structures in detail. The simulation results were compared with experimental data, both qualitatively and quantitatively, and good agreement was obtained.

6. Acknowledgment

The authors gratefully acknowledge the computing time on the IBM SP2 provided by NASA-Ames Research Center. The results have been analyzed in the Environmental Fluid Mechanics Laboratory at Stanford University. This work was supported by the National Science Foundation through Grant DMS-93181166 (program officer: Dr. M. Steuerwalt).

References

R. Bergeron. Measurement of a scientific workload using the IBM hardware performance monitor. In *The 10th High Performance Networking and Computing Conference*, Orlando, Florida, 1998.

A. Cui. *On the Parallel Compuation of Turbulent Rotating Stratified Flows*. PhD thesis, Department of Mechanical Engineering, Stanford University, 1999.

B.P. Leonard. A stable and accurate convective modeling procedure based on quadratic upstream

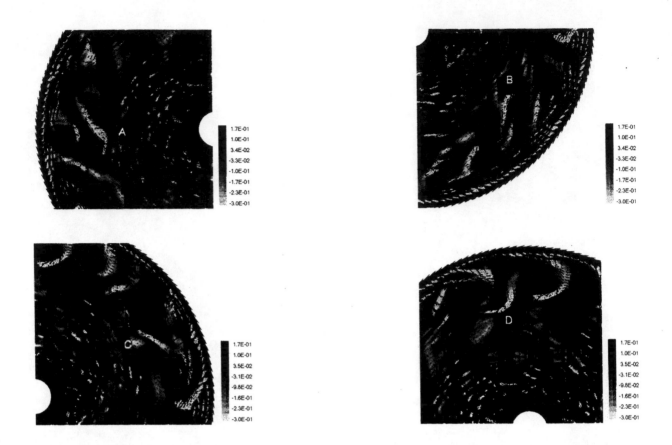

Figure 7: Expanded top view of the vertical vorticity and the velocity fields at four different locations at y/H=0.9 and t=200s (Case NM).

interpolation. *Computer Methods in Applied Mechanics and Engineering*, 19: 59–98, 1979.

B.P. Leonard. Third order multi-dimensional Euler/Navier-Stokes solver. *AIAA ASME SIAM APS First National Fluid Dynamics Congress*, pages 226–231, 1988.

S. Narimousa and T. Maxworthy. Two-layer model of shear-driven coastal upwelling in the presence of bottom topography. *Journal of Fluid Mechanics*, 159: 503–531, 1985.

S. Narimousa and T. Maxworthy. Coastal upwelling on a slopping bottom: the formation of plumes, jets and pinched-off cyclones. *Journal of Fluid Mechanics*, 176: 169–190, 1987.

L. L. Yuan, R. L. Street, and J. H. Ferziger. Large-eddy simulations of a round jet in crossflow. *Journal of Fluid Mechanics*, 379: 71–104, 1999.

Y. Zang, R. L. Street, and J. R. Koseff. A non-staggered grid, fractional step method for time-dependent incompressible Navier-Stokes equations in curvilinear coordinates. *Journal of Computational Physics*, 114(1): 18–33, 1994.

Y. Zang and R.L. Street. Numerical simulation of coastal upwelling and interfacial instability of a rotating and stratified fluid. *Journal of Fluid Mechanics*, 305: 47–75, 1995.

Y. Zang, R.L. Street, and J.R. Koseff. A dynamic mixed subgrid-scale model and its application to turbulent recirculating flows. *Physics of Fluids A*, 5(12): 3186–3196, 1993.

Nonhydrostatic and Quasi-Hydrostatic Simulations of a Coastal Buoyant Jet

Patrick C. Gallacher[1] and Steven A. Piacsek[2]

[1]Ocean Sciences Branch (NRL 7331), Oceanography Division, Naval Research Lab, Stennis Space Center, MS, 39529, (228) 688-5315, gallacher@nrlssc.navy.mil
[2]Ocean Prediction and Remote Sensing Branch (NRL 7322), Oceanography Division, Naval Research Lab, Stennis Space Center, MS, 39529, piacsek@nrlssc.navy.mil

1. Abstract

In the coastal ocean the combination of strong forcing and weak stratification generate flows for which the hydrostatic approximation is not valid. These phenomena tend to have aspect ratios of order one but they are not necessarily small scale. Examples include tidal boils, solitons, large amplitude internal waves, and buoyant coastal jests.

We conducted idealized experiments using quasi-hydrostatic and nonhydrostatic models to simulate the "lock exchange" problem in two dimensions. In this problem two fluids of different densities are separated by a barrier. When the barrier is removed two plumes form, flowing in opposing directions. The resulting plumes are similar in structure and dynamics to the buoyant plumes observed in the coastal ocean. The quasi-hydrostatic and nonhydrostatic simulations are qualitatively similar and agree with laboratory data.

2. Introduction

The coastal ocean is subjected to strong forcing. Tides and buoyant jets from rivers and bays can produce currents of several meters per second. Large amplitude internal waves, solitons, bores and intense fronts are generated by currents flowing over abrupt changes in topography. The contrast in temperature and roughness between the land and the ocean cause large heat fluxes, strong winds, and large wind stress curls. These, in turn, force strong convection, create fronts, large currents, areas of strong convergence and divergence. The dynamics and the kinematics of the coastal ocean are significantly more three dimensional than in the open ocean.

Much of the theory and models of the ocean are based on the largely two-dimensional, horizontal, structure of the large scale ocean. These models and assumptions are not necessarily adequate or appropriate for the coastal regime. We are examining the validity of the hydrostatic approximation in coastal regimes and looking at alternative formulations of the dynamics.

The models most commonly used in ocean modeling are hydrostatic. In the hydrostatic approximation all the terms in the vertical momentum equation are neglected except for the vertical pressure gradient and buoyancy terms. In oceanography this approximation is generally derived from the "long-wave" approximation that is a consequence of the, usually, small aspect ratio of the ocean. The aspect ratio is $\alpha = H/L$ where H is the depth and L is the horizontal length scale. For the wind-driven, large-scale ocean circulation, H is the Ekman depth and is O(100m) whereas the horizontal scale of the ocean gyres is O(100km). Thus $\alpha \approx 10^{-3}$ and the hydrostatic approximation is valid. In coastal regimes the depth is O(10-100m) and the lengthscale of the fronts and waves are O(10m – 1km) so α is O(1-0.1) and the hydrostatic approximation is much weaker.

Numerical solutions to the fully nonhydrostatic equations are expensive and time consuming. For an incompressible fluid a Poisson equation must be solved for the pressure. Solving a Poisson equation on an irregular grid with a free surface is very slow. For a compressible fluid a Poisson equation does not need to be calculated. This significantly reduces the number of calculations per time step. However, the timestep must be small enough to allow for sound waves. In the atmosphere the solution to the compressible equations can be sped up substantially by employing an artificial viscosity to slow the sound waves and by separating the terms governing the sound waves from the hydrodynamical terms. The sound wave terms are solved using the smaller timestep appropriate for the (reduced) speed of sound and the complete equations are solved only on the longer hydrodynamical timesteps. There are some limitations to these methods; however, they significantly speed up the calculations without seriously degrading the solution of the hydrodynamics (Klemp and Wilhelmson, 1978, Skamarock and Klemp, 1992, Hodur, 1997.). Attempts to use these methods in the ocean have not met with complete success (Mahadevean et al., 1996).

An approximation that is intermediate between the hydrostatic approximation and the fully nonhydrostatic equations was developed by Orlanski (1981). This "quasi-hydrostatic" approximation is derived from the equations of motion by expanding the equations in powers of the aspect ratio. When only the zeroth order terms are retained the resulting approximation is the hydrostatic equations. When the next order is included the result is the quasi-hydrostatic equations.

Numerically the quasi-hydrostatic approximation calculates a vertical acceleration as a correction to the hydrostatic basic state. The vertical hydrostatic velocity is calculated from the continuity equation. This is used to generate a correction to the vertical pressure gradient which modifies the horizontal momentum equations. Thus this is a perturbation about the hydrostatic solution.

3. Models

The nonhydrostatic model is a 2-D channel model with a free surface with no heat flux through the surface. The boundary conditions at the bottom of the channel are no slip for the horizontal velocity components and zero for the normal component. The temperature boundary condition is no flux. There are closed boundaries at the ends. The model uses fourth order finite difference methods in space and Adams-Bashforth in time. The eddy diffusivity is split into a horizontal and vertical component. Each component has a constant background value and a part that varies to maintain horizontal and vertical grid cell Reynolds numbers of 10. The Poisson equation for the pressure is solved using SOR.

For this study we used a new version of the DieCast ocean model (Dietrich, 1997, Dietrich and Lin, 1999). This is a three dimensional model but for these experiments we use it as a 2-D channel model. The DieCast model employs a modified Arakawa A-grid in the horizontal plane and z levels in the vertical plane and it has a rigid lid. The finite difference scheme is fourth-order accurate. Time integration is accomplished with a modified leap frog scheme. The vertical acceleration is calculated in a manner similar to that of Orlanski (1981) except that the advective and diffusive terms in the vertical momentum equation are also included. Thus the vertical acceleration is computed from the continuity equation and the buoyancy. Advection and diffusion are then calculated and the pressure is estimated from the vertical integration of the vertical acceleration. The pressure is then used correct the horizontal and vertical velocities.

4. Experiments and Results

The numerical experiments simulate the lock exchange problem. In this problem two water masses of different density are separated by a barrier. When the barrier is removed two plumes form and spread in opposite directions (Turner, J. S., 1973). The low density plume propagates over the top of the denser fluid and a high density plume propagates under the lighter fluid. The mean velocity of the plumes can be approximated from hydraulic theory, using Bernoulli's equation combined with the continuity equation and the fact that the total pressure force plus the momentum flux per unit span is constant. However, to understand the details of the plume structure and evolution requires a more complete set of equations. To this end we compare the results obtained using quasi-hydrostatic and nonhydrostatic models to simulate

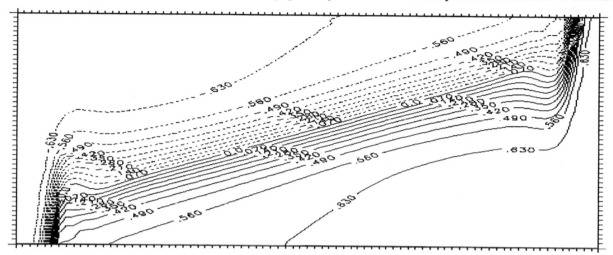

Figure 1. The center 80 m of the 2-D channel for the nonhydrostatic simulation. 40 minutes after the lock was removed. The two plumes have formed and the rotors at the front of the plumes is starting to develop. The contours in this figure are in psu (see text).

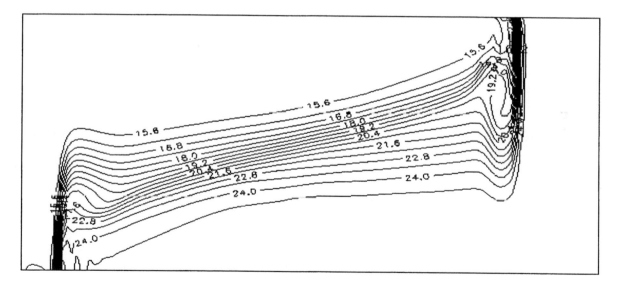

Figure 2. This is the quasi-hydrostatic simulation after 40 minutes. The results are qualitatively similar to the nonhydrostatic simulation. The contours in this figure are temperature in degrees Celsius (see text)

the evolution of the plumes.

For these experiments we simulated a two dimensional channel 20 kilometer long and 50 meters deep with closed ends. The numerical domain contained 2000 points in the horizontal and 51 points in the vertical. The density jump at the barrier was simulated with a hyperbolic tangent function with a width of eight grid points. The density difference across the barrier was 1 kg m^{-3}. In the nonhydrostatic simulation the density was determined by temperature. In the quasi-hydrostatic model salinity was the dynamic variable. The models had been developed separately and it was convenient to maintain the original variables. However, the temperature and salinity were scaled to yield the same density structure and all the other parameters of the simulations were the same for both the quasi-hydrostatic and the nonhydrostatic simulations.

In both cases the plumes develop circulation patterns that are characteristic of buoyantly driven plumes. There is head region consists of a turbulent rotor with a recirculation of fluid around it consisting of a downwelling of fluid in front of the plume and an upwelling behind the turbulent rotor. The mixing is greatest just behind the rotor and the flow becomes more laminar with increasing distance behind the head region. The thickness of the head region is greater on the deeper side and the flow behind the head is more laminar than on the shallow side. The results agree qualitatively with laboratory measurements (Simpson, 1997).

5. Conclusions

For the density difference and the aspect ratio used in these initial experiments the quasi-hydrostatic simulation agreed well with the nonhydrostatic simulation. In both cases plumes develop and propagate away from the lock location. At 40 minutes rotors are beginning to develop at the heads of the plumes. The simulations are continuing to determine the complete evolution of the plumes.

Further simulations are underway to determine the density jump and aspect ratio at which the quasi-hydrostatic approximation breaks down. We have more results and animations available on our web site. Contact the first author for information on the location of the site.

6. Acknowledgements

We wish to thank Paul Martin and David Deitrich for supplying codes and for valuable discussions. This work was sponsored by the Naval Research Laboratory through the core project "Nonhydrostatic Coastal Ocean Modeling" under ONR program element 0601153N.

7. References

Dietrich, D. E., 1997, Application of a modified "A" grid ocean model having reduced numerical dispersion to the Gulf of Mexico circulation, *Dynam. Atmos. Oceans*, **27**, 201-217.

Dietrich, D. E. and C. A. Lin, 1999, Effects of hydrostatic approximation and resolution on the simulation of convective adjustment, submitted to Tellus.

Hodur, R. M., 1997, The Naval Research Laboratory's coupled ocean/atmosphere mesoscale prediction system (COAMPS), *Mon. Wea. Rev.*, **125**, 1414-1430.

Klemp, J. B. and R. B. Wilhelmson, 1978, The simulation of three-dimensional convective storm dynamics, *J. Atmos. Sci.*, **35**, 1070-1096.

Mahadevean, A., Oliger J., Street R., 1996 A nonhydrostatic mesoscale ocean model .2. Numerical implementation. *J. Phys. Oceanogr.* **26**, 1880-1898.

Orlanski, I., 1981, The quasi-hydrostatic approximation, *J. Atmos. Sci.*, **38**, 572-582.

Simpson, J. E., 1997, Gravity currents in the environment and laboratory, Cambridge University Press, Cambridge, UK, pp. 244.

Skamarock, W. C. and J. B. Klemp, 1992, The stability of time-split numeric methods for the hydrostatic and nonhydrostatic elastic equations, *Mon. Wea. Rev.*, **120**, 2109-2127.

Turner, J. S., 1973, Buoyancy Effects in Fluids, Cambridge University Press, Cambridge, UK, pp.~367.

Internal Friction in Shelf and Coastal Seas

Mark E. Inall[1] and Tom P. Rippeth[2]

[1]Scottish Association for Marine Science, Dunstaffnage Marine Laboratory, Oban,
Scotland PA34 4AD
[2]School of Ocean Sciences, University of Wales Bangor, Menai Bridge, Anglesey, Wales LL59 5LY
mei@dml.ac.uk , t.p.rippeth@bangor.ac.uk

1. Abstract

Over the past 5 years a number of experiments have been made in the shelf and coastal waters of the NW European Shelf to test the hypothesis that the internal wave field has associated with it significant frictional dissipation. The methods used were Acoustic Doppler Current Profilers (ADCPs), a Free-falling Light Yoyo shear microstructure profiler (FLY), and moored thermistor chains. In the cases examined the interaction of the barotropic tide with topography in the presence of stratification appeared to be a primary generating mechanism of internal waves at tidal and higher frequencies, including solitary internal waves and internal undular bores. From over 145 km of shear microstructure data (1200 profiles), measurements consistently showed enhanced energy dissipation levels (of the order 1×10^{-3} W m^{-3}) within the pycnocline associated with enhanced fine scale shear, itself associated with internal wave activity. On the shelf vertical eddy diffusivities within the thermocline were on average 3 orders of magnitude above the molecular value, and decreased shoreward of the shelf break. In a fjordic coastal sea environment high dissipation values found near the sill did not extend far into the interior, the results indicating an additional energy sink; possibly critical slope boundary mixing. Variability in dissipation rates was found at a semi-diurnal (M2) frequency. Our broad conclusions are that internal waves are effective vertical stirrers in NW European shelf and coastal seas. Direct observations have shown that turbulent kinetic energy dissipation rates and vertical eddy diffusivities within the pycnocline are enhanced in the vicinity of striking topographic features such as the shelf break and sills.

2. Introduction

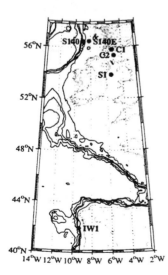

Figure 1 Location map showing station positions. Contours at 150, 500, 1000, 2000, and 3000

Recent years have seen a dramatically increased interest in the action of tides on the ocean system. From the deep ocean, (e.g. Munk and Wunsch, 1998) through shelf (Inall et al., 2000) and coastal seas, (Simpson et al., 1996) to semienclosed fjords (Stigibrandt and Aure, 1989) it has become increasingly clear that the loss of barotropic tidal energy to the internal wave field has an important role to play in the vertical mixing of the water column. The NW European Shelf is a region of seasonal stratification and strong semi-dirunal and diurnal barotropic tides: an ideal place to follow the path of energy from the external to the internal tide, through the internal wave field, and ultimately to dissipation and mixing. However, this is a difficult path to follow, scales range from 100s of km to 10s of mm and many of the processes are inherently three dimensional and nonlinear. For these reasons our approach has been predominantly observational: the renowned first mate of *RRS Challenger*, worried that we might suffer data withdrawal symptoms, once berated us, "You've sucked all the data out of this spot, let's go!". Unfortunately, we know all too well he was wrong; what we present here are the few glimpses we have gained of the inexorable path of energy to smaller and smaller scales.

3. Observations and Analysis Techniques

Six locations have been recently instrumented (Figure 1) with a combination of moored and/or hull mounted ADCPs, moored thermistor strings, and the FLY shear microstructure profiler (see Inall et al., 2000 for details). S140 was located 5 km inshore of the shelf break in 140 m, and S140E a further 50 km on-shelf in the same depth of water. S1 was in the Irish Sea in 90 m. IW1 was 5 km shoreward of the Iberian shelf edge in 167 m. C2 was 5 km inside the sill of the Clyde sea (a fjordic sea loch) in 45 m, and C1 a further 50 km inside the sea loch in the deep basin (142 m). Typically ADCP and thermistor data were collected at 2 minute intervals and with 5 m resolution, with a FLY profiler repeat cycle of approximately 6 minutes. FLY yo-yo'ing was maintained for at least 13 hours at each site, and, at S140 and S140E, during both spring and neap tides. Where possible ADCP and thermistor moorings were maintained for at least 14 days to allow tidal analysis to discriminate between S2 and M2 tidal constituents. Stations S1 and IW1 have only 2 days of ADCP data associated with them. Baroclinic energy densities were calculated from the depth average of the baroclinic velocity spectra, and assuming the frequency dependent kinetic/potential energy partition relationship for internal waves. Turbulent kinetic energy dissipation rates were calculated from the spectra of the square of the shear microstructure following the method of Dewey (1987) with modifications following Inall (1998).

4. Shear, Dissipation and Diffusion

Table 1 gives a summary of dissipation rates (integrated across the thermocline) and vertical eddy diffusion coefficients, calculated according to (Osborn, 1980)

$$K_\rho = \Gamma \frac{\varepsilon}{N^2},$$

where, $\Gamma = R_f /(1 - R_f)$, R_f is the flux Richardson number, ε the energy dissipation rate per unit volume, and N^2 is the local buoyancy frequency. R_f is assumed to take a constant value of 0.2. Instrumental errors in measuring ε are estimated to be ~50% of the value. In order to estimate sampling errors a standard bootstrap method was employed, increasing our uncertainty in ε and K_ρ to ~65% of the estimated value.

SITE	$\int \varepsilon$ (W m^{-2})	K_ρ (cm^2 s^{-1})	N^2 $10^{-4}s^{-2}$	E_{TOT} (J m^{-3})	E_{LF} (J m^{-3})	E_{HF} (J m^{-3})
S140$_1$ (1995, neaps)	3.7 x 10^{-3}	2.0	8.0	2.0	1.0	1.0
S140$_2$ (1995, springs)	1.3 x 10^{-2}	13.0	4.1	6.4	5.4	1.0
S140$_3$ (1996, neaps)	2.8 x 10^{-2}	6.1	1.0	1.8	1.3	0.5
S140$_4$ (1996, springs)	1.5 x 10^{-2}	1.6	0.6	1.6	1.1	0.5
S140E$_1$ (1996, neaps)	3.6 x 10^{-3}	0.7	1.0	0.9	0.7	0.2
S140E$_2$(1996, springs)	4.0 x 10^{-3}	0.7	1.1	0.7	0.5	0.2
C1	0.9 x 10^{-4}	0.22	2.1	0.4	0.35	0.07
C2	1.0 x 10^{-3}	0.47	6.9	2.0	1.7	0.32
S1	2.7 x 10^{-3}	1.9	0.06	0.5	0.5	0
IW1	2.4 x 10^{-3}	0.71	3.2	2.3	1.9	0.4

Table 1. Dissipation rate integrated vertically over the thermocline, diapycnal eddy diffusivity averaged over the thermocline, mean buoyancy frequency squared and depth averaged baroclinic energy density estimated by integrating the velocity spectra over 3 bands; f to N (E_{TOT}), f to 0.7 cph (E_{LF}), and 0.7 cph to 4 cph (E_{HF}).

Overall there is no clear tendency for more energetic sites to be more dissipative. The strongest correlations in Table 1 are between K_ρ and E_{TOT}, and K_ρ and E_{LF} ($r^2=0.87$ for both). A simple comparison between fine scale shear and dissipation rate at S140$_{1 \text{ and } 2}$ showed general correspondence between the two (Inall et al, 2000). S140 (1995) shows strong spring/neap modulation in ε and E_{TOT}. The absence of such modulation in S140 (1996) or S140E is probably as a result the very strong K1 component during this time and the 13 hour duration of the FLY time series. The low correspondence between ε and E_{HF} ($r^2=0.37$) suggests that enhanced dissipation (e.g. S140$_2$) occurs predominantly as a result of increased energy levels at lower wavenumbers. This idea is supported by the observations at S1, where very weak stratification still experienced enhanced dissipation levels (and therefore strong mixing).

With the exception of S140$_1$, less than 30% of the total energy lies in the high frequency band. This shows the significant impact of the solitary internal waves (SIWs) observed during S140$_1$ (Inall et al., 2000), and is discussed further in Section 5.

The proportion of energy dissipated within the thermocline (not shown) was consistently significant compared to the total dissipation: varying from 30% (S140$_1$) to as great as 70% (C1). The other main sink of energy was in the bottom boundary layer (BBL). Our results confirm the cubic dependence of BBL dissipation on U (Simpson et al., 1996), and show the increased importance of internal damping in regions of weak flow (viz. C1).

In both C2/C1 and S140/S140E(1996) proximity to the generation region was associated with significantly greater mixing. Within the semi-enclosed sea loch, however, a four-fold reduction in E_{TOT} was observed between C2 and C1, compared with a two-fold decrease over the same distance on the open shelf; an observation which points to a greater efficiency of energy removal in the semi-enclosed system.

5. Energy Spectra

Baroclinic energy spectra were formed by removing the depth mean flow from each bin, taking the spectra for U and V, then averaging these spectra over the water column, excluding those within the surface well mixed layer. Spectra from four of the locations are shown in Figures 2 to 4.

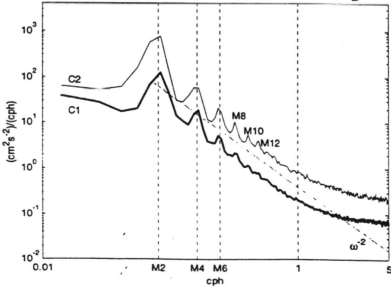

Figure 2. Baroclinic energy spectra from C1 and C2 ADCP data, using nfft=2160, with dt=120 s. A line of arbitrary amplitude and slope ω^{-2} is shown.

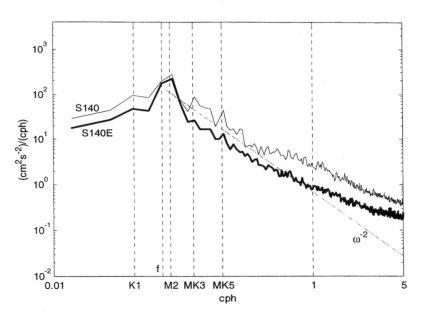

Figure 3. As in Figure 2, now for S140 and S140E (1996), with nfft=2160, dt=120 s.

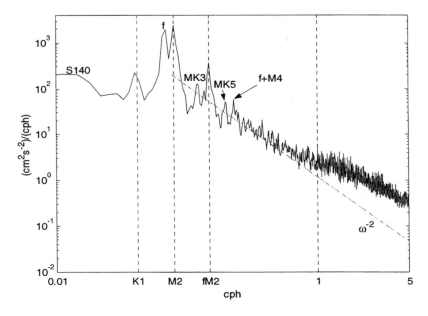

Figure 4. As in Figure 2, now for S140(1995), with nfft=8192, dt=120 s.

The most striking feature is that between f and N the spectra are far from continuous, as in the canonical Garrett and Munk (GM) spectrum (a line of slope ω^{-2} is shown in preference to the GM spectrum). Higher harmonics up to M12 are apparent, including various interactions between M2 and K1 (S140$_{3\ and\ 4}$) and, remarkably, f (S140$_1$). The second characteristic feature is the shoulder in the shelf edge spectra and the departure from the GM slope at between 0.7 and 1 cph, which we associate with SIW activity (see Inall et al., 2000). Above ~4 cph the instrumental noise floor is reached and the spectra begin to whiten.

At both sites in the Clyde Sea (Figure 2) there is a maximum at the M2 tidal frequency, indicating that the tide is the main energy input into the internal motions. Furthermore, higher harmonics are evident at both sites. On the Malin Shelf in 1996 (Figure 3) the maxima are at K1, inertial, and M2 frequencies. Higher harmonics are also evident at both sites, including interaction frequencies between M2 and K1 (MK3, 2MK5). During the strong wind conditions experienced in 1995 on the Malin Shelf (Figure 4) energy maxima occurred at inertial and M2 frequencies.

6. Discussion

We have presented a series of observations taken over the past 5 years at contrasting stratified sites in the NW European shelf seas. Internal wave activity is clearly present at each of the sites, as is enhanced dissipation within the thermocline, the latter leading to pycnocline diffusivities ranging in value from 0.2 to 13.0 cm^2s^{-1}. These values can be contrasted with values of 0.04 to 0.5 cm^2s^{-1} observed at a sites in the English Channel close to a shelf sea front, and where internal wave activity was observed to be minimal (Sharples et al., 2000).

Comparison of dissipation values from sites near striking topographic features (S140 at the shelf edge, and C2 at the Clyde Sea entrance sill) with corresponding sites some distance away (S140E and C1, respectively) show enhanced dissipation and vertical mixing close to the features. This suggests mixing "hotspots" and areas of enhanced form drag in shelf and coastal seas close to topographic features. The sharp decrease in energy at C1 in the deep basin of the Clyde Sea suggests a more efficient removal of energy in the semi-enclosed system compared with the less restricted shelf sea.

Before progress can be made in accurately modelling circulation and stratification in shelf seas, the climatology of mixing must be established and the major mixing processes identified and parameterised. Comparisons between models of vertical exchange (containing state-of-the-art closure schemes) and dissipation measurements made in the thermally stratified region of the Irish Sea have demonstrated the need for improved parameterisation of internal mixing within these models (Simpson et al., 1996, Burchard et al., 1998). In order to proceed a number of fundamental issues must be resolved. These include an improved understanding of the energy transfer mechanisms within the internal wave spectrum, and the processes responsible for the dissipation of internal wave energy. Some clues about the generation and transfer mechanisms are available to us through our measurements.

Baroclinic energy spectra do not exhibit a smooth continuum on continental slope and shelf areas. Internal K1 and M2 oscillations are generated over topography, extracting energy directly from the barotropic tide. As discussed above, higher frequency (harmonic) oscillations are energetic at all locations studied. We can suggest of three possible causes. Firstly, nonlinear disintegration of the internal tide/solibore near S140 has been modelled and internal overtides generated in the process (Sherwin et al., 1996, Small et al., 1998). At both IW1 and S140 it has been demonstrated that, on occasion, internal tidal bores are generated some distance off-shore (perhaps by a nearby seamount) and disintegrate on the shoaling continental slope. Secondly, it is possible that the internal overtides are directly excited by the barotropic overtides, also present at all the locations studied. A third possibility is that the internal overtides are generated by wave-wave interaction. A clear difficulty we have is in separating the barotropic and baroclinic signals, since the ADCP data do not span the entire water column. The first and third mechanisms may be related, however at present we feel unable to distinguish between the three possible mechanisms. The presence of MK3 and 2MK5 internal overtides at S140E and fM2 and fM4 at S140(1995) does, however, provide strong evidence to suggest that diurnal tidal energy (trapped as a baroclinic mode), and energy from inertial oscillations is being fed into the internal wave field, and thus contributing to mixing across the shelf and increased damping of these phenomena.

7. References

Burchard, H, O. Petersen, T.P. Rippeth (1998), Comparing the performance of the Mellor-Yamada and the k-epsilon turbulence models. Journal of Geophysical Research , 103, 10543-10,554.

Dewey, R. K., W. R. Crawford, A. E. Gargett and N. S. Oakey (1987), A microstructure instrument for profiling oceanic turbulence in coastal bottom boundary layers. Journal of Atmosphere and Ocean Technology, 4, 288-297.

Guizien, K., E. Barthelemy and M. E. Inall (1999), Internal tide generation at a shelf-break by an oblique barotropic tide: observations and analytical modelling. Journal of Geophysical Research, 104, 15655-15668.

Inall, M. E. (1998), Software to Process and Image Dissipated Energy Rates. UCES report U98-7, University of Wales Bangor, UK.

Inall, M. E., T. P. Rippeth and T. J. Sherwin (2000). Impact of nonlinear waves on the dissipation of internal tidal energy at a shelf break. Journal of Geophysical Research, (In press).

Osborn, T. R. (1980), Estimates of the local rate of vertical diffusion from dissipation measurements. Journal of Physical Oceanography, 10, 83-89.

Munk, W. and C. Wunch (1998). Abyssal recipes II: energetics of tidal and wind mixing. Deep-Sea Research I, 45, 1977-2010.

Sharples, J., C. M. Moore, T. P. Rippeth, P. M. Holigan, D. J. Hydes and N. Fisher (2000). Phytoplankton distrubution and survival in the thermocline. Submitted to Limnology and Oceanography.

Sherwin, T. J., A. C. Dale, M. E. Inall and D. R. G. Jeans (1996), Linear and non-linear internal tides around the European Atlantic shelf. Proceedings of the Sixth International Offshore and Polar Engineering Conference, Los Angeles, USA, 131-137.

Simpson, J. H., W. R. Crawford, T. P. Rippeth, A. R. Crawford and J. V. S Cheok (1996). The Vertical Structure of Turbulent Dissipation in Shelf Seas. Journal of Physical Oceanography, 26, 1579-1590.

Small, J., Z. Hallock, G. Pavey, and J. Scott (1998), Observations of large amplitude internal waves at the Malin Shelf edge during SESAME 1995. Continental Shelf Research, 19, 1389-1436.

Stigebrandt, A and J. Aure (1989). Vertical mixing in basin waters of fjords. Journal of Physical Oceanography, 19, 917-926.

Effects of Submarine Canyon Topography On Spin-up Over The Continental Shelf

Ramzi S. Mirshak and Susan E. Allen

Earth and Ocean Sciences, University of British Columbia, Vancouver, B.C., Canada, V6T 1Z4
mirshak@ocgy.ubc.ca, allen@ocgy.ubc.ca

1. Abstract

The spin-up of homogeneous and stratified fluids are investigated in a rotating cylindrical tank containing a smooth valley-like interruption in an otherwise axisymmetric topography. The laboratory setup is designed to mimic a submarine canyon cutting into the topography of the coastal ocean. The forcing is induced by varying the rotation rate of the tank. An axisymmetric (canyon-free) case is used as a benchmark and results from these laboratory experiments are compared to theoretically predicted spin-up rates. A solution to an Ekman layer in a homogeneous fluid over a steep slope is compared to laboratory results. For the stratified scenario, Ekman layer arrest occurs slowly as other dynamics are clearly present at early time. It is found that the introduction of a submarine canyon to the system accelerates spin-up rates, especially in the stratified system. Radially outward flow present in the canyon as a result of vortex stretching enhances classical spin-up mechanisms.

2. Introduction

When a current in a rotating system has anticyclonic vorticity, Ekman pumping will cause transport into its horizontal boundary layers. This transport causes vortex stretching in the interior and the system evolves toward a curl-free velocity field. Such a scenario is easily realized in a laboratory with a cylindrical tank placed on a rotating table. By impulsively increasing the rotation rate of the tank, fluid which was in solid body rotation with the tank will suddenly acquire an anticyclonic character. Analysis of the boundary layer response to the induced current makes possible predictions of how the boundary layer will cause the interior flow to evolve, or spin-up.

Extensive early work examined laboratory spin-up in a cylinder (see the review article by Benton and Clark, 1974).The problem we study becomes more complex as we add axisymmetric topography to the tank (Figure 1). As a result, solutions to an Ekman layer on a shallow slope as well as a steep slope become important. Pedlosky (1987) examines an Ekman layer on a shallow slope, but neglects steep slopes as they are rarely encountered in geophysical flows.

MacCready and Rhines (1991) describe how buoyancy effects play a role in upwelling favourable sloped boundary layer dynamics. In time, buoyancy becomes as important as the Ekman layer is effectively "shut-down", insulating the interior flow from the frictional effects of the boundary. Due to the complexity of the momentum equations with density stratification, however, the results do not apply to boundary layers over steep slopes. In laboratory trials, we are able to qualitatively identify the change in flow field evolution as the bottom boundary layers shut-down.

Our laboratory setup is designed to examine coastal flow in and around submarine canyons, common features which cut into the continental shelf from the continental slope. Canyons act as strong conduits for upwelling in the coastal ocean (e.g. Hickey, 1997). with important implications on water mass distribution and the cycling of nutrients.

3. Experimental Set-up

Laboratory experiments were performed in a cylindrical tank on a rotating table which holds rotation rates constant to within ± 0.001 rad·s^{-1}. The topography within the tank mimics that of a

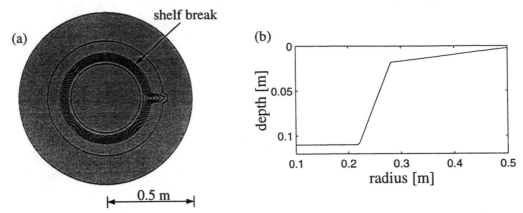

Figure 1: Topography used in models. (a) Contour plot of the laboratory experiment for a scenario including a canyon. Water depth is 2cm at the shelf break and 11 cm at the tank centre. (b) Water depth used in the analytic and numeric modelling of laboratory results is plotted as a function of radius.

generic coastal ocean, albeit at a 10-fold vertical exaggeration: an abyssal plain in the tank centre adjoins the continental slope, leading to a continental shelf and ending in a coastline at the tank edge. To study the effects of a submarine canyon, a 22° slice of the continental slope is removed and replaced by a topographic section that mimics the bathymetry of a submarine canyon (Figure 1.)

For a typical experiment, the tank was filled while rotating over a period of approximately 90 minutes, and the tank was left to spin-up for about 10 hours, allowing it to achieve solid-body rotation. The tank was then accelerated from an initial rotation rate, $\Omega_o = 0.2$ rad·s^{-1}, to its final rotation rate, $\Omega_f = 0.26$ rad·s^{-1}, over 27.3 seconds. This length of time is sufficient to allow development of an Ekman layer along the bottom, while leaving the interior rotating approximately at its original rate.

Particle tracers were placed on the fluid surface and velocities were calculated using cross-correlation particle image velocimetry using MatPIV, a particle image velocimetry package for Matlab written by Johan Kristian Sveen. PIV techniques are discussed in detail by Raffel et al. (1998). Frames with a pixel density of 240x320 were captured at a frequency of 5 frames per second, providing a continuous time series of velocity data.

4. Homogeneous Spin-up Without a Canyon

In the absence of stratification, the spin-up process is governed by Ekman layer dynamics. Radially outward transport is generated in the bottom boundary layer. Continuity dictates that the flow must be balanced by a flux from the interior into the boundary layer. Assuming velocity variations parallel to the bottom boundary are negligible, the momentum equations for a boundary layer on a slope of angle γ can be manipulated to give

$$w\frac{\partial u}{\partial z} - fv\cos\gamma = -\frac{\partial p}{\partial x} - g\cos\gamma + \nu\frac{\partial^2 u}{\partial z^2}, \tag{1}$$

$$w\frac{\partial v}{\partial z} + f\left(u\cos\gamma - w\sin\gamma\right) = +\nu\frac{\partial^2 v}{\partial z^2}, \tag{2}$$

$$\frac{1}{2}\frac{\partial w^2}{\partial z} + fv\sin\gamma = -\frac{\partial p}{\partial z} - g\sin\gamma + \nu\frac{\partial^2 w}{\partial z^2}. \tag{3}$$

The continuity equation is

$$\frac{\partial u}{\partial x} + \frac{\partial v}{\partial y} + \frac{\partial w}{\partial z} = 0. \tag{4}$$

The above equations are for a right-handed coordinate system rotated through an angle γ where $\hat{x}$ is in the up-slope direction, $\hat{y}$ is in the along-slope direction and $\hat{z}$ is normal to the surface, where (u, v, w) give the velocity in the (x, y, z) direction, p is the pressure field, f is the Coriolis frequency, g is gravity and ν is the kinematic viscosity. The time derivative is neglected as the boundary layer is assumed to be in a quasi-steady state with the interior flow, which responds on a much larger timescale. The y-derivative of pressure is removed as polar symmetry is assumed.

It is useful to introduce the scaling, $z = \delta\zeta^*$, $w = \delta(V/L)w^*$, $u = Vu^*$, $v = Vv^*$ and $x = Lx^*$, where $V = \Delta\Omega L$ is the geostrophically balanced interior flow, L is the length scale, and $\delta = \sqrt{2\nu/(f\cos\gamma)}$ is the Ekman layer depth. The asterisks denote non-dimensional variables. The momentum and continuity equations are further treated with the non-dimensional parameters, $R = V/(fL\cos\gamma)$ and $\tan\theta = \delta/L$, where R is a Rossby number and $(\tan\theta)$ is a ratio of the length-to-depth scales used in the problem. This allows us to scale the pressure field as $p = VLf\cos\gamma p^* - (x^*\tan\gamma + \zeta\tan\theta)g/(fV)$. Incorporating these scalings, the momentum equations become (dropping the asterisks)

$$Rw\frac{\partial u}{\partial \zeta} - v = -\frac{\partial p}{\partial x} + \frac{1}{2}\frac{1}{\cos\gamma}\frac{\partial^2 u}{\partial \zeta^2}, \tag{5}$$

$$Rw\frac{\partial v}{\partial \zeta} + u - w\tan\gamma\tan\theta = \frac{1}{2}\frac{1}{\cos\gamma}\frac{\partial^2 v}{\partial \zeta^2}, \tag{6}$$

$$\frac{R\tan\theta}{2}\frac{\partial w^2}{\partial \zeta} + v\tan\gamma = \cot\theta\frac{\partial p}{\partial \zeta} + \tan\theta\frac{\partial^2 w}{\partial \zeta^2}. \tag{7}$$

For the laboratory setup, $L = 0.5$m, $f = 0.52$s^{-1} and $\nu = 10^{-6}$m^{2}s^{-1}. These values give $\tan\theta = O(R^4)$, allowing us to ignore contributions of this order. The results of (7) allow us to determine the vertical variation of the pressure field, which is not of interest for this problem and the equation is dropped from our analysis. Assuming that $\partial p/\partial x$ is balanced by the geostrophic velocity in the interior, and introducing the asymptotic expansion,

$$(u, v, w) = \sum_{n=0}^{\infty} R^n(u_n, v_n, w_n),$$

gives, to first order,

$$\begin{bmatrix} 1 - v \\ u \end{bmatrix} = \frac{1}{2}\frac{1}{\cos\gamma}\frac{\partial^2}{\partial \zeta^2}\begin{bmatrix} u \\ v \end{bmatrix}, \tag{8}$$

which has a classic Ekman spiral solution

$$\begin{bmatrix} u \\ v \end{bmatrix} = e^{-\sqrt{2\cos\gamma}\zeta}\begin{bmatrix} -\sin\left(\sqrt{2\cos\gamma}\zeta\right) \\ 1 - \cos\left(\sqrt{2\cos\gamma}\zeta\right) \end{bmatrix}. \tag{9}$$

Continuity is used to determine the flux out of the boundary layer:

$$w = -\int_0^{\infty}\frac{\partial u}{\partial x}d\zeta = -\frac{\partial^2 p}{\partial x^2}. \tag{10}$$

If one assumes potential vorticity is conserved in the interior, then at lowest order,

$$\frac{\partial}{\partial t}\nabla \times \vec{u}_H^i = \frac{w^i}{H}, \tag{11}$$

985

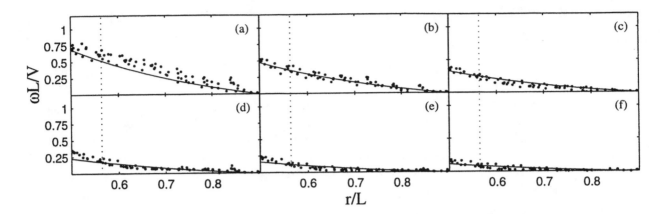

Figure 2: Comparison of laboratory results (dots) to theoretical predictions (solid line) for the spin-up of a homogeneous fluid. The thin vertical dotted line represents the location of the shelf break. Time slices are shown at (a) 0 seconds, (b) 20 seconds, (c) 40 seconds (d) 60 seconds, (e) 80 seconds and (f) 100 seconds. $\omega = v/r$ is the angular velocity.

where H is the water depth, and $\vec{u}_H^i$ corresponds to the horizontal velocity field. The superscript, i denotes that these are values for the interior and are in a cylindrical, non-rotated coordinate system. The vertical flux is directly proportional to the cosine of the slope angle, i.e. $w^i = w \cos \gamma$. Laboratory results suggest that (11) is not separable, and the equation is solved numerically using the Euler method. The theoretical results are compared to data collected in the laboratory (Figure 2).

The data show excellent correlation with theoretical predictions over the continental shelf and shallow continental slope. The initial velocity field used for theoretical comparison was determined by a least squares fit to the velocity data at $t = 0$, forcing a no-slip condition at the coastline.

5. Stratified Spin-up Without a Canyon

The presence of stratification greatly increases spin-up time. Although an analytical model for this problem cannot be easily attained due to buoyancy effects in the equations of motion on a steep slope, laboratory results are compared with a simple diffusion model based on the work of MacCready and Rhines (1991). These authors predict the shutdown time, for the bottom boundary, $\tau = (1/\sigma + S)/[(1+S)S^2 f \cos \gamma]$, where $S = (N \sin \gamma / f \cos \gamma)^2$ is a Burger number, σ is the Prandtl number and N is the Brunt-Väisälä frequency.

For laboratory simulations, the shutdown timescale over the continental shelf is approximately 18 seconds ($f = 0.52s^{-1}$, $\gamma = 4.2°$, $N = 2.2s^{-1}$, $1/\sigma = 0$), less than the time used in ramping the velocity. We are using salt to generate the density field in our tank, and as such, we treat $1/\sigma$ as zero. For our purposes, flow evolution over the abyssal plain is negligible. Assuming ν to be $10^{-6} m^2 s^{-1}$ and the depth at the tank centre of $O(10^{-1} m)$, the spin-up time scale for stratified fluid at the tank center (by diffusion) is about 3 hours.

Following MacCready and Rhines (1991), the along-slope velocity over a shallow slope approximately obeys,

$$\frac{\partial v}{\partial t} = \nu \cos^2 \gamma \left(\frac{1/\sigma + S}{1 + S} \right) \frac{\partial^2 v}{\partial z^2} + \cos^2 \gamma \nu \nabla_H^2 v, \qquad (12)$$

where z is vertical (i.e. not normal to the slope) and ∇_H^2 represents the horizontal components of the Laplacian operator. (Horizontal diffusion is not included in the model of MacCready and

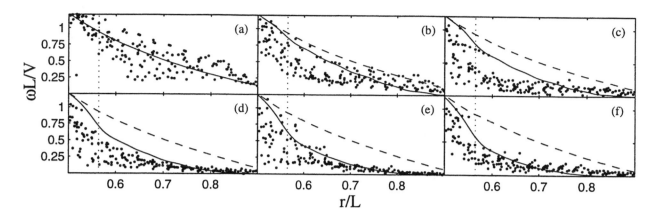

Figure 3: Comparison of laboratory results (dots) to theoretical predictions for the spin-up of a stratified fluid. The solid line represents a diffusion model with an isotropic diffusion coefficient and the dashed line represents the same model using the diffusion coefficient suggested by MacCready and Rhines (1991). The thin vertical dotted line represents the location of the shelf break. Time slices are shown at (a) 0 seconds, (b) 40 seconds, (c) 80 seconds (d) 120 seconds, (e) 160 seconds and (f) 200 seconds.

Rhines.) This equation is solved numerically, a diffusion model is run where kinematic viscosity is isotropic (i.e. $\partial v/\partial t - \nu\nabla^2 v = 0$).

Laboratory data do not compare extremely well to theoretical predictions (Figure 3). It should be noted that in these results, it is assumed that the initial flow field is invariant in the vertical. This is not of serious concern on the shelf, where the flow is shallow and equilibrates quickly. The upward trend seen in these plots as one travels towards the tank centre levels out to a normalized value near 1. These data appear quite noisy early in time but settle into a more easily defined velocity field.

The laboratory flow does not appear to follow either of these solutions. This can be explained by analysis of the laboratory velocity profiles. Ekman shutdown does not appear to be complete until about 40 seconds, and other dynamics are taking place early in the spin-up process. Later in time, however, the flow is evolving even more slowly than that predicted by isotropic diffusion, suggesting an increasing importance to the solution of MacCready and Rhines (1991).

6. Effects of a canyon

Introduction of a canyon alters rates of spin-up considerably, since a rotating flow passing over such variable bathymetry experiences significant changes in the vorticity field due to enhanced vortex stretching (e.g. Hickey, 1997). For the spin-up scenario presented in the laboratory, a canyon increases the upwelling favourable flux of water from adjacent to the continental shelf onto the continental slope, mixing the vorticity field. Submarine canyons are known to enhance shelf-break upwelling, which in theory should decrease spin-up timescales. Figure 4 compares spin-up rates seaward and shoreward of the shelf break for homogeneous and stratified laboratory trials.

For the homogeneous case with a canyon present, spin-up rates increased in the immediate vicinity of the shelf break but this increase appears to taper quickly in space (Figure 4). This can be linked to the fact that the Ekman transport, and therefore the canyon independent spin-up process, is impeded on the steep continental slope much more than it is on the continental shelf. The effect of a canyon in a stratified fluid also clear. Due to the highly non-linear character of flow, buoyancy forces have a lesser effect in the canyon than on the "fast spin-up" process. The mixing of vorticity by diffusion is much slower than the advective processes. Visually it seems clear that the effect of a canyon on spin-up in the stratified case has a stronger spatial signal than that

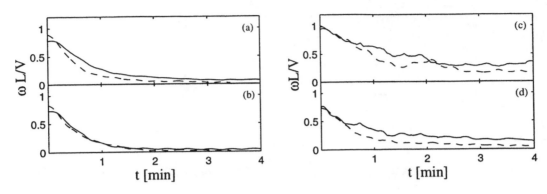

Figure 4: Time evolution of angular velocity for lab results in the absence (solid lines) and presence (dashed lines) a canyon. (a) Homogeneous fluid at $r = 27.9cm$ ($r/L = 0.56$). (b) Homogeneous fluid at $r = 30.7cm$ ($r/L = 0.61$). (c) Stratified fluid at $r = 27.1cm$ ($r/L = 0.54$). (d) Stratified fluid at $r = 31.6cm$ ($r/L = 0.63$).

for the non-stratified case. A simple nonlinear regression shows that if we model the data as an exponential decay, (not shown,) then in all locations but that shown in Figure 4b, the canyon cuts the spin-up timescale in half.

7. Conclusions

The spin-up of a homogeneous fluid on a slope can be modelled using lowest order terms, even at moderate Rossby numbers. The temporal Rossby number, $\Delta f/f$, is 0.23 yet the lowest order, non-trivial terms of our asymptotic expansion show good agreement with our laboratory findings. The introduction of stratification adds complexity to the problem, as buoyancy cannot be ignored. Over several shutdown timescales, we see the spin-up rate over the continental slope change considerably, arriving in a final state in approximate agreement to the "slow diffusion" model of MacCready and Rhines (1991). In early time the flow field evolves quite rapidly, especially over the more shallow, shoreward edge of the continental shelf.

The introduction of a submarine canyon to the topography changed spin-up rates by a factor of 2. In the laboratory experiments less than 10% of the shelf break is within the submarine canyon, yet a very large, easily measurable effect was found. In the ocean, approximately 50% of the shelf break is found within submarine canyons, suggesting that canyons may have a considerable effect on spin-up of the coastal ocean.

Acknowledgements

The authors are grateful to R. Pawlowicz for many useful discussions and N. Yonemitsu for his insights into developing laboratory methods. This work was supported by a National Science and Engineering Research Council of Canada Strategic Grant.

References

Benton, E. and Clark, A: 1974, Spin-up, *Ann. Rev. Fluid Mech.* **6**, 257-280.

Hickey, B.: 1997, The response of a narrow canyon to strong wind forcing, *J. Phys. Oceanogr.* **27**(5), 697-726.

MacCready, P. and Rhines, P.: 1991, Buoyant inhibition of Ekman transport on a slope and its effect on stratified spin-up, *J. Fluid Mech.* **223**, 631-661.

Pedlosky, J.: 1987, *Geophysical Fluid Dynamics, 2nd Ed.*, Springer-Verlag. pp. 710.

Raffel, M., Willert, C., Kompenhans, J.: 1998, *Particle Image Velocimetry: A Practical Guide*, Springer-Verlag. pp. 253.

Vertical Mixing and Horizontal Transport in Stratified Flow at a Near Coastal Site

Jeffery D. Musiak[1], Mark T. Stacey[2], Deanna Sereno[2], Thomas M. Powell[1], Stephen G. Monismith[3], Derek A. Fong[3], Michael Purcell[4]

[1]Department of Integrative Biology #3140, UC Berkeley, Berkeley, CA 94720-3140
[2]Department of Civil and Environmental Engineering, UC Berkeley, Berkeley, CA 94720-1710
[3]Environmental Fluid Mechanics Laboratory, Dept of Civil and Environmental Engineering, Stanford University, Stanford, CA 94305-4020
[4]Oceanographic Systems Laboratory, Woods Hole Oceanographic Institution, Woods Hole, MA 02543
musiak@socrates.berkeley.edu, mstacey@socrates.berkeley.edu, sereno@uclink4.berkeley.edu, zackp@socrates.berkeley.edu, monismit@stanford.edu, dfong@stanford.edu, mpurcell@whoi.edu

1. Abstract

Frequent stratification (and restratification) episodes, strong along-shore tidal flows and variable local bathymetry characterize near coastal environments. These features are thought to control vertical mixing and horizontal transport in such near shore regions. To better understand this environment, a dye-dispersion study was performed in an area off San Clemente Island, CA in March 1999, along with detailed measurements of the flow and vertical mixing. The major result of this work is that observed horizontal dispersion rates of towed fluorometer data are about 2 orders of magnitude larger than generally accepted values. Even when scale dependant dispersion (Stacey et. al, 2000) is applied to the problem, the coefficient of the dispersion term are 0.08 cm$^{2/3}$ s^{-1}, substantially larger than observed values.

2. Introduction

The purpose of this study is to characterize stratified flows in near-coastal environments. It is essential to understand the physics of such flows because they determine the transport and dispersion of scalars, such as contaminants, nutrients, and biota near-shore. Vertical stratification and the interaction of along-shore tidal flows with the local bathymetry are important aspects if these coastal flows. When the water column is stratified, vertical dispersion will be reduced and the transport of scalars may be limited to layers. Further, where the stratified flows interact with the bottom, mixing at the boundary can create horizontal density variations, which may drive offshore intrusions, which can transport scalars cross-slope.

The ADCP velocity data collected during the study indicate that the flow during this period was predominantly along isobath, although instances of significant cross-isobath flow occurred. Therefore, the dye is largely advected along-isobath and constrained by the stratification to the bottom boundary layer. The lateral dispersion of the dye within the boundary layer is well approximated by a solution to the dispersion equation with a scale-dependent dispersion coefficient (Stacey et. al, 2000), which is to be expected in this environment where the velocity structures are characterized by a broad range of lengthscales. Interestingly, there is evidence of offshore transport of dye in a lens at a depth of about 10 meters. This depth is consistent with the location of the strongest thermocline and would suggest the presence of density-driven intrusions created by the interaction of the stratified tidal currents with the sloping bottom. Vertical density/microstructure profiles reinforce this interpretation. These profiles indicate that the water column may be divided into three main sections: 1) A surface layer affected by wind events; 2) a near bed layer, dominated by bottom stress; and, 3) an intermediate section which can be mixed by shear at the base of the thermoclines.

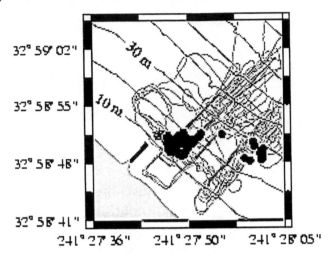

Figure 1. Plan view of test site showing bathymetry contoured at 10 meter intervals, the shore and pier in the lower left corner, the source marked by the star off of the end of the pier.

3. Experimental Setup

A series of dye experiments were performed the week of 24 - 26 March 1999 at the San Clemente Island site, see Figure 1. Each day, a zero-momentum, zero-buoyancy, near-bed source of Rhodamine WT (30% solution diluted with seawater to 2%) at 15 meters depth was turned on at the beginning of a particular tidal phase. The velocity field was measured using a 600 kHz RDI acoustic Doppler Current profiler mounted on a small boat. Sets of transects were made every several hours along six lines which were perpendicular to the isobaths. Each of these transects was approximately 600 meters in length with an along-shore spacing of 100 to 400 meters. Two microstructure profilers were also deployed from this boat to measure the density field and to determine the vertical mixing which was occurring. One profiler was a modified Ocean Sciences OS100 used in downward profiling mode and the other was a self-contained autonomous microstructure profiler (SCAMP), made by Precision Measurement Engineering. These measurements were used to determine the thickness of the bottom boundary layer (BBL) or the thickness of the layer to which the dye was constrained. Microstructure profiles were normally taken at the beginning, middle and end of a line, but occasionally at the beginning, end and four intermediate points. We will focus our discussion here on the morning of 26 March 1999 during a period typified by along-isobath flow from Northwest to Southeast.

4. ADCP Observations

The tidal currents for the period 25 to 27 March are nearly reversing on flood and ebb with an along-isobath (45° - 315° True) maximum component of 15 cm s^{-1} and maximum across-isobath component of 5 cm s^{-1}. Here 'reversing' means that the direction of the ebb current is 180° different from the flood direction and the magnitudes are nearly equal. The flow during the morning of 26 March 1999, is towards the Southeast (45° True) at approximately 10 cm s^{-1}, the across-isobath component is practically 0 cm s^{-1}). The ADCP directional shear indicates a BBL thickness of 7 meters.

5. Dye Observations

The dye measurements consisted of towed fluorometers from two vessels: the R/V HSB was transecting near the source (100-200 meters downstream) and the R/V ECOS was transecting further downstream (400-500 meters downstream). Each vessel followed a fixed-grid sampling plan which involved setting the tow body at a particular depth and driving two parallel transects (one towards shore, one away from shore) which extended in the inshore direction to just outside the isobath at the depth the fluorometers were sampling. The fluorometer depth was then adjusted and the transects were repeated (see Figure 1). The result was a three-dimensional cross-section of the plume during the period of the measurements.

6. Horizontal Advection

On the morning of 26 March the dye release began at 0845 PST along with the ADCP/microstructure transecting while the dye detection tows began later that morning at 1100 PST. Focusing in Figure 1 on the near-source vessel, HSB, the dye is detected primarily along the isobath of the source (at a depth of about 15 meters). This result indicates that in the near-field, the dye is advected primarily along-isobath, as would be expected based on the ADCP observations. In the data from the far-field vessel, the ECOS, the dye is detected further offshore, indicating significant cross-isobath advection.

The local bathymetry is also shown in Figure 1 (contour lines at 10 meter intervals); two characteristics of the plume are evident. First, uniform slope and parallel isobaths characterize the region extending from the source to a few hundred meters downstream. This is the region of along-isobath advection of the dye, which would be expected. Further downstream, however, at a distance of approximately 600 meters from the source, a sill shoals significantly compared to the near-source region. This sill is just downstream of the location of the ECOS transects and we hypothesize that the cross-isobath advection of dye is due to the interaction of the flow with this sill creating cross-isobath flow at depth.

7. Vertical Distribution

Collapsing the data into the cross-isobath - vertical plane produces the dye distribution displayed in Figure 2. This figure illustrates the location of the transect measurements and the location relative to the bed of the dye detections (looking upstream to the Northwest). It is clear that the vast majority of the dye detections are contained in the near-bed region, which indicates that the dye is being retained in the bottom boundary layer. The near-field data, from the HSB, is centered around the location of the source, which is located at a depth of 15 meters and a horizontal position of 150 meters on this figure. In the ECOS data, however, the dye detection is seen to occur much deeper and in the offshore direction, but still within the bottom boundary layer, from 12 to 18 meters depth and a horizontal location of 150 to 270 meters. This indicates that the cross-isobath flow evident in the horizontal advection of the dye is also a down-slope flow. We conclude that the sill located at about 600 meters downstream of the source is influencing the near-bed flow just upstream of it, producing down-slope flow in the bottom boundary layer. Figure 2 also shows that the dye is trapped in a bottom boundary that is approximately 7 meters thick.

Although most of the dye is retained in the bottom boundary layer, there are two notable exceptions, at depths of about 10 and 12 meters. At these depths, lenses of dye are seen to extend from the bottom boundary layer into the interior of the flow. The locations of these potential intrusions are consistent with the location of the thermoclines and are suggestive of density-driven intrusions resulting from the elevated mixing in the bottom boundary layer. At this point, however, a quantitative analysis of this dynamic is limited by the sparse data set, but the velocity and density (see Figure 4) transects are consistent with this interpretation.

8. Horizontal Dispersion

Focusing on the near-source portion of the data set, from the HSB, we can examine the extent of horizontal dispersion within the bottom boundary layer. In Figure 2, we see that the lateral extent of the dye within the bottom boundary layer at a distance of about 200 meters downstream of the source is approximately 150 meters. This lateral extent would suggest a Fickian dispersion coefficient of more than 11 m^2 s^{-1}, a value that is two orders of magnitude larger than would be expected in a turbulent boundary layer. Using a scale-dependent dispersion analysis (Stacey, et al. 2000), the coefficient on the dispersion term would be 0.8 cm$^{2/3}$ s^{-1}, which is also much larger than the values previously observed, which were consistently about 0.01 cm$^{2/3}$ s^{-1} in the coastal ocean (Brooks 1960, Okubo 1971, Stacey et al. 2000). The scale-dependent analysis in Stacey et. al. (2000) was applied to the current data to estimate

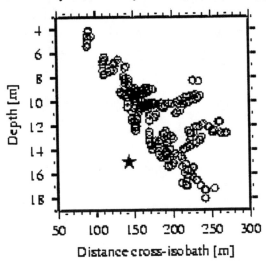

Figure 2. Lateral cross section of dye hits measured from an arbitrary horizontal datum. The source is marked with a star at a depth of 15 meters depth and 140 meters distance.

the dispersion coefficient in a reference frame centered along the plume centerline to remove any meandering or unsteadiness effects in the plume structure. The fact that the horizontal dispersion appears to exceed the expected value by a large amount indicates that over the period of the measurements - which took place over about 1.5 hours - the plume was meandering within the bottom boundary layer. Based on the scale of the dye distribution, we would estimate this meander lengthscale to be about 60 meters on either side of the centerline (along-isobath), which at a distance of 200 meters indicates an angle of about 15°.

9. Plume Summary

The plume structure in this stratified coastal flow is dominated by the bottom boundary layer. The dye, which is released in the near-bed region, is largely constrained to remain in the bottom boundary layer.

Within this layer, it advects along isobaths in the near field, until it is forced downslope by a sill in the bathymetry at about 600 meters downstream. Vertical dispersion is capped by the stratification above the bottom boundary layer, but evidence of density intrusions appear in the form of lenses extending into the interior of the flow. Finally, the horizontal dye distribution within the bottom boundary layer appears to be dominated by extensive meandering of the plume centerline, with a maximum meandering angle of about 15°.

Subsequent to the March 1999 study, an autonomous underwater vehicle (REMUS) was used to sample a similar plume at the same location. Figure 3 shows the dye concentration data collected by REMUS. In this case the flow was to the Northwest at approximately 7 cm s^{-1} along-isobath with the source located on the 15 meter isobath on the right side of Figure 1. This data set was collected in less than 20 minutes and each individual plume crossing was accomplished in less than 20 seconds so the meandering detected in the towed data set does not appear. The plume width expands from 10 to 30 meters at downstream ranges of 30 and 130 meters and the maximum concentration decreases from 15 to 4 ppb at the same ranges.

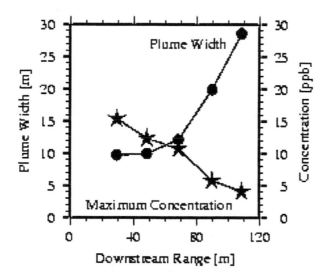

Figure 3. Plot of REMUS dye plume crossing data. The lateral plume width in meters (circles) is shown as a function of range downstream from the source and the maximum dye concentration measured as a function of range is also shown (stars).

10. Microstructure Observations and Discussion

The microstructure profiles show that the water column may be divided into three main sections: 1) A surface layer where, during wind events, active mixing takes place; 2) a near bed layer where mixing is predominantly driven by bottom stress; and, 3) an intermediate, often quiescent, section which is punctuated by areas of shear induced mixing and may contain multiple mixing events. These layers are seen in Figure 4. This cast was taken at 0932 PST on 26 March 1999. The segments were calculated by cumulatively summing the Thorpe displacement and taking the zero turning points as the section boundaries. The resultant kinetic energy dissipation rate ranges from 2.3 x 10^{-8} to 1.6 x 10^{-7} m^2 s^{-1}, while the vertical diffusivity (K$_z$) has a range of 2.7 x 10^{-4} to 1.3 x10^{-3} m^2 s^{-1}. The calculated kinetic energy dissipation rates (epsilon) are calculated by fitting the Bachelor spectrum (Imberger and Ivey 1991), and the flux Richardson number was computed as in Ivey and Imberger (1991), and K$_z$ = R$_f$/(1 - R$_f$) x epsilon/N^2, where N^2 is the Brunt-Viasalla frequency.

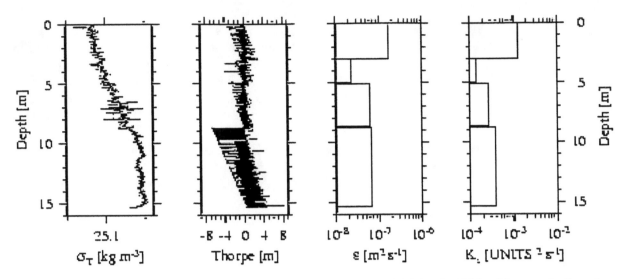

Figure 4. Typical microstructure profile taken at 0932 PST, 26 March 1999. The vertical scale on all plots is depth in meters. Panels a, b, c and d are: density, Thorpe displacement, turbulent kinetic energy dissipation rate and vertical eddy diffusivity.

11. Conclusions

The conclusions drawn from this work are as follows: 1) In the near-shore environment, the flow may be approximated as along-isobath, though there are periods of across-isobath flows. 2) When stratification is strong enough to limit vertical mixing across interfaces, dye released in a layer is necessarily constrained within that layer. 3) The interaction of stratification with a sloping bottom can generate lenses of bottom layer water at the stratification interface which extend seaward possibly transport scalars such as contaminants, nutrients or biota offshore. 4) Observed horizontal dispersion rates of towed fluorometer data (which took 1.5 hours to characterize the plume) are about 2 orders of magnitude larger than generally accepted values. If scale dependant dispersion (Stacey et. al, 2000) is applied to the problem, the coefficient of the dispersion term would be 0.08 $cm^{2/3}$ s^{-1}, substantially larger than observed values. And, 5) that the kinetic energy dissipation rate observed for this period is in the range of 2.3 x 10^{-8} to 1.6 x 10^{-7} m^2 s^{-3}, while the vertical diffusivity has a range of 2.7 x 10^{-4} to 1.3 x10^{-3} m^2 s^{-1}.

13. References

Brooks, N. H. Diffusion of Sewage Effluent in an Ocean-Current. Proc. First International Conference on Waste Disposal in the Marine Environment., UC-Berkeley, 1960.

Imberger, J. and Ivey, G.N. *On the Nature of Turbulence in a Stratified Fluid. Part II: Application to lakes.* Journal of Physical Oceanography, Vol. 21, No. 5, May 1991.

Ivey, G.N. And Imberger, J. *On the Nature of Turbulence in a Stratified Fluid. Part I: The Energetics of mixing.* Journal of Physical Oceanography, Vol. 21, No. 5, May 1991.

Okubo, A. Ocean Diffusion Diagrams. Deep-Sea Research, 18, 789-802, 1971.

Stacey, M. T., A. E. Cowen, T. M. Powell, E. Dobbins, S. G. Monismith and , J. R. Koseff. *Plume Dispersion in a Stratified, Near-Coastal Flow: Measurements and Modeling.*CSR, x.20, 637-663. 2000.

TIDAL FLOW ACROSS A FINITE REGION OF ROUGHNESS

G. Pawlak and P. MacCready

School of Oceanography
University of Washington
Seattle, Washington 98195-7940

Abstract

The transfer of fluid to and from mixing regions at the boundaries of a basin plays a key role in oceanic boundary mixing as well as in coastal and estuarine processes. Experimental observations of the oscillating flow of a fluid over a 2D region of roughness of finite extent are presented which suggest a mechanism for this transfer of mass and momentum. Particle imaging velocimetry along with flow visualization reveal that large scale flow patterns are generated near the region of roughness. Two flow regimes are observed for differing ratios of along-coast tidal excursion, L, to the length of the roughness region, D. For $L/D > 0.5$, a weak inflow is produced in the vicinity of the roughness region, with a corresponding alongslope flow away from the region. For $L/D < 0.5$, a strong outflow jet is established near the center of the roughness region along with an inward alongslope flow. Results are presented for a range of L/D. A model is presented that accounts for the contrasting flow regimes. Effects of stratification and slope are examined using a numerical model.

1   Introduction

The oscillatory flow past a rough boundary is a prevalent feature in a number of oceanographic scenarios from estuarine environments to continental slopes. At the core of the problem of flow over a rough boundary is the issue of flow separation. Separation introduces vorticity into larger scales, which can, in turn, generate residual flows, particularly in tidal cases where eddies are created systematically and may linger near the generation site.

The existence of large scale vortex structures in the separated wake of bathymetrical features is well documented in oceanographic literature. In particular, emphasis has focused on the generation of headland eddies in shallow coastal seas. Most notably, observations and numerical studies by Signell and Geyer [1991] have illuminated the role of flow separation in the generation of these eddies and examined their associated mean flow patterns and 3D structure. For higher aspect ratio flows in deeper waters, where frictional damping is decreased, eddies may exist for more than a tidal cycle and this will have important effects on residual flow patterns. We will show that in weakly damped cases, tidal flow past an isolated separation zone such as a headland will generate either a shoreward flow for long tidal excursions (relative to the scale of the separation zone), or an offshore-directed jet for short tidal excursions.

Considering a roughness region of *finite* extent introduces an additional length scale, *D*. This is a measure of the region over which large scale vorticity structure is generated. We will address how the ratio of the tidal excursion to the alongshore roughness scale, L/D, affects the generation of residual flows through the dynamics of the resulting vorticity field. The ratio L/D can be interpreted as a Keulegan-Carpenter number, which is a key parameter in oscillatory flow past a cylinder. (Keulegan and Carpenter, [1958]).

In this paper, we will first examine the establishment of residual flow pattern resulting from flow past an isolated region of separated flow through observations from laboratory experiments. Numerical experiments will then examine the effects of stratification and slope on flow separation and internal wave generation.

2   Laboratory Experiments

Laboratory experiments have identified two residual flow regimes for tidal flow past an isolated region of roughness for flows in which the tidal excursion is comparable to the extent of the roughness region. The experiments were carried out in a shallow plexiglas tank measuring 76 cm x 244 cm x 20 cm (see figure 1). Flow diagnosis was achieved using a Particle Imaging Velocimetry (PIV) system (Pawlak and Armi [1998], Fincham and Spedding [1997]) which yields two components of velocity in a planar field.

A set of triangular ridges was mounted along the long vertical wall of the tank. The set of ridges was connected by a fine wire rope traverse to a computer-controlled motor programmed to approximate a

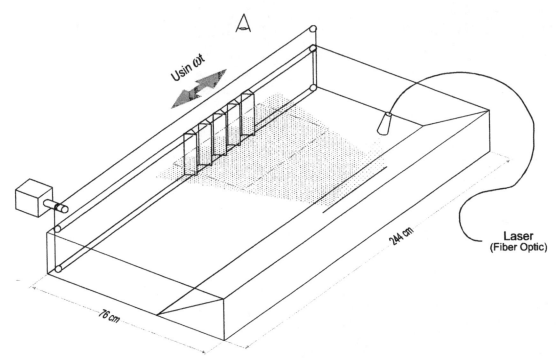

Figure 1: Experimental facility.

sinusoidal velocity at a period, T, with a maximum velocity, U. Experiments were conducted over a range of tidal excursions with the ratio of tidal excursion to patch size, L/D, varying from 0.2 to 1.2. Size and number of ridges was also varied, maintaining a fixed width, D.

Images covered an area of approximately 28cm x 18cm with the alongshore coordinate given as x and the offshore coordinate as y. Since the topography is oscillated, the lab frame of reference of the observations is quasi-Lagrangian, following the body of water in the tidal prism.

3 Flow regimes

For longer tidal excursions, a weak inflow was observed offshore of the region of roughness in the mean velocity field. Velocity vector fields along with mean flow magnitude and vorticity for $L/D = 1.2$ are presented in figure 2a. Velocities and vorticities are normalized by the rms tidal velocity, U_{rms} and U_{rms}/δ, respectively. Along with the inflow, the significant feature in the mean flow field is the outflow observed along the x boundary directed away from the region of roughness.

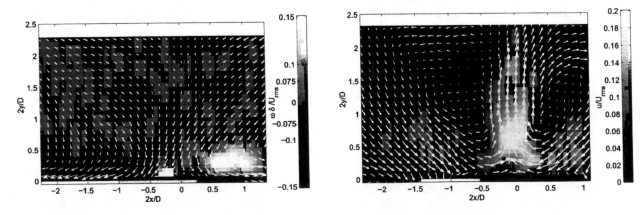

Figure 2: Mean vorticity for: a) L/D=1.3 ; b) L/D=0.3

Examinations of the realtime image sequences along with their corresponding velocity fields indicate that chief contribution to the offshore inflow occurs in the region downstream of the roughness elements (with respect to the tidal flow).

For the case of a tidal excursion smaller than the width of the roughness region, a marked difference is observed in the tidally averaged flow. Mean velocity and vorticity fields are shown in figure 2b for $L/D = 0.3$. A strong outflow jet is prominent immediately offshore of the obstacles. Associated with this offshore flow are diagonal inflows at opposite ends of the patch region. Mean velocities in the jet for the case shown show a maximum of about $0.3U_{rms}$ along the centerline. The outflow observed along the boundary at higher L/D is no longer evident at $L/D = 0.3$.

For cases examined with $0.3 < L/D < 1.2$, the mean flow patterns show a rather smooth progression between the offshore jet and inflow. This is illustrated in figure 3 which shows the maximum offshore flux versus tidal excursion L/D at a range of offshore positions, y/δ. These values are obtained between zero crossings around the jet in the offshore flow cases and by taking a mean across $\pm D/2$ for the inflow cases. The flux is normalized using $U_{rms}\delta$. The strong offshore velocities at low L/D diminish linearly with increasing L/D, yielding subsequently to the inflow case.

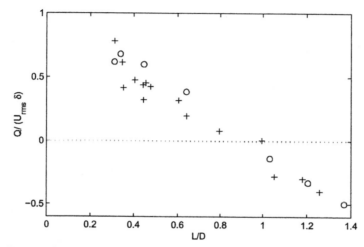

Figure 3: Maximum offshore flux as a function of tidal excursion, L/D. Large ridge experiments are indicated by + and small ridges by **o**.

4   Vortex Dynamics

From observations of realtime and phase averaged vorticity sequences within the two regimes of flow, we have developed a vortex dynamics argument, summarized in 4, which accounts for the variation in the residual flow field. The illustrations in figure 4 are shown within a lab frame of reference with the obstacles moving.

For simplicity, the cartoon ignores effects of earlier cycles on the vorticity field. Examining first the long tidal excursion case, in the initial portion of the cycle, positive (light gray) vorticity is generated as flow separates in the lee of each roughness element. This vorticity is shed downstream of the patch as the flow develops, into a growing region of circulation. The trailing vortex patch also moves to the right by self advection with its image across the boundary. Just prior to the reversal of the tide at $\phi = \pi$, the positive vorticity at each roughness element induces a separation zone upstream with an associated region of negative (dark gray) vorticity. As the reversing tide strengthens, negative vorticity increases and remaining positive vorticity is advected offshore over the new region of opposite sign circulation. As the roughness patch moves back to the left, generating a growing region of negative vorticity, the original positive vorticity is advected to the right. For higher L/D, the tidal excursion is long enough so that the roughness region moves past the entire original positive vorticity region, by the end of the full tidal cycle. At the completion of the cycle, two regions of opposite sign vorticity exist, which induce an inflow in the center. This inflow is balanced by the outflow along the boundaries due to the self advection of each patch of vorticity away from the origin.

The low L/D case is illustrated in figure 4b. Again, earlier tidal cycles are neglected for simplicity. The

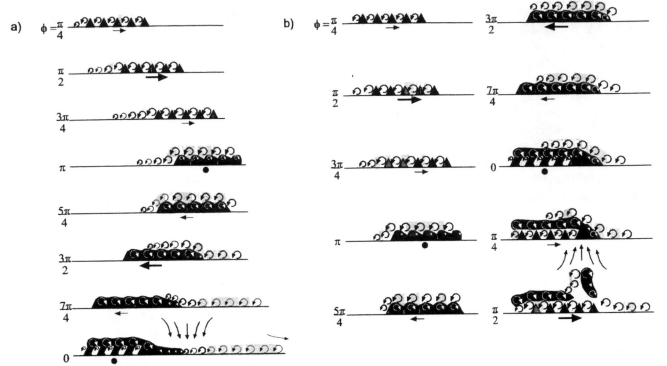

Figure 4: Vortex dynamical description of flow regimes

tidal cycle develops in the same manner as for high L/D, with generation of positive vorticity, followed by negative vorticity on the turn of the tide and advection of the original patch to the right. In the short tidal excursion limit, however, the tidal range is not long enough for the roughness region to move past the entire original patch of positive vorticity. In this case, the end of the tidal cycle results in an accumulation of both signs of vorticity offshore of the rough patch. This results in the formation of vortex pairs from the tails of each patch, which self-advect in the offshore direction creating the jet centered at zero in the mean flow field in figure 2b.

The offshore extent of the flow is limited by the amount of vorticity fed into the jet, the dissipation of vorticity and the inflow induced by vorticity along the boundary. The jet weakens offshore until it reaches a stagnation point balancing the inflow induced by the outer vortices, and the remaining vorticity is fed back into the weak recirculation offshore of the rough patch. The evolution of the offshore flow versus L/D is illustrated in figure 5, showing vorticity fields for $0.3 < L/D < 1.0$. The distinct jet and recirculation zones are most clearly evident for the case of $L/D = 0.4$ (fig. 5b). As L/D increases and the amount of vorticity fed into the jet decreases and the offshore stagnation point moves closer to the boundary, as evidenced in fig. 5d. Above $L/D = 1.0$ (figure 2) the recirculation region vanishes altogether.

We can expect the vorticity near the rough boundary to scale as $\bar{U}/\delta$, where $\bar{U}$ is the mean tidal velocity. For a sinusoidal tide, the mean tidal velocity is given by

$$\bar{U} = \frac{L}{T} = \frac{2U_{max}}{\pi} \qquad (1)$$

in which U_{max} is the peak tidal velocity. The tidal excursion is then related to U_{max} by $L = U_{max}T/\pi$. An individual eddy of scale δ and vorticity $\bar{U}/\delta$ will self advect along a boundary at

$$V_\omega = \frac{\Gamma}{2\pi\delta} \qquad (2)$$

where $\Gamma = \pi\omega\delta^2 = \pi\bar{U}\delta$ is the circulation. In half of a tidal cycle, the eddy will then travel a distance

$$L_\omega = \frac{V_\omega T}{2} = \frac{U_{max}T}{2\pi} = \frac{L}{2} \qquad (3)$$

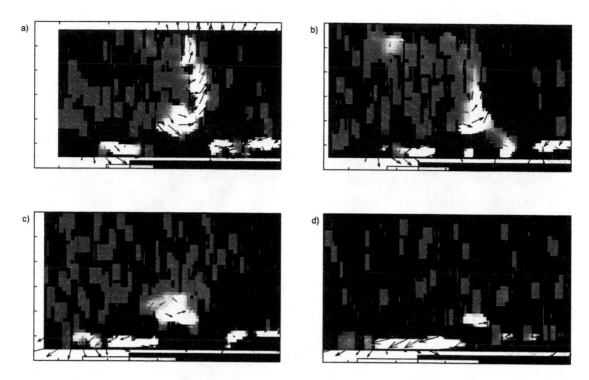

Figure 5: Vorticity fields for $0.3 < L/D < 1.2$.

If we assume that the vortex patch consists of eddies of scale δ, then at $t = T/2$, the patch will have a length $D + l/2$. At $t = T$, the vortex patch will have moved a distance L.

To a first approximation, we might expect, then, the transition between the two flow regimes discussed above to occur at $L = D$, when all of the vorticity from the previous cycle has moved past the roughness region. The transition occurs gradually, however, as the outflow induced by the inner vorticity is offset by the inflow from the vorticity which does finish the cycle outside of the rough region.

5 Numerical Experiments

Numerical experiments conducted using the Hallberg Isopycnic Model (HIM, Hallberg and Rhines, [1996]) have addressed the effects of stratification and internal wave generation on the flow separation along a sloping boundary. Linear analysis of the constant velocity flow of stratified fluid across an inclined wavy boundary (Thorpe, [1996]) reveals the existence of a high and low speed cutoff in the wave generating flow regime. The high velocity limit is related to a critical transition in the flow. The low velocity cutoff occurs when internal waves propagation intersects the slope. Recent analysis by MacCready and Pawlak [2000] has extended Thorpe's solution beyond these cutoffs for a wavy boundary and for a single ridge. Numerical modelling has examined the separating flow regime for flow past a single ridge.

The model is hydrostatic, solving the shallow water equations in a number of layers of different density. A 10km x 10km x 200m domain is used, with a horizontal resolution of 100m and an initial vertical spacing of 5m (40 layers). The simulations are nonrotating using a quadriatic bottom drag and Richardson number dependent mixing. Flow is re-entrant in the x direction with a free slip wall along the y=10 km boundary.

Figure 6a shows model results for the case of a Gaussian ridge with an along channel scale of 1 km. The along channel velocity (-0.5 ms^{-1}) and the stratification ($N = 10^{-2}s^{-1}$) is such that the flow is within the wave generation regime. Strong interface displacements are evident in the the lee of the ridge.

Numerical results of flow below the low speed cutoff (-0.125 ms^{-1}, $N = 10^{-2}s^{-1}$) are shown in figure 6b. Interface displacements are very weak, consistent with the lack of wave generation. Tracer patterns indicate significant horizontal flow separation and developement of a growing eddy in the lee of the ridge. Examination of variations with ridge height show a higher tendency for flow separation in the low velocity, non-wave generating regime.

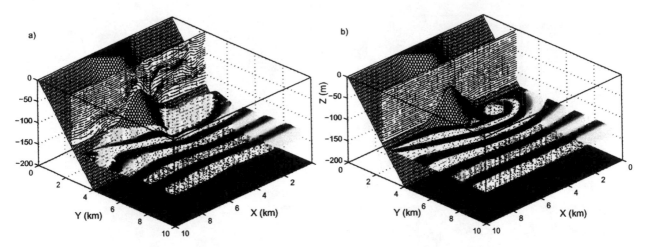

Figure 6: Numerical model results: a) Within wave generation regime. b) Below low velocity cutoff

The numerical model has also allowed analysis of variation of drag for the unidirectional flow case. This analysis suggests that a drag coefficient of one (based on the frontal area of the ridge is appropriate. This agrees well with the vorticity and flux scaling using U and δ in section 3.

6 Summary

We have examined flow past a region of roughness for weakly damped flow. Experiments have revealed two distinct flow regimes for tidally forced flow. For large tidal excursions ($L/D > 1$), an inflow is established offshore of the rough region, with outflow along the boundaries. For shorter tidal excursions ($L/D < 1$), an outflow jet is generated offshore of the patch. These contrasting cases and the linear transition between them can be accounted for using a simple vortex dynamical model. Numerical modeling has been used to examine the interaction between flow separation and internal wave generation for unidirectional flow along a slope.

References

Fincham, A. and Spedding, G. (1997). Low cost, high resolution DPIV for measurement of turbulent fluid flow. *Exp. in Fluids*, 23:449–462.

Hallberg, R. and Rhines, P. B. (1996). Buoyancy driven circulation in an ocean basin with isopycnals intersecting the sloping boundary. *J. Phys. Oceanogr.*, 26:913–940.

Keulegan, G. H. and H., L. (1958). Forces on cylinders and plates in an oscillating fluid. *J. Res. Nat. Bur. Stand.*, 60(5):423–440.

Pawlak, G. and Armi, L. (1998). Vortex dynamics in a spatially accelerating shear layer. *J. Fluid Mech.*, 376:1–35.

Pawlak, G. and MacCready, P. (2000). Stratified flow along rough slopes: horizontal exchange with offshore waters. *J. Phys. Oceanogr.* in prep.

Signell, R. P. and Geyer, W. R. (1991). Transient eddy formation around headlands. *J. Geophys. Res.*, 96(C2):2561–2575.

Thorpe, S. (1996). The cross-slope transport of momentum by internal waves generated by alongslope currents over topography. *J. Phys. Oceanogr.*, 26:191–204.

13

OCEANIC FLOWS

Lagrangian Measurements of Internal Waves and Turbulence in the Deep-Cycle Layer in the Central Equatorial Pacific

Ren-Chieh Lien,[1] Eric A D'Asaro,[1] and Michael J McPhaden[2]

[1]Applied Physics Laboratory, College of Ocean and Fishery Sciences, University of Washington, Seattle, WA 98195
[2]Pacific Marine Environmental Laboratory, National Oceanic and Atmospheric Administration, Seattle, Washington, 98115

lien@apl.washington.edu, dasaro@apl.washington.edu, mcphaden@pmel.noaa.gov

1. Abstract

Lagrangian frequency spectra of vertical velocity and temperature reveal the diurnal cycle of night-time enhancement of internal wave energy and turbulence in a shear-stratified layer below the surface mixed layer in the central equatorial Pacific. Internal waves and turbulence are separated by the buoyancy frequency N in the observed Lagrangian frequency spectra. Estimates of the turbulence kinetic energy dissipation rate (ε) from the observed vertical acceleration spectra show a day to night fluctuation of nearly one decade during a period of strong easterly wind. The spectral level of the time rate of change of temperature in the turbulence inertial subrange provides an estimate of the thermal diffusion rate, χ, which varies by more than four decades in a four-day period. The estimated eddy diffusivity $K_\rho = 0.2\varepsilon N^{-2}$ follows closely with the estimated thermal diffusivity $K_h = 0.5\chi(\partial_z\bar\theta)^{-2}$. The bulk estimate of the turbulent heat flux in the deep-cycle layer, $O(100 \text{ W m}^{-2})$, is comparable to the surface heat flux.

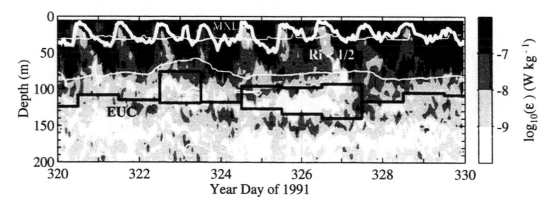

Figure 1: Contours of $\log_{10}\varepsilon$ observed at equator 140°W during the Tropical Instability Wave Experiment (TIWE) (Lien et al., 1995). The thick white curve shows the base of the surface mixed layer. Two thin white curves delineate the depth range where Ri < 1/2. The black stair shows the depth of the Equatorial Undercurrent (EUC), defined as the depth where $\partial_z U = 0$.

2. Introduction

Microstructure measurements from the upper central equatorial Pacific ocean show intensified turbulence and internal wave energy at nighttime in a shear-stratified low Richardson-number layer, called the deep-cycle layer, extending below the surface mixed layer (Fig. 1). Observed properties of turbulence and internal waves in the deep-cycle layer have been described extensively in previous studies (for example, Gregg et al., 1985; Hebert et al., 1992; Moum and Caldwell, 1985; Peters et al., 1988; Wijesekera and Dillon, 1991; Hebert et al., 1992; McPhaden and Peters, 1992; Lien et al., 1995; Lien et al., 1996; Caldwell et al., 1997). During moderate to strong easterly wind, the nighttime dissipation rate in the deep-cycle layer exceeds the daytime value by at least a factor of 10 and greatly enhances turbulence momentum and heat fluxes.

It is generally believed that waves and turbulence in the deep-cycle layer are dynamically linked, although their generation mechanisms are yet not well understood. There are two fundamentally different theories for the observed nighttime enhancement of internal waves and turbulence in the deep-cycle layer. One theory suggests that internal waves are generated during nighttime convection within or at the base of the surface mixed layer, propagate downward into the deep-cycle layer, trigger shear instability, and break into turbulence (Gregg et al., 1985; Wijesekera and Dillon, 1991; Skyllingstad and Denbo, 1994; Peters et al., 1994). The other theory suggests that both the enhanced internal waves and turbulence are generated locally in the deep-cycle layer via the shear instability (Moum et al., 1992; Sutherland, 1996; Mack and Hebert, 1997; Sun et al., 1998; Wang et al., 1998; Clayson and Kantha, 1999). To distinguish these two mechanisms, simultaneous observations of internal waves and turbulence are needed.

3. Lagrangian Measurements in the Deep-Cycle Layer

Measurements were made using neutrally buoyant deep "Lagrangian floats" (DLF) (Fig. 2a). These are designed to accurately follow water motions at high frequencies through a combination of a density that matches that of seawater and a high drag. Float deployments in a variety of flows, both wavelike and turbulent, show the float to be approximately Lagrangian (D'Asaro et al., 1996).

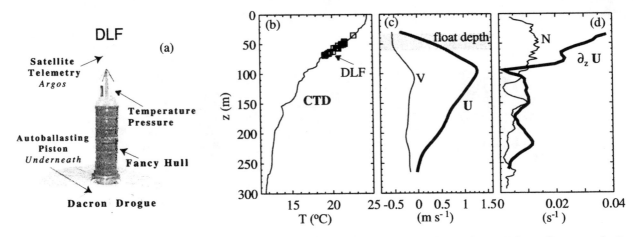

Figure 2: (a) Deep Lagrangian Float (DLF). The hull of the DLF is about 0.7 m long and the drogue opens up to about 1 m in diameter. The thin curve in (b) is the background temperature profile taken from CTD measurements and the squares are the temperature measured by the DLF. The velocity profiles in (c) were taken from the shipboard ADCP. The stratification N and shear in (d) were computed from the CTD and ADCP.

Two DLFs were deployed at the equator 140°W at 45-m and 55-m depths on September 29, 1998, by PMEL/NOAA during routine mooring operations. Unfortunately, the DLF deployed at 55-m depth failed for unknown reasons. The DLF deployed at 45-m depth successfully took 8 days of measurements. It sampled every 300 s in the first half day while measuring the vertical profile of temperature and ballasting the float. In the following 4 days, it sampled every 30 s, resolving both internal waves and part of the turbulence inertial subrange. It then switched to a 300-s sampling rate in the last 3.5 days. In the following analysis, only measurements taken at the 30-s sampling interval, which resolve both internal waves and turbulence, will be discussed.

The CTD profile taken by the NOAA/TAO group showed a buoyancy frequency N of about 0.013 s^{-1} between 30- and 60-m depths (Fig. 2d) where the DLF fluctuated during the 8-day sampling period (Fig. 3b). Temperature measurements taken by the DLF agreed with the CTD profile (Fig. 2b). The South Equatorial Current (SEC) flowed westward at a speed > 0.4 m s^{-1}, and the Equatorial Undercurrent (EUC) flowed at a speed of 1.3 m s^{-1} centering at 90-m depth (Fig. 2c). The vertical shear of the mean zonal flow was 0.03–0.035 s^{-1} between 30- and 60-m depth (Fig. 2d), and the gradient Richardson number was close to 0.25. During these 4 days, the easterly wind was 6–9 m s^{-1} and the vertical shear of zonal flow across the mixed layer, based on current meter measurements at 10- and 25-m depths, was greater than 0.06 s^{-1} (Fig. 3a). The variance of the vertical velocity of the DLF showed a clear enhancement at nighttime (Fig. 3c). Temperature measured by the DLF also showed enhanced high-frequency variances at nighttime associated with the elevated vertical-velocity variance (Fig. 3d).

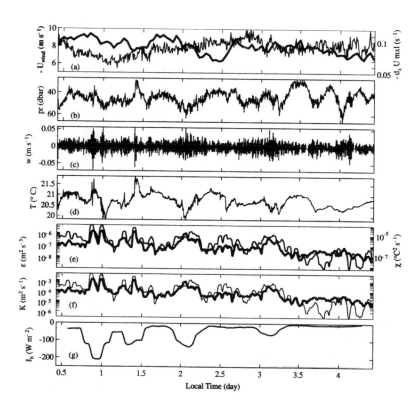

Figure 3: Time series of (a) easterly wind speed (thick curve) and the vertical shear of zonal velocity across the surface mixed layer (thin curve) computed using current-meter measurements at 10- and 25-m depths, (b) pressure measured by the DLF, (c) vertical velocity of the DLF, (d) temperature measurements of the DLF, (e) estimates of ε and χ computed from the wavelet spectra of vertical acceleration and the time rate of change of temperature of the DLF, (f) estimates of eddy diffusivity $K_\rho = 0.2\varepsilon N^{-2}$ and thermal diffusivity $K_h = 0.5\chi(\partial_z\theta)^{-2}$, and (g) the estimate of heat flux $J_h = -\rho C_p K_h \partial_z \theta$ 6-hr running-mean averaged in the deep-cycle layer. The time axis is the local time elapsed from September 29 0000Z.

4. Diurnal Variation of Lagrangian Frequency Spectra

D'Asaro and Lien (2000) show that internal waves and turbulence in a stratified flow can be readily separated by their Lagrangian frequency. Internal waves exist at $\omega \leq N$, and turbulence exists at

$\omega \geq N$. Lagrangian frequency spectra of vertical velocity $\Phi_w(\omega)$ have a universal spectral form, white below N and ω^{-2} beyond N. The vertical acceleration spectrum in the inertial subrange is white, i.e., $\Phi_a(\omega) = \beta_a \varepsilon$, where $\beta_a = 1.8$ is a universal constant (Lien et al., 1998).

On the basis of the dimensional analysis, the Lagrangian frequency spectrum of the time rate of change of temperature $\Phi_{\dot\theta}(\omega)$ in the inertial subrange should be proportional to the thermal diffusion rate χ. Following Tennekes and Lumley's (1972) procedure of deriving $\Phi_w(\omega)$, we derive the exact form $\Phi_{\dot\theta}(\omega) = \beta_\theta \chi$ in the turbulence inertial subrange, where $\beta_\theta = 0.75$.

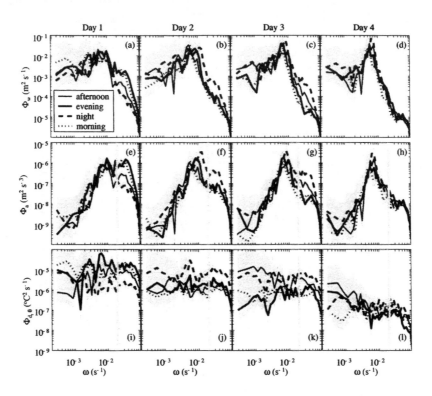

Figure 4: Lagrangian frequency spectra of vertical velocity $\Phi_w(\omega)$ (the top row), vertical acceleration $\Phi_a(\omega)$ (the middle row), and the time rate of change of temperature $\Phi_{d_t\theta}(\omega)$ (the bottom row). Spectra were computed in a 6-hr bin dividing each day into four time zones: 1200Z – 1800Z (afternoon) (thin curves), 1800Z – 2400Z (evening) (thick solid curves), 2400Z – 0600Z (night) (thick dashed curves), and 0600Z – 1200Z (morning) (thick dotted curves). Grey vertical lines in the middle and bottom rows show the frequency in the turbulence inertial subrange at which wavelet spectral levels are used to compute ε and χ in Fig. 3e.

To reveal the diurnal variation of internal waves and turbulence, we compute $\Phi_w(\omega)$, $\Phi_a(\omega)$, and $\Phi_{\dot\theta}(\omega)$ in four time zones of each day; 1200Z – 1800Z (afternoon), 1800Z – 2400Z (evening), 2400Z – 0600Z (night), and 0600 – 1200Z (morning). Except for the fourth day, observed spectra show a significant nighttime enhancement at $\omega \geq N$. The time of the day when spectra reach the maximum varies from day to day, e.g., evening in the first day, night in the second and third days. Spectra show no significant day/night difference at low frequencies, $\omega \leq N$. $\Phi_w(\omega)$ shows a distinct peak near N which is probably the effect of turning point (Desaubies, 1975). $\Phi_a(\omega)$ shows a spectral plateau in the inertial subrange. The rapid roll-off near the Nyquist frequency is due to the combination of the effect of float's finite size (Lien et al., 1998) and the smoothing effect in computing acceleration. The spectral level at the plateau in the inertial subrange is proportional to ε. $\Phi_{\dot\theta}(\omega)$ shows a white spectral shape in the inertial subrange ($\omega \geq N$) as expected, and the spectral level is proportional to χ.

5. Turbulence Properties in the Deep-Cycle Layer

We performed a wavelet analysis on observations of vertical acceleration and time rate of change in temperature (Percival and Guttorp, 1994). Wavelet spectral density was calculated by dividing wavelet variances by the corresponding frequency band at each time. Estimates of ε and χ were computed by dividing wavelet spectral levels of vertical acceleration and the time rate of change of temperature at the wavelet frequency of 0.02 s^{-1} by β_a and β_θ, respectively (Fig. 3e). The estimated χ varies from 2×10^{-9} to 4×10^{-5} °K^2 s^{-1}, four decades of variation. The estimated ε varies from 3×10^{-8} to 2×10^{-6} W kg^{-1}. Estimates of ε and χ fluctuate in unison during the first three days and show an elevated nighttime mixing. The bit noise of the pressure reading of the DLF sets the lower bound of the estimate of ε of $\sim 3 \times 10^{-8}$ W kg^{-1}.

The eddy diffusivity is computed as $K_\rho = 0.2\varepsilon N^{-2}$ (Osborn, 1980), and the thermal diffusivity is computed as $K_h = 0.5\chi(d\bar{\theta}/dz)^{-2}$ (Osborn and Cox, 1972). A constant $N = 0.013 s^{-1}$ and a constant $d\bar{\theta}/dz = 0.1$°K m^{-1} measured from the CTD profile are used to compute K_ρ and K_h. Estimates of K_ρ and K_h follow closely with each other with a factor of two difference, except for the last day when the estimated ε might be contaminated by the bit noise (Fig. 3f). Furthermore, we compute the 6-hr running average of the heat flux $J_h = -\rho C_p K_h d\bar{\theta}/dz$, where C_p is the heat capacity. It again shows a nighttime enhanced heat flux $O(100$ W m$^{-2})$. The peak heat flux in the first night reaches to a maximum value of 200 W m^{-2}.

6. Summary

Four-day measurements of a Lagrangian float reveal the nighttime enhancement of ε and χ in the deep-cycle layer. Spectral levels of vertical velocity, vertical acceleration, and the time rate of change of temperature increase at nighttime in the turbulence inertial subrange, but remain unchanged at frequencies below N. Estimates of ε and χ from observed Lagrangian frequency spectra of vertical acceleration and the time rate of change of temperature are consistent with previous observations from microstructure measurements at the same location. Our estimate of heat flux, $O(100$ W m$^{-2})$, is comparable to the surface heat flux, but exceeds previous microstructure observations, $O(50$ W m$^{-2})$. This is consistent with the result of Wang and McPhaden (2000), who found that the estimated turbulent heat flux in the upper central equatorial Pacific was enhanced during La Niña and reduced during El Niño.

7. References

Clayson, C. A., and L. H. Kantha, 1999: Turbulent kinetic energy and its dissipation rate in the equatorial mixed layer. *J. Phys. Oceanogr.*, **29**, 2146–2166.

Caldwell, D. R., R.-C. Lien, J. N. Moum, and M. C. Gregg, 1997: Turbulence decay and restratification in the equatorial ocean surface layer following nighttime convection. *J. Phys. Oceanogr.*, **27**, 1120–1132.

D'Asaro, E. A., D. M. Farmer, J. T. Osse, and G. T. Dairiki, 1996: A Lagrangian float. *J. Atmos. Oceanic Technol.*, **13**, 1230–1246.

D'Asaro, E. A., And R.-C. Lien, 2000: Lagrangian measurements of waves and turbulence in stratified flows. *J. Phys. Oceanogr.*, **30**, 641–655.

Desaubies, Y. J. F., 1975: A linear theory of internal wave spectra and coherences near the Väisälä frequency. *J. Geophys. Res.*, **80**, 895–899.

Gregg, M. C., H. Peters, J. C. Wesson, N. S. Oakey, and T. J. Shay, 1985: Intensive measurements of turbulence and shear in the equatorial undercurrent. *Nature*, **318**, 40–144.

Hebert, D., J. N. Moum, C. A. Paulson, and D. R. Caldwell, 1992: Turbulence and internal waves at the equator. Part II: Details of a single event. *J. Phys. Oceanogr.*, **22**, 1346–1356.

Lien, R.-C., D. R. Caldwell, M. C. Gregg, and J. N. Moum, 1995: Turbulence variability at the equator in the central Pacific at the beginning of the 1991–93 El Niño. *J. Geophys. Res.*, **100**, 6881–6898.

Lien, R.-C., M. J. McPhaden, and M. C. Gregg, 1996: High-frequency internal waves in the upper central equatorial Pacific and their possible relationship to deep-cycle turbulence. *J. Phys. Oceanogr.*, **26**, 581–600.

Lien, R.-C., E. A. D'Asaro, and G. Dairiki, 1998: Lagrangian frequency spectra of vertical velocity and vorticity in high-Reynolds-number oceanic turbulence. *J. Fluid Mech.*, **362**, 177–198.

Mack, A. P., and D. Hebert, 1997: Internal gravity waves in the upper eastern equatorial Pacific: Observations and numerical solutions. *J. Geophys. Res.*, **102**, 21081–21100.

McPhaden, M. J., and H. Peters, 1992: Diurnal cycle of internal wave variability in the equatorial Pacific Ocean: Results from moored observations. *J. Phys. Oceanogr.*, **22**, 1317–1329.

Moum, J. N., and D. R. Caldwell, 1985: Local Influences on shear flow turbulence in the equatorial ocean. *Science*, **230**, 315–316.

Moum, J. N., D. Hebert, C. A. Paulson, and D. R. Caldwell, 1992: Turbulence and internal waves at the equator. Part I: Statistics from towed thermistors and a microstructure profiler. *J. Phys. Oceanogr.*, **22**, 1330–1345.

Osborn, T. R., 1980: Estimates of the local rate of vertical diffusion from dissipation measurements. *J. Phys. Oceanogr.*, **10**, 83–89.

Osborn, T. R., and C. S. Cox, 1972: Oceanic fine structure. *Geophys. Fluid Dyn.*, **3**, 321–345.

Peters, H., M. C. Gregg, and J. M. Toole, 1988: On the parameterization of equatorial turbulence. *J. Geophys. Res.*, **93**, 1199–1218.

Peters, H., M. C. Gregg, and T. B. Sanford, 1994: The diurnal cycle of the upper equatorial ocean: Turbulence, fine-scale shear, and mean shear. *J. Geophys. Res.*, **99**, 7707–7723.

Percival, D. B., and P. Guttorp, 1994: Long-memory processes, the Allan variance and wavelets. In *Wavelets in Geophysics* (eds. E. Foufoula-Georgiou and P. Kumar), pp. 325–343. Academic.

Sun, C., W. D. Smyth, and J. N. Moum, 1998: Dynamic instability of stratified shear flow in the upper equatorial Pacific. *J. Geophys. Res.*, **103**, 10323-10337.

Sutherland, B. R., 1996: Dynamic excitation of internal gravity waves in the equatorial ocean. *J. Phys. Oceanogr.*, **26**, 2398–2419.

Skyllingstad, E. D., and D. W. Denbo, 1994: The role of internal gravity waves in the equatorial current system. *J. Phys. Oceanogr.*, **24**, 2093–2110.

Tennekes, H., and J. L. Lumley, 1972: *A First Course in Turbulence*, MIT Press.

Wang, D., J. C. McWilliams, and W. G. Large, 1998: Large-eddy simulation of the diurnal cycle of deep equatorial turbulence. *J. Phys. Oceanogr.*, **28**, 129–148.

Wang, W. and M.J. McPhaden, 2000: The surface layer heat balance in the equatorial Pacific Ocean, Part II: Interannual variability. *J. Phys. Oceanogr.*, in press.

Wijesekera, H. W., and T. M. Dillon, 1991: Internal waves and mixing in the upper equatorial Pacific Ocean . *J. Geophys. Res.*, **96**, 711–7125.

Internal Solitons in the Andaman Sea

H. Michallet[1], L. Crosnier[1], E. Barthélemy[1] and F. Lyard[2]

[1] LEGI (CNRS-INPG-UJF),BP53, 38041 Grenoble Cedex 9, France
[2] LEGOS/GRGS, 18 av. Edouard Belin, 31400 Toulouse Cedex, France
eric.barthelemy@hmg.inpg.fr, michalle@hmg.inpg.fr, laurence.crosnier@hmg.inpg.fr, florent.lyard@cnes.fr

Abstract

The novel method of Pelinovsky *et al.* (1994) is implemented numerically to predict the occurence of solitary-wave-like pulses in coastal areas. It combines a set of tools that mimic the different stages from the ocean tide, to the internal tide and to its transformation into nonlinear waves. We show that in the south region of the Andaman Sea solitary like pulses stem from an internal tide created at a shelf break 2000m deep just off the Nicobar Islands. These waves gently shoal while propagating eastward and build up in large waves which produce signatures on SAR images.

1 Introduction

SAR images of the Andaman sea region, as the one shown in Fig. 1, show strong evidence of internal wave activity. It has been demonstrated long time ago that these signatures are due to nonlinear internal waves (Osborne & Burch, 1980). Nevertheless, the location where these solitary like pulses or solitons are generated is still a subject of controversy. Alpers et al. (1997) suspect that the curvature of the wave front indicates a focal point from which the waves originate (Dreadnought Bank in Fig. 1). A simple energetic argument would suggest that a wave of 5 meters in amplitude and of a length of several hundreds of kilometers can not be generated at a single point. It is one of the goals of the present paper to show that the internal non linear waves have actually their origin at the shelf break about 300 kilometers westward.

Recently, Holloway *et al.* (1999) have presented a generalized KdV model to describe the internal tide transformation on the Australian north west shelf. The governing equation includes both quadratric and cubic nonlinearities, rotation, bottom friction and slowly varying topography effects. The model produces some of the observed features of the internal wave field over the shelf. The internal tide is assumed to be a sinusoidal long wave and its transformation is evaluated on a transect. The refraction of the internal wave is therefore not taken into account in the model of Holloway *et al.* (1999). Wave fronts in the Andaman Sea exhibit strong curvatures (Fig. 1) suggesting that refraction effects should be accounted for.

We consider an equivalent two-layer system in our model in order to forecast the occurence of solitary-wave-like pulses in coastal areas. The data required for predicting the internal tide are detailed in the next section. We then present the formation and the refraction of the solitary like pulses. The computations require to successively run three modules. The first one computes the linear internal tide at topographic singularities. The second computes internal rays and the third computes the internal tide evolution towards non linear waves along the rays.

2 Generation of the internal tide

The linear tide is computed using a similar parametrization to that of Baines (1982, see Barthélemy *et al.*, 2000). It has been used by Guizien *et al.* (1999) to describe the internal tide on the Malin Shelf. This parametrization requires the amplitude and the direction of the barotropic forcing. This direction, aligned with the local wave vector, is given by the orientation of the major axis of the barotropic current ellipse. The current ellipses are obtained with a global oceanic tidal model

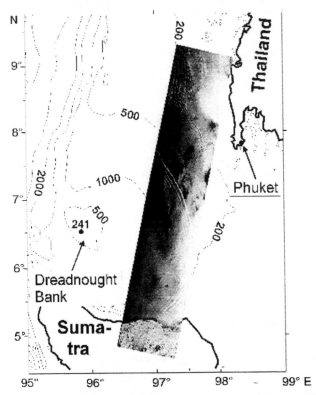

Figure 1: SAR strip inserted into a map of the Andaman Sea, from Alpers et al. (1997): "visible are sea surface manifestations of two internal solitary wave packets [...] separated in time by one tidal cycle". The image was acquired on May 4, 1996, 03:53 UTC, that is roughly 1:30 after low tide at Port Blair (Andaman Islands).

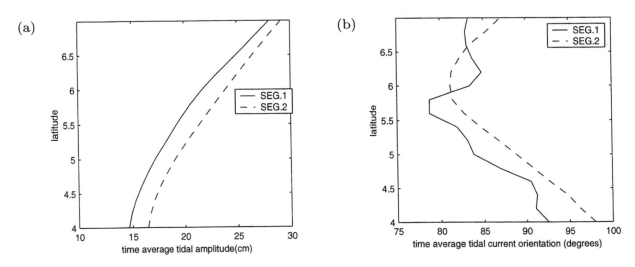

Figure 2: Barotropic forcing along line segments stretching from 91°E, 4°N to 91°E, 7°N (SEG.1) and from 93°E, 4°N to 92°E, 7°N (SEG.2). Surface tidal elevation (a) and orientation of the ellipse major axis of the tidal current to the latitude along the segments (b). (Results from FES95, Le Provost *et al.*, 1998.)

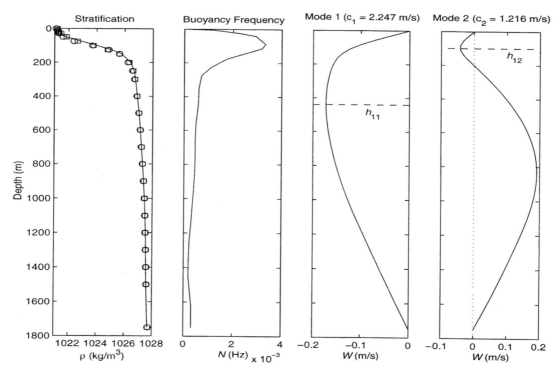

Figure 3: Density profiles (Levitus, 1982) at 95.5°E, 6.5°S in winter (—); at 92.5°E, 6.5°S in winter (□) and in summer (○). (The depths of the measurements are indicated by the symbols.) The Brunt-Väisälä frequency and the vertical velocities of the two first internal modes are also represented. h_{11} is the depth of the interface in the internal tide module, h_{12} is the depth of the interface in the ray and KdV computations.

(FES95, see Le Provost *et al.*, 1998). Some results are presented in Fig. 2. The current is oriented almost parallel to the shelf (Fig. 2b). In other words the tide is roughly propagating from the south to the north with an amplitude of about the same on the two segments considered (Fig. 2a). In the area of interest (between 4°N and 7°N) the mean value of 85° is chosen. The orientation of the current ellipse major axis slightly varies from day to day but this variation is neglected in our model especially with regards to the other approximations made to compute the internal tide.

An equivalent two-layer system is determined from the continuous stratification. The internal tide generation module relies on this two layer approximation. The density profiles presented in Fig. 3 are the average profiles provided by Levitus (1982). We note that this average stratification is not varying very much over the seasons. The associated Brunt-Väisälä frequency N (where $N^2 = -g/\rho \, \mathrm{d}\rho/\mathrm{d}z$) and the vertical velocity profiles of the two most energetic internal modes are also presented in Fig. 3 (see e.g. Holloway *et al.*, 1999, for the method to obtain the decomposition into internal modes). At the shelf break, maximum vertical velocities induced by the tide occur at $h_{11} \simeq 440$ m. These transmit energy that generate a linear baroclinic tide which evolves into nonlinear waves. In turn the latter propagate onto the shelf at the depth of the thermocline defined as the depth of the maximum of the Brunt-Väisälä frequency (note in Fig. 3 that it is approximately $h_{12} \simeq 100$ m the depth of the maximum vertical velocities of the second internal mode). For the linear internal tide module the relative density difference between the two layers is computed so to match the first mode phase speed according to:

$$c_1 = \left[g \frac{\Delta \rho}{\rho} \frac{h_1 h_2}{h_1 + h_2} \right]^{1/2} ,$$ (1)

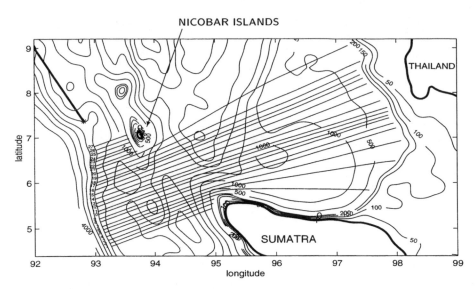

Figure 4: Some calculated rays in the shelf region. The rays start at the shelf break, they are perpendicular to the orientation of the mean shelf break represented by the thick solid line. Note the faning of the rays producing curved wave fronts such as those of Fig. 1 and that the Nicobar Islands and Sumatra act as screens for some of the rays.

where h_1 (h_2) and ρ_1 (ρ_2) are the thickness and density of the upper (lower) layer. With $h_1 = 440$ m (and $h_2 = 1310$ m), we obtain $\Delta\rho/\rho = 0.0015$. On the other hand, the relative difference in density used in the ray and KdV modules is $\Delta\rho/\rho = 0.0057$. This value is computed by averaging the densities in the upper and lower parts of the profile ($h \leq h_{12}$ for ρ_1 and $h \geq h_{11}$ for ρ_2). Note that this is matching (1) with $h_1 = 100$ m. The estimation of the equivalent two-layer system is actually a sensitive part of the model. Instantaneous density profiles would be required to predict accurately the soliton formation on a particular date.

3 Ray Tracing Method

The internal tide evolution is predicted simultaneously by a ray method (Pelinovsky & Shavratsky, 1976; Watson & Robinson, 1991; Pelinovsky *et al.*, 1994) and a nonlinear KdV model. The internal tide is quasi-linear in the vicinity of the shelf break. It refracts and evolves nonlinearly while propagating onshelf towards the coast. It is assumed here that the bottom topography is spatially smooth. Under this assumption the geometrical "optics" approximation for the internal waves is used. In contrast with surface waves internal waves may also refract because of the inhomogeneous ocean density. Smooth changes in the stratification will result in smooth changes of the phase speed and the wave characteristics (Pelinovsky & Shavratsky, 1976). Therefore if the horizontal length scales of both the ocean stratification and bottom topography are much larger than the internal waves length scales then these latter will continuously adapt.

A map of rays is given in Fig. 4. To compute such a map we used the Smith and Sandwell (1997) ocean topography providing a 3' resolution. This resolution is far too large for ray tracing purposes (Dingemans, 1997). The bathymetry is smoothed with a high pass filter: all features of less than 40 km length scales are eliminated. The internal tide characteristics delivered by the internal tide module show that the baroclinic wave crest is approximately aligned with the shelf break. We therefore prescribe in the ray module that all rays start at the 2000 m isobath perpendicular to the mean shelf break.

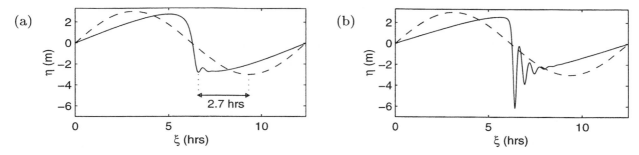

Figure 5: Evolution of the internal tide along ray 14 in Fig. 4: interfacial displacements η vs $\xi = t - \int_0^s \frac{dx}{c(x)}$. The two-layer stratification is $h_1 = 100$ m and $\Delta\rho/\rho = 0.57$ %. a) Initial sinusoidal interfacial displacement but also unaltered tide that would travel at the mode 1 speed ($--$); interfacial displacement at $x = 390$ km ($-$). b) Initial ($--$) and at $x = 540$ km ($-$).

4 Generation of the solitary waves

The solitary-like pulses generation model includes cubic nonlinearities but is not the modified KdV equation that predicts limiting amplitude waves (see Michallet & Barthélemy, 1998). It takes into account the shoaling and the ray separation. The numerical scheme used and described by Zabusky and Kruskal (1965) is a finite difference and explicit scheme.

One example of the internal tide deformation is presented in Fig. 5. The initial sinusoidal wave at the break is estimated by the internal tide module to be 3 m in amplitude (dashed line in Fig. 5). The wave is then progressively steepening and the initial stage of soliton formation is shown after a 390 km propagation (solid line in Fig. 5a). The maximum number of well separated solitary like pulses is apparently 3 as shown in Fig. 5b (solid line) with a maximum amplitude of about 6 m. This stage corresponds to the train in the upper part of the image in Fig. 1. Notice also that the solitary wave like pulses are ahead of the unaltered internal tide that would have travelled at the linear phase speed of the mode 1. The time lag is about 2.9 hours at the end of the ray.

5 Discussion and Conclusion

Alpers et al. (1997) suggest that the internal non-linear waves originate from spots as shallow reefs or seamounts in the Andaman Sea. The curvature of the wave fronts can also be explained by the faning behaviour of the rays that expand leeward the contraction created by the strait between the Nicobar Islands and Sumatra. Arrival times can also give a clue of where the waves are generated. The travel time of a long linear wave is $\int_0^s dx/c_1(x)$, where s is the curvilinear coordinate on a ray and $c_1(x)$ the phase velocity along the same ray. The travel time of the long crested non-linear wave front in Fig. 1 is estimated to be 62.5 hrs (65.3 hrs for the linear wave minus 2.8 hrs for the non-linear phase lag) that is about 5 tidal cycles. On May 4 the SAR image was taken 1.5 hrs after low water. This indicates that if the wave front of Fig. 1 had been generated at the shelf break it would have been generated roughly at low tide also (1.1 hrs after to be precise). It is well known that non-linear waves in two-layer systems with a shallow upper layer stem from depressions generated by low tide flow over the shelf break (e.g. Renouard & Zhang, 1988). We therefore have a set of indications that tend to point at the shelf break off the Nicobar Islands as the generation site. This hypothesis needs to be tested against much more images and even in-situ measurements.

We have presented in this paper preliminary results of a numerical model which mimics the different stages of the internal solitary waves formation on a continental shelf. The parametrization of the internal tide is very simple but also very schematic: it relies on a large set of assumptions.

Some of these could be relaxed. Alternatively a complete 3D hydrostatic numerical model of the internal tide could be used (Xing & Davies, 1998). The ray tracing part of the model is efficient and economic, while the non-linear model equation to predict the solitary like pulses could be improved. Indeed it is a second order KdV type which cannot predict the broadening of the pulses that is expected when the waves shoal meeting critical conditions (*e.g.* Helfrich *et al.*, 1984; Holloway *et al.*, 1999). Besides, the numerical scheme implemented may be time consuming when the depth of the thermocline is small since the spatial resolution must be high to compute narrow pulses. However, the total computing time on a PC computer is about one minute per ray for the conditions presented in this paper.

Acknowledgements

The authors acknowledge the support of IFREMER (contract 99.2064.003 TMSI/IDM/COM) and are indebted to W. Alpers for introducing them to the world of SAR images of internal waves.

References

ALPERS, W., WANG-CHEN, H., & HOCK, L. 1997. Observation of Internal Waves in the Andaman Sea by ERS SAR. *Page http://earth1.esrin.esa.it/florence/papers/data/alpers3/index.html of: 3rd ERS Symp. (ESA).*

BAINES, P. J. 1982. On internal tide generation models. *Deep Sea Res.*, **29**(3), 307–338.

BARTHÉLEMY, E., KABBAJ, A., & GERMAIN, J.-P. 2000. Long surface wave scattered by a step in a two-layer fluid. *Fluid Dyn. Res.*, **26**, 235–255.

DINGEMANS, M. W. 1997. *Water wave propagation on uneven bottoms. Part 1: Linear wave propagation.* Advanced Series on Ocean Engineering, vol. 13. World Scientific.

GUIZIEN, K., BARTHÉLEMY, E., & INALL, M. E. 1999. Internal tide generation at a shelf break by an oblique barotropic tide: Observations and analytical modeling. *J. Geophys. Res.*, **104**(C7), 15655–15668.

HELFRICH, K. R., MELVILLE, W. K., & MILES, J. W. 1984. On interfacial solitary waves over slowly varying topography. *J. Fluid Mech.*, **149**, 305–317.

HOLLOWAY, P. E., PELINOVSKY, E., & TALIPOVA, T. 1999. A generalized Korteweg-de Vries model of internal tide transformation in the coastal zone. *J. Geophys. Res.*, **104**(C8), 18333–18350.

LE PROVOST, C., LYARD, F., MOLINES, J. M., GENCO, M. L., & RABILLOUD, F. 1998. A hydrodynamic ocean tide model improved by assimilating a satellite altimeter-derived data set. *J. Geophys. Res.*, **103**(C3), 5513–5529.

LEVITUS, S. 1982. *Climatological Atlas of the World Ocean.* Washington D.C.: National Oceanic and Atmospheric Administration.

MICHALLET, H., & BARTHÉLEMY, E. 1998. Experimental study of interfacial solitary waves. *J. Fluid Mech.*, **366**, 159–177.

OSBORNE, A. R., & BURCH, T. L. 1980. Internal solitons in the Andaman Sea. *Science*, **208**, 451–460.

PELINOVSKY, E. N., & SHAVRATSKY, S. K. 1976. Distribution of nonlinear internal waves in an inhomogeneous ocean. *Bull. (Izv.), Acad. Sci. USSR Atmospheric and Oceanic Physics*, **12**(1).

PELINOVSKY, E. N., STEPANYANTS, YU. A., & TALIPOVA, T. G. 1994. Simulation of nonlinear internal wave propagation in horizontally inhomogeneous ocean. *Phys. Atmosph. and Ocean*, **30**(1), 77–83.

RENOUARD, D., & ZHANG, X. 1988. Baroclinic waves generation by barotropic waves passing over a shelf. *Dyn. Atmosph. and Oceans*, **13**, 123.

SMITH, W. H. F., & SANDWELL, D. T. 1997. Global sea floor topography from satellite altimetry and ship depth soundings. *Science*, **277**, 1956–1962.

WATSON, G., & ROBINSON, I. S. 1991. A numerical model of internal wave refraction in the Strait of Gibraltar. *J. Phys. Oceanogr.*, **21**(2), 185–204.

XING, J., & DAVIES, A. M. 1998. A three-dimensional model of internal tides on the Malin-Hebrides shelf and shelf edge. *J. Geophys. Res.*, **103**(C12), 27821–27847.

ZABUSKY, N. J., & KRUSKAL, M. D. 1965. Interaction of "solitons" in a collisionless plasma and the recurrence of initial states. *Phys. Rev. Lett.*, **15**(6), 240–243.

Nonlinear waves in a rotating stratified ocean

S.P.Nikitenkova[1] and Yu.A.Stepanyants[1,2]

[1]Nizhny Novgorod State Technical University, Russia
[2]IAP RAS, Nizhny Novgorod, Russia
spn@waise.nntu.sci-nnov.ru

Nonlinear wave dynamics in a stratified ocean under the influence of the Earth's rotation is discussed. We present a review of stationary solutions of several models of nonlinear dispersive waves in rotating fluids. These models are based on a generalization of Ostrovsky's equation for cubic-nonlinear media. They are applicable to the description of long weakly nonlinear wave processed in geophysical fluids dynamics: atmospheric and oceanic waves, plasma waves in ionosphere and other waves. The approximate solutions of stationary equation, describing specific wave processes in rotating media, are constructed. The approach, based on the joining together of two asymptotic solutions of the investigated equation, is used. First an asymptotic solution is obtained as a result of disregarding high frequency dispersion, the second one is a result of disregarding low frequency dispersion. The obtained solutions may be considered as the periodic sawtooth piece-wise linear wave, which smoothed out by inserting KdV solitons of positive polarity in the top of sawtooth wave and solitons of negative polarity in the cavity. The new integral invariant of this equation is obtained. It allows closure of the system of approximate equations and avoids excessive optional parameters. The obtained analytical solutions demonstrate good agreement with the numerical ones. The analytical solutions are used as initial data for numerical computation within the frame of non-stationary equation. This allowed to set the extent of solutions stationarity and ones stability with respect to small perturbations. The solution, good agreeing with limits of usefulness of the theory, remained stationary during long time and somehow tendension of its destruction was not observed.

A theoretical and experimental study of wind-driven convection at density fronts

D.I. Osmond and R.W. Griffiths

Research School of Earth Sciences, Australian National University, Canberra, ACT 0200,
Australia.
david@rses.anu.edu.au Ross.Griffiths@anu.edu.au

1. Abstract

Winds in the vicinity of ocean density fronts will drive a surface Ekman layer which may cause dense water to flow across the front and over the top of the lighter water, thus creating gravitational instabilities. This process has been postulated to generate convection and may be important for the formation of new water masses.

We design and conduct a preliminary experiment using a rotating table to try to investigate this method of generating convection. A two layer density stratification was spun so that the parabolic interface between the two layers outcropped on the lid. The system was then forced anticyclonically by a differentially rotating lid, thus driving an Ekman current radially inwards and across the density front. Laser induced fluorescence was used to infer the time dependent density field. Preliminary results indicate that water of an intermediate density is formed through mixing, although baroclinic instabilities complicate the flow and its analysis. We make a rough estimate that approximately 10% of the anomalous Ekman mass flux directed across the front is turned into mixed fluid.

2. Introduction

The Coriolis force allows the existence of stable ocean density fronts by balancing the horizontal density gradients with vertical velocity gradients. This is known as the thermal wind balance. When winds blow across these fronts it is possible for the denser water on one side of the front to be blown across and over the top of the less dense water on the other side, thus driving convection.

The subantarctic front (SAF) is a density front in the Southern Ocean. It is located beneath the strong westerly winds associated with the mid-latitudes, and is thus subject to the conditions above that lead to convection. North of the SAF, Subantarctic Mode Water (SAMW) and Antarctic Intermediate Water (AAIW) are being formed, by convection resulting from vertical density instabilities. Whether or not the cross-frontal Ekman transport mentioned above is a significant mechanism for generating this convection is a matter of some controversy, particularly for the case of AAIW (Ribbe and Tomczak, 1997). McCartney (1977) proposed that most convection in the mid-latitudinal regions is related to oceanic heat loss. As the ocean loses heat to the atmosphere, its surface cools, and the resulting density inversion can cause deep convection. This was given support by work showing a good relationship between oceanic heat loss, and maximum convection depths (England et al., 1993; Hirst and Godfrey, 1993). Other groups (Piola and Georgi, 1982; Emery and Meincke, 1986) have proposed that its formation is related more closely to the cross-frontal mixing mentioned above.

With the increasing trend of using ocean general circulation models (OGCMs) to predict the Earth's climate, there is concern as to whether these models are adequately able to simulate this form of convection when their resolution is often not much greater than the width of the ocean fronts (Bryden, 1983). Some finer resolution models have been developed to look more closely at this process (Ribbe and Tomczak, 1997), however there has been little theoretical or experimental work in this area.

In this paper we present some preliminary results related to our experimental work. We follow a similar design to that of Narimousa and Maxworthy (1985), who were concerned principally with the motion of the front, rather than the generation of convection. We use a stratified two-layer fluid system, brought to solid-body rotation in a cylindrical tank with lid, so that the parabolic interface between the layers outcrops on the lid. We thus initially only use centripetal force to maintain the front, unlike the situation on Earth, and that used by Narimousa and Maxworthy (1985) where the front is maintained through a geostrophic balance. The surface of the fluid was then anticyclonically forced to generate an Ekman current that was directed radially inwards, thus creating the required convection.

3. Theory

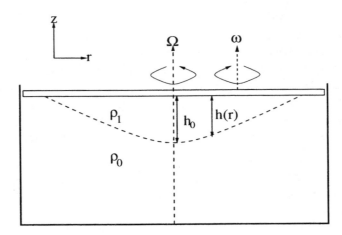

Figure 1: Side view of the experimental tank.

The theory presented in this section commences in a similar way to that of Narimousa and Maxworthy (1985). Referring to the geometry indicated in Figure 1, we start with a stratified two-layer fluid system rotating as a solid body with speed Ω. The upper layer has density ρ_1, while the lower has density ρ_0. We ensure that the upper layer is of sufficiently small volume, and the tank rotation rate is fast enough, so that the interface, $z = -h$, outcrops on the lid, and is given by the equation

$$h = h_0 - \gamma r^2 \tag{1}$$

where h_0 is the central thickness of the upper layer, and where

$$\gamma = \frac{\Omega^2}{2g} \tag{2}$$

is the steepness of the parabola. Note that the z axis is directed upwards.

We then start differentially rotating the lid, by an amount ω slower than the tank. In a time of $O(\Omega^{-1})$, an Ekman layer forms. The Coriolis force causes a component of this Ekman layer to be directed radially inwards. This can be understood physically by considering a fluid particle adjacent to the lid, which is slowed by the lid, and thus feels a reduced centrifugal force, resulting in the pressure gradient accelerating it inwards. Eventually, after a time t_s, a geostrophic balance is reached between the moving fluid and the pressure field. The interface remains parabolic in the form given by (1), however now γ is given by the equation

$$\gamma = \frac{\Omega^2}{2g}\left(1 + \frac{2\omega\rho_0}{\Omega\Delta\rho}\right) \tag{3}$$

The time it takes to reach this steady state is derived by Narimousa and Maxworthy (1985) to be

$$t_s \approx \frac{g'h_0}{\Omega(.07\omega r_f)^2} \tag{4}$$

where $g' = g\Delta\rho/\rho$ is the reduced gravity. This time can be thought of as Richardson number times the inertial period, and implies the stationary state is reached when the kinetic and potential energy is balanced.

Since the upper layer is now rotating at the same speed as the lid, there is no longer any forcing of the upper layer. As hinted to before, this is not a true steady state, as there continues to be forcing on the part of the lower layer exposed to the lid, which continues to drive an Ekman current inwards towards the front. Thus we expect to see two phases to our flow. One where there is an radially inwards Ekman current across the entire lid, which is when we expect to see the most rapid generation of mixing, and which persists up till the steady state time scale t_s, and then a subsequent slower mixing rate beyond that time. We expect the t_s to also signify the time after which the interface of the parabola has reached its new steeper form as given by (3).

Let us now attempt a theory to predict the rate of production of mixed fluid, and also the total amount of mixed fluid produced until the upper layer has reached its steady state. The simplest assumption to make is that the rate of mixing, q_m, is proportional to Ekman flux across the front. Thus

$$q_m = k_1\pi r_f^2\omega d\Delta\rho \tag{5}$$

where r_f is the radius of the front, $d = \sqrt{\nu/\Omega}$ is the Ekman layer thickness, and k_1 is an unknown scaling constant. This definition of mixing rate has units of mass per time. The total production of mixed fluid is proportional to the product of the mixing rate and the steady state time.

$$M = k_2 q_m t_s \tag{6}$$

where k_2 is another unknown scaling constant. We have neglected the fact that the radius of the front changes with time, and thus we shall have to absorb this approximation into the factor k_2, which will then depend on the ratio of the initial to final radius of the front.

4. Experiment

A preliminary experiment has been performed in a rotating tank using a two layer system. The upper layer was of density $\rho_1 = 1000\text{kg/m}^3$ and thickness 1.2cm, while the lower had $\rho_0 = 1015\text{kg/m}^3$ and thickness 8.3cm. The tank was spun at a relatively high speed (2 radians per second), so that the parabolic interface between the layers out-cropped on the lid, with a central thickness of approximately 3.2cm. After solid body rotation had been reached, the system was anticyclonically forced by differentially rotating the lid at 0.03 radians per second slower than the tank, to create a Ekman transport directed radially inwards across the interface. With this set-up, we have an Ekman formation time of about 1 second, while the time predicted to reach steady state was approximately 23 minutes.

Visualisation of the changing density field was achieved by mixing a sodium fluorescein dye into the lower layer, and then illuminating the fluid with a vertical sheet of laser light. The concentration of the fluorescein dye can be inferred from the intensity of the emitted light, and this in turn can be used to calculate the density of the fluid.

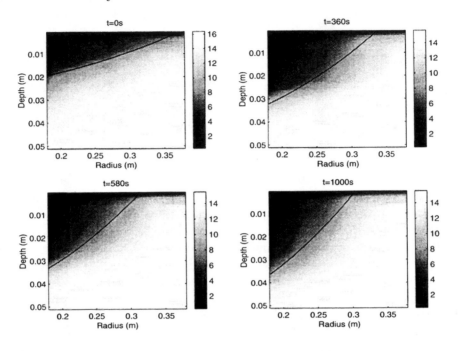

Figure 2: Excess density anomaly ($\rho - 1000\text{kg/m}^3$) of the fluid in the tank at various times. In each plot a parabola has been fitted to the interface between the two fluid layers using a least squares method.

Figure 2 shows a few snapshots of the fluid density anomaly ($\rho - 1000\text{kg/m}^3$) in the tank. Pictured is a vertical profile along a radius of the tank, zoomed in on the region where the interface outcrops onto the lid. The images were constructed from footage taken by a video camera in the same reference frame as the tank. The density of the fluid was inferred from the intensity of light, and each image was constructed by averaging 500 hundred frames, or 40 seconds of video footage, in an effort to reduce noise. In the pictures, darker shading is visible towards the top left corner of each picture representing the upper layer. At each snapshot in time, a parabola is fitted using a least squares method to the interface between the two layers (as defined by the isopycnal with density mid-way between those of the two layers), subject to the constraint that the parabola's axis must be the same as that of the tank. The upper plot of Figure 3 indicates how the the coefficient γ of the parabola changes with time.

Perhaps the most striking feature of this plot is the oscillations with a dimensionless period of about .017, or 240s. This is very close to the frequency of the lid (210s), and it indicates that we have a mode 1 instability associated with the front, that essentially results in the upper fluid layer being aligned off axis. This instability complicates the interpretation of our experiment, however we can minimise its influence by filtering our results.

From equation (2), we expect the initial coefficient of the parabola to be given by $\gamma = \frac{\Omega^2}{2g} \approx 0.2$. This is in excellent agreement with our experimental result. We expect the coefficient of the parabola in the final steady state to be given by (3), or $\gamma = \frac{\Omega^2}{2g}\left(1 + \frac{2\omega\rho_0}{\Omega\Delta\rho}\right) \approx 0.6$. The upper plot of Figure 3 shows the coefficient of the parabola increasing steadily to this value, which it reaches in a dimensionless time of about 0.6, at which point the rate of increase seems to slow, however the instability does complicate things. This time is a bit less than the unitary dimensionless time derived by Narimousa and Maxworthy (1985), however their geometry was different to ours, so it is not surprising the time doesn't coincide exactly. The important point will be to see if future experiments achieve steady state at similar dimensionless times.

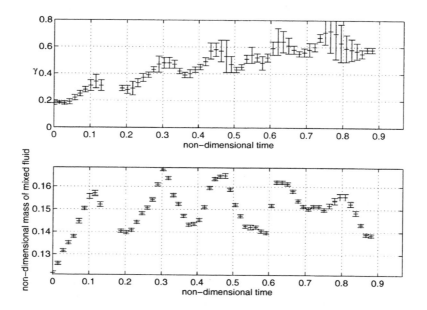

Figure 3: Above: Coefficient γ of the best fitting parabola to the density field. Below: Non-dimensional mass of mixed fluid. In both plots the time has been non-dimensionalised by t_s, given by equation (4), while the mass of mixed fluid in the lower plot has been non-dimensionalised by the Ekman mass flux across the initial position of the interface in a time t_s, (6).

If there was no mixing present in the system, there would simply be the uniform upper layer density, ρ_1, above the parabola, and the uniform lower layer density, ρ_0, beneath. By subtracting the measured density field from this hypothetical zero mixing field, and integrating over the volume of the tank, we can get an idea of the amount of mixing that has occurred. This measurement has units of mass, and after non-dimensionising by the anomalous Ekman mass flux produced in the time t_s, given by (5), the result is plotted as a function of time in the lower half of Figure 3. Again we have non-dimensionalised time by t_s, (4). It is clear from the graph that there is a sizeable amount of mixed fluid before the forcing even begins. Although some of this mixed fluid is dye that has diffused, or from mixing that occured during spin-up, most of it is an artificial product arising through inaccuracies in converting the intensity of emitted light to density, resulting in small deviations from the expected uniform density in regions far from the interface. This is a systematic error, however, as it is constant at all times, so we may simply subtract the amount of mixed fluid at $t = 0$ from values recorded at later times to correct for this.

The mass of the mixed fluid is also greatly influenced by the instability. By filtering out the oscillation due to this we are able to determine that the amount of mixed fluid rises steadily for a non-dimensional time of 0.4, less than the time expected from the time it took for the parabola to reach steady state. During this time the amount of mixed fluid increased its non-dimensional mass by an amount of about 0.04. This suggests that k_1 in (5) has a value of about $0.04/.4 = 0.1$, or in other words approximately 10% of the Ekman transport is actively mixed.

As the time increases past the non-dimensional time of 0.6, when the parabola has almost reached its steady shape, the amount of mixing starts decreasing quite rapidly. This is due to the fact that the entire radius is not visible in our field of view. As the mixed fluid forms at the front, it slowly flows down the parabolic interface to distribute itself evenly along the isopycnal, and in the process leaves our field of view. Our calculations of the mass of mixed fluid thus misses all this fluid, which may explain why the rate of mixed fluid did not continue rising steadily until the parabola reached its steady state, as we were losing mixed fluid from the left of the picture as fast as the it is being produced at the front. Future experiments will be designed so that the entire radius is visible to the camera, although this will reduce the resolution of the picture near the front.

5. Conclusion

We have developed an experimental set-up to generate convection at density fronts by rotating a two layer density stratification, and then anticyclonically forcing the surface with a lid. The preliminary experiment suggested about 10% of the Ekman flux across the front was transformed into the new mixed layer, however the interpretation was greatly obscured by a mode 1 instability that formed. It is hoped that subsequent experiments will verify the scaling formula derived for the rate of production of mixed fluid (5), in addition to more accurately determining the figure of 10% quoted above, and that this will enable us to estimate the ability of the wind to generate quantities of a new water mass at ocean density fronts.

Acknowledgments

The authors would like to thank Dr Xavier Chavanne for his early work on the experiment, and Mr Derek Corrigan for setting up and building parts of the experimental apparatus.

6. References

Bryden, H. (1983). The southern ocean. In Robinson, A., editor, *Eddies in Marine Science*, pages 265–277. Springer, Berlin.

Emery, W. and Meincke, J. (1986). Global water masses: summary and review. *Oceanol. Acta.*, 9:383–391.

England, M., Godfrey, J., Hirst, A., and Tomczak, M. (1993). The mechanism for antarctic intermediate water renewal in a world ocean model. *J. Phys. Ocean.*, 23:1553–1560.

Hirst, A. and Godfrey, J. (1993). The role of indonesian throughflow in a global ocean gcm. *J. Phys. Ocean.*, 23:1057–1086.

McCartney, M. (1977). Subantarctic mode water. In Angel, M., editor, *A Voyage of Discovery: George Deacon 70th Anniversary Volume*, pages 103–119. Pergamon, Oxford.

Narimousa, S. and Maxworthy, T. (1985). Two-layer model of shear-driven coastal upwelling in the presence of bottom topography. *J. Fluid Mech.*, 159:503–531.

Piola, A. and Georgi, D. (1982). Circumpolar properties of antarctic intermediate water and subantarctic mode water. *Deep-Sea Res.*, 29:687–711.

Ribbe, J. and Tomczak, M. (1997). On convection and the formation of subantarctic mode water in the fine resolution antarctic model (fram). *J. Mar. Systems.*, 13:137–154.

Effects of a Cape Upon an Intermediate Current

S. Sadoux, A. Fincham and D. Renouard

Equipe Coriolis, Laboratoire des Ecoulements Géophysiques et Industriels (LEGI)
UJF-CNRS-INPG, Grenoble, France.

Abstract

To study the effects of a cape upon an intermediate water current, experiments were performed on a 13m diameter rotating tank, which was filled with a stable linearly stratified fluid. These experiments focussed on a simplified model of Cape Saint Vincent at depth 1000m (i.e. a 70° cape). When the upstream current is unstable, there is periodic anticyclonic lens production at the cape. Most likely, the detachment process of these lenses from the cape involves the presence of a coupled cyclone located above the intermediate current level. The nondimensional characteristics of the laboratory anticyclonic lenses agree very well with nondimensionalised in situ observations.

1. Introduction

Intermediate water currents are observed in various parts of the world, and are known to play a major role in the exchanges between sea basins. They may lead to isolated eddies such as the Mediterranean Eddies (or Meddies) in the Atlantic Ocean or the Levantine Intermediate Water Eddies (or Leddies) South of Sardinia. The submesoscale eddies detached from the Mediterranean Undercurrent transport salty and warm water of Mediterranean origin and act like point sources of this water mass in the Northeast Atlantic basin (Armi and Stommel 1983). It seems that topography has a significant influence on the lens generation process and that capes (Swallow, 1969) are preferred places for Meddy production. Considering a surface or a subsurface current, D'Asaro (1988) suggested that the lateral friction at the coast was responsible for an anticyclonic coastal layer, which, together with the overshooting of the current at the cape, was responsible for eddy generation. However, he did not mention any condition for the upstream current nor for the cape angle. Baey et al. (1995) showed that there may be anticyclonic lens production even along a plane vertical wall, depending on whether the intermediate water current was stable or not. A preliminary study examined the effect of the cape angle and showed that there is lens generation at the cape only when the upstream current is itself unstable (Sadoux et al, 2000).

The present set of experiments tries to find the mechanisms which make the cape a preferred (but not only) place for lens generation and to provide information about the anticyclonic lenses thus generated. Section 2 describes the data collected in the rotating tank. The analysis, comparison and discussion of the results are presented in section 3 and finally section 4 summarises them.

2. Data and methods

The LEGI-Coriolis 13m diameter, 1.2m deep cylindrical tank was filled with a linearly stratified fluid. The rotation period T, the density gradient $d\rho/dz$ and thus both the Coriolis parameter $f=4\pi/T$ and the Brunt-Väisälä frequency $N=(-g/\rho_0 . \partial\rho/\partial z)^{1/2}$ could be adjusted to cover a wide range of the relevant parameters. The intermediate water is introduced into the rotating tank directly at its equilibrium level via an injector (fig1). The volume flow rate (Q) of the intermediate current can be adjusted. The velocity and interface level measurements (made with a rack of ultrasonic density probes) close to the injector showed its effectiveness in obtaining an intermediate current that is in geostrophic balance downstream of the injector (Sadoux et al. 2000).

Use was made of a non-invasive Correlation Imaging Velocimetry (CIV) system developed by Fincham and Spedding (1997) and recently extended to quasi-3D measurements (Fincham 1997). Polystyrene beads of diameter ~0.7mm were seeded during spin-up throughout the tank over the whole depth. A laser beam was swept vertically by an oscillating mirror and reflected by a submerged 45° mirror fixed in the tank to illuminate the particles. The laser sheet was moved vertically to scan a fixed volume of water ($2.75 \times 2.02 \times 0.43 m^3$) and a digital camera was placed directly over the flow to capture images. At each level on a grid with Δx=3.6cm, Δy=4.2cm and Δz=1.7cm resolution, the horizontal components of the velocity field could be determined with an accuracy O(1-2%). Thus, we can compute derived quantities, such as the vertical component of vorticity or the horizontal divergence at each level, providing a 3D time resolved picture of the parameters governing the flow.

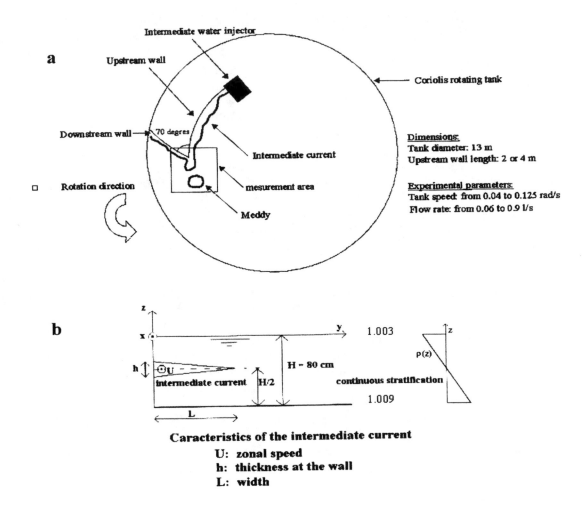

Fig. 1- (a) Top view of the rotating platform with intermediate water injector and cape model; (b) Side view with a sketch of the density profile.

Previous studies (Baey et al. 1995; Sadoux et al. 2000) of the stability of an intermediate water current flowing along a plane vertical wall and initially in geostrophic equilibrium showed that the relevant physical parameters of the flow are the Rossby (or alternatively the Burger), the Froude and the Ekman numbers, defined respectively as *Ro=U/fL (Bu=UNh/f²L²), Fr=U/Nh* and *Ek= ν/fh²*, with *U, H* and *L* defined as in fig.1, *ν* is the kinematic viscosity and *f* is the Coriolis parameter.

3. Analysis and discussion

The upstream current conditions were either unstable (i.e. anticyclonic lens generation along the upstream wall, $Ro<0.2$) or stable (no spontaneous eddy production along the upstream wall, $Ro>0.6$). In the latter case, a vortex is created downstream of the cape due to the overshooting of the current at the end of the upstream wall. The subsequent re-attachment to the downstream wall is due to the Coriolis force. The anticyclone diameter increased with time but this vortex never detached. For a stable current with Rossby number in the range [0.2 - 0.6] there is dipole formation at the cape and the negative to positive vorticity ratio increased with increasing Rossby number. For $Ro<0.2$, there was periodic anticyclonic lens production at the cape. The formation period, the vorticity and spin-up times of the lenses generated at the cape agree very well with in-situ observations.

In all experiments for which there were several anticyclonic lenses produced, the Froude and Rossby numbers for the upstream current shortly before the cape, are respectively in the range [0.05 – 0.1] and [0.04 – 0.15]. These values correspond to conditions along a plane vertical wall where the current is unstable and due to a mixed baroclinic-barotropic instability, it generates anticyclonic lenses periodically.

Fig.2 shows the formation and detachment of three lenses, like "meddies", when the upstream current is unstable ($Ro=0.13$). The vorticity field is averaged over the intermediate current depth. It is noticeable that, even close to the cape, the lenses produced along the upstream or downstream walls always move away from the wall along a line that is practically perpendicular to the wall. However, the lenses formed at the cape initially moved away from the cape along a line that is an extension of the upstream wall. As is clear in Fig. 2, as soon as a lens detaches from the cape another one immediately forms and the process repeats itself periodically.

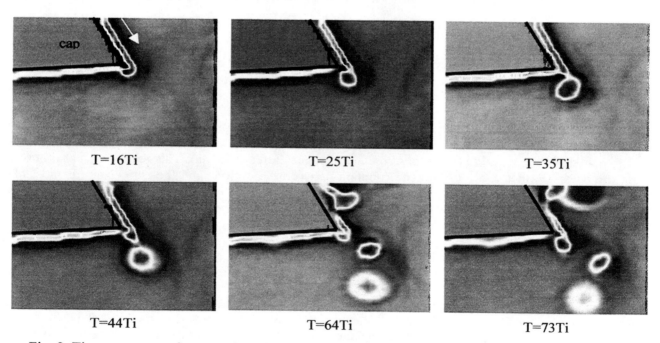

Fig. 2. Time sequence of averaged vertical vorticity showing the formation and detachment of three lenses in an unstable upstream conditions experiment ($Ro=0.13$; $Ek=2.10^{-4}$; T_i inertial period).

These lenses are at first surrounded by a cyclonic ring at the level of the current (fig. 3a), which tends to vanish with time, they are also accompanied by an upper cyclone and sometimes by a (weaker) lower cyclone. In fact, most of the former cyclone is located above the intermediate current, such that its signature at the level of the intermediate current is weak. These features are induced by permanent counter-currents (fig. 3b) above and below the level of the intermediate water, which appear at the beginning of the experiment. Assuming the intermediate current is in geostrophic and hydrostatic equilibrium and using the same formalism as in fig 1b, the intermediate current velocity can be written as: $U=-g/f.\partial h/\partial y$ with $\partial h/\partial y$ the slope of the intermediate current interfaces. Thus, with the same assumptions in the layers surrounding the current, we obtain velocities u of opposite sign, defined in a first approximation as: $u=g'/f.\partial h/\partial y$ (with $g'=g\partial\rho/\rho$ the reduced gravity) above and below the intermediate current. The effect of the stratification is to concentrate the counter-currents in layers close to the intermediate current, where the influence of the slope of the interfaces are the most important. Practically, and likely due to bottom friction, the lower counter-current is much weaker than the upper counter-current, so that the upper cyclonic lense is much more visible than its lower counter-part.

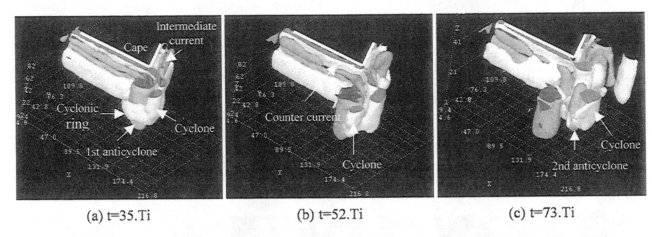

(a) t=35.Ti   (b) t=52.Ti   (c) t=73.Ti

Fig. 3. Three-dimensional isosurface vorticity field showing the generation of meddies. Dark: anticyclonic vorticity; Light: cyclonic vorticity. These pictures correspond to those in fig. 2 at the same times (Ro=0.13; Ek=2.10^{-4}; T_i inertial period, isosurface: $|\omega_z|$=0.2ω_{max})

The anticyclone extends from the level of the intermediate current until the uppermost level of the illuminated volume, so that the anticyclonic signature has a much larger vertical extent than the density anomaly that is confined to the level of the intermediate current (fig. 3a). This feature was also observed in the ocean (Paillet et al. 1999). The coupling between the cyclone and the anticyclone is most likely responsible for the self-propagation of this dipolar structure away from the cape. As this movement proceeds, the cyclonic part weakens and tends to separate from the anticyclonic part. Further downstream from the cape only the anticyclone can be observed (fig. 3c).

From fig. 4, one can notice that the lenses maximum vorticity when they separate from the cape is O(-0.4f), this is always equal to or larger than the upstream current's vorticity (the ratio of the lens vorticity to the current vorticity varies from 1 to 2.5). The vorticity values measured here are close to most previous estimates by other authors. Pingree (1995) estimated a value of -0.45f for a meddy found in the Tagus Abyssal Plain and Schultz Tokos et al. (1994) a value of -0.40f for meddy Aska. The vorticity of both the anticyclonic lens and the associated cyclone attain their respective maximum values at the detachment time and the detachment is in phase for both vortices. In the tank, when the cyclonic lens detaches, the ratio of cyclonic vorticity to anticyclonic vorticity is O(0.7) and it remains practically constant during the whole lifetime of the cyclone, which is of the order of 15 to 30 T_i . The anticyclone seems to have a much longer lifetime as proved by several lenses that could be followed for over 60 T_i or until they left the measurement area. In the ocean, meddies have also been tracked for several hundreds of inertial periods.

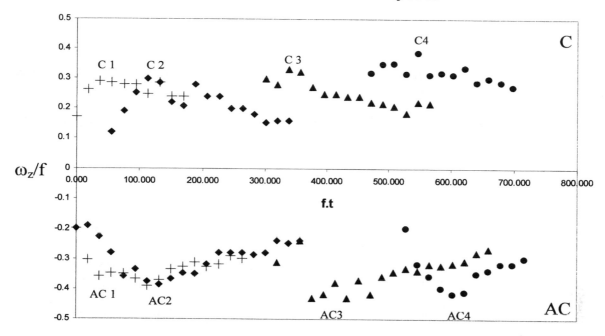

Fig. 4. Maximum vertical vorticity vs. time both normalised by f for 4 different meddies (AC1 to AC4) and their attached cyclones (C1 to C4).

4. Summary and conclusions

Using the LEGI « Coriolis » 13 m diameter rotating tank, we studied the interaction of an intermediate current and a cape. We focused on the mechanisms leading to the formation and detachment of anticyclonic lenses (meddies) as well as on the lens dynamics after its detachment. Meddy generation occurred only when the coastal current has the appropriate intrinsic instability properties (i.e. $Ro<0.2$). The detachment of such an anticyclonic vortex always involved a companion cyclone. Recent float data sets providing information about the characteristic radius, rotation period, translation velocity from the cape and relative vorticity of meddies generated at Cape St. Vincent showed a very good agreement with our data, and also indicated that cyclones are associated with the anticyclones (Serra et al., 2000).

Acknowledgements

The support by CNRS-SDU and grants EPSHOM-CMO N°15/93 and MAST III-CANIGO (MAS3-CT96-0060) are gratefully acknowledged.

References

Armi, L., and H. Stommel, 1983: Four Views of a Portion of the North Atlantic Subtropical Gyre. *J. Phys. Oceanogr.*, **13**, 828-857.

Baey, J-M., D. Renouard, and G.C. D'Hières, 1995: Preliminary results about the stability of an intermediate water current. *Deep-Sea Res.*, **42**, 2063-2073.

D'Asaro, E., 1988, Generation of submesoscale vortices : a new mechanism. *J. Geophys. Res.*, **93**, C-6, 6685-6693

Fincham, A., and G. Spedding, 1997: Low cost, high resolution DPIV for measurement of turbulent fluid flow. *Exp. Fluids*, **23**, 449-462.

Fincham, A., 1997: 3D measurement of vortex structures in stratified fluid flows. IUTAM Symposium of "Simulation and identification of organised structures in flows", Lyngby (Denmark).

Klinger, B., 1994, Baroclinic eddy generation at a sharp corner in a rotating system. *J. Geophys. Res.*, **99**, 12,515-12,531

Paillet, J., B. Le Cann, A. Serpette, Y. Morel, and X. Carton, 1999: Real-Time Tracking of a Galician Meddy. *Geophys. Res. Lett.*, **26**, 1877-1880.

Pingree, R.D., 1995: The droguing of Meddy Pinball and seeding with ALACE floats. *J. Mar. Biol. Assoc. U. K.*, **75**, 235-252.

Sadoux, S., J.-M. Baey, A. Fincham, and D. Renouard, 2000: Experimental study of the stability of an intermediate water current and its interaction with a cape. *Dyn. Atmos. Oceans*, **31**, 165-192.

Schultz Tokos, K., H.-H. Hinrichsen, and W. Zenk, 1994: Merging and Migration of two Meddies. *J. Phys. Oceanogr.*, **24**, 2129-2141.

Serra, N., S. Sadoux, I. Ambar and D. Renouard, 2000: Observations and laboratory modelling of meddy generation at Cape St. Vincent, *J. Phys. Oceanogr.* (Submitted)

Swallow J.C., 1969. A deep eddy off Cape St. Vincent. *Deep Sea Res.*, **16**, 285-295.

Overturning of Soliton-Like Internal Wave: Observation on the Pechora Sea Shelf

Andrey N. Serebryany[1] and G. I. Shapiro[2]

[1] N.N. Andreyev Acoustics Institute, Shvernik Str.4, Moscow 117036, Russia
[2] P.P. Shirshov Institute of Oceanology, Nakhimovsky prospekt, 36, Moscow 117851, Russia
aserebr@dataforce.net

1. Abstract

The evidence of internal wave overturning obtained from field observations is considered. Observations were carried out on the shallow shelf in the East-Southern part of the Barents Sea, so called the Pechora Sea on August of 1998. The measurements were made by line temperature sensors and CTD "yo-yo" soundings from anchored vessel in a site with depth of 16 m. The train of internal waves propagated along the sharp near-bottom thermocline (among them was the overturning one) and it was observed just before appearance of the phenomenon of internal tidal bore. The train consisted of three waves, rank - ordered in amplitude (from 3.5 m to 2.0 m). There we observed occurrence of a large temperature inversion (of 0.5 degree and 2-meter thickness) on the vertical temperature profile obtained during the moment of arrival of the crest of internal wave. The features of the event observed point out that the mechanism of advective instability is responsible for the observed internal wave breaking. Two examples from observations in other seas which underlay different character of the breaking for internal elevation waves (forward overturning of the crest) and internal depression waves (backward overturning of the trough) are presented.

2. Introduction

It is not frequent to observe overturning of internal waves in the sea. We know only a few reports on direct observations of this phenomenon. The first are those of Woods (1968), who photographed "billows" of small scale on thin layers within the seasonal thermocline. Haury et al. (1979) obtained the evidences of overturning of internal waves of greater scale (amplitudes of 10 m and lengths of 60-70 m) over Stellwagen Bank in Massachusetts Bay by means of using of downward sonar simultaneously with synchronic CTD profiling. There are few more evidences on internal waves overturning in works of others authors (Pingree, 1988; Peters et al, 1995; Pinkel et al, 1997). In our opinion this deficit in observations is connected not with the fact that this process is rare in nature, but with the difficulty of carrying out of sophisticated field observations of internal waves which are necessary to study such processes at sea. Our opinion is based on the works of Serebryany (1985,1990,1996) where it was shown (on the basis of long-period observations of internal waves on the shelves of the former Soviet Union) that "horizontal asymmetry" connected with steepness of wave profile is a prominent and widespread feature of internal waves in shallow water. Steepness of internal wave profile is associated with wave overturning and is its predecessor. We had opportunity to observe internal wave overturning during our recent measurements in the Barents Sea on August 1998 during expedition of r/v "Akademik Sergey Vavilov". This paper will present the results of this observation.

3. Observations

We carried out internal wave observations in the shallow East Southern part of the Barents Sea, so called the Pechora Sea. The measurements were made in coastal zone of island Dolgy from anchored vessel by line temperature sensors and CTD yo-yo soundings. Island Dolgy is a narrow island in length of 40 km oriented in north-west direction. An area around it is a shallow shelf with depths of 15-25 m. The research vessel was anchored approximately at a 1-km distance from the shore on south west side of the island in the site with 16-m depth. The semidiurnal tidal variations of the sea level have amplitudes up to 1 m in the study area. Our observations continued during 7 hours and covered partially the period both of tide and ebb (local time of high water was 15 p.m., while the beginning of observations was at 11 a.m.). The presence of warm and fresh water diffuse from the regions of south coast forms in the study area a strong stratification of two-layer type. Despite of quite strong tidal currents, shallow water and frequently observed (it will be shown latter) situations with occurrence of events of mixing this region preserves during the most part of time its stratification close to the two-layered fluid.

For internal wave measurements we used vertical displacement meter (Konyaev, Serebryany, 1991), which consists of two identical line sensors each of 10 m length, shifted vertically by 2 m relative to each other. The meter continuously measures mean temperature and vertical gradient in the layer permitting us to obtain data on vertical displacements of the interfaces. We underlay especially the main properties of line temperature consisting in the meter to measure averaged temperature of the spanned layer of the water. Response of the line sensor to vertical displacements of the water layers is proportional to the vertical temperature gradient averaged over the length of the sensor, and it is more stable then the response of the point sensor (Konyaev, Sabinin, 1973).

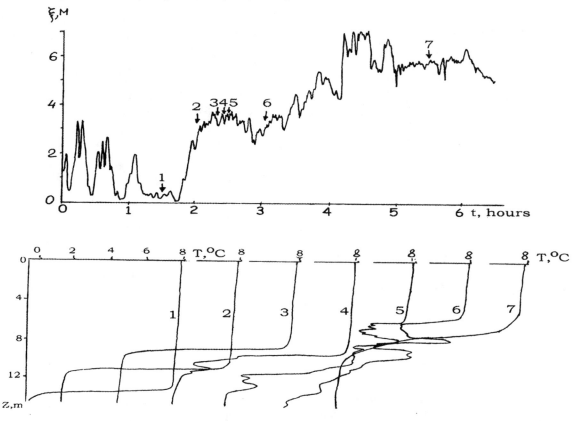

Fig. 1. Record of the internal tidal bore observed on the shelf near island Dolgy in the Southern-East part of the Barents Sea. Casts of vertical temperature profiles, which were obtained in the different phases of the bore's propagation, are shown at the bottom of the figure.

The vertical temperature profile at the station was characterised by a very sharp thermocline near the bottom (mean vertical gradient was more then 5 degrees/m). Upper homogeneous layer spanned from the sea surface (with temperature of $8\,^\circ$C) downward to the depth of 14 m. The temperature of the near-bottom thin layer was almost $0\,^\circ$C. The prominent event we observed in this region was an internal bore in the form of sharp step which propagated shoreward on the bottom thermocline (Fig.1). In the moment of propagation of internal bore front the thermocline shifted 3 meters upwards, but in despite of this the two-layered type of stratification has been preserved. Half our after passing of the bore the two-layered stratification became significantly changed and the temperature inversions had appeared. Further, after 4 hours have passed, the lifetime of these rich fine temperature structures finished and the thermocline became again like an interface between two-layered fluid and had shifted 3-4 meters further upwards. Just before occurrence of the bore we observed a train of soliton-like internal waves propagating across the position of our observation. The train consisted of three sort-period waves, rank-ordered in amplitude. The common picture of the observed event is typical for the phenomenon of internal bore which was observed previously on shelves of different seas (for example, Ivanov and Konyaev, 1976; Serebryany, 1985; Holloway, 1987; Serebryany and Holloway, 1995). In particular, sometimes a train-predecessor travels ahead of a step-like front of the internal bore (Serebryany, 1985, 1993) like in our case. The specific feature of the bore discussed here, which distinguishes it from the bores observed in other regions, is the generation of intense intrusions, that can be assumed as a product of significant mixing induced by strong tidal currents in shallow water.

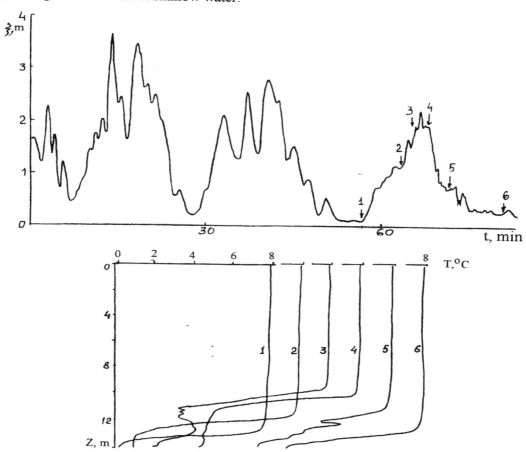

Fig.2. The train of soliton-like internal waves travelling ahead of internal bore front. The cast of vertical temperature profiles of " yo-yo" sounding is shown for the time of the propagation of the third wave. Profile N 3 shows the evidence of internal wave overturning near the crest of the wave.

Let us consider in more detail the main object of our attention in this paper, the observed train of three internal waves, which was a predecessor of the following internal bore (see Fig.2). In the beginning of our observations there was a very strong thermocline in 1-2 m above the bottom. A packet of intense internal waves was observed on this thermocline. The packet consists of three waves, rank-ordered in amplitude (heights are 3.5 m, 2.8 m, 2.0 m). The periods are 21, 25 and 25 minutes, respectively. The waves observed had sharpened crests and smoothen troughs. At the same time the crest of the two leading waves deformed by the shorter-period oscillations with period of 3 minutes. The third wave of the packet has an unusual profile in the form of narrowed crest on the wide pedestal. Fast "yo-yo" soundings by CTD, which were made during passing of this wave, gave us possibility to understand the cause of this feature. At the time of the passing of the first and second wave of the packet the vertical temperature profile changed its form due to vertical displacements of the thermocline up and down caused by the internal waves. During this time the thermocline preserved its smoothed profile (without any signs of the fine structure). In contrast to this, occurrence of a clearly seen temperature inversion on the vertical temperature profile was observed during the moment of passing the crest of last (the third) internal wave of the packet, as seen in profile 3 shown in Fig.2. The inversion had the following parameters: strength of inversion was $0.5\,^{o}$C, thickness was 2 meters. The inversion was in depth between horizons of 12 and 14 meters. Just after the crest of the internal wave had passed the inversion disappeared (the evidence of it is clearly seen on profile 4). After passing of this unusual wave the thermocline returned to its initial position near the bottom, having smoothing profile.

4. Discussion and conclusion

Many features of intense internal waves described above pointed out on their soliton-like character (Serebryany, 1990,1993; Ostrovsky and Stepanyants, 1989), that allow us to treat them like internal solitons. Firstly, this is the characteristic form of the observed internal wave profiles, and secondly, the rank-ordering of waves of the train in amplitude. In addition it is clearly seen the tendency for the two leading waves of the train in relation between the height of the wave and its horizontal scale which is typical for solitons. Higher first wave has less horizontal scale to compare with the second wave having less height, but wider horizontal scale. It will be easy to make estimations of soliton parameters for hydrological conditions in our case in the frame of the Korteveg- de Vries equation two-layered fluid model, but because we have some evidences of strong shear in the study area (personal communication of V. Gorbatsky, who carried out observations of currents by ADSP in the region close to our study area) that demands from us including data on currents for the best approximation of observed data with modal ones, we are limiting ourselves only in the frames of qualitative analysis.

Of importance is a question on what mechanism was responsible for internal wave breaking in our case? There are two main types of instability leading to internal wave breaking (Thorpe 1978,1999; Munk, 1981, Phillips, 1977). The first one is advective instability, which is associated with large-amplitude internal waves or waves with steep isopicnal slopes. The second type is shear instability. This instability can take place even without any background wave motion. In our case we have simultaneously presence of intense internal waves with steep slopes (we believe that the observed waves are soliton-like) and strong shear current. Detail consideration of the observed occasion and comparison with above-mentioned mechanisms suggests that in our case the advective instability played the main role. The local density inversion (in our records this density inversion was traced by temperature inversion) was created by particles near wave crest, which was advected forward in the direction of internal wave propagation. The presence (amplification) of the ambient shear just before the arrival of the internal bore front could enhance the advection of the particles near the crest which lead to the observed overturning in the third wave of the train, which probably "felt" influence of currents of the approaching bore.

In addition to what was discussed above, we now show more examples of events of breaking internal waves these were obtained by one of the authors (AS) in his observations in other seas and under different conditions. The first example (shown on Fig. 3) is a record demonstrating internal waves propagating on a near-bottom thermocline in the coastal zone of the Sea of Japan (Serebryany, 1990). The record was made by line temperature sensor, the same as it was used in the observation in the Barents Sea discussed above. On the fig. 3 we can see a train of strong non-linear internal waves propagating shoreward. Strong nonlinearity of these waves is clearly seen from characteristic distortions of their profiles, in particular steepening of their front faces. The steepening of a front face is a typical feature of non-linear internal wave elevations (Serebryany, 1996), but the example presented here is unique, due to the fact that steepened waves transformed into group of step-like waves. Therefor it is possible to consider this train as periodical internal bores. It is interesting to note that the profile of the third wave is significantly changed to compare with its neighbours. And this is clearly a feature pointing out that the internal wave has been broken. It is interesting to compare this broken wave with the one from our observation in the Pechora Sea. Both examples are broken waves of internal elevation waves. In both cases profiles of breaking waves have common features suggesting that there is overturning of wave to forward.

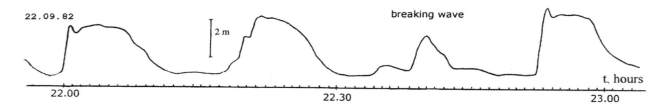

Fig.3. Example of internal wave breaking observed on the shelf of the Sea of Japan (Serebryany, 1990). Measurements were made by line temperature sensor. Strongly nonlinear wave elevations moving along the near-bottom thermocline degenerate into periodic internal bores. The third wave has broken. It seems that here the mechanism of advective instability with forward overturning of the crest is responsible for internal wave breaking, similarly to the discussed above event in the Pechora Sea.

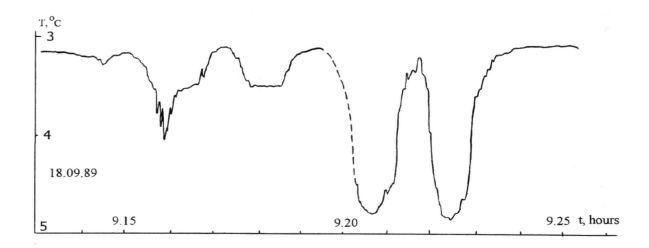

Fig.4. Example of internal wave breaking observed in one of the fjords of Kamchatka, Pacific Ocean (measurements of A.N. Serebryany, September 1989). Measurements were made by point temperature sensor on the horizon of strong thermocline. The two leading wave depressions of the observed group have broken troughs. The profile of the first wave suggests a backward overturning of the trough.

Another example was observed in the input part of one of fjords of Kamchatka, Pacific Ocean. The measurements in contrast to all discussed examples were made by point temperature sensor in a layer with strong thermocline. Whilst such method of internal wave observations commonly is less appropriate for measuring of internal wave parameters to compare to the line sensor, but in our case it gives useful information on process of internal wave breaking. The most interesting feature of this example is that the waves observed were depression waves. The profile of the first wave of the observed train shows evidences of the overturning of the wave in the back.

The main purpose of our paper was to establish new factual data on the breaking of internal waves on a shelf and attract attention of the scientific community to this important phenomenon that in reality exists in the sea.

5. Acknowledgements

The authors are grateful to Dr. J. Da Silva for his help in correction the text. This work was partially supported by Russian Foundation for Basic Research (grant N 98-05-64712) and by grant of Russian Ministry of Science and Technology.

6. References

1. Ivanov. V.A., Konyaev K.V., (1976). Bore on thermocline. Izvestia Academy of Sciences of USSR. Atmospheric and Oceanic Physics, 12: 416–423.
2. Haury L., G.Briscoe, M. Orr, (1979). Tidal generation internal waves in Massachusetts Bay. Nature. 278: 312-317.
3. Holloway P.E., (1987). Internal hydraulic jumps and solitons at a shelf break region on the Australian northwest shelf. J. Geophys. Res. 92: 5405-5416.
4. Konyaev, K.V., Sabinin K.D., (1973). New data on internal waves in a sea obtained using distributed temperature sensors. Dokl. Acad. Sci. USSR, 209:856-864.
5. Konyaev K.V., Serebryany A.N., (1991). Vertical displacement meter for stratified bodies of water (In Russian). Inventor's Certificate USSR N 16688875, 01 K 13/00. Bulletin of Inventions, State Committee on Iventionrs and Discoveries under GKNT of the USSR, VNIPI, Moscow, 29: 182.
6. Munk. W., (1981). Internal waves and small-scale processes. In: B. Warren and C. Wunch (Eds.), Evolution of physical oceanography. MIT Press, 264-291.
7. Ostrovsky L.A. and Yu.A. Stepanyants, (1989). Do internal solitons exist in the ocean? Rev. Geophys. 27: 293-310.
8. Peters, H., M. C. Gregg and T.B.Sanford, (1995). Detail and scaling of turbulent overturns in the Pacific Equatorial Undercurrent. J. Geophys. Res. 100: 18349-18368.
9. Phillips, O.M.,(1977). The dynamics of the upper ocean . Cambridge University Press. Cambridge.
10. Pingree , R.D., (1988). Internal tidal oscillations and water colomn instability in the upper slope region of the Bay of Biscay. In: Small scale turbulence and mixing in the ocean. (J.C.J. Nihoul and B.M.Jamart, eds), Elsevier, Amsterdam, p. 387.
11. Pinkel R. et al., (1997). Solitary waves in the western Equatorial Pacific Ocean. Geoph. Res. Lett. 23: 1603-1606.
12. Serebryany, A.N., (1985). Internal waves in the coastal zone of a tidal sea. Oceanology, 25: 744-751.
13. Serebryany A.N., (1990). Nonlinearity effects in internal waves on a shelf. Izvestia Academy of Sciences of USSR. Atmospheric and Oceanic Physics, 26: 206-212.
14. Serebryany A.N., (1993) Manifestation of soliton properties in internal waves on a shelf. Izvestia Academy of Sciences. Atmospheric and Oceanic Physics, 29: 229-238.
15. Serebryany A. N., Holloway P.E., (1995). Observations of nonlinear internal waves on a shelf break: variety of processes of internal tidal transformation and observed huge internal surf. In: Proceedings of IAPSO XXI General Assembly. N 19, Honolulu, Hawaii, USA, p. 230.
16. Serebryany A.N., (1996). Steepening of the leading and back faces of solitary internal waves-depressions and its connections with tidal currents. Dynamics of Atmospheres and Oceans. 23: 2075-2091.
17. Thorpe S.A., (1978). On internal gravity waves in the accelerating shear flow. J. Fluid. Mech. 88: 623-639.
18. Thorpe S. A., (1999). On the breaking of internal waves in the ocean. J. Phys. Oceanography, 29: 2433-2441.
19. Woods J. D., (1968). Wave-induced shear instability in the summer thermocline. J. Fluid Mech., 32: 791-800.

Change of Internal Wave Polarity on a Shelf: Observations and Experimental Evidences

Andrey N. Serebryany

N.N. Andreyev Acoustics Institute, Shvernik Str. 4, Moscow 117036, Russia

aserebr@dataforce.net

1. Abstract

The effect of change of internal wave polarity which takes place for internal waves which propagate in the shoreward direction, from deep to shallow water, is discussed. The results of a special experiment carried out on the shelf of the Sea of Japan with the purpose of collecting data on the effect and associated accompanied processes are analysed. There, it was revealed a "zone of transition" (vicinity of turning point) where the nonlinearity coefficient change it's sign in the coastal part of the shelf. Evidences on spatial and temporal variability of the turning point zone were obtained. Internal waves with different polarities as well as internal waves near the turning point were observed. It is shown that semidiurnal internal tidal waves propagated shoreward passing through the zone of transition significantly affected on thermocline which periodically leads to its alternating shift to the more shallow or deeper regions.

2. Introduction

One of the most prominent features of intense internal waves in the sea is characteristic asymmetrical form of wave profile which is connected with their nonlinearity. It is well known that the form of internal waves depends on the vicinity of the thermocline to the boundaries - the sea surface or bottom. All large-amplitude internal waves observed in the deep ocean (this is a case when thermocline is closer to the sea surface) have forms of troughs or depression waves (Ostrovsky, Stepanyants, 1989, Serebryany, 1995). On the contrary large internal waves observed in shallow water often manifest themselves as elevation waves because the thermocline becomes closer to the bottom (Lafond, 1966; Ivanov et al, 1981, Serebryany, 1985, 1990). In the frame of the KdV model which gives a reasonable description of internal wave dynamics (Osborne, Burch, 1980; Ostrovsky, Stepanyants, 1989) it is easy to demonstrate that internal wave polarity is dependent on the sign of the nonlinearity coefficient α, which in its turn depends on the above mentioned peculiarities and the position of thermocline. The KdV equation in the case of a two-layer fluid is given by

$$\frac{\partial \eta}{\partial t} + \alpha \eta \frac{\partial \eta}{\partial x} + c_0 \frac{\partial \eta}{\partial x} + \beta \frac{\partial^3 \eta}{\partial x^3} = 0 \; ; \qquad \alpha = \frac{3 c_0 (h_1 - h_2)}{2 h_1 h_2}; \quad \beta = \frac{c_0 h_1 h_2}{6}$$

where β - is dispersion coefficient, t- time, x-horizontal coordinate , η - vertical interface displacement, h_1 - thikness of the upper layer, h_2 – thickness of the lower layer.

The internal soliton solution to the KdV equation is $\eta(x,t) = \eta_0 \sec h^2 [(x - ct) / L]$, where the scale length $L_s = (\frac{12 \beta}{\alpha \eta_0})^{\frac{1}{2}}$. In the case when the thermocline is closer to the surface $h_1 < h_2$, and consequently $\alpha < 0$ and internal soliton is wave of depression, while $h_1 > h_2$ (thermocline is closer to the bottom), $\alpha > 0$

and internal soliton is a wave of elevation. Therefore, the "polarity" of internal waves is governed by hydrological conditions.

In the case of arbitrary stratification α and β are calculated on the basis of eiganfunctions W of the boundary problem for internal wave as follows:

$$\alpha = -\frac{3c_0 \int_{-H}^{0} \rho (\frac{dW}{dz})^3 dz}{2 \int_{-H}^{0} \rho (\frac{dW}{dz})^2 dz} \qquad \beta = \frac{-c_0 \int_{-H}^{0} \rho W^2 dz}{2 \int_{-H}^{0} \rho (\frac{dW}{dz})^2 dz}$$

In the case of a shelf internal waves propagating shoreward, i.e. from the region of continental slope (thermocline is closer to the surface) to the coastal zone (where thermocline is closer to the bottom), the change of internal wave polarity is observed. Internal depression waves propagating to the shore must at some place on the shelf (the so called "turning point", point where the thickness of the mixed layer is equal to the thickness of the bottom layer) be transformed into elevation waves. Hypothetically this situation must be very widespread due to the regularity of the process of internal tide propagation to the shore throughout shelves of the World Ocean. To illustrate that "the effect of internal wave polarity change" exists in the nature we return to our result which has been published previously (Serebryany,1990). During our measurements on shelf of the Sea of Japan in 1982 we observed two trains of intense internal waves which, within an interval of 12 hours, propagated to the shore, crossing our measuring system deployed in the coastal zone in a position where the depth 30-meter (see Fig.1). The striking feature of these events was that each train consisted of internal waves with different polarities. A

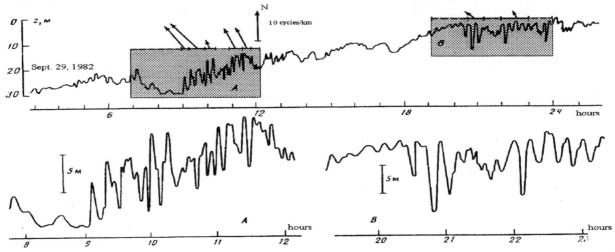

Fig.1. Internal wave trains of different polarity separated by a 12 hour time interval (Serebryany, 1990). Observations in the coastal zone of the Sea of Japan in September of 1982. Both trains propagate shoreward (the arrows are wave vectors indicating the northwest direction of internal wave propagation). Measurements were made by a spatial antenna of line sensors which allowed lengths (100-300 m) and heights (up to 10 m) of the internal waves to be determined.

train of elevation waves were observed first and a train of depression waves followed. This unusual phenomenon observed in one single position on the shelf during one semidiurnal tidal circle was observed because there was distortion of regularity of semidiurnal movement mean position of thermocline in the coastal zone. The generation of the first train was connected with the passing of face front of the internal tidal wave when the mean position of the thermocline was near the bottom. Several hours later the thermocline did not fall down to the bottom as it usually happens, but preserved its high position near the sea surface up to the emergence of the next train of soliton-like internal waves. Because these internal waves propagated on the subsurface thermocline, the polarity of these waves was inverted as compared with the polarity of waves of the previous train, and depression waves were observed. We believe that the distortion in the semidiurnal vertical displacement of the thermocline was initiated by local upwelling induced by wind in the coastal zone. A similar phenomenon was observed in the Rio-Antirio strait of the Ionian Sea by Salusti et al, 1989.

Although on theoretical grounds the effect of change of internal wave polarity on the shelf is expected to be a widespread phenomenon, so far data on this effect obtained in field observations are very rare. The aim of this paper is to present new data on this subject, which was obtained in our field observations, which revealed some new features on the effect of change of internal wave polarity.

3. Observations. Revealing of zone of change of internal wave polarity.

We carried out special experiment on internal waves investigation on shelf of the Sea of Japan where new data on the effect of change of internal wave polarity were obtained. Our observations included measurements of internal waves by line temperature sensors (Konyaev, Sabinin, 1973; Klevkov et al, 1990) from towed and anchored vessel, yo-yo CTD soundings, surveys on cross-shelf sections and etc. The experiment continued 2 days and included the 4 following stages. At the first stage we made a CTD survey on a 30 km section oriented across the shelf and covered space from the coastal zone to a point above the continental slope. Soundings were made at 9 stations spaced 2 miles apart. Just after the survey, we started the second stage. We conducted long-time towing along a line that passed over the CTD stations. During a period of 24 hours the research vessel with towed line temperature sensor performed 10 non-stop repeated runs along the track. The line temperature sensor was deployed in a layer with thermocline and continuously measures mean temperature in the layer, permitting to obtain data on vertical displacements of the thermocline. As a result we obtained 10 space sections with detail information on thermocline relief in upper layer of the sea, internal waves and its variability in time for 2 semidiurnal tidal cycles. The towing was finished by CTD survey in the same 9 stations again. After that research vessel was anchored in coastal waters near the point of St.1. In this position measurements from the anchored vessel were continued by the line temperature sensor along with repeated CTD sounding during period of 13 hours.

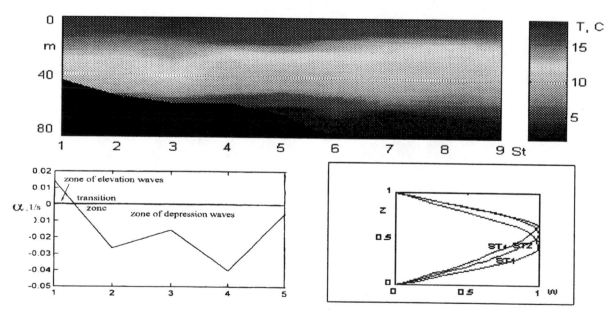

Fig.2. Isotherm distribution on the cross-shelf section for CTD survey. Variability of the nonlinearity coefficient α and internal wave eigenfuctions W in the coastal zone.

Figure 2 shows isotherms in a cross-shelf section for the CTD survey after the towing. We can see the tendency of deepening of the upper thermocline (which was in the boundaries of 10-30 m depth) above shelf in the area between stations 4 and 6. Some deepening was also observed for this section in the coastal zone between stations 1 and 2. It is interesting to follow how the nonlinear coefficient changes on this section. To obtain this dependence we firstly calculated the internal wave eigenfunctions in each point of the survey for the 1st mode, using obtained CTD profiles, by numerical solution of the boundary problem for the internal waves (program of V.V. Goncharov). Then the coefficients of nonlinearities for 5 coastal stations were calculated. The results are shown on Fig. 2, left down part . We can see that above all area of shelf besides position of St.1 α is negative. In the shallow water on a distance between St.1 and St.2 α change its polarity to positive sign. Thus there is a zone of transition of internal wave polarity ,where turning point occurs in the coastal waters between St.1 and St.2. It is also interesting to note that the maximum of corresponding eigenfuction becomes closer to the bottom if we follow shoreward from one station to another (see right down part of Fig.2).

4. Packets of intense internal waves on transactions across the shelf. Influence of tidal internal waves on position of the zone of internal wave polarity change.

Long-period towing provided more detailed information on spatial variability of thermocline in the upper layer. Fig. 3 shows thermocline relief as it was recorded on the run 3 and run 5 of the towing. The main features which we can observe in each run are common and were repeated for all runs performed. We see that the shallow zone of the shelf (shallower St. 4) is an area of intense short-period internal waves with amplitudes up to 10-15 meters. These waves propagated shoreward. The evidences of that were obtained comparing records of the internal wave packet registered on two successive runs with opposite direction. The deeper part of the shelf closer to shelf break (seaward from point of St.4) is a zone of small temporal change of the horizontal thermocline structure. This part consists of a long positive trend of the thermocline up-to the sea surface and an area above of large depth where the thermocline is almost horizontally homogeneous. Following to successive records of all runs (not shown on a figure) we note an interesting feature. In the shallow water the inclination of the thermocline between St.2 and St.1 changes radically during a 5-hour interval so that a drop of the thermocline depth was observed on the record of run 3 during moving vessel to the sore, while there it was observed a rise of the thermocline to the surface

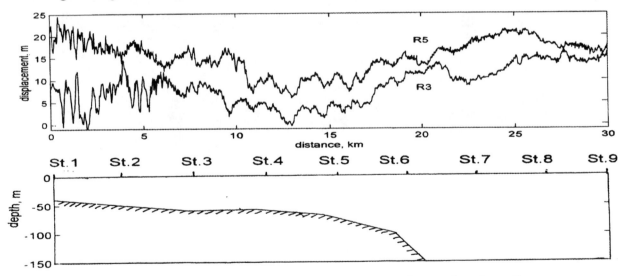

Fig. 3. Cross-shelf sections obtained by towed line sensor for run 3 and run 5.

on the record of run 5 . So, the mean position of thermocline in coastal water (near St.1) undergo vertical oscillations with amplitudes up to 15-20 meters. Moreover, the packets of short internal waves are seen on this long rising (for run 5) or deepening (for run 3) of the thermocline. To explain this effect we used record of moored station measurements which were obtained in position of St.1 after the end of the towing. We found that our approaches to St.1 almost coincides with time of "high internal water"(in the case of run 5) and coincided with time of "low internal water" (in the case of run 3). So the oscillations of the thermocline position discussed here is connected with approach of internal tidal waves in coastal waters of the shelf. Previously it was shown that on spatial transects made by CTD survey we found a zone of change of polarity of internal waves between St.1 and St.2. The new result obtained from towing shows that in the region of the inner shelf we registered intense short-period internal waves which propagated shoreward on the background of the internal tidal (semidiurnal) waves which moved to the shore as well. The trains of internal waves were involved in vertical displacements created by the long-period internal waves. So in the case of "low internal water" (run 3) internal waves have the tendency to change their polarity near St.1. Moreover trough of internal tide propagated to the shore can shift position of the turning point from coastal waters towards deeper water (our estimates show that the shift can reach up to several kilometres), while a crest of internal tide also shifts the turning point position into the opposite direction to the more shallower point in coastal zone.

5. Observation of the change of internal wave polarity on mooring station.

As it was said previously, after finishing the towing, the vessel returned to position of St.1, and carried out mooring measurements of internal waves during 13 hours. During this stage we obtained temperature line sensor record of semidiurnal internal wave (Fig.4) for a time interval between two troughs. The measured amplitude of the internal tide was 16 m. It is a very significant value for 40 m depth of the sea in the position of observation. Casts of temperature profiles shows how the internal tide transforms the vertical structure of temperature. In particular, during passing of rear-slope of internal tide the thermocline was significantly deepened. This is the key for understanding the clearly seen variability in the vertical asymmetry in profiles of intense short-period internal waves. In different phases of the internal tide we can see the appearance of internal waves of different polarities. On the front slope of the internal tide we observed solitary depression wave with amplitude of 10 m and time scale of 30 minutes. On the back slope there was amplification of short period wave intensity. There is a very interesting feature of this record connected with transition of thermocline depth through the turning point (where thermocline passed the equidistant position between the surface and the bottom). In the beginning of this fragment at 7.30 a.m. the solitary wave depression was observed with 6-m height. Half an hour after, firstly a 8- meter depression of the thermocline emerged and after that a train without some features of polarities was observed. Then the thermocline deepened further and some time after more appeared short-period internal waves were observed (6-20 minute period) with features of elevations waves. Vertical profiles of temperature for this period (shown in the inset of Fig.4) confirmed the deepening of the thermocline induced by the tidal wave.

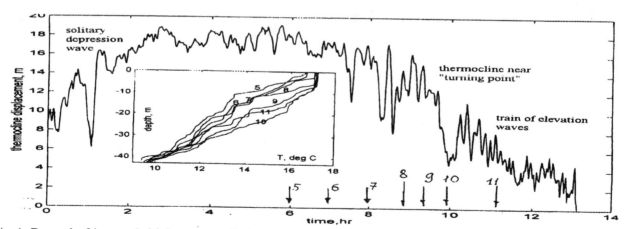

Fig.4. Record of internal tidal wave on St.1 made by line temperature sensor. Vertical temperature profiles for the period when the thermocline passed through the turning point shown in the inset.

6. Conclusion

1039

Our observations have shown complexity of the processes connected with internal wave propagation on a shelf when internal waves propagate in the zone of turning point. Numeric modelling of this process describing evolution of depression waves near turning point and their transformation to elevation waves was made by several authors (Knickerbrocker, Newell, 1980; Liu et al., 1998; Vlasenko, 1993). All these investigations were based on assuming that solitary internal waves propagated shoreward on horizontally homogeneous thermocline. As it was seen from observations presented here the real picture is more complex due to simultaneously occurrence of internal waves of two scales (internal tides and short-period waves exhibited as solitary waves or packets of intense waves) involved in this process. Internal tidal wave has a role of the cause creating slow change of environmental parameters (in particular, nonlinearity coefficient) and which is very important for transformation of solitary waves propagating in the zone of turning point. In reality internal tides produce periodically shifting of a position of boundary of the turning point towards the shore and back. On the another hand, internal tides propagating in the coastal zone itself play a role in the process of changing of its polarity due to decreasing of the water depth. All these circumstances make a complicated picture of internal wave dynamics on a shelf that, indicating that there is scope for more investigations. For the case of a shelf of non-tidal seas (Ivanov et al, 1981; Ivanov, Serebryany, 1985) we can assume that behaviour of solitary internal waves near the turning point will be quite well described by the numerical modelling mentioned above.

7. Acknowledgements

The author is grateful to Dr. J. Da Silva for his help in correction the text. This work was partially supported by Russian Foundation for Basic Research (grant N 98-05-64804).

References

1. Ivanov, V.A., Konyaev, K.V., Serebryany, A.N., (1981). Groups of intense internal waves on the shelf zone of the sea. Izv. Acad. Sci. USSR, Atmos. Ocean.Phys., 17:1302-1309.
2. Ivanov, V.A., Serebryany, A.N., (1985). Short-period internal waves in the coastal zone of a nontidal sea. Izv. Acad. Sci. USSR, Atmos. Ocean.Phys., 21:648-656.
3. Klevkov A.I., Nazarov A.A., Serebryany A.N., (1994). Towed recorder of temperature (In Russian). Inventor's Certificate USSR N 1342196, 01 K 7/16. Bulletin of Inventions, State Committee on Inventions and Discoveries of Russia, VNIPI, Moscow, 22.
4. Konyaev, K.V., Sabinin K.D., (1973). New data on internal waves in a sea obtained using distributed temperature sensors. Dokl. Acad. Sci. USSR, 209:856-864.
5. Knickerbrocker, C. J. and Newell A.C., (1980) Internal solitary waves near a turning point. Phys. Lett. 75A: 326-330.
6. LaFond E.C., (1966). Internal waves. In.:The Encyclopedia of Oceanography. Ed. By R.W. Fairbridge. Reinhold Publishing Corporation. New York.: 109-113.
7. Liu A.K., Y.S. Chang, M.K., M.K. Hsu and N.K. Liang, (1998). Evolution of nonlinear internal waves in the East and South China Seas. J. Geophys. Res. 103: 7995-8008.
8. Osborn A. R., T.L. Burch, (1980). Internal solitons in the Andaman Sea. Science. 208:451-460.
9. Ostrovsky L.A. and Yu.A. Stepanyants. (1989). Do internal solitons exist in the ocean? Rev. Geoph. 27: 293-310.
10. Salusti E., A. Lascaratos and K. Nittis, (1989). Changes of polarity in marine internal waves. Field evidence in Eastern Mediterranien Sea. Ocean. Modelling , 82: 10-11.
11. Serebryany, A.N., (1985). Internal waves in the coastal zone of a tidal sea. Oceanology, 25:744-751.
12. Serebryany A.N., (1990). Nonlinearity effects in internal waves on a shelf. Izvestia Academy of Sciences. Atmospheric and Oceanic Physics, 26: 206-212.
13. Serebryany A.N., (1995). Huge internal waves in the ocean. In: Proceedings of International Symposium "Ocean Cities 95". Monaco: 376-381.
14. Vlasenko V.I., (1993). Modelling of baroclinic tides in the shelf zone of Guinea. Izvestia Academy of Sciences. Atmospheric and Oceanic Physics, 29: 673-680.

14

ATMOSPHERIC FLOWS

Three-dimensional Aspects of Nonlinear Stratified Flow Over Topography Near the Hydrostatic Limit

T.R. Akylas

Department of Mechanical Engineering, M.I.T., Cambridge, MA 02139, USA

A common mechanism by which internal waves are generated in nature is flow over topography. The goal of this work is to improve our theoretical understanding of this generation mechanism with particular emphasis on three-dimensional (3-D) nonlinear disturbances. To this end, an asymptotic theory is developed to describe steady, finite-amplitude internal-wave disturbances induced by stratified flow over locally confined topography that is more elongated in the spanwise than the streamwise direction. The nonlinear 3-D equations of motion then can be handled via a matched-asymptotics procedure: in an 'inner' region close to the topography, the flow is nonlinear but weakly 3-D, while far upstream and downstream the 'outer' flow is governed, to leading order, by the fully 3-D linear hydrostatic equation, subject to matching conditions from the inner flow.

Based on this approach, three particular flow configurations are discussed:

(*a*) Non-resonant flow over finite-amplitude topography in a channel of finite depth. In this instance, it is assumed that the flow Froude number, F, is not close to any of the critical Froude numbers ($F_1 > F_2 > \cdots$) associated with the channel long-wave modes:

$$\cdots < F_M < F < F_{M-1} < \cdots < F_1.$$

The downstream response consists of an infinite number ($n \geq M$) of oblique wavetrains, each oriented at angle $\pm \tan^{-1} (F_n / (F^2 - F^2_n)^{1/2})$ to the flow direction, forming multiple supercritical wakes. The amplitudes of these wakes are not affected seriously by nonlinearity in the near-field flow. On the other hand, 3-D effects inhibit breaking of the flow over the topography, and the critical steepness for overturning is higher than in the analogous 2-D flow.

(*b*) Uniformly stratified, resonant flow in a channel of finite depth. When the flow speed is close to the speed of one of the long-wave modes,

$$F \approx F_M,$$

the flow is resonant. Furthermore, when the flow is uniformly stratified, small-amplitude topography induces a finite-amplitude response under resonance conditions. The downstream response again comprises wakes, qualitatively similar to those found in the non-resonant case; but, in this instance, the generation mechanism is of a different nature: nonlinear interactions in the flow over the topography play an important part, and the amplitudes of the downstream wakes are much stronger than linear theory would predict.

(*c*) Vertically unbounded, uniformly stratified flow. Here the flow may be regarded as resonant for all flow speeds because the spectrum of long-wave modes is continuous. Moreover, according to linear theory, the 3-D wave pattern induced by locally confined topography remains locally confined. It is found that, owing to the same nonlinear mechanism as in (*b*) above, multiple wakes are generated downstream so, in contrast to linear theory, the nonlinear wave pattern is not locally confined.

The theoretical predictions are supported by field observations. Gjevik & Marthinsen (1978), in particular, analysed satellite photographs of atmospheric internal-wave patterns generated by isolated islands in the Norwegian Sea. Apart from the familiar lee waves, they observed a prominent oblique wavetrain east of the island of Jan Mayen that is strikingly similar to those predicted theoretically. A full account of the theory can be found in Akylas & Davis (2000).

This work was supported by AFOSR F49620-98-1-0388 and NSF DMS-9701967.

References

Akylas, T.R. & Davis, K.S. 2000. "Three-dimensional aspects of nonlinear stratified flow over topography near the hydrostatic limit", *Journal of Fluid Mechanics, sub judice.*

Gjevik, B. & Marthinsen, T. 1978. "Three-dimensional lee-wave pattern. *Quart. J. Roy. Met. Soc.* **104**, 947–957.

Characteristics of Urban Heat Island in a City Located at the Bottom of a Basin

Takashi Asaeda[1], Takeshi Fujino[1], and Steven W. Armfield[2]

[1]Department of Environmental Science & Human Technology, Saitama University, Saitama, Japan
[2]Department of Mechanical Engineering, The University of Sydney, Sydney, NSW, Australia
asaeda@post.saitama-u.ac.jp

1. Abstract

Observation was made around the city located on the shore of the lake in the bottom of a basin, intended to obtain the wind field structure of the local circulation and the drainage in the relation to the heat island phenomena. In daytime, upslope winds as a result of subsidence form an entire circulation in the basin, which provides the anomalous distribution in the local humidity and sensible heat; accumulation of humidity over the top of the mountain range and of sensible heat widely over the basin. This accumulated sensible heat maintains the temperature rising and drying of the lake breeze until the arrival of the sea breeze from the outside the basin or the drainage from the mountain slope. The time scale of the circulation is given by the square of the circulation height divided by the turbulent viscosity. In the evening a drainage forms along the cooled mountain slope although the local circulation still exists. The thickness and the velocity of the drainage scales were obtained both for the drainage along the mountain slope and subsequently for the intrusion after arriving at the flat plain of the bottom of the basin. This provides much smaller time scale than the circulation time scale. The lag in the arrival time of the cooler drainage between the field at the bottom of the mountain range and the city center provides the instantaneous temperature difference, which had similar magnitude as the difference due to heating from the ground surface during the travelling over the urban area.

2. Introduction

Although the heat island effect is normally considered to be a result of human activities, large scale topographic effects must be also taken into account. Cities located at the bottom of basins suffer intense heat stress during the day, but at night are subject to a cool drainage from the surrounding mountains, which again acts to alleviate the heat island effect . For a decade, nocturnal cooling and daytime heating at the bottom of these basin topographies were intensively studied (Banta 1984; Kondo 1986). Due to the topographic blocking of the synoptic wind aloft, adiabatic heating due to the subsidence of the stable layer is experienced in the confined basin. The heated daytime air is replaced by a lake of cold nocturnal air at night (Whiteman 1982). During the day upslope winds, resulting from subsidence, form a circulation over the entire basin, providing an anomalous distribution of local humidity and sensible heat with an accumulation of humidity over the top of the mountain range and of sensible heat widely over the basin (Kimura and Kuwagata 1995). This accumulated sensible heat maintains the warm temperature in the basin until the nocturnal cold drainage arrives.

Regardless of the location, heat island phenomena are generally expected around the urban area. The heat island intensity has been empirically obtained solely as a function of the housing density (Johnson et al. 1991; Oke et al. 1991), or population density (Oke 1981) in the area. The close relation of the surrounding topography of the city with its climate, however, suggest that the basin topography will have a significant effect on the heat island phenomena. Meteorological characteristics of cities in basins are not fully understood, making it difficult to evaluate the relative effects of the topography and the artificial heat stresses.

In this paper, we will present the results of the study of a relatively small city located in a basin topography, with the aim of providing a detailed description of the wind structure, which may be used for the evaluation of the relation of the topographic effects and the artificial thermal stress.

3. Observation

Field data were collected in and around Nagahama City (35°24'N, 136°14'E), which is located on the NE shore of Lake Biwa, the largest lake in Japan. Lake Biwa is 673 km² in area, 60 km long in NE-SW direction and 20 km wide (Fig. 1). The section which includes Nagahama city occupies most of the basin and is surrounded by mountain ranges of 500 to 1000 m height. The atmospheric phenomena in this region are expected to be primarily influenced by the basin geometry and to be confined within the basin. Nagahama city is far enough from the Japan sea and Pacific Ocean so that the interaction of the local climate with the sea breezes is assumed to be relatively less significant. The city has a population of 58 000, with 40 % of the people concentrated in the densely populated central residential area, most of which is covered with near uniform 2-storey slate roofed houses of about 7 m height. The measurements were conducted, from July 27th to 29th 1996, for solar radiation, atmospheric radiation, air temperature, relative humidity, atmospheric pressure, wind speed and direction, surface temperature of asphalt roads, roofs, and paddy, and lake water temperature. Most of instruments were placed along a street running through central Nagahama and on the NTT tower located near to the street. The locations are shown in Fig. 1. The street runs perpendicular to the lake shore, in the direction of the lake breeze and other major winds. The tower instruments were mounted 58 m above the ground. Additional data were obtained from radio sondes released 15 km to the north of the city centre several times during the observation period. On these days Japan was covered by the Pacific high pressure system, resulting in typical sunny days for this season. The wind velocity at 5000 m was always less than 10 m s⁻¹.

4. Observational results

a. The diurnal time

Figures 2a-c show the variation of wind vectors, air temperature, specific humidity at 58 m on the NTT tower. Heights greater than 13 m are above the canopy layer. The air temperature at the tower continued to rise for most of each day, peaking at around 18:00 LST and then dropping rapidly. Considering the wind vectors, on each day of the study at 6:00 LST a SE land breeze is blowing. At mid-morning, between 8:00 LST and 10:00 LST, a lake breeze commences ranging from SW to WNW. The lake breeze continues until just after 18:00 LST on the 27th, 15:00 LST on the 28th and just before 18:00 LST on the 29th. On each day the lake breeze is associated with a continual increase in temperature and reduction in specific humidity for the period during which it is blowing. The continued increase of the tower temperature beyond 12:00 LST, when the nearby surface temperatures peak, indicate that the major component dominating air temperature is not the onsite sensible heat flux but rather thermal advection by the lake breeze.

The potential temperature and specific humidity profiles taken by radio sonde on the 29th are shown in Fig. 3. Although a mixed layer has not formed during the day it is apparent that a low temperature gradient region has formed near the ground, extending up to 1500 m by 18:00 LST.

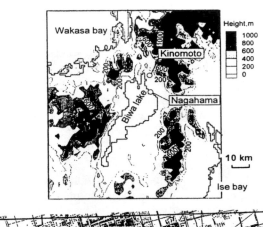

Fig.1. Surrounding topography of Nagahama city, and locations of instruments.

Correspondingly, the specific humidity profile at 15:00 LST shows a region, extending up to 1500 m, in which the specific humidity has reduced during the course of the day. As Kimura and Kuwagata(1995) reported, this profile was produced by the thermally induced local circulation over the basin, which accumulates latent heat over the mountainous region, and accumulates sensible heat over the lake, conveying the high temperature and low moisture air towards ground level inside the basin.

b. The cooling stage

At the tower, the temperature dropped dramatically after 18:00 LST on the 27th, at 16:30 and 21:00 LST on the 28th, and at 17:30 LST and 21:00 LST on the 29th. The vertical temperature profile shown in Fig. 3a indicates that even at 18:00 LST there is no significant sudden change in the temperature of the air above the ground, and it is therefore seen that the cooling observed above was restricted to the surface only, similar to the drainage flow formed by a density anomaly. As shown in Fig. 2b, corresponding to the first fall in temperature, the wind direction changed from the lake breeze to an ESE wind at 18:00-19:00 LST on 27th, to a NNW wind at 16:00 LST on 28th, and to a SW wind at 18:00 LST on 29th before the apparent predominance of an ESE wind afterwards. Judging from the map, the possible origins of these winds re Ise Bay for ESE wind, WakasaBay for the NNW wind and Osaka Bay for the SW wind.The mountain ranges surrounding the lake are about 1000 m high in the eastern region and about 1200 m high in the southern regions. Observed temperatures at 1212 m in the eastern range were 21.8 °C, 22.1 °C and 21.0 °C at 12:00 LST on these days. Assuming dry adiabatic conditions, this corresponds to 32 °C at the city level.

The secondary temperature drop at 21:00 LST on 28th and 29th occurred with the starting of ESE wind. Comparison of these temperature drops and their time indicates that the ESE wind on 27th is the drainage originated from sea-breeze, and on other days, the secondary drop corresponds to the drainage caused by the intensive cooling along the mountain slope although the first drop was due to the arrival of the sea-breeze from different direction.

5. The time scales of the circulation and the drainage

The decay time of the local circulation over the basin, t_C, scales with the square of the circulation height(~1500 m), H_c, divided by the average turbulent viscosity, ν, where it is assumed to be the same order of the turbulent thermal diffusion under the extremely turbulent condition. The vertical distribution of the turbulent viscosity is estimated from the observed data, assuming the horizontal velocity fluctuation being equal to the vertical components. Although there is some variation, the average value in the layer throughout the day is about 30 m² s⁻¹. Thus $t_C \sim H_c^2/\nu \sim 20$ hrs, which agrees with the fact that the circulation was recognized even at 18:00 LST, and indicates that the circulation will last until late evening even though the surface layer is then occupied by the drainage.

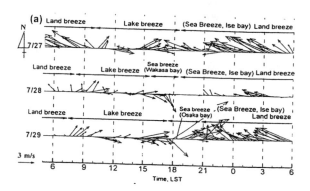

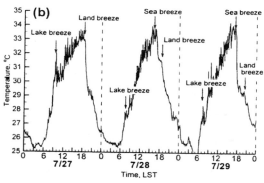

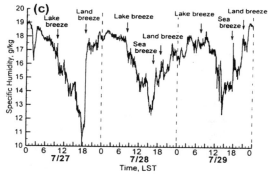

Fig.2. Variations of (a) wind vectors, (b) air temperature, and (c) specific humidity on the tower, 58 m high.

The drainage flow is generated by the air above the mountain slope being cooled, resulting in a vertical layer of cooled air of thickness $O(h_T)$, where $h_T \sim (Kt)^{1/2}$, where K is the turbulent thermal diffusivity and t is the time elapsed. The gravity force acts to accelerate the air only over the thickness h_T and the buoyancy will be balanced by unsteady advection, $O(\nu v/h_T^2)$. Thus, the velocity scales as $v \sim \alpha \Delta T g t \gamma /\sigma$, where α is the thermal expansion, ΔT is the temperature difference between the inside and the outside the drainage, γ is the average slope of the mountain range, and σ is the turbulent Prandtl number, ν /K (Patterson and Imberger 1980). The drainage on the mountain slope will grow until the advection of heat, $O(v \Delta T/l_M)$ and the conduction $O(K \Delta T/h_T^2)$ balance. Thus, a growth time scale for the drainage, T_D, is given as $T_D \sim (\sigma l_M/\alpha \Delta T g)^{1/2}$, where l_M is the length of the mountain slope. The scales for the velocity, v, the thickness, h_T, and the time to achieve full development at the bottom of the slope, t_M, are given by $v \sim (\alpha \Delta T g l_M/\sigma)^{1/2}\gamma$, $h_T \sim (K\nu l_M/\alpha \Delta T g)^{1/4}$, and $t_M \sim (\sigma l_M/\alpha \Delta T g)^{1/2}/\gamma$. The cool drainage travels across the flat bottom of the basin at velocity $u(\sim vh_T/h_P)$, where h_P is the thickness of the drainage intrusion. In the flat field, the intrusion layer is driven by a gravity-induced horizontal pressure gradient of $O(\alpha \Delta T g h_P/ut_P)$, where t_P is the elapsed time for any fluid particle after it arrives at the flat field and thus ut_P is the penetration distance into the field. In the region of the intrusion close to the mountain slope the advection term $\alpha(u^2/ut_P)$ balances the pressure gradient. Subsequently the viscous term $\alpha(\nu \, u/h_P^2)$ balances with the pressure gradient. Comparison of the magnitudes of these two terms provides the transition time of $T_t \sim K\nu^{-4/3}l_M^{4/3}(\alpha\Delta Tg)^{-1/3}$. After the transition, the thickness of the intrusion gradually increases with traveling time, such that $h_P \sim K^{3/10}\nu^{1/10}l_M^{3/10}(\alpha\Delta Tg)^{-1/10}\gamma^{2/5}t_p^{1/5}$ (Patterson and Imberger 1980). At the distance of l_P ($l_P=ut_p$), thus, $h_P \sim (K\nu)^{3/16}l_M^{3/16}l_P^{1/4}\gamma^{1/4}(\alpha\Delta Tg)^{-3/16}$. Accordingly, the velocity scale is given by $u \sim K^{9/16}\nu^{7/16}l_P^{-1/4}l_M^{9/16}\gamma^{3/4}(\alpha\Delta Tg)^{7/16}$. The time scale for traveling, t_P, is $t_P \sim K^{9/16}\nu^{7/16}\gamma^{-3/4}l_P^{5/4}(\alpha\Delta Tg)^{-7/16}l_M^{-9/16}$. In the present experiment, the turbulent diffusivity is slightly less than that of the entire circulation, such that $K \sim \nu \sim 10 \text{ m}^2 \text{ s}^{-1}$, and $h_T \sim 5000$ m, $l_P \sim 5000$ m, $\gamma \sim 0.2$, and $\Delta T \sim 3$ °C. Thus the viscosity becomes predominant only after $T_t \sim 9$ min, when the intrusion has penetrated 1.2 km. Therefore, at the tower where the observations were performed, the balance is between the pressure difference and the viscosity, and $h_P \sim 100$ m, and $u \sim 2.2 \text{ m s}^{-1}$, providing quantities comparable to the observed results. The total time scale for the drainage is the sum of these processes, which is $O(1)$ hour. This is much smaller than the time scale for the decay of the local circulation and thus the drainage will be fully established well before the local circulation has decayed.

6. The effects on the heat island intensity

Although the city is small the urban area is covered with slate roofs and asphalt pavements, while the surrounding area is predominantly paddy fields, and therefore some heat island phenomena are expected. Figure 4 shows the three days temperature measurements at locations P4 and P10, which lie on the main street, running almost in the same direction as the lake breeze. P4 lies within the urban area and P10 in the paddy field region.

During the daytime, the breeze temperature rises from 6:00 LST to approximately 16:00 LST, on each of the days, the temperature then drops rapidly, with the reduction occurring slightly earlier and being more rapid at P10, in the paddy field about 2 km away from the edge of the main residential area. The temperature difference between the residential area and the paddy field on the 27th is shown in Fig. 5a, where it is seen that for most of the day the difference is around 2 °C or less. However between 18:00 LST and 19:00 LST the difference is considerably greater and is over 4 °C for a short time at 18:30 LST. Fukuoka (1983) showed that the heat island effect for a city of this size would produce a temperature difference of about 1.8 °C. This would account for the variation of about 2 °C observed over the greater part of the day, but does not account for the sudden increase in temperature differential at 18:00 LST. The temperature variation may be correlated with the wind-speed in the lake-mountain direction, shown in Fig. 2a. The wind speed initially peaks at 14:20 LST, corresponding to the lake breeze. Subsequently the lake breeze decays by the arrival of the Ise Bay sea breeze at 17:30 LST leading to very low

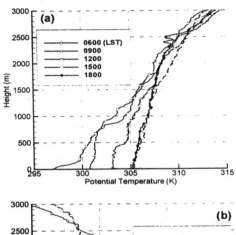

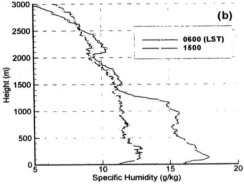

Fig.3. (a) Potential temperature, and (b) specific humidity profiles at 15 km north of Nagahama on 29th July, 1996.

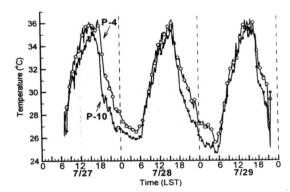

Fig.4.　Variations of air temperature at the center of the city(P4) and the paddy field(P10). (Circles:P4; Squares:P10)

wind speed in the period 17:30 LST to 18:40 LST. The wind speed subsequently increases significantly, peaking just after 19:40 LST and then decaying. The sudden increase at 19:40 LST corresponds to the arrival of the drainage which reinforces the weak Ise Bay sea breeze.

The sea breeze reached P10 at 18:00 LST, when the temperature suddenly started to fall there, while the drainage front reached P10 at about 19:40 LST, and is associated with the secondary fall in temperature observed at that time. The temperature difference observed between P4 and P10 is thus partly a result of the difference in arrival time of the sea breeze and drainage fronts at these two locations. Additionally the heat released from the ground surface in the urban, as well as continuing decline of the drainage temperature, will further enhance this difference.

The horizontal temperature gradient of the drainage is negligibly smaller than that of the vertical gradient. Thereby, is approximately satisfied. Translating temperature into the vertically averaged value inside the layer and integrating this equation from P10 to P4, gives,

$$\frac{1}{h_p}\int_{P10}^{P4}\int_0^{h_p}\frac{\partial uT}{\partial x}dzdx = \frac{1}{h_p}(-\int_{P10}^{P4}\int_0^{h_p}\frac{\partial T}{\partial t}dzdx + \int_{P10}^{P4}\int_0^{h_p}\frac{\partial}{\partial z}(K\frac{\partial T}{\partial z})dzdx).$$

The temperature difference between P4 and P10 is then obtained as follows,

$$T_{P4} - T_{P10} \approx -\frac{l_u}{u}\left(\frac{dT}{dt}\right) + \frac{l_u}{uh_p}\frac{H}{\rho_a C_p}.$$

where $dT/dt < 0$ indicating both terms in the right hand side are positive. Thus, the temperature difference is intensified by $-l_u/u(dT/dt)$ in addition to the heating from the ground surface during the passage over the urban area, given by $l_u H/(u\,h_P\,\rho_a C_p)$, where l_u is the urban travel distance of urban area between P10 and P4, which is 2 km, and thus the time elapsed is $O(l_u/u)$.

Figure 6a shows the temperature difference due to the lag in the arrival time, estimated by the falling rate of the mountain drainage temperature times the traveling time, $-l_u/u(dT/dt)$, where the wind velocity at the city center was utilized. Since the wind was fluctuating the averaged value over 10min. was utilized. Figure 6b, on the other hand, indicates the heating rate from the ground over the urban area, $l_uH/(u\,h_P\,\rho_a C_p)$, with H estimated by $H = \rho_a C_p a^2/N u \, \Delta T F_h(z/z_0, R_{iB})$, where ρ_a is the density of air, C_p is the specific heat of air, a is a constant $(= \kappa/(\ln z/z_o))$, z is the height concerned, z_0 is the roughness of the housing area which is assumed to be $O(0.5)$ cm (Kondo and Yamazawa 1986), N is a constant (=0.74), F_h is the function given by the stability of the layer (Louis 1979). Also shown on Fig. 6c is the sum of these two components of the temperature

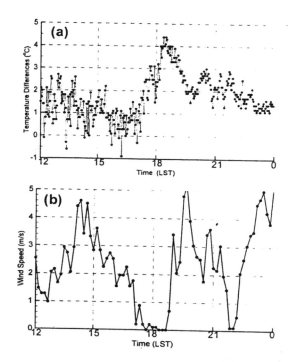

Fig.5. (a) Air temperature difference between P4 and P10, and (b) wind speed variation on the tower on 27th July, 1996.

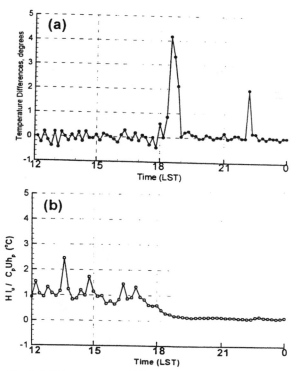

Fig.6. (a)Temperature difference due to the lag in arrival time, (b) temperature rise due to the sensible heat flux during traveling from P10 to P4

difference. Prior to the arrival of the drainage front the wind is weak due to the clash of the still existing circulation and the Ise Bay sea breeze. During this period the accumulated heat forms a major component of the total temperature difference. Subsequent to the arrival of the drainage front the time lag in its arrival at P4 forms the major component of the temperature difference.

Although the match is not exact, the sum of the temperature difference due to time-lag and the heating rate from the ground surface essentially agrees with the observed temperature difference between the city center and the paddy field as shown in Fig. 6a. The temperature difference due to the heating rate from the ground is also in reasonable agreement with the empirically obtained value of 1.8 °C (Fukuoka 1983) for a city of this size.

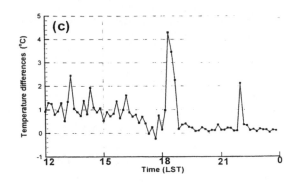

Fig.6. (c) the sum of temperature differences due to the time lag and the sensible heat flux.

6. Conclusions

Observations were obtained in and around the city, located on the shore of lake Biwa in the bottom of a basin, to obtain the wind field structure of the local circulation and the drainage in relation to the heat island phenomena. During the day a circulation forms over the entire basin, producing an anomalous distribution of local humidity and sensible heat with accumulation of humidity over the top of the mountain range and accumulation of sensible heat widely over the basin, drying effect of the lake breeze until the arrival of the drainage from the mountain slope. The time scale of the decay of the circulation is 20 hours, indicating that the circulation will persist into the night.

In the evening a drainage forms along the cooled mountain slope, although the local circulation still exists. The thickness and the velocity of the drainage were scaled at the flat field of the basin bottom. The drainage and circulation will be expected to coexist for some period in the evening, with the circulation partially blocking the drainage and enhancing the temperature difference associated with the advance of the cooler drainage front.

7. References

Banta, R.M., 1984: Daytime boundary-layer evolution over mountaineous terrain Part I: Observation of the dry circulation. *Mon. Wea. Rev.*, **112**, 340-356.

Duckworth, F.S., and J.S. Sandberg, 1954: The effect of cities upon horizontal and vertical temperature gradients. *Bull. Amer, Meteor. Soc.*, **35**, 198-207.

Fukuoka, Y., 1983: Physical climatological discussions on casual factors of urban temperature, *Mem. Fac. Intergraded Arts Sci.*, **8**, Hiroshima Univ., 157-178.

Johnson,G.T.,Oke,T.R.,Lyons,T.J., Steyn,D.G., Watson,I.D., and Voogt,J.A.,1991: Simulation of surface urban heat islands, Part 1: Theory and tests against field data. *Bound.-Layer Meteor.*, **56**, 275-294.

Kimura, F. and Kuwagata, T., 1995: Horizontal heat fluxes over complex terrain computed using a simple mixed-layer model and a numerical model. *J. Appl. Meteor.*, **34**, 549-558.

Kondo,J., and Yamazawa,H., 1986: Aerodynamic roughness over an inhomogeneous ground surface. *Bound.-Layer Meteor.*, **35**, 331-348.

Louis,J.F., 1979: A parametric model of vertical eddy fluxes in the atmosphere. *Bound.-Layer Meteor.*, **17**, 187-202.

Oke,T.R., 1973: City size and the urban heat island. *Atmos.Environ.* **7**, 769-779.

Oke, T.R., 1981: Canyon geometry and the nocturnal urban heat island: comparison of scale model and field observations. *J. Climatorol.*, **1**, 237-254.

Oke,T.R.,Johnson,G.T.,Steyn,D.G., and Watson,I.D.,1991: Simulation of surface urban heat islands under 'Ideal' conditions at night, Part 2: diagnosis of caution. *Bound.-Layer Meteor.*, **56**, 339-358.

Patterson, J., and Imberger, J, 1980: Unsteady natural convection in a rectangular cavity. *J.Fluid Mech.*, **100**, 65-86.

Whiteman, C.D.,1982: Breakup of temperature inversions in deep mountain valleys: Part I. observations. *J. Appl. Meteor.*, **21**, 270-289.

Vortex Dynamics in Strongly Stratified Flow over 3D Obstacles

Ian Castro[1], Simon Vosper[2], Martin Paisley[3] and Paul Hayden[4]

[1]School of Engineering Sciences, University of Southampton, Highfield, Southampton SO17 1BJ, UK
i.castro@soton.ac.uk
[2]School of the Environment, University of Leeds, Leeds LS2 9JT, UK
[3]School of Mathematics, University of Staffordshire, Stafford ST18 0AD, UK
[4]EnFlo, School of Mechanical & Materials Engineering, University of Surrey
Guildford GU2 5XH, UK

1. Abstract

Results of laboratory and numerical experiments on the stratified flow over single, squat obstacles of various shapes are presented. The obstacle height is in most cases of the same order as the base diameter and the major controlling (flow) parameter is the Froude number, defined here as $F_h=U/Nh$, where U is the (uniform) upstream velocity, h is the obstacle height and N is the buoyancy frequency; attention is concentrated on the case $F_h=0.1$, representing stratification sufficiently strong that lee-wave motions do not play a significant role in the flow dynamics. For right-circular cones it is shown that the sectional contributions to the total fluctuating side force (lift) show significant phase variations up the height of the obstacle, which are not always reflected in the developed vortex street further downstream. For some obstacle shapes, the vortex lines linking the von Karman eddies at different heights can be significantly tilted, particularly in the upper part of the wake. Vortex convection speeds do not appear generally to vary greatly with height and, as found in previous work, the shedding frequency remains constant with height, despite the strong variation of cross-stream obstacle width. By comparison with results of experiments on more weakly tapered obstacles, it is suggested that the stratification enhances the shedding instability, which would otherwise be very weak for squat obstacles, but does not annihilate the ability of the flow at one level to influence that at another.

2. Introduction

It has been known for decades that if the upstream density stratification is stable and sufficiently strong, the flow behind three-dimensional obstacles can contain periodic vortex shedding, akin to the classical situation of homogeneous flow over two-dimensional bluff bodies. This phenomenon has been frequently observed at atmospheric scales. There are, for example, some spectacular satellite images of the vortex street behind isolated islands (most recently the Landsat7 image of the cloud patterns behind Alejandro Selkirk island in the southern Pacific, captured on 15th September 1999), which often reveal vortex spacing ratios very close to the classical (von Karman) result from inviscid theory. Such flows have been reproduced in the laboratory (e.g. Brighton, 1978, Castro *et al*, 1983, Vosper *et al*, 1999) and there have also been a number of numerical simulations (e.g. Smolarkiewicz & Rotunno, 1989, Rotunno *et al*, 1999, Vosper, 2000, Paisley, 2000). Despite considerable study there remain a number of unsolved technical questions. How is it, for example, that the shedding frequency seems usually to be invariant with height despite the fact that the spanwise width of the body (the scale which sets the shedding frequency in the 2D homogeneous case) generally varies strongly with height? Precisely how is the total fluctuating lift force (i.e. the spanwise drag) on the obstacle generated? What is the nature of the interaction between the baroclinically generated vorticity and that produced viscously by flow separation from the body? Once the vertical vorticity has appeared (partly *via* tilting of the vortex lines generated in these two ways) how do the vortex lines behave as they convect downstream?

In this paper we address some of these issues by analysis of recent numerical and laboratory experiments. The computations include both (nominally) inviscid and full Navier-Stokes calculations of flow over right-circular cones and cosine-shaped bodies. A wider range of bodies were used for the laboratory experiments, which were undertaken in EnFlo's towing tank at the University of Surrey and broaden our earlier experiments discussed by Vosper *et al* (1999). In particular, the experiments included measurement of vortex convection speeds and phase data at various heights through the wake and we compare this data with corresponding results obtained from the numerical computations. The latter were also used to investigate the vorticity generation, diffusion and convective processes, particularly in the context of the vertical vorticity component, ω_z (which is the only significant component in the wake region), but in this paper space limitations prevent full discussion of this particular topic.

3. Techniques

The inviscid numerical simulations were conducted using NH3D, a three-dimensional finite difference (explicit) model based on the pseudo-inviscid equations in σ (normalised pressure) coordinates and described in detail by Miranda & James (1992). Free-slip lower boundary and sidewall conditions were imposed, radiative upstream and downstream boundary conditions were enforced and the upper boundary was a rigid lid, mimicking conditions in the towing tank used for the laboratory experiments. The model domain consisted of 193 by 51 grid points in the x and y directions, respectively, with 40 vertical levels, and its size was chosen so that, relative to the obstacle size (height h and base diameter L), it had the same width and height as the towing tank. For all computations the horizontal grid length was $L/20$ and the simulations were conducted for two different conical obstacles, with slopes of 1 and 0.5 (i.e. $h=L/2$ and $L/4$, respectively). Time steps were about $2 \times 10^{-3}L/U$ in both cases. Vosper (2000) contains further details

Viscous computations for the same two cones were performed using a full, multi-grid, (implicit) Navier-Stokes code which embodied a simple mixing length turbulence model; this effectively 'switched off' the turbulence wherever the local Richardson number exceeded 1/4. The domain width and height were identical to those of the inviscid calculations, but the downstream boundary was placed somewhat further from the obstacle ($x=10L$). Grid sizes were $160 \times 32 \times 32$ with the horizontal mesh size being, again, typically $L/20$ (and uniform) in the rectangular slab containing the obstacle; outside this region it expanded outwards to the boundaries. The vertical mesh was non-uniform throughout, with the lowest point at 0.01H, expanding to about 0.08H near the top of the obstacle. The time step was $6.25 \times 10^{-2}L/U$ and the Reynolds number (Uh/ν) was 10^5. No-slip boundary conditions were imposed on the surface of the cone (and nowhere else) *via* a standard log-law formulation and the outflow was, again, a radiation boundary. The multi-grid speed-up achieved for these unsteady runs was only around a factor of two (using four grid levels), compared with factors of O(10) for steady flow computations. Convergence to a level where sums of absolute normalised residuals over the whole domain were lower than 10^{-3} was imposed for each time-step, requiring typically 3-4 iterations. Accuracy in the convective term differencing was achieved using a Van-Leer-based scheme. More complete details of the code can be found in Paisley (2000).

Laboratory experiments were performed using the stratified towing tank in the EnFlo laboratory. Mixtures of fresh water and brine were used in filling the tank to create a linear density profile with a Brunt-Väisälä frequency, N, of about $1.57s^{-1}$ and all experiments were undertaken at $F_h=0.1$ by appropriate adjustment of the towing speed, U. The two cones used for comparison with the numerical computations had a base diameter of 500mm and heights of 250mm and 125mm and were towed in an inverted position with their bases at the water surface. Reynolds numbers (based on U and h) were some 3-4000. More complete details of these kinds of experiments are given in Vosper *et al* (1999). For the present purpose, three-component sonic anemometers and/or hot films probes were used to measure local velocity, but since most of the data were used to obtain shedding frequency and phase information, absolute accuracy in velocity was not necessary. Typically, one probe was mounted at a fixed reference location on the edge of the wake (e.g. at an x,y,z location given by $2L$, L, $0.26L$, where 0,0,0 is the centre of the base of the cone and y is in the spanwise direction). For each tow, the second probe was positioned either at the same x,y location but a different z, or the same y,z location and a different x. The resulting pair of velocity traces (for U, say, at the two locations), which always contained large-amplitude quasi-periodic fluctuations because of the vortex shedding, were then cross-correlated with variable time lag, so that phase relationships and vortex convection speeds could be obtained.

Because only a few shedding periods were available during any one tow (typically six or seven at most), and because the wake flow was fully turbulent so that the shedding was not entirely steady, it was found that repeated tows yielded significant scatter in the deduced phase data (or the vortex convection speeds). In many cases, therefore, multiple tows (typically eight or nine) were made with identical conditions and the results averaged to reduce the statistical scatter. A similar post-processing, correlating procedure was possible for selected locations from the results of the numerical computations. The computational times were, like the tow times, not extensive enough to yield more than a few shedding periods. We have reduced the uncertainty in the data by undertaking a degree of spatial averaging. Thus, for example, to obtain the vortex convection speed at height z, the vertical vorticity at two x-locations was cross-correlated but, for each time lag, the correlation was averaged over a y-line spanning the wake - typically from $-1.5L$ to $1.5L$. The results were not significantly dependent on the length of the y-line. It should be emphasised that all our data is likely to suffer from a greater degree of uncertainty than would be typical, say, of similar measurements obtained in wind tunnel experiments, for in that case one usually time-averages over many hundreds of shedding periods.

The numerical results were also used to deduce not only the time-variation of the spanwise drag force (which we hereafter call 'lift') on the cones but also the sectional contributions to this force. These were obtained by using the circumferential pressure field to calculate the lift acting on horizontal 'slabs' of the cones, usually of thickness $0.2h$. The objective was to find which levels contributed most strongly to the lift and how the time-dependent shedding process at different heights affects the lift.

4. Results & Discussion

We begin by showing, in Figure 1, the total lift force for the unit-slope cone, obtained from both the inviscid and the N-S computations. In the inviscid computations the shedding was triggered by imposing a small potential temperature perturbation in a small region upstream of the cone, whereas in the N-S computations shedding was left to arise naturally. Transition from the initial symmetric, steady eddies (attached to the lee of the cone) to the full shedding solution therefore took rather longer in this latter case and the lift trace in the figure has been shifted in time so that the second main peak occurs at the same Ut/L. The peak lift values from the inviscid code are somewhat larger than those obtained using the inviscid code; averaging the moduli of the peak values over the four major cycles shown in fig. 1 gives a difference of about 30%. Reasons for this are unclear but, since the difference is only about 2% for the half-slope cones, it may simply be a result of inadequate 'tow' time. These data, and similar plots of velocity vs. Ut/L at various points downstream, allow the shedding frequency, f, and hence Strouhal

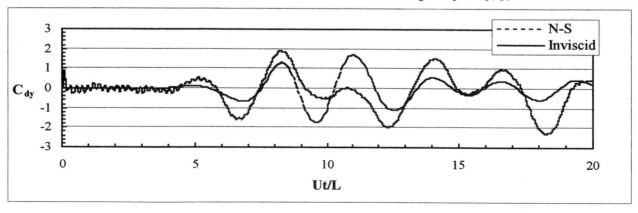

Figure 1. Time traces of the total (spanwise) lift coefficient, obtained from the inviscid and the N-S computations.

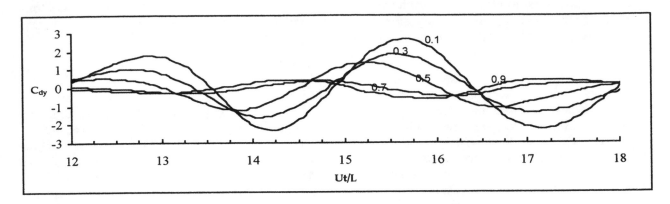

Figure 2. Sectional lift variations. The labels refer to the z/h values at the mid-point of each slab, all of which were $0.2h$ in thickness. Thus the curve labelled 0.1 refers to the sectional lift contribution from the cone section from $z=0$ to $0.2h$. From N-S computations.

number, $St=fL/U$, to be deduced. For the unit slope cone, the inviscid, N-S and laboratory data (solely from velocity measurements in this latter case) gave St=0.35, 0.36 and 0.34, respectively. The corresponding values for the half-slope cone were 0.27, 0.35 and 0.32. Apart from the 0.27 result - rather low probably because of a noticeable modulation in the shedding process for that case - these values are all very consistent with earlier laboratory data for similar bodies (Vosper *et al*, 1999). It is encouraging that the two completely different computational techniques yield such similar results. Note that these St values are higher than those that would be obtained in corresponding flows unrestricted by channel side walls, but because all three techniques used here had the same side-wall location, no blockage corrections have been made.

Figure 2 shows a restricted time-sequence of the five sectional lift contributions covering the $0.2h$ thick slabs, from the N-S computations. There is clearly a significant phase shift with height, with the maximum lift occurring earliest near the top of the cone. Remarkably similar results were obtained from the inviscid computations; this is demonstrated in figure 3, which shows the phase lag measured with respect to the time at which the total lift is a maximum and normalised by the shedding period, T_P. The figure includes corresponding results obtained for the half-slope cone, which show the same trend but with a rather wider variation in phase over the cone height. Careful study of a video of the inviscid computations showed that the time for maximum lift at each height correlated closely with the point at which the vortex was 'shed' at that level, just as in homogeneous flow over cylinders. Note that the phase shifts probably cannot be explained solely on the basis of the variation in local obstacle diameter with height. Assuming that an effective axial convection speed of the shedding eddies is U, convection over a distance equal to half the base diameter only implies a shift of about $0.14T_P$ for a $0.8h$ change in height. But, crudely, shedding presumably occurs from around the separation line, which is not too far from the $\theta=135°$ point (with θ measured from the forward stagnation point), so the appropriate axial distance will be significantly less than half the base diameter and the 'convective' phase shift correspondingly much less than $0.14T_P$. There is therefore a genuine phase variation with height in the shedding and this must lead to inclined vortex lines in the near wake at least; figure 3 suggests increasing inclination towards the top of the obstacle.

Now on the basis of laboratory experiments Hunt *et al* (1997) have suggested that inclined vortex lines are soon tilted into the vertical, at least for stratified flow past inclined circular cylinders. We have deduced the vertical vortex line tilts in the wake *via* the spatial correlation techniques outlined earlier. Figure 4 shows selected data, obtained from the inviscid computations and the laboratory experiments. Note first that there is reasonable agreement for the unit slope cone between the calculated and measured data, with neither set showing a significant phase shift with height until at least z/h=0.5. It was difficult to

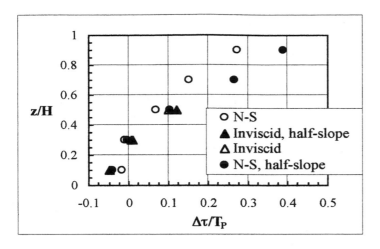

Figure 3. Phase for maximum lift contributions, with respect to the time at which the total drag is a maximum.

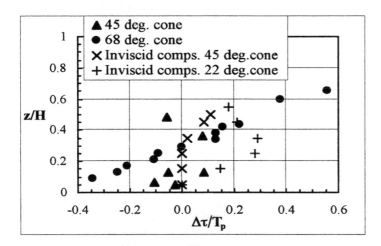

Figure 4. Phase data obtained in the wake (x/L=1.5-2.0) from the inviscid computations and the laboratory experiments.

obtain sensible data at greater z, with any technique. Note secondly, however, that a steeper cone (68° base angle) in the laboratory, and the half-slope cone from the computations, both appear to yield significant tilt in the vortex lines. Other body shapes studied in the laboratory - e.g. triangular flat plates normal to the flow and with the same base angles as the cones - gave similar results. We must conclude, first, that body shape can affect the degree of vortex line tilt in the wake but, second, that the tilt may be negligible even for a case where *at the body itself* there is significant phase variation in the vortex formation process.

These statements about vortex line tilts, deduced from data on time lags for maximum correlation (as in figure 4) rely on the assumption that the vortex convection speed, U_c, is invariant with height. This is not entirely true; measurements from point-wise data in the laboratory and from point-wise and spatially-averaged data from the computations (see Section 2), showed some non-negligible variations in U_c with height, but these were generally within ±10% of U and significant trends were difficult to discern. It is possible that the variations were a result simply of inadequate sampling (only a few shedding periods, as noted earlier) but they could in any case not account for the $\Delta\tau$ variations (shown in fig.4) and thus the vortex phase tilts. Note that the largest tilt implied by figure 4 (for the steepest cone) is in excess of 70° to the vertical. One might ask how such vortex line tilts are possible in a strongly stratified fluid, where significant vertical velocities are largely suppressed and where the vertical vorticity dominates the total vorticity vector. Perhaps the vortices induce variations in the local pressure and density gradients, so that horizontal vorticity is produced baroclinically in a way which ensures that the total vertical velocities remain negligible. Analysis of the vorticity equation is continuing, using the computed fields, but space does not allow further discussion of this point.

That such vortex line tilts *do* occur in the wake is suggested by visualisation of the vertical vorticity fields in axially-oriented vertical slices through the wake and also by horizontal slices. Figure 5 is an example of the latter, for the half-slope cone and computed using the inviscid code. It is clear that the peak vorticity regions are somewhat further downstream for z=0.32h than at z=0. The vertical fields (not shown) suggested that there is significantly more tilt in the case of the half-slope cone, in agreement with the implications of fig. 4, but recall that these are 'snapshots' at a particular time and may thus not be representative of the 'average' conditions in the wake.

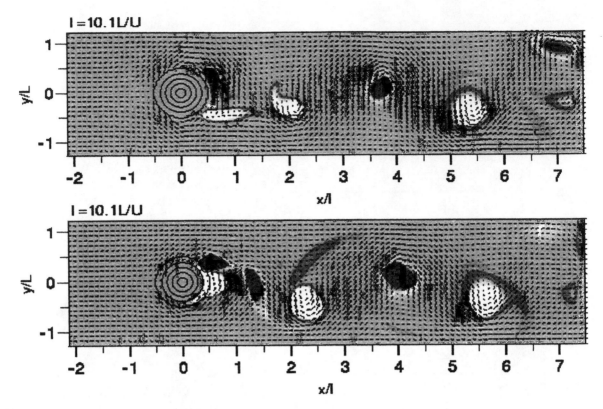

Figure 5. Vertical vorticity contours at z/h=0 (top) and 0.32 (bottom) at Ut/L=10.1. Half-slope cone.

5. Conclusions

We have illustrated some of the features of the well-known vortex street wakes which exist behind three-dimensional obstacles in strongly stratified flow. Many questions remain, but it seems clear that for, conical obstacles at least, there are vertical variations in the phase of shedding at the body which are not strongly dependent on body slope, and that these variations may disappear further downstream, in a way which perhaps *does* depend on body shape. Vortex convection speed, like the shedding frequency, seems not to depend strongly on height, irrespective of body shape. It is emphasised that for more definitive conclusions, significantly longer 'tow' times would be required, whether these are from real laboratory experiments (requiring extremely long tanks) or from very long computational times.

6. References

Brighton PWM (1978) Strongly stratified flow past three-dimensional obstacles. *Quart. J. Roy. Met. Soc.* **104**, 289-307.

Castro IP, Snyder WH & Marsh GL (1983) Stratified flow over three-dimensional ridges. *J. Fluid Mech.* **135**, 261-282.

Hunt JCR, Feng Y, Linden PF, Greenslade MD & Mobbs SD (1997) Low-Froude-number stable flow past mountains. *Il Nuova Cimento* **20**, 261-272.

Miranda PMA & James IN (1992) Nonlinear three-dimensional effects on gravity wave drag: splitting flow and breaking waves. *Quart. J. Roy. Met. Soc.* **118**, 1057-1081.

Paisley MF (2000) Multigrid solution of the incompressible Navier Stokes equations for density-stratified flow past three-dimensional obstacles. *J Comp Phys.* To appear

Rotunno R, Grubisc V & Smolarkiewicz PK (1999). Vorticity and potential vorticity in mountain wakes. *J. Atmos. Sci.* **56**, 2796-2810.

Smolarkiewicz PK & Rotunno R (1989) Low Froude number flow past three-dimensional obstacles. Part I: baroclinically generated lee vortices. *J. Atmos Sci.* **46**, 1154-1164.

Vosper SB (2000) Three-dimensional numerical simulations of strongly stratified flows past conical orography. *J. Atmos. Sci.*, in press.

Vosper SB, Castro IP, Snyder Wh & Mobbs SD (1999). Experimental studies of strongly stratified flow past three-dimensional orography. *J. Fluid Mech.* **390**, 223-249.

On the form of a Eulerian internal wave spectrum in the atmosphere

Igor Chunchuzov

Obukhov Institute of Atmospheric Physics,
3 Pyzhevskii Per, 109017 Moscow, Russia
Contact address: 42-80 Rideau Terr. Ottawa K1M 2C6, Canada

1. Abstract

The model of Eulerian internal wave spectrum in the atmosphere is developed and the asymptotic form for the spectrum is obtained at large wavenumbers. By assuming a Gaussian probability function for wave-induced displacements of fluid parcels the analytic relationship is found between correlation functions for the wave fields in Lagrangian and Eulerian frames of variables. This relationship describes the distortion of the form of the wave spectrum while transferring from the Lagrangian to the Eulerian system. The advective nonlinearity of fluid motion equations, existing only in the Eulerian frame of variables, generates a high wavenumber tail in the Eulerian wave spectrum, with the form that does not depend on the detailed form of the wave spectrum in the Lagrangian system. The asymptotic forms for the Eulerian three-dimensional (3-D) and one-dimensional (1-D) wavenumber spectra are obtained for both displacement and velocity components. The nonlinear formation mechanism for the 3-D Eulerian wavenumber spectrum is proposed which explains a high anisotropy of the form of the spectrum in wavenumber space.

2. Introduction

The statistical characteristics of the random wave fields, such as correlation functions and power spectra, differ from each other when viewed in Eulerian or Lagrangian co-ordinate systems (Allen and Joseph, 1989, hereinafter AJ'89). Such difference arises due to the nonlinearity of the advective term $(v\nabla)v$, that exists in the Eulerian fluid motion equations, but not in the Lagrangian motion equations (Lamb, 1932). In a broad-band spectrum of internal waves generated by a wide variety of random sources in the atmosphere some of them may have horizontal phase velocities comparable in value with the fluid parcel velocities. The waves with the vertical wavenumbers that lay within the m^{-3}-tail of the observed vertical wavenumber spectrum for the wave-induced wind speed fluctuations in the atmosphere have low enough horizontal phase velocities to strongly interact due to advective nonlinearity (Hines, 1991b). The strong nonlinear interactions between waves in the Eulerian system generate a high-wavenumber tail in the wave spectrum both in the ocean (AJ'89) and the atmosphere (Hines, 1991b, Chunchuzov, 1996; Eckermann, 1999). To find an asymptotic form of the Eulerian spectral tail is the objective of this work. Another approach to the same problem was recently proposed by Hines (2000).

When solving this task we are faced with the problem of how to take strictly into account the effect of strong wave interactions in the Eulerian system on the formation of the equilibrium internal wave (IW)spectrum. To describe strictly the influence of the advective nonlinearity on the form of the IW spectrum in the ocean, AJ'89 have developed a rigorous theoretical approach based on the relationship found in their work between correlation functions of the random internal wave field in the Lagrangian and Eulerian frames of variables. This approach resulted in a k^{-5} power law at high wavenumber k for the Eulerian 3-D wavenumber spectrum of the vertical displacements, and in a m^{-5} power law for the Eulerian vertical wavenumber spectrum at high vertical wavenumbers m. Within some range of wavenumbers the obtained form for the high-wavenimber tail was in a good agreement with that in the observed vertical displacement tow spectra in the ocean. The same form for the atmospheric Eulerian IW spectrum was obtained by Chunchuzov (1996, hereinafter Ch'96) after applying AJ's approach to the atmospheric model, which contains both ducted and upward propagating internal waves inherent to the atmospheric conditions.

Recently, Eckermann (1999) numerically simulated the process of advection of air parcels by a linear superposition of hydrostatic gravity waves. As parcel displacements increase in amplitude the advection of fluid parcels by gravity waves causes a nonsinusoidal distortion of the vertical profile of the Eulerian displacement field compared to the quasi-sinusoidal vertical profile of the Lagrangian displacement field. The nonsinusoidal steepening of the profile of the wave field in Eulerian frame of variables resulted in the m^{-3} vertical wavenumber spectrum for both vertical displacements and horizontal velocities.

When obtaining the relationship between Eulerian and Lagrangian correlation functions of the wave field both AJ'89 and Ch'96 used at some step an integration by parts and omitted the end-point term in this procedure . Generally this term is not zero and substantially affects the asymptotic form of the resultant IW spectrum (Chunchuzov, 2000, hereinafter Ch'2000). Here we modify properly the approach of AJ'89 to obtain a correct asymptotic form for the Eulerian spectral tail..

3. The relationship between Eulerian and Lagrangian correlation functions for the Gaussian wave fields

In a Lagrangian description each fluid parcel is identified with a certain three-dimensional parameter denoted by vector $r=(r_1, r_2, r_3)$. The vector r may play the role of the position of certain parcel under some reference condition, which may be undisturbed or static condition for the fluid parcels. In the Lagrangian system the location $x=(x_1,x_2,x_3)$ of the same parcel at any arbitrary time t is considered as a function of r and t (Lamb, 1932). Thus the selected value r for each parcel remains unchanged during a dynamic evolution in time of the system of fluid parcels. We'll denote the Lagrangian displacement vector at the time t of the parcel with the undisturbed position r by $s(r,t)$. Contrary to a Lagrangian system, where we describe the change of fluid parcel location in time, the fluid motion in the Eulerian system is described within a fixed volume of the space, so that we consider the time evolution of the hydrodynamic fields, such as velocity, displacement and etc., at any fixed point of space labeled x. The Eulerian displacement will be denoted by $s_E(x,t)$, where the Eulerian label x refers to the fluid parcel which happens to be at the point x at the time t, so a given value for the Eulerian label x does not always refer to the same fluid parcel.

If $F(r,t)$ is an arbitrary hydrodynamic field in the Lagrangian frame of variables, then the same field in the Eulerian frame of variables $F_E(x,t)$ may be presented as a weighted average of the Lagrangian field (AJ'89)

$$F_E(x,t) = \int d^3r \, J(s) \, F(r,t) \, \delta(x-y), \qquad (1)$$

where $\delta(x-y)$ is a three-dimensional delta function,

$$y = r + s(r,t), \qquad (2)$$

and $J(s)$ is the Jacobian determinant for the variable transformation (2) expressed through the spatial derivatives of the displacement components s_i , i=1,2,3, as follows:

$$J(s) = \Sigma \varepsilon_{\alpha\beta\gamma} \, [\delta_{1\alpha} + \partial s_1(r,t)/\partial r_\alpha] \, [\delta_{2\beta} + \partial s_2(r,t)/\partial r_\beta] \, [\delta_{3\gamma} + \partial s_3(r,t)/\partial r_\gamma], \qquad (\alpha,\beta,\gamma=1,2,3), \qquad (3)$$

where $\varepsilon_{\alpha\beta\gamma}$ is the anti symmetric unit tensor of the third rank, $\delta_{\alpha\beta} =1$ for $\alpha=\beta$ and $\delta_{\alpha\beta} =0$ for $\alpha \neq\beta$, and the sum is taken in (3) over the repeating indices α,β and γ. With the use of a Fourier transform $\delta(x-y)= (2\pi)^{-3}\int d^3k \, \exp\{ik \, (x-y)\}$ the relationship (1) between Eulerian and Lagrangian quantities can be written in the form

$$F_E(x,t) = (2\pi)^{-3} \int d^3r \int d^3k \, \exp\{ik \, (x-r-s(r,t))\} \, J(s) \, F(r,t) \qquad (4)$$

The relationship (4) was derived in AJ'89 and then in Ch'96 to express the correlation function for the Eulerian field $F_E(x,t)$ through the correlation functions for the Lagrangian fields $F(r,t)$ or $s(r,t)$. Consider the relationship (4) under incompressible fluid approximation ($J(s) = 1$) for which a fluid parcel density remains unchanged under its adiabatic motion (Lamb, 1932) . Under such approximation the deviation $J'(s)=J(s)-1= \rho_s/\rho - 1$ of the Jacobian from the unity, which describes relative perturbations in density ρ of the parcel displaced from the static conditions (for which $s_i=0$ and $\rho = \rho_s$), is small in absolute value as compared to the unity and may be neglected . The small term J' is associated with a fluid compressibility and as seen from (3) contains a sum of terms, one of which is the linear term divs, whereas the others are certain quadratic and cubic products of various displacement derivatives $\partial s_i(r,t)/\partial r_j$.

If displacements $s(r,t)$ are caused by internal waves of small amplitude ($|\partial s_i(r,t)/\partial r_j| \ll 1$) and satisfy a Boussinesq approximation, then the influence of fluid compressibility on the internal wave field may be neglected (Lighthill, 1978). In this case the major contribution to the Eulerian field (4) is given by the first term in the Jacobian $J=1+J'$, whereas the second term J' gives a small correction $\sim |\rho_s/\rho - 1| \ll 1$ associated with the effects of fluid compressibility.

Let $F(r,t)$ and $s(r,t)$ be random Gaussian fields within a finite volume V of the stratified atmosphere. The volume V will be taken later as arbitrarily large. The fields are assumed to be stationary (statistically) in time, homogeneous both in any horizontal direction that is parallel to the ground surface $r_3 = x_3 = 0$, and in the vertical. The latter condition requires the vertical dimension of the chosen space volume V be less than the characteristic vertical scales of variation of the undisturbed atmospheric parameters, such as the density and temperature under static conditions, but be much greater than the vertical correlation length of the random Lagrangian fields $F(r,t)$ and $s(r,t)$. From the relationship (4) with $J=1$ the two-point correlation function for the Eulerian field $F_E(r,t)$ may be written as follows

$$\langle F_E (x-X/2, t') \, F_E (x+X/2, t'')\rangle \equiv B_E (X,\tau), \qquad (5)$$

$$B_E (X,\tau) = (2\pi)^6 \int d^3r' \int d^3r'' \int d^3k' \int d^3k'' \, \exp\{ik'(x+X/2-r') - ik''(x-X/2-r'')\} \, M_F(r', r'', t',t'', k',k''), \qquad (6)$$

$$M_F (r', r'', t',t'', k',k'') \equiv \langle F(r',t') \, F(r'',t'') \, \exp\{-i[k's (r',t') - k''s (r'',t'')]\}\rangle, \qquad (7)$$

where the angular braces mean a statistical averaging, X is the vector between the two arbitrary points of the space x-X/2 and x+X/2, and $\tau=t'-t''$ is the time difference between the moments t' and t''. Introducing new variables $R=r'-r''$ and $R_1=(r'+r'')/2$ in the integral (6) and taking into account that function (7) depends on R and τ only (according to the assumptions about the stationarity and homogeniety of the fields $F(r,t)$ and $s(r,t)$), the integration over R_1 results in the delta-function $\delta(k'-k'')$ after the volume V becomes arbitrarily large. When integrating (7) over R_1 the variation of the function (7) with R_1 within the volume V has been neglected and the value of this function was taken at the height $z=x_3$ of the point midway between the two selected points of the space (the Eulerian and Lagrangian positions of the fluid parcels are equivalent in the undisturbed atmosphere with $s_i=0$). As a result the Eulerian correlation function becomes

$$B_E(R,\tau)=(2\pi)^{-3}\int d^3 R \int d^3k' \, \exp\{ik' (X-R)\} \, M_F(R,\tau,k'), \qquad (8)$$

where $M_F(R,\tau,k)$ is given by expression (7) taken at $k'= k'' \equiv k$ and the integrals in (8) are taken from $-\infty$ to ∞.

The general methods for calculating the correlation functions similar to those given by (7) are described , for example, in Klyatskin (1980). In case of Gaussian random fields these methods allow us to express (7) through second-order moments of the displacement field. If F(r,t) is the vertical displacement field $s_3(\mathbf{r},t)$, then (7) may be expressed in the form given by(Ch'2000):

$$M_F(\mathbf{R},\tau,\mathbf{k}) \equiv M_s(\mathbf{R},\tau,\mathbf{k}) = G_s(\mathbf{R},\tau,\mathbf{k}) \exp\{-\Sigma D_{ij}(\mathbf{R},\tau) k_i k_j\}, \qquad (9)$$

where

$$G_s(\mathbf{R},\tau,\mathbf{k}) = \{C_{33}(\mathbf{R},\tau) + [\Sigma D_{3j}(\mathbf{R},\tau) k_j]^2\}, \qquad (10)$$

$C_{ij}(\mathbf{R},\tau) = \langle s_i(\mathbf{r'},t') s_j(\mathbf{r''},t'') \rangle$ are the correlation functions for different components of the Lagrangian displacements, $D_{ij}(\mathbf{R},\tau) \equiv C_{ij}(R=0,\tau=0) - C_{ij}(\mathbf{R},\tau)$, and the sum Σ in (9)-(10) is taken over all repeating indices i and j.

If $F(\mathbf{r},t) = \partial s_1 / \partial t \equiv v_1(\mathbf{r},t)$ is one of the components of the horizontal Lagrangian velocity $\mathbf{v}_\perp = (v_1, v_2)$, then the correlation function for the first component of Eulerian horizontal velocity $B_E(\mathbf{R},\tau)$ is given by expressions (8)-(9), where instead of the function $G_s(\mathbf{R},\tau, \mathbf{k})$ stands the function $G_{V1}(\mathbf{R},\tau,\mathbf{k})$ given by:

$$G_{V1}(\mathbf{R},\tau,\mathbf{k}) = \{- \partial^2 C_{11}(\mathbf{R},\tau)/\partial\tau^2 - \Sigma (k_j \, \partial C_{1j} (\mathbf{R},\tau)/\partial\tau)^2\}. \qquad (11)$$

A similar expression may be obtained for the second velocity component v_2 by replacing the subscript 1 with 2 in the expression (11). The obtained expressions (9) - (11) are general relationships between Eulerian and Lagrangian correlation functions for displacement and velocity fields obtained under the assumption that these fields are Gaussian in the Lagrangian frame of variables (in the Eulerian frame the same field is not Gaussian due to the nonlinear transform (4)). These expressions allow us to obtain various spatial and temporal spectra for the Eulerian displacement and velocity fields.

4. Eulerian wavenumber spectrum for the vertical displacements and horizontal velocities.

In the Lagrangian frame of variables the interaction between gravity wave modes takes place due to only dynamic nonlinearity, which is associated with the nonlinearity of the buoyancy restoration forces arising in stably stratified fluid in response to the fluid parcel displacements, and the nonlinearity of the adiabatic state equation $p/\rho^\gamma = const$, where p and ρ are the pressure and density of the fluid parcel and γ is the ratio of the specific heat at constant pressure to the specific heat at constant volume. To obtain the form of the Lagrangian correlation functions $C_{ij}(\mathbf{R},\tau)$ and the function $M_F(\mathbf{R},\tau,\mathbf{k})$ in (9) we consider a simple model of stably-stratified atmosphere under static condition ($s_i = 0$) which is taken to be without mean wind, molecular viscosity and rotation. We assume that the Lagrangian displacements in the atmosphere $s(\mathbf{r},t)$ are caused by a high number of internal wave modes with small random amplitudes ($\mu \equiv \max |\partial s_i / \partial r_j| << 1$) and random phases. The existing stratification of Brunt-Vaisaala (BV) frequency N(z) in the atmosphere may form wave ducts for linear waves. As a result there are both trapped and upward propagating wave modes in the atmosphere . To take into account the contribution of both trapped and upward propagating wave modes to the resultant IW spectrum we choose the two layer atmospheric model: $N(z) = N_1$ for $0 < z < h$, and N_2 for $z > h$, where h is the height of the lower atmospheric layer and $N_2 < N_1$. In the opposite case of uniform atmosphere with $N_2 = N_1$ only upward propagating waves are present in the wave field.

The Eulerian 3-D wavenumber spectrum may be expressed through Lagrangian correlation functions as follows:

$$S_{3E}(\mathbf{k}) = \int d^3X \, B_E (\mathbf{X},0) \exp\{-i\mathbf{k}\mathbf{X}\} = = \int d^3R \, M_F(\mathbf{R},\tau=0, \mathbf{k}) \exp \{-i \mathbf{k} \, \mathbf{R}\}, \qquad (12)$$

To calculate the form of the spectrum (12) at high wavenumbers we don't need to know a detailed form of the Lagrangian correlation functions and corresponding Lagrangian spectra, because the advective nonlinearity of the Eulerian motion equations masks the form of the Lagrangian spectrum and produces in the Eulerian system the high-wavenumber spectral tail with its own asymptotic form (AJ'89). We assume that some equilibrium energy distribution among modes was established in the Lagrangian system due to energetic balance between the energy input from random internal wave sources with a maximum energy at some non-zero vertical and horizontal lengthscales, designated as m_0^{-1} and k_0^{-1}, the nonlinear energy transfer due to the dynamical nonlinearity from the source scale toward smaller scales, and the wave energy dissipation at small lengthscales. The influence of the advective nonlinearity on the form of the Eulerian spectrum (12) depends on value of the exponential factor in the expression (9). The quadratic form in the exponent is of order of the mean square scalar product $<(ks)^2>$ for a given wavenumber vector $k= (k_1,k_2,k_3)$ of the Eulerian spectrum. This form is positive definite and limited by the value

$$2\Sigma\, C_{ii}(0,0)\, k_i^2 = 2(v_1^2\, k_\perp^2 + v_v^2\, k_3^2) \equiv q^2 \qquad (13)$$

where $k_\perp^2 = k_1^2 + k_2^2$, and v_v^2 and v_1^2 are the mean square values of the Lagrangian vertical and horizontal displacement components, respectively.

To obtain the asymptotic form of the spectral tail for $q^2 >> 1$ we note that the contribution to the integral (13), coming from the exponential factor, is negligibly small for all values of R_i except their small values, for which the correlation functions $C_{ij}(R,0)$ are close in value to their extreme values $C_{ij}(0,0)$. For small values of R_i we can expand the correlation functions $C_{ij}(R,0)$ in both the exponential factor and the multiplier $G_s(R,0,k)$ into a power series on R_i up to the quadratic terms. The expansion allows us to conduct the integration over R_i in (12) and obtain the asymptotic form of the spectrum (12) at high values of q^2 (Ch'2000). The analysis of this form reveals the following features inherent to the high-wavenumber tail of the Eulerian spectrum.

At high values of q^2 the asymptotic behavior of the 3-D wavenumber spectrum for both Eulerian vertical displacements and horizontal velocities is well described by the two first terms of the asymptotic expansion, one of which decays as k^{-5}, where k is the value of the wavenumber vector k, and the second one as k^{-3}. Although the k^{-3}-term is the leading term at $k \to \infty$, there is some range of the wavenumber values at the tail within which the k^{-5}-term exceeds in magnitude the k^{-3}-term. Within the range of dominance of the k^{-5}-term the spectrum depends only on the values of the parameter $M \equiv v_v\, m_0$ (which is the r.m.s. vertical displacement v_v normalised on the characteristic vertical lengthscale m_0^{-1} of the Lagrangian wave field), and the anisotropy parameter $\chi \equiv 2v_1/v_v = k_0/m_0$ (which is the ratio between horizontal and vertical Lagrangian displacements). The parameter χ is thought to be much greater than unity due to suppression of the vertical parcel displacements by the gravity forces in a stably-stratified atmosphere. For a weak wave interaction approximation to be valid for the Lagrangian wave field the parameter M is taken much less than unity. This approximation breaks down along with the assumption that Lagrangian wave field is a Gaussian one as M approaches some maximum value, which for one specific form of the Lagrangian spectrum is about 0.5 (Ch'2000).

The intensity of the spectral tail rapidly increases with the value of M up to its maximum, whereas the wavenumber range of dominance of the k^{-5} power law narrows with the increasing M. In the 3-D wavenumber space the intensity of the Eulerian spectrum at its tail ($q^2 >>1$) is a certain function of the direction of the wavenumber vector k with respect to the vertical axis k_3. For some high (but fixed) value of k_3 the Eulerian spectral density is localised within a certain range of low horizontal wavenumbers $k_\perp$ for which $k_\perp^2 < 4e_0\, k_3^2$, where e_0 is the mean square horizontal gradient of the vertical Lagrangian displacements. Thus, the nonlinear wave-wave interactions form at high vertical wavenumbers a certain anisotropy of the form of the Eulerian 3-D wavenumber spectrum independently of the detailed form of the Lagrangian spectrum. The surfaces of constant values of the spectral density are stretched along the k_3-axis. The wave packet composed of the waves with the wavenumber vectors ending on the surface of constant spectral density forms the anisotropic inhomogeneities in the Eulerian displacement or velocity field with the ratio between the characteristic horizontal and vertical lengthscales of order χ/M. This ratio is higher at $M < 1$ than the anisotropy parameter χ for the Lagrangian wave field. The high anisotropy of the inhomogeneities with small vertical lengthscales shows that the nonlinear wave-wave interactions tend to produce in the Eulerian spectrum the spectral components with higher vertical and smaller horizontal wavenumbers than those which are within the bandwidth of the Lagrangian 3-D wavenumber spectrum.

The obtained vertical (1-D) wavenumber spectrum for both vertical displacements and horizontal velocities decays as k_3^{-1} with the increase of k_3, although there is a certain wavenumber range at the tail within which the k_3^{-3}-form dominates. The intensity of the horizontal velocity spectral tail increases with the value of M and reaches the value of order $10^{-2} N^2$ at M $=2\ 10^{-1}$. At the same time the range of dominance of the k_3^{-3}-form narrows with the increase of M so that the tail tends to decay as k_3^{-1}. In the case of upward propagating waves this range may be several times greater than for ducted waves. The -1 power law decay produces a growing with k_3 shear spectrum and results in infinite vertical gradients of the vertical displacement and horizontal velocity fields. However, in the realistic atmosphere the existing dissipation of the internal wave energy is assumed to limit the values of the spatial gradients of the Eulerian wave field. In the middle atmosphere the wave energy dissipation may be caused by the wave breaking processes associated with the wave-induced convective or shear instabilities (Hines, 1991b). The instabilities switch on at some critical values of the vertical gradients of the potential temperature or horizontal velocity that satisfy the instability criteria. The wave breaking processes are thought to transfer the wave energy into turbulent motions with the vertical wavenumbers greater than the critical wavenumber for which the instability switch on. At the same time the turbulence generated due to the wave .instabilities may act on the stable wave components with k_3 less than the critical wavenumber through a turbulent diffusion of those waves, thereby producing more rapid decay of the spectral tail with k_3 than those obtained in the absence of the dissipation.

5. References

Allen, K.A., and R.I. Joseph, 1989: A canonical statistical theory of oceanic internal waves. *J. Fluid Mech.*, **204**, 185-228.

Chunchuzov, I.P., 1996: The spectrum of high-frequency internal waves in the atmospheric waveguide. *J. Atmos. Sci.*, **53**, 1798-1814.

Chunchuzov, I.P., 2000. On the asymptotic form of the Eulerian internal wave spectrum at large wavenumbers. *J. Fluid Mech* (submitted).

Eckermann, S.D., 1999: Isentropic advection by gravity waves: quasi-universal M^{-3} vertical wavenumber spectra near the onset of instability. *Geophys. Res. Lett.*, **26**, 201-204.

Hines, C.O., 1991b: The saturation of gravity waves in the middle atmosphere. Part II: Development of Doppler-spread theory. *J. Atmos Sci.*, **48**, 1360-1379.

Hines, C.O., 2000. Theory of the Eulerian tail in the spectra of atmospheric and oceanic waves., *J. Fluid Mech* (submitted).

Klyatskin, V.I. 1980: *Stokhasticheskie uravneniya i volny v sluchaino-neodnorodnykh sredakh*, Nauka, Moscow, 336 pp.

Lamb,H., 1932: *Hydrodynamics.*-6 th ed. Cambridge University Press.

Lighthill, J., 1978: *Waves in Fluids*. Cambridge University Press, 504 pp.

Analysis and Modelling of Atmospheric Internal Waves Observed in Synthetic Aperture Radar Ocean Images

Igor Chunchuzov[1], Paris W. Vachon[2], and Xiaofeng Li[3]

[1]42-80 Rideau Terrace, Ottawa, Ontario, Canada K1M 2C6
[2]Canada Centre for Remote Sensing, 588 Booth St., Ottawa, Ontario, Canada K1A OY7
[3]NOAA Science Center, Camp Springs, MD 20746, USA
paris.vachon@ccrs.nrcan.gc.ca

1. Abstract

The spatial patterns of atmospheric internal waves (AIW's) can locally modulate the ocean surface wind speed, which in turn is imprinted on the ocean surface roughness. This spatial roughness variability can be detected in high-resolution Synthetic Aperture Radar (SAR) images of the ocean surface. We consider several cases that illustrate the opportunity for using SAR images to estimate small-scale wind speed variations in the atmospheric surface layer over large ocean areas. By using two- and three-layer atmospheric models, we can gain insight to wave-induced fluctuations of wind speed and horizontal wavelength as functions of atmospheric temperature and wind speed stratification. The models were driven by atmospheric sounding data from nearby meteorological stations or were run parametrically.

2. Introduction

Four case studies of SAR observations of AIW's are presented to demonstrate SAR's capability to measure associated near surface wind field variations [see Chunchozov et al., 2000]. The first two cases consider lee-wave generation by an isolated ridge and show that the pattern shape, wavelength, and wind speed variations estimated from SAR images can provide information on the stratification in the lower atmosphere, such as the depth of the atmospheric surface layer and mean temperature changes within the stable inversion layer. The third case concerns an internal wave packet that was detected nearly simultaneously by two different SAR sensors, allowing us to estimate the temporal parameters of the wave packet as well as its spatial parameters. The estimated parameters were in reasonable agreement with those calculated from a three-layer atmospheric model driven by sounding data from a coastal weather station. The fourth case is an image of AIW's that also shows their generation source, in this case an atmospheric front.

3. Lee Waves generated by an Isolated Ridge

The ocean surface around the oil production platform at Hibernia, about 315 km east of St. John's, Newfoundland, was imaged three times by the ERS-2 and RADARSAT SAR's on 2 and 3 Feb. 1998 (Fig. 1). The platform is visible as a bright point. Also visible are backscatter patterns consisting of dark lines that resemble a ship's wake. Only the edge of the pattern is visible in Fig. 1a (the wake was near the far edge of ERS-2's SAR swath). The spacing between the dark lines is from 1 to 2.5 km. We assume that this pattern is the ocean surface imprint of atmospheric lee waves generated by the wind blowing over the Hibernia platform. Our assumption is supported by comparison of the characteristic shapes and scales of the wake-like patterns observed in the images with those obtained from a linear model of atmospheric lee-wave generation by an isolated ridge, as described by Gjevik and Marthinsen (1978) and Chunchuzov et al. (2000). The model assumes a strong temperature inversion at some height above the ocean surface and allows a non-zero wind shear within the inversion layer. The stable layer serves as a wave-guide, allowing horizontal wave propagation far from the platform. Since the patterns appear to have kept their form for nearly 11.5 hours, we are likely dealing with stationary lee waves.

The only sounding data available were from the weather station at St. John's and were not useful to determine the detailed lower layer structure at Hibernia. Nevertheless, we can use our assumption of an inversion layer with strong stability to explain the observed shape of the wave patterns and the amplitude of radar cross-section oscillations within the wake pattern. The wind speed oscillations across the "arms" of the wake, as estimated using a scatterometer wind retrieval model, have amplitudes of 0.6 m/s to 1.5 m/s at a distance of 60 km from the platform. We assumed an isolated ridge with a height of 165 m (the height of the platform), a surface layer thickness ranging from 170 m to 200 m, and a thin inversion layer (as compared to the vertical wavelength) with a relative increase in potential temperature ranging from 0.67% to 1.5%. It follows from the model that the amplitude of the surface wind speed fluctuations associated with the atmospheric lee waves would be about 0.5 m/s at a downwind distance of 60 km from the ridge.

The form of the phase lines depends on the Froude number $F \equiv V_0 / (\varepsilon g h_0)^{1/2}$, where ε is the relative increase of potential temperature in the inversion layer and (V_1 / V_0) is the ratio of wind speeds above and below the inversion layer. The equations for the phase lines (see Gjevik and Marthinsen, 1978; Chunchuzov et al., 2000) show that for $F > 1$, only diverging waves exist on the lee side of the ridge. Since only diverging wave crests are seen in the images of Fig. 1, we calculated phase lines for $F > 1$ and for V_0 in the range of 5 to 7 m/s, as shown in Fig. 2 for $y > 0$. The local wavelength, that is, the spacing between the phase lines along a certain azimuth $\alpha = \arctan(y/x)$, decreases with α. For $\alpha = 26°$, the wavelengths in Figs. 2a and 2b are about 2.5 km, which is the spacing between the dark portions of the wake of Fig. 1c. Also, the phase line pattern is similar to the wave pattern seen in the SAR images. For the parameters of Figs. 2a and 2b, $F \sim 1.36$ and the amplitudes of the wave-induced wind speed variations near the ocean surface, as estimated from the model for $\alpha = 26°$, are from 0.3 m/s to 0.7 m/s, comparable to estimates from Fig. 1c.

The radar cross-section oscillations across the wake arms in Fig. 1c may be caused by both the wave-induced variations in surface wind speed and the change in radar look direction relative to the local wind vector across the pattern. The radar look direction with respect to the mean wind vector is about $-45°$. For an axial-symmetric ridge, the wind speed perturbations induced by lee-waves are the same for the directions α and $-\alpha$ relative to the mean wind vector. However, the corresponding modulation in radar cross section across the wave crests in the direction $\alpha > 0$ is much stronger than those of the symmetric wave crests in the direction $-\alpha$. This is evident from Figs. 1b and 1c for which only one-half of the wake pattern is readily visible.

The same model was used to explain the shape and parameters of the lee wave pattern generated by mountain peaks on St. Lawrence Island and detected in a RADARSAT SAR image (not shown here). There was a strong, thin inversion layer at a height of about 1000 m, with an air temperature increase of 2 to 4°C, and a maximum buoyancy frequency of $N \approx 1.1(10)^{-2}$ s^{-1}, about 2.5 times larger than above the inversion layer. In this case, the Froude number was smaller that unity and the model showed the existence of both diverging and transverse lee waves. Both of these types of lee waves were visible in the RADARSAT SAR image.

4. Atmospheric Internal Waves off Nova Scotia

Examples of AIW's in successive SAR images, such as those shown in Fig. 3, are rare. These airborne and spaceborne SAR images show the same wave group and a stationary Canadian Coast Guard vessel that was imaged successively within 73 seconds. Relative to the vessel, the wave phase speed C was estimated to be 2.8 m/s, towards the northwest. The mean wavelength over the four main crests was about 1100 m, so the wave frequency ω was about 0.016 rad/s. Sounding data from Yarmouth, about 300 km from the imaged area, show that an inversion layer existed at a height of 300 m with a potential temperature increase $\Delta\theta$ of 5.7K. The mean wind speed within the lower layer of 500 m thickness was about 8 m/s from the southwest (220°), based on sounding data from Sable Island on 27 March 1996 at 00:00 UTC. A meteorological buoy that was moored close to the ship measured 203°. The mean wind speed vector V_0 was nearly perpendicular to the direction of the wave phase velocity C.

The potential temperature profile $\theta(z)$ was approximated with three layers of buoyancy frequency N: N_1 for $0 < z < H$, N_2 for $H < z < H + 2\Delta H$, and N_3 for $z > H + 2\Delta H$, where $N_2 > N_{1,3}$, and H and $2\Delta H$ are the height of the lower layer and the thickness of the inversion layer, respectively. $V_0(z)$ was taken as slowly varying with height z above the surface $z = 0$. Taking $N_3 \approx (10)^{-2}$ s^{-1}, $\theta \approx 281$K, $\Delta\theta \approx 5.7$K from the observed potential temperature profile, and the SAR-observed wavenumber $k \approx 5.71\cdot(10)^{-3}$ m^{-1}, it can be shown that the ratio $N_3^2 / \alpha_0 k \approx 0.024$, where $\alpha_0 = g\,\Delta\theta\, /\, \theta$ is the stability parameter, and may be neglected in the dispersion relation for a three-layer model (Gossard and Hooke, 1975). As a result, the intrinsic wave frequency $\Omega(k) = \omega(k) - k\cdot V_0$ and the wave phase speed C may be estimated with well-known formulas obtained for a deep-water approximation (Gossard and Hooke, 1975): $\Omega \approx (\alpha_0 k\, /\, 2)^{1/2} = 0.024$ s^{-1}, $C \approx 4.2$ m/s. The model calculations of ω and C are within 30% of those estimated from the SAR images.

Another case of AIW generation off Nova Scotia is shown in Fig. 4. The detailed structure of an atmospheric front was clearly visible in the image. A synoptic-scale front was further offshore, based on bracketing surface analysis charts (not shown here), but the front seen in the RADARSAT image was not resolved in those charts. The SAR image shows small-scale wind speed fluctuations in the vicinity of the front, which appear as a sharp dark band with a wave-like pattern consisting of dark crests along one side. The dark crests are inclined to the front, similar to wave crests from a moving ship. The spacing between the crests is from 1 to 3 km. The radar cross-section modulation across the front is likely caused by a local strong wind shear. The bright area below the dark band corresponds to higher wind speeds, whereas lower winds existed in the darker area above the front. According to buoy measurements, the mean surface wind in the bright area was about 8.5 m/s towards the west, essentially parallel to the frontal boundary. Apparently, the instability of the wind shear across the front was an AGW source; the dark crests that adjust to the frontal band are the ocean surface imprints of the generated waves. The observed wave pattern is about 80 km in extent and follows the front's shape.

5. Conclusions

These case studies show that high-resolution SAR images can provide us with detailed information on spatial wind field variations associated with AIW's over large ocean areas. The SAR images, along with sounding data available from nearby stations, have allowed us to identify the generation mechanisms for the internal waves observed around Hibernia, St Lawrence Island, and off Nova Scotia. AIW patterns in SAR images are indicators of stable, stratified atmospheric layers at low altitudes (usually less than the observed wavelengths) relative to the ocean surface. The shape of the SAR-observed AIW pattern, the wavelengths, and the wind speed variations allow us to estimate atmospheric stratification parameters in the lower atmosphere, such as the depth of the surface layer and mean temperature changes within the stable layer. The combination of SAR images with local sounding data is an important task for future SAR studies of AIW's and to better address their generation mechanisms.

6. References

Chunchuzov, I.P., P.W. Vachon, and X. Li, 2000. Analysis and modelling of atmospheric gravity waves observed in RADARSAT SAR images. In press, *Rem. Sens. Env.*

Gjevik, B., and T. Marthinsen, 1978. Three-dimensional lee-wave pattern. *Quart. J. Roy. Met. Soc.*, **104**: 947-957.

Gossard, E.E., and W.H. Hooke, 1975. Waves in the Atmosphere, *Elsevier*, New York, 456pp.

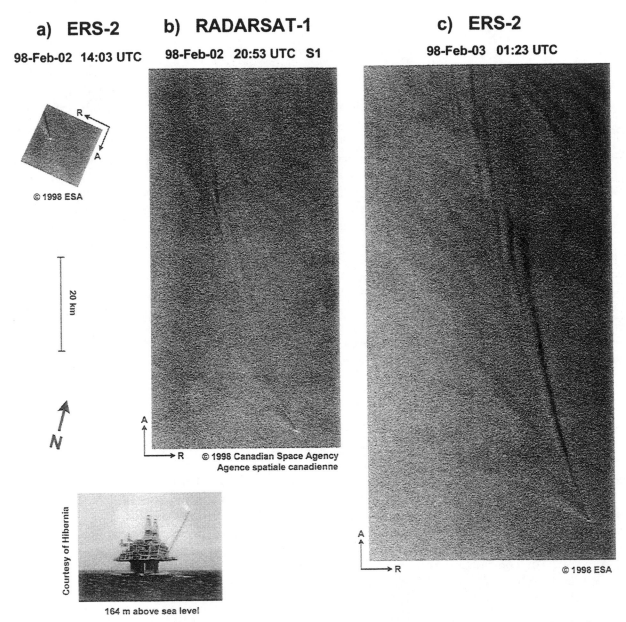

Figure 1: ERS-2 and RADARSAT SAR images of an atmospheric wake from the Hibernia platform.

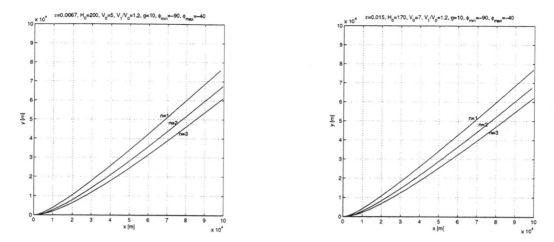

Figure 2: Calculated phase lines for the atmospheric wake from the Hibernia platform.
Left: $\varepsilon = 0.0067$; $h_0 = 200$ m; $V_0 = 5$ m/s; $(V_1 / V_0) = 1.2$.
Right: $\varepsilon = 0.015$; $h_0 = 170$ m; $V_0 = 7$ m/s; $(V_1 / V_0) = 1.2$.

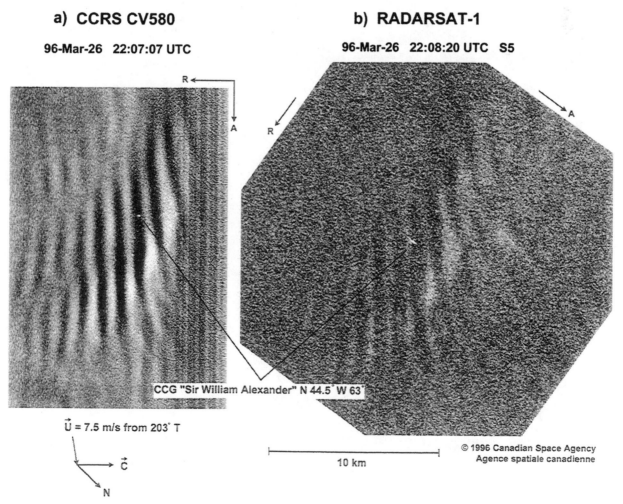

Figure 3: CCRS CV-580 and RADARSAT SAR images of atmospheric gravity waves off Nova Scotia.

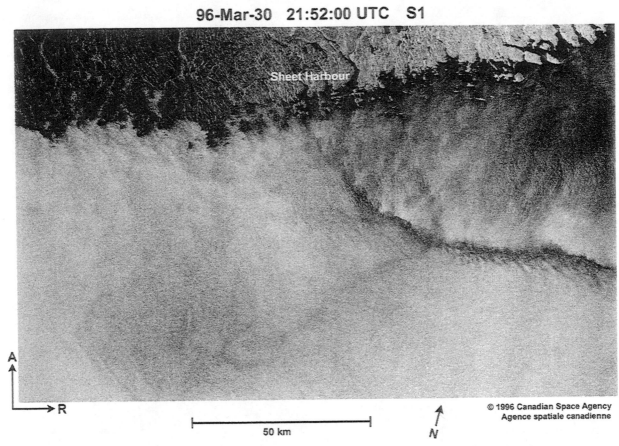

Figure 4: RADARSAT SAR image of an atmospheric front off Nova Scotia.

Gravity Waves and Vortices in the Wake of Large Islands

Dieter Etling

Institute of Meteorology and Climatology, University Hannover,
30419 Hannover, Germany
etling@muk.uni-hannover.de

1. Abstract

Observations of gravity waves and vortices in the lee of the island Jan Mayen are combined with temperature and wind data to investigate the behavior of stable stratified flows in the vicinity of isolated obstacles. The conditions for the formation of waves or vortices are analyzed and compared with numerical and theoretical investigations available in the literature.

2. Introduction

The influence of isolated three-dimensional obstacles on stable stratified flows has been subject to many experimental and numerical work. Without going into detail it may be stated, that for high Froude numbers (say $Fr > 1$) gravity waves are formed in the wake of the obstacle, whereas for low Froude numbers (say $Fr < 0.5$) vortex streets can be observed. With respect to the atmosphere, these phenomena can be made visible through cloud patterns in the wake of large islands. But although these islands can be considered as isolated three dimensional obstacles, they are quite flat (aspect ratio 1:10) as compared to their laboratory counterparts. Hence the application of the classical mechanism of viscous boundary layer separation, as in the case of Karman vortex streets behind cylinders, to atmospheric situations seems doubtful.

In the last years various new mechanisms of vortex street formation in the atmosphere have been proposed, e.g. gravity wave breaking, hydraulic jump, baroclinic vorticity production, flow splitting (see e.g. papers by Schär and Duran, 1997; Schär and Smith, 1993; Rotunno et al., 1999). Most of these theories have been tested against numerical simulations with highly idealized background flows with constant wind and Brunt-Väisälä frequency. But in geophysical situations, vertical variations in the velocity and stratification of the approach flow make the interpretation in forms of simple Froude number arguments not always straight foreward.

3. Waves and Vortices

In order to test the various arguments on the physical mechanism of wake formation versus real atmospheric flow situations, we have collected data on the appearance of waves and vortices in the wake of the island of Jan Mayen, where these phenomena occur quite often. Over a period of four years (1995-1998), days with waves or vortices have been identified from satellite pictures. On few occasions, waves and vortices have been observed simultaneously in the island wake (Fig. 1) which does not fit in the simple regime diagram as proposed so far based on Froude number.

From the satellite pictures we obtain following climatology:

gravity waves:	total	71	cases
vortex street:	total	83	cases
waves and vortices:	total	7	cases

This climatology provides a kind of lower estimate on the occurrence of waves and vortices, as only one satellite picture per day was available for inspection. But for the purpose of relating the formation of waves and wakes to background wind and temperature profiles, this sample seems reasonable. More observations on vortex streets can be found e.g. in Etling (1989). Some examples of three-dimensional lee waves are given in Wurtele et al. (1996).

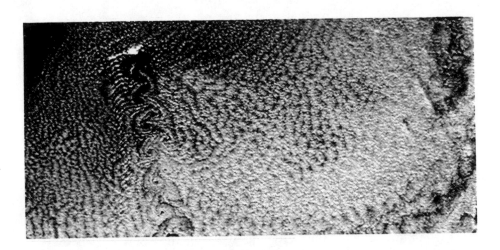

Fig. 1 Satellite picture of clouds in the vicinity of the island of Jan Mayen. The flow direction is from top to bottom. The formation of internal gravity waves and a vortex street in the wake of the island (located at the top left margin) can clearly be seen from the cloud pattern.

4. Environmental flow conditions

In studies on gravity waves or wake vortices it is quite common, to consider a simple approach flow with constant flow speed U and constant Brunt Väisälä-frequency N defined with potential temperature θ by

$$N = \left(\frac{g}{\theta} \frac{\partial \theta}{\partial z} \right)^{1/2}$$

With these flow variables and the mountain height H a Froude number Fr is usually defined as

$$Fr = \frac{U}{NH}$$

All studies on isolated obstacles in stratified flows show, that the formation of gravity waves (in the form of 3-D ship waves) or leeside vortices (in the form of Karman vortex street) can be related to the magnitude of the Froude number. Simplified one could state, that vortices form under low Froude number, say $Fr < 0.7$, and gravity waves for say $Fr > 0.7$. These simple arguments hold for laboratory experiments and numerical simulations under constant U and N. But in the atmosphere, these conditions are never met. In order to provide some insight into real flow conditions, we have obtained vertical profiles of air temperature and wind speed for the days when waves or vortices have observed. Two typical examples for conditions of waves and vortices are presented in Fig. 2. Although no two radiosonde observations are identical, the gross features may be described as follows:

gravity waves: moderate stratification, no capping inversion in the boundary layer. Strong winds, usually speed in increasing with height (forward shear)

wake vortices: nearly well mixed boundary layer with capping inversion at a height well below the mountain top (2200m for Jan Mayen). Strong temperature jump at the inversion with stable stratified layer aloft. Wind speed usually less than in the wave cases.

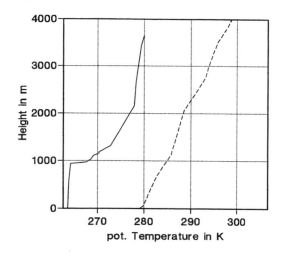 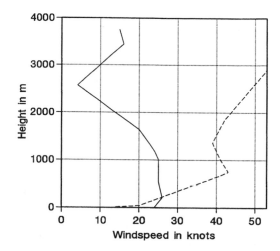

Fig. 2 Vertical profiles of potential temperature θ (left) and wind speed U (right) for the case of observed gravity waves (dashed line) and vortex street (solid line). The height of the island Jan Mayen is about 2200m.

5. Comparison with theoretical and numerical studies

Numerical studies on wake vortices have been performed among others by Schär and Smith (1993), Schär and Durran (1997) and Rotunno et al. (1999). Theoretical and numerical work on lee waves can be found in Miranda and James (1992) and Wurtele et al. (1996). For idealized flow conditions with constant wind speed U and constant Brunt-Väisälä-frequency N the results of these studies can be summarized as follows: Gravity waves are formed for values of the Froude number about $Fr>0.7$, which means moderate stratification and/or strong wind. For $Fr<0.7$ vortex streets are suspected to form in the island wake. The physical mechanism for vortex formation is attributed due to gravity wave breaking for $0.7>Fr>0.5$ and due to flow splitting/hydraulic jump for $Fr<0.5$.

Concerning the environmental flow conditions for observed cases of waves and vortices in the wake of Jan Mayen, more or less uniform Brunt-Väisälä is found in the wave cases as shown in Fig. 2. In this example, $N≈0.013$ s^{-1} and $Fr≈0.73$, if we take an average wind speed of $U≈20$ ms^{-1}. This value of Fr confirms theoretical and numerical estimates on conditions for lee wave formation.

In the case of vortex streets, nearly always a neutral stratified layer can be observed near the ground with a strong temperature jump and stably stratified layer (inversion) aloft. The height of the neutral layer is typically 0.3 - 0.6 H, where H is the island height, like the case shown in Fig. 2. This makes the specification of a Froude-number somewhat arbitrary. For the case in Fig. 2 one would get $N≈0.021$ and $Fr≈0.22$ for the layer above the inversion. Even if the whole layer from the surface to the island top ($H≈2200$m) is taken into account, one gets $N≈0.015$ and $Fr≈0.43$. Both estimates give Froude numbers below 0.5 which indicate vortex street formation.

Concerning the environmental conditions, the pronounced temperature jump at the inversion makes the two-layer hydraulic flow concept of Schär and Smith (1993) suitable for the physical mechanism of vortex street formation. In this case, the creation of wake vorticity is thought to be due to flow splitting (dividing streamline) at the upstream mountain side and/or hydraulic jump at the lee side of the island. For this mechanism to operate, the temperature jump, i.e. the height of the lower layer, must be well below the mountain height H. This is indeed nearly always observed for the cases of vortex streets investigated in this study. But as the real atmospheric situation is not a strict two-layer system as in the analysis of Schär and Smith, but more a combination of a lower layer of constant temperature (density) and an upper layer with continuous stable stratification (Fig. 2), also other mechanisms like gravity wave breaking (Miranda and James, 1992; Schär and Durran, 1996) or baroclinic vorticity production (Rotunno et al, 1999) must be considered for the formation of atmospheric wake vortices. Further numerical simulations for real topography and with observed wind and temperature profiles would be helpful to clarify the discussion on the physical mechanism of wake vortices and lee waves.

6. References

Etling, D.: On atmospheric vortex streets in the wake of large islands. Meteorol. Atmos. Phys. **41**, 157-164.

Miranda, P.M. and I.N. James, 1992: Non-linear effects on gravity-wave drag: splitting flow and breaking waves. Q. J.R.Meteorol. Soc., **118**, 1057-1082.

Rotunno, R., Grubsic, V. and R.K. Smolarkiewicz, 1999: Vorticity and potential vorticity in mountain wakes. J. Atmos. Sci., **56**, 2796-2810.

Schär, C. and R.B. Smith, 1993: Shallow-water flow past isolated topography. J. Atmos. Sci., **50**, 1373-1400.

Schär, C. and D.R. Durran, 1997: Vortex formation and vortex shedding in continuously stratified flows past isolated topography. J. Atmos. Sci., **54**, 534-554.

Wurtele, M.G., Sharman, R.D. and A. Datta, 1996: Atmospheric lee waves. Annu. Rev. Fluid Mech., **28**, 129-176.

Models of Atmospheric Coastal Trapped Disturbances

Peter L. Jackson[1], Kevin J. Tory[1] and Chris J.C. Reason[2]

[1]Environmental Studies, University of Northern British Columbia, Prince George, B.C., Canada V2N 4Z9
[2]School of Earth Sciences, University of Melbourne, Parkville, Vic., Australia 3052
peterj@unbc.ca, k.tory@bom.gov.au, cjr@met.unimelb.EDU.AU

1. Abstract

Numerical simulations of the 15-17 May 1985 Coastally Trapped Disturbance (CTD) event along the west coast of North America are compared with the schematic model of CTD evolution developed by Skamarock et al. (1999) (SRK99) which was based upon more idealized simulations. It is shown that the general evolution of the simulated May 1985 CTD is consistent with the SRK99 schematic model. It is further shown that secondary effects not contained in the SRK99 simulations, such as diurnal radiation variations, can account for the variable CTD initiation and propagation observed both in nature and in the present numerical simulations. The modeled CTD is found to change dynamical characteristics from an initial Kelvin wave / bore similar to that discussed in Ralph et al. (2000) to a gravity current, and this change is consistent and coincident with a sharp change in translation speed of the disturbance.

2. Introduction

Coastally Trapped Disturbances (hereafter CTDs) are mesoscale systems that are laterally confined against a coastal mountain barrier by the Coriolis effect and vertically confined by stable stratification. CTDs propagate along the coastal mountain barrier such that the barrier is on the right (left) in the northern (southern) hemisphere. Propagation is generally energetic but relatively short-lived (typically 2 to 3 days on the North American west coast). Typical length scales are 1000 km alongshore, 100 km across-shore, and 0.5 km in the vertical (Reason, 1994). CTDs along the west coast of North America are generally coastal ridges of higher pressure in the marine layer and result in a wind reversal from the more typical northerly to southerly flow (e.g. Dorman, 1985, 1987; Mass and Albright, 1987; Reason and Dunkley, 1993).

There has been dispute in the literature on the correct dynamical interpretation of CTDs. They have been interpreted as Kelvin waves of various types (Dorman, 1985, 1988), as trapped gravity currents (Dorman, 1987; Mass and Albright, 1987), and as the forced mesoscale response to purely synoptic-scale evolution (Mass and Albright, 1988; Mass and Bond, 1996; Mass, 1995). Using an analytical shallow-water approach, Reason and Steyn (1992) address the relative importance of boundary layer processes (i.e. Kelvin wave and gravity current dynamics) and synoptic-scale processes. A recent analysis of more detailed observations from the 10-11 June 1994 event (Ralph et al. 1998; Ralph et al. 2000) identified the CTD response as a mixed Kelvin wave / bore occurring in the inversion layer above the marine boundary layer (MBL).

In their synoptic climatology, Mass and Bond (1996) found that offshore (easterly) flow at 850 hPa was a robust feature accompanying the initiation stages of CTDs. In order to examine the importance of offshore flow on CTD initiation and propagation, Skamarock et al.(1999) (hereafter SRK99), utilized a non-hydrostatic numerical model in 2- and 3-D simulations with idealized topography and background synoptic conditions. The model used was inviscid and purely dynamical – it did not include surface fluxes, diurnal radiation effects or offshore advection of heated air. They examined the formation and propagation of a CTD resulting from the gradual introduction and subsequent removal of a tapered zone of offshore flow over the middle of their model domain under different marine boundary layer conditions and stratifications. They found that the offshore / downslope flow can lead to adiabatic warming and evacuation of the MBL near the coast causing formation of a surface meso-trough. This results in a displacement offshore of the climatological northerly jet and in onshore flow to the south of the meso-trough feature. The onshore flow to the south results in convergence of marine air and an increase in the MBL depth causing the formation of a meso-ridge along the coast. The meso-ridge is accompanied by southerly flow and propagates to the north as Kelvin wave-like CTD which decays exponentially offshore.

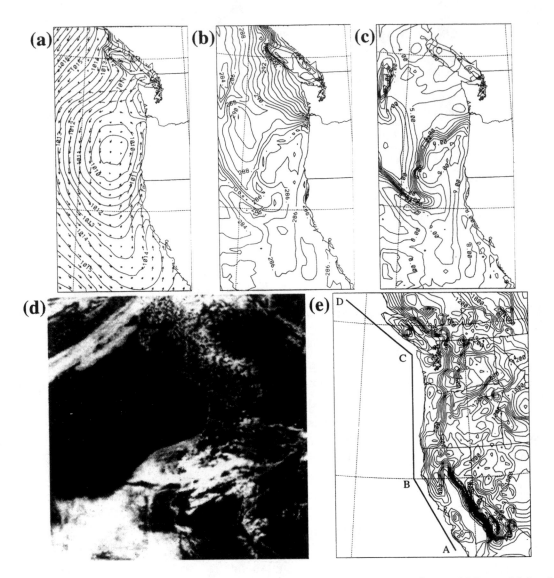

Figure 1: Structure of the mature CTD at 00 UTC 17 May 1985. Panels a-c are from grid 2, model level 4 (216 m ASL) of the RAMS simulation with realistic terrain and radiation. The grid has been truncated along the eastern edge and the noisy fields over the complex terrain blanked out for clarity. a) sea level pressure (contour interval is 0.5 hPa) and 216 m wind (every third vector is displayed, the spacing between vectors represents 10 m s^{-1}. b) potential temperature (contour interval is 1 K). c) mixing ratio (contour interval is 0.5 g kg^{-1}). d) infra-red satellite image from 23 UTC 16 May (reproduced from Mass and Albright, 1987). e) grid 2 model terrain. Line ABCD indicates the location of alongshore potential temperature gradient used subsequently.

In this study, we consider the CTD event of 15-17 May 1985 along the west coast of North America. This event, originally documented by Mass and Albright (1987), is a strong mesoscale trapped event with abrupt transitions in many meteorological parameters. Its propagation along the Oregon / Washington coasts has previously been interpreted as a trapped gravity current (Mass and Albright, 1987; Jackson *et al.* 1999). We discuss how the RAMS model results of the strong 15 May 1985 event compare with the general model of CTD evolution presented in SRK99. We also show how factors not included in the relatively simple numerical models used in SRK99 such as diurnal radiation variations with associated diabatic and advective effects, lead to changes in how CTDs are manifested, and are related to the unsteady propagation of these events observed in nature. It is further suggested that the 15 May 1985 event is best described as a mixed Kelvin wave / bore initially and then becomes more like a gravity current in its final stages, and that this change in dynamical character can explain the reduced propagation speed seen in RAMS simulations.

3. Methods

The RAMS modeling system is described fully in Pielke *et al.* (1992). The RAMS configuration used for the simulations discussed here are described more fully in Guan *et al.* (1998) but will be briefly summarized here. The model used was non-hydrostatic with horizontally variable initial conditions and time-dependent lateral boundary conditions from NCEP analyses on the coarse grid. Solar and terrestrial radiation were permitted on all grids (except the run in which the radiation was turned off). An Arakawa type C grid stagger was used for the two nested grids – grid 1 at 100 km horizontal resolution, and grid 2 at 25 km resolution. A third nested grid, at 6.25 km horizontal resolution was experimented with but not found to lead to further insights at the scale addressed here. All grids had 32 vertical levels with a spacing of 75 m near the surface stretching by a factor of 1.2 for each successive level until a maximum separation of 1000 m was reached, resulting in a vertical domain of 16.5 km.

In this paper we make use of three different simulations of the 15-17 May 1985 CTD event which occurred along the west coast of North America using the grid 2 topography shown in Fig. 1e: (1) normal radiation cycle ('Rrad'), (2) radiation offset by 12 hours ('Rrad+12'), (3) no radiation ('Rnorad'). The simulation with a normal radiation cycle is the same as that presented in Jackson *et al.* (1999). That paper, together with Guan et al. (1998), provides an extensive validation of the ability of RAMS to represent the event.

In comparing the details of various simulations, we have found it very helpful to examine time sequences of the coast-parallel horizontal potential temperature gradient. The leading edge of a CTD is associated with a maximum horizontal temperature gradient (Fig. 1b). Further, the value of the maximum coast-parallel horizontal potential temperature gradient is related to the steepness and non-linearity of the leading edge of the disturbance. In Fig. 2 we take sequences of the horizontal potential temperature gradient along the offshore slice defined by the line 'ABCD' in Fig. 1e (parallel to the y-axes of Fig. 2) at different times into the simulation (time increasing along the x-axes) at model level 4 (216 m above sea level, hereafter ASL) and contour these values. The surface wind reversal position is indicated as a heavy dashed line on these plots (Fig. 2). The resulting figures summarize evolution, intensity, and propagation speed for an entire CTD simulation in one figure, facilitating comparison of differences between simulations. The CTD leading edge along the coast and its movement through time is marked by the locus of maximum contoured values. The slope of the locus of maximum contoured values corresponds to the translation speed – the more nearly vertical the faster the translation. The higher the contour value, the sharper the gradient at the leading edge, and presumably the more non-linear the disturbance.

4. Discussion and Conclusions

For a structural snapshot of the mature CTD, refer to Fig. 1 which depicts the modeled sea level pressure and the 216 m elevation, wind, potential temperature and mixing ratio, as well as an IR satellite image. At 00 UTC 17 May, the disturbance is just south of the Columbia River, and is marked by a narrow coastal ridge with southerly flow in Fig. 1a. A strong thermal gradient is evident at the leading edge of the disturbance (Fig. 1b) with its offshore scale and decay, indicating trapping, apparent from Fig. 1a. The close association between the simulated moisture field and the observed satellite cloud pattern can be seen by comparing Figs. 1c and d.

Fig. 2 shows the contour plots of coast-parallel potential temperature gradient time sequences for the three simulations. There is a distinct change in translation speed in Fig. 2a, indicated by the change in slope of the locus of maximum coast-parallel potential temperature gradient. In the normal radiation simulation shown in Fig. 2a, the early more rapidly propagating part corresponding to a translation speed of 17 m s^{-1} prior to hour 42, we call phase I, and the later, less rapidly propagating part with a translation speed of 5.8 m s^{-1} we call phase II of the CTD.

By following the locus of maximum coast-parallel potential temperature gradient (i.e. the location of the MBL 'step') in Fig. 2a (Rrad), it is apparent that the CTD begins to initiate near simulation hour 12 at 180 km along the section and propagates northward for about 8 hours before a climatological strengthening of the northerly flow component due to daytime heating of the continent in the late afternoon backed the offshore flow ahead of the CTD into a more northerly direction and stalled the propagation. Overnight (after hour 30, 06 UTC 16 May), the flow to the north of the CTD veered anticylonically, returning to an offshore direction, strengthening the coastal lee troughing and resulting in more rapid northward CTD propagation as the CTD accelerated rapidly into the coastal trough. During the daytime and early evening hours (hours 18-28) when the CTD is stalled by the strengthened northerly flow, the CTD leading edge lags the coastal pressure minimum by as much as 300 km (see Jackson *et al.*, 1999 Fig. 5). Overnight, during the period of rapid propagation, the CTD 'catches up' to the coastal pressure minimum. This behavior is consistent with the results of Thompson *et al.* (1997) who showed that the northward extent of coastal wind reversal (of a different case simulation) was limited by the position of the leading pressure trough. In the Rrad simulation, this phase relationship was disrupted by diurnal effects, and returned after the CTD accelerated ageostrophically into the coastal trough. Beginning at hour 43 at 1200 km along the transect (phase II), the coast-parallel potential temperature gradient increases and its slope (i.e. the disturbance translation speed) decreases to 5.8 m s^{-1}. This is accompanied by a steepening of the leading edge of the CTD with nearly vertical isentropes extending to the surface, suggesting a gravity current structure.

In the CTD climatology of Bond *et al.* (1996), it was found that the leading edge of CTDs as inferred from surface marine buoy observations, are sharper at more northern locations, suggesting wave steepening near the surface and a transition to gravity current characteristics. Also, Reason and Steyn (1992) suggest that observed abrupt transitions in CTD translation speed could be due to non-linear wave steepening. SRK99 also report non-linear steepening of the disturbance at the leading edge, which in their simulations occurs shortly after initiation in their experiments with a MBL present due to complete evacuation of the MBL by the offshore flow.

The coastal surface pressure north of the CTD leading edge decreases in response to the offshore flow ahead of the CTD. In SRK99, the offshore flow resulted in an evacuation of the MBL, which in combination with adiabatic warming acted to lower the coastal surface pressure. In our simulations, although the MBL depth is reduced in the offshore flow, a shallow MBL is maintained due to diabatic and frictional effects over the ocean. The MBL depth reduction and surface pressure decrease can be due both to entrainment of warm offshore flow with cyclonic PV into the marine layer (e.g. Reason and Jury, 1990), and to a suppression of the MBL. In addition to adiabatic warming, the advection above the MBL of the radiationally heated continental boundary layer also contributes to lowering of coastal surface pressure in our simulations (although not in the SRK99 simulations). In an analysis of the contributions to lowering of surface pressure ahead of the CTD we find that it is primarily the combination of a reduction in the MBL depth and warm advection above the MBL in the offshore flow that results in the coastal lee trough. This lee trough reverses the alongshore pressure gradient to the south resulting in ageostrophic northward acceleration of the CTD.

In order to assess the importance of diurnal diabatic effects, which were not included in the SRK99 model, two additional simulations were made: one with the radiation cycle offset by 12 hours (Rrad+12 – Fig. 2b), and the second with radiation turned off altogether (Rnorad – Fig. 2c). By comparing Figs. 2a with 2b one can see quite significant differences in evolution caused by differences in the timing of the solar heating cycle. Specifically, the coast-parallel potential temperature gradient at the CTD leading edge seems to weaken during times of peak heating (e.g. Fig. 2b between hours 28-36), and the translation speed also seems to decrease during these times. Radiation is important in developing the coast-parallel potential temperature gradient – in Fig. 2c in which the radiation is turned off – the CTD leading edge has a much smaller potential temperature gradient and the disturbance translation speed is generally less. Solar radiation acts to increase the coast-perpendicular thermal gradient near the surface by differentially heating the continental surface compared with the marine surface. In the presence of offshore flow in the north this results in a northward pointing coast-parallel thermal gradient since the warmed continental air is advected over the coastal zone. In other words, differential off shore warm air advection leads to rotation of the along shore potential temperature gradient from the normal southward pointing direction (i.e. warm air in the south) to northward pointing (i.e. warm air in the north). The importance of diurnal diabatic effects on the evolution and intensity of CTDs is highlighted by the dramatic differences seen between Fig. 2c and Figs. 2a-b - these diabatic effects are not included in SRK99 or in simpler numerical or analytic models of CTD.

The change in translation speed between phase I and phase II, coincident with the non-linear wave steepening and transition from a bore to a gravity current which is denoted by the change in slope of the locus of maximum coast-parallel potential temperature gradient, depends on the timing of the diurnal solar cycle. Even with the same synoptic forcing, the transition which occurs near hour 43 in simulation Rrad (note the change in slope of the locus of maximum horizontal potential temperature gradient at this time in Fig. 2a) is delayed by approximately 17 hours in the Rrad+12 simulation (the change in slope now appears to occur near hour 60 in Fig. 2b). In the Rnorad simulation (Fig. 2c) non-linear wave steepening and a transition from a bore to a gravity current do not appear to occur and the disturbance propagates more steadily. This occurs for several reasons. In the Rnorad simulation the coastal trough is not as deep since there is no contribution to the troughing from the advection of radiationally heated continental air by the offshore flow. Therefore the ageostrophic acceleration of the flow into the trough is less and the coast-parallel thermal gradient is less so that northward propagation is slower and non-linear steepening does not occur. Also, in the Rnorad simulation, the MBLI strength is much weaker since there is no offshore advection of radiationally heated air above the MBLI to intensify it. Consequently the Rnorad system behaves much less like a two-layer system and more like a weakly continuously stratified system so that shallow-water wave dynamics (such as non-linear wave steepening) are less important.

The impact of the diurnal solar radiation cycle on CTD evolution is multifaceted. During the day, heating over the land lowers pressure there and enhances the opposing northerly coastal jet decreasing the CTD translation speed. Offshore advection of radiationally heated air ahead of the CTD, warms the air to the north and is largely responsible for the coast-parallel temperature gradient and hence the coast-parallel pressure gradient which forces the CTD. In SRK99 these gradients were created somewhat artificially without offshore warm advection, by complete evacuation of the MBL by the offshore flow and by adiabatic warming of the air as it flows down the coastal mountains. These two impacts of the diurnal cycle tend to counteract each other, with enhancement of the northerly jet slowing and weakening CTDs while advection of warm air offshore enhances CTDs. The two impacts are however not entirely in phase, with enhancement of the northerly jet occurring from mid-morning to late evening (Ralph et al. 2000, Fig. 7) while offshore advection of air heated during the day occurs during the night as well. This favors northward CTD propagation between late evening and late morning. This is consistent with the climatology of Bond et al. (1996) which found that the initiation of wind reversals tended to occur during night or morning.

The transition between phase I and phase II and the presence of gravity current-like propagation occurs during times of diminished solar radiation – the non-shaded times in Fig. 2, whereas propagation as a bore during phase I can occur during times of peak solar radiation intensity. This also lends support to the idea that phase I propagation is like a bore or mixed Kelvin wave / bore with the zone of strong thermal gradient located aloft where it can not be as easily affected by solar radiation.

5. Acknowledgements

Support for this project came from the U.S. Office of Naval Research Coastal Meteorology Accelerated Research Initiative grants N00014-96-1-0745, N00014-97-1-0342. RAMS was developed under the support of the National Science Foundation (NSF) and the U.S. Army Research Office (ARO).

6. References

Bond, N.A., C.F. Mass, J.E. Overland, 1996: *Mon. Wea. Rev.* **124**, 430-445.

Dorman, C.E, 1985: *Mon. Wea. Rev.*, **113**, 827-839.

Dorman, C.E., 1987: *J. Geophys. Res.*, **92**, 1497-1506.

Dorman, C.E., 1988: *Mon. Wea. Rev.*, **116**, 2401-2406.

Guan, S., P.L. Jackson, C.J.C. Reason, 1998: *Mon. Wea. Rev.*, **126**, 972-990.

Jackson, P.L., C.J.C. Reason, S. Guan, 1999: *Mon. Wea. Rev.*, **127**, 535-550.

Mass, C.F., M. D. Albright, 1987: *Mon. Wea. Rev.*, **115**, 1707-1738.

Mass, C.F., M. D. Albright, 1988: *Mon. Wea. Rev.*, **116**, 2407-2410.

Mass, C.F., 1995: *J. Atmos. Sci.*, **52**, 2313-2318.

Mass, C.F., N.A. Bond, 1996: *Mon. Wea. Rev*, **124**, 446-461.

Pielke, R.A., and 10 co-authors, 1992: *Meteor. Atmos. Phys.*, **49**, 69-91.

Ralph, F.M., and 7 co-authors, 1998: *Mon. Wea. Rev.*, **126**, 2435-2465.

Ralph, F.M., and 5 co-authors, 2000: *Mon. Wea. Rev.*, **128**, 283–300.

Reason, C.J.C., M.R. Jury, 1990: *Quart. J. Roy. Meteor. Soc.*, **116**, 1133-1151.

Reason, C.J.C., D.G. Steyn, 1992: *J. Atmos. Sci.*, **49**, 1677-1692.

Reason, C.J.C., 1994: *Meteor. Atmos. Phys.*, **53**, 131-136.

Reason C.J.C., R. Dunkley, 1993: *Atmos. Ocean*, **31**, 235-258.

Skamarock, W.C., R. Rotunno, J.B. Klemp, 1999: *J. Atmos. Sci.*, **56**, 3349-3365.

Thompson, W.T., T. Haack, J.D. Doyle, S.D. Burk, 1997: *Mon. Wea. Rev.*, **125**, 3211-3230.

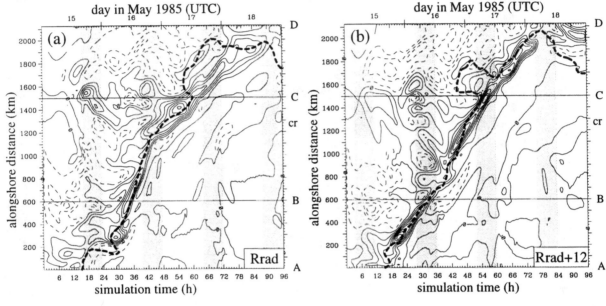

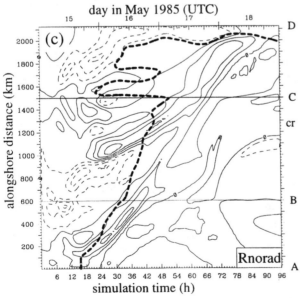

Figure 2: Contours of the alongshore temperature gradient along the heavy line ABCD shown in Fig. 1e (216 m above the surface). The ordinate is distance from south to north, and the abscissa is increasing time into the simulation starting at 00 UTC 15 May 1985. Cape Mendocino is near "B", Juan de Fuca Strait is near "C", and the Columbia River is denoted by "cr" along the right edge of the figures. The shaded regions indicate the 8 hours of maximum solar radiation centered upon local noon. The heavy dashed line indicates position of the surface wind reversal. a) With the realistic coastal topography shown in Fig. 1e (Rrad); b) As in (a) except the model radiation diurnal cycle is offset by 12 hours (Rrad+12); c) As in (a) except with model radiation turned off (Rnorad). Contour interval is 2.5 K (100 km)$^{-1}$.

Experiments on Raindrop energy Dissipation at the saline water surface

Chan Ji Lai [1], Ming Ching Li [1]

[1]Department of Hydraulics and Ocean Engineering, Cheng Kung University, Tainan, Taiwan
70101

laicj@mail.ncku.edu.tw,n8886102@ccmail.ncku.edu.tw

1.Abstract

Experiments are conducted to examine the interaction of raindrops with saline water surface. As rain falls on the surface, turbulent mixing produces density mixing layer. A High Frame Rate Area Scan digital camera is used to visualize this process. It's resolution enables the falling velocities and diameters of raindrops, as well as the instantaneous velocity of a particle near the surface can be obtained from flow visualization technique. A salinometer is used to measure fluid density and detect the depth of the mixing layer. Experiments show that the depth of the mixing layer is hold nearly at 6 ~ 7cm. It does not vary much for the rainfall intensity and duration range (about 13-23mm/min), as long as the velocity and diameter of raindrops are kept nearly constant. In the mixing layer the kinetic energy decays exponentially and can be determined by $u/u_* = 0.015 \cdot (Z/D)^{-3/7}$ and $u/u_* = 0.032 \cdot e^{-6/7(Z/D)}$.

2.Introduction

Rain-sea interaction is a complex process, even the interaction of a single drop with a static receiving fluid is not simple. When raindrops strike the sea surface, they generated Rayleigh jets, cavity, vortex rings and splash near the surface. They also change water surface salinity, temperature. Kinetic energy of raindrops transfers and produces turbulent mixing layer. Some field observations show that they could calm down surface gravity waves, affect sea surface roughness and limit the accuracy of radiometry on water temperature and sea surface winds.

Rainfall and sea surface interaction studies can be categorized into three ways. (1)Simplified model that includes observation of a single drop impact with the quiescent water surface. For example, Siscoe & Levin(1971) explored the splash and Rayleigh jet that were generated by a single drop hit the quiescent receiving fluid; Engel(1966) studied theoretically and experimentally the impact cavity depth caused by raindrop; Chapman & Critchlow(1967), Durst(1996) explored the vortex ring penetrate depth for various raindrop patterns. (2)The mechanism of rain-wave, e.g., Simplis(1990) explored the effect of rain in damping surface waves in laboratory; Yang et al.(1996) studied the wave heights damping and strengthening by rainfalls for waves in gravity and in capillary-gravity capillary ranges respectively.

(3)Turbulent mixing layer studies, e.g., Hopfinger & Linden (1982) used oscillating grid generated turbulence to explore the mechanism of energy transfer and stratification of upper-ocean; Green & Houk(1979) explored the variation of temperature and salinity profile caused by turbulent mixing that were generated by raindrop hit the quiescent fluid.

3. Equipment and procedures

Observation of raindrop and the turbulent mixing density layer were made at the experimental setup shown in Fig.1 and 2. This setup includes a special designed rain generator, a model sea tank, a flow visualization system and a salinometer. Their functions are described as follows.

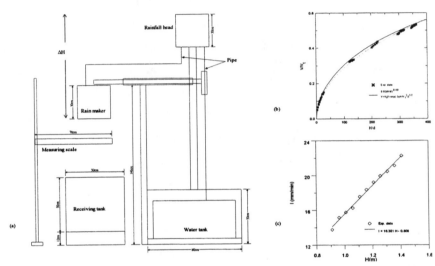

Figure 1.　Experimental layouts

3.1 Rain generator and model sea.
The rain generator was composed of rain modules and a head tank. The rain modules were closed boxes and pressurized by the head tank. There were 27 hypodermic needles in the box. Each needle produced circular raindrops at a diameter of 2.1mm simultaneously. Adjusting the height varied the intensity of rainfall, as indicated in Fig.1(a). Ranges of the rain intensity I were from 13.7 to 22.3 mm/min. The 2.1mm raindrop was designed according to the study of Laws & Parson (1943), they suggested that 73% of natural raindrop diameters were 2.2 mm. The model sea was a 50cmx50cm glass tank filled with saline water, and the rain receiving cell was 8x4 cm². Because of height limit, the raindrop velocity near water surface V could only reach 45% to 51% of theoretical terminal velocity V_t. Velocimetry through visualization gave their relationship as:

$$\frac{V}{V_t} = 0.03 \cdot \left(\frac{H}{d}\right)^{0.49} \tag{1}$$

, in which H is the head of water in the rain module, d is raindrop diameter. Assuming a raindrop keeps spherical during falling, the theoretical velocity of the raindrops is:

$$V = V_t \left[1 - \exp\left(\frac{-2gH}{V_t^2} \right) \right]^{\frac{1}{2}}$$ (2)

Both equations can give good prediction to V as shown in Fig. 1(b).

3.2 Salinity measurement instrumentation

A salinometers(type MK-403) with three probes were used to measured the vertical salinity profile of the model sea. They were placed 10cm from the rain cell. Salinity profiles were taken after at time 5, 10, 15, 20, 30, 40, 60 min after rainfall started.

3.3 Flow visualization technique

The flow visualizing system is shown in shown in Fig.2. It was composed of a high frame rate area scan digital camera, Dalsa256, an Innova90, Ar$^+$ laser as the illuminant and an image processing system for quantifying flow image. The speed of the camera was 80 frame/sec at a resolution of 256×256 pixels. Aluminum powder was used as the tracer.

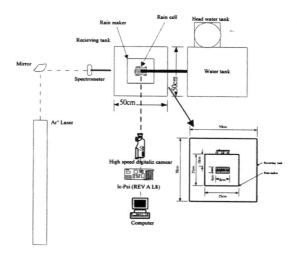

Figure 2.   Schematic diagram of flow-visualization and salinity measurement

4. Results and analysis

4.1 Evolution and depth of density Mixing layer

As raindrops penetrate saline water surface, the fresh water patches firstly move vertically but quickly extend laterally because of the density effect. Mixing layer develops and turbulence decays and diffuses downward. As shown in Fig.3 the salinity profiles for various rainfall duration and intensities. The ordinate Z(cm) is the depth downward from the water surface. The diagrams for the moderate rains, I=15.7-20.5mm/min, show that the salinity of the upper layer at an instant vary only slightly and a distinct

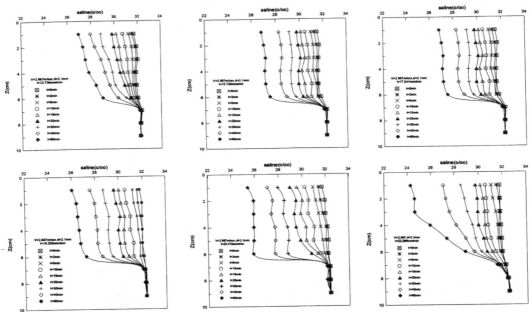

Figure 3.   Salinity of mixing layer with rainfall intensity duration

interface occurs at the depth of 6-7cm. At a higher intensity, I=22.3mm/min, the interface is deeper but has smaller gradient. From this observation, we define a mixing depth D where the value of dS/dz is the largest. The density difference $\Delta S/\Delta S_{max}$ for the moderate rainfall intensities are plotted against Z/D in Fig.4(a). The same plot for data that have the same rainfall intensity, I=19.2mm/min, but have different near surface velocities are plotted in Fig.4(b). It is clear from Figs.4(a) and (b) that increase rainfall intensity or raindrop velocity cause salinity distribute move evenly at Z/D from 0.7 to 1.0. Since the mixed layer develops with time, the density difference at every depth s_d, i.e., s-s_0 is normalized with s_0. It is plotted with rainfall depth "I × t", and is shown in Fig.5. It is not surprise that S_d/S_0 varies linearly rainfall depth.

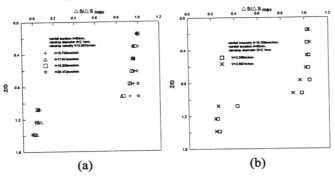

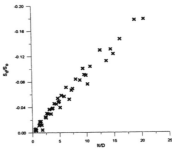

Figure 4.   Normalized salinity with mixing depth and velocity

Figure 5.   Normalized salinity with It/D

4.2 Decay of Kinetic Energy

The kinetic energy of raindrop is transferred as drop patches spread in the upper layer. By averaging the visualized velocities from 64 images, the mean square velocity at a depth Z, $u(Z)$ is obtained. This is used to represent the kinetic energy of the mixed water patches. To evaluate the decay rate of the energy, the rainfall energy flux of Green & Houk(1979) is interpreted as the energy source. Green & Houk(1979) suggested that the rainfall energy flux is calculated by

$$KE_f = \rho u_*^3 = \frac{1}{2}\rho I V^2$$
(3)

and they define u_* are frictional velocity. The normalized energy, $u(Z)/u*$ is plotted with depth Z/D and is shown in Fig. 6. Regressions of the data suggest that the normalized energy follow an exponential function, or a power law. These two functions are $u/u_* = 0.015 \cdot (Z/D)^{-3/7}$ and $u/u_* = 0.032 \cdot e^{-6/7(Z/D)}$. It indicates that at the upper part, i.e., Z/D < 0.2, energy decay follow the power function. When Z/D>0.9 the energy decays more exponentially. In between, the energy decay follows both functions. It is because the mixing layer near water surface is subject to the direct impact of rain-drops. It should vary more closely to the power function or the decay law of Hopfinger and Linden(1982). Near the interface the energy reduced faster because of the sudden attenuation of turbulent eddy by interfacial stresses.

5. Discussion

Using the special designed rain generator and the model sea, we were be able to observe the interaction of raindrops with saline water. Although the falling velocity of the raindrops at the saline water surface was not the terminal velocity, we are confident at the facility because the observed raindrops fit Eqs1 and 2 well. Our energy decay observation also show in the same variation as those obtained by Hopfinger and Linden(1982), whom used grid generator as the kinetic energy input device.

Our results indicate that at certain moderate rainfall intensity, the mixing layer develops at a maximum depth of 6-7 cm. For higher rainfall intensity our results are not conclusive owing to the area limitation of the model sea. Further studies should be conducted in a larger model sea to waive this limitation.

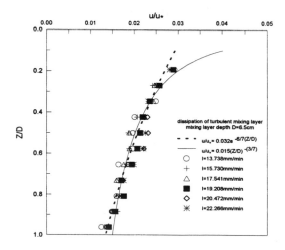

Figure 6.   Normalized decay law of velocity in mixing layer

6. Conclusions

Our experiments were aimed to explore the mixing depth of raindrops on saline water surface, and the kinetic energy dissipation in the layer. A special designed system is used for this laboratory observation. Without the waves and wind interaction and in the range of rainfall intensity between 13 ~ 23 mm/min, this observation concludes that:

1. At moderate rainfall intensity, the mixing layer develops at a maximum depth, D, of 6-7 cm. A distinct density interface can be seen at this depth.

2. Raindrop kinetic energy decays from surface to the density interface. At 0.2<Z/D<0.9, the kinetic energy follow the power and exponential functions $u/u_* = 0.015 \cdot (Z/D)^{-3/7}$ and $u/u_* = 0.032 \cdot e^{-6/7(Z/D)}$. At Z/D<0.2, the upper part of the layer, the kinetic energy follows the power function. At Z/D>0.9 the kinetic energy decay rapidly and follows the exponential function.,

7. References

1. Chapman, D.S. and Critchlow, P.R., "Formation of vortex rings from falling drops", Journal of Fluid Mech., Vol.29, part1, pp177-185, 1967.

2. Durst, F., "Penetration length and diameter development of vortex rings generated by impacting water drops", Experiments in fluid, 21, pp110-117. 1996.

3. Engel, O.G., "Crater depth in fluid impacts", Journal of applied physics, Vol.37, No.4, pp1798-1808,1966.

4. Green, T. and Houk, D.F., "The mixing of rain with near-surface water", Journal of Fluid Mech., Vol. 90,part3,pp.569-588,1979.

5. Hopfinger, E.J. and P.F. Linden, "Formation of thermoclines in zero-shear turbulence subjected to a stabilizing buoyancy flux", Journal of Fluid Mech. Vol. 114,pp.157-173,1982.

6. Linden, P.F., "The interaction of a vortex ring with a sharp density interface: a model for turbulent",Journal of Fluid Mech.,Vol.60 part3, pp.467-480,1973.

7. Siscoe, G.L. and Levin, Z., "Water-drop-surface-wave interactions", Journal of geophysical research, Vol.76, No.21, pp5112-5116, 1971.

8. Tsimplis, M.N. ,"The effect of rain in calming the sea" ,Journal of physical oceanography, Vol. 22,pp.404-412.1992.

9. Yang, Zhzizhang, Shih Tang, and Jin Wu, "An Experiment study of rain effects on fine structures of wind waves", Journal of physical oceanography, Vol.27, pp419-430,1996.

Self-Similar Solutions for the Formation of the Non-Linear Lateral Convection in a Stratified Fluid

Atsushi Mori[1], Hiroshi Niino[2]

[1]Astronomy and Earth Science, Tokyo Gakugei University, Japan,184-8501
[2]Marine Meteorology, Ocean Research Institute, University of Tokyo, Japan, 164-8639
mori@buran.u-gakugei.ac.jp, niino@ori.u-tokyo.ac.jp

1. Introduction

Lateral convection is one of the most basic phenomenon in the geophysical fluid. Land and sea breeze circulations and heat / cool island circulations are typical examples of lateral convections caused by differential heating of the earth's surface. The linear dynamics of land and sea breeze circulations (e.g., Rotunno, 1983; Niino, 1987) and steady heat / cool island circulations (e.g., Malkus and Stern, 1953; Kimura, 1975) have been extensively studied. However, theoretical studies on unsteady non-linear dynamics of these circulations have been very limited. This paper reports our efforts to clarify the non-linear formation process of a lateral convection by means of theoretical analysis using self-similar solutions and a numerical simulation.

2. Formulation

The configuration considered in this paper is shown in Figure 1. A Boussinesq fluid in which the basic temperature increases linearly with height occupies semi-infinite space above an infinite horizontal plane. The bottom plane is non-slip, and the right half of the bottom ($y_* \geq 0$ in the figure) is thermally insulated. Initially there is no motion in the fluid. At a certain instant, the temperature on the left half of the bottom ($y_* < 0$) is lowered by ΔT from its initial value of T_{0*} and maintained thereafter.

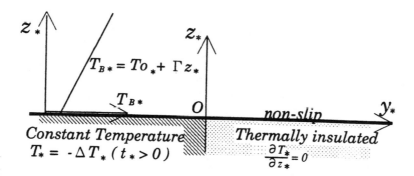

Figure 1: Schematic configuration of the problem.

The horizontal vorticity equation and the internal energy equation may be written as follows:

$$\frac{\partial \zeta_*}{\partial t_*} = -\frac{\partial \zeta_*}{\partial y_*}\frac{\partial \psi_*}{\partial z_*} + \frac{\partial \zeta_*}{\partial z_*}\frac{\partial \psi_*}{\partial y_*} + \alpha g \frac{\partial T_*}{\partial y_*} + \nu \nabla_*^2 \zeta_*, \tag{1}$$

$$\frac{\partial T_*}{\partial t_*} = -\frac{\partial T_*}{\partial y_*}\frac{\partial \psi_*}{\partial z_*} + \frac{\partial T_*}{\partial z_*}\frac{\partial \psi_*}{\partial y_*} + \Gamma \frac{\partial \psi_*}{\partial y_*} + \kappa \nabla_*^2 T_*, \tag{2}$$

where $\zeta_*, \psi_*, \alpha, g, \nu, \kappa$ and Γ are vorticity, streamfunction, coefficient of thermal expansion, gravity acceleration, kinematic viscosity, coefficient of thermal diffusion and vertical gradient of the basic potential temperature field $T_{B*}(z)$, respectively. Vorticity ζ_* is expressed by the streamfunction ψ_* as

$$\zeta_* = -\nabla_*^2 \psi_*. \tag{3}$$

T_* is the temperature deviation from $T_{B*}(z_*) = T_{0*} + \Gamma z_*$. The asterisk denotes dimensional variables. The boundary conditions at the bottom ($z_* = 0$) are given by

$$\psi_* \;=\; 0, \tag{4}$$

$$\frac{\partial \psi_*}{\partial z_*} \;=\; 0, \tag{5}$$

$$\begin{cases} \dfrac{\partial T_*}{\partial z_*} \;=\; 0 \quad (y_* \geq 0), \\ T_* \;=\; -\Delta T_* \quad (y_* < 0). \end{cases} \tag{6}$$

3. Flow Regimes and Self-Similar Solutions

After a suitable nondimensionalization, it can be shown that three distinct flow regimes are realized in the present configuration depending on the nondimensional elapsed time t, the nondimensional stratification parameter Γ' and Prandtl number Pr, which are defined as follows:

$$t \;=\; \frac{t_*}{\left(\frac{\sqrt{\kappa}}{\alpha g \Delta T}\right)^{\frac{2}{3}}}, \tag{7}$$

$$\Gamma' \;=\; \alpha g \Gamma \left(\frac{\sqrt{\kappa}}{\alpha g \Delta T}\right)^{\frac{4}{3}}, \tag{8}$$

$$Pr \;=\; \frac{\nu}{\kappa}. \tag{9}$$

Figure 2 shows such a flow regime diagram on the $t - \Gamma'$ plane for a particular Prandtl number. In the most general situation, the flow experiences two regime transitions as time elapses: from Diffusion to Gravity Current Regime and from Gravity Current to Gravity Wave Regime.

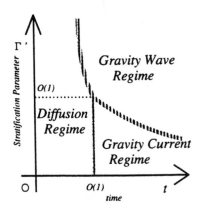

Figure 2: Three flow regimes realized in the present configuration.

For each regime the solutions in the following form can be shown to exist:

$$\eta \;=\; R_\eta(t)\, \eta_S \left(Y(y,t), Z(z,t), Pr\right) \tag{10}$$

$$\;=\; R_\eta(t)\, \eta_S \left(\frac{y}{\ell(t)}, \frac{z}{\delta(t)}, Pr\right), \tag{11}$$

where η is any of dependent variables ζ, ψ and T. $R_\eta(t)$ is a function of time t and represents the magnitude of that quantity η. $\ell(t)$ and $\delta(t)$ are the characteristic horizontal and vertical lengthscales respectively. η_S is the self-similar solution in the sense that it is a function of scaled coordinates $Y \equiv y/\ell(t)$ and $Z \equiv z/\delta(t)$ and of Pr but is not an explicit function of t. Thus, we are assuming that, if η, y and z are suitably scaled, the spatial pattern of η does not change with time.

4. Numerical Simulation

In order to examine the realizability of each flow regime, two different types of numerical experiments are performed. One is an ordinary time integration based on the nondimensional form of basic equations (1) and (2) and boundary conditions (4)-(6). The other is a direct calculation of self-similar solution.

4.1 Ordinary Time Integration

The finite-difference schemes for the nonlinear terms are carefully chosen so as to conserve the temperature deviation T, vorticity ζ, energy, and enstrophy. The calculation domain was taken to be large enough so that the upper and sidewall boundaries do not affect the results. The calculation was started from a state of rest by suddenly cooling the left half of the bottom.

The time evolution of the streamfunction in Gravity Wave Regime is shown in the left hand side of Figure 3. As time elapses, the flow intensifies and increases its size both in the horizontal and vertical directions. The panels on the right hand side, on the other hand, show the same streamfunction under the similarity scaling. The patterns of the scaled streamfunction turn out to change very little with time. Thus, the self-similar solution for Gravity Wave Regime is found to be realized in nature.

As for the other regimes, similar numerical integrations have been made. The results confirmed that the self-similar solutions for these regimes are also realized.

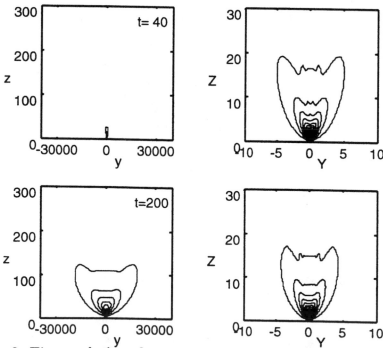

Figure 3. Time evolution of streamfunction for Gravity Wave Regime.
The external parameters are $Pr = 1$, $\Gamma' = 10$. The calculation domain is $-75000 < y < 75000$ and $0 < z < 600$. The left panels show the non-scaled streamfunction ψ at $t = 40$ and 200 with the contour interval of 10. The right panels show the scaled streamfunction corresponding to the left panels. The contour interval is 0.01.

4.2 Direct Calculation of Self-Similar Solutions

Assuming the self-similar solutions (10) and (11), and neglecting small terms, one can derive transformed equations for $\eta_S(Y, Z, Pr)$ from equations (1) and (2). Three transformed equations for different flow regimes are numerically solved to obtain the self-similar solutions.

Figure 4 shows the self-similar streamfunction (ψ_S) thus obtained for Gravity Wave Regime. It is very similar to the right panels of Figure 3.

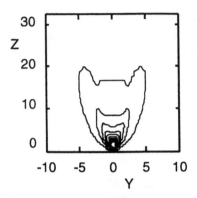

Figure 4. Self-similar solution ψ_S for Gravity Wave Regime
The external parameters are $Pr = 1$. The calculation domain is $-60 < Y < 60$ and $0 < Z < 300$.
The contour interval is 0.01.

5. Discussion

5.1 Physical Mechanism for Each Regime

The time dependencies of δ, ℓ, ψ obtained theoretically by the requirement of existence of self-similar solutions have been verified by the numerical experiments (Table 1).

	D	GC	GW
δ	$t^{\frac{1}{2}}$	$t^{\frac{1}{2}}$	$t^{\frac{1}{2}}$
l	$t^{\frac{1}{2}}$	$t^{\frac{5}{4}}$	$t^{\frac{3}{2}}$
ψ	$t^{\frac{3}{2}}$	$t^{\frac{3}{4}}$	$t^{\frac{1}{2}}$

Table 1. Time dependency for each physical quantity.
D: Diffusion Regime, GC: Gravity Current Regime, GW: Gravity Wave
Regime.

Note that the characteristic vertical lengthscales for all of the three regimes are proportional to $t^{\frac{1}{2}}$. In dimensional form, they are given by $\sqrt{\kappa t}$, the thermal diffusion lengthscale. The characteristic horizontal scale for Diffusion Regime is also given by the diffusion lengthscale. Thus, in this regime, diffusion process dominates over the other effects such as nonlinear effects and the effect of stratification.

In Gravity Current Regime, $\ell(t)$ is proportional to $t^{\frac{5}{4}}$. An order-of-magnitude argument suggests that this lengthscale results from a horizontal propagation of a gravity current the dimensional depth of which is given by $\delta_*(t_*) = \sqrt{\kappa t}$: the horizontal propagation speed of the gravity current is proportional to $\sqrt{g'\delta_*(t_*)}$, where $g' = g\alpha\Delta T$ is the reduced gravity. An integration of this with respect to time t_* gives the horizontal lengthscale

$$\ell_*(t_*) \sim \sqrt{g'\sqrt{\kappa t_*}} \cdot t_* = \sqrt{g'}\kappa^{\frac{1}{4}}t_*^{\frac{5}{4}}. \tag{12}$$

In Gravity Wave Regime, $\ell(t) \sim t^{\frac{3}{2}}$. In dimensional unit, the group velocity of a hydrostatic gravity wave the vertical scale of which is $\sqrt{\kappa t_*}$ is given by $N\sqrt{\kappa t_*}$, where $N = \sqrt{\alpha g \Gamma}$ is Brunt-Väisälä frequency. An itegration of this with respect to time gives the horizontal lengthscale

$$\ell_*(t_*) \quad \sim \quad \sqrt{\alpha g \Gamma}\sqrt{\kappa t_*} \cdot t_* = \sqrt{\alpha g \Gamma} \kappa^{\frac{1}{2}} t^{\frac{3}{2}}. \tag{13}$$

Thus, the horizontal lengthscale in Gravity Wave Regime is determined by the horizontal propagation of the internal gravity wave.

5.2 Regime Transition

The physical mechanism described above suggests that a transition between two regimes occurs when their horizontal lengthscales become of the same order. This idea gives estimates for the times of the regime transitions (Table 2).

Diffusion Regime	$\rightarrow$	Gravity Current Regime	$t_* \sim \left(\frac{\sqrt{\kappa}}{\alpha g \Delta T}\right)^{\frac{2}{3}}$
Gravity Current Regime	$\rightarrow$	Gravity Wave Regime	$t_* \sim \frac{\Delta T^2}{\Gamma^2 \kappa}$
Diffusion Regime	$\rightarrow$	Gravity Wave Regime	$t_* \sim \frac{1}{\sqrt{\alpha g \Gamma}}$

Table 2. Time of the regime transition (see also Figure 2).

5.3 Formation of Cool Island Circulation

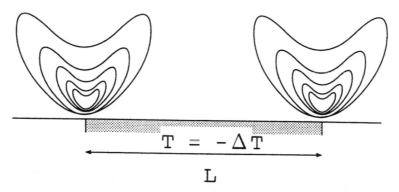

Figure 5. Conceptual figure for the formation of a cool island circulation.

The process by which the steady lateral convection such as a cool island circulation is formed may be interpreted in terms of the flow regimes studied here. According to our study, the size of the circulation increases without limit as time elapses. On the other hand, previous theoretical studies on steady heat or cool island circulations show that the circulation are confined to a finite region near the island (e.g., Kimura 1975).

Let us consider the case of $\Gamma' \sim 1$ and $Pr = 1$ (see Figure 2). When the temperature of a finite region of the lower boundary, whose lengthscale is L, is suddenly lowered by a certain amount, two circulations start to develop from both edges of the cool island (see Figure 5). Though the flow patterns of the circulations are thought to be described by Diffusion Regime at first, soon a regime transition to Gravity Current Regime occurs. Two gravity currents start to flow outward of the cooling region. The effect of the stratification, however, dominates the nonlinearity eventually, and the regime transition to Gravity Wave Regime occurs. The circulation grows both inward and outward from the edge. Only after the circulations from both edges meet at the center, the steady cool island circulation is established. The time t_{L*} required to set up the steady circulation is obtained by equating the lengthscale (13) to L:

$$\sqrt{\alpha g \Gamma} \kappa t_{L*}^{\frac{3}{2}} \quad \sim \quad L,$$

$$t_{L*} \sim \left(\frac{L}{\sqrt{\alpha g \Gamma \kappa}} \right)^{\frac{2}{3}}. \tag{14}$$

The vertical diffusion lengthscale δ_L at this time is given by

$$
\begin{aligned}
\delta_L &\sim \sqrt{\kappa} \left(\frac{L}{\sqrt{\alpha g \Gamma \kappa}} \right)^{\frac{2}{3}\frac{1}{2}} \\
&= \left(\frac{L\kappa}{\sqrt{\alpha g \Gamma}} \right)^{\frac{1}{3}} \tag{15} \\
&= \left(\frac{\alpha g \Gamma L^4}{\kappa^2} \right)^{-\frac{1}{6}} L, \tag{16}
\end{aligned}
$$

which coincides with the depth of a steady cool island circulation obtained by the previous study (Kimura 1975), reinforcing our interpretation of the formation process of the lateral convection.

6. Summary

Formation processes of non-linear lateral convections caused by a differential heating of the lower boundary have been studied theoretically and numerically. A theoretical consideration suggests that three flow regimes exist in the problem: Diffusion Regime, Gravity Current Regime and Gravity Wave Regime. In each regime, the existence of a self-similar solution has been predicted. The results of the numerical simulations show that each flow regime and corresponding self-similar solution are in fact realized depending on the elapsed time and nondimensional parameters. The formation process of a steady cool island circulation has been interpreted in the light of the self-similar solutions.

Reference

1. Kimura, R. 1975. Dynamics of steady convection over heat and cool islands *J. Meteorological Soc. Japan* **53**,440-457

2. Malkus, J. S. and Stern, M. E. The flow of a stable atmosphere over a heated island, I *J. Meteorol.*, **10**, 30-41

3. Niino, H. 1987. Linear theory of land and sea breeze circulation. *J. Meteorological Soc. Japan* **65**,901-920

4. Rotunno, R. 1983. On the linear theory of the land and sea breeze. *J. Atmos. Sci.* **40**, 1999-2009

Relationship between Gas Transfer and Increased Surface-Area

Tadanobu Nakayama

Water and Soil Environment Division, National Institute for Environmental Studies,
Tsukuba, 305-0053, Japan
nakat@nies.go.jp

1. Abstract

The relationship was evaluated between the increase of surface area and the gas transfer coefficient across the interface in two-layer flows by using cross-correlation coefficients evaluated from two sets of ultrasonic depth-measuring instruments in comparison with VTR. It was clarified that the surface area has little effect on gas transfer in smooth-bed flow against previous studies. Furthermore, it became clear that smaller-scale eddies contribute greatly to the greater gas transfer in open-channel flow than those in wind-wave. These findings can be used for evaluating gas transfer in actual river only by the spectrum of surface-wave.

2. Introduction

It has been pointed out that there has a close relationship between the turbulence (and coherent) structures in air/water layers and the gas transfer mechanism across the interface. Akai *et al.* (1977) examined the difference of auto-correlation functions of surface-wave fluctuations when the surface shapes change in two-layer flows about the suggestion by Hanratty and Engen (1957). On the other hand, when the gas transfer coefficient K_L was evaluated, the surface-renewal model (Equation (1)) proposed by Danckwerts (1951), *etc.* have been often used on the assumption that the surface area scarcely changes, except for some suggestions that the surface-renewal rate can be directly given by using the generation period of surface-renewal eddies, for example, Rashidi *et al.* (1991) and Komori *et al.* (1993).

$$K_L = \sqrt{D_m \cdot r} \qquad (1)$$

where D_m (cm²/s) is the molecular diffusivity of the gas in the liquid, and r (1/s) is the mean frequency of surface renewal. By the way, Nakayama and Nezu (1999) have experimentally verified that the gas transfer coefficient K_L in open-channel flows is much larger than that in wind waves even though the surface-wave fluctuations in both flows are same with each other due to the difference of enhanced surface area. Furthermore, Dobbins (1964) and Thackston and Krenkel (1969) have applied the renewal model and proposed a formula including the effect of Froude number to account for enhanced surface area C_A due to surface distortions in open-channel flow, as follows:

$$K_L = C_A \sqrt{D_m \cdot r} \ , \quad C_A = 1 + 0.3 Fr^2 \ or \ 1 + Fr^{1/2} \qquad (2)$$

In the same manner, Rashidi *et al.* (1991) have extended the renewal model to evaluate K_L including the effect of the "*patch*" (the area that looks like rising at the free surface) area and frequency by visualization technique on the assumption that there occur no waves.

In this way, the previous studies were conducted on a specific wind speed or water velocity. And in these studies about gas transfer, increased area of free surface is closely related to promotion of gas transfer. However, it is not clear about the relationship between the increasing surface area and the gas transfer coefficient in two-layer flows, and it is doubtful whether the surface area increases greatly. So, in this study, the effect of increase of surface area and other factor on gas transfer was evaluated by conducting the simultaneous measurements of two depth meters.

3. Experimental Apparatus and Procedures

Experiments were conducted in tilting wind-water tunnel of 16m long and 40cm wide. Coordinate axis in the streamwise direction is defined as x. As for the vertical direction, the upward direction from the bottom is defined as y. Instantaneous velocities for the streamwise and vertical components are $u(t)$ and $v(t)$, respectively. The simultaneous measurements by two sets of depth meters were conducted in the following. The LDA system (DANTEC-made) was fixed at the center of channel ($y/H=0.9$) 9m downstream of the channel entrance for measuring the instantaneous velocity. At the same time, one ultrasonic depth-measuring instrument (KEYENCE-made) was set above the free surface as a fixed probe, and the other was moved horizontally as a movable probe, both of which were synchronized with the LDA. The sampling time was

Table 1. Hydraulic conditions for air-water interactions.

open-channel flow

case	H (cm)	Uw,mean (cm/s)	Fr	U*b (cm/s)
d1f1	4.0	6.8	0.10	0.44
d1f2	4.0	20.2	0.32	1.22
d1f3	4.0	50.2	0.80	2.53
d1f4	4.0	92.9	1.50	4.64
d1f5	4.0	123.5	2.00	6.06
d2f1	8.0	11.2	0.32	0.56

wind-water wave (Valve-Closed)

case	H (cm)	Ua,max (m/s)	Uw,mean (cm/s)	U*a (cm/s)
d2wa	8.0	0.94	0.0	3.84
d2wb	8.0	1.79	0.0	7.56
d2wd	8.0	3.63	0.0	17.51
d2wf	8.0	5.46	0.0	28.67
d2wh	8.0	8.30	0.0	50.29
w3f0	4.0	8.41	0.0	37.99

wind/stream combined flow

case	H (cm)	Ua,max (m/s)	Uw,mean (cm/s)	Fr	U*a (cm/s)	U*b (cm/s)
w1f1	4.0	1.49	20.30	0.32	4.52	1.25
w2f1	4.0	4.39	20.26	0.32	18.45	1.20
w3f1	4.0	8.41	20.59	0.33	40.20	1.22
w1f2	4.0	1.49	50.47	0.81	3.20	2.57
w2f2	4.0	4.39	51.83	0.83	13.66	2.61
w3f2	4.0	8.41	59.24	0.95	38.57	2.61
w1f3	4.0	1.49	98.27	1.57	1.82	4.67
w2f3	4.0	4.39	98.64	1.58	12.49	4.77
w3f3	4.0	8.41	101.84	1.63	32.19	4.93

60sec, and sampling frequency was about 150Hz. Furthermore, Dissolved oxygen meter was used for measurement of dissolved oxygen (DO) concentrations. Water was firstly deoxygenated by putting enough sodium sulfite. Then DO measurement was conducted and gas transfer coefficient K_L was calculated by the time-gradient of the measured value of DO concentration. About the details of DO measurement, please see Nakayama and Nezu (1999) and Nakayama (2000a). Hydraulic conditions for this experiment are shown in Table 1. Experiments are divided into three conditions; (A) bottom-shear generated flow (open-channel flow), (B) wind-shear generated flow and (C) combined wind/stream flow. The parameters are defined as follows, H : the flow depth, $U_{a,max}$: the maximum wind velocity, U_{*a} : the friction velocity in the air layer calculated from the log-law, U_{*b} : the friction velocity in the water layer, and Fr $(=U_m/\sqrt{gH})$: Froude number, respectively. As for (B) wind-induced flow, winds of several speeds were blown over a still water on the basis of roughness Reynolds number, as pointed by Nakayama and Nezu (2000b). As for (C) combined wind/stream flow, the stream condition was changed to three patterns, so called, Fr=0.32 (sub-critical flow), 0.80 (near-critical flow) and 1.50 (super-critical flow). The wind condition was changed to three patterns, that is to say, $U_{a,max}$(m/s)=1.49 (smooth region), 4.39 (incompletely rough region) and 8.41 (rough region).

4. Theoretical Considerations

In the present study, we consider the increased area C_A by using the intensity of surface-wave fluctuations η' $(\equiv\sqrt{\overline{\eta^2}})$ instead of Equation (2), as follows:

$$C_A = 1 + A\left(\frac{\eta'}{H}\right)^2 \tag{3}$$

where A is a constant coefficient. Nakayama and Nezu (1999) expressed the following equation (4) by considering the effect of surface wave on the surface renewal frequency r and tle length scale l. From the above mentioned, K_L is expressed by the surface-renewal model in this way.

$$K_L \propto \left(\frac{D_m}{\sigma}\right)^{1/2} \rho_w^{7/8}(gv_w)^{3/8}\left(1+A\left(\frac{\eta'}{H}\right)^2\right)\eta'^{3/4} \propto \left(1+A\left(\frac{\eta'}{H}\right)^2\right)\eta'^{3/4} \tag{4}$$

Therefore, the following relation is obtained:

$$K_L \propto \eta'^{3/4} \ for \ A \ll H^2, \quad K_L \propto \eta'^{11/4} \ for \ A \gg H^2 \tag{5}$$

On the assumption that the wind wave has a small amplitude and that proceeds to the positive streamwise-direction, the surface-wave fluctuations at the different positions in the streamwise direction can be expressed as follows:

$$\eta_1(0,t) = A\cos(-\omega t), \ \eta_2(x,t) = A\cos(kx-\omega t) \tag{6}$$

where $k=2\pi/\lambda$, $\omega=2\pi f$, A : amplitude, λ : wave length, k : wave number, f : frequency, and ω : angular

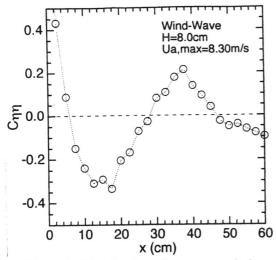

Figure 1. Distribution of cross-correlation coefficient $C_{\eta\eta}$ of surface-wave fluctuations.

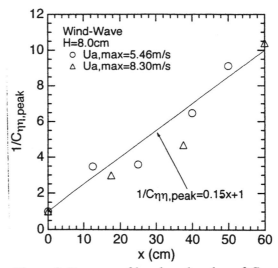

Figure 2. Reverse of local peak value of $C_{\eta\eta}$.

frequency, respectively. The intensities of surface-wave fluctuations at two points can be given in the following.

$$\eta_1'^2=\frac{1}{T}\int_0^T \eta_1(0,t)^2 dt=\frac{A^2}{2}, \quad \eta_2'^2=\frac{1}{T}\int_0^T \eta_2(x,t)^2 dt=\frac{A^2}{2} \quad (T\to\infty) \quad (7)$$

Therefore, the cross-correlation coefficient between the different points can be given as follow:

$$C_{\eta_1\eta_2}(x)=\frac{\int_0^T \eta_1(0,t)\cdot\eta_2(x,t)dt}{T\cdot\eta_1'\cdot\eta_2'}=\cos(kx) \quad (T\to\infty) \quad (8)$$

The above equation means that the cross-correlation coefficient is sine wave in the amplitude of unit if the surface wave can be assumed to sine wave.

5. Comparison between VTR Image and Cross-Correlation Measurement

Firstly, it is necessary to examine whether the distribution of correlation coefficients is almost equal to the real free-surface shape before evaluating the surface area by using the depth meters. Figure 1 shows the distribution of cross-correlation coefficient $C_{\eta\eta}$ of surface-wave fluctuations in 2-D wind waves when one depth meter is fixed at $x=0$ in the center of the channel and the other is moved to the streamwise direction. It can be seen that the peak value decreases as x increases in spite of the quasi-periodical space. Akai et al. (1977) have pointed out that the auto-correlation function versus lag time in 2-D waves takes the same distribution as Figure 1, which shows that "*Taylor's frozen-turbulence hypothesis*" is effective in wind waves. Though the amplitude of $C_{\eta\eta}$ does not decrease in the streamwise direction as expressed in Equation (8) on the assumption that the wind wave can be regarded as a small amplitude wave, the value really does decrease. Therefore, it is necessary to add the damping correction to $C_{\eta\eta}$ in order to evaluate the surface area from the cross-correlation coefficient. Figure 2 shows the reverse of $C_{\eta\eta,peak}$ (local peak value of $C_{\eta\eta}$) versus x. Linear relations can be seen in both two cases, and the approximate line evaluated by the least-square method is also described in this Figure . Figure 3 is the corrected value of $C_{\eta\eta}$ by using the line in Figure 2, together with the approximate curve. The distribution of $C_{\eta\eta,new}$ is quite similar to Equation (8), which means that the damping correction is fairly correct. Figure 4 shows the distribution of $\eta=AC_{\eta\eta,new}$, where A is a significant wave height, together with the surface shape estimated from VTR (phase-averaged value of more than at least 30 samples). The distributions estimated from VTR and calculated by cross-correlation are well coincident with each other for periods and curvatures, which means that this method is very effective.

6. Variations of Water Surface

Figure 5(a) shows the shape of water surface in open-channel flow at $Fr=1.50$. There occur randomly a lot of disturbances in spite of small amplitude. Figure 5(b) shows the shape of water surface in wind waves of $U_{a,max}=8.41$m/s. Though there exist 2-D waves with quite a longer wave-length, there are less disturbances than those in open-channel flow. Figure 5(c) shows the shape of water surface in two-layer flows ($Fr=1.50$

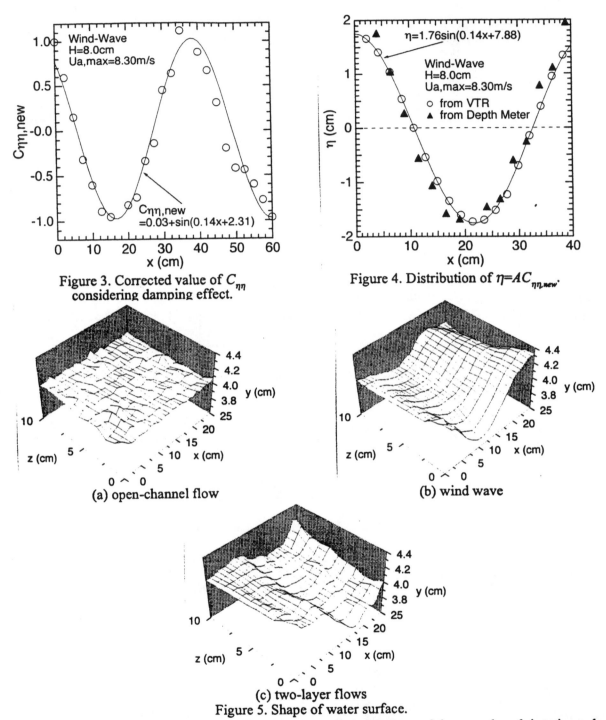

Figure 3. Corrected value of $C_{\eta\eta}$ considering damping effect.

Figure 4. Distribution of $\eta = AC_{\eta\eta,new}$.

(a) open-channel flow

(b) wind wave

(c) two-layer flows

Figure 5. Shape of water surface.

and $U_{a,max}$=8.41m/s). There occurs small disturbances over wind waves and the wave length is twice as long as in wind waves due to the effect of greater convection. Figure 6 shows the increasing rate of surface area $C_A = A/A_0$ in open-channel flow and wind wave. The surface area was calculated by the triangular meshes. It can be seen that the increasing rate is almost zero in both flows because the previous formula in Equation (2) are for the actual river with rough bed. Furthermore, the increasing rate in wind wave is a little greater than that in open-channel flow, which is inconsistent with the experimental data by Nakayama and Nezu (1999) and Equation (5). Therefore, the effect of surface area on the gas transfer can be almost ignored in smooth open-channel flow against previous studies.

7. Evaluation of Another Effects on Gas Transfer

It has been pointed out that the -5 power law in wind waves proposed by Phillips (1958) is mostly effective

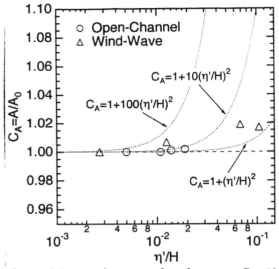

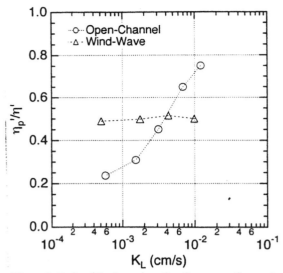

Figure 6. Increasing rate of surface area $C_A = A/A_0$.

Figure 8. Ratio of the intensity of surface-wave fluctuations by the higher frequency component $\eta_p{}'$ to the total intensity η'.

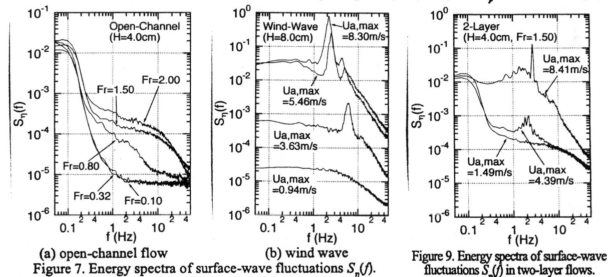

(a) open-channel flow   (b) wind wave

Figure 7. Energy spectra of surface-wave fluctuations $S_\eta(f)$.

Figure 9. Energy spectra of surface-wave fluctuations $S_\eta(f)$ in two-layer flows.

instead of a little modification. By the way, Nezu (1977) pointed out the slope of power law in open-channel flow changes from -5 in sub-critical flow to -3 in super-critical flow as the Froude number increases. Figures 7(a) and (b) show the energy spectra of surface-wave fluctuations $S_\eta(f)$ in open-channel flow and wind waves. For calculating the spectra, the ensemble average was conducted over about 40 samples. In wind waves, the gradient is milder at the higher frequency region by the scatter of supersonic waves due to the larger amplitude of waves. In open-channel flow, the -5 power law is effective in the smaller Froude number, and the energy shifts to the higher frequency region as the Froude number increases. Figure 8 shows the ratio of the intensity of surface-wave fluctuations by the higher frequency component $\eta_p{}'$ to the total intensity η' versus K_L, where $\eta_p{}'$ is defined as follow:

$$\eta_p{}'^2 = \int_{f_p}^{\infty} S_\eta(f)df \qquad (9)$$

where f_p is the transitional frequency from the -5 power law to the -3 power law in open-channel flow, and the upper limit of dominant frequency in wind waves, respectively. It can be seen that $\eta_p{}'/\eta'$ is almost constant in wind waves and that the value gradually approaches one as K_L increases in open-channel flow. This implies that the relation $K_L \sim \eta'^{3/4}$ is effective when S_η takes the -5 power law regardless of open-channel flow or wind waves, and that the gas transfer is more promoted ($K_L \sim \eta'^{1/4}$) in open-channel flow than that in wind wave due to the predominance of the energy of the smaller-scale surface-wave in open-channel flow at the higher Froude number. Figure 9 shows S_η in two-layer flows (Fr=1.50). It can be seen that the effect of wind velocity becomes greater over the hole frequency region as the wind becomes faster. Figure 10 shows the distribution of $\eta_p{}'/\eta'$ in two-layer flows, where f_p is the upper limit of the predominant wave motion. The value $\eta_p{}'/\eta'$ increases as the velocity of water layer becomes faster, which means that the

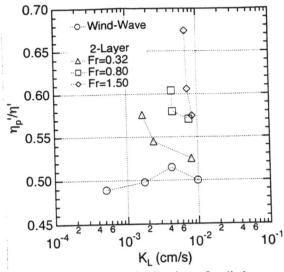

Figure 10. Distribution of η_p'/η' in two-layer flows.

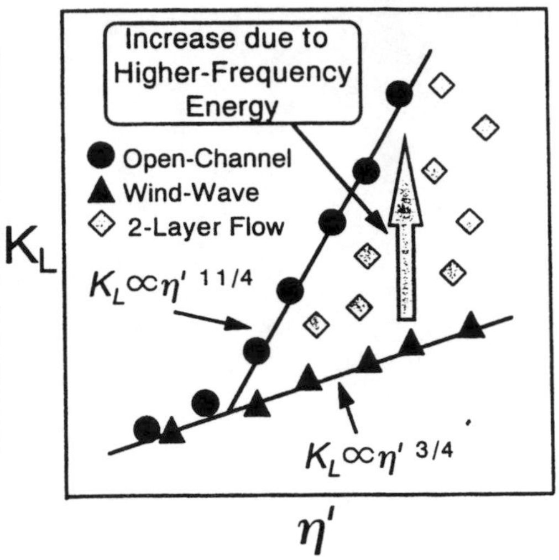

Figure 11. Conceptual model about the relationship between K_L and η'.

energy rate of higher-frequency component increases. The increasing rate is larger as the wind is smaller. In this way, the value η_p'/η' becomes a good measure of the contributions of higher-frequency component in two-layer flows. Figure 11 shows the conceptual model about the relationship between K_L and η'. As for two-layer flows, the values are located between the two lines depending on the rate of higher-frequency energy. This relationship is very effective because it is not necessary to use the relation between friction velocities and K_L in this situation, which does not depend on the shear conditions.

8. Conclusions

In this study, the effect of increase of surface area and other factor on gas transfer was evaluated by conducting the simultaneous measurements of two depth meters. As a result, it was found that the effect of enhanced surface area on the gas transfer can be almost ignored in smooth open-channel flow. The energy of the smaller-scale surface-wave fluctuations contributes greatly to the rapid increase of gas transfer.

9. Acknowledgements

This study was partially supported by Showa Shell Sekiyu Foundation for Promotion of Environmental Research.

10. References

[1] Akai, M., Inoue, A. and Aoki, S. : Structure of a co-current stratified two-phase flow with wavy surface, *Theor. Appl. Mech.*, Vol.25, pp.445-456, 1977.
[2] Danckwerts, P.V. : Significance of liquid-film coefficients in gas absorption, *Indust. and Eng. Chem.*, Vol.43, No.16, pp.1460-1467, 1951.
[3] Dobbins, W.E. : BOD and oxygen relationships in streams, *J. Sanitary Eng.*, ASCE, Vol.90, SA3, pp.53-78,1964.
[4] Hanratty, T.J. and Engen, J.M. : Interaction between a turbulent air stream and a moving surface, *AIChE J.*, Vol.3, No.3, pp.299-304, 1957.
[5] Komori, S., Nagaosa, R. and Murakami, Y. : Turbulence structure and mass transfer across a sheared air-water interface in wind-driven turbulence, *J. Fluid Mech.*, Vol.249, pp.161-183 1993.
[6] Nezu, I. : Turbulent structure in open-channel flows, *Ph.D. Thesis presented to Kyoto University*, 1977 (in Japanese).
[7] Nakayama, T. and Nezu, I. : Relationship between turbulence structures and gas transfer across air-water interface, *Journal of Hydraulic Engineering*, JSCE, No.635/II-49, pp.85-95, 1999 (in Japanese).
[8] Nakayama, T. : Turbulence and coherent structures across air-water interface and relationship with gas transfer, *Ph.D. Thesis presented to Kyoto University*, 2000a.
[9] Nakayama, T. and Nezu, I. : Turbulence structures of wind water waves, *Journal of Hydraulic Engineering*, JSCE, No.642/II-50, 2000b (in Japanese).
[10] Phillips, O.M. : The equilibrium range in the spectrum of wind-generated ocean waves, *J. Fluid Mech.*, Vol.4, pp.426-434, 1958.
[11] Rashidi, M., Hetsroni, G. and Banerjee, S. : Mechanisms of heat and gas transport at gas-liquid interfaces, *Int. J. Heat Mass Transfer.*, Vol.34, No.7, pp.1799-1810, 1991.
[12] Thackston, E.L. and Krenkel, P.A. : Reaeration prediction in natural streams, *J.Sanitary Eng.*, ASCE, Vol.95, SA1, pp.65-93, 1969.

15

JOHN E. SIMPSON SESSION

Flow and Spreading of Three-dimensional Negatively Buoyant Surface Jets Discharged on a Sloping Bottom

Masamitsu Arita[1], Masanori Nakai[1] and Jun Umemoto[1]
[1]Department of Civil and Environmental Engineering, Tokyo Denki University
Hatoyama-machi, Hiki-gun, Saitama, 350-0394, Japan

1. ABSTRACT

The flow and spreading mechanism of three-dimensional negatively buoyant surface jets discharged on a sloping bottom was experimentally investigated by flow visualization and exhaustive thermometry. The flow gradually varies, through its flow-down process, from the jet-like characteristic to the buoyancy-dominating characteristic which has great lateral spreading in surface and bottom layers and intense constriction in a middle layer. In addition, a hypothesis which can explain the special features in the buoyancy-dominating region was presented through physical consideration.

2. INTRODUCTION

Negatively buoyant surface jets discharged on a sloping bottom are often observed in lakes, reservoirs, and seas, for example, inflow of river water with a lot of suspended sand particles into reservoirs, cool water release from power plants to coastal seas. Such flows spread in total depth as far as a certain point and then plunge into a bottom layer due to their negative buoyancy.

A lot of studies on this phenomenon have been performed for the two-dimensional case, as described below. Researchers have paid attention to plunging of the flows into a bottom layer (Fukuoka, Fukushima and Nakamura(1980), Akiyama and Stefan(1984), Arita and Tsukahara(1996) etc.). The behavior of positively buoyant jets on a inclined bottom after plunging have been also examined both theoretically and experimentally by a number of researchers (Turner(1973)). Recently, in addition, numerical analyses and field observations on the buoyant inclined jets have been carried out (Fukushima(1988), Ishikawa, Nagao and Nagashima(1996)). Accordingly, the characteristics of two-dimensional negatively buoyant surface jets released on a sloping bottom have been made clear to some extent.

On the other hand, a few studies have been made for the three-dimensional case (Hauenstein and Dracos(1984), Tsihrintzis and Alavian(1996), Arita et al.(1998, 1999)). Although the authors theoretically and experimentally treated the three-dimensional case and showed an outline of its behavior, they could not clarify the details of the flow mechanism.

In this study, the flow and spreading mechanism of three-dimensional negatively buoyant surface jets released on a sloping bottom was experimentally investigated, confining scope of the study to the upstream side of a plunging point, by flow visualization and exhaustive thermometry.

3. OUTLINE OF THE PHENOMENON

Fig.1 shows an outline of the flow and definition sketches. A three-dimensional negatively buoyant surface jet with the initial densimetric Froude number F_o discharges on a sloping bottom of the slope S and plunges into a bottom layer at distance L_p from an outlet. After that, the flow runs down on the sloping bottom as a three-dimensional positively buoyant inclined jet. Herein, $F_o = U_o / \{(\Delta \rho_o / \rho_o)gH_o\}^{1/2}$, and U_o, $\Delta \rho_o (= \rho_o - \rho_a)$, ρ_o, ρ_a, H_o, and g denote the initial velocity, the initial density difference, the initial density of the jet, the density of ambient water, the initial flow depth, and gravitational acceleration, respectively (see Fig.1). In the following, the jet treated here, 'three-dimensional negatively buoyant surface jet released on a sloping bottom', is simply called 'the negatively buoyant jet'.

We have obtained some knowledge on the negatively buoyant jets (Arita et al. (1998, 1999)). In the upstream side of a plunging point, spreading of the negatively buoyant jet will be jet-like with large F_o and small S, while, it will be buoyancy-dominating with small F_o and large S. In addition, the flow gradually varies, through the flow-down process, from the jet-like characteristic to the buoyancy-dominating characteristic.

4. EXPERIMENT

A water tank which is 6.0 m in length, 2.5 m in width, and 0.6 m in depth was used in this experiment. A channel for jet release was connected to the tank, and an acrylic plate for a sloping bottom was set in the tank. A multi-port pipe for water intake was equipped in the downstream side of the tank to keep a constant water depth.

In the experiment, cool water jets with 5.0 cm in width and 4.0 cm in depth were released

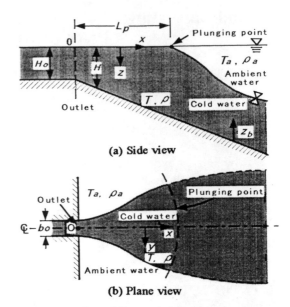

(a) Side view

(b) Plane view

Fig.1 Outline of flow and definition sketches

on the sloping plate from the channel. Cross-sectional spreading of the jets was visualized, using a slit beam, by fluorescent dye with Al flakes and was photographed by a video-camera. In addition, exhaustive thermometry was carried out in some cross-sections using a lot of thermistor-type thermometers to obtain time-averaged temperature distributions for 30 seconds. The initial densimetric Froude number F_o and the bottom slope S were changed for each case : the former was scattered in the range of $2 \leq F_o \leq 13$ and the latter is set to 1/5, 1/10, and 1/40.

5. RESULTS

Figs.2 and 3 show the visualized photographs and their sketches in three cross-sections in Run1(F_o =6.5, S=1/5). Herein, x and H_o express a distance from the outlet and the initial flow depth, respectively. This case was chosen for easy recognition of the lateral spreading phenomenon ; the water depth is relatively large because of the large bottom slop S.

In Figs.2(a) and 3(a) (x/H_o=1.25 : near the outlet), the spreading width is nearly uniform in the depthwise direction. The spreading mechanism is thought to be almost same as that of non-buoyant jets. In Figs.2(b) and 3(b) (x/H_o=5.0), the bottom layer slightly widens and weak constriction emerges in the middle layer, with a downward flow from the middle layer to the bottom layer. In Figs.2(c) and 3(c) (x/H_o=10.0 : near the plunging point), both the spreading in the bottom and surface layers develops, and intense constriction appears in the middle layer.

In Figs.2(c) and 3(c), the great spreading in the bottom layer is caused by the buoyancy effect, as reported by the authors (Arita et al.(1998)). On the other hand, the large spreading in the surface layer was observed for the first time in this experiment. We cannot simply explain this phenomenon from the buoyancy-dominating characteristic. Although it seems to be unreasonable that this spreading is regarded as buoyant spreading, we call it 'buoyant spreading', because it occurs simultaneously with the great spreading in the bottom layer generated by the buoyancy effect. In addition, a pair of longitudinal eddies observed both in the surface and bottom layers produce periodic, horizontal entrainment in the middle layer (see Fig.3(c)).

The above results can be summarized as follows. Figs.2 and 3 (a)-(c) exhibit the jet-like characteristic, the transient state, and the buoyancy-dominating characteristic, respectively.

To quantitatively understand the cross-sectional spreading, exhaustive thermometry was carried out in a lot of cross-sections. Figs.4(a), (b), and (c) depict the distributions of dimensionless temperature

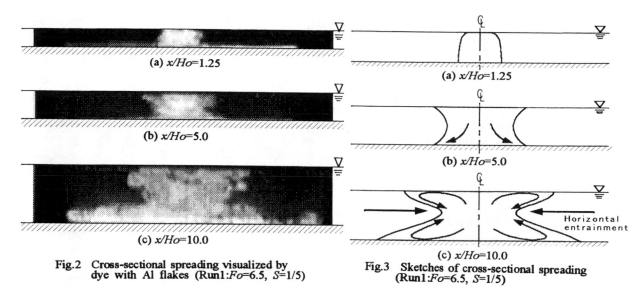

Fig.2 Cross-sectional spreading visualized by
dye with Al flakes (Run1:F_0=6.5, S=1/5)

Fig.3 Sketches of cross-sectional spreading
(Run1:F_0=6.5, S=1/5)

difference $\Delta T/\Delta T_0$ in cross-sections in Run 2, 3, and 4 : F_0 was changed to 12.3, 6.3, and 3.1 and S was fixed to 1/10. Herein, $\Delta T = T_a - T$ and $\Delta T_0 = T_a - T_0$ express temperature difference at any point and that at the outlet respectively, furthermore, T, T_0, and T_a represent temperature at any point, the initial temperature of discharged water, and the temperature of ambient water respectively.

In Fig.4(a) (for large F_0), in the range of $x/H_0 \leqq 10.0$, the negatively buoyant jet gradually spreads with horizontal entrainment of ambient water, and its spreading width is almost uniform in the depthwise direction. The spreading pattern, which is same as that of non-buoyant jets, corresponds to Fig.2(a) and Fig.3(a). At x/H_0=15.0, the bottom layer certainly expands and weak constriction occurs in the middle layer.

In Fig.4(c) (for small F_0), the negatively buoyant jet behaves like a non-buoyant jet at x/H_0=1.5. However, large spreading in the bottom layer and weak constriction in the middle layer appear at x/H_0=2.5, and the former develops and the latter disappears at x/H_0=3.75. The features in both the cross-sections can be explained as follows. The bottom layer spreads by the buoyant force due to density excess, and a downward flow from the middle layer to the bottom layer occurs and produces the weak constriction (at x/H_0=2.5). After that, water masses in the surface layer enter the bottom layer by the downward flow, and then, the weak constriction vanishes (at x/H_0=3.75). At x/H_0=5.0, great spreading in the surface and bottom layers and intense constriction in the middle layer, which correspond to Fig.2(c) and Fig.3(c), are observed. The constriction in this cross-section is physically different from that at x/H_0=2.5, as discussed in the following chapter. The flow characteristics in the above four cross-sections are as follows. x/H_0=1.5 and 5.0 belong to the jet-like characteristic and the buoyancy-dominating characteristic respectively, and x/H_0=2.5 and 3.75 are thought to be in the transient state.

In Fig.4(b) (for medium F_0), the results exhibit intermediate features between Fig.4(a) and Fig.4(c). In particular, the shape of contour-lines at x/H_0=2.5, 'weak constriction in the middle layer', is similar to those in Fig.2(b) and Fig.3(b). Accordingly, this cross-section can be judged to be in the transient state (x/H_0=3.75 also belongs to the transient region).

6. DISCUSSION

In this chapter, we discuss the experimental results and propose a hypothesis on the flow and spreading mechanism of the negatively buoyant jets.

Fig.5 summarizes the spreading process of the negatively buoyant jets. The negatively buoyant jet behaves like a non-buoyant jet near an outlet (cross-section ①) and then changes into the transient state. In the transient region, spreading in a bottom layer develops and a downward flow from middle

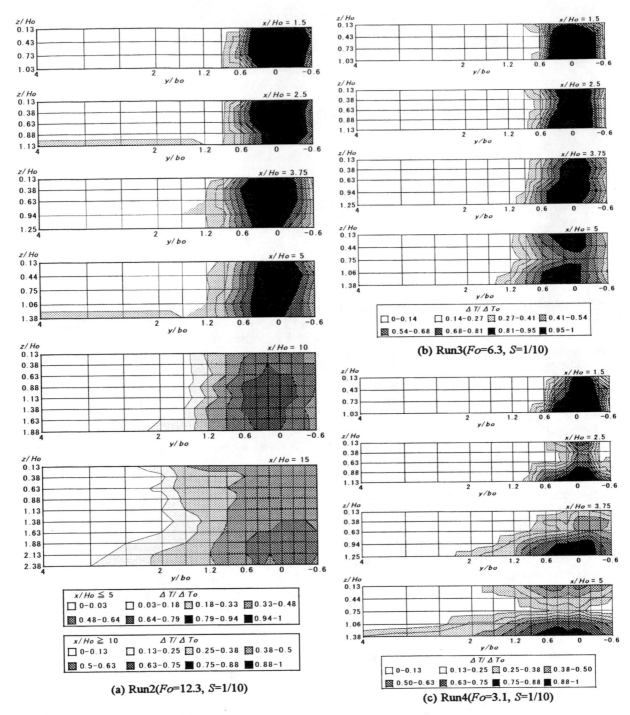

Fig.4 Contour-lines of dimensionless temperature difference $\Delta T/\Delta T_0$ in cross-sections

and surface layers to a bottom layer originates. With the downward flow, weak constriction momentarily emerges in a middle layer (cross-section ②) and vanishes (cross-section ③). In succession, the negatively buoyant jet exhibits the buoyancy-dominating characteristic : spreading in a surface layer also grows up and intense constriction in a middle layer appears (cross-section ④). After that, the negatively buoyant jet reaches a plunging point and then goes toward a bottom layer (cross-section ⑤,⑥).

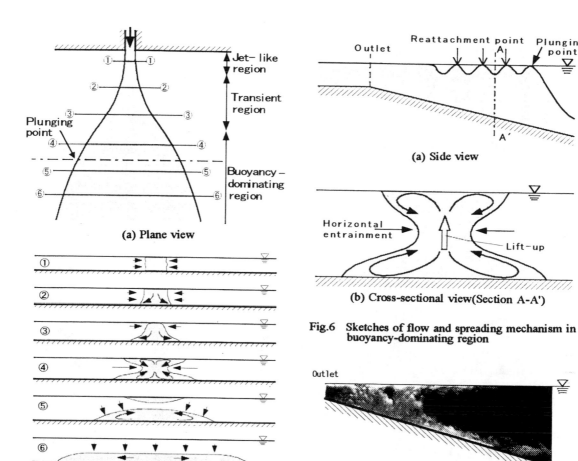

(a) Plane view

(a) Side view

(b) Cross-sectional view

Fig.5 Sketches of streamwise variation of flow spreading

Fig.6 Sketches of flow and spreading mechanism in buoyancy-dominating region

(b) Cross-sectional view(Section A-A')

Fig.7 Pulsating flow (Fo=3.0, S=1/3)

When the negatively buoyant jet enters the buoyancy-dominating region, it largely loses the inertial force and starts to plunge by the negative buoyancy. At the time of slightly plunging, however, entrainment occurs from ambient water to the flow near a water surface, and the pressure in ambient water just over the flow drops due to large entrainment velocity. Then, the negatively buoyant jet rises up and reattaches on a water surface : so-called Coanda effect. Consecutively, the negatively buoyant jet starts to plunge again and repeats the same process. After that, the negatively buoyant jet completely loses the inertial force and then plunges into a bottom layer (see Fig.6(a)). In this study, the wavy flow composed of a series of the plunging and reattachment, which is previously visualized (Soga(1995) : see Fig.7), is called 'pulsating flow'. As a point to notice, in the two-dimensional case, reattachment of a negatively buoyant jet on a water surface does not exist, because ambient water cannot laterally move and entrainment velocity is very small. In this case, accordingly, the pulsating flow is not generated.

Herein, we consider the flow behavior in a cross-section in the pulsating flow region (the buoyancy dominating region). Water masses in a middle layer will be pumped up to a surface layer by reattachment of the negatively buoyant jet and will be widely expanded near a water surface. Horizontal entrainment in a middle layer occurs as compensation of the pumping-up phenomenon, and thus, the cross-sectional flow will be like Fig.6(b). According to the above discussion, we propose a hypothesis on the flow and spreading mechanism for the buoyancy-dominating region ; large spreading in a surface layer is caused by the pumping-up of water masses in a middle layer due to reattachment of the negatively buoyant jet on a water surface.

The pulsating flow plays an important role in the flow and spreading mechanism of the negatively buoyant jets, as described above, and also influences on determination of a plunging point. In the two-dimensional case, once a negatively buoyant jet slightly plunges, it goes toward a bottom layer without reattachment on a water surface. In the three-dimensional case, on the other hand, the negatively buoyant jet forms the pulsating flow composed of the plunging and reattachment. Consequently, the pulsating flow makes it to enlarge the distance between a plunging point and an outlet. In addition, a plunging point fluctuates in the streamwise direction for time in the three-dimensional case, and it can be attributed to the pulsating flow (in the two-dimensional case, fluctuation of a plunging point is hardly observed).

7. CONCLUSION

In this study, the flow and spreading mechanism of three-dimensional negatively buoyant surface jets released on a sloping bottom was experimentally investigated. The concluding remarks obtained are as follows.

1) In the flow-down process, the negatively buoyant jets exhibit the jet-like characteristic near an outlet and then change into the transient state. In the transient region, a bottom layer largely spreads with a downward flow from middle and surface layers to a bottom layer. In succession, the negatively buoyant jets have the buoyancy-dominating characteristic, so spreading in a surface layer also develops and intense constriction appears in a middle layer.

2) The flow and spreading mechanism of the negatively buoyant jets was physically discussed to present a hypothesis on it for the buoyancy-dominating region. In the hypothesis, existence of the pulsating flow and its great contributions to spreading and plunging were pointed out.

8. REFERENCES

Akiyama, J. and Stefan, H.G. (1984) : Plunging flow into a reservoir : Theory, J. Hydr. Engrg., ASCE, Vol.110, No.4, pp.484-499.

Arita, M., Nakai, M., Watanabe, T. and Umemoto, J. (1998) : An experimental study on three-dimensional negatively buoyant surface jets discharged on a slopping bottom, Proc. Hydr. Engrg., JSCE, Vol.42, pp.535-540 (in Japanese).

Arita, M., Nakai, M., Watanabe, T. and Umemoto, J. (1999) : A study on three-dimensional negatively buoyant jets discharged on a sloping bottom, Annual Report Res. Inst. Tech., Tokyo Denki University, No.18, pp.3-12 (in Japanese).

Arita, M. and Tsukahara, C. (1996) : Experimental study on the plunging conditions of the negative surface buoyant jet, J. Japan Soc. Fluid Mech., Vol.15, No.5, pp.409-416 (in Japanese).

Fukuoka, S., Fukushima, Y. and Nakamura, K. (1980) : Study on the plunge depth and interface form of density currents in a two-dimensional reservoir, Proc. JSCE, No.302, pp.55-65 (in Japanese).

Fukushima, Y. (1988) : Analysis of inclined wall plume by turbulence model, J. Hydr. and Sanitary Engrg, JSCE, No.399, pp.65-74 (in Japanese).

Hauenstein, W. and Dracos, T. (1984) : Investigation of plunging density currents generated by inflows in lakes, J. Hydr. Res., Vol.22, No.3, pp.157-179.

Ishikawa, T., Nagao, M. and Nagashima, S. (1996) : Entrainment coefficient of saline plume on the slope of lake Ogawara, Proc. Hydr. Engrg., Vol.40, pp.595-600 (in Japanese).

Soga, A. (1995) : Study on the behavior of gravity flows in reservoirs, Thesis in partial requirements of master of engineering degree at Tokyo Denki University (in Japanese).

Tsihrintzis, V. A. and Alavian, V. (1996) : Spreading of three-dimensional inclined gravity plumes, J. Hydr. Res., Vol.34, No.5, pp.695-710.

Turner, J. S. (1973) : Buoyancy effects in fluids, pp.178-186, Cambridge Univ. Press.

Gravity current propagation in a rotating dissipative system, theory

M. Baldi[1,2], G. Morra[1], and G.A. Dalu[1,2]

1 - Institute for Atmospheric Physics, IFA-CNR, I - 00133 Tor Vergata Rome, Italy
2 - Department of Atmospheric Science, CSU, Fort Collins, CO 80523

mailing address: M. Baldi
IFA-CNR, via del Fosso del Cavaliere 100
I - 00133 Rome, Italy
email: baldi@atmos.ifa.rm.cnr.it

1. Abstract

Weak large scale flows are favorable to mesoscale flows with a distinctive diurnal patterns as sea land breezes, Simpson (1994). We present an analytical evaluation of the sea breeze inland penetration as a stratified density current in a dissipative rotating system. The flow is mainly confined within the CBL, and the dynamics is driven by the buoyancy gradients generated by differential diabatic sensible heat fluxes. As the convective boundary layer, CBL, grows during the day over land, the sea breeze density current deepens and penetrates inland through damped inertia-gravity oscillations.

2. The diabatic forcing and the CBL growth

In the initial value problem, the atmosphere, initially uniformly stratified, is perturbed by the vertical divergence of the diabatic source, $Q(x, z, t)$:

$$Q(x,z,t) = Q_0\, q(t)\, r(x,z) \quad \text{where} \quad q(t)\, r(x,z) = \sin(\omega\, t)\, He(H - z)\, He(x - L) \tag{1}$$

$q(t)$ and $r(x, z)$ are the time behavior and spatial distribution of the diabatic source, respectively. H is the CBL depth and L is the inland density current penetration. $He(x - L)$ is the Heaviside step function equal to 1 when $x < L$ and equal to 0 when $x > L$. During the daytime the CBL, $H(x, t)$, grows monotonically from sunrise to sunset (Green and Dalu, 1980):

$$H(x,t) = \frac{2}{N_0^2} \int_{t_{sunrise}}^{t} Q\, dt' \tag{2}$$

$$H(x,t) = \frac{1}{2} H_0 \left[1 - cos(\omega\, t)\right] He(H - z)\, He(x - L) \Rightarrow$$

$$\Rightarrow \frac{1}{2\, s} \frac{\omega^2}{s^2 + \omega^2} H_0\, He(H - z)\, He(x - L); \quad t < t_{sunset}$$

$$H(x,t) = H_0\, He(H - z)\, He(x - L) \quad \text{with} \quad H_0 = \frac{4\, Q_0}{\omega\, N_0^2}; \quad t > t_{sunset}$$

$$\text{where} \quad \omega = \frac{2\pi}{\text{day}}; \quad \Theta_z = 3\,[\text{K/km}] \quad \text{and} \quad N_0 = \left(g\frac{\Theta_z}{\Theta}\right)^{\frac{1}{2}}; \tag{3}$$

s is the Laplace transformed time t, ω is the Earth rotation speed, Θ is the environment potential temperature, and Θ_z is its vertical gradient, N_0 is the Brunt-Väisälä frequency.

3. The sea breeze as a density current

The flow is driven by the buoyancy horizontal gradient induced by the diabatic source, Eq. (1). The propagation speed of front of the density current is governed by the following set of equations:

$$\left(\frac{\partial}{\partial t}+\lambda\right) u_{front} - f\,v_{front} + \overline{g'}\frac{\partial h_g}{\partial x} = 0 \quad \Rightarrow \quad (s+\lambda)\,u_{front} - f\,v_{front} + \overline{g'}\frac{\partial h_g}{\partial x} = 0 \tag{4}$$

$$\left(\frac{\partial}{\partial t}+\lambda\right) v_{front} + f\,u_{front} = 0 \quad \Rightarrow \quad (s+\lambda)\,v_{front} + f\,u_{front} = 0 \tag{5}$$

$$\frac{\partial h_g(x,t)}{\partial t} + u_{front}\frac{\partial h_g(x,t)}{\partial x} = 0 \quad \Rightarrow \quad (s+\lambda)\,h_g + u_{front}\frac{\partial h_g}{\partial x} = 0 \tag{6}$$

$p = s + \lambda$, and s is the time Laplace transformed; $f = 2\,\omega\sin(\text{latitude})$ is the Coriolis parameter; λ^{-1} is the lifetime of the mesoscale flow a Rayleigh friction coefficient which represents frictional losses. $h_g(x,t)$ is the depth of the density current. g' is the reduced gravity, $\overline{g'}$ is the vertically averaged reduced gravity, and h_g is the density current profile:

$$g' = \frac{H}{h_g}N_0^2\,He(h_g - z)\,(h_g - z); \quad \overline{g'} = \frac{1}{2}N_0^2\,H = N_0'^2\,h_g \tag{7}$$

The density current is driven by the buoyancy horizontal gradient. From Eq.s (4 and 5) the velocities of the front are:

$$u_{front} = -\overline{g'}\frac{\partial h_g}{\partial x}\frac{p}{p^2 + f^2}$$

$$v_{front} = \overline{g'}\frac{\partial h_g}{\partial x}\frac{f}{p^2 + f^2} \tag{8}$$

In the dam breaking problem, the asymptotic in time velocities and aspect ratio are:

$$u_{front} = -\overline{g'}\frac{\partial h_g}{\partial x}\frac{\lambda}{\lambda^2 + f^2} \quad v_{front} = \overline{g'}\frac{\partial h_g}{\partial x}\frac{f}{\lambda^2 + f^2} \quad \text{when} \quad t >> f^{-1} \tag{9}$$

$$A = \overline{\frac{\partial h_g}{\partial x}} \approx \frac{h_{go}}{R_0'} \qquad R_0' = h_{go}\frac{N_0'}{\sqrt{\lambda^2 + f^2}} \tag{10}$$

1106

In Eq. (9), the first term is the drainage velocity, and the second term is the across front velocity which goes into geostrophic balance, when the dissipation λ can be neglected. In Eq. (10), derived from Eq.s (6 and 9), the aspect ratio A of the density current equals the ratio between the depth of the density current h_{g0}, Eq. (28), and the Rossby radius R_0'.

Recalling the definition of convolution product

$$\{f(t) \, * \, g(t)\} = \int_0^t dt \, f(t-t') \, g(t')$$

Eq. (8), Laplace inverse transformed in time, shows that the dynamics of the density current develops through inertia oscillations with a pulsation equal to f and a damping equal to λ:

$$u_{front} = -\left\{\overline{g'} \frac{\partial h_g}{\partial x} \quad * \quad \exp(-\lambda t) \cos(f t)\right\}$$

$$v_{front} = \left\{\overline{g'} \frac{\partial h_g}{\partial x} \quad * \quad \exp(-\lambda t) \sin(f t)\right\} \tag{11}$$

Using Eq. (6) in Eq. (8), the forcing can be expressed in term of the density current depth:

$$u_{front} = \frac{p}{\sqrt{p^2 + f^2}} \left(\overline{g'} h_g\right)^{\frac{1}{2}} \qquad v_{front} = -\frac{f}{\sqrt{p^2 + f^2}} \left(\overline{g'} h_g\right)^{\frac{1}{2}} \tag{12}$$

From Eq. (12), the Froude number is of the order of 1:

$$Fr = \frac{u_{front}^2 + v_{front}^2}{\overline{g'} h_g} = 1 \tag{13}$$

In the dam breaking problem, the asymptotic in time velocities are:

$$u_{front} = \frac{\lambda}{\sqrt{\lambda^2 + f^2}} \left(\overline{g'} h_g\right)^{\frac{1}{2}} \qquad v_{front} = -\frac{f}{\sqrt{\lambda^2 + f^2}} \left(\overline{g'} h_g\right)^{\frac{1}{2}} \quad \text{when} \quad t \gg f^{-1} \tag{14}$$

The drainage velocity is proportional to the dissipation λ, while the across front velocity is proportional to the Coriolis parameter f. In a non rotating system, the propagation speed is proportional to the square root of the reduced gravity by the depth of the density current:

$$u_{front} \left(\overline{g'} h_g\right)^{\frac{1}{2}} \quad \text{when} \quad f = 0 \tag{15}$$

In the sea breeze problem, the density current propagates into a growing CBL between sunrise and sunset (Eq. 5), the velocities are:

$$u_{front} = \frac{p}{\sqrt{p^2 + f^2}} N_0' h_{ss} \frac{1}{2s} \frac{\omega^2}{s^2 + \omega^2} \qquad v_{front} = -\frac{f}{\sqrt{p^2 + f^2}} N_0' h_{ss} \frac{1}{2s} \frac{\omega^2}{s^2 + \omega^2} \tag{16}$$

where h_{ss} is the depth of the sea breeze at sunset, $t = t_{sunset}$. Eq. (16), Laplace inverse transformed in time, shows how the dynamics develops through inertia oscillations of pulsation f combined with the pulsation ω of the CBL:

$$u_{front} = N_0' h_{ss} \left\{ \frac{1}{2}[1 - cos(\omega t)] \quad * \quad exp(-\lambda t) f J_1(f t) \right\} \qquad (17)$$

$$v_{front} = - N_0' h_{ss} \left\{ \frac{1}{2}[1 - cos(\omega t)] \quad * \quad exp(-\lambda t) f J_0(f t) \right\} \qquad (18)$$

$J_0(f t)$ and $J_1(f t)$ are the Bessel functions of order 0 and 1 respectively. The inland sea breeze penetration L is

$$L = \int_0^t u_{front} \, dt' \qquad (19)$$

The dynamics within the density current is governed by the following set of equations:

$$\left(\frac{\partial}{\partial t} + \lambda \right) u - f v + g' \frac{\partial h_g}{\partial x} = 0 \quad \Rightarrow \quad (s + \lambda) \, u - f v + g' \frac{\partial h_g}{\partial x} = 0 \qquad (20)$$

$$\left(\frac{\partial}{\partial t} + \lambda \right) v + f u = 0 \quad \Rightarrow \quad (s + \lambda) \, v + f u = 0 \qquad (21)$$

$$\frac{\partial u}{\partial x} + \frac{\partial w}{\partial z} = 0. \qquad (22)$$

Eq.s (20-22) are solved using Laplace transform theory. As boundary conditions, we assume that the vertical momentum component vanishes at the ground and at the top of the CBL:

$$\text{B.C.s} \qquad w(x, z, t)|_{z=0} = 0 \quad \text{and} \quad w(x, z, t)|_{z=H} = 0 \qquad (23)$$

From Eq.s (20-23), the momentum components (u_g, v_g, w_g) within the gravity current, $z < h_g$, are:

$$u_g = u_{front} \, He(x - L) \, He(h_g - z) \frac{h_g - z}{h_g}$$

$$v_g = v_{front} \, He(x - L) \, He(h_g - z) \frac{h_g - z}{h_g} \qquad (24)$$

$$w_g = - \int_0^z dz \, \frac{\partial u_g}{\partial x}$$

Given the lower and the upper boundary conditions, (23), the return flow, $0 < z < H$, is governed by the following set of equations:

$$u_r = -\frac{1}{H}\int_0^{h_g} dz\, u_g; \qquad v_r = -\frac{1}{H}\int_0^{h_g} dz\, v_g; \qquad w_r = -\int_0^{h_g} dz\, \frac{\partial u_r}{\partial x} \qquad (25)$$

From Eq.s (25), The propagation speed $u_{front_{warm}}$ of the warm front over the sea side is half of the propagation speed of the cold sea breeze front over land.

$$u_{front_{warm}} = u_r(x, z = H, t) = -\frac{1}{2}u_{front} \qquad (26)$$

Finally, below the CBL and within the density current, $0 < z < H$, the momentum components are:

$$u(x,z,t) = u_g + u_r; \qquad v(x,z,t) = v_g + v_r; \qquad w(x,z,t) = w_g + w_r \qquad (27)$$

From Eq. (27), the turning height h_{g0}, height at which the onshore velocity vanishes to become offshore, is:

$$h_{g0} = \frac{3}{8}H \qquad (28)$$

Acknowledgements:

The Authors acknowledge the support of the Italian Space Agency, ASI.

4. References

Dalu G.A. and J.A.S. Green, 1982: Energy theory of propagation of gravity current. Mesoscale Meteorology, Theories and Observations and Models. NATO-ASI Lilly and Gal-Chen Editors, pp 211-216.

Fodor G., 1965: *Laplace Transform in Engineering*. Hungarian Academy of Science, pp 758. Budapest.

Green J.A.S. and G.A. Dalu, 1980: Mesoscale energy generated in the boundary layer. *Quart. J. R. Met. Soc.*, **106**, 721-726.

Pielke, R.A., 1984: *Mesoscale Meteorological Modeling*. Academic Press, New York, N.Y., 612 pp.

Simpson, J.E., 1994: *Sea breeze and local winds*. Cambridge University Press, Great Britain, 234 pp.

Simpson, J.E., 1997: *Density Currents in the Environment and the Laboratory* Cambridge University Press, Great Britain, 244 pp.

Two–layer flow of mixible fluid

V.Yu.Liapidevskii

Lavrentyev Institute of Hydrodynamics, Novosibirsk 630090, Russia
liapid@hydro.nsc.ru

1. Abstract

A mathematical model of two–layer flow taking into account mixing and generation of short waves at the interface is developed. Peculiarities of entrainment processes at the front of basic stratified flows such as mixing layers, turbulent bores and gravity currents are described by this model.

2. Introduction

A problem of mathematical modeling of entrainment processes is of considerable importance in two–layer shallow water theory. Mixing and nonhydrostatic pressure distribution in two-layer flow are responsible for such phenomena as a formation of wave bore and its transition into turbulent one as well as for downstream control of amount of entrained fluid in mixing layers and buoyant jets (Chu and Baddour, 1984; Lawrence, 1993; Wilkinson and Wood, 1971; Wood and Simpson, 1984).

To simulate such flows a mathematical model of two–layer flow of mixible fluid based on the hydrostatic assumption is developed (Liapidevskii, 1994). An intermediate layer where mixing between homogeneous layers takes place is considered in the model as the third one. Three–layer flow is preferable to two-layer scheme of flow since the governing equations consist of conservation laws. Therefore, the well–known contradiction in the shallow water theory of two–layer flows may be overcome and internal hydraulic jumps are uniquely determined. It is shown that the mathematical model which contains no empirical constants represents the main peculiarities of entrainment and downstream control in mixing layers and gravity currents.

Nonhydrostatic terms may be included in the equations in a nontraditional way. The governing system remains hyperbolic and the entrainment process prevents the development of shear instability in the model. The model describes also a formation of soliton–like solutions in two–layer flow and a transition from a "smooth" bore into "turbulent" one when its amplitude increases.

3. Mathematical model

Three-layer shallow water equations in the Boussinesq approximation $[(\rho^- - \rho_0)/\rho_0 \ll 1]$ may be written in the form (Liapidevskii, 1994):

$$(h + 0.5\eta)_t + (hu + 0.5\eta v)_x = 0, \quad u_t + (0.5u^2 + bh + \bar{b}\eta + p/\rho_0)_x = 0,$$

$$w_t + (0.5w^2 + p/\rho_0)_x = 0, \quad (bh + \bar{b}\eta)_t + (bhu + \bar{b}\eta v)_x = 0,$$

$$((H - h - \eta)w + \eta v + hu)_t + ((H - h - \eta)w^2 + \eta v^2 +$$

$$+ hu^2 + Hp/\rho_0 + 0.5\bar{b}\eta^2 + \bar{b}\eta h + 0.5bh^2)_x = 0, \tag{1}$$

$$((H - h - \eta)w^2 + \eta(v^2 + e) + hu^2 + \bar{b}\eta^2 + 2\bar{b}\eta h + bh^2)_t +$$

$$+ ((H - h - \eta)w^3 + \eta v(v^2 + e) + hu^3 + 2p\bar{Q}/\rho_0 + 2\bar{b}\eta hu +$$

$$+ 2\bar{b}(h + \eta)\eta v + 2bh^2u)_x = 0.$$

$$\eta_t + (\eta v)_x = 2\sigma q. \tag{2}$$

Here H is the channel depth, h, η are the depths of the lower layer and the intermediate one, respectively, u, v, w are the mean horizontal velocities in the layers, $b = (\rho^- - \rho_0)g/\rho_0 > 0$ is the given buoyancy of the lower layer, $\bar{b} = (\bar{\rho} - \rho_0)g/\rho_0$ is the buoyancy in the intermediate layer, ρ^-, ρ_0 are the densities of the lower and upper layers, $\bar{\rho}$ is the mean density of the intermediate layer, p is the pressure under the channel lid, $\bar{Q} = hu + \eta v + (H - \eta - h)w = \bar{Q}(t)$ is the total flow rate, q is the velocity of "large eddies" in the intermediate layer. The only empirical coefficient $\sigma \simeq 0.15$ is determined by the analysis of mixing in shear flows of homogeneous and stratified fluids (Ovsyannikov et al. 1985). It is responsible for scaling horizontal and vertical motions and may be eliminated from the system by replacing independent variables.

4. Traveling waves

If a flow is steady in a frame of reference moving with the constant velocity D, the following relations for solutions of (1)–(2) are satisfied

$$h(u - D) + 0.5\eta(v - D) = Q^-, \quad (H - h - \eta)(w - D) + 0.5\eta(v - D) = Q^+,$$

$$bh(u - D) + \bar{b}\eta(v - D) = m,$$

$$0.5(w - D)^2 + p/\rho_0 = J^+, \quad 0.5(u - D)^2 + bh + \bar{b}\eta + p/\rho_0 = J^-,$$

$$h(u - D)^2 + \eta(v - D)^2 + (H - h - \eta)(w - D)^2 + 0.5\bar{b}\eta^2 + \bar{b}h\eta + 0.5bh^2 + p/\rho_0 H = F,$$

$$h(u - D)^3 + \eta(v - D)((v - D)^2 + q^2) + (H - h - \eta)(w - D)^3 + 2p\bar{Q}/\rho_0 + 2\bar{b}\eta h(u - D) +$$

$$+ 2\bar{b}(h + \eta)\eta(v - D) + 2bh^2(u - D) = E. \tag{3}$$

The constants $Q^\pm$, m, $J^\pm$, F, E may be calculated from upstream flow conditions. Relations (3) hold both for continuous and discontinuous solutions. All dependent variables may be expressed from (3) as functions of one variable, say, u. Equation (2) takes the form:

$$d\eta(u)(v(u) - D)/d\xi = 2\sigma q(u). \tag{4}$$

5. Gravity current

Consider the steady–state gravity current (D=0) realized by Simpson and Britter (1978) and by Garcia and Parsons (1994). Figure 1 shows the sketch of the flow. At the head of the flow (dashed curve) there is a smooth interface between the fluids of different density. No mixing occurs in this section, and in shallow water approximation this part of gravity flow is represented by an internal hydraulic jump (0 – 1). In the section (1 – 2) an intense entrainment of fluid from upper and lower layers occurs. The transition (2 – 3) is the hydraulic jump generated by downstream control EF. It is absent for the maximal entrainment flow regime (see below). The fluid with density ρ^- is discharging at the flow rate Q_3 along of the horizontal bottom to compensate the entrained fluid.

To determine the basic flow parameters, we use steady-state solutions of (3). Relations (3) hold both for a continuous solution in the section (1–2) and at the internal hydraulic jumps (0–1) and (2–3). The Froude number of upstream flow $\mathrm{Fr} = w_0/\sqrt{bH}$ and the total head difference $\Delta J = (J^- - J^+)/(bH)$ are assumed to be the basic dimensionless parameters. At the internal hydraulic jumps entrainment can be ignored, which produces additional relations $\eta_1 v_1 = 0$ and $\eta_2 v_2 = \eta_3 v_3$. One can choose the flow rate in the lower layer $Q = -hu = \eta v/2$ as an independent parameter which characterizes the state of the flow in the section (1–2). By virtue of (3), $(b - 2\bar{b})Q = 0$,

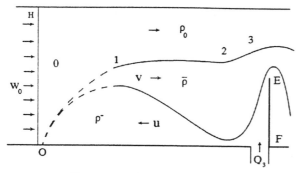

Figure 1: Gravity current.

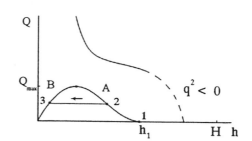

Figure 2: (h, Q)-diagram for gravity current.

and, therefore, for $Q > 0$ we have $\bar{b} = b/2$. For Froude numbers from the interval $0.3 < \mathrm{Fr} < 0.5$ and sufficiently small positive values of the parameter ΔJ $(0 < \Delta J < 0.05)$, the dependence $h = h(Q)$ is depicted in Figure 2.

The dashed curve shows a physically inadmissible branch of solution (3) with $q^2 < 0$. For $Q < Q_{max}$ there are two branches A and B, which merge for $Q = Q_{max}$. The solution is transformed by a hydraulic jump from state 0 to state 1 for $Q_1 = 0$ and $h_1 > 0$, i.e., $u_1 = v_1 = 0$ and $\eta_1 > 0$. The part of the curve B between points 1 and 2 corresponds to the possible states in the section (1–2) of the flow (Fig. 1), where the quantity Q monotonically increases due to entrainment. The thickness of the lower layer h decreases, and the total thickness of the homogeneous and mixed layers $h + \eta$ remains almost constant, which was noted in the experiments. Next, the transition (shown by the arrow) from state 2 to state 3 on the curve A is possible by means of a hydraulic jump for $Q_3 = Q_2$. This transition is the internal hydraulic jump of the second mode, because system (1)-(2) is hyperbolic in state 3, i.e., there are four different roots of the characteristic polynomial, two of them being positive and the other two being negative. For $Q = Q_{max}$ the critical flow corresponds to a regime of maximal entrainment. This regime is realized when the transition (2–3), which is due to additional control at the channel exit, is absent. For given Fr and ΔJ, the parameters at all sections of gravity current can be calculated (Liapidevskii, 1998).

Similarly to (Benjamin, 1968), the theoretical analysis of the gravity-flow structure performed in (Simpson and Britter, 1978) was based on the use of the total conservation laws of mass and momentum and also the Bernoulli integral in the upper layer for direct determination of the (0–3) transition. The presence of the mixing layer is taken into account by the experimentally found "universal" velocity profile in the state (3). The Froude number Fr and the dimensionless flow rate $Q_d = bQ_3/w_0^3$ were chosen as governing parameters.

The quantity Q_d is as a matter of fact the functional of a steady-state flow, and it is impossible to specify it *a priori*. Therefore, the hypothesis of the internal constant Richardson number Ri_L in the interlayer between homogeneous layers, which is based on experimental observations, was also used as the closure relation:

$$\mathrm{Ri}_L = \frac{b\eta_3}{(w_3 - u_3)^2} = 0.35 \pm 0.1. \tag{5}$$

For given Fr and Ri_L all basic flow parameters behind the front of gravity flow including Q_d, can be uniquely defined.

It is shown in (Liapidevskii, 1998) that within the range of experimentally observed values $Q_d = 0.1\text{--}0.3$, the Richardson number Ri_L is close to that postulated in (5). The range of Froude numbers $0.3 < \mathrm{Fr} < 0.5$ corresponds to the experiments (Simpson and Britter, 1978; Garcia and Parsons, 1994). For $\mathrm{Fr} > 0.5$ and positive values of ΔJ, the solutions of (3) – (4) with the above mentioned properties do not exist. Note that the case where $\mathrm{Fr} = 0.5$ and $\Delta J = 0$ is unique, because the transition $(0-1)$ in this case is described by Benjamin's solution ($\eta_1 = 0$ and $h_1 = 0.5H$) (Benjamin, 1968).

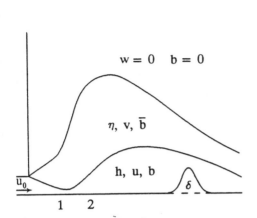

Figure 3: Mixing layer.

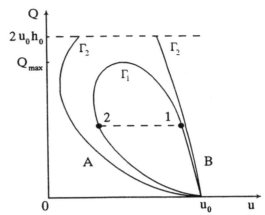

Figure 4: (u, Q)-diagram for mixing layer (A – subcritical flow, B – supercritical flow, Γ_1 is for $\mathrm{Fr} = 2$, Γ_2 is for $\mathrm{Fr} = 3$.)

6. Mixing layer and submerged jet

Further examples of simple turbulent shear flows, namely mixing layer and submerged jet, may be obtained by discharging a dense fluid along of the horizontal bottom in a light fluid ambient in a two-dimensional channel (Fig. 3). Such flows have been investigated theoretically and experimentally in a number of works, for example by Wilkinson and Wood (1971) and Chu and Baddour (1984). System (3) – (4) may be used to describe a stationary mixing layer for $D = 0, \eta_0 = 0$, $\mathrm{Fr} = u_0/\sqrt{bh_0} > 1$. The dependence $Q = \eta v = Q(u)$ from (3) is similar to that shown in Figure 2. It is depicted in Figure 4 for $\mathrm{Fr} < 5$ (the curve Γ_1) and for $\mathrm{Fr} > 5$ (the curve Γ_2). There are two branches A and B corresponding to subcritical and supercritical flows, respectively. If $\mathrm{Fr} > 5$ the mixing layer reaches the bottom and a submerged jet is realized.

If the downstream control is absent ($\delta = 0$), the critical flow with the maximal entrainment $Q_{\max}$ is developed. When increasing the height of the obstacle the transition (1–2) by a hydraulic jump occurs and the total entrainment in supercritical flow decreases. Notice that no additional hypothesis should be used to describe the maximal entrainment regime by (3), (4).

7. Turbulent bore

A turbulent bore may be generated upstream of an obstacle towed along the bottom with the constant velocity D in the thinner lower layer ($h_0 \ll H$, $\eta_0 = 0$, $\mathrm{Fr} = D/\sqrt{bh_0} > 1$) of the two-layer fluid at rest (Fig. 5). In this case the relations (3), (4) are satisfied for solutions of (1), (2) with $w \equiv 0$, $p \equiv 0$.

The relationship $Q = \eta(D - v) = Q(u)$ is shown in Figure 6 for $\mathrm{Fr} = 2$. Along the curve A the energy $e = e(u) < 0$ and this branch is not considered here. Along B we have $\eta \to 0$, $h \to h_0$, $Q \to 0$, $v \to D$, $q \to D$ when $u \to 0$. The part of the curve B where $e(u) > 0$ is shown in Figure 6 by solid line. The wave profile may be found from (4).

Solutions of (3), (4) are shown in Figure 5 for $\mathrm{Fr} = 2$ (dotted line). Solutions of corresponding unsteady problem (1) – (2) are shown in Figure 5 by solid line.

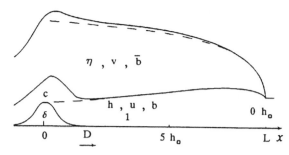

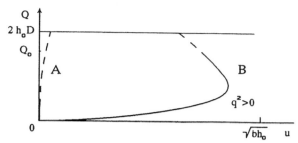

Figure 5: Internal turbulent bore (Fr = 2).

Figure 6: (u, Q)-diagram for turbulent bore (Fr = 2).

For $Fr > Fr_*$ ($Fr_* \simeq 2.1$) the intermediate layer reaches the bottom ($h_1 = 0$, $Q_1 \doteq 2h_0D$) and the transition from the mixing layer to a submerged jet occurs.

The mathematical model (1) – (2), developed initially for stratified fluid, may be applied to a homogeneous fluid (Liapidevski, 1999). For $\rho_0 = 0, \bar{\rho} = \rho^-, b = \bar{b} = g$ it describes the evolution of an upper turbulent layer generated by surface wave breaking. The model has many common features with the model of a turbulent bore developed in (Svendsen and Madsen, 1984).

8. Nonhydrostatic effects

In the models with hydrostatic pressure distribution discussed above, the wave–like structure of small amplitude bores can not be described. To simulate a wave bore structure and its transition into turbulent bore, nonhydrostatic effects should be taken into account. Two–layer shallow water equations for homogeneous fluid (k=1) and for stratified fluid (k=2) may be written in the form:

$$h_t + (hu)_x = -\sigma q, \quad \eta_t + (\eta v)_x = k\sigma q,$$

$$u_t + uu_x + bh_x + \bar{b}\eta_x + p_x^* = 0,$$

$$v_t + vv_x + \bar{b}(h_x + \eta_x) = \frac{\sigma q}{\eta}(u - kv),$$

$$q_t + vq_x = \frac{\sigma}{2\eta}\left(u^2 - 2uv + kv^2 - kq^2 - (k-1)b\eta\right). \tag{6}$$

Here $\rho_0 = 0, \bar{\rho} = \rho^-, b = \bar{b} = g$ for $k = 1$ and $w \equiv 0$, $p \equiv 0$ for $k = 2$ ($h_0 \ll H$).

The instantaneous depth $\zeta(t, x)$ of the lower layer and the vertical velocity $w(t, x)$ at the interface are introduced to find the nonhydrostatic term p^*. The flow is hydrostatic, when the condition $h(t, x) \equiv \zeta(t, x)$ is fulfilled. Suppose that

$$p^* = g(h - \zeta). \tag{7}$$

For the variables ζ, w we have the following equations:

$$\zeta_t + u\zeta_x = w, \quad w_t + uw_x = \frac{2p^*}{h}. \tag{8}$$

System (6) – (8) describes the evolution of the turbulent layer and the nonhydrostatic effects at the front of nonlinear waves. The structure of undular and turbulent bores was investigated in (Liapidevskii, 1999). For $k = 1$ (homogeneous fluid), stationary solutions of (6) – (8) give the following structure of traveling waves depending on the Froude number $Fr = D/\sqrt{gh_0}$ (D is the wave velocity, h_0 is the initial depth of fluid at rest, Fig. 7 and Fig. 8):

a) $1 < Fr < 1.4$. There is a soliton-like wave train structure with a thin upper turbulent layer;

b) $1.4 < Fr < \infty$. Mixing starts at the toe of the wave with a finite rate. The structure of flow at the front is like to that in turbulent mixing model (1) – (2) without dispersion effects ($p^* \equiv 0$).

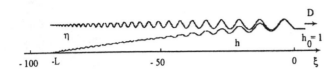

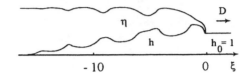

Figure 7: Undular bore in homogeneous fluid (Fr = 1.2).

Figure 8: Turbulent bore in homogeneous fluid (Fr = 2).

9. Conclusions

The three–layer shallow–water equations are applied for simulation of shear flows of stratified and homogeneous fluid governed by mixing and entrainment processes. The front structure of the basic flows such as mixing layers, gravity flows and turbulent bores is considered. The following peculiarities of the flows are explained by the model:

The maximal entrainment flow regime in mixing layers and gravity flows is described without any additional hypothesis about stability of the flow. The layer Richardson number corresponding to equilibrium conditions in the mixing layer and gravity flow is found.

The possibility of downstream control of mixing process in a stationary mixing layer as well as a structure of internal hydraulic jump generated by downstream control and the transition from high rate entrainment process in supercritical flow to short wave generation at the interface in subcritical flow is explained in the frame of the model.

Transition of an undular bore into a turbulent monotone bore when its amplitude increases is described for homogeneous and stratified fluids.

The work was supported by Russian Foundation of Basic Research under grant No. 00-01-00850.

10. References

Benjamin, T. B. (1968) Gravity currents and related phenomena. *J. Fluid Mech.*, **31**, pp. 209–248.

Chu, V.H. & Baddour, R.E. (1984) Turbulent gravity-stratified shear flows. *J. Fluid Mech.*, **138**, pp. 353–378.

Garcia, M. H. & Parsons, J. D. (1994) Mixing at the front of a gravity current. *Proc. 4th Int. Symp. on Stratified Flows*, (Grenoble, June 29 – July 2, 1994), Vol. 3 .

Lawrence, G.A. (1993) The hydraulics of steady two-layer flow over a fixed obstacle. *J.Fluid Mech.*, **254**, pp. 605–634.

Liapidevskii, V.Yu. (1994) Mixing and blocking effects in two-layer flow over an obstacle. *Proc. 4th Int. Symp. on Stratified Flows*, (Grenoble, June 29 – July 2, 1994), Vol. 4 .

Liapidevskii, V.Yu. (1998) Gravity flow structure in a miscible fluid. *J. Appl. Mech. Tech. Phys.*, **39**, pp. 393–398.

Liapidevskii, V.Yu. (1999) Structure of a turbulent bore in a homogeneous liquid. *J. Appl. Mech. Tech. Phys.*, **40**, pp. 238–248.

Ovsyannikov, L.V., Makarenko,N.I. et al. (1985) Nonlinear problems in a theory of surface and internal waves. Nauka (chap.4) (in Russian).

Simpson, J. E. & Britter, R. E. (1978) Experiments on the dynamics of a gravity current head. *J. Fluid Mech.*, **88**, pp. 223–240.

Svendsen, I.A. & Madsen, P.A. (1984) A turbulent bore on a beach. *J.Fluid Mech.*. **148**, pp. 73–96.

Wilkinson, D.L. & Wood, I.R. 1971 A rapidly varied flow phenomenon in a two-layer system. *J. Fluid Mech.*, **47**, pp. 241–256.

Wood I.R., & Simpson J.E. Jumps in layered miscible fluids. *J. Fluid Mech.*, **140**. pp. 329–342.

A Laboratory Study of the Velocity Structure in an Intrusive Gravity Current

Ryan J. Lowe, Paul F. Linden and James W. Rottman

Department of Mechanical and Aerospace Engineering,
University of California, San Diego, La Jolla, California, 92093-0411, USA
rlowe@ucsd.edu, pflinden@mae.ucsd.edu, jrottman@mae.ucsd.edu

1. Abstract

Laboratory experiments were performed in which an intrusive gravity current was observed using shadow-graph and particle tracking methods. The intrusion was generated in a two-layer fluid with a sharp interface by mixing the fluid behind a vertical lock-gate and then suddenly withdrawing the gate from the tank. The purpose of the experiments is to determine the structure of the velocity field inside the intrusion as well as the stability characteristics of the interface. Experiments were conducted over a range of Reynolds numbers between 3200 and 8000, where the Reynolds number is defined in terms of the intrusion front speed and half the total fluid depth in the tank. Soon after the removal of the lock-gate the speed of the front of the intrusive gravity current reached a constant speed. The observed structure of the flow inside the intrusion shows a "head region" where the flow is nearly uniform, followed by a region of intense mixing and high velocities and finally followed by another region of fairly uniform velocity with a speed slightly faster than the front speed. The results show that the maximum centerline velocity is about 50% greater than the front speed and corresponds to the position in the intrusion where the strongest Kelvin-Helmholtz billows form.

2. Introduction

A gravity current is the mainly horizontal motion of a fluid of one density into a fluid of another density driven by buoyancy. An intrusive gravity current is a type of gravity current that flows along the interface between two fluid layers of different densities and has a density intermediate between that of the two layers.

A common method for generating gravity currents in the laboratory is the so-called lock release, in which a volume of fluid (the lock) in a tank contained behind a barrier is suddenly released into a fluid of a different density. Previous observations have shown that a gravity current produced this way initially advances at a constant speed for several lock lengths before its speed starts to decrease (see Keulegan, 1958; Barr, 1967; Huppert & Simpson, 1980; and Rottman & Simpson, 1983). Benjamin (1968) proposed a theory for steadily advancing gravity currents. With the assumptions that the fluid is inviscid, uniform velocity inside a gravity current and no mixing between the fluid in the gravity current and the surrounding fluid, Benjamin derived a relationship between the front speed and the far downstream depth of the gravity current. Furthermore, for the special case of an energy-conserving gravity current he was able to derive an accurate approximate expression for the shape of the current. Using similar methods, Holyer & Huppert (1980) extended Benjamin's analysis to intrusive gravity currents.

In reality, mixing does occur in all observed gravity currents due to the formation of Kelvin-Helmholtz billows on the interface separating the fluids. Mixing results when the billows grow in size and subsequently collapse behind the gravity current "head region", which must invalidate Benjamin's assumption that the velocity is uniform within a gravity current. Simpson & Britter (1979) considered the effect of mixing in an inviscid-boundary gravity current, and showed that the velocity is large behind the steadily advancing front, in order to supply the additional volume flux necessary to balance the losses due to mixing. Using a tank with a moving floor, Simpson & Britter were able to create a stationary gravity current with minor viscous boundary effects and measured the mean vertical velocity profile at a single fixed location far behind the front.

Few experiments have measured the complete two-dimensional velocity profile inside a gravity current. Kneller, Bennett & McCaffrey (1999) measured the velocity structure inside a gravity current advancing over a rigid boundary, using Laser-Doppler anemometry (LDA). With LDA the velocity can be measured at only one point in the flow at a time. Kneller, et al. produced a composite velocity map by measuring the velocity at a different point in each of 35 nearly identical runs. This method averaged over any of the time-dependent features, so a complete instantaneous velocity structure is still desirable. Moreover, viscous boundary effects complicate their measured velocity structure, so it is difficult to isolate the effects of the mixing.

In the experiments described in this paper we obtained detailed measurements of the two-dimensional velocity structure within several Boussinesq intrusive gravity currents using particle tracking velocimetry. Each velocity profile was compared with a corresponding shadowgraph image to relate the velocity structure to the mixing processes. Results show that the velocity varies significantly behind an intrusion front and that the internal velocity structure is governed by the Kelvin-Helmholtz billows. The interface thicknesses were measured to be sufficiently thin so we expect these results to be relevant to gravity currents in general.

3. Experimental Procedure

The experiments were performed in a rectangular Plexiglas tank of 182 cm length, 23 cm width and 30 cm depth. Each intrusion was generated by first filling the tank to a depth of 10 cm with salt water of density ρ_2 (Figure 1). A 10 cm layer of fresh water of density ρ_1 was then carefully added on top of the saline layer using a porous float. The interface thickness between the two layers of fluid was measured from the shadowgraphs and was less than 1 cm in all cases, so that all experiments were performed on intrusions with effectively sharp interfaces. Once filled, a vertical gate was inserted a distance $L_0 = 30$ cm from one end of the tank to form a lock, and the fluid behind the gate was mixed to an intermediate density $\bar{\rho} \approx (\rho_1 + \rho_2)/2$. To initiate the experiment, the gate was smoothly withdrawn vertically, causing the fluid behind the lock to flow along the two-layer interface as an intrusive gravity current.

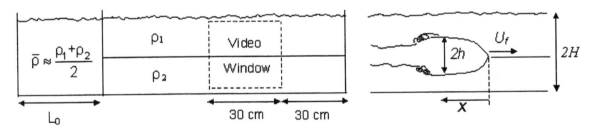

Figure 1: *Left*: The experimental setup before the intrusion is released into a two-layer fluid. *Right*: A sketch of an intrusion front defining the nomenclature used in the text.

The flow characteristics of the intrusions were determined by using either a shadowgraph to visualize the density fields or particle tracking velocimetry (PTV) to quantify the velocity fields. The shadowgraphs were created by covering the face of the tank with a sheet of drafting vellum and positioning a 300 W projector 4 m behind the tank. Each shadowgraph was photographed every 0.25 s using a 35 mm camera. A typical shadowgraph image from these experiments is shown in Figure 2a.

For PTV, the fluid of density $\bar{\rho}$ behind the lock was seeded with approximately 4 g of Pliolite VT, an opaque resin with an average density of 1.022 g cm^{-3}. The particles were sieved to have diameters between 425 and 600 μm and were soaked in a wetting agent to reduce the effect of surface tension. The particles in the center of the tank were illuminated by a 1.5 cm wide sheet of light. The motion of the particles was recorded in a laboratory frame of reference with a CCD camera and recorded onto super-VHS video tapes. The video window was 30 cm wide and located a distance of 30 cm from the end wall, as indicated by the dashed line in Figure 1. A computer system with a frame-grabber card and the image-processing software

Digimage was then used to process the recordings off line. Approximately 500 particles were tracked in the video window and the velocity field was determined at points on a 16 x 32 grid.

When using PTV it was necessary to match the refractive indices of the different fluids in order to minimize the refraction of the projected light due to the mixing of the fluids. To achieve this, a small amount of 2-propanol was added to the fresh water layer to match its refractive index to the dense saline layer. These refractive indices were measured using a digital refractometer. The addition of 2-propanol, which has a density of 0.760 g cm^{-3}, slightly reduced the density of the light fluid layer.

Experiments were conducted at six different values of the reduced gravity, $g' = \frac{1}{2}g(\rho_2 - \rho_1)/\rho_1$, corresponding to a range of Reynolds numbers $Re_H = U_f H/\nu$ between 3200 and 8000, where U_f is the intrusion front speed, H is the half the total fluid depth in the tank and ν is the kinematic viscosity (Table 1). These Reynolds numbers are all well above the value Simpson and Britter (1979) determined for Reynolds number independence. Densities ρ_1 and ρ_2 were chosen such that the fluid of density $\bar{\rho}$ within the intrusion closely matched the 1.022 g cm^{-3} density of the Pliolite, to ensure that the particles were approximately neutrally buoyant. As a result, it was necessary to add some salt to the upper layer to raise its density above that of fresh water.

Table 1: Experimental parameters

Run	ρ_1 (g cm^{-3})	ρ_2 (g cm^{-3})	g' (cm s^{-2})	Fr_H	Re_H
A	1.0164	1.0287	5.936	0.46	3200
B	1.0085	1.0301	10.506	0.45	4400
C	1.0044	1.0363	15.578	0.48	5700
D	1.0029	1.0399	18.096	0.46	6000
E	0.9985	1.0465	23.589	0.47	7000
F	0.9867	1.0544	33.635	0.46	8000

4. Results and Discussion

The front speeds U_f for each intrusion were measured to be constant during the period they passed through the video window. Table 1 lists the Froude numbers defined by $Fr_H = (U_f/g'H)^{1/2}$. These values show no systematic variation with Re_H, and are only slightly lower than the theoretical value $Fr_H = 1/2$ for an energy-conserving Boussinesq intrusion. This discrepancy can be partially attributed to the unavoidable finite thickness of the interface between the light and heavy fluids. Benjamin's theoretical shape for an energy-conserving gravity current (1968, §231, equations (4.32-3)) is plotted as a dashed line on the shadowgraph image in Figure 2a. It provides an accurate representation of the intrusion head, which illustrates the robust nature of Benjamin's energy-conserving front condition. Despite the obvious energy losses behind the head, these experiments confirm that the head of a lock-release gravity current behaves similarly to an energy-conserving gravity current. This agreement implies that the head is largely insensitive to the complicated flow dynamics near the wake.

Figure 3 shows a vector map of the velocity field within the intrusion head for $Re_H \approx 6000$ plotted in a frame of reference moving with the current front. The data has been time-averaged over 1.50 seconds using velocity data sampled every 0.25 seconds. A contour map of the instantaneous streamfunction is also shown to further illustrate the flow pattern. A dominant feature of the flow are the two vortices clearly visible in the upper and lower halves of the intrusion at a distance $x/H \approx 1.6$. A comparison with the corresponding shadowgraph image in Figure 2a reveals that this vortices correspond to the largest Kelvin-Helmholtz billows. These vortices advect fluid away from the centerline which roll up and entrain ambient fluid. When the billows subsequently collapse, the resulting mixed fluid has lost its forward momentum and is left behind in the wake. As a result, the diluted fluid mixture does not penetrate into the intrusion head.

A core of high velocity fluid is apparent behind the largest Kelvin-Helmholtz billows, which is necessary

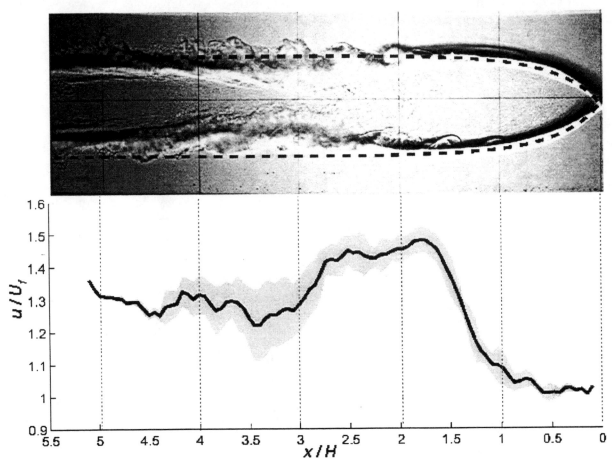

Figure 2: (a) A shadowgraph image of the intrusion in Run D (see Table 1). Benjamin's energy conserving current shape is plotted as a dashed line; (b) the horizontal component of fluid velocity on the intrusion centerline as a function of x. The standard deviation for this measurement is indicated by the shaded region.

to supply the dense fluid lost to the mixing processes. The velocities are much smaller within the intrusion head in front of the Kelvin-Helmholtz billows, and thus more closely match the front speed. This velocity structure explains why Benjamin's energy-conserving model works so well for lock-release gravity currents with large energy dissipation in the wake. In the head region, Benjamin's energy-conserving assumptions are indeed justified because the flow field is close to uniform and the dense fluid driving the motion remains largely undiluted. In this manner the fluid in the gravity current head propagates as a nearly uniform pocket of fluid, largely insensitive to the dissipation in the wake. Both Hallworth, Huppert, Phillips & Marks (1996) and Hacker, Linden & Dalziel (1996) observed using concentration measurements that the dense fluid within the head of a gravity current flowing over a rigid boundary remains largely undiluted throughout the constant velocity phase, but could not provide a physical explanation for this behavior.

The horizontal velocity component u along the intrusion centerline, nondimensionalized with the front speed U_f, is plotted against the distance behind the front x/H in Figure 2b, beneath the shadowgraph image of the corresponding flow with the same horizontal axis scale. From $x/H \approx 0 - 1$ the horizontal velocity component closely matches the front speed and there is little flow relative to the front. After $x/H \approx 1$ the velocity rapidly increases until it attains a maximum velocity approximately 50% greater than the front speed at $x/H \approx 1.75$. Comparison with the shadowgraph image reveals that this maximum velocity occurs slightly behind the location where the strongest Kelvin-Helmholtz billows are located. Beyond this point, the velocity decreases until a near uniform velocity approximately 30% greater than the front speed is attained as the interface restabilizes downstream.

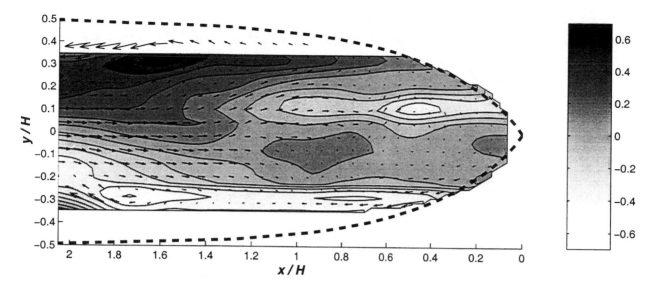

Figure 3: The velocity field inside the intrusion in Run D (see Table 1), as measured using PTV. The dashed lines represent Benjamin's energy-conserving current shape. The arrows represent fluid velocity (the length of the arrow on the left boundary at $y/H = 0$ has a magnitude of 0.46 U_f). The contours are lines of constant streamfunction nondimensionalized by $U_f H$ and plotted at a contour interval of 0.05.

Kneller, Bennett and McCaffrey (1999) also found that the maximum velocity in a gravity current with $Re_H \approx 7200$ flowing over a rigid boundary was 51% greater than the front speed and occurred at a distance $x/H \approx 1.2$ behind the front. The magnitude of this maximum velocity is nearly identical to the measured values in our experiments, which suggests that the viscous effects of a boundary does not significantly alter the internal dynamics of the flow. Due to the no-slip boundary, however, they did find that this maximum velocity occurred at a height $y \approx 0.2h$ above the boundary, where h is the current height, which confirms that the viscous boundary effects are confined to a relatively thin region of the flow.

Simpson & Britter (1979) did not investigate how the velocity varied behind a gravity current front using their stationary gravity current apparatus, but they did calculate an 'overtaking speed' U_o, which they define as the mean velocity of the dense fluid supplying the head. They determined U_o indirectly by measuring the flux Q per unit width of the dense fluid needed to arrest a gravity current front and by assuming that the flow in the wake has both uniform velocity U_o and depth d. This gives $U_o = Q/d$ which they measured to be $U_o/U_f = 0.16 \pm 0.04$ in their experiments. This 'overtaking speed' is often cited as the flow speed within the wake region of a gravity current even though Simpson and Britter comment that it is quite possible for the maximum velocity to be much greater. Our measurements reveal that the velocity varies significantly behind a gravity current front so to define a single 'overtaking' speed does not capture the complexity of the flow structure.

5. Summary and Conclusions

These experiments reveal that the velocity structure within a lock-release intrusive gravity current is dominated by the stability characteristics of the upper and lower interfaces. For each run, the maximum velocity was found to be approximately 50 % greater than the front speed, which occurred near the position in the intrusion where the largest Kelvin-Helmholtz billows form. In this region, the fluid within the intrusion is detrained into the wake, so velocities higher than the front speed are required to balance the mass transport lost through mixing. The diluted fluid mixture in the wake does not to penetrate into the head of the intrusion, which explains why Benjamin's energy-conserving gravity current is robust for gravity currents with obvious energy dissipation in the wake.

These experiments also compare favorably to velocity measurements within a well-documented high Reynolds number sea-breeze front described by Simpson, Mansfield & Milford (1977). They found that the maximum velocity in the sea-breeze was approximately 50 % faster than the front speed and occurred at a distance $x/H \approx 1.5$ behind the front, where in the atmospheric example H is the inversion height. These sea-breeze measurements are similar to the results in our experiments, which suggests that the experiments capture some of the features of these atmospheric flows.

6. References

Barr, D.I.H., 1967. Densimetric exchange flows in rectangular channels. *Houille Blanche*, **22**, 619–631.

Benjamin, T. B., 1968. Gravity currents and related phenomena. *J. Fluid Mech.*, **31**, 209–248.

Britter, R. E. & Simpson, J. E., 1981. A note on the structure of an intrusive gravity current. *J. Fluid Mech.*, **112**, 459–466.

Hacker, J., Linden, P. F. & Dalziel, S. B., 1996. Mixing in lock-release gravity currents. *Dyn. Atmos. Oceans*, **24**, 183–195.

Hallworth, M. A., Huppert, H. E., Phillips, J. C. & Sparks, R. S. J., 1996. Entrainment into two-dimensional and axisymmetric turbulent gravity currents. *J. Fluid. Mech.*, **308**, 289–311.

Huppert, H. E., & Simpson, J. E., 1980 The slumping of gravity currents. *J. Fluid Mech.*, **99**, 785-799.

Keulegan, G. H. 1958. The motion of saline fronts in still water. Natl Bur. Stnd. Rep. 5813.

Kneller, B. C., Bennett, S. J., & McCaffrey, W. D., 1999. Velocity structure, turbulence and fluid stresses in experimental gravity currents. *J. Geophys. Res.*, **104**, 5381–5391.

Rottman, J. W. & Simpson, J. E., 1983. Gravity currents produced by instantaneous releases of a heavy fluid in a rectangular channel. *J. Fluid Mech.*, **135**, 95–110.

Simpson, J. E. & Britter, R. E., 1979. The dynamics of the head of a gravity current advancing over a horizontal surface. *J. Fluid Mech.*, **94**, 477–495.

Simpson, J. E., Mansfield, D. A. & Milford, J. R., 1977. Inland penetration of sea-breeze fronts. *Quart. J. Roy. Met. Soc.*, **103**, 47–76.

Dynamics of fronts of density currents in the presence of background rotation

A. Mahalov[1], J.R. Pacheco[1], S. Voropayev[1], H.J.S. Fernando[1], J.C.R. Hunt[2]

[1]Arizona State University, Department of Mathematics, Tempe, AZ 85287, USA
[2] Department of Space and Climate Physics
University College London, W.C.1, London, UK

1. Abstract

The effects of background rotation with angular velocity $f/2$ are studied for buoyancy driven currents of initial height h_0 whose density exceeds by $\Delta \rho$ the ambient value of ρ_0. Our aim is to find how viscous density currents adjust in time under effects of background rotation focusing on time evolution of fronts of density currents. Rotation reduces the front velocity, $U_F^f = F(ft)U_F^0$, of the density current which is compared to a non-rotating case, U_F^0, by the function $F(ft)$ where $F \to 1$ as $ft \to 0$ and $F \to 0$ as $ft \to \infty$. When the parameter $\mu = ft$ becomes of order one, there is a transition to the geostrophic asymptotic regime. We present numerical results for the transition curve for the density current front radial position for axisymmetric density currents on a rigid surface in a rotating frame. The transition is from a non-rotating power law to a long-time solution. The results of laboratory experiments are found to agree with the results of numerical simulations.

2. Experiment

The experiments on axisymmetric rotating gravity currents were conducted in a Plexiglas tank of dimensions $75 \times 75 \times 25$ cm filled with water. The experimental apparatus is depicted in Figure 1. A pulley system was mounted above the tank to raise a bottomless cylinder (inner radius $R_0 = 5.4$ cm, wall thickness 0.15 cm) containing dense salt water and release this water smoothly into the tank. The tank and pulley system were placed on a rotating table capable of rotating with the angular frequency $\Omega = f/2 = 1.5$ s^{-1}. Mounted above the tank was a super-VHS video camera used to capture the fluid motion. The tank was filled with distilled water (depth 15 cm), and a cylinder was placed on the bottom of the tank with its center coinciding with the center of the tank. A known quantity of salt-water solution with density $\rho > \rho_0$, where ρ_0 is the tank water density, colored with dark blue thymol-blue dye, was placed inside the cylinder. Layers of salt-water solution of initial height $h_0 = 4.3$cm and initial radius $R_0 = 5.4$cm were used in all the laboratory experiments presented in this paper. In experiments with rotating fluid the tank was then rotated (30–40min), allowing the fluid to spin up to a rigid body rotation. With the camera recording, the motor was then switched on raising the cylinder and releasing the dense fluid. The position of gravity front as a function of time was recorded using a video camera and the propagation velocities of the front were determined.

2..1 Non-rotating fluid

After dense water is released from a cylinder, the flow evolved into an axisymmetric gravity current. The front of this current propagates with a relatively large velocity from the origin and typical horizontal size

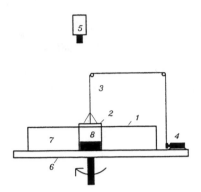

Figure 1: Schematic of the experimental set up. (1) tank, (2) bottomless cylinder, (3) thin·wire, (4) DC motor, (5) video camera, (6) rotating table, (7) distilled water, (8) salt dyed water.

(radius R) of the flow increases with time t, whereas typical vertical size (thickness h) remains approximately uniform along the radius while decreasing with time. The propagation velocity of the current dR/dt strongly depends on the excess of buoyancy Δb in the current and decreases when Δb decreases. Here $\Delta b = g\Delta\rho/\rho_0$, $\Delta\rho = \rho - \rho_0$ and g is the gravitational acceleration. Also at large values of Δb the Reynolds number, Re $= (2RdR/dt)/\nu$, is very large (Re $= 30000$–80000, ν is the kinematic viscosity of water), but only the fluid inside the current is turbulent, because of the stable buoyancy force at the upper surface of the gravity current. Visual observations showed that, except at the front in the initial stages when $ft \ll 1$, there is no significant mixing with the surrounding fluid. The flow remains stable with numerous small-scale vortices at the front. The typical horizontal size l of these vortices increases when the horizontal size R of the current increases in such a way that $l \propto R$. Neglecting mixing of the current with the surrounding fluid, the front propagation velocity in a non-rotating fluid may be scaled (this scaling follows from the balance of the horizontal pressure gradient and inertia term) as

$$dR/dt = U_F^0 = C_1(2h\Delta b)^{1/2}, \tag{1}$$

where constant C_1 is of order unity (it takes into account specific geometry of the current and bottom friction). The conservation of mass gives

$$h_0 R_0^2 = h R^2. \tag{2}$$

From (1), (2) one immediately derives the estimate

$$(R^2 - R_0^2)/R_0^2 = \frac{2C_1 t(2\Delta b h_0)^{1/2}}{R_0}. \tag{3}$$

The measured values of R for different times t in six experiments with different values of Δb were plotted in non-dimensional form and scaled, from which an estimate of $C_1 = 0.6$ was found.

2..2 Rotating fluid

After dense water is released, the initial flow pattern in a rotating fluid is approximately the same as in a non-rotating case. The flow is stable and the current has an almost axisymmetric discoid shape. With time, however, the flow behavior changes significantly, compared to a non-rotating case. The main difference is that, after a relatively short time interval, the radial propagation velocity of the front rapidly decreases and

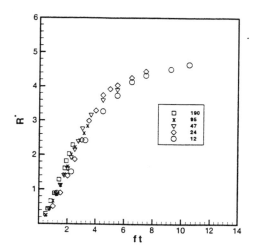

Figure 2: Time evolution of the function R^* given by Eq. (5) for an axisymmetric gravity current in a rotating fluid ($\Omega = f/2 = 1.5$ s^{-1}) after the release of dense fluid obtained in laboratory experiments. Different symbols are the data for different values of Δb which are given in units of cm/s^2 in a legend. The data are plotted in the non-dimensional coordinates: $R^* = \dfrac{f(R^2 - R_0^2)}{2C_1 R_0 (2\Delta b h_0)^{1/2}}$ and ft.

after that the horizontal size R of the current changes insignificantly. Besides this, noticeable (anti-cyclonic) azimuthal velocity arises in the flow. The results of measurements demonstrate that at moderate and small values of Δb the front velocity dR/dt rapidly drops to a small value and the flow reaches an intermediate regime. The critical size of the current at which the transition between the initial and intermediate regimes occurs depends on the value of Δb and increases when Δb increases. Neglecting again the mixing of current with the surrounding fluid, the front propagation velocity U_F^f in a rotating fluid may be scaled as

$$dR/dt = U_F^f = U_F^0 F(ft),\tag{4}$$

where U_F^0 is the front velocity in a non-rotating fluid given by (1) and $F(ft)$ is a function of ft. From (4), (2) we obtain

$$R^* = \frac{f(R^2 - R_0^2)}{2C_1 R_0 (2\Delta b h_0)^{1/2}} = \int_0^{ft} F(x)dx = \Phi(ft).\tag{5}$$

The results of measurements for five experiments with different values of Δb are given in the non-dimensional form in Figure 2. The experimental data was plotted in Figure 2 in accordance with (5). Note that since F is finite for all times, Φ continues to grow, but vary much more slowly after $t \approx f^{-1}$.

3. Numerical analysis and the front condition

In this section we present numerical simulations of axisymmetric gravity currents in a rotating frame. The numerical results are compared with the experimental data presented in Section 2. (see Figure 2).

In the present numerical study, the problem is analyzed using the shallow-water approximation. In this context, the shallow-water theory has often been used to study the evolution of gravity currents. Using the shallow-water approximation, Rottman and Simpson (1983) obtained results in channels of rectangular cross-section. Non-rotating axisymmetric gravity currents have also been investigated in Bonnecaze *et al.* (1995). The corresponding flow in a rotating system was studied in Ungarish and Huppert (1998).

If we define the following depth-averaged quantities

$$U = \frac{1}{h} \int_{z_b}^{h+z_b} u \, dz, \; V = \frac{1}{h} \int_{z_b}^{h+z_b} v \, dz \tag{6}$$

the two-dimensional depth-averaged equations of motion can be written as:

$$\frac{\partial h}{\partial t} + \nabla \cdot h\mathbf{U} = 0 \tag{7}$$

$$\frac{\partial h\mathbf{U}}{\partial t} + \mathbf{U} \cdot \nabla h\mathbf{U} = -f\mathbf{e_z} \wedge h\mathbf{U} - \Delta bh\nabla(h + z_b) - \nabla h\mathbf{T} - \mathbf{T_b} \tag{8}$$

Here h is the water depth, $\mathbf{U} = (U, V)$ represents the Cartesian depth-averaged velocity components in the x and y directions, z is the vertical direction, z_b is the bottom elevation ($z_b = 0$ in our case), $f = 2\Omega$ is the Coriolis parameter, t is the time, $\Delta b = g\Delta\rho/\rho_0$ is the reduced gravity acceleration; $\mathbf{T_b} = (\tau_{bx}, \tau_{by})$ are the bottom shear stress components and $\mathbf{T} = (T_{xx}, T_{xy}, T_{yy})$ are the depth-averaged effective stress components. In our formulation, the effective stress components are neglected and the shear stresses on the bottom surface are approximated by using the Chezy formulas $\tau_{bx} = \frac{\Delta b}{C^2}U(U^2 + V^2)^{1/2}$ and $\tau_{by} = \frac{\Delta b}{C^2}V(U^2 + V^2)^{1/2}$, where C is the Chezy constant (Vreugdenhill 1993). A new flux-splitting technique was used to numerically solve the governing equations (Pacheco 1999; Pacheco and Pacheco-Vega 2000).

The effect of background rotation generates a remarkable difference in the behavior of gravity current fronts. In the non-rotating case, the front travels radially outwards at constant velocity. This velocity of the front (front condition) given by Eq. (1), has previously been studied both theoretically and experimentally. On the other hand, the velocity of the density-current front in the presence of background rotation is hindered by the Coriolis effect. In the hydrostatic analysis performed by Ungarish and Huppert (1998), it is assumed for simplicity that the speed of the inner's front in relation to the height was unaffected by rotation, although this is not valid when a front becomes a geostrophic front. Our approach to the simulation of density current fronts differs from Bonnecaze *et al.* (1995) and Ungarish and Huppert (1998) in two ways. First we set the computational domain to a size large enough to contain the gravity current (the computational domain size is larger than the Rossby radius of deformation and initial condition length-scale is smaller than the Rossby radius of deformation). In this way, the density-current front never reaches the computational boundary. Second, we impose a small height (δh) extending from the location of the front to the edge of the computational boundary. Setting the computational film height in the numerical simulations is equivalent to wetting the surface in the experiment. Then, the total height h never becomes zero and imposing a condition for the velocity is not required. Typically, the computational film height was set to 0.1% of the maximum density-current height at every time step. One of the main advantages of our formulation is the capability to track the position of the front directly from the numerical simulation without imposing a front condition.

Numerical simulations are carried out with initial conditions matching the experimental parameters presented in Section 2.. The parameters chosen for the run are $\Delta b = 24$ cm/s^2, $h_0 = 4.3$ cm, $R_0 = 5.4$ cm. We have chosen a circular grid layout to minimize any numerical perturbations introduced by the orientation of the grid. The speeds of propagation obtained in our simulations are scaled following the balance of horizontal pressure gradient and inertial terms through a constant C_1 described in Section 2.. The value of the constant coming out from the numerical computation was found to be $C_1 = 2.8$.

The effects of background rotation on the flow are presented in Figure 3, where the velocity field is plotted as a function of time for $f = 3$ s^{-1}, and $\Delta b = 24$ cm/s^2. The background rotation is clockwise causing

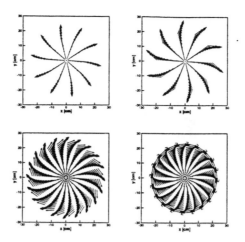

Figure 3: Velocity vector plots of the axisymmetric density–driven current at different times after the release of the dense fluid. The numerical conditions are: $f = 3$ s^{-1}, $\Delta b = 24$ cm/s^2 and the background rotation is counter clockwise.

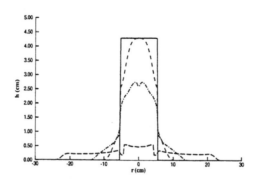

Figure 4: Cross–section view of the axisymmetric density–driven current at different times after the release of the dense fluid. Numerical conditions: $f = 3$ s^{-1}, $\Delta b = 24$ cm/s^2. Horizontal axis – radius; vertical axis – height

the flow to rotate in counter clockwise direction satisfying the conservation of angular momentum. The results of experiments (described in Section 2.) confirm this behavior. Figure 4 depicts the height of the rotating density current as a function of time for the same parameters. The position of the density current front at different times for both numerical and experimental runs is plotted in non–dimensional variables R^* vs. ft in Figure 5. The variance of the experimental data can be attributed to the uncertainty associated with the measurements of the position of the front, mixing, etc. The numerical results obtained with the shallow-water equations match the experimental data.

After an initial transient phase, the effect of rotation, for experiments and numerical simulations, is seen to slow the outward propagation of the gravity current as compared to the non-rotating case. Initially, the behavior is similar to the non-rotating case. However, after a transient time, the effect of rotation modifies the gravity current and tends to slow its radial propagation. The experimental and numerical results shown in Figure 5 are presented for different buoyancy values. The curves are extended sufficiently long in time to demonstrate the cross-over to slower spreading in agreement with the theory (Mahalov and Marcus 1995; Babin, Mahalov, and Nicolaenko 1998; Babin, Mahalov, and Nicolaenko 1997).

It is here that we grateful acknowledge the comments of Dr. K.–L. Tse which improved the quality of the manuscript. This research was supported by the AFOSR Grant No. F49620-93-1-0172, the NSF Environ-

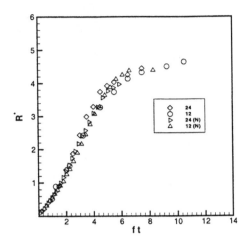

Figure 5: Comparison with laboratory experiments for the non–dimensional function R^* as a function of the non–dimensional time ft of the axisymmetric density–driven current for different values of Δb [cm/s^2]. The legend (N) indicates numerical results.

mental Geochemistry and Biochemistry Initiative Grant No. 97-08452 and the Office of Vice President for Research.

4. References

Babin, A., A. Mahalov, and B. Nicolaenko (1997). Global Regularity and integrability of 3D Euler and Navier-Stokes Equations for Uniformly Rotating Fluids. *Asympt. Anal. 15*(2), 103–150.

Babin, A., A. Mahalov, and B. Nicolaenko (1998). On Nonlinear Baroclinic Waves and Adjustment of Pancake Dynamics. *Theor. and Comp. Fluid Dyn. 11*(3/4), 215–235.

Bonnecaze, R. T., M. A. Hallworth, H. E. Huppert, and J. R. Lister (1995). Axi–symmetric particle–driven gravity currents. *J. Fluid Mech. 294*, 93–121.

Mahalov, A. and P. Marcus (1995). Long Time Averaged Rotating Shallow Water Equations. W. Hui, Y.-K. Kwok, and J. Chasnov (Eds.), *Proc. of the First Asian Computational Fluid Dynamics Conference*, Volume 3, pp. 1227–1230.

Pacheco, J. R. (1999). *On the numerical solution of film and jet flows.* Ph. D. thesis, Dept. Mechanical and Aerospace Engineering, Arizona State University, Tempe, AZ.

Pacheco, J. R. and A. Pacheco-Vega (2000). Flux difference splitting for thin film flows, Submitted. *J. Fluids Engrg.*.

Rottman, J. W. and J. E. Simpson (1983). Gravity currents produced by instantaneous releases of a heavy fluid in a rectangular channel. *J. Fluid Mech. 135*, 95–110.

Ungarish, M. and H. Huppert (1998). The effects of rotation on axisymmetric gravity currents. *J. Fluid Mech. 362*, 17–51.

Vreugdenhill, C. B. (1993). *Numerical Methods for Shallow-Water Flows.* Dordrecht, Netherlands: Kluwer Academic Publishers.

Internal wave excitation by interfacial gravity currents

A. P. Mehta[1] and B. R. Sutherland[2]

[1] Dept. of Mechanical and Aerospace Engineering, University of California, San Diego, La Jolla, California, 92093
[2] Dept. of Mathematical Sciences, University of Alberta, Edmonton, Alberta, T6G 2G1, Canada
apmehta@mae.ucsd.edu, Bruce.Sutherland@ualberta.ca

1   Introduction

The dynamics of intrusions along the interface of a two-layer fluid have been examined in a variety of experiments in the past. In particular, Maxworthy (1980) and Britter and Simpson (1981) investigated the behaviour of solitary waves excited by an intrusion in a two-layer fluid with a thin and thick (diffused) interface. The dynamics of the intrusion and excited waves was found to depend upon the structure of the density profile.

As a step toward understanding the dynamics of a gravity current in more complex stratified systems, we examine the dynamics of intrusions and waves in a three-layer fluid. A three-layer fluid introduces dynamics not present in a two-layer fluid because of the more complex dispersion relation of internal waves. A two-layer fluid has been found to develop naturally into a three-layer fluid through interfacial mixing by the passage of successive intrusions (Sutherland 2000).

In a series of lock-release experiments, we examine the behaviour of the flow within a symmetric three-layer salt-stratified fluid, in which the density of the middle layer is the average of the outer two layers. At a certain depth of the middle layer, an intrusive gravity current is found to excite an internal 'double-humped' solitary wave in front of the intrusion head, and the current itself stops propagating. Trailing the intrusion are large-amplitude trapped internal waves. The characteristics of these waves are examined as a function of the middle-layer depth and density difference between the three layers (Mehta and Sutherland 2000).

2   Experiments

The experiments are performed in a glass tank measuring $197\,\mathrm{cm}$ long, $17.5\,\mathrm{cm}$ wide and $48.5\,\mathrm{cm}$ tall. In setting up a three-layer experiment with a middle-layer depth of d and total depth $H = 18\,\mathrm{cm}$, the bottom layer is filled with salt water of density ρ_1 to a depth $(H - d)/2$. A weaker salt water solution of density $\rho_m = \frac{1}{2}(\rho_0 + \rho_1)$ is layered on top through a sponge float until the depth of this layer is d. Finally, fresh water is layered on top until the total depth of stratified fluid in the tank is H.

A water-tight gate is inserted $10\,\mathrm{cm}$ from one end of the tank through a thin vertical guide. The fluid behind the gate is dyed and thoroughly mixed to create a homogeneous fluid with density approximately equal to ρ_m. When the lock fluid is almost stationary the gate is rapidly extracted. The lock fluid then collapses to form an intrusion along the interface at mid-depth.

Only one intrusion is generated for each of the experiments with $d = 3$ and $4\,\mathrm{cm}$ because a solitary wave is observed on the first run. In some experiments with $d = 2\,\mathrm{cm}$, intrusions are successively released throughout a number of runs, as described by Sutherland (2000). The mixing caused by the intrusions acts to widen the middle-layer. To analyse the characteristics of the intrusions and interfacial waves, the experiments are recorded on a digital video camera focusing on a $20\,\mathrm{cm}$ wide window of the tank extending between $80\,\mathrm{cm}$ and $100\,\mathrm{cm}$ from the lock-end of the tank. The DigImage software package (Dalziel 1993) is used to take velocity, wavelength, amplitude, and other measurements determined from digitized time-series images.

3 Theory

The intrusion is found to be approximately spanwise-uniform across the width of the tank, and therefore the significant dynamics can be described by theory for two-dimensional flow. We examine the predictions of simple two- and three-layer models in order to develop insight into the dynamics of trapped internal waves, gravity currents and solitary waves in a three-layer fluid.

The steady-state speed of a bottom-propagating dissipative gravity current, of density ρ_m, intruding into a finite-depth fluid of density ρ_0 was predicted theoretically by Benjamin (1968). Symmetry arguments are used to extend this theory to predict the speed, $u_{(gc)}$, of an intrusive gravity current along the interface of a two-layer fluid:

$$\frac{u_{(gc)}^2}{g\sigma\Delta d} = \frac{1}{4}\frac{(H-\Delta d)(2H-\Delta d)}{H(H+\Delta d)}. \tag{1}$$

where Δd is the total depth of the tail of the gravity current sufficiently far behind the head, H is the total fluid depth (the upper and lower layers each have depth $H/2$) and $\sigma \equiv (\rho_1 - \rho_0)/\rho_m$ is the relative density difference. The speed, C_{gc}, of an intrusive gravity current in an infinitely deep fluid is given by (1) in the limit $H \to \infty$:

$$C_{gc} = \sqrt{g\sigma\Delta d/2}. \tag{2}$$

For ease of interpreting the discussion below, a schematic of an intrusive gravity current in a three-layer fluid is shown in Figure 1. By extending the results of Klemp $et\ al.$ (1997), the speed of an intrusive bore in a three-layer fluid is found to be

$$\frac{u_{(br)}^2}{g\sigma(d+\Delta d)} = \frac{1}{4}\frac{(2H-2d-\Delta d)(H-d-\Delta d)(d+\Delta d)}{H[H(2d+\Delta d)-(d+\Delta d)(2d-\Delta d)]}. \tag{3}$$

In the limit of an infinitely deep fluid ($H \to \infty$) (3) becomes

$$C_{br} = \sqrt{\frac{g\sigma}{2}\frac{(d+\Delta d)^2}{2d+\Delta d}}. \tag{4}$$

Interfacial internal waves are found to trail the intrusion if the middle layer is sufficiently wide. The wave characteristics are compared with those derived analytically for a three-layer fluid system of total depth H and middle layer depth d. Analytic solutions are found if the ambient density profile is assumed to be stepwise-continuous and the system is assumed to be spanwise uniform and of infinite horizontal and vertical extent. If the displacement from equilibrium of the upper and lower interfaces is assumed to be small compared with the wavelength of the disturbances, linear theory can be applied, allowing normal mode solutions for the displacements. For inviscid, irrotational, incompressible, non-diffusive flow, the motion in each layer can be described by velocity potentials for the upper, middle and lower layers. The boundary conditions require continuity and zero stress across the interfaces and vanishing vertical velocities at the upper and lower boundaries of the domain. In the simple case of an infinitely large domain, the eigenvalue problem yields the dispersion relation, given implicitly by

$$(\omega^2)^2\left[1 - \frac{\sigma^2(1-\gamma)}{16}\right] - (\omega^2)\left[\frac{1}{2}g\sigma k\right] + \left[\frac{1-\gamma}{16}(g\sigma k)^2\right] = 0. \tag{5}$$

where $\gamma = \exp(-2kd)$. The two roots of the quadratic equation for ω^2 correspond to the dispersion relations for the even and odd modes. In experiments, the wave-train behind the head of the gravity current is observed to have the structure of even modes with moderately small wavenumbers.

For fixed k, the frequency of the even mode is larger than that of the odd mode. In the limit $d \to 0$, the dispersion relation of the even mode is the same as that for internal waves in a two-layer fluid. In particular

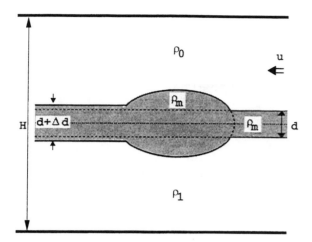

Figure 1: Schematic of an intrusive gravity current in a three-layer fluid. The density of the intrusion is the same as the density of the middle layer.

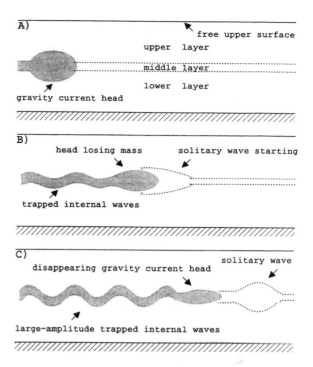

Figure 2: Schematic showing the excitation of internal waves and solitary waves during the collapse of an interfacial gravity current.

the phase speed of the even and odd modes are $C_e = \sqrt{g\sigma/2k}$ and $C_o = \sqrt{g\sigma d/2}$ respectively. The phase speed of the odd mode is typically much smaller than that of the even mode if the depth d of the middle layer is relatively small compared with the total fluid depth H.

For $kd > 0.4$ the phase speed relation between the infinite-depth and finite-depth fluids is approximately the same. Finite depth effects are most pronounced for the even modes with $kd \ll 0.4$: in a finite-depth fluid the phase speed approaches a constant value (dependent upon H) as the wavenumber becomes small, whereas the phase speed is unbounded in an infinitely deep fluid.

A large amplitude disturbance on relatively shallow water may develop to form a coherent structure in the form of a solitary wave. An internal solitary wave in a two-layer fluid is an elevated hump if the depth of the upper layer is greater than the depth of the lower layer. It is a wave of depression if the depth of the upper fluid is less than that of the lower fluid. Extending these concepts to a symmetric three-layer fluid, a solitary wave develops in the form of a double-humped wave propagating along the middle layer. The experiments show that the two disturbances are phase-locked propagating as a single disturbance with the symmetry of odd (varicose) internal wave modes. A representation of the solitary wave dynamics is given by adapting the large-amplitude solitary wave theory that combines results of Korteweg and deVries (KdV) and "modified KdV" theory (Miles 1981; Funakoshi 1985; Funakoshi and Oikawa 1986). With rigid upper and lower boundary conditions and for a Boussinesq fluid, the large-amplitude KdV theory predicts the speed of a large-amplitude internal solitary wave (Michallet and Barthélemy 1997). The symmetry of the double-humped solitary waves is exploited to derive a simple extension of this theory to a three-layer system. Explicitly

$$u_{(\text{sw})} = \sqrt{\left(\frac{g\sigma H}{16}\right)} \left[1 - 8\frac{(A_{sw} + H/4 - d/2)^2}{H^2}\right]. \tag{6}$$

where A_{sw} is the amplitude of the solitary wave. In the limit $H \to \infty$, the solitary wave speed is

$$C_{(\text{sw})} = C_o \left[1 + \frac{a}{d}\right]. \tag{7}$$

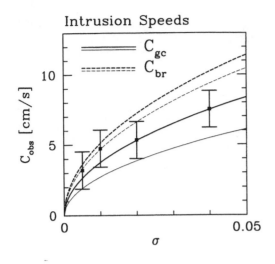

Figure 3: Observed speed of intrusion compared with theoretical predictions given by a 3-layer gravity current theory (solid line) and a 3-layer theory for bore propagation speeds (dashed line). In each case the middle layer thickness is $d = 2\,\mathrm{cm}$. The increase in width of the middle layer is estimated using $\Delta d = 0.8\,\mathrm{cm}$ (thick lines) and $\Delta d = 0.4\,\mathrm{cm}$ (thin lines).

4   Analysis of Experiments

In the case of a two-layer fluid, the trapped internal waves behind the gravity current are of small amplitude and persist for one or two wavelengths. However, in a three-layer fluid, trailing the gravity current are large-amplitude internal waves. If the middle layer is sufficiently thick a double-humped solitary wave is excited in the interfacial layer propagating in front of the gravity current head. Upon the creation of the solitary wave, the gravity current stops propagating. The schematic in Figure 2 illustrates this transition.

The intrusive gravity current speed is found to be a strong function of the relative density difference, σ, and a weak function of the middle layer thickness, d. The observed intrusion speed is compared with theory in Figure 3. In the absence of mixing, one would expect the width of the middle layer to increase by $\Delta d \simeq H\ell/L \sim 0.8\,\mathrm{cm}$, where ℓ is the lock-length and L is the length of the tank. With these estimates, the prediction given by (1) moderately under-predicts the speed of the current in weakly stratified experiments. The prediction is quite good in more strongly stratified cases for which $\sigma > 0.02$. The theoretical speed of an internal bore, given by (3), moderately over-predicts the observed speed. The discrepancy with the bore theory is explained because the theoretical bore speed of Klemp *et al.* (1997), assumes an infinite mass of intruding fluid behind the hydraulic jump, whereas in the experiments the intrusions have finite mass.

Though internal waves are always observed behind the gravity current, their number and amplitude are large if the width, d, of the middle interface is large. The resonant excitation of internal waves is clearly demonstrated in Figure 4 which shows false-colour images of time-series of a vertical cross section of the tank during the passage of a successive series of intrusions. The middle layer is dyed and the intrusion is dyed with a different colour so the that the motion of both is visualised.

Figure 5 compares the experimentally determined phase speed with that predicted by linear theory for a range of wavenumbers. For all three values of d, the observed phase speed is smaller than that predicted by theory. The discrepancy is attributed to sensitivities of the dispersion relation to the thickness of the upper and lower interfaces. The phase speed of the waves is consistently smaller than the intrusion speed. As with the intrusion, the speed of the waves decreases as a function of increasing d.

If the middle layer is sufficiently wide, the intrusion is observed to stop propagating and a double-humped solitary wave is generated. The speed of the wave is found to vary approximately as the square root of the relative density difference. The observed horizontal distance, L_{sw}, at which the solitary wave separates from the gravity current head (which in turn stops propagating) are given in the last two columns of Table 1. For fixed σ, the solitary wave appears at a further distance d along in the tank when $d = 3\,\mathrm{cm}$ than it does when $d = 4\,\mathrm{cm}$. If d is fixed, the solitary wave appears further along in the tank for larger σ.

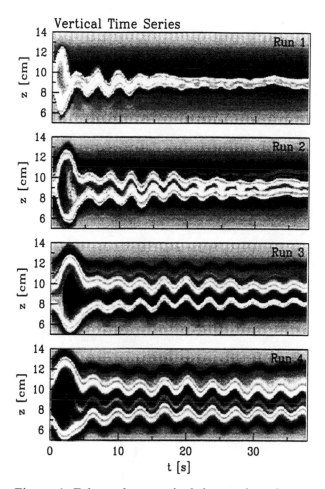

Vertical Time Series

Figure 4: False-colour vertical time series taken for successive runs in an experiment. The middle layer is dyed to visualize the vertical motion of the intrusion and trailing internal waves.

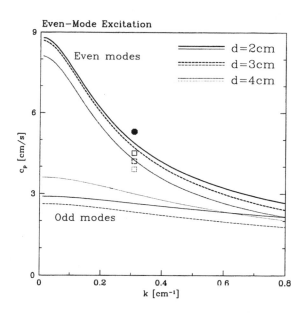

Even–Mode Excitation

Figure 5: Phase speed versus wavenumber calculated for a three-layer fluid with $\Delta\rho/\rho_m = 0.02$, $D = 0.5\,\mathrm{cm}$, and $H = 18\,\mathrm{cm}$. The relationships are shown for middle layer depths of $d = 2\,\mathrm{cm}$ (solid line), $d = 3\,\mathrm{cm}$ (dashed line) and $d = 4\,\mathrm{cm}$ (dotted line). The even (odd) modes are plotted as thick (thin) lines. The positions of the plotted squares correspond to the observed wavenumber and phase speed of internal waves trailing behind the intrusion in experiments with $d = 2$ (solid), 3 (dashed) and 4 cm (dotted). The solid circle denotes the observed speed of the intrusion for the case $d = 2\,\mathrm{cm}$.

σ	A_{iw}		L_{sw}	
	$d = 3\,\mathrm{cm}$	$d = 4\,\mathrm{cm}$	$d = 3\,\mathrm{cm}$	$d = 4\,\mathrm{cm}$
0.0025	0.44	0.45	110	80
0.005		0.42		95
0.01	0.39	0.41	90	97
0.02	0.37	0.32	140	97
0.03	0.34	0.36	180	110
0.04		0.32		112
0.05		0.19		120

Table 1: The average amplitude of trailing internal waves and the horizontal distance (±2 cm) from the lock at which the solitary wave separates from the gravity current head. For $\sigma = 0.05$, the solitary wave does not appear before the gravity current head reaches the end of the tank and is reflected.

5 Conclusions

We have examined the propagation of an intrusion in a three-layer fluid as it is controlled by two nondimensional parameters $\epsilon = \sqrt{\frac{d}{H}}$ and $\sigma = \frac{\Delta \rho}{\rho_m}$.

For $\epsilon \ll 1$ small amplitude internal waves trail the intrusion. The waves persist for only one or two periods behind the head of the intrusion. These waves are generated during the process of collapse of the lock fluid, but are not continuously excited by the propagating intrusion. If $\epsilon \simeq 0.3$ large amplitude trapped internal waves are continuously excited in the tail behind the head of the intrusion. For $\sigma = 0.0025$ and $\epsilon = 0.3$ the measured amplitude of the waves starts at roughly 0.2 cm followed by a rapid decay and the gravity current head propagates at roughly 2 cm/sec. As σ increases, the speed of the gravity current head also increases.

The characteristics of the internal waves agree well with linear theory predictions for sinuous waves in a three-layer fluid. The phase speed of sinuous waves decreases as a function of the middle-layer thickness. We propose that large amplitude waves are continuously excited when the width of the middle layer is sufficiently large that the sinuous wave phase speed is comparable with the intrusion speed.

If $\epsilon > 0.4$, large amplitude internal waves are still excited behind the intrusion and a solitary wave is generated ahead of the intrusion. With a lock length of 10 cm, $\epsilon \simeq 0.5$ and $\sigma = 0.0025$, the solitary wave appears 8 lock-lengths from the gate. When σ is increased to 0.05 (20 times greater) the measured amplitude of the waves is 2 times larger with no noticeable decay; the speed of propagation of the gravity current head is four times faster, and the solitary wave appears further along in the tank at 12 lock-lengths.

References

Benjamin, T. B. 1968. Gravity currents and related phenomena. *J. Fluid Mech.*, 31:209–248.

Britter, R. E. and Simpson, J. E. 1981. A note on the structure of the head of an intrusive gravity current. *J. Fluid Mech.*, 112:459–466.

Dalziel, S. B. 1993. Rayleigh-Taylor instability: experiments with image analysis. *Dyn. Atmos. Oceans*, 20:127–153.

Funakoshi, M. 1985. Long internal waves in a two-layer fluid. *J. Phys. Soc. Japan*, 54:2470–2476.

Funakoshi, M. and Oikawa, M. 1986. Long internal waves of large amplitude in a two-layer fluid. *J. Phys. Soc. Japan*, 55:128–144.

Klemp, J. B., Rotunno, R., and Skamarock, W. C. 1997. On the propagation of internal bores. *J. Fluid Mech.*, 331:81–106.

Maxworthy, T. 1980. On the formation of nonlinear internal waves from the gravitational collapse of mixed regions in two and three dimensions. *J. Fluid Mech.*, 96:47–64.

Mehta, A. and Sutherland, B. R. 2000. Interfacial gravity currents: Part II - wave excitation. (in preparation for submission to *Phys. Fluids*).

Michallet, H. and Barthélemy, E. 1997. Ultrasonic probes and data processing to study interfacial solitary waves. *Exp. Fluids*, 22:380–386.

Miles, J. W. 1981. On internal solitary waves II. *Tellus*, 33:397–401.

Sutherland, B. R. 2000. Interfacial gravity currents: Part I - mixing and entrainment. (in preparation for submission to *Phys. Fluids*).

Analysis of Density Currents Using the Non-Staggered Grid Fractional Step Method

J. Rafael Pacheco[1], Arturo Pacheco-Vega[2] and Sigfrido Pacheco-Vega[3]

[1] Mathematics, Arizona State University, Tempe, AZ 85287
[2] Aerospace and Mechanical Engineering, University of Notre Dame, Notre Dame, IN 46556
[3] Civil Engineering, University of British Columbia, Vancouver, B.C., Canada V6T 1Z3
rpacheco@asu.edu, apacheco@nd.edu, pacheco@civil.ubc.ca

1. Abstract

A new approach for the solution of time-dependent calculations of buoyancy driven currents is presented. The density distribution is not uniform throughout the flow field, however the incompressibility condition and Boussinesq approximation are assumed to be valid because the time variation of density is not significant. This method employs the idea that density variation can be pursued by using markers distributed in the flow field. The analysis based on the finite difference technique with the non-staggered grid fractional step method is used to solve the flow equations written in terms of primitive variables. The physical domain is transformed to a rectangle by means of a numerical mapping technique. The problems analyzed include two-fluid flow in a tank with sloping bottom and colliding density currents. The numerical experiments performed showed that this approach is efficient and robust.

2. Introduction

Density currents, also called gravity currents, occur in both man-made and natural situations. These currents may be generated by density difference where in some cases is only of few percent. Most density currents are primarily horizontal flows. However, not all gravity currents in the environment flow along horizontal surfaces. Important examples of gravity currents down an incline plane often encounter in nature are avalanches. Also, the sloping surface of a mountain plays a vital part in the formation of the currents which form in the ocean at the edge of the continental shelf. There are also instances where there may be different kinds of interaction between two gravity currents. For example, the collision between two mesoscale frontal flows has been observed in the atmosphere and it is found that the mixing of the rising air at the two fronts produces a strong zone of convection. There is also evidence, from sedimentary deposits, of the collision of currents on the ocean bed (Simpson 1997).

Numerical models of gravity currents are powerful tools to understand and elucidate their dynamics. Using a suitable model is possible to examine the whole range of parameters and to reproduce the basic results of laboratory experiments in order to identify differences between the flows in the laboratory and the environment. Several different models have been employed to examine gravity currents. Among the numerical techniques available to analyze density current surges, finite-difference and finite elements are the most commonly used. Due to their simple formulation and ease of programming, finite difference methods are preferred. One early example of the marker-and-cell numerical technique to study the transient evolution

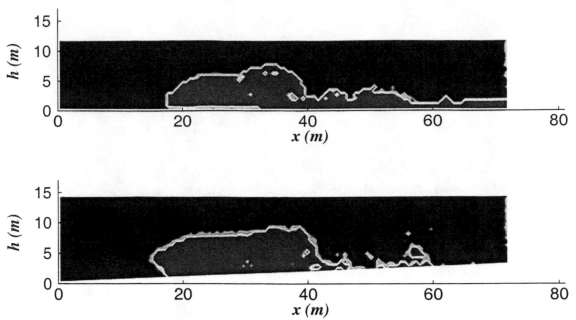

Figure 1: Contour plot of the density of gravity currents flowing down slopes of $0°$ and $5°$.

of a two-dimensional gravity current surge after starting from rest was first introduced by Daly and Pracht (1968). Their time-explicit finite-difference technique is limited to rectangular grids. On the other hand, finite-element techniques are able to treat irregular grids and have been used to numerically analyze density currents flowing down slope (Kawahara and Ohmiya 1985).

In this paper, we present results obtained with a finite-difference method to analyze two-dimensional gravity currents. The numerical method is attractive because it is second-order accurate in both space and time, and its accuracy is unaffected by grid orientation. The validation of the method, not shown here due to limited space available, was done by successful comparison of our results with those of Daly and Pracht (1968) and Kawahara and Ohmiya (1985). We apply the proposed method to analyze a tank with sloping bottom for different slope values and the collision of gravity currents. Finally, we will show that our results are in qualitative agreement with those reported in the literature.

3. Governing equations

In this work, two- and three-phase flows in which the densities of the Newtonian fluids are ρ_0 and ρ_1 and ρ_2, are analyzed in a two-dimensional domain Ω. Although the density distribution is not uniform in the entire flow field, the time variation of density is regarded as insignificant, thus the incompressibility condition and Boussinesq approximations are then assumed to be valid (the difference between the fluids is neglected in the momentum equations, and only appears in density relations). The density distribution of fluid particles is computed by means of markers attached to the fluid. The equations governing the flow are: where

$$\frac{\partial u_j}{\partial x_j} = 0 \quad \text{in} \quad \Omega, \tag{1}$$

$$\frac{\partial u_i}{\partial t} + \frac{\partial}{\partial x_j}(u_j u_i) = -\frac{1}{\rho_0}\frac{\partial p}{\partial x_i} + \nu\frac{\partial^2 u_i}{\partial x_j \partial x_j} + \frac{\rho}{\rho_0}g_i \quad \text{in} \quad \Omega, \tag{2}$$

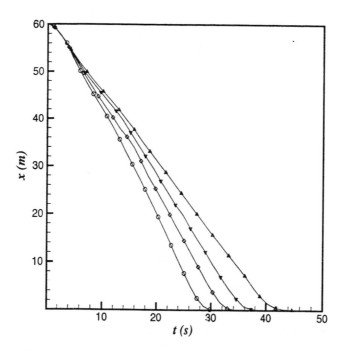

Figure 2: Schematic of the position of the front for different sloping angles. $-\triangle-$, $0°$; $-\bigtriangledown-$, $2.5°$; $-\diamond-$, $5°$; $-\circ-$, $10°$.

where $i, j = 1, 2$; u_i represents the Cartesian velocity components; p is the pressure (relative to zero ambient p_a); ρ and ρ_0 represent density and reference density; ν is the kinematic viscosity; g_i represents the gravity components. A number of markers are distributed in the flow field to distinguished fluid properties. Three kind of markers are used corresponding to the fluids of densities ρ_0 and ρ_1 and ρ_2. The position of the markers are moved according to

$$x_i^{n+1} = x_i^n + \Delta t u_i^n,$$
(3)

where x_i^{n+1} is the position of the marker at time n and Δt is the increment in time. If we denote m by the number of markers in a cell, the density of cell (i) can be obtained as follows:

$$\rho^{(i)} = \frac{m_0 \rho_0 + m_1 \rho_1 + m_2 \rho_2}{m_0 + m_1 + m_2}$$
(4)

where $\rho(i)$ means the density of the cell (i). The non-staggered-grid layout is employed in this analysis. The pressure and the Cartesian velocity components are defined at the cell center and the volume fluxes are defined at the midpoint of their corresponding faces of the control volume in the computational space. We use a semi-implicit time-advancement scheme with the Adams-Bashforth method for the explicit terms and the Crank-Nicholson method for the implicit terms as described by Zang et al. (1994) and Pacheco and Peck (1998). The details of the method of solution can be found in Pacheco and Pacheco-Vega (2000) and Hunt et al. (2000).

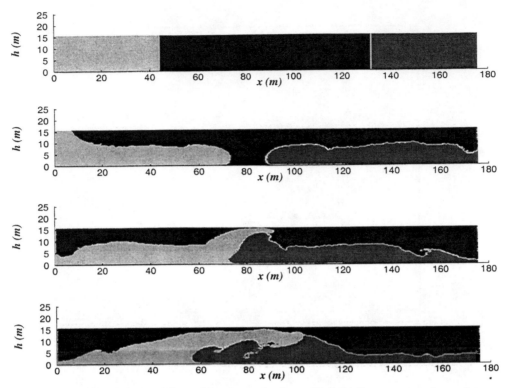

Figure 3: Schematic of the position of the fronts in the collision of two unequal gravity currents.

4. Analysis of gravity currents in a tank with slope

The typical structure of two gravity current visualized by means of isocontours of density is seen in Figure 1 first flowing on a horizontal surface and second flowing down slope of 5 degrees. The numerical mesh employed in this simulation consist of (240×40) grid points and the density of the fluids are $\rho_0 = 1.0$ and $\rho_1 = 1.1$. The gravity acceleration $g = 9.8$m/s and viscosity $\nu = 0$ are used. The time interval governed by the CFL condition was set to 0.75 (see Pacheco 2000). The horizontal dimension of the tank is 72 m. The dense fluid occupies the right portion of the tank and it is released from rest at a point 60 m from the left boundary. At this location, the height of the tank is 12 m. The boundary condition at the top is free of shear-stress whereas the conditions at the remaining walls are no-slip.

The initial velocity distribution is zero everywhere in the tank. Among the characteristic features of intrusion fronts that are apparent from Figure 1, the head volume increases, both by direct entrainment and also by addition from the following flow. The position of the front along the slope is presented in Figure 2 for different slope values. It is known that although the gravitational forces increase with slope, so does the entrainment, both into the head and into the flow behind it; thus there is a slight variation in the speed of the front. These features obtained from the computation are similar to those observed in experiments (Britter and Linden 1980).

5. Analysis of colliding gravity currents

In this section, the head-on collision of two gravity currents of different densities of equal size is analyzed for three different fluids of viscosity $\nu = 0.1$ and with gravitational acceleration $g = 9.8$ m/s. The numerical mesh employed in this simulation consist of (480×80) grid points. Four stages in the collision starting from

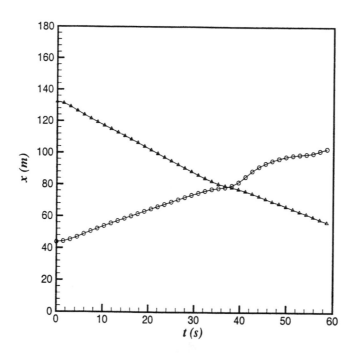

Figure 4: Schematic of the position of the fronts in the collision of two unequal gravity currents. $-\circ-$, $\rho_1 = 1.1$; $-\diamond-$, $\rho_2 = 1.05$.

rest are presented in Figure 3. The position of the fronts as function of time are also illustrated in Figure 4. The density of the gravity current moving from the left is $\rho_1 = 1.05$ and the gravity current moving from the right is $\rho_2 = 1.1$ flowing in a parallel-sided water channel of size 176 m long by 16 m high. The form of the front after collision is shown in Figure 3. From this figure, it can be seen that the current from the left is reflected as a deep bore, whereas that from the right reappears as a weak one. Also, the gravity currents met and they continued to travel in the same direction as before, with slight change in their velocity values but also with the appearance of disturbances reflected in the form of undular bores (see Figure 4). The results presented here show the same trend with the laboratory experiments reported in (Simpson 1997)

6. Concluding remarks

In the current report we have presented results that were obtained in numerical simulation studies of two-dimensional gravity currents for both, flows down an inclined plane and gravity currents that collide. The mathematical problem is formulated in primitive variables and solved using the fractional step method for non-staggered grids adapted from Zang *et al.* (1994). The numerical method accommodates non-orthogonal grids. The application of these schemes allows to reproduce the basic features of these flows from laboratory experiments. As a closing statement, it can be said that because of the highly stable and convergent nature of this method, even for very large time steps, it will prove to be useful tool in the solution of these type of time-dependent fluid dynamics problems.

The authors would like to thank Professor Sergey Voropayev for helpful discussions on this work and to Mr. Bruce Tachoir for access to computer facilities.

7. References

Britter, J. E. and P. F. Linden (1980). The motion of the front of a gravity current travelling down an incline. *J. Fluid Mech. 99*, 531–543.

Daly, B. J. and W. E. Pracht (1968). Numerical study of density–current surges. *Phis. Fluids 11*, 15–30.

Hunt, J. C. R., J. R. Pacheco, A. Mahalov, , S. I. Voropayev, and H. J. S. Fernando (2000). Effects of rotation and sloping terrain on fronts of density currents, Submitted. *J. Fluid Mech.*.

Kawahara, M. and K. Ohmiya (1985). Finite element analysis of density flow using the velocity correction method. *Int. J. Numer. Methods Fluids 5*, 981–993.

Pacheco, J. R. (2000). The solution of viscous incompressible jet flows using non-staggered boundary fitted coordinate methods, In print. *Int. J. Numer. Methods Fluids*.

Pacheco, J. R. and A. Pacheco-Vega (2000). Numerical simulation of transient viscous free-surface flows, Submitted. *J. Comput. Phys.*.

Pacheco, J. R. and R. E. Peck (1998). Non-staggered grid boundary-fitted coordinate method for free surface flows. *1st International Symposium on Computational Technologies for Fluid/Thermal/Chemical Systems with Industrial Applications*, Volume 337-1, San Diego, California, pp. 49–59.

Simpson, J. (1997). *Gravity Currents*. Cambridge: Cambridge University Press.

Zang, Y., R. I. Street, and J. F. Kossef (1994). A non-staggered grid, fractional step method for time dependent incompressible Navier-Stokes equations in curvilinear coordinates. *J. Comput. Phys. 114*, 18–33.

Mixing and structure in a double diffusive gravity current

Chris R. Rehmann[1], Jin H. Hwang[1] and Patrick R. Jackson[1]

[1]Civil and Environmental Engineering, Univ. of Illinois at Urbana-Champaign, Urbana, IL, USA 61801
rehmann@uiuc.edu, jinhwang@uiuc.edu, prjackso@uiuc.edu

1. Abstract

Laboratory experiments on warm, salty arrested currents injected beneath a cold, fresh opposing flow were performed to examine the contributions of mechanical and double diffusive processes to vertical mixing. Comparing the time scale of the double diffusive instability to the eddy turnover time indicates conditions under which interfacial scouring by turbulent eddies should be important. The ratio of the discharges of dense and light water decreases by a factor of 4 as the density ratio increases, but no systematic effect of the stratification strength was observed. Temperature and salinity profiles measured along the length of the current have several features observed in previous experiments on salt wedges and double diffusive flows. Profiles near the outlet have layers for low density ratios and high Richardson numbers.

2. Introduction

Double diffusive processes can contribute to vertical mixing in many parts of the ocean. One example is on continental shelves where during the summer warm, salty water from the continental slope can intrude into the colder, fresher shelf water. During a field experiment south of New England, Rehmann and Duda (2000, hereafter RD) followed a particularly prominent intrusion of about 5 m thickness that moved up the shelf along the seafloor. The thermal eddy diffusivity reached very high levels ($O(10^{-3} \text{ m}^2/\text{s})$) near the bottom, and an approximate temperature budget showed that this vertical flux was mainly responsible for the heat transfer between the slope water and the shelf water.

A difficulty in interpreting these results is that the analysis of RD ignores contributions from diffusive layering. The near-bottom water had a density ratio $R_\rho = \beta \Delta S / \alpha \Delta T$ of approximately 3, where ΔT and ΔS are the temperature and salinity changes across the interface and α and β are the thermal and haline expansion coefficients. Since laboratory experiments show an increase in heat flux at low R_ρ (e.g., Turner 1979, p. 275), double diffusive convection may be important. For this reason, we developed a laboratory model to isolate and analyze the relative contribution of mechanical and double diffusive processes to vertical mixing.

Several previous experiments have examined the competition between mechanical and double diffusive processes in various flows. For example, Atkinson (1994) studied a grid-stirred diffusive system and found that while double diffusion did not change the entrainment across the interface, the fluxes of heat and salt exceeded those in unstirred systems. Although the flux is molecular-diffusive as in unstirred cases, the scouring of the interface by turbulence reduces the interfacial thickness and increases the fluxes. Maxworthy (1983) studied gravity currents formed by either releasing a volume of fluid or injecting fluid at a constant rate into quiescent water. For an injection of fluid creating a diffusive stratification, stress at the double diffusive interface retarded the motion of the current. Yoshida et al. (1987) postulated that this retarding effect was due to the large initial density difference; for the smaller initial density differences used in their experiments, the upgradient buoyancy flux caused by double diffusion accelerated the current.

We describe results of laboratory experiments to quantify the effects of shear on mixing at a diffusive interface. A goal of the experiments is to determine the conditions under which interfacial shear and mechanically generated turbulence affect the fluxes across the interface. In this paper we discuss measures of bulk mixing and properties of temperature and salinity profiles measured along the length of a gravity current with stratification favorable for diffusive layering.

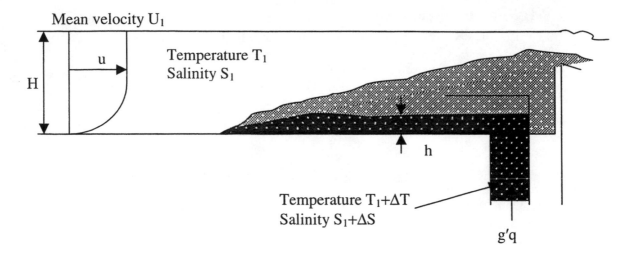

Figure 1. Definition sketch for the double diffusive, arrested current. A warm, salty current with discharge per unit width q and depth h is injected into an opposing flow of cold, fresh water with velocity U_1 and depth H.

3. Analysis

To model the bottom intrusion observed by RD, we inject warm, salty water beneath an opposing flow of colder, fresher water, as shown by the definition sketch in figure 1. By adjusting the discharges of both the dense and light water, the dense current can be arrested at a specific location. In this steady state, the amount of dense fluid mixed out of the front is equal to the dense water discharge per unit width q. Dimensional analysis applied to this flow is similar to that presented by García and Parsons (1996) except that $\alpha \Delta T$ and $\beta \Delta S$, the fractional changes in density due to temperature and salinity, become important independent variables. Because the Prandtl number $Pr = \nu/D_T$ and Lewis number $\tau = D_S/D_T$ (where ν is the kinematic viscosity and D_T and D_S are the diffusivities of temperature and salt) are fixed in these experiments, the ratio of dense water discharge (or mixing rate) and the light water discharge can be expressed as

$$\frac{q}{U_1 H} = f(R_\rho, Ri, Ra_T, Re),$$ (1)

where $Ri = g'h/U_1^2$ is the Richardson number, $g' = (\beta \Delta S - \alpha \Delta T)g$ is reduced gravity, $Ra_T = g\alpha \Delta T h^3/\nu D_T$ is the thermal Rayleigh number, and $Re = U_1 H/\nu$ is the Reynolds number.

Values of the density ratio and the Richardson number at which the scouring effects of eddies near the interface are significant can be estimated using the time scale analysis of Atkinson (1994). In his analysis, Atkinson (1994) compared an eddy turnover time scale $t_e \sim \ell/u$ to the time scale of the instability, which is based on the model of Linden and Shirtcliffe (1978):

$$t_c = \left\{ \frac{1}{\pi D_T} \left(\frac{\nu Ra_c}{g\alpha \Delta T (1 - \tau^{1/2})^3} \right)^2 \right\}^{\frac{1}{3}}$$ (2)

where the critical Rayleigh number Ra_c is taken to be 1640 (Atkinson 1994). Simulations of sheared, stratified, homogeneous turbulence show that the time scale of the large eddies is about 10% of the shear rate (Holt et al. 1992), and experiments on salt wedges at stratifications similar to those used in the present experiments suggest that the shear rate is approximately $2U_1/H$. With these estimates and an

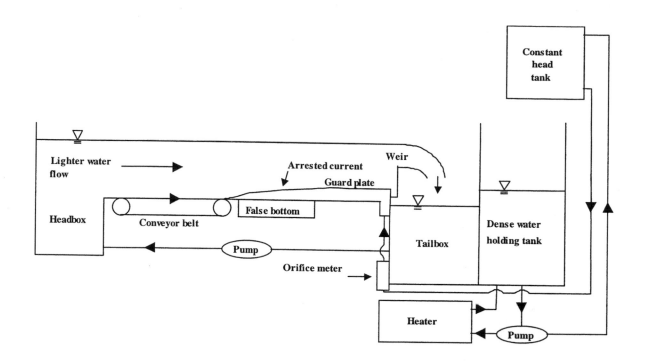

Figure 2. Schematic of the experimental facility. The conveyor belt, which facilitates arresting the current, was not used in these experiments because of mechanical problems.

average value of the Reynolds number, one can find that the eddy time scale and instability time scale are comparable when

$$\mathrm{Ri} \approx 6(R_\rho - 1). \tag{3}$$

For Richardson numbers less than the values predicted by equation (3), mechanically generated turbulence should have a significant effect on the dynamics. For example, this analysis suggests that in the intrusion observed by RD, which had $R_\rho \approx 3$ and $\mathrm{Ri} \approx 1$, eddies scoured the interface before instabilities could develop. Future work will involve applying this criterion to our flow as well as testing the various assumptions on which it is based.

4. Experimental facility and procedures

The experimental facility, shown in figure 2, was modeled after that of Britter and Simpson (1978) and used by García and Parsons (1996) in their experiments on mixing in saline gravity currents. It consists of a tailbox, dense fluid holding tank, constant head tank, and a test section that is 3.2 m long, 0.3 m wide, and 0.5 m deep. Water in the tailbox is circulated through the test section with a 1.5-HP pump; the water enters the headbox, passes through several honeycomb flow straighteners, and then flows through the test section and over an adjustable weir. A Venturi meter placed before the headbox allows the flow rate of the lighter water to be measured. After heating, water in the holding tank is continuously stirred and pumped to the test section. It flows from the constant head tank, through either a Venturi meter or a small-bore orifice meter, and into the test section. Before entering the test section, the dense water passes through an expansion that prevents flow separation and beneath a 30-cm square guard plate that avoids "short-circuiting", or entrainment of the dense water directly into the opposing flow of lighter water.

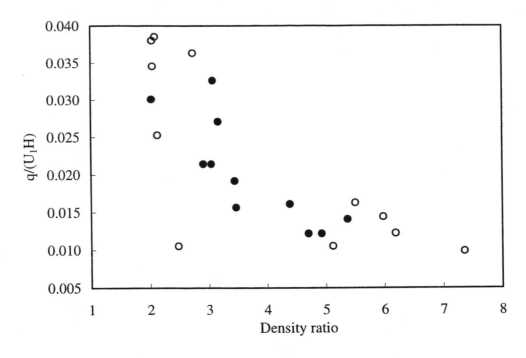

Figure 3. Ratio of discharges of dense and light water as a function of density ratio: ○, Ri < 1; ●, Ri > 1.

Experiments proceed in the following way. The tailbox and holding tank are filled, and the temperature and salinity of the water are set to achieve the target value of the density ratio. After the opposing flow of colder, fresher water is established, the dense fluid is introduced into the test section and allowed to advance, usually to the end of the stationary floor. The dense water flow rate is adjusted until the current becomes stationary, and when the steady state is achieved, the dense water flow rate is recorded, and temperature and salinity profiles are measured with a conductivity-temperature probe. In these experiments the total depth H was nearly constant at 23 cm, while the velocity U_1 of the light water varied from 2.8 to 4.6 cm/s. The dense water discharge per unit width was between 60 and 400 cm^2/s.

5. Experimental results and discussion

In this section results will be presented from experiments with $2 < R_\rho < 8$ and $0.4 < Ri < 1.7$. These Richardson numbers correspond to values of the Froude number $Fr = U_1/(g'H)^{1/2}$ of 0.3 to 0.6. All values are based on the layer depth (defined as the position of 50% excess density), temperature difference, and salinity difference measured 5 cm from the outlet. The current was arrested in all cases, but the length of the intrusion varied from 65 to 130 cm. Bulk mixing results will be discussed first, and then some of the details of the temperature and salinity profiles will be presented.

The bulk mixing results are summarized in figure 3, in which the ratio of the discharges of the dense and light water is plotted as a function of the density ratio. The data are scattered, but they show a decreasing trend from a maximum of about 4% at relatively low density ratio ($R_\rho = 2$) to 1% at higher density ratios. Measurements at $R_\rho \approx 13$ suggest that the discharge ratio q/U_1H will not fall much below 1%. The observed range of values is similar to that in other laboratory experiments; for example, the values measured by Sargent and Jirka (1987) increased from 0 to 4% from the tail to the tip of their salt wedges with a Froude number of 0.45. In contrast, field measurements of salt wedges with lower Froude numbers and much higher Reynolds numbers yield discharge ratios of close to 100% (e.g., Arita and Jirka 1987).

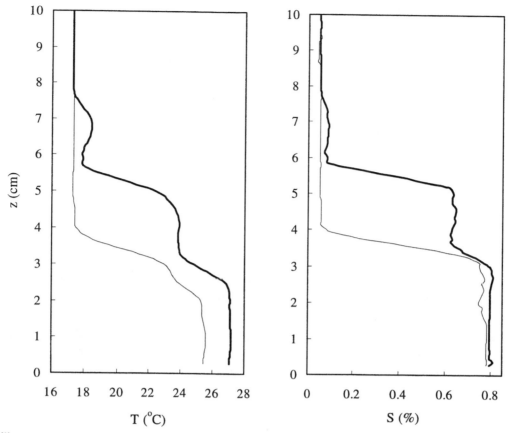

Figure 4. Temperature and salinity profiles from an experiment with $R_\rho = 2.9$ and $Ri = 1.06$. Bold lines indicate profiles measured at 5 cm from the outlet, while the lighter lines indicate profiles measured at 80 cm from the outlet.

The discharge ratios in figure 3 show no systematic dependence on the Richardson (or Froude) number even though Arita and Jirka (1987) predicted that the discharge ratio should increase as the Froude number decreases. Their theory also predicts the dependence of the relative salt circulation on the relative position along the salt wedge, which we have not yet included in our analysis. The variation of q/U_1H with R_ρ superficially resembles the behavior of the ratio of the salt flux F_S and heat flux F_T in double diffusion experiments with bottom heating (e.g., Turner 1979, p. 276). In such experiments with heat and salt, αF_T is roughly 7 times greater than βF_S at large density ratios, but the fluxes approach each other as the density ratio decreases toward the limit for gravitational stability. Progress toward determining the dependence of the discharge ratio on the various dimensionless parameters could be made by modifying the theory of Arita and Jirka (1987) to include double diffusive fluxes across the interface.

Temperature and salinity profiles near the outlet and about 50 cm from the tip of the current are shown in figure 4 for a case with $R_\rho = 2.9$ and $Ri = 1.06$, values similar to those in the observations of RD. Several features are apparent. As in experiments on salt wedges, the lower layer thickness h decreases as the tip of the current is approached, and as in other double diffusion experiments, the interface thicknesses in the profiles of temperature (i.e., the component with the large diffusivity) are larger than those in profiles of salinity. Also, the temperature difference decreases more quickly than the salinity difference. As the tip of the current is approached, local values of R_ρ increase, while local values of Ri decrease. Thus, according to the ideas in section 2, double diffusive fluxes across the interface should become less important closer to the tip. An objective of future work is to quantify the heat and salt fluxes across the interface by evaluating budgets of temperature and salinity for specific control volumes along the length of the current.

Another feature of the profiles in figure 4 is the double-layer structure evident in both the temperature and the salinity profiles near the outlet. Layers are a salient feature of double diffusion experiments with bottom heating (e.g., Turner 1979, pp. 262-266): Heating drives convection that mixes a layer near the bottom, and a series of layers and interfaces develops. In the present experiments layers are typically observed at distances of 5 and 20 cm from the outlet in cases with $R_\rho < 5$ and $Ri > 1$. In all cases the analysis in section 2 suggests that the Richardson number is low enough for scouring by turbulent eddies to be important. The layering could be due to double diffusion or to an artifact of the flow in the vicinity of the guard plate. Future work includes systematic experiments to examine the cause of the layering.

6. Summary

To isolate and study some processes contributing to vertical mixing in the coastal ocean, we performed laboratory experiments on arrested currents that were favorable for diffusive layering. Comparing the time scale of the double diffusive instability to the eddy turnover time yields a criterion for interfacial scouring to be important. The ratio of the discharges of dense and light water decreases by a factor of 4 as the density ratio increases, but these preliminary experiments show no systematic effect of the Richardson (or Froude) number. Temperature and salinity profiles measured along the length of the current have several features observed in previous experiments on salt wedges and double diffusive flows. Profiles near the outlet have layers for low density ratios and high Richardson numbers.

7. References

Arita, M. and Jirka, G. H. 1987 Two-layer model of saline wedges. II: Prediction of mean properties. *J. Hydraul. Eng.*, **113**, 1249-1263.

Atkinson, J. F. 1994 Interfacial fluxes at a grid-stirred diffusive interface. *Int. J. Heat Mass Transfer*, **37**, 2089-2099.

Britter, R. E. and Simpson, J. E. 1978 Experiments on the dynamics of a gravity current head. *J. Fluid Mech.*, **88**, 223-240.

García, M. H. and Parsons, J. D. 1996 Mixing at the front of gravity currents. *Dyn. Atmos. Oceans*, **24**, 197-205.

Holt, S. E., Koseff, J. R., and Ferziger, J. H. 1992 A numerical study of the evolution and structure of homogeneous stably stratified sheared turbulence. *J. Fluid Mech.*, **237**, 499-539.

Linden, P. F. and Shirtcliffe, T. G. L. 1978 The diffusive interface in double-diffusive convection. *J. Fluid Mech.*, **87**, 417-432.

Rehmann, C. R. and Duda, T. F. 2000 Diapycnal diffusivity inferred from scalar microstructure measurements near the New England shelf/slope front. *J. Phys. Oceanogr.*, **30**, 1354-1371.

Sargent, F. E. and Jirka, G. H. 1987 Experiments on saline wedges. *J. Hydraul. Eng.*, **113**, 1307-1324.

Turner, J. S. 1979 *Buoyancy Effects in Fluids*. Cambridge Univ. Press, Cambridge, U. K., 368 pp.

Yoshida, J., Nagashima, H., and Ma, W.-J. 1987 A double diffusive lock-exchange flow with small density difference. *Fluid Dyn. Res.*, **2**, 205-215.

The non-Boussinesq lock exchange problem and related phenomena

James W. Rottman[*], Ryan Lowe and Paul F. Linden
University of California, San Diego, La Jolla, CA, USA

The results of an experimental study of the non-Boussinesq lock exchange problem are described. The experiments were performed in a rectangular channel using water and a sodium Iodide solution as the two fluids, which gave a maximum density difference of about 60%. The main purpose of these experiments is to resolve some recent controversy about how gravity currents evolve from a flow at rest to the well-known steady-state gravity current made famous by Benjamin (1968). It has been argued, based on two-dimensional shallow-water theory, that Benjamin's steady-state energy-conserving gravity current cannot evolve from the lock-exchange (or any physically reasonable) initial conditions. The experiments show that this is not true. A shallow-water theory for the non-Boussinesq problem is derived that is valid for the lock-exchange problem for large times after the flow is initiated. This theory requires the formulation of a two-layer theory for hydraulic jumps in non-Boussinesq fluids. The results of the model are compared with our lock-exchange experiments and with two previous non-Boussinesq sets of lock exchange experiments, both of which use a combination of exotic gases or gases and liquids as the working fluids, with good qualitative agreement.

[*] Corresponding author: Department of Mechanical and Aerospace Engineering, University of California, San Diego, 9500 Gilman Drive, Dept. 0411, La Jolla, CA 92093-0411. Telephone: +1 858-534-7002, Fax: +1 858-534-7599, Email: jrottman@mae.ucsd.edu.

Effects of the boundary condition on the two-dimensional structure of the head of an inertial gravity current

Luis P. Thomas[1] and Stuart B. Dalziel[2]

[1]Instituto de Física Arroyo Seco, Facultad de Ciencias Exactas, Universidad Nacional del Centro de la Provincia de Buenos Aires (UNCPBA), Pinto 399, 7000 Tandil, Argentina.
[2]Department of Applied Mathematics and Theoretical Physics, University of Cambridge, Silver Street, Cambridge CB3 9EW, UK.
lthomas@exa.unicen.edu.ar, s.dalziel@damtp.cam.ac.uk

1 Abstract

Detailed measurements of the flow within and around the head of lock-release gravity currents running both over a no-slip bottom and along a free surface are obtained by using particle tracking velocimetry. We present measurements of the velocity, vorticity, stress, shear and divergence fields, and streamlines of the head in order to determine the two-dimensional time-averaged structure of the current during its slumping phase. For a bottom current, the stagnation point is found to be located below the foremost point (or nose) of the head, and dense fluid is seen to be supplied from the centre of the head to the leading edge. As a consequence of this location for the stagnation point, the current overruns less fluid than previously estimated because some of this fluid is being diverted back forwards and around the current.

We compare these results with those for a current along a free surface, and find additional unexpected effects related to the surface tension gradients established on the liquid free surface.

2 Introduction

Inertial gravity currents have been studied extensively, motivated largely by their relevance in the environmental and geophysical contexts. Even though the real flows are frequently three-dimensional, experimental studies have focused on a two-dimensional view of the current (see Simpson 1997 and references cited therein). The close agreement in the description of the gross features between earlier experimental studies and the analytical and two-dimensional numerical results indicates clearly that the large-scale dynamics is fundamentally of a two-dimensional character.

It has long been known that the head of a gravity current plays a key role in determining the advance of the current. The flow within the head is responsible for maintaining the size and form of the head as fluid is removed and diluted through shear instabilities on the back of the head. Most previous experimental studies have concentrated on determining the relationships characterizing the head as a function of flow parameters such as the fractional depth and Reynolds number (see Simpson, 1997). To our knowledge, the only published study of the velocity structure within the head is that of Alahyari & Longmire (1996). Here we provide time-averaged two-dimensional velocity fields both within the head of the current and in the ambient fluid for horizontal miscible gravity currents during the slumping phase following a lock-release. The gravity currents both along the floor of the tank and along the free surface are studied.

3 Experimental set-up

The gravity currents were produced in a Perspex tank (200 cm long, 20.3 cm wide and 25 cm deep) by means of a classical lock-release system. The tank was filled with fresh water to a depth $H=20$ cm and a vertical gate was inserted at a distance $x_0=50$cm from the rear wall. Salt was dissolved into the water to create a small density difference $\Delta\rho$ between the two parts of the tank, and a small quantity of sodium fluorescein and Pliolite particles were added for flow visualisation. Prior to their addition, the particles were allowed to soak briefly in a solution containing a high concentration of wetting agent to facilitate their suspension in the water. The particles were then washed carefully with fresh water before adding them to the tank. In spite of this treatment, some particles remained attached to the free surface and they were not used for calculating the velocity field.

The experimental set-up used for the particle tracking was fairly standard. A 1kW photographic halogen lamp with a linear filament and a spherical lens generated a vertical light sheet along the center line of the tank. This light sheet, approximately 6mm thick, entered through the tank floor. A CCD video camera, fitted with zoom lens, was fixed 4.30m from the tank and focused on the light scattered by the particles within the light sheet between $x \approx 130$cm and $x \approx 170$cm. The fluorescent dye within the current allowed the instantaneous current profile to be seen. From this we calculated the mean front velocity U from a least squares fit to the front position, and we could determine the time-average shape of the current. The behaviour of the current profile and constant front velocity confirmed the current to be in the slumping phase as it passed through the viewed region of the tank.

The velocity field was determined by tracking the particles from digitized video images using Dig*Image* (Dalziel 1992, 1993). Subsequently, the data was shifted from the fixed camera frame of reference into the frame of reference moving with the head of the current by subtracting the instantaneous location of the front from the particle positions at each step in time.

4   Results

Figure 1 shows the time-average image obtained from a dense gravity current advancing over a solid boundary for $Re = Uh/\nu \approx 1200$, where h is the maximum depth of the head and ν is the kinematic viscosity of water. Three different intensity contours are superimposed, suggesting the density structure of the head. The characteristic raised nose and enlarged head of the gravity current are clearly visible, as are the billows at the back of the head. The depth of the head is close to 10cm or half the channel depth, as found by previous authors (see Simpson 1997). The elevation of the nose is observed to vary between $\eta \approx 1.3$cm and $\eta \approx 1.6$cm during the passage of the head through the recording windows. At the same time we see that the small amount of ambient fluid overrun by the head mixes inside, indicating that the lower value for the elevation

Figure 1: Time averaged image of a bottom current with $\Delta\rho$ =0.07%, U=1.54cm/s and Reynolds number about 1200. Three curves superimposed represent estimate of the density distribution of the current.

corresponds to a lobe in the illuminated slice while the upper value corresponds to a cleft. The average horizontal velocity measured behind the nose of the current is in the range of values observed by Britter & Simpson (1978) and Simpson & Britter (1979), who measured the mean velocity along a vertical line in the tail using a hot film probe.

Figure 2 shows the flow field (in the frame of reference of the head) for the same current as shown in figure 1. The time-averaged velocity field (vectors) is superimposed on a greyscale representation of the time-averaged fields of the in-plane magnitude of velocity (figure 2a), vorticity (figure 2b) and shear strain (figure 2c). As expected, the ambient fluid with uniform velocity far from the gravity current is decelerated near the floor ahead the current and accelerated as it passes over the head of the current. Further downstream, the velocity of the ambient fluid tends to a constant value and is uniform with depth.

Also visible is a small flux of fluid towards the nose within the current. This flux balances the flux associated with the generation of fluid of intermediate density that is then swept downstream of the head.

Figure 2b demonstrates that the vorticity in the ambient fluid remains close to zero everywhere, as may be expected from an inviscid response to the passage of the current. The generation of vorticity is confined to the boundary between the fluids, and the solid bottom of the channel. Positive vorticity arises due to the shear between the current and the ambient fluid and is carried towards the left by the mean flow. At the same time, negative vorticity is generated by the passage of the current over the floor of the tank as the result of the no-slip boundary condition there, this condition being responsible also for the presence of the velocity vectors directed towards the left near the floor. The non-zero shear strain in the ambient flow (figure 2c) suggests there is viscous dissipation in the ambient fluid above the nose of the current. However, more careful analysis of the flow shows that the Reynolds stresses (not shown here) represent the dominant mechanism for momentum transfer in this region. The low time-average strain at the front suggests the velocity of the recirculation approximately matches that of the ambient flow there. Downstream of the nose the shear strain increases with the acceleration of the ambient fluid as it squeezes past the head. Kelvin-Helmholtz instabilities grow in this strongly sheared region, disrupting the structure of the flow and leading to relatively high levels of dissipation.

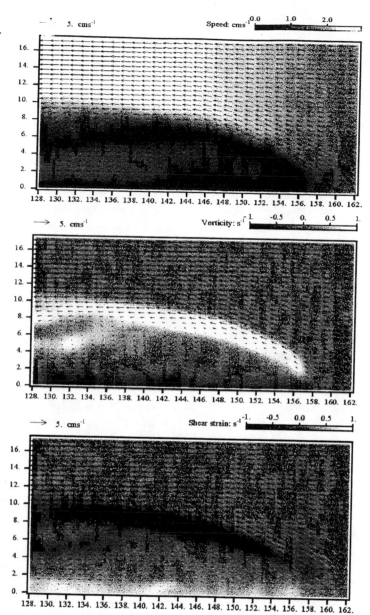

Figure 2: Flow fields for a bottom current with Re≈1200. (a) Velocity and in-plane speed; (b) velocity and vorticity; (c) velocity and shear strain

Contours of the time-average streamfunction ψ are presented in Figure 3. As expected, the streamlines tend towards the horizontal at the top of the field of view (the departure from horizontal is due to the region in which the measurements were taken not extending all the way to the free surface at $y=20$cm. Two circulation cells within the head are present; the larger and stronger upper cell continually replenishes the fluid at the nose of the gravity current, ensuring the strong density gradients are maintained. The presence of billows towards the rear of the gravity current head is signaled by the approximately circular streamlines at that point. The weak lower circulation cell is created by the boundary layer on the bottom dragging fluid back to the left. This cell appears to thicken slightly towards the nose of the current, an effect that is probably due to a flux of negative vorticity carried by the nose-ward flow within the head.

Of particular interest is the position of the ambient fluid stagnation streamline near the nose of the current. Until recently, it was thought that this streamline intersected the foremost point of the nose of the current (*e.g.* Simpson 1997). However, direct numerical simulations reported by Hartel *et al.* (2000) suggest that the stagnation point lies on the underside of the raised nose, although still forwards of the point where the gravity current first makes contact with the ground.

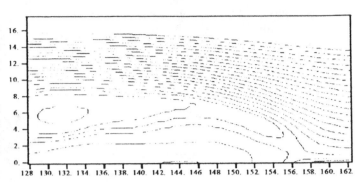

Figure 3: Streamlines for a bottom current with Re≈1200

While the resolution of the velocity measurements for this experiment cannot determine the precise location of this stagnation point, the stagnation streamline appears to travel under the nose before it disappears into the base of the current. This finding is reinforced by a careful analysis of the individual particle paths. Therefore, the volume of fluid overrun by the current is less than previously estimated because part of this fluid is diverted back around the current.

We may estimate the thickness of the boundary layer in the rear of the head by using dimensional arguments. The fluid there has been in contact with the bottom since the current was released a time $(x_f-x_0)/U$ ago, where x_f is the location of the front. This time scale leads to the boundary layer thickness $\delta=\sqrt{(vx_f/U)}$ ~1cm, which is consistent with the measurements presented in figure 2 but at the limit of their resolution.

The structure of a buoyant current running along the free surface of the water has some fundamental differences from gravity currents over a non-slip surface. Figure 4 shows the time-averaged shape of a surface current at $Re≈1300$. As expected, the current propagates with a Froude number $Fr=U/(h\ g')^{1/2}$ slightly higher ($Fr=0.69$) than that ($Fr=0.65$) for bottom currents at comparable Reynolds numbers, where $g'≈(\Delta\rho/\rho)g$ is the reduced gravity. The Froude number for this surface current coincides with the reported by previous studies (see Hartel *et al.* 2000, Simpson 1997), but it is slightly lower than the theoretical value for an inviscid flow predicted by Benjamin (1968).

Benjamin's (1968) theoretical prediction for the shape of an energy-conserving gravity current is superimposed on figure 4. Despite the reasonable agreement with the profile observed for a current along the free surface, some important differences remain. First, the present surface current exhibits a raised nose, albeit with an elevation substantially less than that for the equivalent bottom current shown in figure 1. As explained by Simpson (1997), the presence of a nose means that the liquid surface does not impose a strictly free boundary condition. Thus, as such a current is overrunning a layer of ambient fluid, an unstable stratification is created which drives the formation of lobes and clefts and the associated turbulence through the head. The particle paths also confirm a thin layer of

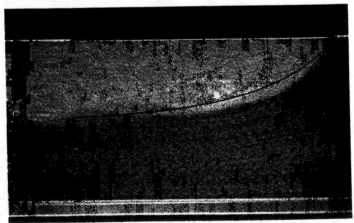

Figure 4: Time averaged profile of a surface current with Re≈1300. The black curve superimposed represents Benjamin's prediction for the shape of the current

ambient fluid overrun by the gravity current very near the liquid-air interface. Second, the current deepens more rapidly near the front than suggested by Benjamin's solution. This deviation coincides with the large but weak circulation cell inside the head. Compared with the equivalent cell in figure 1, the recirculation cell in the surface current is larger and extends further forwards. The source of the circulation within the cell is the diffusion and entrainment of the vorticity resulting from the shear between the current and the ambient fluid.

Comparison between figures 1 and 4 suggests a general reduction of the level of turbulence caused by the relaxation of the no-slip boundary condition at the upper boundary. A reduction is also found in the turbulence generated at the broad interface between ambient and the dense fluid at the bottom of the current. This reduced shear-driven turbulence is understood by noting that the enlarged principal recirculation cell inside the head may be maintained more easily (smaller shear strain) as it is not diffusing vorticity to the upper boundary. Some of ambient fluid is still entrained into the head by the cell within the current, but less than in the bottom gravity current with similar Reynolds number.

Figure 5 shows that the velocity within most of the head is close to the front speed, and that the velocity of the recirculating fluid within the principal cell is relatively small. The flux of fluid towards the front is also smaller than for the bottom current as the flux in the boundary layer on the surface is much lower. The boundary layer between the ambient fluid and that of the current is thinner than for the bottom current, due to the lower turbulence levels resulting in less mixed fluid being generated and swept downstream of the front.

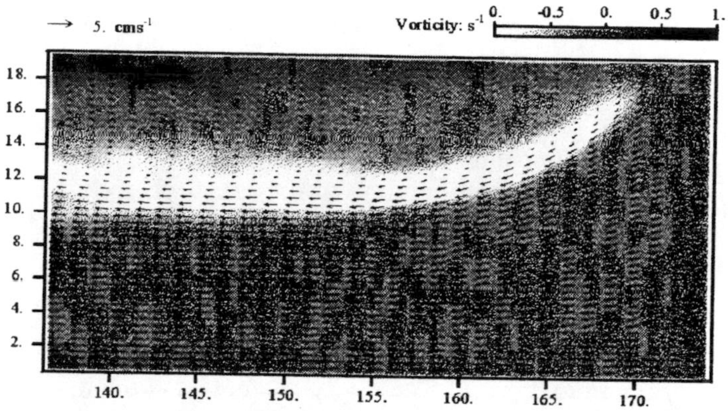

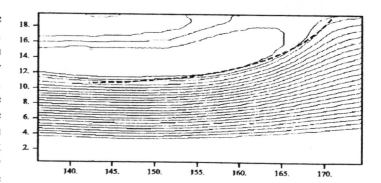

Figure 5: Velocity and vorticity fields for a surface current with Re≈1300

The time-averaged vorticity field is also displayed in figure 5. As with figure 2c, the ambient fluid far from the head remains essentially irrotational and vorticity production is confined in a layer between the current and the ambient. However, the maximum values of vorticity are slightly lower and confined to a more structured region. The roll-up of this vorticity into Kelvin-Helmholtz billows, observed in the bottom current, is not visible in figure 5 as the development of the instability is forced further downstream due to the smaller perturbations tripping this instability.

The features seen in figures 4 and 5 are reflected in the streamline plot in figure 6. The dominance of the principal recirculation cell is balanced by its weakness indicated by the wide spacing of the streamlines within it. The boundary between the current and the ambient fluid is clearly marked by the change in spacing of the streamlines at a position corresponding approximately to that predicted by Benjamin (1968) (indicated by the dashed line). For a stress-free surface, we expect the stagnation streamline to coincide with the free surface. However, as the surface here is not stress free, as witnessed by the elevated nose seen in figure 4, we expect the

Figure 6: Streamlines for a surface current with Re≈1300. The dash curve superimposed represents Benjamin's prediction for the shape of the current

stagnation point to be just above and behind the nose. However, the structure of the streamlines does not bear this out, probably because of a combination of the averaging procedure and the limited resolution of the velocity measurements.

5 Conclusions

The gravity currents running over solid bottom (no-slip boundary) displayed the expected features in agreement with previous experimental and numerical results, and we verified experimentally that the stagnation point is below the foremost point of the head. Dense fluid is supplied from the centre of the head to the leading edge by two main counter-rotating rolls whose intensities and positions depend on the boundary condition. Another interesting feature is the generation of negative shear strain in the ambient fluid just upstream of the nose, which indicates there is viscous dissipation not only inside the head but in the ambient fluid. The gravity currents running along the free surface display a generally good agreement with Benjamin's theoretical shape. However, the experimental results suggest that the liquid free surface may hold an intermediate boundary condition between a full slip and a full non-slip condition that has been overlooked previously. We detected changes in the expected shape of the head probably beyond those discussed in this paper due to random experimental fluctuations in the surfactant concentration between the current and the ambient fluid, leading to an imbalance of surface tension. Even though the results presented here depend critically on our experimental conditions, we believe that surface effects may be present in both natural and experimental situations, and must be taken into account for a satisfactory representation of the gravity current running along a fluid interface.

References

Alahyari A; Longmire EK (1996) Development and structure of a gravity current head. Experiments in Fluids 20: 410-416.

Benjamin TB (1968) Gravity currents and related phenomena. J. Fluid Mech. 31: 209-248.

Britter RE; Simpson JE (1978) Experiments on the dynamics of a gravity current head. J. Fluid Mech. 88: 223-240.

Dalziel, S.B. (1992) Decay of rotating turbulence: some particle tracking experiments; Appl. Scien. Res. 49, 217-244.

Dalziel, S.B. (1993) Rayleigh-Taylor instability: experiments with image analysis; Dyn. Atmos. Oceans, 20 127-153.

Hartel C; Meiburg E; Necker F (2000) Direct numerical simulation of lock-release gravity currents. Submitted to J. Fluid Mech.

Simpson JE; Britter RE (1979) The dynamics of the head of a gravity current advancing over a horizontal surface. J. Fluid Mech. 94: 477-495.

Simpson JE (1997) Gravity currents: In the environment and the laboratory. 2nd Ed. Cambridge University Press, Cambridge, UK.

LPT is a researcher of Consejo Nacional de Investigaciones Científicas y Técnicas (CONICET), Argentina. LPT acknowledges the support of UNCPBA and CONICET. SBD acknowledges the support of Yorkshire Water plc.

16

TURBULENCE AND MIXING

Thermohaline Buoyancy and Mixing

Raouf E. Baddour

Civil and Environmental Engineering, University of Western Ontario, London, Canada N6A 5B9
rbaddour@julian.uwo.ca

1. Abstract

Turbulent mixing in a thermohaline environment is studied with an equation of state, which is nonlinear in temperature and linear in salinity. Expressions for calculating local and integrated buoyancy forces are formulated and applied in modelling jets and internal hydraulic jumps. The results revealed that nonlinear buoyancy effects are not confined to cold climate conditions, but are noticeable in a wide range of temperature and salinity. Nonlinear effects are found significant when thermal-buoyancy and saline-buoyancy are in opposite directions.

2. Introduction

Thermohaline buoyancy plays an important role in many environmental and oceanographic applications. Circulation and mixing caused by temperature and salinity gradients are commonly modelled using a linearized equation of state, *Whitehead* (1995). This study was conducted to study the limitations of this approximation and develop tools to model thermohaline mixing problems.

3. Thermohaline Equation of State

The buoyancy of a flow with variable temperature and salinity is governed by an equation of state. Some of the earliest equations of state for seawater can be traced back to the work of *Knudsen, Forch and Sörensen* in 1902. More recently, *Millero and Poisson* (1981) developed a precise equation of state for seawater. Under normal atmospheric pressure, this equation is given by:

$$(1) \quad \rho(T,S) \; = \; f_0(T) + f_1(T)\,S + \; f_2(T)\,S^{\frac{3}{2}} + CS^2$$

where ρ = density in kg/m^3, T = temperature in $^\circ C$, S = Salinity in *ppt*, f_0, f_1 and f_2 are only functions of temperature and C is a constant. This equation was shown by *Millero and Poisson* to accurately fit water density data in the range $0<T<40^\circ C$ and $0<S<40$ ppt. The terms proportional to $S^{3/2}$ and S^2 were not included on physical grounds, but on purely statistical grounds. These two terms are indeed much smaller than the other terms in Equ 1, and a simpler equation of the form:

$$(2) \quad \rho(T,S) \; = \; f_0(T) + f_1'(T)\,S$$

can be used for modelling thermohaline buoyancy without significant loss of accuracy. Equ 2 recognises that the density dependence on temperature is nonlinear but assumes that the density dependence on salinity is linear. Note that f_0 is the density of pure water and f_1' is adjusted in Equ 2 to obtain density values similar to *Millero and Poisson's* full equation throughout the range of temperature and salinity stated above. Expressing f_0 and f_1' as polynomials we have:

(3) $\quad \rho = \sum_{i=0}^{n} a_i T^i + S \sum_{i=0}^{m} b_i T^i$

A fifth order polynomial (n=5) defines accurately the function f_0, and according to *Bigg (1967)*:a_0 = 999.842594 , a_1 = 6.793952 x 10^{-2}, a_2 = - 9.095290 x 10^{-3}, a_3 = 1.001685 x 10^{-4}, a_4 = - 1.120083 x 10^{-6} and a_5 = 6.536332 x 10^{-9}. The function f_1' is, on the other hand, well approximated by a 2nd order polynomial (m=2) and b_0 = 0.8069236, b_1 = - 3.042878 x 10^{-3} and b_2 = 3.280458 x 10^{-5}, *Baddour (1994)*. The linear form of the equation of state is recovered with n=1 and m=0, i.e

(4) $\quad \rho = a_0 + a_1 T + b_0 S$

When Equ 4 is used, the coefficients a_0, a_1 and b_0 are chosen to best fit the equation of state over a small range of temperature and salinity.

4. Thermohaline Buoyancy

Buoyancy is proportional to the density difference $\Delta \rho = \rho - \rho_r$, where the subscript r refers to a reference state of the surrounding water. When modelling thermohaline phenomena, it is desirable to relate buoyancy directly to temperature difference $\Delta T = T - T_r$ and salinity difference $\Delta S = S - S_r$. This can be achieved by transforming the variables of the equation of state from (T, S, ρ) to $(\Delta T, \Delta S, \Delta \rho)$. Hence by moving the origin of the equation of state from $(0,0,0)$ to (T_r, S_r, ρ_r) and adopting the sign convention that positive buoyancy acts upwards, it can be shown that:

(5) $\quad B = -\dfrac{g}{\rho_r} \Delta \rho = -\dfrac{g}{\rho_r} \left(\sum_{i=1}^{n} \alpha_i \, \Delta T^i + S_r \sum_{i=1}^{m} \beta_i \, \Delta T^i + \Delta S \sum_{i=0}^{m} \beta_i \, \Delta T^i \right)$

where g is the gravity constant. The coefficients α_i and β_i are related to a_i, b_i and T_r and given by :

$\alpha_i = \sum_{j=i}^{n} \dfrac{j!}{i!\,(j-i)!} \, a_j T_r^{j-i} \qquad i \in [1,n]$

$\beta_i = \sum_{j=i}^{m} \dfrac{j!}{i!\,(j-i)!} \, a_j T_r^{j-i} \qquad i \in [0,m]$

For a linearized equation of state (n=1, m=0), Equ. 5 reduces to:

(6) $\quad B_l = -\dfrac{g}{\rho_r}\left(a_1 \Delta T + b_0 \Delta S \right)$

where B_l will be referred to as linear buoyancy. The thermohaline buoyancy is conveniently separated into linear and nonlinear components, i.e.

(7) $B = B_l + B_{nl}$

where B_{nl} will be referred to as nonlinear buoyancy. It will be examined in the following in terms of the mixing parameter

(8) $\gamma = \dfrac{\Delta T}{\Delta T_0} = \dfrac{\Delta S}{\Delta S_0}$

where ΔT_0 and ΔS_0 are temperature and salinity scales, respectively. For example, in the case of a thermohaline jet, ΔT_0 and ΔS_0 are the initial temperature and salinity differences between the jet and the surrounding water. Hence, the physical domain of γ is in the range $0<\gamma<1$ with $\gamma=0$ defining the fully-diluted state of the jet and $\gamma = 1$ the non-diluted state. It can be seen from (6) and (8) that γ is also equal to the buoyancy ratio B_l/B_0 , which is the tacit assumption made when the equation of state is linearized. Substituting from (6), (7) and (8) into (5), it can be shown that the nonlinear buoyancy is:

(9) $B_{nl} = -\dfrac{g}{\rho_r}\gamma(\gamma-1)\left(\alpha_2\Delta T_0^2 + \beta_2 S_r \Delta T_0^2 + \beta_1 \Delta T_0\Delta S_0\right) + O(\Delta T_0^3) + O(\Delta T_0^2 \Delta S_0) + O(\Delta T_0^4) + O(\Delta T_0^5)$

All the terms in Equ 9 vanish at $\gamma = 0$ and $\gamma = 1$. Normalized values of all the terms contributing to B_{nl} are presented in Fig. 1. The dominant second-order term, B_{nl2}, reaches a peak value at $\gamma = 0.5$ and B_{nl} at $\gamma \approx 0.5$

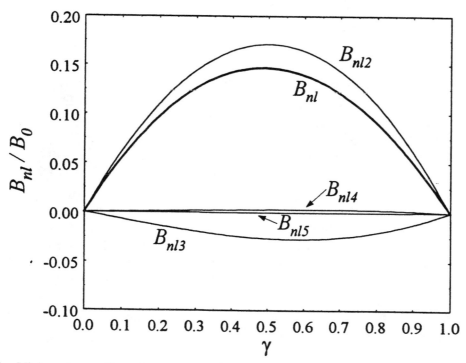

Figure 1. High-order nonlinear buoyancy variations with γ : T_r=20°C, S_r=30 ppt, ΔT_0= 15°C, ΔS_0= 5 ppt

Fig. 2 shows variations of B_{nl} with γ for different thermohaline conditions at moderate ($T_r=20^\circ C$) and low ($T_r=0^\circ C$) temperatures. The results show that the nonlinear buoyancy can be of same magnitude as the initial buoyancy, B_0, over a wide range of temperature. Nonlinear effects were significant when the buoyancy due to temperature and buoyancy due to salt were of comparable magnitude and in opposite directions.

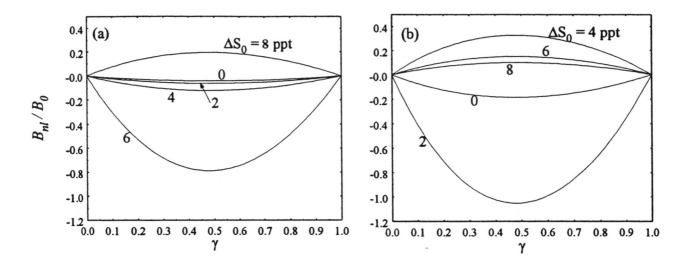

Figure 2.   Nonlinear buoyancy variations with mixing parameter: S_r=30 ppt, ΔT_0= 15°C.
(a) T_r=20°C ; (b) T_r=0°C

5. Thermohaline jets

The basic properties of buoyant jets were reviewed by *List (1982)*. For round jets, the mean excess temperature ΔT, and mean excess salinity ΔS, are approximately given by the Gaussian profiles:

$$(10) \qquad \Delta T = \Delta T_m \, e^{(-\frac{r^2}{b_T^2})} \quad ; \quad \Delta S = \Delta S_m \, e^{(-\frac{r^2}{b_S^2})}$$

where m denotes a centre line value, r the radial distance, and b_T and b_S are characteristic radii of temperature and salinity, respectively. The distribution of thermohaline buoyancy corresponding to these Gaussian profiles was studied using Equ 5. Fig 3 shows typical buoyancy profiles in thermohaline jets. The Gaussian profile of buoyancy, which corresponds to a linearized equation of state, is also shown for comparison. In Fig. 3a the nonlinear effects are significant because the buoyancy induced by heat is in a direction opposite to the buoyancy induced by salt. The opposite occurs in Fig. 3b, and nonlinear effects are relatively small.

The mean buoyancy force integrated over the cross-section area of a jet is important in determining the jet momentum. For a round jet, the buoyancy force is calculated as

$$(11) \qquad G = \int B \, dA = \int_0^\infty B \, (2\pi r) \, dr$$

and substituting from (10) into (5) and integrating gives:

$$(12) \quad G = -\frac{\pi b^2 g}{\rho_r} \left(\sum_{i=1}^{n} \frac{\alpha_i \Delta T_m^i}{\left(\frac{i}{\lambda_T^2}\right)} + S_r \sum_{i=1}^{m} \frac{\beta_i \Delta T_m^i}{\left(\frac{i}{\lambda_T^2}\right)} + \Delta S_m \sum_{i=0}^{m} \frac{\beta_i \Delta T_m^i}{\left(\frac{i}{\lambda_T^2} + \frac{1}{\lambda_S^2}\right)} \right)$$

where b is the characteristic radius of the velocity profile and $\lambda_T = b_T/b$ and $\lambda_S = b_S/b$ are about 1.2. Closure of the jet model was accomplished by invoking the entrainment hypothesis by *Morton, Taylor and Turner (1956)*. More details may be found in *Baddour (1994)* and *Zhang (1997)*, where thermal and thermohaline jet models were found capable of reproducing the essential features of jets, including those with reversing buoyancy.

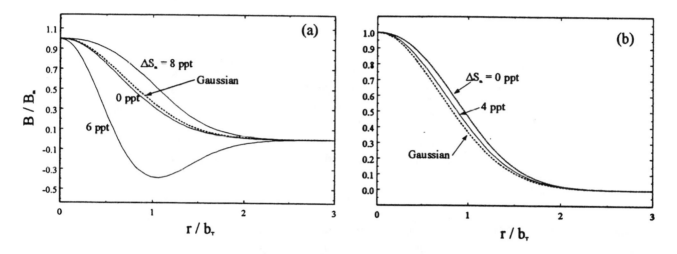

Figure 3.   Buoyancy profiles in thermohaline jets: S_r=30 ppt, T_r=20°C.
(a) ΔT_m= 15°C ; (b) ΔT_m= -15°C

6. Thermohaline internal hydraulic jumps

The thermohaline buoyancy equation was also applied in modelling internal hydraulic jumps. The objective was to study the miscible behaviour of thermohaline jump and extend the work on density jump by *Wilkinson and Wood (1971)*, and thermal jump by *Baddour (1991)*. In non-dimensional form, the governing equation of an expanding thermohaline jump reduces to:

$$(13) \quad Fr_0^2 = \frac{1}{2}\left(\frac{\beta r}{\mu^2 - \beta r}\right)\left(1 - \phi[\beta(r^2 - 1) + 1]\right)$$

where Fr_0 = initial densimetric Froude number, $r = h_1/h_0$ = depth ratio, $\mu = Q_1/Q_0$ = volume flux ratio or dilution, $\beta = b_1/b_0$ = width ratio and $\phi = B_1/B_0$ = buoyancy ratio. All the ratios are defined across the jump with subscript 1 denoting conditions after the jump, and subscript 0 before the jump. For a saline jump, the buoyancy is linear, and $\phi = \Delta S_1/\Delta S_0 = 1/\mu$. The miscible behaviour of the jump was studied by examining the properties of Equ 13. Typical results are shown in Fig. 4, where depth ratio is plotted against dilution for thermohaline and saline jumps. The jump solutions obtained have the form of a loop, with an upper subcritical branch ($Fr<1$) and a lower supercritical branch ($Fr>1$). The two branches meet at a critical point where $Fr = 1$ and $\mu = \mu_{max}$. As seen in Fig. 4, nonlinear buoyancy increases the size of loop and potentially creates deeper and more dilute flow downstream of the jump.

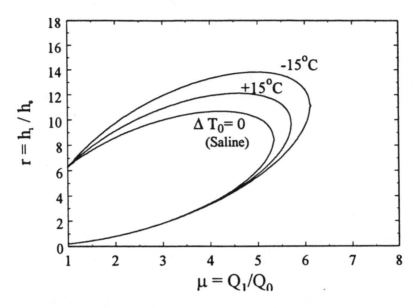

Figure 4. Miscible behaviour of thermohaline jump: $Fr_0 = 10$, $\beta = 5$, $S_r = 5$ ppt, $T_r = 5°C$, $\Delta S_0 = -5$ppt.

7. Concluding remarks

Themohaline buoyancy was formulated through a polynomial transformation of the equation of state. When heat and mass are conserved, maximum nonlinear buoyancy occurred when the mixing parameter $\gamma \approx 0.5$. Thermohaline buoyancy was also applied in modelling jets and miscible hydraulic jumps. The results showed that nonlinear effects were not confined to cold climate conditions, but were noticeable throughout the range of temperature and salinity. The nonlinear effects were particularly significant when thermal-buoyancy and saline-buoyancy were acting in opposite directions.

Support provided by the Natural Sciences and Engineering Research Council of Canada is gratefully acknowledged

8. References

Baddour R.E. (1991) Thermal hydraulic jump: theory and experiment .J. Fluid Mech., 226, 243-256

Baddour R.E. (1994) Thermalsaline bubble plumes. *Recent Advances in the Fluid Mech of Turbulent Jets and Plumes* , Eds P.A. Davies and M.J.V. Neves, Kluwer Academic Publ., 117-129

Bigg, P.H. (1967) Density of water in SI units over the range 0-40oC. *Brit. J. Appl. Phy.*, 18, 521-525

List E.J. (1982) Turbulent jets and plumes. *Annu. Rev. Fluid Mech.* 14: 189-212

Millero, F.J. and Poisson, A. (1981) International one-atmosphere equation of state of seawater. *Deep Sea Research*, 28A, 625-629

Morton, B.R., Taylor, G.I. and Turner, J.S. (1956) Turbulent gravitational convection from maintained and instantaneous sources. *Proc. R. Soc. Lond.*, A 231: 466-478.

Whitehead, J.A. (1995). Thermohaline ocean processes and models. *Annu. Rev. Fluid Mech.* 27: 89-113

Wilkinson D. L and Wood I. R (1971) A rapidly varied flow phenomenon in a two-layer flow. *J. of Fluid Mech.*, 47, 241-256

Zhang, H. (1997) Saline, thermal and thermal-saline buoyant jets. *PhD Thesis*, University of Western Ontario, London, Canada

Laboratory Experiments on Turbulent Lengthscales and Diffusivities in Stratified Fluids of Different Prandtl Number

M. E. Barry, G. N. Ivey and K. B. Winters[1]

Centre for Water Research, University of Western Australia, Nedlands 6907, Western Australia.
[1] Also at Applied Physics Laboratory, University of Washington, Seattle 98105-6698, USA.
barrym@cwr.uwa.edu.au, ivey@cwr.uwa.edu.au, winters@cwr.uwa.edu.au

1. Abstract

Linearly salt stratified fluids of different Prandtl number were subjected to turbulent stirring by a horizontally oscillating vertical grid in a closed laboratory system. The experimental setup allowed the independent measurement of an rms turbulent lengthscale L_t, turbulent diffusivity for mass K_ρ, rate of dissipation of turbulent kinetic energy ϵ, stratification strength N and viscosity ν, for a wide range of turbulence intensities, $\epsilon/\nu N^2$. The behaviour of both L_t and K_ρ was characterised in terms of this turbulence intensity and two regimes were identified.

In the more energetic of these regimes (Regime E, where $300 < \epsilon/\nu N^2 < 10^5$), quantitative expressions for both L_t and K_ρ were identified. In this regime, L_t was found to be a function of only ν, κ and N, whilst K_ρ was a function of ν, κ and $(\epsilon/\nu N^2)^{1/3}$. From these expressions for L_t and K_ρ, a scaling relation for the root mean square turbulent velocity, U_t, was derived. This scaling relation showed good agreement with other data sets.

In the weaker turbulence regime (Regime W, where $10 < \epsilon/\nu N^2 < 300$) a quantitative relationship was found for K_ρ as a function of ν, κ and $\epsilon/\nu N^2$.

Comparison was made between our expressions for K_ρ and the model of Osborn (1980). For $10 < \epsilon/\nu N^2 < 1000$, the model of Osborn (1980) differs from our experimental results by approximately a factor of 2. For higher turbulence intensities the model and experimental results diverge, such that at $\epsilon/\nu N^2 \approx 10^4$, there is approximately an order of magnitude discrepancy between the model and our measurements.

2. Introduction

A clear understanding of the irreversible vertical transport of mass in a stably stratified turbulent flow is fundamental to quantifying the dynamics of density stratified fluids. The rate at which this transport occurs has historically been modelled as a turbulent diffusivity for mass, K_ρ. Since K_ρ influences the distribution of heat, mass, contaminants and biota throughout a turbulent fluid (eg Tennekes and Lumley, 1972), an understanding of this quantity is essential to the management of aquatic systems such as lakes, estuaries and the oceans.

The simplest model describing turbulent transport in homogeneous isotropic turbulence relates a turbulent diffusivity K to a turbulent velocity scale U and a turbulent integral lengthscale L (Tennekes and Lumley, 1972),

$$K \sim U \times L. \tag{1}$$

This expression for K is considered to represent a bulk eddy diffusivity. Taylor (1935) found that the rate of dissipation of turbulent kinetic energy per unit mass, ϵ, is,

$$\epsilon \sim \frac{u^3}{l}, \tag{2}$$

where u is the fluctuating component of velocity and l is a linear dimension defining the scale of the turbulent field. If we assume that U, L, u and l are well represented by their root mean square velocity and length scales U_t and L_t respectively, (1) and (2) can be combined to give,

$$K \sim \epsilon^{1/3} L_t^{4/3}. \tag{3}$$

Currently, the most widely used model for estimating K_ρ in geophysical flows was developed by Osborn (1980) for use in the ocean thermocline,

$$K_\rho \leq 0.2 \frac{\epsilon}{N^2}. \tag{4}$$

Field experiments have been undertaken that estimate K_ρ in lakes and oceans by using tracer techniques and the model of Osborn (1980) (for example Ledwell et al., 1993; Wuest et al., 1996; Polzin et al., 1997). These experiments, however, have typically spanned a small range of turbulence intensities. Whilst several laboratory experiments have examined the behaviour of stratified grid turbulence (eg Ruddick et al., 1989; Park et al., 1994; Rehmann, 1995; Liu, 1995; Holford and Linden, 1999), no controlled laboratory or field experiments have been executed that directly measure K_ρ and quantitatively describe it in terms of fluid and flow properties over a wide range of turbulence intensities. The current work addresses this issue.

3. Experiments

The experimental setup (Figure 1) allowed the independent measurement of K_ρ, ϵ, N, ν and an rms turbulent lengthscale L_t. Turbulence was generated by the horizontal motion of a rigid vertical grid mounted on a pneumatic drive. Under the power of the pneumatic drive, this grid was able to move continually back and forth in the horizontal direction along the entire 500 mm length of the tank at a preselected constant velocity, U_g.

Vertical temperature and conductivity profiles were logged simultaneously using a single fast response FP07 thermistor and 4-electrode fast response conductivity probe (CT), set on a vertical computer controlled traverser. In addition, two L-shaped horizontally oriented fast response FP07 thermistors were mounted on a traversing rack near the centre of the tank. A force transducer was mounted on the apparatus such that it was the sole active link between the pneumatic drive and the grid. Both water and water-glycerol mixtures were used in the experiments and the absolute viscosity, μ, of the fluids was measured using a Haake Viscotester, VT550, incorporating a Haake Sensor System PK100D.

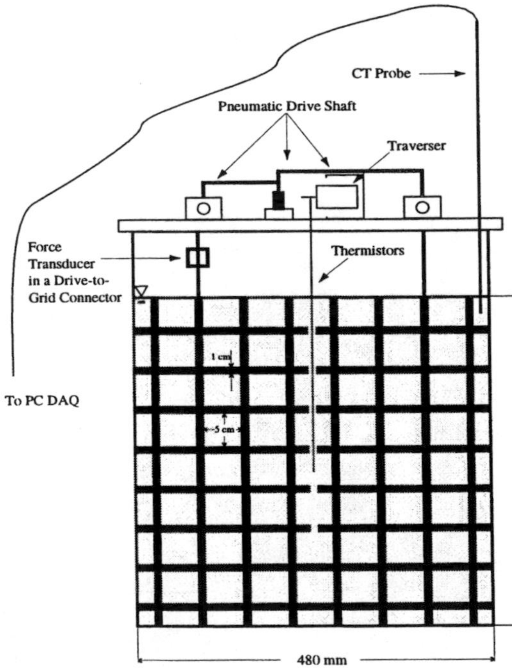

For each experiment, the tank was filled with a linearly salt stratified fluid to a depth of approximately

Figure 1: Experimental setup

480 mm. As a result of the filling process, a small mean vertical temperature gradient also resulted, however the contribution to the fluid density from temperature was far outweighed by the

contribution from salinity. After all fluid motions resulting from the filling process had dissipated, two vertical density profiles of the fluid were taken using the mounted CT. Oscillatory grid motion was then initiated at a preselected constant grid speed to generate turbulence in the fluid. During this time, the time series signals from the force transducer and the horizontally oriented stationary thermistors were logged. We refer to this mixing time as a single mixing event. At the termination of a mixing event, the vertical density profile was twice re-sampled after allowing the fluid to adiabatically resort itself. The above routine was then repeated up to ten times in a given experiment. A summary of the initial conditions for all experiments is shown in the table. Experiments 1 to 8 were executed in salt stratified water, and experiments 9 and 10 in salt stratified water-glycerol solution.

Experiment Number	N^2 (rad^2/s^2)	U_g (cm/s)
1	0.0945	7.4
2	0.1415	7.4
3	0.0217	9.0
4	0.3631	4.5
5	0.5501	7.0
6	0.8423	7.0
7	0.5015	5.2
8	1.1943	4.2
9	0.0569	8.2
10	0.1139	7.5

The rms turbulent lengthscale, L_t, was computed from the stationary thermistor timeseries record by diving the rms temperature fluctuation by the local vertical temperature gradient from the CT profiles,

$$L_t = \frac{\left(\overline{T'^2}\right)^{1/2}}{\frac{d\overline{T}}{dz}}. \tag{5}$$

In a closed stratified system, a turbulent diffusivity K_ρ will manifest itself as a temporal change in the system's background potential energy, E_b, where E_b is the minimum potential energy attainable through adiabatic redistribution of ρ (Winters et al., 1995). Hence, we used the CT profiles (which were the adiabatically resorted profiles taken before and after a mixing event) to compute a time and volume average K_ρ,

$$K_\rho = \frac{\left(Ag \int_0^H \rho z dz\right)_{final} - \left(Ag \int_0^H \rho z dz\right)_{initial}}{Vg\Delta t \left(\frac{d\rho}{dz}\right)_{average}}, \tag{6}$$

where A is the horizontal area of the tank, V is the volume of the fluid, Δt is the duration of the mixing event and $(d\rho/dz)_{average}$ is the background density gradient averaged over a mixing event.

The rate of dissipation of turbulent kinetic energy, ϵ, was calculated from a power balance in the experimental system,

$$\sigma \times F_D \times U_g = \epsilon \times mass + \frac{\Delta E_b}{\Delta t}, \tag{7}$$

where σ is the grid solidity and F_D is the measured drag force. We used (7) to compute a time and volume average ϵ, since all other quantities were measured directly.

4. Results

We have interpreted our rms turbulent lengthscale and turbulent diffusivity results in terms of a turbulence intensity $\epsilon/\nu N^2$, as this parameter is widely used in characterising turbulent flows. For all figures, $*$ and $\circ$ show the results from the water and water-glycerol experiments respectively.

In Figure 2, L_t is plotted against L_{co} for $\epsilon/\nu N^2 > 300$, where L_{co} is the convective lengthscale, $L_{co} = (\nu\kappa)^{1/4}/N^{1/2}$. L_{co} has been used in the analysis of laminar horizontal intrusions into stratified fluids (Ivey and Corcos, 1982) and decaying stratified turbulence (Pearson and Linden, 1983). In the current experiments, $L_t = 37L_{co}$ for $\epsilon/\nu N^2 > 300$. We refer to this range in $\epsilon/\nu N^2$ as the energetic regime, Regime E. Our expression for L_t suggests that in this regime, a turbulent overturn can lose its identity by the diffusion of both momentum and density. Further, it shows that L_t is independent of ϵ, as ϵ was varied by more than an order of magnitude in this regime. We suggest that L_{co} is a fundamental lengthscale of the turbulence in Regime E. For $\epsilon/\nu N^2 < 300$, which we refer to as the weaker turbulent regime, Regime W, this relationship no longer holds.

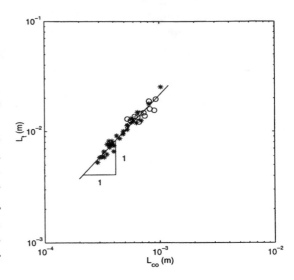

Figure 2: The rms turbulent lengthscale L_t vs L_{co} for all experiments with $\epsilon/\nu N^2 > 300$.

In Figure 3 we have plotted K_ρ/κ, K_ρ/ν and $K_\rho/(\nu^{2/3}\kappa^{1/3})$ vs $\epsilon/\nu N^2$. The Figure shows that normalisation of K_ρ by either κ or ν does not collapse the data from the experiments of different Prandtl number fluids. Figure 3c, however, shows excellent collapse. We note that this collapse of K_ρ in Regime E is predicted by substitution of our expression for L_t from the best fit in Figure (2) into (3).

Regardless of the normalisation of K_ρ, however, we note that Figure 3 demonstrates a smooth evolution of K_ρ over more than four orders of magnitude of $\epsilon/\nu N^2$. Further, even for the weakest turbulence intensity at $\epsilon/\nu N^2 = 10$, K_ρ is approximately three orders of magnitude greater than molecular diffusivity, κ.

Our turbulent diffusivity data is separable into two regimes, with the division between these regimes also at $\epsilon/\nu N^2 \approx 300$. We again refer to these regimes as Regimes E and W. From Figure 3c our collapsed data shows that in Regime E,

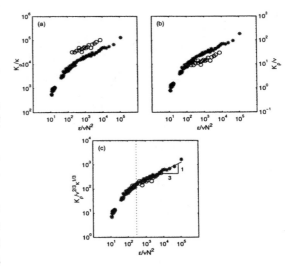

Figure 3: K_ρ normalised by (a) κ (b) ν and (c) $\nu^{2/3}\kappa^{1/3}$ for all experiments. The dotted line is at the transition between Regimes E and W. The solid line in (c) is slope 1/3 (see (8)).

$$K_\rho = 20\nu^{2/3}\kappa^{1/3}\left(\frac{\epsilon}{\nu N^2}\right)^{1/3}. \tag{8}$$

We do not have data from the water-glycerol experiments in Regime W. However, the turbulent diffusivity data from the water experiments is attenuated throughout this regime and this again suggests that the turbulence has undergone a transition in character. We fit a linear regression to the data in this regime,

$$K_\rho = 0.65\nu^{2/3}\kappa^{1/3}\left(\frac{\epsilon}{\nu N^2}\right). \tag{9}$$

Given the rms lengthscale and turbulent diffusivity results, we predict a time and volume averaged rms turbulent velocity scale, U_t in Regime E via (1),

$$U_t \sim \left(\frac{\epsilon}{\nu N^2}\right)^{1/3} (\nu N)^{1/2} Pr^{-1/12}. \tag{10}$$

This scale prediction is in excellent agreement with the velocity measurements of Saggio and Imberger (2000) and Itsweire et al. (1986) for $\epsilon/\nu N^2 > 300$.

5. Discussion

It is useful to recast our results in terms of prior models for K_ρ. Of particular interest is the comparison between our results and the prediction of K_ρ due to Osborn (1980),

$$K_\rho \;\leq\; 0.2\frac{\epsilon}{N^2}, \tag{11}$$

$$\text{ie} \quad \frac{K_\rho}{\nu^{2/3}\kappa^{1/3}} \;\leq\; 0.2\frac{\epsilon}{\nu N^2}Pr^{1/3}. \tag{12}$$

In order to compare (12) to our results, we have selected a value of $Pr = 7$ for heat stratified water. Figure 4 shows normalised diffusivities from the current experiments, and $K_\rho/\nu^{2/3}\kappa^{1/3}$ predicted from (12) with $Pr = 7$ as a solid line. The upper and lower bound dotted lines represent a factor of 2 higher and lower than this prediction.

Our results show that for the grid turbulence in these experiments, (12) is a reasonable estimate of the turbulent diffusivity over only a limited range of approximately $10 < \epsilon/\nu N^2 < 1000$. In this range (12) is within a factor of 2 of the diffusivity measured in these experiments. Above this range, (12) is an overestimate of the measured K_ρ, and when $\epsilon/\nu N^2 \approx 10^4$, it is approximately an order of magnitude greater than the experimental results.

The derivation of (12) assumes a steady-state homogeneous turbulent kinetic energy balance, defines K_ρ in terms of an advective buoyancy flux, and assumes an approximately constant flux Richardson number, $R_f = 0.15$. It can be shown that these experiments were executed such that the first two assumptions were as close to being satisfied as possible. We conclude then that the choice of R_f as a constant is likely to be the primary cause of the divergence between (12) and the K_ρ measured in these experiments for $\epsilon/\nu N^2$ greater than approximately 1000.

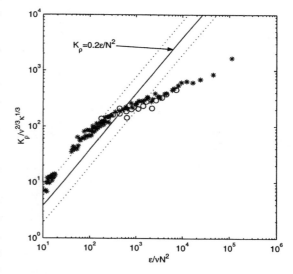

Figure 4: Normalised experimental diffusivity results from all experiments and the prediction of Osborn (1980); —, Osborn (1980), $Pr = 7$, $\cdots$, twice and half of the Osborn (1980) prediction.

In order to achieve agreement between the prediction of Osborn (1980) and these experimental results in Regime E, R_f could be written as some function of ϵ, N^2 and a characteristic turbulent lengthscale L. By analysing laboratory data, Ivey and Imberger (1991) suggested such a dependence. Alternatively, we suggest that for $\epsilon/\nu N^2 > 300$, K_ρ is better expressed directly as a function of $(\epsilon/\nu N^2)^{1/3}$ and a constant of proportionality, rather than forcing it to be a function of ϵ/N^2 and some variable flux Richardson number to be determined. Further, using a formulation involving R_f requires knowledge of ϵ, N^2 and L. However, by using (8) or (9), K_ρ can be evaluated by measuring only ϵ and N^2, without knowledge of a turbulent lengthscale.

6. References

Holford, J. M. and Linden, P. F. (1999). Turbulent mixing in a stratified fluid. *Dynamics of Atmospheres and Oceans*, 30:173–198.

Itsweire, E. C., Helland, K. N., and Van Atta, C. W. (1986). The evolution of grid-generated turbulence in a stably stratified fluid. *Journal of Fluid Mechanics*, 162:299–338.

Ivey, G. N. and Corcos, G. M. (1982). Boundary mixing in a stratified fluid. *Journal of Fluid Mechanics*, 121:1–26.

Ivey, G. N. and Imberger, J. (1991). On the nature of turbulence in a stratified fluid. Part I: The energetics of mixing. *Journal of Physical Oceanography*, 21:650–658.

Ledwell, J. R., Watson, A. J., and Law, C. S. (1993). Evidence for slow mixing across the pycnocline from an open-ocean tracer-release experiment. *Nature*, 364:701–703.

Liu, H.-T. (1995). Energetics of grid turbulence in a stably stratified fluid. *Journal of Fluid Mechanics*, 296:127–157.

Osborn, T. R. (1980). Estimates of the local rate of vertical diffusion from dissipation measurements. *Journal of Physical Oceanography*, 10:83–89.

Park, Y.-G., Whitehead, J. A., and Gnanadeskian, A. (1994). Turbulent mixing in stratified fluids: layer formation and energetics. *Journal of Fluid Mechanics*, 279:279–311.

Pearson, H. J. and Linden, P. F. (1983). The final stage of decay of turbulence in stably stratified fluid. *Journal of Fluid Mechanics*, 134:195–203.

Polzin, K. L., Toole, J. M., Ledwell, J. R., and Schmitt, R. W. (1997). Spatial variability of turbulent mixing in the abyssal ocean. *Science*, 276:93–96.

Rehmann, C. R. (1995). *Effects of stratification and molecular diffusivity on the mixing efficiency of decaying grid turbulence*. PhD thesis, Depertment of Civil Engineering, Stanford University, California, USA.

Ruddick, B. R., McDougall, T. J., and Turner, J. S. (1989). The formation of layers in a uniformly stirred density gradient. *Deep-Sea Research*, 36:597–609.

Saggio, A. and Imberger, J. (2000). Mixing and turbulent fluxes in the metalimnion of a stratified lake. *In preparation*.

Taylor, G. I. (1935). Statistical theory of turbulence. In *Proc. of The Royal Society of London, Series A*, volume 151, page 421.

Tennekes, H. and Lumley, J. L. (1972). *A First Course in Turbulence*. Massachusetts Institute of Technology, USA.

Winters, K. B., Lombard, P. N., Riley, J. R., and D'Asaro, E. A. (1995). Available potential energy and mixing in density-stratified fluids. *Journal of Fluid Mechanics*, 289:115–128.

Wuest, A., van Senden, D. C., Imberger, J., Piepke, G., and Gloor, M. (1996). Comparison of diapycnal diffusivity measured by tracer and microstructure techniques. *Dynamics of Atmospheres and Oceans*, 24:27–39.

A New Class of Self-Similar Turbulence: Super-exponential Rayleigh-Taylor Flow

R. E. Breidenthal

Aeronautics and Astronautics, University of Washington, Seattle, WA USA 98195-8156

1. Abstract

A new class of forced, self-similar turbulence is proposed. This class is simply related to all other known self-similar turbulent flows. In unforced turbulence, the large-scale vortex rotation period is essentially equal to the vortex age, a direct consequence of dimensional analysis. As the vortex ages, it entrains irrotational fluid or fluid of opposite sign vorticity and hence rotates more slowly. For exponentially forced turbulence, with a constant e-folding time, the rotation period of the vortex is a constant, the imposed e-folding time. The entrainment rate is correspondingly reduced. A third case is called super-exponential forcing, where the e-folding time is itself a function of time. If the e-folding time declines linearly with time, then a self-similar flow is achieved, in which the vortex rotation period declines by a constant fraction at each rotation. This super-exponential flow is the mirror image of unforced turbulence, where the rotation period increases by a constant fraction at each rotation. As a consequence, it is predicted to have special characteristics, such as a small entrainment rate. This flow may be important in geo- and astrophysics as well as in inertial-confinement fusion.

2. Introduction

When light fluid is accelerated into heavy fluid, the stratified interface between them becomes unstable (Rayleigh 1900, Taylor 1950). For a constant acceleration, the resulting turbulent Rayleigh-Taylor flow grows at a rate proportional to the hydraulic speed, rapidly entraining the pure, irrotational fluid into the turbulence and mixing it. At Reynolds numbers greater than about 10^3, i.e. above the mixing transition, mixing is entrainment-limited. Thus the "product thickness" of the mixed fluid must be proportional to, and of the same order as, the layer thickness (Breidenthal 1981).

In many situations, however, the acceleration is not constant. The initiation of a volcanic eruption in a magma chamber presumably has a variable acceleration of light, vesicular magma into heavier fluid. Violent astrophysical events and inertial confinement fusion (Nuckolls et al. 1972) are other examples. Because the entrainment and mixing in these processes can have important dynamic consequences, it is of great practical interest to understand the effect of variable acceleration. The amount of mixing in Rayleigh-Taylor flow has not yet been measured for either the constant or variable time-varying acceleration, but our uncertainty is much greater in the variable acceleration case, for the reasons discussed below.

In general, acceleration is known to have a strong effect on turbulent entrainment. In boundary layers, positive acceleration tends to stabilize or relaminarize the flow (Narasimha & Sreenivasan 1979). Negative acceleration has the opposite effect. In the free jet, acceleration inhibits entrainment (Breidenthal 1986 and 1987, Kato et al. 1987, Zhang & Johari 1996, Johari & Paduano 1997). Acceleration is the only known method for controlling the far-field mixing rate in the jet.

The exponential jet is a self-similar flow where the nozzle injection speed increases exponentially in time. In a jet with constant nozzle speed, the large-scale vortices have a rotation period essentially equal to their chronological age. An obvious consequence of dimensional analysis, this is true in general for all turbulent flows that do not have any external time scale imposed on them. However, in the exponential jet, the rotation period is compelled to be the e-folding time of the acceleration (Breidenthal 1986, Zhang & Johari 1996).

The exponential jet provides one important hint about the control of turbulence. When the large-scales vortices have an external e-folding time scale imposed on them, their entrainment rate changes.

A second important hint is that ordinary, unforced turbulence is self-similar, in that the rotation period increases by a constant factor at each vortex rotation. It is natural to ask if another kind of self-similar flow is possible, a kind of mirror image, where the rotation period *decreases* by a constant fraction at each rotation.

3. Super-exponential Rayleigh-Taylor flow

Consider Rayleigh-Taylor flow with an effective acceleration $g' = g\Delta\rho/\rho = g'_0\exp(t/\tau)$. Here g'_0 is the acceleration at time $t = 0$ and τ is the e-folding time. Suppose $\tau = \tau_0 - \beta t$, where τ_0 is the e-folding time at $t = 0$. If $\beta = -1$, we have the constant acceleration case of classical RT flow. If $\beta = 0$, the acceleration is exponential with a constant e-folding time. For $\beta > 0$, the vortex rotation period declines by a constant factor at each rotation for all $t < \tau_0/\beta$. At $t = \tau_0/\beta$, the vortex rotation rate vanishes, and the flow becomes singular.

For large $\beta > 0$, the baroclinic torques induced by the acceleration at any instant are so large compared to the existing vortical field from earlier torques that the "old" vorticity becomes negligible in comparison with the new. As a consequence, the instantaneous vortex sheet hardly gets a chance to roll up. Since the turbulent entrainment process occurs by this gulping mechanism (Roshko 1976), the entrainment rate is predicted to vanish in the limit of large β.

An experiment to test this prediction has not yet been accomplished. However, a related experiment has already shown a similar result. Eroglu & Breidenthal (1998) observed the vortex dynamics of a special kind of transverse jet. It consisted of a streamwise array of nozzles that increased in width exponentially in the downstream direction. Furthermore, at each nozzle, the injection speed likewise increased exponentially in the streamwise direction, so that the ratio of local nozzle width to injection speed was a constant, called the nozzle time. A second time scale was imposed on the flow, the e-folding time of the primary stream past the exponential array. The ratio of these two times was defined to be an acceleration parameter α. As α increased above one, the vortex roll-up was substantially reduced. The volume of fluid within the vortex declined by about a factor of ten as α increased from zero to about three. Since the mixed fluid can only reside within the vortex at high Peclet number (Broadwell & Breidenthal 1982), the amount of mixing is reduced accordingly.

This experiment is analogous to the proposed super-exponential RT flow. In both cases, there are two time scales imposed on the vortex, the rotation periods for both the current rotation and the next one. The ratio of the current to the next rotation period is the acceleration parameter $\alpha = 1 + \beta$. At large α, the next rotation period is less than the current one.

4. Relation to other self-similar flows

All self-similar flows seem to be related to each other as members in a family, differing only by the value of the parameter β. As we have seen, ordinary, unforced turbulence has $\beta = -1$. Turbulence forced at a single imposed time, such as the exponential jet (Zhang & Johari 1996) or the sinusoidally-forced shear layer, has $\beta = 0$ (Oster & Wygnanski 1982, Roberts 1985). The transverse exponential jet or the super-exponential RT flow has $\beta > 0$.

Figure 1 illustrates the evolution of the vortex rotation period $\tau_v = \tau$ as a function of time t, both normalized by the initial rotation period $\tau_v = \tau_0$ at t = 0. In each of the three cases, the rotation period is a linear function of time originating at the same point. The only difference between the different family members is the slope of the line, $-\beta$.

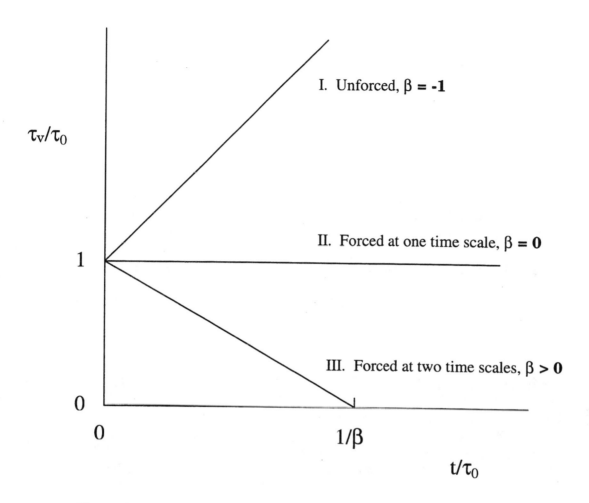

Figure 1. Temporal evolution of the vortex rotation period τ_v for self-similar flows.

5. Conclusions

A new class of self-similar turbulence is proposed. In it, the large-scale vortex rotation period is forced to decline by a constant factor at each vortex rotation. It is thus related to all other self-similar flows, both forced and unforced, where the rotation period is either constant or increasing by a constant factor at each rotation.

In analogy with earlier work on accelerating flows, a proposed "super-exponential" Rayleigh-Taylor flow is predicted to exhibit a small entrainment rate at large accelerations. If this prediction is confirmed by experiment, it may prove useful in understanding certain geophysical eruptions and in achieving ignition in inertial-confinement fusion.

6. Acknowledgements

The author is grateful to Guy Dimonte, Mitsuru Kurosaka, and George Bergantz for stimulating discussions.

7. References

Breidenthal, R. E. 1981 Structure in turbulent mixing layers and wakes using a chemical reaction, *J. Fluid Mech.* **109,** 1.

Breidenthal, R. E. 1986 The turbulent exponential jet, *Phys. of Fluids* **29**, 2346.

Breidenthal, R. E. 1987 Turbulent mixing in accelerating jets, *IUTAM Symposium on Turbulence Management and Relaminarization*, H.W. Liepmann, R. Narasimha (Eds.) Springer-Verlag, New York, 459.

Broadwell, J. E. & Breidenthal, R. E. 1982 A simple model of mixing and chemical reaction in a turbulent shear layer, *J. Fluid Mech.* **125**, 397.

Eroglu, A. & Breidenthal, R. E. 1998 Exponentially Accelerating Jet in Cross-Flow, *AIAA J.* **36,** 1002.

Johari, H. & Paduano, R. 1997 Dilution and mixing in an unsteady turbulent jet, *Exp. Fluids* **23**, 272.

Kato, S. M., Groenewegen, B. C. & Breidenthal, R. E. 1987 On turbulent mixing in nonsteady jets, *AIAA J.* **25**, 165.

Narasimha, R. & Sreenivasan, K. R. 1979 Relaminarization of fluid flows, *Adv. Appl. Mech.* 221.

Nuckolls, J. H. *et al.* 1972 Laser compression of matter to super-high densities: Thermonuclear (CTR) applications, *Nature* **239**, 139.

Oster, D. & Wygnanski, I. 1982 The forced mixing layer between parallel streams, *J. Fluid Mech.* **123,** 91.

Rayleigh, Lord 1900 *Scientific Papers II*, Cambridge, England, 200.

Roberts, F. A. 1985 Effects of a periodic disturbance on structure and mixing in turbulent shear layers and wakes, Ph.D. thesis, Caltech, Pasadena, CA.

Roshko, A. 1976 Structure of turbulent shear flows: A new look, *AIAA J.* **14**, 1349.

Taylor, G. I. 1950 *Proc. R. Soc. London*, Ser. A **201**, 192.

Zhang, Q. & Johari, H. 1996 Effects of acceleration on turbulent jets, *Phys. Fluids* **8**, 2185.

Applicability of the rotating annular flume for entrainment experiments

A. W. Bruens[1] , R. Booij[1], C. Kranenburg[1], J.C. Winterwerp[1,2]

[1]Fluid Mechanics Section, Faculty of Civil Engineering and Geosciences, Delft University of Technology, P.O. Box 5048, 2600 GA Delft, The Netherlands.
[2]WL|delft hydraulics, P.O. Box 117, 2600 MH Delft, The Netherlands
a.bruens@ct.tudelft.nl

1. Abstract

This paper discusses how the rotating annular flume can be used for stratified flow research by minimising its secondary currents. This flume is used to study the entrainment of fresh - saline and fresh - turbid water layers, where either of the two layers is turbulent.

2. Introduction

In nature, water systems are often stratified; examples are warm - cold water, saline - fresh water and turbid - clear water. For engineering and oceanographic applications, mixing at the interface of these fluids plays a critical role. In case of stable stratification, three types of mixing can be distinguished: If the upper, less dense layer is more turbulent, it entrains material from the lower, dense layer. This results in an increase in density of the upper layer and a decrease in thickness of the lower layer (referred to as case 1). If, on the other hand, the lower, dense layer is more turbulent, it entrains material from the upper less dense layer. This results in a decrease in density of the lower layer and an increase in thickness of the lower layer (case 2). If both fluids are equally turbulent, equal volumes of fluid are transferred between the layers, the density of the upper layer increases, the density of the lower layer decreases and the interface becomes less distinct (case 3).

For a long time, laboratory experiments on stratified flows have been carried out in order to enhance the understanding of the mixing process. In the 1960's, the first entrainment experiments in annular flumes were conducted. The advantage of annular flumes is the absence of in- and outflow conditions, as present in straight flumes. The flow in annular flumes is usually driven by a rotating top lid. The disadvantage of these flumes is their curvature; fluid with higher tangential velocity near the lid is driven away from the centerline of the flume and a secondary flow is generated in the flume. In order to minimise these secondary currents, a so-called *rotating* annular flume can be deployed in which the flume itself can rotate in a direction opposite to that of the top lid.

Such a rotating annular flume is also in use at Delft University of Technology. It has a width of 0.3 m, a height of 0.4 m and a mean diameter of 3.7 m. During previous years, the flow was driven by a top lid. In case the flume was filled with a stable two-fluid system, turbulence was mainly generated at the top lid and the upper, less dense layer became turbulent and entrained material from the lower, more dense layer (case 1).

Recently, the top lid was replaced by a rotating base plate to drive the fluid. In case the flume is filled with a stable two-fluid system, turbulence is mainly generated at this base plate and the lower, dense layer becomes turbulent and entrains material from the upper, less dense layer (case 2).

This paper describes the optimisation of the operational conditions of the flume, including the ratio of the rotational speeds of top lid and flume as well as the ratio of rotational speeds of base plate and flume. For both configurations an example of the application for stratified flow research (i.e. entrainment experiments on case 1 and 2) is presented. The experimental results are discussed and compared with an integral entrainment model.

The objective of this paper is to show that sufficiently weak secondary currents can be obtained in annular flumes and that rotating annular flumes are therefore very suitable for stratified flow research.

3. Optimisation of the rotating lid case

To optimise the ratio of the rotational speeds of top lid and flume, extensive clear water measurements (reported in Booij, 1994) were executed using laser-Doppler velocimetry (LDV). The measurements showed that near optimum conditions the pattern of the secondary flows depends strongly on the exact ratio of the rotational speeds U_l/U_f , where U_l is the rotational speed of the top lid and U_f the rotational velocity of the flume. For the aspect ratios used generally in rotating annular flumes the following relation between the optimum ratio and the aspect ratio was found:

$$\frac{U_l}{U_f} + 1 \approx -1.17 \frac{H}{B} \tag{1}$$

where B is the width of the flume and H is the level of the lid above the bottom. However, the high cost of this kind of investigation prohibits the experimental determination of the optimum ratio of rotational speeds for all different flow cases encountered. Moreover, the opacity of sediment-laden fluid and variations of the refraction-index when density differences are induced by variations in the salt content, impedes the use of LDV. This indicates the importance of flow computations for rotating annular flumes. Measured flow patterns can be used for the validation of the computational model to be used. For the present study the numerical model PHOENIX is used. The axi-symmetry allows a computation in a (tapered) slice of the flume. It proved possible to reproduce both the main flow and the secondary flow with a standard $k - \epsilon$ model. The main characteristics of the main flow and the secondary flow can be reproduced sufficiently well for all measured flow cases and the correct optimum ratio of rotational velocities U_l/U_f could be predicted. Figure 1 shows a comparison between measurements and reproduction of the flow at an optimum ratio for a nearly square cross-section. Though computational and experimental results differ in detail, it is concluded that the computational model is suited to simulate the flow in rotating annular flumes of various geometries.

4. Application of the rotating lid conditions

This configuration was applied to study the entrainment processes of a dense, non-turbulent lower layer by a less dense, turbulent upper layer (case 1). Such conditions are met in the case of wind-induced entrainment of stratified lakes, or the entrainment of patches of fluid mud by a turbulent tidal flow.

Experiments were carried out for salinity-induced and sediment-induced stratification. In the latter case, the lower layer was formed by not- to weakly consolidated fluid mud. This was achieved by a limited consolidation time of a well-mixed slurry of cohesive sediment within the flume. These experiments were conducted at relative small values of the overall Richardson number $Ri*$ $(= \frac{\Delta g H}{u*}$, where Δ is relative density difference, g is gravity, H is the thickness of the turbulent layer, and $u*$ is the shear velocity), when viscous effects do not play a role, and at higher values of $Ri*$, when viscous effects become important. In the latter case, the lower layer is dragged with the flow in the upper layer, and little turbulence is produced at the interface between upper and lower layer. This implies that in the flume, turbulence is produced mainly at its side walls.

The results of these experiments are presented in Figure 2, showing the non-dimensional initial entrainment rate $E*$ $(= w_e/u*$, where $w_e = dH/dt)$ as a function of $Ri*$. The large scatter in the data points at low $Ri*$ is caused by the rapid entrainment process and large-amplitude internal waves at the interface, which hamper accurate readings. For more details the reader is referred to (Winterwerp & Kranenburg 1997) .

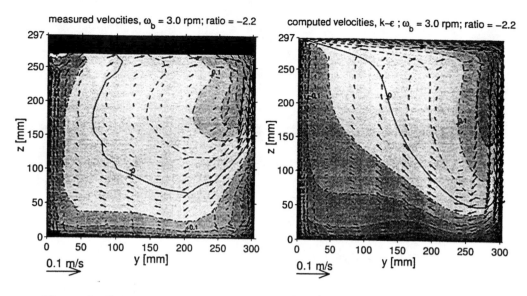

Figure 1: Comparison between measurements and reproduction of the flow.

These experiments are further analysed with an overall entrainment model. This model is derived from a formal integration of the turbulent kinetic energy equation over the turbulent (upper) layer. It contains some empirical coefficients that were obtained from data on salinity- and temperature-induced stratification experiments, presented in the literature, and terms that account for the energy required to keep the sediment particles in suspension and for a possible yield strength in the mud. For more details the reader is referred to Kranenburg and Winterwerp (1997).

For low and high values of Ri_*, this entrainment model yields the following simple laws of entrainment:

$$E_* = \left[\frac{c'_s + c_s}{c_q + Ri_*} \right]^{0.5} \qquad \text{for small } Ri_* \tag{2}$$

$$E_* = \frac{c_w}{\left[2\lambda \frac{H}{B} \right]^{0.5} (c_q + Ri_*)} \qquad \text{for large } Ri_* \tag{3}$$

where c'_s, c_s, c_q and c_w are model coefficients and λ is a side wall friction coefficient. Equation 2 yields the well-known relation $E_* \propto \frac{1}{\sqrt{Ri_*}}$, whereas equation 3 yields $E_* \propto \frac{1}{Ri_*}$. Note that the latter relation is only applicable in flumes of limited width. These relations are also plotted in Figure 2, showing that the trend of the experimental data is predicted properly.

It is concluded that the initial entrainment behaviour of fluid mud is similar to the entrainment rate in salinity-induced stratified flow, and is predicted properly with the entrainment model. This implies that the fluid mud behaves as a viscous fluid.

5. Optimisation of the rotating base plate case

In order to simulate the process of entrainment of a non-turbulent, upper layer by a dense, turbulent lower layer (case 2), the top lid of the rotating annular flume was replaced by a rotatable base plate. This base plate is fixed to the supporting gear, originally used to drive the top lid, consisting of eight vertical, streamlined rods with a chord of 0.1 m and a maximum thickness of 0.004 m. This base plate drives the fluid in the flume and turbulence is mainly generated at this plate. The operational procedure for entrainment experiments in the adapted annular flume is as follows: The flume is filled with a lower, dense layer and an upper, less dense

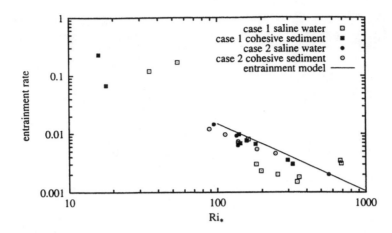

Figure 2: Entrainment rates versus Ri* for experiments on case 1 and on case 2.

layer. The flume and the base plate are initially set to rotate at the same speed in the same direction, resulting in a rigid body rotation of the flume and fluids. An entrainment experiment is then started by changing the rotational direction of the base plate. Due to inertia, the lower layer maintains its initial speed and due to the friction between base plate and this layer, turbulence is generated at the base plate. Because of buoyancy, turbulence is damped near the interface between the two layers. The turbulent lower layer starts to entrain material from the upper non-turbulent layer.

For this new configuration, equation 1 is no longer valid and new operational conditions, with small secondary currents and a near-uniform distribution of tangential velocities near the density interface, had to be assessed. The set-up of the study was as follows: A new formula for the ratio of the rotational speeds of base plate and flume was obtained theoretically from the integral momentum equation. This theoretically derived equation was validated with numerical simulations with the PHOENICS software package, as well as with dye experiments in the flume.

Initially, during the rigid body rotation, the velocity of the fluids (U), flume (U_f) and base plate (U_b) were equal ($U = U_b = U_f$). Once the base plate was set to rotate in opposite direction, entrainment started. The following assumptions are made: 1) The upper layer is flowing at the same speed as the flume. 2) Due to the velocity difference between rotational speed of flume (U_f) and base plate (U_b) a shear flow develops in the lower layer. 3) Due to rotation of base plate and flume, a core exists in the lower layer in which hardly any velocity gradients exist. This core appeared to span approximately 90 % of the flow in the lower layer and is surrounded by boundary layers where velocity gradients are high. This assumption is based on earlier observations. 4) The amount of momentum that is transferred from the upper layer into the lower layer due to entrainment dominates over the momentum transfer by inter-facial shear stresses. The integral balance equation of momentum for the lower layer then becomes:

$$\frac{\mathrm{d}}{\mathrm{d}t}\left(\rho_b H B U_c\right) = B\tau_b - 2H\tau_f + B\rho_w w_e U_f \tag{4}$$

where ρ_b is mean bulk density of the lower layer, H is the thickness of the layer, B is the width of the flume, U_c is the velocity of the core, τ_b is the bottom shear stress, τ_f is the flume side wall shear stress, ρ_w is mean bulk density of the upper layer. Velocities are given with respect to a non-rotating reference frame. The last right-hand term represents the amount of momentum that is transferred from the upper layer in the lower layer due to entrainment.

The terms containing the entrainment rate are small compared to the other terms and therefore dropped from the equation. We restrict ourselves herein to the case where the rotational speed of the base plate has become constant. The bulk of the suspension is contained in the core. For annular flumes with a top

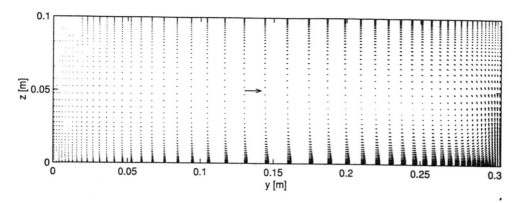

Figure 3: Secondary flow velocities calculated with PHOENICS, $h = 0.1$ m, $U_b = 0.24$ m/s, $U_f = -0.26$ m/s; the arrow in the centre represents 0.05 m/s.

lid, secondary currents where shown to be minimum for a zero velocity of this core ($U_c = 0$) with respect to the non-rotating reference frame (Booij, 1994; Spork, 1997), it is assumed that this is also the case for the present configuration. Finally, by assuming a quadratic friction law to parameterise the shear stresses, equation 4 becomes:

$$\left(\frac{U_b}{U_f}\right)^2 = 2\frac{\lambda_f H}{\lambda_b B} \qquad (5)$$

where λ_b is the base plate friction factor and λ_f is the side wall friction factor.

To validate this theoretical formula for the operational ratio U_b/U_f, simulations with the numerical model PHOENICS have been carried out. As it is not yet possible to simulate stratified flows with PHOENICS easily, only homogeneous conditions (one layer) were simulated. Numerical simulations were carried out for rotational velocities of flume and base plate according to equation 5 and for deviating rotational velocities, B is equal to 0.3 m, λ_b is set to $1.4 \cdot 10^{-3}$ and λ_f is set to $1.8 \cdot 10^{-3}$ (Kranenburg & Winterwerp, 1997). Figure 3 shows the results of a numerical simulation for a case where the ratio of U_b/U_f from equation 5 is applied. Secondary flow velocities were largest at the bottom near the outer wall (right-hand side of the plot). In this region flow velocities did not exceed 0.03 m/s, i.e. 10% of the tangential flow velocity, indicating that secondary flow velocities were sufficiently weak in case equation 5 was applied.

Another way of validating equation 5 was to carry out experiments with dye in the annular flume. Two types of experiments have been carried out. In the first series the flume was filled with a layer of fresh water, in the second series the flume was filled with a layer of saline and a layer of fresh water. Dye was injected in the flume, visualising the flow pattern. The apparatus from which dye was injected, was connected to one of the streamlined rods and it rotated at the same speed as the base plate. The dye showed a trace in nearly tangential direction, indicating that secondary flow velocities were very small. The largest deviation from the tangential direction was found at the base plate near the outer wall of flumes, as found with PHOENICS (Figure 3, see also Bruens (2000)). Hence, using equation 5 the rotational speed of flume and base plate can be set such that secondary currents are sufficiently weak for carrying out entrainment experiments.

6. Application of the rotating base plate conditions

The optimum ratio found in the previous section was applied for entrainment experiments on case 2 conditions. Such conditions are met in the field in case of a tidal flow in stably stratified estuaries, where the lower dense layer consists of saline water or of a concentrated mud suspension .

Experiments were carried out for salinity-induced and sediment-induced stratification. In the latter case, the lower layer was formed by settling of cohesive sediment from a well-mixed suspension. Consolidation times prior to each experiment were limited, such that no strength was developed in the concentrated layer, otherwise the mud layer could resist the tidal pressure gradient and entrainment processes of case 1 take place.

Experiments were carried out for Ri_* varying between 60 and 600. The generation of turbulence in the lower layer, the entrainment of material from the upper layer and the subsequent increase in thickness of the lower layer were clearly visible at the glass side walls.

It was expected that the flow velocity in the upper layer (U_{up}) would be equal to the rotational speed of the flume ($U_{up} = U_f$). During the experiments, it became clear that this was not the case. The deviation between the two velocities can be explained by the drag by the streamlined rods which rotated in a direction opposite to the flume, and possibly inter-facial shear. A considerable flow velocity in the upper layer was measured. This influenced the entrainment rate (resulting in a decrease in entrainment rate).

The results of the experiments are also presented in Figure 2. As can be seen from equation 2, the non-dimensional entrainment rate is a function of the aspect ratio $\frac{H}{B}$. This ratio differed significantly for the experiments on case 1 ($\frac{H}{B}$ =0.83) and the experiments on case 2 ($\frac{H}{B}$ =0.5). The effect of the streamlined rods counteracts the effect of a lower aspect ratio and this explains the agreement between the experiments on case 1 and case 2.

At present, the experiments are further analysed with two numerical flow models. In one of the models a $k - \epsilon$ turbulence model is included. The other model includes a Prandtl mixing-length turbulence model. In both models, the effect of the streamlined rods is taken into account.

7. Conclusions

From this study the following conclusions can be drawn: 1) An extensive measurement program of the flow pattern in the annular flume with top lid leads to proper operational conditions (small secondary currents) for this configuration. 2) A flow computation program, validated by the measured flow patterns, can be used to find operational conditions for different flow cases, for example the annular flume with base plate. 3) Results of entrainment experiments carried out in the flume with top lid and base plate are in good agreement with entrainment theory.

References

BOOIJ, R. 1994. *Measurements of the flow field in a rotating annular flume*. Communications on hydraulic and geotechnical engineering, nr 94-2.

BRUENS, A. W. 2000. *Laboratory experiments on the entrainment by a Concentrated Benthic Suspenion*. Tech. rept. 3-00. Delft University of Technology.

KRANENBURG, C., & WINTERWERP, J.C. 1997. Erosion of fluid mud layers. I: Entrainment model. *Journal of Hydraulic engineering, ASCE*, **123**, 504–511.

SPORK, V. 1997. *Untersuchung der Transporteigenschaften von Flusschweb in einem Kreisgerinne, Tech. Rep Rheinisch Westfalische Technische Hochschule Aachen*.

WINTERWERP, J. C., & KRANENBURG, C. 1997. Erosion of Fluid Mud Layers. II: Experiments and Model Validation. *Journal of Hydraulic Engineering, ASCE*, **123**, 512–519.

Transition from waves to turbulence
in a forced stratified flow

George F. Carnevale[1], Marco Briscolini[2], Paolo Orlandi[3]

[1]Scripps Institution of Oceanography, La Jolla, CA, 92093, USA
[2]IBM Italia S.p.A., Via Shangai 53, Roma, Italy
[3] Dept. Meccanica, University of Rome, La Sapienza, Roma, Italy

1. Abstract

Much of the variability of the density and velocity of the oceans on scales greater than 10 m in the vertical is associated with internal wave activity. At scales below about 1 m and down to a viscous or diffusive cutoff, the flow appears to be dominated by isotropic turbulence. Between these wave and turbulence ranges there is a transition range, sometimes called the "buoyancy range," in which waves and turbulence compete. The nature of the dynamics in this range is a controversial matter. It would be useful to have a numerical model of flow in this range. Here an attempt is made by using an isotropic grid with a subgrid-scale model with its cutoff wavenumber in the inertial range. The forcing is supplied only at large-scale in the form of a standing internal wave. This model results in a break in the energy spectra from the anisotropic k^{-3} buoyancy range to the small-scale $k^{-5/3}$ isotropic inertial range. The density structures that form during wave breaking events and during periods of high strain rate are examined.

2. Introduction

A schematic representation of the internal wave spectrum in the ocean is shown in figure 1 (based on Holloway 1981). ϕ is the spectrum of vertical shear, and λ represents vertical wavelengths. Our goal is to study the buoyancy range, which extends from about 10 m down to about 1 m in wavelength. To this end we modeled the forcing, which we consider to be the waves in the Garret-Munk (GM) range, as a single standing wave of wavelength 20 m in the vertical and horizontal (cf. Bouruet-Aubertot, Sommeria, & Staquet, 1996). We modeled the inertial range dynamics with the eddy viscosity model of Kraichnan (1976) as modified by Lesieur and Rogallo (1989). The grid spacing in our simulations was at 15 cm. We believe that we were able to achieve a representation of the buoyancy range with the transition to the inertial range occurring at about wavelenght 1 m.

3. Numerical Simulation

In this numerical experiment it appears that the expected spectral signature of a transition between a buoyancy range at large-scale and the inertial range at small-scale occurs only for periods during which there is active breaking. In figure 2, we show enlargements of the images of the $\rho = \rho_0$ isosurface at two times identified during a breaking event. The first shows curling over and spilling down of the heavier over lighter fluid, and the later image suggests mixing by the appearance of many small scale structures along the two parallel lines of the breaking wave. The corresponding spectra for all three components of kinetic and for the potential energy are shown in figure 3. First we notice that although the spectra are highly anisotropic from the forcing scale (20 m) down to about the 1 m scale, there is a 'return' to isotropy for the smaller scales. This is particularly evident in the kinetic energy spectra for t=11.82 T_F (panel c). In panels (a) and (c), we have made an attempt to draw the best fit inertial range spectra to determine the appropriate Kolmogorov constants (C_K) corresponding to these spectra. We did this for the $E_v(k)$ spectra, obtaining the best fit 'by eye' from enlarged portions of the small scale spectra. The result that was used to draw the inertial range model spectra in panels (a) and (c) is (C_K) = 1.4. In panels (b) and (d), the potential energy spectra are drawn. In these panels the small scales were fit to the Corrsin-

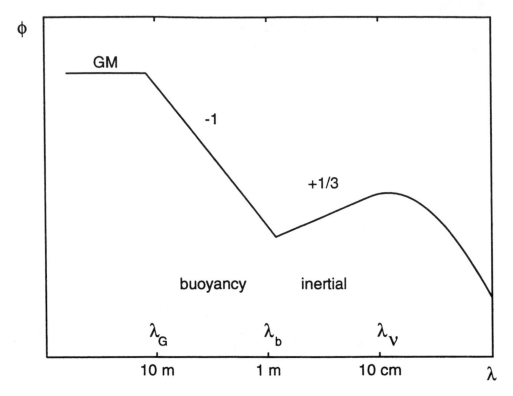

Figure 1: Schematic of the oceanic horizontal shear spectrum. The horizontal axis is labeled in terms of wavelength for convenience, but it is actually the k_z wavenumber axis. The slopes corresponding to the k_z^{-1} buoyancy range and the $k_z^{-1/3}$ inertial range are labeled by the exponents.

Obykov spectrum to determine the appropriate Corrsin constant. In panels (b) and (d) the Corrsin constants used to draw the model Corrsin-Obykov spectrum were $C_o = 0.83$ and 0.8 respectively. In all panels the model buoyancy range spectrum drawn is $0.2N^2k^{-3}$. Thus the Kolmogorov constant found here is somewhat smaller than the empirical values of 1.5 and the Corrsin constant is somewhat larger than the empirical value of 0.67. Nevertheless, the values are remarkably close to the empirical values, given that the spectral width of the inertial range here only covers scales from about 1 m to about 0.3 m (corresponding to a 0.15 m mesh spacing).

Examining the full density field more thoroughly, we also find interesting structures of a rather different nature. These can be represented well by the deformations of the density surfaces that are the flat nodal surfaces of the forcing wave. The combination of the large-scale background straining motion and small-scale eddies produces localized deformations of the nodal surface that can result in overturning and mixing in a manner different from the overturns discussed in the last section. The structures formed appear to be eruptions on the density isosurface where there are localized intrusions of heavy fluid into lighter fluid and vice versa. We shall refer to them as 'spouts.'

An example of these structures is given in figure 4, where we show a side view of the nodal surface. The scale of these structures range from about 1 to 4 m and they are very anisotropic as seen in the figure. Here we see that some of the 'spouts' are elongated in the x direction while there is one that is nearly symmetric in x and y and appears to be a finger of light fluid penetrating into the deeper fluid below. They are usually produced at points where the vertical strain is the strongest at times when the strain is vertically dilational. During the vertically compressional phase of the motion, these structures are compressed back toward the unperturbed nodal plane, but at the same time they are extended horizontally by the horizontally dilational component of

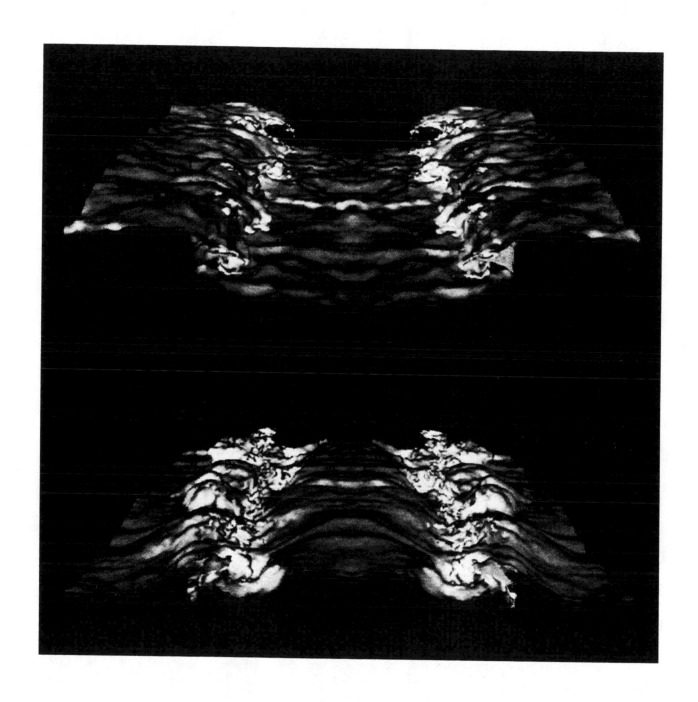

Figure 2: A breaking event visualized on the $\rho = \rho_0$ isopycnal, corresponding to times (a) 11.68 and (b) 11.82 T_F where T_F is the forcing period).

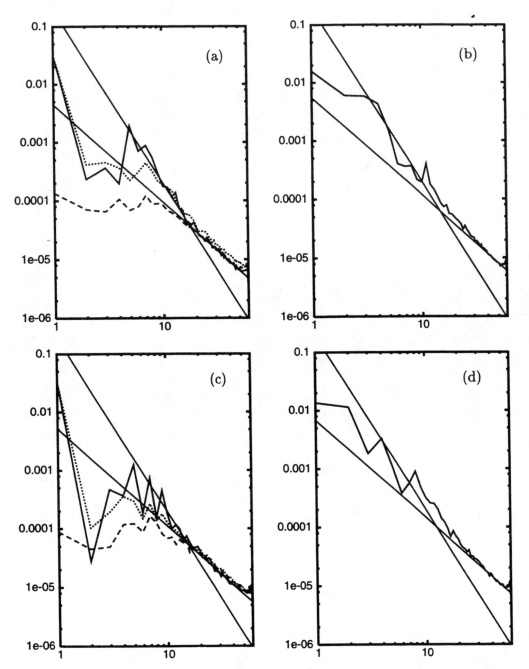

Figure 3: a) Kinetic energy spectra for all three components of the velocity at time $t = 11.68T_F$. The thick long dashed, solid and short dashed lines correspond to the energy spectra for the u,v, and w components respectively. The thin solid lines correspond to the Kolmogorov spectrum $(1/3)C_K\epsilon^{2/3}k^{-5/3}$ with $C_K = 1.4$ and the saturation spectrum $0.2N^2k^{-3}$. b) Potential energy spectrum at time $t = 11.68T_F$. The thick solid line corresponds to the potential energy spectrum. The thin solid lines correspond to the Corrsin-Obykov spectrum $C_o\epsilon_{pe}\epsilon^{-1/3}k^{-5/3}$ with $C_o = 0.83$ and the saturation spectrum $0.2N^2k^{-3}$. c) As in (a) but for t=11.82 T_F and $C_K = 1.4$. d) As in (b) but for t=11.82 T_F and $C_o = 0.80$.

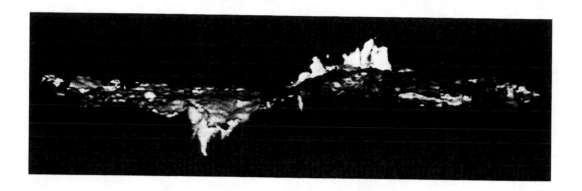

Figure 4: Visualization of the isosurface corresponding to one of the nodal planes of the forcing at time 16.04 T_F. The view is taken along the a horizontal axis.

the strain. This results in convectively unstable fluid which then produces small scale mixing.

References

Bouruet-Aubertot, P., Sommeria, J. & Staquet, C. 1996 Stratified turbulence produced by internal wave breaking: two-dimensional numerical experiments. (4th International Symposium on Stratified Flows, Grenoble, France, 29 June-2 July 1994). *Dyn. Atmos. Oceans* **23**, 357-69.

Holloway, G. 1981 Theoretical approaches to interactions among internal waves, turbulence and finestructure. in Nonlinear Properties of Internal Waves, AIP conference proceedings No. 76, (ed. B.J. West. AIP, New York.)

Kraichnan, R.H. 1976 Eddy viscosity in two and three dimensions. *J. Atmos. Sci.*, 33, 1521-1536.

Lesieur, M. & R. Rogallo, 1989 Large-eddy simulation of passive scalar diffusion in isotropic turbulence. *Phys. Fluids A*, 1, 718-722.

Overturns in stably stratified homogeneous sheared turbulence

Peter J. Diamessis and Keiko K. Nomura

Mechanical and Aerospace Engineering, University of California - San Diego, La Jolla, California, 92093-0411, USA
pdiamess@ucsd.edu, knomura@ucsd.edu

1   Introduction

Density overturns (hereafter, referred to as OTs) are three-dimensional features associated with mixing in naturally stratified fluids. Since field microstructure observations are usually limited to one-dimensional (1-D) vertical profiles of temperature (or density) and single realizations (snapshots) of the OTs, no concrete picture yet exists on their dynamical evolution and spatial structure: Are the OTs actively turbulent regions [1, 2] or remnants (fossils) of previous rare but powerful events [3] ? What is their actual contribution to diapycnal mixing [4] and to the available potential energy (APE) of the overall flow [2] ? How do OT dynamics correlate to the large scale vertical shear, strain, and stratification [5] ? Detailed laboratory and numerical studies are needed to help resolve these issues [6].

In this paper, we are concerned with homogeneous stratified turbulence. Laboratory studies of homogeneous turbulence in a salt-stratified water tunnel [7, 8, 9, 10] have examined the evolution of OT lengthscales. Recently, Keller and Van Atta (hereafter referred to as KV) [11] examined these lengthscales for a stratified homogeneous shear flow of air along with the behavior of the APE and diapycnal mixing for various values of the Richardson number, Ri. Stratified homogeneous turbulence has also been studied by direct numerical simulation (DNS) [12, 13, 14], the most detailed study of lengthscale evolution being that of Itsweire et al. (hereafter referred to as IBKF) [15] for a sheared flow. However, none of the above studies have directly examined the 3-D spatial structure or dynamical evolution and significance of OTs. In this paper, we present results of our investigation which address these issues. The study also assesses the effectiveness of the method of Thorpe-sorting vertical density profiles in obtaining the state of minimum potential energy of the flow.

2   Direct Numerical Simulations

DNS of homogeneous sheared turbulence with uniform stable stratification was performed for this study [16]. Relevant nondimensional parameters include the turbulent Reynolds number, Re_λ, the Shear number, Sh, the Schmidt number, Sc, and the gradient Richardson number, $Ri = N^2/S^2$. In our notation, N denotes the Vaisala frequency, S the mean velocity gradient, and x, y, and z, the streamwise, spanwise, and vertical directions, respectively. The governing equations describing the flow are the Navier-Stokes equations with the Boussinesq approximation for the density, ρ. The computational domain is a finite cube containing 128^3 grid points. Initial parameter values for the results presented here are $Re_{\lambda_o} = 20$, $Sh_o = 3.2$, and $Sc = 0.7$. Four different values of Ri are considered: $Ri = 0.05$, 0.2, 0.5, and 1. The critical Ri for this flow is $Ri_{cr} \approx 0.1$. In the results presented, time is non-dimensionalized by S.

3   Analysis and Results

The background state of potential energy (BSPE) is the state of minimum potential energy a stratified fluid can attain through adiabatic restratification [17]. In this state, the density field consists of uniform horizontal layers with a value of ρ monotonically decreasing with z. For a DNS dataset, the BSPE can be obtained to a very good approximation by resorting the entire discrete set of values of ρ and monotonically redistributing them on the computational grid [17]. We regard this state as the volume-sorted BSPE. For a limited set of vertical density profiles, an approximation to the BSPE can be obtained by resorting the individual profiles into profiles monotonically decreasing with height. We regard this as the Thorpe-sorted BSPE which is believed to be an accurate representation of the true BSPE under certain conditions. Two distinct lengthscales can be obtained by computing the rms value of the nonzero (particle) vertical displacements that are required in each of the two sorting methods: the average Thorpe scale $\langle L_T \rangle$, averaged over the set of available density profiles [15, 11], and L_V, which results from the volume-sorting method. In the latter case, if the rms is computed for all particles in the flow (including those with zero displacements), it can be shown that L_V is equal to the overturn (or Ellison [15, 11]) scale.

The method of Thorpe-sorting a vertical density profile provides a method for educing OT structures. Figure 1 shows a representative instantaneous $\rho(z)$ profile, the corresponding sorted profile and profiles of the vertical density gradient $\partial\rho/\partial z$ and Thorpe displacement $d(z)$ [8]. The OTs correspond to regions of $d(z) \neq 0$ with a signature of a reverse "Z" in the $d(z)$ profile [1, 8, 11]. Immediately outside the boundaries of these regions, $d(z) = 0$ for some distance z. Note that all $\partial\rho/\partial z > 0$ observations in the field occur within the interior of the reverse-Z regions. In addition, the values of ρ inside a given overturn are not found anywhere else in the profile [2]. In order to identify OTs for visualization and conditional statistics, we can define a discrete function $I_O(\vec{x})$ which assumes the values of 0,1, or 2, if a point in our flow lies outside, on the boundaries of, or inside the $d(z) \neq 0$ regions, respectively. As demonstrated by our results, this method is effective in capturing local configurations of heavy fluid over light, i.e., OTs.

Figure 2a shows the evolution of the fraction of the flow volume occupied by OTs for all four runs. For $Ri = 0.05 < Ri_{cr}$, the effect of buoyancy is not felt at the scale of the OTs and they grow to occupy approximately 50% of the volume by the end of the simulation. For $Ri \geq Ri_{cr}$, at some time beyond the initial growth which depends on the value of Ri, the turbulence cannot overcome the buoyancy force and the volume occupied by the OTs decreases and eventually diminishes to a zero value. The evolution of $\langle L_T \rangle$ in Figure 2b is similar and also consistent with the results of both IBKF and KV. At early times, all four runs exhibit similar initial growth from zero in regards to OT size. This implies that the generation mechanism of the OTs is shear-turbulence driven and begins at the small scales. The growth in $\langle L_T \rangle$ observed for $Ri < Ri_{cr}$ soon turns into a decay for the supercritical runs and all OTs vanish by $Nt \approx 2\pi$. Figure 2c shows the evolution of the lengthscale ratio, $\langle L_T \rangle/L_V$. For the cases of $Ri = 0.05$ and 0.2, the ratio remains at a value of nearly unity. For the cases with stronger stratification, $Ri = 0.5$ and 1, the ratio begins to depart from unity at about $Nt = \pi$ as $\langle L_T \rangle$ decreases at a much greater rate than L_V. This is in qualitative agreement with IBKF but the opposite of KV's observations. The reason may be subtle differences between the set-up of the simulation and experimental facility (initial conditions, boundaries etc.). The departure of the ratio from unity indicates that the average perturbation of an isopycnal decays slower than the size of an overturn, i.e., the overturning APE decays faster than that of larger scale motions [11]. Such motions may include internal waves which are more likely to occur for higher N. L_V is thus not an accurate indicator of average OT size.

Figure 3 displays $y - z$ and $x - z$ plane-view cuts of isosurfaces of $I_O(\vec{x}) = 1$, i.e. OT boundaries, for $Ri = 0.2$. We see that the OTs exhibit elongated structure in the $x - z$ view with an elliptical or more complex cross-section in the $y - z$ (streamwise) view. Their longitudinal axis is inclined from the streamwise direction and their vertical height lies in the range $[\langle L_T \rangle, 3\langle L_T \rangle]$. The strongest $\nabla\rho$ occurs outside the OTs, often between two adjacent OTs and close to their boundaries. For the Ri=0.05 flow, where the overturns comprise a significant portion of the total volume, the OT structures exhibit greater vertical extent and are longer and more inclined from the horizontal, while the opposite is observed in the Ri=0.5 and 1 flows.

Figure 2b indicates that overturning is shear-turbulence driven and begins at the small-scales. In our DNS, there are no breaking large-scale internal waves and no oscillations in any vertical large-scale strain [18] which could create OTs. Based on our previous analysis [16], intense vortex structures with tube-like geometry are responsible for generating $\partial\rho/\partial z > 0$ and the associated OT structure. Persistent rotational motion of some vertical extent is thus sufficient to raise heavy fluid over light. A zoomed-in plane-view cut of the flow field across a representative OT structure is shown in Figure 3c. The underlying vortex structure resembles the Burgers' vortex [19] with a rotation-dominated core which instigates overturning by wrapping around isopycnals while compressive straining at the periphery results in strong $\nabla\rho$. Neighboring vortex structures can significantly enhance these straining regions resulting in even stronger $\nabla\rho$ as indicated in Figures 3a,b. Thus, the OTs in this flow are a result of stirring induced by vortex tubes which may act simultaneously or sequentially on the isopycnals. Note that at higher Ri, the observed OTs are not simply smaller because of collapse due to stronger buoyancy forces, but also because the strength of the generating vortex structures is diminished by the counteracting effects of baroclinic torque [16].

According to Dillon [2], the accuracy of the Thorpe-sorted BSPE in representing the true BSPE of the flow is ensured when the turbulence is horizontally homogeneous and turbulent stirring is the only generating mechanism of OTs. As our DNS flow satisfies both these conditions, we test the validity of Dillon's claim. Using both the Thorpe-sorted and volume-sorted estimates of the BSPE, we can obtain two different estimates of the APE (E_p) which is defined by [17]: $E_p = Ri \int_V \rho(z - z_*)dV$ (z_* is the position of the fluid particle associated with density $\rho(x, y, z)$ in the evaluated BSPE [17, 11]). Figure 4 shows that the Thorpe-sorted BSPE calculation can underestimate the true E_p by one or more orders of magnitude. Similar statements can be made for other quantities in the APE evolution equation (see below) which could lead to errors in closing the APE budget.

We now investigate the contribution of OTs to the APE budget which, for a homogeneous flow, is given by [17, 11]:

$$\frac{dE_p}{dt} = \Phi_z - \Phi_d + \Phi_i \qquad (1)$$

where Φ_z, Φ_d and Φ_i are the buoyancy flux, diapycnal flux and mean molecular flux, respectively (see [17]). We note that in the $Ri = 0.05$ case, because of the high fraction of flow volume occupied by the OTs, their behavior is not distinguishably different from that of the total flow. Figure 5a shows the APE evaluated for the total flow volume and that occupied by the OTs for the supercritical Ri flows. As indicated, the OTs never contribute to more than 40% of the overall flow APE, their contribution diminishing with time. Thus, the APE is primarily contained in larger scale displacements of fluid from its equilibrium position (possibly internal waves at a later time), which are not necessarily associated with overturning. Consistent with this result, KV found that the contribution to the overall density variance $\langle \rho'^2 \rangle$ in their experiments originated from larger scale motion rather than OTs. Figure 5b shows the contribution of the OTs to the buoyancy flux, Φ_z, i.e., the rate of exchange of APE with kinetic energy (KE). Again, the major contribution to Φ_z originates from larger scale motions, not OTs, the difference being greater with increasing Ri. For $Ri = 1$ at $St = 3$, which corresponds to the time of most intense restratification, the behavior of OTs does not appear to be distinctly different from that of the whole flow. Finally, Figure 5c shows the time evolution of the diapycnal flux, Φ_d. Evidently, diapycnal mixing is quite weak within the OTs as would be expected from Figures 1b and 3 which show that the strongest $\nabla\rho$ are associated with stable (negative) gradients and not unstable ones. This is also consistent with observations of KV. However, our results also indicate that the strongest $\nabla\rho$ occurs immediately outside and between adjacent OT structures. In summary, the major contribution to the APE, buoyancy flux, and diapycnal mixing of the overall flow is not directly from OT regions.

4 Conclusions

Through DNS, we have examined various issues related to the 3-D structure, interpretation and dynamical significance of overturning events in stratified homogeneous sheared turbulence. The statistics of the associated lengthscales are in agreement with experimental and field results. Visualizations of the overturning regions show elongated structure inclined from the horizontal plane due to advection by the mean shear and the vortex structures that generate them. For higher Ri, as time elapses, the OTs become less space filling, smaller in vertical extent, and their longitudinal axis becomes horizontal. The method of Thorpe-sorting vertical profiles of the density is effective in educing overturning structures and estimating their associated lengthscales. It does not provide, however, an accurate representation of the background state of the flow for the estimation of energetic quantities. Sorting the entire flow volume to produce nearly uniform layers of fluid density, monotonically decreasing with height, is the appropriate method for this. The interior of overturns contributes to only a small fraction of the APE, buoyancy flux and diapycnal flux of the total flow. However, significant mixing occurs just beyond the boundaries of these events. Thus, the OTs may, indirectly, be an indicator of mixing and the underlying flow structures.

References

[1] T. M. Dillon. Vertical overturns: A comparison of Thorpe and Ozmidov length scales. *J. Geophys. Res.*, 87, no. C12:9601–9613, 1982.

[2] T. M. Dillon. The energetics of overturning structures: Implications for the theory of fossil turbulence. *J. Phys. Oceanogr.*, 14:541–549, 1984.

[3] C. H. Gibson. Alternative interpretations for microstructure patches in the thermocline. *J. Phys. Oceanogr.*, 18:374–383, 1982.

[4] T. M. Dillon and M. M. Park. The available potential energy of overturns as an indicator of mixing in the seasonal thermocline. *J. Geophys. Res.*, 15, no. C5:541–549, 1987.

[5] M. H. Alford and R. Pinkel. Observations of overturning in the thermocline: The context of ocean mixing. *J. Phys. Oceanogr.*, 5:805–832, 2000.

[6] M.C. Gregg. Diapycnal mixing in the thermocline. *J. Geophys. Res.*, 92, no. C5:5249–5286, 1987.

[7] D. C. Stillinger, K. H. Helland, and C. W. Van Atta. Experiments on the transition of homogeneous turbulence to internal waves in a stratified fluid. *J. Fluid Mech.*, 131:91–122, 1983.

[8] E.C. Itsweire. Measurements of vertical overturns in a stably stratified flow. *Phys. Fluids*, 27:764–766, 1984.

[9] E.C. Itsweire, K.N. Helland, and C.W. Van Atta. The evolution of grid-generated turbulence in a stably stratified fluid. *J. Fluid Mech.*, 162:299–338, 1986.

[10] J. J. Rohr, E. C. Itsweire, K. N. Helland, and C. W. Van Atta. Growth and decay of turbulence in a stably stratified shear flow. *J. Fluid Mech.*, 195:77–111, 1988.

[11] K. H. Keller and C. W. Van Atta. An experimental investigation into the vertical temperature structure of homogeneous stratified shear turbulence. *J. Fluid Mech.*, To appear, 2000.

[12] O. Metais and J. R. Herring. Numerical simulations of freely evolving turbulence. *J. Fluid Mech.*, 202:117–148, 1989.

[13] T. Gerz and U. Schumann. Length scales of sheared and unsheared stratified homogeneous turbulence deduced from direct simulations. In *Seventh Symposium on Turbulent Shear Flows*, Stanford, USA, 1989.

[14] F. G. Jacobitz, S. Sarkar, and C.W. Van Atta. Direct numerical simulations of the turbulence evolution in a uniformly sheared and stably stratified flow. *J. Fluid Mech.*, 342:231–261, 1997.

[15] E.C. Itsweire, J.R. Koseff, Briggs D.A., and J. H. Ferziger. Turbulence in stratified shear flows: Implications for interpreting shear-induced mixing in the ocean. *J. Phys. Oceanogr.*, 23:1508–1522, 1992.

[16] P. J. Diamessis and K. K. Nomura. Interaction of vorticity, rate-of-strain and scalar gradient in homogeneous sheared turbulence. *Phys. Fluids*, 12:1166–88, 2000.

[17] K. B. Winters, P. N. Lombard, J. J. Riley, and E. A. D'Asaro. Available potential energy and mixing in density stratified fluids. *J. Fluid Mech.*, 289:115–128, 1995.

[18] G. F. Carnevale, M. Briscolini, and P. Orlandi. Buoyancy to inertial range transition in forced stratified turbulence. *J. Fluid Mech.*, Submitted for publication, 2000.

[19] K. K. Nomura and G. K. Post. The structure and dynamics of vorticity and rate of strain in incompressible homogeneous turbulence. *J. Fluid Mech.*, 377:65–97, 1998.

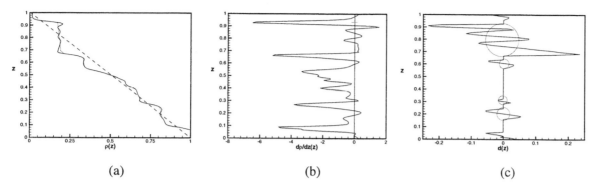

(a)   (b)   (c)

Figure 1: Thorpe-sorting of a sample vertical density profile $\rho(z)$ for $Ri = 0.05$ ($St = 8$). (a) Measured profile (solid line) with Thorpe-sorted profile (dotted line) and mean profile (dashed line). (b) Profile of $\partial\rho/\partial z(z)$. (c) Profile of displacement $d(z)$ (dotted circles indicate OTs).

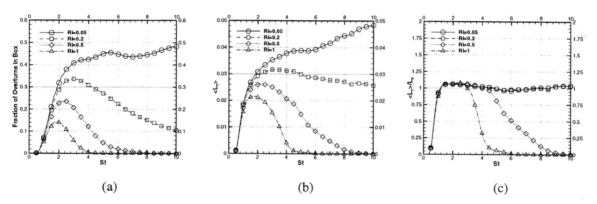

(a)   (b)   (c)

Figure 2: Timeseries of: (a) Fraction of flow volume occupied by overturns. (b) Average Thorpe scale $\langle L_T \rangle$. (c) Lengthscale ratio $\langle L_T \rangle / L_V$.

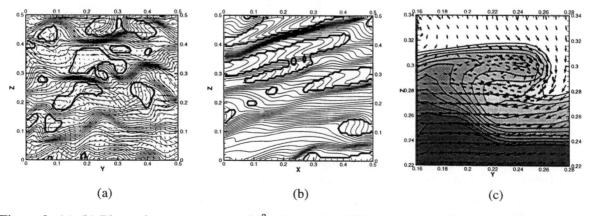

(a)   (b)   (c)

Figure 3: (a)-(b) Plane-view cuts across a 64^3 subdomain of $Ri = 0.2$ flow ($St = 6$). Thick lines represent overturn boundaries and thin lines are isopycnals. (a) $(y - z)$ plane at $x = 0.16$ and (b) $(x - z)$ plane at $y = 0.15625$. (c) Close-up view in $(y - z)$ plane at $x = 0.25$ for $Ri = 0.05$ flow ($St = 2$). Velocity field is plotted in (a) and (c). Dashed lines in (c) are contours of streamwise vorticity.

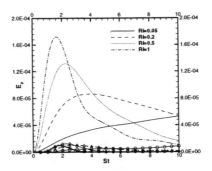

Figure 4: Time evolution of computed APE based on different estimates of background state of potential energy (BSPE). Plain lines: BSPE obtained through volume-sorting flow domain. Lines with symbols: BSPE obtained through Thorpe-sorting the set of individual vertical density profiles.

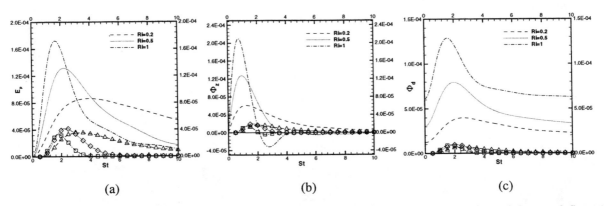

(a)   (b)   (c)

Figure 5: Comparison of APE and associated evolution equation quantities evaluated for total flow (plain-lines) vs. for volume occupied by overturns (lines with symbols): (a) APE, E_p. (b) Buoyancy flux, Φ_z. (c) Diapycnal flux, Φ_d.

Turbulence Measurements in a Narrow Rectangular Channel for Two-Layer Stratified Flow

T. Feng and K. Shiono

Department of Civil and Building Engineering, Loughborough University, LE11 3TU, UK
Tel: (+44) 01509 222936, Fax: (+44) 01509 223981, E-mail: K.Shiono @lboro.ac.uk

1. Abstract

This paper describes a measuring technique for turbulent velocity and salinity concentration both together in two-layer density stratified flow using a combined laser Doppler anemometer (LDA) with laser induced fluorescence (LIF). This is a non-intrusive probe technique in fluid. Fluorescent dye, Rhodamine 6G, was used as the surrogate for saline water density. Experiments were conducted in a narrow rectangular channel under three different density conditions to investigate the effect of stratification on flow development.

2. Introduction

Most measurements of solute and suspended solids concentration in laboratory flumes and estuaries have been carried out using an intrusive method, placing a probe into the flow or taking discrete samples from the flow (e.g. Wood & Liang, 1989). In estuaries, simultaneous turbulence measurements of velocity and salinity concentration have been carried out using an intrusive method (e.g. West et.al.,1985 and West & Shiono, 1988). Papanicolaou & List (1988) introduced a non-intrusive Laser Induced Fluorescence (LIF) method to measure turbulent fluctuations of solute concentration and, more recently, Lemoine et al. (1997) used a combination of both LIF and LDA to measure simultaneous turbulent fluctuations of velocity and tracer concentration in grid generated turbulence flow. Shiono et. al. (1998) attempted to measure turbulent fluctuations of velocity and dye concentration in an open rectangular channel using a combination of LDA and LIF.

3. Instrumentation

LIF/LDA

A TSI three component fibre optic LDA together with a data acquisition system (Engineering and Physical Sciences Research Council (EPSRC) loan pool), was adapted to a LIF system. The LIF system was use to measure the concentration of dye, Rhodamine 6G, as a surrogate for saline water density. A LIF device is based on the photoluminescence of a fluorescent solution. According to spectrometry theory, the colour of fluoresced light is yellow-orange with a wavelength of 570 nm when Rhodamine 6G solution is illuminated by a green laser beam with a wavelength of 514 nm. The fluoresced light together with the all scattered light was collected from the focal point by the probe head. A colour separator filtered the orange light with a long wave pass filter (Corion LL550F7325, provided by TSI). The filtered orange light was transmitted into a photo multiplier to produce an analogue output voltage. A multi-channel analogue to digital convertor, called "DataLink", was used for sampling the analogue signals of the concentration and the LDA data. This system, together with three signal processors controlled by the TSI FIND computer programme, enabled the velocity and concentration signals in a real-time sequence to be recorded simultaneously.

Calibration between the concentrations of salinity and dye were carried out using a number of saline water samples mixed with the dye. Both the LIF system and a standard technique using the Sodium-Potassium-Lithium flame photometry were used to estimate the concentrations of dye and salinity in the samples and, as a result, a calibration curve was obtained. In order to compare the salinity concentrations between the flame photometer and LIF in the channel flow, a number of samples were also taken during the experiments. Fig. 1 shows the salinity concentrations of both LIF and flame photometer. Both methods agree well.

A micro-probe electric conductivity sensor (ECS), (Precision Measurements, USA), was used to investigate turbulent fluctuation response of the LIF. A series of simultaneous measurements have been carried out using both methods at the same point in the rectangular channel flow. Fig. 2 shows an example of the records of turbulence fluctuations of saline water density obtained from both methods. Both fluctuations are very similar with small discrepancies. The discrepancies would be expected owing to that the measurement points were not the same since the probe of ECS was in the water and that there are also some effects of the submerged ECS probe head on the flow at the point of the LIF measurement.

4. Experimental channel

The open rectangular channel made of perspex with dimensions of 100mm width and 250mm height was constructed in a flume with dimensions 12m long, 0.3m wide and 0.3m deep. The bed slope of the channel was set to 1:2000. There were two ducts in the first 2.5m of the open channel separated by a thin rigid plate at 50mm height from the bottom of the channel in order to make two-layer density-stratified flow. The lower duct was used to discharge saline water and the upper duct was for fresh water. The flow rates were 75 l/min in the both ducts. The same total discharge and the same water depth were kept when the density differences between saline water and fresh water changed to $1kg/m^3$, $3kg/m^3$, and $5kg/m^3$. The water depth was 105mm.

Because there was a lack of space in the laboratory installing a large saline water storage tank conducting the experiment for long hours, an alternative method was adopted to last saline water for the experiment. A relatively small amount of concentrated saline water stored in a small tank was injected into the pipe line connected to the lower duct. A serious of tests was carried out in order to achieve the concentrated saline water being uniformly mixed in the whole cross section at the lower duct exit and it was achieved. The fluorescent dye, Rhodamine 6G was also injected at a constant concentration flow rate from the bottom of the upstream lower duct and a serious of discharge tests was also carried out and the dye being uniformly mixed at the exit of the lower duct was achieved.

The measurements were carried out in a half cross section at 3 locations along the channel (i.e. 1.5m, 3.2m and 6.4m downstream) for the rectangular channel.

5. Results

a) Mean flow

The distributions of mean longitudinal velocity and secondary current vectors at 1.5m and 6.4m downstream from the inlet for the fresh water flow and $5kg/m^3$ density difference at the inlet are shown in Fig. 3. At 1.5m, it is noticeable slower velocity in the mid water depth region at which the flow was divided by the thin plate. The inlet flow structure therefore still remains however the flow proceeds downstream, at 6.4m this region disappears. The location of maximum velocity moves from the water surface at 1.5m to the mid water depth at 6.4m. The flow structure at 6.4m is similar to the fully developed flow structure as shown by Nezu and Nakagawa (1993), hence the flow is more or less the fully developed flow. For the stratified flow conditions, much more distinct slower velocity in the mid depth region appears and the faster flow area increases near the water surface as density difference at the inlet increases, which implies that when the density stratification increases the mixing reduces. At the 6.4m test section, the distribution of velocity is not quite the same as that in the fresh water flow condition, there still exists the bugle of the flow pattern in the mid depth region, hence the development of the flow is still in progress.

b) Secondary flow structure.

Vectors of secondary flow along the channel for the fresh water flow case are also shown in Fig. 3 a). At 1.5m downstream from the inlet, there is a clear pattern in mid depth region showing the direction of the secondary flow towards the centre of the channel. This shows still remaining of the secondary flow arisen by the inlet ducts which the secondary flow pattern is a typical duct flow case. As the flow runs downstream, at 6.4m, this secondary flow appears to be re-directed to upwards and becomes similar to that as shown in Nezu and Nakagawa (1993). Hence again, the flow is fully developed.

For the 5kg/m^3 density difference at 1.5m and 6.4m downstream, it can be clearly seen from Fig. 3 b) that the secondary flow structure changes from small outwards secondary currents to large when the density difference is 5kg/m^3, which naturally shows inhibiting mixing when the stratification presents. The secondary flow pattern corresponds well with the mean flow structure, that is, the bulge in the flow pattern corresponds with the strong secondary currents

c) Density structure

For the 3kg/m^3 and 5kg/m^3 density differences, the distributions of density at 1.5m and 6.4m are shown in Fig. 4. At 1.5m downstream, the contour lines are more or less horizontal over the water depth for both cases except the near the corner of the channel, which indicates that the density structure is more or less 2-D stable stratification flow. As the flow runs downstream, the horizontal contour lines start tilting vertically, in particular, for the 3kg/m^3 difference case. This suggests that the wall-generated turbulence mix salinity vertically and transversely, rather than mixing by only the bed-generated turbulence. For the 5kg/m^3 difference case, the distribution of contour lines tends to be more horizontal, which indicates that mixing caused by the wall-generated turbulence is not yet strong, or the wall-generated turbulence may be reduced due to stratification.

d) Production of turbulence kinetic energy.

The main mixing mechanisms in this channel may be due to either the bed-generated turbulence or the wall-generated turbulence or both. An understanding of production of turbulent kinetic energy (TKE) gained from the mean flow is to give insight into mixing mechanisms due to turbulence in stratified flow. The productions of TKE for the fresh water and 5 kg/m^3 difference cases were worked out from the data and plotted in Fig. 5. For the fresh water case, the distributions of production of TKE at 1.5m and 6.4m indicate that the production arising from the bed-generated turbulence increases along the channel however its production due to the wall-generated turbulence does not follow the trend of its bed one. The production due to the wall-generated turbulence is largest at 1.5m and its magnitude reduces along the channel. At 6.4m, the production due to the bed-generated turbulence is more or less the same as its production due to the wall-generated turbulence. For the stratified flow conditions, its production due to the bed-generated turbulence becomes smaller at 6.4m compared with its magnitude for the fresh water case. It is noticed that its production due to the wall-generated turbulence is smaller at the 1.5m section and increases along the channel.

The production of turbulent kinetic energy due to buoyancy was also calculated and was compared with that due to all the Reynolds stresses as a ratio. The ratio of the production due to the buoyancy to its due to the Reynolds stresses at 6.4m for the 5kg/m^3 difference case is also shown in Fig. 5. The value is less than 0.1 in most of the area, but is larger in the mid depth area and near the water surface at the centre of the channel, which would be reflected by small production due to the Reynolds stresses. This result shows that the TKE production due to the buoyancy is not a significant contribution to the total TKE production in most of the area, but is significant in the mid depth and water surface region at the centre of the channel. The local gradient Richardson number, a typical stratification parameter, is defined by the ratio of the production of TKE due to buoyancy to that due to the Reynolds stresses. Numerical modellers commonly use the Richardson number as 2-D flow in their numerical models, which takes only the TKE production due to the bed-generated turbulence into account, however in a 3-D flow region, the wall-generated turbulence is also a significant contribution to the turbulent kinetic energy production. This suggests that, in a 3-D flow region, the definition of the gradient Richardson number should also take the wall-generated turbulence into account.

6. Conclusions

The laser induced fluorescence (LIF) enabled us to measure turbulent fluctuations of salinity using fluorescent dye as a surrogate for salinity in a narrow rectangular open channel for stratified flow conditions. As a result, clear evidence of the effect of stratification on the development of both mean velocity and secondary flow was identified. Secondary flow pattern in stratified flow was different from that in homogeneous flow and the development of the secondary flow was slower owing to the stratification. From the analysis of TKE production, the following results were obtained. The TKE production due to buoyancy always is negative to the production of TKE. The contributions due to the Reynolds stresses are the main sources for TKE production. The contribution of the buoyancy to the total TKE production is one order smaller than those contributed by the Reynolds stresses in most of the area however it is significant near the water surface.

References
1. Lemoine, F, Wofff, M. and Lebouche, M, (1997), Experimental investigation of mass transfer on a grid generated turbulent flow using combined optical methods, International Journal of Heat and Mass Transfer, Vol. 40, No. 14, pp.3255-3266.
2. Papanicolaou, P.N. and List, E.J., (1988), Investigations of Round Vertical Turbulent Buoyant Jets, Journal of Fluid Mechanics, Vol.195, pp. 431-391.
3. Nezu, I. and Nakagawa, H., (1993), Turbulence in open channel flows, IAHR Monograph. A.A. Balkema/Rotterdam/Brookfield.
4. Shiono, K, Feng, T. and Muto, Y. (1998), Reynolds stress and flux measurements in open channel flow using a laser induced fluorescence technique, Proceedings of the Seventh International Symposium on Flow Modelling and Turbulence Measurements, National Cheng Kung University, Taiwan, pp 117-124.
5. West, J. R., Knight, D. W. and Shiono, K., (1985), "A note on the determination of vertical turbulent transport coefficients in a partially mixed estuary", Proceedings of Institution of Civil Engineers, Part 2, 79, pp.235-246.
6. West, J. R. and Shiono, K., (1988), Vertical turbulent mixing processes on ebb tides in partially mixed estuaries, Estuarine, Coastal and Shelf Science, 26, pp.51-66.
7. Wood, I.R. and Liang, T. (1989), Dispersion in an open channel with a step in the cross-section, Journal of Hydraulic Research, IAHR, Vol.27, No.5, pp.587-601.

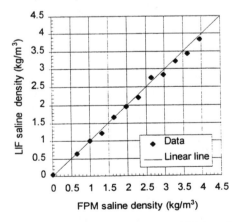

Fig. 1 Comparison between PFM and LIF concentrations

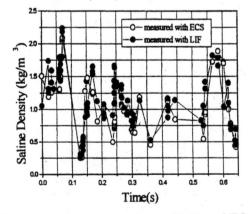

Fig. 2 Turbulent fluctuations of LIF and ECS

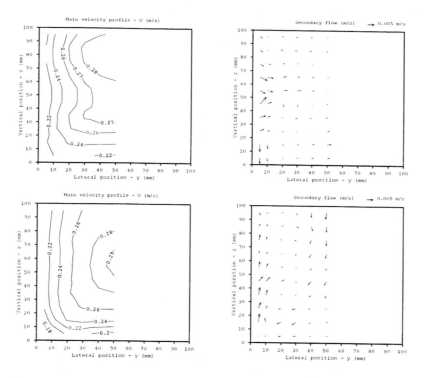

Fig.3 a) Main velocity and secondary currents, top: at 1.5m and bottom: at 6.4m
for the fresh water case.

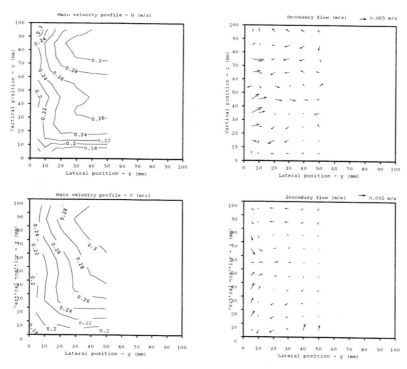

Fig.3 b) Main velocity and secondary currents, top: at 1.5m and bottom: at 6.4m
for the 5kg/m^3 difference case.

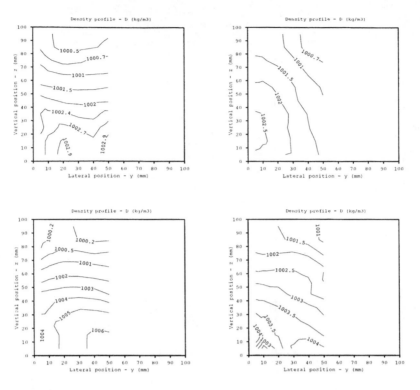

Fig. 4 Salinity concentration distributions, top left: at 1.5m and top right: at 6.4m for 3kg/m^3 and bottom left: at 1.5m and bottom right: at 6.4m for 5kg/m^3.

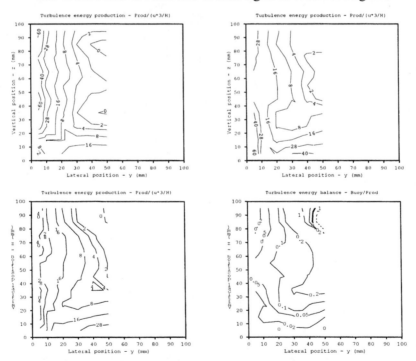

Fig. 5 Distributions of the production of TKE, top left: at 1.5m and right: at 6.4m for fresh water case and bottom left: at 6.4m for 5kg/m^3 and right: the ratio of buoyancy/ productions.

Algebraic Parametrizations for the Triple Correlations in Modelling the Shearless Turbulence Mixing Layer

Vladimir Grebenev [1], Boris Ilyushin [2]

[1]Institute of Computational Technologies, Russian Academy of Science SD,
Lavrentjev ave. 6, Novosibirsk 630090, Russia
[2]Institute of Thermophysics, Russian Academy of Science SD,
Lavrentjev ave. 1, Novosibirsk 630090, Russia
vova@lchd.ict.nsc.ru, ilyushin@ict.nsc.ru

1. Abstract

In this article we introduce a concept based on the differential constraints method to examine the closure procedure in Turbulence Models. We show how this concept may be applied to study the problem on interaction and mixing between two semi-infinite homogeneous turbulent flow fields of different scales. To describe correctly this physical model, we expose a new third-order closure model of turbulence. We find an invariant set and construct a parametric family of selfsimilar solutions. In application to Turbulence Models, it is shown that the equation describing the obtained invariant set (manifold) coincides with the algebraic expression for the triple correlation of the vertical velocity fluctuation or the so-called tensor-invariant model (Hanjalic & Launder, 1972).

2. Introduction

The method of differential constraints advanced by Yanenko (1964), (Sidorov, Shapeev & Yanenko, 1984) for constructing explicit solutions to different kinds of nonlinear partial differential equations makes it possible to obtain the gradient–type algebraic expressions for unknown functions. This provides us a concept for examining the closure procedure for momentum equations in Turbulence Models. Moreover, the method gives a reasonable tool for obtaining algebraic expressions. The exposition is demonstrated on an example chosen from Free Turbulence Flows Theory. The analysis has been carried out in the article shows that a concept of differential constraints allows us to interpret algebraic expressions as the equations of invariant sets (manifold) generated by corresponding differential equations.

The plan of the article is as follows. In Section 3 we expose a new third-order closure model of turbulence based on using an approach which was developed in (Ilyushin, 1999, 2000). This approach has been employed in (Ilyushin, 1999) to obtain a closed model of turbulence that does not imply equality to zero of the fourth-order cumulants. The closure procedure was performed at level of the fifth moments. We also mention that the method proposed by Ilyushin (1999, 2000) also includes a physically reasonable technique for constructing approximate algebraic parametrizations of higher moments. We apply the model to study a classical problem on the dynamics of the shearless turbulence mixing layer.

Our next result is devoted to examining an algebraic expression for the triple correlation of the vertical velocity fluctuations $\langle w^3 \rangle$. In Section 4 we show that the set of smooth functions:

$$D = \{\langle w^2 \rangle, \langle w^3 \rangle, \hat{\tau} : \mathcal{H}^1(\langle w^2 \rangle, \langle w^3 \rangle, \hat{\tau}) \equiv \langle w^3 \rangle + \delta \hat{\tau} \langle w^2 \rangle \langle w^2 \rangle_z = 0\}$$

is invariant under the flow generated by the differential equation for $\langle w^3 \rangle$. As a consequence, it is established that the differential constraint $\mathcal{H}^1$ coincides with the algebraic expression for $\langle w^3 \rangle$ or the so-called tensor-invariant model (Hanjalic & Launder, 1972).

Hence,

$$e_h = \frac{c_1 - 1}{c_1 + 2}\langle w^2 \rangle, \quad E = \frac{3c_1}{2(c_1 + 2)}\langle w^2 \rangle, \quad \tau = \frac{3c_1}{2(c_1 + 2)}\frac{\langle w^2 \rangle}{\epsilon}.$$

By the obtained relations, in the case of absence stratification i.e. $N \equiv 0$ we can rewritten the equation as:

$$\frac{\partial \langle w^2 \rangle}{\partial t} = -\frac{\partial \langle w^3 \rangle}{\partial z} - \frac{c_1}{c_1 + 2}\frac{\langle w^2 \rangle}{\tau},$$

$$\frac{\partial \epsilon}{\partial t} = \frac{\partial}{\partial z}\left[c_d \tau \langle w^2 \rangle \frac{\partial \epsilon}{\partial z}\right] - c_{\epsilon_2}\frac{\epsilon}{\tau},$$

$$\frac{\partial \langle w^3 \rangle}{\partial t} = \frac{\partial}{\partial z}\left[\frac{\tau}{c_3}\left(6\langle w^3 \rangle\frac{\partial \langle w^2 \rangle}{\partial z} + 4\langle w^2 \rangle\frac{\langle \partial w^3 \rangle}{\partial z}\right)\right] - 3\langle w^2 \rangle\frac{\partial \langle w^2 \rangle}{\partial z} - c_2\frac{\langle w^3 \rangle}{\tau}.$$

It follows from the formula for C (Ilyushin, 1999) that the contribution of the second term in the algebraic model for the cumulant C is leading. Thus the governing equations are:

$$\frac{\partial \langle w^2 \rangle}{\partial t} = -\frac{\partial \langle w^3 \rangle}{\partial z} - \alpha\frac{\langle w^2 \rangle}{\hat{\tau}}, \tag{1}$$

$$\frac{\partial \langle w^3 \rangle}{\partial t} = \frac{\partial}{\partial z}\left[\kappa\hat{\tau}\langle w^2 \rangle\frac{\partial \langle w^3 \rangle}{\partial z}\right] - 3\langle w^2 \rangle\frac{\partial \langle w^2 \rangle}{\partial z} - \gamma\frac{\langle w^3 \rangle}{\hat{\tau}}, \tag{2}$$

$$\frac{\partial \epsilon}{\partial t} = \frac{\partial}{\partial z}\left[\delta\hat{\tau}\langle w^2 \rangle\frac{\partial \epsilon}{\partial z}\right] - \varrho\frac{\epsilon}{\hat{\tau}}, \tag{3}$$

where $\alpha = 2/3$, $\kappa = 6c_1/c_3(c_1 + 2)$, $\gamma = 2c_2(c_1 + 1)/3c_1$, $\delta = 3c_1 c_d/2(c_1 + 2)$, $\varrho = 2c_{\epsilon_2}(c_1 + 2)/3c_1$, $\hat{\tau} = \langle w^2 \rangle/\epsilon$.

4. Invariant sets

We briefly recall a special terminology of Symmetry Analysis. For detailed description of extra materials see, for example (Ibragimov, 1985).

Consider the system of evolution equations $\mathcal{F}$:

$$u_t^i = \mathcal{F}^i(t, x_1, \ldots, x_n, u^1, \ldots, u_\lambda^k, \ldots,)$$

where $i = 1, \ldots, m$, $u_\lambda^k = \partial^\lambda u^k/\partial x_1^{\lambda_1} \ldots \partial x_n^{\lambda_n}$.

A set(manifold) $\mathcal{H}$ given by equations:

$$h_i(t, x_1, \ldots, x_n, \ldots, u^1, \ldots, u^m, \ldots, u_\lambda^k, \ldots) = 0$$

is said to be invariant set (manifold) of the system $\mathcal{F}$ if

$$V_{\mathcal{F}}(h^i)\Big|_{[\mathcal{H}]_0} = 0,$$

$$V_{\mathcal{F}} = \frac{\partial}{\partial t} + \sum_{i=1}^{m}\mathcal{F}^i\frac{\partial}{\partial u^1} + \sum_{i=1}^{m}D^\alpha(\mathcal{F}^i)\frac{\partial}{\partial u_\alpha^i},$$

where $\alpha = (\alpha_1, \ldots, \alpha_n)$, $D^\alpha = D_{x_1}^{\alpha_1}\ldots D_{x_n}^{\alpha_n}$. Here $[\mathcal{H}]_0$ denotes the equations $\mathcal{H}$ and its differential prolongations with respect to $x_1, \ldots, x_n$.

The invariant condition can be written in the following equivalent form:

$$D_t(h_i)\Big|_{[\mathcal{F}]_0}\Big|_{[\mathcal{H}]_0} = 0.$$

In Section 5 we discuss the existence of selfsimilar solutions. It is well-known that if an operator admits invariant sets, then there exist a solution to an overdetermined system under suitable assumptions on operators and the form of invariant sets.

3. Modelling the turbulent transport in a shearless mixing layer

The subject of the study is the problem on interaction and mixing between two semi-infinite homogeneous turbulent flow fields of different scales. As the flow evolves these two different turbulent fields penetrate and diffuse into one another. The typical example is the turbulent buoyant jet from a smoke cigar issuing into the atmospheric turbulent layer. To describe correctly the physical model, it is proposed to consider the hypothesis of equality to zero of the fifth-order cumulants under the condition of nonzero fourth-order cumuants. The starting point is the following system of average equations:

$$\frac{\partial e_h}{\partial t} = -\frac{\partial \langle e_h w \rangle}{\partial z} - \frac{c_1}{\tau}\left[e_h - \frac{2}{3}E\right] - \frac{2}{3}\epsilon, \qquad \frac{\partial \epsilon}{\partial t} = \frac{\partial}{\partial z}\left[c_d \tau \langle w^2 \rangle \frac{\partial \epsilon}{\partial z}\right] + \frac{c_{\epsilon_1}}{\tau}\beta g \langle w\theta \rangle - c_{\epsilon_2}\frac{\epsilon}{\tau},$$

$$\frac{\partial \langle w^2 \rangle}{\partial t} = -\frac{\partial \langle w^3 \rangle}{\partial z} + 2\beta g \langle w\theta \rangle - \frac{c_1}{\tau}\left[\langle w^2 \rangle - \frac{2}{3}E\right] - \frac{2}{3}\epsilon.$$

In the absence of mean shear velocity the horizontal component e_h of the turbulent kinetic energy takes the form:

$$e_h = (\langle u^2 \rangle + \langle v^2 \rangle)/2.$$

As usual, the sign $\langle \cdot \rangle$ denotes average values, $\langle u^2 \rangle$, $\langle v^2 \rangle$, $\langle w^2 \rangle$ are the one-point velocity correlation of the second-order, $\tau = E/\epsilon$ the time scale of turbulence. Here E, ϵ are the kinetic energy and spectral flux of the turbulent kinetic energy. The volumetric expansion coefficient is $\beta = 1/\Theta$, where Θ and θ are the mean and variance potential temperature respectively. The constants involved in the model with lower case letters are denoted by c_{**}. We complete the system by the transport equation for the triple correlation of the vertical velocity fluctuation:

$$\frac{\partial \langle w^3 \rangle}{\partial t} = -\frac{\partial C}{\partial z} - 3\langle w^2 \rangle \frac{\partial \langle w^2 \rangle}{\partial z} + 3\beta g \langle w^2\theta \rangle - c_2 \frac{\langle w^3 \rangle}{\tau}.$$

Algebraic parametrizations for the fourth-order cumulant C, the triple correlation $\langle w^2\theta \rangle$ and the vertical heat flux $\langle w\theta \rangle$ can be written as [4]:

$$C = -\frac{\tau}{c_3}\left[6\langle w^3 \rangle \frac{\partial \langle w^2 \rangle}{\partial z} + 4\langle w^2 \rangle \frac{\partial \langle w^3 \rangle}{\partial z}\right],$$

$$\langle w^2\theta \rangle = -\frac{\tau}{c_4}\left[\langle w^3 \rangle \frac{\partial \Theta}{\partial z} - 2\beta g \langle w\theta^2 \rangle\right], \qquad \langle w\theta^2 \rangle = -\frac{\tau}{c_5}\langle w^2 \rangle \frac{\partial \langle \theta^2 \rangle}{\partial z},$$

$$\langle w\theta \rangle = -\frac{\tau}{c_{\theta_1}}\langle w^2 \rangle \frac{\partial \Theta}{\partial z} \equiv -\frac{\tau N^2}{\beta g c_{\theta_1}}\langle w^2 \rangle, \quad N^2 = \beta g \frac{\partial \Theta}{\partial z}$$

$$\langle \theta^2 \rangle = -\frac{\tau}{c_r}\langle w\theta \rangle \frac{\partial \Theta}{\partial z} = -\frac{\tau N^2}{\beta g r}\langle w\theta \rangle = \left(\frac{\tau N^2}{\beta g}\right)^2 \frac{\langle w^2 \rangle}{c_{\theta_1} r},$$

where $r = \tau/\tau_\theta$, τ_θ is the time scale of potential temperature variance, N the Brunt-Vaisala frequency. Using the balance approximation between exchange mechanism and dissipation, the equation for the horizontal component e_h of the turbulent kinetic energy is simplified and has the form:

$$-c_1\left[e_h - \frac{2}{3}\left(e_h + \frac{\langle w^2 \rangle}{2}\right)\right] = \frac{2}{3}\left(e_h + \frac{\langle w^2 \rangle}{2}\right).$$

As the first result that uses the above notion we prove that the set

$$D = \{\langle w^2 \rangle, \langle w^3 \rangle, \hat{\tau} : \mathcal{H}^1(\langle w^2 \rangle, \langle w^3 \rangle, \hat{\tau}) \equiv \langle w^3 \rangle + \delta \hat{\tau} \langle w^2 \rangle \langle w^2 \rangle_z = 0\} \tag{4}$$

is invariant under the flow generated by equation (2).

Theorem 1 *Let the triple $\langle w^2 \rangle$, $\langle w^3 \rangle$, ϵ be a sufficiently smooth solution of (1)-(3) and let $\kappa = \delta$. Assume also that $\hat{\tau}_z = 0, \hat{\tau}_t = (2\alpha\delta - \gamma\delta + 3)/\delta$, then (i) the equation (2) admits the invariant set D; (ii) the system (1)-(3) on the invariant set D is equivalent to:*

$$\langle w^2 \rangle = (2\alpha\delta - \gamma\delta + 3)\epsilon/\delta, \qquad \langle w^3 \rangle = -\delta\hat{\tau}\langle w^2 \rangle\langle w^2 \rangle_z, \tag{5}$$

$$\frac{\partial \epsilon}{\partial t} = \frac{\partial}{\partial z}\left[\delta\hat{\tau}^2\epsilon\frac{\partial \epsilon}{\partial z}\right] - \varrho\frac{\epsilon}{\hat{\tau}}. \tag{6}$$

Theorem 1 has a special interest in view of its application to Turbulence Models.

Corollary 1 *The equation $\mathcal{H}^1(\langle w^2 \rangle, \langle w^3 \rangle, \hat{\tau}) = 0$ that defines an invariant set of (1)-(3) coincides with the algebraic triple correlation model or the tensor-invariant model* (Hanjalic, & Launder, 1972)

Other words, the algebraic expression represents the equation of an invariant set (manifold) generated by the differential equation for the triple correlation.

Corollary 2 *There no exists differential constraints of the form*

$$\mathcal{H}^n \equiv \langle w^3 \rangle - H^n(\langle w^2 \rangle, \langle w^3 \rangle, \langle w^3 \rangle_1, \ldots \langle w^3 \rangle_n, \hat{\tau}) = 0$$

for $n > 1$ where $\langle w^3 \rangle_n$ denotes the n-order derivative, H^n is a sufficiently smooth function.

5. Selfsimilar solutions

Theorem 1 enables us to reduce (1)-(3) to the algebraic differential expressions (5), (6) which are more simple system for analyzing. Using the obtained reduction we give the selfsimilar description for (1)-(3). We recall that a solution of the equation (or the system of equations) is said to be selfsimilar for the equation if this solution is invariant under the parametric group of scale transformation.

Appropriate selfsimilar solution to our problem is a solution of the form:

$$\epsilon_a = \frac{h(\xi)}{(t + t_0)^{3\mu + \nu}}, \quad \langle w_a^2 \rangle = \frac{f(\xi)}{(t + t_0)^{2\mu}}, \quad \langle w_a^3 \rangle = \frac{q(\xi)}{(t + t_0)^{3\mu}}, \tag{7}$$

$$\xi = \frac{z - z_0}{L}, \quad L = \lambda(t + t_0)^\nu, \quad z_0 = \lambda_0 L + \lambda_1, \quad t_0 > 0,$$

where λ, λ_i are model constants and t_0 is a parameter. A straightforward calculation yields that if we choose $\nu = 1 - \mu$, then the original system is transformed to the system of ordinary differential equations for the profiles f, q and h:

$$2\mu f + (1 - \mu)(\xi + \lambda_0)f_\xi - g_\xi - \alpha h = 0, \tag{8}$$

$$\kappa\left(\frac{f^2}{h}q_\xi\right)_\xi - 3ff_\xi - (\xi + \lambda_0)q_\xi - \gamma\frac{qh}{f} + 3\mu q = 0, \tag{9}$$

$$\delta\left(\frac{f^2}{h}h_\xi\right)_\xi - (\xi + \lambda_0)h_\xi + (2\mu + 1)h - \varrho\frac{h^2}{f} = 0. \tag{10}$$

The free similarity exponent μ has to be determined from a solution of the obtained nonlinear eigenvalue problem. This is a typical situation appearing in nonlinear diffusion problems where a conservation law does not exist. The boundary conditions are determined by the physical model: the functions $f(\xi)$, $q(\xi)$, $h(\xi)$ tend to given positive limits as ξ tends to $\pm\infty$.

To solve the problem we use the existence of an invariant set obtained in Theorem 1. For this purpose, we study the equation for $\hat{\tau}$ and show that $\hat{\tau} = (\varrho - \alpha)(t + t_0)$ is a solution to the equation. As the result, the system (8)-(10) admits a reduction. Therefore we have the following boundary value problem:

$$\delta(w_c^2 h h_\xi)_\xi + (1 - \mu)(\xi + \lambda_0)h_\xi = 0, \quad w_c = \varrho - \alpha, \quad \mu = \frac{\alpha}{2(\varrho - \alpha)}, \tag{11}$$

$$h(-\infty) = a_- t_0^{2\mu+1}, \quad h(+\infty) = a_+ t_0^{2\mu+1}, \tag{12}$$

where $a_\pm = \lim_{z\to\pm\infty} \epsilon(z, 0), a_\pm > 0$. We prove the existence and uniqueness results in a class of positive functions to the boundary value problem for $h(\xi)$, expose in details the qualitative properties of the solution. As a remark we note that this solution is essentially different from the well-known Barenblatt's solutions (Barenblatt, 1996) to the porous medium equation.

Theorem 2 *Let $\kappa = \delta$, $\delta = 3/(\rho - \gamma)$ and $\gamma = (3/2)\alpha$, assume that $\rho - \gamma > 0$. Then there exists a solution $\langle w_a^2 \rangle$, $\langle w_a^3 \rangle$, ϵ_a of system (1)-(3) which represents the selfsimilar description of evolution of the shearless turbulence mixing layer.*

Acknowledgments

This research was partially supported by the Russian Foundation of Basic Research (grant no. 98-01-00719). This work was financially supported by INTAS (proposal no. 97-2022)

References

[1] Barenblatt G. I. 1996. *Scaling, selfsimilar and intermediate asymptotics*. Cambridge Texts in Applied Mathematics, 14.

[2] Hanjalic K., Launder B. E. 1972. *A Reynolds stress model of turbulence and its application to thin shear flows*. J.Fluid Mech., 52, pp. 609–638.

[3] Ibragimov N. H. 1985. *Transformation groups applied to mathematical physics*. Reidel.

[4] Ilyushin B. B. 1999. *Model of fourth–order cumulants for prediction of turbulent transport by large-scale vortex structures*. J. Appl. Mechan. Tech. Phys., 40, N.5, pp. 871–876.

[5] Ilyushin B. B. 2000 *Higher-moment diffusion in stable stratification*. In: Closure strategies for turbulent and transition flows. (Ed. Launder B. E., Sandham N. D.), Cambrigde, (in the press).

[6] Sidorov A. F., Shapeev V. P., Yanenko N. N. 1984. *The differential constraints method and its application to gas dynamics*. Nauka, Novosibirsk (in Russian).

[7] Yanenko N. N. 1964. *The compatibility theory and methods of integration of systems of nonlinear partial differential equations*. In: Proceedings of All-Union Math. Congress, pp. 613–621, Nauka, Leningrad (in Russian).

Mixing Efficiency in Unstably Stratified Flows

Joanne M. Holford and S. B. Dalziel

Department of Applied Mathematics and Theoretical Physics, Silver Street,
Cambridge, CB3 9EW, U. K.

1. Abstract

Mixing is an important consequence of small-scale motion, unresolved in most theoretical or numerical models, which irreversibly changes the background stratification, and removes available energy from the fluid flow. One useful measure of mixing in a flow is the instantaneous mixing efficiency η, defined as the ratio of the change in background potential energy to the change in available energy (kinetic and potential).

In many stratified flows, η is a function only of the bulk parameters, for example the overall Richardson number in a stably stratified flow. In other flows, η varies either with the detailed structure of the stratification or with details of the perturbing flow. An extreme initial condition is that of an initially unstable stratification, which develops Rayleigh-Taylor instability. In this instability, the large initial available energy is greater that the maximum possible increase in background potential energy, and the maximum value of η must be strictly less than 1. Below this maximum value, there is generally an increase in η with the Atwood number (non-dimensional density difference).

Here we investigate the variation in η that results from an initial unstable two-layer density stratification, in which the interface is tilted at some angle. If the interface is horizontal, we have classical Rayleigh-Taylor instability, whereas if it is vertical, we have a lock exchange flow. Any tilt to the interface encourages the subsequent flow to organise into an overturning motion, while the added shear at the interface modifies the growth of the Rayleigh-Taylor instability.

Results are presented from multiple realisations of laboratory experiments, using LIF techniques to estimate the potential energy and particle tracking to estimate the kinetic energy as the flow evolves.

2. Introduction

Mixing is the process by which fluid parcels from different regions are brought together on sufficiently small scales to allow molecular diffusion to homogenise the fluid properties. It is an important process in many situations, for example, as a control on reactance rates in a chemically active mixture. In a stratified fluid, density variations may drive motion, and the mixing process may irreversibly remove energy from the flow, by increasing the background potential energy (PE), *i.e.* the minimum PE attainable through adiabatic motions (given by a Thorpe reordering of fluid parcels, Thorpe (1977) and Winters *et al.* (1995)). In addition, transient density variations contribute to the available PE, which may be exchanged with the kinetic energy (KE) of the flow. For stratified flows, a global measure of irreversible mixing of density is the increase in background PE. This may be expressed as a fraction of the energy permanently lost to the fluid motion as the mixing efficiency η. In many situations, it is desirable to be able to parametrise the mixing that occurs in terms of the bulk properties of the flow.

In initially stably stratified flows, an important parameter is the bulk Richardson number Ri, which is a measure of the overall flow stability relative to the perturbation strength. Laboratory experiments, including those of Linden (1979) and Huq & Britter (1995), show an increase in η with Ri at low Ri, but a range of behaviour at higher Ri. Experiments show that η can vary with the structure of the stratification and with the character of the stirring (see Holford & Linden 1999a,b). In Rayleigh-Taylor

(RT) instability, the main parameter is the Atwood number A, which is representative of both the available and background PE. The experiments of Linden & Redondo (1991) show that η increases with the Atwood number, and further studies show that mixing is insensitive to small variations in the initial conditions, providing that a large-scale overturning does not occur (see Linden, Redondo & Youngs (1994) and Dalziel, Linden & Youngs (1999)).

In this paper we investigate the evolution of an unstable two-layer density stratification when an initial tilt of the interface, to an angle θ from the horizontal, induces a large-scale overturning. The experiments are described in section 3, and background theory is discussed in section 4. In section 5, the experimental results are presented and discussed.

3. Experimental Set-up

Experiments have been carried out in a tank of length $L = 40$cm, width $W = 20$cm and height $H = 50$cm (internal dimensions). At mid-height, a removable barrier, parallel to the floor, divides the tank. The tank was originally designed to study the evolution of the early stages of RT instability, and is described in detail in Dalziel (1993) and Dalziel *et al.* (1999). In the present experiments, the whole tank is mounted with the floor at an angle θ to the horizontal, so that the barrier is removed downhill.

The tank is filled with fluid of density ρ_2 beneath the barrier, the barrier is inserted, and then the tank is topped up with fluid of density $\rho_1 > \rho_2$ above the barrier. The fluids used are a dilute solution of propanol in water, and salt solution, where the concentrations of propanol and salt are chosen to match the refractive indices of the two layers. De-aerated water is used to reduce the number of air bubbles brought out of solution in the low pressure region in the wake of the barrier. A floating lid, weighted at one end to ensure that it floats parallel to the floor, prevents surface waves while allowing the upper layer fluid to descend to take up the volume of the barrier when it is removed. The Atwood number A is given by $A = (\rho_1 - \rho_2)/(\rho_1 + \rho_2)$, which is related to the reduced gravity g' by $g' = 2Ag$, where g is the acceleration due to gravity. The densities of the two layers are measured in an Anton Paar DMA602 densitometer.

The barrier is hollow, and two sheets of fabric are fed together through it from outside the tank, separating at the end of the barrier to return around the outside to the edge of the tank, where they are attached. As the barrier is pulled out, both sheets of fabric are pulled through the hollow barrier, at twice the speed of the barrier. The dominant disturbance due to this method of initialising the flow is a slightly asymmetric jet behind the barrier, caused by the fluid adjusting to the removal of the finite volume of the barrier. The most unstable mode of this jet gives a well-defined, repeatable wavelength that grows preferentially in the subsequent evolution. Despite this drawback, the magnitude of the initial disturbance is much less than the strong vortex sheet created by the removal of a solid barrier.

The experiment is illuminated from below by a vertical light sheet approximately 5mm thick, and viewed from the side with a video camera. The flow is visualised either by seeding the whole flow with small (<0.5mm in diameter) neutrally buoyant particles, or by dying the upper layer with sodium fluorescein, a fluorescent dye. The motion of the particles is followed from frame to frame from a video of the experiment, giving Lagrangian velocity information which is then interpolated onto a regular grid, (Dalziel 1992). The dyed images are corrected for divergence of the light sheet, and attenuation of the light by the dye, to give an estimate of the fluid density (Dalziel *et al.* (1999)). Both methods give a good degree of temporal and spatial resolution (within the vertical plane), and are non-intrusive.

4. Theory

In RT instability at a horizontal unstable interface, the linear instability is rapidly overtaken by a nonlinear self-similar growth. Dimensional analysis then suggests that the width h of the perturbed region increases as

$$h = \alpha A g t^2 ,$$

while the velocity scale increases as

$$u \propto \alpha A g t .$$

For Boussinesq fluids, α has a typical value of $\alpha \approx 0.06$, independent of A. Together these scaling predict an initial increase in the KE proportional to t^4.

As the flow evolves, vorticity ϖ can be created and destroyed within the flow through the relative rotation of pressure and density surfaces, according to

$$\frac{D\varpi}{Dt} = \varpi.\nabla u - \hat{z} \wedge \nabla b + \nu \nabla^2 \varpi ,$$

where b is the buoyancy $b = -g(\rho - \rho_0)/\rho_0$. For two-dimensional, inviscid flow in the vertical along-slope plane, the rate of change of circulation κ in the plane is

$$\frac{d\kappa}{dt} = \oint n_x b \, dl ,$$

where n_x is the horizontal component of the normal to the tank walls. For the initial conditions in the present tilted experiments, the initial evolution is

$$\frac{d\kappa(0)}{dt} = 2 A g L \sin(\theta) ,$$

confirming that an anticlockwise circulation develops. For fluid in a tank of depth H, the characteristic timescale is for RT instability and overturning is $\tau = (H/Ag)^{1/2}$.

5. Results

Two sequences of images in a vertical plane, from similar experiments with $\theta = 5°$ and $A = 2.5 \times 10^{-3}$, are shown in landscape arrangement in figures 1 and 2. At early times (a, $t/\tau < 1/2$) the motion is dominated by the wake of the barrier. There is a net circulation in the plane tending to overturn the stratification clockwise, and the disturbances on the interface are sheared in the direction of the barrier removal. As local instabilities develop on the interface the disturbances become more symmetrical, although the interface is affected by a large-scale overturning (b, c, $0.5 < t/\tau < 2$). This overturning circulation rapidly dominates, reaching a peak at around $t/\tau = 4$ (d). Thereafter the fluid sloshes from one side of the tank to the other with a period of about 10τ. Snapshots at the time when the flow next has minimum KE (e, $t/\tau = 6$) and maximum KE (f, $t/\tau = 8.5$) are shown. Significant small-scale motion, leading to a divergence of the planar flow above the noise threshold, is only observed around the time of the first KE minimum. The phase of the sloshing mode relative to the start of the experiments varies somewhat with the details of the initial disturbance for $\theta = 5°$, but is much more uniform in experiments with $\theta \geq 10°$.

Estimates of the global energy balance can be made from these measurements. Figure 3a shows estimates of the KE evolution for the flow in figure 1. The mean flow KE is calculated by smoothing the velocity field to estimate the large scale overturning field, which is predominantly confined to this plane. The difference between the resolved flow in this plane and the overturning is then the fluctuation or small-scale RT unstable flow field. The KE of this fluctuation flow field does indeed grow like t^4 until $t/\tau = 2$, when it saturates. Since the fluctuation field is approximately horizontally homogeneous, an

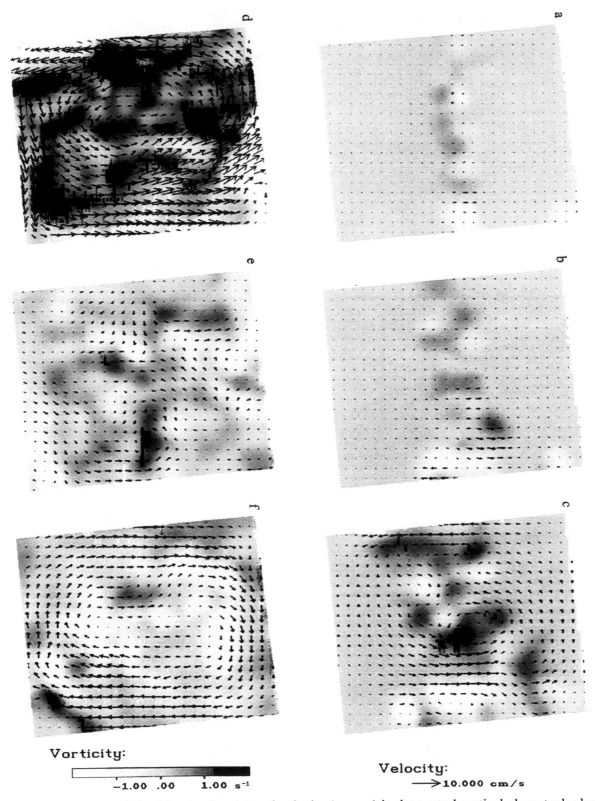

Vorticity:

−1.00 .00 1.00 s⁻¹

Velocity:

⟶ 10.000 cm/s

Figure 1 Sequence of vorticity (greyscale) and velocity (arrows) in the central vertical along-tank plane, at times t/τ = 0.4, 0.9, 1.8, 3.5, 6.0 and 8.5, in an experiment with $\theta = 5°$ and $A = 2.4 \times 10^{-3}$. Gravity acts towards the left and the barrier is removed upwards.

Figure 2 Sequence of the density field in the central vertical along-tank plane, at times $t/\tau = 0.4$, 0.9, 1.8, 3.5, 6.0 and 8.5, in an experiment with $\theta = 5°$ and $A = 2.6 \times 10^{-3}$. The scale ranges from white (ρ_1) to black (ρ_2). Gravity acts towards the left and the barrier is removed upwards.

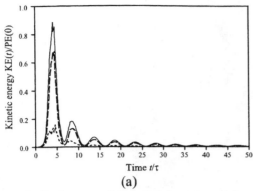 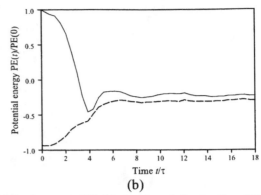

(a)	(b)

Figure 3 Estimates of the global energy: (a) total KE (solid line), mean KE (dashes) and fluctuation KE (dots), and (b) total PE (solid line) and background PE (dashes).

estimate of the total KE can be made by adding the horizontal fluctuation KE to the resolved KE from the flow in the vertical plane.

The total and background PE are calculated from integration of the LIF data, either directly or after reordering. A final non-dimensional PE of about -0.25 is attained, after approximately 10τ, which equates to a mixing efficiency for the whole experiment of $\eta = 0.6$. In the early stages of the experiment, the instantaneous mixing efficiency is somewhat higher, at about $\eta = 0.8$. Hence for this small angle of inclination, the high values of η consistent with RT instability are observed.

The authors wish to thank the technical staff D. Page-Croft, B. Dean and C. Mortimer. JMH wishes to acknowledge the financial support of AWE Aldermaston through a William Penney Fellowship.

References

Dalziel, S. B. (1992) Decay of rotating turbulence: some particle tracking experiments.. *Appl. Sci. Res.*, **49**, 217 – 244.

Dalziel, S. B. (1993) Rayleigh-Taylor instability: experiments with image analysis. *Dyn. Atmos. Oceans*, **20**, 127 – 153.

Dalziel, S. B., Linden, P. F. & Youngs, D. L. (1999) Self-similarity and internal structure of turbulence induced by Rayleigh-Taylor instability. *J. Fluid Mech.*, **399**, 1 – 48.

Holford, J. M. & Linden, P. F. (1999a) The development of layers in a stratified fluid. In *Proc. of 5th IMA Conf. on Strat. Flows, Dundee, 'Mixing and Dispersion in Stably Stratified Flows'*, OUP, 165 – 179.

Holford, J. M. & Linden, P. F. (1999b) Turbulent mixing in a stratified fluid. *Dyn. Atmos. Oceans*, 30, 173 – 198.

Huq, P. & Britter, R. E. (1995) Turbulence evolution and mixing in a two-layer stably stratified fluid. *J. Fluid Mech.*, **285**, 41 – 67.

Linden, P. F. (1979) Mixing in stratified fluids. *Geophys. Astrophys. Fluid Dyn.*, **13**, 3 – 23.

Linden, P. F. & Redondo, J. M. (1991) Molecular mixing in Rayleigh-Taylor instability. Part I: Global mixing. *Phys. Fluids A*, **3**, 1269 – 1277.

Linden, P. F., Redondo, J. M. & Youngs, D. L. (1994) Molecular mixing in Rayleigh-Taylor instability. *J. Fluid Mech.*, **265**, 97 – 124.

Thorpe, S. A. (1977) Turbulence and mixing in a Scottish Loch. *Phil. Trans. R. Soc. Lond. A*, **286**, 125 – 181.

Winters, K. B., Lombard, P. N., Riley, J. J. & D'Asaro, E. A. (1995) Available potential energy and mixing in density-stratified fluids. *J. Fluid Mech.*, **289**, 115 – 128.

TURBULENT "FLARES" IN A STRATIFIED WATER COLUMN: STATISTICS AND VERTICAL TRANSPORT

V. Kushnir[1], B. Shteinman[2], Y. Kamenir[3]

[1]Marine Hydrophysical Institute National Academy of Science of Ukraine, 2 Kapitanskaya Str., Sevastopol 99011, Ukraine
[2]Israel Oceanography and Limnological Research, Yigal Allone Kinneret Limnological Laboratory, P.O. Box 345, Tiberias 14102, Israel
[3]Deparment of Life Sciences, Bar Ilan University, Ramat Gan 52900, Israel

1. Introduction

The sharp vertical gradients of density are formed in natural and artificial reservoirs under influence of intensive solar heating and wind hashing of the top layer. During the summer period, such gradients reach up to 10^{-4} -10^{-5} g/cm^4 in the top layers of 15-25 m in the Black Sea and 10-15 m layers in the Lake Kinneret. These vertical gradients of density appreciably complicate the vertical exchange of pulse and passive substations (temperature, salinity, nutrients, oxygen) owing to necessity to overcome the Archimed's forces.

On the other hand, the energy of internal waves and eddy-wave structures of various scales concentrates in the layers with sharp density gradients. Due to this, favorable conditions for development of hydrodynamical instability zones are created. These zones of local hydrodynamical instability are formed as local turbulent structures - *flares* of a turbulence, which may be the basic mechanism of the vertical exchange of pulse and conservative substations between layers of the water column divided by sharp vertical density gradients. The definition of the statistical characteristics of such turbulence *flares*, and fluxes of pulse and conservative substations formed by them will allow carrying out parameterization of the vertical exchange in the specific layers. It has the important meaning for creation of physics-ecological models of the natural and artificial basins, which take into account the specified feature of vertical structure of the density distribution in the water column.

The analysis of the specified problem of the vertical exchange in the water column with sharp density gradients is executed in the present work on the basis of experimental data on vertical profiles of currents and density.

2. Materials and Methods

The data was collected in the Black Sea, with vertical resolution of 1 m, and also in Lake Kinneret, with vertical resolution of 0.1 m (Kushnir, 1998; Kushnir et al., 1999). The results of similar researches, executed at the Loch Ness (Thorpe, 1977), also were used. The calculation of the coefficient of the vertical diffusion is executed on the basis of semi-empirical models of Ozmidov (1965) and Mellor & Yamada (1974).

3. Results and Discussion

The processing of the specified experimental data has allowed to receive synchronous estimations of the Brunt-Vaisala frequency N and vertical gradients of horizontal current speed E. The common diagram of E-N dependence for the specified water conditions is shown on Fig.1. It is necessary to note a rather high correlation between N and E values, which means that at increase of the vertical density gradient (and, hence, N), the vertical gradients of horizontal current speed and, hence, the turbulent energy are also increased. It confirms the key moment of the present work about concentration of energy of internal waves and eddy-wave structures in layers with high density gradients.

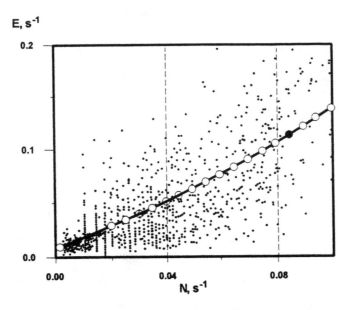

Figure 1. Correlation between vertical current shifts E and Brunt-Vaisala frequency N in the Black Sea (R=0.704), Lake Kinneret (R=0.642), Loch Ness (R=0.820), with the average regression line

The dimensionless function $\log (N/N_m) = f (z/z_m)$, where N_m is the maximal value of the Brunt-Vaisala frequency at depth z_m, were calculated for conditions of the Black Sea, Lake Kinneret and Loch Ness, on the basis of experimental data.

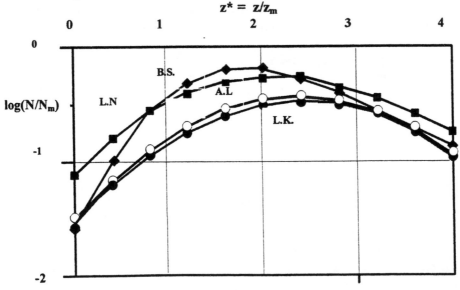

Figure 2. Regression dependence of $\log(N/N_m)$ on z/z_m

The regression lines for dependence of $\log(N/N_m)$ on (z/z_m) are shown in Fig.2 for the Black Sea (B.S., R=0.707), Lake Kinneret (L.K., R=0.643) and Loch Ness (L.N., R=0.872). The average regression lines (A.L.) of the type $\log n = b_3 z^3 + b_2 z^2 + b_1 z + b_0$ for the specified basins are shown in this Figure.

Dimensionless regularity of another type - logRi = f (z/z$_m$), where Ri - is the Richardson number, and standard deviations of logRi also were calculated for the specified water basins, and are presented on Fig. 3 a and 3 b. The main feature of these functions is the identical character and shape. This confirms the similarity of physical processes structuring the top water layer in natural basins during the summer heating

z / z $_m$

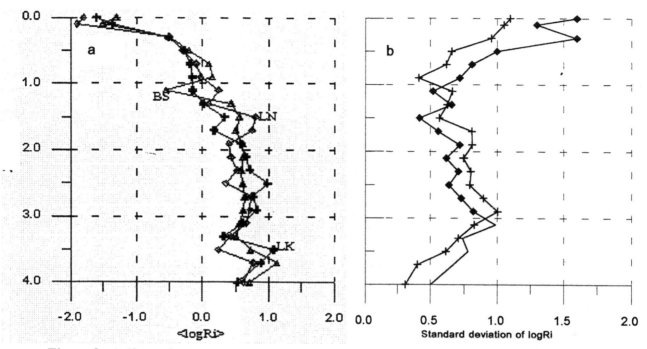

Figure 3. a) dimensionless parameter logRi = f (z/z$_m$); b) standard deviation of logRi.

The calculated asymmetry γ_a and excess γ_e coefficients of the experimental estimates of logRi crowd near zero values. So, the probability distribution of logRi values corresponds to quasi-normal (Gaussian) form described by the first three members of a series containing Ermit's polynomials.

Coefficients of vertical pulse diffusion K$_z$ and their statistics are calculated on the base of Ozmidov's (1965) semi-empirical model:

$$K_z = C_0 \varepsilon^{1/3} L_O^{4/3},$$
(1)

where C$_o$ = 0.1 is a constant, $\varepsilon = 7.5 \nu E^2$ is the rate at which energy is dissipated per unit volume, ν is kinematic viscosity, E^2 is the square of the mean horizontal current vertical shift, $L_O = \varepsilon^{1/2} N^{-3/2}$ is the Ozmidov's scale.

Ratio (1) is transformed easily to the following form:

K$_z$ = 0.75ν/Ri
(2)

The vertical turbulent diffusion can be developed at condition

$$L_O > L_K = \nu^{3/4} \varepsilon^{-1/4} \text{ (Kolmogorov's scale)}.$$

We found a ratio for L$_O$ and L$_K$, at which the maximal (critical) value of Richardson number for vertical turbulent diffusion development is equal to 7.5; the value of K$_z$/ν = 0.1, which is about equal to the coefficient of molecular thermal diffusivity.

The regression for the relationship between <log Ri> and $z_* = z/z_m$ (Fig 3.a) has the following form: $< \log Ri >= x_0 = -0.247z_*^2 + 1.484z_* - 1.348$. Taking this ratio into account, the average values of the vertical diffusive coefficient are expressed as follows:

$$< K_z >= 0.75v10^{-X_0} \tag{3}$$

$<K_z>$ values and standard logRi deviation at $z_* = 0$ (Lake Kinneret and Black Sea surface layer) are equal to 0.17cm^2/s and 1.11, respectively. The highest $<K_z>$ estimate (at 95% probability) corresponds to log Ri = -3.57 and is equal to 27.87 cm^2/s.

$<K_z>$ values obtained in the near surface layer of Lake Kinneret are comparable to similar estimates obtained from Kullenberg's (1971) semi-empirical ratio for the top water layer:

$$K_z = 10^{-8} C_K W^2 E N^{-2},$$

(4)

where $C_K = 2$ (constant), W is wind speed. This ratio can be transformed to the following form:

$$K_z = 10^{-8} C_K W^2 N Ri^{0.5}.$$

(5)

For the Lake Kinneret conditions, the average wind speed in the summer months of 1996-1997 was about 3.8 m/s, with maximal values of 11.5 m/s. These values correspond to the average value $<K_z> = 0.27$ cm^2/s, and the maximum value of 31.82 cm^2/s calculated using ratio (5). Therefore, independent estimates of the vertical diffusion coefficient appear to be close enough to the ratio obtained using equation (3). Thus, the average background of the vertical turbulent diffusion is a very slowed down process, with the rate of the vertical exchange some 15-20 times higher than the molecular diffusion in the near surface layer.

Local turbulent flares play the main role in the vertical exchange that works on the background of a much slowed-down process. From our analysis above, we deduced that the maximal K_z value in the near surface layer (27.7 cm^2/s) is about 165 times higher than the average values, and some 2800 times higher than the rate of molecular diffusivity. The statistical analysis of variation of the vertical diffusion coefficients is especially important in this situation.

As we have noted above, it is possible to use the common relationship for near-normal probability distributions of experimental logRi values in the following form:

$x = \log Ri$, $< \log Ri >= x_0 = -0.247z_*^2 + 1.484z_* - 1.348$, $X = (x - x_0)/\sigma$

$$W(X) = \frac{1}{\sigma\sqrt{2\pi}} e^{-0.5X^2} [1 - \frac{\gamma_a}{6} H_3(X) + \frac{\gamma_e}{24} H_4(X)], \tag{6}$$

where $H_n(X)$ are Ermit's polynomials, $H_3 = X^3 - 3X$, $H_4 = X^4 - 6X^2 + 3$.

Then, using the common rules of nonlinear transformations of stochastic estimates, we found the following general ratio describing the probability distribution of the $Y = K_z/v$ values:

$$\log Ri = x = \log(0.75/Y) = -0.125 - \log Y,$$

$$W(Y) = \frac{0.1732}{\sigma^2 Y} e^{-0.5Z^2} [1 - \frac{\gamma_a}{6} H_3(Z) + \frac{\gamma_e}{24} H_4(Z)], \quad Z = (0.125 + x_0 + 0.4343 \ln Y)/\sigma. \tag{7}$$

The W(Y) distributions (7) are characterized by a significant positive asymmetry, which is displayed in the relatively slow reduction of W(Y) with increase of Y.

It is possible to use the W(Y) distribution to determine the probability of occurrence of local turbulence flares, in which the vertical diffusion coefficient exceeds the kinematic viscosity by a given amount. For example, we set the range of the K_z size changing from 0.1 to 1 cm^2/s; such values are typical in hydrodynamic models. The probability of occurrence of appropriate local turbulence areas is defined by integration of W(Y) within Y limits from 10 to 100. The general picture is the following: the probability of the local turbulent flares development is equal to 30-40% within the top quasi-homogeneous layer, 5-8% in the density jump layer, and 1-3% in the deep layers.

The coefficient of vertical diffusion of conservative pollutants K_s was calculated using the following common ratio

$$K_s = K_z R_f Ri^{-1},$$ (8)

where R_f is flux Richardson number.

Empirical ratio for R_f has the following form (Mellor & Yamada, 1974).

$$R_f = 0.725(Ri + 0.186 - \sqrt{Ri^2 - 0.316Ri + 0.0346})$$ (9)

for conditions of expressed density stratification.

As $K_z = 0.75\nu Ri^{-1}$, the ratio (9) is easily transformed to the following form:

$$\frac{K_s}{\nu} = S = \frac{K_z}{\nu}[0.725 + 0.1798\frac{K_z}{\nu} - 0.725\sqrt{1 - 0.4213\frac{K_z}{\nu} + 0.0615(\frac{K_z}{\nu})^2}].$$ (10)

Analysis of this ratio has shown that value of $K_s/\nu = S$ depends from $K_z/\nu = Y$ as

$$S = 0.325Y^{1.95} \text{ at } 0.1 < Y < 4.5,$$ (11)

where the upper limit (Y = 4.5) corresponds to the Richardson number Ri equal to 0.17; that is the value smaller then critical Ri = 0.25, at which the hydrodynamic instability begins, and:

$$S = Y, \text{ at } Y > 4.5,$$ (12)

which is in accordance with advanced turbulence conditions and means that the vertical transport of conservative pollutants is executed by turbulent pulsations.

The density of probability distribution of the S-size is calculated on the basis of general rules of nonlinear transformation of stochastic values:

$$Y = (3.77S)^{0.513} \text{ at } 3.65 \ 10^{-3} < S < 6.1, \quad Y = S, \text{ at } S > 6.1;$$

$$W_1(S) = \frac{0.089e^{-0.5Z^2}}{\sigma^2 S}[1 - \frac{\gamma_a}{6}H_3(Z) + \frac{\gamma_e}{24}H_4(Z)]; \quad Z = \frac{0.375 + x_0 + 0.223\ln S}{\sigma};$$

$$H_3(Z) = Z^3 - 3Z; \quad H_4(Z) = Z^4 - 6Z^2 + 3, \text{ at } 3.65 \ 10^{-3} < S < 6.1;$$

$$W_2(S) = \frac{0.1732e^{-0.5T^2}}{\sigma^2 S}[1 - \frac{\gamma_a}{6}H_3(T) + \frac{\gamma_e}{24}H_4(T)]; \quad T = \frac{0.125 + x_0 + 0.434\ln S}{\sigma};$$

$$< \log Ri >= x_0 = -0.247z_*^2 + 1.484z_* - 1.348.$$ (13)

The results of calculation of average coefficients of vertical diffusion of conservative pollutant M(Ks) and M(Kz) have shown that, in accordance with usual representations, the efficiency of vertical diffusion of conservative pollutants is considerably smaller then the efficiency for pulse: 4-6 times in the near-surface layer ($z_* = 0$); 1.3-2.9 times in the density jump layer ($z_* = 1$); and 2.6 -10 times in the deep-water layer ($z_* = 3$).

The performed analysis of characteristics of the vertical diffusion in summer natural waters has shown that the effective vertical exchange ($K_z=0.1-1$ cm^2/s) is carried out mainly by separate flares of local turbulence. These local turbulent events may be borne by many random causes: shifts of the current speed in internal waves, eddy-wave coherent structures of billows type other dynamic processes various scales. The average vertical exchange works under turbulent diffusion action more actively in the upper layer of Lake Kinneret, for example (K_z=0.2-0.8 cm^2/s). The vertical diffusion of the conservative substrates (oxygen, nutrients) acts more sluggishly: K_s is equal to 0.1-0.15 cm^2/s in the surface layer; 0.015-0.04 cm^2/s in thermocline (z = 10-15 m) and 0.005-0.015 cm^2/s in the deep-water layers (z = 25-40 m).

The discontinuity layer provides a strong barrier to oxygen transport from the lake surface to the depths of more than 10 m. It prevents also transport of nutrients from the deep-water to the euphotic layer of Lake Kinneret. The consequences of this hindrance will be the drastic reduction of the dissolved oxygen concentrations, and accumulation of nutrients in layers below the pycnocline. Hydrochemical measurements, carried out in June 1997, confirmed this: the dissolved oxygen concentration decreased from 9-11 mgO$_2$l^{-1} in the surface layer to 1.9-0.8 mgO$_2$l^{-1} in the near-bottom waters. The ammonia concentration increased from 8-9 µg l^{-1} in the top layer of the lake to 83 µg l^{-1} in the near-bottom layer

4. Conclusion

1. The performed analysis of characteristics of the vertical diffusion in summer Lake Kinneret has shown that the effective vertical exchange (K_z=0.1-1 cm^2/s) is carried out mainly by separate flares of local turbulence.

2. Estimations of the turbulent flares probability and average values of the vertical diffusion coefficients for pulse and conservative pollutants can be obtained using the relationships obtained here, in view of statistical character of the vertical transport in natural waters.

3. The methods outlined here for the determination of the turbulent diffusion characteristics can be used in solving a broad class of problems connected with statistical characteristics and impacts of the vertical turbulent diffusion.

5. References

KULLENBERG, G. (1971): Vertical diffusion in shallow water. – Tellus 23, 129-135.

KUSHNIR V.M. (1998): Turbulent fluxes parameterization in the upper Black Sea layer.- UFZ-Bericht Nr.23/1998. Third Workshop on Physical Processes in Natural Waters. 31.8-3.9.1998 in Magdeburg, 22-27.

KUSHNIR V.M.,SHEINMAN B.S.,DANILOVA I.A. (1999): Vertical nutrient fluxes during sharp density stratification. EMI Report Series, No 10, 78-82.

MELLOR G.L.,YAMADA N.A. (1974): A hierarchy of turbulence closure models for planetary boundary layer. J. Atmos. Sci. 31. 1791-1806.

OZMIDOV, R. V. (1965): Turbulent exchange in steadily stratified Ocean. – Izv. AS USSR. Physics of Atmosphere and Ocean. 1, 853-859. (in Russian).

THORPE, S. A. (1977): Turbulence and mixing in a Scottish Loch. – Phil. Transaction of Royal Soc. London 286, 125-181.

The Formation of Step-Like Structure in Near-Surface and Near-Bottom Pycnoclines

Iossif Lozovatsky[1,2], Alexander Ksenofontov[3] and H.J.S. Fernando[1]

[1]Environmental Fluid Dynamics Program, Mechanical & Aerospace Engineering, Arizona State University, Tempe, AZ, 85287-9809, USA
[2]P.P. Shirshov Institute of Oceanology, RAS, 117851 Moscow, Russia
[3]Kabardino-Balkarski State University, 360022, Nalchik, Russia
i.lozovatsky@asu.edu, ksenofontov_a@mail.ru, j.fernando@asu.edu

1. Abstract

A one-dimensional model of unsteady, stratified tidal flow in the presence of background rotation was employed to simulate the formation of step-like density structure under the influence of boundary forcing. Richardson number dependent turbulent diffusivities based on oceanographic microstructure measurements was used for the closure of equations. Upon introduction of a constant surface shear stress, periodic formation and evolution of thin but distinct steps were observed in near surface and near bottom pycnoclines during first three to four cycles of inertial oscillations. The lifetime of these small structures was less than a few hours. Later, several thin quasi-homogeneous layers merge to form larger steps, which became a persistent feature of the mean density profile. A new series of steps was generated thereafter. The details of fine-structure formation were significantly dependent on a combination of factors, including the initial magnitude of the Richardson number, boundary stress, rotation and persistent background shear. It was found that the period between the initialization of boundary forcing and the onset of fine structure is a function of several non-dimensional parameters. The results with tidal forcing exhibited novel features of evolution of step-like structure.

2. Introduction

Well-defined quasi-homogeneous mixed layers separated by narrow sharp density interfaces are common in seasonal oceanic thermoclines and in the pycnocline aloft the bottom boundary layer. *Phillips* (1972) suggested that a stably-stratified turbulent layer can become unstable when the mixing efficiency or flux Richardson number R_f decreases with the gradient Richardson number Ri beyond a critical value. Theoretical and numerical studies of this type of instability have been given by *Posmentier* (1977), *Barenblatt et al.* (1993), *Kranenburg* (1996) and *Balmorfth et al.* (1998). *Ruddick et al.* (1989) and Park et al. (1998) showed the possibility of step-like layer formation in series of laboratory experiments. Recently, *Lozovatsky et al.* (1998) emphasized the role of rotation on the generation, formation and evolution of the layered structure. In the present study, we explore the combined effects of wind stress and tidal forcing on the formation of upper and near bottom pycnoclines rich in fine-structure.

3. Model

a) Basic equations

The model (*Lozovatsky and Ksenofontov* 1994) consists of system of equations describing one-dimensional momentum balance (1 and 2), buoyancy transfer (3), and the balance of turbulent kinetic energy (4)

$$\frac{\partial u}{\partial t} = \frac{\partial}{\partial z} K \frac{\partial u}{\partial z} + f(v - v_T) + \frac{\partial u_T}{\partial t}, \qquad \frac{\partial v}{\partial t} = \frac{\partial}{\partial z} K \frac{\partial v}{\partial z} - f(u - u_T) + \frac{\partial v_T}{\partial t}, \qquad (1), (2)$$

$$\frac{\partial b}{\partial t} = \frac{\partial}{\partial z} K_b \frac{\partial b}{\partial z},\tag{3}$$

$$\frac{\partial e}{\partial t} = \frac{\partial}{\partial z} K_e \frac{\partial e}{\partial z} + K V_z^2 (1-Rf) - \varepsilon,\tag{4}$$

which are closed by a hypothesis (*Lozovatsky et al.* 1993) on turbulent diffusivities

$$K = K_0 / \sqrt{1+Ri/Ri_{cr}} \quad \text{and} \quad K_b = K /(1+Ri/Ri_{cr}),\tag{5}$$

where K_b is the mass diffusivity, K is the eddy viscosity and K_0 is defined as

$$K_0 = l_0 \sqrt{e}, \quad l_0 = 1.3 \times \sqrt{e/V_z^2},\tag{6}$$

where e is the turbulent kinetic energy per unit mass, t the time, z the vertical coordinate directed downward, $b = g(\rho-\rho_0)/\rho_0$ the buoyancy, ρ and ρ_0 are the density and its reference value, g the gravity, f the Coriolis parameter, $K_e = 0.73K$ the turbulent energy diffusivity; $\varepsilon = 0.1e^2/K$ the kinetic energy dissipation rate, V_z^2 the respective squared mean vertical shear, $Ri = N^2/V_z^2$ and $R_f = (K_b/K)Ri$ are the gradient and flux Richardson numbers, $Ri_{cr} = 0.1$ and N^2 the squared buoyancy frequency. The Ekman components of the velocity vector u and v are time and depth dependent variables; the components u_T and v_T induced by tidal forces are depth independent.

The closure (5)-(6) implies that the Ozmidov scale

$$L_N = \varepsilon^{1/2}/N^{3/2}\tag{7}$$

serves as an asymptotic approximation of the turbulence scale l in the case of very strong stratification ($Ri \gg Ri_{cr}$). Because the choice of basic turbulent scales can influence the fine-structures predictions of this model, it is of interest to discuss the relationship between the Ozmidov scale and other buoyancy scales that could be used to parameterize vertical mixing in stably stratified flows.

b) Turbulent scales

Oceanic microstructure can be characterized by velocity, length and time scales of motions. In a stably stratified water column, eddies with characteristic rms velocity $e^{1/2}$ and length scale l can overturn against the stable stratification, provided that the inertia forces of eddies e/l exceed the corresponding buoyancy forces N^2l, or when $l \ll L_b$, where $L_b = e^{1/2}/N$. As pointed out by *Hunt* (1985), L_b is a rational choice for the turbulence lengthscale in stratified non-sheared flow. Kinematically based lengthscales that have been used for stratified turbulence include the Ellison scale $L_E = \Theta_b/N^2$, where Θ_b is the rms of buoyancy fluctuations, and the Thorpe scale L_{Th}. The latter signifies the scale of overturning in a turbulent region and is calculated by reordering a density profile containing inversions to obtain a stable profile with monotonic variation of density. Laboratory experiments of *DeSilva and Fernando* (1992) show how L_{Th} of a growing turbulent patch increases with time and then achieves a maximum value proportional to L_b. Recently *Lozovatsky and Fernando* (2000) argued that the Thorpe scale, in either growing or decaying patches, is a function of the mixing Reynolds number and patch Richardson number. The rapid generation of a turbulent layer, its growth when the turbulence scale $l \ll L_b$ or L_N (active turbulence), the onset of buoyancy effects distinguished by the retardation of growth at $l = L_b$ and the subsequent decay of l in equilibrium with decaying L_N are the essentials of *Gibson's* (1980) fossil turbulence theory. When the overturning scale $l \sim L_N$ decays to the Kolmogorov scale $\eta = (v^3/\varepsilon)$, the dissipation rate decreases to $\varepsilon \leq (25-30) \times v N^2$; here v is molecular viscosity, and the flow becomes completely fossilized.

If the length scale that characterizes the shear production $L_{sp} = l_0/1.3 = \sqrt{e/V_z^2}$ is larger than L_b, that is if $Ri \gg 1$, then the length scale demarcating between the inertial subrange and the large scale of overturning motions becomes L_b, and given that $\varepsilon \sim e^{3/2}/L_b$, it is possible to write $L_b \sim L_N$. On the other hand, if $Ri << 1$, then $L_{sp} << L_b$, and $\varepsilon \sim e^{3/2}/L_{sp}$. In this case, the Ozmidov scale cannot be directly used to interpret stratified turbulence. An alternative buoyancy scale, known as the Bolgiano-Obukhov scale L_*,

$$L_* = \varepsilon^{5/4} \chi_T^{-3/4} (g\alpha_T)^{-3/2} , \tag{8}$$

where χ_T is the temperature (or other buoyancy-related scalar) dissipation rate, α_T the coefficient of thermal expansion has also been used in stratified turbulence studies. The derivation of this lengthscale assumes the existence of a wavenumber subrange in stably stratified spectra where the turbulence is locally axi-symmetric and horizontally homogeneous and large eddies are affected by buoyancy.

To establish a relationship between the Ozmidov L_N and Bolgiano-Obukhov L_* scales, assume that the buoyancy fluctuations are produced by turbulent motions within a stratified layer at the scales on the order of L_{pr}. If so, the buoyancy variance $\overline{\Theta_b^2} = \overline{(g\rho'/\rho_o)^2}$, which relates to the temperature variance $\overline{\Theta_T^2}$ as

$$\overline{\Theta_T^2} = \overline{\Theta_b^2} /(g\alpha_T)^2 , \tag{9}$$

can be defined as

$$\overline{\Theta_b^2} = N^4 L_{pr}^2 . \tag{10}$$

The temperature dissipation χ_T in the buoyancy subrange can be parameterized in terms of the turbulent kinetic energy e, the variance of temperature $\overline{\Theta_T^2}$ (or buoyancy $\overline{\Theta_b^2}$) fluctuations, and the production scale L_{pr} as

$$\chi_T = c_T \frac{\sqrt{e_{tr}}}{L_{pr}} \overline{\Theta_T^2} , \tag{11}$$

where c_T is a non-dimensional constant.

Substitution of (9), (10) and $\varepsilon = c_\varepsilon e^{3/2}/L_{pr}$ in (11) gives

$$\chi_T = c_\chi \frac{N^4 \varepsilon^{1/3} L_{pr}^{4/3}}{(g\alpha_T)^2} , \; c_\chi = \frac{c_T}{c_\varepsilon^{1/3}} . \tag{12}$$

If we use (12) as the temperature dissipation in the buoyancy subrange and substitute it in (8), the following relationship can be obtained between the Bolgiano-Obukhov, Ozmidov and production lengthscales

$$L_* = c_L L_N^2 / L_{pr} , \tag{13}$$

where

$$c_L = a_* \left(c_\varepsilon / c_T^3 \right)^{1/4} . \tag{14}$$

If the scale of turbulent production L_{pr} is proportional to the Ozmidov scale L_N, (14) suggests possible linear dependence between L_* and L_N. A test of this hypothesis is shown in Fig. 1 using the microstructure measurements taken on a shallow Black Sea shelf (*Lozovatsky et al.* 1999). Although there is wide scatter of individual samples, correlation between L_N and L_* is clearly evident. The best least-square fit gives a linear relation between Ozmidov and Bolgiano-Obukhov scales as

$$L_* = 2.92 \times L_N . \tag{15}$$

Peters et al. (1995) found that $c_\varepsilon \approx 4$ and $c_T \approx 7$ for turbulent patches in the equatorial Pacific and *Lozovatsky* (1987) obtained $a_* = 2.7$. Substitution of these values in (14), gives $c_L \approx 0.88$, which is much smaller than that obtained in (15). This discrepancy can be reconciled by assuming $L_{pr} \approx 0.3 \times L_N$. Since the production scale is usually associated with the Thorpe displacement scale for turbulent overturns, or with a shear production scale $L_{sp} = \varepsilon^{1/2}/V_z^{3/2}$, L_{sp} is related to L_N as

$$L_N = Ri^{-3/4} \times L_{sp}, \qquad (16)$$

and since $L_{sp} \approx 0.3 \times L_N$, the local Richardson number can be established as $Ri \approx 0.2$. This is in agreement with the observations made in stratified inner layer on the Black Sea shelf (*Lozovatsky and Fernando, 2000*).

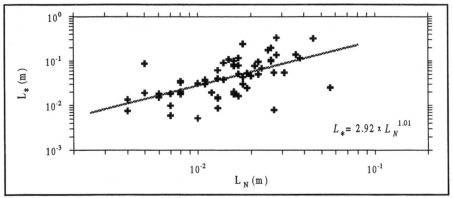

Fig. 1. The dependence between Ozmidov L_N and Bolgiano-Obukhov L_* scales in a stratified layer on the Black Sea shelf.

The discussion given above shows that the use of Ozmidov scale in our numerical model is a reasonable approximation for the turbulent lengthscale l in strongly stratified layers. The scale L_{sp} works mainly in homogeneous layers and the intermediate scale $L_R = \varepsilon^{1/2}/NV_z^{1/2}$ is a key player in the transition region between quasi-homogeneous boundary layers and neighboring pycnoclines (*Lozovatsky, 1996*).

c) Dependence on the initial and boundary conditions

The following initial and boundary conditions were imposed in solving Eqs. (1) - (6):

$$t = 0: \quad u = u^0(z), \quad v = v^0(z), \quad \rho = \rho^0(z), \quad e = e^0(z), \quad u_T = u_A^\circ \sin(\omega_T t - \varphi_1), \quad v_T = v_A^\circ \sin(\omega_T t - \varphi_2) \qquad (17)$$

$$z = 0: \quad K\frac{\partial u}{\partial z} = \frac{\tau_x}{\rho_0} = u_*^2, \quad K\frac{\partial v}{\partial z} = 0, \quad K_b\frac{\partial b}{\partial z} = 0, \quad K_e\frac{\partial e}{\partial z} = -P_e, \qquad (18)$$

$$z = H: \quad u = v = 0, \quad u_T = v_T = 0, \quad K_b\frac{\partial b}{\partial z} = 0, \quad K_e\frac{\partial e}{\partial z} = 0 \qquad (19)$$

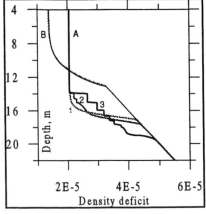

Fig. 2. The influence of V_{zin} (see text).

Here $z = 0$ is the sea surface and $z = H$ is the bottom boundary. In solving the equations, stable conservative numerical schemes with high order approximation for spatial and temporal derivatives satisfying conservation laws were used. The grid step of 2 cm and time step of 4 min were chosen to achieve fine scale resolution for hydrophysical profiles.

The closure hypotheses (5)-(6) require vertical shear to be non-zero at any depth during all time of the calculation. Therefore, a sustained "background" shear V_{zin} was introduced, which imposed specific hydrodynamic conditions on modeling. The development of vertical profiles under the influence of boundary forcing in this model significantly depends on the non-dimensional parameters f/N_{in} and on $Ri_{in} = N_{in}^2/V_{zin}^2$, which is the initial Richardson number. If $Ri_{in} \gg Ri_{in}^{cr}$ for a given f/N_{in}, the pycnocline formed below the upper quasi-homogeneous layer does not contain any fine structure (Fig.2, curve 1, set A, no tidal forcing). For $Ri_{in} \le Ri_{in}^{cr}$, a few prominent steps are generated in the pycnocline after 60 hours of the onset of calculation (curve 2). For small Ri_{in}, sudden generation of step-like structure started after 36 hours of calculations (curve 3). The influence of V_{zin} on the development of the pycnocline started after a few hours of boundary mixing from the initiation of the model, when the wind induced current shear decreased below V_{zin}. Before this, up to $t = 10$ h, all profiles evolved almost identically (Fig. 2, set B) and only later they depart from each other. A critical time t_{cr} at which the background shear begins to play an important role in turbulence generation appears to be a function of the ratios $u_*^2/e^0 V_{zin}$ and f/N_{in}. An explicit form of this dependence has not been established yet. The actual value of the initial Richardson number, which is critical for layer formation, can differ depending on the combination of $u_*^2/e^0 V_{zin}$ and f/N_{in}. For calculations shown in Fig. 2, $Ri_{in}^{cr} \approx 6$. The initial and boundary conditions for calculations shown in Fig. 2 were the same as those specified in the next section.

4. Tidal Current Experiment

The initial linear density profile in these calculations was set as $\rho^0(z) = \rho_0 + z(d\rho/dz)_{in}$ with the constant density gradient $(d\rho/dz)_{in} = 2.5 \times 10^{-3}$ kg/m^4 and $\rho_0 = 1025$ kg/m^3; the corresponding initial $N_{in}^2 = 2.45 \times 10^{-5}$ s^{-2}. The "background" shear $V_{zin} = 2 \times 10^{-3}$ s^{-1} ensured that $Ri_{in} = N_{in}^2/V_{zin}^2 = 6.1$. Surface wind stress and turbulent energy flux were calculated using the bulk formulae corresponding to a constant wind speed of 8 m/s; $u_* = 9.2 \times 10^{-2}$ m/s. The amplitudes of semidiurnal $\omega_T = 2\pi/12.4$ hr^{-1} tidal component are 5 cm/s, the Coriolis parameter $f = 10^{-4}$ s^{-1} and the water depth is 42m. The results of calculations are shown in Fig. 3, 4 for the time period 15 to 180 hours after the onset of winds.

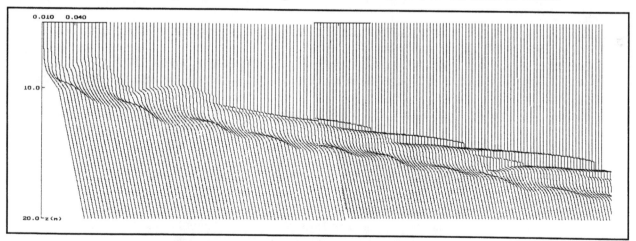

Fig. 3. Formation of the upper pycnocline under constant wind stress.

The model clearly reproduces an upper well-mixed homogeneous layer, which gradually deepens under sustained wind stress. The fine structure in the pycnocline is modulated by the periodic amplification of vertical shear associated with inertial oscillations. Phases of the generation of new steps also change with periods of thin-layer merging. As a result, a pycnocline with persistent fine structure is formed. In the bottom layer (Fig. 4), where tidal friction produces vertical mixing near the very bootom, the development of turbulent boundary layer is limited by inertial - buoyancy balance. The height of the homogeneous near bottom layer is stabilized after about 140 hours of calculations, achieving almost 8-m thickness. The pycnocline aloft this mixed layer is somewhat weak in fine structure, compared to the upper part of the water column affected by the wind stress. The interaction between the tidal $\tau_T = 12.4$ h and inertial $\tau_f = 17.4$ h oscillations generates long period beats with frequency $\omega_{bt} = \omega_T - \omega_f$.

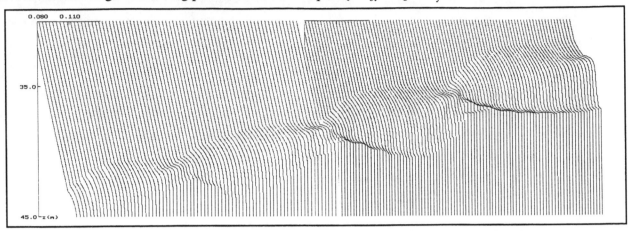

Fig. 4. Evolution of the near bottom mixed layer and pycnocline aloft in the presence of a tidal current.

The evolution of the homogeneous layer and density gradients in the near bottom pycnocline are strongly influenced by such beats that have a period of $\tau_{bt} \approx 42$ h. The present version of model does not contain any parameterization for the bottom roughness, and accounting for it will be the next step of our efforts.

References

Balmorfth, N.J., S.G.L. Smith and W.R. Young, 1998: Dynamics of interfaces and layers in a stratified turbulent fluid, *J. Fluid Mech.*, **355**, 329-358.

Barenblatt, G.I., M. Bertsch, R. Dal Passo, V.M. Prostokishin, and M. Ughi, 1993: A mathematical model of turbulent heat and mass transfer in stably stratified shear flow. *J. Fluid Mech.*, **253**, 341-358.

De Silva, I.P.D., and H.J.S. Fernando, 1992: Some aspects of mixing in a stratified turbulent patch, *J. Fluid Mech.*, **240**, 601-625.

Gibson, C.H., 1980: Fossil temperature, salinity and vorticity turbulence in the ocean, *Marine Turbulence*, edited by J.C.J. Nihoul, pp. 221-257, Elsevier, Amsterdam.

Hunt, J.C.R., 1985: Diffusion in stably stratified boundary layer, J. *Climate and Appl. Meteor.*, **24**, 1187-1195.

Kranenburg, C., 1996: On gradient-transport turbulence models for stably stratified shear flow. *Dyn. Atm. and Oceans*, **24**, 257-259.

Lozovatsky, I.D., Turbulence decay in stratified and homogeneous marine layers, 1996: *DAO*, **24**, 15-25.

Lozovatsky, I. D., and A. S. Ksenofontov, 1994: A differential model of the vertical structure of hydrophysical fields in stratified tidal flow on a shelf, *Marine Hydrophysical Journal*, No.1, 36-42.

Lozovatsky, I.D., A.S. Ksenofontov, A.Yu. Erofeev and C.H. Gibson, 1993: Modeling of the evolution of vertical structure in the upper ocean by atmospheric forcing and intermittent turbulence in the pycnocline, *J. Marine Sys.*, **4**, 263-273.

Lozovatsky, I.D., A.L. Berestov, and A.K. Ksenofontov, 1998: Phyllips theory of turbulence generated fine-structure: Numerical and stochastic modeling, John Hopkins Conf. Envir. Fluid Dyn., Book of Abstr., 102-103.

Lozovatsky, I.D., T.M. Dillon, A.Yu. Erofeev, and V.N. Nabatov, 1999: Variations of thermohaline and turbulent structure on the shallow Black Sea shelf in the beginning of autumn cooling, *J. Marine Sys.* **21**, 255-282.

Lozovatsky, I.D., and H.J.S. Fernando, 2000: Turbulent mixing on a shallow shelf, *J. Phys. Oceanogr.*, (sub justice).

Park, Y. G., J. A. Whitehead, and A. Gnanadeskian, 1994: Turbulent mixing in stratified fluids: layer formation and energetics. *J. Fluid Mech.*, **279**, 279-311.

Peters, H.M., Gregg, M.C., and T.B. Sanford, 1995: Detail and scaling of turbulent overturns in the Pacific Equatorial Undercurrent, *J. Geophys. Res.*, **100**, 18,349-18,368.

Phillips, O.M., 1972: Turbulence in a strongly stratified fluid - is it unstable? *Deep-Sea Res.*, **19**, 79-81.

Posmentier, E.S., 1977: The generation of salinity fine-structure by vertical diffusion. *J. Phys. Oceanogr.*, **7**, 298-300.

Ruddick, B.R., T.J. McDougall, and J.S. Turner, 1989: The formation of layers in a uniformly stirred density gradient. *Deep-Sea Res.*, **36**, 597-609.

Dynamics of Layered Structures in the Final Stage of Turbulence Decay in a Stably Stratified Fluid

Vladimir Maderich[1], Vladimir Nikishov[2]

[1]Institute of Mathematical Machine and System Problems NASU, Kiev, Ukraine
[2]Institute of Hydromechanics NASU, Kiev, Ukraine
vlad@immsp.kiev.ua

Abstract

The dynamics of layered structures in the final stage of turbulence decay in a stably stratified fluid are considered. Such buoyancy-driven motions are distinguished together with internal waves and quasi-horizontal vortices. Layered structures exist at small internal Froude and Reynolds numbers and large Prandtl (Schmidt) numbers. The linear analysis of the velocity perturbations was carried by using multi-scale methods. An interaction between structures was studied numerically as a possible mechanism for the formation of microstructure layers. The transformation of intrusion in the field of quasi-horizontal vortices was considered.

1. Introduction

Turbulent mixing is a general process of mass and energy transfer in geophysical flows. It is known that buoyancy forces result in a restriction of vertical scales of vortices in a stably stratified medium. A spatio-temporal intermittency of turbulent vortices leads to their collapse. This collapse causes a counter-gradient flux of mass that results in a partial restoring of the undisturbed stratification (restratification) and thus decreases the diapycnal transport. For these reasons the structure of the collapsed turbulence is of considerable importance to the mixing process. In a number of experiments, it was found that the fields of internal waves, quasi-horizontal vortices, and layered structures coexist in the final stage of turbulence decay. The aim of this paper is to describe mechanisms of the formation and evolution of layered structures.

2. Scaling

A scaling analysis of the Boussinesq equations was provided by Riley *et al.* (1981). Table 1 summarized the scaling amplitudes of time t, pressure p, horizontal velocity $\mathbf{V}_H$, vertical velocity w and buoyancy b for this isotropic scaling, depending on Froude number $\mathbf{F} = V_H / l_v N$ for large Reynolds number $\mathbf{Re} = V_H l_v / \nu$. Here $\delta = l_v / l_H$ is the aspect ratio; l_v, l_H are the vertical and horizontal scale of motion, respectively, and N is the Väisälä frequency. We extended this scaling to include the layered structure dynamics that is driven by the buoyancy field with amplitude $b_0 = l_v N^{-2}$ and with condition of strong anisotropy ($\delta \ll 1$) and small $\mathbf{Re}$ and $\mathbf{F}$. We assumed that balance between buoyancy and

Table 1. Amplitude scales for flows

Type of motion	t	p/ρ_0	$\mathbf{V}_H$	w	b
Waves (F<<1,Re>>1, $\delta \sim 1$)	N^{-1}	$V_g l_v N$	V_g	V_g	$V_g N$
Vortices (F<<1,Re>>1, $\delta \sim 1$)	$l_H V_0^{-1}$	V_0^2	V_0	$V_0 \mathbf{F}^2 \delta$	$V_0^2 l_v^{-1}$
Layered structures (F<<1,Re>>1, $\delta \sim 1$)	$\nu l_v^{-2} N^{-2} \delta^{-2}$	$l_v^2 N^2$	$l_v^3 N^2 \nu^{-1} \delta$	$l_v^3 N^2 \nu^{-1} \delta$	$l_v N^2$

viscosity is important for these processes. The results are included in Table 1. The corresponding dimensionless Boussinesq system of equations for linearly stratified undisturbed fluid is then

$$\mathbf{F}^2(\partial \mathbf{V}_H / \partial t + \mathbf{V} \cdot \nabla \mathbf{V}_H) = \underline{-\nabla_H p + \partial^2 \mathbf{V}_H / \partial z^2} + \delta \nabla_H^2 \mathbf{V}_H, \tag{1}$$

$$\delta^2 \mathbf{F}^2(\partial w / \partial t + \mathbf{V} \cdot \nabla w) = \underline{-\partial p / \partial z + b} + \delta^2(\partial^2 w / \partial z^2 + \delta^2 \nabla_H^2 w, \tag{2}$$

$$\underline{\nabla_H \cdot \mathbf{V}_H + \partial w / \partial z} = 0, \tag{3}$$

$$\underline{\partial b_T / \partial t + \mathbf{V} \cdot \nabla b_T + w} = \varepsilon_T (\partial^2 b_T / \partial z^2 + \delta^2 \nabla_H^2 b_T), \tag{4}$$

$$\underline{\partial b_S / \partial t + \mathbf{V} \cdot \nabla b_S + w} = \varepsilon_S (\partial^2 b_S / \partial z^2 + \delta^2 \nabla_H^2 b_S), \tag{5}$$

Here b_T and b_S are temperature and salinity components of the buoyancy $b = b_T + b_S$,

$$\varepsilon_T = \frac{v \chi_T l_H^2}{N_T^2 l_V^6}, \varepsilon_S = \frac{v \chi_S l_H^2}{N_S^2 l_V^6},$$

χ_T is the temperature conductivity, χ_S is the diffusivity, $N_T^2 = \alpha g dT_n / dz$, $N_S^2 = -\beta g dS_n / dz$, (index "n" denotes unperturbed values), g is the gravity. The parameters $\varepsilon_T, \varepsilon_S$ describe the relation between effects of diffusion and buoyancy forces. The main terms in the equations are underlined. For one component fluid ($\varepsilon_T = \varepsilon_S = \varepsilon$) the value of the nondimensional parameter ε yields the relation between the vertical and horizontal scales of the most slowly decaying mode given by Pearson and Linden (1983). It is easy to show that $\varepsilon = \mathrm{Pr}^{-1}\mathbf{F}^{-2}$. Therefore if the Froude number $\mathbf{F}$ is small, layered structures, in which buoyancy and velocity fields are interrelated, can exist at large Prandtl (or Schmidt) numbers. If Pr=$O(1)$, the time scale of layered structures in the table replaced by the diffusion scale $(l_V^2 \chi^{-1})$, and in first approximation, the buoyancy field does not depend on the velocity field.

3. Linear analysis of diffusion effects

In this section we consider the evolution of layered structures in a temperature and salinity stratified fluid. It is assumed that double-diffusion instability effects are absent. The linearized system of equations (1)-(5) in dimensional form can be reduced to a single equation for the vertical velocity

$$L_1 L_2 L_3 \Delta \vec{V} = (N_T^2 L_3 + N_S^2 L_2) \left(\nabla \frac{\partial W}{\partial z} + \frac{\vec{g}}{g} \Delta W \right).$$

Here $\vec{V} = (U, V, W)$ is the velocity vector, g' is the vector of gravity acceleration L_1, L_2, L_3 are the operators $L_1 = \partial / \partial t - v\Delta$, $L_1 = \partial / \partial t - \chi_T \Delta$, $L_1 = \partial / \partial t - \chi_S \Delta$. We assume that a solution exists in the form of the normal modes $W = W(t) \exp(i \vec{k} \vec{r})$. Then the equation for the dimensionless amplitude $\tilde{W}(t) = W(t) / W_0$ (further, we omit "~") is

$$\frac{d^3 W}{dt^3} + (1 + a_T + a_S) \frac{d^2 W}{d\tau^2} + (a_T + a_S + a_T a_S) \frac{dW}{d\tau} + (\theta_T + \theta_S) \frac{dW}{d\tau} + a_T a_S W + (a_S \varepsilon_T + a_T \varepsilon_S) W = 0,$$

where W_0 is a characteristic value of the velocity vertical component, $a_T = \chi_T / v$, $a_S = \chi_S / v$, $\tau = vk^2 t$ is dimensionless time, parameters $\theta_T = m^2 N_T^2 / (v^2 k^6)$, $\theta_S = m^2 N_S^2 / (v^2 k^6)$ describes the ratio of the buoyancy to the viscous forces, $m^2 = k_1^2 + k_2^2$.

Using the method of many scales we introduce the different scales of time $T_0 = \tau$, $T_1 = \theta_T \tau$, $T_2 = \theta_T^2 \tau$, $T_3 = \theta_S \tau$, $T_4 = \theta_S^2 \tau$, $T_5 = \theta_T \theta_S$ (Nikishov, Khristyuk, 1999). The solution is sought in form

$$W = W_{00} + \theta_T W_{10} + \theta_T^2 W_{20} + \theta_S W_{01} + \theta_S^2 W_{02} + \theta_T \theta_S W_{11} + \ldots,$$

where $W_{ij} = W_{ij}(T_0, T_1, T_2, T_3)$. Finally, we obtain for the vertical component of velocity (in the dimension form)

$$W = A\exp\left[\left(-\nu k^2 + \frac{1}{k_T}\frac{\omega_T^2}{\nu k^2} + \frac{1}{k_T^3}\frac{\omega_T^4}{\nu^3 k^6} + \frac{1}{k_S}\frac{\omega_S^2}{\nu k^2} + \frac{1}{k_S^3}\frac{\omega_S^4}{\nu^3 k^6} + \frac{k_T + k_S}{k_T^2 k_S^2}\frac{\omega_T^2 \omega_S^2}{\nu^3 k^6}\right)t\right]$$

$$+ B\exp\left[\left(-\chi_T k^2 - \frac{1}{k_T}\frac{\omega_T^2}{\nu k^2} - \frac{1}{k_T^3}\frac{\omega_T^4}{\nu^3 k^6} + \frac{1}{k_T^2 k_{ST}}\frac{\omega_T^2 \omega_S^2}{\nu^3 k^6}\right)t\right]$$

$$+ C\exp\left[\left(-\chi_S k^2 - \frac{1}{k_S}\frac{\omega_S^2}{\nu k^2} - \frac{1}{k_S^3}\frac{\omega_S^4}{\nu^3 k^6} + \frac{1}{k_S^2 k_{ST}}\frac{\omega_T^2 \omega_S^2}{\nu^3 k^6}\right)\right] + O(\theta_T^3, \theta_S^3, \theta_T \theta_S^2, \theta_T^2 \theta_S, \theta_T^3 \tau, \theta_S^3 \tau, \theta_T \theta_S^2 \tau, \theta_T^2 \theta_S \tau)$$

Here $\omega_T = m N_T / k$, $\omega_S = m N_S / k$, $k_T = 1 - a_T$, $k_S = 1 - a_S$, $k_{ST} = a_S - a_T$. The first solution represent viscous decay mechanism and others – the diffusion mechanism. The decay rates of the last solutions have minimums defined by balance of buoyancy, viscous and diffusion effects that were studied for one component fluid earlier by Linden and Pearson (1983).The decay rate of the temperature perturbations increases in the presence of the salinity stratification. On the other hand, the presence of the temperature stratification retards the decay of the salt perturbations. The reason is concerned with the difference between coefficients of salt diffusion and thermal conductivity. At the end of the final stage the temperature perturbations are decayed and temperature profile is restratified. The presence of the salinity perturbations results in the collapse but arising temperature perturbations and corresponding forces retard the development of the collapse (anti-collapse effect).

4. The linear analysis of shear flow effects

In this section we consider effect of shear flow on the layered structures. Linearized equations of motion in Boussinesq approximation, heat transport that describe the behaviour of small perturbations are used. It is supposed that characteristic variation time of the perturbation parameters is smaller in comparison with the characteristic period of the flow variation and the space variations of flow are small along the horizontal direction. In the other words, the flow is stationary and homogeneous along the horizontal direction. In addition, it is considered the perturbations having the small vertical scales, that is, shear of velocity can be taken as a constant. The corresponding equation for the vertical velocity perturbations in an infinite shear flow ($\vec{U} = (0, 0, Gz)$) can be derived from the Boussinesq system of equation

$$L_1 L_2 \Delta w + N^2 \Delta_H w = 0,$$

where $L_1 = d/dz - \chi_T \Delta$, $L_2 = d/dz - \nu \Delta$, $G = const$. Following Phillips (1966) the elementary perturbation is considered in the next form

$$w = W(t)\exp\left[i\left(\vec{k}\vec{r} - k_1 Gzt\right)\right].$$

It is noted that in the beginning wave vector of the perturbation possesses components k_1, k_2, k_3. As time elapses, it turns to vertical direction in response to shear and vertical component k_3 increases $(G<0)$, $k_3 >> k_1$, $k_3 >> k_2$. In other words, the vertical scale becomes smaller than horizontal ones. The system of solutions (modes) are found by an asymptotic method for the various relationship between Λ_i, where $\Lambda_1 = m^2 N^2 / k_1^2 G$, $\Lambda_2 = \nu k^3 / k_1^2 G$, $\Lambda_3 = \chi_T k^3 / k_1^2 G$. For the case of a dominant viscosity contribution $\Lambda_2 >> 1$ it described the next relationships

$$W_1 = \mu^{-1} \exp\left[\phi_1(\tau) + o(\Lambda_2^{-1})\right], \qquad W_2 = \mu^{-2} \exp\left[\phi_2(\tau) + o(\Lambda_2^{-1})\right],$$

where

$$\phi_1(\tau) = \Lambda_2 \int \mu \, d\tau - \Lambda_1 \Lambda_2^{-1} \int \mu^{-2} \, d\tau, \quad \phi_2(\tau) = \Lambda_3 \int \mu \, d\tau - \Lambda_1 \Lambda_2^{-1} \int \mu^{-2} \, d\tau,$$

$$\tau = (k_3 - k_1 Gt), \quad \mu = a^2 + \tau^2, \quad a = m / k.$$

The equation for the amplitude buoyancy perturbation can be derived in a similar manner. The equation for buoyancy is

$$L_2 \Delta L_1 b + N^2 \Delta_H b = 0.$$

The buoyancy perturbation b has the same form as w

$$b = B(t)\exp\left[i(\mathbf{k} \cdot \mathbf{r} - k_1 Gtz)\right].$$

Unlike the case of the absence of mean shear, the equation for the amplitude B differs from the equation for the velocity amplitude. The solutions are

$$B_1 = \mu^{-2} \exp\left[\phi_1(\tau) + o(\Lambda_2^{-1})\right], \quad B_2 = \exp\left[\phi_2(\tau) + o(\Lambda_2^{-1})\right].$$

The decay rate of the solution B_2 is less than that of B_1, as it was with W_1 and W_2. In distinction from non-shear case the decay rates of the solutions W_2 and B_2 are different. The presence of shear flow implies a new mechanism of energy exchange between velocity perturbations and basic flow. It causes the above-mentioned difference of the decay of the velocity and scalar perturbations.

5. Non-linear dynamics of layered structures

In addition to the above factors, interactions with waves and vortices are of importance in the evolution of layered structures. In the first approximation, we restrict our consideration to the effect of vortex motions with velocities $V_h = (v_x(x,y), v_y(x,y))$ on the evolution of layered structures. In the case of one-component fluid $(\varepsilon_T = \varepsilon_S = \varepsilon)$ and ($\mathbf{F}<<1$, $\delta <<1$) the system of equations (1)-(5) can be reduced to a single equation for an auxiliary function $Q(x,y,z,t)$:

$$\frac{\partial^5 Q}{\partial t \partial z^4} - \left(\frac{\partial^2 Q}{\partial x^2} + \frac{\partial^2 Q}{\partial y^2}\right) - \varepsilon \frac{\partial^6 Q}{\partial z^6} + \gamma(v_x(x,y)\frac{\partial^5 Q}{\partial x \partial z^4} + v_y(x,y)\frac{\partial^5 Q}{\partial y \partial z^4}) = $$

$$= \left(\frac{\partial^2 Q}{\partial x^2} + \frac{\partial^2 Q}{\partial y^2}\right)\frac{\partial^5 Q}{\partial z^5} - \frac{\partial^2 Q}{\partial x \partial z}\frac{\partial^5 Q}{\partial x \partial z^4} - \frac{\partial^2 Q}{\partial y \partial z}\frac{\partial^5 Q}{\partial y \partial z^4},$$

(6)

where $\mathbf{V}_H$, w, b are expressed in terms of Q by

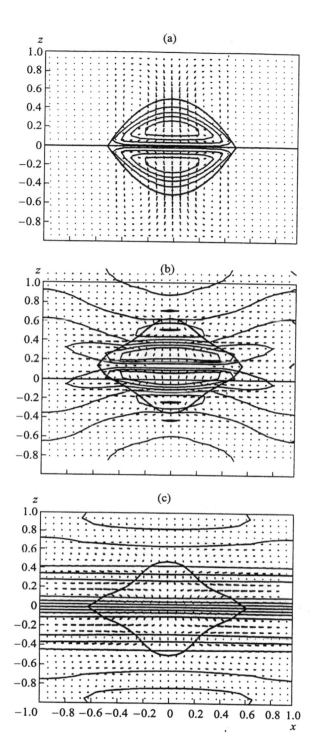

Fig. 1 Vertical section in the x0z-plane:
t=0 (a); t=1000 (b); t=10000 (c)

$$\mathbf{V}_H = \gamma \mathbf{N}_h + \nabla\left(\frac{\partial Q}{\partial z}\right), \quad w = -\nabla_H^2 Q, \quad b = \frac{\partial^4 Q}{\partial z^4}.$$

The parameter $\gamma = \nu l_H V_0 /(l_v^4 N^2)$ describes the contribution of vortex motions to buoyancy advection. The three-dimensional non-linear equation (6) was solved by the pseudospectral method. At first we consider the formation of layered structures as a result of interactions of an ensemble of collapsing intrusions. We assume that there is a regular array of identical intrusions, so that we can restrict our consideration to a periodic problem for one of them in the absence of vortex motions $(\gamma = 0)$. Figure 1 shows the vertical section of the patch in the x0z-plane at different dimensionless times with $\varepsilon = 10^{-6}$. The figure depicts isolines of the buoyancy field, the contours of the intrusion marked by passive tracer, and the vector field of intrusion velocity. Gradations of density isolines in Figs. 1b and 1c are reduced (compared to Fig. 1a) to reveal qualitative changes. As follows from the figure, complicated patterns of flows and buoyancy occur within and beyond the intrusion. The well mixed core collapses, while fluid elements in the outer part of an intrusion remain at an equilibrium level. Ultimately, the "array" of mixed patches transforms to weakly mixed layered structures similarly to experiments. Changes in the shape of the intrusion contour do not follow density field transformations. Figure 1c shows that the intrusion flow ceases completely before it reaches the boundary of calculation domain. This is explained by the fact that the density field both within and beyond intrusions is rearranged by flows in such a way that the buoyancy distribution ahead of and behind of front of intrusion flattens ("mechanism of blocking"). This mechanism can be important in the merging of mixed patches in layers.

Finally, we discuss the results of an experiment in which the transformation of layered structures under the action of a circular vortex with a vertical axis was modelled. A spatially periodic problem was solved. The vertical axes vortex was placed in centre of computational region. Figure 2 shows the evolution of potential energy of a unit column of fluid

$$\pi = \frac{1}{2}\int_{-1}^{1} b^2(x, y, z)dz,$$

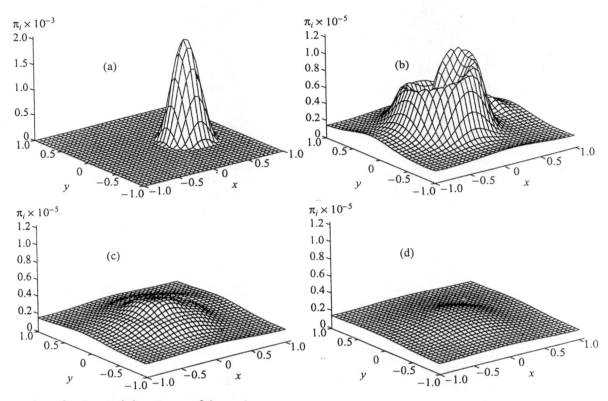

Fig. 2 Potential energy of intrusion in the vortex field: t=0 (a); t=1000 (b); t=2000 (c); t=4000 (d).

in the vortex field at $\varepsilon = 10^{-6}, \gamma = 10^{-3}$, that correspond to the situation when the period of revolution of fluid elements in the vortex is comparable with characteristic time of the evolution of the intrusion. As follows from Fig. 3 the process of transformation consist of three stages. In the first stage, a layered structure is curved into spiral by a vortex. In the second one, the spiral branches coalesces because, on the one hand, the potential energy within the spiral branches decreases as a result of collapse and diffusion, a on the other hand, the potential energy between the spiral decrease more slowly at the cost of rearrangement of the density field through the above mentioned mechanism of blocking. In the third stage, the layered structure converts to a disk whose centre coincides with the centre of the vortex. Diffusing, it rotates with the vortex as a rigid body. For more details see Galaktionov and Maderich (1999).

6. References

Galaktionov A., Maderich V. 1999 Dynamics of the layered structures in the final stage of turbulence decay in the stably stratified fluid. *Izvestiya, Atmosph. Oceanic Physics*, 35, No 6, p.751-758.

Nikishov V., Khristiuk R. 1999 On decay of the velocity perturbations in the stratified fluid. *Applied Hydromechanics*. 1(73), p.24-31.

Pearson H. J., Linden P.F. 1983 The final stage of turbulence decay in stratified fluid. *J. Fluid Mech.*, 134, p. 195-203.

Phillips O.M. 1966 The dynamics of the upper ocean. Cambridge University Press.

Riley J. J., Metcalfe R.W., Weissman M.A. 1981 Direct numerical simulations of homogeneous turbulence in density stratified fluids. *Proc. AIP Conf. on Nonlinear Propogation of Internal Waves*,(West, B. J. Ed.), p.79-112.

Entrainment measurements at a density interface

G. Mancini[1] - A. Cenedese[1]

[1] Department of Hydraulics, Transportation and Roads, University of Rome "La Sapienza"

Via Eudossiana 18, 00184 Rome, Italy

Phone: +39 06 44585033
+39 06 44585217
E-mail giu@dits.ing.uniroma1.it

Abstract

A laboratory experiment was performed to simulate the deepening of a convective mixed layer in a stratified lake. The aim of this paper is to analyse the turbulence in the mixed layer, and to provide an instrument to measure the entrainment at the interface by means of lagrangian trajectories. Experimental results are used in conjunction with transilient turbulence theory for the study of a penetrative convection phenomenoun. Lagrangian trajectories, reconstructed by means of Particle Tracking Velocimetry, allow "large eddy" effects on the mixed layer mixing to be included. Transilient matrix is then used to identify the turbulent transfer between different layers.

Introduction

The role of lakes as an important alternative to the too often polluted and exploited subterranean resources has been increasing. Eutrophication phenomena, however are extremely important in lakes causing an increase of water treatment costs or, in the worst case, impairing the use the water resource. It is known (*Denman e Gargett,* 1995) that eutrophication is sensibly related to the dynamic features of the lakes and not only to the nutrients inputs. From the hypolimnium the internal load of nutrients, through several mechanisms of transport and dispersion, can reach superficial layers where it increase primary production. Stratified lakes dynamic however is extremely complex and its still incomplete knowledge often brings to conflicting results.

The present experiment simulated a penetrative convection phenomenon in a stratified lake with aiming at analyzing mixing mechanisms inside the upper layer and transport through the interface. During penetrative convection there is no turbulent kinetic energy (TKE) production by shear so the similarity is effective only in the real case where no mean motion is due to wind or differential density distributions over the horizontal. Particle Tracking Velocimetry (PTV) was employed to reconstruct the field of motion. Specifically this technique allows the lagrangian tracking of tracer particles placed in the fluid. The simulation features, with a growing thickness of mixed layer (ML) depth and a continuous decrease of heat flux at the surface, make not possible to consider the analyzed system in a steady state. However, the time scale t* of the studied convective phenomena is definitively smaller than the time for significant changes in ML mean temperature and depth. On the basis of these consideration it is possible to consider the present experiment as a series of steady states, so with a quasi-steady variation of the analyzed variables (*Cenedese et Querzoli,* 1994). Under this hypothesis, even measuring the physical quantities in different times during the experiment, it is possible to non dimensionalize the variables with the relative length and velocity scale (z* and t* respectively) obtaining results not conditioned by phenomenon evolution.

Experimental set up

A tank with glass sidewalls of dimension 40 x 40 x 41 cm in the two horizontal and vertical directions respectively was constructed for the for laboratory experiments. A two layers stratification was obtained with the upper layer 8 °C hotter than the water below (more details on the experiment can be found in *Cenedese et Mancini*, 1999). The free surface was cooled by using a shell and tube exchanger. The mixed layer depth increased during the experiment (5500 s) from 12 to 18 cm. Particle trajectories were determined by PTV on a vertical plane of 26 cm depth by 20 cm width, so including epilimnion, metalimnion and part of the hypolomnion. About 1200 particle barycentres and 600-800 trajectories were validated on each video frame with a minimum detectable displacements of 0.35 mm.

Six thermocouples, located at different depths in the tank, acquired the changes of the temperature with time. Four temperature profiles were also taken in the middle of the tank by a mobile thermocouple with a spatial resolution along the vertical direction of 0.5 cm.

 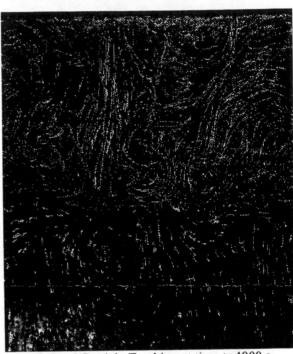

Figure 1 Particle Tracking at time t=2000 s   **Figure 2** Particle Tracking at time t=4000 s

Flux across the interface

The impact of thermals on the interface causes the growth of the mixing layer through the entrainment of denser water from the layer below. This flux is extremely important for phytoplankton dynamics because it is associated with a nutrient flux from the richer layers closer to sediments. Due to the presence of a density gradient beneath, the hits of thermals at the base of the mixed layer excite both interfacial and internal waves which break causing patches of intense mixing.

A measurement of entrainment is the deepening rate w_e of ML, whose expression in terms of heat flux was given By Stull (1988):

$$w_e = -\frac{\overline{w'T'}(-h)}{\Delta T} \tag{1}$$

where h is the depth of the interface, $\overline{w'T'}$ is the kinematic heat flux ad ΔT is the temperature difference between the entrained water temperature and ML mean one.

Deardoff (1983) obtained an expression for the entrainment rate based on turbulent kinetic energy balance, buoyancy flux equations and velocity fluctuations variance in the entrainment area. The TKE balance equation was closed through some empirical functions. Deardoff experimental results on the entrainment zone of the convective mixed layer showed that the non dimensional entrainment velocity can be expressed by:

$$\frac{w_e}{w*} = 0.25 Ri*^{-1}$$ (2)

where $w*$ is the convective velocity scale and $Ri*$ is the Richardson number:

$$Ri* = \left[\frac{gh\Delta\rho}{\rho_0 w*^2} \right]^{1/2}$$ (3)

It can be noted, however that equation (2) can be derived directly from (1) when heat flux at the interface is evaluated as the 25% of the free surface one ($-\overline{w'T'}(-h) = -0.25 \cdot \overline{w'T'}(0)$). In any case it remains the uncertainty on the proper value for the density difference $\Delta\rho$.

In the present experiment the authors found a linear behavior both for the mixed layer growth and the heat flux at the interface (*Cenedese et Mancini*, 1999). From these results the theoretical pattern of the entrained fluid mean temperature, satisfying Stull expression, was obtained (Figure 3).

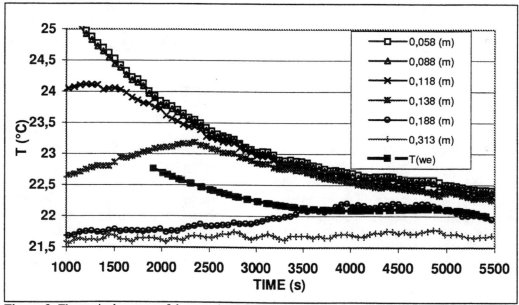

Figure 3. Theoretical pattern of the entrained fluid mean temperature. Temperatures at different depths are also plotted vs. time.

Translient Matrix

When studying turbulent convective phenomenon such penetrative convection it can be considered that dispersion is mostly due to transport by large organized structures while diffusion can be neglected. A way to deal with this topic was proposed by Stull (1984) through the formulation of translient turbulence theory. Unlike the other first order closure the translient turbulence theory allows large size eddy (up to the mixed layer depth) to transport fluid across finite distances before the smaller eddies cause the mixing with the surrounding fluid (*Inclàn et al.*, 1996).

If we subdivide the analyzed volume into N horizontal layers of equal thickness Δz we can identify with the index i the i-th layer, centered at a depth $z = (i-0.5)\Delta z$. Stull defined c_{ij} as the fraction of fluids being transported by turbulence from a source layer j into a destination layer i during a time interval Δt. c_{ij} can so be interpreted as the probability that a particles at a time t and depth iΔz can be found after the time interval Δt at a depth jΔz.

The squared matrix C(t, Δt) of all such elements is called a *Transilient Matrix* (Stull, 1993; Cuxart et al., 1994). Translient matrix accounts for all the mixing processes resolved by the grid spacing, from the smallest eddy traced by the pollen particle on the sheet to the medium and large coherent structures over the entire mixed layer depth.

It is assumed that transported fluids parcel maintain their original characteristics in terms of heat, tracer and momentum so the same matrix can be used to describe the changes in temperature as well as the changes in nutrients concentration over the entire depth of the lake.

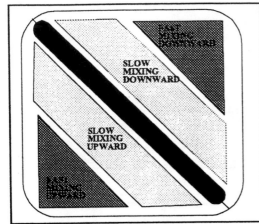

Figure 4 Physical meaning of translient matrix

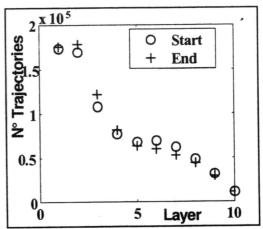

Figure 5 Comparison between particles arrivals and departures at each layer

Translient matrix is usually displayed as a contour plot of the element values. This kind of representation allows a immediate visual description of particles transition probability as a function of the source and destination depths. The absolute value of the generic matrix element represents the fluid quantity involved in the mixing process while its relative location characterizes the mixing features.

Elements in the lower left corner and in the upper right corner represent a rapid transport done by large scale vortex in the upward and downward direction respectively. Elements closer to the diagonal identify a slower transport performed by mean and small scale vortex which move particles to a relatively shorter distance. Finally diagonal coefficients represent particles which remain inside the original layers during the time interval Δt.

The matrix coefficients must satisfy the conservation of fluid mass and state that means that the same amount of water which reaches the i-th layer must leave it during the same time interval.

In order to satisfy this constrain each row and each column of a translient matrix for layers of equal depth must sum to 1.

This constrain is sufficiently satisfied by the reconstructed trajectories which show a similar number of incoming and out coming particles at each layer (Figure 5). The results seem to confirm the effectiveness of the employed tracking technique. Penetrative convection is a completely 3D phenomenon which causes most of the particle to leave the thin sheet at a certain depth so allowing only few of the structures to be fully described by the tracked trajectories. However it is possible to observe a statistical compensation between the number of arrivals and departures at any layers which allows to satisfy (4). To construct the translient matrix only the trajectories longer than Δt were used. When large Δt are considered the 2D technique is only able to detect large coherent structures, advectively transporting fluid parcel on the shot plane. The trajectories representative of the smallest structure, with marked 3D curvature, leave the light sheet before reaching Δt.

Unlike Stull results, the mixing caused by a series of small eddies is not fully taken into account by the translient matrix here described. It is therefore necessary to turn to a stereoscopic technique to track also the component normal to the shot plane of the single camera.

Translient matrix is displayed in Figure 6 for four time interval Δt non dimensionalised by the time scale t*. As time interval Δt increases the transilient matrix changes because the amount of turbulent mixing varies. When Δt is small compared with the time scale t* (Δt/t* = 0.25) particles have not enough time to move to a depth significantly different from the departure one. The contour lines show an high probability in a narrow area nearby the diagonal which indicates the absence of mixing.

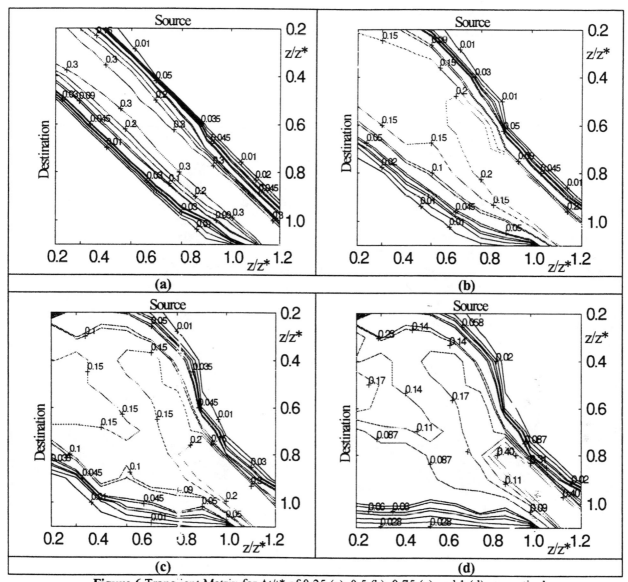

Figure 6 Translient Matrix for Δt/t* of 0.25 (a), 0.5 (b), 0.75 (c) and 1 (d) respectively.

When Δt increases (Δt = 0.5-0.75 t*), this area spread out towards the layers where particles show the maximum acceleration (*Cenedese et Mancini*, 1999) due to presence of descensional thermals. Above the diagonal the contour lines turn upwards showing small values as a consequence of slow mixing downward. Finally, when the interval over which the translient matrix is calculated, is of the same order of magnitude of the time scale of the phenomenon (Δt = t*), particles scatter in a uniform way over the entire depth of the mixed layer. All the area of the matrix that represents positions inside the ML shows sufficiently similar values. In the layers below, in the presence of a stable density gradient, mixing is extremely small and translient matrix coefficients remain virtually unchanged from the diagonal ones.

Conclusion
The experiment carried out appears to simulate well penetrative convection inside a stratified lake. Entrainment process, mixing and dispersion inside the mixed layer were analyzed. It was discussed the

possibility to parameterize the transport across the interface when a changing density gradient is present underneath. In this case, the difficulty to apply the equations in literature were underlined in relation to the temperature variation of the entrained fluid. Through the lagrangian information obtained by analysis of image (PTV) it was possible to apply translient theory. Particularly a description of mixed layer dispersion was provided by means of translient matrix. It was however noted that the employed 2D technique is not able to catch a completely 3D phenomenon such as penetrative convection. For time interval close to the time scale indeed, the information on mixing and transport provided by translient matrix is not complete because of the selectivity of the tracking.

Bibliography

Denman, K.L., Gargett, A. E. 1995 Biological-physical interaction in the upper ocean: The role of vertical and small scale transport processes. *Annual Review of Fluid Mechanics*, **27**, 225-255

Deardorff J.W., 1983, "A multi-limit mixed-layer entrainment formulation", *J. Phys. Oceanogr.*, **13**: 988-1002.

Inclàn M.G., Forkel R., Dlugi R., Stull R.B., 1996: Application of translient turbulent theory to study interactions between the atmospheric boundary layer and forest canopies. *Boundary-Layer Meteorology.*, **79**, 315-344.

Cenedese A. and Querzoli G. 1994, "A laboratory model of turbulent convection in the atmospheric boundary layer", *Atmos. Env.* **28**: 1901-1913.

Cenedese A and Mancini G. 1999, "Application of Particle Tracking Velocimetry to the study of Penetrative Convection". in Proc.of the 8th International Conference on Laser Anemometry, Advances and Applications Rome September 6-8, 1999: 381-389.

Stull, R.B., 1984: Transilient Turbulence Theory. Part I: The concept of eddy mixing across finite distances. *J. Atmos. Sci.*, **41**, 3351-3367.

Stull, R.B. 1988 An Introduction to boundary layer meteorology. *Cambridge University Press*, 368 pp.

Stull, R.B., 1993: Review of non-local mixing in turbulent atmospheres: Transilient turbulence theory. *Bound-Layer Meteor.*, **62**, 21-96.

Turbulent patch identification in microstructure profiles

Jaume Piera [1,2], Elena Roget [1], Jordi Catalan [2]

[1]Environmental Physics. Department of Physics. University of Girona, Campus de Montilivi, Girona. Catalonia, Spain. E-17071
[2]Department of Ecology. University of Barcelona, Diagonal 645 Barcelona 08028. Catalonia, Spain

jpiera@porthos.bio.ub.es, roget@fc.udg.es, catalan@porthos.bio.ub.es

Abstract

In this paper, a new method for turbulent patch identification is proposed, based on a wavelet denoising procedure and semiquantitative analysis of Thorpe displacement (d_T). The method has been implemented for achieving two main objectives: (1) *global applicability* in a wide range of density gradients, which is especially important for modelling biological-physical interactions and (2) *robustness* as the uncertainties derived from noise should not change significantly the final result.

The method has been tested using a theoretical profile and finally validated with field data. These results have been compared to other criteria for patch identification yielding a high level of coincidence.

1. Introduction

One of the objectives in analysing microstructure density profiles, is to identify turbulent patches and computing its characteristic vertical length (L_p). Patch identification is an important issue in turbulence characterisation, as mixing occurs in patches produced by multiple mechanisms over a wide range of space and time scales.

Turbulent physical characterisation, based on vertical microstructure records, are usually focused on the main thermocline, avoiding problems related to instrumental noise (e.g. Gregg, 1987; Moum, 1996). However, some biological-physical processes should be characterised in a wider range of background conditions with different turbulent regime. These differences can generate vertical differences in population dynamics and selective processes among planktonic algae (Reynolds, 1992) or zooplankton distribution (Haury et al. 1990). For this reason, a new method for turbulent patch identification is proposed, that has been implemented for being applicable in a wide range of density gradients

2. Resolution limits on turbulent patch detection

Turbulent patches identification is usually based on Thorpe displacement (d_T) profiles. Thorpe displacement are computed from density profiles, and represents the vertical distance that an individual fluid particle (i.e. a single density value) has to be moved in order to generate an stable density profile. The simplest eddy model is a solidbody rotation where a cylindrical overturning eddy in an initially linear density profile yields a Z-shaped $\rho_{(z)}$ segment. We can express the length of the theoretical displacement d_T as a function of the stable density gradient $\partial\rho/\partial z$, and the magnitude of the density fluctuation ρ' (the difference between the measured and the stable profiles):

$$d_T \approx \frac{\rho'}{\partial\rho/\partial z} \qquad (1)$$

From (1) we can compute the relative error of d_T as

$$\frac{E_{d_T}}{d_T} \approx \frac{E_{\rho'}}{\rho'} + \frac{E_{\partial\rho/\partial z}}{\partial\rho/\partial z} \qquad (2)$$

Since the density gradient computation is based on a greater number of measurements than the density fluctuation, we can assume that the relative error in density fluctuation is much higher than that in monotonic density. Then, from (1) and (2)

$$E_{d_T} \approx \frac{E_{\rho'}}{\partial \rho / \partial z} \qquad (3)$$

The lower bound for a measurable patch has been related to the minimum measurable displacement. The use of a safety margin suggest that this value should not be smaller than $2 E_{d_T}$

$$L_{p(min)} > 2 \left| \frac{E_{\rho'}}{\partial \rho / \partial z} \right| \qquad (4)$$

that in terms of associated buoyancy frequency can be expressed as

$$L_{p(min)} > 2 \frac{g}{N^2} \frac{|E_{\rho'}|}{\rho_0} \qquad (5)$$

The resolution limits on patch size provide crude lower bounds on measurable signals in low stratified environments. Improving the patch size resolution is only possible by reducing $E_{\rho'}$. The main contribution on $E_{\rho'}$ is the noise derived from the instrumentation, which can also yield patterns in the density profiles that may generate false turbulent structures. In order to achieve the highest resolution in patch detection is necessary to find a method for optimal signal recovering. This method should minimise the noise from the density profile, without loosing the small density perturbations derived from the overturn motions at low density gradients.

3. Optimal method for noise reduction.

In the last few years, there has been considerable interest in the use of wavelet transforms for removing noise from data. When data are intermittent in nature, as is the case of density fluctuations, wavelet basis is highly advantageous over either Fourier or real-space analysis (Pen, 1999).

The proposed method for noise reduction is derived from a wavelet-based thresholding algorithm (Donoho and Johnstone, 1994; Donoho 1995). This method can be decomposed in three steps (figure 1):

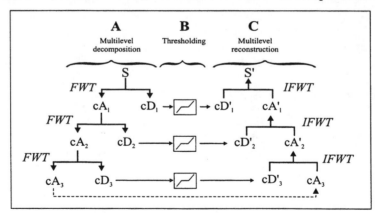

Figure 1. Schematic diagram of the denosing method: S original signal, S' denoised signal.

A. Multilevel decomposition. Fast wavelet transform, *FWT,* (Mallat, 1988) can be applied for decomposing a signal in two different parts, one that keeps the global features (the approximation coefficients) and the other with the local features (detail coefficients). Applying recursively such decomposition to the measured data (Cohen et al.1993), is possible to obtain empirical wavelet coefficients associated to different levels of local characterisation. Figure 1A graphically represents an example of this hierarchical decomposition. In this example, the level of decomposition has set to 3, yielding one series of approximation coefficients (cA_3) and a set of three different detail coefficient signals ($cD_{1,2,3}$).

B. Thresholding. In order to reduce the noise contribution, a threshold is applied to the detail coefficients, thereby suppressing those coefficients smaller than a certain amplitude (figure 1B).

C. Multilevel reconstruction. A denoised profile can be recovered from the transformed coefficients, applying recursively the Inverse Wavelet Transform (*IWT*) over each level of decomposition (figure 1C).

3.1 Sensitivity analysis. Theoretical test

With no accepted statistical model of overturning, there is little guidance to confirm when density fluctuations are caused by overturning motions or by instrumental noise. A theoretical profile has been designed for testing the error contribution to the d_T, calculated from a denoised density profile. The test has been focused on the worst field conditions, low buoyancy frequencies and small overturn sizes, in order to determine the resolution limits for patch detection. The theoretical profile is based on the solid-body rotation model, as it is easy to check the changes on the final Z-shaped structures. The profile model comprises five segments, each with a different associated buoyancy frequency. Hypothetical overturns were simulated in each segment. In the fifth segment (the most critical), two overturns of different length were simulated. The following table summarises the features of these segments.

Segments			Overturns	
Number	Interval depth (m)	N (rad/s)	depth (m)	size (m)
1	0.00 - 1.50	$1.6\ 10^{-2}$	0.75	0.2
2	1.50 - 2.00	$1.2\ 10^{-2}$	1.75	0.2
3	2.00 - 2.75	$1.0\ 10^{-2}$	2.35	0.2
4	2.75 - 4.25	$7.0\ 10^{-3}$	3.50	0.3
5	4.25 - 7.25	$3.0\ 10^{-3}$	5.00	0.4
			6.50	0.3

The different noise levels have been simulated adding a zero mean gaussian white noise to the theoretical density profile. The first profile has been constructed adding a noise signal with variance equal to $6.25 \cdot 10^{-8}$ $kg^2 \cdot m^{-6}$. The variance has been calculated from laboratory test measurements, using the density error variance equation proposed by Gregg (1979). Assuming certain uncertainty from this variance, a factor of 50% and 100% has been applied to the standard deviation, yielding two new density profiles with noise variance of $1.40 \cdot 10^{-7}$ and $5 \cdot 10^{-7}$ $kg^2 \cdot m^{-6}$ respectively.

The test of sensitivity has been developed in two steps. In the first step, the method of denoising has been applied to the density profiles with different noise variance. Multilevel wavelet transform has based on orthogonal and compactly supported wavelets (*Daubechies*) and the level of decomposition has been set to 9.

A soft threshold function (Donoho, 1995) has applied to detail coefficients:

$$cD' = \text{sgn}(cD) \cdot (cD - thr) \cdot I(cD > thr) \qquad (6)$$

With this function, the coefficients smaller than the threshold *thr* are suppressed while the rest of the coefficients are shrunk an equivalent of the threshold value. The threshold value has been selected as (Donoho and Johnstone, 1994)

$$thr = \sigma \sqrt{2\log(n)} \qquad (7)$$

where *n* is the number of samples and σ is a rescaling factor estimated from the noise level present in the signal. The estimation of the noise level has based on first level of detail coefficients (cD1) well suited for zero mean gaussian white noise in the denoising 1-D model (Misiti et al. 1996).

$$\sigma = \frac{median\left(|cD_1|\right)}{0.6745} \qquad (8)$$

Once the density profiles have been denoised, the Thorpe displacements have been computed comparing the result calculated from the theoretical profile, to the Thorpe displacements calculated from the denoised density profiles.

Figure 2 shows the graphical results of this test. Figure 2A represents the theoretical density profile used for the test. Circle lines indicate the position of each overturn and horizontal dotted lines the limits of each segment. The theoretical d_T profile is shown in 2B. Figures 2C-D shows the error derived from the different levels of noise. As a reference, in each figure there are the extremes values (dotted line) obtained without applying the denoising method. Comparing the denoised results (C-D) from the theoretical (B) we can see that all the overturns from the segments 1-4 can be identified. In the case of the most critical segment, although noise has been reduced considerably, the effect of the noise yields a significant error of displacements.

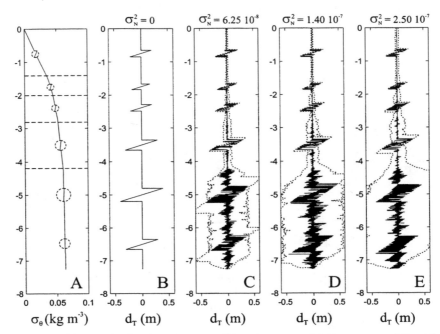

Figure 2. A) Theoretical density profile for sensitivity test. B) Thorpe displacement, computed from the theoretical profile. C-D) Thorpe displacement computed from noisy profiles with increasing levels of noise.

4. Local gradient classification

Wavelet denoising has demonstrated a powerful tool, but even with such efficient method, too high displacement errors are still present at low density gradients. A complementary method has been implemented for turbulent patch detection, based on semiquantitative analysis of d_T, which can be decomposed in the following parts

Data classification. Thorpe displacement at each point of the profile is compared to its potential error, which is computed from the den density error and the local density gradient (eq. 3). This comparison yields three possible states

state	Condition
Z	$d_T = 0$
U	$|d_T| < E_{dT}$
S	$|d_T| > E_{dT}$

Computing index. Two statistical indexes have been defined from this data classification. Displacement index (I_D) is computed as the quotient between the number of points on state S and the number of points considered, and represents the percentage of samples that, we can assure, have d_T different than zero. Uncertain index (I_U) is computed as the quotient between the number of points on state U and the number of points considered, and gives an estimation of the measurement uncertainty. I_D and I_U have been computed over 50 points, which is reasonable for statistical robustness and spatial resolution (50 samples corresponds approximately to 5 cm for 1 mm resolution, which is a common value for microstructure instrumentation).

Patch identification. Segments with values of I_D equal to zero can be supposed to delimit the turbulent patches. Patches are identified as the segments with strict positive I_D values. Figure 3 shows the results of the indexes computed from the sensitivity test profiles. I_D values are represented as solid areas, while I_U values are in dotted lines. Note that under the solid rotation model I_D profiles are affected by a characteristic gap that can affect patch identification in low density gradients. This effect however is not expected in field data, with much more complex dynamics. Comparing the theoretic I_D (fig 3B) with the indexes computed from the noisy profiles we can see that all the profiles are very similar in the first four segments. The fifth segment has the same pattern in low noise level (figs 3C and 3D) and starts to change when noise level (fig 3E). These results suggest that I_D can be a robust parameter for patch identification.

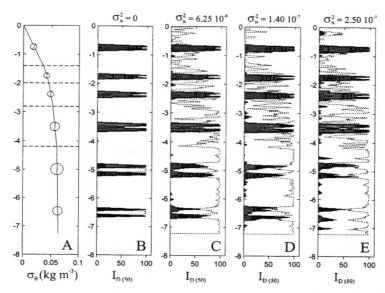

Figure 3. I_D (solid grey) and I_U (dotted) profiles. A) Theoretical density profile. B) Theoretical I_D and I_U profiles. C-D) I_D and I_U profiles computed from noisy profiles with increasing levels of noise.

5. Test data

A set of microstructure profiles has been used to test the proposed method. The data were obtained in the summer of 1999, at Banyoles lake (Spain). All measurements were made from sensors mounted on vertical microstructure profiler. These include temperature, conductivity and horizontal velocity fluctuations (using airfoil probes). Salinity and density were determined from temperature and conductivity following Chen and Millero (1986). Thorpe displacement was calculated from potential density profiles and a total of 575 turbulent patches were identified from the epilimnion (2-10 m). where the associated buoyancy frequency N range from 0.009 to 0.020 rad/s.

Following Moum (1996) criterion, we have tested which of these patches have well defined upper and lower boundaries. Two conditions are required for this criterion: $L_{Tmax} < L_p$, where L_{Tmax} denotes the maximum Thorpe displacement throughout the patch, and $\int d_T(z)\,dz$ over L_p is equal to 0.

Figure 4 shows the comparison between L_{Tmax} and L_p, showing that the first condition is valid for 100% of the identified patches. The second condition has been tested considering that noise can affect the final result. Applying the criterion $\int d_T(z)\, dz < 0.05$ m, 94.1% of the patches verified this inequality.

We can see that using the proposed method, there are a high percentage of validated patches.

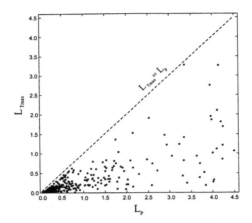

Figure 4. Comparison of L_p and L_{Tmax}.

6. Conclusions

Wavelet-based thresholding algorithm is a powerful tool for reducing noise contribution in Thorpe displacement calculation, although at very low density gradient error on d_T is too high.
Displacement index, derived from the local gradient classification method, is a robust parameter for turbulent patch identification.

References

Chen,C.T. and Millero,F.J. (1986). Precise thermodynamic properties for natural waters covering only the limnological range. *Limnol. Oceanogr.* vol 31(3): 657-662.

Cohen, A.; Daubechies, I.; Jawerth, B. and Vial, P. (1993). Multiresolution analysis, wavelets and fast wavelet transform on an interval. *Comptes Rendus Acad. Sci. Paris (A)*. t. 316: 417-421.

Donoho, D.L. and Johnstone, I.M. (1994). Ideal spatial adaptation by wavelet shrinkage. *Biometrika* vol 81: 425-455.

Donoho, D.L. (1995). De-Noising by soft-thresholding. *IEEE Trans. On Inf. Theory*. Vol 41(3): 613-627.

Gregg, M.C. (1979) The effects of bias error and system noise on parameters computed from C, T, P, and V profiles. *J. Phys. Oceanogr*. 9: 199-217.

Haury, L.R.; Yamazaky, H. And Itsweire, E.C. (1990) Effects of turbulent shear flow on zooplankton distribution. *Deep sea Res.* vol 37(3): 447-461.

Misiti, M.; Misiti, Y.; Oppenheim, G. and Poggi, J.M. (1996). *Matlab Wavelet Toolbox User's Guide*. The MathWorks, Inc. 626 pp.

Mallat, S. (1989) A theory for multiresolution signal decomposition: the wavelet representation. *IEEE Pattern Anal. And Machine Intell*. vol 11(7): 674-693.

Moum, J. N. (1996) Efficiency of mixing in the main thermocline. *J. Geophys. Res.* vol 101: 12057-12069.

Pen, U.-L. (1999). Application of wavelets to filtering of noisy data. *Phil. Trans. R. Soc. Lond. A* vol 357:2561-2571.

Reynolds, C.S. (1992) Dynamics, selction and composition of phytoplankton in relation to vertical structure in lakes. *Arch. Hydrobiol. Beih. Ergebn. Limnol.* vol 35: 13-31

Fundamental Studies on the Application of the $k - \varepsilon$ Model to Surface Mixed Layer Deepening of DIM-type Entrainment

Xin Qian and Tadaharu Ishikawa

Department of Environmental Science and Technology, Interdisciplinary Graduate School of Science and Engineering, Tokyo Institute of Technology, Yokohama, Japan 226-8502
qian@depe.titech.ac.jp

1. Abstract

This paper presents fundamental studies on the application of the $k - \varepsilon$ model to surface mixed layer deepening of DIM-type entrainment caused by the wind-induced current. Numerical experiments are carried out as a one-dimensional(vertical) situation in a horizontally infinite water basin and the results are compared to theoretical and experimental studies. This study shows that $k - \varepsilon$ model successfully reproduces the DIM entrainment, and entrainment coefficient E[U.] agree with the laboratory experiment by Kranenburg(1984). The non-dimensional velocity and density profiles of the mixed layer agree with those from theoretical results. Turbulent kinetic energy produced by the wind shear stress is converted to potential energy with a mixing efficiency of 0.2. This agrees with the value proposed by Imberger(1985).

2. Introduction

In recent years $k - \varepsilon$ model has been applied to several kinds of density currents, and the numerical results are compared with experimental data (Yoon et al., 1995; Tsubono et al., 1997). However, because the verification have been made individually for specified situations, its general performance has not been shown in the sense that the model output is or isn't consistent with the general knowledge of fluid mechanics such as the entrainment law of the densimetric interface.

The formulation of the entrainment velocity at the interface of a two-layered fluid system is one of the fundamental studies of fluid mechanics. It has been the subject of many laboratory experiments and field measurements, and the results are summarized into entrainment laws. In the case of vertical mixing of stratified water in lake and bay caused by wind stress, the entrainment law can be classified into two types(Price et al. 1978). One is Dynamic Instability Model(DIM) which is used to estimate the entrainment velocity when the turbulent energy generated by the shearing stress in a stratified fluid is the dominant source of the vertical mixing. The other is Turbulent Erosion Model(TEM) which is valid when some external stirring is the dominant sources of energy.

The DIM entrainment is usually seen in ocean or other closed water bodies before water level gradient has been set up. If the wind shear stress and total buoyancy are kept constant during the process of surface mixed layer deepening, the entrainment coefficient can be expressed as the following formula.

$$E[U_.] \propto Ri[U_.]^{-\frac{1}{2}} \tag{1}$$

where $E[U_.] = We/U_*$, We is entrainment velocity, U_* is the shear velocity at the water surface, $Ri[U_*] = \delta g h / U_*^2$, $\delta = \Delta\rho / \rho_0$, $\Delta\rho$ is density difference between the layers, ρ_0 is reference density, g is gravitational acceleration, h is mixed layer thickness. This equation was firstly proposed by Pollard et al.(1973) and supported by Price et al.(1978) with the data obtained in the Gulf of Mexico. Kundu(1981) presented some theoretical background that this entrainment law is natural if some dynamic similarity is developed. Kranenburg(1984) carried out an excellent laboratory experiment in a flume of finite length in which he simulated a situation where the presence of endwalls was not noticeable. The experimental results clearly supported the above formula.

In this study, in order to examine whether the DIM entrainment can be reproduced by the $k - \varepsilon$ model, numerical experiments are carried out as a one-dimensional(vertical) situation in a horizontally infinite water basin and the results are compared to experimental and theoretical studies.

3. Mathematical Equations

The ideal DIM entrainment appears in horizontally infinite water basin. So, considering it as a vertical one-dimensional phenomenon we can write the governing equations as follows:

$$\frac{\partial u}{\partial t} - \frac{\partial}{\partial z}(v \frac{\partial u}{\partial z}) = 0 \tag{2}$$

$$\frac{\partial \delta}{\partial t} - \frac{\partial}{\partial z}(v_\delta \frac{\partial \delta}{\partial z}) = 0 \tag{3}$$

$$\frac{\partial k}{\partial t} - \frac{\partial}{\partial z}(v_k \frac{\partial k}{\partial z}) = P_r + G - \varepsilon \tag{4}$$

$$\frac{\partial \varepsilon}{\partial t} - \frac{\partial}{\partial z}(v_\varepsilon \frac{\partial \varepsilon}{\partial z}) = C_1 \frac{\varepsilon}{k}\{P_r + (1-C_3)G\} - C_2 \frac{\varepsilon^2}{k} \tag{5}$$

where t is time, z is vertical co-ordinate(upward: +); u is horizontal velocity; δ is relative density difference; k is the turbulent kinetic energy; ε is rate of viscous dissipation; v_0 is molecular kinematic viscosity of water; v is effective eddy viscosity; v_k, v_ε and v_δ are effective diffusivities of k, ε, δ which can be given as:

$$v = v_0 + C_\mu \frac{k^2}{\varepsilon}, \quad v_k = v, \quad v_\varepsilon = 0.77v, \quad v_\delta = 1.2v \tag{6}$$

P_r is the production of turbulent kinetic energy, and G is the production of potential energy. The P_r, G and empirical constants of turbulent model can be given as:

$$P_r = v(\frac{\partial u}{\partial z})^2, \quad G = -gv_\delta \frac{\partial \delta}{\partial z}, \quad C_1 = 1.44, \ C_2 = 1.92, \ C_3 = 1.0, \ C_\mu = 0.09 \tag{7}$$

4. Boundary Conditions and Numerical Method

DIM type entrainment phenomenon can be simulated as the following process: the buoyancy is concentrated near the water surface, and the all layers are quiescent initially. As the wind blows, wind-induced current develops. Water below the mixed layer is entrained upward as mixed-layer deepens. Buoyancy is conserved during this period of time. At water surface the wind shear stress U_*^2 is applied to the velocity equation. For all other quantities(δ, k, ε), the gradient normal to the surface plane are set to be zero. Because the water below the mixed layer remains quiescent in the deepening process of the surface mixed-layer, it is reasonable to take the gradient of all quantities normal to the bottom plane as zero.

Integration of governing equations (2)–(5) over the control volume using implicit scheme gives the discretized equations, which are solved by TDMA(Tri-Diagonal Matrix Algorithm). The vertical grid size Δz and total water depth H are 0.3m and 12.0m respectively, and the time step Δt is set to be 10sec.

At initial time, the u of all layers are set to be zero since the fluid is quiescent, and the total buoyancy B is concentrated at the first grid from the water surface. The initial values of k and ε are set to be small enough to keep the simulation process steady.

The experimental conditions and results are listed in Table 1.

Table 1. The experimental conditions and results

Case	U_* (m/s)	B (m²/s²) ×10³	$Ri[U_*]$	We(m/s) ×10⁴	$E[U_*]$	$\triangle u$ (m/s)	$E[\triangle u]$
1	0.0058	6.480	192.6	2.3	0.040	0.175	0.00131
2	0.0070	6.480	132.6	3.5	0.050	0.179	0.00196
3	0.0080	6.480	101.3	4.5	0.056	0.174	0.00259
4	0.0090	6.480	80.0	5.8	0.064	0.177	0.00325
5	0.0095	6.480	71.8	6.2	0.065	0.189	0.00328
6	0.0030	6.480	720.0	6.9	0.023	0.162	0.00043
7	0.0040	4.766	297.9	1.4	0.035	0.148	0.00095
8	0.0040	5.189	324.3	1.4	0.035	0.154	0.00090
9	0.0058	5.189	154.3	2.8	0.048	0.149	0.00188
10	0.0097	5.342	57.4	6.3	0.065	0.157	0.00398
11	0.0064	5.342	130.4	3.2	0.051	0.051	0.00203
12	0.0058	5.342	158.8	2.8	0.048	0.048	0.00176
13	0.0070	8.241	168.2	3.1	0.044	0.189	0.00164
14	0.0040	8.241	515.5	1.1	0.028	0.179	0.00061
15	0.0030	8.241	915.7	6.5	0.022	0.167	0.00039
16	0.0090	8.241	101.7	5.1	0.057	0.198	0.00257
17	0.0140	8.241	42.1	1.1	0.078	0.213	0.00516
18	0.0160	8.241	32.2	1.4	0.089	0.216	0.00662
19	0.0045	8.241	406.9	1.3	0.029	0.181	0.00072

5. Results and Discussion

(1) Similarity of Vertical Distribution

The vertical distribution of relative density difference and velocity of Case 2 are plotted in Fig.1 and Fig.2 respectively. It can be observed that besides the profiles at t=1hr which are affected by the initial condition, the profiles after t=1hr keep approximately the similar shape and have the same entrainment velocity while the surface mixed-layer deepens downward.

Vertical distributions which are nondimensionalized by the maximum value of the profiles respectively are presented in Fig. 3-1 and Fig. 3-2. The vertical coordinates are nondimensionalized by the mixed-layer depth h. The profiles at different times overlay each other. It shows that the non-dimensional quantities follow the similar distribution and have no relation with time t .

(2) Entrainment Law

The depth of mixed-layer versus time is plotted in Fig. 4. It is observed that the mixed-layer, except during the initial time

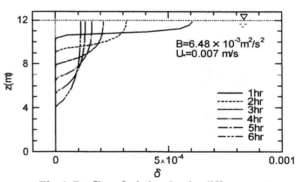

Fig. 1. Profiles of relative density difference δ

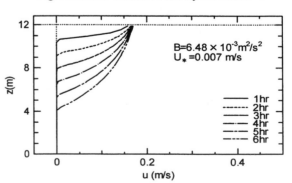

Fig. 2. Profiles of velocity u

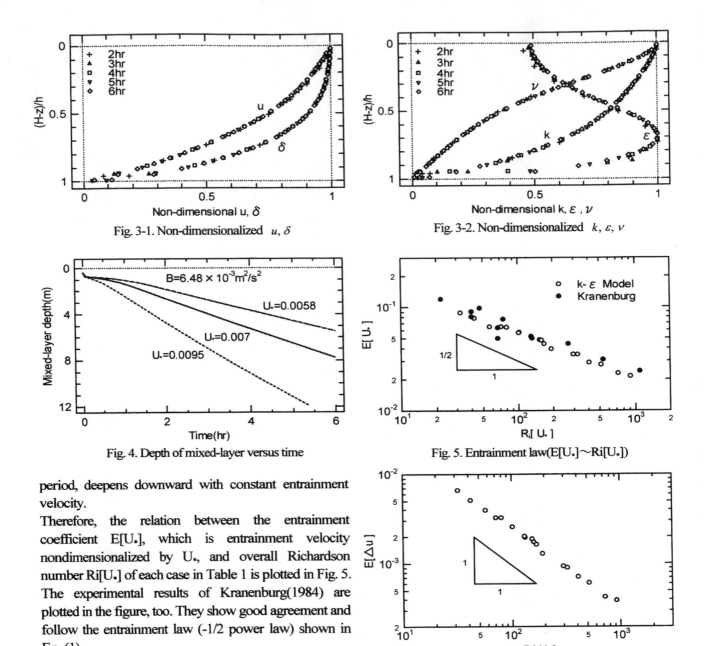

Fig. 3-1. Non-dimensionalized u, δ

Fig. 3-2. Non-dimensionalized k, ε, ν

Fig. 4. Depth of mixed-layer versus time

Fig. 5. Entrainment law($E[U_*] \sim Ri[U_*]$)

period, deepens downward with constant entrainment velocity.

Therefore, the relation between the entrainment coefficient $E[U_*]$, which is entrainment velocity nondimensionalized by U_*, and overall Richardson number $Ri[U_*]$ of each case in Table 1 is plotted in Fig. 5. The experimental results of Kranenburg(1984) are plotted in the figure, too. They show good agreement and follow the entrainment law (-1/2 power law) shown in Eq. (1).

Fig. 6. Entrainment law($E[\Delta u] \sim Ri[U_*]$)

(3) *Dynamic Similarity*

The vertical distribution of $u, \delta, k, \varepsilon$ follows the similar shape respectively. It implies that there is dynamic similarity in the mixed-layer.

Fig. 6 shows the relation between the entrainment coefficient $E[\Delta u]$ which is entrainment velocity nondimensionalized by the maximum velocity Δu of the profile and overall Richardson number $Ri[U_*]$ of each case in Table 1. They follow the entrainment law(-1 power law) obviously as shown in Eq. (8).

$$E[\Delta u] \propto Ri[U_*]^{-1} \qquad (8)$$

Eq. (8) can be rewritten in the form of Eq. (9).

$$\Delta \rho \, g h We \propto \rho_0 \, U_*^2 \Delta u \qquad (9)$$

Turbulent kinetic energy produced by the wind shear stress is converted to potential energy. Eq. (9) suggests that the increasing rate of potential energy is proportional to the rate of the work done by the wind shear stress(Niller and Kraus 1977). Therefore, it can be concluded that the results of $k - \varepsilon$ model show a similarity of the total energy conversion(averaged in mixed layer).

Ishikawa and Tanaka(1990) presented a similar profile of velocity u and relative density difference δ with a hypothesis about the similarity of energy conversion at each point within the mixed-layer(it was called local similarity hypothesis). They stressed that, if the ratio of potential energy production (G) to turbulent kinetic energy production (Pr) is constant within the mixed-layer(if ratio G/Pr is constant, no matter what value G and Pr are), the velocity profile and relative density difference profile can be predicted solitarily. The profiles vary with the value of turbulent Prandtl number(ν / ν_δ).

The comparison of similar profiles obtained with the use of $k - \varepsilon$ model and those from Ishikawa and Tanaka(1990) are presented in Fig. 7. In both of them, the turbulent Prandtl number were set to be 0.83($\nu_\delta = 1.2\nu$). As seen in the figure, they have good agreements.

Then, in Fig. 8, the vertical distribution of G, Pr, nondimensionalized by the maximum value in each profile respectively, and coefficient $C_0(=G/P_r)$ from the results of the $k - \varepsilon$ model are plotted. The vertical coordinate are normalized by the mixed layer depth h. It can be observed that at the base of the mixed layer, C_0 remains constant and has no relation to the experimental conditions. However, C_0 is half of the value of Ishikawa and Tanaka(1990).

(4) Mixing Efficiency

For practical purposes like predicting the entrainment velocity, the total mixing efficiency of the mixed-layer is more important than the vertical distribution of C_0. Therefore, the energy components of mixed-layer calculated from the results of $k - \varepsilon$ model are provided in Fig. 9. As shown in the figure, the kinetic energy and potential energy of mixed-layer increase in straight line with time t after t=1hr.

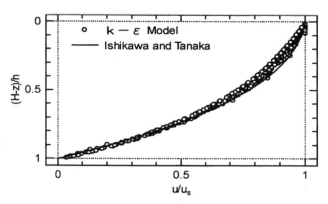

Fig. 7-1. Non-dimensionalized velocity distribution

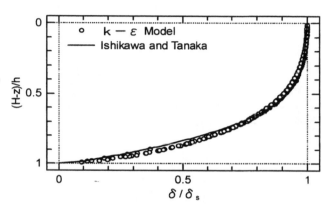

Fig. 7-2. Non-dimensionalized relative density difference distribution

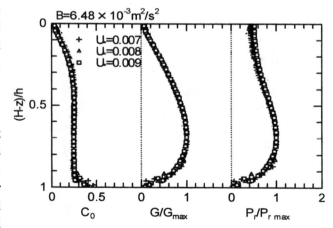

Fig. 8. Distribution of C_0, non-dimensionalized Pr and G

It can be noticed that the fluid below the mixed layer in Fig. 2 remains quiescent, so the energy transferred from mixed layer to the water under it can be ignored. Therefore, the mixing efficiency $C_0(=G/P_r)$ can be calculated from three components showed in Fig. 9 as ③/(①-②). The C_0 of each case shown in Table 1 are plotted in Fig. 10. It can be concluded that the C_0 is near 0.2 and does not change much with the overall Richardson number. This value agrees with that proposed by Imberger(1985), which is based on laboratory experiment and numerical model.

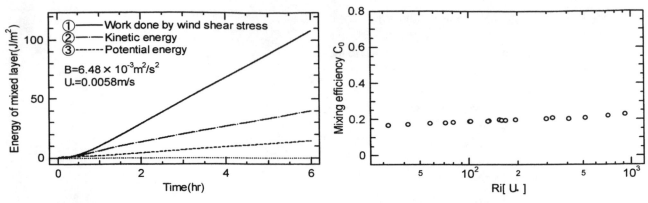

Fig. 9. Energy components of mixed layer   Fig. 10. Mixing efficiency of the mixed layer

6. Conclusions

The numerical simulation of DIM entrainment process by the use of $k - \varepsilon$ model has been undertaken with ideal conditions. The conclusions can be made as follows:
(1) The vertical distribution of all quantities ($u, \delta, k, \varepsilon$) follow nearly similar shape respectively;
(2) The entrainment law of DIM entrainment obtained in this study agrees with the experimental results provided by Kranenburg(1984);
(3) The non-dimensional velocity profile and relative density difference profile agree with that of theoretical studies (Ishikawa and Tanaka 1990);
(4) Turbulent kinetic energy produced by the wind shear stress is converted to potential energy with a mixing efficiency of 0.2. This agrees with the value proposed by Imberger(1985).
The above conclusions suggest that the $k - \varepsilon$ model works well in the numerical simulation of turbulent stratified flow containing DIM entrainment process.

References

Imberger, J. (1985), The Diurnal Mixed Layer, *Limnol. Oceanogr.*, Vol.30(4), pp.737-770.

Ishikawa, T., and Tanaka, M.(1990), Theoretical Study on the DIM Type Entrainment, *J. Hydrau., Coast. Environ. Eng., JSCE*, No.417/II-13, pp. 99-108.

Kranenburg, C.(1984), Wind-Induced Entrainment in a Stably Stratified Fluid , *J.F.M.*, Vol.145, pp. 253-273.

Kundu, P.K.(1981), Self-similarity in stress-driven entrainment experiments, *J. Geophy. Res.*, Vol. 86, No. C3, pp.1979-1988.

Niller, P.P. and Kraus, E.B.(1977), One-dimensional Models of the Upper Ocean, *Modelling and Prediction of the Upper Layers of the Ocean*, E.B.Kraus, pp.143-172, Pergamon Press.

Pollard, R.T., Rhines, P.B. and Thompson, R.O.(1973), The Deepening of the Wind Mixed Layer, *Geophys. Fluid Dynam.*, Vol.3, pp.381-404.

Price, J.F., Moores, C.N.K. and Leer, J.C.V.(1978), Observation and simulation of storm-induced mixed layer deepening, J. Phys. Oceanogr., Vol.8,pp.582-599.

Tsubono, T., Nakashiki, N., Matsunashi, S., Sakai, S., and Maruyama, K.(1997), Numerical Simulation of a Horizontal Buoyant Jet Discharged from a Multiple Pipe, *Annual J. of Hydrau. Eng., JSCE*, Vol 41, pp.295-302.

Yoon, J.S., Nakatsuji K., and Muraoka, K.(1995), Density Interface Movement and Mixing in a Two-Layered Stratified Flow System Exposed to Wind Stress-Hydraulic Experiments and Numerical Experiments-, *Annual J. of Hydrau. Eng., JSCE*, Vol 39, pp.811-818.

Turbulence anisotropy in stratified uniform shear flow

S. Sarkar

Department of Mechanical and Aerospace Engineering, University of California at San Diego, La Jolla, California, 92093-0411, USA. ssarkar@ucsd.edu

1 Abstract

Direct numerical simulation of uniform shear flow is used to study the anisotropy of fluctuating motion in a stably stratified medium with uniform mean shear. Turbulence is found to be three-dimensional over a wide range of gradient Richardson numbers in the two flows investigated here: vertical mean shear($d\overline{U}/dz$) and horizontal mean shear ($d\overline{U}/dy$). The role of the turbulent Froude number in establishing the regime of stratified turbulence observed here is described. The fluctuating velocity gradients are examined. The vertical gradient of streamwise velocity is found to dominate the other components of turbulent dissipation in both horizontal and vertical shear flows.

2 Introduction

Stably stratified shear flow with horizontal mean shear, $d\overline{U}/dy = S_h$, was compared with vertical mean shear, $d\overline{U}/dz = S_v$ using DNS (direct numerical simulation) in our previous studies, Jacobitz and Sarkar (1998); Jacobitz and Sarkar (2000). The turbulent kinetic energy was found to be much larger when the mean shear is horizontal essentially because the turbulent production in such a case does not directly involve the gravity-suppressed vertical velocity and the associated vertical buoyancy flux is larger because turbulence remains three-dimensional. However, gravity was found to affect the overall dynamics, for example, when $Ri_g = N^2/S_h^2$ was larger that a critical value of $Ri_g \simeq 1.5$, the turbulence was found to decay. The coupling between fluctuations in horizontal velocity, vertical velocity and density is key to understanding the observed behavior and motivates the present study of turbulence anisotropy. Presumably, the coupling leads to qualitative differences in the vertical mixing due to different types of fluctuations supported in the stably-stratified ocean such as internal waves Gregg (1989), buoyancy-affected but three-dimensional turbulence, the potential vorticity mode Riley et al. (1981); Muller et al. (1988) and fossil turbulence Gibson (1987).

In the case of vertical shear flow, it is well-known that, with increasing Richardson number, the turbulent energy and associated vertical mass transport is suppressed. However, the effect of stratification on the anisotropy of the fluctuating velocity is not clear. Ocean spectra, for example, D'Asaro and Lien (2000) often show internal wave activity at low wave numbers followed by three-dimensional turbulence. In the case of decaying grid turbulence, the laboratory experiments of Pearson and Linden (1983); Lienhard and Van Atta (1990); Fincham et al. (1996) and DNS of Metais and Herring (1989) indicate that, although the vertical component is reduced with respect to the other components, it is only after a very long time that the state is close to the two-dimensional (more accurately two-component) limit of horizontal turbulence. In the case of uniform vertical shear, the laboratory studies of Rohr et al. (1988) and DNS of Gerz et al. (1989); Holt et al. (1992); Jacobitz and Sarkar (1997) indicate that the two-component limit is not reached. The results of Itsweire et al. (1993) find significant deviation of small-scale isotropy due to stratification. Laboratory investigations of wakes by Chomaz et al. (1993); Spedding et al. (1996) and jets by Voropayev et al. (1991) show the formation of predominantly horizontal eddying motion. The studies of Fincham et al. (1996); Spedding et al. (1996) suggest that the vertical variability of the collapsed horizontal structures lead to dominant velocity gradients in the vertical direction.

1245

3 The governing equations

The density, ρ, the velocity, u_i, and the pressure, p, denote fluctuations with respect to the mean density $\bar{\rho}$, the mean velocity $\bar{U}_i$, and the mean pressure $\bar{p}$. The uniform mean density gradient, $\partial\bar{\rho}/\partial x_3 = S_\rho$, imposes a stable stratification which is hydrostatically balanced by a corresponding mean pressure gradient. Uniform mean shear, $\partial\bar{U}_1/\partial x_3 = S_v$ or $\partial\bar{U}_1/\partial x_2 = S_h$, provides the forcing for turbulence. The effect of rotation is neglected since, for the scales considered here, the Rossby number $Ro >> O(1)$.

After the customary Boussinesq assumption, the equations governing the evolution of the fluctuating variables are as follows,

$$\frac{\partial u_i}{\partial x_i} = 0 \tag{1}$$

$$\frac{Du_1}{Dt} + u_j\frac{\partial u_1}{\partial x_j} = -S_v u_3 - S_h u_2 - \frac{1}{\rho_0}\frac{\partial p}{\partial x_1} + \nu\frac{\partial^2 u_1}{\partial x_j \partial x_j} \tag{2}$$

$$\frac{Du_2}{Dt} + u_j\frac{\partial u_2}{\partial x_j} = -\frac{1}{\rho_0}\frac{\partial p}{\partial x_2} + \nu\frac{\partial^2 u_2}{\partial x_j \partial x_j} \tag{3}$$

$$\frac{Du_3}{Dt} + u_j\frac{\partial u_3}{\partial x_j} = -g\frac{\rho}{\rho_0} - \frac{1}{\rho_0}\frac{\partial p}{\partial x_3} + \nu\frac{\partial^2 u_3}{\partial x_j \partial x_j} \tag{4}$$

$$\frac{D\rho}{Dt} + u_j\frac{\partial \rho}{\partial x_j} = -S_\rho u_3 + \alpha\frac{\partial^2 \rho}{\partial x_j \partial x_j} \tag{5}$$

where ν and α are molecular transport coefficients. Examination of Eqs. (1)-(5) shows a highly anisotropic structure. Mean shear directly forces only the streamwise velocity while the other velocity components are forced by the fluctuating pressure gradient. Gravity and density fluctuations directly influence only the vertical component, u_3. The mean density gradient appears only in the density fluctuation equation and not the mean momentum equation.

In the absence of stratification, all three components of the fluctuating velocity in a shear flow are experimentally observed to have comparable magnitudes with the following ordering: streamwise > spanwise > cross-stream. In the case of uniform vertical shear, equilibrium values of the energy partition into the three components that are experimentally measured when $Ri_g = 0$ are:

$$\overline{u_1^2}/2K = 0.53 \quad , \quad \overline{u_2^2}/2K = 0.27 \quad , \quad \overline{u_3^2}/2K = 0.20\,. \tag{6}$$

Despite the fact that mean shear forces only a single velocity component, the other two velocities are induced to have comparable magnitudes by the fluctuating pressure gradient since the fluctuating pressure is linked to *all* velocity components by the following Poisson equation,

$$\frac{\nabla^2 p}{\rho_0} = -2S_v\frac{\partial u_3}{\partial x_1} - \frac{\partial u_j}{\partial x_i}\frac{\partial u_i}{\partial x_j} + \frac{g}{\rho_0}\frac{\partial \rho}{\partial x_3} \tag{7}$$

The buoyancy term in the momentum equation introduces an additional nondimensional parameter into the problem. If the density fluctuation is estimated by $\rho \simeq (\partial\bar{\rho}/\partial x_3)l_3$ where l_3 is the appropriate vertical length scale, then the the turbulent Froude number,

$$Fr_t = u'/Nl_3 \tag{8}$$

appears naturally as the relevant parameter because the ratio of the two terms that cause vertical motion, the pressure gradient and buoyant acceleration, is $O(Fr_t^2)$. Buoyancy effects are important when $Fr_t \leq O(1)$.

Here, $N = \sqrt{-gS_\rho/\rho_0}$ is the Brunt-Vaisala frequency while the superscript $'$ denotes the characteristic scale for a fluctuation, for example, u' is a typical magnitude of velocity perturbation. In the case of sheared turbulence, the gradient Richardson number, $Ri_g = N^2/S^2$, is a convenient choice for parametric studies because it quantifies the ratio of mean buoyant forcing to mean shear forcing. Setting aside the issue of convenience, it should be emphasized that it is the Froude number, Fr_t, which fundamentally determines the dynamical coupling between stratification and fluctuating motion.

4 DNS results on the velocity anisotropy

It is clear that the vertical component of turbulence is suppressed with increasing stable stratification since turbulence has to do work against gravity. This gravity-induced reduction of vertical motion eventually leads to global suppression of turbulence in stratified shear flow. For example, in the DNS cases to be considered here, the turbulent kinetic energy, K, decays when $Ri_{g,cr} \simeq 0.18$ is exceeded in vertical shear flow and $Ri_{g,cr} \simeq 1.5$ is exceeded in horizontal shear flow. Reduction of the vertical component is often thought to imply that turbulence tends to the two-component limit with the vertical velocity fluctuation much smaller than the horizontal velocity fluctuations. Fig. 1(a) shows the evolution of vertical energy partition $\overline{u_3^2}/2K$

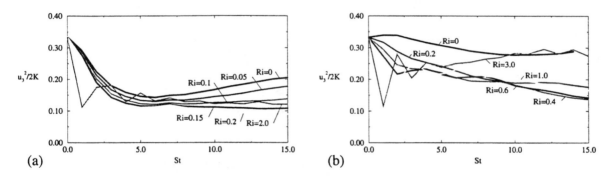

Figure 1: Evolution of the vertical energy partition $\overline{u_3^2}/2K$ as a function of the gradient Richardson number Ri in (a) vertical shear flow and (b) horizontal shear flow.

in vertical shear flow. In the case with $Ri_g = 0$, after an initial transient, the experimentally observed value shown in Eq. (6) is asymptotically approached. The vertical energy partition decreases somewhat with increasing Richardson number. However, the two-component limit is certainly not reached. Fig. 1(b) shows that, in horizontal shear flow too, the turbulence does not reach a two-component state.

5 Theoretical scalings applicable to the velocity components

In order to understand our results, we reconsider the governing equations to derive simple order-of-magnitude estimates applicable when buoyancy substantially effects the state of fluctuating motion. If the other term in Eq. (4) that balances buoyancy is the unsteady term then,

$$\frac{u_3'}{\tau_3} = O(g\frac{\rho'}{\rho_0}), \tag{9}$$

where τ_3 is the characteristic time scale. Similarly, if the unsteady term balances the forcing by mean density gradient in Eq. (5) then,

$$\frac{\rho'}{\tau_3} = O(u_3'S_\rho) \tag{10}$$

Multiplying Eq. (9) and Eq. (10) leads to the following relation for the time scale, $\tau_3 = 1/N$. The magnitude of u_3 is set by the fluctuating pressure gradient in the vertical momentum balance and, estimating the pressure by $p = O(\rho_0 u'^2)$, leads to $u_3'/u' = O(Fr_t)$. Recall that the Froude number, Fr_t, is defined by Eq. (8). The nonlinear terms do not invalidate these scalings as long as they are of the same or lesser order as the unsteady term. Thus, the vertical velocity has a characteristic time scale, N, imposed by stratification. The streamwise velocity fluctuation on the other hand, has a characteristic time scale, $1/S$, imposed by the mean shear. It should be noted that the fluctuating pressure gradient couples the vertical and horizontal motions by imposing the time scale, $1/S$, on u_3 and, similarly, $1/N$ on u_1 and u_2. It can be anticipated that with increasing values of $Ri_g = N^2/S^2$, the vertical shear-induced correlation between u_1 and u_3 as well as the horizontal shear-induced correlation between u_1 and u_2 is hampered because of the increasing disparity between the characteristic time scales, $1/S$ and $1/N$. The reduction in shear stress, $\overline{u_1 u_3}$ and $\overline{u_1 u_2}$, and associated production of turbulent kinetic energy, K, leads to eventual decay of velocity fluctuations for sufficiently large stratification. Indeed, the direct cause of turbulence decay in a stratified medium is the reduced production and not the buoyancy flux. In summary, the regime of stratified sheared turbulence which occurs when $Fr_t \leq O(1)$ and *all* terms (except the viscous term) are of the same order in the vertical momentum equation, is characterized by the following scalings for the fluctuating variables:

$$\frac{u_3'}{u_1'} = O(Fr_t) \quad , \quad \frac{\rho'}{\rho_0} = \frac{u'^2}{gl_3} \quad , \quad N\tau_3 = O(1) . \tag{11}$$

It is emphasized that although the motion described by Eq. (11) has a characteristic time scale, $O(1/N)$ for the vertical velocity, this mode does *not* necessarily represent a propagating linear internal wave.

In the preceding arguments, the assumption that the unsteady term balances the buoyancy term in Eq. (4) leads to the constraint that $\tau_3 = O(1/N)$. A plausible alternative is to fix the time scale, τ, in all equations to be the horizontal advection time scale, l_1/u_1'. Furthermore, if $Fr_t << 1$, the dominant balance in the u_3 equation *must* be between the fluctuating pressure gradient and the buoyancy term with the unsteady term being of higher order. As shown by Riley and Lelong (2000), such a balance leads to the potential vorticity mode characterized by

$$\frac{l_3}{l_1} = O(\alpha) \quad , \quad \frac{u_3'}{u_1'} = O(\alpha Fr_t^2) \quad , \quad \frac{\rho'}{\rho_0} = O(\frac{u'^2}{gl_3}) . \tag{12}$$

According to both Eq. (11) and Eq. (12), the fluctuating velocity approaches the two-component limit, $u_3'/u_1' \to 0$, *assuming* $Fr_t \to 0$ with increasing stratification.

6   The turbulent Froude number

Since the relative magnitude of vertical and horizontal components is controlled by the turbulent Froude number, it is of interest to obtain the evolution of Froude number from our DNS. It is found that Fr_t asymptotically reaches a constant in the simulations. The dependence of the asymptotic value of the vertical Froude number, $Fr_w = w'/NL_e$ on the gradient Richardson number is given in Fig. 2. Here w' is the r.m.s vertical velocity fluctuation while $L_e = \rho_{\text{rms}}/(d\bar{\rho}/dx_3)$ is the Ellison scale. The most striking aspect of Fig. 2 is that, after a rapid initial decrease, the Froude number becomes relatively *independent* of Ri_g with $Fr_w \simeq 0.6$ in vertical shear flow and $Fr_w \simeq 0.75$ in horizontal shear flow. There appears to be no tendency for $Fr \to 0$ explaining our DNS result that the fluctuating motion does not approach the two-component limit even for large values of Ri_g corresponding to strongly-decaying turbulence. Why does the turbulent Froude number not approach zero with increasing values of N? The unsteady term and the shear-forcing term must be of the same order in the streamwise momentum balance, Eq. (2), giving,

$$\frac{u_3}{u_1} = O(\frac{1}{S\tau_1}) \tag{13}$$

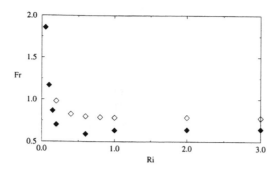

Figure 2: The variation of Fr_t as a function of gradient Richardson number in vertical shear flow (filled symbols) and horizontal shear flow (unfilled symbols).

The l.h.s of Eq. (13) was derived to be $O(Fr_t)$ and, since u_1 is forced by the mean shear, the r.h.s. is $O(1)$. Thus,

$$Fr_t = O(1).\tag{14}$$

7 Anisotropy of the velocity gradient

Stratification imposes anisotropy on the velocity gradients and, consequently, the turbulent dissipation. In the following, the relative contribution of the nine components $\epsilon_{\alpha\beta}$ to the total value ϵ is considered:

$$\epsilon_{\alpha\beta} = \nu\overline{\frac{\partial u_\alpha}{\partial x_\beta}\frac{\partial u_\alpha}{\partial x_\beta}}\tag{15}$$

Note that there is no summation over any Greek index. Table 1 shows the relative contributions for zero and large values of Ri_g. In the unstratified case with $Ri_g = 0$, the largest gradient corresponds to the shearing direction, the 1-2 component in horizontal shear flow and the 1-3 component in vertical shear flow. However, for large Ri_g, the 1-3 component, which is the vertical gradient of the streamwise fluctuation, dominates all other components. This observation is similar to the recent experimental observations in stratified wakes and grid turbulence.

(a)

$Ri_g = 0.00$	$\alpha = 1$	$\alpha = 2$	$\alpha = 3$
$\beta = 1$	0.045	0.049	0.068
$\beta = 2$	0.218	0.060	0.190
$\beta = 3$	0.186	0.116	0.069

$Ri_g = 3.00$	$\alpha = 1$	$\alpha = 2$	$\alpha = 3$
$\beta = 1$	0.005	0.003	0.009
$\beta = 2$	0.099	0.058	0.271
$\beta = 3$	0.414	0.078	0.062

(b)

$Ri_g = 0.00$	$\alpha = 1$	$\alpha = 2$	$\alpha = 3$
$\beta = 1$	0.045	0.065	0.045
$\beta = 2$	0.193	0.069	0.113
$\beta = 3$	0.219	0.192	0.060

$Ri_g = 2.00$	$\alpha = 1$	$\alpha = 2$	$\alpha = 3$
$\beta = 1$	0.009	0.007	0.001
$\beta = 2$	0.087	0.021	0.023
$\beta = 3$	0.470	0.361	0.020

Table 1: Contribution of the component $\epsilon_{\alpha\beta}$ to the dissipation rate ϵ at $St = 11$ in the (a) horizontally sheared flow, and (b) vertically sheared flow.

8 Conclusions

In the case of uniformly sheared flow with either horizontal ($d\overline{U}/dy$) or vertical ($d\overline{U}/dz$) shear, horizontal and vertical velocity fluctuations are found to remain coupled over the range of Richardson numbers, $0 < Ri_g < 3$, studied here. As a consequence of the coupling, first, horizontal mean shear induces vertical mixing, second, the vertical mixing is larger when the mean shear is horizontal instead of vertical since the turbulent production in that case is not directly inhibited by gravity, and, third, the suppression of vertical fluctuations eventually leads to the overall decay of all velocity fluctuations for sufficiently large values of Ri_g. The anisotropy of fluctuating gradients is also found to be affected by stratification. At high Ri_g, in both horizontal and vertically sheared flows, the component, $\partial u_1/\partial x_3$, dominates, while the streamwise gradients, $\partial u_i/\partial x_1$, becomes small.

The turbulent Froude number, Fr_t, is found to approach a $O(1)$ constant at high values of Ri. Thus, the limit of two-component turbulence which requires asymptotically small Froude number is *not* approached in the case of turbulence forced by uniform shear. There are other counter-examples such as the far-wake and horizontal jet where Fr_t progressively decreases. In such situations the two-component limit may be approached. In geophysical flows with a variety of mechanisms available for forcing fluctuating motion, both three-dimensional and two-dimensional turbulence are potentially realizable in a stratified medium with the former responsible for most of the energetic vertical mixing.

Acknowledgements

The support of NSF grant OCE-9818912 is acknowledged. The simulations were performed by Dr. F. Jacobitz while at UCSD.

References

J. M. Chomaz, P. Bonneton, A. Butet and E. J. Hopfinger, *Phys. Fluids*, **11**, 2799-2806 (1993).

E. A. D'Asaro and R.-C. Lien, *J. Phys. Oceanogr.*, **30**, 641-655 (2000).

A. M. Fincham, T. Maxworthy, G. R. Spedding, *Dyn. Atmos. Oceans*, **23**, 155-169 (1996).

T. Gerz, U. Schumann, and S. E. Elghobashi, *J. Fluid Mech.*, **200**, 563-594 (1989).

C. H. Gibson, *J. Geophys. Res.*, **92**, 5383-5404 (1987).

M. C. Gregg, *J. Geophys. Res.*, **94**, 9686-9698 (1989).

S. E. Holt, J. R. Koseff, and J. H. Ferziger, *J. Fluid Mech.*, **237**, 499-539 (1992).

E. C. Itsweire, J. R. Koseff, D. A. Briggs, *J. Phys. Oceanogr.*, **23**, 1508-1522 (1993).

F. G. Jacobitz, S. Sarkar, and C. W. Van Atta, *J. Fluid Mech* **342**, 231-261 (1997).

F. G. Jacobitz and S. Sarkar, *Phys. Fluids*, **10**, No. 5, 1158-1168 (1998).

F. G. Jacobitz and S. Sarkar, *Flow, Turbulence and Combustion*, in press (2000).

J. K. Lienhard and C. W. Van Atta, *J. Fluid Mech.*, **210**, 57-112 (1990).

O. Metais and J. R. Herring, *J. Fluid Mech.*, **202**, 117-148 (1989).

P. Müller, R. C. Lien and R. Williams, *J. Phys. Ocean.*, **18**, 401-416 (1988).

H. J. Pearson and P. F. Linden, *J. Fluid Mech.*, **134**, 195-204 (1983).

J. J. Riley, R. W. Metcalfe, and M. A. Weissman, In *Nonlinear Properties of Internal Waves*, ed. B. J. West, 79-112, AIP (1981).

J. J. Riley amd M. P. Lelong, *Ann. Rev. Fluid Mech.*, **32** 613-657 (2000).

J. J. Rohr, E. C. Itsweire, K. N. Helland, and C. W. Van Atta, *J. Fluid Mech.*, **195**, 77-111 (1988).

G. R. Spedding, F. K. Browand, and A. M. Fincham, *J. Fluid Mech.*, **314**, 53-103 (1996).

S.I. Vorpayev, Y. D. Afansyev, and I. A. Filippov, *J. Fluid Mech.*, **227**, 543-566 (1991).

The efficiency of mixing in sheared, stratified turbulence: inferences from direct simulations and oceanographic observations

W.D. Smyth, J.N. Moum and D.R. Caldwell
College of Oceanic and Atmospheric Sciences
Oregon State University, Corvallis OR 97331-5503
smyth@oce.orst.edu, moum@oce.orst.edu, caldwell@oce.orst.edu

1. Abstract

We investigate the time evolution of mixing in turbulent overturns, using a combination of direct numerical simulations (DNS) and microstructure profiles obtained during two field experiments. Our focus is on the flux coefficient Γ, the ratio of the rate of working against gravity by turbulence to the kinetic energy dissipation rate ϵ. In observational oceanography, a constant value $\Gamma = 0.2$ is often used to infer the buoyancy flux and the turbulent diffusivity from measured ϵ. Both simulations and observations indicate that Γ varies systematically in time, decreasing by an order of magnitude or more over the life of a turbulent overturn. The results suggest useful parameterizations for both Γ and turbulence age in terms of the ratio of Ozmidov scale to Thorpe scale.

2. Introduction

In this paper, we investigate the efficiency of mixing by turbulent overturns in the ocean thermocline. In particular, we are interested in variations of the flux coefficient, Γ, in time over the life cycle of a turbulent event. (The flux coefficient is closely related to mixing efficiency: it is the ratio of work done against gravity to energy dissipated via friction.) Our approach employs a combination of microstructure observations and direct numerical simulations.

In oceanic applications, Γ is often treated as a constant, usually with the value 0.2, and used to estimate heat and salt fluxes from measurements of the kinetic energy dissipation rate, ϵ (e.g. Smyth et al., 1996). However, an accumulation of observational evidence suggests that Γ is, in fact, significantly variable (Gargett and Moum, 1995; Moum, 1996a; Ruddick et al., 1997). Here, we investigate the possibility that Γ evolves systematically in time as turbulent overturns grow, break and decay.

We investigate the time-dependence of Γ using two very different approaches: direct numerical simulations (DNS) and field observations of turbulent microstructure. These two methods were chosen because their respective strengths and weaknesses are complementary. The time dependence of Γ is easy to assess in DNS output, but the validity of DNS as a model of ocean turbulence is limited to low Reynolds number and specified initial and boundary conditions. In contrast, microstructure measurements sample genuine ocean turbulence, but neither Γ nor time (relative to onset) can be measured directly. These limitations of the observational data can be circumvented by means of two assumptions:

1. The ratio of the Ozmidov to the Thorpe length scale, $R_{OT} = L_O/L_T$, varies monotonically in time and can therefore be used to indicate the evolutionary stage of an observed overturn (e.g. Wijesekera and Dillon, 1997).

2. Γ can be approximated by $\Gamma_d = \kappa C N^2/\epsilon$, where κ is the scalar diffusivity, C is the Cox number (to be defined later) and N is the Brunt-Vaisala frequency (Osborn and Cox, 1972; Oakey, 1982).

Insofar as assumptions (1) and (2) are valid, the time dependence of Γ can be assessed using observational data. Here, DNS results will be used to examine the time dependence of Γ directly, and also to test assumptions (1) and (2) above. Having established the range of validity of these assumptions, we then proceed to examine the relationship between Γ_d and R_{OT} in the observational data.

DNS and observational methods are described in section 3. In section 4, we describe mixing in the simulated flows. Preturbulent overturns are shown to mix very efficiently, to the extent that a substantial fraction of the net mixing occurs before the onset of turbulence. As turbulence begins to decay, the flux coefficient asymptotes to 0.2. We then ask whether or not the same behaviour is evident in oceanic observations. In sections 5 and 6, we assess the validity of the two assumptions (described above) needed for the interpretation of the observational results. The observed evolution of the flux coefficient is then described in section 7. The results confirm that the flux coefficient decreases dramatically as turbulence evolves. Section 8 summarizes our conclusions.

3. Methodology

3.1 Direct numerical simulations of breaking Kelvin-Helmholtz billows

Our simulations are done in a domain with periodic boundary conditions in the two horizontal dimensions and zero flux conditions at the upper and lower boundaries. The full Navier-Stokes equations are solved, with buoyancy effects represented via the Boussinesq approximation. Spatial derivatives are evaluated using Fourier transforms in the horizontal dimensions, second-order centered differences in the vertical. Time advancement is via a second-order Adams-Bashforth method. Each simulation is initialized with a parallel flow in which shear and stratification are concentrated a horizontal layer surrounding the plane $z = 0$:

$$\tilde{u}(z) = \frac{u_o}{2} \tanh \frac{2z}{h_o}; \qquad \tilde{\theta}(z) = \frac{\theta_o}{2} \tanh \frac{2z}{h_o}, \tag{1}$$

plus a small perturbation to initiate instability. The flow develops a train of Kelvin-Helmholtz billows which subsequently merge and break down into turbulence via a sequence of secondary instabilities. The dimensions of the computational domain are chosen on the basis of linear stability analysis to accommodate two wavelengths of both the primary and the secondary instability.

The constants defining the initial conditions (1) can be combined with the kinematic viscosity $\nu = 1.0 \times 10^{-6} m^2 s^{-1}$, the gravitational acceleration $g = 9.8 m s^{-2}$ and the diffusivity κ to form three dimensionless groups whose values determine the stability of the flow at $t = 0$: the initial Reynolds number $Re_o \equiv u_o h_o / \nu$, the initial bulk Richardson number $Ri_o \equiv g \theta_o h_o / u_o^2$, and the Prandtl number $Pr \equiv \nu / \kappa$. Values of these parameters are given in table 1.

Extensive comparison with oceanographic measurements has shown that, while Reynolds numbers achieved in the simulations are at the small end of the observed range, most other turbulence statistics tested are consistent with observations (Smyth et al., 2000)). These include measures of large eddy geometry, as well as statistics relating background stratification, kinetic energy, and dissipation rates. We conclude that our simulated overturns provide an acceptable model for turbulent events in the thermocline. Further information is given in Smyth (1999) and Smyth and Moum (2000b).

3.2 Observations of turbulent overturns in the ocean thermocline

Two observational datasets are used in the present study. The first was collected during the FLUX STATS experiment (FLX91) in May 1991 off the coast of northern California. Measurements made by the free-falling profiler Chameleon included pressure (depth), temperature, conductivity, temperature-gradient fluctuations using an FP07 microbead thermistor, horizontal velocity-gradient fluctuations using airfoil shear probes, and vertical velocity fluctuations using a Pitot tube (Hebert and Moum, 1994; Moum, 1996a,b). From 400 profiles, 3425 overturns were selected using principles similar to those of Moum (1996b). A second set of 1155 events was selected from the Tropical Instability Wave Experiment (TIWE), conducted at the equator at 140°W in December 1991 (Lien et al., 1995). The overturns were all located in the upper thermocline between 60 and 200m depth, and spanned both the upper and lower flanks of the Equatorial Undercurrent.

Simulation	Pr	Re_o	L_x (m)	L_y (m)	L_z (m)	Δx (10^{-2}m)	h_o (m)	u_o (10^{-3}m/s)	θ_o (10^{-6}K)	Symbol
1	7	1354	2.73	0.34	1.36	0.53	0.20	8.34	2.00	•
2	4	1967	3.29	0.41	1.63	0.64	0.24	10.00	2.41	*
3	1	4978	5.24	0.65	2.62	1.03	0.38	13.27	3.83	○

Table 1: Parameter values describing a sequence of three simulations of breaking Kelvin-Helmholtz billows. L_x, L_y and L_z are the domain dimensions, and Δx ($= \Delta y = \Delta z$) is the grid interval. Initial conditions are characterized by the length scale h_o, the velocity scale u_o and the temperature scale θ_o. Pr is the Prandtl number; Re_o the initial Reynolds numbers. For all simulations, the initial bulk Richardson number was $Ri_o = 0.08$. All simulations described here employed array sizes of $512 \times 64 \times 256$.

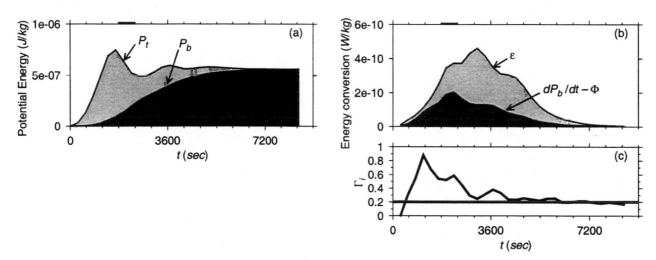

Figure 1: Evolution of various quantities describing work done against gravity for the $Pr = 7$ simulation. (a) The upper (lower) curve denotes the total (background) potential energy. Shaded bars at the tops of (a) and (b) mark the approximate time of the onset of turbulence. (b) Volume-averaged perturbation kinetic energy dissipation rate (upper curve) and rate of irreversible potential energy increase due to fluid motions (lower curve). The latter is dP_b/dt minus Φ, the rate of potential energy increase that would occur in a state of rest. The ratio of the lower to the upper ordinate is Γ_i. (c) Γ_i.

4. Flux coefficient evolution in simulated flows

In figure 1, we show various aspects of potential energy evolution for the case $Pr = 7$. The total potential energy is denoted as P_t, while P_b indicates the background potential energy, i.e. the minimum potential energy achievable via reordering of the density field (Winters et al., 1995). The difference $P_t - P_b$ is the available potential energy. Early in the simulation, most of the work done against gravity is reversible, i.e. it contributes to the available potential energy (figure 1a). The latter grows to a maximum near $t = 1600s$, then decreases rapidly (i.e. the wave breaks). The background potential energy grows monotonically and, ultimately, becomes equal to the total potential energy as vertical motions decay.

In figure 1b, we see that the rate of irreversible work done against gravity peaks quite early in the simulation; in fact, it peaks as the billow is breaking. The dissipation of kinetic energy, in contrast, peaks near $t = 3000s$, after the transition to turbulence is complete. This offset between maximum irreversible work and maximum kinetic energy dissipation leads to large values of the instantaneous flux coefficient, $\Gamma_i = (dP_b/dt - \Phi)/\epsilon$, early in the simulation (figure 1c). This highly efficient mixing occurs in the braids connecting adjacent Kelvin-Helmholtz billows. After the onset of turbulence, Γ_i decreases and appears to asymptote to the canonical value 0.2.

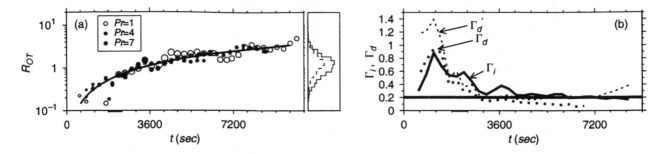

Figure 2: (a) Evolution of the ratio of the Ozmidov scale to the Thorpe scale. At selected times during each simulation, 512 vertical profiles were taken through the simulated flowfields and analyzed as if they were microstructure profiles (Moum, 1996b; Smyth et al., 2000). Each plotted symbol represents the median of R_{OT} obtained from a particular simulation at a particular time. The shaded bar at the top marks the approximate location of the transition to turbulence. The solid curve represents (2). The histograms at the right represent the probability distributions of R_{OT} in the two observational datasets: TIWE (solid) and FLX91 (dashed). (b) Comparison of the instantaneous flux coefficient Γ_i and its approximation Γ_d for simulation 1. Thick, solid curves: Γ_i. Thin dashed curves: Γ'_d, computed using the unaltered ϵ field. Thick dashed curves: Γ_d computed after applying noise field and ϵ threshold to DNS profiles. The horizontal line indicates the standard value 0.2. Shaded bars mark the approximate time of the transition to turbulence.

5. R_{OT} as an indicator of turbulence age

In figure 2a, we demonstrate that R_{OT} represents an effective clock for turbulent events (assumption #1 in the Introduction), using the DNS database. Young, preturbulent overturns are characterized by $R_{OT} < 1/2$. Shortly after transition, the ratio increases to order unity. As turbulence decays, R_{OT} increases further to values substantially greater than 1. These results are entirely consistent with the conclusions of Wijesekera and Dillon (1997), which were derived from observational data by using entropy as a time measure. A convenient alternative expression of the time dependence shown in figure 2a is given by

$$t_N \equiv \int_{t_o}^{t} \frac{\hat{N}(t')}{2\pi} dt' = 0.2 + 3.2 \log_{10} R_{OT} \pm 0.5, \tag{2}$$

which produces an estimate of the time, in buoyancy periods, since the maximum R_b was reached (at t_o, shortly after the transition to turbulence). The estimate is also valid when $t_N < 0$, i.e. for preturbulent overturns. The error estimate 0.5 pertains to the DNS case #1 ($Pr = 7$). The uncertainty will be larger if this formula is applied in more general situations.

6. Γ_d as a surrogate for the flux coefficient

We now test the second of the two assumptions described in section 2. This requires assessing the usefulness of Γ_d as a surrogate for Γ_i. For this calculation, the DNS data is altered in two ways to facilitate comparison with observational results: a weak, random noise field is added to ϵ, and profiles for which $\epsilon < 4 \times 10^{-10} m^2 s^{-2}$ are discarded. The flux coefficient is then computed as $\Gamma_d = \kappa C N^2 / \epsilon$. The evolution of Γ_d is shown in figure 2b. To assess the effect of noise, we also show Γ'_d, which is calculated from the untreated ϵ fields. Γ'_d and Γ_i follow similar evolutionary patterns, the main differences being $\Gamma'_d > \Gamma_i$ during the preturbulent phase and the tendency of Γ'_d to increase during the final stages of turbulence decay. The large discrepancy found in the preturbulent phase is not surprising, as the assumptions inherent in the Osborn-Cox formulation are invalid during this phase. The increase observed late in the simulation is related to the inaccuracy of the isotropic approximation of ϵ in this very weak turbulence (Smyth and Moum, 2000a). Nevertheless, the correspondence is reasonable while turbulence is strong, and even prior to transition Γ_d gives a qualitative indication of the large flux coefficient that characterizes that early phase.

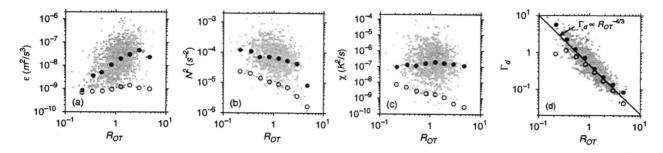

Figure 3: Γ_d and related quantities as functions of the length scale ratio $R_{OT} = L_O/L_T$, for turbulent overturns observed in TIWE and FLX91. (a) Volume-averaged perturbation kinetic energy dissipation rate. (b) Squared Brunt-Vaisala frequency. (c) Temperature variance dissipation rate. (d) Γ_d. The ordinate is interpreted as a surrogate for time. Shaded circles represent individual turbulent events from TIWE. Symbols represent bin averages taken over appropriate ranges of R_{OT}. Open circles (bullets) correspond to the FLX91 (TIWE) cruise.

Both the addition of the noise field and the acceptance criterion result in larger mean values of ϵ, and thus values of Γ_d that are smaller than Γ_d'. The result is improved agreement with Γ_i in the preturbulent phase, although this improvement is unrelated to the flow physics. After transition, the increase in apparent dissipation rates leads to underestimates of Γ_i. Unlike both Γ_i and Γ_d', Γ_d does not asymptote to 0.2, but rather continues to decrease. We will see that this behavior is evident in the observational data also.

7. "Evolution" of Γ_d in observations

We have now assessed the validity of the two assumptions needed in the interpretation of the observational data. Accordingly, we next examine the relationship between Γ_d and R_{OT} in the microstructure data, interpreting the results in terms of the time evolution of the flux coefficient. The plotted points in figure 3 represent bin averages of the TIWE and FLX91 data with respect to R_{OT}. In the background, we show the individual events from which the bin averages were derived (for clarity, individual observations are shown for TIWE only).

For each dataset, the "evolution" shown in figure 3 corresponds qualitatively to our expectations. The TIWE results are generally more energetic than their counterparts from FLX91, mainly because of the strong background shear of the Equatorial Undercurrent. In each case, the dissipation rate ϵ grows initially, then decays. The bulk stratification N^2 decreases monotonically, as one would expect in an entraining turbulent layer. The scalar variance dissipation rate χ remains approximately constant in time for the TIWE data, while decreasing for the FLX91 data. This is consistent with our finding that preturbulent overturns generate strong temperature gradients and thus large χ (Smyth et al., 2000).

Unlike the quantities discussed previously, Γ_d shows considerable uniformity between the TIWE and FLX91 cases. In each case, Γ_d decreases monotonically over most of the evolution. Results for early times are likely to be influenced by the nonstationarity and inhomogeneity, both of which degrade the validity of the Osborn-Cox formulation. There is no indication of the asymptotic approach to a value near 0.2 as seen in figure 2b. Instead, the evolution of Γ_d exhibits an approximate power law behavior, with slope near -4/3, in both the FLX91 and TIWE datasets. This apparent discrepancy at late times is consistent with the result from DNS calculations shown in figure 2b, where we saw how the noise threshold decreases the apparent value of Γ_d when turbulence is weak.

8. Conclusions

We have employed a combination of numerical and observational methods to investigate mixing as it evolves over the lifetime of a turbulent overturn. The DNS data enable us to test assumptions that are needed for the interpretation of the observations, while the observational data allow access to realistic parameter regimes that present-day computers cannot simulate. First, we assessed the dependence of Γ_i on time in the simulated flows. Second we used the simulated flows to test the usefulness of R_{OT} as a surrogate for time, and of Γ_d as a surrogate for Γ_i (assumptions 1 and 2 of the Introduction). Based on these results, we examined the dependence of Γ_d on R_{OT} using the observational data, and compared the results with expectations based on the time dependence of Γ_i in the simulations.

The result of these analyses is a self consistent picture, supported by both model and observations, in which the flux coefficient decreases dramatically over the lifetime of a turbulent overturn. For application to observations, this evolution may be parameterized as $\Gamma_i = 0.33 R_{OT}^{-0.63}$ (Smyth et al., 2000). The preturbulent phase (in which mixing is highly efficient) may be of secondary importance in circumstances where turbulence persists over long times, such as the Equatorial Undercurrent. In other cases, however, turbulence-driving shear is likely to be more intermittent, with the result that the initial stage of billow development contributes a more significant fraction of the net mixing.

Acknowledgements: This research was funded by the National Science Foundation. Computations were performed at Oregon State University's Environmental Computing Center.

References

Gargett, A. and J. Moum, 1995: Mixing efficiencies in turbulent tidal fronts: results from direct and indirect measurements of density flux. *J. Phys. Oceanogr.*, **25**, 2583–2608.

Hebert, D. and J. Moum, 1994: Decay of a near-inertial wave. *J. Phys. Oceanogr.*, **24**, 2334–2351.

Lien, R.-C., D. Caldwell, M. Gregg, and J. Moum, 1995: Turbulence variability at the equator in the central pacific at the beginning of the 1991-1993 El Nino. *J. Geophys. Res.*, **100**(C4), 6881–6898.

Moum, J., 1996a: Efficiency of mixing in the main thermocline. *J. Geophys. Res.*, **101**(C5), 12,057–12,069.

Moum, J., 1996b: Energy-containing scales of turbulence in the ocean thermocline. *J. Geophys. Res.*, **101**(C6), 14095–14109.

Oakey, N., 1982: Determination of the rate of dissipation of turbulent energy from simultaneous temperature and velocity shear microstructure measurements. *J. Phys. Oceanogr.*, **12**, 256–271.

Osborn, T. R. and C. S. Cox, 1972: Oceanic fine structure. *Geophys. Fluid Dyn.*, **3**, 321–345.

Ruddick, B., D. Walsh, and N. Oakey, 1997: Variations in apparent mixing efficiency in the North Atlantic Central Water. *J. Phys. Oceanogr.*, **27**, 2589–2605.

Smyth, W., 1999: Dissipation range geometry and scalar spectra in sheared, stratified turbulence. *J. Fluid Mech.*, **401**, 209–242.

Smyth, W., D. Hebert, and J. Moum, 1996: Local ocean response to a multiphase westerly windburst. part 2: Thermal and freshwater responses. *J. Geophys. Res.*, **101**, 22495–22512.

Smyth, W. and J. Moum, 2000a: Anisotropy of turbulence in stably stratified mixing layers. *Phys. Fluids*, (in press).

Smyth, W. and J. Moum, 2000b: Length scales of turbulence in stably stratified mixing layers. *Phys. Fluids*, (in press).

Smyth, W., J. Moum, and D. Caldwell, 2000: The efficiency of mixing in turbulent patches: inferences from direct simulations and microstructure observations. *J. Phys. Oceanogr.*, (submitted).

Wijesekera, H. and T. Dillon, 1997: Shannon entropy as an indicator of age for turbulent overturns in the oceanic thermocline. *J. Geophys. Res.*, **102**(C2), 3279–3291.

Winters, K., P. Lombard, J. Riley, and E. A. D'Asaro, 1995: Available potential energy and mixing in density-stratified fluids. *J. Fluid Mech.*, **289**, 115–128.

Mixing in a stably stratified shear layer: two- and three-dimensional numerical experiments.

C. Staquet

LEGI, B.P. 53, 38041 Grenoble Cédex 9 France

Chantal.Staquet@hmg.inpg.fr

Abstract

A direct method for analyzing diapycnal mixing in a stably stratified fluid (Winters *et al.*, 1995) has been applied to the stably stratified shear layer. The diapycnal flux and mixing efficiency are computed as functions of time, whatever the turbulent activity in the fluid. The mixing properties of two-dimensional and three-dimensional numerical simulations of the Boussinesq equations are analysed and compared. The interest of the former simulations is to enlight the fundamental role of three-dimensional effects in fluid mixing and to quantify it. We focus on the influence of stratification (measured by the minimum Richardson number J) and changes in Prandtl number on the overall mixing that occurs as the computed flows evolve from unstable initial conditions.

In three dimensions, the flow dynamics exhibits three successive stages, each with different mixing properties. During the first stage, a primarily two-dimensional Kelvin-Helmholtz instability develops and the mixing efficiency is high (the flux Richardson number Rf_b ranges between 0.37 and 0.68, decreasing as J increases). The second stage is characterized by the development of small scale three-dimensional instabilities. These motions result in significantly higher diapycnal flux than during the first stage but in only moderate mixing efficiency ($R_f \simeq 0.32$), as the rate of kinetic energy dissipation is also high during this stage. Finally, the turbulent activity is progressively expulsed toward the outer regions of the shear layer and decays in time while the central region relaminarizes. During this final stage, R_f approaches an asymptotic value close to 0.25 and the diapycnal diffusivity displays a clear functional dependence on the gradient Richardson number Ri_b of the form Ri_b^{-2}.

As expected, the two-dimensional flows are unable to reproduce the mixing properties of the flow, except during the first stage. During the subsequent turbulent regime, both the diapycnal flux and the dissipation rate of kinetic energy are too small (because, for the latter quantity, of the nonlinear enstrophy conservation constraint). The final stage consists in a quasi-stationary weakly turbulent regime, for which the diapycnal diffusivity behaves as Ri_b^{-1}. It should be noted that, despite these differences, R_f relaxes toward the 0.25 value found in three dimensions.

Evolution of vertically (or horizontally) sheared grid turbulence in density stratified flow

Edward J. Stewart and Pablo Huq[†]

College of Marine Studies, University of Delaware, Newark, DE, USA 19711
[†]huq@udel.edu

1. Introduction

The goal of this paper is to report the effect of shear, and the direction of shear, on rates of vertical buoyancy flux in stably stratified grid-generated turbulence. Results from an experimental study of turbulent, density stratified, sheared flow are presented. The flow field is a combination of decaying grid-generated turbulence, stable density stratification, and shear production of turbulence. Turbulent mixing is at the heart of many industrial processes. For example, rapid mixing is essential in the chemical engineering industry to optimize yields from reacting chemicals. Density stratification is common in the ocean and atmosphere. Variations in temperature and salinity in the ocean, and temperature and humidity in the atmosphere, result in density gradients. Stable stratification influences the dynamics as a kinetic energy sink because energy is sapped by work against gravity. Thus, turbulent mixing rates in a density-stratified fluid can be severely attenuated relative to the case without density stratification. Velocity shear, common in the environment, is a source of energy, and therefore turbulent mixing rates are greater when shear is present. However, turbulent mixing rates depend on the relative strengths of shear and density stratification, and on initial conditions as expressed by the ratio of turbulent potential to vertical kinetic energies.

2. Experiment

Experiments are conducted using a recirculating water channel 400 cm long, 40 cm deep and 25 cm wide with a measurement section 200 cm long. Shear ($S = dU/dx_i$) can be generated efficiently using a mesh of variable density. The mesh can be orientated in both directions across the tank to produce either vertical shear (dU/dz) or horizontal shear (dU/dy) of magnitudes of about 0.25 s^{-1}. For the experiments, values of N (the buoyancy frequency) were up 0.4 s^{-1}, which leads to a large domain space of Nx/U and Sx/U values up to about 8. Here, Nx/U and Sx/U are equal to Nt and St, the dimensionless strain rates used to gauge the importance of stratification and shear. Concentration measurements are made by a conductivity probe with a spatial resolution of 0.04 cm. Velocity measurements are obtained using a hot-film anemometer, and a quartz-coated cylindrical x-probe. The conductivity and hot-film probes can be operated concurrently so as to yield flux measurements.

3. Results

The evolution of the buoyancy flux coefficient $\overline{\rho w}/\rho'w'$ with dimensionless buoyancy strength Nt is presented in Figure 1 for four ranges of the dimensionless shear strength St. Best-fit fourth-order polynomials have been included for each range of St to aid in the recognition of data trends. For data where shear effects are not important, including both the $St < 1.5$ and $1.5 < St < 3.5$ cases, data agree well with previous shear-free studies (e.g., Itsweire et al., 1986; Yoon and Warhaft, 1990; Huq and Britter, 1995). Near the grid when $Nt \approx 0$, the flux coefficient is small and negative. In this region, the velocity field is dominated by the kinetic energy introduced by the turbulence-generating grid located at $x = 0$. Buoyancy effects have yet to become important, and the density field is virtually uncorrelated with the velocity field, hence the small magnitude of buoyancy flux coefficients. A sufficient amount of activity of the density field is required to generate buoyancy flux. The flux is less than zero in this region because one of the effects of the turbulence-generating grid is to stir the initial density and velocity gradients. The effect of this initial perturbation is that a large number of fluid parcels have been displaced from their equilibrium positions, which then eventually migrate back, resulting in some restratification of the flow. This restratification process is manifested in a negative buoyancy flux.

From the initially small value of buoyancy flux for the low shear data, $\overline{\rho w}/\rho'w'$ rises quickly to reach a maximum value of about 0.4 at $Nt \approx 1$. The magnitude of the maximum buoyancy flux coefficient is a function of Schmidt number. That is, for salt-stratified water, the peak should be near 0.4 (Stillinger *et al.*, 1983) and for heat-stratified air, near 0.7 (Sirivat and Warhaft, 1983).

As Nt values increase beyond two, the velocity and scalar fields begin to decouple. A result of the decoupling is the collapse of the mean buoyancy flux coefficient. Physically, the density and velocity fields are both very active; this collapse of the buoyancy flux coefficient is not indicative of the extinction of turbulent motions as has been implied by some studies (Stewart, 1969). The region of flux collapse, instead, is a path to the restratification process indicated by the counter-gradient flux.

For Nt values greater than about 2.5, the data in weakly sheared flow ($St < 3.5$) show substantial counter-gradient buoyancy flux. This is because buoyancy fluctuations are quite large in magnitude and also are not being dissipated sufficiently quickly. Little or no counter-gradient temperature flux is seen in heated air experiments (*e.g.*, Lienhard and Van Atta, 1990; Jayesh *et al.*, 1991) because heat is orders of magnitude easier to dissipate than salt (Schmidt numbers are 7 and 700 for heat and salt, respectively), and there is little need for the conversion of potential energy into kinetic energy to maintain balance in the flow. Gerz *et al.* (1989) use the term "sufficiently large Prandtl numbers" to describe the necessary conditions for counter-gradient buoyancy flux to arise. The sign of the flux term has changed from negative to positive in the turbulent kinetic energy equation and now acts as a source term. After this point ($Nt \approx 2$), the density fluctuations begin to decay slowly. The re-stratified fluid parcels will again attempt to diffuse and smooth the density gradient. The result is a return of the flux coefficient through zero to positive values.

Introducing a mean velocity gradient has a dramatic effect on the evolution of the buoyancy flux coefficient. When the dimensionless shear rate St becomes large, the dominant forcing of the velocity field is no longer the turbulence-generating grid, but the velocity gradient. Shear production can become large enough to change the sign of the rate of change of kinetic energy in the TKE balance. Thus, velocity variances no longer decay in the longitudinal direction, but can remain steady and even increase.

For data with moderately large St values (the triangles in Figure 1, $3.5 < St < 5.0$), the magnitude of the buoyancy flux coefficient remains relatively constant with increasing values of Nt. There is a small amount of variation, shown by the fourth-order polynomial fitted to the data. The line shows an increase in $\overline{\rho w}/\rho'w'$ for small Nt, reaching a maximum of just over 0.2 at about $Nt = 2$, after which the flux decays to a local minimum value of 0.1 at about $Nt = 5$. Finally, the flux coefficient increases again to attain a value of about 0.2 at $Nt = 8.2$. The energy input by this level of shear is evidently sufficient to keep the density field fairly well mixed. For $3.5 < St < 5.0$, the flow appears to be in equilibrium; the effect of shear production is approximately balancing the effect of stratification with the consequence of a nearly constant level of vertical buoyancy flux.

The most strongly sheared data ($St > 5.0$) show a markedly different evolution to that of the previous cases. Increasing from a value of -0.2 at $Nt = 1$, $\overline{\rho w}/\rho'w'$ reaches values of nearly 0.5 at the large values of $Nt = 7$. For this data set, the velocity field is very active and strongly influenced by shear production. For data in the weakly sheared flow, the buoyancy flux maximum is near $Nt = 1$, when the velocity fluctuations induced by the turbulence-generating grid and the density fluctuations are most correlated. In contrast, for strongly sheared flow, the flux coefficient reaches an asymptote at large Nt values near the passive value of the vertical flux coefficient for the salt-stratified flow field, $\overline{\rho w}/\rho'w' \approx 0.45$. These observations imply that the density field must be sufficiently strong to be correlated with the strongly sheared velocity field. For low-St data and $Nt \approx 1$, the motions of the active density field drive the vertical velocity component; however, for the large-St data, with an active density field ($Nt > 3$), the vertical velocity component, which is driven by strong shear, drives the density field. Both of these scenarios, where one field is forcing the other, produce large values of the vertical buoyancy flux coefficient.

Cospectra for several data points are plotted in Figure 2; note the use of log scaling for the x-axis while the ordinate is linear. The magnitude of the mean vertical buoyancy flux coefficient for each of the three lines shown is about 0.3. For $Nt = 1.7$ and 4.3, data are chosen so that shear effects are minimal ($St < 0.5$). For $Nt = 1.7$ the flux value is 0.33, and a negative value (where transport is counter-gradient) of -0.32 exists for $Nt = 4.3$. The cospectrum plot reveals that the largest resolved scales are those that contribute most to the value of the flux coefficient. For wavenumbers larger than $k\eta \approx 1$ (i.e., the smaller scales), there is negligible contribution to the buoyancy flux. For the data with considerable counter-gradient buoyancy flux ($Nt = 4.3$), the cospectrum obtains similar magnitudes as the $Nt = 1.7$ data (and the absolute value of the mean flux is similar), but it is negative for all wavenumbers. Additionally, there is counter-gradient transport at the smaller scales ($0.8 < k\eta < 1.3$).

In general, the effect of shear is to increase the magnitude of the vertical buoyancy flux coefficient for a given value of Nt as has been shown in Figure 1. The result is that no mean counter-gradient flux occurs when St is large and Nt values are greater than unity. The data of Figure 2 for which $Nt = 1.8$ and $St = 5.9$ reveals that at some scales of the flow, however, transport may be counter-gradient. The value of the flux coefficient $\overline{\rho w}/\rho' w'$ is equal to 0.27. This cospectrum reveals that the mean flux can be large and down gradient, but transport is counter gradient at $k\eta = 0.15$. Therefore, even though shear has the effect of increasing the magnitude of the buoyancy flux coefficient and preventing the typical (shear-free) collapse of $\overline{\rho w}/\rho' w'$ at $Nt \approx 3$, some amount of counter-gradient flux is present in the flow.

The vertical buoyancy flux coefficients are presented in Figure 3 for both shear orientations as they evolve with Nt. For the vertically sheared data, understanding of the effect of shear on $\overline{\rho w}/\rho' w'$ could only be made if the data are segregated by the relative effect of shear (i.e., dividing the data into ranges of St, as in Figure 1). In Figure 3 no such segregation is made and $Nt \approx St$ for all data shown. Thus, when $Nt > 3$, shear effects have begun to dominate the flow, so the data shown in Figure 3 is a blending of two trends shown in Figure 1. This blending of trends is emphasized in the figure by using a solid line for the low-St region where stratification effects dominate and a dotted line for the shear-dominated high-St region. The vertical buoyancy flux coefficient in horizontally sheared flow behaves differently. For $Nt < 3$, the data are close to the data from vertically sheared flow, but as Nt increases, the flux coefficient is noticeably lower in magnitude for the data in horizontal shear. For example, at $Nt \approx 5$, the flux coefficient in horizontally sheared flow is about one third the magnitude than in vertically sheared flow. Thus, when shear effects become dominant in the flow field, the vertical buoyancy flux coefficient shows very high values when shear is oriented vertically, but is only about half as large when the shear is orthogonal to the density gradient. This trend is opposite that of Jacobitz et al. (1998) who predict an increase in the vertical flux coefficient when the velocity gradient is orthogonal to the density gradient.

The problem of the evolution of the vertical buoyancy flux coefficient can be examined in the sense of an initial value problem. Specifically, numerical simulations require a value of the flux coefficient at $x = 0$, which is usually either 1 (full correlation between w and ρ) or 0 (no correlation). Often the chosen initial condition is close to 1 (e.g., Gerz and Schumann, 1991; Gerz and Yamazaki, 1993; Hanazaki and Hunt, 1996), and less often, it is near 0 (e.g., Gerz et al., 1989; Jacobitz and Sarkar, 1998). A natural way to consider the initial value problem is in terms of the initial ratio of potential to kinetic energies, as has been done by Holt et al. (1992). Therefore, a natural check on the difference between flux coefficients measured in vertically and horizontally sheared flow noted above in the discussion of Figure 3 is to plot this ratio of energies for the two data sets. The ratio of potential to vertical kinetic energy is plotted in Figure 4 as it evolves in Nt for each data set. The important region to compare on this figure is that indicative of the initial conditions (*i.e.*, low values of *Nt*). In this region, there is a difference of about an order of magnitude between the horizontally and vertically sheared flows. Therefore, the data compared in Figure 3 are not "apples and apples." Instead, the data in horizontally sheared flow initially have much less vertical kinetic energy relative to potential energy in comparison to the data measured in vertical shear. In this case, shear effects will take longer to develop and quantities based on the vertical velocity component should be smaller in general. In the numerical simulations, the initial conditions are set such that the relative magnitudes are the same for both shear orientations. Experimentally, such equal initial conditions are probably not physically realizable. The likely impossibility of physically identical initial conditions in the laboratory must be considered in any meaningful numerical simulations of such a flow field.

4. References

Gerz, T., U. Schumann and S. E. Elghobashi (1989) Direct numerical simulation of stratified homogeneous turbulent shear flows. *J. Fluid Mech.* **200**, 563-594.

Gerz, T. and H. Yamazaki (1993) Direct numerical simulation of buoyancy-driven turbulence in stably stratified fluid. *J. Fluid Mech.* **249**, 415-440.

Hanazaki, H. and J. C. R. Hunt (1996) Linear processes in unsteady stably stratified turbulence. *J. Fluid Mech.* **318**, 303-337.

Holt, S. E., J. R. Koseff and J. H. Ferziger (1992) A numerical study of the evolution and structure of homogeneous stably stratified sheared turbulence. *J. Fluid Mech.* **237**, 499-539.

Huq, P. and R. E. Britter (1995) Turbulence evolution and mixing in a two-layer stably stratified fluid. *J. Fluid Mech.* **285**, 41-67.

Itsweire, E. C., K. N. Helland and C. W. Van Atta (1986) The evolution of grid-generated turbulence in a stably stratified fluid. *J. Fluid Mech.* **162**, 299-338.

Jacobitz, F. G. and S. Sarkar (1997) The effect of nonvertical shear on turbulence in a stably stratified medium. *Phys. Fluids* **10(5)**, 1158-1168.

Jacobitz, F. G, S. Sarkar and C. W. Van Atta (1997) Direct numerical simulations of the turbulence evolution in a uniformly sheared and stably stratified flow. *J. Fluid Mech.* **342**, 231-261.

Jayesh, K. Yoon and Z. Warhaft (1991) Turbulent mixing and transport in a thermally stratified interfacial layer in decaying grid turbulence. *Phys. Fluids A* **3 (5)**, 1143-1155.

Lienhard, J. H. and C. W. Van Atta (1990) The decay of turbulence in thermally stratified flow. *J. Fluid Mech.* **210**, 57-112.

Sirivat, A. and Z. Warhaft (1983) The effect of a passive cross-stream temperature gradient on the evolution of temperature variance and the heat flux in grid turbulence. *J. Fluid Mech.* **128**, 323-346.

Stewart, R. W. (1969) Turbulence and waves in a stratified atmosphere. *Radio Sci.* **4**, 1269-1278.

Schumann, U. and T. Gerz (1995) Turbulent mixing in stably stratified shear flows. *J. Appl. Meteorol.* **34**, 33-48.

Stillinger, D. C., K. N. Helland and C. W. Van Atta (1983) Experiments on the transition of homogeneous turbulence to internal waves in a stratified fluid. *J. Fluid Mech.* **131**, 91-122.

Yoon, K. and Z. Warhaft (1990) The evolution of grid-generated turbulence under conditions of stable thermal stratification. *J. Fluid Mech.* **215**, 601-638.

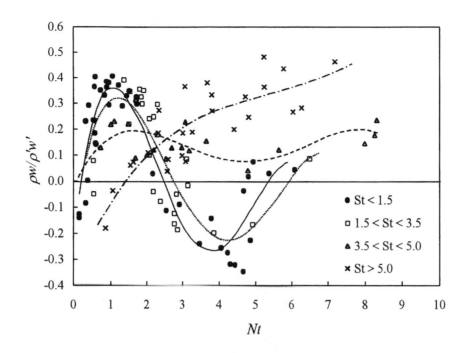

Figure 1: Evolution of the vertical buoyancy flux coefficient with *Nt* for four ranges of *St*. A best-fit fourth-order polynomial is included for each of the *St* ranges. The solid line is for *St* < 1.5; the dotted curve, 1.5 < *St* < 3.5; the dashed curve, 3.5 < *St* < 5.0; and the dash-dot curve, *St* > 5.0.

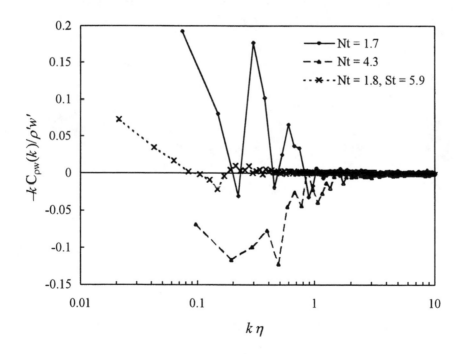

Figure 2: Normalized cospectra for the vertical buoyancy flux against the dimensionless wavenumber. Values of the mean vertical buoyancy flux coefficients are about 0.3 for each data set. The solid and dashed lines are for shear-free flow (*St* < 0.5), and the dotted line is for strongly sheared flow.

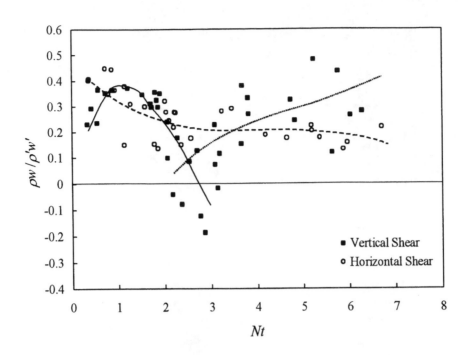

Figure 3: Evolution of the vertical buoyancy flux coefficient with Nt for vertically sheared data and horizontally sheared data. For all data presented, $0.5 < Nt/St < 1.5$, so shear effects increase with increasing Nt. The dashed line is a third-order polynomial to show the trend of data in horizontally sheared flow. The vertically sheared data is of two trends: shear-free (low-St) data (solid line) and strongly sheared (high-St) data (dotted line).

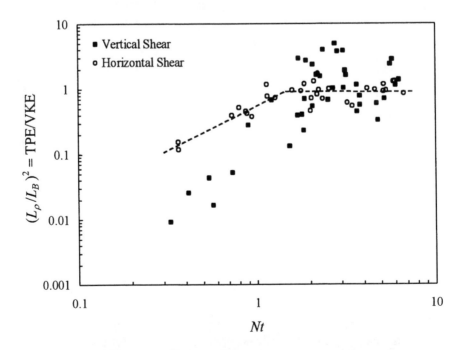

Figure 4: Evolution of the ratio of total potential to vertical kinetic energy with density stratification Nt. (Note that this ratio can be related to the square of ratio of the Ellison lengthscale L_ρ to the buoyancy lengthscale L_B.). The trend for data in horizontally sheared flow is indicated by the dashed lines.

Mixing efficiency in decaying stably stratified turbulence

Derek Stretch[1], Keiko K. Nomura[2], and James W. Rottman[2]

[1]School of Civil Engineering, University of Natal,
Centenary Building, King George V Avenue, Durban, 4041, South Africa
[2]Department of Mechanical and Aerospace Engineering, University of California, San Diego
9500 Gilman Drive, La Jolla, CA 92093-0402, USA
stretchd@eng.nu.ac.za, knomura@mae.ucsd.edu, jrottman@mae.ucsd.edu

1. Introduction

Mixing efficiency in stratified flows is a measure of the proportion of turbulent kinetic energy that goes into increasing the potential energy of the fluid by irreversible mixing. This is an important issue in the parameterization of mixing in geophysical flows. The laboratory experiments of Britter (1985), Rottman & Britter (1986) and Rehmann & Koseff (2000) have attempted to measure the mixing efficiency of grid turbulence in a uniformly stratified fluid. These experiments have been done mostly by towing a grid horizontally through water that has been stratified using either salt or heat. The mixing efficiency in these experiments is measured as a function of the Richardson number $Ri = (NM/U)^2$, in which N is the buoyancy frequency of the fluid, M is the grid mesh length, and U is the towing speed. The mixing efficiency itself is measured as the flux Richardson number R_f, defined as the ratio of the change in potential energy of the fluid to the amount of work done towing the grid through the tank. The Reynolds numbers Re for these experiments, based on the tow speed and grid mesh length, range from 1,000 to 10,000. The Schmidt number Sc is about 700 for the salt-stratified experiments and the Prandtl number Pr is about 7 for the heat-stratified experiments.

The results of these experiments are fairly consistent; there appears to be no strong dependence on the molecular diffusivity (although there are some uncertainties about this conclusion). For $Ri < 1$ the mixing efficiency increases approximately as $Ri^{1/2}$. For larger Ri the mixing efficiency appears to approach a constant value of about 6although since none of the laboratory experiments can achieve values of Ri much greater than about 10 there is some uncertainty about whether the mixing efficiency will remain constant or not for larger Ri. Some different types of experiments have suggested that R_f should decrease for sufficiently large Ri. There have been many attempts to develop scaling arguments to describe this mixing efficiency behavior. The $Ri^{1/2}$ behavior can be explained using simple energy arguments. The behavior at large Ri is not well understood.

In the research described here, direct numerical simulations (DNS) of transient turbulent mixing events are carried out in order to study the detailed physics of the mixing efficiency. In particular, DNS results of decaying, homogeneous, stably-stratified turbulence are reviewed and used to determine the mixing efficiency as a function of the initial turbulence Richardson number.

2. Numerical Methods

Most of the numerical experiments described here were carried out with the pseudo-spectral DNS code used by Riley, Metcalfe & Weissman (1981) and is described in detail by those authors. This code simulates a flow field that is periodic in all three spatial co-ordinates, with uniform background density gradient.

Some additional results have been obtained using the DNS code described in Gerz, Schumann & Elgobashi (1989) and Diamessis & Nomura (1999). For the same flow conditions, this code produced results in agreement with those obtained with the previously described code.

2..1 Initialization

For all our numerical experiments, the turbulent flow field was initialized as a Gaussian, isotropic and solenoidal velocity field in the usual way using random Fourier modes with a specified energy spectrum. The turbulence was then allowed to decay until approximately 99% of the initial turbulence energy had dissipated. Decay times of about ten times the initial time scale of the turbulence L_0/u_0 were typically required, where L_0 and u_0 are the initial length and velocity scales as determined by the specified initial spectrum. The stable stratification for each transient experiment was specified by the initial Richardson number, which was varied in the range $0 < Ri < 40$. The Richardson number for these simulations is defined as $Ri = (NL_0/u_0)^2$.

The energy spectrum of the initial turbulence was chosen to have the exponential form (see *e.g.*, Townsend, 1976) :

$$E(k) = C \, u_0^2 \, L_0^5 \, k^4 exp[-\frac{1}{2} k^2 L_0^2]$$
(1)

where C is a constant scaling factor.

For most of the simulations, the initial energy was exclusively kinetic in form *i.e.*, the initial density fluctuations (and hence PE_0) were set to zero. Since one of our main objectives is to compare the simulation results with experimental measurements, the appropriate modelling of the initial conditions is necessary. Experimental measurements downstream of grid generated turbulence in stratified fluids suggest that the PE close to the grid (say at $x/M = 10$) is typically only a small fraction of the KE, approximately 10% (possibly increasing with increasing stratification). On this basis it seems that the above initialization scheme is reasonable, however Hunt, Stretch & Britter (1988) have indicated that the flow evolution can be sensitive to the PE initial conditions. As a preliminary test, two sets of simulations were done with non-zero initial density fluctuations with PE_0 equal to 24% and 95% of the initial turbulent kinetic energy.

2..2 Evaluating Mixing Efficiency

The main diagnostics describing the energetics of the decaying flow fields were archived from each run for subsequent analysis: these included the horizontal and vertical kinetic energy (HKE, VKE), potential energy (PE) and dissipation rates. In addition the time-integrated contributions of each of these aspects of the energy decay were also archived for subsequent analysis.

For the numerical simulations, the turbulence remains homogeneous (but not isotropic) for all times. This includes the buoyancy fluxes and dissipation rates. This implies that the mean fields are decoupled from the turbulence in this idealized problem, so that there is no change in the background potential energy. This model problem should be applicable to the homogeneous region of the flow fields investigated in the experiments. However, the turbulence in the experimental flows must be non-homogeneous near the upper and lower boundaries. It is in these regions that the gradients in the density flux produces changes to the background mean density profile, and hence in the PE of the fluid column. To compare the simulations with the experiments, we use the time-integrated buoyancy flux from the homogeneous region to represent the changes that are reflected in the non-homogeneous regions in the experiments. That is, in the numerical simulations the integral flux Richardson number R_f (or mixing efficiency) is defined as the time integral of the buoyancy flux divided by the change in turbulent kinetic energy over the same time period. We note that local irreversible mixing processes within the homogeneous region, represented by the local dissipation of scalar fluctuations (by molecular diffusion), do not contribute directly to changes in the background mean density field. They do however contribute indirectly by influencing the development of the buoyancy flux.

3. Results

The resolution of the simulations varied from 32^3 for the initial series of numerical experiments, and was later increased to 64^3. This allowed for about a factor of two increase in the Reynolds number $Re = u_0 L_0/\nu = 100$ and 200, respectively, in which ν is the kinematic viscosity. Most of the simulations reported here were carried out for Prandtl numbers $Pr = 0.5$. Limited investigation of Prandtl number effects were carried out by varying the Prandtl number in the range $0.1 < Pr < 2$. Higher Prandtl numbers could not be achieved without problems in resolving the scalar field: Reynolds numbers were reduced to $Re = 50$ for the $Pr = 2$ cases. Dissipation spectra were used to evaluate resolution issues. These values of Pr are substantially smaller than those for the laboratory experiments.

There is some arbitrariness in relating the different definitions of Ri used in the DNS and laboratory experiments. This relationship could be established using existing grid turbulence data at, say, $10M$ downstream from the grid. However, since our interest initially is in the trends of R_f and its maximum magnitude, we will assume the two definitions of Ri are approximately equal.

Figure 1 is a plot of R_f versus Ri for a selection of the DNS and laboratory results. To keep the figure simple, and since all the laboratory data is fairly consistent, we have plotted only the results from the laboratory experiments of Rottman & Britter (1986) and Rehmann & Koseff (2000). The results from three sets of numerical simulations are shown in the plot. These simulations correspond to the initial conditions: (1) $Re = 100$, $Pr = 0.5$ and $PE_0/VKE_0 = 0$; (2) $Re = 100$, $Pr = 0.5$ and $PE_0/VKE_0 = 24\%$; and (3) $Re = 100$, $Pr = 0.5$ and $PE_0/VKE_0 = 94\%$. The DNS results for other values of Pr used did not differ greatly from those shown. The DNS results for all three initial conditions compare well qualitatively with the experimental data. Quantitatively, the best comparison with the experimental results is for the DNS case for which $PE_0/VKE_0 = 94\%$. The other two initial conditions appear to produce mixing efficiencies that are much higher than was measured in the laboratory.

It appears, then, that the initial conditions are the controlling feature of the mixing efficiency in this kind of flow. However, our numerical simulations do not span a large enough range of Pr to definitively rule out any significant Pr effects. Looking at the simulations in more detail we note that most of the interesting dynamics, and in particular the contributions to integrated buoyancy flux, are completed by about 2 - 3 initial time scales of the turbulence. We suspect that these mixing efficiency results can be reproduced by inviscid, non-diffusive Rapid Distortion calculations. If this is true, it would rule out completely the differences in Pr or Sc as an explanation for the observed differences in mixing efficiency between the DNS and laboratory experiments.

Acknowledgements. DDS would like to acknowledge the support of Prof. J. Riley (University of Washington) during the time that some of this research was carried out. Prof. Riley provided the DNS code used for some of this work and many interesting discussions. Don Slinn at UW also assisted by carrying out some of the higher Reynolds number simulation runs. Peter Diamessis helped with the calculations done at UCSD.

4. References

Britter, R. E. 1985 Diffusion and decay in stably-stratified turbulent flows. In *Turbulence and Diffusion in Stable Environments*, ed. J. C. R. Hunt, Claredon, Oxford, 3-13.

Diamessis, P. J. and Nomura, K. K. 1999 Interaction of vorticity, rate of strain, and scalar gradient in stably stratified homogeneous sheared turbulence. *Turbulence and Shear Flow Phenomena - First International Symposium*, Santa Barbara, California", 715–720.

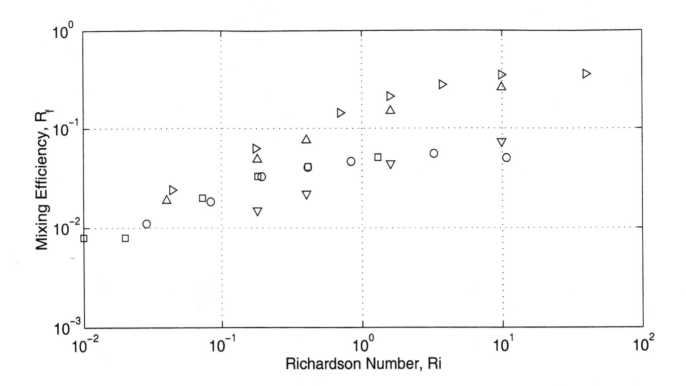

Figure 1: The mixing efficiency Ri_f plotted versus Ri. □, experimental data from Rottman & Britter (1986); ○, salt-stratified data from Rehmann & Koseff (2000); ▷, DNS with $Re = 100$, $Pr = 0.5$ and $PE_0/VKE_0 = 0$; △, DNS with $Re = 100$, $Pr = 0.5$ and $PE_0/VKE_0 = 24\%$; ▽, DNS $Re = 100$, $Pr = 0.5$ and $PE_0/VKE_0 = 94\%$.

Gerz, T. and Schumann, U. & Elghobashi, S. 1989 Direct simulation of stably stratified homogeneous turbulent shear flows. *J. Fluid Mech.*, **200**, 563–594.

Hunt, J. C. R., Stretch, D. D. & Britter, R. E. 1988 Length scales in stably stratified turbulent flows and their use in turbulence models. In *Stably Stratified Flow and Dense Gas Dispersion*, Proc. IMA Conf., Chester, UK, 9-10 April 1986.

Riley, J. J., Metcalfe, R. W. & Weissman, M. A. 1981 Direct numerical simulations of homogeneous turbulence in density-stratified fluids. In *Non-linear properties of internal waves*, Proc. AIP Conference, La Jolla Institute, 1981 (ed. by B.J. West).

Rottman, J. W. & Britter R. E. 1986 The mixing efficiency and decay of grid-generated turbulence in stably stratified fluids. *Proc. of the 9th Australasian Fluid Mechanics Conference*, Univ. of Auckland, Auckland, New Zealand, 8 - 12 Dec, 1986.

Rehmann C. R. & Koseff J. R. 2000 Mean potential energy change in weakly and strongly stratified grid turbulence. Submitted to *J. Fluid Mechanics*.

Townsend, A. A. 1976 *The structure of turbulent shear flow*. Cambridge University Press.

AUTHOR INDEX

VOLUME I pp 1-614
VOLUME II pp 615-1270